A HISTORY OF THE SOUTH

Volume X

THE EMERGENCE OF THE NEW SOUTH

1913–1945

A HISTORY

OF

THE SOUTH

Volume X

EDITORS

WENDELL HOLMES STEPHENSON

E. MERTON COULTER

The Emergence
of the
New South

1913-1945

BY GEORGE BROWN TINDALL

LOUISIANA STATE UNIVERSITY PRESS
THE LITTLEFIELD FUND FOR SOUTHERN
HISTORY OF THE UNIVERSITY OF TEXAS

PUBLISHERS' PREFACE

A HISTORY OF THE SOUTH is sponsored by Louisiana State University and the Trustees of the Littlefield Fund for Southern History at the University of Texas. More remotely, it is the outgrowth of the vision of Major George W. Littlefield, C.S.A., who established a fund at the University of Texas in 1914 for the collection of materials on Southern history and the publication of a "full and impartial study of the South and its part in American history." Trustees of the Littlefield Fund began preparations in 1937 for the writing of the history that Major Littlefield contemplated. Meanwhile, a plan had been conceived at Louisiana State University for a history of the South as a part of that institution's comprehensive program to promote interest, research, and writing in the field of Southern history.

As the two undertakings harmonized in essentials, the planning groups united to become joint sponsors of *A History of the South.* Wendell Holmes Stephenson, then professor of American history at Louisiana State University, and the late Charles W. Ramsdell, professor of American history at the University of Texas, were chosen to edit the series. They had been primarily interested in initiating the plans, and it was appropriate that they should be selected to edit the work. Upon the death of Professor Ramsdell in 1943, E. Merton Coulter, professor of history at the University of Georgia, was named his successor.

Volumes of the series are being published as the manuscripts are received. This is the ninth published volume; it follows Volume IX. When completed, the ten-volume set will represent more than twenty-five years of historical planning and research.

vii

AUTHOR'S PREFACE

OF LATE the diagnosis of the "emerging South" or the "changing South" has become a flourishing minor industry—as Edwin M. Yoder, Jr., has noted in the Greensboro *Daily News*—an enterprise in which countless pundits and symposiasts have acquired something of a vested interest. The idea that the everlasting South might somehow undergo change is rehearsed with all the freshness of newborn discovery, although the concept itself has long since become a commonplace. Indeed a realization that change had become the Southern way of life began to prevail during the period with which this volume deals. For a generation before 1913 economic and social evolution had moved with such deliberate speed that most Southerners in their everyday life did not face a constant necessity for adjustment. After World War I the pace quickened to such a degree that the consciousness of change was inescapable even in the most remote quarters.

In the period arbitrarily bounded by the years 1913 and 1945 one encounters on every hand recurrent themes of emergence. In national life under Woodrow Wilson and Franklin D. Roosevelt Southern leaders reached positions of influence unequaled since the Civil War. In regional life the Southern people moved into a far more diversified, pluralistic society. For many Southerners the stresses of change set off defensive reactions against the new and unfamiliar, but for many others change offered at last an escape from poverty, both economic and cultural.

Poverty was, of course, a relative matter; what was perhaps more significant was a growing sense of Southern deficiencies and a growing impulse to lift the region's standards. That impulse lay behind the struggles for economic development: the drive for industry, farm programs, the labor movement. And it lay behind the struggles for cultural development: education, scholarship, the renaissance in literature, and above all, the growth of critical attitudes which, among other things, gave rise to an almost insurmountable documentation of contemporary problems. Moreover, one need not search far below the surface before he encounters the origins of a Second Reconstruction, which would emerge not long after 1945.

It might have been better to have dropped that shopworn phrase "New South," but I have been no more able to dispense with it than the author of the preceding volume in *A History of the South*. In the title it signifies a period, not a doctrine, yet much of what happened in the first half of the twentieth century fulfilled the nineteenth-century creed of the New South. "South" here, as in the preceding volume, means the eleven former Confederate states plus Kentucky and Oklahoma. In the sources, however, one encounters other definitions which must be accepted on occasion. The "Census South" includes the states of Delaware, Maryland, and West Virginia, and the District of Columbia. And "Southeast," at least where statistics are given, conforms to the definition in Howard W. Odum's *Southern Regions of the United States:* eleven states, excluding Texas and Oklahoma which Odum linked with Arizona and New Mexico to form his "Southwest."

It is manifestly impossible to acknowledge adequately the generosity of all the librarians, scholars, and editors who have eased my task. One especially heavy obligation is to Rupert B. Vance, who had to abandon research for this volume because of other responsibilities. Professor Vance turned over to me his accumulation of notes, clippings, outlines, and drafts—two of the chapter titles are his—and later read most of the finished manuscript. Others who read parts of the manuscript at various stages and offered valuable suggestions are John Wells Davidson, Gilbert C. Fite, John Hope Franklin, Dewey W. Grantham, Jr., C. Hugh Holman, Arthur S. Link, August Meier, H. L. Mitchell, Joseph L. Morrison, James W. Patton, Louis D. Rubin, Jr., Theodore Saloutos, Anne Firor Scott, James A. Tinsley, and C. Vann Woodward.

I am further indebted to the student assistants who helped with research and the preparation of footnotes: William C. Allred, Marvin L. Cann, Susan Speare Durant, Jack P. Maddex,

Donald Saunders, and Maud Thomas Smith. My favorite research assistant and critic, however, was Blossom McGarrity Tindall, who with Bruce and Blair endured more patiently than the author deserved his chronic obsession with this book.

I was assisted in completing the research and writing by fellowships from the Guggenheim Foundation, the Social Science Research Council, and the Institute for Advanced Study; by grants from the faculty research funds of Louisiana State University and the University of North Carolina, from the Cooperative Program in the Humanities, and from the Institute for Research in Social Science which also extended the services of its typing pool; and by leaves of absence from both Louisiana State University and the University of North Carolina. Beverly Jarrett, who prepared the copy for the printer, also prepared the index.

G.B.T.

Chapel Hill, 1967

CONTENTS

LIST OF ILLUSTRATIONS

CHAPTER I

IN THE HOUSE OF THEIR FATHERS

HALF a century of Southern political isolation ended with the inauguration of President Woodrow Wilson on March 4, 1913. Whether Democratic or Republican, government for years "had been steadily conservative, Eastern, urban, industrial." [1] Whatever hopes and aspirations the agrarians and petty middle classes, Southern and Western, held had been classified as heresies: free trade, populism, Bryanism, and the conspiracy to debase the coinage with silver. Only the rise of a nationwide progressive movement finally had broken the spell of the bloody shirt and the full dinner pail, split the Republican party, and permitted the Democrats to win in 1912. It was the victory of a minority party—Arizona was the only state outside the South in which Wilson polled a majority—but that served only to accentuate the position of the South as the main support of the winner. [2]

Even the setting of the inauguration evoked a Southern mood. It was "one of the most perfect March days Washington had ever known." A gentle breeze blew across the Capitol as the former Rebel, Chief Justice Edward Douglass White of Louisiana, administered the oath. Southerners crowded into Washington for the triumph, "brought along their full lung development and let it loose every few minutes." Three hundred thousand marchers took four hours to pass down Pennsylvania Avenue; they represented the victorious Democracy from coast to coast, but reporters noted

[1] Ray Stannard Baker, *Woodrow Wilson: Life and Letters* (New York, 1937), III, 439.

[2] Edgar Eugene Robinson, *The Presidential Vote, 1896–1932* (Stanford University, 1934), 14, 51, 52. Wilson won majorities in the eleven former Confederate States, but only pluralities in Kentucky and Oklahoma.

1

that a vociferous "Rebel Yell" broke out whenever a Southern figure rode by or a band blared *Dixie!* "Thousands of voices sang the words of it in unison." If any Southern observer caught the portent of top-hatted and gray-gloved Negroes among the Tammany braves, that detail seems not to have been recorded.[3]

The Democratic hosts acclaimed the first native Southerner elected President since Abraham Lincoln. Wilson had lived in the North since maturity, but the background of birth in Virginia and early years in Georgia and the Carolinas had left its imprint on his speech, character, and personality. He said once that "the only place in the country, the only place in the world where nothing has to be explained to me is the South." Staunton, Virginia, his birthplace, called him back for a sentimental celebration before the inauguration; citizens of Columbia, South Carolina, bought his boyhood home and invited him to use it as a summer residence.[4]

✕ His election was a kind of vindication for the South. The South, "beaten, bleeding, prostrate" half a century before, one reporter reflected, had "come back to rule the Union." In Washington, he said, "you feel it in the air . . . you listen to evidence of it in the mellow accent with which the South makes our English a musical tongue; you hear strange names of men to whom leadership and importance are attributed, and if you ask, you almost invariably learn that they are from the South."[5] Five of the ten cabinet members were men born below the Potomac, and William Jennings Bryan, the Secretary of State, was an idol of the Southern masses. William Gibbs McAdoo, Secretary of the Treasury and James C. McReynolds, Attorney-General, were hyphenated New Yorkers, born and raised in Georgia and Tennessee. David F. Houston, former Texan, North Carolina-born, took leave from Washington University to become Secretary of Agriculture. The Secretary of the Navy was Josephus Daniels, publisher of the

[3] New York *World*, March 5, 1913; New York *Times*, March 5, 1913; Washington *Bee*, March 8, 1913; Josephus Daniels, *The Wilson Era: Years of Peace, 1910–1917* (Chapel Hill, 1944), 104.

[4] Arthur S. Link, *Wilson: The Road to the White House* (Princeton, 1947), 3–4; Arthur S. Link, *Wilson: The New Freedom* (Princeton, 1956), 2, 24–26, 66–67.

[5] Judson C. Welliver, "The Triumph of the South," in *Munsey's Magazine* (New York), XLIX (1913), 740.

Raleigh *News and Observer* and a Bryanite progressive. Albert Sidney Burleson of Texas left the House of Representatives after eight terms to become Postmaster General. In other administrative and diplomatic positions the South had "a vastly larger proportion of big and influential posts than it has held since the Civil War." [6] At the President's right hand, and one of the most influential members of the Wilson circle at least until 1919, though without official position, was Colonel Edward M. House of Texas.

At the other end of Pennsylvania Avenue the "mellow accent" of the South was, if anything, even more prevalent. In the Senate more than half of the Democratic majority were Southerners, in the House more than two fifths; but even more significant was the Southern hold on major committee chairmanships: all but two of fourteen in the Senate and all but two of thirteen in the House.[7] The Democratic majority leader in the House was Oscar W. Underwood of Alabama, succeeded in 1915 by Claude Kitchin of North Carolina; in the Senate, John W. Kern of Indiana, a native of Virginia, succeeded after his death in 1917 by Thomas S. Martin of Virginia.

The sudden accession of the South to national leadership provoked a variety of reactions and conjectures. For Southern Democrats, who had wandered so long in the political wilderness, it meant that they were, in the often repeated words of Benjamin H. Hill, back in the house of their fathers. For many Northerners, it raised a fearsome vision of the South once again "in the saddle." But some anticipated the culmination of a great national reconciliation. "The first and most important meaning, perhaps is that *the period of reconstruction is ended*," said one writer.[8] "The return of the Democrats to power breaks down sectionalism," said another.[9] Still another predicted that "the necessity of taking a national view of national problems, under the lead of a man whose

[6] *Ibid.*, 733. For a substantial list see pp. 734–36.
[7] *Official Congressional Directory*, 63 Cong., 1 Sess., 131–40; 2 Sess., 161–70, 185–94.
[8] Welliver, "Triumph of the South," *loc. cit.*, 740.
[9] A. Maurice Low, "The South in the Saddle," in *Harper's Weekly* (New York), LVII (February 8, 1913), 20.

3

view is eminently national, is certain to broaden the South and its public men in a most desirable way." [10]

But these confident assertions did not quiet apprehensions about the course of policy. "It was the prevailing Progressive theory," a contemporary later wrote, "that the Democratic party would not be permanently progressive because of what was regarded as the ultra-conservatism of the South." [11] Conservatism, a progressive journalist warned, would be the dominant attitude of the new Congress. "And nowhere has the drift been more noticeable than in the professional congressmen returned, term after term, by the undisturbed Democracy of the South." [12] The best hope, a Progressive party Congressman from California submitted, was "Democratic ruction with Wilson and Bryan on one side and southern reactionaries on the other." [13]

Casual observers, tossing off clichés about the conservative South, overlooked the events of recent years. Without the hypnotic power of the "Solid South" idea, it would have been abundantly clear that the region was not a monolithic unit politically. More careful attention to the record of the previous decade would have revealed the rise of progressive factions and a cycle of progressive governors whose achievements rivaled those of contemporaries in the North.[14] A review of the preceding Congress, in which the House was already under Southern leadership, would have shown "the accomplishment of more progressive legislation than in any Congress since the problems of the industrial revolution had come to bloom." [15] A survey of the Southern press might

[10] Unidentified speaker quoted in Welliver, "Triumph of the South," *loc. cit.*, 738.

[11] Donald R. Richberg, *My Hero: The Indiscreet Memoirs of an Eventful But Unheroic Life* (New York, 1954), 81.

[12] George Kibbe Turner, "What Wilson Is Up Against," in *McClure's Magazine* (New York), XL (1912–1913), 162.

[13] William Kent to Gifford Pinchot, November 9, 1912, in William Kent Papers (Yale University Library, New Haven), quoted in John Wells Davidson, "The Response of the South to Woodrow Wilson's New Freedom, 1912–1914" (Ph.D. dissertation, Yale University, 1954), 84.

[14] C. Vann Woodward, *Origins of the New South, 1877–1913,* in Wendell Holmes Stephenson and E. Merton Coulter (eds.), *A History of the South* (Baton Rouge, 1951), 369–95; Dewey W. Grantham, Jr., *The Democratic South* (Athens, Ga., 1963), 42–62.

[15] Anne Firor Scott, "Southern Progressives in National Politics, 1906–1916"

have turned up the Little Rock editor who believed Wilson's election assured farmers and workers "a just share of the fruits of their labor" and indicated the determination of the people forever to *"emancipate themselves from the slavery of political bosses and the over-lords of industrial privilege."* [16] Or one might have discovered the opinion expressed in William E. Gonzales' Columbia *State* that "progressivism . . . has become a veritable tidal wave." [17]

The progressive movement had put down sturdy roots in the South, a region to which modern capitalism had come late, where it had yet only begun to secure a foothold, and where many of the political leaders and the preponderance of small businessmen remained under the spell of an agrarian mystique that rendered them skeptical of finance-capitalism, protectionism, trusts, railroads, and the symbolic menace of "Wall Street." [18] Deeply impregnated with the traditional ideas of states' rights, white supremacy, and free trade, Southern agrarians shaded off into several degrees of radicalism in fighting the battles of the farmers for democracy, railroad regulation, warehouses, and rural credits —a broad range of programs that looked to governmental intervention. Not a few of the small businessmen, closely identified with the farming communities from which their incomes rose, supported such battles. If they were alarmed at the threat of governmental regulation, they felt themselves drawn to Woodrow Wilson by sectional and party loyalties and by his enunciation of the New Freedom which paralleled their own concern to deny special privilege and restrain the growth of trusts. In the spirit of the New South they sought economic development first; but, unreconciled to the concentration of wealth in the East, they believed as strongly as the agrarian radicals that Wall Street financiers controlled economic power to their disadvantage. Freeing

---

(Ph.D. dissertation, Harvard University, 1957) , 137. For a dissenting view see Turner, "What Wilson Is Up Against," *loc. cit.,* 160–67.

[16] Little Rock *Arkansas Democrat,* November 6, 1912, quoted in Davidson, "Response of the South to Woodrow Wilson's New Freedom," 83.

[17] Columbia (S. C.) *State,* June 17, 1912, quoted in Scott, "Southern Progressives in National Politics," 79.

[18] See William G. Carleton, "The Southern Politician—1900 and 1950," in *Journal of Politics* (Gainesville, Fla.) , XIII (1954) , 226.

small scale enterprise from victimization by the larger corporate interests, they felt, was a proper function of government, one that would contribute to the vital interests of the South.[19]

The progressive cause in the South, founded chiefly on the aspirations of the middle-income groups to own and develop productive property, drew strength from merchants, mechanics, farmers, small manufacturers, and the brokers and factors who serviced the farm economy, many of whom combined in one person the functions of capitalist and laborer. Their basic ideology in its radical aspects had been populism, a cause that did much to break up the older suspicions of governmental action without undermining the belief in a system of private property, competition, and profit.

But if Southern progressives could reconcile their traditional independence with positive governmental programs to benefit farmers or restrict big business, many of them persisted in viewing labor unions and social legislation as alien to the issues to be fought out. Shopkeepers and farmers generally held the accepted view that working men, thrifty and honest, could in due course acquire the ownership of productive property. Arguments for workmen's compensation, regulation of hours and wages, or the restriction of child labor often left them unmoved because the conditions of urban labor were either unknown or judged by traditional standards. A frustrated agent of the National Child Labor Committee summarized their outlook in 1914: "The doctrine that social justice and human rights rise above parental and property rights does not yet determine either the law or custom of these states," he wrote. Somehow Southerners "lived under the idea that God fixes man's lot and that things were about right anyway." At times, he said, "we do show a disposition to cry out against the bad rich, but I call to your attention the fact that in our opinion most of the bad rich live next to Wall Street, and certainly north of the Mason and Dixon line. We believe in investigating the New York insurance companies and even the rail-

[19] Robert H. Wiebe, "Memorandum on Southern Businessmen's Response to the Progressive Period" (Typescript in author's possession) ; and Dewey W. Grantham, Jr., "The Anticorporation Movement and Progressivism: The Case of the South" (Typescript in author's possession) , lend support to this view.

roads, but to appoint an inspector to look into conditions in our mill villages is thought to be a reflection upon the word and character of good men." [20]

Progressivism in the South was traditionalistic, individualistic, and set in a socially conservative milieu. Southern progressives, in their battles against monopoly and the corporations, still looked back to the agrarian arcadia, to an economy of small property, independent farmers, storekeepers, and at least relatively small-scale manufacturers. Yet a substantial minority of Southerners belonged to the social justice wing of progressives who looked beyond the loosening of economic restrictions to positive action against social ills. Their focus was in the Southern Sociological Congress, which drew into its councils a dedicated group of social workers associated with churches and private charities, social-minded ministers, education leaders, and a scattering of urban reformers and clubwomen devoted to the cause of social service.[21] Primarily a clearing house for the forces of uplift, the Congress disseminated through papers and speeches at its annual meetings from 1912 to 1920 both inspiration and information about the latest developments in social welfare, public health, penology, organized charities, child labor, care of the handicapped, the peace movement, mental hygiene, woman suffrage, race relations—the whole catalog of social problems that agitated the more advanced progressives.[22]

The most significant aspect of the movement, its historian has suggested, was its rationale: "Preached with moral and religious, rather than theoretical sanctions, the idea of social amelioration stimulated the thinking of many men and women in the South who would not have been aware of similar national organizations." [23] The mission of the Congress, Arkansas Governor

[20] W. H. Swift, "Why It Is Hard to Get Good Child Labor Laws in the South," in *Child Labor Bulletin* (New York), III (1914–1915), 73–74, 76. Swift was field representative for the North and South Carolina child labor committees.

[21] For a survey of their activities, see Scott, "Southern Progressives in National Politics," 12–44. See also Virginia Wooten Gulledge, *The North Carolina Conference for Social Services: A Study of Its Development and Methods* (n. p., 1942).

[22] E. Charles Chatfield, "The Southern Sociological Congress: Organization of Uplift," in *Tennessee Historical Quarterly* (Nashville), XIX (1960), 328–47.

[23] E. Charles Chatfield, "The Southern Sociological Congress: Rationale of Uplift," *ibid*, XX (1961), 64.

Charles H. Brough declared, was "preaching the crusade of the new chivalry of health and sanity in dealing with every vital problem of civic and social welfare, and supplementing the 'pew religion' of the different creeds . . . by the 'do religion' of twentieth-century efficiency." [24] A distinctive feature of every meeting was the session on the church and social service. One finds in the annals of this and later social reform movements a fundamental conditioning influence of the churches which gave to middle-class liberalism in the South a unique moral-religious tone.

Religion also conditioned and stiffened the character of Woodrow Wilson, who had grown up in Southern Presbyterian manses. In the new President the progressives had assets at first unrealized: his high conception of the Presidential office, his program, and his organizational skills. If the South was in the saddle, it soon became apparent that Woodrow Wilson held the reins. Powerful forces bent even reluctant Southerners to his leadership. He offered the party its first real opportunity since the Civil War to establish a record of achievement. The spirit of party regularity, especially strong in the South, brought along conservative men like the elder Senator John H. Bankhead of Alabama, one of the five old Confederates still in Congress, who regarded a political party as "something like an army in which the colonels must follow the lead of the general." [25] Conservative Southerners were further inhibited by progressive factions at home. "If I oppose Wilson," Senator Thomas S. Martin complained, "his claquers in Virginia all cry out, 'Tom Martin is a reactionary' and hound me." [26]

Progressive factions had scored indifferent success in local elections, but they had been the core of Wilson's support, and hope sprang high with his success. "The people are in the saddle," Birmingham editor Frank Glass exulted after his nomination;

---

[24] Charles H. Brough, "The Objective of the Congress," in James E. McCulloch (ed.), *Democracy in Earnest* (Washington, 1918), 13.

[25] Daniels, *Wilson Era: Years of Peace*, 43; Davidson, "Response of the South to Woodrow Wilson's New Freedom," 96.

[26] Daniels, *Wilson Era: Years of Peace*, 524; "McGregor" [Alexander J. McKelway], "The Progressive South," Typescript in Alexander J. McKelway Papers (Division of Manuscripts, Library of Congress), surveys progressive factions but must be used with caution.

". . . they are going to down bosses and bossism. They are going to restore rule of the people for the benefit of the people." The South, "now partly enlightened and aroused, must be kept alive and awake, so that the minds of southern reactionaries in Congress shall be illuminated," William E. Gonzales wrote in the Columbia *State*. "Traitors to Wilson should receive no aid or comfort." [27] Hope rose higher after Wilson's announcement that he would "pick out progressives, and only progressives," and after a thinly veiled attack on the Virginia machine.[28] But the hope that progressive factions would win Federal patronage was quickly dashed. Upon the urging of Postmaster General Burleson, Wilson determined that his legislative program should take priority; therefore, he pursued a policy of cultivating Party leaders in Congress first of all. "I'd rather trust a machine Senator when he is committed to your program," he finally told Josephus Daniels, "than a talking Liberal who can never quite go along with others because of his admiration of his own patented plan of reform." [29]

The appointment of Edward K. Campbell, an Alabama railroad and corporation lawyer, to the United States Court of Claims on the recommendation of Oscar W. Underwood provided one early omen. A supporter complained that the choice "would be the coldest chill you could give to your friends in this state," but Wilson could only respond that it was "inevitable in the circumstances." [30] In North Carolina the symbolic act was the choice of Alston D. Watts, private secretary to Senator Furnifold M. Simmons, as Collector of Internal Revenue for the western district. Even where progressives won recognition, as with the appointment of Josephus Daniels, so many left the state that one of those remaining found that "the one result seems to have been about as fatal as the other." [31] Bryan summarized Wilson's plight

[27] Frank P. Glass to Woodrow Wilson, July 6, 1912, in Woodrow Wilson Papers (Division of Manuscripts, Library of Congress) ; Columbia *State*, November 9, 1912, both quoted in Scott, "Southern Progressives in National Politics," 167, 168–69.
[28] Link, *Wilson: The New Freedom*, 25–26, 157.
[29] Josephus Daniels to Franklin D. Roosevelt, February 9, 1939, in Franklin D. Roosevelt Papers (Franklin D. Roosevelt Library, Hyde Park, N.Y.) . Another version of Wilson's statement appears in Daniels, *Wilson Era: Years of Peace*, 525.
[30] Link, *Wilson: The New Freedom*, 162.
[31] Clarence Poe to Josephus Daniels, August 6, 1914, in Josephus Daniels Papers (Division of Manuscripts, Library of Congress) .

in a letter to one of the Virginia Wilsonians: "The President appreciates the work done by those who assisted him, but he is not at liberty to disregard the representatives whom the people have sent to Washington as his co-laborers. . . . He is doing the best he can and I am sure that the success he is having in carrying out the principles of the party will overcome any personal disappointments that may be felt." [32]

Wilson denied many loyal supporters the rewards of patronage, but he secured the adherence of the senior Democrats and committee chairmen. By his skill and persistence in cultivating Congressional leaders, more than by patronage, he welded them into an effective organization. The outcome was less the predicted division between Wilson and "southern reactionaries" than a division between Wilsonians and a "radical" wing led by such men as Robert L. Henry and Joseph H. Eagle of Texas, Claude Kitchin of North Carolina, Otis Wingo of Arkansas, J. Willard Ragsdale and Asbury F. Lever of South Carolina, and James K. Vardaman of Mississippi. In the end the most significant pressures on the administration came not from reactionaries but from the "radical" agrarians.[33]

Tariff reform, the first item in Wilson's program, was happily suited to inspire unity among the traditionally low-tariff Southerners.[34] The leaders of the two pertinent committees, Underwood and Simmons, both championed the "competitive tariff" that Wilson urged, which meant the removal of protection from trusts, but some consideration for small competing firms. It was not so extreme as the "tariff for revenue only and not for the

[32] William Jennings Bryan to Henry St. George Tucker, November 21, 1913, in Tucker Family Papers (Southern Historical Collection, University of North Carolina, Chapel Hill).

[33] Arthur S. Link, "The South and the 'New Freedom': An Interpretation," in *The American Scholar* (New York), XX (1950–1951), 314–24. For dissenting views see Richard M. Abrams, "Woodrow Wilson and the Southern Congressmen, 1913–1916," in *Journal of Southern History* (Baton Rouge), XXII (1956), 417–37; and Howard W. Allen, "Geography and Politics: Voting on Reform Issues in the United States Senate, 1911–1916," *ibid.*, XXVII (1961), 216–28.

[34] The following account of Wilson's legislative program leans heavily upon the previously cited studies by Davidson, Link, and Scott, and Dewey W. Grantham, Jr., "Southern Congressional Leaders and the New Freedom, 1913–1917" (M.A. thesis, University of North Carolina, 1946), 11, 126. See also Arthur S. Link, *Woodrow Wilson and the Progressive Era, 1910–1917* (New York, 1954), 35–57.

benefit of special interest" about which Underwood and other Southerners had orated. Still, the Democrats proposed the most drastic reduction since the Civil War.[35] The outcome was never seriously in doubt. Underwood, "placid ever, urbane even in attack, tender even in his tyrannies,"[36] dominated the debate by his mastery of detail and brought the measure through with an overwhelming majority. In the Senate, traditional bone yard of tariff reform, Simmons guided the bill to passage with the help of a sensational attack by Wilson on the lobbyists. The only important Southern opposition to reductions came from Texas wool, Louisiana sugar, and Southeastern textile interests, but only the sugar Congressmen bolted their party on the final vote.[37]

Southerners led in another drastic departure, a provision in the Underwood-Simmons Act for the first income tax under the Sixteenth Amendment. Drafted and guided through the House by Cordell Hull of Tennessee, it was altered under pressures from John Nance Garner of Texas in the House and Vardaman in the Senate to include a graduated surtax on large incomes. Opponents raised objections in the press and Congress on the grounds that it was class legislation and a sectional raid on Eastern wealth, but Hull disclaimed any intention of redistributing the wealth and justified it on the principle that Eastern wealth derived from all sections of the country: "I deny the right of wealth anywhere to segregate itself and then upon the plea of segregation to exempt itself from its fair share of taxes."[38]

[35] Evans C. Johnson, "Oscar W. Underwood: The Development of a National Statesman, 1894–1915" (Ph.D. dissertation, University of North Carolina, 1953), 414; Oscar W. Underwood, *Drifting Sands of Party Politics* (New York, 1928), 181–82; J. Fred Rippy (ed.), *F. M. Simmons, Statesman of the New South: Memoirs and Addresses* (Durham, 1936), 5–7.

[36] Representative Victor Murdock of Kansas, in *Congressional Record*, 63 Cong., 1 Sess., 5238.

[37] J. Carlyle Sitterson, *Sugar Country: The Cane Sugar Industry in the South, 1753–1950* (Lexington, Ky., 1953), 348; Lewis W. Parker to Oscar W. Underwood, February 4 and April 10, 1913, in Oscar W. Underwood Papers (Alabama Department of Archives and History, Montgomery); W. J. Thackston to William Watts Ball, February 26, 1913, in William Watts Ball Papers (Manuscript Collection, Duke University, Durham, N. C.).

[38] Cordell Hull, *The Memoirs of Cordell Hull* (New York, 1948), I, 48–50, 70–71, 73–74; Harold B. Hinton, *Cordell Hull: A Biography* (New York, 1942), 135–37, 139–44; Sidney Ratner, *American Taxation: Its History as a Social Force in Democracy* (New York, 1942), 324–26. Hull's major speech defending the income tax is in *Congressional Record*, 63 Cong., 1 Sess., 503–15.

Before the tariff bill had cleared the Senate, the administration had underway its measure for banking and currency reform. The complicated story of political maneuver and accommodation behind the Federal Reserve Act cannot be retraced here, but the major peculiarities that distinguished the final measure from the conservative Republican Aldrich plan were largely the result of Southern influences. The dominant figure in its passage was the pugnacious little redheaded Congressman from Lynchburg, Virginia, Carter Glass, assisted by a Washington and Lee economist, H. Parker Willis. Glass's chief contribution was the plan, which appealed to the traditional Southern fear of centralization, for the establishment of regional reserve banks. Wilson, however, insisted upon a central board of governors, with minority banker representation, as the capstone of the system.

It was on the banking bill that the agrarian radicals first asserted themselves. With several members on the House committee, and with support from rules chairman Henry, Senate banking chairman Robert L. Owen, and Bryan, they secured Wilson's acceptance of provisions to exclude banker representatives from the board, to make Federal Reserve Notes obligations of the Federal government, and to provide short-term, ninety-day farm as well as commercial credit facilities.[39]

Wilson signed the bill two days before Christmas. As the triumphant Democrats prepared for the holidays, Alabama's orotund champion of cotton, J. Thomas Heflin, rose on the floor of the House. "Mr. Speaker," he said, "let the calamity howlers howl. Let the croakers croak, and the chronic kickers kick. Labor is employed, wages good, the earth has yielded abundantly, the Democratic Party is in control, God reigns, and all is well with the Republic." [40]

Agrarian demands for an antitrust provision in the banking act

[39] Participants' accounts of the framing of the law appear in Robert L. Owen, *The Federal Reserve Act* (New York, 1919) ; H. Parker Willis, *The Federal Reserve System: Legislation, Organization, and Operation* (New York, 1923) ; and Carter Glass, *An Adventure in Constructive Finance* (Garden City, N.Y., 1927). A rejoinder to the last is Samuel Untermeyer. *Who Is Entitled to the Credit for the Federal Reserve Act? An Answer to Senator Carter Glass* (New York, 1927). An answer by Glass, "Vapor vs. the Record," is in the Carter Glass Papers (University of Virginia Library, Charlottesville, Va.).

[40] *Congressional Record,* 63 Cong., 2 Sess., 1455.

yielded to a promise that the question would come up separately in 1914. The Wilson antitrust program finally took form in the Federal Trade Commission (FTC) and Clayton Anti-Trust Acts of 1914, the latter being drafted by the House judiciary chairman from Alabama. While they supported the antitrust principle, Southern members made few contributions to the evolution of the legislation. They had no leading part in the most significant development, granting the FTC authority to define "unfair trade practices" and issue cease-and-desist orders. The radicals, however, in alliance with organized labor, secured a stipulation in the Clayton Act which supposedly exempted farm and labor organizations from the antitrust laws but actually only declared them not to be, *per se,* unlawful combinations in restraint of trade. The provision, written by Representative E. Y. Webb of North Carolina, was later described by Wilson's biographer as "one of the most artful dodges in the history of American politics." [41]

To that point none of the major reforms had significantly eased the problem of rural credits. The agrarians won important goals in the bank reform battle, as well as further concessions in the Cotton Futures Act and the Cotton Warehouse Act of 1914, the latter providing for Federal licensing of warehouses whose certificates presumably would be more acceptable as collateral.[42] But these measures did not fulfill the farmers' pressing need for credit. In 1914 the average cost of chattel loans to farmers ran from 9.9 per cent in Tennessee to 15.6 per cent in Oklahoma. State averages for mortgage loans ran from 8.4 per cent in South Carolina and Oklahoma to 9.6 per cent in Arkansas and Florida. Short-term rates often went above 60 per cent. Nor did bank rates tell the whole story. In Eastern North Carolina a 1914 survey showed that merchant credit covered approximately 60 per cent of all purchases by small farmers at an average rate of 20 per cent for six- to eight-month loans.[43] An anonymous farmer expressed the matter more

[41] Link, "The South and the 'New Freedom': An Interpretation," *loc. cit.,* 320; W. P. Newton, "Henry D. Clayton and Anti-Trust Legislation" (M.A. thesis, University of Alabama, 1953).

[42] A more general measure on the same lines was the Warehouse Act of 1916. Legislation regulating cotton futures is summarized in James E. Boyle, *Cotton and the New Orleans Cotton Exchange* (Garden City, N. Y., 1934), 88–90.

[43] Herbert Quick, "The Rural Credits Firing Squad," in *Saturday Evening Post* (New York), CLXXXVIII (April 15, 1916), 30; Lewis Henry Haney, "Farm Credit

succinctly: "They charge from 25 per cent to grand larceny." [44]
Agrarian leaders had long since concluded that only governmental action could provide a solution. "No commercial system
can be made to meet the requirements of agriculture," Senate
agriculture chairman Duncan U. Fletcher of Florida said.[45] No
measure "will be worth the paper it is written on which does not
provide for government aid," a Texas agrarian declared, but "it
will be the effort of the banking fraternity . . . to prevent any
rural credits bill which will get the farmer out from under their
direct, indirect and remote control." [46] In the spring of 1913
Congress authorized the President to appoint a Rural Credits
Commission to accompany an unofficial commission of the Southern Commercial Congress in studying European systems of agricultural credit and co-operation. The recommendations of both
groups went into a bill worked out by Senator Fletcher for a
system of privately controlled land banks under Federal charter.
However, in 1914 a joint subcommittee of the House and Senate
banking committees submitted the Hollis-Bulkley bill providing
that the government should subscribe to the capital of the banks and
purchase their bonds if the public did not. The second bill more
nearly embodied agrarian demands, but it ran headlong into the
laissez-faire assumptions that informed the early Wilson program.
In this condition the situation stood until 1916, when Wilson
yielded to House agriculture chairman Asbury F. Lever's demand
that the Federal government should control the land banks and
provide a capital of $500,000 to each of them. With the President's
support, the Federal Farm Loan Act passed easily. It established
twelve regional banks to make long-term loans to farmers on the

Conditions in a Cotton State [Texas]," in *American Economic Review* (Cambridge,
Mass.), IV (1914), 47–66; Garret W. Forster, "The Effects of the Present Credit Sys-
tem on Southern Agriculture," in *Social Forces* (Chapel Hill), X (1931–1932), 427;
Charles Lee Raper, "The Use of Credit by the North Carolina Farmers," in *South
Atlantic Quarterly* (Durham), XIII (1914), 119–21.

[44] Quoted in Clarence H. Poe, *How Farmers Co-operate and Double Profits* (New
York and London, 1915), 44.

[45] Quoted in Theodore Saloutos, *Farmer Movements in the South, 1865–1933*
(Berkeley and Los Angeles, 1960), 222.

[46] Joe H. Eagle to Carter Glass, July 1, 1915, copy in Claude Kitchin Papers
(Southern Historical Collection, University of North Carolina).

security of land and improvements. The Act was an important factor in Wilson's sweep of the agricultural states in November.

Other concessions to agrarian demands came more readily in the Smith-Lever Act of 1914 and the Smith-Hughes Act of 1917. The first, providing Federal grants-in-aid for county agricultural extension agents under the supervision of land-grant colleges, grew out of a farm demonstration program that Seaman A. Knapp had started in Texas in 1903 and that had subsequently spread to many other localities under the auspices of the General Education Board, the Department of Agriculture, and various business and banking groups. The bill, sponsored by A. F. Lever in the House and Georgia's Hoke Smith in the Senate, passed without significant opposition. The extension system was remarkably successful, and resulted in a unique collaboration of Federal, state, and county governments with private agencies.[47]

Hoke Smith's interest in vocational education led him also to promote a program to extend into secondary schools the principle of Federal aid to vocational education. His bill for an eventual appropriation of seven million dollars a year won the endorsement of business, agricultural, labor, and educational groups. It was uncontroversial and passed easily in 1917, sponsored by Georgia's Dudley M. Hughes in the House; thus the principle of Federal grants-in-aid was extended into another area of community life.[48]

Meanwhile, Southern efforts were a factor in expanding the dollar-matching idea to the building of highways. In the first decade of the new century numerous Southern Congressmen had taken the initiative by introducing and supporting Federal highway bills. In 1907 John H. Bankhead of Alabama had won election to the Senate with Federal aid for roads as the leading plank in his platform. By 1916 lingering constitutional scruples yielded to the prospect of additional moneys and the argument of national

[47] Dewey W. Grantham, Jr., *Hoke Smith and the Politics of the New South* (Baton Rouge, 1958), 256–64. See also Joseph C. Bailey, *Seaman A. Knapp: Schoolmaster of American Agriculture,* in Columbia University *Studies in the History of American Agriculture,* No. 10 (New York, 1945), 141–68, 244–80; Grant McConnell, *The Decline of Agrarian Democracy* (Berkeley and Los Angeles, 1953), 24–30; and Alfred C. True, *A History of Agricultural Extension Work in the United States, 1785–1923* (Washington, 1928), 50–65.

[48] Grantham, *Hoke Smith,* 264–67.

15

defense. Wilson was persuaded by Bankhead and Kenneth Mc-Kellar of Tennessee, and in 1916 he supported passage of the Bankhead-Shackelford Federal Highways Act providing the distribution of $75,000,000 over five years to states with responsible highway departments that met certain Federal standards.[49]

While Southern agrarian pressures contributed significantly to the enlarged responsibilities of the Federal government, Southern leadership played little part in the extension of labor legislation by the Furuseth Sailor Act, the Kern-McGillicuddy Workmen's Compensation Act for government workers, or even the Keating-Owen Child Labor Act, co-sponsored by Owen of Oklahoma. In 1916 William C. Adamson of Georgia took the lead in the adoption of an eight-hour law for railroad workers at the behest of an administration faced with a crippling railroad strike, an unyielding management, problems of national defense, and an approaching election.

The child labor controversy revealed a division in Southern opinion—but a willingness of many to follow Wilson's lead. Nearly all the opposition to child labor legislation, based technically on constitutional scruples, came from the South. Yet it is clear from the final vote in 1916 that the opposition centered in the Southeastern textile states and that in the showdown a majority of Southern members in both houses supported Federal child labor legislation. Not only that, but two North Carolinians, Alexander J. McKelway, secretary of the National Child Labor Committee, and Josephus Daniels, wielded a significant influence in persuading Wilson that social justice progressives would regard the Child Labor Act as an important test of his humanitarian concerns.[50]

[49] Charles L. Dearing, *Federal Highway Policy* (Washington, 1941), 78–86, 262–65; "Senator Bankhead's Authorship of Bankhead Cotton Control Act [*sic*]" January 1, 1941, Typescript, and Montgomery *Advertiser*, April 1, 1944, clipping, in John H. Bankhead, Jr., Papers (Alabama Department of Archives); James F. Byrnes, *All in One Lifetime* (New York, 1958), 31–32. Numerous items on highway development are in John H. Bankhead, Sr., Papers (Alabama Department of Archives).

[50] In the final vote, Southern Representatives went 62 to 46 for the measure and Southern Senators, 11 to 10 for. Without the Border States of Kentucky and Oklahoma the figures would be 45 to 46 and 9 to 10 against. *Congressional Record*, 64 Cong., 1 Sess., 2035, 12313. Abrams, "Woodrow Wilson and the Southern Congressmen." *loc. cit.*, 431; Alexander J. McKelway to Woodrow Wilson, July 17, 1916,

So it happened that Wilsonian progressivism became associated with the names of Southerners: the Underwood-Simmons Tariff, the Glass-Owen Federal Reserve Act, the Clayton Anti-Trust Act, the Smith-Lever Act, the Smith-Hughes Act, the Bankhead-Shackelford Federal Highways Act, the Adamson Eight Hour Act, the Keating-Owen Child Labor Act. Confounding the prophets of rebellion, the senior Democrats placed at Wilson's disposal their endowments of experienced leadership, mature knowledge, and parliamentary skill. The outcome was the fulfillment, if not in the purest form at least in large measure, of the contemporary agrarian programs through tariff, banking, currency, credit, anti-trust, educational, and good-road legislation. In the process the more radical agrarians contributed to a gradual shift of the administration toward a more dynamic program of positive Federal action. If their program emphasized the class interest of farmers and succeeded largely because of Wilson's need to woo the Rooseveltian progressives in 1916, "the Southern progressives could claim as much credit as could several other major groups for the amazing metamorphosis in Democratic policy that occurred from 1913 to 1916." [51]

Equally as important as Southern influence on Wilson was his influence on Southern politics. The effect was to "Wilsonize" the Southern Democratic party much as it had been "Bryanized" before, but with the result of thinning down the reform urge by reliance upon a relatively conservative leadership in Congress. The militant tone of progressivism was tempered not alone by the adherence of belated Wilsonians; it "was blunted by the widespread faith in industrial progress." [52] The South, William E. Dodd suggested, "had got just enough of the new industrialism and the profits of big business to disturb the thinking of her

---

in McKelway Papers; Jonathan Daniels to Woodrow Wilson, July 17, 1916, in Woodrow Wilson Papers (Division of Manuscripts, Library of Congress); Elizabeth H. Davidson, *Child Labor Legislation in the Southern Textile States* (Chapel Hill, 1939), 249–71.

[51] Link, "The South and the 'New Freedom': An Interpretation," *loc. cit.*, 324. See also Theodore Saloutos, *Farmer Movements in the South*, 213–35.

[52] Dewey W. Grantham, Jr., "Prohibition and the Progressive Movement in the South" (Typescript in author's possession), 8.

leaders." [53] The middle-class leaders who gave progressivism its predominant tone had fought largely against monopoly and railroad practices that they thought inhibited economic development. They were not hostile to the factory and corporation as such; and facing the need for outside capital and the complexity of corporate regulation, they gradually turned their attention toward good government and public services in education, good roads, public health, and care of the handicapped. In their zeal for efficiency and the rationalization of state taxes and finances the progressives manifested important features of business development itself.

The anticorporation drive was further diluted by the cold, pure springs of prohibition. Given the moral disrepute of saloons, prohibitionists were able somehow to equate the "liquor traffic" with rural and progressive suspicion of the trusts and "special interests." When reform pressures mounted, prohibition offered an easy outlet. "In a peculiarly satisfying way," said one historian, "the growing agitation over the liquor question . . . absorbed the yearnings for reform and fulfillment of a people whose God had become Progress but whose basic ideas remained fundamentally conservative." [54]

Yet if for many Southerners prohibition became the sum of progressivism, it added strength in most states to other progressive causes and contributed probably more often to the victory than the defeat of progressive candidates. The major exception was Virginia, where the Anti-Saloon League allied itself to the Martin-Flood machine, and where in 1916 Methodist Bishop James Cannon "sat enthroned as the supreme ruler of Capitol Hill" in Richmond while the legislators approved the Mapp Act for state-wide prohibition.[55]

In at least three states alcohol became the chief factional issue dividing the Democratic party, one that almost completely dissolved all others and weakened the force of progressivism. In

[53] William E. Dodd, *Woodrow Wilson and His Work* (Garden City, N.Y., 1920), 112.

[54] Grantham, *The Democratic South*, 63.

[55] Virginius Dabney, *Dry Messiah: The Life of Bishop Cannon* (New York, 1949), 54–56, 98–102; Richard L. Watson, Jr. (ed.), *Bishop Cannon's Own Story: Life as I Have Seen It* (Durham, 1955), 126–27, 146–50, 162–63.

Texas the election of the wringing-wet conservative Governor Oscar B. Colquitt in 1910 left the progressives seemingly demoralized; yet Texas in 1912 sent to the Senate Morris Sheppard, soon to be the "Father of National Prohibition," a man who more than any other individual personified the union of prohibition and progressivism. Sheppard's acceptance speech in 1913 "bristled with the ideas of 'progressive Democracy,' " and at his death in 1941 he was one of the most advanced New Dealers in the Senate.[56] In 1910 bifactional division over prohibition so disrupted Tennessee's Democratic party as to give the state a two-term Republican governor, Ben W. Hooper, but also a season of moderate reform sponsored by independent Democrats and progressive Republicans in the legislature, and the progressive "boy Senator," Luke Lea, who in 1913 joined Hoke Smith in a bold if foredoomed rebellion against the seniority system in the upper house.[57] In 1914 the issues of railroad regulation and progressivism in Alabama yielded to campaigns that turned altogether on local option versus statewide prohibition. Despite the victories of local optionists Charles Henderson for governor and Oscar W. Underwood for senator, the Alabama legislature enacted statewide prohibition over a veto and carried through reforms in the primary election laws, education, and public health, the establishment of a public service commission, a drainage law, and tax revision.[58]

Elsewhere, if the movement had no such importance in determining factional alignments and dominating campaigns, it scored one victory after another. In 1915 South Carolina closed its dispensary system and permitted thereafter only the importation of a gallon of whisky a month, then reduced that to two quarts and in 1917 to one quart a month for "medicinal" purposes. Convivial Charleston found the action "beyond the bounds of reason" and

[56] Escal Franklin Duke, "The Political Career of Morris Sheppard, 1875–1941" (Ph.D. dissertation, University of Texas, 1958).

[57] Paul E. Isaac, *Prohibition and Politics; Turbulent Decades in Tennessee, 1885–1920* (Knoxville, 1965), 182–231; Woodward, *Origins of the New South,* 391–92; Grantham, "Southern Congressional Leaders and the New Freedom," 10–11, 39–40; Grantham, *Hoke Smith,* 239–41.

[58] Albert Burton Moore, *History of Alabama and Her People* (Chicago and New York, 1927), I, 1933–41; James Benson Sellers, *The Prohibition Movement in Alabama, 1702–1943* (Chapel Hill, 1943), 176–85.

19

"interfering with the enjoyment of life, liberty, and the pursuit of happiness." [59] Arkansas joined the prohibition states before the end of 1915. The action of Florida in 1918 and Kentucky in 1919 drove the saloon from the South, except for the exercise of local option in the French and Delta parishes of Louisiana.[60] For the better part of three decades prohibition and progressivism usually traveled the same road. Their paths did not diverge until well into the 1920's.

The complex fabric of Southern politics in the teens presented still another baffling pattern, the diverse threads of class division and hostility woven across the basic warp and woof of economic and moral issues. Ever since the farmers' movement of the 1890's had taught plebeian voters the power of their numbers, "redneck" revolts had erupted wherever artful leaders arose to exploit the frustrations of poverty and ignorance—the Southern firebrands, heirs to the tradition of Tom Watson, "Pitchfork Ben" Tillman, Cole Blease, and James K. Vardaman, all of whom remained on the scene in the teens. Skilled in a luxuriant and often vindictive oratory, salted with the rustic idiom, they flouted upper-class proprieties, appealed to narrow prejudices against the rich, the city folk, often against Catholics and Jews, usually against Negroes. They offered if nothing else a kind of catharsis and vicarious fulfillment for their followers. Arrayed against them were usually the "best people" of established family or of middle-class aspirations, the professional men and educators, who preferred to act with urbanity and decorum. It was a division that confused contemporaries and historians alike, for it was chiefly a difference of style. The only consistency was a cleavage between respectabil-

[59] Charleston *News and Courier*, February 21, 1916, and Charleston *Evening Post*, April 12, 1916, quoted in Robert Milburn Burts, "The Public Career of Richard I. Manning" (Ph.D. dissertation, Vanderbilt University, 1957), 286. See also *ibid.*, 234, 377–79. The dispensary had been on a county option basis since 1907.

[60] Peter H. Odegaard, *Pressure Politics: The Story of the Anti-Saloon League* (New York, 1928), 165; Charles Merz, *The Dry Decade* (Garden City, N.Y., 1931), 308. Even so, the only bone-dry states in the South before national prohibition were Georgia, Arkansas, and Oklahoma; the others had such loopholes as Mississippi's tolerance of home-made wine, Tennessee's of home-made whiskey, and South Caroline's "medicinal" quart a month. Merz, *Dry Decade*, 20–22; Daniel Jay Whitener, *Prohibition in North Carolina, 1715–1945* (Chapel Hill, 1945), 176.

ity and audacity rather than a fundamental division on program.[61]

In 1914 a curious alliance redeemed South Carolina from the four-year demoralization of Bleaseism. Coleman Livingstone Blease, "Our Coley," stood without peer as the classic example of the political mountebank, a man with a flair that won not only the rural plebeians but what the old master, Tillman, called "that damned factory class." His oratory, a contemporary said, was "that of Billy Sunday, headed in the opposite direction. . . . A receptive listener will leave the hall after his address with more intense hatreds, less faith in his fellowmen, decreased respect for law, a diminished veneration for the church and for moral ideals, and a greater ignorance of the real causes of conditions at which he might justly complain." [62] Opposing labor legislation, school attendance laws, and medical examinations for school children, openly advocating lynching, he dragged the state through four years of petty bickering and turbulence.[63]

In the statewide reaction against Blease even Tillman repudiated his successor. He reluctantly supported re-election of Senator Ellison D. "Cotton Ed" Smith over Blease and tacitly backed Richard I. Manning for governor against the Bleaseite John G. Richards. Manning also drew the support of middle-class progressives, the leading daily papers, and "Bourbon" respectables. A successful lawyer, planter, and businessman, cultivated and gracious, grandson of one governor and nephew of another, Manning belonged to one of the state's established families. But men of the old school who expected a return to quiescent days were soon disillusioned. "We are progressive Democrats," their candidate told the new legislature, "and we must have the courage to do

[61] Paul Lewinson, *Race, Class, and Party: A History of Negro Suffrage and White Politics in the South* (London and New York, 1932), 189, called the plebeian-respectable cleavage "perhaps the clearest and most consistent political division" in the South from 1900 to 1930.

[62] W. K. Tate, "After Blease—A New Program for South Carolina," in *Survey* (East Stroudsburg, Pa.), XXXIII (1914–1915), 577.

[63] Burts, "Public Career of Richard I. Manning," 166–67; Ernest McPherson Lander, *A History of South Carolina, 1865–1960* (Chapel Hill, 1960), 49–63; Daniel W. Hollis, *The University of South Carolina* (Columbia, 1951–1956), II, 248–62.

justly to each and every class of our citizens even if this requires legislation hitherto untried by us." [64]

Manning's four-year record formed an almost complete muster roll of progressive reforms. He revised the state's tax structure, equalized assessments, caught industrial plants that had previously escaped their share, increased revenues more than $65,000, and made possible a reduction in the levy. Common schools received increased appropriations, and in 1915 the first compulsory attendance law was passed, on a local-option basis. Labor legislation forbade payment in kind from company stores, required weekly pay checks from textile mills, established a sixty-hour week, a laborer's lien, a Board of Arbitration for labor disputes, and outlawed the labor of children under fourteen in textile mills. For farmers Manning undertook to improve markets and agricultural education, and unsuccessfully attempted to provide state loans for tenants to purchase their own land. He replaced Blease's appointee at the state hospital, established a state Board of Charities and Corrections, a highway commission, a school for the feeble-minded, and a girls' industrial school. In 1918 the state inaugurated a secret ballot for the Democratic primaries in all but the smaller rural communities. "Under his administration," Manning's biographer concluded, "the state received its strongest single, concentrated impetus in social and economic progress since the Civil War." [65] The impetus continued under his successor, R. A. Cooper, who raised school appropriations further, and moved on to establish statewide compulsory education and a budget system for state finances.[66]

Two years after Manning's election, Arkansas followed the Wilsonian example with its own scholar in politics. Charles H. Brough, a Johns Hopkins Ph.D. and former student of Wilson himself, resigned a professorship of economics and sociology at the state university to win election as governor in 1916.[67] In a state

---

[64] Tate, "After Blease—A New Program for South Carolina," *loc. cit.*, 577; James C. Derieux, "Crawling toward the Promised Land," in *Survey,* XLVIII (1922), 176.

[65] Burts, "Public Career of Richard I. Manning," 201–31, 275–86, 358–65, 385–88, 527–30.

[66] Derieux, "Crawling toward the Promised Land," *loc. cit.*, 179.

[67] Charles W. Crawford, "From Classroom to State Capitol: Charles H. Brough

that had experienced the volatile "one gallus" democracy of Jeff Davis, Brough admirably personified the respectability of progressivism. A spellbinder of the pompous school, a prominent Baptist layman, and a congenital joiner, Brough was also a leader in the good-roads movement and in the Southern Sociological Congress. He presided over an extensive program of fiscal reorganization, progressive reform, and the extension of state activities, similar in its major aspects to Manning's program.[68]

In 1918, Alabama's Lieutenant Governor Thomas E. Kilby, a wealthy Anniston steel manufacturer, candidate of the Anti-Saloon League, rode into the governor's office on a wave of enthusiasm for the Eighteenth Amendment. His victory revitalized Alabama progressivism, and Kilby proceeded methodically to redeem elaborate campaign pledges. Presented originally as a potential "business governor," he directed the establishment of a state budget system and the reorganization of the tax system to equalize assessments and tap new sources of revenue. His reforms included reorganization of the public school system and the highest appropriations for public education to that time, the establishment of a state welfare department, a reorganization of the prison system, construction of a new penitentiary, sizable increases in appropriations for public health, a workmen's compensation law, a $25,000,000 bond issue for good roads, and a program to develop the port of Mobile.[69]

The pervasive influence of the progressive urge was strikingly manifested in the rise of Mississippi's Theodore G. "The Man" Bilbo, the "Pride of Poplarville," erstwhile schoolteacher and

---

and the Campaign of 1916," in *Arkansas Historical Quarterly* (Fayetteville), XXI (1962), 213-30.

[68] David Y. Thomas, "Charles Hillman Brough," in Harris E. Starr (ed.), *Dictionary of American Biography* (New York, 1944), Supplement 1, XXI, 123-24; David Y. Thomas (ed.), *Arkansas and Its People: A History, 1541-1930* (New York, 1930), I, 290-94; Charles Hillman Brough Papers (University of Arkansas Library, Fayetteville). Roman J. Zorn, "Arkansas Manuscripts: The Collected Papers of Charles Hillman Brough and Harmon L. Remmel," in *Arkansas Historical Quarterly*, XII (1953), 278-82, gives a brief summary of Brough's career.

[69] Moore, *History of Alabama and Her People*, I, 950-54. Kilby's own, more detailed, summary of his accomplishments is in Alabama *House Journal*, 1923, I, 13-139. See also Mrs. L. B. Bush, "A Decade of Progress in Alabama," in *Social Forces*, II (1923-1924), 539-45; and Emily Owen, "The Career of Thomas E. Kilby in Local and State Politics" (M.A. thesis, University of Alabama, 1942).

Baptist exhorter, a man whose political career began under the cloud of attempted bribery and progressed through accusations of fornication, adultery, graft, and slander. William Alexander Percy, whose family enjoyed a status comparable to the Mannings' in South Carolina, called him "a slick little bastard," "a pert little monster, glib and shameless, with a sort of cunning common to criminals which passes for intelligence." [70] After Vardaman's departure for Washington in 1913, Bilbo rose rapidly to the leadership of the agrarian masses, excoriating alien corporations and the native aristocrats of the Delta. Elected lieutenant governor in 1911, he was chosen governor in 1915 after a bitter and scandalous quarrel with his predecessor, Earl Brewer. The voters, a hostile editor declared, had decided "that they would rather wallow in filth than walk on clean ground." [71]

But Bilbo was a progressive governor. His programs paralleled those of the ultra-respectables Manning, Brough, and Kilby, and marked the climax of the progressive era in Mississippi. One of his first goals was an end to the "anomalous, paradoxical and illogical tax system of eighty bodies regulating taxation." [72] A new tax commission, established over the opposition of Delta representatives who found state equalization "undemocratic," "Dangerous and revolutionary," raised assessments in eighteen counties, fourteen of them in the Delta. Valuations of railroads and other public service corporations rose $40,000,000. An authority on state finances later called Bilbo's tax equalization "the very cornerstone" of Mississippi's fiscal machinery. [73]

The extension of governmental functions for the first time gave Mississippi a state government beyond the legal forms. Bilbo's innovations included a highway commission, a pardon board, a board of bar examiners, state limestone crushing plants that

[70] William Alexander Percy, *Lanterns on the Levee: Recollections of a Planter's Son* (New York, 1941), 148. An alleged attempt to bribe Bilbo had been instrumental in the defeat of Percy's father, Le Roy Percy, by James K. Vardaman in a senatorial election in 1911.

[71] Fred Sullens in Jackson *Daily News*, August 8, 1915, quoted in Albert D. Kirwan, *Revolt of the Rednecks: Mississippi Politics, 1876–1925* (Lexington, Ky., 1951), 28. See also *ibid.*, 241–58.

[72] Bilbo's inaugural address in Mississippi *House Journal*, 1916, 170.

[73] *Ibid.*, 1240–42; Charles G. Hamilton, "Mississippi Politics in the Progressive Era, 1904–1920" (Ph.D. dissertation, Vanderbilt University, 1958), 316–18.

supplied farmers at cost, a state tuberculosis sanitarium, a reformatory for whites, antilobbying, blue sky, tick eradication, antivice, and uniform negotiable instrument laws, "bone dry" prohibition, the abolition of public hangings, the substitution of salaries for fees in county offices, compulsory school attendance (Mississippi in 1918 was the last state to adopt it), a fund to equalize school expenditures in the various counties, the extension of consolidated schools, and night schools for adult illiterates. In the four Bilbo years, according to the Federal commissioner of education, Mississippi made more educational progress than any other state—even though it remained near the bottom in all indices.[74] Bilbo's record would have been impressive for any state, and even his opponents acknowledged that "under his administration more forward-looking legislation was enacted than in any previous gubernatorial regime." [75] Even so, it was less than he recommended.[76]

Bilbo, however, was unique in this positive phase of progressivism. No other leader of the plebeian masses in the teens had either a program or a record to equal his. He had inherited Vardaman's following; and Tillman, now allied to the Charleston conservatives, was in ill health and died in 1918.[77] Tom Watson, on the other hand, remained the master of the rural masses in Georgia and practically dictated the Democratic nominees for governor from 1906 through 1920, but his agrarian radicalism was overshadowed by a strange alteration of character that sent him off into scurrilous attacks on minorities.[78] In Florida, Sidney J. Catts, Baptist minister and insurance salesman, a "strange mixture of idealism and demagogy," rose suddenly from the obscurity of De-Funiak Springs to the governorship in 1916 on a tidal wave of pro-

[74] Hamilton, "Mississippi Politics in the Progressive Era," 359. See also Wallace Buttrick, "Pearl River, an Educational Idea in Action," in *Outlook* (New York), CXXVIII (1921), 655–57.

[75] Reinhard H. Luthin, *American Demagogues: Twentieth Century* (Boston, 1954), 53; Kirwan, *Revolt of the Rednecks*, 259–72; Hamilton, "Mississippi Politics in the Progressive Era," 311–59.

[76] Unidentified clipping, in W. D. Robinson Scrapbook (Southern Historical Collection, University of North Carolina).

[77] Francis B. Simkins, *Pitchfork Ben Tillman: South Carolinian* (Baton Rouge, 1944), 455–56, 497–500, 502, 506–507, 524–27, 545–46.

[78] C. Vann Woodward, *Tom Watson: Agrarian Rebel* (New York, 1938), 370–450.

hibition and anti-Catholic prejudice like that unleashed by Watson in the neighboring state. Almost as suddenly, Catts subsided into obscurity again after 1920, having forever disrupted the old fight of corporation and anticorporation factions that dominated Florida politics in the previous decade.[79]

In the Southwest, where society and the economy were "less bound by concepts of tradition and status," [80] rural grievances for a season bred a program of agrarian socialism, only to give way finally to the cult of personality that haunted plebeian politics. As early as 1909 Socialist party organizers among Oklahoma tenant farmers produced a Renters' Union in McLain County. A similar organization, started at Waco, Texas, in 1911, merged with the Oklahoma group two years later as the Land League. The rise of the renters' unions paralleled that of other groups: the Farmer's Protective Association and two ultra-radical groups in eastern Oklahoma and western Arkansas: the Working Class Union and the strangely named Jones Family, both touched by syndicalist doctrines.[81]

Mobilizing the rural discontent through these organizations, speaking at country schoolhouses and churches, denouncing the "electric light cities," organizing summer encampments, pursuing

[79] John Richard Deal, "Sidney Johnston Catts, Stormy Petrel of Florida Politics" (M.A. thesis, University of Florida, 1949), quotation from p. 222; William T. Cash, *History of the Democratic Party in Florida* (Tallahassee, 1936), 122–35. Catts was unique in that he won election as an Independent and Prohibition Party nominee after losing the Democratic nomination in a disputed primary.

[80] Stuart M. Jamieson, *Labor Unionism in American Agriculture* (Washington, 1945), 261.

[81] *Ibid.*, 256, 262; Carey McWilliams, *Ill Fares the Land: Migrants and Migratory Labor in the United States* (Boston, 1942), 211–12, 217–18; Oscar Ameringer, *If You Don't Weaken: The Autobiography of Oscar Ameringer* (New York, 1940), 228–32, 236–37, 256–59, 271–74; Ralph W. Steen, *Twentieth Century Texas: An Economic and Social History* (Austin, 1942), 47–53; Benjamin H. Hibbard, "Tenancy in the Southern States," in *Quarterly Journal of Economics* (Cambridge, Mass.), XXVII (1912–1913), 494–95. In 1915 a Federal investigation of tenancy conditions in the Southwest produced over three hundred pages of testimony in five days of hearings, which detailed stories of annual moves, frugal diets, efforts to economize, and struggles to rear children. It received little public attention then or later. "The Land Question in the Southwest," in *Industrial Relations*, Final Report and Testimony Submitted to Congress by the Commission on Industrial Relations (Washington, 1916), IX, 8949–9056; X, 9057–9290. See also Charles W. Holman, "The Tenant Farmer, Country Brother of the Casual Worker," in *Survey*, XXXIV (1915), 62.

the oldtime evolutionary methods of unrelenting agitation and education, publishing newspapers under such fiery editors as Oscar Ameringer, Patrick Nagle, and H. G. Milner in Oklahoma, and Tom Hickey in Texas, the Socialists seemed by the teens on the way to challenging the Democratic hegemony.[82] Texas, a Hamilton County judge complained, was being "turned from a state of patriotic home owners into a state of rebellious discontented tenants"; and Tom Hickey's *Rebel Farmer* hinted darkly that Mexico's revolution might spread north of the Rio Grande.[83]

Continued agitation soon made tenancy an important political issue for the first time in the South, despite efforts of the daily press to play it down. But the Socialists were not destined to reap the harvest. In Texas a formidable figure arose in the person of James E. Ferguson to seize upon the issue, make himself Democratic governor in 1914, and launch a colorful political career. A banker in Temple, he posed first as the businessman's candidate, held aloof from the prohibition issue that had dominated previous Democratic primaries, and ran largely on a rural appeal. With a program of fixing tenant rentals at not more than one third of the grain and one fourth of the cotton produced, improved schools, penitentiary reform, and state-controlled warehouses, "Farmer Jim" avoided the cities for the countryside and inundated his progressive-prohibitionist opponent, Thomas H. Ball, under a deluge of billingsgate. Ball, he charged, belonged to the elite Houston club "with its pool tables and billiard tables, bar, yellow niggers with white aprons," and thereby derived "a profit from the sale of whiskey."[84]

[82] Ameringer, *If You Don't Weaken*, 227–80; David A. Shannon, *The Socialist Party of America: A History* (New York, 1955), 34–36, 106; James R. Scales, "Political History of Oklahoma, 1907–1949" (Ph.D. dissertation, University of Oklahoma, 1949), 148–52, 174. An examination of Professor Gilbert C. Fite's notes on Oklahoma socialism was useful in gaining an impression of the scope and character of the movement.

[83] *The Rebel Farmer*, January 27, 1912, February 28, 1914, both cited in James A. Tinsley, "The Progressive Movement in Texas" (Ph.D. dissertation, University of Wisconsin, 1954), 171–72.

[84] Quoted in Tinsley, "Progressive Movement in Texas," 313. On the campaign see also *ibid.*, 305–13; Seth S. McKay, *Texas Politics, 1906–1944, with Special Reference to the German Counties* (Lubbock, Tex., 1952), 54–59; and Rupert N. Richardson, *Texas: The Lone Star State* (2nd ed., Englewood Cliffs, N. J., 1958), 289–90.

Things went smoothly enough during Ferguson's first term. Most of his program went through, but the tenant law proved unenforceable and was eventually declared unconstitutional. Nevertheless, he easily won re-election in 1916 only to be removed from office the following year. Piqued by the state university officials' failure to show a seemly deference, Ferguson in 1917 vetoed the institution's appropriation, whereupon friends of the university opened investigations into gubernatorial irregularities. Impeached on twenty-one articles and convicted on ten, he was not only removed but banned from holding office again on charges of appropriating state funds to his own use, illegally depositing state funds in his own bank, and securing sizeable "loans" from the brewing interests, among other things. Texas progressivism, already disrupted by prohibition—and one might add socialism—"was dealt its death blow by demagoguery." [85]

In Oklahoma, on the other hand, the Socialists in 1910 had more paid-up members than any other state. By 1913 they had 342 locals, and during 1914 the "red card membership" grew to nearly 10,000. Neglected by the party leaders at the time and historians of the movement since, they represented an indigenous growth, akin to populism, which was based not upon an industrial proletariat but chiefly upon the submerged tenants in the eastern cotton counties south of the Canadian River, the most "southern" part of the state.[86] "Socialism as we find it in this state," said the *Daily Oklahoman*, "is more of a protest against tenantry and money sharks than a demand for collectivism. . . . [The struggling tenant farmer] only knows that something is wrong, radically wrong, with a system which condemns him to a life of toil and grinding poverty and he expresses his contempt for the same by affiliating with a party which holds out a vain hope." [87]

[85] Tinsley, "Progressive Movement in Texas," 314; McKay, *Texas Politics*, 60–61, 75; Richardson, *Texas: The Lone Star State*, 290–93; John A. Lomax, "Governor Ferguson and the University of Texas," in *Southwest Review* (Dallas), XVIII (1942–1943), 11–29; J. Evetts Haley, *George W. Littlefield, Texan* (Norman, Okla., 1943), 224–50.

[86] Shannon, *Socialist Party of America*, 34–36; Oklahoma City *Social Democrat*, December 31, 1913; H. M. Sinclair, "The Real Democracy of the Socialist Party," in *Harlow's Weekly* (Oklahoma City), V (April 25, 1914), 21–22, 63; Scales, "Political History of Oklahoma," 174.

[87] Oklahoma City *Daily Oklahoman*, quoted (without date) in *Harlow's Weekly*, IX (November 20, 1915), 385.

In their 1914 platform Oklahoma's Socialists set forth the major principles of Debs socialism but featured especially a "Renters' and Farmers' program" for state aid to tenants and co-operatives, state banks, warehouses, and grain elevators, and other forms of assistance to farmers. Collapse of the cotton market in 1914 added to the discontent, and a full state ticket polled over fifty thousand votes. Two years later, despite Wilson's appeal to the advanced progressive and peace elements, the Socialists ran up a vote of 42,262 for their Presidential candidate.[88] But soon, in the excitement of World War I, they acquired a stigma of disloyalty they could not cast off. Finally, in Oklahoma as in Texas, the remnants of their strength were drawn off in 1923 by a popular leader, Jack Walton, whose promise proved as illusory as Ferguson's.

Another deviant group, the Bull Moose Progressives up the bayous of Louisiana, stood in sharp contrast to the tenant-labor radicals of the Southwest. Led by John M. Parker, Jr., a New Orleans cotton broker, they based their appeal chiefly upon the dissatisfaction of sugar growers with Democratic tariff reductions. In 1910 Parker took an active part in the election of an antimachine governor and in 1912 went over to the support of his personal friend, Theodore Roosevelt. When the Democrats came into power, "violating the well known Democratic traditions, that a revenue tax should be kept on sugar," Parker wrote in 1914 that he had determined "forever to put Democracy behind me." The Louisiana Progressives, he said, stood for three things: reasonable tariff protection for farmers, laborers, and manufacturers; absolute Federal control of the Mississippi River and its tributaries; and white supremacy—the Progressive party, he claimed, was "the first White Man's Party ever inaugurated in the South." [89]

Upholding this delimited version of Roosevelt's New Nationalism, the party in 1914 and 1916 elected the South's only third-

[88] Sinclair, "Real Democracy of the Socialist Party," *loc. cit.*, 63; Shannon, *Socialist Party of America*, 34; Rand School of Social Science, *American Labor Year Book, 1917–1918* (New York, 1918), 336–38.

[89] Daniel D. Moore, "A Bull Moose Democrat," in *World's Work* (New York), XLIII (1921–1922), 23–25; John M. Parker, Jr., to James Beary, January 27, 1914, and Parker to M. E. Norman, August 14, 1913, in John M. Parker Papers (Southern Historical Collection, University of North Carolina). See also Parker to George W. Perkins, October 11, 1913, in John M. Parker Papers (Department of Archives, Louisiana State University, Baton Rouge).

party Congressman, Whitmell P. Martin of Thibodeaux, "as a Progressive protectionist." [90] Early in 1916 Parker ran as the Progressive candidate for governor on a platform that included condemnation of bosses, abolition of unnecessary offices, the short ballot, improvement of public roads, and an early constitutional convention. Despite the hopeless task of overcoming traditional Democratic strength and insidious charges that the "Progressive party is the sickly, dying wake of the Pickaninny Republican party," Parker carried eighteen parishes, three wards in New Orleans, and ran up 48,068 votes against 80,801 for Ruffin G. Pleasant.[91] The showing was so spectacular that the Progressives gave Parker their nomination for vice president later in the year. After Roosevelt declined to run, however, Parker threw his support to Woodrow Wilson although the Progressives in the Third District resolved that the re-election of Wilson "would mean the continued enforcement of the free trade theories of the Underwood bill." [92] Within the next two years the Party disintegrated; but Whitmell P. Martin won re-election as a Democrat in 1918, and Parker went on in 1920 to win the Democratic nomination for governor.

While the planter-business and tenant-labor variations on the progressive theme were minority deviations, they pointed up the wide range of program and support that came within the scope of the reform spirit. North Carolina perhaps best illustrated the tendency for even conservative elements to fall under the progressive spell. The drive for reform there seemed to flag after 1907 until it experienced a revival under the administration of Governor Locke Craig, a "machine" candidate supported by the organization of Senator Simmons. One of Craig's most insistent demands

[90] Whitmell P. Martin to John R. Mann, February 3, 1915, in Parker Papers (University of North Carolina). Martin served until 1929, but after 1918 as a Democrat. Elting E. Morison (ed.), *The Letters of Theodore Roosevelt* (Cambridge, Mass., 1954), VIII, 1077 n.

[91] John M. Parker to George W. Perkins, April 24, 1916, and "Extract from Overton's Speech of April 3, 1915," mimeographed, in Parker Papers (University of North Carolina); Benjamin Spencer Phillips, "The Administration of Governor Parker" (M.A. thesis, Louisiana State University, 1933), 12–17.

[92] New Orleans *Times-Picayune*, October 24, 1916, p. 3; Morison (ed.), *Letters of Theodore Roosevelt*, VIII, 1077, 1080 n.

was further action against freight-rate discriminations, which the 1913 legislature undertook together with a series of other progressive measures: ratification of the Seventeenth Amendment, a new corrupt practices act, stricter antitrust laws, extension of the Corporation Commission's authority to include electric power and gas companies, expansion of employer liability for railroad workers, prohibition of night labor in factories for children under sixteen (though without provision for inspection), reforms in the judiciary, and state approval of a six-month public school term.[93] If, despite vigorous efforts by the Farmers' Union, Clarence Poe of the *Progressive Farmer,* Josephus Daniels, Josiah Bailey, Walter Clark, and other progressive leaders, the reform movement subsided in the legislative session of 1915, it was to surge forward again under Governors Thomas W. Bickett and Cameron E. Morrison after World War I in vigorous state action for highways, schools, and public welfare.[94]

In every Southern state new responsbilities were being assumed in the Wilson years. "Oh, the South is looking up!" a reporter exclaimed after traversing the region in 1916. "There are economic and social and even political movements in parts of it that amount to a spiritual renaissance."[95] Whatever poetic license that statement may have abused, one thing was certain: that by 1920 new responsibilities of government had become a familiar part of the political landscape, and if state services lagged somewhat in the South for want of taxable wealth, they did not lag for want of widespread public support.[96] If militant progressivism had been diluted by the adherence of belated Wilsonians, by the need for capital, by chasing after the elusive goal of prohibition, and by plebeian-respectable divisions, it had conquered the old dictum that that government is best which governs least, whatever political rhetoric might be heard to the contrary, and left the more ex-

[93] Joseph F. Steelman, "The Progressive Era in North Carolina, 1884–1917" (Ph.D. dissertation, University of North Carolina, 1955), 363–64, 555–62, 715.

[94] *Ibid.,* 378–80, 386, 394.

[95] Frederick W. Davenport, "The Pre-Nomination Campaign: The Southern Renaissance," in *Outlook,* CXII (1916), 430.

[96] For an excellent account of the impact of progressivism on a Southern city, see William D. Miller, *Memphis during the Progressive Era, 1900–1917* (Memphis and Madison, Wis., 1957).

treme doctrines of limited government as dead as William Lowndes Yancey and Robert Barnwell Rhett.

Progressivism, an amalgam of agrarian radicalism, business regulation, good government, and urban social justice reforms, became in the end a movement for positive government. Out of two decades of progressive ferment (three, if the populists be counted) the great fundamental residue of the progressive era in Southern government was the firm establishment and general acceptance of the public service concept of the state. In this sense, progressivism had become the fashion.

CHAPTER II

WORLD WAR I:
SOUTHERN HORIZONS EXPAND

WHEN the thunderbolt of war struck Europe in
August, 1914, it came to most Americans "like lightning out of a clear sky." [1] Across the South its reverberations shattered a midsummer's dream of comfort and security.
For a decade the cotton belt had enjoyed a happy conjunction of
rising production and rising prices. On the eve of war, cotton
fetched thirteen cents a pound; and a bumper crop of more than
sixteen million bales, the largest yet known, was being laid by to
ripen.[2] Suddenly, instead of prosperity, the cotton belt faced
desolation.

Whatever feelings of shock or sympathy Southerners might have
harbored, their immediate concern was the disruption of export
markets. On August 3 the major cotton exchanges failed to open.
"In New Orleans and in Memphis and in Galveston people are
losing their heads," John Sharp Williams told the Senate the next
day. "Cotton has gone off $10 a bale." [3] For three months the ex-
changes remained closed; and farmers, with no reliable barometer
of prices, were left at the mercy of spot buyers offering eight cents
or less, even below five cents at some interior points. Some found
their crop unmarketable at any price, hauled it to town and then

[1] R. N. Page to Walter Hines Page, November 12, 1914, quoted in Arthur S. Link,
Wilson: The Struggle for Neutrality (Princeton, 1960), 7. The writer was a Congressman from North Carolina and the recipient his brother, the United States
Ambassador in London.
[2] U.S. Bureau of the Census, *Historical Statistics of the United States, Colonial
Times to 1957* (Washington, 1960), 301, columns K-302 and K-303.
[3] *Congressional Record*, 63 Cong., 2 Sess., 13220.

back home again.[4] The price collapse destroyed about half the value of the crop, a loss of some $500,000,000, which dragged down both the growers and the businessmen who serviced the cotton trade.

"The South was as surprised and taken as unaware of conditions which we are now facing," a Georgia Congressman said, "as was the world over the outbreak of the most disastrous war in history."[5] The response of agricultural leaders was to bring forth again the panaceas that reappeared with every market crisis, most of them compounded from familiar prescriptions: either more adequate credit plus storage while the farmer waited for better prices, or crop limitation and diversification. None of the ideas had much effect, but the agitation gave renewed impetus to one hopeful movement, a Farmers' Union program for state aid to cotton warehouses. In Texas the movement reached quick fruition in a special legislative session during August, with legislation for temporary state lease of emergency storage space and a more permanent provision for a system of state-incorporated warehouses. South Carolina soon afterward enacted a similar law.[6] In Alabama Senator Bankhead unsuccessfully proposed state warehouses with credits of $40,000,000 to enable farmers to hold the crop. The emergency, he said, left "no time for abstract discussion of paternalism and other such doctrines of government."[7] Atlanta's Coca-Cola millionaire Asa G. Candler personally offered loans at six cents and threw up an enormous warehouse to provide storage for a quarter-million bales. The warehouse idea, said the Lyons, Georgia, *Progress,* would revolutionize marketing and "finally do away

[4] Boyle, *Cotton and the New Orleans Cotton Exchange,* 127–31; *The Oklahoma Farmer-Stockman* (Oklahoma City), XXVII (September 10, 1914), 3.

[5] Dudley M. Hughes, in *Congressional Record,* 63 Cong., 2 Sess., Appendix, 1263.

[6] Tinsley, "Progressive Movement in Texas," 153–58; George P. Huckaby, "Oscar Branch Colquitt: A Political Biography" (Ph.D. dissertation, University of Texas, 1946), 407–408; Address to the Legislature, August 24, 1914, in Oscar B. Colquitt Papers (University of Texas Library, Austin); Steen, *Twentieth Century Texas,* 59–60; John L. McLaurin, "How South Carolina Is Warehousing Cotton," in *Manufacturers' Record* (Baltimore), LXVIII (July 22, 1915), 38. See also *Progressive Farmer* (Raleigh), XXXII (1917), 777; XXXVI (1921), 262.

[7] John H. Bankhead to the People of Alabama, October 3, 1914, and Birmingham *Age-Herald,* October 5, 1914, clipping, in John H. Bankhead, Sr., Papers.

with the ruinous system of selling the entire crop at harvest time for what it will bring on a glutted market."[8] By 1919 Louisiana, Arkansas, Georgia, and North Carolina also had state systems, but the movement had little if any immediate effect upon the market.[9]

Other formulas proved even less effective. One of the more futile was a Farmers' Union effort to encourage the use of cotton sacks and other products in place of jute and linen. The daughters of Postmaster General Burleson, Senator Hoke Smith, and Speaker Champ Clark agreed to wear cotton gowns only.[10] In Texas and nearby states a movement developed for the acquisition of a steamship to carry cotton to Europe; the effort finally failed in 1916.[11] By October, 1914, there had sprung up a spontaneous nationwide "buy a bale" movement, which enlisted the aid of citizens in "baling out the South" by purchasing cotton. New York City erupted with signs that invited people to "Buy a Bale of Cotton" and "Help the South." Gimbel Brothers offered ten thousand bales at ten cents a pound, apparently the first time a department store ever sold raw cotton.[12] A movement for limitation or even elimination of the 1915 crop won strong support, especially in South Carolina and Texas, but failed when several Southern governors expressed a preference for a national law and Wilson rejected the idea. Three thousand bank presidents pledged financial

[8] Charles H. Candler, *Asa Griggs Candler* (Emory University, Ga., 1950) , 308–14.

[9] McLaurin, "How South Carolina Is Warehousing Cotton," *loc. cit.*, 38; *Progressive Farmer*, XXXIV (1919) , 513.

[10] Reuben Dean Bowen, mimeographed letter, October 19, 1914; Bowen to Horace W. Vaughan, James Young, Sam Rayburn, and Jack Beall, October 20, 1914; Bowen to Josephus Daniels, November 13, 1914; Bowen to Woodrow Wilson, November 12, 1914; Bowen to Editor of the New York *Times*, November 14, 1914, in Reuben Dean Bowen Papers (Manuscripts Department, Duke University) ; Saloutos, *Farmer Movements in the South*, 241–42.

[11] Reuben Dean Bowen to William Gibbs McAdoo, December 29, 1914; Bowen telegram to McAdoo, January 27, 1915; Bowen to Morris Sheppard, December 27, 1914; Sheppard to Bowen, January 26, 1915, in Bowen Papers; Saloutos, *Farmer Movements in the South*, 244–45.

[12] "Buy a Bale of Cotton," in *Literary Digest* (New York) , XLIX (1914) , 669; *Manufacturers' Record*, LXVI (October 22, 1914) , 42; (October 8, 1914) , 41, 44; (November 19, 1914) , 45; (December 3, 1914) , 50, 53; Saloutos, *Farmer Movements in the South*, 242; Burts, "Public Career of Richard I. Manning," 190–91.

support to those who would reduce acreage, but as in similar efforts before and after, crop limitation on a voluntary basis was impossible.[13]

The chief hope for effective relief lay in Federal action, but the efforts of agrarians in that direction set them once again at odds with the administration.[14] A conference of Southern farm leaders, businessmen, and politicians gathered in Washington on August 24–25 to hear proposals for currency inflation and a bold new plan for "valorization" of cotton, or government purchase at a set price; but Treasury Secretary McAdoo recoiled from such "perfectly wild and ridiculous schemes." He suggested instead a program to encourage short-term credits by issuing emergency national bank note currency to Southern banks. It was tried but proved inadequate. Meanwhile, various schemes stirred Congress, but administration opposition to "special privilege" legislation prevented the passage of any proposal for relief. Before Congress adjourned in October, Hoke Smith led a filibuster that prolonged the Senate session for two days, but to no avail. He and his associates, the New York *Times* pontificated, were "determined to hurl back the foul imputation that the Democratic Party has at last become a sane, coherent, and orderly organization." [15]

The administration, however, did have a program. It shrank from "radical" experiments but set forth one drastic measure, written by McAdoo, for a government fleet of merchant ships to assure continued exports. The measure evoked little enthusiasm among farmers seeking immediate relief and was defeated by a bipartisan opposition of conservatives. Another proposal, prepared by Agriculture Secretary Houston and introduced by Representative Lever of South Carolina, the Cotton Warehouse Act, was

[13] Wade Stackhouse to Reuben Dean Bowen, September 14 and October 17, 1914; and Bowen to Charles St. Clair, September 14, 1914, in Bowen Papers; Saloutos, *Farmer Movements in the South*, 241.

[14] The following account of the cotton crisis leans heavily upon Link, *Wilson: The Struggle for Neutrality*, 91–102, 598–616, and Arthur S. Link, "The Cotton Crisis, the South, and Anglo-American Diplomacy, 1914–1915," in J. Carlyle Sitterson (ed.), *Studies in Southern History in Memory of Albert Ray Newsome, 1894–1951* (Chapel Hill, 1957), 122–38. See also Saloutos, *Farmer Movements in the South*, 238–48; W. P. G. Harding, *The Formative Period of the Federal Reserve System* (Boston and New York, 1925), 19–24; and Grantham, *Hoke Smith*, 277–91.

[15] New York *Times*, October 24, 1914.

passed a few days before adjournment. The only other action of the administration was to support the plan of Festus J. Wade, a St. Louis banker, for a private loan fund of $135,000,000 subscribed mostly by Northern and Middle Western banks; but only seven loans ultimately were made, for a total of $28,000. The cotton distress eased only as renewed British purchases began to stabilize the market. On November 16 the New York and New Orleans cotton exchanges reopened at around 7½ cents and gradually climbed to about 9 cents where they remained from March to August, 1915. After that they rose steadily to much higher wartime and postwar peaks.

The worst was over, but the crisis had not entirely passed. In February, 1915, Germany commenced its submarine blockade of Britain and the British responded with a complete blockade of Germany. They discreetly omitted cotton from their contraband list, but excluded it from German ports all the same. Seizures began in March and the apprehension of the cotton belt aroused renewed panic. On May 22 Senator Hoke Smith issued a warning that unless the blockade ended "the exportation of munitions of war will be stopped, and the action of Congress may go much further." A. Frank Lever wrote the President after a conference of South Carolina farm leaders "that unless some assurance for the future can be given . . . the counsel of wise, conservative leaders will be swept aside by an uncontrollable hysteria such as must develop in men who find themselves facing disaster." During the summer of 1915, John Sharp Williams declared, every politician in the South was forced to be anti-British—even in the face of public revulsion against German U-boat activity.

The possibility of a Southern coalition with pro-German and neutralist elements was not lost on the British. As they moved to strengthen their blockade, therefore, they also moved to mollify the cotton belt. A decision finally to put cotton on the contraband list as an important ingredient of explosives prompted careful planning in conferences with the American government. The British timed the announcement, in August, to coincide with massive British purchases on the New York and Liverpool cotton exchanges. Secretary McAdoo announced that the treasury was ready to deposit $30,000,000 in Southern banks, and the Federal Reserve

Board shortly thereafter announced a preferential rediscount rate for loans on agricultural commodities. The British carried out a promise to peg the market at ten cents, and wartime demands soon carried it higher. The British announcement brought the expected flurry of denunciations. "The cotton producers of North Carolina and the entire South," declared the Greensboro *Daily News*, " . . . want the Administration to be as emphatic in dealing with England on this score as it has been in dealing with Germany on others." [16] But the excitement faded, and the anti-British agitation receded.

All through that year of discontent in the cotton belt larger events moved in another direction as Wilson evolved his basic policies of response to the war. Two crucial decisions unfolded by the end of the summer of 1915 with respect to submarine warfare and preparedness. From the beginning the administration had objected to the departure from the traditional rules of search and seizure in submarine warfare. It strongly reaffirmed that position after the sinking of the *Lusitania* in May, 1915—so strongly that Secretary of State Bryan resigned in protest. After the *Lusitania* incident there was more than a dim premonition of American involvement in the war and the quarrels over neutral commerce contributed to a growing demand for a stronger army and navy. During 1915 Wilson decided for increased preparedness and although he did not formally announce his intentions until November 4, developing plans were public knowledge. As the Wilson policies unfolded they evoked widely divergent responses from Southerners; but on foreign policy, as on domestic policy, a substantial majority of Southern Congressmen continued to sustain the President.

From the beginning of the war Southern opinion was broadly sympathetic to the Allied cause, if generally committed to nonintervention. Despite the cotton crisis, a national survey of editors in November, 1914, indicated a stronger disposition toward the Allies in the South than in any other region. Out of 103 Southern editors who responded, 47 described themselves as pro-Ally and 71 found their communities predominantly pro-Ally. Unlike the

[16] Greensboro *Daily News*, August 27, 1915, quoted in Alex Mathews Arnett, *Claude Kitchin and the Wilson War Policies* (Boston, 1937), 142.

Midwest, the South had few pockets of German-American population, and only 5 editors and 4 communities showed up as pro-German.[17] The preponderant heritage of British ancestry and culture in the white South predisposed this region more than any other to the British side, but opinion was influenced also by approval of British democracy and a sense of outrage at the German invasion of Belgium and, later, the submarine warfare. John Sharp Williams had been offended by the Junker spirit when he was a student in Germany and became persuaded early in the war that the "Prussian-Junkerthum" would not rest "until it has asserted Germanic supremacy throughout the world." [18] The *Progressive Farmer* warned its readers against letting the cotton crisis crowd out attention to German atrocities, and in the very midst of the cotton frenzy a North Carolinian asked, "Is not Germany with her cynical disregard of the rights of others going to force us into war anyway? I know that many who are talking a great deal, it would seem in the interest of Germany, are not representing a lot of us in the South." [19] In Augusta, Georgia, a Baptist minister asked, "Is cotton of so great a value that for it we will sacrifice our manhood, our independence and our moral poise? I am profoundly convinced that the price of cotton is a fundamental moral question, and by it God is testing the souls of our people." [20]

By and large the newspapers of the region became anti-German and pro-preparedness. On September 3, 1914, Marse Henry Watterson nailed to the masthead of the Louisville *Courier-Journal* the phrase "To Hell with the Hohenzollerns and Hapsburgs," and kept it there through the war.[21] In Memphis the *Commercial Appeal* adopted a consistent pro-Ally tone. During the fall of 1915

[17] "American Sympathies in the War," in *Literary Digest*, XLIX (1914), 939–41, 974–78. Among 367 replies, 103 were from the South.

[18] John Sharp Williams to John Ross, January 5, 1915, quoted in George C. Osborn, *John Sharp Williams, Planter Statesman of the Deep South* (Baton Rouge, 1943), 255.

[19] James M. Norfleet to "Editor Herald," August 24, 1915, in Claude Kitchin Papers (Southern Historical Collection, University of North Carolina), cites *Progressive Farmer* of "recent date."

[20] Rev. Dr. M. Ashby Jones, quoted in *Manufacturers' Record*, LXVII (August 5, 1915), 45.

[21] Joseph F. Wall, *Henry Watterson: Reconstructed Rebel* (New York, 1956), 299.

the editor, C. P. J. Mooney, sponsored a preparedness parade in which twenty thousand men took an hour and eight minutes to pass.[22] The Baltimore *Manufacturers' Record* found it incredible that "cotton demagogues" could be guilty of "such a piece of folly" as to arouse antagonism against the British. "They are fighting the battle of this country and of every other country against a militarism the success of which would throw civilization back for 100 years." [23] Virginia and North Carolina newspapers for the most part supported preparedness.[24] Georgia papers, with the outstanding exception of Hearst's Atlanta *Georgian,* sided with the Allies.[25] Even the Atlanta *Journal,* long a Hoke Smith organ, broke with the Senator on his anti-British crusade. In the "life and death struggle between democratic government and Prussian autocracy," the *Journal* chose "English liberty." [26] The Georgia legislature resolved in favor of the preparedness program, and when Representative Schley Howard went to Atlanta to speak against preparedness, he heard so many shouts at every mention of Wilson's name that he pocketed his speech and proceeded to eulogize the President.[27] In May, 1916, a survey of Southern businessmen showed them to believe, by a margin of 265 to 15, that public sentiment approved preparedness.[28]

Other manifestations, however, revealed a widely prevalent rural-progressive opposition to war and militarism like that in many parts of the West. "I have seen the horrors and sufferings of battle," a Confederate veteran wrote in 1915, "and I have seen something less obvious, but more lasting and pernicious in its evil effects. . . . My chief objection to militarism is that . . . it per-

---

[22] Miller, *Memphis during the Progressive Era,* 188.

[23] *Manufacturers' Record,* LXVIII (July 9, 1915), 33. See also *ibid.,* LXVII (June 17, 1915), 39; LXVIII (July 15, 1915), 38–39; (November 11, 1915), 39.

[24] Arthur Kyle Davis (ed.), *Virginia War Letters, Diaries, and Editorials,* in *Publications of the Virginia War History Commission,* Source Vol. III (Richmond, 1925), xxiv–xxx and *passim;* Arnett, *Claude Kitchin and the Wilson War Policies,* 66.

[25] Louis T. Griffith and John E. Talmadge, *Georgia Journalism, 1763–1950* (Athens, Ga., 1951), 142.

[26] Grantham, *Hoke Smith,* 287.

[27] John Bach McMaster, *The United States in the World War* (New York, 1918), I, 233; Byrnes, *All in One Lifetime,* 35–36.

[28] *Outlook,* CXIII (1916), 226–27.

verts the judgment of otherwise good and reasonable men, and dulls their sensibility to the sufferings and rights of others, and encourages the spirit of aggression and conquest." [29]

A deep suspicion permeated the rural South that preparedness was a scheme for the profit of munitions makers and financial interests. As early as the spring of 1915 a Texas Farmers' Union leader protested the developing war prosperity for the "powder trust, the manufacturers of high explosives, the steel trust" while cotton farmers had to sell at thirty dollars a bale.[30] Later in the year the district unions of the Texas Farmers' Union petitioned their members of Congress to vote against preparedness: "We cannot understand how sensible men urge 'Preparedness' as a prevention of war when all the facts of history contradict them." [31] From Mobile a timber cruiser wrote Senator Bankhead that in his travels through Alabama, Mississippi, and Arkansas, he had found "a great majority of the people opposed to the great military propaganda that is now exciting this country." [32] To a preparedness advocate Bankhead wrote: "this propaganda of unreasonable and unnecessary preparedness has its origin with the manufacturers of munition and war supplies that are being exported to Europe at immense profits." Fearing an early end of the war, "they must have a home market." [33] It was "the lesson of all history," said Martin Dies, Sr., of Texas, "that the spirit of liberty, equality, and free government could not live in the military atmosphere." He warned against war scares, sensational stories in the press, inflammatory motion pictures, and "the Teddy Roosevelts, who are

[29] B. F. Hall to Claude Kitchin, November 2, 1915, in Kitchin Papers. In 1928 a Mississippi folklorist wrote, "I have never heard the cynical epithet 'rich man's war and poor man's fight' applied to the Civil War in a public speech, nor have I seen it in a popular history, but I have heard it many times from the lips of ex-Confederate soldiers." Arthur Palmer Hudson, *Specimens of Mississippi Folklore* (Ann Arbor, Mich., 1928) , v.

[30] D. E. Lyday in *Farmers' Fireside Bulletin*, April 6, 1915, cited in Saloutos, *Farmer Movements in the South*, 245–46. The letter ran under the heading, "Is Government Run to Enrich War Munitions Manufacturers at Expense of Producers of Food and Clothes?"

[31] Saloutos, *Farmer Movements in the South*, 246.

[32] Walter O. Ernest to John H. Bankhead, December 11, 1915, in John H. Bankhead, Sr., Papers.

[33] John H. Bankhead to S. O. Williams, February 16, 1916, *ibid.*

41

never truly happy unless they can see blood and bellow like a bull in a slaughter pen." [34]

One striking phenomenon was that political leaders like Vardaman, Watson, Blease, and Catts stood among the most vigorous opponents of preparedness and war: "you represent the big interests and are very anxious for war," Catts wrote the *Manufacturers' Record,* "not because of any patriotic sentiment but because it will *bring dollars* into your coffers and theirs." [35]

In the Congress North Carolina's Claude Kitchin, the new Democratic majority leader in the House, emerged as the leader of the antimilitarist forces. He opposed "the big Navy and big Army program of the jingoes and war traffickers," Kitchin wrote to Bryan; "some of our usually level-headed people have gone mad over 'national preparedness.' " [36] "You are dead right on the question of 'preparedness,' " Vardaman assured Kitchin, "and I hope and pray to Almighty God that . . . others . . . may be constrained to follow you and save the farmers and wealth producers of this Republic from being plundered in the interest of the manufacturers of munitions of war." [37] The result of the opposition organized by Kitchin was a defeat for the administration's original proposals. Most Southerners, however, were willing to accept what Senator Bankhead called a "reasonable preparedness." [38]

[34] William Gellerman, *Martin Dies* (New York, 1944), 19. Texas was the only Southern state with a German-American population large enough to influence attitudes. Governor Oscar B. Colquitt relied on the antiprohibitionist German vote and hoped to capitalize on anti-Wilson sentiment in the senatorial election of 1916. He was greatly embarrassed during this campaign by the revelation of his negotiations with German-American leaders regarding a proposal to purchase the New York *Sun* and convert it into a pro-German, anti-Wilson organ. Huckaby, "Oscar Branch Colquitt," 424–37. Colquitt to L. H. Gibson, April 3, 1916; N. C. Schlemmer to Colquitt, April 25, 1916; Alphonse G. Koeble to Colquitt, April 25, 1916; Colquitt to Koeble, April 26, 1916; George Sylvester Viereck to Johann von Bernstorff, February 6, 1915, in Colquitt Papers.

[35] Sidney J. Catts to *Manufacturers' Record,* March 27, 1917, in *Manufacturers' Record,* LXXII (April 12, 1917), 45.

[36] Claude Kitchin to William Jennings Bryan, September 10, 1915, in William Jennings Bryan Papers (Division of Manuscripts, Library of Congress).

[37] James K. Vardaman to Claude Kitchin, October 22, 1915, in Kitchin Papers. For many other expressions of support for Kitchin's position, see Arnett, *Claude Kitchin and the Wilson War Policies,* 66–68.

[38] John H. Bankhead to Walter O. Ernest, December 11, 1915; Bankhead to A. S. Hough, March 7, 1916, in John H. Bankhead, Sr., Papers.

The antimilitarist opposition, therefore, focused on War Secretary Garrison's proposal for compulsory service to build up a large standing "Continental Army" under Federal control, backed up by a substantial reserve. The membership of the House Military Affairs Committee, under James Hay of Virginia, had been conveniently "packed" with antimilitarist Representatives and brought forward an alternative plan emphasizing the National Guard. The Hay proposal, somewhat altered in the Senate, finally passed after Secretary Garrison resigned to be replaced by Newton D. Baker of Cleveland.[39]

The bill for an increased navy had less difficulty because of the general feeling expressed by Secretary Daniels that there was "no danger of militarism from a relatively strong navy such as would come from a big standing army." [40] Yet Kitchin lamented upon the passage of the bill: "The United States today becomes the most militaristic naval nation on earth." [41]

Forced to compromise on the defense program, Kitchin and his group determined that the burden should rest on the people they held responsible. The income tax was their weapon. Kitchin was "persuaded to think," he wrote Bryan, "that when the New York people are thoroughly convinced that the income tax will have to pay for the increases in the army and navy . . . preparedness will not be so popular with them as it now is." [42] Secretary McAdoo preferred to finance the program by regressive taxes: excises, retention of the sugar duty, a lower income tax exemption, and a doubling of the basic income tax rate. But the radicals, aided by Kitchin's control of the Ways and Means Committee and a groundswell of popular support, won the victory. The Revenue Act of 1916 conceded retention of the sugar tax and raised the

---

[39] Link, *Woodrow Wilson and the Progressive Era*, 180–89; Arnett, *Claude Kitchen and the Wilson War Policies*, 47–92; George C. Herring, Jr., "James Hay and the Preparedness Controversy, 1915–1916," in *Journal of Southern History*, XXX (1964) , 383–404.

[40] Josephus Daniels to William Jennings Bryan, August 18, 1915, in Bryan Papers. See also Osborn, *John Sharp Williams*, 264; Oscar B. Colquitt to Dallas *News*, January 15, 1916; Colquitt to E. J. McCall, February 19, 1916, on forming a navy "strong enough to protect our commerce on the high seas," in Colquitt Papers.

[41] New York *Times*, August 16, 1916.

[42] Claude Kitchin to William Jennings Bryan, January 31, 1916, in Kitchin Papers.

basic income tax from 1 to 2 per cent; but it lifted the surtax to a maximum of 13 per cent on incomes over $2,000,000, imposed a graduated estate tax, a special tax on munitions profits, and new taxes on corporation capital and on surplus and undivided profits.[43] The new income and inheritance taxes constituted the most clearcut victory of the agrarian radicals in the entire Wilson era, a victory further consolidated and advanced after war came.

It was on the issue of German submarine warfare that opposition to the Wilson war policies finally foundered, but until 1917 an active protest continued. The sense of outrage at the *Lusitania* sinking in May, 1915, was blunted in the South by the cotton crisis. Two Virginia leaders, Senator Martin and Representative Flood, paid a personal call on Secretary of State Bryan to warn that public opinion opposed warlike gestures.[44] When Bryan quit in protest at the severity of Wilson's stand, Senator Vardaman hailed his refusal "to be drawn into the brutal conflict which disgraces the civilization of Europe today just to gratify the speculative spirit vanity greed and stupidity of a few American citizens." [45] Toward the end of a long summer of cotton crisis and negotiations with Germany, a Greensboro, North Carolina, attorney observed that "people all over this section of the country are saying very little about Germany's conduct but are condemning England in almost violent terms." But he noted, too, that in the beginning "most of the people were in sympathy with England because our ancestors are supposed to have come from that country and we speak the same language." [46]

Later, as the administration tried to stiffen its attitude toward the sinkings, Representative Jeff: McLemore of Texas and Senator Thomas P. Gore of Oklahoma created a serious embarrassment in

[43] Ratner, *American Taxation*, 344–61.

[44] Link, *Wilson: The Struggle for Neutrality*, 416–17.

[45] James K. Vardaman to William Jennings Bryan, telegram, June 1, 1915, in Bryan Papers. Wilson's course in the *Lusitania* crisis, however, won general support in the public expressions of Southern Congressmen, governors, and the major newspapers. Timothy G. McDonald, "Southern Democratic Congressmen and the First World War, August 1914–April 1917: The Public Record of Their Support for or Opposition to Wilson's Policies" (Ph.D. dissertation, University of Washington, 1962), 94–99, 110.

[46] John A. Barringer to Claude Kitchin, August 27, 1915, in Kitchin Papers.

the midst of the preparedness controversy by offering resolutions warning American citizens against traveling on belligerent vessels. The administration was able to stop them only by the most strenuous efforts and with the support of most Eastern and Southern Democrats.[47] A common opinion on the issue was expressed by the editor of the Jacksonville *Times-Union*. Any citizen who took passage on an armed merchantman, he said, should do so on his own responsibility "and his government should not be expected to involve itself in a war with Germany or the Allies or anybody else to vindicate the rights of a fool like this." [48] Wilson's policy of pressure on the German government, however, elicited a pledge in May, 1916, that German submarines would for the time being observe the rules of search and seizure, and the controversy subsided until the renewal of all-out submarine warfare in 1917.

Throughout the controversies of 1915 and 1916 the name of Wilson retained its appeal as the rallying point for good Democrats. "The South is satisfied, highly satisfied, with the Wilson Administration," a national political reporter asserted early in 1916. Most of the Southerners who questioned the war policies took care to avoid a break with Wilson.[49] Senator Bankhead for one wrote that he preferred to trust Wilson's judgment, based upon superior sources of information, rather than transfer the conduct of foreign relations to Congress, "where there are more jingoes than statesmen." [50] By the end of 1916 tension within the Party had eased for a number of reasons: the end of the preparedness controversy, the success of Wilson's submarine policy, his efforts at mediation, the developing domestic program of progressivism, rising farm prices, and a successful Presidential campaign.

But early in 1917 the final war crisis broke sharply into the euphoria. The resumption of unrestricted submarine warfare and

---

[47] Link, *Woodrow Wilson and the Progressive Era*, 211–14.

[48] Jacksonville *Times-Union*, March 3, 1916, quoted in John H. Bankhead, Sr., to A. S. Hough, March 7, 1916, in John H. Bankhead, Sr., Papers. Hough had signed the editorial.

[49] Frederick M. Davenport, "The Pre-Nomination Campaign: The National South," in *Outlook*, CXII (1916), 388.

[50] John H. Bankhead, Sr., to A. S. Hough, March 7, 1916, in John H. Bankhead, Sr., Papers.

the publication of the Zimmermann Note, in which the German Foreign Secretary proposed an alliance with Mexico, shattered complacency and set the administration on a course toward war. Southern Democrats in the House sustained Wilson's decision for an armed neutrality by an overwhelming margin of 108 to 24.[51] In the Senate only Vardaman and William F. Kirby of Arkansas joined "that little group of willful men" who stood against the proposal.[52] A trip across Mississippi confirmed the opinion of one journalist that the South was behind Wilson in breaking relations with Germany, and that attitudes had shifted markedly after publication of the Zimmermann Note.[53] "The people of the South are thinking more Nationally than perhaps they have ever done before," another wrote.[54] "The patriotism of the South," wrote still another, who traversed the Southeast in early April, "plus its trust in the President, plus its present attitude toward the war, are factors which, with proper leadership in Washington, can be developed into a mighty element of our National strength during the coming conflict. . . . Public opinion in the South is ready for the test." [55] When the decision for war came in April, only five Southern Representatives and Senator Vardaman voted against it.[56]

Despite the overwhelming vote for war, a widespread if largely latent rural-progressive opposition continued up to the time of the

[51] McDonald, "Southern Democratic Congressmen and the First World War," 257b. This count includes all the former slave states.

[52] *Ibid.*, 227. Further evidence of sentiment for Wilson's policies appeared in resolutions of support by the Arkansas, Oklahoma, and Tennessee legislatures and the Kentucky senate. New York *Times*, March 6, 7, 1917.

[53] *Outlook*, CXV (1917), 446. On Southern editorial support of the break, see New York *Times*, February 1, 4, 1917.

[54] *Outlook*, CXV (1917), 496.

[55] Harold T. Pulsifer, "The South and the War," *ibid.*, 648. In Virginia, two local historians wrote later, "Most citizens had such confidence in their President and Congress that they willingly and unquestioningly accepted their leaderships." E. J. Sutherland and J. H. T. Sutherland, "Dickerson County in War Time: A Community History," in Arthur Kyle Davis (ed.), *Virginia Communities in War Time: First Series*, in *Publications of the Virginia War History Commission*, Source Vol. VI (Richmond, 1926), 87.

[56] *Congressional Record*, 65 Cong., 1 Sess., 261, 412–13. The five representatives were Kitchin, McLemore, Edward B. Almon and John L. Burnett of Alabama, and Fred H. Dominick of South Carolina. The last was Cole Blease's law partner.

declaration. Without organization, it found articulation chiefly in areas where the Farmers' Union was strong.[57] If the national union had acted more quickly, President H. Q. Alexander of the North Carolina Farmers Union contended, it could have had the national executive board and at least a half dozen state presidents in Washington to protest the action of Congress. "We are driven to war by the munitions mongers, the bankers, speculators, the jingo press and the devil," he wrote to an associate, "and all for their profit, while all that is expected of the farmers is that they furnish the men to do the fighting and then pay the great bulk of the war taxes for the next hundred years. It is an infamous shame and an outrage upon our people and I expect to say so on every rostrum from which I speak this summer." [58] About two thirds of the Farmers Union locals in North Carolina expressed approval of Alexander's stand, and numerous letters to Claude Kitchin in support of his vote against war indicated that the feeling went far beyond the Farmers Union members.[59] "My work puts me in touch with farmer audiences in country school houses nearly every night in the week," President John A. Simpson of the Oklahoma union wrote to Senator Owen. "We always discuss the war question and universal military service. I know nine out of ten farmers are absolutely opposed to both. We farmers are unalterably opposed to war unless an enemy lands on our shores." His judgment was reinforced by numerous antiwar resolutions from Union locals in Oklahoma and Texas. Weeks afterward, Simpson expressed hope for the defeat of every "War Lord" in Congress: "I believe that every

[57] See, however, an expression by the Miami *Metropolis* of "the real reason back of the call to arms—the protection of Wall Street dollars," quoted in *Manufacturers' Record*, LXXII (April 5, 1917), 63. It is interesting to notice also that a celebrated hero of the war, Sergeant Alvin C. York, a Tennessee mountaineer, had to overcome religious scruples against war at the beginning. Mark Sullivan, *Our Times: The United States, 1900–1925* (New York, 1935), VI, 514–15; Frederick Palmer, *Newton D. Baker: America at War* (New York, 1931), I, 343.

[58] H. J. Alexander to Reuben Dean Bowen, April 9, 1917, in Bowen Papers.

[59] Charles P. Loomis, "Activities of the North Carolina Farmers' Union," in *North Carolina Historical Review* (Raleigh), VII (1930), 451–52. The war issue brought on a rancorous controversy within the Union but the membership increased during 1917. Charles P. Loomis, "The Rise and Decline of the North Carolina Farmers' Union," *ibid.*, VII (1930), 325; Arnett, *Claude Kitchin and the Wilson War Policies*, 239–40.

one of them is guilty of treason and should be dealt with as traitors." [60]

Once a decision came, however, the rally of Southern communities to the support of war services, bond drives, and a thousand other patriotic ventures overwhelmed the antimilitarism. Whether intimidated or acquiescent, most of the peace advocates retreated into silence after April, 1917. In Scott County, Virginia, a local historian asserted, public opinion within sixty days "changed from strong opposition to the war to active and hearty co-operation in carrying it on." [61] A year later in Oklahoma John Simpson was vigorously denying charges of disloyalty. "I have always urged obedience and loyalty to the government," he insisted.[62]

In the development of war legislation the Southerners who dominated Congress and the Southern members in general abandoned states' rights and backed with almost complete unanimity measures that handed sweeping war powers to the national government. On eight major war issues—conscription, the Espionage Act, the Sedition Act, the Lever Food Act, the Railroad Act of 1918, the Overman Act, and antifilibuster resolutions in 1917 and 1918—members from the former Confederate states registered a total of only twenty-one negative votes. "I challenge any lawyer here," Alabama's William B. Bankhead said in the House, to produce a single judicial dictum "that the Constitution . . . in time of war can stand in the way of any measures necessary for the saving of the life and very sovereignty of the government itself when in desperate peril." [63]

[60] John A. Simpson to Robert L. Owen, March 31, 1917; Simpson to Reuben Dean Bowen, April 3, 1917; Resolution of Coppell Local Farmers' Union of Dallas County, April 2, 1917; Resolution of Fannin County Farmers' Union, April 4, 1917; Resolution of Kaufman County Farmers' Union, April 7, 1917; Resolution of Shadowland Local Farmers' Union of Red River County, April 5, 6, 1917; Simpson to Bowen, April 28, 1917, in Bowen Papers.

[61] Robert Milford Addington, "Scott County in War Time," in Davis (ed.), *Virginia Communities in War Time: First Series*, 505.

[62] John A. Simpson to Oklahoma City *Daily Oklahoman*, telegram, June 5, 1918; two unidentified clippings stating charges of disloyalty; H. Arthur Morgan to Oklahoma City *Daily Oklahoman*, June 10, 1918, enclosing resolution of the Association of State Farmers' Union Presidents passed in New Orleans, June 5, 1917, defending Simpson's loyalty, in John A. Simpson Papers (University of Oklahoma Library).

[63] I. A. Newby, "States' Rights and Southern Congressmen During World War I," in *Phylon* (Atlanta), XXIV (1963), 34–50, quotation on p. 34.

The task of fostering and channeling the patriotic outpouring fell to state councils of defense which organized a grass-roots machinery for the various civilian war programs: Liberty Loan, War Savings, and Red Cross drives; "meatless Tuesdays," "victory gardens," conservation of fuel, "education" in the causes of the war. Louisiana organized councils in every parish and in five hundred local communities; South Carolina had a corps of two hundred "Four Minute Men" to exhort public gatherings; an Oklahoma "Loyalty Bureau" circulated pledges in which citizens promised to report "disloyal" acts or utterances.[64]

The war effort demanded not only passive acceptance but active support in thought and deed. "There is no middle ground," the South Carolina council's handbook declared. "Our citizens who are not pro-American are pro-German. Those who are not for us are against us." [65] W. F. Dorsey, a former mayor of Atlanta, warned that "disloyalists might expect to be branded on the forehead and on either cheek, and the rope would be the end of traitors, in legal process of law or otherwise." [66] The Dalton *Citizen* was more lenient. "The time is coming," it said, "when German sympathizers will be run out of every community where they are known." [67] Pent-up emotions erupted in absurd rumors of poisoned water works, attempted arson, "a systematic and concerted spreading of germs by the Kaiser's minions" during the influenza epidemic of 1918, German spies posing as geologists in Oklahoma oil fields.[68] At "Mr. Jefferson's University" in Charlottesville a

---

[64] William P. Beer, "Louisiana State War Activities," in *Proceedings of the Mississippi Valley Historical Association* (Cedar Rapids, Iowa), X (1918–1919), 109–10; Burts, "Public Career of Richard I. Manning," 408–16; O. A. Hilton, "The Oklahoma Council of Defense and the First World War," in *Chronicles of Oklahoma* (Oklahoma City), XX (1943), 18–42.

[65] *South Carolina Handbook of the War*, quoted in James A. B. Scherer, "The Necessity of America's Part in the War," in McCulloch (ed.), *Democracy in Earnest*, 44. The author of the handbook, Dr. George B. Cromer of Newberry, was a citizen of German descent.

[66] Atlanta *Constitution*, June 1, 1918, quoted in H. C. Peterson and Gilbert C. Fite, *Opponents of War, 1917–1918* (Madison, Wis., 1957), 223.

[67] Quoted in *Manufacturers' Record*, LXXIII (April 25, 1918), 41.

[68] W. P. Connell to John M. Parker, March 29, 1917, in John M. Parker Papers (University of North Carolina); *Manufacturers' Record*, LXXIII (January 10, 1918), 49, on an alleged plot to burn Norfolk; William M. E. Rachal, "A Plague on Us: The Influenza Epidemic of 1918," in *Virginia Cavalcade* (Richmond), I (Spring,

professor of journalism, Leon R. Whipple, was dismissed for making a pacifist speech at Sweet Briar. "Every hour that he remains," Carter Glass exploded in a telegram to President Edwin A. Alderman, "is a profanation of the history, the traditions, and the aspirations of the institution." [69]

In Oklahoma the reaction against radicalism caused the most extreme cases of war hysteria and repression, provoked in large part by the "Green Corn Rebellion" of August, 1917. A wretched movement of some two thousand Seminole County farmers and tenants whom syndicalists persuaded to march on Washington and end the war by seizing the government in the name of the people, the "rebellion" derived its name from a plan to subsist on roasting ears along the way. Posses of citizens easily scattered the rebels in about four days and eighty-six participants were finally convicted in Federal court. The sequel was what the Socialist editor Pat Nagle called a "reign of terror" upheld by the state's press and the "Democratic machine." "We are fighting to uproot autocracy that the world may be safe for democracy," a visiting minister proclaimed at Tulsa in December. "We must also guarantee that safety by destroying Socialism. It is but another form of autocracy." Amid the furor, the Socialist party of Oklahoma, whose leaders had tried to dissuade the rebels, formally dissolved itself.[70]

The more numerous victims of war hysteria were "slackers" rather than "disloyalists." A common punishment was to paint their places of business with yellow paint. One Oklahoma farmer had his wheat forcibly taken by the local food administration, which deducted three hundred dollars from his payment check for Liberty Bonds; another "slacker" was brought in by a local war council, his car auctioned off, and the proceeds invested for him in Liberty Bonds. By the end of the war there was a widespread

---

1952), 34; Quinn Brisben, "Illegal Superpatriotic Activities in Oklahoma during the First World War" (Unpublished seminar paper, Department of History, University of Oklahoma, 1955, copy in possession of Professor John S. Ezell).

[69] Peterson and Fite, *Opponents of War*, 106–107; Dumas Malone, *Edwin A. Alderman: A Biography* (New York, 1940), 319–25.

[70] Charles C. Bush, "The Green Corn Rebellion" (M.A. thesis, University of Oklahoma, 1932); Peterson and Fite, *Opponents of War*, 40–42, 171–76; Ameringer, *If You Don't Weaken*, 351–57; Hilton, "Oklahoma Council of Defense and the First World War," *loc. cit.*, 33; Shannon, *Socialist Party of America*, 108.

practice in Oklahoma of publishing the names of "slackers" in the papers, with invitations for citizens to boycott them. Use of the German language was discouraged or forbidden.[71] In March, 1918, a poll of twelve hundred school systems showed that about one in seven had dropped German language instruction. The higher patriotism of the South was reflected in the fact that about 40 per cent of its systems had dropped German.[72] In New Orleans Berlin Street became General Pershing Street.[73]

While mobs hunted spies and chased rumors, the Federal government stalked bigger game. Under the Espionage and Sedition acts criticism of government leaders and war policies was in effect outlawed. One of the most important weapons was the arbitrary power wielded by Postmaster General Burleson to exclude disloyal publications from the mails. Soon after the passage of the Espionage Act he excluded Tom Hickey's *The Rebel Farmer,* and other Socialist and antiwar publications went the same way.[74] In Georgia Tom Watson carried forward a personal vendetta against Wilson and his policies, opposed the war, and undertook a court test of conscription. "Shall I, at my time of life, become an opportunist, a conformist, in order to avoid harsh criticism?" he asked. "The masses—especially the rural masses—are with me." In August, 1917, his personal organ, the *Jeffersonian,* was barred from the mails and Federal judge Emory Speer privately asserted that he had evidence "which indicated the most widespread disobedience and threatened resistance to the Selective Draft Enactment, all fomented by the matter printed by Mr. Watson." [75]

In South Carolina Cole Blease stated that every American killed in the war would be charged against Wilson and Congress "as an unwarranted sacrifice in the sight of Almighty God, of fresh young

[71] Incidents, taken chiefly from *Harlow's Weekly,* in Brisben, "Illegal Superpatriotic Activities in Oklahoma."

[72] John Higham, *Strangers in the Land: Patterns of American Nativism, 1860–1925* (New Brunswick, N. J., 1955) , 208.

[73] It had been named in honor of a Napoleonic triumph. Thomas Ewing Dabney, *One Hundred Great Years: The Story of the* Times-Picayune *from Its Founding to 1940* (Baton Rouge, 1944) , 387.

[74] Donald Johnson, "Wilson, Burleson, and Censorship in the First World War," in *Journal of Southern History,* XXVIII (1962) , 46–58.

[75] Woodward, *Tom Watson,* 453–58; Speer as quoted in Morison (ed.) , *Letters of Theodore Roosevelt,* VIII, 1235 n.

American manhood." A "hand primary" of farmers who heard him at Pomaria in July, 1917, showed that every one would have voted against war. David R. Coker, chairman of the state defense council, referred to Blease, Watson, and the "long-haired Vardaman" as a trio "who are deluding themselves into thinking they can ride into office over the dying patriotism of the South." Blease in turn accused the "mangy" Coker of "trying to go to the United States Senate or the Governor's chair over the dead bodies of your boys." Much of the debate involved factional politics. Blease complained that his supporters were excluded from the state's war machinery, but as patriotic sentiment jelled he moderated his tone. Meanwhile, two of his prominent supporters ran afoul of Federal law. William P. Beard, publisher of the Abbeville *Scimitar*, went to prison for an editorial charging that the war fulfilled pre-election pledges by Wilson to get support from the money powers. John P. Grace, an Irish-American politico who upset the patrician torpor of Charleston with a plebeian following and a Bleaseite alliance, found outlet for his anti-British feeling in his own Charleston *American*. Temporarily denied mailing privileges during 1917, it again circulated by mail before the war ended, although its associate editor was convicted of conspiracy connected with the scuttling of a German vessel in an unsuccessful attempt to block access to the Charleston Navy Yard.[76]

Vardaman of Mississippi stood to his guns and stubbornly refused to recant his opposition to war. "I am well physically," he wrote shortly after the declaration of war, "but I have been more distressed and suffered more heartache in the past two months than all the balance of my life put together. It seems to me the world has gone crazy. Where it will all end God only knows." [77] He kept up a consistent opposition to war measures, including the conscription, food control, and espionage bills, and met increasing charges back home that "Herr Von Vardaman" was "a Kaiser-loving betrayer of the American people," whose vote against conscription placed him "in the army of slackers." [78]

[76] Burts, "Public Career of Richard I. Manning," 438–45; David Duncan Wallace, *The History of South Carolina* (New York, 1934), III, 445–47; John P. Grace to Fred J. Wilson, January 20, 1918, in John P. Grace Papers (Manuscripts Department, Duke University).

[77] James K. Vardaman to Mary L. Bryan, May 18, 1917, in Bryan Papers.

[78] Kirwan, *Revolt of the Rednecks*, 279, 281, 285–86.

Throughout the war other echoes of the antiwar spirit resounded in minority criticism of war measures. Conscription, said Representative George Huddleston of Alabama, was un-American and supported chiefly by business and high finance elements who claimed that "We have too much discontent, too many Socialists, too much freedom of speech, too many ranting demagogues and labor agitators." He feared "They would suppress all this with the iron hand of the military." [79] Senator Thomas W. Hardwick of Georgia was saddened by the "spirit of intolerance, the spirit of suppression, the spirit of oppression, if you please, that seems to me to lurk in these times." [80] When the Sedition Act came up in 1918, he argued that the country would be stronger by preserving its basic freedoms than by surrendering or hedging them about. "If we are fighting freedom's battles, let us fight in a cause worthy of freemen." [81]

On one major point, revenue policy, the agrarian-progressive group succeeded. After the United States' entry into the war, Kitchin and others led a strong public sentiment for further levies upon great wealth and war profits. The Revenue Acts of 1917 and 1918 reduced tax exemptions from $3,000 to $1,000 for unmarried persons and from $4,000 to $2,000 for married persons. The normal levy went up to 6 per cent on the first $4,000 and 12 per cent on all incomes above that, but surtaxes raised the maximum to 77 per cent on incomes above $1,000,000, to 65 per cent on excess profits, and to 25 per cent on inheritances. "Who Will Pay the Taxes?" Kitchin asked. "Wealth, and not poverty," he answered.[82]

The most significant immediate effect of the war on the South was to create situations of dynamic change in an essentially static society. In all, nearly a million Southerners entered the army, left their local environments, and mixed with men from other regions. Carter Glass recalled that Wilson told Virginia's Governor Henry C. Stuart: "There should be intermingling of troops from all the States. We should submerge provincialism and sectionalism and party spirit in one powerful flood of nationalism, which would

---

[79] *Congressional Record*, 65 Cong., 1 Sess., 1094.   [80] *Ibid.*, 6742.
[81] *Ibid.*, 2 Sess., 4637.
[82] Ratner, *American Taxation*, 362–99; Arnett, *Claude Kitchin and the Wilson War Policies*, 249–70.

carry us on to victory." [83] Thousands went overseas not only into battle but to far-flung posts from England to Russia, from Gallipoli to Japan.[84] Moreover, the Southern climate was the magnet for a majority of the army training camps. Six of the fifteen National Army camps and thirteen of the sixteen National Guard cantonments were in the Southern states (the others were in New Mexico and California). Only two Southern states lacked at least one camp, but Florida had naval installations and Tennessee important war industries.[85] The immeasurable impact of war camps on Southern communities may be illustrated by the case of Spartanburg, an Upcountry textile town in South Carolina, where the building of Camp Wadsworth brought "a dynamic energy which startled and transformed the tempo of life in that town and expanded its horizons to the uttermost parts of the earth. . . . Spartanburg saw a city rise on its borders with a population larger than its own." [86] The city raised a fund of $27,500 for War Camp Activities and a Hostess House appeared at the camp; but the pressure overtaxed local recreation facilities, rents soared, soldiers stood in block-long lines at soda fountains, and local merchants garnered a rich harvest.[87]

Naval installations galvanized coastal communities into unaccustomed activity. In the Hampton Roads area, seat of the Newport News Shipbuilding and Drydock Company, the government developed the greatest naval complex in the United States, including one of the two embarkation points for troops going to Europe. Within the space of a few months Norfolk, population 67,452 in 1910, had an influx of more than 100,000 newcomers. It became "almost overnight the center of government activities involving the expenditure of millions and transforming its outlying districts into hives of industry crowded with busy workers. . . . Business of all kinds . . . expanded beyond facilities to handle it." [88] Lesser

[83] *Congressional Record*, 65 Cong., 2 Sess., 1827–28.
[84] David (ed.), *Virginia War Letters, Diaries, and Editorials,* xii.
[85] Colonel Leonard P. Ayres, *The War with Germany: A Statistical Summary* (Washington, 1919), 28; Palmer, *Newton D. Baker,* I, 238.
[86] Spartanburg Unit of the Writers' Program of the Works Progress Administration in South Carolina, *A History of Spartanburg County* (Spartanburg, 1940), 233.
[87] *Ibid.,* 236–58.
[88] Norfolk *Virginian-Pilot,* December 29, 1918, quoted in Thomas Jefferson Wertenbaker, *Norfolk: Historic Southern Port* (Durham, 1931), 341, see also 331–

bases down the coast included Charleston, Key West, and the Parris Island marine station. On the Gulf, the Pensacola and New Orleans bases were reactivated, the former as the navy's chief air station.[89]

Shipbuilding brought to life other coastal communities. Outside the Newport News Shipbuilding and Drydock Company, which expanded by $9,500,000 and built everything up to the largest battleships, the South's peculiar contribution was the wooden ship.[90] The pioneer in this field was Henry Piaggio, an Orange, Texas, lumberman whose first ship reached Europe in September, 1917. By November a cluster of shipyards on the Orange waterfront had about 35 vessels under construction, and by early 1918 the government had contracted for 150 ships in Southern yards, mostly along the Gulf. On the Mississippi coast alone, at Gulfport, Biloxi, Pascagoula, and Moss Point, more than three million dollars was invested in the industry, partly because of a state tax exemption. By the end of the war a chain of shipyards from Virginia to Texas was launching wooden, steel, and concrete ships.[91]

Army cantonments and wooden ships, both of which utilized mainly Southern pine, created a runaway expansion in lumber production.[92] By mid-April, 1917, more than 70 per cent of all

---

54; Marvin W. Schlegel, *Conscripted City: Norfolk in World War II* (Norfolk, 1951), 2–3; Benedict Crowell and Robert F. Wilson, *The Road to France: The Transportation of Troops and Military Supplies, 1917–1918* (New Haven, 1921), I, 297; Arthur Kyle Davis, "Norfolk City in War Time," in Davis (ed.), *Virginia Communities in War Time: First Series*, 291–357.

[89] Frank B. Freidel, *Franklin D. Roosevelt* (Boston, 1952), I, 204–205; Daniels, *Wilson Era: Years of Peace*, 299–302; Josephus Daniels, *The Wilson Era: Years of War and After, 1917–1923* (Chapel Hill, 1946), 104, 122, 198–99; Beer, "Louisiana State War Activities," *loc. cit.*, 108–109.

[90] "Ships on the Ways," *Fortune* (Jersey City, N. J.), XIV (November, 1936), 176.

[91] Hamilton P. Easton, "The History of the Texas Lumbering Industry" (Ph.D. dissertation, University of Texas, 1947), 287–90; E. T. Hollingsworth, Jr., "The Wooden Ship—The South's Contribution to the New American Merchant Marine," in *Manufacturers' Record*, LXXIV (October 17, 1918), and *ibid.*, LXXII (August 9, 1917), 55–61; LXXIII (January 2, 1918), 76; (January 31, 1918), 78c; (March 21, 1918), 60; LXXV (May 22, 1919), 98.

[92] At Camp Taylor, Kentucky, barracks arose from timber which had stood in Mississippi a week before, New York *Tribune*, August 5, 1917, quoted in Sullivan, *Our Times*, V, 311.

yellow pine sawmills west of the Mississippi had withdrawn entirely from the public market. By August the government had already purchased more than 700,000,000 board feet of yellow pine. A Southern Pine Emergency Bureau, created by the Southern Pine Association, co-operated with the War Industries Board in compiling statistics and mobilizing sawmills. When faced with a ship timber shortage in 1918, it sent out a corps of speakers to exhort 68,000 workers in ninety-eight mills from Florida to Texas, a campaign that the bureau said almost tripled shipments in forty-five days. Between May, 1917, and February, 1919, the bureau handled shipments of nearly two million board feet.[93]

The war, one writer remarked, launched the South on "a kind of week-end economic debauchery, with its inevitable gloomy Monday when normal peacetime conditions returned." [94] But the ubiquitous war prosperity gave the region a taste of affluence such as it had never before experienced and lifted economic expectations to levels from which they would never again completely recede. Industry expanded, farm prices rose, and workers, even sharecroppers, became acquainted with the feel of folding money. Continuing economic demand after the war postponed the "gloomy Monday" until well into 1920. And even that did not entirely stop the thrust of industrial expansion.

Even the demand for explosives, drastically curtailed at the end of the war, gave a lasting momentum to the development of hydroelectric power and chemical manufactures. One major contribution was the construction of a nitrate plant and Wilson Dam at Muscle Shoals, Alabama, unfinished at the end of the war but later the nucleus of the Tennessee Valley Authority. At the confluence of the James and Appomattox rivers a small dynamite factory grew almost overnight into the enormous DuPont powder mills, giving birth in 1915 to a turbulent boom town named

[93] James Boyd, "It Is War," chapter in "Southern Pine Association History," typescript in Drawer 77, Southern Pine Association Papers (Department of Archives, Louisiana State University), 4–6, 19–22; Easton, "History of the Texas Lumbering Industry," 285–92; Grosvenor P. Clarkson, *Industrial America in the World War: The Strategy behind the Line, 1917–1918* (Boston, 1923), 421–25; Bernard M. Baruch, *American Industry in the War: A Report of the War Industries Board* (New York, 1941), 225–26.

[94] Paul Seabury, *The Waning of Southern "Internationalism"* (Princeton, 1957), 20.

Hopewell.[95] Near Nashville in 1917–1918 the Old Hickory powder plant developed a complex that spread over an area of four and a half square miles. Seventy times larger than the biggest plant before the war, it produced five hundred thousand pounds of explosives per day at the Armistice. After the war both plants turned to rayon production which, like explosives, utilized cellulose.[96] Government subsidy also initiated a more diversified wood chemical industry. Of eight government-sponsored plants built during the war, four were in Tennessee, and three of these became the nuclei of significant expansions later at Lyles, Memphis, and Kingsport. The last became the nucleus of an Eastman Kodak subsidiary, the Tennessee Eastman Corporation, manufacturers of cellulose acetate film and yarn.[97] On the Gulf Coast a new producer joined the Union and Freeport Sulphur companies: the Texas Gulf Sulphur Company, which opened the Big Hill sulphur dome in Matagorda County with a new plant, townsite, and rail connections.[98]

Established industries likewise entered an era of expansion that carried into the next decade. Wartime demands halted a threatened depression in textiles and set the Southern industry upon growth that carried it ahead of New England in the 1920's. As early as 1916 the Avondale Mills in Alabama were reporting gross earnings of more than 100 per cent.[99] One mill in Georgia declared dividends of 100 per cent for several years; another cleared a million dollars in the last year of the war.[100] Mill villages began to take on an improved appearance, a new coat of paint and

[95] Thomas B. Robertson, "Hopewell and City Point in the World War," in Davis (ed.), *Virginia Communities in War Time: First Series,* 215–34; John Ihlder, "Hopewell: A City Eighteen Months Old," in *Survey,* XXXVII (1916–1917), 226–30.

[96] Clarkson, *Industrial America and the World War,* 407–10; Baruch, *American Industry in the War,* 186–87.

[97] Williams Haynes, *American Chemical Industry* (New York, 1945–1954), III, 136–37.

[98] Clarkson, *Industrial America in the World War,* 397–98; Williams Haynes, *The Stone That Burns: The Story of the American Sulphur Industry* (New York, 1942), 135–54. See also Robert H. Montgomery, *The Brimstone Game: Monopoly in Action* (New York, 1940), 52–60.

[99] Braxton Bragg Comer to Mrs. D. L. McDonald, January 24, 1917, in Braxton Bragg Comer Papers (Southern Historical Collection, University of North Carolina).

[100] *Manufacturers' Record,* LVII (March 11, 1920), 108.

repairs, perhaps a new church or YMCA, and company welfare activities flourished.[101] Higher wages created a taste for new clothes, picture shows, tin lizzies. The taste of prosperity was sweet and the memory of it lingered into the lean years that followed.

In the Kentucky mountains war prosperity reached some of the most isolated communities. Harlan County, for example, in 1913 was still largely a backwoods community of log cabins and subsistence farmers, almost roadless and isolated from the outside world. But rich coal seams were known to exist underneath the hills and war demands brought in the capital to develop them. With 169 mines in 1911, Harlan had 1,496 by 1915 and 9,260 by 1923; Pike County increased from 1,094 in 1910 to 7,212 in 1923; Perry from 113 in 1913 to 5,908 in 1923. The coal fever reached a climax immediately after the war, when American and European needs were at a peak. After the removal of price controls on April 1, 1920, prices shot up from $2.58 a ton to a high of around $14 at the mine; some diggers in 1920 earned $50 a day and some subcontractors as much as $2,000 a month.[102]

If the war contributed little to the expansion of oil production in the Southwest, it did alleviate the problem of overproduction. The new Cushing field in Oklahoma reached a maximum daily production in 1914–1915 of some three hundred thousand barrels of high grade petroleum, about a third of the national output. Only the sudden wartime demand, coupled with the growing automobile industry, took up the increase. In the end, as Viscount Curzon was to put it, "The Allies floated to victory on a wave of oil." [103] The popular new "domestic blends" for cigarettes— Camels, Chesterfields, and Lucky Strikes—arrived just in time to exploit war nerves and patriotism, in the face of shortages in

[101] Harriett L. Herring, *Welfare Work in Mill Villages: The Story of Extra-Mill Activities in North Carolina* (Chapel Hill, 1929), 118–21 and *passim*.

[102] Homer L. Morris, *The Plight of the Bituminous Coal Miner* (Philadelphia and London, 1934), 20–21; Malcolm H. Ross, *Machine Age in the Hills* (New York, 1933), 51–53; Edward E. Hunt et al. (eds.), *What the Coal Commission Found: An Authoritative Summary by the Staff* (Baltimore, 1925), 77–81. See also Harry M. Caudill, *Night Comes to the Cumberlands: A Biography of a Depressed Area* (Boston, 1963), 93–144.

[103] Carl Coke Rister, *Oil! Titan of the Southwest* (Norman, Okla., 1949), 134, 334–45.

Turkish tobacco. Smokes for servicemen became a patriotic necessity and the consumption of cigarettes soared from 166 per capita in 1914 to 426 in 1919.[104]

Even the Southern iron and steel industry around Birmingham, whose growth had lagged since the turn of the century, received some stimulus, although its potentialities were yet unrealized. The fault—laid by some to inferior ores, by others to the lack of Southern markets, by still others to outside control by United States Steel—was attributed by the corporation's leaders to the threat of antitrust action for its acquisition of the Tennessee Coal and Iron Company in 1907. After a 1915 decision for the company in a lower court, the *Manufacturers' Record* conducted a long and vigorous campaign to persuade U.S. Steel that it should expand its capacity in the South; but the campaign was without success until the Supreme Court indicated in 1917 that the suit would be postponed during the war.[105] With that, the company allocated $11,000,000 to construction of the new Fairfield Works, a blooming mill, combination bar and structural mill, and plate mill.[106] Still, at the end of the war the blast furnace industry in the three states of Alabama, Tennessee, and Georgia had declined relatively in employment from 17.8 per cent of the nation's wage earners in 1900 to 11.4 per cent in 1919, and in production from 10 to 8 per cent of the value added. In steelworks and rolling mills, however, the picture had improved somewhat. Alabama's wage earners increased from 2,204 in 1900 to 8,121 in 1919—a rate above the national average.[107] Meanwhile, the war induced two important

[104] Joseph Clarke Robert, *The Story of Tobacco in America* (New York, 1949), 229–36.

[105] *Manufacturers' Record,* LXVIII (September 30, 1915), 71–72; (October 7, 1915), 50; (October 21, 1915), 38–39; LXIX (January 13, 1916), 37–38; (January 27, 1916), 35, 52; (March 23, 1916), 43; LXXI (January 4, 1917), 59–60; (January 18, 1917), 45; (February 15, 1917), 47; (April 5, 1917), 63; (May 24, 1917), 43.

[106] *Manufacturers' Record,* LXXII (June 14, 1917), 41; (July 19, 1917), 59; B. E. U. Lutz, "Iron and Steel Development of the South," in *The South's Development: Fifty Years of Southern Progress* (Baltimore, 1924), 293 (this was a special issue of *Manufacturers' Record*).

[107] Herman H. Chapman, *Iron and Steel Industries of the South* (University, Ala., 1953), 116–17; U. S. Bureau of the Census, *Abstract of the Census of Manufactures,* 1919 (Washington, 1923), 658.

new minor producers into the field, the Dixie Steel Corporation of New Orleans and the Texas Steel Company of Rusk.[108]

The taste of prosperity was sweetest of all to the subjects of King Cotton. The war, "which seemed a curse to the cotton states," a trade editor said, "has been turned, horrible as it is to others, into one great blessing to all of Dixie." [109] By the end of 1916 financial writers and Southern editors were alive with assurance that "King Cotton is now restored to his throne, and from fields nodding drowsily in white through the summer he draws royal revenues." [110] Cotton, one writer said, joined with the nitrate beds of Chile, the coke ovens of the Appalachians, and the sulphur of Louisiana and Texas to spread death and destruction in Europe.[111] Before the Armistice the government purchased over five hundred thousand bales of cotton linters for use in making explosives,[112] but the fact that prices continued to rise in 1919 bore out the conclusion that the prosperity came "more as a result of domestic business activity, general inflation, and moderately small crops than from actual war demand." [113] The years 1917–1919 were the best cotton had ever seen. The average price for those years was twenty-seven cents, and the thirty-five-cent cotton of 1919 was the most valuable crop ever produced, worth over two billion dollars.[114]

"The Negro tenants are rolling in wealth," an observer reported from the Georgia Black Belt, and the rare wealth inspired marveling reports of debt settlements, forty-five-dollar suits, six-dollar shirts, eight-dollar shoes, and most spectacular of all, the automobile invasion of the rural South.[115] Everywhere one heard

[108] *Manufacturers' Record,* LXXII (July 19, 1917), 59; LXXIII (June 27, 1918), 64.

[109] H. E. Harmon, editor of *The Cotton Seed Oil Magazine* (Atlanta), quoted in "Cotton's Magical Rise Enriching the Nation," in *Literary Digest,* LIII (1916), 1577.

[110] *Ibid.,* 1517.   [111] Clarkson, *Industrial America in the World War,* 401.

[112] Baruch, *American Industry in the War,* 181–84.

[113] A. B. Genung, "Agriculture in the World War Period," in *Farmers in a Changing World: The Yearbook of Agriculture, 1940* (Washington, 1940), 285; Benjamin H. Hibbard, *Effects of the Great War Upon Agriculture in the United States and Great Britain* (New York, 1919), 48–49.

[114] James H. Street, *The New Revolution in the Cotton Economy: Mechanization and Its Consequences* (Chapel Hill, 1957), 41; Genung, "Agriculture in the World War Period," *loc. cit.,* 285.

[115] Charles Lewis, "Thirty Cent Cotton and the Negro," in *Illustrated World,*

the reproach of the comfortable at the improvidence of the poor. "They are like little children to whom some good fairy has paid a visit, leaving unexpected and unlooked-for treasure," said the Savannah *Press*. "Our people can't stand prosperity," an Arkansan asserted.[116] South Carolina tenants "engaged in a perfect orgy of money spending," and North Carolina countrymen fell victim "to the hordes of agents who radiate from the small towns and have just the things the farmer needs, usually at exhorbitant prices." [117]

But, a social worker asserted, "The extravagance of working people is not altogether waste; it represents the awakening of new desires which call for industry and thrift, and with them come more rational expenditures for better food, cook stoves, household implements, comfortable beds, and, very soon, better housing." [118] Together with waste, after long years of deprivation, there came solid gains. "The tremendous paying of old debts was harvest time for the merchants," a traveler reported after the war; everywhere he found "new houses, new barns, new roof paint, better roads, school houses, churches, and better farm machinery . . . certain neighborhoods where for the first time there have been glimpses of the comforts which are the common necessities of life in the North: home water supply, plumbing, proper lighting, washing machines, better furniture, musical instruments, telephones." [119] From 1914 to 1918 per capita savings in banks, trust companies, and war savings rose from $18.45 to $26.73.[120]

May, 1918, p. 470, quoted in Rupert B. Vance, *Human Factors in Cotton Culture: A Study in the Social Geography of the American South* (Chapel Hill, 1929) , 138; "Cotton's Magical Rise Enriching the Nation," *loc. cit.,* 1519, 1521; Harris Dickson, *The Story of King Cotton* (New York and London, 1937) , 170; Victor I. Masters, *The Call of the South: A Presentation of the Home Principle in Missions, Especially as It Applies to the South* (Atlanta, 1918) , 107.

[116] "Cotton's Magical Rise Enriching the Nation," *loc. cit.,* 1521–22.

[117] David R. Coker, "Open Letter to Farmers" (1917) , quoted in George Lee Simpson, Jr., *The Cokers of Carolina: A Social Biography of a Family* (Chapel Hill, 1956) , 194; W. H. Swift, *Child Welfare in North Carolina* (New York, 1918) , 170.

[118] Hastings H. Hart, "Social Reconstruction in the South," in J. E. McCulloch (ed.) , *"Distinguished Service" Citizenship* (Washington, 1919) , 58.

[119] Ray Stannard Baker in New York *Evening Post*, March 8, 1921, quoted in Vance, *Human Factors in Cotton Culture,* 139. See also Stephen Graham, *The Soul of John Brown* (New York, 1920) , 150–51 and *passim*.

[120] Hart, "Social Reconstruction in the South," *loc. cit.,* 152. The figures include West Virginia in the South.

Social impulses also rallied. The war "has had an amazing effect upon the morale of the Southern people which, I believe, has set them forward in their social progress twenty-five years at a single bound," said a national welfare leader. "Their horizon has been tremendously widened; their mental vision has been sharpened, and their moral perceptions quickened." [121] Health and welfare work related to the cantonments marked new milestones in the field of social service. Important beginnings in both lines owed much to Raymond B. Fosdick of New York, civilian chairman of both army and navy commissions on training camp activities. Among other activities, Fosdick directed a campaign of pressure and persuasion against casehardened generals and mayors to suppress prostitution.[122] Through the summer and fall of 1917 authorities shut down red-light districts across the South, including the notorious Storyville in New Orleans, despite Mayor Martin R. Behrman's vigorous defense of "the God-given right of men to be men"—an incident celebrated in the annals of jazz for its effect of dispersing the musicians from the whorehouses.[123] Army and navy programs of medical prophylaxis were supplemented in 1918 by the appropriation of $1,000,000 for each of two years to be used by state health departments in the control of venereal diseases; a further boost to public health services was given by the revelations of deficiencies in medical and psychological examinations and by Red Cross and Public Health Service efforts to eliminate health hazards around military establishments.[124]

The positive aspect of Fosdick's welfare campaign involved the

[121] *Ibid.*, 50.

[122] Raymond B. Fosdick, *Chronicle of a Generation: An Autobiography* (New York, 1958), 135–48.

[123] *Ibid.*, 146–48; *Survey*, XXXVIII (1917), 349–50; XXXIX (1917–1918), 97; Herbert Asbury, *The French Quarter: An Informal History of the New Orleans Underworld* (New York, 1936), 451–52.

[124] Frank H. Gardner, "The Government's War on Venereal Diseases," in McCulloch (ed.), *"Distinguished Service" Citizenship*, 89; Hart, "Social Reconstruction in the South," *ibid.*, 50; Fosdick, *Chronicle of a Generation*, 162–63; Henry P. Davison, *The American Red Cross in the Great War* (New York, 1920), 46; Rockefeller Foundation, *Annual Report, 1923* (New York, 1923), 134. In the case of Camp Wadsworth the building of roads to the camp stimulated local interest in the good-roads movement. Professor Lewis P. Jones, Wofford College, to author, September 10, 1960, citing Spartanburg newspapers of 1917.

provision of leisure time activities through the War Camp Community Service, which mobilized community recreational facilities, and through the Commission on Training Camp Activities, which co-ordinated the work of agencies like the YMCA, YWCA, Knights of Columbus, Jewish Welfare Board, and the American Library Association.[125] Before the war, except in a few urban centers, social work had been "a washed out, broken down, sour, dilapidated field. Like much of our tenant robbed land, it wouldn't grow anything." [126] During the war, the Red Cross revitalized the field through the work of its Gulf and Southern divisions, each headed in succession by a young Northern social worker named Harry Hopkins.[127] In the name of soldier morale the Red Cross Home Service undertook to keep the men in touch with their families, nourished a "wet weather growth of lady bountifuls and patrioteers," and advanced professionalization·through six-week Home Service Institutes which had graduated eighteen hundred students by mid-1919.[128] "Such impetus was given to the social welfare program in the period after 1917," a student of the movement concluded, "that that year probably would mark the beginning of the new era in the South." [129]

If there was little occasion for programs to "Americanize" immigrants in a region of native-born citizens, the South experienced its own peculiar kind of "Americanization" in the fires of patriotism. Sectional loyalty receded at least temporarily before the universal cry for unity. Throughout the war the *Manufacturers' Record*, exponent of Southern industrial development, proclaimed itself also an "Exponent of Americanism." One of the

[125] Fosdick, *Chronicle of a Generation*, 148–52; T. S. Settle, "The Proper Use of Leisure Time," in McCulloch (ed.), *"Distinguished Service" Citizenship*, 68–71; Joseph H. Odell, "The New Spirit of the New Army. . . . An Account of What Atlanta, Georgia, Is Doing for a Cantonment," in *Outlook*, CXVII (1917), 496–97.

[126] Burr Blackburn, "What the Southern Division Did for the South," in *Survey*, LV (1925–1926), 760.

[127] Robert E. Sherwood, *Roosevelt and Hopkins: An Intimate History* (New York, 1948), 26.

[128] Blackburn, "What the Southern Division Did for the South," *loc. cit.*, 760; Lyda Gordon Shivers, "The Social Welfare Movement in the South: A Study in Regional Culture and Social Organization" (Ph.D. dissertation, University of North Carolina, 1935), 67–71.

[129] Shivers, "Social Welfare Movement in the South," 371A.

sad but inevitable things about the war, a Florida newspaper lamented in 1918, was that all Americans thereafter would be called Yankees.[130] The Tulsa *World* in the first postwar year ventured the opinion "that there exists in the South at the moment a more alert and apprehensive American spirit than exists in any other section of the country."[131] Indeed the idea of a peculiarly pure Americanism in the South, with overtones of Anglo-Saxon racism and anti-radicalism, became an established article of the regional faith.

The war temper of the Southern people found expression in the Democratic primaries of 1918, in which many of the leaders who opposed the administration policies went down to defeat. Jeff: McLemore lost every county in the Texas Seventh District; James L. Slayden withdrew in another Texas district when the President criticized him for failure to support the administration. Senators Hardwick of Georgia and Vardaman of Mississippi fought it out against the weight of open Presidential opposition, and both lost. It was the political end of both men. Blease and Watson chose that inopportune year to attempt political comebacks, Blease for the Senate and Watson for the House, but both were defeated. Of the Southerners who had voted against the declaration of war, only Kitchin and Edward B. Almon of Alabama returned to the next Congress. Although Wilson failed to eliminate Alabama's Representative Huddleston or Tennessee's Senator John K. Shields, he had achieved a successful "purge" of his party.[132] It provided an important foundation for the solid support that Wilson's peace policies got from Southern Democrats in the subsequent months.

But a fateful irony pursued the elections of 1918. Republican victories in November offset Wilson's strength in his own party. And while the "Americanization" of the South minimized sec-

[130] Thomas A. Bailey, *The Man in the Street: The Impact of American Public Opinion on Foreign Policy* (New York, 1948), 114.

[131] Quoted in *Manufacturers' Record*, LXXVI (October 16, 1919), 82.

[132] Seward W. Livermore, *Politics Is Adjourned: Woodrow Wilson and the War Congress, 1916–1918* (Middletown, Connecticut, 1966), 138–40, 160–65; Frederick L. Paxson, *America at War, 1917–1918* (Boston, 1939), 427; Woodward, *Tom Watson*, 461–63; Walter Prescott Webb, "Introduction," in Ellen Maury Slayden, *Washington Wife: The Journal of Ellen Maury Slayden* (New York, 1963), xii–xiii, see also 331–32. Woodrow Wilson to Thomas W. Gregory, January 26, 1918, in Thomas W. Gregory Papers (Division of Manuscripts, Library of Congress) requested that Vardaman's recommendations for appointments be given no consideration.

tionalism in the region, Republicans won Congress by reviving sectionalism elsewhere. From the beginning of the Wilson administration an undercurrent of suspicion had accompanied the South's return to power. In 1914 Democratic losses in the East accentuated the Western and Southern character of Wilson's support. His "policies had been outlined by a Western Democracy," one observer claimed, not altogether correctly, "while the bulk of his Congressional majorities were from the South." [133] Indeed Claude Kitchin expressed the wish that a few Southerners would yield committee chairmanships "for the sake of good politics"—even though sectional imbalance had been greater under Republican control.[134]

The Presidential election of 1916 further strengthened sectional divisions. In Wilson's victory the electoral college registered a coalition of the South and West against the East and Midwest. "It is the combination which made Jefferson and Jackson," the progressive historian William E. Dodd exulted. "It is the South and the West united; the farmers, small businessmen and perhaps a large sprinkle of Union labor against the larger industrial, transportation and commercial interests. With a few substitutions the factors of the equation of 1916 might be exchanged for that of 1828 or 1800. . . ." [135] At the same time, Dodd wrote elsewhere, "Those who were behind the President were ridiculed as provincial Southerners, as sectionalists seeking only sectional interests." The new tariff, bank reforms, "and all the other laws that bore adversely upon industry in the North were but outdroppings of the old Confederate animus." [136] The charge was spread that the income tax was sectional in nature, a raid on Northern wealth for expenditures in the South.[137] Josephus Daniels was depicted

---

[133] Edgar E. Robinson, "A Future for the Democratic Party," in *New Republic,* II (1915) , 46–48, quotation from p. 4.

[134] Claude Kitchin to M. F. Conroy, October 1, 1915, in Kitchin Papers.

[135] William E. Dodd to Edward Mandell House, November 10, 1916, in Edward Mandell House Papers (Yale University Library) . Courtesy of Dr. John Wells Davidson.

[136] Dodd, *Woodrow Wilson and His Work,* 144, 189. See also Livermore, *Politics Is Adjourned,* 9–10.

[137] David F. Houston, "The Issue of Sectionalism," memorandum enclosed with Houston to Woodrow Wilson, September 29, 1916, in Woodrow Wilson Papers (Division of Manuscripts, Library of Congress) . See also Dodd, *Woodrow Wilson and His Work,* 138.

as a narrow-minded Bryanite, using the Navy Department to promote democracy, pacifism, trust busting, and prohibition. "A vote for Wilson," one campaign slogan went, "is a vote for Daniels." [138]

Until 1918 sectionalism remained an undercurrent. Then it surfaced. The issue came on cotton, which never went under wartime controls; the program limited price-fixing to commodities purchased by the government in such quantities as to interfere seriously with civilian needs.[139] But the favored status of cotton was easily attributed to Southern influence in Washington and the impression was furthered by vigorous representations of Southern Congressmen and the Farmers' Union against controls. "The farmer rarely ever has an inning," Senator Gore wrote, "and so far as I am concerned he shall not be deprived of the legitimate fruits of his inning." [140] It would be "absolutely unfair, unjust, and inequitable for the Government to control the higher prices of cotton," the Georgia legislature resolved in July, 1917, "unless it will aid the farmers when in distress and fix a minimum . . . price above the cost of production." [141]

The Lever Food Control Act of August, 1917, provided for government controls on food, fuel, fertilizers, and agricultural implements; reference to cotton was eliminated in the Senate. Wheat became the first crop to be regulated, with the price fixed in both 1917 and 1918 at $2.20 a bushel. Cotton meanwhile rode the wartime inflation, while Southern "senators and representatives . . . formed a solid bloc in defense of unregulated cotton, rushed to the White House at every rumor of impending price control, and issued defiant statements calculated to reassure the homefolk but highly irritating to the rest of the country." [142] The sectional

[138] Burton J. Hendrick, "The Case of Josephus Daniels," in *World's Work*, XXXII (1916), 281–96.

[139] The following account is based chiefly upon Seward W. Livermore, "The Sectional Issue in the 1918 Congressional Elections," in *Mississippi Valley Historical Review* (Cedar Rapids, Iowa), XXV (1948–1949), 29–60, and his *Politics Is Adjourned*. See also Selig Adler, "The Congressional Election of 1918," in *South Atlantic Quarterly*, XXXVI (1937), 447–65.

[140] Thomas P. Gore to Reuben Dean Bowen, June 23, 1917, in Bowen Papers.

[141] Quoted in Saloutos, *Farmer Movements in the South*, 253.

[142] Livermore, "The Sectional Issue in the 1918 Congressional Elections," *loc. cit.*, 40.

issue of wheat and cotton reached a climax just at the time of the 1918 elections. Meanwhile, although it was clearly not decisive, Claude Kitchin replaced Josephus Daniels as the Republican whipping boy in the East. A partisan press campaign castigated his revenue policies as designed, in the words of the New York *Sun,* "to pay for the war out of taxes raised north of the Mason and Dixon Line." As one slogan put it, "The only way to be rid of Kitchinism is to elect Republicans to Congress!" [143]

In the outcome, the Democrats lost twenty-three House seats; two in the East, eleven in the Old Northwest, and ten in the wheat belt west of the Mississippi. Democratic Senators went down in Illinois, Kansas, Missouri, and Colorado, as well as in New Hampshire and Delaware. "Despite the fact that the West was enjoying unparalleled prosperity," Seward W. Livermore concluded after a study of the elections, "the administration permitted its opponents to manufacture a bogus economic issue out of the price-fixing situation and to use it in such a way as to undermine confidence in the impartiality of the government at a critical time in the nation's history. Failure to meet the charges of cotton profiteering was a political blunder compared to which Wilson's appeal [for a Democratic Congress to support his war and peace policies] was a minor matter." [144]

And so "the black sin of sectionalism," which the Memphis *Commercial Appeal* accused "South-hating" journals of using to political ends, presented Wilson an opposition Congress at the crucial moment of the peace negotiations.[145] In the long and confused maneuvers and debates that dragged out from July, 1919, when Wilson presented the treaty to the Senate, until the final rejection in March, 1920, the issue finally boiled down to a decision among three groups: the irreconcilable isolationists, the reservationists headed by Henry Cabot Lodge of Massachusetts who favored ratification only with reservations designed to protect American sovereignty and interests, and the Wilsonians who favored ratification of the treaty as it stood. With few exceptions

[143] Arnett, *Claude Kitchin and the Wilson War Policies,* 270–85, quotations from pp. 274, 283.
[144] Livermore, "The Sectional Issue in the 1918 Congressional Elections," 58.
[145] *Ibid.,* 60.

the Southern Senators stood with Wilson and a majority of them vigorously defended the proposed League. When the Senate attached the Lodge reservations to the treaty in November, only three Southern Senators refused to follow Wilson in declining to accept it on that basis: Smith of Georgia, Shields of Tennessee, and Gore of Oklahoma.[146] A renewed attempt at ratification with reservations lost in March. "One striking fact stands out like a lighthouse," a historian of the event concluded. "With the exception of [three] every single one of the twenty-three senators who stood loyally with Wilson in March came from south of the Mason and Dixon line. Only four of the 'disloyal' twenty-one represented states that had seceded in 1860–1861." [147]

One cannot escape the conclusion that the outcome was the consequence of partisan loyalties. The Republicans followed their leaders, mostly irreconcilables or reservationists. The Southern Democrats remained fiercely loyal to Wilson and contemptuous of what they regarded as blind partisan hostility toward the President. "The South is heart and soul for the Treaty," the Greenville, South Carolina, *Piedmont* declared. "It hasn't read it, but it has read some of the speeches of them darned Republicans." [148] One close student of the period found that "forty per cent of the state resolutions endorsing the League during 1917–1919 were passed by southern states, and public opinion in the South was almost solidly behind the League." [149] But ironically, the last-ditch Wilsonians had united with the irreconcilables to reject compromise and defeat ratification.

The force of Wilson's idealism struck deeply. "Men sometimes disparage idealists," John Sharp Williams told the Mississippi legislature a few days after the treaty's final defeat, "but they are coarse grained jackasses who do so and do it because they are coarse grained. But the idealists point the way and cheer men's souls." [150]

[146] Dewey W. Grantham, Jr., "The Southern Senators and the League of Nations, 1918–1920," in *North Carolina Historical Review*, XXVI (1949), 195.

[147] Thomas A. Bailey, *Woodrow Wilson and the Great Betrayal* (New York, 1945), 272. Three more "disloyal" votes came from Oklahoma and Kentucky, *Congressional Record*, 66 Cong., 2 Sess., 4599.

[148] Quoted in Bailey, *Woodrow Wilson and the Great Betrayal*, 48.

[149] Grantham, "Southern Senators and the League of Nations," *loc. cit.*, 199.

[150] Quoted in Osborn, *John Sharp Williams*, 449.

Two years later Carter Glass lamented the lack
"when the greatest Christian statesman of all time su
nations of the earth to enter into a Covenant which contained ...
very essence of the Sermon on the Mount and was the consumma-
tion, as far as Christian nations could contrive, of the sacrifice on
Calvary." [151]

As Southerners emerged onto the threshold of the 1920's the
experience of war had in many ways altered and enlarged their
perspectives. Southern politicians had moved into the orbit of
national politics. Sectionalism had retreated before nationalism
and an even wider vision of international co-operation. Parochial-
ism had diminished in the face of extensive contacts with the
outside world. Southern farms and cities had realized a taste of
prosperity beyond their previous experience, one that gave a lasting momentum to industrial if not to agricultural development.
Both the war effort and the new prosperity had spurred activity in
social work and public health, and the increased revenues of state
governments inspired the development of highways, public
schools, and other state services in the new decade. In race relations the war had contributed to significant developments that
must be considered in another chapter: the Great Migration of
Negroes to the North, paradoxical reactions that in some ways
eased and in others worsened the problems of Negroes, and finally,
the interracial movement of the 1920's.

Above all, the experience of the war years brought a new realization of change, the significance of which touched most keenly the
sensitive young writers of a coming revival in Southern letters.
"With the war of 1914–1918," one of them said later, "the South
re-entered the world—but gave a backward glance as it stepped
over the border: that backward glance gave us the Southern
renascence, a literature conscious of the past in the present." [152]
Some Southerners responded eagerly to change, others defensively;
but most, like the rising authors, reacted with ambivalence. Whatever their response, the consciousness of change had become one of
the abiding facts of the twentieth-century South.

[151] Carter Glass to John Stewart Bryan, November 3, 1921, in Carter Glass
Papers.
[152] Allen Tate, "The New Provincialism," in *Virginia Quarterly Review* (Charlottesville), XXI (1945), 272.

CHAPTER III

NORMALCY AND THE
ATLANTA SPIRIT

AMONG the major prophets of an industrial New South Richard Hathaway Edmonds was the only one who witnessed the congenial New Era of the 1920's. Publisher and editor of the Baltimore *Manufacturers' Record* since 1882, a contemporary of Henry W. Grady, he lived on to become the patriarch of Southern boosters.[1] There was "no other section in this or any other land known to mankind," he wrote in 1913, "of such boundless potentialities, predestined by nature to be the focusing point of the world's greatest material activities and of the mightiest influences for shaping the world's affairs." [2] "The South," he informed his readers in 1929, the year before his death, was "writing an Epic of Progress and Prosperity in Letters of Gold." [3]

If allowances must be made for Edmonds' obsession with Southern development and his penchant for propaganda, he was not a false prophet. Since 1880 Southern industry had slowly and steadily increased its proportion of the national output. The persistent forces of economic change, quickened by the First World War, easily survived a brief postwar slump in 1920–1921. In the piping times of normalcy that followed, an accelerated expansion and diversification of industry rapidly altered the face of the land.[4]

---

[1] For studies of Edmonds see Yoshimitsu Ide, "The Significance of Richard Hathaway Edmonds and his *Manufacturers' Record* in the New South" (Ph.D. dissertation, University of Florida, 1959) ; and Norman Ferris, "75 Years of Development Reporting," in *Industrial Development and Manufacturers' Record* (Atlanta) , CXXVII (December, 1958) , 6–9, 12–19.

[2] *Manufacturers' Record*, LXIII (March 27, 1913) , Part II, 3.

[3] *The Blue Book of Southern Progress*, 1929 (Baltimore, 1929) , 11–14.

[4] *Statistical Abstract of the United States*, 1922 (Washington, 1923) , 220–30. From

One significant token of industrial emergence was the election of a Southerner as president of the National Association of Manufacturers in 1921. Serving until 1931, John E. Edgerton, a textile manufacturer of Lebanon, Tennessee, became one of the chief spokesmen for the national business community during that decade, closely advised and assisted by Gus W. Dyer, professor of economics at Vanderbilt University.[5] In more significant ways Southern industry's coming of age pulled Southern business, as Wilson had pulled Southern politics, toward the national orbit. "The new industry of the South is part and parcel of a larger economy," a North Carolina economist declared in 1930. It belonged to "a pecuniary society, whose economic ramifications extend over an ever widening area."[6] The numbers of people it touched were rapidly increasing, the scope of its markets enlarging, the variety of its products growing. Moreover, Southern manufacturing was drawn ever more closely into a national structure of financial and corporate control through the processes of consolidation and the entry of new capital from outside.

But for most Southerners the overriding theme of the 1920's was, very simply, expansion. In the Southeast, economic renaissance was "largely a byproduct of technical electrical progress," a trade editor asserted in 1928. "An electric spark has fired the South to build a new civilization."[7] The Southern states as a whole had an estimated potential of 5,550,000 horsepower in their rivers, more than a third of the waterpower available 90 per cent of the time east of the Rockies.[8] The greatest part of the potential was along the Appalachian slopes where mountain rivers flowed

---

1919 until 1927 the number of wage earners in manufacturing rose by 9 per cent for the South while declining by 9 per cent for the rest of the nation. Large increases occurred in South Carolina (37 per cent), North Carolina (30 per cent), Georgia (25 per cent), Tennessee (21 per cent), and Alabama (11 per cent); the number declined slightly in the other Southern states. Clarence Heer, *Income and Wages in the South* (Chapel Hill, 1930), 6, 23.

[5] James W. Prothro, *Dollar Decade: Business Ideas in the 1920's* (Baton Rouge, 1954), relies heavily upon Edgerton's pronouncements. For a brief sketch see *Manufacturers' Record*, XCVI (August 22, 1929), 45.

[6] Heer, *Income and Wages in the South*, 3, 4.

[7] L. W. W. Morrow, "The Interconnected South," in *Electrical World* (New York), XCI (1928), 1077, 1084.

[8] Calvin B. Hoover and B. U. Ratchford, *Economic Resources and Policies of the*

toward the Atlantic or Gulf through narrow valleys that could readily be dammed—all in proximity to coal that could be used for supplementary steam power.[9]

Electrical development began in local systems during the 1880's, but large-scale development may be dated from 1904 when James B. Duke met William S. Lee, an engineer who infected the tobacco tycoon with his own zeal for power development. The result was the organization of the Southern (later Duke) Power Company in 1905. Beginning with the acquisition of a local plant near Charlotte, the company pursued Lee's plans for developing the entire Catawba-Wateree River system. A plant at Great Falls, South Carolina, commissioned in 1907, was the first link in a chain of dams and plants that within two decades extended from the upper reaches of the Catawba at Bridgewater, North Carolina, to a site on the Wateree near Camden, South Carolina—"a mighty river completely harnessed to perform the service of mankind." In 1925 ten hydroelectric stations had a total capacity of 483,000 horsepower and supplied energy for three hundred cotton mills as well as the towns and cities of the Piedmont Carolinas. By 1930 an installed capacity of 695,000 horsepower made Duke Power the largest operating company in the South, capable of producing more energy, one writer calculated, than all the slaves of the Old South.[10]

The characteristic growth elsewhere involved a process of consolidation and the wholesale entry of outside capital. The Alabama system, for instance, grew from two smaller companies: the Cherokee Development and Manufacturing Company, established

---

South (New York, 1951), 14. Estimate made in 1941.

[9] Rupert B. Vance, *Human Geography of the South* (Chapel Hill, 1932), 282–83; Walter H. Voskuil, *The Economics of Water Power Development* (Chicago and New York, 1928), 80–81.

[10] John Kennedy Winkler, *Tobacco Tycoon: The Story of James Buchanan Duke* (New York, 1942), 263–66; John W. Jenkins, *James B. Duke, Master Builder: The Story of Tobacco, Development of Southern and Canadian Water-Power and the Creation of a University* (New York, 1927), 173–239; Thomas W. Martin, "Hydro-Electric Development in the South," in *South's Development*, 245; Thorndike Saville, "The Power Situation in the Southern Power Province," in *Annals of the American Academy of Political and Social Science* (Philadelphia), CLIII (1931), 118; J. G. K. McClure, quoted in Clarence Poe, "America Discovers Dixie," in *Review of Reviews* (New York), LXXIII (1926), 380.

in 1900 to develop the Tallapoosa River, and the original Alabama Power Company, organized by Captain William Patrick Lay in 1906 to develop the Coosa. Consolidation resulted from the promotional activities of a Canadian engineer, James Mitchell, who got the co-operation of Lay, Thomas W. Martin, a Montgomery lawyer, and others in securing English capital to consolidate some fifteen companies and reserve the likely water-power sites in the state. Early in 1912 they organized the Alabama Traction Light and Power Company, Ltd., under the laws of Canada and projected a twenty-year development plan to harness the rivers of the state. The plans were carried through at first under Mitchell's presidency and after 1920 under Martin's. By 1926 Alabama was producing more power than any other Southern state.[11]

Meanwhile the company became the nucleus of even wider consolidation. In 1924 control passed to the Southeastern Power and Light Company, a holding company organized under the laws of Maine. And soon thereafter other subsidiaries came in: the Georgia Power Company, the Mississippi Power Company, and the Gulf Power Company in North Florida. In 1929 still another level rose on the pyramid of control when the Commonwealth and Southern Corporation acquired Southeastern; Commonwealth's other holdings were in Pennsylvania and Ohio.[12]

The process of growth and consolidation recapitulated nineteenth-century railroad development.[13] In the years 1924–1929

[11] Thomas Wesley Martin, *Forty Years of Alabama Power Company, 1911–1951* (New York, 1952), 12–32, 44; Thorndike Saville, "The Power Situation in the Southern Appalachian States," in *Manufacturers' Record*, XCI (April 21, 1927), 70–72.

[12] Martin, *Forty Years of Alabama Power Company*, 25–26, 42–43. The Securities and Exchange Commission later ordered Commonwealth and Southern dissolved under provisions of the Public Utility Holding Company Act of 1935 but approved the organization of The Southern Company as a successor. The Southern Company was, in effect, a reconstituted Southeastern Power and Light, controlling the same integrated group of Alabama, Georgia, Mississippi, and Gulf power companies as its chief subsidiaries. Its first full year of operation was 1948.

[13] On over-all power development, see in addition to works cited above, Joseph Hyde Pratt, "In the Southern Appalachians," in *Survey*, LI (1923–1924), 611–12, 654; Carroll E. Williams, "The South's Hydro and Steam Electric Power Development," in *Manufacturers' Record*, XCIV (November 29, 1924), 51–63; Morrow,

combinations absorbed a total of 635 electric properties in the Southern states east of the Mississippi. By the end of the decade seven management groups controlled 84 per cent of the output in those states, and three of them controlled 71 per cent: Commonwealth and Southern (33 per cent), Electric Bond and Share Company (23), and Duke Power Company (15.3). Duke, however, was not affiliated with any of the holding companies.[14]

Meanwhile, from 1921 to 1930 generating capacity expanded by 156 per cent, whereas it rose only 58 per cent in the non-Southern states. By 1929 the South had 5,460,000 kilowatts of generating capacity, or 17.3 per cent of the national total, and 2,112,000 kilowatts of hydroelectric capacity, or 25.9 per cent of the total.[15]

A strategic innovation of the period was the device of interconnections, widely publicized as "Super-Power," the great "region builder." The process started with a link in 1914 that permitted the transfer of surplus power from the Georgia Railway and Power plant at Tallulah Falls to the Duke system. A striking demonstration of its wider possibilities occurred in 1921 and 1922 when power from the government's Muscle Shoals plant permitted Alabama Power to release energy into Georgia. This in turn relieved a shortage resulting from a severe drought in Eastern North Carolina and represented an interchange over a distance of eleven hundred miles. By 1930 the system had grown to include a total of twenty-nine operating companies, reportedly the most extensive interconnection east of the Rockies.[16]

The growth of power was most significant to manufacturing development around the fringes of the Appalachians, especially in the Piedmont Industrial Crescent from Virginia to Alabama. It contributed to the thrust of powered processes like textiles and to the development of electrochemical processes like aluminum. By the end of the 1920's industrial power rates were lower in the

---

"Interconnected South," *loc. cit.*, 1077–84. Miles C. Shorey, "An Empire Builder and His Achievements," in *Manufacturers' Record*, XCV (May 2, 1929), 74–77, is a profile of Harvey C. Couch, founder of the Arkansas Power and Light Company.

[14] Saville, "Power Situation in the Southern Power Province," *loc. cit.*, 116–17.

[15] Hoover and Ratchford, *Economic Resources and Policies of the South*, 136.

[16] Martin, "Hydro-Electric Development in the South," *loc. cit.*, 255–56; Saville, "Power Situation in the Southern Power Province," *loc. cit.*, 116; Morrow, "Interconnected South," *loc. cit.*, 1078–80.

South than elsewhere in the country, and the Southeast used more electric power per wage earner than the Northeast.[17] By 1927 about half of all Southern industries had been electrified, with lumber a somewhat larger consumer than textiles.[18] In the Carolinas alone, one writer asserted, electricity powered about 90 per cent of the cotton and tobacco factories and 50 per cent of the furniture and knitting mills.[19]

The textile machinery set whirling by the war roared on through 1919 and 1920 without slackening pace. All through the Piedmont Crescent promoters were seeking new mills. Gaston County, North Carolina, adopted the slogan "Organize a mill a week." [20] It was magnificently unrealistic, but the county had 105 mills by 1923 and in 1929 was the leading textile county in the South, third in the nation.[21] Construction reports for the whole South showed 221 new mills and expansions in 1921, 480 in 1922, and 469 in the first nine months of 1923.[22] As early as 1913 Southern textile mills overtook New England in their consumption of cotton. During the 1920's they passed one milestone after another: supremacy in wage earners and value of product, 1923; in active spindles and value added by manufacture, 1925; in total spindles and total wages, 1927; and in looms, between 1927 and 1931.[23] After 1921 more than half the sales of the Saco-Lowell

[17] Saville, "Power Situation in the Southern Power Province," *loc. cit.,* 112, cites Preston S. Arkwright, President of Georgia Power Company, as source for the statement that the average industrial rate for sixty-eight typical cities across the United States was 1.544 cents per kilowatt hour and for the South, 1.359 cents. However, figures for a selected group of cities showed domestic rates in 1931 for thirty kilowatt hours to be 2.42 cents in the South and 2.01 cents in the rest of the country. Figures cited in Wilson Gee, *Research Barriers in the South* (Chapel Hill, 1932), 61. See also Hoover and Ratchford, *Economic Resources and Policies of the South,* 134.

[18] Voskuil, *Economics of Water Power Development,* 78.

[19] Jenkins, *James B. Duke,* 183.

[20] Benjamin U. Ratchford, "Toward Preliminary Social Analysis: II. Economic Aspects of the Gastonia Situation," in *Social Forces,* VIII (1929–1930), 360.

[21] *Manufacturers' Record,* LXXXIV (October 25, 1923), 115; Howard W. Odum, *Southern Regions of the United States* (Chapel Hill, 1936), 70.

[22] *Manufacturers' Record,* LXXXIV (October 25, 1923), 115.

[23] Jules Backman and M. R. Gainsbrugh, *Economics of the Cotton Textile Industry* (New York, 1946), 33, 173; Jack Blicksilver, *Cotton Manufacturing in the Southeast: A Historical Analysis* (Atlanta, 1959), 93; *Cotton Textile Industry: A Report on the Conditions and Problems of the Cotton Textile Industry,* Senate Document No. 126, 74 Cong., 1 Sess., 28, 52, 56.

textile machinery shops went to Southern mills.[24] And the advance was qualitative, with the South diversifying into dyeing and finishing plants, automobile tire fabrics, woolen and knit goods, rayon, hosiery, and apparel plants, and raising the quality of its products.[25]

Contrary to popular impression, the rise of Southern textiles did not result from a wholesale migration of either plants or capital from New England. An investigation by alarmed New Englanders indicated that 83.8 per cent of Southern spindles were still owned or controlled by Southern capital in 1922, only 14.2 per cent by Northern and 2 per cent by Western.[26] A substantial movement of Northern capital occurred in the summer of 1923, however, and through the following year involved about $100,000,000 for the purchase or building of Southern mills. From 1921 to 1929, according to another source, 51 mills with over 1.3 million spindles moved from New England into the South.[27] Still, as late as 1931, a study of the four major Southern textile states revealed only 51 non-Southern firms with 80 branches. They controlled only about 15 per cent of all the spindles and 12 to 13 per cent of the looms; but the proportion rose markedly as one progressed from North Carolina to Alabama, which suggested a larger Northern influence in the newer development.[28]

But the South bought its textile ascendancy at a heavy cost of troubles. The business slump of 1920–1921 inaugurated a prolonged period of difficulty. Some recovery came in 1923, but in 1924 the industry as a whole experienced "the most unfavorable return to manufacturers since prewar years"; and the low returns

[24] George Sweet Gibb, *The Saco-Lowell Shops: Textile Machinery Building in New England, 1813–1949* (Cambridge, Mass., 1950), 473, 668.

[25] Benjamin Franklin Lemert, *The Cotton Textile Industry of the Southern Appalachian Piedmont* (Chapel Hill, 1933), 8–9; Blicksilver, *Cotton Manufacturing in the Southeast*, 93–94.

[26] Massachusetts Department of Labor and Industries, *Report of a Special Investigation into Conditions in the Textile Industry in Massachusetts and the Southern States* (Boston, 1923), 18.

[27] Carroll E. Williams, "Southern Mills Add More Than 1,000,000 Spindles in Two Years," in *Manufacturers' Record*, XC (October 28, 1926), 99–104; Solomon Barkin, "The Regional Significance of the Integration Movement in the Southern Textile Industry," in *Southern Economic Journal* (Chapel Hill), XV (1948–1949), 308.

[28] Lemert, *Cotton Textile Industry of the Southern Appalachian Piedmont*, 153–56.

continued until the Great Depression turned them into losses.[29] Circumstances of intense competition and over-production made lower costs imperative, from the viewpoint of management, and gave the Southern industry its fateful advantage—lower wages and longer hours in a labor-intensive industry. An inquiry in 1922 showed that average hourly earnings of 40.9 cents in Massachusetts mills contrasted sharply with earnings of 32.5 cents in Virginia and 21 cents in Alabama.[30] In 1926 representatives of sixty Northern firms active in Southern textiles answered a questionnaire on the growth of Southern industry: in every case they made reference to cheaper labor, and many added revealing complaints at labor conditions in the Northeast "which made a mockery of orderly business management." [31] The abundant electrical power offered lower rates and eliminated the need to tie up capital in power plants; and the Southern Railway, double-tracked from Washington to Atlanta shortly after the war, provided ready access to the electrified Piedmont.[32]

Obsolescence penalized the New England mills. The South had newer plants and machinery, although the cost advantage of proximity to cotton was less significant than it seemed; for the center of cotton production, especially in the longer staples and better grades, was moving westward.[33] By the end of the 1920's probably no more than a third of the Southern mills could meet their requirements from their own states.[34]

[29] Stephen Jay Kennedy, *Profits and Losses in Textiles* (New York, 1936), 10, 128; Backman and Gainsbrugh, *Economics of the Cotton Textile Industry*, 135–39, 141–42; Herman E. Michl, *The Textile Industries: An Economic Analysis* (Washington, 1938), 103; Blicksilver, *Cotton Manufacturing in the Southeast*, 99.

[30] Massachusetts Department of Labor, *Report of a Special Investigation*, 2.

[31] "Northern and Western Interests Give Reasons for Establishing Textile Plants in the South," in *Manufacturers' Record*, XC (October 28, 1926), 95–98. See also Broadus Mitchell, "A Survey of Industry," in William T. Couch (ed.), *Culture in the South* (Chapel Hill, 1935), 89–90.

[32] Massachusetts Department of Labor, *Report of a Special Investigation*, 2; Frederick M. Halsey, "The Southern Railway: Its Development and Future," in *Moody's Magazine*, XIX (1916), 245; E. C. Ferriday, "Double-Tracking the Southern Railway," in *Manufacturers' Record*, LXXIV (November 7, 1918), 84–85.

[33] Massachusetts Department of Labor, *Report of a Special Investigation*, 2; *Cotton Textile Industry*, Senate Document No. 126, 74 Cong., 1 Sess., 114–18.

[34] Claudius T. Murchison, *King Cotton Is Sick* (Chapel Hill, 1930), 42; Lemert, *Cotton Textile Industry of the Southern Appalachian Piedmont*, 93.

Over-all surveys of reputable experts confirmed the judgment that lower costs provided a significant differential in favor of Southern mills. In 1923 a representative of the engineering firm Lockwood, Green and Company estimated a difference of 14 per cent in favor of the South, with 85 per cent of that attributed to wages.[35] Another study in 1926 showed a Southern advantage of 16.8 per cent over Massachusetts, with more than 67 per cent attributed to labor. Taking into account the expense of company mill villages, the advantage was still nearly 13 per cent.[36]

The result was devastation for New England; "the columns of the textile press reporting the discontinuance and liquidation and abandonment of New England mills, read like wartime casualty lists," one observer said.[37] From 1923 to 1933 New England lost 40 per cent of its mills and almost 100,000 of its 190,000 wage earners; Southern employment rose from 220,000 to 257,000 and its share of total employment from 46 to 68 per cent.[38] Southern textiles avoided the wholesale bankruptcies of New England, but during the years 1926–1932 probably fewer than half of the Southern mills were on a regular dividend basis for common stocks. The market prices of twenty-five leading Southern mill issues dropped from an average of $144.50 in 1923 to $71.48 in July, 1930.[39] The very process of expansion produced a rank growth of difficulties. "In terms of overproduction, declining prices and profits, liquidation, the stretch-out, and embittered labor relations," Jack Blicksilver has written, "cotton millmen after 1923 were to reap the whirlwind of seeds so blithely sown during the halcyon years, 1900–1923." [40]

In the upper Piedmont, while textiles moved ahead, tobacco entered the cigarette revolution. James B. Duke had earlier

[35] Blicksilver, *Cotton Manufacturing in the Southeast*, 81.

[36] *Mechanical Engineering*, October, 1926, cited in Paul Blanshard, *Labor in Southern Cotton Mills* (New York, 1927) , 34.

[37] Quoted, from unidentified writer, in Dane Yorke, *The Men and Times of Pepperell: An Account of the First One Hundred Years of the Pepperell Manufacturing Company* (Boston, 1945) , 91.

[38] Blicksilver, *Cotton Manufacturing in the Southeast*, 92–93.

[39] Michl, *Textile Industries*, 104; Robert Sidney Smith, *Mill on the Dan: A History of Dan River Mills, 1882–1950* (Durham, 1960) , 113–91; Murchison, *King Cotton Is Sick*, 34.

[40] Blicksilver, *Cotton Manufacturing in the Southeast*, 50.

envisioned the possibilities, but it was Robert J. Reynolds who ushered in a new era. Freed from the American Tobacco empire by the antitrust decision of 1911, Reynolds determined to "give Buck Duke hell" for earlier humiliations. In 1913 he brought forth a new blend, predominantly bright leaf with a touch of burley and Turkish, but with an Oriental name—Camel—in the established tradition. The next year, with an advertising campaign which cost nearly a million and a half dollars ("Tomorrow there will be more Camels in this town than in all Asia and Africa combined!"), sales reached nearly .5 billion cigarettes and 2.4 billion in 1915; in 1921 Camels accounted for more than half the cigarette sales in the country. Reynolds' innovation was imitated by Liggett and Myers' Chesterfields in 1915 and American's Lucky Strike ("It's Toasted") in 1916. The popular new "domestic blends" arrived just in time to capitalize on the war, but the growth continued through the 1920's; Lorillard belatedly introduced a new "standard brand," Old Golds, in 1926. The production of more than 125 billion cigarettes in 1930 represented an increase of 1,339 per cent in twenty years; other tobacco products, except snuff and smoking mixtures, experienced a decline.[41]

The spectacular accompaniment of the cigarette revolution was the increase of advertising, directed by such leaders as Reynolds' William Cole Esty and American's Albert Lasker ("Reach for a Lucky instead of a Sweet"). In 1926 Reynolds spent $19,000,000 for advertising; in 1928 American launched a $12,300,000 campaign for Luckies alone; in the depression year of 1931 Reynolds spent $1,000,000 in seven days to promote his new cellophane wrapping, and the industry as a whole put out $75,000,000 during the year. Cigarette production remained largely in the hands of the Big Three (American, Reynolds, and Liggett and Myers), who had about 90 per cent of the production in 1927, and was concen-

[41] Robert, *Story of Tobacco in America*, 229–36; Richard B. Tennant, *The American Cigarette Industry: A Study in Economic Analysis and Public Policy* (New Haven, 1950), 75–84; Winkler, *Tobacco Tycoon*, 259–60; "R. J. Reynolds Tobacco Company," in *Fortune's Favorites: Portraits of Some American Corporations, an Anthology from Fortune Magazine* (New York, 1931), 195–217; Reavis Cox, *Competition in the American Tobacco Industry, 1911–1932: A Study of the Partition of the American Tobacco Company by the United States Supreme Court*, in Columbia University *Studies in History, Economics, and Public Law*, No. 381 (New York, 1933), 41.

trated in North Carolina, whose share of the output rose from 51 per cent in 1920 to 64 in 1930.[42]

During the 1920's another Southern consumer product, Coca-Cola, moved well on the way toward becoming a national institution. First concocted in 1886 by an Atlanta druggist, it made one fortune for its proprietor, Asa Griggs Candler, before controlling interest passed in 1919 to a syndicate organized by Ernest Woodruff, an Atlanta banker and businessman. Under Woodruff's son Robert, who became president in 1923, the company entered new markets and raised its profits within a decade to nearly the level of the purchase price; stock values increased tenfold. Before 1919 the nickel "dope" found its chief markets in the South; as late as 1930 a business writer expressed doubt that Northern office managers would ever accept the Southern custom of morning and afternoon breaks for the "pause that refreshes." But Robert Woodruff transformed Coca-Cola into a national symbol, eventually known around the world. "Candler put us on our feet," a company old-timer said later, "but Woodruff gave us wings." [43] It was not until the 1930's that Pepsi-Cola, invented by a New Bern, North Carolina, druggist about 1896, began to give any important competition.[44]

Beyond Atlanta, at the end of the Piedmont Crescent, the Birmingham district offered a contrast to the surging growth in other fields. Despite advantages in the cost of materials and labor, Southern iron and steel lagged behind its potential. The region's percentage of pig iron production declined from 13.2 in 1905 to

[42] Cox, *Competition in the American Tobacco Industry*, 67, 227; Robert, *Story of Tobacco in America*, 236–40, 260. By 1949 the three states of North Carolina, Virginia, and Kentucky produced 95 per cent of American cigarettes, North Carolina alone more than half. William H. Nicholls, *Price Policies in the Cigarette Industry: A Study of "Concerted Action" and Its Social Control, 1911–1950* (Nashville, 1951) , 17.

[43] "The Coca-Cola Company," in *Fortune's Favorites*, 329–50; E. J. Kahn, Jr., *The Big Drink: The Story of Coca-Cola* (New York, 1960) , 55–68. For expressions of fascination at the phenomenal Southern capacity for the drink, see Ursula Branston, *Let the Band Play "Dixie"! Improvisations on a Southern Signature Tune* (London, 1940) , 19, 31, 43, 47–48, 105, 243, and *passim*. On later development, see "Bob Woodruff of Coca-Cola," in *Fortune*, XXXII (September, 1945) , 139–43, 220, 223–24, 226, 228, 230.

[44] John J. Riley, *A History of the American Soft Drink Industry: Bottled Carbonated Beverages, 1807–1957* (Washington, 1958) , 127, 134, 143.

11.6 in 1929, although the percentage of rolled iron and steel rose slightly, from 2.65 in 1901 to 4.86 in 1926, largely because of the war-inspired Fairfield Works; and employment in that field went up from 2,204 at the turn of the century to 8,121 in 1919 and 9,253 in 1929.[45] "In a competitive struggle for southern markets," a careful student of the problem concluded, "Birmingham mills with their lower costs would have come off best."[46] But unlike textiles, iron and steel were not in a competitive situation. Republic Steel had entered the South prior to 1900 and a few independents continued to operate, including the war-born Texas and Gulf States steel companies, but the supreme giant was the Tennessee Coal and Iron Company, subsidiary of United States Steel since 1907.[47] With its dominance of the coal and ore fields, it held the key to expansion but operated under a control that placed regional interests in a subordinate position; any Southern expansion would be at the expense of Northern capacity already developed.

Another explanation of the reluctance to exploit Southern advantages was the relative lack of markets in the region, but that in turn derived at least partially from pricing policies undertaken to protect the established plants. From about the turn of the century until 1924 the industry levied prices on a "Pittsburgh Plus" basis—that is, the Pittsburgh price plus freight from there—so that Pittsburgh mills could lay down steel anywhere in the Birmingham market area at prices equally attractive. Steel fabricators near Pittsburgh could buy their raw material for less and tended to congregate near that source. The Federal Trade Commission turned up case after case of Southern fabricators operating under the disadvantage: the Vulcan Rivet Company of Bessemer paying twenty-five cents more per hundred pounds of steel bars than competitors in Pittsburgh; the American Bolt Company of

[45] Edward C. Eckel, "The Iron and Steel Industry of the South," in *Annals of the American Academy of Political and Social Science,* CLIII (1931), 61; O. C. Ault, "Is Industry Decentralized in the South?" in [Mercer G. Evans (ed.)], *The Industrial South* (Atlanta, 1928), 33; Chapman, *Iron and Steel Industries of the South,* 116–17.

[46] George W. Stocking, *Basing Point Pricing and Regional Development: A Case Study of the Iron and Steel Industry* (Chapel Hill, 1954), 104.

[47] Sketches of the major companies' histories appear in Chapman, *Iron and Steel Industries of the South,* 142–46.

Birmingham suffering a price differential on raw materials estimated at 8¾ per cent of its selling price; the Harriman Manufacturing Company, plowmakers of Chattanooga, with a disadvantage of 9½ per cent. Even after the FTC outlawed Pittsburgh Plus in 1924, Birmingham operated for another fourteen years under the burden of a "multiple basing point" system that arbitrarily maintained its steel prices at three to five dollars a ton above Pittsburgh.[48]

Except for food processing, which was largely for the local market, lumbering was the most ubiquitous of Southern industries.[49] After 1900, with the decline of the Great Lakes cutover region, the South quickly became the area of greatest lumber production, but at the cost of an exploitation that showed little regard for selective logging, reforestation, or the fate of communities stranded by the cutout. By 1921 a total area of probably 100,000,-000 acres had been devastated in the coastal plain from South Carolina to Texas—equal to half the total area of Texas or the combined areas of Georgia, Alabama, and Mississippi, and not counting denuded mountainsides in the Appalachians.[50] In the South as a whole the cutover area was more than 156,000,000 acres by 1920.[51] In 1924 a report to the Southern Pine Association estimated a supply good for only twenty to twenty-five years and the Secretary of Agriculture suggested ten as a more realistic figure. Yet the industry stubbornly refused to die. Postwar demands for construction materials found the Southern states a continuing source of supply through the natural replenishment of

[48] Stocking, *Basing Point Pricing and Regional Development*, 50–57, 62–98; Chapman, *Iron and Steel Industries of the South*, 371–75, 378–85, 415–16. For the FTC order against Pittsburgh Plus pricing, see 8 *FTC Decisions*, 1, 59, published in full in *Manufacturers' Record*, LXXXVI (July 31, 1924) , 69–73.

[49] Suggestive beginnings in a neglected area were made in Ralph N. Traxler, "Food Processing—A Problem?" (Paper read to the Southern Historical Association, Atlanta, November, 1959) . See also Emory Business Executives' Research Committee, *A Look at Georgia Manufacturing Industries* (Atlanta, 1959) .

[50] F. W. Farley and S. W. Greene, *The Cut-Over Pine Lands of the South for Beef-Cattle Production*, U. S. Department of Agriculture Bulletin No. 827 (Washington, 1921) , 2; Robert S. Lambert, "Logging the Great Smokies," in *Tennessee Historical Quarterly* (Nashville) , XX (1961) , 350–63; Robert S. Lambert, "Logging on Little River, 1890–1940," in *East Tennessee Historical Society Publications* (Knoxville) , XXXIII (1961) , 32–42.

[51] Rupert B. Vance, *Human Geography of the South* (Chapel Hill, 1932) , 124.

pine, "the fastest growing tree outside the tropics." Where major operators cut out the virgin timber and moved on, little "peckerwood" mills sprang up in the second growth and smaller stands.[52]

First alarm, and then recognition of the possibilities in controlled growth, together with the activities of forestry leaders like William L. Bray in Texas, Joseph Hyde Pratt in North Carolina, and Henry Hardtner in Louisiana, aroused public concern and brought about legislation for conservation.[53] Meanwhile, the larger operators turned to sustained yield operations. In 1922 the Crossett Lumber Company of Arkansas, one of the biggest, employed its first graduate forester.[54] In 1925 a trained forester entered the employ of the Great Southern Lumber Company of eastern Louisiana to develop what the company said was the largest private hand-planted reforestation area in the world; in 1928, 7,000,000 pine seedlings were put out.[55] Both Crossett and Great Southern stabilized their operations further by using waste and by-products for boxes, ladder rungs, strips, dowel pins, wood chemicals, and finally pulp and paper. Trade associations of the pine and hardwood producers worked toward stabilization by means of standardized grading and "open competition" through the dissemination of statistics. The Southern Pine Association, whose members produced 45 per cent of the Southern pine, established in 1925 uniform grade marking in accordance with Commerce Department standards.[56]

[52] *Ibid.*, 139; Stanley F. Horn, *This Fascinating Lumber Business* (Indianapolis and New York, 1943), 36–40.

[53] Easton, "History of the Texas Lumbering Industry," 418; Bolling Arthur Johnson, "Past, Present and Future of Forestry and Lumbering in the South," in *The South's Development*, 322; Stanley Todd Lowry, "Henry Hardtner, Pioneer in Southern Forestry: An Analysis of the Economic Bases of His Reforestation Program" (M.A. thesis, Louisiana State University, 1956); W. W. Ashe, "Forest Conditions in the Southern States and Recommended Forest Policy," in *South Atlantic Quarterly*, XXII (1923), 295–303; Charles H. Schaeffer, "The State Forestry Department," in *Alabama Historical Quarterly* (Montgomery), I (1930), 224–31; Reuben B. Robertson, "Recent Developments in Southern Forestry," in *Georgia Review* (Athens), V (1951), 362–68.

[54] Carolyn Blanks, "Industry in the New South: A Case History," in *Arkansas Historical Quarterly*, XI (1951), 167.

[55] Charles W. Goodyear, *The Bogalusa Story* (Buffalo, 1950), 163–66.

[56] Lee M. James, "Restrictive Agreements and Practices in the Lumber Industry, 1880–1939," in *Southern Economic Journal*, XIII (1946–1947), 115–25; Albert F. Israel, "How Trade Bodies Can Serve Producer and Consumer as Shown by the

With stabilization the South achieved the distinction "of having been a continuous major source of lumber production longer than any other section of the country." [57] From 1909 to 1925 it was the leading lumber region and in 1940 regained the lead with its 13,515,000 board feet, 46.5 per cent of the nation's total. By 1940 five states had more than a thousand lumber mills each: North Carolina, Virginia, Georgia, Alabama, and Mississippi.[58]

Furniture making, an important adjunct to lumbering, had progressed from its beginnings with crude "plunder" in the 1880's to a quality product "attractively designed, well constructed by skilled workers, and . . . finished equal to the same class made in any other section." [59] In 1922 the Southern Furniture Exposition Building, ten stories high with 228,000 square feet of exhibit space, made its debut in High Point, North Carolina. Within a few years it added four more floors and became one of the country's leading furniture marts. Southern furniture production increased from 14.3 per cent of the nation's total in 1919 to 15.8 in 1929; with more than half coming from Virginia and North Carolina.[60]

Major signs of future diversification for both industry and agriculture were the beginnings of the paper and chemical industries. As early as 1914 there were twenty-five paper mills in the eleven former Confederate states, mostly producing negligible quantities of quality papers, but with processes not suited to resinous woods like the predominant Southern pine.[61] The begin-

---

Southern Pine Association," in *Manufacturers' Record*, LXXXVI (August 7, 1924), 104–105. See also *Manufacturers' Record*, LXXXVII (April 2, 1925), 97–99; Ruth A. Allen, *East Texas Lumber Workers: An Economic and Social Picture, 1870–1950* (Austin, 1961), 32–33; James W. Silver, "The Hardwood Producers Come of Age," in *Journal of Southern History*, XXIII (1957), 427–53.

[57] Horn, *This Fascinating Lumber Business*, 96.

[58] *Ibid.*, 31–33; Vance, *Human Geography of the South*, 123–44.

[59] Charles F. Scribner, "Southern Furniture Plants Apply Modern Management with Success; The Plant, Its Arrangements and Service Facilities," in *Management and Administration* (Camden, N.J.) X (1925), 83.

[60] Harold Emerson Klontz, "An Economic Study of the Southern Furniture Manufacturing Industry" (Ph.D. dissertation, University of North Carolina, 1948), 32, 36–37.

[61] Olin Terrell Mouzon, "The Social and Economic Implications of Recent Developments within the Wood and Paper Industry in the South" (Ph.D. dissertation, University of North Carolina, 1940), 142. Except where otherwise indicated, the

nings of mass production came with the introduction from Germany of the sulphate process for making brown kraft wrapping papers and bags from either resinous or nonresinous woods. The pioneer was North Carolina's Roanoke Rapids Paper Company in 1909, closely followed by an Orange, Texas, plant.[62] In 1913 Moss Point, Mississippi, a lumber center stranded by the cutout and by the opening of a deep water port at Gulfport, undertook to recoup its fortunes with a sulphate mill, thus setting a pattern for many cutover areas.[63] By 1920 there were nine Southern plants using the new process and by 1930 seventeen kraft mills across the pine belt from Virginia to Texas, in all forty-eight Southern paper mills. By that time the South had secured approximately half the nation's papermaking capacity and was approaching a new expansion in the 1930's. Meanwhile, related industries, the Celotex mills in Louisiana and the Masonite Corporation at Laurel, Mississippi, turned out insulating and building boards from sugar cane waste and wood chips.[64]

The critical moment for the chemical industry arrived with World War I, heralded by its pioneer propagandist, Dr. Charles H. Herty.[65] Equipped with mineral resources that ran from arsenopyrite to zirconia ores in the *Manufacturers' Record* cata-

---

following account of the paper industry is drawn from *ibid.*, 104–58. See also C. E. Curran, "The Paper Industry in the South," in J. E. Mills (ed.), *Chemical Progress in the South* (New York, 1930), 140–41.

[62] Curran, "Paper Industry in the South," *loc. cit.*, 141.

[63] Ed Lipscomb, "A New Kind of Agriculture Comes to the Piney Woods," in *Nation's Business* (Washington), XXV (August, 1937), 35–36.

[64] Robert M. Boehn, "Manufacture of Insulation Board and Pressed Wood by the Masonite Process," in Mills (ed.), *Chemical Progress in the South*, 167–70; Elbert C. Lathrop, "The Utilization of Bagasse in the Manufacture of Celotex," *ibid.*, 171–72; John Hebron Moore, "William H. Mason, Southern Industrialist," in *Journal of Southern History*, XXVII (1961), 169–83.

[65] Charles H. Herty, "The Psychological Moment in Southern Development," in *Manufacturers' Record*, LXXIII (April 25, 1918), 48. This was a special issue connected with a Southern tour sponsored by the American Electrochemical Society. Herty, a former professor of chemistry at the state universities of Georgia and North Carolina, had become president of the American Chemical Society (1915–1916), editor of the *Journal of Industrial and Engineering Chemistry* (1917–1921), president of the Synthetic Organic Chemical Manufacturers' Association (1921–1926), and advisor to the Chemical Foundation (1926–1928). D. H. Kelleffer, "Charles Holmes Herty," in Robert Livingston Schuyler (ed.), *Dictionary of American Biography*, XXII, Supplement Two, 300–302.

logs, the South offered additional lures in forest and agricultural products, electricity, climate, and water.[66] With foundations already established in petroleum, sulphur, pulp, vegetable oils, and fertilizers, the industry began to reach out into other fields so diverse as to defy summary. In one basic field, sulphur, both Freeport and Texas Gulf consolidated their positions in the 1920's by exploring and opening new mounds, while Union, the original producer, exhausted its Louisiana mine in 1924. Through the two remaining corporations the South accounted for nearly all the domestic production, and through a cartel with Sicilian producers, took 75 per cent of the world market.[67] In Tennessee the production of sulphuric acid was expanded by the Tennessee Copper & Chemical Corporation, which already had the largest plant for the purpose, and by the Ducktown Chemical & Iron Company.[68]

Three of the war-inspired wood chemical plants in Tennessee continued in the 1920's to produce methanol, acetic acid, and ethyl acetate.[69] At Hopewell, Virginia, in 1927 Allied Chemical put $50,000,000 into an air-nitrogen plant.[70] As early as 1893 the Mathieson Chemical Company had started alkali production at Saltville, Virginia. Attracted by the appearance of viscose rayon, kraft paper, and oil refining, the ammonia-soda alkali industry began to look further South and acquired holdings at Corpus Christi and Baton Rouge; plants materialized in the 1930's.[71] Improvements in resins and turpentine diversified uses and saved that industry from declining markets. A single holding company, the Swann Corporation of Alabama, founded in 1929 and later absorbed into Monsanto Chemical Company, controlled com-

[66] Richard K. Meade, "Economic and Mineral Resources of the South and Their Relation to Chemical Manufactures," in *Manufacturers' Record*, LXXVI (December 25, 1919), 93–96. See also special issue on the chemical potentialities of the South, *ibid.*, LXX (September 14, 1916).

[67] Montgomery, *Brimstone Game*, 73–74; Haynes, *American Chemical Industry*, IV, 74–80; Haynes, *Stone That Burns*, 155–236. The exhaustion of the Union's mine in 1924 did not permanently end production in Louisiana; in 1933 Freeport opened a new operation at Grand Ecaille in the Mississippi River Delta. *Ibid.*, 237–56.

[68] Haynes, *American Chemical Industry*, IV, 81–82.

[69] *Ibid.*, III, 136–37; IV, 128–30.

[70] "The Industrial South," in *Fortune*, XVIII (November, 1938), 54.

[71] *Ibid.*; Haynes, *American Chemical Industry*, IV, 90–94.

panies producing ferromanganese, ferrosilicon, ferrochrome, calcium and silicon carbide, mono- and tri-calcium phosphate, and electrical power, among other things. Swann Research, Incorporated, introduced the combine to diphenyl, xylose, and various textile chemicals.[72] By 1927 the South had twenty types of major chemical production producing 25.6 per cent of all their value in Southern plants.[73] Dr. Herty attempted a summary: "nitrogen fixation, rayon, paper, caustic soda, chlorine, refractories, glass, products from natural gas, barium compounds, synthetic organic chemical compounds—and most of these . . . manufactured from cheap raw materials." [74]

The manufacture of rayon, which used cellulose as its raw material, began in 1917 at the American Viscose Corporation plant at Roanoke, Virginia, which until about 1941 had the world's largest capacity. Wartime cellulose plants for explosives at Hopewell and Nashville subsequently became rayon plants for the Tubize Artificial Silk Company and DuPont. In 1928 and 1929 new plants rose in Elizabethton, Tennessee; Asheville, North Carolina; Rome, Georgia; and Covington, Waynesboro, and Richmond, Virginia. By 1930 American production reached 117,500,000 pounds, of which 81,200,000 was in the South and 42,000,000 in Virginia alone, where rayon by 1933 led all industries in the number of wage earners.[75]

The most successful exploitation of the new fiber was undertaken by Burlington Mills, the creation of J. Spencer Love, a young war veteran who jumped first into the postwar boom at Gastonia, then sold his mill at a profit, and in 1923 moved to Burlington, where a co-operative Chamber of Commerce under-

[72] C. H. Penning, "The Swann Corporation," in Mills (ed.), *Chemical Progress in the South*, 150–52.

[73] Lauren B. Hitchcock, "Chemical Resources and Industries of the South," in *Annals of the American Academy of Political and Social Science*, XLIII (1931), 76, 79, 81.

[74] *Chemical Markets*, XXIII (1928), 464, quoted in Haynes, *American Chemical Industry*, IV, 29.

[75] William Haynes, *Cellulose: The Chemical That Grows* (Garden City, N.Y., 1953), 59–73; Haynes, *American Chemical Industry*, IV, 378–81; Robert E. Hussey and Philip C. Scherer, Jr., "The Rayon Industry in the South," in Mills (ed.), *Chemical Progress in the South*, 134–39; Thomas W. Douglas, *The Rayon Yarn Industry in Virginia* (Charlottesville, 1950), 10–11, 44.

wrote his issue of stock. In 1924 Burlington used 106 pounds of rayon for "garish bedspreads that were not notable contributions to fashion or good taste, even in the Flapper Era." But sales reached $1,800,000 in 1927, when Love entered dress goods, and held up through the Depression. Burlington Mills, "a bubble that didn't break," by 1935 had fourteen plants producing $20,000,000 worth of goods and absorbed more than 11 per cent of all rayon shipped to the weaving trade.[76]

The aluminum industry was drawn South by bauxite which was found in Georgia, Arkansas, Alabama, and Tennessee, electrical power, and growing markets. At Alcoa, adjoining Maryville, Tennessee, the Aluminum Company of America built a plant that began a daily production of 25,000 to 30,000 pounds in 1914. Fifteen years later, with the addition of carbon, sheet, and aluminum bronze powder plants, the operation had a payroll of three thousand and had advanced Blount County from one of the ten poorest in the state to the tenth richest in taxable wealth. Across the mountains at Badin, North Carolina, Andrew Mellon's monopoly in 1915 absorbed the beginnings of a French-owned mill when the war dried up the sources of French capital. There Alcoa completed a major plant with seven pot rooms and an entirely company-built town: streets, water supply, schools, churches, and club accommodations. At the same time Alcoa became a major producer of electricity, chiefly for its own requirements.[77]

If "Super Power" was the basic "region builder" in the Southeast, petroleum assumed that role in the Southwest. "Indeed oil," said one of its historians, "Southwestern oil for the most part, has become industrial America's lifeblood, without which our fast-moving economy would be paralyzed." [78] The oil fever induced by Spindletop in 1901 became endemic in subsequent decades;

[76] "And Who Will Weave It?" in Fortune, XVI (1937), 44–48, 114, 116, 118; Burlington Bandwagon (Burlington), I (Summer, 1948), 18; Thirty Years of the Burlington Story (New York, 1954).

[77] L. P. Mason, "Making Aluminum in East Tennessee," in Manufacturers' Record, LXVI (July 9, 1914), 47–48; J. D. Porter, "Aluminum in the South," in Mills (ed.), Chemical Progress in the South, 163–66; Charles C. Carr, Alcoa: An American Enterprise (New York, 1952), 93–95, 100–102, 179–80; Harvey O'Connor, Mellon's Millions, the Biography of a Fortune: The Life and Times of Andrew W. Mellon (New York, 1933), 91–92.

[78] Rister, Oil!, 392–93.

temperatures rose alternately in Texas and in Oklahoma, which took the lead in 1906. In 1914 Oklahoma's new Cushing and Healdton fields moved into peak production, pouring oil into hastily improvised pools and tanks and forcing drastic price cuts until wartime requirements had created a period of acute shortage in 1915, with consumption rising faster than production until another glut late in 1920.[79] In Texas the wartime spectacle was the Ranger boom, starting with a well brought in October 21, 1917, that produced 93,053 barrels before the end of the year and more than 3,000,000 in 1918.[80] In rapid succession came other Texas fields: Desdemona, Sour Lake, Humble, Goose Creek, Hull, Mexia, Burkburnett. During 1920 the combination of high prices and new discoveries attracted an increasing number of drillers: of 33,911 new wells in the United States, 24,273 were producers—both figures set new records.[81]

Despite a price collapse late in 1920 new fields continued to spout petroleum. In 1919 Louisiana assumed third place with the Homer field, and other discoveries followed over the next few years.[82] Oklahoma's bonanza of 1920, the Burbank field, was located on Osage Indian lands and produced not only oil but a new American folk character, the poor Indian stricken with wealth.[83] In 1921 southwest Arkansas suddenly began production, "oozing human interest and mud" as well as oil from the El Dorado pool. Within the year it sprouted five hundred wells and disgorged more than ten million barrels, only to be surpassed the next year by Smackover. Located in a scantily populated and almost inaccessible quarter, Smackover had one of the wildest histories of haphazard waste. Pending frantic efforts to establish transportation, operators impounded their oil chiefly in earthen storage where it evaporated, overflowed in the rain, or was set afire by lightning—one fire lasted a month.[84] So it went through the

[79] *Ibid.*, 119–39.   [80] *Ibid.*, 143–57.

[81] Myron W. Watkins, *Oil: Stabilization or Conservation? A Case Study in the Organization of Industrial Control* (New York and London, 1937), 40–42.

[82] Rister, *Oil!*, 215–18.

[83] *Ibid.*, 190–206; Isaac F. Marcosson, *The Black Golconda: The Romance of Petroleum* (New York and London, 1934), 197–206; John Ise, *The United States Oil Policy* (New Haven and London, 1926), 397–98.

[84] Gerald Forbes, "Brief History of the Petroleum Industry in Arkansas," in *Arkansas Historical Quarterly,* I (1942), 31–35; Marcosson, *Black Golconda,* 216; G. S.

1920's, the glut compounded by the rise of new fields in California. In 1926 Borger, Texas, appeared on the oil map and Oklahoma brought in the Greater Seminole pool. In 1928 Oklahoma City began to sprout wells around the state capitol.[85]

The oil finds produced boom towns as raw and tempestuous as the legendary mining and cattle towns of the previous century. If they were not the only evidences of economic growth and transition in the twenties, they "were the fiercest and most convulsive." [86] Together with the drilling-crew roughnecks, engineers, and geologists, the boom towns lured a motley crew of bootleggers, prostitutes, racketeers, and specialists in phony oil stocks. Fort Worth became the center for several ingenious schemes: one group found a Robert E. Lee (soon designated "General") to endorse its stocks; another offered Frederick A. Cook, alleged discoverer of the North Pole. A Federal district attorney estimated that, around the country, swindlers bamboozled more than a million persons with promotion and merger schemes.[87]

Nevertheless, the oil fields soon went the way of the mining frontier; development became more complex and expensive but more stable and orderly. If the wildcatter with a $5,000 well in the Healdton pool of 1914 had prospered, he might have put in one of the East Texas wells of the early 1930's at about $25,000; but unless he had become quite wealthy he would have been closed out of Oklahoma City, where the first well cost $168,000 and later drillings from $90,000 to $125,000. Various barriers excluded the small independent: greater depth of the wells, rising prices of machinery and leases, the waste of funds in excessive drilling, the growing importance of scientific exploration and technology, and, more significantly, the rise of the integrated "majors" that controlled refineries, pipelines, marketing, and drilling.[88]

Gibb and E. H. Knowlton, *History of the Standard Oil Company (New Jersey): The Resurgent Years, 1911–1927* (New York, 1955), 415–16.

[85] Rister, *Oil!*, 231–57. [86] *Ibid.*, 207.

[87] Gerald Forbes, "Southwestern Oil Boom Towns," in *Chronicles of Oklahoma*, XVII (1939), 393–400; Marcosson, *Black Golconda*, 312–29; Oliver Knight, *Fort Worth: Outpost on the Trinity* (Norman, Okla., 1953), 198; Steen, *Twentieth Century Texas*, 99.

[88] Gerald Forbes, "The Passing of the Small Oil Man," in *Southern Economic Journal*, VII (1940–1941), 205–15. Two studies analyze the economic factors in the

The development of refining lagged behind the production of crude oil, although the region made a respectable showing. In 1929 petroleum production in the South was about 59.3 per cent of the national total, mostly in Texas, Oklahoma, Arkansas, and Louisiana; but those four states also had 145 refineries, about 40 per cent of the total number, with 37 per cent of the daily crude oil capacity and 42 per cent of the cracking capability. More than half of the refineries were in Texas, mostly in the coastal strip from Corpus Christi to the Sabine River, and chiefly at Port Arthur; oil and oil products constituted two thirds of the tonnage leaving Texas ports.[89] To the east, the Standard Oil Company of Louisiana refinery at Baton Rouge had arisen in 1909 at the terminus of the interstate pipeline that "threaded a golden course through the very heart of the Mid-Continent-Louisiana oil regions," tapping Arkansas and Oklahoma. It grew into one of the world's largest refineries, covering two thousand acres with its tank farms.[90]

The pipelines were a basic instrumentality of integration. Before the end of the 1920's they interlaced the Southwest with a network that drained the crude oil into the tank farms and refineries of the majors, a flow checked neither by criticism nor by Federal and state legislation designating the lines as common carriers. As late as 1931, more than 60 per cent of the larger pipeline companies carried no outside oil and the other 40 per cent served a grand total of 129 shippers.[91] Natural gas lines, as well, grew into a major enterprise in the 1920's. The first long-distance transmission was on the Magnolia Gas Company's 216-mile line to

---

integration movement: John G. McLean and Robert William Haigh, *The Growth of Integrated Oil Companies* (Boston, 1954) ; and Melvin G. deChazeau and Alfred E. Kahn, *Integration and Competition in the Petroleum Industry* (New Haven, 1959).

[89] Vance, *Human Geography of the South*, 344–47.

[90] Gibb and Knowlton, *Standard Oil (New Jersey): Resurgent Years*, 67–68, 173, 560–61; Frank A. Howard, "Standard Oil Company, the Largest Industrial Investor in the South," in *Manufacturers' Record*, XCVII (February 13, 1930) , 56–59; John L. Loos, *Oil on Stream! A History of the Interstate Oil Pipe Line Company, 1909–1959* (Baton Rouge, 1959) .

[91] George S. Wolbert, Jr., *American Pipe Lines: Their Industrial Structure, Economic Status and Legal Implications* (Norman, Okla., 1952) , 8, 43–44; Gibb and Knowlton, *Standard Oil (New Jersey): Resurgent Years*, 464–65; Loos, *Oil on Stream!*, 82–99.

Beaumont from Northeastern Texas, completed in 1925. By 1931 lines ran from the Louisiana fields around Monroe to New Orleans, Atlanta, Memphis, and St. Louis and from the Texas fields around Amarillo to Denver, Des Moines, Chicago, and Indianapolis. Like oil, gas was controlled by the larger corporations.[92]

The oil majors flourished even in the face of official hostility. Standard Oil of New Jersey, the great symbol of the trust monster in the early days, felt with particular severity the strictures of Texas law. Its chief subsidiary, the Waters-Pierce Oil Company, was dissolved in 1907 and others were banished in 1913.[93] But the ouster did not prevent other majors, nor eventually Jersey Standard itself, from operating in the state.

Of the three new majors that sprang out of Spindletop, the Gulf Oil Company was from the beginning dominated by the Mellons of Pittsburgh and Sun Oil Company by the Pews of Philadelphia.[94] And the Texas Company, although organized by an indigenous group led by J. S. Cullinan, was dependent upon investment groups in Chicago and New York. As a result, in 1913 the company replaced Cullinan as president with E. S. Lufkin, an Easterner, and transferred the headquarters from Houston to New York.[95] Another early major, the Magnolia Petroleum Company, a collection of former Standard subsidiaries, eventually passed under the control of the Standard Oil Company of New York.[96]

The experience of the Humble Oil & Refining Company best illustrated the inexorable pressures for integration and the sometimes contradictory results of outside control. Ultimately the giant of the Southwest, Humble grew paradoxically out of efforts to resist domination by the majors. Rebuffed in bids to secure legislation favorable to the independents, a group led by Ross S. Sterling and William S. Farish combined in 1917 under the name of

---

[92] "Gas Balloon," in *Fortune*, IV (August, 1931), 51–52, 109–12; "Natural Gas," *ibid.*, XXII (August, 1940), 58, 96.

[93] Rister, *Oil!*, 187–88.

[94] *Ibid.*, 70 n; Craig Thompson, *Since Spindletop: A Human Story of Gulf's First Half Century* (Pittsburgh, 1951); O'Connor, *Mellon's Millions*, 93–108.

[95] Marquis James, *The Texaco Story: The First Fifty Years, 1902–1952* (New York, 1953), 35.

[96] Marcosson, *Black Golconda*, 232–34.

Sterling's predecessor company, the original Humble, and set out to play the game of the majors. Ambitious plans and the search for capital, however, eventually led Farish to the offices of Jersey Standard.[97] In January, 1919, Humble representatives agreed to sell half the stock, to be held at first in the name of Jersey's President Walter C. Teagle; additional shares bought in the market gave Standard a majority, and thus the company returned to Texas in 1919. A state court determined in 1923 that Jersey Standard did not "control or manage" Humble, and a state law in 1924 finally legalized the holding and voting of stock in a Texas company by a "foreign" company.

Standard, in fact, did not hold a taut rein on its affiliate. Voting control stayed in the hands of the Texans, and the company "remained essentially a Texas company, administered by native or naturalized Texans" from its headquarters in Houston. "Take us over, hell!" Sterling had exploded to a needling independent in 1919. "We're going to take over the Standard." During his lifetime, two men from Humble became presidents of Jersey Standard, one of them William S. Farish.

But Humble's autonomy was unique in the Standard empire. In the Louisiana and Arkansas fields the chief affiliate was the Standard Oil Company of Louisiana, organized in 1909 primarily to operate the Baton Rouge refinery. In 1913 it was the most profitable of all Standard affiliates, but was soon overshadowed by an Oklahoma subsidiary, the Carter Oil Company.[98] Originally a West Virginia firm, Carter established a Western division at Tulsa in 1915 under J. Edgar Pew, who temporarily left the family's Sun Oil enterprise and before his resignation in 1918 checkerboarded Oklahoma and Kansas with leases, giving Carter a momentum that sent it well ahead of both Louisiana and Humble in crude oil production during the 1920's.[99]

[97] The account of Humble is taken chiefly from Henrietta Larson and Kenneth Porter, *History of Humble Oil & Refining Company: A Study in Industrial Growth* (New York, 1959). See also Gibb and Knowlton, *Standard Oil (New Jersey): Resurgent Years*, 411–13; James, *Texaco Story*, 41–43; and Warner E. Mills Jr., "The Public Career of a Texas Conservative: A Biography of Ross Shaw Sterling" (Ph.D. dissertation, The Johns Hopkins University, 1956), 31–37.

[98] Gibb and Knowlton, *Standard Oil (New Jersey): Resurgent Years*, 67–70.

[99] *Ibid.*, 59–67, 414–25; Larson and Porter, *History of Humble Oil & Refining Company*, 696.

93

As early as 1924 the growth of the majors had reached the point that in Oklahoma thirteen companies and in Texas ten accounted for more than half the production.[100] In the interstices left by the giants, new wildcat millionaires and new independents continued to rise. Some, like the Phillips Petroleum Company, became majors.[101] Others surrendered and submitted to lines of control that reached as far as London and The Hague.[102] One of the most successful early wildcatters in Oklahoma, Ernest W. Marland, a native of Pennsylvania, expanded into successive new fields from beginnings around Ponca City in the first decade of the century. By the 1920's Marland was on the way to becoming a new major but, like the early Humble, needed capital. After flirtation with the Royal Dutch-Shell interests he turned at last to J. P. Morgan and Company in 1923. But as the Morgan interest rose, Marland's influence waned and his grandiose scheme of a pipeline to the Gulf was squelched because it would compete with Morgan allies in the Standard empire. Before the decade was over, Marland had been eased out, his company merged with the moribund Continental Oil Company, and his name replaced with "Conoco" on the red triangles of filling stations across the country.[103]

But if outside capital brought absentee control that could bridle the growth of a Marland Oil or a Birmingham, it more often released the galloping expansion that brought new payrolls, construction contracts, real estate developments, and other assets—profits, too, in many cases. In 1929 individual tax returns indicated that Southerners realized cash dividends of $372,000,000 from domestic corporations, or 7.8 per cent of the total, little enough in relation to population but not inconsiderable in comparison to the region's 10.2 per cent of the value added by manufactures.[104]

The economic revolution brought urban as well as industrial

---

[100] Ise, *United States Oil Policy*, 262–63, citing *Oil Weekly*, March 13, 1925, p. 35, and February 20, 1925, Supplement, 2. The figures are for the last quarter of 1924.

[101] Rister, *Oil!*, 197.

[102] *Ibid.*, 201n–202n, on Amerada Petroleum Company; Kendall Beaton, *Enterprise in Oil: A History of Shell in the United States* (New York, 1957), 113–70, 348, and *passim*.

[103] John Joseph Mathews, *Life and Death of an Oilman: The Career of E. W. Marland* (Norman, Okla., 1951), 165–76, 190–98.

[104] Hoover and Ratchford, *Economic Resources and Policies of the South*, 116, 193.

growth. During the 1920's the South's urban population grew more rapidly than any other region's, from 25.4 per cent of the total in 1920 to 32.1 per cent in 1930.[105] One of the most striking characteristics of the urban growth, however, was the importance of the small town. Electrical power and the automobile permitted industries to scatter over broad areas, and before the end of the 1920's a pattern of commuting from farm to mill was already established in the Piedmont.[106] Moreover, raw-material or labor-oriented industries like mining, lumber, paper, chemicals, food, and furniture had no intensive urbanizing effect. Thus many of the people listed in the census as rural worked in industry. At the same time the growing towns manifested the countrified manners of their new inhabitants.

Nor was manufacturing the only cause of urban development. By 1929, 47 per cent of the wholesale business in the Southeast and 57 per cent of that in the Southwest was done in cities of one hundred thousand or more, and one economist estimated that three fourths of all retail trade was done in towns of ten thousand or more.[107] But the administrative, banking, financial, transportation, and various professional and service functions tended to concentrate in the larger centers.[108] The number of Southern cities of one hundred thousand or more increased from seven to twelve in the decade before 1920 and from twelve to nineteen in the decade that followed.[109] During the 1920's they included five of the seven fastest growing metropolitan centers in the nation: in order, Miami, Los Angeles, Oklahoma City, Houston, San Diego, Tampa–St. Petersburg, and Tulsa.[110]

But the New South philosophy had deeply implanted the idea

[105] T. Lynn Smith, "The Emergence of Cities," in Rupert B. Vance and Nicholas Demereth (eds.), *The Urban South* (Chapel Hill, 1954) , 33.

[106] Glenn Gilman, *Human Relations in the Industrial Southeast: A Study of the Textile Industry* (Chapel Hill, 1956) , 131.

[107] Walter J. Matherly, "The Emergence of the Metropolitan Community in the South," in *Social Forces*, XIV (1935–1936) , 324.

[108] Causes of urbanization are treated in some detail *ibid.*, 323–25; Walter J. Matherly, "The Urban Development of the South," in *Southern Economic Journal*, I (February, 1935) , 23–26; Rudolf Heberle, "The Mainsprings of Southern Urbanization," in Vance and Demereth (eds.), *Urban South*, 6–23; and T. Lynn Smith, "Emergence of Cities," *loc. cit.*, 27, 31.

[109] Smith, "Emergence of Cities," *loc. cit.*, 27, 31.

[110] Matherly, "Emergence of the Metropolitan Community in the South," *loc. cit.*, 319.

of deliverance through industry. "The very words 'new factory' and 'new pay roll,' " Allen Raymond observed, "cast a spell over all this area." Cities and towns vied with each other "in offering free land, or exemptions from taxation over short periods of years, or other bonuses if industrial concerns will only locate within their borders." [111] Dalton, Georgia, advertised in 1924 the low assessments on manufacturing property in the community; Gainesville offered free sites and tax exemptions, the latter permitted by state legislation in 1923.[112] In Tennessee communities openly defied the state constitution to carry out such offers.[113] Sometimes the promotion was limited to informational service, as in the Spartanburg, South Carolina, Industrial Commission that from 1927 to 1931 provided each of thirty-six new concerns "a carefully prepared factual analysis of their needs and the ability of the community to meet them." [114] Sometimes the promoters offered development capital on a strictly business basis through loans and the purchase of preferred stock as in the Louisville Development Foundation, established in 1916.[115]

Kingsport, Tennessee, provided the unusual example of an entire town built by industrial promotion, combined for once with community planning. A sleepy mountain village in the Holston Valley until 1909 when the Clinchfield Railway went through to tap the Kentucky coal fields, Kingsport got brick and portland cement plants the next year. In 1915 the Kingsport Improvement Corporation, a group of investors with several thousand acres of fields and pastures for industrial development, hired Dr. John Nolan, a professional engineer, to plan a new city of broad boulevards, parkways, winding residential roads, and sites for industry and community services. In 1917 the town acquired a

[111] Allen Raymond in New York *Herald-Tribune*, June 1, 1930.

[112] R. P. Brooks, "Taxation of Manufacturing in Georgia," in *Southern Manufacturer's Tax Bill, Bulletin of the* (University of Kentucky) *Bureau of Business Research*, No. 13 (Lexington, Ky., 1947), 21.

[113] Robert E. Lowry, "Municipal Subsidies to Industries in Tennessee," in *Southern Economic Journal*, VII (1940–1941), 320.

[114] L. H. Duncan to Dr. Arthur E. Morgan, May 20, 1933, copy in Howard W. Odum Papers (Southern Historical Collection, University of North Carolina). Duncan directed the Commission.

[115] Ernest J. Hopkins, *Louisville Industrial Foundation: A Study in Community Capitalization of Local Industries* (Atlanta, 1945).

charter drawn up by the Rockefeller Foundation Bureau of Municipal Research. By that time it already had a power plant, a hosiery mill, extract, pulp, and paper factories, and the beginnings of a wartime cellulose plant that became in 1920 the nucleus of Tennessee Eastman. During the 1920's it added the Kingsport Press, a foundry, and plants producing textiles, book cloth, belting, glass, and silk goods, thus acquiring a diversified and in some cases co-ordinated group of industries—a unique community that "existed first in its entirety in the minds of its builders." [116]

Industrial promotion was the small town shibboleth, but it developed on a broader scale as well. In 1925 a Southern Exposition, challenging "the nation's attention to study its exhibits of raw materials and the variety of its agricultural and manufactural [sic] products," filled the Grand Central Palace in New York from May 11 to 23. It was conceived and planned by William G. Sirrine, an engineer who had earlier promoted the biennial Southern Textile Exposition at Greenville, South Carolina. And according to the Manufacturers' Record, it was "an unequalled opportunity for drawing capital to the South." [117] The major railroads and power companies supported continuing programs of advertising, information, and occasionally financial services. Duke from the beginning promoted hydroelectric power as a service to textiles and offered financial assistance to cotton mills served by the company.[118] Alabama Power organized an industrial development department in 1920 and Georgia Power followed in 1921.[119] In 1920 L. O. Crosby ("I believe in God and Mississippi"), a lumberman of Picayune, conceived the idea of a state development board which collaborated with the state Chamber of

---

[116] Howard Long, *Kingsport: A Romance of Industry* (Kingsport, 1928), 81–106 and *passim.;* The Rotary Club [of Kingsport], *Kingsport: The Planned Industrial City* (Kingsport, 1946); *Manufacturers' Record,* LXIX (January 13, 1916), 53; LXXI (May 17, 1917), 65; LXXXIII (March 8, 1923), 67–72; LXXXVIII (December 10, 1925), 77.

[117] *Manufacturers' Record,* LXXXVII (April 16, 1925), cover page; (April 23, 1925), 126–27; (May 7, 1925), 77, and many other references during 1924 and early 1925; *ibid.,* (May 14, 1925), 73–75; Charlotte *Observer,* May 6, 1926.

[118] Jenkins, *James B. Duke,* 177–80.

[119] Martin, *Forty Years of Alabama Power Company,* 32; Kennedy, *Profits and Losses in Textiles,* 98–102; William D. Ross, Jr., "Industrial Promotion by Southern States" (Ph.D. dissertation, Duke University, 1951), 218.

_____rce, announced that "Mississippi Is Awake," and crusaded for agricultural, industrial, and tourist development.[120] State programs of a rudimentary sort, chiefly information and advertising, had their beginning, if an exact date can be set, with the Alabama Department of Commerce and Industries in 1923 (the Industrial Development Board after 1927), followed by the Florida Board of Immigration, which got an appropriation of $50,000 in 1925 to advertise state resources; the North Carolina Division of Commerce and Industry, 1925; the Virginia Division of Publicity and Advertising, the South Carolina Natural Resources Commission, and the Kentucky Progress Commission, 1928.[121]

Amid the bustle of the 1920's one journalist offered a new definition of the Southerner. "The average Southerner," he wrote, "is a born booster, and the mood is contagious." [122] "Down in Dixie they tell you, and always with cheerful pride, that the South is the new frontier," a traveler wrote in 1927. "There is a thrill in the air; big tomorrows seem to be coming around the corner. . . . Everywhere are new roads, new automobiles, new hot dog stands, tea shops, movie palaces, radio stores, real estate subdivisions, tourist camp grounds." [123] Economic development, an Alabama economist declared, had "started on a career in the South one fears to prophesy about, because such prophesy may turn out to be ridiculous in understatement." [124] Governor Harry F. Byrd of Virginia said in 1929, "The South is being pointed to today as the West was in a former period—as the land of promise." [125]

[120] Craddock Goins, " 'This Man Crosby'—A Southern Empire Builder," in *Manufacturers' Record*, XCIII (March 8, 1928), 70–71.

[121] Albert Lepawsky, *State Planning and Economic Development in the South* (Washington, 1949), 8; Ross, "Industrial Promotion by Southern States," 270; C. Frank Dunn, "Progress Commission Launches Broad Program," in *Kentucky Progress Magazine* (Louisville), I (1928–1929), 31, 77–80.

[122] George Marvin, "Progress and the Parthenon," in *Outlook*, CXXXIX (1925), 653.

[123] Bruce Bliven, "Away Down South: Casual Notes of a Traveler in the Land of the New Frontier," in *New Republic*, X (1927), 296.

[124] George Lang, *The South in the National Economic Setting*, Address to the Alabama Bankers' Association, Mobile, May 18, 1928 (Tuscaloosa, 1928), 58.

[125] Carroll E. Williams, "Governor Byrd in Role of State Business Agent Speeds Virginia's Industrial Expansion," in *Manufacturers' Record*, XCV (February 21, 1929), 45.

"The clamor of Chambers of Commerce," a Northern reporter said, "the seductive propaganda of city and state industrial development boards, the rattling knives and forks and pepful jollities of Rotarians, Kiwanians, Lions, and Exchange clubs are filling the erstwhile languorous wistaria-scented air with such a din these days that every visitor must recognize immediately a land of business progress." [126] Houston alone had not only the clubs mentioned but the Optimists, "The Dirty Dozen," and in all thirty luncheon clubs adding zest to the civic spirit.[127] In Ranger, Texas, the Rotarians contributed something new to the wild frontier by serving as vigilantes to break up the gambling and whisky dives in 1922.[128] In 1925 the Charlotte, North Carolina, Rotary Club, founded in 1916, emphasized juvenile court work while the Lions experienced "baptismal emersion [sic] into . . . unselfish service." They sponsored a boy scout band, assisted a school and hospital, entertained the Billy Sunday workers and the Salvation Army band, presented Mr. Sunday a set of cuff links, "protested against the Child Labor law and advanced many projects for municipal betterment." [129]

In hundreds of towns "from the Potomac to Mobile Bay, from Hatteras to the Rio Grande," a Greensboro writer noted in 1924, "there is no God but Advertising, and Atlanta is his prophet." [130] Atlanta was indeed the metropolitan center and source of the new middle-class spirit, the original capital of the "New South," source of the South's more notorious contributions to twentieth-century American culture—Coca-Cola and the Ku Klux Klan—but also the home of the interracial movement, several colleges, a symphony orchestra (organized in 1923), and annual performances by the Metropolitan Opera Company.[131] An English visitor who arrived at fair time in the first autumn of postwar prosperity (1919) found multitudes of "resplendently enameled, capacious, smoothrunning, swift-starting" automobiles giving out "a multiform chorus of barking, howling, and hooting." On either side sky-

[126] Allen Raymond in New York *Herald-Tribune,* June 1, 1930.
[127] Henry F. Pringle, "Heat at Houston," in *Outlook,* CXLIX (1928), 374.
[128] Rister, *Oil!,* 155.   [129] Charlotte *Observer,* May 18, 1925.
[130] Gerald W. Johnson, "Greensboro, or What You Will," in *The Reviewer* (Richmond), IV (1923–1924), 169.
[131] Hal Steed, *Georgia: Unfinished State* (New York, 1942), 286–89.

scrapers climbed heavenward in severe lines, "and where heaven should be the sky signs twinkled." The sidewalks thronged with youth "whose hilarious faces and gregarious movements show a camaraderie one would hardly observe in the colder North." [132]

More than anything else the railroads made Atlanta. Situated at the hub of lines radiating across the Southeast, in 1924 it had 8 systems, 13 major trunk lines, and originated 350 merchandise and package cars daily, not counting car lots. With 150 passenger trains every day, the railroads during the previous year had hauled in 80,000 delegates to attend 300 conventions. About 600 outside firms maintained their offices and 150 warehouses in Atlanta. Among the 35 major office buildings, 9 just completed, the Hurt Building purported to be the eighth largest in the country. In 1923, with the $6,000,000 Biltmore Hotel, a dozen buildings of five to seventeen stories, and nearly two thousand dwellings and apartments, Atlanta's construction amounted to more than $27,000,000. Moreover, the city was the fire insurance capital of the Southeast, with fifty home and foreign companies and headquarters of the Southeastern Underwriters Association and the Southern Adjustment Bureau.[133]

Atlanta was scarcely challenged as the metropolitan capital of the Southeast either by New Orleans, actually larger in population, which staged its own skyscraper boom next door to the French Quarter and opened new highway and bridge routes to the East, or by Nashville, much smaller in population but claiming with its collection of colleges proportionately more students than any other city in the country.[134] For a while Nashville was bidding to become the Southern financial center through Caldwell and Company ("We Bank on the South"), which Luke Lea and Rogers Caldwell had started as a commission house for state and local bond issues and expanded into a tremendous empire of financing,

[132] Graham, *Soul of John Brown*, 122–24.
[133] J. H. Reed, "Atlanta: An Inspiring Story of Growth in Trade, Industry, Finance, Education, and Music," in *Manufacturers' Record*, LXXXV (February 28, 1924), 76–84; Merle Thorpe, "Georgia Rolls Up Her Sleeves," in *Nation's Business*, XII (April, 1924), 29–30.
[134] George Marvin, "Mistress of the Mississippi," in *Outlook*, CXXXIX (1925), 568–71; Dabney, *One Hundred Great Years*, 408–409; Marvin, "Progress and the Parthenon," *loc. cit.*, 653–56.

banks, insurance companies, manufacturing enterprises, newspapers, and politics.[135]

Farther west oil was the city builder. Oil-field boom towns rioted with excitement in their season, but the development of pipelines, refineries, and administrative offices contributed to more permanent metropolitan centers. Oklahoma's largest oil city was Tulsa, which had the early advantages of a modern hotel, the headquarters for Carter Oil, and the terminus of the Gulf Pipe Line Company. A former Creek Indian town, a rural village in 1901, Tulsa sported a population of 70,000 by 1920, a threefold increase over 1910. Even into the mid-1930's its "boom-town fever and mining-camp restlessness" persisted. Elsewhere, too, in Oklahoma City, Bartlesville, Ponca City, Enid, Ardmore, Seminole, the state was more or less "sold out to the Babbitts—the go-getters and the boosters." [136]

Texas oil towns included Wichita Falls, Amarillo, Odessa, Kermit, Hobbs, Tyler, Longview, and Kilgore. The twin cities of Dallas and Fort Worth were among the fastest growing metropolises of the 1920's. Dallas, home of the region's Federal Reserve Bank, led the state in wholesale trade—$729,000,000 in 1929.[137] But Houston emerged as the foremost city in both population and manufacturing. Its story was essentially the story of the Houston Ship Channel, a development of Buffalo Bayou approved in principle by Congress in 1899 and opened to ocean-going vessels in 1914. By 1925 the channel was thirty feet deep, reached fifty-five miles to the outer bar, and was flanked by refineries and other enterprises. In the year ending June 30, 1926, 1,240 ocean-going vessels handled at Houston a cargo valued at $457,823,882, including exports of oil, cotton, livestock, lumber, and steel. By 1939 Houston was exceeded only by New York and Philadelphia among American ports.[138] While it outdistanced its competitors, it was

[135] John B. McFerrin, *Caldwell and Company: A Southern Financial Empire* (Chapel Hill, 1939).

[136] Angie Debo, *Tulsa: From Creek Town to Oil Capital* (Norman, Okla., 1943), 97; Rister, *Oil!*, 401–402; B. A. Botkin, "Folk-Say and Space," in *Southwest Review* (Dallas), XX (1934–1935), 333.

[137] James Howard, *Big D Is for Dallas: Chapters in the Twentieth-Century History of Dallas* (Austin, 1957), 14–15, 60–61.

[138] Writers' Program of the Works Progress Administration in the State of Texas, *Houston: A History and Guide* (Houston, 1942), 132–38; Burt Rule, "Factors in the

but the most important in a string of man-made inland ports from Corpus Christi to Lake Charles, Louisiana, including Orange, Beaumont, and Port Arthur in the Sabine Port District.[139] Farther east Mobile, with a $10,000,000 harbor development in the 1920's, served as the outlet for the Warrior-Tombigbee Waterway, completed in 1915 and reaching within fifteen miles of Birmingham.[140]

Everywhere urban growth brought an inevitable retinue of realtors, the prime source and symbol of the booster mystique. So far as Alabama was concerned, it seemed to Clarence Cason, the industrial development was from the local point of view a real estate boom. The modern realtor, he argued, had replaced the fabled planter as the arbiter of local destinies.[141] Greensboro, North Carolina, in the early 1920's annexed the adjacent mill villages and reported a population of 43,525 in the corporate limits. None could escape the knowledge, Gerald W. Johnson declared, "except the wholly illiterate." In the middle of town the seventeen-story Jefferson Life Building spurted up "suddenly and unreasonably . . . like Memnon among the dunes. . . ." At a whispered inquiry to the Chamber of Commerce, members would "fall upon you ecstatically, snowing you under with pamphlets, casting recklessly into the air handfuls of popping statistics like Chinese firecrackers, hustling you into a motor car to exhibit to you endless miles of asphalt and endless rows of unlovely skeletons of houses in process of construction." [142]

Growth of Texas' Largest City," in *Manufacturers' Record*, CII (May, 1933), 16–17, 42; Richardson, *Texas: Lone Star State*, 357.

[139] Vance, *Human Geography of the South*, 347–48.

[140] Charles G. Summersell, *Mobile: History of a Seaport Town* (University, Ala., 1949), 52, 63. On the development of inland waterways, especially on the Mississippi River, see A. E. Parkins, *The South: Its Economic-Geographic Development* (New York and London, 1938), 148–49; Harold Sinclair, *The Port of New Orleans* (Garden City, N.Y., 1942), 306–307; Clarence B. Douglas, "Development of Inland Waterways System," in *Manufacturers' Record*, CII (February, 1933), 18–19.

[141] Clarence E. Cason, "Alabama Goes Industrial," in *Virginia Quarterly Review*, VI (1930), 168.

[142] Johnson, "Greensboro, or What You Will," *loc. cit.*, 169–71. See also Albert S. Keister, "A City in Depression—Greensboro, North Carolina," in *Social Forces*, XIII (1934–1935), 92–93.

In some places the real estate fever erupted into an epidemic. In 1921 Henry Ford submitted an offer for the purchase of the Federal hydroelectric and nitrate facilities at Muscle Shoals and announced intentions to build a great industrial center, seventy-five miles long. To the people of the Valley the offer was "like commutation of a death sentence." Speculators platted town lots, opened offices in leading cities, ran special trains from New York, and took prospects up in airplanes to view the countryside. Thousands were hoodwinked on the belief that, as Senator George Norris said, they were "getting on a ground floor of a new American wonderland." But Norris, proponent of public power, blocked the sale and Ford finally withdrew the offer in 1924. Speculators who stayed in too long lost everything.[143]

If Northern capital and industrial development, real or fancied, stirred most communities, not a few discovered a likely cash crop in Yankee millionaires looking for playgrounds. South Carolina's Low Country, in the doldrums since the 1890's, found a market for plantation houses among wealthy Northerners who came down to enjoy the winter climate and shoot waterfowl in the abandoned rice fields. "Indeed," a Charleston editor reported in 1929, "the odor of genteel Yankee wealth, while not suffocating, is pervading." At many a dinner he found Berkeley corn liquor "the perfect solvent of the sectional difference," and "personally witnessed not less than half a billion dollars worth of Republican Yankees warring against 'the experiment noble in motive.' "[144] And in other likely resorts the idle rich disported themselves in or out of season: at Camden and Aiken, in Pinehurst and Southern Pines, along the Mississippi and Alabama Gulf Coasts, at Thomasville, Georgia, in Virginia manor houses, in Natchez, and in the neighborhood of Lexington, Kentucky, which was by the 1930's "almost

[143] Preston J. Hubbard, *Origins of the TVA: The Muscle Shoals Controversy, 1920–1932* (Nashville, 1961), 28–47, 138–43; Leslie S. Wright, "Henry Ford and Muscle Shoals," in *Alabama Review: A Quarterly Journal of Alabama History* (University, Ala.), XIV (1961), 196–209; George W. Norris, *Fighting Liberal: The Autobiography of George Norris* (New York, 1945), 256–59; Karl Schriftgiesser, *This Was Normalcy: An Account of Party Politics during Twelve Republican Years, 1920–1932* (Boston, 1948), 228–30. Martin Clary, *The Facts about Muscle Shoals* (New York, 1924), is an example of the promotional literature.

[144] William Watts Ball to Yates Snowden, March 22, 1929, in Ball Papers.

entirely taken over by absentee landlords from the East who want to have some acres of Bluegrass on which to raise horses." [145]

Some communities could assimilate *nouveaux* Yankees to the genteel tradition, or even insult them with tales of grandmother's silverware.[146] Others found that the influx swept them into raging tornadoes of change. Asheville, "Land of the Sky," and much of Western North Carolina had been ripening a boom ever since the chill tonic millionaire, E. W. Grove, had built the Grove Park Inn in 1913, with appurtenant subdivisions. In the early 1920's Grove leveled off a small mountain to make downtown business property and made more with the dirt that was removed. By 1925 Asheville was, in Thomas Wolfe's eyes, "Boom Town, where everyone is full of Progress and Prosperity and Enterprise, and 100,000 by 1930, and Bigger and Greater Asheville." Buncombe County in 1926 led the state in real estate valuations just as the bubble began to break.[147]

But the realtors staged their supercolossal in southernmost Florida, where an American Riviera sprang from the mangrove swamps and sand dunes.[148] In 1925 T. H. Weigall, a foot-loose Englishman drawn to Miami in search of quick wealth, found a

[145] Barry Bingham, quoted in Jonathan Daniels, *A Southerner Discovers the South* (New York, 1938), 324–25.

[146] One Yankee lady, after some years of suffering in silence, suggested to William Watts Ball that if Charleston desired a good Northern press, "all citizens in conversation with northerners able to use a typewriter should carefully avoid the following words: Yankee, Sherman, carpet bag, silverware, grandfather and grandmother, nigger, and other words which occur to them." Mrs. S. E. Stauffer to Ball, November 15, 1935, in Ball Papers.

[147] Elizabeth Nowell (ed.), *The Letters of Thomas Wolfe* (New York, 1956), 101–102; Jonathan Daniels, *Tar Heels: A Portrait of North Carolina* (New York, 1941), 223–24; George W. McCoy, "Asheville and Thomas Wolfe," in *North Carolina Historical Review*, XXX (1953), 200–17. See also Louis D. Rubin, Jr., *Thomas Wolfe: The Weather of His Youth* (Baton Rouge, 1955), 76–95.

[148] For fuller descriptions see Frank B. Sessa, "The Real Estate Boom in Miami and Its Environs [1923–1926]" (Ph.D. dissertation, University of Pittsburgh, 1950), parts of which appeared as "Miami on the Eve of the Boom, 1923," in *Tequesta: The Journal of the Historical Association of Southern Florida* (Coral Gables), No. 11 (1951), 3–25, and "Miami in 1926," *ibid.*, No. 16 (1956), 15–36; Kenneth Ballinger, *Miami Millions: The Dance of the Dollars in the Great Florida Land Boom of 1925* (Miami, 1936); Frederick Lewis Allen, *Only Yesterday: An Informal History of the Nineteen-Twenties* (2nd ed., New York, 1957), 170–89; and Kenneth Roberts, *Florida* (New York and London, 1926).

scene of "real estate madness . . . *in excelsis*." Amid the din of automobile horns, drills, hammers, and winches, he later wrote, everybody "seemed to be shaking hands, offering cigars, studying mysterious diagrams of 'desirable subdivisions.'" Miami, they assured him, was "One hell of a place," the "finest city, sir, in the U.S.A., and I don't mean mebbe." [149] The mob scene into which Weigall stepped was one of the supreme spectacles of those palmy years, a full dress rehearsal for the Great Bull Market of 1929. Journalists who reported it nearly exhausted their stock of superlatives: "the most fantastic land boom since the Mississippi Bubble," "the greatest migration since the Crusades," "something . . . to which the history of developments, booms, inrushes, speculation, investment yields no parallel." [150]

The Florida boom stemmed from a long line of promoters who had flung railroads down the east and west coasts, developed drainage and agriculture in the Palm Beach hinterland, and created millionaires' playgrounds long before. It sprang more immediately from the activities of Carl G. Fisher, founder of the Indianapolis Speedway and the Prestolite Company, who in 1913 financed the completion of a bridge across Biscayne Bay and inaugurated the more bizarre phases of promotion at Miami Beach. He dredged up the bottom of the bay to fill swamps and make artificial islands, incorporated the town of Miami Beach in 1915, and after World War I opened a campaign of hotel building and high-pressure advertising; he conceived the Miami Beach bathing beauty when Mrs. Fisher excited public consternation by wearing one of the first fitted bathing suits.[151]

By 1924 the combination of Coolidge prosperity and the proliferation of Ford's "tin lizzies" gave people extra money and made Florida an accessible place to spend it. From 1915 Fisher vigorously promoted the "Dixie Highway" from northern Michigan to Miami; by 1925 it was officially open and fed by other roads from the populous Northeast.[152] Every winter after the Armistice

[149] T. H. Weigall, *Boom in Florida* (London, 1931), 34, 35.

[150] George W. Seaton and Miami *News*, quoted in Alva Johnston, *The Legendary Mizners* (New York, 1953), 217–18; New York *Times*, March 22, 1925.

[151] Alfred Jackson Hanna and Kathryn Abbey Hanna, *Florida's Golden Sands* (Indianapolis, 1950), 329, 334–35.

[152] Kathryn Abbey Hanna, *Florida: Land of Change* (2nd ed., Chapel Hill, 1948)

more and more "snowbirds" appeared in Florida from the North.[153] If the nineteenth-century development created what Henry James called a "hotel civilization" and Miami Beach followed the pattern, a new "subdivision civilization" offered the opportunity of sun worshipping to the lower middle classes, and soon the more hypnotic bait of speculative profits.

The Florida boom had a glamor that made it unique in the history of inflationary mass manias. In the words of Burton Rascoe, it "was the only one that was founded upon an aesthetic ideal." [154] The prototype of the Florida subdivision, Coral Gables, was the embodiment of a vision that had gestated for years in the mind of George E. Merrick, a local fruit grower, realtor, and amateur poet. By 1921 he was ready with sixteen hundred acres on the outskirts of Miami and a plan for new model city "wherein nothing would be unlovely," an American Venice planned not only for comfort and convenience but for aesthetic quality, with waterways, wide plazas, fountains, swimming pools, golf courses, a great hotel, and the University of Miami. All was to be in a Spanish-Italian architecture that Merrick labeled "Mediterranean," and all construction required prior approval by an architectural board. As the boom advanced, development accelerated and spread over an area of ten thousand acres. At the height of its promotion Coral Gables commanded the services of three thousand salesmen, gondoliers imported from Italy, author Rex Beach, and orchestra leaders Paul Whiteman and Jan Garber. From a float in the Venetian Pool, William Jennings Bryan, adopted son of Florida, magnified the miracle of Miami for a salary variously reported at $50,000 to $100,000, and Gilda Gray, the original "shimmy" girl, shook her chemise to distract attention from the prices.[155]

389; W. D. L. Robinson, "Complete the Dixie Highway as a Measure of National Defense," in *Manufacturers' Record*, LXXI (June 7, 1917), 72–73.

[153] Homer B. Vanderblue, "The Florida Land Boom," in *Journal of Land and Public Utility Economics* (Madison, Wis.), III (1927), 115–17, 128–29.

[154] Burton Rascoe, "Introduction," in T. H. Weigall, *Boom in Paradise* (American edition of *Boom in Florida*; New York, 1932), xi.

[155] Mary T. Moore, "Coral Gables History" (Coral Gables, 1950, mimeographed), 1–5; Weigall, *Boom in Florida*, 75–76, 96–99, and *passim*; Sessa, "Real Estate Boom in Miami and Its Environs," 21–22; M. R. Werner, *Bryan* (New York, 1929), 267.

Northward from Miami the boom spirit spread up the Gold Coast into a hundred other subdivisions, each elaborating its own variations on Merrick's theme. Even staid old Palm Beach was caught up in the hurricane of expansion. Architect Addison Mizner transmogrified it after the First World War into a more opulent and grandiloquent Coral Gables. Carried to Florida by ill health in 1918, Mizner soon found dozens of wealthy patrons eager to pay for the privilege of being insulted by a transcendent genius and for having him foist off on them gigantic pleasure domes in what Alva Johnston summarized as the Bastard-Spanish-Moorish-Romanesque-Gothic-Renaissance-Bull-Market-Damn-the-Expense Style.[156]

At mid-decade the boom reached its apex. Miami became the scene of frantic excitement, with thousands pulled in by the fantastic but often true stories of sudden wealth.[157] In the speculative fairyland of fast turnover and quick fortunes, the careless plunger was, if anything, more likely to gain than the prudent investor, and the "binder boys" perfected to a fine art the practice of making money on little or no investment. The principle was to pay a nominal "binder" fee on promise of a later down payment and then to reap a profit by selling binders which might pass through a dozen hands and, in complex legal snarls, might or might not convey legal title.[158]

Up the peninsula from the Gold Coast the mania spread as far as Jacksonville, the gateway to the boom, which reaped a harvest from the entire state.[159] The twin cities of Tampa–St. Petersburg ran a close second to Miami in growth. There the miracle worker was D. P. Davis, who dredged up "Davis Islands" from Tampa Bay and then set out to enlarge an island off St. Augustine, exhibiting as bait for morbid speculators the coffin in which the bones of Pedro Menendez de Aviles, founder of the city had lain for three

[156] Johnston, *Legendary Mizners*, 25, 211–99; Addison Mizner, *The Florida Architecture of Addison Mizner* (New York, 1928).

[157] Gertrude M. Shelby, "Florida Frenzy," in *Harper's*, CLII (1925–1926), 177–86.

[158] Vanderblue, "Florida Land Boom," *loc. cit.*, 119–120; Kenneth Roberts, "Tropical Parasites," in *Saturday Evening Post* (Philadelphia), CXCIX (January 2, 1926), 80; Charles Donald Fox, *The Truth about Florida* (New York, 1925), 173–74, 241–49.

[159] Frank Parker Stockbridge and John Holliday Perry, *Florida in the Making* (New York, Jacksonville, and Kingsport, 1926), 184.

centuries.[160] To the spectacular, others added the downright fraudulent. The championship of cozenage would probably be closely contested between Charles Ponzi, who developed a subdivision "near Jacksonville," which was sixty-five miles away, and the promoters of Manhattan Estates near "the prosperous and fastgrowing city of Nettie," which was an abandoned turpentine camp.[161]

The ubiquitous tales of fraud eventually took their toll of confidence, and sober heads began to calculate that there were enough lots within ten miles of Miami to provide homes for two million people. Caution was reinforced by the warnings of business and financial observers. Then the transportation system collapsed under the burden. In the summer of 1925 the Florida East Coast and Seaboard railways declared an embargo on all but the most essential freight pending urgent repairs; and before they were completed, an overturned ship blocked the channel to Miami harbor. A stock market break in February and March, 1926, cast further gloom over the scene.[162] In July a reporter announced bluntly, "The Florida boom has collapsed. The world's greatest poker game, played with building lots instead of chips, is over." The roads north, she said, were black with "a strangely quiet exodus," and she found a Georgian on his doorstep by the highway who was convinced that "they's mo' comin' out o' Florida than evah went down." [163] The boom was already dead before the *coup de grâce* came in the form of a hurricane that roared over the Gold Coast and the Everglades on September 19, 1926. The storm destroyed 4,000 homes and damaged another 9,000 in the area from Ft. Lauderdale to Miami, twisted an unfinished skyscraper's skeleton askew, killed 115 people in the Miami area, drowned at least 300 at Moore Haven, and finally crossed the Gulf to strike again at Pensacola.[164]

Yet the boom could not be written off as an unmitigated failure.

[160] *Ibid.*, 191–92, 204–205; John van Schaik, Jr., *Cruising Cross Country, or the Journeyings of an Editor* (Boston and Chicago, 1926) , 327.

[161] Vanderblue, "Florida Land Boom," *loc. cit.*, 260–61.

[162] Sessa, "Real Estate Boom in Miami and Its Environs," 258–317.

[163] Stella Crossley, "Florida Cashes in Her Chips," in *Nation*, CXXIII (1926) , 11–12.

[164] Joseph H. Reese, *Florida's Great Hurricane* (Miami, 1926) , 12–13, 21–22.

Florida still had what Frederick Lewis Allen called its "unanswerable argument," the climate. It was still closer to the nation's population centers than California. The full story of the boom, one historian suggested, included "not only scenes of brass bands, armies of real estate salesmen, and lands under water, but of subdivision development, community incorporation, and physical and financial expansion." New hotels, downtown office buildings, homes in the suburbs were in many cases left empty, and public utilities overextended, but ready for a future in which Florida could grow into them. Transportation had been improved by new harbor facilities, extension of the Seaboard into Miami, double-tracking of the Florida East Coast, a network of paved highways and streets, even the beginnings of airlines. America's "last frontier" was fully publicized and put firmly on the map. These gains were wiped out neither by the heritage of debt nor the coming of the hurricane, and Florida was left "in a position where it could one day vie with Southern California for honors both as a resort and as a commercial center." [165]

Lost in the hubbub of the market places and the din of the factories were a few voices of dissent and a few flurries of disquietude at the New South Triumphant, but they came mostly from the bookish kind whom practical men could easily ignore. "In another five years," Alabamian Sara Haardt wrote in 1925, ". . . the old glow of such lovely towns as Tuscaloosa, Athens, Marion, and Eufaula will have vanished, and the Pittsburghs and Newarks of the South will rise in their stead." [166] *Can we afford to be rich?,"* writers Mary and Stanley Chapman asked. "We must look well into our consciences before we answer this question, for the loss of our spiritual grace is too high a price to pay for any material gain." [167] "Surely," the editors of an obscure little magazine in New Orleans protested, "the spirit of blatant superficiality, provincial self-complacency, and hypocritical righteousness was never more rampant than in the South today." [168] In Asheville,

[165] Sessa, "Real Estate Boom in Miami and Its Environs," 163, 353–57.

[166] Sara Haardt, "Alabama," in *American Mercury,* VI (September, 1925), 196.

[167] Maristan [Mary and Stanley] Chapman, "The South's Spiritual Grace," in *South Atlantic Quarterly,* XXI (1922), 297.

[168] *The Double Dealer: A National Magazine from the South* (New Orleans), I (1921), 126.

Thomas Wolfe wrote his baffled mother in 1923, they "shout 'Progress, Progress, Progress'—when what they mean is more Ford automobiles, more Rotary clubs, more Baptist Ladies Social Unions." There should be rather "beauty and spirit which will make us men instead of cheap Board of Trade boosters, and blatant pamphleteers." [169]

In the studies at Vanderbilt, almost in the shadow of Caldwell and Company, "the Morgan of the South," Fugitive poets percolated a revolt, while the mill villages of the Piedmont fermented an entirely different kind of rebellion. Both boiled over almost simultaneously with the Great Depression and provoked a painful reappraisal of New South industrialism and all its corollaries. But for the time being the Atlanta spirit reigned supreme in the Babbitt warrens of the New South. Later reports of its death would be highly exaggerated.

[169] John Skelly Terry (ed.), *Thomas Wolfe's Letters to His Mother* (New York, 1943), 49–50.

CHAPTER IV

AGRICULTURE AND THE
RECURRENT CRISIS

WHILE towns and cities flourished and grew, the South remained what it had been, predominantly a farm region. "The very land itself," a reporter wrote in 1930, "seems new to a Northern visitor, with its vast resources scarcely tapped, with its mile after mile of cheap fertile land and fast growing forest," and with its "typical symbol of toil . . . a patient Negro, driving a mule, and marching endlessly behind a plow for crops which never quite brought freedom from economic slavery." [1] In 1930, the region's population was still 67.9 per cent rural, and 42.8 per cent of its work force still worked on farms, at a per capita income of $189 in contrast to the $484 for nonfarm occupations.[2]

Briefly, after the war, the farmers' hopes soared on wings of prosperity. Wartime inflation was followed by the two-billion-dollar cotton crop of 1919, and prices continued to rise in the first half of 1920. Then with the historic regularity of the cotton cycle, farmers expanded their production and brought in the biggest crop since 1914, a crop not yet harvested before the most drastic price collapse in cotton history. Cotton, which rose to a high of 41.75 cents at New Orleans in April, 1920, and remained near 40 cents through July, slid to 13.5 cents in December.[3] The average

[1] Allen Raymond in New York *Herald-Tribune,* May 29, 1930.

[2] Smith, "Emergence of Cities," *loc. cit.,* 33; Hoover and Ratchford, *Economic Resources and Policies of the South,* 34; Edgar Z. Palmer, "Sources and Distribution of Income in the South," in *Southern Economic Journal,* II (1935–1936) , 50, 52.

[3] Boyle, *Cotton and the New Orleans Cotton Exchange,* 186–87; U.S. Bureau of the Census, *Historical Statistics of the United States,* 301–302, columns K-301 and K-303.

111

price for bright tobacco fell from 44 cents in 1919 to 21.1 in 1920, with a corresponding drop in burley from 33 to 13.4 cents. Auctions at Lexington, Kentucky, ended in riot, and disturbances elsewhere forced markets to close.[4] Across the cotton belt, from the Carolinas to Texas, night riders threatened to stop the picking and movement of cotton, burned gins and mercantile houses that refused to heed the warnings.[5] "I found many fields of cotton unpicked," a traveler wrote, "some that would never be picked at all." [6] From Georgia towns came reports of Negroes "walking the streets . . . begging for work at any price." [7]

Sharp and devastating as it was, the sudden slump was less prolonged in the South than in the corn and wheat belts. In 1921 and 1922 cotton prices reacted to improved markets and short crops and rose to an average of 28.69 cents in 1923, then broke sharply again in 1925 and 1926 and rose but little before the end of the decade. Only in the years 1922–1924 did the farmers' average return per acre rise above half its inflated level of 1919. Tobacco hit a peak annual average of 22.8 cents in 1922 and remained at fairly satisfactory levels for the rest of the decade, although it saw 20 cents again only in 1927 and 1928.[8]

Yet the crisis of 1920–1921 inflicted permanent scars. In the opinion of a South Carolina planter the South had lost its first opportunity since the Civil War to accumulate capital and break the chain of farmers who "owe the merchants and the bankers who in turn owe the jobbers, the large city banks, and the Federal Reserve Bank." Instead of holding a proportion of their profits, the farmers spent their money, bought new lands at inflated prices, and mortgaged themselves to the limit. "Hundreds of millions of dollars have been drawn into the South to finance this crop [1920], whereas our own resources should have been conserved for this

[4] James H. Shideler, *Farm Crisis, 1919–1923* (Berkeley 1957) , 49.

[5] *Ibid.,* 50; New York *Times,* October 7, 11, 28, November 1, 1920; and January 24, 1921.

[6] Ray Stannard Baker, in New York *Evening Post,* March 10, 1921, quoted in Vance, *Human Factors in Cotton Culture,* 137.

[7] Howard W. Odum to T. J. Woofter, Jr., January 4, 1921, in Odum Papers. See also Woofter to Odum, January 7, 1921, *ibid.*

[8] U. S. Bureau of the Census, *Historical Statistics of the United States,* 301–302, columns K-303, K-309; Vance, *Human Factors in Cotton Culture,* 125.

purpose." [9] It was a familiar refrain. "No part of the country needs the discipline of systematic saving or a realization of the importance of a little accumulation as does the rural South," one observer remarked; but another felt impelled to add that "no section has less opportunity to learn these principles as long as its cash income, dependent on cotton, is subject to violent fluctuations." [10]

The spreading malady of low prices, foreclosures, and bankruptcies called forth once again the old agrarian nostrums. As early as the spring of 1919 postwar apprehensiveness had sent some sixty members of Congress traveling through the cotton belt urging farmers to reduce cotton acreage and warning of efforts by "cotton bears" to undermine prices.[11] In May, 1919, a "Cotton Acreage Reduction Convention" brought together more than two thousand delegates in New Orleans to organize the American Cotton Association and recommend that farmers cut their acreage and withhold two million bales until prices of 36–40 cents returned.[12] When the prices broke in 1920 the outcry mounted. In December a convention of bankers, merchants, and farmers from twelve states assembled at Memphis with Louisiana's Governor John M. Parker in the chair. The group proposed to cut acreage a third to a half, and devised a plan of organization to reach every school or election district in the cotton belt, to circulate pledges, and to penalize nonsigners by withholding credit. There was a surprisingly active follow-up and the 1921 crop was a short one, but probably more as a result of bad weather and the boll weevil than of the Memphis convention.[13]

Another reflex, conditioned by years of agitation, was the cry for

[9] David R. Coker to Columbia *State* and Charleston *News and Courier*, quoted in Simpson, *Cokers of Carolina*, 195.

[10] E. E. Miller, "Cotton a National Crop," in *Review of Reviews*, LXXIV (1926), 72; Vance, *Human Factors in Cotton Culture*, 240.

[11] *Manufacturers' Record*, LXXV (March 20, 1919), 82. See also *ibid.* (January 30, 1919), 75; (February 6, 1919), 97; *Progressive Farmer*, XXXIV (1920), 1502; Birmingham *Age-Herald*, August 15, 1920.

[12] Robert Preston Brooks, "The American Cotton Association," in *South Atlantic Quarterly*, XIX (1920), 97–104; *Progressive Farmer*, XXXIV (1919), 1496; *Manufacturers' Record*, LXXVI (October 2, 1919), 125; (November 20, 1919), 95.

[13] *Manufacturers' Record*, LXXVI (November 20, 1919), 85–86; LXXVII (December 16, 1920), 109–10; (January 6, 1921), 144; (February 17, 1921), 91.

credit. Farm leaders turned immediately to the Federal Reserve Board and the Treasury Department, but from the orthodox heads of those agencies, W. P. G. Harding and David F. Houston, they got the pertinent but fruitless advice that the real need was markets and that the government could not support crop-holding operations. In addition, the Federal Reserve Board late in 1919 had adopted a policy of raising rediscount rates to check the postwar inflation. Although the policy was later relaxed, it became the basis for charges of a deliberate "credit conspiracy" to depress farm prices. Charles Barrett of Georgia, President of the Farmers' Union, dubbed Harding and Houston the "deflation twins" who "were working as the pliant, if not eager tools of mysterious, invisible, but immensely powerful interests, that were determined to enshrine the dollar at the expense of the man." Harding, who was from Birmingham, became the chief scapegoat, a "traitor to his section" according to one senator. As a result of the outcry Harding became lodged in the rural mind as the leader of a "Great Conspiracy," the "Crime of '20." The charges were wildly exaggerated, if not wholly false, and the farmers won neither a policy of inflation nor a governmental support for crop holding.[14]

The clamor for credit sounded a faint echo of populism. A new group, the American Cotton Association, expressed new themes of business agrarianism.[15] The Association was the brainchild of its first president, J. Skottowe Wannamaker, a self-made planter, banker, and businessman of South Carolina, and Harvie Jordan, a Georgia planter who had been a leader of the earlier Southern Cotton Association.[16] The production of cotton, Wannamaker

[14] Arthur S. Link, "The Federal Reserve Policy and the Agricultural Depression of 1920–1921," in *Agricultural History* (Chicago), XX (1946), 166–75; Harding, *Formative Period of the Federal Reserve System*, 187–96; David F. Houston, *Eight Years in Wilson's Cabinet, 1913 to 1920, with a Personal Estimate of the President* (New York, 1926), 103–105; Shideler, *Farm Crisis*, 56–57; Charles S. Barrett, *Uncle Reuben in Washington* (Washington, 1923), 78–79; George W. Armstrong, *The Unpardonable Sin of Frenzied Finance* (Dallas, 1922).

[15] The new themes of business agrarianism are pursued at some length in McConnell, *Decline of Agrarian Democracy*, and more briefly summarized in Richard Hofstadter, *The Age of Reform: From Bryan to F.D.R.* (New York, 1955), 109–14 and *passim*.

[16] For sketches of Wannamaker and Jordan see *Progressive Farmer*, XXXV (1920), 110–220.

told the first convention in 1919, had "blessed mankind wherever the sun shines except in the South; to the South it has proved a curse." The main reasons were unscientific farming, the crop lien system, and the unsatisfactory marketing system.[17] The Association's agenda included some of the old panaceas like rural credits, holding operations, acreage limitation, and diversification; but it emphasized improvements along businesslike lines: cooperative marketing, direct selling, better compression and baling, warehouses, shelters at compresses and freight platforms, grading, commercial courses in the agricultural colleges, statistics, the control of pests, improved seeds, and the opening of foreign markets.[18] The *Manufacturers' Record,* reviewing the program, bestowed its accolade: "The American Cotton Association is undertaking to handle cotton along business lines. That is all it is attempting to do." [19]

Grandiose in conception, the Association played a brief role chiefly as the vehicle for a co-operative marketing movement that swept the entire country in the early 1920's and, in its Southern phase, evoked a crusading fervor reminiscent of the cotton mill campaigns and the Southern Education Movement. It was not a new idea that cotton farmers were at the mercy of highly competitive markets which they neither controlled nor fully understood. Studies by the Department of Agriculture corroborated the farmers' suspicions that they were victimized, if not always by sharp-dealing, certainly by a system that led to widespread price irregularities in various markets or even in the same market. Controlled experiments established further that a better understanding of grades and staples improved the prices they could secure.[20] Some remedy had been sought by the promulgation of official standard grades under the Cotton Futures Acts of 1914 and 1916 with subsequent refinements up to the Cotton Standards Act of 1923, and

[17] Brooks, "American Cotton Association," *loc. cit.,* 98–99.

[18] *Ibid.,* 104–108; "Address of J. S. Wannamaker, Esq., President of the American Cotton Association at the First Annual Convention of the American Cotton Association, Montgomery, Alabama, April 13–16, 1920," in E. J. Gay Papers (Department of Archives, Louisiana State University); Harvie Jordan, "Cotton Marketing Reform Essential to All Cotton Interests," in *Manufacturers' Record,* LXXVI (October 2, 1919), 125; *Manufacturers' Record,* LXXVII (April 22, 1920), 119.

[19] *Manufacturers' Record,* LXXVI (November 20, 1919), 95.

[20] Robert Hargrove Montgomery, *The Cooperative Pattern in Cotton* (New York, 1929), 9–42, discusses the investigations in some detail.

further by the publication of weekly bulletins after 1919 on spot prices and market conditions.[21]

Meanwhile, a widespread propaganda had laid foundations for a co-operative movement in the South. It began at least as early as the Granger movement of the 1870's and continued in the Farmers' Alliance and Farmers' Union in subsequent years. Farm periodicals preached the benefits of co-operation in season and out, and in 1915 Clarence Poe, editor of the *Progressive Farmer* brought out a book, *How Farmers Co-Operate and Double Profits*, based on extensive studies of the movement in Europe and America. Among more remote examples Poe recounted successful ventures like the Eastern Shore of Virginia Produce Exchange, with a $5,000,000 annual business; the Catawba (North Carolina) Co-operative Creamery Company; and the Scott Cotton Growers Association of Arkansas, which had handled 7,554 bales in 1913, its first year of business.[22] In 1917 the Department of Agriculture began a series of marketing demonstrations in collaboration with the Southern agricultural colleges to show the benefits of proper varieties, efficient handling, and large-scale marketing. By 1921 the movement had developed eighty-five local organizations in six states, most of which later joined statewide co-operatives.[23]

The great impulse to the co-operative gospel, however, came from the first regular annual meeting of the American Cotton Association at Montgomery, Alabama, in 1920. "The story of that April convention," one enthusiastic participant wrote, "records one of the most dramatic episodes of Southern history." [24] A young spellbinder, Aaron Sapiro, a California lawyer who had risen from poverty to success as promoter of marketing associations

[21] George O. Gatlin, *Cooperative Marketing of Cotton*, U.S. Department of Agriculture Bulletin No. 1392 (Washington, 1926), 4.

[22] Poe, *How Farmers Co-operate and Double Profits*, 113–32. Another outstanding example was the Florida Citrus Exchange, dating from 1909. James T. Hopkins, *Fifty Years of Citrus: The Florida Citrus Exchange, 1909–1959* (Gainesville, Fla., 1960).

[23] Wilson Gee and Edward Allison Terry, *The Cotton Cooperatives in the Southeast*, in University of Virginia Institute for Research in the Social Sciences Monographs, No. 17 (New York and London, 1933), 36; Gatlin, *Cooperative Marketing of Cotton*, 3. The states were Texas, Oklahoma, Arkansas, Mississippi, and the Carolinas.

[24] Montgomery, *Cooperative Pattern in Cotton*, 45.

in raisins, eggs, and other specialties, infected the delegates with his own enthusiasm. Casually invited to Montgomery by an assistant secretary, he suddenly emerged there onto a larger stage. His program was thorough and complex, but essentially a call for regional commodity marketing associations; ironclad contracts with the producers ("horse-high, bull-strong, and pig-tight") to deliver their crops over a period of years; and "orderly marketing," which included the establishment of standards and grades, efficient handling and advertising, and a businesslike organization with professional technicians and executives.[25] The most significant thing about the plan, Sapiro said later, was that it "turned the interest of the average farmer from a wild sort of indefinite political hankering to some real intelligent attention to the economic phases of his problem." [26]

In the aftermath of Montgomery the co-operative agitation crowded the American Cotton Association off the scene. Fired by Sapiro's eloquence, the delegates ignited an irresistible enthusiasm across the region, promoted state co-operative laws, and set up associations for cotton and many other commodities. Sapiro traveled indefatigably across the cotton and tobacco belts, giving as many as ten speeches a week to groups of receptive farmers. At Abilene, Texas, more than 2,500 people followed him nearly a mile through the streets seeking an adequate meeting place, which they found in the First Baptist Church, and listened for three hours, alternately silent and cheering.[27] Clarence Poe followed an almost equally exhausting regimen, scheduling tours in six states and helping to organize co-operatives in tobacco, cotton, and peanuts.[28]

Twenty-one delegates from Oklahoma left Montgomery to organize the first statewide cotton co-operative. By April 1, 1921,

[25] Merle Crowell, "Nothing Could Keep This Boy Down," in *American Magazine* (New York), XCV (April, 1923), 16, 136, 138, 143, 144, 146; Shideler, *Farm Crisis*, 99–101. The program as presented at Montgomery is given in Montgomery, *Co-operative Pattern in Cotton*, 49–69.

[26] Quoted in Shideler, *Farm Crisis*, 101.

[27] Saloutos, *Farmer Movements in the South*, 261–64; Montgomery, *Cooperative Pattern in Cotton*, 102–28; *Progressive Farmer*, XXXV (July 10, 1920), 1313; (November 6, 1920), 1884; XXXVI (April 23, 1921), 473; (April 30, 1921), 494.

[28] Clarence Poe, "One Year of Co-operative Marketing," in *Progressive Farmer*, XXXVIII (1923), 379.

117

the Oklahoma Cotton Growers Association had 35,000 members and in August received the first bale of cotton.[29] During the 1921 season active associations in eight states handled 5.2 per cent of the year's cotton production. Three years later fifteen co-operatives marketed 8 per cent of the crop. They failed to secure the monopoly to which many aspired in the "holy-roller" organizing campaigns, but at the end of the 1920's they handled nearly 10 per cent of the crop.[30] Beginning in 1921 the state associations federated under the American Cotton Growers Exchange in Memphis, headed by Carl Williams of Oklahoma, which maintained domestic and foreign sales offices and provided statistical, accounting, financing, and advisory services.[31]

In tobacco the movement scored a brilliant success at first. Tobacco growers had marketing problems like those in cotton, with the additional complaint that the major tobacco companies thimblerigged the sales. Throughout the period 1912–1930, for example, three domestic manufacturers purchased 70 to 80 per cent of the burley crop and in 1927 accounted for 70 per cent of the domestic purchases of flue cured. Another perennial problem was the irregularity of grades and prices in the hasty warehouse actions. Federal officials had prepared a grading system under the Warehouse Act of 1916, but it did not correspond to the manufacturers' system, and farmers were unable to get Federal standards accepted before 1929.[32]

The promise of more orderly procedures and even the possibility of a farmers' countermonopoly, therefore, spurred the establishment of three major organizations in tobacco. Kentucky's Burley Tobacco Growers' Cooperative Association was organized largely through the leadership and financial assistance of Robert

[29] Gee and Terry, *Cotton Cooperatives in the Southeast*, 41; *Manufacturers' Record*, LXXVIII (August 19, 1920), 113.

[30] Gee and Terry, *Cotton Cooperatives in the Southeast*, 44, table. See also Ward W. Fetrow and R. H. Elsworth, *Agricultural Cooperation in the United States*, Farm Credit Administration Bulletin No. 54 (Washington, 1947), 34–39.

[31] Gee and Terry, *Cotton Cooperatives in the Southeast*, 198–205; *Manufacturers' Record*, LXXIX (May 19, 1921), 91. By 1929 it included all the large-scale associations except the Staple Cotton Growers' Association of the Mississippi Delta. *Progressive Farmer*, XLIV (September 7, 1929), 938.

[32] Robert, *Story of Tobacco in America*, 202, 212; T. J. Woofter, Jr., *The Plight of Cigarette Tobacco* (Chapel Hill, 1931), 52.

W. Bingham, publisher of the Louisville *Courier-Journal*. In 1921 a campaign enlisted 55,700 growers, representing 76 per cent of the 1920 crop. The group sold 68 per cent of the burley crop in 1921 and 75 per cent in 1923. Membership exceeded 100,000 in 1924, and over six consecutive years the pool handled more than 100,000,000 pounds annually. A Dark Tobacco Growers' Cooperative Association with members in Kentucky, Tennessee, and Indiana eventually counted over 70,000 members.[33]

In North Carolina Clarence Poe and Governor Cameron Morrison sponsored the Tobacco Growers' Cooperative Association, widely known as the Tri-State Association (Virginia, North Carolina, and South Carolina). The Association was incorporated in 1922 with more than 64,000 members who pledged 57 per cent of the combined flue-cured, dark fire-cured, and dark air-cured leaf, and some burley. It had 80,000 members before the end of 1922. In all, with some members in smaller non-Southern organizations, the tobacco co-operatives at their climax in 1923 included almost 300,000 growers and controlled 46 per cent of the leaf. Thereafter they faded rapidly; in 1930 the Federal Farm Board could find only two active associations, in Maryland and Wisconsin, handling about 2 per cent of the total leaf.[34]

The tobacco co-operatives succumbed to a number of afflictions. One was the antagonism of the American and Imperial Leaf Companies. Among the three domestic majors, only Reynolds and Liggett and Myers were consistently large buyers. Another problem was the hostility of the tobacco trade: the warehousemen, creditors, time merchants, and others who benefited from the established auction system. In many direct and subtle ways they worked to undermine confidence in the associations and to entice growers into breaking their contracts. Members often reasoned that they

[33] Aaron Sapiro, "Rolling Their Own: How the Tobacco Growers Won Their Independence," in *Survey*, L (1923), 15–19, 54; Robert, *Story of Tobacco in America*, 203–204; Nicholls, *Price Policies in the Cigarette Industry*, 215–17. The Bingham Cooperative Marketing Act (1922) of Kentucky was "perhaps the best expression of the effort to codify the legal experiences of the cooperatives." Saloutos, *Farmer Movements in the South*, 263.

[34] Robert, *Story of Tobacco in America*, 204–205; Nicholls, *Price Policies in the Cigarette Industry*, 215. Nannie May Tilley, *The Bright-Tobacco Industry, 1860–1929* (Chapel Hill, 1948), 449–88, recounts the story of the Tri-State Association.

could hit the market at its peak and secure better prices than the associations did. As a result, one student observed, "disloyalty among the members was rampant from the beginning, making it impossible for [the associations] to weather adversity."[35] The final blow came with the discovery of corruption and mismanagement in the Tri-State Cooperative. The revelation that the director and the head of the leaf department were secretly associated in a redrying company, handling co-op leaf at a handsome profit to themselves, sapped confidence irretrievably and brought the association into receivership in 1926.[36]

The fall of the Tri-State delivered a severe shock to the entire movement, causing reduced deliveries to the cotton as well as the tobacco associations. "That thing has cost me ten thousand dollars already in tobacco marketing," a disgruntled farmer wrote his senator. "The talk of Congress about aiding cooperative marketing as a means of raising the price [o]f cotton brings out a sort of cold sweat on me. One who has not been through it can never know how it feels to cooperate in going busted."[37]

Among supply and purchasing co-operatives, however, there was one outstanding success. The Southern States Cooperative of Richmond, Virginia, organized in 1923 as the Virginia Seed Service, gradually expanded into general supplies, developed a chain of service stores and other subsidiaries, and grew steadily from a volume of $100,000 in its first year to more than $67,000,000 and a membership of 194,236 in 1946. Another notable success later was the Farmers' Cooperative Exchange (FCX) of the Carolinas, formed in North Carolina in 1934, which achieved a volume of over $15,000,000 in 1946.[38]

During the Depression and New Deal years the co-operative movement experienced some revitalization; it regained its foothold

[35] Nicholls, *Price Policies in the Cigarette Industry*, 219. See also Clarence Poe, "Old 'Credit System' Must Be Changed," in *Progressive Farmer*, XXXIX (1924), 93.

[36] *Progressive Farmer*, XLI (1926), 152; Clarence Poe, "Breaking Up the Tobacco Coops," *ibid.*, 1015.

[37] Millard F. Morgan to Furnifold M. Simmons, December 27, 1926, in Furnifold M. Simmons Papers (Manuscripts Department, Duke University).

[38] Joseph S. Rowland, Jr., "The Southeast in the Cooperative Movement" (M.A. thesis, University of North Carolina, 1947), 26–28; W. G. Wysor, *The History and Philosophy of Southern States Cooperative* (Richmond, 1940).

in tobacco and expanded into other fields. By 1941–1942 there was a diversity of marketing associations in the Southeast—in tobacco, cotton, livestock, fruits and vegetables, nuts, dairy products, wool and mohair, poultry and poultry products, grains, dry beans, rice, and a few other fields, in the order of their membership—in all, 492,340 farmers. Yet, that late, not more than one of every twelve farmers was doing business through co-operatives in contrast to one of five in the nation and one of three in some areas. "Whatever standard is applied," a student concluded in 1944, "cooperative organization in the Southeast as a whole and in each of the Southeastern states is weak to the point where it is ineffectual as a device for dealing with the complex, multiple problems of farmers in an agriculture in which technology is ascendant." [39]

Problems other than the fickle markets also bedeviled the farmers. "Today the world's largest consumer of raw cotton is the boll weevil," Rupert Vance asserted in 1929.[40] The devastation was deep, widespread, often sudden and capricious. One example will suffice. Greene County, Georgia, where the weevil first appeared in 1916, ginned 20,030 bales in 1919, but only 13,414 in 1920, only 1,487 in 1921, and 333 in 1922. Greene County was but one milestone along a trail that had lengthened across the Deep South for three decades.[41] The weevil invaded Texas about 1892; by 1913 he was half way across Alabama; he reached Georgia in 1916, penetrated South Carolina in 1917, and blanketed the cotton South by 1923. The worst year was 1921, when the weevil damaged more than 30 per cent of the crop and completely wiped out the long staple Sea Island cotton of South Carolina.[42] His invinci-

[39] Charles M. Smith, "Observations on Regional Differentials in Cooperative Organization," in *Social Forces*, XXII (1943–1944), 439. For greater statistical detail see Fetrow and Elsworth, *Agricultural Cooperation in the United States*, 203–207.

[40] Vance, *Human Factors in Cotton Culture*, 89. In Louisiana the mosaic disease nearly wiped out the sugar industry as well. It was conquered in the late 1920's and early 1930's only by the introduction of new varieties of cane from the Dutch East Indies and India. Sitterson, *Sugar Country*, 346, 358, 379–80.

[41] Arthur F. Raper, *Preface to Peasantry: A Tale of Two Black Counties* (Chapel Hill, 1936), 201–202.

[42] Vance, *Human Factors in Cotton Culture*, 95–97; Eugene Butler, "Fifty Years of Cotton Growing," in *Progressive Farmer*, LI (1936), 12; *Manufacturers' Record*, LXXXVII (March 19, 1925), 85; maps in Raper, *Preface to Peasantry*, 205; and *Progressive Farmer*, XXIX (1914), 204.

bility was celebrated in the interminable stanzas of a folk song. The farmer "buried him in hot sand. . . . 'I'll stand it like a man' "; "lef' him on de ice . . . 'mighty cool and nice' "; "fed him on paris green . . . 'the best I ever seen,' " "It is my home," was his refrain, "It's jes' my home." [43]

It proved almost impossible to evict him. In 1918 Professor B. R. Coad of the experiment farm at Tallulah, Louisiana, announced an effective insecticide, calcium arsenate. Production was difficult and only 75,000 acres were treated in 1919, but the market was adequately supplied by the late 1920's and crop dusting by airplane had by then passed the experimental stage.[44] But application often proved difficult when obstinate farmers insisted that the weevil represented a judgment of God.[45] Meanwhile other remedies developed, involving chiefly the spacing of plants and measures to insure quicker ripening. Eventually the weevil became just another of the farmer's risks, like the weather, and insecticides another of his costs, like fertilizer. With the assistance of two hot, dry summers in 1925 and 1926, bumper crops reappeared with the usual consequences of overproduction.

The boll weevil, however, was not an unmitigated disaster—or so the cotton belt Pollyannas professed. As he moved eastward, he left behind a trail of campaigns for diversified farming. John M. Parker of Louisiana, for example, almost gave up as a cotton planter and in 1913 undertook the successful raising of cattle and hogs on his farm near St. Francisville, together with a campaign against the cattle tick.[46] "You have got the right sow by the ear," John Sharp Williams wrote to his son in Mississippi, "whenever

[43] John A. Lomax and Alan Lomax, *Folk Song U.S.A.* (New York, 1947), 237.

[44] Vance, *Human Factors in Cotton Culture*, 101–107; Street, *New Revolution in the Cotton Economy*, 40, 102–103; Haynes, *American Chemical Industry*, III, 110–19; IV, 333–37; Butler, "Fifty Years of Cotton Growing," *loc. cit.*, 12, 54; *Manufacturers' Record*, LXXXVI (September 4, 1924), 100; LXXXVII (March 19, 1925), 85–86; Gilbert C. Fite, "Recent Progress in the Mechanization of Cotton Production in the United States," in *Agricultural History*, XXIV (1950), 23.

[45] T. J. Woofter, Jr., *Southern Race Progress: The Wavering Color Line* (Washington, 1957), 61.

[46] John M. Parker to W. E. Vasbiner and F. M. Clark, June 16, 1913; Parker to W. F. Ward, April 14, 1915; Parker to W. B. Williams, February 6, 1922; all in John M. Parker Papers (University of North Carolina).

you think of increasing your stock of horses and cattle, and your stock of hay and pasturage . . . but the minute you get the idea that you can raise cotton . . . under boll weevil conditions that minute you are hurting your pocket-book." [47] During the teens the Alabama Black Belt came alive with campaigns for diversification. Newspapers publicized it, farm organizations discussed it, business leaders promoted it, county agents pushed it, George Washington Carver of Tuskegee Institute preached it to Negro farmers, model farms demonstrated it. In 1915 a Central Alabama Diversified Farm Association reported the organization of a Potato Growers' Association, a campaign against cattle ticks, plans for packing houses in Montgomery and Andalusia, creameries in Montgomery and Selma, bank loans for livestock, and an increase in grain and truck crops. Wartime food production programs added impetus. In 1918 the Union Stock Yards of Montgomery opened with a daily capacity of 2,500 cattle, 5,000 hogs, and 5,000 sheep. In 1919 the citizens of Enterprise erected a monument in "profound appreciation of the Boll Weevil and what it has done as the Herald of prosperity." In 1921 even the state's automobile dealers sponsored a diversification campaign. But while the movement laid the foundation for a future development of livestock in the Black Belt, "the volume of discussion was more indicative of the fear of the boll weevil than of actual progress toward diversification." [48]

The diversification campaign, a perennial Southern growth, sprang up again during the 1920's in a cattle-raising program for Colquitt County, Georgia; an Arkansas "Live at Home" movement sponsored by the farm and home demonstration agents in 1926; the "Cow, Hog and Hen" program of the Ashburn, Georgia, *Wiregrass Farmer;* the advice of the Savannah *Morning News* that

[47] John Sharp Williams to John Sharp Williams, Jr., February 19, 1914, quoted in George C. Osborn (ed.), "Plantation Letters of a Southern Statesman," in *Agricultural History,* XXI (1947), 125.

[48] Glenn N. Sisk, "Alabama Black Belt: A Social History, 1875–1917" (Ph.D. dissertation, Duke University, 1951), 159–478; Shirley Graham and George D. Lipscomb, *Dr. George Washington Carver, Scientist* (New York, 1944), 153–60; Christy Borth, *Pioneers of Plenty: The Story of Chemurgy* (Indianapolis and New York, 1939), 315–29; Vance, *Human Factors in Cotton Culture,* 101.

the "boll weevil can't chew tobacco." [49] "For many years the dangers of adhering to a single crop system have been proclaimed," the *Progressive Farmer* observed. "The cry of 'Wolf! Wolf!', however, has fallen largely on unresponsive minds and ears stuffed with cotton." [50] In an area where, according to one whimsical journalist, "cotton is Religion, Politics, Law, Economics, and Art," the folkways and economy were too stubbornly set to the routine of staple production.[51] The routines of tenancy yielded with difficulty to other arrangements; the marketing, supply, and credit systems were geared to staple crops. The commercial leaders of the community "may meet . . . and proclaim that there must be a reduction of cotton acreage," said a Texas lawyer, but go "to the mortgage records and see the work that is really being done. . . . Not one word is said in private conference with farmers about reduction of cotton acreage." [52]

Obstinate folkways hampered the war on the cattle tick, bearer of Texas fever. The struggle to make the South safe for livestock began in 1906 with a measure introduced by Representative Joseph E. Ransdell of Louisiana. At the beginning of the work 966 counties, including 741,515 square miles, went under quarantine and authorities imposed compulsory dipping of cattle. Over the years the work advanced despite balky farmers who refused to round up their scrub cattle and on occasion dynamited the vats and took pot shots at the dipping agents. But by the end of 1931 only 137 counties in the lower South remained under quarantine; a major hindrance to cattle and dairying development was on the way out.[53]

Still, the preachments of a hundred years quickly dissipated at some temporary upturn in prices. Diversification was beginning to

[49] "The Industrial South," in *Fortune*, XVIII (November, 1938), 123; Gus M. Oehm, "Arkansas Farmers Learning to 'Live at Home,'" in *Manufacturers' Record*, LXXXIX (April 8, 1926), 78–79; Griffin and Talmadge, *Georgia Journalism*, 148.

[50] *Progressive Farmer*, XXXVIII (1923), 350.

[51] Quoted in Vance, *Human Factors in Cotton Culture*, 296.

[52] T. N. Jones, letter in Dallas *News*, February 17, 1928, quoted in *ibid.*, 189–90.

[53] Adras P. Laborde, *A National Southerner: Ransdell of Louisiana* (New York, 1951), 29–30; Vance, *Human Geography of the South*, 159–62; Sisk, "Alabama Black Belt," 473–74; Charles W. Holman, "Rescuing the South from the Cattle Tick," in *Review of Reviews*, LXVIII (1923), 289–95; J. Stanley Clark, "Texas Fever in Oklahoma," in *Chronicles of Oklahoma*, XXIX (1951–1952), 429–43.

leave the verbal stage, but it took the form of new specialties like peanuts, cattle, truck farming, and fruit growing, rather than a "live at home" subsistence farming. In 1931 the Charlotte *Observer* pictured North Carolina farmers growing staple crops for the depressed market while they imported butter and milk from Minnesota, wheat from Kansas, corn from Iowa, and vegetables from Ohio and Maryland.[54]

The chronic distresses of Southern agriculture increasingly negated the Jeffersonian vision of the independent yeoman farmer, but the image persisted. "Farming is the best business in the world, the highest order of business, the most honest occupation," John Sharp Williams assured his son.[55] "One of the best forms of insurance against revolution is a large and contented rural population," wrote an Arkansas historian.[56] A rural sociologist proclaimed the "inherent environmental superiority of the country as a place in which to breed men and women of upstanding and outstanding character," but in preface to a catalog of shortcomings in education, illiteracy, tenancy, and poverty that utterly belied his assertion.[57]

It was a perennial irony that such invocations of the agrarian myth accompanied the steady drift of farmers into the dependent status of tenancy and sharecropping. In 1880 tenants operated 36.2 per cent of all Southern farms; by 1920, 49.6 per cent; in 1930, 55.5 per cent.[58] Nor were the farmers "speaking of the grandeur of farm life any more," wrote President Charles S. Barrett of the Farmers' Union. "They are not telling of the glorious independence from want and care Uncle Reuben enjoys. But they are tell-

[54] Charlotte *Observer*, September 7, 1931. On the obstacles to diversification see Vance, *Human Factors in Cotton Culture*, 179–92; Vance, *Human Geography of the South*, 154–59; Street, *New Revolution in the Cotton Economy*, 9–10, 30–34. Anthony Ming Tang, *Economic Development in the Southern Piedmont, 1860–1950: Its Impact on Agriculture* (Chapel Hill, 1958), emphasizes the importance of industry and urbanization in providing markets for a diversified agriculture.

[55] John Sharp Williams to John Sharp Williams, Jr., January 14, 1913, in Osborn (ed.), "Plantation Letters of a Southern Statesman," *loc. cit.*, 118.

[56] David Y. Thomas, "Tenancy as Related to the Negro Problem," in *Manufacturers' Record*, LXXVII (June 17, 1920), 127.

[57] Wilson Gee, "The Rural South," in *Social Forces*, II (1923–1924), 713–14.

[58] Charles S. Johnson, Edward R. Embree, and W. W. Alexander, *The Collapse of Cotton Tenancy: Summary of Field Studies and Statistical Surveys, 1933–1935* (Chapel Hill, 1935), 4–5.

ing their children that he is a slave to the distributor of his products, the manipulator of markets." [59] To the general disillusionment of the landowners, Arthur Raper remarked, was added the dejection "of those white and Negro tenants who lost their meager savings of years by trying to finish payments during the deflation period on land bargained for at high prices. . . . To the vast majority the urge for home ownership is gone. They are fatalists of the first order." [60] Jeff Wilson, a tenant character in Dorothy Scarborough's novel of cotton in the Brazos Valley, expressed the feeling pungently: "If I was to start to hell with a load of ice, there'd be a freeze before I got there." [61]

It was not for want of serious concern that no effective program developed to check the deterioration of the rural community. From the time of Theodore Roosevelt's Rural Life Commission in 1908, much ink and wind were expended in a diffuse "Country Life Movement," an effort by agricultural, religious, and educational leaders to preserve the vision of farming as a way of life.[62] From the first decade of the century scholarly monographs detailed the growth and magnitude of the problem.[63] Tenant agitations in Texas inspired early studies there; the census bureau and agriculture department devoted bulletins to it; scholarly and agricultural journals opened their pages to students of the problem.[64] Southern tenancy moved "steadily toward the peasant type of European countries," wrote E. C. Branson of the University of North Carolina; "it is villeinage that begins to approach the sixteenth century type." [65] "The greatest single economic and social prob-

---

[59] Barrett, *Uncle Reuben in Washington*, 124.

[60] Raper, *Preface to Peasantry*, 215.

[61] Dorothy Scarborough, *In the Land of Cotton* (New York, 1923), 162.

[62] Orrin L. Keener, *Struggle for Equal Opportunity: Dirt Farmers and the American County Life Association* (New York, 1961).

[63] E. M. Banks, *Economics of Land Tenure in Georgia* (New York, 1905); Robert Preston Brooks, *The Agrarian Revolution in Georgia, 1865–1912* (Madison, Wis., 1914).

[64] For examples see E. A. Boeger and E. A. Goldenweiser, *A Study of the Tenant System of Farming in Yazoo-Mississippi Delta*, U.S. Department of Agriculture Bulletin No. 337 (Washington, 1916); E. A. Goldenweiser and Leon Truesdell, *Farm Tenancy in the United States* (College Station, Tex., 1921); J. T. Sanders, *Farm Ownership and Tenancy in the Black Prairies of Texas*, U.S. Department of Agriculture Bulletin No. 1068 (Washington, 1922).

[65] E. C. Branson, "Farm Tenancy in the Cotton Belt: How Farm Tenants Live," in *Social Forces*, I (1922–1923), 213; E. C. Branson, "Farm Tenancy in the South: II.

lem . . . throughout the South is farm tenancy," wrote his col-league, S. H. Hobbs.[66]

Yet little of this penetrated the public consciousness. Its chief result for the time was academic; the study of rural conditions became the entering wedge for the new discipline of sociology in Southern universities. Any real attention to the problem depended upon making scholarly work assimilable by the newspapers, a discerning journalist admonished, unless there should appear "a Charles Dickens whose genius might put the tenant farmer so starkly before Mr. Babbitt's imagination that he would be galvanized into a fury of activity." [67]

The times were not propitious for social reform. Serious efforts to secure state programs for tenant land purchases failed in the legislatures of both North and South Carolina.[68] Nor, it turned out, were the times altogether propitious for schemes to reclaim cutover, swamp, and other waste lands for agriculture—despite the urban land booms. The reclamation idea usually appeared in terms of economic development, but was often rationalized as a new safety valve for the dispossessed. In 1920 the Southern states included some 65,504,000 acres, or more than two thirds of all the land in the United States, unfit for cultivation without drainage, including nearly half the area of Florida and a good third of Louisiana.[69] An important beginning of reclamation came in the North Carolina Drainage Law of 1909; by the end of the 1920's all Southern states except Alabama had similar legislation and had brought nearly 22,500,000 acres into drainage districts.[70] The

The Social Estate of White Farm Tenants," in *ibid.*, 451. See also E. C. Branson (ed.) , *Home and Farm Ownership*, North Carolina Club Year-book, 1921–1922 (Chapel Hill, 1922) .

[66] Samuel H. Hobbs, Jr., *North Carolina: Economic and Social* (Chapel Hill, 1930) , 119.

[67] Gerald W. Johnson, "Mr. Babbitt Arrives at Erzerum," in *Social Forces*, I (1922–1923) , 208.

[68] Elwood Mead, "Community Farming," in *New Republic*, XLI (1924–1925) , 329–30; *North Carolina Land Conditions and Problems: The Report of the State Land Commission* (Raleigh, 1923) ; Burts, "Public Career of Richard I. Manning," 513–16; *Manufacturers' Record*, LXXXIV (November 29, 1923) , 57–58.

[69] Ray P. Teele, *The Economics of Land Reclamation in the United States* (Chicago and New York, 1927) , 45–47.

[70] S. H. McCrory, "Progress of Drainage in the Southeastern States," Address before the National Drainage Congress, Atlanta, November 10, 1920, in William B.

most ambitious single project was Florida's effort to control water levels in the Everglades by lowering Lake Okeechobee. Most of the project was completed in the ten years 1916–1926, with eight major canals totaling 486.9 miles accompanied by extensive levees and pumping operations. The drainage opened a new empire of sugar cane and truck farming, but scant opportunity for hard-pressed tenants. It established instead the winter base for an army of migratory workers who provided in their squalor a stark contrast to the migratory Yankees of the Gold Coast.[71]

Much less successful were the scattered efforts to colonize the cutover lands.[72] In 1917 and 1918 the Southern Pine Association sponsored conferences on the problem at New Orleans and Savannah, with interested lumbermen, public officials, and forestry and agricultural experts in attendance; and the Mississippi experiment station produced a comprehensive bulletin on the outlook for cattle growing.[73] But the discussions provoked no action by lumbermen who, a disappointed association officer said, did not fully grasp the idea of stabilizing society through farm home ownership.[74]

The Southern Settlement and Development Organization in Baltimore, set up at a conference of Southern governors there in 1912, undertook over-all guidance of land development agitation. It won the support of Southern railroads, businessmen, and land-

Bankhead Papers (Alabama Department of Archives); U.S. Bureau of the Census, *Drainage of Agricultural Lands, Fifteenth Census: 1930* (Washington, 1932), 28.

[71] L. LeMar Stephen, "Historico-Economic Aspects of Drainage in the Florida Everglades," in *Southern Economic Journal*, X (1943–1944), 197–211; Donald H. Grubbs, "The Story of Florida's Migrant Farm Workers," in *Florida Historical Quarterly* (St. Augustine), XL (1961–1962), 105.

[72] Goodyear, *Bogalusa Story*, 160–62, recounts one such failure by the Great Southern Lumber Company in eastern Louisiana. In 1916 the Southwestern Settlement and Development Company undertook to subdivide and sell off some eight million acres in East Texas and west Louisiana formerly owned by the Houston Oil Company. Easton, "History of the Texas Lumbering Industry," 223.

[73] James Boyd, "Cut-Over Lands," in "Southern Pine Association History" (typescript), 9; "Proceedings of the Cut-Over Land Conference of the South at New Orleans, La., April 11–12–13, 1917" (typescript); and "Lumbering—The Forerunner of Industrial Progress" (typescript), all in Case 9, Drawer 1, Southern Pine Association Papers. Farley and Greene, *The Cut-Over Pine Lands of the South for Beef-Cattle Production.*

[74] A. G. T. Moore to William B. Bankhead, February 8, 1924, in William B. Bankhead Papers.

owners for a general program of economic development and informational services for corporations interested in the region. It emphasized the establishment of subsidiary state development boards to promote drainage and reclamation.[75] Under Executive Vice President Clement S. Ucker, a former Interior Department official, the organization turned its attention to the development of a Federal reclamation program on a national scale, comprehending swamp and cutover lands as well as the arid lands of the West. Representative William B. Bankhead of Alabama repeatedly introduced a bill endorsed by a Forestry, Reclamation and Home-Making Conference at New Orleans in 1923, but got only an authorization of $100,000 and an actual appropriation of $15,000 in 1926 for an investigation of possibilities in the South.[76] After working fifteen years for a Federal program, Ucker wrote, "I have about come to the conclusion that this generation doesn't want it. Maybe we are ahead of our time."[77]

Interior Department advisors who made the investigation proposed experiments with a limited number of farm colonies similar to a group of settlements near Wilmington, North Carolina, where Hugh McRae, an imaginative engineer and businessman, had developed since 1905 a group of successful colonies on the principle of compact rural communities and intensive truck farming in small tracts. Elwood P. Mead, one of the investigators, had inspired a similar program under a California land settlement act of 1917 and had subsequently joined McRae and others in promoting the idea. In December, 1927, Mead assembled delegates from nine Southern states in a conference at Washington to endorse the scheme. The group sponsored a bill to set up in each of

[75] Origins and activities of the organization are summarized in H. H. Richardson to William Jennings Bryan, January 7, 1922, in Bryan Papers. See also "Meeting of the Cut-Over Land Committee Held at the Grunewald Hotel, New Orleans," December 12, 1916, in Southern Pine Association Papers.

[76] Paul K. Conkin, *Tomorrow a New World: The New Deal Community Program* (Ithaca, N.Y., 1959), 104–105; "Proceedings of the Forestry Reclamation and Home-Making Conference," held at the Roosevelt Hotel, New Orleans, November 19, 20, 21, and 22, 1923 (Typescript in Southern Pine Association Papers); "Synopsis of Address of Representative W. B. Bankhead on the Subject of '*Reclamation and Homemaking in the South*'" (typescript), and "Drainage and Reclamation: Southern Settlement and Development Organization" (bound folder of correspondence), in W. B. Bankhead Papers.

[77] Clement S. Ucker to Francis G. Tracy, August 26, 1924, copy in William B. Bankhead Papers.

twelve Southern states one organized rural community of at least two hundred families. It never came to a vote, but the concept of organized rural communities aroused widespread discussion and support. It prepared the way for New Deal rural community experiments within a few years.[78]

The South, a graveyard of farm organizations since the Civil War, buried yet another in the 1920's. The Farmers' Union, founded in Texas in 1902, carried the populist spirit into the twentieth century. It swept across the South within a few years, like the Farmers' Alliance, but declined almost as quickly while it secured a more permanent footing in the wheat belt. From 1914 to 1919 Southern membership dropped from 61,817 to 28,135 while the national rose from 103,276 to 131,425.[79] An Association of State Farmers' Union Presidents in the cotton states gave the organization a claim to spokesmanship for Southern farmers until after World War I, but its brave front disguised a basic weakness.[80] The organization grew rapidly, said a North Carolina state president, and then the pendulum "swung the other way." Disappointment at the defeat of extravagant hopes nourished in the mushroom growth, failure of the co-operatives sponsored by the Union, and the poor results of the Union's acreage reduction and crop-holding operations all contributed to its decline. The final blow came with the postwar deflation and the subsequent rise of the new co-operative movement that absorbed the energies of many farm leaders.[81] Charles S. Barrett of Union City, Georgia,

[78] Conkin, *Tomorrow a New World*, 105–107; *Manufacturers' Record*, XCI (February 17, 1927), 85; XCIII (February 2, 1928), 91; (May 10, 1928), 71; David R. Coker, "Defense of the Plan for Establishment of Federally-Financed Farm Colonies in the South," *ibid.*, XCVII (March 20, 1930), 54–55; Hugh McRae to Furnifold M. Simmons, June 7, 1928, and Simmons to Richard H. Edmonds, May 24, 1929, in Simmons Papers; Charlotte *Observer*, April 24, 1929.

[79] Robert L. Tontz, "Memberships of General Farmers' Organizations, United States, 1874–1960," in *Agricultural History*, XXXVIII (1964), 155. See also Commodore B. Fisher, *The Farmers' Union*, in University of Kentucky *Studies in Economics and Sociology*, No. 2 (Lexington, Ky., 1920), 15.

[80] John A. Simpson to Thomas J. Heflin, February 14, 1919, copy in Bowen Papers.

[81] Saloutos, *Farmer Movements in the South*, 184–212, deals chiefly with the period before 1913. See also Robert Lee Hunt, *A History of Farmer Movements in the Southwest, 1873–1925* (College Station, Tex., 1935), 41–143; Fisher, *Farmers' Union*, 44–45; Loomis, "Rise and Decline of the North Carolina Farmers' Union,"

first elected national president in 1906, remained the head of what had become a Western organization until 1928, when he was displaced by C. E. Huff of Kansas who was in turn succeeded in 1930 by John A. Simpson of Oklahoma, a state that formed a bridge between the Southern and Western phases of Union history.[82]

The Union left a legacy of contributions to the warehouse movement, the co-operative idea, public education, and rural credits, but its collapse left the region without an effective over-all farm organization during the 1920's. The American Farm Bureau Federation did not reach that status until the 1930's. In contrast to the unreconstructed populists of the Farmers' Union and the nostalgic idealists of the Country Life Movement it represented the "businesslike" attitudes of commercial agriculture. Founded at a meeting in Chicago in 1920, the Farm Bureau built its organization from the county "bureaus" that had sprung up to support the county agents of the Extension Service. It occupied a unique position, closely allied to an important Federal agency. Its philosophy stemmed in part from association with business leaders who supported the bureaus and in larger part from the predominance of the more successful commercial farmers in its membership, a situation that reflected in turn the county agents' practice of concentrating on the larger farmers with whom they could show greater results.

Eight Southern states sent delegates to the founding convention in 1920; three already had state federations. By the time of the Atlanta convention in 1921 only three Southern states lacked at least formal organizations.[83] In Texas the Farm Bureau absorbed the

---

loc. cit., 305–25, and Loomis, "Activities of the North Carolina Farmers' Union," *loc. cit.*, 443–62; William Tucker, "Populism Up-to-Date: The Story of the Farmers' Union," in *Agricultural History*, XXI (1927), 201. The above interpretation is supported by two veteran leaders of the Union. Gladys Talbott Edwards to the author, May 7, 1959, and C. E. Huff to the author, July 24, 1959.

[82] Theodore Saloutos and John D. Hicks, *Agricultural Discontent in the Middle West, 1909–1939* (Madison, Wis., 1951), 236–38; Gilbert C. Fite, "John A. Simpson: The Southwest's Militant Farm Leader," in *Mississippi Valley Historical Review*, XXXV (1948), 567–70.

[83] Orville M. Kile, *The Farm Bureau through Three Decades* (Baltimore, 1948), 49, 111; Orville M. Kile, *The Farm Bureau Movement* (New York, 1921), 280–82; *Progressive Farmer*, XXXV (1920), 901. In 1920 Virginia, North Carolina, Georgia, Tennessee, Mississippi, Texas, Oklahoma, and Kentucky were represented. In 1921 only South Carolina, Mississippi, and Louisiana lacked formal organizations.

Texas branch of the American Cotton Association and proceeded to organize marketing co-operatives for cotton, wool, hay, and sweet potatoes, each with a proviso for deducting Farm Bureau dues from members' sales. Late in 1921 the Texas Bureau claimed 70,000 members in 130 counties.[84] In Alabama, where the "Farmers' Union had never been popular with the large planters and farmer business men," the Extension Service hired a man specifically to organize a state bureau, which in turn sponsored marketing organizations for eight commodities, from watermelons to cotton.[85] Elsewhere, especially in Arkansas, Georgia, and Mississippi, the bureaus figured significantly in the co-operative movement, and it was the Farm Bureau that promoted the federation of cotton associations under the American Cotton Growers' Exchange.[86] The group suffered from its very success, for energies flowed into the co-operative movement, and it maintained stable organizations through the 1920's only in Alabama and Tennessee. In 1930 Southern membership was only 25,476 in a total of 321,196.[87] For the time, the Farm Bureau had its most secure base in the corn belt, but it was destined for a more significant future in the South.

Toward the end of the 1920's the granddaddy of all farm organizations, the National Grange, quietly reappeared in the South whence it had disappeared in the 1890's. Its leader, Louis J. Taber, began an organizing campaign that re-established the Virginia State Grange in 1928 and reorganized North Carolina in 1929, South Carolina in 1930, Tennessee and Arkansas in 1934, and Texas in 1935. The national convention at Winston-Salem in

---

[84] Montgomery, *Cooperative Pattern in Cotton*, 76–79, 102–28; Kile, *Farm Bureau Movement*, 137; Saloutos, *Farmer Movements in the South*, 257.

[85] Theodore Saloutos, "The Alabama Farm Bureau Federation: Early Beginnings," in *Alabama Review*, XIII (1960), 185–98; Gee and Terry, *Cotton Cooperatives in the Southeast*, 58–62; Gladys Baker, *The County Agent*, in University of Chicago *Studies in Public Administration*, XI (Chicago, 1939), 141–42.

[86] *Manufacturers' Record*, LXX (May 19, 1921), 91; *Progressive Farmer*, XLIV (1929), 938.

[87] Tontz, "Memberships of General Farmers' Organizations," *loc. cit.*, 156. See also Ralph Russell, "Membership of the American Farm Bureau Federation, 1926–1935," in *Rural Sociology: Devoted to Scientific Study of Rural Life* (Baton Rouge), II (1937), 30–31.

1932 was the first in the South since the Atlanta meeting of 1890.[88]

If concern with co-operatives and other businesslike approaches to agricultural problems drew farmers ever further away from populism, it was still inevitable that farm problems should invite political solutions. In national politics the most effective response to the agricultural crisis of the early 1920's was the formation of the Farm Bloc, a coalition of Western Republicans and Southern Democrats that put through an impressive, if fairly moderate, program of legislation over a three-year period. The Farm Bloc originated on May 9, 1921, at a meeting in the office of Gray Silver, Washington representative of the Farm Bureau. Eleven Senators, including five from the South, attended the first meeting and the group soon mustered some twenty-five Senators led by Arthur Capper of Kansas. In the other wing of the Capitol a similar bloc of nearly a hundred appeared under the leadership of Representative L. J. Dickinson of Iowa. Only a negligible number in either group came from east of the Mississippi and north of the Ohio, but the only Southern states not represented in either house were Tennessee and North Carolina.[89]

Between 1921 and 1923 Farm Bloc legislation added an important capstone to the agrarian program of the Wilson period. In 1921 the Bloc threw its force behind the passage of five important measures: the Emergency Tariff, which included protection for farm commodities; a three-year extension of the War Finance Corporation to assist co-operative, storage, and export operations; the Packers and Stockyards Act to preserve competition among packers; the Grain Futures Trading Act; and the Federal Highways Act. In 1922 the Farm Bloc supported the Fordney-McCumber Tariff; another grain futures act; the Capper-Volstead Co-operative Marketing Act, exempting agricultural co-operatives

[88] "Reminiscences of Louis J. Taber," in Oral History Research Office (Columbia University), 213; Stuart Noblin, *The Grange in North Carolina, 1929–1954: A Story of Agricultural Progress* (Greensboro, N.C., 1954), 4–6; Charles M. Gardner, *The Grange—Friend of the Farmer* (Washington, 1949), 280; *Progressive Farmer*, XLVII (1932), 9.

[89] Phillips Bradley, "The Farm Bloc," in *Social Forces*, III (1924–1925), 714–18; William G. Carleton, "Gray Silver and the Rise of the Farm Bureau," in *Current History* (New York), XXVIII (1955), 343–50.

from the antitrust laws; and enlargement of the Federal Reserve Board to include a "dirt farmer." The last major reform was the Intermediate Credit Act of 1923, which extended agricultural credits under the Federal Reserve System to nine months and established a system of Intermediate Credit Banks for loans of six months to three years.[90]

For several years the Farm Bloc challenged the leadership of a business-minded Republican administration, brought forth condemnation of "developing factionalism" from President Harding, and alarmed Eastern commercial interests with the "meddlesome experimental discriminations of politics dominated from the West."[91] After 1923 it succumbed to a number of adversities: administration opposition; death of the sympathetic Agriculture Secretary Henry C. Wallace in 1924; Senator Capper's Presidential ambitions; Gray Silver's departure from Washington in 1924; the LaFollette third-party movement of 1924; and more than anything else, the lack of sustained Southern interest and support.[92] Several factors were involved in that: the Farm Bureau was not yet strong in the South; revival of the War Finance Corporation gave Southerners substantially what they wanted, aid to co-operatives and exports; recovery of cotton and tobacco prices from 1922 until 1925 relieved the pressures of agitation; and Southern agrarians were suspicious of Western Republican support for protective tariffs.

For better than a century the cotton and tobacco South had been the irreducible core of low tariff sentiment, for the simple reason that producers of export commodities wanted an active foreign trade. In the 1920's, despite increasing world competition, a large proportion of Southern products entered world markets. In the period 1926–1929 about 58 per cent of the American cotton, 40 per cent of the tobacco, one sixth of the petroleum, a third of the sulphur, and half of the naval stores were exported. According to a well-informed estimate, Southern exports of about $1,476,-000,000 in that period constituted 30 per cent of all American

[90] Bradley, "Farm Bloc," loc. cit., 715; Shidler, Farm Crisis, 152–279; Harding, Formative Period of the Federal Reserve System, 222.

[91] Bradley, "Farm Bloc," loc. cit., 717.

[92] Shideler, Farm Crisis, 151, 165, 235, 279; Kile, Farm Bureau through Three Decades, 120.

exports and equalled roughly 20–25 per cent of the value of all economic production in the South. "It was no great exaggeration to say," two economists wrote, "that at that time the South had to export or die." [93]

Yet protectionism had begun to appear around the fringes of the cotton, tobacco, and petroleum economies. Industrialism brought to the South its retinue of tariff advocates; manufacturers of texiles, chemicals, fertilizers, lumber, and other products were increasingly eager to exclude foreign competition. The South needed "reasonable protection to industry," Senator Walter George of Georgia declared in 1926.[94] Independent oil men, alarmed at the development of foreign resources by the majors, came to the protectionist position as well. The strikingly new feature of the situation was a growing propaganda for protection to agricultural commodities.

Leadership was undertaken by John H. Kirby, a Houston lumberman who was among the first of a prolific breed of ultra-conservative Texas millionaries. In the fall of 1920 he declared that the Democratic party was "honeycombed with socialism" and announced his withdrawal from the "party which for eight years has increased [the people's] taxes and reduced their liberties." [95] A month later he presided over the organization of the Southern Tariff Association in Houston. A second meeting, held in Atlanta during January, 1921, on the call of sixteen governors, heard an address by Calvin Coolidge and proclaimed that the association represented "every important Southern industry" and truly reflected "the thought and aspirations of the people of the South." [96] Next the association set up a Washington headquarters under Vance Muse and promoted a series of tariff meetings across the South during the summer and fall. Republican Speaker Nicholas

[93] Hoover and Ratchford, *Economic Resources and Policies of the South*, 425–27.
[94] William J. Robertson, *The Changing South* (New York, 1927), 201.
[95] *Manufacturers' Record*, LXXVIII (November 4, 1920), 145.
[96] Albert Phenis, "South Makes Urgent Demand for Protective Tariff," in *Manufacturers' Record*, LXXIX (February 3, 1921), 115. The claim to represent "every important Southern industry" was scarcely substantiated by the list of contributors, which included sugar, sulphur, peanut, and sheep- and goat-raising associations, in addition to a number of individuals. "Membership Subscription to the Southern Tariff Association to January 31, 1921," in Drawer 37, Southern Pine Association Papers.

J. Longworth was so impressed as to announce that "protection sentiment fairly seethes today throughout the South." [97] The following year, while the Fordney-McCumber Tariff was under consideration, the association concentrated upon protection for agriculture, centering its fight around vegetable oils. The act that followed, said Kirby, was the first "applying the principle that the farmer is entitled to the same treatment in tariff legislation as the manufacturer." There had been "a complete and permanent change in tariff sentiment in the South," he asserted.[98]

The Emergency Tariff Act of 1921 had included such Southern products as peanuts, wheat, corn, meat, wool, sugar, and long-staple cotton. Schedule seven of the Fordney-McCumber Act of 1922 listed more than two hundred agricultural products, from huckleberries to reindeer meat; it was the first tariff in nearly a century that gave "the South a square deal with other sections of of the country," according to Kirby. It would add a quarter-billion dollars "to the value of farm products of the South above the price of competitive products in foreign markets." [99]

Some farm leaders rallied to the cause, "protesting against this pernicious doctrine of free trade for the farmer when he wants to sell his product and protection when he wants to buy his supplies." [100] G. T. McElderry, president of the moribund Alabama Farmers' Union, decided that "the time is at hand now when the business interests and farmers must join hands," accepted the chairmanship of the tariff association's Organization Committee in 1923, secured support from Farmers' Union remnants in other states, and sponsored five men in Ford cars to canvass Alabama and

[97] *Congressional Record,* 67 Cong., 1 Sess., 3614.

[98] "Statement Issued by John H. Kirby, President, Southern Tariff Association, on Effect of the McCumber Fordney Tariff Measure on the South," Washington, August 22, 1922, in Drawer 37, Southern Pine Association Papers.

[99] Shideler, *Farm Crisis,* 156–57, 184; Frank W. Taussig, *The Tariff History of the United States* (7th ed.; New York and London, 1923), 452, 455; "Statement Issued by John H. Kirby, President, Southern Tariff Association, on Effect of the Mc-Cumber Fordney Tariff Measure on the South," in Drawer 37, Southern Pine Association Papers.

[100] John H. Kirby, "The Tariff with Special Reference to Its Effects upon the Economic Progress of the South." Address delivered . . . before . . . the Louisiana Bankers Association at Shreveport, Louisiana, April 18, 1923, in Drawer 37, Southern Pine Association Papers.

organize tariff clubs "as a safeguard against meddling by tariff theorists." [101] The Florida Chamber of Commerce, and citrus and vegetable growers of the state, entered the movement, and by 1929 Kirby's association was organizing state conferences with the support of state commissioners of agriculture. The Louisiana meeting resolved "that a crisis exists in American agriculture for which no relief is possible or permanent without adequate tariff duty." A Southwide meeting at Washington attracted such notables as Georgia's agriculture commissioner Eugene Talmadge, who enthusiastically supported the tariff panacea; A. Steve Nance, Georgia labor leader; and Edward A. O'Neal, president of the Alabama Farm Bureau.[102]

However, the seething activity was deceptive. A decade of agitation brought few cotton or tobacco farmers into the protectionist fold, and an overwhelming majority of Southern Congressmen held fast to their low-tariff principles. They often acted to include Southern products in pending bills, but then voted against the bills. In 1922, for example, only 15 per cent of the Southern Representatives voted for final passage of the Fordney-McCumber Act.[103] Furthermore, even the Farm Bureau, which had joined the hue and cry for farm tariffs, discovered in a study by its Department of Research that farmers would gain about $125,000,000 income from the 1922 tariff but pay out about $426,000,000 more for goods they bought.[104]

It was in this situation that the first McNary-Haugen bill appeared in 1924. The bill embodied a plan worked out by George Peek and Hugh S. Johnson of the Moline Plow Company to secure "equality for agriculture in the benefits of the protective tariff." Complex as it would have been in operation, it was relatively simple in conception: in short, a plan to dump farm surpluses

[101] G. T. McElderry to Reuben Dean Bowen, July 16, 1923, in Bowen Papers; G. T. McElderry, "Southern Farmers Turning to a Protective Tariff," in *Manufacturers' Record*, LXXXV (February 21, 1924), 83.

[102] *Manufacturers' Record*, XCV (April 4, 1929), 80; (June 27, 1929), 59–60; J. A. Arnold to H. C. Berckes, July 5, 1929, in Drawer 37, Southern Pine Association Papers. Arnold was Vice President and Executive Manager of the Southern Tariff Association.

[103] Hoover and Ratchford, *Economic Resources and Policies of the South*, 423.

[104] Shideler, *Farm Crisis*, 187.

overseas at world prices. Farmers would assume the loss in an "equalization fee," but would profit by rises in the domestic price which theoretically should reach a level of the world price plus the tariff on the given crop.[105] McNary-Haugenism remained the favorite Western solution to the farm problem through the 1920's, but it aroused conflicting regional interests. The cotton South was more complacent during the price recovery of 1922–1925 and viewed with misgiving any program that proposed to entrench protection. Moreover, the plan would not work for predominantly export crops. Cotton farmers required to pay an equalization fee for dumping some 58 per cent of their crop on the export market could scarcely recoup their losses from a rise in the domestic price of the other 42 per cent.

Consequently a combination of Southern and Eastern votes defeated the first McNary-Haugen bill in 1924. A second bill in 1925 never reached a vote. The scheme evoked little interest in the South until 1926, when the cotton cycle produced another crisis. Bumper crops in 1925–1926 set a new record for a two-year period, sent the average price plunging from 19.6 cents in 1925 to 12.5 in 1926, and prompted a rapprochement between the agrarian South and West.[106] Some Western leaders, notably Chester Davis of Montana and Henry A. Wallace of Iowa, had already begun to talk of a "marriage of cotton and corn" as the only means of effective agricultural legislation.[107] In December, 1925, C. O. Moser, Secretary of the American Cotton Growers' Exchange, expressed a more friendly attitude toward Federal legislation than the cotton co-operatives had shown before. In March, 1926, George Peek conferred with co-operative leaders in Memphis, and directors of the exchange agreed to a meeting later that month in which they formed an alliance with McNary-Haugen supporters in Washington. The outcome was a new McNary-Haugen bill

[105] One may trace the evolution of McNary-Haugenism in John D. Black, *Agricultural Reform in the United States* (New York, 1929), 232–54; and in Darwin N. Kelly, "The McNary-Haugen Bills, 1924–1928: An Attempt to Make the Tariff Effective for Farm Products," in *Agricultural History*, XIV (1940), 170–80.

[106] Peter Molyneaux, *The Cotton South and American Trade Policy* (New York, 1936), 51; Vance, *Human Factors in Cotton Culture*, 107; U.S. Bureau of the Census, *Historical Statistics of the United States*, 301, columns K-302, K-303.

[107] Kile, *Farm Bureau through Three Decades*, 132.

which proposed for cotton the more orderly handling of exports through the co-operatives and a Federal corporation. Southern leaders appeared before committees in support of the measure yet it lost in the House during May with fewer than thirty cotton state Democrats voting for it.[108]

The continuing slide of cotton prices, meanwhile, brought another cotton convention. Governor H. L. Whitfield of Mississippi called the meeting at Memphis in October, 1926, with the anticipation that "a time of great necessity" had brought the psychological situation "that causes the people to quit the old systems of business and adopt new ones." The new system, it transpired, was another holding effort—but the boldest yet—with cotton pools of four million bales to be formed by the co-operatives in collaboration with bankers who would refuse loans to farmers unless they reduced cotton acreage by 25 per cent and planted food and feeds. Southern governors were asked to proclaim "Cotton Reduction Acreage Week" in October, and a committee of bankers and agricultural leaders appeared in each state. The program had a more thorough follow-up even than that of 1921, and had the support of a special committee of three cabinet members with War Finance Corporation director Eugene Meyer as chairman and $30,000,000 of credit available. Little of the money was used, but whatever the cause, six million fewer acres were harvested in 1927 and the average annual price rose above twenty cents again for the last time before the next war.[109]

But the Memphis program did not halt the budding courtship of cotton and corn. Shortly after the 1926 elections the Corn Belt Committee, an organization sponsoring the McNary-Haugen plan, called a joint meeting of corn-hog, wheat, cotton, tobacco, and rice representatives in St. Louis. The meeting renewed activity for a

[108] Fite, *George N. Peek,* 151–62; Murray Reed Benedict, *Farm Policies of the United States, 1790–1950: A Study of Their Origins and Development* (New York, 1953), 224–25; Saloutos and Hicks, *Agricultural Discontent in the Middle West,* 391.

[109] *Proceedings of Cotton Convention Held at Memphis, Tenn., Wed., Oct. 13th, 1926, pursuant to Call of Gov. H. L. Whitfield of Miss., Joined by the Governors of Fourteen Cotton Growing States* (n.p., [1926]), 3, 8–11; *Manufacturers' Record,* XC (November 18, 1926), 79–80; Saloutos, *Farmer Movements in the South,* 268–69; U.S. Bureau of the Census, *Historical Statistics of the United States,* 301, column K-301.

united front and recommended revival of the Farm Bloc "to express and work for the economic interests of agriculture." [110] Farmers of both West and South were "suffering from a common calamity," Clarence Poe declared in the *Progressive Farmer*. They needed a new coalition to end their political isolation.[111] A drastically revised McNary-Haugen program followed the St. Louis conference. The new plan included cotton, tobacco, and rice among the "basic crops" covered and proposed an equalization fee for cotton to collect funds for a holding movement, with operation of the plan dependent upon a vote of farmers representing half the production. For the first time, with Southern support, a McNary-Haugen bill passed both houses of Congress in 1927, only to be vetoed by President Coolidge; another bill was vetoed in 1928.[112]

The successive bills had moved progressively away from the original plan of dumping surpluses and toward orderly marketing through the co-operatives. Their purpose, said B. W. Kilgore, board chairman of the American Cotton Growers' Exchange, was the same as that of the Cotton Textile Institute and other trade associations—stabilization of production and markets.[113] But the new emphasis did not move all to support the plan. Leaders of the cotton trade, like W. L. Clayton of Houston, argued that "irrespective of [the] merits of the plan as applying to other agricultural products," especially those consumed mostly in the domestic market, "it must be abortive if applied . . . to cotton." [114] Shortly after the St. Louis conference the New York *Times* reported that some Southern Representatives were "shying away from the principle of the bill on the assumption that it will commit them to a high tariff." [115] Cordell Hull of Tennessee

[110] Fite, *George N. Peek*, 169–72; Benedict, *Farm Policies of the United States*, 226; Saloutos, *Farmer Movements in the South*, 269.

[111] Clarence Poe, "South and West Unite for Farm Relief," in *Progressive Farmer*, XLII (1927), 5.

[112] Fite, *George N. Peek*, 173–81, 193; Black, *Agricultural Reform in the United States*, 235–36.

[113] B. W. Kilgore to J. M. Gamewell, February 9, 1927, in Simmons Papers.

[114] New Orleans *Cotton Trade Journal*, February 19, 1927, quoted in Saloutos and Hicks, *Agricultural Discontent in the Middle West*, 398. The *Cotton Trade Journal* was consistently suspicious of both the co-operatives and McNary-Haugenism.

[115] New York *Times*, November 18, 1926, quoted in Saloutos and Hicks, *Agricultural Discontent in the Middle West*, 397; Fite, *George N. Peek*, 163, 166.

presented their viewpoint in debate on the 1927 bill. The farmer's continuing needs, he argued, were low costs of production, of living, and of transportation, plus wider and better foreign markets for his surplus. But protectionist spokesmen for two generations had "taught the western farmer almost as a part of his religion the economic falsehood that typical high tariffs benefit all classes and sections alike." The result was an unfortunate choice of economic isolation in 1921 when a realistic appraisal showed that the war had left the United States a creditor nation with unrivaled productive capacity while other nations were exhausted and prostrated. "America had but to adopt a system of moderate or competitive traiffs for revenue, cooperate in maintaining the international exchange, credit and trade situation, insist on liberal trade relations and fair trade methods, and extend her commerce in all lines throughout the world." As to the farm plan, he concluded, "I am not disturbed, therefore, about the 'newness' or the 'drastic nature' of the pending bill, but rather by the certain belief that it will not offer permanent relief to agriculture and will perpetuate the Fordney tariffs." [116]

The failure of McNary-Haugenism, therefore, resulted in part from Southern fear of the tariff but also from Eastern fear of an increased cost of living. Strong opposition, Senator Simmons charged, came from Secretary Mellon and other Eastern industrialists and financiers "in the face of the fact of their enjoying for nearly a hundred years the exclusive privilege of taxing all the people of this country for the purpose of increasing their profits." [117] But the Eastern viewpoint had the crucial advantage of dominating the Coolidge administration. The issue was "primarily one between the agricultural sections of the country and the industrial," B. W. Kilgore said. "The president has run true to his provincial form and sided with his sector, the Industrial East, against the great and sorely distressed agricultural areas." [118]

In a broader sense, however, McNary-Haugenism did not fail. It made the farm problem into an issue of national policy and for the first time defined it in the fundamental terms of surpluses, heretofore attacked only tangentially. When a national program finally

[116] *Congressional Record,* 69 Cong., 2 Sess., 3899, and 3895–3899.
[117] Reprinted in Rippy (ed.), *Simmons: Memoirs and Addresses,* 494.
[118] Quoted in Saloutos, *Farmer Movements in the South,* 270.

emerged, the export scheme became only a minor and at first neglected feature. In its essence the program was the old Southern remedy prescribed with every cotton crisis and most recently in the Memphis conventions of 1920 and 1926—acreage reductions combined with holding operations. Moreover, the evolution of the McNary-Haugen plan revived the idea of bipartisan alliance between South and West, which became in the next decade a dominant influence in the development of a national farm policy. The "marriage of cotton and corn" finally came under the auspices of the American Farm Bureau Federation. Edward A. O'Neal of Alabama, elected its national president in 1931, officiated at the nuptials.

CHAPTER V

THE AGE OF SEGREGATION

WOODROW WILSON became President in the semi-centennial year of the Emancipation Proclamation, but his inauguration brought no new birth of freedom for American Negroes. It brought instead the deepening shadows of segregation and proscription. In 1912 his campaign organization cultivated the votes of Negroes and Wilson promised "absolute fair dealing . . . in advancing the interests of their race," but the statement was deliberately vague and the minority of Negroes who supported him were destined to bitter disappointment. The President's racial philosophy was more plainly revealed in the benevolent clichés that sprang so readily to his lips. "I know myself as a Southern man how sincerely the heart of the South desires the good of the negro and the advancement of his race on all sound and sensible lines," he told a delegation from the University Commission on Southern Race Questions. Segregation, he wrote to a church editor, was "distinctly to the advantage of the colored people themselves." [1] In the best tradition of Southern paternalism, he clearly wished Negroes no harm, but the whole question was peripheral to his concerns and he drifted willingly in the current of the times.

Under Wilson the rising tide of segregation swept on through the Federal government. Postmaster General Burleson broached the subject at one of the first cabinet meetings, proposing separation to eliminate alleged friction between white and Negro railway mail clerks. "Mr. Burleson thought the segregation would be a great thing as he had the highest regard for the negro and wished

[1] New York *Times*, December 16, 1914, p. 10; Woodrow Wilson to H. A. Bridgman, September 8, 1913, quoted in Link, *Wilson: The New Freedom*, 251.

to help him in every way possible," Josephus Daniels confided to his diary. The proposal was not challenged and Wilson expressed a wish to have the matter "adjusted in a way to make the least friction." [2] He never blueprinted an over-all plan, but the practice of segregation spread rapidly through government offices, shops, rest rooms, and lunchrooms, especially in the post office and treasury departments. In September, 1913, an investigator concluded that segregation was being given "systematic enforcement" and was "becoming known as the policy of the present government." [3]

Colored Democrats failed even to get appointments previously reserved for Negroes. Ironically Secretary McAdoo's plan to advance segregation by making the Treasury's Registry Division an all-Negro unit foundered when vigorous opposition from Southern Senators led Adam E. Patterson, a Negro Democrat of Oklahoma, to withdraw from the nomination as Register. Thereafter Wilson challenged his Southern supporters on the issue only once, in 1914, by forcing the reappointment of Robert H. Terrell as a municipal judge in Washington. The choice of a Negro Democrat, James L. Curtis, as minister to Liberia in 1915 did not provoke serious opposition. Otherwise, among some thirty Negroes who held appointments at the time of the inauguration Wilson retained only about eight.[4] Hitherto, the Charlotte *Observer* commented, Federal departments had stood apart from the trend of events, "viewing the negro as Reconstructionists viewed him and not as the country has come to view him." Government had finally

[2] E. David Cronon (ed.), *The Cabinet Diaries of Josephus Daniels, 1913–1921* (Lincoln, Neb., 1963), 33.

[3] May Childs Nerney to Oswald Garrison Villard, September 30, 1913, quoted in Link, *Wilson: The New Freedom*, 247. The subject is treated extensively *ibid.*, 243–52; in Kathleen L. Wolgemuth, "Woodrow Wilson and Federal Segregation," in *Journal of Negro History* (Lancaster, Pa., and Washington, D. C.), XLIV (1959), 158–73; and in Constance McLaughlin Green, *Washington: Capital City, 1879–1950* (Princeton, 1963), 207–33, which shows that segregation began to develop in governmental offices before Wilson.

[4] Kathleen L. Wolgemuth, "Woodrow Wilson's Appointment Policy and the Negro," in *Journal of Southern History*, XXIV (1958), 457–71; George C. Osborn, "Woodrow Wilson Appoints a Negro Judge," in *ibid.*, 481–93. The Wolgemuth article includes a tabular summary which, however, omits the removal of Robert Smalls as Collector of Customs at Beaufort, S.C. and the retention of Mrs. Mary C. Booze as Postmistress at Mound Bayou, Miss. New York *Times*, April 13, 1913; Eugene P. Booze to Joseph P. Tumulty, May 8, 1916, in Wilson Papers.

accepted the universal rule. "Nothing but what was bound to occur has occurred." [5]

The new climate in Washington stirred a heightened aggressiveness among the devotees of caste. Every man "who dreams of making the Negro race a group of menials and pariahs is alert and hopeful," a Negro journal admonished Wilson. "Vardaman, Tillman, Hoke Smith, Cole Blease and Burleson are evidently assuming that their theory of the place and destiny of the Negro race is the theory of your administration." [6] Congressional hoppers teemed with Southern bills to require segregation in the civil service, in Washington streetcars and residential areas; to forbid interracial marriages; to exclude Negroes from the armed services; there was even a resolution by "Cotton Ed" Smith of South Carolina to repeal the Fourteenth and Fifteenth Amendments. [7] None passed, but proposals for Jim Crow and antimarriage measures in Northern states gave credence to the Charlotte Observer's comment that "the country has fairly come to be of one mind upon the so-called negro problem." [8]

In the South the earlier wave of laws for Jim Crow railway cars was followed by a new wave of municipal laws for residential segregation, beginning at Baltimore in 1910. [9] In the early teens Clarence Poe of the Progressive Farmer proposed to extend the segregation principle to rural land ownership. His idea inspired widespread discussion and secured the endorsement of the North Carolina Farmers' Union. [10] But for the most part additional

[5] Charlotte Observer, October 9, 1913.

[6] The Crisis: A Record of the Darker Races (New York), VI (1913), 232.

[7] The Crisis, VI (1913), 62, 168; VII (1913–1914), 283–84; IX (1914–1915), 246, 291; XIII (1916–1917), 39–41.

[8] Charlotte Observer, October 9, 1913; The Crisis, VI (1913), 19; IX (1914–1915), 246–47; Reuben Dean Bowen to J. C. Shaffer, February 20, 1915, in Bowen Papers.

[9] Gilbert T. Stephenson, "The Segregation of the White and Negro Races in Cities," in South Atlantic Quarterly, XIII (1914), 1–18; Gilbert T. Stephenson, "The Segregation of the White and Negro Races in Cities by Legislation," in National Municipal Review (Worcester, Mass.), III (1914), 496–504; B. H. Nelson, The Fourteenth Amendment and the Negro since 1920 (Washington, 1946), 23–33, 96–98. On the unhappy conditions Negroes experienced in Jim Crow cars see a series by T. Montgomery Gregory, "The 'Jim Crow' Car," in The Crisis, XI (1915–1916), 87–89, 137–38, 195–98.

[10] The plan is summarized in Clarence Poe, "Rural Land Segregation between Whites and Negroes: A Reply to Mr. Stephenson," in South Atlantic Quarterly, XIII

segregation laws represented spasmodic elaboration into new or overlooked areas, as Jim Crow laws for taxicabs in Mississippi in 1922, Jacksonville in 1929, Birmingham in 1930, or for buses in South Carolina as late as 1937.[11] The spread of segregation was as much a matter of individual practice and growing custom as it was of legislation, and it was often capricious and inconsistent in application.[12] Few indeed were the primitive communities like the Carr's Fork neighborhood of the Kentucky mountains where as late as 1921 white and black freely visited each other's churches, the separate Negro church being a recent innovation, and a visitor saw a small black boy roll into bed with the white boys of the family on whose farm he worked. Even in that remote quarter people were learning that such behavior was bad form.[13]

[The Wilson years saw the consolidation of segregation,] but they also saw the beginnings of a movement, the Great Migration, "which after emancipation was the great watershed in American Negro history." [14] Causes of the Negro exodus from the South were deeply rooted in past hopes and grievances, but the immediate occasion was World War I. War industries in the North depleted the ranks of common labor at a time when the war prevented replacement by foreign immigration. Before the end of 1915 the agents of Northern employers ventured southward in search of domestic immigrants and found eager clients. The cotton crisis of 1914–1915, the ravages of the boll weevil, floods over much of the Deep South in 1915 and 1916 unsettled large areas and contributed to the migratory urge.[15] By the early summer of

---

(1914), 207–12; and Clarence Poe, "What Is Justice between White Man and Black in the Rural South," in *Lectures and Addresses on the Negro in the New South*, Phelps-Stokes Fellowship Papers, No. 1 (Charlottesville, Va., 1915), 37–55.

[11] C. Vann Woodward, *The Strange Career of Jim Crow* (New York, 1955), 102–104; Charles S. Johnson, *Patterns of Negro Segregation* (New York and London, 1943), 168; Albert N. Sanders, "State Regulation of Public Utilities by South Carolina, 1879–1935" (Ph.D. dissertation, University of North Carolina, 1956), 448.

[12] Bertram W. Doyle, *The Etiquette of Race Relations in the South* (Chicago, 1937).

[13] W. K. Bradley, "Negroes in the Kentucky Mountains," in *The Crisis*, XXII (1921), 69–71.

[14] August Meier, *Negro Thought in America, 1880–1915: Racial Ideologies in the Age of Booker T. Washington* (Ann Arbor, 1963), 170.

[15] The voluminous literature of the Great Migration is catalogued in F. H. Ross and Louise V. Kennedy, *A Bibliography of Negro Migration* (New York, 1934).

1916 the Pennsylvania and Erie railroads had inaugurated programs to transport trainloads of Negroes from the Southeast, and before the end of the year several railroads and the major steel corporations had developed camps from which to distribute the new immigrants.[16]

According to one informed estimate, however, no more than 10 to 20 per cent of the Negro workers went North at the direct solicitation of labor agents. The rest were impelled by word of mouth, by friends who went ahead, by Negro journals and papers that supported the movement. "To die from the bite of frost is far more glorious than at the hands of a mob," the Chicago *Defender* suggested.[17] As the momentum gathered the exodus became a spontaneous mass movement, without organization and without leadership. "The Negroes just quietly move away without taking their recognized leaders into their confidence any more than they do the white people about them," one observer reported. "A Negro minister may have all his deacons with him at mid-week meeting, but by Sunday every church officer is likely to be in the North." [18]

For many Negroes migration was a kind of mute protest, but the movement inspired the articulation of unvoiced grievances. "The treatment accorded the Negro always stood second, when not first, among the reasons given by Negroes for leaving the South," a contemporary investigator wrote. "I talked with all classes of colored people from Virginia to Louisiana . . . and in every instance the matter of treatment came to the front voluntarily. This," he concluded, "is the all-absorbing, burning question among Negroes." [19]

The wartime migration set the pattern and established the channels for a continuing northward movement of Negroes. From the first census in 1790 until 1910 the center of Negro population

[16] Francis D. Tyson, "The Negro Migrant in the North," in U.S. Department of Labor, Division of Negro Economics (ed.) , *Negro Migration in 1916–1917* (Washington, 1919) , 95.

[17] Quoted in John Hope Franklin, *From Slavery to Freedom: A History of American Negroes* (New York, 1947) , 464.

[18] W. T. B. Williams, "The Negro Exodus from the South," in Division of Negro Economics (ed.) , *Negro Migration in 1916–1917*, p. 95.

[19] *Ibid.*, 101. For a different view see Charles S. Johnson, "How Much Is the Migration a Flight from Persecution?", in *Opportunity*, I (1923) , 272–74.

had drifted steadily southwestward. In 1920 for the first time it moved 21.5 miles northeastward, from the neighborhood of Fort Payne, Alabama, to the vicinity of Rising Fawn, Georgia.[20] In all, the Southeast lost some 323,000 native Negroes by migration during the 1910's, or some 4.9 per cent of the native Negro population in 1910, and 615,000 during the 1920's or 8.2 per cent of the native Negro population at the beginning of that decade. By 1930, 26.3 per cent of all Negroes born in the Southeast were living elsewhere, a total of some 1,840,000. Of the nation's total Negro population 89 per cent lived in the South in 1910, 85.2 per cent in 1920, and only 78.7 per cent by 1930.[21]

The ambivalent reactions of whites to the movement nearly everywhere conformed to the same progression from amused toleration to outraged alarm. "The northern drift . . . will lower negro congestion in certain sections of the South," said the Vicksburg *Herald*. "Such a change promises ultimate benefit."[22] A hundred thousand blacks should be sent into Mexico to conquer the "mongrel breed" and at the same time rid the South of that many Negroes, said the Macon *Telegraph*, but its tone changed abruptly as the migration grew. "Everybody seems to be asleep about what is going on right under our noses," the *Telegraph* warned presently. "That is, everybody but those farmers who have wakened up of mornings recently to find every male Negro over 21 on his [sic] place gone—to Cleveland, to Pittsburgh, to Chicago, to Indianapolis." Labor agents, the paper charged, were part of an organized plan "to rifle the entire South of its well-behaved, able-bodied Negro labor."[23]

Macon soon had a license fee of $25,000 for all labor agents, each of whom also had to be recommended by ten local ministers,

[20] Louise V. Kennedy, *The Negro Peasant Turns Cityward: Effects of Recent Migrations to Northern Cities*, in Columbia University *Studies in History, Economics, and Public Law*, No. 329 (New York, 1930), 28.

[21] Rupert B. Vance, *All These People: The Nation's Human Resources in the South* (Chapel Hill, 1945), 117–19; Maurice R. Davie, *Negroes in American Society* (New York, 1949), 92.

[22] Vicksburg *Herald*, August 19, 1916, quoted in Emmett J. Scott, *Negro Migration during the War*, in Carnegie Endowment for International Peace, *Preliminary Economic Studies of the War*, No. 16 (New York, 1920), 153.

[23] Macon *Telegraph*, n.d., quoted *ibid.*, 156; Macon *Telegraph*, n.d., quoted in *The Crisis*, XIII (1916–1917), 22.

ten manufacturers, and twenty-five businessmen. Other communities passed similar laws—Montgomery enacted an outright prohibition—and supplemented the laws by extralegal action. At Albany, Georgia, policemen tore up the tickets of migrants about to leave; at Savannah on one occasion they arrested every Negro found in the railway station; at Greenville, Mississippi, officers dragged Negroes from trains and prevented others from boarding; in Hattiesburg a passenger agent refused to sell tickets until overruled by his superior.[24] "Unhappily," a Charleston editor lamented when the migration continued into the 1920's, "we have plenty of Southerners whose disposition is identical with that of the ancient Egyptians—they would chase the Negroes to the Red Sea to bring them back." [25]

When neither intimidation nor force sufficed to stem the tide, more indulgent attitudes began to surface. "If you thought you might be lynched by mistake," the Columbia *State* asked its readers, "would you remain in South Carolina?" [26] "Does the South want to keep its great supply of Negro labor?" an upcountry paper asked. "If not, there is no need of a change in the South's treatment of the Negro; if it does, there must be a change." [27] "We should exercise influence with our landlords and our merchants," a Georgia paper declared, "to see that a fairer division of profit is made with the negro." [28] In some communities white leaders began to give ear to Negro grievances; "hard-headed business men began to give consideration to what the Negro was thinking, and the two most important factors in Southern life sat down together for the first time since emancipation." [29]

[24] Scott, *Negro Migration during the War,* 72–78; Sisk, "Alabama Black Belt," 446. Stories appeared in the Southern press about the mistreatment of Negroes in the North and about many who had returned in disillusionment to the Sunny South. Some of them, according to rumor, were disguised labor agents who soon disappeared back into the North with new recruits. Division of Negro Economics (ed.), *Negro Migration in 1916–1917,* p. 28.

[25] William Watts Ball to Clarence Poe, May 5, 1923, in Ball Papers.

[26] Quoted in W. E. B. Du Bois, "The Migration of Negroes," in *The Crisis,* XIV (1917), 66.

[27] Greenville (S.C.) *Piedmont,* n.d., quoted in *The Crisis,* XIV (1917), 24.

[28] Columbus *Enquirer-Sun,* December 2, 1916, quoted in Scott, *Negro Migration during the War,* 155.

[29] Robert Russa Moton, *What the Negro Thinks* (Garden City, N.Y., 1929), 60.

A YMCA representative, who raised funds in the Mississippi Delta during the war, later recalled "the wonderful unity that had come to these Delta communities. As white and black crowded together to hear of the war they were not race conscious. For a moment something greater than race had been laid upon their hearts." [30] "The dominant race is just a bit less dominant at present," one Negro Mississippian remarked.[31] In Birmingham and Mobile, Confederate veterans led parades of Negro draftees to their trains. In communities across the region Negroes assisted in war services, bond drives, and other patriotic ventures.[32] George E. Haynes, a professor at Fisk University, became director of a Division of Negro Economics in the Department of Labor and organized 11 state and 225 local committees to consider the problems of Negro labor.[33]

Yet neither the open road north nor the war spirit offered any magic liberation from the bonds of dependency. Both had contradictory effects: amelioration on the one hand and heightened tensions on the other. Migrants created in Northern ghettoes "urban equivalents of what the South had called the 'black belt,' " and faced the hostility of white workers who feared their competition.[34] At East St. Louis, Illinois, Negro competition for jobs sparked a race riot on July 2, 1917, in which nine whites and about thirty-nine Negroes lost their lives.[35] Nor did experience in the armed services do much to raise Negro expectations. Those who undertook to volunteer early in the war were for the most

[30] Quoted in R. L. Duffus, "Counter-Mining the Ku Klux Klan," in *World's Work*, XLVI (1923), 276; "Reminiscences of Will W. Alexander" (in Oral History Research Office), 155–56; James Weldon Johnson, *Along This Way: The Autobiography of James Weldon Johnson* (New York, 1933), 332–33.

[31] Scott, *Negro Migration during the War*, 90.

[32] George Edmond Haynes, "Negroes Move North: I. Their Departure from the South," in *Survey*, XL (1918), 121; Moore, *History of Alabama and Her People*, I, 942; Emmett J. Scott, *Scott's Official History of the American Negro in the World War* (Chicago, 1919), 416, 419, 421; Scott, *Negro Migration during the War*, 79–84; Kate M. Herring, "How the Southern Negro Is Supporting the Government," in *Outlook*, CXX (1918), 452–53; *The Crisis*, XVI (1918–1919), 131–32.

[33] U.S. Department of Labor, Division of Negro Economics, *The Negro at Work during the World War and during Reconstruction* (Washington, 1921), 12–19.

[34] Quotation from Sullivan, *Our Times*, V, 488.

[35] Elliott M. Rudwick, *Race Riot at East St. Louis, July 2, 1917* (Carbondale, Ill., 1964), 4.

part discouraged, but complaints were general that draft b
the South enrolled Negroes out of proportion to their numbers. In
the nation at large approximately 31 per cent of the Negro draft
registrants were accepted in contrast to 26 per cent of the whites.[36]
Violent protests from white leaders against stationing Negro
troops in Southern camps led the army to send thousands of
Southern Negroes and most Northern Negroes into Northern
camps, although administrative difficulties eventually dictated
abandonment of the plan. Negroes served in segregated units,
mostly labor battalions, and for the most part under white officers.
Incidents of discrimination and racial conflict were matters of
frequent protest, and the appointment of Emmett J. Scott, formerly Booker T. Washington's secretary, as Special Assistant to the
Secretary of War only provided a lightning rod for the harmless
discharge of complaints.[37] At Houston, Texas, in September,
1917, police harassment of Negro soldiers at Camp Logan brought
on a full-fledged race riot in which seventeen whites were killed. In
the aftermath thirteen Negro soldiers were hanged, forty-one given
life sentences, and forty held pending further investigations.[38]
At Spartanburg, South Carolina, the solution to growing tensions
that threatened to bring on a riot was hasty embarkation of the
Negro soldiers for Europe. American prejudice pursued Negroes
on into France where, however, they encountered drastically different attitudes.[39]

Within a few weeks of the Armistice in 1918 a wave of rumors
revolving in part about Negro soldiers who had been "French-
woman ruined" began to sweep Southern communities.[40] During
the first postwar year newspapers North and South reported

[36] Franklin, *From Slavery to Freedom*, 447–48; Seligman, *Negro Faces America*,
136–37. Scott, *Official History of the American Negro in the World War*, 67–69,
gives the numbers called from each state by race.

[37] Scott, *Official History of the American Negro in the World War*, 72–77, 92–93,
426–30, 445–53.

[38] Franklin, *From Slavery to Freedom*, 252. *The Crisis*, XV (1918), 14–19, contains
the account of an investigation by Martha Gruening for the NAACP.

[39] Scott, *Official History of the American Negro in the World War*, 79–81,
440–45; Robert Russa Moton, *Finding a Way Out: An Autobiography* (Garden
City, N.Y., 1921), 256–60.

[40] James K. Vardaman, quoted in "Our Own Subject Race Rebels," in *Literary
Digest*, LXII (1919), 25.

rumors of plots, revolts, and insurrections. After a series of premonitory clashes in the spring, the worst being an encounter between white sailors and Negroes in Charleston on May 10, the summer of 1919 "ushered in the greatest period of interracial strife the nation had ever witnessed." Before the end of the year some twenty-five race riots took place, and more were threatened.[41] What James Weldon Johnson called "The Red Summer" began early in July when whites invaded the Negro section of Longview, Texas, seeking a schoolteacher who had allegedly accused a white woman of a liaison with a Negro man. They met resistance, but burned a number of shops and homes and ran several Negroes out of town before the militia restored order.[42] The following week a more violent outbreak took place in Washington, where an inflammatory press campaign manufactured a crime wave out of routine reports and aroused mobs with charges of Negro attacks on white women. For four days gangs of white and Negro rioters waged race war in the streets of the capital until Federal troops and driving rains ended the affrays.[43] These were but preliminaries to the Chicago riot of late July, arising out of rumors about an incident at a Lake Michigan beach, in which 38 people were killed and 537 injured.[44] At Knoxville in August a mob supposedly bent on a lynching, released prisoners from the jail, seized confiscated whisky, and looted shops in the Negro section.[45] In September a lynch mob nearly killed the mayor of Omaha for refusing to hand over a prisoner.[46]

The climactic disorders occurred in the rural area around Elaine, Arkansas. The convulsions of that October in Phillips County are still clouded by the prejudice and hysteria that

[41] Franklin, *From Slavery to Freedom*, 472. Arthur J. Waskow, *From Race Riot to Sit-In, 1919 and the 1960's* (Garden City, N.Y., 1966), offers the fullest and best general account.

[42] *The Crisis*, XVIII (1919), 297–98.

[43] "Washington Riots," in *The Independent* (New York), XCIX (1919), 147; "Washington Riots," in *Nation*, CIX (1919), 143; "Race Riots in Washington and Chicago," in *Current History and Forum*, X (1919), 453–54.

[44] Chicago Commission on Race Relations, *The Negro in Chicago: A Study of Race Relations and a Race Riot* (Chicago, 1922).

[45] Seligman, *Negro Faces America*, 177–79.

[46] Wichita (Kan.) *Protest*, n.d., reprinted in Robert J. Kerlin (ed.), *The Voice of the Negro, 1919* (New York, 1920), 85–86.

surrounded them, but they clearly turned on tenant grievances.[47] Negro tenants in the area had formed a semisecret fraternal order, the Progressive Farmers and Household Union of America, to seek itemized statements and quicker settlements from landlords. They sought legal aid and even discussed withholding their cotton or charging landlords with peonage. "The Union wants to know why it is that the laborers cannot control their just earnings which they work for," a leaflet demanded. "There are many of our families suffering because our men are forced to act as children." [48]

Such alarming manifestations of self-reliance set the countryside abuzz with reports of plotting and insurrection. A shooting incident between Negroes and a party spying out one of their meeting places precipitated sporadic fighting across the southern end of the county. White men poured in from other parts of Arkansas and from neighboring Mississippi and Tennessee. Finally, Governor Brough personally accompanied a force of Federal troops from Camp Pike who rounded up Negro refugees from the canebrakes and put them in a stockade.

According to official reports five whites and twenty-five Negroes died, but white men in the area told one reporter that more than a hundred Negroes had been killed. Newspapers across the country ran lurid headlines about black insurrection in Arkansas, and that became the official version of what happened. The tenant union, according to the statement prepared by a committee of local planters, was "established for the purpose of banding Negroes together for the killing of white people." Inexplicably "some of the ring-leaders were found to be the oldest and most reliable of the Negroes." [49] Governor Brough himself blamed it on Northern "agitators," and described it "advisedly" as a "damned rebellion." [50] Another investigator reported to a Negro paper, however, that he was able to discover "no basis for the belief that a

[47] The most satisfactory account is in Waskow, *From Race Riot to Sit-In*, 121–74. Other general accounts are O. A. Rogers, Jr., "The Elaine Race Riots of 1919," in *Arkansas Historical Quarterly*, XIX (1960), 142–50; J. W. Butts and Dorothy James, "The Underlying Causes of the Elaine Riot of 1919," *ibid.*, XX (1961), 95–104; and Walter F. White, *A Man Called White: The Autobiography of Walter F. White* (New York, 1948), 47–51.

[48] Leaflet quoted in "Statement," in Brough Papers.   [49] *Ibid.*

[50] Seligman, *Negro Faces America*, 288; Graham, *Soul of John Brown*, 326.

massacre was planned by the Negroes and, in point of fact, it was the Negroes who were massacred." It was no insurrection, said the former Republican postmaster of Little Rock, whose law firm represented the union, "only a preconceived plan to put a stop to the Negro ever asking for a settlement."[51]

Within a month sixty-five Negroes were hastily indicted and tried. A court sentenced eleven to death and fifty-four to prison terms of one to twenty years. One more death sentence came later, but the litigation dragged through a complicated series of appeals until 1923. Six of the twelve sentenced to death won release by order of the state supreme court because of irregularities. The other six won a retrial in a landmark decision of the United States Supreme Court on the grounds that they were denied due process of law by the lack of adequate counsel and by trial in surroundings of hysteria and mob threat. The retrial never took place; in January, 1924, Governor McRae ordered their release.[52]

After the Elaine massacres the time of troubles began to pass, although several minor clashes occurred the following year, the largest brought on by Negro efforts to vote in Ocoee, Florida. The final major riot of the postwar era occurred in 1921 at Tulsa where rough elements of both races had gravitated to the oil boom. The ingredients of trouble, according to the state adjutant general, were "an impudent negro, a hysterical girl, and a reporter for a yellow newspaper." Inflammatory accounts of an apparently trivial incident led to rumors of a lynching, and an armed Negro mob gathered at the jail to prevent it. A white mob gathered, a shot was fired, and the riot ensued. The Negroes fell back into their own section which the whites attacked, looted, and burned to the ground. Forty-four blocks of Negro property were reduced to a rubble like that of a Rheims or a Louvain.[53] But the race riots

[51] U. S. Bratton to David Y. Thomas, March 1, 1920, quoted in Rogers, "Elaine Race Riots of 1919," *loc. cit.*, 150.

[52] J. S. Waterman and E. E. Overton, "The Aftermath of Moore v. Dempsey," in *Arkansas Law Review and Bar Association Journal* (Fayetteville), VI (1951–1952), 1–7; *The Crisis*, XXVI (1923), 163; XXVII (1923–1924), 72–76, 124; XXIX (1924–1925), 272; Moore v. Dempsey, 216 U.S. 86 (1923).

[53] Baker, *Negro-White Adjustment*, 96–100; *Literary Digest*, LXIX (1921), 8–9; *The Crisis*, XXII (1921), 114–16; Amy Comstock, " 'Over There': Another View of the Tulsa Riots," in *Survey*, XLV (1921), 460.

petered out in 1923; the last serious affair was at Rosewood, Florida, where a white mob in search of an alleged Negro rapist ran amuck through the Negro community, burned six houses and a church, and left five Negroes and two whites dead. The Nashville *Banner* suspected "Florida's large Northern population, permanent and seasonal." Southerners did "sometimes visit summary punishment upon a guilty person," the paper admitted, but "we do not kill the innocent by wholesale." [54]

Two salient facts stood out in the postwar pattern of rioting. One was that they were not solely a regional phenomenon, and Southern papers often reported Northern disorders with complacent relish. The clashes, said the Memphis *Commercial Appeal*, "should be a warning to the Negroes of the South that the supposed benevolent treatment of their race in the Northern states is largely a myth." The cause, said the Houston *Chronicle*, covering an opposite viewpoint, was "an old, old, story . . . of silly pampering." The uniform had given Negroes "an unprecedented degree of protection and consideration while high wages and allotments have tended to make them shiftless and irresponsible." [55] Another signal fact was the bristling new spirit of resistance, even retaliation, among Negroes. Negroes had fought back in organized fashion not only in Washington and Chicago but in Charleston, Longview, Knoxville, Elaine, Tulsa, and Rosewood; and the casualties included substantial numbers of whites.

If some could believe with the Dallas *News* that the guilt "attaches itself mostly to the white race," more whites agreed with South Carolina's Representative James F. Byrnes that race antagonism was "due to the incendiary utterances of the would-be leaders of the race now being circulated through negro newspapers and magazines." Armed with editorials and statements of protest from *The Crisis*, the Chicago *Messenger*, and the Chicago *Defender*, Byrnes demanded that the Department of Justice proceed against their Negro editors under the Espionage Act.[56] In re-

[54] *Literary Digest*, LXXVI (1923), 11–12.

[55] Quoted in "What the South Thinks of Northern Race Riots," *ibid.*, LXII (1919), 17.

[56] Dallas *News*, quoted in "Mob Fury and Race Hatred as a National Danger," *ibid.*, LXIX (1921), 8; *Congressional Record*, 66 Cong., 1 Sess., 4302–4305.

sponse to his demand for investigation, the department reported three months later "a well-concerted movement among a certain class of negro leaders . . . to constitute themselves a determined and persistent source of radical opposition to the Government, and to the established rule of law and order." Particulars included "first, the ill-governed reaction toward race-rioting; second, the threat of retaliatory measures in connection with lynching; third, the more openly expressed demands for racial equality . . . fourth, the identification of the Negro with such radical organizations as the I. W. W. and an outspoken advocacy of the Bolshevik or Soviet doctrines." [57]

Through the year of racial unrest a professor at the Virginia Military Institute clipped and pasted together an impressive compendium of protest from Negro papers, North and South.[58] Readers who turned to Robert T. Kerlin's book found that the militancy reached beyond a few radical editors in the North. "Any Negro who says that he is satisfied to be let alone with his broken political power, his miserable Jim Crow restrictions, his un-American segregation, his pinched and emasculated democracy, and his blood-curdling inquisition of lynching simply lies," exclaimed the Newport News *Star*.[59] There will be no peace, declared an Atlanta paper, "until all classes and conditions of men shall have equal opportunities in the race for life, liberty and the pursuit of happiness." [60] "The 'Black Mammy' . . . is going," a Methodist paper asserted in New Orleans, "and we bid her an affectionate good-by and a long farewell." [61] "It does not take an

---

[57] New York *Times*, November 23, 1919, IX, 1, 3. To the last charge a group of Negro editors responded that no Negro to their knowledge had been arrested in the current campaign against "Reds" and the I. W. W. Seligman, *Negro Faces America*, 144.

[58] Kerlin (ed.), *Voice of the Negro*. Kerlin lost his job in 1921 because of a public appeal on behalf of the Negroes condemned after the Elaine riots. Robert T. Kerlin, "Open Letter to the Governor of Arkansas," in *Nation*, CXII (1921), 847–48; New York *Times*, September 9, 1921; Robert T. Kerlin to S. C. Mitchell, December 8, 1921, in S. C. Mitchell Papers (Southern Historical Collection, University of North Carolina).

[59] Newport News *Star*, October 3, 1919, reprinted in Kerlin (ed.), *Voice of the Negro*, 28.

[60] Atlanta *Independent*, October 18, 1919, *ibid.*, 34–35.

[61] New Orleans *Southwestern Christian Advocate*, n.d., *ibid.*, 29.

I. W. W. to clinch the argument that the majority of Negroes in the United States cannot vote," an Oklahoma editor informed his governor. "It does not take an anarchist to ride with us on the railroad for us to know . . . we do not get what you get by paying the same identical amount. It does not take a Bolshevist to inform us that . . . a separate status as citizens is designed for the black man." [62]

The growing spirit of protest was but one among a cluster of tendencies in the Negro world that received their generic name in 1925 when a special "Harlem" issue of *Survey Graphic* reappeared in revised book form as *The New Negro*. The capital of the movement was in upper Manhattan, where Negro immigrants had created a new black belt in Harlem. Definitions of the New Negro varied: some emphasized achievement in literature and the arts; others the rise of a group economy in the ghettoes, together with the development of middle-class standards of education and refinement; still others the proud, self-assertive Negro, fretful at discrimination and injustice. But out of their very separation it was apparent that American Negroes were evolving a sense of race pride, solidarity, and self-realization that would give a formidable support to future demands for recognition; "we are witnessing the resurgence of a people," said Alain Locke, a "rise from social disillusionment to race pride." [63]

The Great Migration laid the social basis for the emergence of the New Negro, and just as it got underway in 1915 Negro history passed a significant landmark with the death of Booker T. Washington. The outstanding leader of American Negroes for two decades, Washington had come to be the symbol of conciliation, compromise, and economic development; but the position of Great Leader that he occupied was never again to be filled. Major Robert R. Moton, who replaced him at Tuskegee Institute, permitted the old controversies that swirled around his predecessor to die of neglect. [64] But among the race leaders the time

[62] Oklahoma City *Black Dispatch*, October 10, 1919, *ibid.*, 63–66.

[63] Alain Locke (ed.) , *The New Negro: An Interpretation* (New York, 1925) , xi, 11; Meier, *Negro Thought in America*, 256–78.

[64] He "came increasingly to move toward an ideology which incorporated and expressed the Negro protest in cautious but no uncertain terms." Gunnar Myrdal, *An American Dilemma: The Negro Problem and Modern Democracy* (New York,

seemed propitious for a new spirit of co-ordination and unity. To that end a conference of Negro leaders who represented a variety of viewpoints convened at the home of Joel E. Spingarn at Amenia, New York, in 1916. The Amenia Conference produced no ringing manifesto and no agreement on methods and procedures, but it found a consensus on the goals of Negro enfranchisement, the abolition of lynching, the enforcement of laws protecting civil rights, and the encouragement of all forms of education, general and vocational. Officially the conference was disassociated from the young National Association for the Advancement of Colored People, founded at New York in 1910; but the initiative clearly came from the leaders of that group, and the meeting occurred at the home of its president.[65]

It soon became clear that the NAACP was filling the vacuum left by Washington's death and that its commanding figure, the editor of its journal, W. E. B. Du Bois, was the new major voice of the race. If Du Bois alone could not speak with the authority of Washington, and if he lacked Washington's contact with the masses of the Negro people, before a decade had passed there could be little doubt that the organization he represented stood as the most influential force in Negro leadership. From its base in the North, but with a leadership made up largely of native Southerners like James Weldon Johnson, William Pickens, Robert W. Bagnall, and Walter White, the NAACP could operate free from at least some of the strictures of white supremacy. Negro migrants offered a growing clientele who furnished "channels for the distribution of 'dangerous doctrine' to their fellows of the South." [66]

In 1916 the NAACP leaders further advanced the convergence in racial ideology and leadership by the *"coup d'état"* of securing a former Washingtonian as their Field Secretary.[67] James Weldon

1944) , 743. See also Moton, *Finding a Way Out*; Moton, *What the Negro Thinks*; and William Hardin Hughes and Frederick D. Patterson (eds.) , *Robert Russa Moton of Hampton and Tuskegee* (Chapel Hill, 1956) .

[65] Francis L. Broderick, *W. E. B. Du Bois: Negro Leader in a Time of Crisis* (Stanford University, Calif., 1959) , 119–20.

[66] *Ibid.*, 119–22; Franklin, *From Slavery to Freedom*, 446–47; Horace Mann Bond, "Negro Education since Washington," in *South Atlantic Quarterly*, XXIV (1925) , 115–30.

[67] Joel E. Spingarn, quoted in Meier, *Negro Thought in America*, 255; Johnson, *Along This Way*, 309.

Johnson, a native of Jacksonville and graduate of Atlanta University, had already gained success in New York as librettist, poet, and novelist, and had served in consular posts in Venezuela and Nicaragua. In his new position he set out vigorously to expand the struggling organization. In 1913 the NAACP had only 14 branches and only 1 in the South, at Lynchburg, Virginia. By 1916 it had 67, with 6 in the South. During the period of war and migration the expansion accelerated until by the end of 1919 there were 300 branches, 155 in the South, and 88,448 members, 42,588 in the South.[68] The burgeoning membership and the growing circulation of *Crisis*, its official organ, partly accounted for the sudden discovery of the organization by Southern editors and politicians in the upheavals of 1919. Shortly after the Longview riot, local officials in Austin demanded that the local branch disband, and when National Secretary John R. Shillady, a white man, went down to investigate he was assaulted on the street by a mob that included a county judge.[69] Most of the Southern branches, however, steered a cautious and inconspicuous course; and the 1920 national conference in Atlanta enjoyed the "utmost freedom of speech," heard a routine welcome by the mayor, and got full and factual notices in the Atlanta *Constitution*.[70]

Despite its rapid growth the NAACP remained an elite vanguard, an agency of protest and legal action. The whole New Negro movement, in all its ramifications, was largely a measure of the Negro's urbanization and the rise of a brown middle class. It penetrated but little into the countryside where the "illiterate, indifferent, dependent negro is still typical," the man to whom race "consciousness and racial aspirations mean practically nothing . . . and the spirit of unrest is very little more than the mere realization that he could move if conditions became unbearable."[71] Yet a few perceptive individuals could sense the drive of

[68] *The Crisis*, VI (1913), 90; Robert L. Jack, *History of the National Association for the Advancement of Colored People* (Boston, 1943), 17.

[69] New York *Tribune*, August 23, 1919, quoted in Leon Whipple, *The Story of Civil Liberty in the United States* (New York, 1927), 194–95; Mary White Ovington, *The Walls Came Tumbling Down* (New York, 1947), 171–74; White, *Man Called White*, 46–47.

[70] Ovington, *Walls Came Tumbling Down*, 178–79; Atlanta *Constitution*, May 31, June 1, 2, 3, 1920.

[71] Guy B. Johnson, "The Negro Migration and Its Consequences," in *Social Forces*, II (1923–1924), 405.

dynamic forces for racial uplift. Gazing out the window at a stevedore in Charleston, writer DuBose Heyward said he could "only be profoundly sorry for him for there he sits in the sunshine unconsciously awaiting his supreme tragedy. He is about to be saved." [72] But Heyward himself shortly turned the new outlooks to his own uses not only in the exotic-primitive Negroes of *Porgy* but in a moving chronicle of Negro aspirations and the New Negro in Charleston itself, in *Mamba's Daughters*.

Heyward saw more than dimly a gathering of forces that few whites detected from behind their solid fortress of white supremacy. In the 1920's the new peculiar institution of Negro subordination had reached its apogee as an established reality in law, politics, economics, and folkways—under attack from certain minorities in the North, to be sure, but not effectively menaced and indeed virtually taboo among respectable whites as a subject for serious discussion. The question was settled. [73] "A truce to race problem talks!" the Memphis *Commercial Appeal* commanded. "There is no race problem in the South." [74] Justification, insofar as it came, usually appeared in terms of established faith. "There is just one thing that I love better than the Democratic party . . . the United States . . . my wife or children or myself," John Sharp Williams told the Senate, "and that is the hope of the purity and the integrity and the supremacy of the white race everywhere." [75] "Why apologize or evade?" Senator Walter F. George

[72] Du Bose Heyward, "And Once Again—the Negro," in *The Reviewer* (Richmond) , IV (1923-1924) , 42.

[73] The new Ku Klux Klan of the 1920's was not primarily concerned with white-Negro relations and generally assumed the question had been settled. Outstanding exceptions were the Anglo-Saxon Clubs and the Associated White America Society of Virginia, which purveyed a systematic racist anthropology and secured state laws strengthening the ban on interracial marriages and unsegregated public meetings. See Nancy Armstrong, *The Study of an Attempt Made in 1943 to Abolish Segregation of the Races on Common Carriers in the State of Virginia*, Phelps-Stokes Fellowship Papers, No. 17 (Charlottesville, 1950) , 42-43; John Powell, "The Last Stand," series of articles on the dangers of "mongrelization," in Richmond *Times-Dispatch*, February 15–March 2, 1926; Earnest Sevier Cox, *White America* (Richmond, 1923) ; Earnest Sevier Cox, *The South's Part in Mongrelizing the Nation* (Richmond, 1926) .

[74] Quoted in *The Crisis*, XXIII (1921-1922) , 132.

[75] *Congressional Record*, 65 Cong., 2 Sess., 10981, quoted in Osborn, *John Sharp Williams*, 326.

asked. "We have been very careful to obey the letter of the Federal Constitution—but we have been very diligent in violating the spirit of such amendments and such statutes as would have a Negro to believe himself the equal of a white man." [76] "God Almighty never intended that a white race and a black race should live on terms of social equality," James F. Byrnes revealed.[77] That, if nothing else, settled the question. The very "central theme of Southern history," the leading Southern historian of the day proclaimed, was "a common resolve indomitably maintained" that the South "shall be and remain a white man's country." [78]

One inescapable fact of the white man's country was the Negroes' economic subordination. Negro landowners enjoyed a precarious independence, but their numbers declined from a peak of about 220,000 in 1910 to about 183,000 in 1930, or 13.1 per cent of all Negro agricultural workers. Nearly 80 per cent of the Negro agricultural workers were on the lowest rungs of the tenure ladder—tenants, sharecroppers, and wage laborers. In their separate urban world, too, Negroes found opportunities for independence severely restricted. Of all male nonagricultural workers in 1930 not more than 7 per cent were in professional, managerial, or clerical jobs, and a good majority of those were schoolteachers and preachers.[79] Many of the traditional "Negro jobs" were still falling to whites—a process that dated almost from emancipation. By 1930 Negro carpenters and painters in the South had declined to only 17 per cent of the total. Among the building skills, Negroes retained a strong position only in the trowel trades, constituting about 44 per cent of the bricklayers and 61 per cent of the plasterers. Even unskilled Negro building workers had declined from about three fourths of the total in 1910 to less than two thirds in 1930.[80]

[76] *Liberty*, April 21, 1928, quoted in Walter Wilson, *Forced Labor in the United States* (New York, 1933) , 99.

[77] *Congressional Record*, 66 Cong., 1 Sess., 4305. See also George Gardner, "Racial Differences Are of Divine Origin," in *Manufacturers' Record*, XCIII (March 29, 1928) , 61.

[78] Ulrich B. Phillips, "The Central Theme of Southern History," in *American Historical Review* (New York) , XXXIV (1928–1929) , 31.

[79] Myrdal, *American Dilemma*, 236–37, 296, 305–306.

[80] *Ibid.*, 1101. Figures for the Census South. See also Charles B. Roussève, *The Negro in Louisiana: Aspects of His History and His Literature* (New Orleans, 1937) ,

Nor did Negroes share proportionately in the expanding areas of the economy. Until the teens they had participated in the growth of such "Negro job" industries as lumbering, naval stores, unskilled work in blast furnaces and rolling mills, and railroad construction and maintenance. But most of the expanding areas of the economy after 1910 were for white only, except at the most menial levels. Textiles, furniture, electricity, oil and gas, paper and pulp, chemicals, and various urban fields such as streetcars and busses, telephone and telegraph work, trade, banking, insurance, and brokerage—all were "white work." There were exceptions in tobacco, fertilizers, and longshore jobs, but while the total number of Southern male workers in nonagricultural pursuits expanded by about 2,424,000 from 1910 to 1930, the number of Negro male workers increased only about 293,000 and their percentage of the total dropped from 26.7 to 21.1.[81]

"These are the days of democracies and white proletariats," a British traveler observed in 1920, "and both show themselves less friendly toward Negroes and 'natives' than the old monarchies."[82] The first and greatest handicap to the employment of Negroes, a white Southerner concluded, was "the traditional and deeply rooted race fear and race prejudices of the Southern white workers. . . . They fear Negroes more than they fear exploitation by the factory employers."[83] The trade unions that entered the South before 1930 offered few antidotes for the prejudices of

---

135–36; Charles S. Johnson, "Negro Workers in Skilled Crafts and Construction," in *Opportunity*, XI (1933), 296–300; T. J. Woofter, Jr., "Status of Racial and Ethnic Groups," in *Recent Social Trends in the United States: Report of the President's Research Committee on Social Trends* (New York and London, 1933), I, 577.

[81] For a convenient summary of the status of Negro labor see Myrdal, *American Dilemma*, 279–303, 1079–1124. See also Charles H. Wesley, *Negro Labor in the United States, 1850–1925: A Study in American Economic History* (New York, 1927); Sterling D. Spero and Abram S. Harris, *The Black Worker: A Study of the Negro and the Labor Movement* (New York, 1931); Lorenzo J. Greene and Carter G. Woodson, *The Negro Wage Earner* (Washington, 1930).

[82] Graham, *Soul of John Brown*, 307.

[83] Will W. Alexander, "Negroes and Organized Labor in the South," in *Opportunity*, VIII (1930), 109. For a vivid description of this attitude in operation against a young Negro eager to learn a skilled trade, see Richard Wright, "The Ethics of Living Jim Crow: An Autobiographical Sketch," in Richard Wright, *Uncle Tom's Children* (Penguin Signet Edition, New York, 1947), 2–4.

their members. The American Federation of Labor's official position against discrimination, like many pious affirmations, remained inoperative. On the plea that the Federation had no
power to interfere in the internal affairs of its affiliates, the group
permitted its national unions to discriminate in their constitutions
and rituals and through the device of separate locals.[84] "Indeed,"
a student of organized labor observed in 1936, "the Southern trade
unionism of the last thirty-odd years has been in good measure a
protective device for the march of White artisans into places held
by Negroes." [85]

The building trades unions limited Negro participation in the
expanded construction of the twentieth century. The plumbers
and steam fitters, for example, not only barred Negroes from their
union but secured licensing laws in nine Southern and thirteen
other states by 1925 which in effect excluded Negroes altogether
from their trade.[86] The electricians followed a similar policy. The
carpenters and painters, on the other hand, established separate
locals. Only in the trowel trades were Negroes sufficiently entrenched to demand serious recognition, in the bricklayers' and
plasterers' unions, and it was in those areas that Negro craftsmen
were best able to hold their own.[87] In Charleston, a rare exception, they formed "the backbone of the union movement," but
only because it was otherwise weak.[88]

By 1921 nearly all the Southern railroads had granted recognition to the operating unions. In Georgia by 1920 the operating
workers were 78 per cent organized, the conductors almost to a

[84] The AF of L racial policies are discussed in detail in Wesley, *Negro Labor in
the United States*, 261–80; Spero and Harris, *Black Worker*, 87–115; Herbert R.
Northrup, *Organized Labor and the Negro* (New York and London, 1944), 8–14; and
F. Ray Marshall, *The Negro and Organized Labor* (New York, 1965), 14–33.

[85] George S. Mitchell, "The Negro in Southern Trade Unionism," in *Southern
Economic Journal*, II (1935–1936), 27.

[86] Northrup, *Organized Labor and the Negro*, 23; Spero and Harris, *Black
Worker*, 59.

[87] Northrup, *Organized Labor and the Negro*, 18–47; *The Crisis*, IX (1914–1915),
19. See, however, Northrup, *Organized Labor and the Negro*, 39–40; and Johnson,
Patterns of Segregation, 97, for the establishment of separate white locals in Atlanta
and Jackson, resulting in drastic reductions in the number of Negro bricklayers.

[88] T. Arnold Hill, "Negroes in Southern Industry," in *Annals of the American
Academy of Political and Social Science*, CLIII (1934), 177.

THE EMERGENCE OF THE NEW SOUTH

man.[89] In no other industry of comparable size was unionization so successful in the South, but in no other industry did collective bargaining have "such disastrous results for Negroes." [90] The rise of the railroad unions accompanied a steady decline in Negro employment, especially after World War I. In January, 1918, white switchmen on several lines attempted a wildcat strike against the employment of Negroes in the Memphis yards. The strike failed, but a reign of terror against Negro employees followed, with threatening letters, bushwhackings, and outright murder along the Illinois Central between Memphis and New Orleans. The trainmen's union threatened to tie up Southern lines altogether unless the Railroad Administration revised working rules to eliminate Negroes. When such rules became effective in September, 1919, the regional director of railroads frankly admitted to a protesting delegation of Negroes that he had accepted them because "it was better to inconvenience a few men than to tie up the entire South for an indefinite length of time." Between 1910 and 1930 the proportion of Negro trainmen in ten Southern states dropped from 29.8 to 16.3 per cent, of Negro firemen from 41.3 to 33.1.[91]

Outside the trowel trades there was only one other field in which Negroes benefited conspicuously from a policy of non-discrimination. The International Longshoremen's Association, organized in the 1890's, dominated the Atlantic and Gulf Coast waterfronts and accepted Negroes, including some in its national leadership. There was a long and turbulent history of racial dissonance but also frequent cases of collaboration, and Negroes by the sheer force of numbers usually held their own and more in agreements to share the work. They nearly monopolized the Atlantic ports from Newport News to Jacksonville and signifi-

[89] Marshall, "History of Labor Organization in the South," 115–16.
[90] Northrup, Organized Labor and the Negro, 100.
[91] Spero and Harris, Black Worker, 284–300; The Crisis, XXII (1921), 212–13. For general surveys of the race question in railroad unions see Northrup, Organized Labor and the Negro, 48–99; Spero and Harris, Black Worker, 284–94; and Marshall, "History of Labor Organization in the South," 112–26. Negro workers made some gains in railroad shops after the shop strike of 1922. George S. Mitchell and Horace R. Cayton, Black Workers in the New Unions (Chapel Hill, 1939), 284–309.

cantly increased their proportions on the Gulf. In 1930 they constituted 69.8 per cent of the Texas longshoremen and 95.8 per cent of those in Alabama. Longshoremen were consistently the most completely unionized group of Negro workers.[92]

The access to economic opportunity was constricted, but the imperatives of white supremacy decreed "that the door of hope is forever closed to the Negro, in so far as participation in politics is concerned, and there is no appeal from that decree." [93] "As sons of proud Anglo-Saxon sires," Charles H. Brough of Arkansas declared, "we of the South doubt seriously the wisdom of the enfranchisement of an inferior race." [94] And from his home in Miami, William Jennings Bryan asserted with the certainty of an adopted son that restriction of Negro suffrage was "justified on the ground that civilization has a right to preserve itself." [95]

Before 1913 the Southern states by residential, literacy, and tax requirements had reduced the numbers of Negro voters to negligible proportions by "legal" means. Still, they declared no moratorium on the conventional amenities of intimidation and fraud. A New Orleans Negro said in 1924 that the literacy test could not have been more difficult if he were planning to practice law; the first Negro woman to attempt registration in Birmingham was told to write on a blank sheet of paper what she knew about the Constitution; in Virginia Negroes were entrapped by obscure and misleading questions; almost everywhere they suffered delays and humiliation if they attempted to register. At Columbia, South Carolina, a group of Negro women was forcibly ejected from the registration office in 1920; in Jacksonville four thousand Negroes stood in line from eight to five on election day, without being permitted to vote. When several Negroes attempted to vote at Ocoee, Florida, the community ran riot for three days to check

[92] Northrup, *Organized Labor and the Negro*, 137–53; Marshall, "History of Labor Organization in the South," 152–58; Myrdal, *American Dilemma*, 1097–99; Robert C. Francis, "Longshoremen in New Orleans," in *Opportunity*, XIV (1936), 82–85, 93.

[93] Jackson *Daily News*, quoted in Seligman, *Negro Faces America*, 23.

[94] Charles Hillman Brough, "Work of the Commission of Southern Universities on the Race Question," in *Annals of the American Academy of Political and Social Science*, XLIX (1913), 55.

[95] William Jennings Bryan to Kenneth B. Griffin, February 24, 1923, in Bryan Papers.

their "unholy and presumptuous ambitions . . . to vote." [96] The realities of "legal" disfranchisement were perhaps most vividly illuminated by Cole Blease's droll observation on the 1,100 votes South Carolina recorded for Coolidge in 1924: "I do not know where he got them. I was astonished to know that they were cast and shocked to know that they were counted." [97]

In most parts of the South the Democratic nomination was, in the journalistic cliché, "tantamount to election." In 1930 the Democratic party barred Negroes from its primaries by statewide rule in eight states and by county and city rules in three. North Carolina and Tennessee offered some local exceptions, but only Kentucky and Oklahoma lacked white primaries, and most Negroes in those states remained loyal to active Republican parties.[98]

Local exceptions only proved the rule of political impotence. Nonpartisan municipal elections sometimes offered entrée for those who could get on the books and Negroes sometimes influenced local elections during the 1920's, especially in the towns of Virginia and Texas. On occasion municipal reform movements enlisted Negro support: Nashville in 1921 and Savannah in 1923 offered examples. Occasionally a disputed bond referendum warmed the Negro vote into life. In 1920 Louisville Negroes helped defeat a bond issue from which they stood to gain nothing. In Atlanta, after twice defeating a four-million-dollar school bond issue, Negro voters organized by the NAACP provided the winning margin in 1921 when a fourth of the total was pledged to Negro schools.[99]

Even in the Democratic primaries Negroes sometimes voted in moderate numbers, particularly in Piedmont North Carolina towns where relations rested on "solid foundations of mutual

[96] Lewinson, *Race, Class, and Party*, 117–18; William Pickens, "The Woman Voter Hits the Color Line," in *Nation*, CXI (1920), 372–73; Walter F. White, "Election Day in Florida," in *The Crisis*, XXI (1920–1921), 106–109.

[97] *Congressional Record*, 69 Cong. 2 Sess., 5362.

[98] Lewinson, *Race, Class, and Party*, 112; Ralph Bunche, "The Political Status of the Negro" (Microfilm of typescript in Schomburg Collection, New York Public Library), 406, 408.

[99] Lewinson, *Race, Class, and Party*, 148–51; *The Crisis*, XXI (1920–1921), 117; "The Atlanta Negro Vote," *ibid.*, XVIII (1919), 90–91; White, *Man Called White*, 33, 37–38.

respect and good will." [100] But the only places where they breached the primaries in significant numbers were Memphis and San Antonio. In Memphis the Negro Republican leader, Robert R. Church, regularly delivered the Negro vote in Democratic primaries to Boss Edward H. Crump. In San Antonio Charles Bellinger, "king of the lottery," had enough votes in his pocket to influence city elections from 1918 until his death in 1935, and delivered to the Negro community paved streets, sewers, schools, parks, firehouses, a library, and a public auditorium—as well as bootleggers and gamblers.[101]

Barred from the Democratic primaries, Negroes suffered increasing neglect in Republican councils. A revealing measure of their national status was provided in 1921 by the platitudes with which President Harding ventured to lecture the South on its race relations. "If the South wishes to keep its fields producing and its industries still expanding," he said in a speech at Birmingham, "it will have to compete for the services of the colored man." The key to racial progress was for both races to "stand uncompromisingly against every suggestion of social equality," which would be "but a question of recognizing a fundamental, eternal and inescapable difference." However, the black man should vote "when he is fit to vote" and have equal opportunity "in precisely the same way and to the same extent . . . as between members of the same race." But equal opportunity did not mean that both races "would become equally educated within a generation or two generations or ten generations." It was not necessary "to educate people . . . into something they are not fitted to be." A Negro "should seek to be, the best possible black man, and not the best possible imitation of a white man." [102]

One could not expect "any more tolerant or broadminded

[100] Lewinson, *Race, Class, and Party,* 141.

[101] *Ibid.,* 138–41; George Washington Lee, *Beale Street: Where the Blues Began* (New York, 1934), 240–49. Audrey Granneberg, "Maury Maverick's San Antonio," in *Survey Graphic* (East Stroudsburg, Pa.), XXVIII (1939), 425; Bunche, "Political Status of the Negro," 898–902, 1140–45. In 1926 San Antonio had the unusual distinction of using the same salary scale for white and Negro teachers. Jesse O. Thomas, "New Wine in Old Bottles," in *Opportunity,* IV (1926), 291.

[102] New York *Times,* October 27, 1921. See also account of a fruitless audience of a Southern interracial group with President-Elect Harding, in Woofter, *Southern Race Progress,* 125.

attitude on the part of a man reared outside our section," the *Progressive Farmer* conceded. "The South will have no quarrel with President Harding upon his address," said the Birmingham *News*. Nevertheless, the Houston *Post* feared that "many of the Negroes would misconstrue his language and exaggerate his meaning," and Capitol Hill rang with charges that Harding had advocated "racial equality." "All outside attempts to settle the so-called race problem will fail," a Birmingham resident wrote. "Such attempts tend to upset what might be called the Negro psychology." [103] Negro reaction was equally mixed. James Weldon Johnson hoped the "net result" would be good but found "grave danger in some of the things he said." The Houston *Informer* raised the ultimate question. Harding, it noted, supported the Lily-whites in the Republican party. The paper therefore reserved judgment pending action from Harding the "doer." [104]

Since the 1890's a growing lily-white movement among Southern Republicans had contested the legitimacy of the old "black-and-tan" regulars; by 1928 the division existed in every Southern state except Oklahoma and Kentucky.[105] Republicans often emulated Democrats in pronouncements for white supremacy. In 1916 a Republican candidate for governor of North Carolina championed the idea of rural segregation; in 1920 another stated his opposition to Negro voting. Negroes "have taken no part in the affairs of the Republican party since I have been Chairman," the state chairman wrote in the early 1920's.[106] In Florida a "Republican, white" candidate entered the race for governor in 1920 against regular Republican and Democratic candidates. Arkansas, with a "lily-white" regular, had a "Negro Independent" candidate

---

[103] *Progressive Farmer*, XXXVI (1921), 957; Houston *Post*, quoted in Monroe N. Work (ed.), *Negro Year Book: An Annual Encyclopedia of the Negro,: 1921–1922* (Tuskegee, Ala., 1922), 48–49; Birmingham *News* and Frank Diedmeyer of Birmingham to New York *Herald*, quoted in *The Crisis*, XXIII (1921–1922), 127–28.

[104] James Weldon Johnson and Houston *Informer*, quoted in *The Crisis*, XXIII (1921–1922), 128.

[105] Lewinson, *Race, Class, and Party*, 171.

[106] *The Crisis*, XXII (1921), 101; Charlotte *Observer*, October 25, 1920; "U.S. District Attorney Linney resigns as Chairman of his Party," mimeographed statement to North Carolina Republican State Executive Committee, in Box 658, Daniels Papers.

the same year. In Virginia a "lily-black" candidate opposed the white Republican, Colonel Henry W. Anderson, who ran for governor in 1921 on a promise to exclude Negroes from office-holding.[107]

The factional contests, however, focused upon the grand prize of recognition in the national convention, which carried the best opportunity for patronage. In 1916 the rotten boroughs of the eleven former Confederate states named 35.3 per cent of all the delegates to the Republican national convention and thereafter between 15 and 20 per cent. The proportion of Negroes in the Southern delegations fluctuated between 10 and 21 per cent until 1928, when Herbert Hoover bypassed the black-and-tan factions in the campaign and later in the patronage, attempting "to build up a Republican party in the South such as would commend itself to the citizens of those states." Negroes constituted only 6.2 per cent of Southern delegates in 1932.[108]

"Every four years," W. E. B. Du Bois charged, "the disgrace of the buying up of certain delegates for the Republican convention" discredited a party which "repeatedly refused support or countenance to the better class of colored leaders." [109] When Congress undertook legislation in 1926 to restrict the sale of offices and party assessments on officeholders, Benjamin J. Davis, Negro committeeman from Georgia, complained that the Negro would lose all incentive for politics if he were "denied appointment to Federal office and at the same time prohibited by law from using his influence in the distribution of patronage." Such action would be "nothing less than a new scheme to disfranchise the negro in the South, wearing the guise of good morals in politics." [110]

[107] Alexander Heard, *A Two-Party South?* (Chapel Hill, 1952), 224; Monroe N. Work, "Defeat Lily Whites in Virginia Blow to Efforts to Build Up Party Independent of Negro," in Work (ed.), *Negro Year Book, 1921–1922*, p. 39; Lewinson, *Race, Class, and Party,* 159; *The Crisis,* XXIII (1921–1922), 105.

[108] Heard, *A Two-Party South?*, 118, 290n, and 314n. Actual percentages were: 1912, 25; 1916, 9.5; 1920, 12; 1924, 17.5; 1928, 21; 1932, 6.2. Hoover quoted in Elbert Lee Tatum, *The Changed Political Thought of the Negro, 1915–1940* (New York, 1951), 133.

[109] *The Crisis,* XIX (1919–1920), 297.

[110] Davis, quoted from his Atlanta *Independent,* December 16, 23, 1926, in Samuel Taylor Moore, "Public Office on Easy Payments," in *Independent,* CXVIII (1927),

Federal officeholders and party contributors were almost without exception white men, and often Democrats. Senate investigation in 1929–1930 confirmed common gossip of collaboration between Democrats and Republicans. In 1928, when Mississippi's Negro committeeman Perry Howard went on trial for allegedly selling offices and levying contributions he got letters of endorsement from the chief justice, an associate justice, and the clerk of the Mississippi Supreme Court, and won acquittal by twelve white Southerners to the rejoicing of the state's Democratic press and politicians. "As between the black-and-tan organization that has been in power, and the leaders whom Mr. Hoover will probably select," Governor Bilbo declared, "I prefer the Negroes." [111]

White supremacy was firmly buttressed in institutional arrangements, but the practice of lynching served as a constant reminder that force and violence set the ultimate context. There was no remedy for lynching that might not "result in unmerited hardship to whites and an increase in rape cases as well," an apologist for the practice wrote. "The white man in lynching a Negro does it as an indirect act of self-defense against the Negro criminal as a race." Lynching was necessary "in order to hold in check the Negro in the South." [112] The act was seldom defended so bluntly as an instrument of social control, but often by indirection. By some unfailing rule of psychology a lynching for any cause became, willy-nilly, a defense of white womanhood: "rape is responsible directly and indirectly for most of the lynching in America," James F. Byrnes assured the Congress. [113] "Race is greater than law now and then," said John Sharp Williams, "and

---

204. See also Samuel Taylor Moore, "Republican Patronage in South Carolina: Where Public Office Is a Private Debt," *ibid.*, 149–52; Samuel Taylor Moore, "Mississippi Auction Block—New Style," *ibid.*, 231–34; Frederick Rush, "Republicans for Revenue Only," *ibid.* (1926), 635–39; "Southern Job-Selling," in *Outlook and Independent* (New York), CLIV (1930), 576; Guy B. Hathorn, "C. Bascom Slemp—Virginia Republican Boss, 1907–1932," in *Journal of Politics*, XVII (1955), 250–60.

[111] Lewinson, *Race, Class, and Politics*, 180–84; "The Hoover House-Cleaning for the Southern G. O. P.," in *Literary Digest*, CI (April 13, 1929), 6.

[112] Winfield H. Collins, *The Truth about Lynching and the Negro in the South; in Which the Author Pleads That the South Be Made Safe for the White Race* (New York, 1918), 58, 70.

[113] *Congressional Record*, 67 Cong., 2 Sess., 544.

protection of women transcends all law, human and divine." [114] "Whenever the Constitution comes between me and the virtue of the white women of South Carolina," Cole Blease bellowed to his constituents, "then I say 'to hell with the Constitution!' " [115]

Such a heat of irrational fear and guilt surrounded the subject, a close observer declared, that even the most fair-minded white Southerner would not discuss it for fear of fanning the flames. It was "distorted by the conspiracy of semi-silence into an importance infinitely greater than the actual facts . . . would justify," and nourished by the "fertile soil" of religious fanaticism "from which springs the rule of the mob, whether it be one to burn a Negro or flog a white woman or to wage a campaign for compulsory reading of the Bible or to enact an anti-evolution law." [116]

In such a volatile atmosphere a lynching could become almost a twentieth-century *auto-da-fé*. From the turn of the century the number of lynchings had steadily declined, but the tensions of the First World War reversed the trend and the reversal was attended by aggravated savagery and sadism. Burning at the stake was often prolonged for the benefit of spectators, who sometimes included women and children, although the gasoline age afforded a new and perhaps merciful refinement in the art of immolation. Incredible tortures and humiliations accompanied the spectacles. In May, 1918, to choose one example, mobs outraged by the killing of a white planter stormed across two South Georgia counties for a week, hanged three innocent men, strung up the pregnant widow of one by the ankles, doused her clothing with gasoline, and after it burned away, cut out her unborn child and trampled it underfoot, then riddled her with bullets. A man who finally confessed the original murder was shot, his body unsexed and dragged through the streets of Valdosta.[117] The Gothic horror of these crimes—and German propaganda exploitation of racial violence—

[114] Quoted in *Manufacturers' Record*, LXXVI (October 9, 1919), 86. "Senator Williams was defending lynch law. In doing so, he was disgracing his state and the South."

[115] Quoted in Arthur F. Raper, *The Tragedy of Lynching* (Chapel Hill, 1932), 293.

[116] Walter F. White, *Rope and Faggot, A Biography of Judge Lynch* (New York and London, 1929), 48–49.

[117] Walter F. White, "The Work of a Mob," in *The Crisis*, XVI (1918), 221–23.

ɪɪnally brought forth the condemnation Negro leaders had long
sought from President Wilson. "We are at the moment fighting
lawless passion," he declared. "Germany has outlawed herself
. . . and has made lynchers of her armies. Lynchers emulate her
disgraceful example."[118] In the ten years 1918–1927, according
to one computation, American lynch mobs slaughtered 454 persons, of whom 416 were Negroes, including 11 women, 3 of them
pregnant. Altogether 42 were burned alive, 16 after death, and 8
were either beaten to death or cut to pieces.[119]

The typical lynching county was "characterized in general by
social and economic decadence," a student of the problem reported: below the state average in per capita tax valuation, bank
deposits, income from farm and factory, income tax returns,
ownership of automobiles, and educational facilities. The church
membership was 75 per cent Southern Baptist and Methodist.
There was "generally present a supposed necessity for protecting
white women against sex crimes by the Negro. All these, plus
emotional and recreational starvation and a fear of economic
domination by enterprising Negroes, create the complex of 'keeping the nigger in his place.' "[120] The cause of lynching, a
Georgian concluded, "is that we are the only Government on
earth that has set up several thousand little-bitty, small, weak, distinctive governments. . . . These tiny kingdoms can kill their
subjects like hogs if they want to, and under State rights they
know that there is no law on earth to prosecute them but their
own law; no judge ever prosecutes himself."[121]

Yet the plague of lynchings afforded Negroes one major issue
with which to pierce the veil of hostility and evasion that shrouded
their condition. Leaders of the NAACP, "like the progressives,
assumed that when Americans knew of injustice, their intelli-

[118] Ray Stannard Baker and William E. Dodd (eds.), *The Public Papers of
Woodrow Wilson: War and Peace; Presidential Addresses and Public Papers,
1917–1924* (New York, 1927), I, 238. "It took war, riot, and upheaval to make Wilson
say one small word." [W. E. B. Du Bois], "Postscript of W. E. B Du Bois: Roosevelt,"
in *The Crisis*, XLI (1934), 20.

[119] White, *Rope and Faggot*, 19–21. See also Raper, *The Tragedy of Lynching*,
480–84, for over-all statistics.

[120] James H. Chadbourn, *Lynching and the Law* (Chapel Hill, 1933), 4.

[121] W. E. Wimpy, "Mob Lynching Lynches the Law," in *Manufacturers' Record*,
LXXVI (December 25, 1919), 113.

gence and moral principles would demand reform from legislatures and courts." [122] The earliest sustained work of the NAACP, therefore, was its campaign to arouse the public conscience against lynching. Its basic recourse was to assure maximum publicity through mass meetings, appeals to public officials and the press, and reports of special investigators. The lynching probe became a specialty of Walter F. White, whom James Weldom Johnson had spotted as a promising young leader in the Atlanta school bond agitations and brought into the national office in 1918. Light enough to pass as white, he found it possible to circulate freely and to gather information that sometimes placed public officials in the awkward possession of the lynchers' names. His methods often aroused more indignation than his revelations.[123] Nothing "is more calculated to incite the white South to insensate anger than is the sending of a Negro into the South in the guise of a white man," a Charleston editor wrote. It involved "dangers about as grave as can be conceived." [124]

In 1919 the NAACP broadened its antilynching front. It shed much new light on the subject when it sent two researchers into the Library of Congress to gather data on lynching which appeared as *Thirty Years of Lynching, 1889–1918*. Among other things the report challenged the sexual shibboleth: fewer than one sixth of the mob victims tabulated had been accused of rape or attempted rape. The report came out in connection with a national antilynching conference in New York in May, 1919, with representatives from twenty-five states, including two white representatives of the Mississippi Welfare League and former Governor Emmett O'Neal of Alabama, attending. The conference issued an Address to the Nation, urging citizens "to oppose with all their power the recurrence of the crime and shame of mob lynching," and sparked a campaign for a Federal antilynching law as the only remedy.

In 1921 the NAACP set up a lobbying effort in Washington to

[122] Francis L. Broderick, *W. E. B. Du Bois* (Stanford, 1959) , 93.

[123] White, *Man Called White,* 34–35, 39–43, 49–51, 53–59.

[124] William Watts Ball to Herbert Bayard Swope, January 19, 1927, in Ball Papers. It is noteworthy that Ball refrained from rushing into print with his complaint, for fear of arousing sympathy for lynchers White had recently investigated.

get behind an antilynching bill sponsored by Representative L. C. Dyer of St. Louis, who represented a largely Negro constituency. The bill, first introduced in 1919, proposed to make mob murder or the failure to protect a prisoner a Federal offense and to levy fines against counties in which the offenses occurred. The Dyer bill finally passed the House by 230–119 in 1922, but was defeated in the Senate by a filibuster of Southern senators. The agitation continued until 1925, when committees of both houses conducted hearings on antilynching bills; but the issue did not again reach the floor of either house for a decade.[125]

The Dyer bill did not become law, but it made Congress "a forum in which the facts were discussed and brought home to the American people as they had never been before," James Weldon Johnson later asserted. "Agitation for the passage of the measure was, without doubt, one of the prime factors in reducing the number of lynchings in the decade that followed to less than one third of what it had been in the preceding decade. It served to awaken the people of the Southern states to the necessity of taking steps themselves to wipe out the crime; and this, I think, was its most far-reaching result."[126] Johnson's appraisal was at least partially confirmed by the expressions of leading Southern newspapers on the Dyer bill. "Our representatives were right in holding that the South would itself protect its Negro population and that the law was unnecessary," said the Charleston *News and Courier*. It was "up to the States to make good the promises and professions of their senators and representatives," said the Atlanta *Georgian*. The only way to forestall Federal antilynching legislation, said the Asheville *Times,* was "to be found in the stern handling of lynching parties by Southern courts."[127] Whatever the cause, the number of lynchings declined annually from 83 in 1919

[125] The agitation for a Federal antilynching law is traced in Jack, *History of the National Association for the Advancement of Colored People,* 31–36; Johnson, *Along This Way,* 361–73; White, *Rope and Faggot,* 207–26; White, *Man Called White,* 42–43; Mary Lu Nuckols, "The NAACP and the Dyer Anti-Lynching Bill: A Barometer of Emerging Negro Political Power" (M.A. thesis, University of North Carolina, 1963).

[126] Johnson, *Along This Way,* 373.

[127] All quoted in "It's Up to Us," mimeographed release of the Commission on Interracial Cooperation, enclosed with Josephus Daniels to James Weldon Johnson, January 13, 1923, in Daniels Papers.

to 16 in 1924; it rose to 30 in 1926 but dropped to 11 in 1928, only to rise again at the onset of the Great Depression.[128]

The NAACP legal program secured even less tangible results for the time being. Unable to wield effective political pressures, the organization undertook to revitalize the Reconstruction amendments by turning to the Federal courts. The earliest important victory was a decision in Guinn v. United States (1915) which overturned Oklahoma's grandfather clause, but the state quickly reversed its effect by a new law requiring registrars to enroll all those who voted in 1914 under the old law and other persons only if they should "be satisfied" of the applicants' qualifications.[129] The second major constitutional victory, in Buchanan v. Warley (1917), struck down municipal ordinances requiring residential segregation, but Southern towns stubbornly continued to enact them and achieved the purpose in any case by social pressures and restrictive covenants except in some areas of the older cities where segregation had never been established.[130]

The South would see and hear more of the NAACP and the New Negro, but for the time being a more extensive influence within the region was the interracial movement. Born of a union between paternalism and the progressive urge to social justice, the movement sought a "New Reconstruction," as one of the early leaders extravagantly labeled it, through Negro advancement within the framework of segregation and discreet contacts across the veil of separation.[131] Three pathfinders stood out among the pioneers of the movement: James Hardy Dillard, Willis D. Weatherford, and Mrs. L. H. Hammond. At the first meeting of the Southern Sociological Congress in 1912 Dillard, director of the Jeanes and Slater funds for Negro education, took the lead in starting the University Commission on Southern Race Questions. With representatives from eleven state universities, the group sought to "keep informed in regard to the relations existing between the races" and to get "southern college men to approach the subject with

[128] Work (ed.), *Negro Year Book, 1931–1932,* p. 293.
[129] Charles S. Mangum, Jr., *The Legal Status of the Negro* (Chapel Hill, 1940), 397–99.
[130] *Ibid.,* 147–56; Nelson, *Fourteenth Amendment and the Negro,* 23–33, 96–98.
[131] William O. Scroggs, "The New Reconstruction," in *Lectures and Addresses on the Negro in the New South,* 59–64.

intelligent information and with sympathetic interest." The Commission drew Negro leaders into its counsels, held regular sessions at the annual meetings of the Congress and occasional meetings elsewhere, issued public letters appealing for more thoughtful responses to current problems, and promoted the study of race problems in white universities.[132] In 1912 it induced the Phelps-Stokes Foundation to establish fellowships at the universities of Georgia and Virginia for studies and publications on race questions.[133]

Dillard voiced the watchwords of the rising movement with two aphorisms: from Shakespeare's *Henry IV*, "You are too shallow,/ To sound the bottom of the aftertimes," and from Chaucer's *Good Counsel* an old English proverb, "Do the next thing." The nearest duty, Dillard said, was "good will, cooperation, and practical helpfulness"; the immediate problems were "better homes, a fuller conception of religion, and a more efficient system of education." Ultimate goals would be the responsibility of posterity in any case. "But in the meanwhile there is enough at hand to engage our attention for a time." [134]

Even before the Phelps-Stokes fellowships began, Willis D. Weatherford had pioneered in the study of race relations as student secretary of the YMCA and director of its summer conference at Blue Ridge, North Carolina. In 1910 he produced the first textbook on the subject, *Negro Life in the South*, designed for use in discussion groups of the college YMCA's; in 1919 as the first head of the Southern College of the YMCA at Nashville he inaugurated a course in "Applied Anthropology" which dealt

[132] Benjamin Brawley, *Dr. Dillard of the Jeanes Fund* (New York, 1930), 118–27; Josiah Morse, "The University Commission on Southern Race Questions," in *South Atlantic Quarterly*, XIX (1920), 302–10; *Minutes of the University Commission on Southern Race Questions* (Charlottesville, 1917); *Five Letters of the University Commission on Southern Race Questions*, in Occasional Papers of Trustees of the John F. Slater Fund, No. 24 (Charlottesville, 1927). The absence of segregation at the Memphis meeting in 1919 created a minor furor of protest. Clarence Poe to William Hodges Mann, open letter in *Progressive Farmer*, XXIX (1914), 655; Booker T. Washington to James H. Dillard, June 3, August 14, 1914, and Dillard to Washington, June 8, 1919, in Booker T. Washington Papers (Library of Congress).

[133] *Twenty Year Report of the Phelps-Stokes Fund, 1911–1931* (New York, 1932), 10–11; Morse, "University Commission on Southern Race Questions," *loc. cit.*, 304.

[134] James H. Dillard, "Considerations of Race Adjustments in the South," in *Lectures and Addresses on the Negro in the New South*, 28.

primarily with racial contacts in the South. Thereafter he participated in nearly every important phase of the interracial movement
and wrote several books on race relations and Negro history.[135]

Mrs. L. H. Hammond, the Southern-born wife of the white
president of Payne College for Negroes in Augusta, Georgia,
foretokened the important role of women in the movement. In
1914 she published a moving personal account of the growing
social conscience in the South, particularly among church women,
and in 1918 sponsored the Southern Publicity Committee, supported by the Phelps-Stokes Fund, to gather and disseminate news
about Negro achievements.[136]

The great impulse to interracialism came with the contradictory
developments of the war period. As the South and the nation
teetered on the verge of the "Red Summer" of 1919, what little
interracial contact and morale there was seemed about to dissolve
into violence. In that emergency the Commission on Interracial
Cooperation arose to organize the nascent spirit into a Southwide
movement. In Atlanta, the scene of a local interracial committee
since the 1906 race riot, a group of white leaders who had promoted war work among Negro soldiers and civilians commenced
in January, 1919, a series of discussions on the emergency.[137]
Several Negro leaders soon entered the discussions and on April 9,
1919, the group organized the Interracial Commission.[138] Will
W. Alexander, former Methodist minister in Nashville and war-

[135] Willis D. Weatherford, *Negro Life in the South: Present Conditions and
Needs* (New York, 1911), v; Willis D. Weatherford, *The Negro from Africa to
America* (New York, 1924), 449.

[136] Mrs. Lily Hammond, *In Black and White: An Interpretation of Southern
Life* (New York, 1914); Weatherford, *Negro from Africa to America*, 445.

[137] Early participants included John H. Eagan, Atlanta manufacturer; M. Ashby
Jones, Baptist minister and, it was invariably noted, son of Robert E. Lee's chaplain;
R. H. King, YMCA War Work Council; Plato Durham of Emory University; C. B.
Wilmer, Episcopal minister; Thomas Jesse Jones of the Phelps-Stokes Fund; and
Wallace E. Buttrick of the General Education Board. Edward Flud Burrows, "The
Commission on Interracial Cooperation, 1919–1944: A Case Study in the History of
the Interracial Movement in the South" (Ph.D. dissertation, University of Wisconsin,
1955), 46; Duffus, "Counter-Mining the Ku Klux Klan," *loc. cit.*, 278.

[138] Early Negro participants included Robert R. Moton of Tuskegee Institute;
John Hope of Atlanta University; Isaac Fisher of Fisk University; Bishop Robert E.
Jones of the Methodist Episcopal Church; and John M. Gandy of the Petersburg
Normal and Industrial Institute. Burrows, "Commission on Interracial Cooperation,"
118–20; Duffus, "Counter-Mining the Ku Klux Klan," *loc. cit.*, 278.

time YMCA worker among Negroes, quickly emerged as the guiding genius of the movement in his position as executive director of the Commission.[139]

The immediate needs were the readjustment of Negro soldiers to their communities and the relaxation of tensions. With an initial appropriation from the National War Work Council, the commission organized ten-day conferences of social workers: 824 whites attended classes under Weatherford at Blue Ridge and 509 Negroes under Alexander at Gammon Theological Seminary in Atlanta.[140] To meet the problem of community tensions a temporary staff of one white man and one Negro in each Southern state undertook to reach the centers of tension, draw together community leaders of both races, and through them attempt some amelioration. In the joint wartime efforts, Alexander said, white leaders "had begun to discover . . . the Negro leaders in their own communities and had come to have . . . a very high regard for some of them." The problem, he argued, was to secure as much interracial contact among community leaders as there was among bootleggers, to provide avenues through which grievances could be communicated and rumors scotched.[141] By 1920 more than five hundred state, county, and local interracial committees had sprung up and by 1923 approximately eight hundred.[142]

As the committees developed they recognized "vast areas of interracial injustice and neglect that could not be cleared up in a few months, or even a few years." [143] What started as an emergency measure grew into a permanent organization, and after subsisting two years on funds of the National War Work Council, drew support from a number of foundations, church groups, and other sources during its career of twenty-five years. The second phase of activity emphasized the use of the interracial committees

[139] The most conveniently available general account of the Commission is in Wilma Dykeman and James Stokeley, *Seeds of Southern Change: The Life of Will Alexander* (Chicago, 1962) .

[140] Weatherford, *Negro from Africa to America*, 450.

[141] "Reminiscences of Will W. Alexander," 173–76.

[142] Willis D. Weatherford, "Growing Race Cooperation," in *Survey*, XLV (1920–1921) , 89; Duffus, "Counter-Mining the Ku Klux Klan," *loc. cit.*, 279.

[143] "Educational Program Commission on Interracial Cooperation, Inc.," typescript report prepared for Leo M. Favrot, General Education Board, enclosed with Emily H. Clay to Howard W. Odum, October 24, 1938, in Odum Papers.

to adjust grievances and remove specific irritants. Here and there a few store managers discovered, often to their surprise, that Negroes did not like being addressed as "Uncle" or "John." "For White Only" signs occasionally disappeared; offensive conduct by streetcar conductors was corrected; community services were secured for Negro areas; Negro welfare agencies got support from Community Chest funds in Atlanta, Louisville, Lynchburg, Memphis, Richmond, and elsewhere; legal services were provided; Negroes were aided in collecting insurance after the Tulsa riot of 1921; the problem of treatment in the courts was raised.[144] It was "not very profitable to get people together to talk," Alexander argued. "You probably change the attitudes of people first by bringing them into perfectly human contacts with others. Second, by . . . setting them at work at some common task. . . . The difficulty is to eliminate that delightful sensation of doing something *for* someone." Local communities were the basic units of advancement; "the idea of better relations must be made to take root in the hard soil of their Main Streets." [145]

Lynching was one of the continuing concerns. State and local committees from the beginning developed a technique of contacting white and Negro leaders whenever trouble threatened, and of exerting pressure upon officials to prevent violence. The Kentucky director asserted that county committees in his state prevented five lynchings during the first five years of the Commission's existence, and the Georgia group during 1923 helped to get twenty-two indictments against alleged lynchers and four convictions—during the previous thirty-seven years there had been only one such indictment.[146] The Mississippi bar association published an

[144] Many examples of local and state activities appear in C. Chilton Pearson, "Race Relations in North Carolina: A Field Study of Moderate Opinion," in *South Atlantic Quarterly*, XXIII (1924), 109; H. H. Proctor, "The Atlanta Plan of Interracial Cooperation," in *Southern Workman* (Hampton, Va.), XLIX (1920), 9–12; *Progress in Race Relations: A Survey of the Work of the Commission on Interracial Cooperation for the Year 1923–1924* (n.p., n.d.), 6–14; and Duffus, "Counter-Mining the Ku Klux Klan," *loc. cit.*, 280–84.

[145] *Toward Interracial Cooperation: What Was Said and Done at the First National Interracial Conference* (n.p., 1926), 67–68; Will W. Alexander, "Better Race Relations," in *Southern Workman*, LI (1922), 362–64.

[146] Dr. James Bond of Kentucky, in *Toward Interracial Cooperation*, 70–71; Mary Ross, "Where Lynching Is a Habit," in *Survey*, XLIX (1922–1923), 627.

eighty-page handbook on the prevention of lynching, to which the governor, judges, and members of Congress contributed, and the Interracial Commission undertook to have it studied in the state's high schools.[147] In 1925 the Commission struck a medal for officers who showed "particular bravery or intelligence, or both, in outwitting mobs or defending prisons." Between 1925 and 1932 it was awarded to fifteen sheriffs, one constable, and one jailer in eight states.[148]

The Interracial Commission secured a remarkable diversity of support. NAACP President Joel R. Spingarn endorsed the principle of interracial committees in 1920, and the Negro press generally supported it, although the *Crisis* warned against naming "pussy-footers" to the committees.[149] From the beginning the committee cultivated the support of opinion-making groups. In 1920 a conference of church leaders at Blue Ridge declared that "the real responsibility for the solution of inter-racial problems in the South rests directly upon the hearts and consciences of the Christian forces of our land." [150] With the help of Methodist women, a conference of about a hundred women's leaders in various fields assembled at Memphis in the fall of 1920 to hear a group of leading Negro women, to declare a "deep sense of responsibility to the womanhood and childhood of the Negro race," and to call for a women's department in the Interracial Commission, which developed under Mrs. Luke G. Johnson of Atlanta and later Mrs. Jessie Daniel Ames of Georgetown, Texas.[151] Newspaper editors, assembled state by state, Alexander found to be better informed and more sensitive to the situation than any

[147] *Progress in Race Relations*, 4.

[148] "Reminiscences of Will W. Alexander," 242–46; Burrows, "Commission on Interracial Cooperation," 203; Baker, *Negro-White Adjustment*, 77–79. One sheriff refused the award because he was planning to run for the state legislature. M. Philips Price, *America After Sixty Years: The Travel Diaries of Two Generations of Englishmen* (London, 1936), 196.

[149] Atlanta *Constitution*, June 2, 1920; Frederick G. Detweiler, *The Negro Press in the United States* (Chicago, 1922), 190–92.

[150] *An Appeal to the Christian People of the South Adopted by Church Leaders' Conference, Blue Ridge, North Carolina, August 18–21, 1920* (n.p., n.d.) .

[151] "Reminiscences of Will W. Alexander," 225–41; "Background," "The Memphis Conference," and other typescripts in Jessie Daniel Ames Papers (Southern Historical Collection, University of North Carolina) ; *Southern Workman*, XLIX (1920), 537–38; *The Crisis*, XXI (1920–1921), 249.

other group. Years later he asserted that "the best newspapermen in the South have . . . been the most constructive single influence in changing racial patterns." [152]

Some of the committees even drew in members of the Ku Klux Klan and the movement won endorsements from a number of political leaders. The governors of Arkansas, Kentucky, and North Carolina sponsored state committees; the governors of Oklahoma and Georgia called state conferences. Governor Lee Russell and Senator Pat Harrison of Mississippi, Harry F. Byrd of Virginia, Charles H. Brough of Arkansas, and Richard I. Manning of South Carolina all expressed support.[153] In 1921 the Commission induced Governor Hugh M. Dorsey of Georgia to issue a public statement cataloging 135 examples of atrocities against Negroes in the state over a period of two years: lynching, peonage, Negroes driven from their homes, individual acts of cruelty. "If the conditions indicated by these charges should continue," Dorsey said, "both God and man would justly condemn Georgia more severely than man and God have condemned Belgium and Leopold for the Congo atrocities." [154]

The key to acceptance was avoidance of the segregation issue. The group "never adopted an interracial creed as a condition for membership in our organization," one of its leaders said; another conceded that "unless those forms of separation which are meant to safeguard the purity of the races are present, the majority of the white people flatly refuse to cooperate with Negroes." [155] Church leaders at Blue Ridge in 1920 felt obligated to declare themselves "absolutely loyal . . . to the principle of racial integrity." [156]

[152] "Reminiscences of Will W. Alexander," 201a–205a.

[153] George Madden Martin, "Race Cooperation," in *McClure's Magazine* (New York), LIV (1922–1923), 9–20; *Progress in Race Relations*, 3; "Annual Meeting Commission on Interracial Cooperation April 18–19, 1934—Report of North Carolina and Virginia," typescript in Odum Papers; "Reminiscences of Will W. Alexander," 201a; Pat Harrison to Charles H. Brough, telegram, September 14, [1920], in Brough Papers.

[154] *A Statement from Governor Hugh M. Dorsey as to the Negro in Georgia*, April 22, 1921 (Atlanta, 1921), [27].

[155] M. Ashby Jones, "The Interracial Commission an Experiment in Racial Relations," in *Southern Frontier* (Atlanta), V (1944), 1; T. J. Woofter, Jr., *The Basis of Racial Adjustment* (Boston and New York, 1925), 240.

[156] *Appeal to the Christian People of the South*. For similar statements see M. Ashby Jones, "The Approach to the South's Race Question," in *Social Forces*, I

Alexander from the beginning warned against excessive caution, however. He insisted upon foundation support because raising money in the South "would result in our having to change and adapt the present program so as to meet the prejudices and special interests of those who would furnish the finances." [157] He usually avoided the subject of segregation, but in response to direct questioning at a Sunday School meeting in Birmingham he answered, "I believe in the repeal of unjust laws and it [segregation] is unjust." Education, he confessed, increased the hostility of Negroes to whites. "As the mind is cultivated, one sees more clearly the injustice done." [158]

Despite the emphasis upon *ad hoc* adjustments and interracial contacts a conviction early developed that work for improved conditions "was only to treat the symptoms rather than the disease," that prejudiced attitudes could best be undermined by education and the dissemination of facts. In 1922 another phase of activity began with the establishment of an educational department directed by Robert B. Eleazer, Jr., and after 1926, Arthur F. Raper, both trained sociologists. From their work came a number of useful studies, and over the years Eleazer developed popular studies and pamphlets for general circulation. Colleges and schools co-operated in summer schools and conferences for teachers, essay contests, the distribution of literature, tours of white schools and colleges by George Washington Carver, the Tuskegee chemist, and other speakers, and by Negro choral groups, and the development of interracial contacts between high school and college students.[159] Beginning about 1923 interracial forums of collegians,

---

(1922–1923) , 41; M. Ashby Jones, "The Negro and the South," in *Virginia Quarterly Review*, III (1927) , 9–10; Willis D. Weatherford, "Race Relationship in the South," in *Annals of the American Academy of Political and Social Science*, XLIX (1913) , 172; Brough, "Work of the Commission of Southern Universities on the Race Question," *ibid.*, 59; Hammond, *In Black and White*, 42–45.

[157] Will W. Alexander to S. C. Mitchell, December 10, 1920, in S. C. Mitchell Papers.

[158] *The Crisis*, XXXII (1926) , 91. A group of white ministers thereupon declared him unsuited "to take the lead in the discussion and direction of race relations." *Ibid.*, 165–66.

[159] "Educational Program Commission on Interracial Cooperation, Inc.," *loc. cit.*; "Reminiscences of Will W. Alexander," 219–23; Woofter, *Southern Race Progress*, 169.

not all sponsored by the Commission, sprang up at Knoxville, Lynchburg, Atlanta, New Orleans, Durham, Raleigh, and other centers—the most active at Nashville.[160] Eleazer's press service by the early thirties distributed releases to newspapers and journals with a combined circulation of more than twenty million in "an effort to interpret each race to the other in terms more consistent with the facts," and by 1930 Alexander found thirty-nine courses on Negroes and race relations in Southern white colleges.[161]

Both the interracial contacts and the educational programs had their limitations. But the Commission stubbornly planted the seeds of change in an unpromising soil. If its accomplishments were slight, one participant argued, there did exist "an enormous amount of good will and love of fair play in the minds and hearts of all human beings, if there were only the genius and the will to evoke them as there is to evoke the baser impulses, feelings and sentiments." Someday, he assured a colleague in the work, "there will be a Klan-like movement and organization to do this . . . but it will require zealots and fanatics to initiate and forward it. Wars and crusades shape future history more in a year than the slower processes of education can in half a century, but we are not warriors or crusaders." [162]

[160] College interracialism grew out of a Student Volunteer Conference in Indianapolis during the Christmas holidays, 1923. It was promoted chiefly by the Fellowship of Reconciliation, which by 1929 had a Southern Interracial Secretary, Howard Kester, with offices on the Vanderbilt University campus. The Commission on Interracial Cooperation, the YMCA, and the YWCA also promoted the groups. Baker, *Negro-White Adjustment*, 188–98; Rebecca Caudill, "The Plight of the Negro Intellectuals," in *The Christian Century* (Chicago), XLVII (1930), 1012–14; Robert W. Bagnall, "Lights and Shadows in the South," in *The Crisis*, XXXIX (1932), 124–25; Cranston Clayton, "College Interracialism in the South," in *Opportunity*, XII (1934), 267–69, 288. On interracial activities of other groups see Burrows, "Commission on Interracial Cooperation," 331–42.

[161] Baker, *Negro-White Adjustment*, 222; Will W. Alexander, "Southern White Schools Study Race Questions," in *Journal of Negro Education: Quarterly Review of Problems Incident to the Education of Negroes* (Lancaster, Pa.), II (1933), 140.

[162] Josiah Morse to S. C. Mitchell, February 13, 1927, in S. C. Mitchell Papers. Morse taught philosophy and psychology at the University of South Carolina and participated actively in both the University Commission and the Commission on Interracial Cooperation.

CHAPTER VI

THE SOUTH AND THE SAVAGE IDEAL

THE final great result of Reconstruction," W. J. Cash wrote in 1941, was "that it established what I have called the savage ideal as it had not been established in any Western people since the decay of medieval feudalism. . . . Tolerance, in sum, was pretty well extinguished all along the line, and conformity made a nearly universal law." [1] When the postwar South of the 1920's surged into a strange new world of urban booms and farm distress, it entered an unfamiliar terrain of diversity and change in which there lurked a thousand threats to the older orthodoxies. A comparatively static society found itself suddenly caught up by changes that brought a mixture of hope and fear, of anticipation and nostalgia. After a Southern visit in 1919, Hamlin Garland called the period "an unlovely time of sorry transition." The South, in Howard Odum's words, succumbed to a "state of mind similar to that commonly manifest in war times. . . . There was little freedom of feeling and little freedom of speech in matters relating to religion, race, industry or several social and moral sanctions." [2]

The defensive temper of the 1920's, to be sure, was not altogether a Southern phenomenon. Over the first two decades of the century there had been a growing tendency to associate American nationalism with nativism, Anglo-Saxon racism, and militant Protestantism, a tendency reinforced by wartime "Americanism" and leading to severe restrictions on immigration in 1921 and 1924. The South was in the vanguard of the new creed, with

---

[1] Wilbur J. Cash, *The Mind of the South* (New York, 1941), 134–35.

[2] Hamlin Garland, *My Friendly Contemporaries: A Literary Log* (New York, 1932), 232; Odum, *American Epoch*, 321.

all the enthusiasm of a recent convert.[3] By the 1920's nativism in the South had become a peculiar expression of sectionalism in terms of nationalism. If the test of Americanism was native birth of Anglo-Saxon ancestry (or Scotch-Irish—either sufficed), it followed that the South was the "most American" of all regions, derived from the "best stock." "One of the glories of the South," the *Manufacturers' Record* boasted, "is that its foreign stock is so limited as compared with that of other sections." [4] But if in adopting Anglo-Saxon nativism the white South was largely importing a creed that fulfilled ancient urges, it was soon developing with new intensity the anti-Catholic and anti-Semitic corollaries and re-exporting nativism with the addition of certain historic Southern trappings.

Tom Watson of Georgia, frustrated Populist but still a potent leader of the rural masses, played a leading role in summoning up the demons of malice that infested the period. "Frustrated in their age-long and eternally losing struggle against a hostile industrial economy," Watson's biographer wrote, "the farmers, together with a large depressed urban element, eagerly welcomed exciting crusades against more vulnerable antagonists: against anything strange, and therefore evil." Watson provided the antagonists in abundance: first Negroes, then Catholics and Jews. In publications that issued from his home near Augusta, he began in 1910 to uncover in lurid detail the "sinister wonders" of Catholicism.[5] While he was still waging war on the Pope, the Leo Frank case in 1913 opened the way for a new crusade against "the typical young libertine Jew," the "lascivious pervert" who allegedly had done to death fourteen-year-old Mary Phagan, an employee of the Atlanta pencil factory he managed. Entangled in a net of circumstantial evidence twisted by prejudice and rumor, Frank was found guilty in a trial punctuated by open expressions of hostility in the court-

---

[3] Rowland T. Berthoff, "Southern Attitudes toward Immigration, 1865–1914," in *Journal of Southern History*, XVII (1951), 328–60. See also Higham, *Strangers in the Land*, 164–71, 175, and *passim;* and Julius Turner, *Party and Constituency: Pressures on Congress*, in Johns Hopkins University Studies in Historical and Political Science, LXIX, No. 1 (Baltimore, 1951), 138.

[4] *Manufacturers' Record*, LXXXVIII (November 12, 1925), 65. Fewer than twenty years before, the *Record* had promoted immigration.

[5] Woodward, *Tom Watson*, 416–30.

room and the cry of mobs outside. The hero of the piece was the chief prosecutor, Hugh M. Dorsey, who rode the prosecution to fame and the governor's chair in 1917. The villains were Governor John M. Slaton and his successor, Nathaniel E. Harris. Slaton commuted Frank's death sentence to life imprisonment in 1915 because of the doubt surrounding the case and ended his term a few days later under conditions of near insurrection. Harris tried in vain to identify the lynchers who spirited Frank from a state prison farm and hanged him on a tree at Marietta.[6]

The year of Frank's death brought two other fateful contributions to the growing plague of bigotry. On March 3, 1915, a new motion picture, *The Birth of a Nation*, commenced a record run of forty-seven weeks at the Liberty Theater in New York. The production was a technical triumph of cinema art; "the modern motion picture was born when *The Birth of a Nation* was produced." [7] But it projected a gross distortion of history. Based on *The Clansman*, a novel by Thomas Dixon, native North Carolinian and Baptist minister, directed by David Wark Griffith, a native Kentuckian, and replete with villainous Radicals, sinister mulattoes, blameless Southerners, and faithful darkies, the film brilliantly evoked the Southern mythology of Reconstruction. In its thrilling climax the Ku Klux Klan rode to the salvation of white civilization from a cowardly Negro militia. It was "like writing history with lightning," Woodrow Wilson was reported to have said. "Every man who comes out of one of our theatres is a Southern partisan for life," Dixon wrote to the President's secretary.[8] In the light of the film's wide circulation and popularity,

[6] The story of the case appears *ibid.*, 435–49. For greater detail see Christopher P. Connolly, *The Truth about the Frank Case* (New York, 1915); Charles and Louise Samuels, *Night Fell on Georgia* (New York, 1956); and Harry Golden, *A Little Girl Is Dead* (Cleveland, 1965). See also Nathaniel E. Harris, *Autobiography: The Story of an Old Man's Life, with Reminiscences of Seventy-Five Years* (Macon, Ga., 1925), 350–64, 371, on mob hostility to himself and to Governor Slaton.

[7] Milton MacKaye, "The Birth of a Nation," in *Scribner's Magazine* (New York), CII (1937), 42.

[8] Everett Carter, "Cultural History Written with Lightning: The Significance of *The Birth of a Nation*," in *American Quarterly*, XII (1960), 347–57; Lewis Jacobs, *The Rise of the American Film: A Critical History* (New York, 1939), 175; Thomas Dixon to Joseph P. Tumulty, May 1, 1915, quoted in Link, *Wilson: The New Freedom*, 253n.

one could hardly exaggerate its significance in fixing for a generation the popular image of Reconstruction or in preparing the way for a revival of the Klan.[9]

In the gloom of Thanksgiving night, 1915, two months after the death of Leo Frank, a weird group in white robes climbed Stone Mountain near Atlanta to gather beside a flag-draped altar with a Bible opened to Romans 12. There, at the mystic hour of midnight, "bathed in the sacred glow of the fiery cross, the invisible empire was called from its slumber of half a century to take up a new task." [10] Presiding over the resurrection of the Ku Klux Klan was Colonel William Joseph Simmons, Alabama native, whilom Methodist minister, inveterate joiner and promoter of fraternal societies, a mellifluous orator "as full of sentiment as a plum is full of juice," a dreamer saturated with the legends of the Confederacy and Reconstruction.[11] "They call me 'colonel,'" he once said, "largely out of respect." [12] The origins of the idea for a new Klan remained shrouded in the murky meditations of its founder, who testified to having seen apparitions of Klansmen riding across the walls of his room or through the clouds since boyhood. The immediate occasion, however, was the Atlanta premiere of *The Birth of a Nation*, which came about a week after the Stone Mountain ceremony. The Atlanta *Journal* carried Simmons' first public announcement of the new order next to the theater notice.[13]

---

[9] The film grossed approximately eighteen million dollars, went through endless revivals, and ran continuously in the Southern states for fifteen years after its release. MacKaye, "Birth of a Nation," *loc. cit.*, 40. See also John Hammond Moore, "South Carolina's Reaction to the Photoplay, *The Birth of a Nation*," in Proceedings of the *South Carolina Historical Association* (Columbia, S.C.), XXXIII (1963), 30–40.

[10] W. J. Simmons, testimony in *Hearings before the Committee on Rules. The Ku Klux Klan*, House of Representatives, 67 Cong., 1 Sess. (Washington, 1921), 122; hereinafter cited as *Klan Hearings*. The best general secondary accounts of the revived Klan are David Chalmers, *Hooded Americanism: The First Century of the Ku Klux Klan, 1865–1965* (New York, 1965); Arnold S. Rice, *The Ku Klux Klan in American Politics* (Washington, 1962); and Higham, *Strangers in the Land*, 234–99.

[11] "The 'Invisible Empire' in the Spotlight," in *Current Opinion* (New York), LXXI (1921), 562.

[12] *Klan Hearings*, 67. The title seems to have come from a position in the Woodmen of the World. *Ibid.*, 68; Marion Monteval [pseudonym of Edgar Irving Fuller?], *The Klan Inside Out* (Chicago, 1924), 8.

[13] *Klan Hearings*, 68–69; William Joseph Simmons, *America's Menace; or The Enemy Within; (an Epitome), including "America My America," The Most Power-*

Nor was the task to which the Klan had awakened any more clearly defined than its origins. It was a "living memorial" to the earlier Klan and a fraternal society with the common accouterments of the genus, including an array of Klaliffs, Klokards, Kludds, Kligrapps, and Klokann (the plural of Klokan), an elaborate secret ceremonial and passwords (Ayak, Akia, Kigy, Sanbog), and a mystifying slogan, "Non silba, sed anthar"—all of which the author took care to copyright in his own name.[14] But in a striking departure from its predecessor, a sectionalist white-supremacy group, the new Klan endorsed "100 per cent Americanism" and limited its membership to native-born white Protestants, although at the outset Simmons apparently did not envision the nativist fury that later erupted.[15]

For nearly five years the obscure successor to Nathan Bedford Forrest labored doggedly in his "Imperial Aulik" at the Georgia Savings Bank Building to preserve the Invisible Empire from bankruptcy and oblivion.[16] Here and there the Klan manifested itself: materialized before leaders of a threatened shipyard strike at Mobile in 1918, paraded through Montgomery, haunted suspected draft dodgers and slackers, marched at a reunion of Confederate veterans.[17] Meanwhile, the tide gathered that would lead Simmons on to fortune: wartime "Americanism," postwar Bolshevik scares, and race riots. In 1918 Thomas E. Kilby successfully ex-

---

fully *Appealing Patriotic Poem Ever Penned. A Clarion Call to Patriotic Action* (Atlanta, 1926), 4; Chalmers, *Hooded Americanism,* 29-30, and illustration 4. Thomas Dixon, however, publicly repudiated the new Klan, and Tom Watson seems to have had no direct hand in it; Watson claimed in 1921 that he was not a member and knew Simmons only slightly. Woodward, *Tom Watson,* 446; *Klan Hearings,* 87.

[14] *Kloran, Knights of the Ku Klux Klan: First Degree, Character* (Atlanta, 1916). Copyrighting made the "secrets" available to the public through the Library of Congress. They were circulated in the New York *World,* September 10, 1921.

[15] The exclusion of Negroes, Catholics, Jews, and the foreign born, Simmons maintained, did not indicate hostility to those groups and corresponded to the exclusion of non-Catholics from the Knights of Columbus. *Klan Hearings,* 73.

[16] Benjamin H. Avin, "The Ku Klux Klan, 1915–1925: A Study in Religious Intolerance" (Ph.D. dissertation, Georgetown University, 1952), 67. In 1916 a traitor to the ranks absconded with the treasury and sought to establish a rival order. *Klan Hearings,* 69. A contrary version had it that Simmons stole the idea from one Jonathan P. Frost. Monteval [pseud.], *Klan Inside Out,* 7.

[17] Rice, *Ku Klux Klan in American Politics,* 5–6; William G. Shepherd, "Ku Klux Koin," in *Collier's* (New York), LXXXII (1928), 8–9.

ploited the Catholic issue in Alabama, and in 1920 Tom Watson himself rode a wave of religious prejudice and postwar disillusionment into the Senate while Governor Sidney J. Catts stood firm against the imminent transfer of the Holy See to Florida. In Birmingham a short-lived postwar movement, the True Americans, sought to oust Catholics from county and municipal jobs.[18] Still, the Klan reached the summer of 1920 with probably not more than two thousand members.

Then Simmons made a fateful alliance with Edward Young Clarke and Mrs. Elizabeth Tyler, two publicity experts who had perfected the huckster technique in Red Cross and other wartime drives conducted by their Southern Publicity Association.[19] On June 7, 1920, the Imperial Wizard signed a contract granting Clarke exclusive rights to publicize and propagate the Klan. Out of the $10 klecktoken (initiation fee) the promoter got $8, with which he paid all expenses.[20] Mrs. Tyler dispensed ballyhoo while Clarke directed the organizing drive. First in Georgia and across the South, then in other regions, by shrewd exploitation of prejudice against Negroes, Catholics, Jews, Mexicans, Orientals, Bolsheviks, or whomever local circumstances dictated, they transformed bigotry into big business. By July, 1921, Clarke had at least 214 kleagles (organizers) in the field, working on a commission basis.[21] Within little more than a year he had brought the membership to more than 90,000 and had personally collected a sum reported at $225,568.84.[22]

A sensational exposé by the New York *World,* September 6–26, 1921, and a Congressional investigation in October only brought further publicity and provided Simmons an opportunity to play his oleaginous role of Southern "colonel." In the "idea of selling people their own prejudices," a sardonic editor remarked in

[18] Charles P. Sweeney, "Bigotry in the South," in *Nation,* CXI (1920), 585–86. See also Charles P. Sweeney, "Bigotry Turns to Murder," *ibid.,* CXIII (1921), 232–33.

[19] New York *World,* September 26, 1921; "For and Against the Ku Klux Klan," in *Literary Digest,* LXX (September 24, 1921), 36. Clarke had worked on Will Alexander's staff for the YMCA War Work Council, so that both the Ku Klux Klan and the Interracial Commission, in a sense, sprang from the same origins. Clarke "was ornery, he had a dirty mind and mean disposition," Alexander declared later. "Just mean." "Reminiscences of Will W. Alexander," 209a–211a.

[20] Text of the contract in *Klan Hearings,* 111–12.

[21] Their names appeared in New York *World,* September 9, 1921.

[22] *Klan Hearings,* 87, 155.

Charleston, Simmons had displayed a genius "almost equal to the old bunco game of selling a hick the Capitol." "We might have drawn enough money to the South from Jew or Catholic haters in the rest of the country to have offset the stream that pours from this section into the treasuries of the great insurance companies," he lamented, if that "engaging old reprobate" had not been exposed.[23] But the judgment was premature. In living testimony to the cynical adage that there is no such thing as bad publicity, the Klan battened on exposure. "Congress made us," Simmons later asserted.[24]

Somehow all the heightened fears, frustrations, and disillusionments of the postwar world poured into "this central apotheosis of a tribal spirit," and in the Klan's apocalyptic demonology the alien menace came rapidly to the forefront.[25] America is no melting pot, Simmons warned. "It is a garbage can! . . . My friends, your government can be changed between the rising and setting of one sun. . . . When the hordes of aliens walk to the ballot box and their votes outnumber yours, then that alien horde has got you by the throat." [26] His successor Hiram Evans declared that in most of the immigrants there was "a fundamental inferiority of racial and national strains." Only 55,000,000 real Americans were left, a bare majority of the population. Negroes could not "attain the Anglo-Saxon level"; Jews set themselves apart by "a racial and religious antipathy, unrelenting and unabating since the cross of Calvary"; Catholics accepted "a higher temporal allegiance" to the Pope than to their own government.[27]

As a defensive organization the Klan had a potent drawing power in the changing South of the 1920's. It was "primarily the reaction of the Old South to the advent of the New," one

[23] T. R. W[aring] to William Watts Ball, September 27, 1921, in Ball Papers. Waring was editor of the Charleston *Evening Post*.

[24] Rice, *Ku Klux Klan in American Politics*, 8.

[25] Higham, *Strangers in the Land*, 285.

[26] Address to the Junior Order of United American Mechanics, Atlanta, April 30, 1922, quoted in Charles P. Sweeney, "The Great Bigotry Merger," in *Nation*, CXV (1922), 9. See also William Joseph Simmons, *The Klan Unmasked* (2nd ed.; Atlanta, 1924), which emphasized the nativist theme above all others. See also John M. Mecklin, *The Ku Klux Klan: A Study of the American Mind* (New York, 1924), 122, 128, 157.

[27] Hiram W. Evans, "The Menace of Modern Immigration," in *Official Souvenir of Klan Day at the State Fair of Texas, Dallas, October 24, 1923* (n.p., n.d.). Personal copy loaned to author by Professor Jo Ann Carrigan.

sociologist declared.[28] Under the stress of social competition in hundreds of growing towns, the new immigrant from the country was "made to realize his essential mediocrity," another sociologist observed. "Here is a large and powerful organization offering to solace his sense of defeat by dubbing him a knight of the Invisible Empire for the small sum of ten dollars." [29] "The Klan was a means of giving them an instrument with which they could affect their community and become important," Will Alexander said.[30] The robes, the flaming crosses, the spooky processionals, the kneeling recruits, the occult liturgies all tapped a deep urge toward mystery and brought drama into the dreary routine of a thousand communities.[31]

At the same time the Klan was paradoxically a movement of opposition to the strange and exotic, against shifting moral standards, the declining influence of the churches, the broadmindedness of cities and colleges. It represented a degradation of the millennial hopes aroused by progressivism and the war. "It is going to drive the bootleggers forever out of this land," declared a sympathetic Texan. "It is going to bring clean moving pictures . . . clean literature . . . break up roadside parking . . . enforce the laws . . . protect homes. . . . It means the return of old time Southern chivalry and deference to womanhood; it means that the 'married man with an affinity' has no place in our midst." [32] With a magnificent inconsistency the Klan drive to maintain law and order, defined in terms of its own strait-laced morality, coalesced with an old propensity for night-riding and extralegal violence.[33]

---

[28] Guy B. Johnson, "A Sociological Interpretation of the New Ku Klux Movement," in *Social Forces*, I (1922–1923) , 444.

[29] Mecklin, *Ku Klux Klan*, 108.

[30] "Reminiscences of Will W. Alexander," 211a–212a.

[31] Frank Tannenbaum, *Darker Phases of the South* (New York, 1924) , 16–17. The dullness of small town life was one of the conventional stereotypes of the 1920's, but doubtless also a very real factor in such phenomena as the Klan. In any case, the Klan was chiefly a phenomenon of the small towns or the growing new cities of the South rather than of the rural areas. Mecklin, *Ku Klux Klan*, 96–109.

[32] *Colonel Mayfield's Weekly* (Houston) , quoted in "The Klan as a National Problem," in *Literary Digest*, LXXV (December 2, 1922) , 13.

[33] Especially in the Southwest. See Charles C. Alexander, *Crusade for Conformity: The Ku Klux Klan in Texas, 1920–1930*, in Texas Gulf Coast Historical Association Publication Series, VI (Houston, 1962) ; and Charles C. Alexander, *The Ku Klux Klan in the Southwest* (Lexington, Ky., 1965) .

By 1921 the Klan was a national phenomenon, but its influence was nowhere so pervasive or violent as in the South. Its progress across the region left a trail of threats, brandings, floggings, emasculation, and murder. In the fall of 1921 masked bands paraded the streets of several Florida cities to intimidate Negro voters and the Klan had a part in the election riots at Ocoee.[34] But its violence was directed less against Negroes, Catholics, or Jews than against the unrighteous or the unwary victims of private grudges and sadistic horseplay. In 1921 hooded terrorism reached its height in Texas, where forty-three tarrings were reported in six months. Wayward husbands and wives, wife beaters, bootleggers, an abortionist, and other sinners felt the sting of the Klan's vengeance.[35]

Around the northern Louisiana community of Bastrop the Klan set out to clean up Morehouse Parish by raiding stills, driving out moonshiners and "undesirable women," and threatening those who objected. The reign of terror reached its climax with the disappearance of two citizens of Mer Rouge who, the Exalted Cyclops of Bastrop "officially announced," would "never return," and whose bodies months later came to the surface of Lake La Fourche with marks of beastly torture. Governor Parker had to use the state militia to forestall warfare between Bastrop and Mer Rouge. Two years later he secured legislation requiring the Klan to register its membership rolls with the state.[36] A similar terrorism brought out the Oklahoma militia in 1923.[37] The violence receded thereafter but the widespread sympathy for the movement, its secrecy, and its terrorism cast a pall of fear over Southern communities. Enemies of the Klan, said a Kentucky Klansman,

[34] White, "Election Day in Florida," *loc. cit.*, 106–109. See also *Klan Hearing*, 63–66.

[35] Edward T. Devine, "The Klan in Texas," in *Survey*, XLVIII (April 1, 1922), 10–11; "The Reign of the Tar Bucket," in *Literary Digest*, LXXX (August 27, 1921), 12; New York *World*, September 18, 1921; Albert De Silver, "The Ku Klux Klan—'Soul of Chivalry'," in *Nation*, CXIII (1921), 285–86; Alexander, *Crusade for Conformity*, 9–12; and Alexander, *Ku Klux Klan in the Southwest*, 20–35.

[36] John Rogers, *The Murders of Mer Rouge* (St. Louis, 1923); Robert L. Duffus, "How the Ku Klux Klan Sells Hate," in *World's Work*, XLVI (1923), 174–78.

[37] W. C. Witcher, *The Reign of Terror in Oklahoma* (Fort Worth, 1923); Howard A. Tucker, *History of Governor Walton's War on Ku Klux in the Invisible Empire* (Oklahoma City, 1923).

were uncertain who the members were, or how many. "It is the invisible something that gets their goat." [38] Here and there men of courage faced down the Klan even in its strongholds, but most preferred not to offend. [39] "During the Ku Klux era one was advised that it was better to keep one's mouth shut because one never knew who was around," Howard Odum noted. [40]

Colonel Simmons betrayed a fatal inability to control the monster he had conjured up. No administrator, slovenly in record-keeping, absorbed mainly with the financial reports, he confessed to "a distinctive streak of timidity," a lack of "desire to rule or to govern." [41] In the spring of 1922 his wife, fearing for his health, arranged a six-month leave during which Edward Y. Clarke acted in his place. Intrigues for the succession set in immediately and Clarke proved no more effective than the Colonel in managing the tough customers attracted by the scramble for power and booty. In November, 1922, a palace revolution ousted Simmons; faced with threats of violence, he accepted a sinecure as "Emperor," and finally withdrew altogether, selling his copyright on the Klan for $146,500. [42] The new Imperial Wizard, Hiram Wesley Evans, a former dentist and Exalted Cyclops in Dallas, had entered the Atlanta office as Imperial Kligrapp (national secretary). Plump, round-faced, fortyish, he called himself the "most average man in America." [43] Ostensibly a reform leader, he set out to establish a tight grip on the organization and to curb violence in preparation for political ends that proved to be as poorly defined as Simmons' original purposes. [44]

The hooded order temporarily laid vassal Atlanta, Birmingham, Houston, Dallas, Fort Worth, Tulsa, and Little Rock, all banner Klan cities, and many lesser communities. Thousands of local officeholders owed their places to the Klan and more were stricken

[38] E. H. Lougher, *The Kall of the Klan in Kentucky* (Greenfield, Ind., 1924), 39.

[39] Duffus, "How the Ku Klux Klan Sells Hate," *loc. cit.*, 180; Mecklin, *Ku Klux Klan*, 231.

[40] Odum, *American Epoch*, 321.   [41] *Klan Hearings*, 83.

[42] Loucks, *Ku Klux Klan in Pennsylvania*, 45–48; interview with Simmons, in New York *Times*, September 23, 1937.

[43] Stanley Frost, *The Challenge of the Klan* (Indianapolis, 1924), 21–23.

[44] Hiram W. Evans, "Where Do We Go From Here?", in *Papers Read at the Meeting of Grand Dragons Knights of the Ku Klux Klan at Their First Annual Meeting Held at Asheville, North Carolina, July, 1923* (n.p., n.d.), 7–13.

dumb on the subject. In 1922 the Klan elected Clifford Walker governor of Georgia, sent Earle B. Mayfield to the Senate from Texas, and captured the Oklahoma legislature.[45] In 1924 Evans tried to become the Warwick of Presidential politics, and the Klan issue utterly disrupted the Democratic party—a story that will be told later. In Louisiana the Klan contributed to the victory of Governor Henry L. Fuqua and in Oklahoma to that of Republican Senator W. B. Pine. In 1926 the Klan's power in Alabama forced its most outspoken enemy, Oscar W. Underwood, to shrink from a senatorial contest with Hugo Black and made Bibb Graves governor, but a renewed wave of hooded terrorism in 1927 forced the new administration ultimately to break with its former supporters after a period of masterful inaction.[46] But even where it showed power the Klan never articulated a political program, beyond securing the dismissal of a Catholic now and then or afflicting officials with a salutary blindness to floggings. Diligent search has uncovered only one Klan-inspired law, an Oregon act requiring Catholic children to attend public schools—and it was declared unconstitutional.[47] Nowhere in the South did the Klan perfect a political machine such as that through which David C. Stephenson briefly dominated Indiana.[48] In the three states where its strength most clearly determined statewide elections—Texas in 1922, Georgia in 1922 and 1924, Alabama in 1926—its influence rapidly receded.

In the absence of reliable membership figures, one cannot say precisely when decline set in. In any case, one commentator asserted, its true strength lay in the millions of sympathizers. "It is not enough to say that the great body of uninitiated Klansmen are merely in sympathy with the movement. *They are the Ku Klux*

[45] Duffus, "How the Ku Klux Klan Sells Hate," *loc. cit.*, 181–83. For a discussion of Klan activities in southern politics, state and local, see Rice, *Klux Klan in American Politics*, 38–73. For thorough state by state accounts, see Chalmers, *Hooded Americanism*.

[46] R. A. Patton, "A Ku Klux Klan Reign of Terror," in *Current History and Forum*, XXVIII (1928), 52–55; Birmingham *News*, March 30, 1930; Montgomery *Advertiser*, January 18, 1931; Rice, *Ku Klux Klan in American Politics*, 64–66; Alexander, *Ku Klux Klan in the Southwest*, 182–84, 202–203.

[47] Alexander, *Ku Klux Klan in the Southwest*, 111–12.

[48] Edgar Allen Booth, *The Mad Mullah of America* (Columbus, Ohio, 1927).

movement!" [49] The total membership reached a peak of three million late in 1923, according to one source, or as many as eight million in 1925, according to another. Both sources indicate a Southern proportion approximating the population ratio, but located mostly in the Deep South and Southwest.[50] Decay set in almost as fast as the growth of the order. The split in the leadership prefaced recurrent factional squabbles and schisms. The Klan's moral luster was tarnished by charges of questionable relations between Clarke and Mrs. Tyler and later a sordid scandal leading to the Indiana leader's conviction for murder.[51] The "best people" of many communities had joined what they thought was an agency of reform, but drifted away as the Klan became a cloak for outrage; in that respect, at least, the organization repeated the history of its ancestor.

Most of the major urban dailies of the South kept up a running attack on the Klan and all its works. Politicians became increasingly emboldened to act against it. Some kind of poetic justice was served when "Farmer Jim" Ferguson, the premier rabble-rouser of Texas, put up "Ma" Ferguson as his proxy in the gubernatorial race of 1924 and rode to victory over the Klan's candidate with revelations that "ex-Grand Gizzard Simmons and Clarke were whore lovers and the present Grand Gizzard is a nigger lover." [52] The Klan, devoted above all to nativism, suffered from the decline in nativist excitement after the immigration law of 1924. And already in decline, the movement activated the hostility of Democratic regulars by its opposition to Al Smith in 1928. But above all the supreme weakness was that it had no political program, no dynamic leadership. Unlike kindred movements in postwar Europe, it threw up no Mussolini, no Hitler. By 1930 the total

[49] Johnson, "Sociological Interpretation of the New Ku Klux Klan Movement," *loc. cit.*, 444–45.

[50] Higham, *Strangers in the Land*, 297; Washington *Post*, November 2, 1930. Rice, *Ku Klux Klan in American Politics*, 12, estimated a maximum of four million in 1924. Alexander, *Ku Klux Klan in the Southwest*, 158, estimated three to five million in 1924.

[51] Rice, *Ku Klux Klan in American Politics*, 11–12. In 1924 Clarke pleaded guilty to a charge of violating the Mann Act.

[52] Charles W. Ferguson, "James E. Ferguson," in *Southwest Review*, X (1924–1925), 30.

membership had dwindled to not more than fifty thousand.[53]

The vagueness of the Klan's program was reflected in its nebulous relationship to the Protestantism it purported to defend. A standard ceremonial practice was the hooded processional into some approved church at which the Klansmen would leave an offering, but careful historians have found that neither the major church bodies and periodicals nor fundamentalist leaders ever worked closely with the Klan. Many opposed it vehemently.[54] Yet there were parallels; more than one Klansman found his Anglo-Saxon nativism and fear of the Roman menace reinforced from the Protestant pulpit. One of the classic tributes to the newest "Chosen Race" had come from Methodist Bishop Warren A. Candler of Georgia, in his *Great Revivals and the Great Republic* (1904) which declared the Anglo-Saxons to be divinely appointed for the advancement of evangelical religion in the world, a theme re-echoed time and again by preachers and revivalists.[55] The line of reasoning led directly to sectionalism. Other regions, a Baptist divine noted, had lost "whatever there is of advantage in this un-mixed Anglo-Saxon blood." Romanism had flooded their cities, had "invaded and despoiled the old patriotism and the old culture and political ideals." [56] The logic was inescapable. "The hope of the world is America, the hope of America is evangelical religion of the most orthodox type, the hope of the American church is the Southern Evangelical churches." [57]

The South was indeed a bastion of evangelical Protestantism. It outranked other regions in its proportion of church membership, in denominational colleges, in the general position and influence of the church. Of the total adult population in the Southeast 61.4

---

[53] Rice, *Ku Klux Klan in American Politics*, 12.

[54] Robert Moats Miller, "A Note on the Relationship between the Protestant Churches and the Revived Ku Klux Klan," in *Journal of Southern History*, XXII (1956), 355–68; Norman F. Furniss, *The Fundamentalist Controversy, 1918–1931* (New Haven, 1954), 38.

[55] Warren A. Candler, *Great Revivals and the Great Republic* (Nashville and Dallas, 1904). William G. McLoughlin, Jr., *Modern Revivalism: Charles Grandison Finney to Billy Graham* (New York, 1959), 354–65, summarizes Candler's work and places it in context.

[56] Masters, *Call of the South*, 208.

[57] Edwin Mims, *The Advancing South: Stories of Progress and Reaction* (Garden City, N.Y., 1926), 285.

per cent were church members in 1926—in contrast to 54.3 per cent in the nation as a whole—about three quarters of them Baptists and Methodists. What is more, membership had risen from 10,562,000 in 1906 to 15,678,000 in 1926; the Southern Baptist growth of 34.6 per cent over the two decades was the largest of any major church body in the United States, and urban churches grew even faster than urban population. Nor was membership the full measure of the churches' influence in a society for which they provided the only form of social organization for great numbers of people.[58]

The legendary rank order of denominations from the aristocratic Episcopalians to the democratic Methodists and Baptists did not always prevail, but Southern congregations of whatever sect were more than apt to reflect class distinctions. In striking contrast to fashionable uptown churches in the flourishing cities, rural churches shared the distress of the countryside. In many places the circuit rider had dismounted only to board a Model T. In seventy counties scattered across the South a survey in the early 1920's showed that only 20 per cent of the churches had full-time ministers and that 38 per cent of the ministers served four or more churches. Seven out of ten ministers had no college or seminary training, only 11 per cent had both, more than one in seven of the full-time ministers served at an annual pay of $500 or less, more than half at $1,250 or less.[59] To the categories of uptown and rural churches the industrial evolution added mill churches, largely the products of denominational rivalries in mission programs to proselytize the new proletariat. Somewhere outside the pale were the growing premillennial sects, the "Holy Rollers" to their mocking superiors, who substituted "religious status for social status" and abandoned this hopeless world for sanctification,

[58] Francis B. Simkins, *A History of the South* (2nd ed.; New York, 1953), 411. Kenneth K. Bailey, *Southern White Protestantism in the Twentieth Century* (New York, 1964), offers a useful survey. The isolation of masses of the people posed particular problems for movements like the Interracial Commission, which "didn't know how to reach them" because they had nothing but "poor little churches"—no farm or labor organization. "Reminiscences of Will W. Alexander," 194. See also Odum, *Southern Regions of the United States*, 141–49.

[59] Edmund deS. Brunner, *Church Life in the Rural South: A Study of the Opportunity of Protestantism Based upon Data from Seventy Counties* (New York, 1923), 44, 58–60, 63–65.

regeneration, and the Holy Ghost.[60] And beyond them lay the "vast rural underworld of poor whites and poor Negroes" who danced in the "jooks" on Sunday night without knowledge of the puritan Sabbath.[61]

Yet for all the sectarian schisms a pervasive unity of doctrine covered Southern Christendom "like Joseph's garment, a coat of many colors . . . a flawless ensemble" holding together the varieties of religious experience and social distinction.[62] But doctrine offered a major stumbling block to the reunification of the great Baptist, Methodist, and Presbyterian bodies that had split apart in the nineteenth century. Only in the Methodist church did reunion progress to the point of an actual plan, submitted in 1920 and adopted by the General Conference of the Southern Church but defeated in 1925 for want of a three-fourths majority in the annual conferences. Racial segregation offered one barrier to understanding, but above all was the fear that heresy had subverted the Northern church. "Modernism is prevalent in the Methodist Episcopal Church," Bishop Candler announced. "It is there, and it is strongly intrenched in high places. . . . Let the Southern churches beware of it." [63]

The purest orthodoxy rejected the social gospel for individual salvation. "A nice fresh coat of paint on the pen does not change the nature of the pig," said one Baptist. "Shall a preacher be interested in the community welfare? Certainly, but the greatest service he can possibly render is to bring wrong-hearted men to Jesus." [64] But there were rents in the flawless ensemble of doctrine. A strong theme of religiosity ran through the Southern Sociological Congress and the interracial movement. At one time more than a fourth of the members of the Commission on Interracial Cooperation were ministers. Its first president was a devout

[60] Liston Pope, *Millhands and Preachers: A Study of Gastonia*, in Yale Studies in Religious Education, No. 15 (New Haven, 1942), 70–78, 126–40.
[61] Francis B. Simkins, "The Rising Tide of Faith," in Louis D. Rubin, Jr., and James J. Kilpatrick, Jr. (eds.), *The Lasting South: Fourteen Southerners Look at Their Home* (Chicago, 1957), 92.
[62] Quoted *ibid.*, 97.
[63] Paul N. Garber, *The Methodists Are One People* (Nashville, 1939), 116–20; Warren A. Candler, "Resolute and Revolutionary Rationalism," in Nashville *Christian Advocate*, January 30, 1925, quoted in Mims, *Advancing South*, 284–85.
[64] Masters, *Call of the South*, 161.

layman, a manufacturer who argued that the first claim on industry should be a "living wage." Its guiding spirit, Will W. Alexander, who as a Methodist clergyman organized aid to Nashville's unemployed in 1914, manifested a growing concern with social applications of religion, and emerged finally as the co-ordinator of Southern liberalism, in effect, for a generation. Most of the leaders in college interracialism were students active in religious organizations.[65] All this may have reflected a regional tendency to invoke the judgment of religion on all issues, and it did confirm the judgment that "the power of the church has been in its ideologies and conditioning attitudes and not in its program." [66]

Such a conclusion, however, neglects the evidences of social concern within church groups. Much of that concern found outlet in the prohibition movement, but the Southern Baptist Convention in 1913 set up a Committee on Social Service which defined its concerns as not only alcohol and narcotics, but war, economic or political; vice; and public health, although the emphasis remained on individual regeneration. "Social life is to be cleansed by cleansing the life of the social unit," the Committee declared. "It is not a new distribution of wealth or a new classification of people that is wanted, but new people." The Methodists created a Commission on Temperance and Social Service in 1918; the Episcopal Address to the General Conference at Memphis in 1926 spoke of the right to a living wage, limited hours, restrictions upon child labor, better medical care, parks, and playgrounds—"in short, whatever makes for a richer, fuller life." In 1927 a group of religious leaders led by Bishop James Cannon joined in public appeal to the Southern textile manufacturers for improvement of living and working conditions.[67]

Both the social gospel and the serpent of rationalism had en-

[65] Marion M. Jackson, "The Kingdom of God in a Foundry," in *Survey*, LIII (1924), 255–58, 298; "Reminiscences of Will W. Alexander," 110–27, 136–42, 189a; Robert Moats Miller, "The Attitudes of American Protestantism toward the Negro, 1919–1939," in *Journal of Negro History*, XLI (1956), 224–25.
[66] Odum, *Southern Regions of the United States*, 527.
[67] Shivers, "Social Welfare Movement in the South," 87–95; William Wright Barnes, *The Southern Baptist Convention, 1845–1935* (Nashville, 1954), 247–48; James Cannon, Jr., "Concerning the Appeal to the Industrial Leaders of the South," in *Manufacturers' Record*, XCIII (February 16, 1928), 63–64.

tered the Southern Eden. New doctrines of evolution and the Higher Criticism had crept into the state universities, and Baptist leader Victor I. Masters complained that not even the denominational schools "had altogether an easy time in safeguarding the class rooms from the miasmatic utterances of teachers who have been contaminated by the rationalistic and evolutionary imaginings of the New Religion." [68] Orthodox Southern Methodists, after a decade of struggle to recover their hold on Vanderbilt University, lost in 1914 and retired to new sanctuaries at Southern Methodist in Dallas and Emory in Atlanta—both of which, together with the newer Duke University, by the mid-1920's were drifting toward liberal theology. In Nashville, which William Jennings Bryan labeled "the centre of Modernism in the South," Methodist Bishop Edwin D. Mouzon preached against a literal interpretation of the Scriptures, as did other leading divines like the Episcopalian C. B. Wilmer and the Baptist M. Ashby Jones in Atlanta.[69] In North Carolina, indeed, the Baptists had put at the head of Wake Forest College the very incarnation of the new heresies: William Louis Poteat, ordained Baptist minister, biologist, and evolutionist. Speaking at Chapel Hill in 1925 Poteat enjoined students to search beyond the Bible for truth. "The deepest of all infidelity," he told them, ". . . is the fear lest the truth be bad." [70]

With the dawning knowledge that new theories had infected the schools and even the pulpits, orthodoxy achieved a new militancy in fundamentalism. The movement had acquired a name and definition in a series of pamphlets, *The Fundamentals* (1910), sponsored by two wealthy residents of Los Angeles; it first became organized in the World's Christian Fundamentals Association at Montrose, Pennsylvania, in 1916; by 1920 it was poised for a war on evolution. Armed with the "Five Points" fundamental to the faith—an infallible Bible, the Virgin Birth, the Atonement, the Resurrection, and the Second Coming—the fundamentalists were

[68] Masters, *Call of the South,* 157.

[69] Mims, *Advancing South,* 292–311; Furniss, *Fundamentalist Controversy,* 159–60.

[70] William Louis Poteat, *Can a Man Be a Christian To-day?* (Chapel Hill, 1925), 109. See also Suzanne Cameron Linder, *William Louis Poteat: Prophet of Progress* (Chapel Hill, 1966).

distinguished less by their theology, which many others shared, than by their posture of relentless hostility toward any deviation.[71]

By the process through which complex problems become simplified into symbolic issues, the defense of the faith came to depend upon opposition to Darwinism—and upon the peerless leadership of William Jennings Bryan. "The whole modernistic propaganda rests on evolution," Bryan wrote to Josephus Daniels. "They first reject the miracle and then everything in the Bible that is miraculous or supernatural. As this includes the virgin birth, the deity of Christ and the resurrection, nothing of importance is left. . . . What the world needs is the supernatural Christ of whom the Bible tells, not a mere reformer without authority." The old reformer Bryan still spoke through the new fundamentalist. "Evolution, by denying the need or possibility of spiritual regeneration, discourages all reforms, for reform is always based upon the regeneration of the individual." "Something must be done," he wrote, "to enlarge the moral rudders of the intellectual ships which we are building in our schools or they will be wrecked on the larger temptations of this age." [72]

Among the lesser lights of fundamentalism, J. Frank Norris, minister of a Baptist church in Fort Worth, was the most notorious and the most spectacularly flawed, known chiefly for his truculence and his propensity for controversy. In the early 1920's he specialized in the purification of church colleges, beginning with an agitation against Baylor in 1920 that within three years drove out a sociologist, Grove S. Dow, author of a textbook describing the evolutionary social and biological development of man, and two of Dow's colleagues. Through his magazine, *Searchlight*, topped by an illustration of Satan cowering in the glare, Norris reached out into ever broader fields, challenging Presidents Poteat of Wake Forest and Edgar Young Mullins of the Southern Baptist Seminary, among others. In 1923 he crossed denomina-

[71] Furniss, *Fundamentalist Controversy*, 12-13, 49.

[72] William Jennings Bryan to Josephus Daniels, February 9, *1925*, in Daniels Papers; Bryan to [Dr. Howard A.] Kelly, June 17, 1925, "Bible Instruction in Schools," typescript dated May 1, 1925, in Bryan Papers. Lawrence W. Levine, *Defender of the Faith William Jennings Bryan: The Last Decade 1915-1925* (New York, 1965), supports the above interpretation.

tional lines to indict three Methodist colleges in Texas and staged a flamboyant "trial" before the World's Christian Fundamentals Association in Fort Worth with the testimony of six students that evolution was rife in their institutions. The Methodists were credited with furnishing "more recruits for the war on modern science than any other denomination except the Baptist," but they never took official action on the issue in their assemblies; in 1927, however, their Education Association expressed its opposition "to all legislation that would interfere with the proper teaching of science in American schools and colleges." Still, Professor John A. Rice found it expedient to leave Southern Methodist after attacks from Norris. In all, Norris claimed the scalps of six professors, but his influence among Baptists faded under resentment at his "factious methods and personal behavior." After 1923 the Texas Baptist Convention barred messengers from his church, and after 1926 his influence in the Southern Baptist Convention was gone.[73]

Only Bryan had the qualities of prestige and eloquence to make the movement a popular crusade. As he issued forth from Coconut Grove on his regular speaking assignments, evolution became his chief theme. In 1921, alarmed at evidence of infidelity among students, he sparked a movement for antievolution laws in addresses at the Union Theological Seminary (Southern Presbyterian) in Richmond and at the University of Wisconsin.[74] The first move to enact such a law failed in South Carolina in 1921 when the lower house refused to concur in a senate amendment making it unlawful to use state funds to teach "the cult known as Darwinism" as "a creed to be followed," but antievolution bills mushroomed in other legislatures.[75]

[73] Furniss, *Fundamentalist Controversy*, 121–23, 125–26, 157–58; Virginius Dabney, *Liberalism in the South* (Chapel Hill, 1932), 292.

[74] William Jennings Bryan, *In His Image* (New York, 1922); William Jennings Bryan, "The Menace of Darwinism," in *The Commoner* (Lincoln, Neb.), XXI (April, 1921), 5–8.

[75] Maynard Shipley, *The War on Modern Science: A Short History of the Fundamentalist Attacks on Evolution and Modernism* (New York, 1927), 115. This is the fullest account in print of the struggle for antievolution laws. See also Kenneth K. Bailey, "The Antievolution Crusade of the Nineteen-Twenties" (Ph.D. dissertation, Vanderbilt University, 1954); and Willard B. Gatewood, Jr., *Preachers, Pedagogues and Politicians: The Evolution Controversy in North Carolina, 1920–1927* (Chapel Hill, 1966).

A " ' monkey bill' promises rare sport," a journalist wrote later. "Bryan will come. Perhaps 'the Texas Cyclone,' Rev. J. Frank Norris, will come. Shaking like a leaf, the University president will come. Still more amusing, politicians from the backwoods will rise up to refute 'science falsely so-called.' " [76] The pattern first took form in Kentucky where the Baptist Reverend J. W. Porter of Lexington, author of the broadside *Evolution—A Menace*,[77] launched a campaign for an antievolution law. Bryan, hearing of it, wrote to Porter: "The movement will sweep the country, and we will drive Darwinism from our schools. . . . Strength to your arms!" In January, 1922, Bryan gave a series of speeches in the state, including his Chautauqua lecture, "The Enemies of the Bible," in Lexington and an address to a joint session of the legislature in Frankfort. Bills appeared in both houses. Newspapers thundered and pulpits reverberated, but the Baptists divided on the bills and the Episcopal diocese came out against them. And if he trembled, the resourceful president of the state university, Dr. Frank L. McVey, stood firm. Armed with statements from distinguished clergymen and educators, he denied that evolution made atheists at the university and argued that the proposed law would prevent the effective teaching of science. Finally the house bill lost by 42 to 41, and the senate bill died with adjournment. "We were the first to fight this thing through on behalf of modernity," the editor of the Louisville *Evening Post* boasted, "and we won." [78] Wherever educational leaders and the press acted forcefully, the result was the same.

In 1923 Bryan descended upon Atlanta to present the Georgia House of Representatives an impassioned plea against "the teaching of Darwinism as a fact." Shortly afterward Representative Hal Kimberly presented his classic and comprehensive bibliography: "Read the Bible. It teaches you how to act. Read the hymnbook. It

[76] Rollin Lynde Hartt, "Down with Evolution!", in *World's Work*, XLVI (1923), 611.

[77] Dedicated to his "beloved and womanly wife, on whose brow is stamped the likeness of Him, in whose image she was created, and whose pure and noble blood is untainted by that of insect, reptile, fowl, or beast." Quoted *ibid.*, 605.

[78] *Ibid.*, 605, 607–608; Shipley, *War on Modern Science*, 118–27; Frank L. McVey, *The Gates Open Slowly: A History of Education in Kentucky* (Lexington, Ky., 1949), 224–36.

contains the finest poetry ever written. Read the almanac. It shows you how to figure out what the weather will be. There isn't another book that is necessary for anyone to read." But antievolution bills failed to reach a vote in either house.[79]

Yet the tides of fundamentalism rose in one state after another. Early in 1923 the Oklahoma legislature forbade the use of any textbook offering "a materialistic conception of history, that is, the Darwin theory of creation." Governor Jack C. Walton, who attributed the measure to the Ku Klux Klan, signed it, he said, because he could not veto the bill without vetoing the textbook money.[80] A few months later the Florida lawmakers, influenced by Bryan and his friend President A. A. Murphree of the state university, passed a joint resolution against teaching atheism, agnosticism, or Darwinism "as true" in public schools. It was written by Bryan.[81] In North Carolina and Texas victories came in 1924 by other means; in both cases state boards, impelled by Governors Morrison and Ferguson, ordered the elimination of textbooks or references in textbooks upholding Darwinism. "I'm a Christian mother, . . ." declared "Ma" Ferguson, "and I am not going to let that kind of rot go into Texas textbooks." [82] Still, the legislatures of both states held fast.

The climax came in Tennessee, where events in 1923 augured those two years later. In 1923 the University of Tennessee threw out Professor Jesse W. Sprowls after he had proposed to use in class James Harvey Robinson's *The Mind in the Making,* a favorite fundamentalist target, and discharged five others in the ensuing uproar.[83] When in 1925 an obscure legislator, John Washington Butler, introduced a bill to outlaw the teaching of evolution in public schools and colleges, the educational leaders of the state distinguished themselves chiefly by their silence. Both the public schools and the university had important bills pending. A small

[79] Shipley, *War on Modern Science,* 127–37.

[80] Dabney, *Liberalism in the South,* 289; Furniss, *Fundamentalist Controversy,* 83; Jack C. Walton to William Jennings Bryan, May 26, 1923, in Bryan Papers.

[81] Furniss, *Fundamentalist Controversy,* 83–84; Shipley, *War on Modern Science,* 137–38.

[82] Shipley, *War on Modern Science,* 88, 170–75.

[83] "Report on the University of Tennessee," in *Bulletin of the American Association of University Professors* (Boston), X (1924), 213–60.

but active Baptist lobby hastily mobilized and with little opposition the measure passed by overwhelming majorities. Governor Austin Peay, unwilling to endanger his pending school program, signed the act with the observation that it probably would never be applied.[84]

He reckoned without the civic boosters of Dayton, a group of whom inveigled a guileless young high school teacher, John T. Scopes, into accepting the offer of the American Civil Liberties Union to defend a test case—chiefly to put their town on the map. They succeeded beyond their wildest hopes; the publicity was worldwide, and enduring. Before the opening day of the "monkey trial," July 13, 1925, the streets of Dayton swarmed with sundry oddments of humanity—and other anthropoids—drawn to the carnival: publicity-hounds, curiosity-seekers, professional evangelists and professional atheists, a blind mountaineer who proclaimed himself the world's greatest authority on the Bible, ballyhoo agents for the Florida boom, hot dog and soda pop hucksters, and a miscellany of reporters and publicists.

The twice-told tale of the Scopes trial cannot be repeated here in full, but it was one of the most dramatic battles in the warfare of science and theology.[85] The two stars of the show, Bryan, who had offered his services to the prosecution, and Clarence Darrow, renowned trial lawyer of Chicago and self-confessed agnostic, were united in their determination that the trial should be an exercise in public education. However, when Judge John T. Raulston, a Methodist lay preacher, ruled out scientific testimony on the validity of the Darwinian hypothesis, the defense called Bryan as an expert witness on Biblical interpretation. In his colloquy with Darrow, he repeatedly entrapped himself by his literal-minded interpretations and indeed his profound ignorance of Biblical history and scholarship. Bryan's humiliation, however, had no effect upon the outcome. Scopes was found guilty of teaching evolution,

[84] Kenneth K. Bailey, "The Enactment of Tennessee's Antievolution Law," in *Journal of Southern History,* XVI (1950), 472–90.

[85] The fullest account of the Scopes trial is in Ray Ginger, *Six Days or Forever?: Tennessee v. John Thomas Scopes* (Boston, 1958). See also *The World's Most Famous Court Trial: Tennessee Evolution Case: A Complete Stenographic Report of the Famous Court Test of the Tennessee Anti-Evolution Act, at Dayton, July 10-21, 1925, including Speeches and Arguments of Attorneys* (Cincinnati, 1925).

but the Tennessee Supreme Court on a legal technicality later overruled the fine imposed by Judge Raulston, while upholding the constitutionality of the act. The chief prosecutor accepted the higher court's advice against "prolonging the life of this bizarre case" and dropped the indictment, leaving the defense without a conviction to appeal. Thus, the constitutional issues never reached the Federal courts. With more prescience than he knew, Bryan had described the coming trial as a "duel to the death"; on July 26, 1925, a few days after it closed, he died suddenly.[86]

After Dayton, the rest was anticlimax. No other leader could assume Bryan's mantle, but out of the welter of fundamentalist groups two arose to give the movement momentary focus. In 1926 the Supreme Kingdom brought from obscurity Edward Young Clarke, who now championed Old Testament science. "In another two years," Clarke proclaimed, ". . . there will be lighted in this country countless bonfires, devouring those damnable and detestable books on evolution." Business flourished for a while, but the movement dissolved quickly with the disclosure that Clarke was up to his old game, taking cuts from initiation fees.[87]

More important were the Bible Crusaders, founded in 1926 by George W. Washburn, a Northern millionaire wintering in Florida. Under the leadership of the Reverend T. T. Martin, author of *Hell and the High Schools,* the Bible Crusaders organized mobile bands of the faithful to descend upon state legislators. In Mississippi they secured another antievolution law in 1926, and while they lost in Louisiana to an opposition led by President Thomas D. Boyd of Louisiana State University, they carried their point in part by an order from the state superintendent of education to remove objectionable sections from biology textbooks. In North Carolina, where Presidents Poteat of Wake Forest and Harry Woodburn Chase of the state university had successfully mobilized opposition in 1925, the antievolutionists failed again in 1927. One final victory came in Arkansas where they used the initiative and referendum to circumvent a reluctant legislature. On November

---

[86] The cause of death remains unknown, but probably was diabetes melitis aggravated by fatigue and heat. Levine, *Defender of the Faith,* 356–57.

[87] Shipley, *War on Modern Science,* 45–50; Furniss, *Fundamentalist Controversy,* 61–66.

6, 1928, when the sovereign people of Arkansas delivered their electoral vote to Al Smith, they also voted Darwin out of their public schools.[88]

With that the fundamentalist fury had spent itself. Soon other problems, of life itself rather than its remote origins, preoccupied people and their legislatures. The very victories of the fundamentalists were self-defeating, for they served to publicize heresy. The states that experienced the fiercest controversies became prime markets for books on evolution, and the movement tended to arouse a liberal opinion to the defense of academic freedom.[89] The fundamentalists, usually defeated, suffered the complacent scorn of what Howard Odum called the "learned ignoranti," whose contempt for simple folk often provoked the intolerance of the opposition.[90] As the fundamentalist crusade faded into the background from which it had emerged, a new tone began to appear. Most apparent, said its historian, "was a note of petulance and, occasionally, the feeling of martyrdom."[91] Militant fundamentalists, hopeless of victory in this world, sought refuge in the otherworldly premillennial sects, which grew rapidly in the 1930's.[92]

"We are not half so religious, anyway, as reported," a Montgomery editor declared in 1928. "Our pulpit to-day is very much less of a furnace and more of a sun-parlor than ever before. Unquestionably the big dogs of the Christian church in the South tend more and more to expound ethics and ignore miracles."[93] "The war between science and religion is over," a commentator could write in 1936. "[T]he proponents of religion have been defeated; they have been worse than defeated; they have been converted."[94] There were, to be sure, signs of retreat from conventional attitudes on such matters as dancing, movies, drinking, or

[88] Furniss, *Fundamentalist Controversy*, 57–61, 94–95.   [89] *Ibid.*, 179.

[90] Howard W. Odum, "The Duel to the Death," in *Social Forces*, IV (1925–1926), 189–94.

[91] Furniss, *Fundamentalist Controversy*, 180.

[92] Haskell M. Miller, "Religion in the South," in *Christendom: A Quarterly Review* (Chicago), VII (1942), 309.

[93] Grover C. Hall, "We Southerners," in *Scribner's Magazine*, LXXXIII (1928), 83, 86.

[94] Cleanth Brooks, "The Christianity of Modernism," in *American Review* (New York), VI (1935–1936), 435.

mixed bathing, but there was still little evidence in the older denominations of a pell-mell retreat from orthodoxy as distinguished from fundamentalist militancy.[95]

To a greater degree than the Ku Klux Klan, the fundamentalist crusade contributed to a revival of sectionalism in the 1920's. It stirred the Middle West to some extent, but unlike the Klan it scored victories only in the South—and the Scopes trial took place in the South. It was probably the trial more than any other single event that alerted the masses of Southerners to the growing image of the benighted South that contrasted so starkly with the special images they had of themselves as democratic agrarians, as progressive builders and developers, as "the most American" of all Americans, as defenders of the faith. By contrast they read or heard about journalists' accounts of the circus in Dayton, accounts which ranged from disappointment to ridicule, from Joseph Wood Krutch's judgment that his native Tennessee suffered chiefly from the timidity of its intellectuals and legislators to H. L. Mencken's columns cataloguing "morons," "hill-billies," "peasants," and the "degraded nonsense which country preachers are ramming and hammering into yokel skulls."[96] Metropolitan journalists in general found it difficult to treat the subject seriously.

The image of the benighted South by then was already virtually complete, and it had been rapidly compounded out of multiple elements within less than a decade. After some years of relative neglect, the South had suddenly become an object of concern to every publicist in the country. "It is difficult now," one Southerner wrote in 1924, "to find on the news stands a serious magazine without an article on some phase of life below the Potomac, or a discussion of one idea or another that has come out of the South."[97] After the sectional campaign against the "cotton

[95] Miller, "Religion in the South," loc. cit., 314–15; Edwin M. Poteat, "Religion in the South," in Couch (ed.), Culture in the South, 261–62; Willie Snow Ethridge, "Liberalism Stirs Southern Churches," in Christian Century, XLIX (1932), 317–19; Carter Brooke Jones, "The South Turns Its Back on Methodism," in The American Mercury (New York), XXVIII (1933), 452–54.

[96] Joseph Wood Krutch, "Tennessee's Dilemma," in Nation, CXXI (1925), 110; New York Times, July 17, 1925. For a selection of Mencken's reports from Dayton see Jerry R. Tompkins (ed.), D-Days at Dayton: Reflections on the Scopes Trial (Baton Rouge, 1965), 35–54.

[97] Gerald W. Johnson, "Critical Attitudes North and South," in Social Forces, II (1923–1924), 575.

THE
DOUBLE-DEALER
A NATIONAL MAGAZINE
FROM THE SOUTH
PUBLISHED AT NEW ORLEANS

Vol. II   July, 1921   No. 7

THE HOUSE
By
Arthur Symons

THE ECSTASY
By
Haniel Long

VERSE
By
John McClure

Grace Hazard
Conkling

Etc.

25
Cents

$2.50
Yearly

Cover of *The Double Dealer*, July, 1921

William Jennings Bryan at the Venetian Pool, Coral Gables, Florida, January 14, 1925

Dayton, Tennessee, 1925

Traffic Jam, Northwest Field, Burkburnett, Texas, 1918

demagogues" in 1918, it seemed that torrents of abuse deluged the region. In fact, the infidels had crossed the Mason-Dixon Line to set up headquarters in Baltimore, where H. L. Mencken developed the game of South-baiting into a national pastime at which he had no peer. The sage of Baltimore was, of course, a man of catholic taste in his choice of targets. From the aristocratic heights of *The Smart Set, The American Mercury,* and the *Sunpapers,* he chronicled the doings of *Homo Boobiens* everywhere but with a special solicitude for the Southern breed. Beginning with the barrenness of Southern culture, he went on from there. It was "amazing to contemplate so vast a vacuity," he wrote. "One thinks of the interstellar spaces, of the colossal reaches of the now mythical ether. . . . It would be impossible in all history to match so complete a drying-up of civilization." [98] Once there had been an aristocratic culture of the finest sort, his version of Southern history went, but the Civil War left it bleeding and helpless, and opened the way to the "lower orders" who had no more comprehension of the ancient faith "than any other like group of former plumbers, corner grocers, and crossroads lawyers." They were "eighth-rate men wearing the stolen coats of dead first-rate men. . . ." Their taste was "a compound of elemental fears and appetites—chiefly the fear of ideas, and the appetite for security." [99]

But the root of evil, and Mencken's special target, was the peculiar clerical tyranny of "Baptist and Methodist barbarism" below the Potomac. "No bolder attempt to set up a theocracy was ever made in this world", he announced with typical hyperbole, "and none ever had behind it a more implacable fanaticism." [100] The clerical will to power, culminating in the fundamentalist excesses of the 1920's, also acquired a peculiarly Menckenesque history stemming from the Civil War. The preachers, so numerous among the slackers and cowards, found themselves after the war the only survivors with any pretense of training. With little competition from the cultivated remnants of the Confederacy, they

[98] Henry L. Mencken, "The Sahara of the Bozart," in *Prejudices: Second Series* (New York, 1920), 136–37. For the treatment of Mencken I am indebted to William J. Bosch, "Henry L. Mencken's Image of the South" (unpublished seminar paper, University of North Carolina, 1963).

[99] H. L. Mencken, "Morning Song in C: Major," in *The Reviewer,* II (1921–1922), 3.

[100] H. L. Mencken, Editorial, in *American Mercury,* VII (1926), 32.

soon established a religious, cultural, and political hegemony. Ignorant even in their superiority to the "yowling yokels" over whom they held sway, they spread abroad their own obsessive fear of intelligence, the inquiring mind, and individual freedom. The climax came with prohibition, over which they gloated "in their remote Methodist Tabernacles as they gloat over a hanging." Intoxicated by that success, the Baptist and Methodist shamans of the "Bible Belt" proceeded next "to put down learning by the law." [101]

Professional defenders of the South served only to publicize their tormentor and tickle his risibilities. When Mencken wrote that he knew of New Yorkers who had been in Cochin China, Kafiristan, Paraguay, Somaliland, and even West Virginia, "but not one who has ever penetrated the miasmatic jungles of Arkansas," a former governor retorted with an unconsciously ludicrous letter that offered statistics on agricultural production and a "two volume deluxe illustrated set of *The Folklore of Arkansas*" as evidence of the state's cultural achievements.[102] Mencken merrily gathered and published some of the prize castigations. "By cutting through six inches of fat and drilling through four inches of bone," Fred Sullens raged in the Jackson *Daily News*, "one might possibly find Mencken's brain cavity—but he would not find any grey matter there." "This modern Attila!" Clio Harper cried in the *Arkansas Writer*, "This brachycephalous Caliban! The Black Knight of Slander! An intellectual Houyhnhnm!" [103] All of which only inspired Mencken to further triumphs of calumny against the South, the "bunghole of the United States, a cesspool of Baptists, a miasma of Methodism, snake-charmers, phoney real-estate operators, and syphilitic evangelists." [104]

If Mencken was the guiding genius in creating the new image of

---

[101] H. L. Mencken, *Notes on Democracy* (New York, 1926), 38; H. L. Mencken, Editorial, in *American Mercury*, III (1924), 421; Bosch, "Henry L. Mencken's Image of the South," 16–21. See also H. L. Mencken, "Der Wille zur Macht," in Baltimore *Evening Sun*, September 10, 1928, p. 15.

[102] H. L. Mencken, "Famine," in Baltimore *Evening Sun*, January 19, 1931, p. 17; Charles Hillman Brough, "Response to Mencken," *ibid.*, March 5, 1931, p. 19.

[103] Quoted in *Menckeniana: A Schimpflexicon* (New York, 1928), 43, 128.

[104] Quoted in Charles Angoff, *H. L. Mencken: A Portrait from Memory* (New York, 1956), 126.

the benighted South, he was by no means its only architect. While he wielded his meat-axe in Baltimore men of differing temperaments wielded their own special weapons. Two books published in 1924 significantly elaborated the developing pattern. In *The Southern Oligarchy* William Henry Skaggs, a young progressive mayor of Talladega in the 1880's, a leading Alabama Populist in the 1890's, and subsequently a professional lecturer based in New York, set forth what he called in his subtitle, *An Appeal in Behalf of the Silent Masses of Our Country Against the Despotic Rule of the Few*.[105] In tones of righteous indignation, redolent more of abolition than of Mencken, and in lengthy catalogues of Southern deficiencies like the later fashion of regional sociologists, Skaggs handed down one of the most thoroughgoing indictments of Southern villainy ever published; he detailed at length political corruption, landlordism, illiteracy, peonage, lynch law, partisan and racial proscription, and a hundred other delinquencies. He "brought to his work wide reading, a formidable array of statistics and praiseworthy industry," one reviewer thought. "If he could have presented his material temperately he might have written a great and much needed book." As it was, the book poured vitriol so "liberally upon . . . the Southern princes, potentates and powers" that its impact was dissipated.[106]

In contrast to Skaggs, Frank Tannenbaum, a young professor at Columbia University, brought together in *Darker Phases of the South* a slender collection of essays that constituted one of the most perceptive social critiques of the times, more balanced and charitable but all the more damaging for its restraint. In successive chapters he considered the Ku Klux Klan, mill villages, prisons, tenancy, and the race question. The social setting for the development of the Klan he described as one of "[h]istorical antecedents, passions, prejudices, hates, loves, ennui, the need for constructing a defense mechanism against one's own sins, the attempt to preserve as static what is becoming dynamic, the craving for drama-

[105] William H. Skaggs, *The Southern Oligarchy: An Appeal in Behalf of the Silent Masses of Our Country Against the Despotic Rule of the Few* (New York, 1924).

[106] Silas Bent, "'Criminal Lawlessness' of the American South," in *New York Times Book Review*, November 23, 1924, p. 3; Walter C. Stevens, "Southern Problems," in New York *Evening Post Literary Review*, October 11, 1924, p. 6.

tization and excitement in the face of a dull and monotonous existence. . . ." [107] Boasting of its racial purity, the South had segregated its Anglo-Saxons and buried them in its mill villages. Southern penology offered one long story of brutality, neglect, and indifference. The rural South suffered "a white plague—cotton," the source of poverty, much of the race problem, soil exhaustion, laziness, peonage, ignorance, and a dozen other shortcomings.

The grave social issues that troubled Skaggs and Tannenbaum became perennial topics. One Southern abomination after another was ground through the journalistic mills: Ku Kluxry, the Scopes trial, child labor, lynching, hookworm, pellagra. In 1921 came the first among many revolting disclosures of peonage when one John Williams murdered eleven Negroes on his farm near Covington, Georgia, in the vain attempt to destroy evidence that he was holding them to work out fines he had paid to the county.[108] The same year Governor Hugh M. Dorsey listed nearly two dozen other known cases of peonage in the state; still other examples came to light in Georgia and elsewhere, usually uncovered by Federal investigation.[109] In 1929 Orlando Kay Armstrong, former dean of journalism at the University of Florida, spread out an exposé of forced labor in Florida lumber and turpentine camps. Under a state law of 1919 any person who promised or contracted labor and refused to perform it after an advance was guilty of a misdemeanor. "It is safe to say that most of those men sentenced to the gang on the basis of the 1919 law were recruited under misrepresentation," Armstrong wrote, "were forced to work under intolerable conditions, were caught and held under warrants that asserted a misdemeanor under an unconstitutional law, and sentenced without a semblance of a defense—for fraud!" [110]

[107] Tannenbaum, *Darker Phases of the South*, 5.

[108] Steed, *Georgia: Unfinished State*, 278–85.

[109] *Statement from Governor Hugh M. Dorsey as to the Negro in Georgia*, [5–9]; Wilson, *Forced Labor in the United States*, 102–107.

[110] New York *World*, November 24, 1929. In 1944 the Supreme Court ruled the law unconstitutional after it had struck down a similar debt law in Georgia in 1942. For other disclosures of peonage see Walter Wilson, "Cotton Peonage," in *New Republic*, LXIX (1931–1932), 130–32; Sasha Small, "Uncle Sam Indicts Peonage Boss," in *The Crisis*, XLVIII (1941), 219, 226; Stetson Kennedy, *Southern Exposure* (New York, 1946), 50–56; "Reminiscences of J. Waties Waring" (Oral History Research Office), 202.

Along with the peonage disclosures came revelations that convict leasing and penal brutalities persisted. In 1923 the New York *World* uncovered the story of Martin Tabert, a North Dakotan whipped to death in a lumber camp to which he had been leased after failure to pay a fine for hopping a train in Tallahassee. It was a story of greed, mendacity, brutality, and murder, which included a sheriff who rounded up hoboes for a side payment of twenty dollars each from the lumber company and who returned money sent to cover Tabert's fine, a malignant whipping boss, and a company doctor who reported death from malaria. The *World's* exposé inspired further revelations by Florida papers, a legislative investigation, and mass indignation that brought about the elimination of convict leasing and the establishment of a model penitentiary at Raiford.[111] In 1919 Alabama's Governor Kilby had started an extensive program of prison reform, but he failed to abolish the leasing system which he branded "a relic of barbarism . . . a form of human slavery." In 1923, while indignation was running high over Martin Tabert, representatives of the League of Women Voters and the Jaycees uncovered evidence of beatings, sweatboxes, and other brutalities in convict mining camps. With the help of other civic clubs and the United Mine Workers they launched a long fight against the leasing system. In 1926 the disclosure of several murders in the mining camps added force to their campaign and finally led to the abolition of convict leasing in 1928.[112]

Even the disappearance of this "worse than Siberian system" from the Southern scene did not eliminate the persistent evils that characterized it.[113] Prisoners confined to penitentiaries, penal farms, road camps, and county chain gangs still suffered neglect and brutality, documented repeatedly but with particular effect in two books of 1932: John L. Spivak's *Georgia Nigger,* a fictionalized revelation of chain gang tortures based upon actual investigation, and Robert Elliott Burns's *I Am a Fugitive from a Georgia*

[111] New York *World*, March 29–31, April 1–20, 1923; Hilda Jane Zimmerman, "Penal Systems and Penal Reforms in the South since the Civil War" (Ph.D. dissertation, University of North Carolina, 1947), 387–90.

[112] Zimmerman, "Penal Systems and Penal Reforms in the South," 391–400.

[113] Fletcher M. Green, "Some Aspects of the Southern Convict Lease System in the Southern States," in Fletcher M. Green (ed.), *Essays in Southern History Presented to Joseph Gregoire de Roulhac Hamilton* . . . (Chapel Hill, 1949), 122.

Chain Gang! [114] There was, of course, another side of the pattern—the persistent efforts of public-spirited citizens, women's and civic clubs, and trained criminologists to gain slow and hard-won reforms in all the states. In 1939 Walter Wilson, author of *Forced Labor in the United States,* returned "to the chain gang country" for a personal survey "and discovered that since 1933, and chiefly since 1936, the South has made definite progress toward a more humane and intelligent penal system." But the pattern was still spotty; prison camps ranged from portable steel cages to the neat brick and wooden buildings found in the road camps of North Carolina and Virginia. [115]

In the South itself a band of native muckrakers inadvertently added their own bit to the adverse image of the South. Among them Gerald W. Johnson of the Greensboro *Daily News* wielded perhaps the most trenchant style both before and after he ascended unto the right hand of Mencken on the Baltimore *Sun.* "Too much has been said of the South's need for 'sympathetic criticism,' " he argued. It needed no sympathy for bigotry, intolerance, superstition, and prejudice, but "criticism that is ruthless toward those things—bitter towards them, furiously against them—and sympathetic only with its idealism, with its loyalty, with its courage and its inflexible determination." [116] But he found grounds for hope. The Ku Klux Klan had served the useful function of showing the South "that its lack of keen and relentless self-criticism, the only effective social prophylaxis, has laid it open to invasion by any sort of disease." [117] Even Mencken had to admit that new rebels hatched out day by day. "The very heat of the fundamentalist and Ku Klux fury is hurrying them out of the egg." [118]

[114] Both New York, 1932. See also Tannenbaum, *Darker Phases of the South,* 74–115; and Jesse F. Steiner and Roy M. Brown, *The North Carolina Chain Gang: A Study of County Convict Road Work* (Chapel Hill, 1927) .

[115] Walter Wilson, "Twilight of the Chain Gang," in *Nation,* CL (1940) , 44–46; Blake McKelvey, "A Half Century of Southern Penal Exploitations," in *Social Forces,* XIII (1934–1935) , 112–23; Zimmerman, "Penal Systems and Penal Reforms in the South," 410–24, 429–32, and *passim.*

[116] Johnson, "Critical Attitudes North and South," *loc. cit.,* 578–79.

[117] Gerald W. Johnson, "Fourteen Equestrian Statues of Colonel Simmons," in *The Reviewer,* IV (1923–1924) , 22.

[118] H. L. Mencken, "The South Rebels Again," in Chicago *Tribune,* December 7, 1924, reprinted in Robert McHugh (ed.) , *The Bathtub Hoax and Other Blasts & Bravadoes from the Chicago Tribune* (New York, 1958) , 254.

Indeed the incubator of the 1920's produced a numerous brood of Southern journalists who found a simple formula for fame. Assaults on the barbarities of the benighted South became for that decade a high road to the Pulitzer Prize. Three awards went for attacks on the Klan: in 1923 to the Memphis *Commercial Appeal* under C. P. J. Mooney; in 1926 to the Columbus *Enquirer-Sun* under Julian and Julia Collier Harris; and in 1928 to Grover C. Hall of the Montgomery *Advertiser*. Editorial prizes went in 1925 to Robert Lathan for an editorial in the Charleston *News and Courier* on the decline of Southern statesmanship and in 1929 to Louis I. Jaffe of the Norfolk *Virginian-Pilot* for a campaign against lynching.[119] These were only the most celebrated among the iconoclasts who had shaken off the inclination "to accept traditional romanticism as established fact." [120]

Well before the end of the 1920's most of the elements in a new image of the benighted South had fallen into place, and its influence ran deep. A philosopher and critic, Eliseo Vivas, who later had a change of heart, wrote of what at the time he took the South to be: "it was the Bible belt, the land of the Klu [*sic*] Klux Klan, and I knew, knew with the confidence of a good 'liberal', that nothing but fundamentalism and intolerance could come out of the South. No one around me would have thought it possible to challenge this proposition. It was part of a system of *idées reçues* that constituted the then reigning orthodoxy of my group." [121] "The legend of the barbarism of the South," Donald Davidson wrote in the 1930's, ". . . for a good many years . . . governed the approach of the metropolitan East to the phenomena of life in the so called hinterland. . . . The South—so the tale runs—is a region full of little else but lynchings, shootings, chain-gangs, poor whites, Ku Kluxers, hookworm, pellagra, and a few decayed patricians whose chief intent is to deprive the uncontaminated, spiritual-singing Negro of his life and liberty. But what is more

[119] John Hohenberg (ed.), *The Pulitzer Prize Story: News Stories, Editorials, Cartoons, and Pictures from the Pulitzer Prize Collection at Columbia University* (New York, 1959), 336–37, 348–49.

[120] Gerald W. Johnson, "Southern Image-Breakers," in *Virginia Quarterly Review*, IV (1928), 513. See also Dabney, *Liberalism in the South*, 397–413; Mims, *Advancing South*, 172–96; Gerald W. Johnson, "Journalism below the Potomac," in *American Mercury*, IX (1926), 77–82.

[121] Eliseo Vivas, "Mi Ritrovai per Una Selva Oscura," in *Sewanee Review* (Sewanee, Tenn.), LXVII (1959), 561.

shocking, it is inhabited by believers in God, who pass anti-evolution laws; and more shocking still, it is in thought and deed studiously backward and anti-progressive. . . . Over such pictures the East stormed, or shed crocodile tears, in the clever nineteen-twenties." [122] Davidson's summary was almost definitively complete. About the only things omitted were the tyrannies of prohibition and the mill village.

The growing image of the benighted South provoked a variety of responses. The more defensive Southerners developed their own peculiar image of the benighted North, disfigured by slums, overrun by mongrel hordes, and fatally corrupted by gangsters and their henchmen.[123] Many editors retaliated by tossing stink bombs, chiefly toward Baltimore. But the pattern was broader than that. In Nashville and New York, Fugitive poets pondered the scene. "Was it possible," they asked, "that nobody in the South knew how to reply to a vulgar rhetorician like H. L. Mencken?" [124] Was it not possible that the Southern heritage represented deeper values than either the New South's boosters or its facile critics? And so for a small group of poets and their allies the trauma of Mencken and Dayton redirected thought toward the viable elements of tradition, toward a new consciousness of their Southernness that found outlet in 1930 with John Crowe Ransom's *God Without Thunder,* an unorthodox defense of orthodoxy in terms of religious myth, and the "Agrarian Manifesto," *I'll Take My Stand.*[125]

Others rallied to the defense of their native region in terms not of tradition but of progress. At Vanderbilt, whence the traditionalists held forth, Chancellor Kirkland announced that the answer to Dayton would be the building of new laboratories, and Edwin Mims, head of the English department, hastily assembled a volume on *The Advancing South* that revealed "a veritable war of

[122] Donald Davidson, *The Attack on Leviathan* (Chapel Hill, 1938) , 156.

[123] Griffith and Talmadge, *Georgia Journalism,* 148, offers some examples.

[124] Donald Davidson, *Southern Writers in the Modern World* (Athens, Ga. 1958) , 37.

[125] Louise Cowan, "The Fugitive Poets in Relation to the South," in *Shenandoah* (Lexington, Va.) , VI (Summer, 1955) , 6–7; Randall Stewart, "The Relationship between Fugitives and Agrarians," in *Mississippi Quarterly* (State College, Miss.) , XIII (1960) , 56–58.

liberation" by "constantly enlarging groups of liberal leaders who are fighting against the conservatism, the sensitiveness to criticism, the lack of freedom that have too long impeded Southern progress." [126] In Richmond, Virginius Dabney of the *Times-Dispatch* compiled in his book, *Liberalism in the South,* the genealogy of a Southern liberalism stemming from Thomas Jefferson. In academic groves the critical spirit was emerging in the application of social science research to the problems of the region. Soon the quest for a viable tradition, the realistic and searching inquiries into Southern life would produce the varied themes of regionalism in the 1930's.

Behind it all was the flux of change. "The difficulty of understanding the South is increased by the very variety of conditions in this section," Donald Davidson wrote in 1928. "Here, by and large, are the mingled phenomena of a period of transition. . . . Hence the South is thickly sown with contradictions." [127] The image of the benighted South obscured certain important aspects of Southern diversity and dynamism behind a pattern of monolithic cussedness. Attention focused on the Scopes trial, lynchings, the Klan, and clerical influence in politics, a Southern-born historian noted. "But the awakening of millions of white men and women from a condition little short of serfdom, and their transformation into useful, intelligent, industrious citizens excites no more than passing comment." [128] Together with that process came a subtle assimilation to broader patterns. "Today the South reads Associated Press dispatches, national advertising, and listens each night to national radio programs," Will Alexander observed in the late 1920's. "The heroes of southern boys today are General Pershing, Ford, Edison, and Lindbergh. The Prince Albert coat

[126] Edwin Mims, *Chancellor Kirkland of Vanderbilt* (Nashville, 1940), 268, 316; Mims, *Advancing South,* vii. Gerald Johnson, however, counted only 123 individual liberals in the book and challenged its optimistic tone: "One cannot avoid the feeling that the shattering battleaxe might do more real good to the South than the trumpet and cymbals, seductively as they are used." Review in the *Virginia Quarterly Review,* II (1926), 596.

[127] Donald Davidson, "First Fruits of Dayton: The Intellectual Evolution in Dixie," in *Forum* (Philadelphia), LXXIX (1928), 897.

[128] T. J. Wertenbaker, "Up from the Depths: How the Civil War Brought Emancipation from Slavery not only to the Slaves Themselves but to the Poor Whites as Well," in *Princeton Alumni Weekly,* XXIX (1928–1929), 453–54.

and the goatee have entirely disappeared. The Rotarian, true to the national type, is the voice of the community. What the nation thinks the South is largely thinking; that America is God's country and Calvin Coolidge is a great president".[129] In the new pluralistic society of the South, the savage ideal became another Lost Cause. For better or for worse, the genie of modernism was out of the bottle and it could not be lured back.

[129] Quoted in White, *Rope and Faggot*, 192.

CHAPTER VII

THE METAMORPHOSIS
OF PROGRESSIVISM

ANY serious effort to understand Southern politics in the 1920's must begin with a recognition that the progressive urge did not disappear but was transformed through greater emphasis upon certain of its tendencies and the distortion of others. The impulse for "good government" and public services remained strong; the impulse for reform somehow turned into a drive for moral righteousness and conformity. The Ku Klux Klan and the fundamentalist movement inherited the reform spirit but channeled it into new crusades. Such anomalies of the New South "must be viewed in the light of catastrophic changes which have attended the inevitable adjustment of the old regime to a new order which is as yet inchoate and undetermined," a contemporary Alabaman suggested. "Thus it is that what appears in the present-day South as moral or religious fanaticism . . . is in reality political radicalism. It represents a misguided social revolution." [1]

Prohibition was one example of this, a direct outgrowth of the reform spirit, but increasingly associated with the narrow intolerance of the times. Southern leaders had played decisive parts in the drive for a prohibition amendment, which the American Anti-Saloon League endorsed at its "Jubilee Convention" in November, 1913. That December, when a procession of some four thousand White Ribboners marched on the Capitol to present resolutions for a constitutional amendment, Senator Morris Sheppard of Texas and Representative Richmond P. Hobson of Alabama, hero of Santiago Bay, hastened to introduce them. In the 1914 Congressional campaigns the legislative committee of the

[1] Clarence Cason, *90° in the Shade* (Chapel Hill, 1935), 57–58.

Anti-Saloon League, chaired by Southern Methodist Bishop James M. Cannon, Jr., sent out thousands of speakers, and in 1915 Hobson left Congress to stump the nation for prohibition. In the 1916 election another drive produced the necessary two-thirds majority in both houses of Congress. The wartime spirit of sacrifice, the need to use grain for food, and wartime hostility to German-American brewers added strength to the cause. Senator Sheppard's resolution, reintroduced three months after the declaration of war, became the basis for the Eighteenth Amendment, with only minor changes.[2]

The margin for prohibition was everywhere great, but Southerners in both houses of Congress gave heavier support than the members as a whole and in the lower house supplied the necessary margin for passage.[3] Even that did not fully measure Southern sentiment. Some prohibitionists opposed the amendment out of deference to states' rights; "the wisest and best way to handle the whisky question is through the exercise of the police power of the state," said Alabama's Thomas J. Heflin.[4] Approved by Congress in December, 1917, the amendment quickly passed four Southern legislatures the following month and made a steady progression until Nebraska completed the ratification on January 16, 1919.[5] On the effective date one year later the corpse of John Barleycorn arrived at Norfolk, Virginia, on a special train. While His Satanic Majesty trailed along in deep mourning and anguish, twenty pallbearers carried an enormous coffin to a tabernacle where evangelist Billy Sunday preached the funeral oration to more than ten thousand people.[6]

But John Barleycorn, like Joe Hill, never died. The noble experiment, like the mock obsequies in Norfolk, assumed the character of symbolic action, nowhere more transparently than in the South, a major stronghold of prohibition and a major pro-

---

[2] Merz, *Dry Decade*, 15–42; Andrew Sinclair, *Prohibition: The Era of Excess* (Boston, 1962), 124–25, 154–64; Duke, "Political Career of Morris Sheppard," 215–52.

[3] Merz, *Dry Decade*, 309–14, presents the vote by states. In the Senate the South provided 24 of the 64 votes for and only 5 of the 20 against; in the House 92 of 282 for and 23 of 128 against.

[4] *Congressional Record*, 65 Cong., 2 Sess., 457.   [5] Merz, *Dry Decade*, 315–16.

[6] Dabney, *Dry Messiah*, 133–34.

ducer of illicit booze. The Eighteenth Amendment had not bee. effective eight months before authorities found a still with a daily capacity of 130 gallons near Austin, Texas, on a farm belonging to Morris Sheppard, the "Father of National Prohibition." [7] Saloons and beer parlors operated more or less openly in Bryan's Miami; rumrunners provided the Bahamas enough revenue to get the islands out of debt and furnish a surplus for civic improvements.[8] A reporter at the Houston Democratic convention in 1928 found "northern wets and southern drys fraternizing over the bottle and debating the relative enlivening properties of Johnny Walker and White Mule." [9] Indeed, the technique of extracting white mule enabled many a farmer to escape the burden of rural distress. In 1928 moonshiners in Eastern North Carolina were said to be undermining the rural labor supply by paying workers eight dollars a day to run their stills.[10] The prohibitionists, a Charleston editor said, "by causing the people to instruct themselves in liquor-making have done more to promote the liquor business than they had gained in the fight against it in fifty years." But Charleston tastes had been utterly debased by the "descent from madeira and cognac to Hell Hole Swamp 'corn' ".[11]

Of the illicit liquor plants seized in 1925 more than 70 per cent were in the Southern states; Georgia was the banner state of the entire union.[12] "If there is, as a product of sincere conviction and honest observance of the law, such a reality as the 'Dry South,' " a South Carolina editor remarked, "I have yet to see it, and I have lived and journeyed over it for more than 40 years." [13]

In close sequence to prohibition, the cause of woman suffrage

[7] New York *Times*, August 12, 1920.

[8] Hanna, *Florida's Golden Sands*, 348–49; Weigall, *Boom in Florida*, 154–55; R. A. Haynes to William Jennings Bryan, January 6, 1922; Peoria (Ill.) *Star*, March 7, 1923, clipping, both in Bryan Papers.

[9] Arthur Sears Henning of the Chicago *Tribune*, dispatch from Houston, July 1, 1928, unidentified clipping in Josephus Daniels Papers.

[10] Remarks of Federal Judge I. M. Meekins to grand jury in Elizabeth City, N.C., Wilmington *Morning Star*, October 23, 1928, clipping in Simmons Papers.

[11] William Watts Ball to Thomas F. McDow, August 19, 1933; and Ball to B. P. Adams, April 2, 1935, in Ball Papers.

[12] William Cabell Bruce, "The Eighteenth Amendment," in *Proceedings of the University of Virginia Institute of Public Affairs* (Charlottesville), I (mimeographed, 1927), 207.

[13] R. Charlton Wright, editor of Columbia *Record*, quoted in *ibid.*

achieved its ultimate triumph with the Nineteenth Amendment in 1920. The organized movement had invaded the South in the 1880's and 1890's, but remained relatively dormant until the progressive era.[14] The movement's appeal to human rights, its promise of political virtue and social justice all harmonized with progressive instincts, but potent taboos left it generally weaker in the South than elsewhere: the "chivalric" concern for keeping woman in her domestic "sphere" and out of the "mire of politics"[15] (but not out of the factories and fields, as suffragettes noted) ; the fear that woman suffrage would in some way legitimize Negro suffrage; crafty arguments that the enfranchisement of Negro women would bring Negroes back into politics; and a standard charge that radical leaders directed the movement from the "outside." Disputes over states' rights, with overtones of race, divided the woman suffrage movement itself. Some of the Southern adherents, who preferred state action, seceded from the national group, but most remained and supported the Federal amendment.[16]

As the national movement approached its goal, Southern legislatures gradually yielded. Arkansas in 1917 and Texas in 1918 admitted women to their primaries; Oklahoma adopted statewide woman suffrage in 1918; Tennessee granted a Presidential and municipal suffrage in 1919; Kentucky offered Presidential suffrage in 1920.[17] However, only five Southern states contributed to the ratification of the Nineteenth Amendment: Texas, Oklahoma, Arkansas, Kentucky, and Tennessee. The rest rejected it or failed

[14] The movement's growth may be pursued in Antoinette Elizabeth Taylor, *A Short History of the Woman Suffrage Movement in Tennessee* (Nashville, 1943) , and in numerous articles by Professor Taylor in state historical quarterlies and in the *Journal of Southern History.*

[15] W. H. Laney, quoted in A. Elizabeth Taylor, "The Woman Suffrage Movement in Arkansas," *Arkansas Historical Quarterly,* XV (1956) , 16.

[16] Eleanor Flexner, *Century of Struggle: The Woman's Rights Movement in the United States* (Cambridge, Mass., 1959) , 303–304; Aileen S. Kraditor, *The Ideas of the Woman Suffrage Movement, 1890–1920* (New York, 1965) , 163–218.

[17] Taylor, "Woman Suffrage Movement in Arkansas," *loc. cit.,* 16; A. Elizabeth Taylor, "The Woman Suffrage Movement in Texas," *Journal of Southern History,* XVII (1951) , 210; Carrie Chapman Catt and Nettie Rogers Shuler, *Woman Suffrage and Politics: The Inner Story of the Suffrage Movement* (New York, 1923) , 305–13, 340 n; Nell Battle Lewis in Raleigh *News and Observer,* May 3, 1925.

to act, but the Tennessee legislature had the distinction of completing ratification in August, 1920, amid a fierce struggle during which the embattled champions of masculine prerogative fled the state in a vain effort to prevent a quorum.[18]

Soon afterward the woman suffrage organizations gave way to the new League of Women Voters and women began to participate in political organizations. Georgia, which had rejected the suffrage amendment, sent the first woman to the United States Senate with the nominal interim appointment of Rebecca Latimer Felton in 1922.[19] During the 1920's women served in every Southern legislature except that of Louisiana, and through their organizations subtly but effectively advanced the progressive concepts of social justice and public welfare.[20]

But neither the suffragettes nor the paladins of morality represented the dominant themes of state politics in the 1920's. It was the period of triumph for the "Atlanta spirit," the age of progress. "Conservatism," Maristan Chapman wrote in 1922, "has become a term of reproach." [21] But now the term progress appeared in a different context, more closely associated with the urban middle class, with chambers of commerce and civic clubs. It carried the meaning of efficiency and development rather than reform. The "progressive" community was one that had good government, great churches, improved schools, industry, business, real estate booms. The reform urge diminished; the anticorporation drive all but disappeared. Agrarian battle cries against big business and Wall Street faded with the passing of the Farmers' Union and the rise of "business" methods in agriculture. "A steady barrage of propaganda issues through newspapers, magazines, radios, billboards, and other agencies . . . to the effect that progress must be

[18] Taylor, *Short History of the Woman Suffrage Movement in Tennessee*, 19–22; Catt and Shuler, *Woman Suffrage and Politics*, 422–62.

[19] John E. Talmadge, "The Seating of the First Woman in the United States Senate," *Georgia Review*, X (1956), 168–73.

[20] Anne Firor Scott, "After Suffrage: Southern Women in the Twenties," in *Journal of Southern History*, XXX (1964), 298–318. See also Anne Firor Scott, "The New Woman in the New South," *South Atlantic Quarterly*, LXI (1962), 471–83; Mims, *Advancing South*, 224–56; and Dabney, *Liberalism in the South*, 371–79.

[21] Chapman, "South's Spiritual Grace," *loc. cit.*, 292.

maintained," Lyle H. Lanier wrote in 1930. "It requires little sagacity to discover that progress usually turns out to mean business." [22]

The outlook of what may be called the business progressivism of the 1920's emphasized the old progressive themes of public services and efficiency. "The business class political philosophy of the new South is broad enough to include programs of highway improvement, educational expansion, and health regulation," political scientist H. C. Nixon wrote. "But it does not embrace any comprehensive challenge to laissez faire ideas in the sphere of relationship between capital and labor, and the section is lagging in social support of such matters as effective child labor regulation and compensation legislation." On the theme of efficiency, Nixon found "an influence toward change in the meaning and spirit of government as against the rather political and theoretical conceptions of the country lawyer. . . . [B]usiness methods in government tend to get the right of way over the ideas of checks and balances, and governmental functions tend to expand in response to social or business needs." [23]

These neo-whiggish trends were manifested in a sequence of business progressive governors, a relatively colorless group on the whole, respectable and circumspect in demeanor, "constructive" in their approach to public problems. They stormed no citadels of entrenched "privilege," but carried forward the new public services that had gained acceptance in the progressive era, especially good roads and schools. Good government was for them almost a fetish. Sometimes this attitude took the rhetorical form of political cries for economy, but upon closer examination economy usually meant the elimination of waste rather than the reduction of services.

"Economy," "reduce taxes," "abolish useless offices and reduce salaries," Alabama's Governor Thomas E. Kilby cautioned as he

[22] Lyle H. Lanier, "A Critique of the Philosophy of Progress," in Twelve Southerners, *I'll Take My Stand: The South and the Agrarian Tradition* (New York, 1930), 123.

[23] H. C. Nixon, "The Changing Political Philosophy of the South," in *Annals of the American Academy of Political and Social Science*, CLIII (1931), 248. See also George Fort Milton, "Also There Is Politics," in Couch (ed.), *Culture in the South*, 121–25.

left office in 1923: "These cries may be popular, but . . . they contain a positive and serious menace to the welfare of Alabama and particularly to her educational and health interests and to the unfortunate and helpless wards of the State. Not only do they threaten those interests but they threaten our agricultural and industrial interests as well." [24] That same year the *Southern Textile Bulletin* of Charlotte ran an editorial headed "Expenditures Produce Prosperity." "The man who is educated," it argued, "starts new enterprises or engages in new lines of business that pay taxes." Good roads opened new markets for farmers and improved economic conditions.[25] The state, in short, could spend its way into prosperity!

North Carolina stood at the forefront of the movement, and it was more in the 1920's than in the prewar progressive era that the state won its reputation as "the Wisconsin of the South." [26] During this period it developed under President Harry Woodburn Chase the leading state university in the South, embarked upon the most ambitious highway program in the area, and expanded its activities in education, public health, and welfare. In the active expansion of public services North Carolina set the pace for other Southern states and ranked high in the nation at large. Between 1913 and 1930, taxes in North Carolina rose by 554 per cent, a rate of increase exceeded only by Delaware. Between 1915 and 1925 state expenditures grew by 847 per cent, a rate of increase greater than any other state's, nearly thrice the national average. Between 1920 and 1930 the total state bonded debt soared from $13,300,000 to $178,265,000.[27]

The expansion began in the administration of Governor Thomas W. Bickett, 1917–1921. That period saw, among other things, the creation of a state public welfare system in 1917, the

[24] Alabama *House Journal*, 1923, I, 137.

[25] *Southern Textile Bulletin* (Charlotte, N.C.), XXV (September 13, 1923), 20.

[26] Nell Battle Lewis in Raleigh *News and Observer*, January 20, 1924.

[27] Clarence Heer, "Taxation and Public Finance," in President's Research Committee on Social Trends, *Recent Social Trends in the United States* (New York, 1934), II, 1338–39; Benjamin U. Ratchford, "The Public Finances of North Carolina since 1920," in *South Atlantic Quarterly*, XXVII (1928), 1; Hugh T. Lefler and Albert Ray Newsome, *North Carolina: The History of a Southern State* (Chapel Hill, 1954), 570.

state guarantee of a six-month school term in 1919, and rising expenditures for salaries, public health, and state institutions.[28] In 1919–1920 Bickett sponsored tax reforms that segregated the general property tax for local and county uses, extended the income tax to income from property, and doubled property assessments. Increased income taxes brought receipts in 1926 almost twelve times those of 1920. Inheritance, license, privilege, franchise, automobile, and gasoline levies all rose during the 1920's.[29]

It was Cameron Morrison, however, who in the face of postwar depression led the greatest expansion. In his 1921 inaugural address Morrison called upon the forces of "progressive democracy" to "war for righteousness with the reactionary and unprogressive forces of our State." [30] Overwhelmed by his crusade for highways and schools, the "reactionary" forces faltered, and in 1921 the legislature voted a $50,000,000 bond issue for highways, nearly $6,750,000 for educational and charitable institutions, and $5,000,000 for school buildings. Before the end of Morrison's term it had approved a total of $65,000,000 in highway bonds, $33,718,-700 in expenditures for benevolent and educational institutions, and had more than doubled public school expenditures.[31]

Frank Page, chairman of the highway commission after his return from wartime road engineering in France, kept the program free from political manipulation and graft.[32] By 1928 the

[28] Santford Martin (comp.) and Robert B. House (ed.), *Public Letters and Papers of Thomas Walter Bickett, Governor of North Carolina, 1917–1921* (Raleigh, 1923), v.

[29] Charles Chilton Pearson, "The Present Status of Tax Reform in North Carolina," in *South Atlantic Quarterly*, XVIII (1919), 289–98; Francis Nash, "Revaluation and Taxation in North Carolina," *ibid.*, XIX (1920), 289–301; and Ratchford, "Public Finances of North Carolina since 1920," *loc. cit.*, 1–15.

[30] William H. Richardson (comp.) and David Leroy Corbitt (ed.), *Public Papers and Letters of Cameron Morrison, Governor of North Carolina, 1921–1925* (Raleigh, 1927), 14.

[31] Heriot Clarkson, "A Biographical Sketch of Cameron Morrison," *ibid.*, xxxiii–xxxiv, xl, xli; Willard B. Gatewood, Jr., *Eugene Clyde Brooks, Educator and Public Servant* (Durham, 1960), 155. See also French Strother, "North Carolina's Dreams Come True," in *World's Work*, XLIX (1924–1925), 72–85; William H. Richardson, "North Carolina's Recent Progress," in *American Review of Reviews*, LXVIII (1923), 621–31; and Gerald W. Johnson, "North Carolina in a New Phase," in *Current History and Forum*, XXVII (1927–1928), 843–48.

[32] Josephus Daniels to Marshall Ballard, August 20, 1928, in Daniels Papers.

highway commission had spent $153,546,677, developed a state system of 7,551 miles, of which 3,738 were hard-surfaced, and reclaimed "lost provinces" behind the mountains and the coastal swamps.[33] North Carolina's act of faith was rewarded by increased revenues from gasoline and automobile taxes, enough to cover the cost.[34] The state ended the decade second only to Texas in the South and eleventh in the nation in the total mileage of surfaced roads.[35]

Morrison's successor, Angus W. McLean, successful banker and lawyer of Lumberton, promised the state "an administration characterized by efficiency, economy, and rational progress." He carried forward, even expanded, Morrison's programs, and added an executive budget system and other measures to insure fiscal regularity in the growing activities of the state.[36]

North Carolina was most consistent in the support of progressive programs, but other states moved in the same direction. In Alabama Thomas E. Kilby inaugurated business progressivism during his term as governor, 1919–1923. After a fallow period under Governor William W. "Plain Bill" Brandon, who promised not to increase taxes but continued the Kilby programs, Alabama entered another period of change under the dynamic "little Colonel," Bibb Graves. Elected in 1926, he presided over another forward surge in the last years of prosperity, promoted a $25,000,-000 road bond issue, a State Bridge Corporation, expansion of public schools and colleges, additional support to hospitals, charitable institutions, public health services, child welfare, and further development of the port of Mobile. Additional revenues came

---

[33] Cecil Kenneth Brown, *The State Highway System of North Carolina* (Chapel Hill, 1931), 207, 210; Hobbs, *North Carolina: Economic and Social*, 165. The figures are for January 1, 1928; "hard-surfaced" means concrete, asphalt-concrete, sand-asphalt, and macadam.

[34] Clarence Heer, "The Cost of Government in North Carolina," in *Taxation in North Carolina*, University of North Carolina Extension Bulletin XII (November, 1932), 21.

[35] U.S. Bureau of the Census, *Statistical Abstract of the United States*, 1932, p. 351.

[36] David Leroy Corbitt (ed.), *Public Papers and Letters of Angus Wilton McLean, Governor of North Carolina, 1925–1929* (Raleigh, 1931), 4; Mary Evelyn Underwood, "Angus Wilton McLean, Governor of North Carolina, 1925–1929" (Ph.D. dissertation, University of North Carolina, 1962).

from levies on public utilities, coal and iron operators, tobacco, and a larger franchise tax on corporations. Grover C. Hall, editor of the Montgomery *Advertiser,* summed it up with the comment that "Bibb Graves makes a good governor, but an expensive one." [37]

A striking contrast to "Bibb the Builder" was Austin Peay, governor of Tennessee from 1923 to 1927. A small-town lawyer from Clarksville, the very epitome of colorlessness, he announced for governor in 1922, leaving to others "any pleasure of fine periods in the campaign," and confining himself "to bare facts and statistics, with which my mind is accustomed to deal." After the fashion of business progressive rhetoric, he called for a "clean, honest and courageous Legislature, working under sane direction to repeal laws and reduce government in Tennessee!" [38] Victorious in the Democratic primary, he defeated Alfred Taylor, the state's last Republican governor, in the general election. Alf Taylor cracked jokes and told stories about his dog, "Old Limber." Peay stuck to his statistics and his paradoxical exposition of the state's need for tax reform, reduced expenditures, highways, and schools.[39]

Swept into office by a comfortable majority, Peay summoned expert assistance at his own expense to develop a reorganization bill that regrouped sixty-four scattered agencies under eight commissioners directly responsible to the governor. The resulting efficiency, it was claimed, saved the state over a million dollars in two years.[40] The state tax system was overhauled, with reductions in land taxes but a new privilege tax on corporate earnings, a gasoline tax for highways, and a tobacco tax for an eight-month school term in rural schools. Despite his appeal for the reduction

[37] Moore, *History of Alabama and Her People,* I, 954–62; William E. Gilbert, "Bibb Graves as a Progressive Governor, 1927–1930," in *Alabama Review,* X (1957) , 15–30.

[38] Quoted in T. H. Alexander, "Austin Peay; A Brief Biography," in Mrs. Sallie H. Peay (ed.) , *Austin Peay, Governor of Tennessee, 1923–1925, 1925–1927, 1927–1929: A Collection of State Papers and Public Addresses* (Kingsport, Tenn., 1929) , xxi.

[39] *Ibid.,* xxii–xxiii.

[40] *Ibid.,* xxiv; Arthur Eugene Buck, *Reorganization of State Governments in the United States* (New York, 1938) , 219–24.

of government, Peay directed an expansion of the road system and public schools that cost far more than the savings from his reorganization. By 1929 Tennessee had five thousand miles of surfaced roads in its state system, in contrast to about five hundred in 1920, and all but thirteen of its ninety-five counties had an eight-month school term in contrast to fewer than one third with more than five months in 1920.[41]

The reluctant progressive may be typified by the young Harry Flood Byrd, governor of Virginia, 1926–1930, whose strong points were efficiency and the promotion of industry. He was an FFV, newspaper publisher, apple grower, a self-made businessman, heir to the old "machine"; in one revealing speech he compared government to business: the governor as president of the corporation, the legislature as board of directors, the taxpayers as stockholders, the dividends paid in public services. "The administration of government," he said, "should be efficiently conducted along the lines of well organized business enterprises, but the benefits of government cannot be measured by the yardstick of the dollar. The cost . . . has enormously increased . . . and the need of improved efficiency becomes daily more important." However, a state government should not extend beyond the discharge of functions "public necessities have imposed on it"; "undue extension" of governmental activities should be avoided.[42]

True to his philosophy, Byrd, like Peay, carried through an extensive reorganization. He merged a total of more than one hundred bureaus, boards, and commissions into fourteen departments and inaugurated a short ballot. These reforms, Byrd wrote, were "progressive and modern, and yet they were approved by popular vote in one of the oldest and most conservative of the States."[43] Ironically, but not incidentally, the resultant central-

[41] U.S. Bureau of the Census, *Statistical Abstract of the United States*, 1931, p. 396; Milton, "Also There Is Politics," *loc. cit.*, 121; Stanley J. Folmsbee, Robert E. Curlew, and Enoch L. Mitchell, *History of Tennessee* (New York, 1960), II, 254.

[42] French Strother, "Youth Takes the Helm in Virginia," in *World's Work*, LIII (1926–1927), 140–42; Harry Flood Byrd, "Reorganization of State and County Governments," in *Proceedings of the University of Virginia Institute of Public Affairs*, I, 8, 10.

[43] Arthur Eugene Buck, "A Survey of Virginia State and County Governments," in *Social Forces*, VI (1927–1928), 448–52; Harry F. Byrd, "Better Government at Lower Cost," in *Yale Review* (New Haven), XXII (1932–1933), 72–73.

ization served to strengthen an oligarchy headed by Byrd.[44] Tax reforms segregated land taxes to local uses and reduced taxes on capital investments, and Governor Byrd personally embarked on a campaign to attract industries to the state.[45] At the same time he warred on the oil companies for their alleged price discrimination against Virginia, blocked telephone rate increases, and brought insurance rates under state regulation.[46]

Byrd's long memory of Virginia's struggle with state debts after the Civil War made fiscal prudence the central theme of his political career.[47] His active opposition to a state bond issue for roads in 1923, which was defeated, placed him in the forefront of contenders for the governorship. But he, too, was swept along by the demand for highways, supported a pay-as-you-go system in his campaign, championed tax increases that made possible annual state expenditures of fourteen million dollars on highways, and gave the state nearly five thousand miles of surfaced roads by 1929.[48]

In other states business progressive programs enjoyed greater or lesser success. The slogan of Arkansas' Governor John E. Martineau, "Better Roads and Better Schools," could stand almost as a motto for the decade.[49] In some states progressive governors failed to win the support of state legislatures: Pat Neff and Dan Moody in Texas, for example, and Lamartine G. Hardman in Georgia.[50] In Kentucky suspicious voters in 1924 rejected a bond issue of

[44] The Byrd machine is anatomized in V. O. Key, *Southern Politics in State and Nation* (New York, 1949), 20–22. One state historian, however, says that under Byrd "it ceased to be a machine and became a union of leaders." Hamilton J. Eckenrode, "Virginia since 1865: 1865–1945, A Political History," Typescript in Virginia State Library, 414. Carter Glass, former opponent of the "machine," allied with Byrd after 1925.

[45] Byrd, "Better Government at Lower Cost," *loc. cit.*, 70–71; Harry F. Byrd, "Virginia through the Eyes of Her Governor," in *Scribner's Magazine*, LXXXIII (1928), 687; Abram P. Staples, "Operation of the Segregation Tax in Virginia," in *Manufacturers' Record* XCIX (January 15, 1931), 48.

[46] Virginius Dabney, "Governor Byrd of Virginia," in *Nation*, CXXVI (1928), 632–34.

[47] *Time* (New York), LXXX (August 17, 1962), 14.

[48] Eckenrode, "Virginia since 1865," 386–90, 399; U.S. Bureau of the Census, *Statistical Abstract of the United States*, 1931, pp. 396–98; Strother, "Youth Takes the Helm in Virginia," 143–44.

[49] Thomas, *Arkansas and Its People*, I, 304.

[50] Richardson, *Texas: The Lone Star State*, 314–16, 318–21; E. Merton Coulter, *Georgia: A Short History* (Chapel Hill, 1960), 435.

$75,000,000 intended chiefly for highways and schools.[51] In others there was no strong central figure in the development of policies, but everywhere efficiency and expansion were significant themes in state government. South Carolina politics, a state historian wrote, experienced an era of "vacuity," but the state started the decade with the lowest public school expenditure per pupil in the country and ended it with the highest rate of increase. It climaxed the decade with a $65,000,000 highway bond issue in 1929.[52]

State after state took up administrative and tax reforms, and despite pious talk about economy, state and local governments projected ambitious programs on every hand. Every Southern state adopted some kind of budget system between 1918 and 1929, and general reorganizations were advanced or at least partially adopted in all.[53]

The rate of increase in both state revenues and debt in the South far exceeded that for the rest of the nation.[54] The search for revenue led to a variety of new sources. Gasoline taxes, nonexistent before 1919, produced some $129,000,000 for Southern states in 1929, about one third of their revenues. By 1929 eight Southern states had adopted the income tax, and between 1923 and 1928 revenues from that source rose 137 per cent. Of nine states with a sales tax in 1932, five were Southeastern; of thirteen having cigarette and tobacco taxes, nine were Southeastern. Local government revenues meanwhile benefited from the rise in property assessments and from the segregation of property taxes to local purposes.[55]

[51] McVey, Gates Open Slowly, 209–11.

[52] David Duncan Wallace, South Carolina: A Short History, 1520–1948 (Chapel Hill, 1951), 679–80; United States Office of Education, Biennial Survey of Education in the United States, 1928–1930 (Washington, 1932), II, 28–30.

[53] James W. Martin, Southern State and Local Finance Trends and the War (Nashville and Lexington, Ky., 1945), 55–56; Buck, Reorganization of State Governments in the United States, 45, 50, 76–78, 106–107, 115, 143, 184–85, 196, 213, 219–24, 232–33, 240–46.

[54] Total revenues of Southern states jumped 128 per cent between 1922 and 1932 while those in the rest of the nation rose only 79 per cent; total state and local debt per capita climbed 110 per cent in contrast to 65 per cent for the nation as a whole. Martin, Southern State and Local Finance Trends and the War, 86–99. These figures include West Virginia, exclusion of which would show a slightly higher rate of increase for the South in each case.

[55] Ibid., 6; Hoover and Ratchford, Economic Resources and Policies of the South, 196–97; Odum, Southern Regions of the United States, 127, 360; Heer, "Taxation

There can be no question that the South strained its resources more than any other region to support and expand public services. In both the ratio of tax collections to private income and in per capita state indebtedness the region ranked ahead of all others by 1930. Yet despite the increases the South lagged behind in revenues. In 1932 the general revenues of state and local governments in the thirteen Southern states amounted to $33.26 per capita, less than half the $69.63 per capita for the non-South.[56]

In the development of state government, a student of Tennessee finances identified three main stages before 1929: the "debt" period to 1904, during which debt service dominated expenditures; the school period to about 1921; and the highway period thereafter.[57] This was characteristic of other states. "Good roads," Francis B. Simkins wrote, "became the third god in the trinity of Southern progress"—after industry and education.[58] By 1930 highways and education far outdistanced other state functions. Every Southern state channeled at least 60 per cent of its expenditures to those two purposes and all but three more than 70 per cent. Some idea of the priorities of business progressivism, however, may be derived from the fact that in all but the same three states, the expenditures for highways exceeded those for education.[59]

A rough measure of governmental expansion may be drawn from state handbooks prepared for legislators. The North Carolina manuals indicate that state administrative departments, boards, and commissions increased from twelve in 1913 to twenty in 1921 to sixty in 1929, and state educational, charitable, and correctional institutions from eighteen to twenty-one to thirty-two. New agencies in the 1920's dealt with conservation, promotion of industry,

---

and Public Finance," *loc. cit.*, 1375; James W. Martin, "Industrial Changes and Taxation Problems in the Southern States," in *Annals of the American Academy of Political and Social Science,* CLIII (1931) , 233.

[56] Odum, *Southern Regions of the United States,* 125, 127, 210; Hoover and Ratchford, *Economic Resources and Policies of the South,* 198. The revenue figures omit Federal aid to the states.

[57] Charles P. White, "Problems of Taxation in Tennessee," in *Annals of the American Academy of Political and Social Science,* CLIII (1931) , 238.

[58] Simkins, *History of the South,* 474.

[59] Paul R. Mort, *State Support for Public Education* (New York, 1936) , 274. The three states were Alabama, Florida, and Mississippi.

budgetary and fiscal programs, child welfare, the licensing of various professions, and crime detection, among other things.[60]

The business progressive philosophy, to be sure, had its limitations. Race relations were assumed to be a settled issue. The economic problems of the underprivileged, farm tenants and factory workers, were not its problems; their remedy would come, if at all, through economic growth. In turn, the expansion of services created new problems: the political influence of the new agencies, the highway departments, the road contractors, the trucking lobbies, the teachers' associations. Soon, in the depression, the debts came due with severe repercussions on the extended state and local governments. State services required a pressure and strain to accomplish what was a matter of course in wealthier states. But the continuing development of public services at least partially confirmed the old maxim that yesterday's radicalism is today's moderation. The business progressive philosophy had deep roots in both the progressive movement and the "New South" creed of economic development. It was shaken by the depression and the New Deal, but its policies of expansion and efficiency became by and large the norm of Southern statecraft in the decades that followed.

The period of business progressivism afforded a brief interlude in plebeian politics between its earlier heyday and the new era of Huey Long, Eugene Talmadge, and the later Bilbo. Except for Lee M. Russell, Bilbo's successor in Mississippi, 1920–1924, one can search the list of Southern governors from 1920 to 1928 without finding any who might be labeled classic redneck leaders unless they were Sidney J. Catts of Florida, who left office in 1921, or Miriam Ferguson of Texas who served two years, 1925–1927, as proxy for a husband who had been disqualified from holding state office. At Washington the national image of Southern buffoonery was kept alive by such figures as Senators Tom Watson, Cole Blease, and Thomas J. Heflin, and Representative Willie D. Upshaw, Atlanta's supreme Klansman and prohibitionist.

Mississippi remained the one state most continuously bedeviled

---

[60] Robert D. W. Connor (ed.), *A Manual of North Carolina, 1913* (Raleigh, 1913); Robert D. W. Connor (ed.), *North Carolina Manual, 1921* (Raleigh, 1921); Albert Ray Newsome (ed.), *North Carolina Manual, 1929* (Raleigh, 1929).

by the unabashed style of redneck politics. Highlights in the administration of Lee M. Russell, Bilbo's handpicked successor, were a series of antitrust suits that drove a group of old-line fire insurance companies out of the state and closed down Ford dealers for six weeks, and a seduction suit by the governor's former secretary. The charges were completely discredited, and Bilbo served a brief sentence for contempt in refusing to testify at Russell's trial, allegedly to avoid cross-examination for having engineered the charges against his erstwhile ally. Upon his release, Bilbo announced his candidacy for governor from the jail steps, but lost the 1923 primary. He won again in 1927 but dragged out his second term in fruitless wrangles with the legislature over proposals for highways, education, and other programs.[61] His outstanding achievement was to purge forty-five faculty members and a number of administrators from the state colleges in 1931. "Boys," he told the reporters after that, "we have just hung up a new record." [62] Mississippi, H. L. Mencken concluded after an exhaustive statistical survey that year, was "the worst American state." [63]

Oklahoma in the early 1920's saw a brief resurgence of Southwestern radicalism.[64] The twin problems of the farmers' depres-

[61] Kirwan, Revolt of the Rednecks, 292–306; Clarence E. Cason, "The Mississippi Imbroglio," in Virginia Quarterly Review, VII (1931), 229–40; Frederick W. Jones, "Mississippi's Great Fight for Honor and Prosperity," in Outlook, CXXXI (1922), 209–11; Raymond Gram Swing, "Bilbo the Rabble-Rouser," in Nation, CXL (1935), 123–25; Theodore G. Bilbo, Take Your Choice: Separation or Mongrelization (Poplarville, Miss., 1947), 323–24.

[62] Louis Cochran, "Mussolini of Mississippi," in Outlook and Independent, CLVIII (1931), 203–205, 222–23; James Allen Cabaniss, A History of the University of Mississippi (University, Miss., 1950), 158–67; John K. Bettersworth, People's College: A History of Mississippi State University (University, Ala., 1953), 291–97. The figure of forty-five faculty members comes from A. Wigfall Green, The Man Bilbo (Baton Rouge, 1963), 76. Other sources give as many as 179. John B. Hudson, "The Spoils System Enters College: Governor Bilbo and Higher Education in Mississippi," in New Republic, LXIV (1930), 123–25.

[63] Charles Angoff and Henry L. Mencken, "The Worst American State," in American Mercury, XXIV (1931), 1–16, 175–88, 355–71.

[64] The following account is drawn from Scales, "Political History of Oklahoma," 227–71; Ameringer, If You Don't Weaken, 373–90; and Ernest T. Bynum, Personal Recollections of Ex-Governor Walton: The Inside Story of His Public Career (Oklahoma City, 1924). See also Gilbert C. Fite, "The Nonpartisan League in Oklahoma," in Chronicles of Oklahoma, XXIV (1946), 146–57.

sion and organized labor's struggle with open shop movements brought their leaders together in September, 1921, at Shawnee to form the Farmer-Labor Reconstruction League of Oklahoma. A year later the league adopted a platform with many elements of agrarian socialism and turned up as its leader the handsome mayor of Oklahoma City, Jack C. Walton—former traveling salesman, hotel clerk, railroader, and army officer, a man of brilliantly erratic temperament. Walton campaigned in the extravagant fashion of the plebeian exhorters, added to their style the use of string bands, and became for many a legendary champion of the people —while he left the systematic presentation of a program to the Reconstruction League. Walton carried the Democratic primary by a comfortable plurality and in the general election led an uneasy alliance of regular Democrats, Socialists, Republican farmers, and Wilson-haters to victory over the "right-thinking people." The inauguration turned into a glorious revel that inspired reporters to themes of the roughhewn frontier: "cowpunchers, Indians, share-croppers and miners tottering through the streets of Okahoma City, gorged with slabs of whole steers, cross-sections of titanic hogs, Paul Bunyan helpings of sizzling mutton. And all on the house." [65]

Disillusionment followed soon. In the end Walton's program was a truncated version of business progressivism. The farmers got a minimal program of co-operative, warehouse, and inspection laws. The legislature voted more than a million dollars for "weak school aid," passed the first free textbook law (with an antievolution proviso) , and added $3,000,000 in highway revenues by a one-cent gasoline tax. Walton's vacillation, his indolence, his carelessness with money, pardons, and personal favors, his attempts to build a machine and to control state colleges, all contributed to his downfall. The capstone of his follies was the purchase of a new $48,000 governor's mansion with money provided, apparently in all innocence, by oilman E. W. Marland.[66] In August, 1923, Walton tried to bolster his dwindling authority by a bold step—the declaration of martial law, ostensibly to crush Ku Klux terrorism

[65] Ameringer, *If You Don't Weaken*, 378.

[66] John J. Mathews, *Life and Death of an Oilman: The Career of E. W. Marland* (Norman, Okla., 1951) , 140–42.

but largely to divert attention from his own failures. One result was to incur the enmity of the Klan, which he had earlier courted. The state legislature, turned away once by bayonets, met in October, 1923, to impeach and remove Walton on charges ranging from misuse of state funds to general incompetence. A conservative lieutenant governor succeeded him and the ill-matched political alliance that made him disintegrated.

Louisiana had a different experience. In 1920 the old Bull Moose leader, John M. Parker, returned triumphantly to the Democratic party, won its nomination for governor, and guided the state through a period of business progressivism.[67] Parker's program of constitutional and administrative reforms and expansion of schools and highways, however, seemed only to whet the appetite for more. When the state government returned to its wonted complacency after 1924 a number of issues remained open for exploitation by the colorful and vigorous young Huey P. Long, Jr. Born in 1893 in Winn Parish, which had a long record of plebeian insurgency—antisecessionism, populism, and socialism— Long carried the anticorporation rhetoric on into the 1920's.[68] Starting as a door-to-door peddler, the youthful Long used his savings and money borrowed from an older brother to study law for a year at Tulane. He immediately took and passed the bar examination. In 1918, breathing fire at Standard Oil and other corporate interests, he won election to the state Railroad Commission (later the Public Service Commission), where he built a ten-year record of warring against the utilities, got reductions in telephone, electric, gas, railroad, and streetcar rates, and won the right to regulate Standard's Interstate Pipe Line as a common carrier. In 1920 he supported Parker but later denounced him as a tool of the interests for making a "deal" with Standard Oil and other mineral interests to limit a new severance tax to 2 per cent.

In 1924, at the minimum age of thirty, Long entered the race for governor and although he placed third, showed substantial strength in the northern parishes and thereafter cultivated new contacts in the French parishes. In 1928 his time came. Running

[67] Phillips, "Administration of Governor Parker."
[68] Grady McWhiney, "Louisiana Socialists in the Early Twentieth Century: A Study of Rustic Radicalism," in *Journal of Southern History*, XX (1954), 317.

against an incumbent who was plagued by highway scandals and a nondescript congressman who represented the New Orleans "ring," he exploited the issues left behind by Parker. Parker had got Louisiana "out of the mud," but mostly onto improved dirt and gravel roads with a pay-as-you-go program; Long proposed a bond issue and free bridges. Parker had increased outlays for education; Long promised free textbooks. Parker had briefly upset the New Orleans Choctaws; Long again warred on the "ring." Parker had failed to get natural gas for New Orleans or to curtail gas wastage by carbon black plants; Long promised to do both.

His vivid portrayal of a standpat planter-business alliance with the "ring" contrasted sharply with his own folksiness. He "spoke American instead of bombast," said a writer who at first supported him, "and I liked his similes and metaphors derived from the barnyard and the cornfield." [69] Moreover, his antic wit was compounded with a genius for melodramatic eloquence. "Evangeline is not the only one who has waited here in disappointment," he told a Cajun audience at the Evangeline Oak. "Where are the schools that you have waited for your children to have that have never come? Where are the roads and the highways that you spent your money to build . . . ? Where are the institutions to care for the sick and disabled? Evangeline wept bitter tears in her disappointment. . . . Your tears in this country, around this oak, have lasted for generations. Give me the chance to dry the tears of those who still weep here." [70]

A consequence of the pent-up demand for public services was that the achievement of things accomplished with decorum in other states assumed the form of class struggle in Louisiana and provoked a vituperative hostility on both sides. But the program that Long put through the 1928 legislature was essentially that of a Cam Morrison or an Austin Peay: a $30,000,000 bond issue for roads and bridges, free textbooks financed by an increased severance tax, higher appropriations for state charitable institutions and schools, cheap natural gas for New Orleans. Increased services

[69] Hamilton Basso, "Huey Long and His Background," in *Harper's Magazine*, CLXX (1934–1935), 664.

[70] Quoted in Hodding Carter, "Huey Long: American Dictator," in Isabel Leighton (ed.), *The Aspirin Age* (New York, 1949), 349.

in Louisiana, as elsewhere, required increased revenues; but Long's demand for an occupational tax of five cents a barrel on refined crude oil touched a sensitive pocketbook nerve, and his crude attempts to coerce legislators and newspapermen added to the hostility.

To rid themselves once and for all of this upstart menace the opposition in 1929 got an impeachment on multiple charges of misconduct that included one never-proven accusation that he sought the assassination of an opposition senator. But the effort backfired with shattering effect. Long got fifteen of the thirty-nine senators to sign a round robin stating that they would not vote to convict; the necessary two-thirds vote was therefore impossible. "I used to try to get things done by saying 'please,'" Long said grimly after the adjournment. "That didn't work and now I am a dynamiter. I dynamite 'em out of my path." Before his untimely death six years later he had demolished for all time the old patterns of Louisiana politics and sent tremors of apprehension through the body politic of the nation.[71]

In the national interlude of Republican "normalcy" Southern Congressmen returned to their familiar minority role. The Congressional Democrats were mostly Southerners and remained under Southern leadership: Claude Kitchin of North Carolina, Finis J. Garrett of Tennessee, and John Nance Garner of Texas successively as minority leaders in the House, and Oscar W. Underwood of Alabama and Joseph T. Robinson of Arkansas in the Senate. They represented a party dispirited by defeat and a region isolated by stubborn sectional issues, divided from the West on agriculutral policy and set at odds with the Democratic East by nativist and fundamentalist credos. Senator Thomas J. Walsh, Montana Democrat and a Catholic, lamented "the evident impossibility of any Northern or Western man securing the floor leadership," and decried even more strongly the Ku Klux Klan, "the

---

[71] Huey P. Long, *Every Man a King: The Autobiography of Huey P. Long* (New Orleans, 1933). See also Harnett T. Kane, *Louisiana Hayride: The American Rehearsal for Dictatorship, 1928–1940* (New York, 1941), 36–87; Allen P. Sindler, *Huey Long's Louisiana: State Politics, 1920–1952* (Baltimore, 1956), 45–67; Arthur M. Schlesinger, Jr., *The Age of Roosevelt: The Politics of Upheaval* (Cambridge, Mass., 1960), 42–52; T. Harry Williams, "The Gentleman from Louisiana: Demagogue or Democrat," in *Journal of Southern History*, XXVI (1960), 3–22.

product of the South" with "its center there." In a letter to Bryan he wrote: "The people of the North and West are not going to entrust the destinies of this country to a party, the dominant influence in which springs from a section in which are generally harbored the spirit of intolerance and persecution that disgraced the 16th, 17th, and 18th centuries." [72]

As the decade advanced, an image of Southern political ineptitude unfolded in the Southern press. The South "has today virtually no national program and virtually no national leadership," Robert Lathan of the Charleston *News and Courier* wrote on election day, 1924. "What is it contributing today in the way of political thought? What political leaders has it who possess weight or authority beyond their own States? What constructive policies are its people ready to fight for with the brains and zeal that made them a power in the old days?" [73] Other writers echoed his idea of retreat from the golden age. One reason was the one-party system. "There is no progress without opposition," Douglas Southall Freeman wrote in the Richmond *News Leader*, "and no opposition without dissent. Virginia has long been in danger of political stagnation." [74] Another reason was the irrelevance of the issues. White supremacy was "not a cause upon which to rear an enduring structure of national political leadership," said another writer, nor prohibition, nor anti-Catholicism. Out of the processes of change, however, new issues might arise to "fire the imagination." [75]

Southern Congressional leaders of the 1920's fired the imaginations of few, but they continued to manifest certain patterns of progressivism. For one thing, men like Claude Kitchin, John Nance Garner, and Furnifold M. Simmons struggled to maintain the graduated income tax against reductions in the upper brackets

[72] Thomas J. Walsh to William Jennings Bryan, December 20, 1922, in Bryan Papers. See also remarks of Representative Edward Pou of North Carolina on complaints at Southern domination of minority committee assignments, *Congressional Record*, 67 Cong., 1 Sess., 577–78.

[73] Robert Lathan, "The Plight of the South," in Charleston *News and Courier*, November 5, 1924. The editorial won a Pulitzer Prize.

[74] Quoted in Mims, *Advancing South*, 193.

[75] J. N. Aiken, "The South's Lost Leadership," in *Virginia Quarterly Review*, V (1929), 548–50.

sponsored by Secretary of the Treasury Andrew Mellon.[76] For another thing, the zeal for regional development brought increasing support for Federal aid programs—another aspect of the New South expansionism looking northward for capital.[77]

Most important was the Federal road program, begun in 1916 and extended in 1921. State funds would not have been expended in such quantity but for the incentive of Federal funds, North Carolina's highway chairman said, nor so wisely spent but for Federal standards.[78] Hoke Smith's program of aid to vocational education expanded under the George-Reed Act of 1929, co-sponsored by another Georgia senator.[79] Agricultural programs for boll weevil control, tick eradication, and the like grew with Southern backing. The Federal Barge Lines, an outgrowth of the first World War, found strong support in the Mississippi Valley. In 1928, after the disastrous flood of the previous year, Louisiana's Senator Joseph M. Ransdell sponsored a new Flood Control Act which established Federal responsibility for the problem in the Lower Mississippi Valley.[80] Southern ports looked to Federal aid for their development and expansion. Grants-in-aid from the Public Health Service spurred the establishment of county health units and the operation of state health programs. In 1921 a Texas Senator and an Iowa Representative sponsored the Sheppard-Towner Act, which provided Federal aid for state studies in maternal and infant mortality; and in 1930 Senator Ransdell secured an act for a National Institute of Health to promote

[76] Ratner, *American Taxation*, 410–12, 415–16, 420, 424–25, 428; Arnett, *Kitchin and the Wilson War Policies*, 297; Marquis James, *Mr. Garner of Texas* (Indianapolis and New York, 1939), 100–108; Bascom N. Timmons, *Garner of Texas: A Personal History* (New York, 1948), 97–106; Rippy (ed.), *F. M. Simmons: Memoirs and Addresses*, 65; Raleigh *News and Observer*, April 19, 1925.

[77] Nixon, "The Changing Political Philosophy of the South," *loc. cit.*, 247.

[78] Frank Page, quoted in Austin F. MacDonald, *Federal Aid: A Study of the American Subsidy System* (New York, 1928), 115.

[79] Leon E. Cook *et al.*, "The Federal Government and Vocational Education in the South," in W. Carson Ryan, J. Minor Gwynn, and Arnold R. King (eds.), *Secondary Education in the South* (Chapel Hill, 1946), 78.

[80] James E. Edmonds, "A New Era in the Mississippi Watershed," in *Current History and Forum*, XXXI (1930–1931), 953–60; Laborde, *National Southerner*, 145–46. See also John M. Parker, "After the Flood," in *Outlook*, CXLVI (1927), 148–49.

scientific research on diseases.[81] "It is the South which calls for national aid for roads . . . for agriculture and education and for national health legislation," one Southerner observed. "In short, Southern Congressmen are stretching the welfare clause of the Constitution to cover anything tending to develop their section." [82]

The paramount goal of regional development appeared, too, in Southern attitudes toward the Muscle Shoals project. Sale of the uncompleted wartime nitrate and electric plants to private enterprise was consistently and successfully opposed for a decade by Nebraska's Senator George Norris, a champion of public power. Regardless of whether Southern Congressmen consciously yielded principles on issues of states' rights or private enterprise, a student of the controversy asserted, "it is obvious that they followed a policy of expediency designed to bring economic aid to the South." [83] That was their one consistency in the successive positions they took: first, support for governmental operation to produce cheap fertilizer, then for Henry Ford's offer to transform it into a vast industrial complex, then opposition to acquisition by Alabama Power or the American Cyanamid Company (despite substantial farm support for the latter) , and finally support for the Norris idea of governmental development which seemed to promise the most widespread diffusion of cheap power.

Presidential politics, meanwhile, focused on emotional issues that aggravated sectional conflict within the Democratic party. Many thought William Gibbs McAdoo, Wilson's son-in-law and his Secretary of the Treasury, could revive the Wilsonian coalition

[81] MacDonald, *Federal Aid*, 210–36; Laborde, *National Southerner*, 123, 174; "Remarks of Hon. Jos. E. Ransdell on the occasion of the awarding of the medal of the American Institute of Chemists to Dr. Charles H. Herty," New York City, May 7, 1932, in Joseph E. Ransdell Papers (Department of Archives, Louisiana State University) ; Charles H. Herty to Mrs. Joseph Goldberger, April 19, 1928, in Joseph Goldberger Papers (Southern Historical Collection, University of North Carolina) .

[82] Robert Watson Winston, "The North and the South Today," *Current History and Forum*, XXVII (1927–1928) , 246–47. One student professed to see the development of a new states' rights school "whose adherents are drawn chiefly from the wealthy, urban, industrial East," whence came a large proportion of the votes against Federal aid programs. MacDonald, *Federal Aid*, 239–41.

[83] Hubbard, *Origins of the TVA*, 114. The details may be followed in this work, a thoroughgoing and superior monograph.

of South and West with Eastern progressives. In 1922 McAdoo moved to California and announced his availability "to rescue the Government from the hands of the base and selfish interests now dominating it." [84] Wilsonians flocked to his banner and he started well ahead of the field—only to fall victim to the fickle turns of fate. The scandals of the Harding administration should have helped a Progressive Democrat, but McAdoo as a lawyer had represented Edward L. Doheny, one of the beneficiaries of the dubious Elk Hills-Teapot Dome oil leases. McAdoo had no connection with the scandal, but the taint of oil was hurtful. A more damaging issue, however, was that of the Ku Klux Klan, first injected into the campaign by Oscar W. Underwood.

Underwood, who announced his candidacy in August, 1923, boldly invaded the Klan stronghold of Houston that October for a stinging attack on secret organizations of "class and clan." As a moderate wet Underwood was already unacceptable to the shrouded order; he opposed it on principle anyway. But at the same time old Wilsonians and Bryanites regarded him as "too conservative to make the Democratic party thoroughly progressive" and Senate colleagues found him ineffective as floor leader.[85] An opponent in Alabama stated the nub of the opposition: he was "reactionary and wet." [86] He would become a stalking horse for Wall Street and the wets, Bryan predicted, "for the purpose of getting delegates in the south which will be turned over to John W. Davis or some man of his type." [87] A certain corroboration of this view appeared in the private statement of an Underwood leader

[84] Quoted in Lee N. Allen, "The McAdoo Campaign for the Presidential Nomination in 1924," in *Journal of Southern History*, XXIX (1963), 213.

[85] Josephus Daniels to Mark Sullivan, November 11, 1922, in Daniels Papers; Carter Glass to Bernard M. Baruch, September 23, 1921, in Glass Papers; Frank A. Hampton to J. C. Carr, September 30, 1923, in Simmons Papers. Hampton, secretary to Senator Simmons, called Underwood "the Republican Administration's candidate for the Democratic nomination."

[86] Lycurgus Breckinridge Musgrove, quoted in Lee N. Allen, "The 1924 Underwood Campaign in Alabama," *Alabama Review*, IX (1956), 181. "Prohibition and liberalism go hand in hand in the South, where it was always the reactionaries, the hard-shells, the tools of the interests, who fought prohibition," wrote the Tennessean who became McAdoo's publicity director. George Fort Milton, "The South—and 1924," in *Outlook*, CXXXVI (1924), 30.

[87] William Jennings Bryan to George Huddleston, March 30, 1923, in Bryan Papers. See also Huddleston to Bryan, March 23, 1923, *ibid.*

that the campaign objectives were, first, to stop McAdoo, second, to influence the platform, and last, to nominate Underwood if possible.[88]

The Underwood strategy threw the McAdoo progressives, therefore, into awkward coalition with Klansmen. There is no evidence that McAdoo ever cultivated the Klan, but neither did he repudiate it, although he pointedly stated in Georgia his support of the rights guaranteed by the First Amendment.[89] In five Southern states Underwood and McAdoo contested Presidential primaries; in each McAdoo won. In addition he won three other Southern delegations while Underwood gained only the Alabama delegates and a scattering of votes elsewhere, none in the South. Five Southern states backed favorite sons or remained uncommitted.[90] Underwood therefore sought to embarrass McAdoo with the Klan issue and make himself the legatee of Eastern support for New York's Alfred E. Smith and, perhaps, a bloc of Southern votes if the swing developed toward a Southern man.[91]

His strategy was to revive a plank from the 1856 Democratic platform that had condemned Know Nothing attempts to arouse religious and racial dissensions. By convention time all the major candidates supported such a plank, but at the insistence of the Underwood and Smith forces the question became one of censur-

[88] [F. J. Merkling] to R. B. Evins, June 5, 1924, in Oscar W. Underwood Papers (Alabama Department of Archives). No signature appears on the copy, but the letter seems to be a reply to Evins' letter to Merkling, June 3, 1924. Merkling, former secretary to Senator Thomas S. Martin of Virginia, was assistant campaign manager in the Underwood Washington headquarters. Lee N. Allen, "The Underwood Presidential Movement of 1924" (Ph.D. dissertation, University of Pennsylvania, 1955), 49.

[89] Allen, "McAdoo Campaign for the Presidential Nomination in 1924," 218. A Klan official said the statement was completely acceptable to the order.

[90] Allen, "Underwood Presidential Movement of 1924," 213; Official Report of the Proceedings of the Democratic National Convention, 1924 (Indianapolis, [1924]), 338–40. The primaries were contested in Georgia, Texas, Kentucky, Tennessee, and Florida. Allen judged that the Klan "dominated" the vote in Georgia and Texas and exerted a "commanding influence" in the rest. North Carolina, South Carolina, and Oklahoma were the other McAdoo states. McAdoo's opposition, a South Carolinian said, "reflected the views of manufacturers in the upper part of the state and Charleston bankers in the lower part." William E. Gonzales to D. L. Rockwell, May 22, 1924, in William Gibbs McAdoo Papers (Division of Manuscripts, Library of Congress).

[91] [F. J. Merkling] to R. B. Evins, June 5, 1924, in Underwood Papers.

ing the Klan by name.[92] A minority of the platform committee carried the issue to the floor with vociferous support from Madison Square Garden galleries. Andrew C. Erwin, a Georgia delegate, set off a floor demonstration with a denunciation of the Klan, and Bryan defended the majority plank amid strident heckling. It took more courage, Bryan shouted, to fight the Republican party than the Klan, "which is nearly dead and which will soon pass away." The party should not be diverted from its mission, he cried. "Anybody can fight the Ku Klux Klan, but only the Democratic party can stand between the common people and their oppressors in this land." [93] Alabama was the only Southern state that cast its entire vote to "name the Klan," although a scattering of such votes came from six others, and the motion lost by less than one vote.[94]

The long struggle made a two-thirds majority impossible for either McAdoo or Smith, and the embittered convention began a protracted balloting for its nominee.[95] On the 101st ballot Underwood inherited some of the Smith strength, but the Southern delegates turned instead to West Virginia's favorite son, John W. Davis, a native of that state and a New York lawyer, who finally got a badly tarnished nomination on the 103rd ballot. In the campaign that followed, North Carolina's Democratic state chair-

[92] Allen, "Underwood Presidential Movement of 1924," 259.

[93] *Official Report of the Proceedings of the Democratic National Convention,* 1924, p. 306; see also *ibid.,* 279–309. After the Convention Bryan told Heflin "he had never been so humiliated in his life, and he had tears in his eyes as he said it." Werner, *Bryan,* 280.

[94] The result was announced as 543 9/20 to 542 7/20 against the minority plank, but refined by later computation to 546.15 to 541.85 against. *Official Report of the Proceedings of the Democratic National Convention,* 1924, p. 310; New York *Times,* June 30, 1924. Josephus Daniels was among a minority of McAdoo supporters who voted to name the Klan. Daniels to John W. Davis, August 25, 1924, in Daniels Papers.

[95] "Strangely enough," McAdoo wrote later, "a large part of the South was opposed to the majority rule because of the belief that the two-thirds rule was a protection to it against the power of the corrupt bosses." Instead, he declared, the existing rule favored "reaction and evil since New York, New Jersey, Illinois and Massachusetts with their predominant and non-Democratic representation, are able to obstruct the majority." William Gibbs McAdoo to Lewis C. Humphrey, July 17, 1924; McAdoo to Charles E. Russell, July 19, 1924, in McAdoo Papers. His publicity director claimed that banking, railroad, and public utility interests used the Klan and Doheny labels to defeat McAdoo. George Fort Milton to Joseph Pulitzer, June 2, 1944, in George Fort Milton Papers (Division of Manuscripts, Library of Congress).

man noted a "general apathy."[96] But the South maintained its traditional loyalty and, except for Kentucky, cast a solid electoral vote for Davis.[97]

"Had Beelzebub been the Democratic nominee," Gerald Johnson asserted, "the clergy would have been deprived automatically of the privilege of the franchise, and no doubt many of the laity also would have laid down the ballot unused; but . . . the stalwarts would have rallied by tens of thousands and gallantly gone to hell."[98] A choice almost as bad faced the Southern Democrats in the next campaign. When McAdoo withdrew in September, 1927, "for the sake of party unity," the nomination seemed assured for Al Smith, Catholic son of Irish immigrants, New Yorker, Tammanyite, and wet.[99] A Norfolk editor in that pre-election year scented " 'a fiery sweetness in the air'—a faraway smell of flesh burning at the stake . . . a sound of distant buglers calling the faithful to avenge anew the martyrdom of Ridley and Cranmer, presentiments of a great Protestant girding 'to stablysh Christen quietness.' "[100] The trumpets were sounded by Senators Thaddeus H. Caraway of Arkansas and "Tom-Tom" Heflin of Alabama. Heflin tagged Smith the "Roman candidate," charged that a papal banner flew above the American flag on naval vessels (actually a pennant to indicate divine services), attributed to the "Roman hierarchy" opposition to a cotton bill, and professed a fear of Jesuit plots to poison him. "Choose ye this day whom ye will serve," he demanded, "the God of white supremacy or the false god of Roman social equality."[101]

The ominous persistence of intractable issues troubled more prudent leaders. It would be "a fatal mistake for the Democratic Party to nominate a man with the wet record of Governor Smith,"

[96] John G. Dawson to Josephus Daniels, October 20, 1924, in Daniels Papers.

[97] Robinson, *Presidential Vote*, 50–52.

[98] Gerald W. Johnson, "A Tilt with Southern Wind-Mills," in *Virginia Quarterly Review*, I (1925), 184.

[99] McAdoo, quoted in Roy V. Peel and Thomas C. Donnelly, *The 1928 Campaign: An Analysis* (New York, 1931), 10.

[100] Louis I. Jaffe, "The Democracy and Al Smith," in *Virginia Quarterly Review*, III (1927), 324.

[101] Michael Williams, *The Shadow of the Pope* (New York and London, 1932), 174–77; Edmund A. Moore, *A Catholic Runs for President: The Campaign of 1928* (New York, 1956), 81–86.

Josephus Daniels warned; "it would tear us all to pieces in North Carolina." [102] But as the Houston convention drew near, an assortment of favorite sons offered no alternative. The platform called for enforcement of the Eighteenth Amendment and the convention balanced the ticket with Senator Joseph T. Robinson, an Arkansas Protestant and dry, as Smith's running-mate. All remained fairly harmonious until the Happy Warrior provided the occasion, if not the cause, for revolt by stating in his acceptance a personal desire to liberalize the Volstead Prohibition Act and then by selecting for national chairman John J. Raskob, Catholic, wet, General Motors executive, and at least until recently a Republican.[103] "He obviously is acting on the theory that the South is obliged to vote for him regardless of anything or everything," Carter Glass wrote after a conference with Smith, "and that his sole effort . . . must be directed to getting the vote of certain wringing wet Eastern states." [104]

The convention had scarcely disbanded before the rebels began to mobilize. On July 18 in Asheville, North Carolina, more than two thousand delegates met at the summons of Methodist Bishop James Cannon, Jr., and Dr. A. J. Barton, chairman of the Southern Baptist Board of Temperance, to "organize for the defeat of the wet Tammany candidate for president." [105] Smith's candidacy posed "the greatest moral crisis in the nation's history," Methodist Bishop H. M. Du Bose grimly warned the throng, "and perhaps in the history of mankind." The conference denounced Smith's "repudiation" of the Houston platform, his wet record, his selection of Raskob, and his association with Tammany. It called for anti-Smith organizations in every Southern state.[106]

The Protestant clergy and press entered the campaign to an extent unprecedented in American political history.[107] The

---

[102] Josephus Daniels to Mrs. Nelly Root Hall, September 8, 1927; Daniels to R. F. Beasley, September 8, 1928, in Daniels Papers.

[103] Peel and Donnelly, *1928 Campaign*, 11–12, 33–34; Allen, *Only Yesterday*, 302.

[104] Carter Glass to Harry F. Byrd, August 16, 1928, in Glass Papers.

[105] Raleigh *News and Observer*, June 30, 1928.

[106] Asheville *Times*, July 19, 1928.

[107] A poll of Protestant ministers in Alabama showed that two thirds of the clergymen contacted would speak against Smith either directly or indirectly. Not one said he would support or vote for Smith. Birmingham *Post*, June 30, 1928, cited in Sellers, *Prohibition Movement in Alabama*, 199.

Southern Baptist Convention had already resolved in favor of breaking party lines to oppose a wet candidate and four bishops of the Southern Methodist church actively opposed Smith. Counsels of prudence were overridden. "Our church is strictly a religious and in no wise a political body," Bishop Warren A. Candler declared, but the political bishops insisted that it would be "an unthinkable repudiation of our personal responsibility as Christian citizens, and a base betrayal of those who look to us for moral leadership to retire from the field at this critical juncture." [108] Cannon, organizer and chief of the movement, embarked on an intensive speaking tour of Virginia in September, and then rode the circuit through Texas, Tennessee, Mississippi, Alabama, Georgia, Oklahoma, and Arkansas.[109]

The central theme was Demon Rum, but religion crept inexorably into the campaign. "Catholicism is a degenerate type of Christianity," said the Atlanta *Wesleyan Christian Advocate;* "the Catholic Church is as much a political party as it is a religious body," said the Baptist Reverend T. F. Calloway in Thomasville, Georgia. The penultimate was probably reached by Mordecai F. Ham, itinerant revivalist and pastor of Oklahoma City's First Baptist Church. "If you vote for Al Smith you're voting against Christ and you'll all be damned," he told his congregation.[110]

By rumor, speech, and broadside the Roman menace was flaunted across the South. Alabama's Republican national committeeman confessed to circulating 200,000 copies of a circular attacking Catholic doctrines; on October 1 he had 200,000 more on hand.[111] There were accusations, if not proof, of Republican

[108] Miriam Williford, "The South Carolina Democrats in the 1928 Presidential Election" (M.A. thesis, University of North Carolina, 1950), 95, citing Columbia *State,* May 20, 1928; Williams, *Shadow of the Pope,* 193; Alfred M. Pierce, *Giant against the Sky: The Life of Bishop Warren Aiken Candler* (New York, 1948), 212–13; Dabney, *Dry Messiah,* 182. Robert Gilman Smith, *Politics in a Protestant Church: An Account of Some Happenings in the Methodist Episcopal Church, South, during the Hoover-Smith Race of 1928, and of Some Events in 1929. . . .* (Atlanta, 1930), traces Methodist divisions over the campaign. The anti-Smith bishops were Cannon, Edwin D. Mouzon, John M. Moon, and H. M. Du Bose. Collins Denny joined Candler in repudiating political action.

[109] Dabney, *Dry Messiah,* 183.

[110] Both quoted in Williams, *Shadow of the Pope,* 192–93, 208–209.

[111] Stuart C. Deskins, "The Presidential Election of 1928 in North Carolina" (Ph.D. dissertation, University of North Carolina, 1945), 103. There is no evidence that the Democrats undertook any general effort to discredit Herbert Hoover's

contacts with Klan leadership.[112] In any case Republicans co-operated with the new anti-Smith groups that overshadowed their regular organizations. In Virginia C. Bascom Slemp, Republican national committeeman and former secretary to President Coolidge, arranged contributions of $65,000 to the Cannon group.[113]

The rebellion provoked agonized soul-searching, and no little fright, among Democratic regulars.[114] "Can you wonder that I am heartsick," Carter Glass wrote to Josephus Daniels, "and could fervently wish that I were free from the moral constraints of party regularity?" [115] Daniels, who confessed to "walking through deep waters," called it "a bitter pill for me to swallow Al Smith." [116] Like Glass he swallowed hard and sought issues on which to support the nominee. "I have been profoundly stirred by his stand on Jeffersonian hostility against privilege and his earnest stand for the government ownership, development and operation of Muscle Shoals for cheap water power and . . . cheap fertilizer," he declared; one "could not, even by indirection, seem to approve the scandals and corruption of the Republican administration." [117]

The dose was too much for others. Chattanooga editor George Fort Milton's ingrained distrust of Tammany and "boss rule" in general had been reinforced by his experience as McAdoo's pub-

---

Quaker religion. However, there is one interesting document that cites Quaker pacifism, lack of creed and sacraments, opposition to oaths, and leadership in the abolitionist movement, among other things. [Mrs.] Marie Bankhead Owen, "Hoover's Religion" (mimeographed) , in William B. Bankhead Papers.

[112] Elvy E. Callaway, *The Other Side of the South* (Chicago, 1936) , 150–51. Extremely hostile to Hoover for his failure to cultivate the regular Republican organizations and therefore to be used with caution. The remnants of the Klan, of course, did work against Smith. Rice, *Ku Klux Klan in American Politics*, 85–91.

[113] Hathorn, "C. Bascomb Slemp." *loc. cit.*, 262–64.

[114] Representative William B. Bankhead stirred into unaccustomed activity before the general election out of fear that anti-Smith Alabamans would vote the straight Republican ticket. Bankhead to Harry Holcombe, October 8, 1928, and Bankhead to S. W. Williams, October 15, 1928, in Bankhead Papers.

[115] Quoted in Daniels to Josiah W. Bailey, July 21, 1928, and Daniels to Furnifold M. Simmons, July 26, 1928, in Daniels Papers.

[116] Daniels to Josiah W. Bailey, July 21, 1928, *ibid.*

[117] Josephus Daniels to Frank Smethurst, n.d. [1928], *ibid.;* Daniels to C. W. Carter, December 20, 1928, *ibid.* See also exchange between Daniels and Richard Hathaway Edmonds in *Manufacturers' Record*, XCIV (July 5, 1928) , 45–49.

licity director in 1924. In 1928 he bolted to Hoover. The "collateral aspects" of Smith's appeal, "so wet that whiskey is dry by comparison," he wrote, would be "primarily to appetite, and secondarily to every sort of group complex, inferiority attitude, and resentment to American standards and ideals which could be contrived." Smith appealed to aliens, Northern Negroes, Catholics, Jews, and, Milton insisted, to the reactionary vested interests of the East. The "Old America," the America of Jackson, and of Lincoln and Wilson, should rise up in wrath and defeat the "New America" of Al Smith.[118]

Here and there party professionals yielded to the strain. The most prominent apostate was Senator Furnifold M. Simmons, the architect of Democratic supremacy in North Carolina. He would support the state ticket, Simmons affirmed in August, but not Smith; "the party platform has been repudiated, the party rebuilt, the issues reframed and forces of privilege and license are now dominating and controlling the national machinery." [119] "So help me God, I will vote against Al Smith," Tom Heflin declared, "if they read me out of the Democratic Party and drive me from every Senate committee!!!" [120] In Oklahoma Robert L. Owen, in Texas Thomas Love, in Florida Sidney J. Catts bolted to the "Hoovercrats." [121]

But most party leaders remained regular. Theodore Roosevelt "bolted the Republican party that had made him," warned O. Max Gardner, Democratic candidate for governor of North Carolina. "He did what every bolter has to do, come back in sack cloth and ashes." [122] Simmons was the "traitor, the Benedict Arnold, the Judas Iscariot of the North Carolina Democracy," another stalwart declared.[123] At the same time the regulars pleaded for toleration

[118] George Fort Milton to William Gibbs McAdoo, July 31, 1928, in Simmons Papers.

[119] Quoted in Richard L. Watson, Jr., "A Political Leader Bolts—F. M. Simmons in the Presidential Election of 1928," in *North Carolina Historical Review*, XXXVII (1960), 528.

[120] Quoted in Moore, *Catholic Runs for President*, 178.

[121] Lewinson, *Race, Class, and Party*, 167; Herbert J. Doherty, Jr., "Florida and the Presidential Election of 1928," in *Florida Historical Quarterly*, XXVI (1947–1948), 177.

[122] Quoted in Deskins, "Presidential Election of 1928 in North Carolina," 70–71.

[123] Walter Murphy of Rowan County, quoted *ibid.*, 71–72.

and attacked the political clergy.[124] "When they convert their pulpits into political rostrums," Smith's running mate told his fellow Arkansans, "stop preaching Christ and Him crucified, and engage in preaching Al Smith and him crucified, they work harm to both church and state." [125]

One automatic reflex was to trot out the racial bugaboo. "The campaign should be waged on the sharply-defined issue that the Democratic Party is the white man's party and the Republican Party is the Negro party," a Mississippi editor advised.[126] "Let the thinnest trickle of independent voting . . . be permitted," the Charleston *News and Courier* warned, " and the torrents of independent action will sweep away the solid dam which holds the white people in the same party in South Carolina." [127] In Alabama, Judge Bernard Harwood put the issue more pungently: "The Republican party still smells strongly of the Negro." [128] But the most artful ploy was Bilbo's. Hoover, he said, had danced with Mrs. Mary Booze, postmistress of Mound Bayou, Mississippi's all-Negro town.[129] Hoovercrats retaliated with pictures of a Tammany Negro official and his white secretary.[130] The resurgence of the race issue brought forth a protest inspired by the Interracial Commission and signed by forty-six prominent citizens, but it was a potent factor in holding the Deep South for the Democrats.[131]

Yet the returns registered a deep split in the Solid South.

[124] See, for example, Angus Wilton McLean, "Religious Liberty," address delivered at Bladensboro, N.C., October 3, 1928, in Corbitt (ed.) , *Public Papers and Letters of Angus Wilton McLean,* 474–90.

[125] Arkansas *Gazette,* November 6, 1928, quoted in Thomas Lee Bedford, "Rhetorical Analysis of Joseph T. Robinson" (M.A. thesis, Louisiana State University, 1953) , 16.

[126] Frederick Sullens, quoted in New Orleans *Item,* August 29, 1928.

[127] Charleston *News and Courier,* April 27, 1928, quoted in Williford, "South Carolina Democrats in the 1928 Presidential Election," 17. Williford was convinced that this was the deciding issue in South Carolina. *Ibid.,* 98.

[128] Quoted in Sellers, *Prohibition Movement in Alabama,* 205.

[129] Green, *The Man Bilbo,* 77. "As to religion," Bilbo said, "I don't think either Smith or Hoover has enough to alarm anybody."

[130] New Bern (N.C.) *Times,* October 26, 1928, copy in Simmons Papers.

[131] Moton, *What the Negro Thinks,* 251; Dykeman and Stokeley, *Seeds of Southern Change,* 122. Smith, it has been claimed, considered a strong pro-Negro stand in his campaign but finally rejected the idea. White, *Man Called White,* 100–102. Key, *Southern Politics in State and Nation,* 318–29, demonstrates a strong correlation between Negro population and support for Smith. White voters in the Black Belts were the nucleus of Smith support.

Hoover carried seven Southern states and a majority of the region's popular and electoral votes. Only a hard core of Alabama, Arkansas, Georgia, Louisiana, Mississippi, and South Carolina remained Democratic, Alabama by only 7,083 votes.[132] The election has since been subjected to innumerable analyses and judgments, many focused on the relative significance of the prohibition and Catholic issues. Reports to the Democratic National Committee on the question were inconclusive; some emphasized one and some the other.[133] Bishop Cannon and many of the ministers denied that religion was the issue, and clearly much of the organized effort against Smith came from the Anti-Saloon League groups. But the religious issue so easily crept into the campaign under the cloak of prohibition and was so closely associated with nebulous fears of the alien metropolis that the pattern became too knotty to disentangle.[134]

Such matters obscured the ill-defined economic issues like public power, farm relief, and the tariff. Economic changes in the South nevertheless exerted influence. It was an old saying "that thousands of business people in the South vote one way and pray another in times of Presidential elections." [135] Now Yankees were "swarming into the South like locusts," Will Rogers said, "and the rascals bring their Republican politics with 'em." [136] More significantly, a North Carolina journalist reported, textile barons of the state were moving into the Republican ranks, followed by bankers, merchants, newspaper publishers, and businessmen in general. "Republican rolls, once dedicated to niggers, hill-billies and other such pariahs, begin to smack of the Social Register." [137]

Around the centers of the "Atlanta spirit" a Republican trend

[132] Robinson, *Presidential Vote*, 50–52.

[133] "1928 National Political Digest," Group 17, in Roosevelt Library.

[134] One case in point was a disingenuously worded throw-away distributed by the Alabama Anti-Saloon League: "It is unnecessary to bring into this fight any of Mr. Smith's short-comings other than his wetness." In William B. Bankhead Papers. A more striking case was a letter from a Methodist minister in Palatka, Florida, which began with an indignant denial that religion was the issue and ended with sharp condemnations of Catholic doctrine. W. J. Carpenter to Franklin D. Roosevelt, October 5, 1928, in Florida folder, Group 17, in Roosevelt Library.

[135] *Manufacturers' Record*, XCII (September 8, 1927) , 51–52.

[136] Quoted in Nixon, "Changing Political Philosophy of the South," *loc. cit.*, 247.

[137] Wilbur J. Cash, "Jehovah of the Tar Heels," in *American Mercury*, XVII (1929) , 318.

had appeared in 1920, when Atlanta itself went for Harding—as did the states of Oklahoma and Tennessee. In 1924 Coolidge polled substantially over half as many votes in the South as Davis.[138] One month before the 1928 election Hoover appeared at Elizabethton, Tennessee, to voice his prosperity theme. "In every phase of life the South is moving forward," he declared. "New vistas of betterment are opening." [139] In the election he captured such "progress-conscious" cities as Houston, Dallas, Birmingham, Atlanta, Chattanooga, and Richmond, while Smith held "the more easy-going districts" of San Antonio, New Orleans, Mobile, Montgomery, Savannah, Charleston, and Memphis.[140] "The aristocrat still exists," said a Southern professor at Princeton, "he still sips his mint-julep . . . he derides the antievolution laws, denounces the interference of the preachers in politics, and glorifies the party of Jefferson and Jackson. But it is the great new middle class, the heirs to the vigorous, prosperous, advancing New South, who now decide the elections." [141]

In 1928 many voters for the first time permitted their convictions, moral or economic, to overcome the dictates of party regularity. Their decision seemed to open a new epoch of two-party politics in the South, but unforeseen events halted the process. The Great Engineer fell heir to the Great Depression, enough in itself to discredit politically those who had rallied to his support. Even before that Mrs. Hoover in the spring of 1929 had confirmed the worst fears of many Southerners by inviting Mrs. Oscar DePriest, wife of Chicago's Negro Congressman, to a White House tea. It was "a great blow to the social stability of the South," said Senator Overman of North Carolina; such incidents were "exceedingly injurious to the negro himself and should be discouraged by all who have the welfare of the negro at heart," the lower house of the Georgia legislature resolved.[142] The last word

[138] Robinson, *Presidential Vote*, 50–52; Milton, "Also There Is Politics," *loc. cit.,* 117–18.

[139] New York *Times*, October 7, 1928.

[140] H. C. Nixon, "The Changing Background of Southern Politics," in *Social Forces*, XI (1932–1933) , 15; Nixon, "Changing Political Philosophy of the South," *loc. cit.,* 248.

[141] T. J. Wertenbaker, "Up from the Depths," in *Princeton Alumni Weekly*, XXIX (1928–1929) , 453.

[142] Quoted respectively from Wilmington *Star*, June 18, 1929, and Columbus (Ga.) *Enquirer-Sun*, June 28, 1929, from clippings in Odum Papers.

on the incident perhaps belongs to the author of a letter to the Baltimore *Sun*. It was unfortunate he wrote, "after the extreme effort . . . to keep out de Pope that now they had to let in De Priest." [143]

Within two years the wages of sin were meted out to the Hoovercrats. In 1929 Bishop Cannon's anti-Smith forces in Virginia struck up another alliance with the Republicans on a joint state ticket, and lost. Within another year Cannon himself suffered the humiliation of a Senatorial probe of financial irregularities in the anti-Smith campaign and personal irregularities in bucket-shop speculations.[144] In 1930 Texas voters ended Thomas Love's campaign for governor in the first primary and North Carolina voters replaced the hitherto invincible Senator Simmons with Josiah W. Bailey. Alabama's Democrats read Senator Heflin out of the party and nominated John H. Bankhead, Jr., who defeated Heflin in the general election.[145] Southern Republicans in Congress dropped from the nineteen carried in with Hoover to five.[146]

The campaign of 1928 and its aftermath did usher in a new political epoch, but not a two-party South. It was as if all the peculiar forces of the 1920's—prohibition, fundamentalism, nativism, religious bigotry, and the nascent middle-class Republicanism—had united in one glorious and disastrous finale. All were shaken and discredited by the misfortunes of the administration they helped to install, and their discomfiture cleared the way for a new progressive coalition, the New Deal.

[143] T. A. O'Keefe in Baltimore *Sun*, June 20, 1929, clipping in Odum Papers.

[144] Alvin L. Hall, "Virginia Back in the Fold: The Gubernatorial Campaign and Election of 1929," *Virginia Magazine of History and Biography*, LXXIII (1965), 280–302.

[145] Lewinson, *Race, Class, and Party*, 167; Richard L. Watson, Jr., "A Southern Democratic Primary: Simmons vs. Bailey in 1930," in *North Carolina Historical Review*, XLII (1965), 21–46. Lewinson erroneously stated that Cole Blease bolted the national ticket.

[146] *Biographical Directory of the American Congress, 1774–1961* (Washington, 1961), 361–66.

CHAPTER VIII

THE EMERGENCE OF
PUBLIC SERVICES

T HE decade of business progressivism was harvest time for a succession of popular crusades: the movements for good roads, education, public health, and social welfare. In each case the characteristic themes of business progressivism— expansion and efficiency—accompanied a transition from the missionary era to one of institutionalization and professionalism. The growing functions of public service became the responsibility of permanent agencies, public or private, manned by professional staffs and directing programs that expanded at an accelerated pace.

The good-roads movement, automobile age equivalent of the nineteenth-century railroad movement, still awaits its historian. It is a diffuse story of conventions and associations, the promotion of named highways by aggregations of local boosters, heroic caravans in dusters and goggles, and finally broad-gauged planning of integrated networks with the Federal highways acts of 1916 and 1921 and the development of state systems. For two decades before 1913 "the highways movement had shown premonitory signs of life." [1] After that date a bewildering profusion of good-roads associations and publications sprouted alongside such existing growths as the magazine *Good Roads* (1892), the National Good Roads Association (1900), the American Automobile Association (1902), and the American Road Builders Association (1903). [2]

---

[1] Frederic L. Paxson, "The Highway Movement, 1916–1935," in *American Historical Review*, LI (1945–1946), 240.

[2] *Ibid.*, 239–40; William C. Hilles, "The Good Roads Movement in the United States: 1880–1916" (M.A. thesis, Duke University, 1958), 140.

A meeting at Birmingham in April, 1913, for example, led to the organization of the United States Good Roads Association at St. Louis the following November. Founded chiefly as an agency to promote the elder John H. Bankhead's proposal for Federal aid to highways, it continued propaganda activities into the 1930's, primarily as a Southern organization with headquarters in Birmingham.[3] In July, 1913, the Ozark Trails Association, founded by W. H. "Coin" Harvey, attracted two thousand delegates to its first convention at Jonesboro, Arkansas. Devoted to highway development in the Southwest, it functioned until 1920 and, among other activities, laid out much of the route later followed by U.S. 66.[4] In 1914 a special good-roads issue of the *Manufacturers' Record* heralded a meeting in Atlanta of the American Road Congress, founded at Richmond in 1911. Special issues and sections on good roads thereafter became a regular feature of the publication. Out of the Atlanta meeting grew still another group, the American Association of State Highway Officials, organized at Washington shortly afterward.[5]

Numerous state and area groups testified to the universal interest: a North Carolina Good Roads Association as early as 1901, a Southern Good Roads Association, the Appalachian Good Roads Association, the Chattahoochee Good Roads Association, and others. Even the railroads were sympathetic at first. "I do not regard [good roads] as factors in long-distance transportation," the president of the Southern Railway told a Congressional committee in 1913, "and I welcome them in connection with the development of the areas surrounding our system."[6] A favorite promotional device was the named highway association, which mapped out a specified route and gathered in the community boomers along the way. As early as 1909 the Atlanta *Journal* joined the New York *Herald* in sponsoring a "National Highway" between

---

[3] J. A. Rountree to Thomas L. Cannon, May 22, 1923; and Rountree to John H. Bankhead, Sr., May 24, 1913, in John H. Bankhead, Sr., Papers; Birmingham *Post*, June 21, 1934, clipping in John H. Bankhead, Jr., Papers.

[4] Clara B. Kennan, "The Ozark Trails and Arkansas' Pathfinder, Coin Harvey," in *Arkansas Historical Quarterly*, VII (1948), 299–316.

[5] *Manufacturers' Record*, LXVI (October 22, 1914), special issue; Paxson, "Highway Movement," *loc. cit.*, 239n.

[6] W. W. Finley, quoted in Dearing, *American Highway Policy*, 262.

the two cities; the Atlanta *Constitution* joined in promoting Carl Fisher's Dixie highway from Mackinaw to Miami.[7] Before 1920 the map of the South was crosshatched by such schemes. In 1916 a Bankhead National Highway Association began to promote a road from Washington to El Paso (or more ambitiously, San Diego) via Atlanta and Memphis; the old Senator himself, after a rousing send-off in the Capitol rotunda, motored over the existing roads and ruts from Washington to Atlanta, giving more than a hundred speeches en route.[8] About the same time the New Orleans Association of Commerce hatched out a Jefferson Highway from the Crescent City to Winnipeg.[9] Other more or less ambitious schemes included the Meridian Highway (Nuevo Laredo to Winnipeg), the Dixie Overland Highway (Savannah to Los Angeles), the Charlotte-Wilmington Military High-Way, and the Old Spanish Trail (Tampa via the Gulf Coast to Los Angeles).

During the first decade of the century the rising demand for good roads found outlet chiefly through increased authorizations to counties for road bond issues. A number of wealthier counties seized the opportunity, particularly Mecklenburg County (Charlotte), North Carolina, which stood in the vanguard of the movement for many years.[10] The era of state aid and responsibility, except for scattered exceptions, opened in the second decade of the century. Between 1906 and 1917 all the Southern states created highway commissions; between 1912 and 1924 each designated a state highway system.[11] The demand for Federal aid, supported by Southern Congressmen, led to the first trickle of Federal money under a 1912 appropriation for post roads, sponsored by Furnifold M. Simmons.[12] But the great spur was the enactment of the Federal Highways Act of 1916 and, in some local

[7] Norman J. Radder, *Newspapers in Community Service* (New York, 1926), 68–69.

[8] *The Dixie Manufacturer,* XLIII (May 25, 1917), copy; and *American Motorist,* December, 1917, clipping, in John H. Bankhead, Sr., Papers.

[9] Paxson, "Highway Movement," *loc. cit.,* 242.

[10] Thomas H. McDonald, "Fifty Years of Progress in Highway Improvement in Southern States," in *South's Development,* 273, 275; Hilles, "Good Roads Movement in the United States," 159; Brown, *State Highway System of North Carolina,* 18–29.

[11] Dearing, *American Highway Policy,* 54–55.

[12] Hilles, "Good Roads Movement in the United States," 171–75.

areas, the example of roads built to wartime army camps.[13] The law of 1916 limited grants to rural post roads, but the renewal act of 1921 invited each state to prepare a list of not more than 7 per cent of its roads the improvement of which would "expedite the completion of an adequate and connected system of highways, interstate in character." The resultant scheme of Federal highways threw the named highways into the discard after 1925. Here and there the names survived locally, but the road markers gradually weathered and lost their meaning.[14]

Despite a lingering rural suspicion that highway systems favored intercity connections to the neglect of farm-to-market roads, the movement advanced with little resistance. The only substantial disagreement was between the proponents of bond issues and of pay-as-you-go plans, and in most states the impatient advocates of deficit financing won out. From 1920 to 1929 expenditures for the construction of state-administered highway systems increased by 157 per cent in the South and 123 per cent outside the South. Surfaced rural roads in the region increased from 69,797 miles in 1914 to 121,164 in 1921 and 209,880 in 1930.[15]

The advances were not without pains. Some states, particularly Arkansas, plunged disastrously into debt. "Cities that preserved the finest flavor of the old regime," Donald Davidson lamented, now "had to be approached over brand-new roads where billboards, tourist camps, filling stations, and factories broke out in a modernistic rash among the water oaks and Spanish moss." [16] But the resultant benefits, tangible and intangible, radiated in many directions: in the breakdown of provincial isolation, in the greater mobility of labor, in farm-to-factory commuting, in school buses that moved across improved roads to new consolidated schools, and in bookmobiles that penetrated the rural precincts.

The direct economic consequences were even more striking: automobile agencies, garages, service stations, roadside inns,

[13] Lewis P. Jones to the author, September 10, 1960, cites the example of Camp Wadsworth on the latter.

[14] Paxson, "Highway Movement," *loc. cit.*, 245–46.

[15] Hoover and Ratchford, *Economic Resources and Policies of the South*, 205; U.S. Bureau of the Census, *Statistical Abstract of the United States*, 1932, p. 351.

[16] Davidson, *Attack on Leviathan*, 142.

257

tourism, and trucking. Motor transportation increased by leaps and bounds. Truck deliveries to Texas ports advanced from 0.6 per cent of total deliveries in 1924 to 15 per cent in 1929, 30 per cent in 1930, and 45 in 1931. By 1933 trucks in the South carried over 37 percent of the citrus crops, 31 per cent of the fertilizer, and according to various sources 35–50 per cent of the packinghouse and dairy products, 40–50 per cent of the peanuts, 60 per cent of the crushed stone, sand, and gravel, and 55 per cent of the merchandise. Motor trucks and buses provided a major new industry that gradually came under the same public regulation as railroads.[17]

For education, as for good roads, the fruits were ripening. At the beginning of the teens the Southern Education Movement, first in the procession of twentieth-century crusades, drew to its close. To the more than two thousand people registered for the Sixteenth Conference for Education in the South at Richmond in April, 1913, Robert Curtis Ogden of New York, its chief backer, sent his regrets. He was too ill to attend, and four months later he was dead. At the Louisville meeting a year later the group formed a larger Southern Educational and Industrial Association to study general social and economic as well as educational problems. But the diffusion of interests was fatal, for the new organization largely duplicated the concerns of the Southern Sociological Congress and soon faded from the scene.[18]

The greatest contribution of the Conference had been to put interested philanthropists in contact with Southern educational leadership and to inspire campaigns for educational awakening among the masses through the Southern Education Board, founded in 1902. In 1914 both became defunct, together with the older Peabody Fund which left most of its remaining capital to the George Peabody College for Teachers in Nash-

[17] Milton S. Heath, "Motor Transportation in the South," in *Southern Economic Journal*, I (August, 1934), 17–19; Albert N. Sanders, "State Regulation of Public Utilities in South Carolina, 1879–1935" (Ph.D. dissertation, University of North Carolina, 1956); Clyde C. Carter, *State Regulations of Commercial Motor Carriers in North Carolina*, in University of North Carolina School of Business Administration Studies in Business Administration, III (Chapel Hill, 1958).

[18] Charles William Dabney, *Universal Education in the South* (Chapel Hill, 1936), II, 306–11; Shivers, "Social Welfare Movement in the South," 48–50.

ville.[19] The role of central directorate for Southern education fell to the General Education Board (GEB), itself an outgrowth of the Rockefeller family's interest in the Ogden Movement. Although it developed broader programs over the years, Southern education remained a central concern. From 1902 through 1947 the GEB poured $126,774,765 into its Southern program and nurtured a dedicated corps of fieldworkers who struggled with growing success for universal education.[20] Most of the major innovations in Southern education and much of its continuing momentum stemmed from the activities of the GEB. The crusades of the early twentieth century had served their day. The public schools, at least for whites, were assured of continuing support in principle. The new tasks were those of administration, surveys, planning, curricula, standards, and of filling out the uneven places.

The development of rural schools posed one of the most challenging problems. The town schools of North Carolina were "fairly well supported," Clarence Poe noted in 1913, "but our country schools, having no lobbyists to plead for them . . . have been neglected, shamefully neglected, year after year." [21] The Richmond conference of 1913 emphasized discussions of the question. The advancement of rural schools, the conference secretary wrote, would bolster the forces "gathering to organize country life" by providing "an effective instrument for the organization and constant up-building of community life." [22] The Peabody Fund had already initiated a methodical approach to the problem, however. By 1914 it had helped eleven Southern states in hiring full-time agents for rural schools.[23] In that year the South Caro-

---

[19] Dabney, *Universal Education in the South*, II, 115–22.

[20] Robert D. Calkins, "Historical Review, 1902–1947," in General Education Board, *Annual Report, 1947–1948* (New York, 1948), 8–9. Raymond B. Fosdick, Henry F. Pringle, and Katharine Douglas Pringle, *Adventure in Giving: The Story of the General Education Board* (New York, 1962), is the standard history.

[21] Clarence H. Poe, "What North Carolina's Farmers Expect of the Legislature," in Raleigh *News and Observer*, January 19, 1913.

[22] A. P. Bourland to L. J. Hanifan, October 31, 1913, in Series A, Southern Education Papers (Southern Historical Collection, University of North Carolina).

[23] The GEB assumed support of the agents in 1914. [Abraham Flexner], *The General Education Board: An Account of Its Activities, 1902–1914* (New York, 1915), 180, 187–89; Dabney, *Universal Education in the South*, II, 219–23.

lina agent, William Knox Tate, moved to Peabody College to offer courses in rural education and carry on an active career of speaking and writing for the cause.[24]

In the good-roads era the consolidated school afforded one solution. The consolidation movement began in Lafayette Parish, Louisiana, in 1902. Following the successful experiment there, a state program reduced the total number of rural schools from 2,352 in 1910 to 1,210 in 1935, eliminating many inefficient one- or two-teacher schools.[25] But Mississippi set a faster pace. In eighteen years after 1910 the state developed 969 consolidated schools with 168,523 pupils, costing in all $15,825,000. Mississippians could take some consolation for their other statistical shortcomings from the claim to "lead the nation in the number of Consolidated Schools." [26] Meanwhile, North Carolina by 1927 had acquired 2,876 school buses serving 111,725 pupils; Arkansas in 1930 had nearly 100 new consolidated schools; and South Carolina could boast in 1934 that only 350 one-teacher schools remained in the state.[27]

A parallel development was the increase of state aid to help poorer districts expand facilities, pay teachers, and maintain longer terms. In 1913 North Carolina had a second brief "educational awakening" that resulted in a statewide property tax of five cents for an "equalization fund" to maintain a minimum five-month term. In 1919 the minimum reached six months, and ten years later the legislature was moving toward an eight-month minimum.[28] In 1915 Texas set up a $1,000,000 equalization fund contingent upon a minimum effort by local authorities, a practice

---

[24] Dabney, *Universal Education in the South*, II, 227–28.

[25] W. H. Plemmons, "Extension and Equalization of Educational Opportunity in the South," in Ryan, Gwynn, and King (eds.), *Secondary Education in the South*, 30–31.

[26] Dabney, *Universal Education in the South*, II, 380–81, quoting Mississippi's State Superintendent of Education, W. F. Bond.

[27] Plemmons, "Extension and Equalization of Educational Opportunity in the South," *loc. cit.*, 31–32; Dabney, *Universal Education in the South*, II, 229, 390.

[28] Louis R. Harlan, *Separate and Unequal: Public School Campaigns and Racism in the Southern Seaboard States, 1901–1915* (Chapel Hill, 1958), 128–29; Dabney, *Universal Education in the South*, II, 343; Plemmons, "Extension and Equalization of Educational Opportunity in the South," *loc. cit.*, 33–34; Gatewood, *Eugene Clyde Brooks*, 102–11, 115–21; Fred W. Morrison, *Equalization of the Financial Burden of Education among Counties in North Carolina* (New York, 1925), 10–25.

continued and enlarged in subsequent years. In 1919 Georgia's Barrett-Rogers Law provided $200,000 for aid in consolidation, in 1920 a constitutional amendment required counties to levy a minimum school tax, and in 1927 the state established an equalization fund of $1,000,000. In 1924 South Carolina adopted a "6-0-1" law, providing state support for teachers' salaries for six months if local authorities would provide the seventh. In 1925 Tennessee guaranteed an eight-month term.[29]

The wide chasm between the elementary and college levels presented another problem, a gap scarcely bridged by numerous private academies, "usually meagre in outfit and transient in point of duration," and a few college fitting schools.[30] After 1905 the GEB moved also into that breach by supporting professors of secondary education, eventually in thirteen state universities.[31] Following the example of work begun in 1903 by Professor Joseph S. Stewart at the University of Georgia, they worked chiefly as state agents for high schools, promoting favorable legislation and stirring communities into action.[32] After 1917 further impetus came from the Smith-Hughes Act for Federal aid to vocational education and from the promotion of "farm life schools" in some areas as an opening wedge for secondary education. On the whole, however, the Southern high schools remained more closely wedded than those in other regions to the traditional and classical branches.[33]

[29] Richardson, *Texas: Lone Star State*, 291; Dorothy Orr, *A History of Education in Georgia* (Chapel Hill, 1950), 265, 273, 278; Wallace, *South Carolina: Short History*, 692; Lander, *History of South Carolina*, 129; Andrew David Holt, *The Struggle for a State System of Public Schools in Tennessee, 1903–1936* (New York, 1938), 353–54.

[30] [Flexner], *General Education Board*, 74–76.

[31] In all the Southern states as herein defined, except Oklahoma, and in West Virginia.

[32] Joseph Roemer, "The Development of Secondary Education in the South," in *Proceedings of the Thirty-Seventh Annual Meeting of the Southern Association of Colleges and Secondary Schools* (Birmingham, [1930]), 247–48; Plemmons, "Extension and Equalization of Educational Opportunity in the South," *loc. cit.*, 22; Calkins, "Historical Review," *loc. cit.*, 34–36. In all the GEB contributed approximately $950,000 to the program.

[33] In 1928 four of the five states with the highest percentages of secondary pupils enrolled in Latin, and all five with the highest in algebra were Southern states. Despite much talk of manual training in Southern educational circles, not one ranked among the five highest in that field, and three were at the very bottom of the list. President's Research Committee on Social Trends, *Recent Social Trends in*

The total number of high schools in the region gradually rose from 2,782 in 1914—a figure "entitled to little credence" because it counted many elementary schools with incidental secondary classes—to 3,518 in 1920 and 8,270 in 1930.[34]

By the 1920's the missionary age had passed. Gradually state and local governments took responsibility for the programs inaugurated by the GEB and other foundations: agents for rural, secondary, and Negro schools; surveys and studies of educational needs; special administrative divisions for information and statistics, schoolhouse planning and construction, libraries, standards of teacher training and certification.[35] And if the average cost per pupil in every Southern state lagged behind the national average in 1930, eight Southern states since 1920 had exceeded the national rate of increase in current expenditures for schools, led by Mississippi with 257 per cent, and eight had exceeded the national rate of increase in cost per pupil, led by South Carolina with 149.6 per cent. Nine had exceeded the national rate of increase in length of school term, although none had reached the national average except Oklahoma.[36]

There was reason for pride in the achievement, but one educational leader warned that the South was "in grave danger of ballyhooing itself into further backwardness."[37] To illustrate his point, Edgar W. Knight of the University of North Carolina quoted the speaker of an unidentified Southern legislature: "I should not wonder if the amount of money spent for public

---

the United States, 332. See also Rob Roy Purdy (ed.), Fugitives' Reunion: Conversation at Vanderbilt, May 3–5, 1956, Vanderbilt Studies in the Humanities, III (Nashville, 1959), 103–105, 110–15.

[34] U.S. Commissioner of Education, Report, 1914 (Washington, 1914), II, 411; U.S. Bureau of Education, Biennial Survey of Education, 1918–1920, II, 505; U.S. Bureau of Education, Biennial Survey of Education, 1928–1930, p. 685. Quotation from [Flexner], General Education Board, 73.

[35] Calkins, "Historical Review," loc. cit., 31–38. During the 1910's and 1920's the GEB assisted in statewide surveys of the school systems in Virginia, Florida, Alabama, North Carolina, and Kentucky. General Education Board, Annual Report, 1928–1929, pp. 16–17.

[36] U.S. Bureau of Education, Biennial Survey of Education, 1928–1930, II, 20, 28–30. The national average cost per pupil was $86.69; in the South costs ran from $31.89 in Georgia to $65.48 in Oklahoma. The average length of school term was 172.7 days; in the South it ran from 133.4 in Mississippi to 173.3 in Oklahoma.

[37] Edgar W. Knight, "Recent Progress and Problems of Education," in Couch (ed.), Culture in the South, 224.

schools in this State is as much per capita as any state in the Union." Actually, Knight noted, it was less than half the national average. In the late 1920's, he asserted, the states of the former Confederacy were a region of less than fifth graders, with 260,000 illiterates among their native whites alone. "Except for school textbooks the southern states are the leanest book markets in the United States. As readers of the leading national magazines they rank at the bottom, and as readers of newspapers the country at large makes almost a three-fold better showing than the southern states." Continuing backwardness, Knight declared, "stifles industry, represses effort, discourages enterprise, weakens the desire for excellence and makes us satisfied with second-rate achievements." [38]

The struggle against second-rate achievement presented thorny problems for ambitious college leaders. Before the rise of public high schools many a little "college" was so overshadowed by its preparatory department as to be a high school in reality. In 1913 sixteen out of twenty colleges in South Carolina maintained such departments; realistic standards, they claimed, had to avoid opening an "impassable gap" between colleges and public schools.[39] Only gradually and painfully was a distinction between secondary and collegiate education defined. In 1908 the Association of Colleges and Secondary Schools of the Southern States, founded in 1895, urged a college entrance requirement of fourteen "acceptable units" of high school work; on the basis of that measurement a survey disclosed that in 1913 the degrees of nine among the twenty-eight colleges in the association—presumably the best in the region—represented less than four years of college work.[40] In 1915 South Carolina's high school inspector reported that "any

[38] Edgar W. Knight, "Can the South Attain National Standards in Education?", in *South Atlantic Quarterly*, XXVIII (1929), 2–5; Edgar W. Knight, "Education in the South," in *Outlook and Independent*, CLIV (1930), 47–48, 79.

[39] Hollis, *University of South Carolina*, II, 267–68.

[40] Guy E. Snavely, "A Short History of the Southern Association of Colleges and Secondary Schools," in *The Southern Association Quarterly* (Durham), IX (1945), 499; Elizabeth Avery Colton, "The Approximate Value of Recent Degrees of Southern Colleges," in *Proceedings of the Nineteenth Annual Meeting of the Association of Colleges and Secondary Schools of the Southern States* (Nashville, 1913), 74–77, 83. The "Carnegie unit," promoted by the Carnegie Foundation for the Advancement of Teaching, represented "a year's study in any subject . . . constituting approximately a quarter of a full year's work." R. L. Duffus, *Democracy Enters College: A Study of the Rise and Decline of the Academic Lockstep* (New York and Chicago, 1936), 61.

high school pupil with ten units to his credit can get into the freshman class of any college in the State." [41] But the Southern Association gradually upgraded its requirement to fifteen and then to sixteen units.[42] It was an arbitrary device, "the fitting product of an age which loved mechanical precision," but it served the useful purpose of more systematic distinctions between high school and college.[43] In 1912 the Southern Association established a Commission on Secondary Schools which developed regular standards of accreditation, but not until 1921 did the Association fix a complete set of standards for college members.[44]

Financial resources for higher education meanwhile grew encouragingly. In 1920 the GEB began to distribute a new $50,000,-000 Rockefeller gift for increased faculty salaries; state institutions for the first time shared in the aid. In 1922 the Board established graduate fellowships for "persons in the South in position to exert leadership in public education"; 243 had been granted by 1929.[45] Between 1902 and 1934 eight major foundations gave a total of $87,790,036 to 127 Southern colleges and universities.[46] In 1925 Chancellor James H. Kirkland voiced a new spirit of affluence and hope at Vanderbilt's fiftieth anniversary celebration: "Today we stand side by side with many sister institutions of this great Southland. We feel strength in such fellowship. The isolation of the first years of our history has passed. . . . As we have shared the limitations and poverty of the South, so we hope to share her growing prosperity." [47]

Hundreds of institutions were moving from secondary to higher education; others began to thrust up toward university status, with diversified programs of graduate and professional training, re-

---

[41] William H. Hand, South Carolina high school inspector, quoted in Hollis, *University of South Carolina*, II, 269.

[42] Snavely, "Short History of the Southern Association of Colleges and Secondary Schools," *loc. cit.*, 523.

[43] Duffus, *Democracy Enters College*, 51.

[44] Snavely, "Short History of the Southern Association of Colleges and Secondary Schools," *loc. cit.*, 494, 523.

[45] General Education Board, *Annual Report*, 1920–1921 (New York, 1921), 7–12, 17, 73–87, 90–92.

[46] Ernest Victor Hollis, *Philanthropic Foundations and Higher Education* (New York, 1938), 269.

[47] Mims, *Chancellor Kirkland of Vanderbilt*, 268.

search, and other services. Vanderbilt and Tulane were the leading beneficiaries of philanthropy; in the 1920's the Carnegie and Rockefeller foundations selected them as strategic sites for major medical schools below the Potomac.[48] In 1925 Vanderbilt dedicated its new medical school, a nurses' home, Alumni Memorial Hall, a new auditorium, and inevitably, a stadium, as part of the continuing expansion under Chancellor Kirkland.[49] In 1919, with a million dollars from the Coca-Cola baron, Asa G. Candler, Emory College moved to a new campus in Atlanta's Druid Hills to join a graduate school and schools of theology, law, medicine, nursing, library science, and business administration in Emory University.[50] But there was one arresting omission; it had no stadium. Emory could "well wait for others to come to her safe and sane position" of excluding the "evil" of intercollegiate athletics, Methodist Bishop Warren A. Candler declared. It would be a long wait.[51]

The Candler benefaction was "the largest . . . within our memory by any man of the South," according to one editor, "a dramatic suggestion to men of wealth in the South," according to another.[52] But Emory was dwarfed by the transformation of another Methodist school, Trinity College, into Duke University. In December, 1924, James "Buck" Duke announced the Duke Endowment of $40,000,000, mostly in power and tobacco stocks; $6,000,000 of the principal (for construction) and nearly a third of the income went to the new university which arose in Gothic splendor west of Durham.[53] The existing liberal arts college, with appurtenant schools of law and engineering, added a hospital and medical, divinity, forestry, and graduate schools. It was "a greater transformation, and in a shorter space of time, than had ever

---

[48] Between 1902 and 1934 Vanderbilt received $21,355,655 and Tulane, $5,063,200 from the major foundations. Hollis, *Philanthropic Foundations and Higher Education*, 274. See also *ibid.*, 204, 211, 213, 276.

[49] Mims, *Chancellor Kirkland of Vanderbilt*, 262–79.

[50] Henry Morton Bullock, *A History of Emory University* (Nashville, 1936), 285–88, 294–98, 311–64.

[51] Pierce, *Giant Against the Sky*, 152.

[52] *Wesleyan Christian Advocate* and *Manufacturers' Record*, quoted in Charles H. Candler, *Asa Griggs Candler* (Emory University, Ga., 1950), 401, 402.

[53] Earl W. Porter, *Trinity and Duke, 1892–1924: Foundation of Duke University* (Durham, 1964), 232.

occurred in the South." [54] Before his death in 1925 Duke gave another $17,000,000 to the university and 10 per cent of his residuary estate. "Get the best executives and educators, no matter what they cost," he said. "I want Duke to be a great national institution." [55]

The University of Virginia, long regarded as the leading Southern university, since 1904 the only Southern member of the Association of American Universities, found its leadership challenged in the 1920's.[56] "Its pre-eminence is seriously threatened," President Edwin A. Alderman declared in 1924, "and will be destroyed in a period of five years unless something is done." [57] The threat came not from any retrogression of the institution at Charlottesville, which experienced continuing growth in the 1920's—adding a new medical center among other buildings, an Institute for Research in the Social Sciences, the *Virginia Quarterly Review*— but from the progress of other institutions.[58]

Alderman's own University of North Carolina, which he had attended and once served as professor and president, was the leading challenger. Under Harry Woodburn Chase, a transplanted New Englander who was president from 1919 to 1930, the university grew rapidly in size and prestige. The faculty rose from 78 to 225, annual support from $270,097 in 1918–1919 to $1,342,774 in 1928–1929. The university added new departments of dramatic art, sociology, music, journalism, and psychology; schools of business administration, public welfare, and library science; developed a research library; and in 1922 sponsored the first Southern university press.[59] A climate of creativity prevailed, especially around the Carolina Playmakers under Frederick Koch and the growing sociological empire of Howard Odum; these and other stirrings in the village of Chapel Hill amounted to a minor renais-

[54] Robert H. Woody (ed.), *The Papers and Addresses of William Preston Few* (Durham, 1951), 107.

[55] Jenkins, *James B. Duke*, 276.

[56] Mary Bynum Pierson, *Graduate Work in the South* (Chapel Hill, 1947), 76n, gives a list of members and dates of admission.

[57] Quoted in Malone, *Edwin A. Alderman*, 346.

[58] *Ibid.*, 193–97, 305–307, 346–53, 358–62, and *passim*.

[59] Louis Round Wilson, *Harry Woodburn Chase* (Chapel Hill, 1960), 12–21; Louis Round Wilson, *The University of North Carolina, 1900–1930: The Making of a Modern University* (Chapel Hill, 1957), 305–598.

sance. "Everybody has written a book or an article or a monograph," Edwin Mims marveled, "or is reading the proof of one, or collecting notes for one." [60] In 1922 North Carolina joined Virginia in the Association of American Universities.

In the Southwest the University of Texas discovered that its apparently worthless land holdings in West Texas were a rich source of oil revenues, nearly $5,000,000 of which poured in before the end of 1926 and a total of $64,965,576 by 1948, making the university one of the most heavily endowed state institutions in the nation. With its phenomenal income, Texas developed one of the largest libraries between the Potomac and the Rio Grande, especially rich in Southern historical materials because of generous gifts from Major George W. Littlefield.[61] In 1929 Texas became the third Southern member of the Association of American Universities.[62] Virginia, North Carolina, and Texas, through their institutes for research in social science, led in the academic study of social problems in the South; they were joined soon by other institutions, particularly in institutes for the study of administrative and economic development.[63] In their general growth and expansion they were foremost, but other state universities paralleled their experience.[64]

Southern institutions, however, still lagged behind national standards. In 1927–1928 the state universities of Illinois and Michigan each spent more for their libraries than nine Southern state universities combined; Harvard alone spent more than the state universities of all eleven former Confederate states and had in its library twice as many books as all of them combined.[65] In 1931–1932 salaries for full professors at Southern institutions averaged from $3,131 to $4,370 in contrast to a range of $3,841 to

[60] Mims, *Advancing South*, 115.

[61] Rister, *Oil!* 290, 405; Dabney, *Liberalism in the South,* 345; Haley, *George W. Littlefield,* 258–73.

[62] Duke University was also admitted in 1938. Pierson, *Graduate Work in the South,* 76.

[63] *Ibid.,* 99–101.

[64] Histories of Southern colleges and universities are evaluated in Horace H. Cunningham, "The Southern Mind Since the Civil War," in Arthur S. Link and Rembert W. Patrick (eds.), *Writing Southern History: Essays in Historiography in Honor of Fletcher M. Green* (Baton Rouge, 1965), 395–99.

[65] Knight, "Recent Progress and Problems of Education," *loc. cit.,* 216.

$6,421 in Northern and Western institutions; average teaching loads were respectively 12.8 and 9.9 hours a week.[66]

Education for Negroes, like every other kind of opportunity, fell under the inexorable constraints of white supremacy. In the first two decades of the century the GEB acted on the deliberate expedient of evading and soft-pedaling the subject, and Negro schools steadily fell behind the steaming progress of the education movement.[67] Inescapably the cause of Negro education required "the good will of men of weight and influence." [68] The conviction persisted that education spoiled field hands. "Literacy," a sociologist noted, "is not an asset in the plantation economy." [69] Even where there was a will to act, it was qualified by the rationalizations of inequality. Negro children "more often have to work in the field . . . and it would therefore be impossible for them to be in school as long," a county superintendent in Texas explained. "Furthermore, negroes pay only a very small per cent of the taxes, their teachers are not so competent as the whites, and they certainly have no righteous claim to an equal division." [70] In 1930 a survey of sixty county superintendents in North Carolina elicited as reasons for shorter terms in Negro schools the lack of a special tax, the need for Negroes on the farms, insufficient funds, insufficient attendance, the sentiment of whites, the refusal of white taxpayers to increase the costs of education.[71]

In 1916 the Federal Bureau of Education issued the first systematic study of Negro education, two volumes in which Thomas Jesse Jones unfolded a panorama of deficiency and in-

[66] Gee, *Research Barriers in the South,* 49–81. The figures are for forty-seven Southern and fifty-one non-Southern universities and colleges; they are averages rather than maximums and minimums.

[67] Harlan, *Separate and Unequal,* documents the point at some length.

[68] Leo M. Favrot, *Some Problems in the Education of the Negro in the South and How We Are Trying to Meet Them in Louisiana: An Address . . . before the National Association for the Advancement of Colored People, Cleveland, Ohio, June 25, 1919* (Baton Rouge, 1919) , 8.

[69] Johnson, *Shadow of the Plantation,* 129.

[70] Quoted in H. Y. Benedict and John A. Lomax, *The Book of Texas* (Garden City, N.Y., 1916) , 374–75.

[71] Dennis Hargrove Cooke, *The White Superintendent and the Negro Schools in North Carolina,* in George Peabody College for Teachers *Contributions to Education,* No. 73 (Nashville, 1930) , 63.

equality. At the time only 58.1 per cent of the Negro children six to fourteen were in either public or private schools. Many districts lacked any Negro schools at all, and where they existed, the teacher salaries per pupil in fifteen states averaged $10.32 for whites and $2.89 for Negroes. Negro high schools were almost nonexistent; Jones found 64 in the fifteen states, only 45 with four-year programs. Colored A & M schools subsisted mainly on Federal funds, and many small private schools were "brazen frauds imposing upon the philanthropy of Northern donors." Of the 133 schools teaching courses of college grade, mostly in the South, only 3 "had a student body, teaching force, equipment and income sufficient to warrant the characterization of 'college' ": Howard University, Fisk University, and Meharry Medical College.[72]

The 1916 report, cosponsored by the Phelps-Stokes Fund and written by its director, was itself a product of forces gathering to rescue Negro education. A key figure in the movement was James Hardy Dillard, who in 1908 left a professorship of Latin at Tulane to take charge of the Jeanes Fund for Negro rural schools. The date marked "the year when one of the ablest, bravest and most tactful of Southern gentlemen determined to devote the remainder of his life to furthering the cause of Negro education." [73] "Do the next thing" was the watchword he contributed to the interracial movement; one way to do the next thing in education was shown by Virginia Randolph, teacher of a small Negro school in Henrico County, Virginia. At her own suggestion the county superintendent, Jackson Davis, set her upon visitations in other schools to promote simple projects of sanitation, handicrafts, and homemaking. Dillard agreed to support the work experimentally and gradually extended it through the South. With additional support from other foundations the Jeanes teachers grew in number from 65 in 1909 to 320 in 1932, by which time 66 per cent of their salaries came from public funds. Working at simple day-to-

[72] Thomas Jesse Jones, *Negro Education: A Study of the Private and Higher Schools for Colored People in the United States* (Washington, 1917), II, 9–11, 14–17. The fifteen states included the South as herein defined plus Maryland, Delaware, and the District of Columbia.

[73] Brawley, *Dr. Dillard of the Jeanes Fund*, 52; Dabney, *Liberalism in the South*, 244.

day improvements they often functioned, in effect, as county superintendents of Negro schools.[74] Their example led in turn to the support of state agents for Negro schools. In 1910 Jackson Davis became the first, paid by the Peabody Fund; in 1914 the GEB took up the work and carried it eventually to fifteen states, giving each an official whose full-time responsibility was the promotion and improvement of Negro schools.[75]

As director of the Slater Fund after 1910, Dillard also tackled the problem of secondary education. In 1911 he extended the first offers of aid for "county training schools" for Negroes. The purpose of these, the Alabama state superintendent said in 1916, was to give "the practical training needed by the Negroes of the rural districts." [76] Most began as elementary schools, but the goal was gradually to smuggle Negro high schools into the public systems through the ritual of "industrial" education. By 1927–1928 the number had grown to 328, of which 104 were four-year high schools drawing support from public funds, contributions, foundations, and Federal aid under the Smith-Hughes Act.[77] By 1933 there were 2,003 public high schools for Negroes in Southern and Border States, 807 with four-year programs, but only 367 accredited by any agency.[78] Atlanta did not have one until 1924; in South Carolina Negroes first received public high school diplomas in 1929. As late as 1930 Montgomery, the capital city of Alabama, maintained no senior high school for Negroes; more

[74] Lance G. E. Jones, *The Jeanes Teacher in the United States, 1908–1933: An Account of Twenty-Five Years' Experience in the Supervision of Negro Rural Schools* (Chapel Hill, 1937), 89–92, 142. See also James H. Dillard, "Fourteen Years of the Jeanes Fund," in *South Atlantic Quarterly*, XXII (1923), 193–201.

[75] Ullin W. Leavell, *Philanthropy in Negro Education*, in George Peabody College for Teachers *Contributions to Education*, No. 100 (Nashville, 1930), 100–102; Samuel L. Smith, *Builders of Goodwill: The Story of the State Agents of Negro Education in the South, 1910 to 1950* (Nashville, 1950), 175–78, lists the agents. Thirteen states, including Maryland, had them by 1919; Oklahoma in 1927 and Missouri in 1929. All were white, although some had Negro assistants.

[76] Quoted in Horace Mann Bond, *Negro Education in Alabama: A Study in Cotton and Steel* (Washington, 1939), 267.

[77] *Ibid.;* Dabney, *Universal Education in the South*, II, 438; Edward E. Redcay, *County Training Schools and Public Secondary Education of Negroes in the South*, in John F. Slater Fund *Studies in Negro Education* (Washington, 1935), 24–50.

[78] Redcay, *County Training Schools and Public Secondary Education for Negroes in the South*, 53–54.

than half the Negro high school enrollment for the entire state was in Birmingham; and 38,183 Negroes of high school age still lived in Alabama counties that had no four-year high school.[79]

One of the most effective stratagems to outflank the prejudice and apathy that hobbled Negro education was the school-building program of the Rosenwald Fund. Started in 1912, with Julius Rosenwald's first gift for schools in Alabama, the building program before its end twenty years later contributed to the construction of 5,357 schools in 883 counties of 15 states. In twelve states for which figures were available in 1935–1936 the Rosenwald schools numbered about a fifth of all Negro school buildings. The Fund's chief utility, however, was in the stimulus it gave to public support while neutralizing the opposition of white taxpayers; actually about 64 per cent of the total building cost of the schools came from tax funds, as well as most of the operating costs—the Rosenwald Fund only contributed about 15 per cent, Negroes themselves 17, and sympathetic whites 4 per cent of the total $28,408,520.[80]

If in its first decade the GEB had neglected Negro schools, the pattern changed in the teens as it came quietly to the aid of the Jeanes teachers, state agents, county training schools, and other efforts inaugurated by the smaller foundations. "The year 1920," one historian noted, marked "the beginning of a new era in the history of educational philanthropy for Negroes in the South." [81] In that year the Rosenwald program went into full swing from its new offices in Nashville under S. L. Smith, former Tennessee agent for rural schools; and the GEB began an expansion of its service to Negro schools with enormous new sums donated by John D. Rockefeller. During the period 1923–1924 through 1928–1929 the GEB spent for its Negro school programs more than twice as much as it had during all its first two decades. It had

[79] Willard Range, *The Rise and Progress of Negro Colleges in Georgia, 1865–1949,* in University of Georgia *Phelps-Stokes Fellowship Studies,* No. 15 (Athens, Ga., 1951), 181; Lander, *History of South Carolina, 1865–1908,* 129; Bond, *Negro Education in Alabama,* 257, 267.

[80] Edwin R. Embree and Julia Waxman, *Investment in People: The Story of the Julius Rosenwald Fund* (New York, 1949), 48; Doxey A. Wilkerson, *Special Problems of Negro Education,* in U.S. Advisory Committee on Education *Staff Studies,* No. 12 (Washington, 1939), 32–33.

[81] Leavell, *Philanthropy in Negro Education,* 119.

found, *The Crisis* remarked, some Southern white liberals in deed as well as talk and had become "the salvation of education among Negroes." [82]

Salvation, perhaps, but not transfiguration; the fact that Negro schools through the twenties held about the same proportion of the growing expenditures, however, was ironic evidence of progress.[83] If the Southern states in 1930 spent $44.31 for each white and only $12.57 for each Negro pupil, and if the salaries of white teachers exceeded those for Negroes by nearly three to one, the gap had ceased to widen and in places had even begun to narrow during the 1920's.[84] But whatever tendencies toward equality may have existed, they were delayed by the appearance of new services which invited vast expenditures for whites: transportation, modern buildings, elaborate equipment, and all sorts of auxiliaries. The result, one author asserted in the early 1930's, "has been that Negro children do now receive a smaller proportion of the public funds in the Southern States than they have at any time in past history." [85]

As meager opportunities grew, the 1920's became a decade of emergence for Negro colleges. Indeed, their historian remarked, "it was during this decade that this group of schools began creating for themselves a college atmosphere, so overwhelming had been the elementary and secondary emphasis before that time." [86] The Jones study of 1916 disclosed only thirty-three Negro institutions with a total of 2,634 students taking college and professional

[82] It had appropriated $8,240,060.51 and spent $5,944,062.19 for Negro education by 1923; six years later, it had appropriated $20,986,576.62 and spent $14,246,008.28. General Education Board, *Annual Report, 1922–1923*, p. 47; *1928–1929*, p. 92. "The General Education Board," in *The Crisis*, XXXVII (1930), 229.

[83] Over the decade expenditures for Negro schools remained about the same proportionately, rising slightly from about 10.1 per cent of the total to 10.7 in seventeen states plus the District of Columbia; the total amount more than doubled. Work (ed.), *Negro Year Book*, 1921–1922, p. 240; 1931–1932, p. 204.

[84] Fred McCuistion, *Financing Schools in the South: Some Data Regarding Sources, Amounts, and Distribution of Public School Revenue in the Southern States, 1930* (Nashville, 1930), 25; Work (ed.), *Negro Year Book*, 1931–1932, p. 206.

[85] Horace Mann Bond, *The Education of the Negro in the American Social Order* (New York, 1934), 170–71.

[86] Dwight Oliver Wendell Holmes, *The Evolution of the Negro College*, in Teachers' College, Columbia University, *Contributions to Education*, No. 609 (New York, 1934), 184.

subjects. The postwar years, however, saw a phenomenal growth in college attendance: from 5,231 in 1921–1922, to 13,197 in 1926–1927 and 22,609 by 1931–1932.[87] A turning point in financial support came in 1919, when the GEB appropriated $500,000 to Fisk University and $200,000 each to Morehouse College, Shaw University, and Virginia Union University, and smaller amounts to other Negro colleges. Within ten years endowments aggregating $5,375,000 went to eleven Negro colleges, all but one of which were in the South.[88] At about the same time the GEB extended support for "training teachers" or "critic teachers," "whose tact and diplomacy must have verged on the super-human," to train students for teaching and to promote better methods and procedures in the classrooms of twelve Negro colleges.[89] Meanwhile, an expansion of state support increased the enrollments in public colleges for Negroes from a negligible number to 49.7 per cent of the total in 1932.[90] In 1930 the Southern Association of Colleges and Secondary Schools began to accredit Negro colleges; by 1933 it had nine on the Class A list, with an enrollment of 3,244.[91]

In the late 1920's the Rosenwald Fund and the GEB evolved a plan to develop four strategically located university centers for Negroes: Fisk University and Meharry Medical College in Nashville; Howard University in Washington; and the combination of several smaller institutions into the greater Atlanta and Dillard universities, the latter in New Orleans. Several Negro institutions in Atlanta that dated from the Reconstruction missionary efforts were fortunately located on adjacent campuses. In 1929 John Hope, already president of Morehouse College for men, became

[87] Jones, *Negro Education*, II, 16–17; Fred McCuistion, *Higher Education of Negroes (A Summary)* (Nashville, 1933), 15. Slight variations will be found in the figures given in Arthur J. Klein, *Survey of Negro Colleges and Universities*, U.S. Bureau of Education *Bulletin*, 1928, No. 7 (Washington, 1929), 947.

[88] General Education Board, *Annual Report*, 1919–1920, pp. 79, 83; 1928–1929, p. 31.

[89] General Education Board, *Annual Report*, 1928–1929, pp. 28–29; Fosdick *et al.*, *Adventure in Giving*, 196; Leavell, *Philanthropy in Negro Education*, 132–33.

[90] Holmes, *Evolution of the Negro College*, 197. Figures for fifteen states.

[91] *Ibid.*, 199. The first attempts at standardization had been made by the Association of Colleges for Negro Youth, founded at Knoxville in 1913. Charles S. Johnson, *The Negro College Graduate* (Chapel Hill, 1938), 294–95.

president of Atlanta University, and Spelman College for women also entered the arrangement. Atlanta University emphasized graduate work while the other two continued their undergraduate programs. In 1931 New Orleans University, Straight College, and the Flint-Goodridge Hospital combined into Dillard University with a new campus on Gentilly Road and with Will Alexander of the Interracial Commission as its first president.[92]

The recurrent theme of Negro educational movements during these years was "a feud of almost Kentuckian duration and intensity" between the genteel tradition of Latin and Greek and the "practical" industrial-vocational curriculum first sponsored by Hampton and Tuskegee. Opinions differed strongly. Many people argued cogently that the masses of Negroes needed vocational preparation, but the discussion often resolved itself into "what kind of education the Negro most needed" or was "best fitted for," or what kind was "most worthy of public support." [93] In short, industrial education became a corollary of white supremacy, and in meaning was limited to a few lessons in simple carpentry, gardening, or the household arts which would make the Negro more "useful" to his community.

Thomas Jesse Jones in 1916 found industrial training "ineffective and very limited in quantity" in fully half the cases.[94] As late as 1935 a survey showed that for every dollar spent per white pupil in vocational training only 58 cents was spent per Negro pupil.[95] The Hampton-Tuskegee idea "was probably never tried except in the institutions which first began it," Horace Mann Bond concluded. "Elsewhere, the process of 'industrial education' was ritualized." In the midst of a kaleidoscopic economic world, the Negro industrial schools, according to the president of one, sat "as though sublimely oblivious of the whirling streams around them like medieval monasteries unconscious of the torrent of the Ren-

[92] Holmes, *Evolution of the Negro College*, 192–97; "Reminiscences of Will W. Alexander," 325–49; Embree and Waxman, *Investment in People*, 85–98; *Southern Workman*, LVIII (1929), 207.
[93] Alain Locke, "Negro Education Bids for Par," in *Survey*, LIV (1925), 568.
[94] Jones, *Negro Education*, II, 19.
[95] Wilkerson, *Special Problems of Negro Education*, 100. Figures are for eighteen states.

aissance," still teaching the handicrafts and neglecting vocational guidance or placement. Land grant colleges gave "pretty sloppy" courses in the agricultural and mechanical arts, mainly for teacher-trainees.[96]

The paternalistic spirit of both the genteel classicism and the industrial education ran afoul of the New Negro philosophy. In the mid-twenties, a wave of student and alumni unrest shook one campus after another: Florida A & M, Lincoln University in Missouri, Fisk, Howard, Tuskegee, and Hampton. Demonstrations prompted changes of administration at Howard and at Fisk, where a benign Northern white president seemed unable to cope with the New Negro without the aid of the Nashville police.[97] In 1927 students temporarily closed Hampton with a strike that one observer considered "a half-blind, half-awakened resentment of the parade atmosphere of an interracial showroom, a revulsion from the constant intrusion of a social problem into their daily lives." [98] In 1925 a conference of over a hundred Negro students denounced "the paternalistic attitude so prevalent in Negro colleges and so offensive and uninspiring to their students," and demanded the appointment of Negro presidents at Negro institutions as the only way out. The whole development represented the growing pains of a new generation "in process of moulting the psychology of dependence and subserviency," the beginning of a transition toward the employment of Negro presidents and the introduction of modern programs in liberal arts and sciences.[99] The rise of accrediting agencies and the requirements of standardization in college and secondary education caused the pendu-

[96] Bond, *Education of the Negro in the American Social Order*, 124; Frank Horne, "The Industrial School of the South," in *Opportunity*, XIII (1935), 138, 178.

[97] Locke, "Negro Education Bids for Par," *loc. cit.*, 570; John R. Scotford, "The New Negro Education," in *Christian Century*, XLV (1928), 47–48; Baker, *Negro-White Adjustment*, 159–63; W. E. B. DuBois, "Negroes in College," in *Nation*, CXXII (1926), 229.

[98] "Hampton Tweaks the Reins," in *Survey*, LIX (1927–1928), 206; W. E. B. DuBois, "The Hampton Strike," in *Nation*, CXXV (1927), 471–72.

[99] Locke, "Negro Education Bids for Par," *loc. cit.*, 569, 592. For the personal account of a Negro college president representing the "accommodation" leadership see Joseph W. Holley, *You Can't Build a Chimney from the Top: The South through the Eyes of a Negro Educator* (New York, 1948). See also Horace Mann Bond, "A Negro Looks at His South," in *Harper's*, CLXIII (1931), 100–102.

lum to swing strongly that way.[100] On the whole, it seemed, most Negroes got about the same general kind of education as the whites, the main difference being in the quantity and quality.

The growth of schools and highways paralleled a significant, if lesser, growth of public health services. Successive crusades for the conquest of tuberculosis, hookworm, malaria, pellagra, and syphilis had cumulative effects along many lines: they exploded the legend of an unhealthful climate, implanted the germ theory in the public consciousness, encouraged sanitation and drainage, contributed to the disappearance of the classic "poor white" type, and nourished a public health movement that attacked disease on an expanding front.

Popular imagination was first captured by the Sanitary Commission for the Eradication of the Hookworm Disease, a Rockefeller agency which from 1909 to 1914 contributed to the treatment of 694,494 cases in eleven Southern states.[101] The work continued under the International Health Board (IHB) of the Rockefeller Foundation, which gradually turned it over to burgeoning county health departments and after 1921 confined itself to periodic resurveys, spending $3,783,125.74 on the hookworm program between 1913 and 1933.[102]

Malaria stood second only to hookworm as "probably the most serious obstacle to the development of civilization in the region where they prevail," according to the IHB.[103] Climate and topography conspired to localize both in the South—hookworm in the hot sandy soils, malaria in swamplands and the sluggish lower reaches of river valleys. "The loss of efficiency caused . . . in . . . the malarious section of the South," one student concluded, "is beyond comparison greater than that caused by any other disease." As with hookworm, sickness rather than mortality was the

[100] Frank Horne, "The Industrial School of the South," in *Opportunity*, XIII (1935), 137–38, 178–79. See also W. E. B. DuBois, "Education and Work," commencement address at Howard University, June 6, 1930, reprinted in *Journal of Negro Education*, I (1932), 60–74.

[101] Rockefeller Sanitary Commission for Eradication of Hookworm, *Fifth Annual Report* . . . (Washington, 1915), 43.

[102] Rockefeller Foundation, *Annual Report*, 1933, pp. 138–39.

[103] International Health Board, *Fourth Annual Report*, 126, quoted in Vance, *Human Geography of the South*, 391.

curse; a single death from malaria, in an estimate made in 1919, corresponded to about two to four thousand days of chills and fever.[104] However, IHB experiments in several Arkansas and Mississippi communities from 1916 to 1918 demonstrated the possibility of control at low cost through spraying, drainage, screening, and treatment with quinine. A general campaign may be said to have started in 1917, with work in and about army camps by the U.S. Public Health Service. From 1920 to 1922 the IHB conducted demonstrations in more than a hundred municipalities. By 1926 it was aiding the health departments of seven states and twenty-six counties in rural mosquito control activities.[105] Progress was slow and painful, dependent in the long run upon rising standards of education and prosperity, funds for mosquito control, the screening of homes, and medical care. But testimony to the results was impressive, especially in Mississippi, where the effort was most concentrated. In 1927, a faculty member of Mississippi A & M observed, the school hospital had not a single case—twenty years before it had been crowded with malarious students from the Delta.[106]

Pellagra, third in the Southern trilogy of "lazy diseases," yielded more slowly to medical science. First diagnosed at the Alabama Hospital for the Colored Insane in 1906, it seemed to be spreading rapidly in the years that followed, although it must have prevailed unrecognized for years.[107] Characterized by hard red splotches on the skin and extreme diarrhea, the disease in advanced stages could produce nervous disorders, insanity, and death; but its chief ravages came in an overpowering lethargy. In 1914 the Public Health Service placed Dr. Joseph Goldberger in charge of an investigation into the unknown causes.[108] Disdaining the laboratory for the field, Goldberger quickly found it to be typically a

[104] H. R. Carter, *The Malaria Problem of the South,* U.S. Public Health Service Public Health Report, No. 552 (Washington, 1919) , 3.

[105] Rockefeller Foundation, *Annual Report,* 1917, pp. 184–97; 1919, pp. 186–97; 1923, p. 134; 1933, pp. 144–47, 396–400.

[106] R. W. Harned, quoted in L. Q. Howard, *The Insect Menace* (New York, 1931) , 186–88.

[107] Francis R. Allen, "Public Health Work in the Southeast, 1872–1941: The Study of a Social Movement" (Ph.D. dissertation, University of North Carolina, 1946) , 350–51.

[108] Robert Blue to Joseph Goldberger, February 7, 1914, in Goldberger Papers.

disease of the poor, especially prevalent in rural areas and mill villages, and reached a simple conclusion: it resulted from a dietary deficiency in certain classes of protein food. "It seems probable," the immigrant doctor wrote his wife, "that pellagra can be wiped out in the South by simply getting the people to eat beans, BEANS, BEANS, BEANS, and BEANS!!!" [109] In 1915 experiments with a volunteer "Pellagra Squad" at the Rankin farm of the Mississippi State Penitentiary confirmed his theory. Given all they could eat of that common diet of the Southern poor—the "three M's" (salt meat, meal, and molasses) —six of eleven developed pellagra.[110] Goldberger corroborated the evidence with unsuccessful efforts to infect himself and other subjects, thus proving the affliction to be non-contagious; by dietary experiments that eliminated the disease in several public institutions; and by statistical studies showing its relationship to income levels and food costs.[111]

But the delay between discovery and application was agonizingly long. In 1921 the Public Health Service, acting on knowledge then six years old, warned that the collapse of the cotton market and the ravages of the boll weevil would produce an epidemic among farmers forced into a starvation diet—only to meet a storm of objection and abuse. Even public health officials indignantly denied that there was "hidden hunger" in the South; Senator Harris denied knowledge of a single case in Georgia; the Southern people were "not menaced with famine," Representative Byrnes of South Carolina protested, and they were "not seeking charity." Health officials abruptly dropped their tentative plans for relief measures, and an epidemic followed.[112]

[109] Joseph Goldberger to [Mrs. Joseph Goldberger], September 30, 1915, in Goldberger Papers.

[110] Goldberger to [Mrs. Goldberger], October 29, 30, November 1, 1915; New Orleans *Times-Picayune*, February 5, 1915; Jackson *Daily News*, November 1, 1915; New York *World*, November 2, 1915, in Goldberger Scrapbook, in Goldberger Papers.

[111] Milton Terris (ed.), *Goldberger on Pellagra* (Baton Rouge, 1964), reprints his major papers on the subject. A detailed secondary account is in Robert P. Parsons, *Trail to Light: A Biography of Joseph Goldberger* (Indianapolis, 1943), especially 279–327.

[112] Willford I. King, "Pellagra and Poverty," in *Survey*, XLVI (1921), 629–32; New York *Times*, July 25, 26, 27, 31, 1921; Vance, *Human Geography of the South*, 438–39; Allen, "Public Health Work in the Southeast," 354; E. M. Perdue, "Pellagra in the South Not a Menace Nor Due to Under Nourishment," in *Manufacturers' Record*, LXXX (September 8, 1921), 67–68.

It took a major disaster to bring the work to fruition, a dozen years after the discovery. In 1927, a great Mississippi River flood and an attendant famine brought the "red horror" before the eyes of Red Cross volunteers. On the basis of more recent experiments Goldberger advised the use of yeast, at about two cents a day per person. Nearly six tons were distributed, some four thousand cases were quickly cured, and the Red Cross undertook to spread the Goldberger doctrine of fresh milk, fruits, vegetables, and meat. The incidence of pellagra dropped steadily thereafter, even through the depression years.[113] Finally, in 1937 several researchers almost simultaneously discovered the specific for pellagra, which Goldberger had never identified: nicotinic acid, or niacin, which soon went into general use with other B vitamin additives in strengthening bread.[114]

Meanwhile still another health crusade was in the making. In 1929 a Public Health Service (PHS) survey of venereal disease among Mississippi Negroes found positive reactions in more than 25 per cent of three thousand Wasserman tests, "the first reliable indication that syphilis rather than malaria, pellagra or hookworm, might be the most serious public health problem of the southern states." [115] The same year the PHS and Rosenwald Foundation started a pilot program in six counties from Bolivar, Mississippi, to Albemarle, Virginia; about six thousand persons were treated, but the program ended in 1932. Further development by public health agencies was only spotty until the enactment of a Federal Venereal Disease Control Act of 1938 and a new crusade for the diagnosis and eradication of syphilis.[116]

The hookworm campaign had provided a fortuitous beginning to the health crusades, for that affliction was easily explained and readily understood. The hookworm could be seen with the naked eye; it prepared the mind for acceptance of the germ theory and

[113] Paul de Kruif, "The Rise and Fall of Pellagra," in *Country Gentleman* (Philadelphia), CVII (August, 1937), 10–11, 40–41; William R. Redden, "Health Services in Flood Valuable National Asset," in *Red Cross Courier* (Washington), VII (June 15, 1928), 16.

[114] Paul de Kruif, "Dr. Joseph Goldberger, Great American," in *Charlotte Observer*, June 21, 1942; Allen, "Public Health Work in the Southeast," 356.

[115] Thomas B. Parran, "No Defense for Any of Us," in *Survey Graphic*, XXVII (1938), 198.

[116] Embree and Waxman, *Investment in People*, 113–15; Allen, "Public Health Work in the Southeast," 402.

fostered an understanding of sanitation. Its eradication, in fact, virtually resolved itself "into a problem of popular education against soil pollution." [117] Beginning in 1918 the campaign made the building of sanitary privies an issue of community pride; health officials published lists in the papers and posted maps showing occupants or owners who had installed facilities. The improvements brought measurable reductions in the incidence of dysentery and typhoid fever as well as hookworm infection. [118] The malaria campaigns in turn won eager converts, as much perhaps because they reduced mosquito discomfort as because they reduced infection. The pellagra discoveries prompted lessons in nutrition and farm diversification, with county and home demonstration agents taking up the cause of garden plots and curb markets in the towns. [119]

Most significant of all was the development of county health departments to advance the work on a continuing basis. By 1913 every Southern state had already established some kind of state health agency. After that date county agencies multiplied rapidly; in 1915 the Southeast had 11 of the 14 county departments in the nation and maintained the lead in subsequent years. The International Health Board adopted a policy of encouraging the establishment of county departments as the best means of retaining and extending the hookworm work. By 1920 the number had grown to 94 and by 1925 to 166. [120] In the Mississippi flood disaster of 1927 the American Red Cross directed "the foremost emergency health program ever developed in the country in peace time," mobilized nurses, public health officers, engineers, sanitary inspectors, and water chemists; distributed yeast, fought malaria, immunized refugees against smallpox and typhoid fever, organized programs of instruction in health and sanitation—in all, provided services to

[117] Unidentified International Health Board report, quoted in Vance, *Human Geography of the South*, 385.
[118] Rockefeller Foundation, *Annual Report*, 1916, pp. 78–84; 1918, pp. 181–84.
[119] Vance, *Human Geography of the South*, 433–36.
[120] Allen, "Public Health Work in the Southeast," 346–61, 401; Rockefeller Foundation, *Annual Report*, 1916, pp. 89–90; 1918, p. 98; 1919, p. 74; John A. Fennell and Pauline Mead, *History of County Health Organizations in the United States*, U.S. Public Health Service Public Health Bulletin No. 222 (Washington, 1936), 11–19.

some 650,000 people. As the flood waters drained off, public health leaders at a meeting in New Orleans agreed that counties with health organizations had most effectively met the emergency. They proceeded to work out a program under which the Public Health Service and the Rockefeller Foundation together would supply 25 per cent of the cost of new county departments if the states and counties would assume the rest. By April, 1928, a total of eighty new departments had sprung up in the flooded counties. In all, from 1927 through 1932 the Rockefeller Foundation spent more than half a million dollars in support of departments in those areas; public treasuries spent much more.[121]

Like the highway and education movements the health crusades eventually moved into the phase of institutionalization. At first the effort was to inform the masses of the people about the principles of sanitation, nutrition, and prevention; by 1930 the emphasis had shifted to permanent agencies working on a multiplicity of problems. Various smaller groups made contributions in the process, most notably the Milbank Memorial Fund and the Rosenwald Fund; but the Rockefeller Foundation's International Health Board, like the GEB in education, was the central agency. From 1913 through 1932 it spent more than $1,000,000 for the support of local health departments in the South, in addition to its other activities. Total governmental expenditures for the purpose in Southern states grew from $230,496 in 1902 to $4,217,997 in 1930. The eleven Southeastern states by that time had 347 of the nation's 553 full-time county health organizations.[122]

In 1931 Dr. Charles Wardell Stiles, the nemesis of the hookworm, returned to the scenes of his battles. "Prior to 1910," he said, "a person could stand on the street corner of practically any city or town in the sand lands of the South and in an afternoon . . . see from five to twenty, so-called 'dirt-eaters.' " By

[121] Redden, "Health Services in Flood Valuable National Asset," *loc. cit.*, 15–17; James L. Fiesler, "Seven Great Gains from Out the Great Valley," in *Red Cross Courier,* VII (June 15, 1928), 6–7. Of the eighty new departments, five were in Illinois and two in Missouri; the remainder were in Southern states.

[122] Rockefeller Foundation, *Annual Report,* 1933, pp. 168–69; Dabney, *Universal Education in the South,* II, 262; Allen, "Public Health Work in the Southeast," 401.

1931 it took several days to find one. Among 18,649 school children inspected, a survey uncovered only 40 cases of hookworm infection, and the disease was "lighter in form." Yellow fever had been conquered, malaria and typhoid fever drastically reduced. "No school seen in 1931 compared as a disease center with the majority of rural schools in 1902, when they were all surrounded by polluted soil. This is a marvelous advance." Medical inspection of school children had become widespread. Many rural children still lived in dwellings without outhouses, but even the good-roads movement had had an impact on the problem. "People living along improved highways take a greater pride in their homes." [123]

But the South still lagged in many standard health facilities. Twelve of the Southern states in 1930 had fewer than six hospital beds per 1,000 population; only three states outside the region ranked so low. At the same time the states of the Southeast had 95.1 physicians per 100,000 population while the nation as a whole had 125.2.[124] From 1920 to 1929 only Arkansas, Oklahoma, North Carolina, and Kentucky fell consistently below the national death rate.[125]

In the field of social welfare, closely related to public health, there was similar progress toward professionalization. Along with the rise of associated charities and, later, community chests, came state conferences of social work; beginning with Virginia in 1900 seven Southern states had them before 1913, three more by 1916, and the remainder by 1927.[126] They were the state equivalents of the Southern Sociological Congress but more durable and more effective in gaining specific objectives. Uniting social workers and community-minded laymen, the conferences promoted a broad range of social legislation. The North Carolina Conference for Social Service, for example, from 1913 to 1929 sponsored measures for juvenile courts, a mother's aid system, segregation of the criminally insane, compulsory school attendance, physical examination

[123] Charles Wardell Stiles, manuscript report, quoted in Dabney, *Universal Education in the South*, II, 260–62.

[124] Odum, *Southern Regions of the United States*, 370; Kenneth Evans, "Changing Occupational Distribution in the South with Special Emphasis on the Rise of Professional Services" (Ph.D. dissertation, University of North Carolina, 1938), 113–25.

[125] Vance, *Human Geography of the South*, 376–77.

[126] Shivers, "Social Welfare Movement in the South," 156.

of school children, the establishment of a prison farm for women, a special camp for tubercular prisoners, and a school for delinquent Negro girls.[127]

The war work of the Red Cross and other agencies did much to stimulate the welfare movement. At the end of the war the Red Cross Southern Division under Joseph C. Logan of Atlanta undertook to hold and extend the gains. It developed local chapters and worked for the establishment of family agencies, public welfare departments, recreation services, and community chests; and it encouraged public understanding by "education—education and more education—putting in workers against insurmountable odds, impossible situations, plowing them in and then planting others," until the work finally ended in 1925.[128] The hastily formed Home Service Institutes of the war led the Red Cross in 1920 to help establish the School of Public Welfare at the University of North Carolina under Howard W. Odum and the Atlanta School of Social Work for Negroes under E. Franklin Frazier and, later, Forrester B. Washington. Additional contributions to professionalization came from the schools of social work at William and Mary (1916), Rice (1916), and Tulane (1925). The school at the University of North Carolina was the first designed to meet the needs of rural social workers.[129]

Another achievement of the period was the creation of state public welfare agencies, beginning with North Carolina in 1917; by 1927 they existed in all Southern states except Mississippi—and by 1934 in Mississippi as well.[130] In 1930 welfare expenditures amounted to 3.8 per cent of total state expenditures in the Southeast and 4.2 in the Southwest, or $1,461 and $1,675 respectively per capita.[131] One measure of growing interest was the

[127] *Ibid.,* 174. See also Gulledge, *North Carolina Conference for Social Service.*

[128] Blackburn, "What the Southern Division Did for the South," *loc. cit.,* 760; Shivers, "Social Welfare Movement in the South," 69–73; obituary of Logan in Atlanta *Journal,* March 15, 1928.

[129] Shivers, "Social Welfare Movement in the South," 70–72, 208, 211; Range, *Rise and Progress of Negro Colleges in Georgia,* 178–79.

[130] Shivers, "Social Welfare Movement in the South," 244. Arkansas and South Carolina discontinued their programs in 1926. *Ibid.,* 275–76.

[131] Gordon W. Blackwell, "State Public Welfare in the Southeast: An Aproach to Regional Planning in the Field of State Public Welfare" (M.A. thesis, University of North Carolina, 1933) , 75.

Southern membership in the National Conference of Social Work, which grew from 141 in 1908 to 677, or more than 10 per cent of the total, in 1928, although a more accurate measure of professional personnel was membership in the American Association of Social Workers—only 253.[132] The advance was limited and the expenditures small, but the development laid foundations for the future. In the 1930's, under the rubric of "relief," the field of social work would flourish. By the end of that decade public welfare and public health together would add a third major area of state responsibility to the existing programs for highways and schools.

[132] Howard W. Odum, "How New Is the South in Social Work?", in *Survey*, LX (1928), 329. The figures do not include Arkansas and Oklahoma.

CHAPTER IX

THE CONGO OF THE BOZART

WHEN the stream of Southern history broke upon the social and economic rapids of the 1920's, no gifted critic found reason to prophesy that it would nourish a flowering of Southern literature. Professional Southerners claimed to cherish the sixteen-volume *Library of Southern Literature* which had been collected to "make clear that the literary barrenness of the South has been overstated." [1] But few professional critics cherished any Southern writers except the Virginians Ellen Glasgow and James Branch Cabell, and Miss Glasgow still worked in relative obscurity. Several monuments from an earlier day, like Grace King and Mary Johnston, stood until the 1930's, but their era ended when Thomas Nelson Page, Mary Noailles Murfree, George Washington Cable, and James Lane Allen all died between 1922 and 1925.

In 1917, when H. L. Mencken set about constructing his image of the benighted South in his essay, "The Sahara of the Bozart," it was with the sterility of Southern literature that he began. With devilish glee he anointed one J. Gordon Coogler of South Carolina "the last bard of Dixie" and quoted his immortal couplet:

Alas for the South! Her books have grown fewer—
She never was much given to literature.

"Down there," Mencken avowed, "a poet is now almost as rare as an oboe-player, a drypoint etcher or a metaphysician." As for

[1] Edwin A. Alderman, "Introductory," in Edwin A. Alderman, Joel Chandler Harris, and Charles W. Kent (eds.) , *Library of Southern Literature* (16 vols., New Orleans and Atlanta, 1908–1913) , I, xiv.

"critics, musical composers, painters, sculptors, architects . . . there is not even a bad one between the Potomac mud-flats and the Gulf. Nor an historian . . . sociologist . . . philosopher . . . theologian . . . scientist. In all these fields the south is an awe-inspiring blank—a brother to Portugal, Serbia and Esthonia." The arts, he said, "save in the lower reaches of the gospel hymn, the phonograph and the chatauqua harangue, are all held in suspicion." [2]

But Mencken's metaphor had missed the mark, Gerald Johnson suggested. The South was "not the Sahara, but the Congo of the Bozart. Its pulses beat to the rhythm of the tom-tom, and it likes any color if it's red." If Mencken presumed to doubt, he should explore "the trackless waste of the Library of Southern Literature, where a man might wander for years" through the literary equivalent of Sir Harry Johnson's Sierra Leone: "the mammalian fauna of chimpanzis, monkeys, bats, cats . . . large eared earth-pigs, little known duiker bush-buck, hartebeeste, and elephant." By way of prophecy Johnson quoted one Mattie J. Peterson, the Tar Heel counterpart of Coogler and author of the classic lines:

> *I seen Pa coming, stepping high,*
> *Which was of his walk the way.*

"He who has the vision to see Southern literature coming at all . . ." Johnson said, "needs must see it stepping high, for that is of its walk the way. . . . It may be outlandish. . . . It may be gorgeously barbaric, but it will not be monotonous. For all I know, it may be in some manifestations tremendously evil—it may wallow in filth, but it will not dabble in dirt." [3]

Johnson anticipated a stereotype that long hampered critical

---

[2] Henry L. Mencken, "The Sahara of the Bozart," in *Prejudices: Second Series* (New York, 1920), 136, 137, 139, 153. It was this publication that gave the essay a wider audience. It first appeared, however, in the New York *Evening Mail*, November 13, 1917. Betty Adler and Jane Wilhelm, *H.L.M.: The Mencken Bibliography* (Baltimore, 1961), 56.

[3] Gerald W. Johnson, "The Congo, Mr. Mencken," in *The Reviewer*, III (1923), 891, 892–93. Johnson took some liberties with Miss Peterson's grammar. The original was, "I saw him coming, stepping high/Which was of his walk the way. . . ." Mattie J. Peterson, "I Kissed Pa Twice After His Death," in *Little Pansy, A Novel, and Miscellaneous Poetry* (Wilmington, 1890), 46.

understanding of the new literature, but he identified one of the major forces that motivated it, emancipation from the genteel tradition. Another factor, which became clear only with greater perspective, was that the South had reached a historical watershed, that it stood between two worlds, one dying and the other struggling to be born. The resultant conflict of values, which aroused the Ku Klux and fundamentalist furies, had quite another effect on the South's young writers. "After the war," wrote one of them (Allen Tate), "the South again knew the world, but it had a memory of another war; with us, entering the world once more meant not the obliteration of the past but a heightened consciousness of it; so that we had . . . a double focus, a looking two ways, which gave a special dimension to the writings of our school." [4] The peculiar historical perspective of that generation, Tate said on another occasion, made possible the "curious burst of intelligence that we get at a crossing of the ways, not unlike, on an infinitesimal scale, the outburst of poetic genius at the end of the sixteenth century when commercial England began to crush feudal England." [5]

Increasingly adrift in a sea of rooming houses and filling stations, the old gray stone house of Ellen Glasgow at One West Main in Richmond aptly symbolized Southern literature, poised between two eras. There, in the Victorian twilight at the turn of the century she had commenced a lonely revolt against the "twin conventions of prudery and platitude." [6] In the years since, she had patiently composed her "Novels of the Commonwealth," which comprised a realistic social history of Virginia from the Civil War. The series was completed with *Life and Gabriella* (1916), which made the best-seller list, but Miss Glasgow still enjoyed the critics' "benevolent neglect." [7] She was, her neighbor Cabell said, "that other Virginian woman who wrote books," lost "in the obscuring shadow of the famousness and the large sales of

---

[4] Allen Tate, "*The Fugitive*, 1922–1925: A Personal Recollection Twenty Years After," *Princeton University Library Chronicle*, III (1942), 75.

[5] Allen Tate, "The Profession of Letters in the South," in *Virginia Quarterly Review*, XI (1935), 175–76.

[6] Ellen Glasgow, *A Certain Measure* (New York, 1943), 141.

[7] *Ibid.*, 177; Alice Payne Hackett, *60 Years of Best Sellers, 1895–1955* (New York, 1956), 121.

Mary Johnston," author of cape-and-sword romances—in third place after still another Virginian, Henry Sydnor Harrison.[8]

She had broken with tradition but, she later confessed, still felt "the backward pull of inherited tendencies." With *Barren Ground* (1925), she wrote, however, "I knew I had found myself." That book was the response to a fresh creative impulse. "All that came after . . . was the result of this heightened consciousness and altered perspective." [9] *Barren Ground* brought the critical recognition so long withheld. In the story the central figure, Dorinda Oakley, daughter of an impoverished dirt-farmer, returned from an unhappy love affair to convert the barren farm into a prosperous dairy and to marry a prosaic storekeeper who later died a hero in a train wreck. In the end Dorinda herself became a heroic figure of endurance, one of those who existed "wherever a human being has learned to live without joy, wherever the spirit of fortitude has triumphed over the sense of futility." [10]

For many a reader the novel represented almost a tract for diversified farming, a timely fact that perhaps had something to do with its reception. Vanderbilt's Donald Davidson felt impelled to object that it was almost a piece of fictionalized advice to young Southern women: "Go, become scientific dairymaids, study agricultural manuals and join the uplift." [11] Davidson's colleague, Edwin Mims, regarded it with more favor: "There is not a single progressive movement in the South to-day that may not find enlightenment and inspiration in some one of her novels." [12] But Ellen Glasgow had set off on a new tack. Entering now her most fruitful years, she turned to the satirical comedy of manners in Queenborough, a thinly-disguised Richmond, and brought forth amid growing plaudits *The Romantic Comedians* (1926), *They Stooped to Folly* (1929), and *The Sheltered Life* (1932).

The new release of powers came in an act of return from the

[8] James Branch Cabell, *Let Me Lie* (New York, 1947), 239.

[9] Ellen Glasgow, *The Woman Within* (New York, 1954), 243; Glasgow, *A Certain Measure*, 129.

[10] Glasgow, *A Certain Measure*, 154.

[11] Donald Davidson, "The Artist as Southerner," in *Saturday Review of Literature*, II (May 15, 1926), 782.

[12] Mims, *The Advancing South*, 215.

"long distant view" of Virginia history to the more familiar ground of her class and environs. For all the "blood and irony" of her realism, Ellen Glasgow remained a Virginia gentlewoman, inhabiting a new world she had not made. Now she turned to communities "in which the vital stream was running out into the shallows," to social orders that had outlived their functions, a declining aristocracy whose "spirit of adventure had disintegrated into an evasive idealism, a philosophy of heroic defeat" and the thinning stock of rural pioneers whose "fortitude had degenerated into a condition of moral inertia." [13] Like the younger writers of the day she looked backward and forward, and turned her irony both ways. "I do not like the twin curses of modern standardization and mass production," she said in 1931. "I do not like filling stations and smoke stacks in place of hedges. Yet I like even less the hookworm and pellagra and lynching of the agrarian scene, the embattled forces of religious prejudice and the snarling feature of our rural dry-nurse prohibition." [14]

After *Vein of Iron* (1935), which featured a stoical heroine like Dorinda Oakley, the long-delayed award of a Pulitzer Prize came with her last novel, *In This Our Life* (1941), written in the shadow of a lingering illness. Before she died in 1945, Ellen Glasgow found herself again, as she had begun, a rebel against the prevailing fashion. Looking over "the multitude of half-wits, the whole idiots, and nymphomaniacs, and paranoiacs, and rakehells in general, who populate the modern literary South," she began to suspect that one "was as little likely to encounter truth in the exposed features of the new barbarism as under the mask of civilized conduct." [15] Readers hardened to a new generation of writers would find her earlier work sentimental and strongly tinged with old-fashioned romance. They would find little evidence of the experimental techniques essayed by younger writers. But she had introduced a multitude of new types, new classes, new characters, new themes to Southern literature; and there was still good reason to endorse a judgment passed in 1930: "The novelist

[13] Glasgow, *A Certain Measure*, 153, 155.

[14] Quoted in Grace Stone, "Ellen Glasgow and Her Novels," in *Sewanee Review*, L (1942), 297.

[15] Glasgow, *A Certain Measure*, 15, 69.

who gives the most nearly complete picture of the South is undoubtedly Ellen Glasgow." [16]

The novels of Ellen Glasgow's neighbor, James Branch Cabell, offer a puzzle for chroniclers of regional literature. In 1920 he shared with two obscure poets the distinction of being the only Southern writers worth mentioning in Mencken's "Sahara of the Bozart." An abortive attempt to suppress *Jurgen* (1919) in New York suddenly thrust Cabell into notoriety, and after 1920 he enjoyed a subterranean reputation as the writer of "sexy" books together with critical acclaim and a following that grew almost into a cult of "exquisites." Probably the best-known Southern writer of the period, he was little concerned with the movements and themes that animated his contemporaries: "Ellen Glasgow and I are the contemporaneous products of as nearly the same environment as was ever accorded to any two writers," he said. "From out of our impressions as to exactly the same Richmond-in-Virginia, she has builded her Queenborough, and I my Lichfield; yet no towns have civic regulations more widely various." [17]

After an early career of light romances for *Harper's* and other magazines, several Virginia genealogies, and two novels that gently mocked Virginia conventions—*The Cords of Vanity* (1909) and *The Rivet in Grandfather's Neck* (1915) —he retreated more and more into the dream world of Poictesme, a medieval province of his own invention. There began the lengthy "Biography of the Life of Manuel," of which *Jurgen* comprised one installment. If Ellen Glasgow's novels might be entitled, as he suggested, "The Tragedy of Everywoman, As It Was Lately Enacted in the Commonwealth of Virginia," his own might be called "The Fantasy of Everyman, As It Was Once Enacted in the Province of Poictesme." Everyman—were he Manuel the Redeemer whose own history and legend developed in *Figures of Earth* (1921) and *The Silver Stallion* (1926) or one of his descendants, some of them in Lichfield—was moved to feats of chivalry, gallantry, and poetry, traversed the realms of time and space, entered heaven and hell, pursued and possessed the seductive females of history and myth. Finding only disillusionment, he returned at last to a prosy and

---

[16] Eudora Ramsay Richardson, "The South Grows Up," in *The Bookman*, LXX (1930) , 546.

[17] Cabell, *Let Me Lie*, 247-48.

matronly wife, to middle-aged comfort and routine, much as Cabell himself descended from his study to dinner with his Priscilla. "Art," he once wrote, "is in its last terms an evasion of the distasteful." [18] Only in the deliberate cultivation of myth and dream did man transcend mortality. Yet these, too, ultimately failed to satisfy his appetite for certainty and purpose.

Remote as Poictesme seemed, its genesis was in the Virginia of Cabell's youth. The growth of the myth of Manuel bore a striking resemblance to the rise of the myth of the Confederacy, which Cabell experienced as a youth and described years later in *Let Me Lie* (1947). Each myth, though false to its origins, had its uses, as Cabell saw it, in bolstering the morale and virtue of its adherents, and finally merged indistinguishably with reality.[19]

No other Southern writer during the 1920's equaled the achievement of Richmond's patricians, but all across the barrens of Mencken's "Sahara" new shoots began to stir in the soil; by mid-decade they had flowered into a literary revival. It may be too much to claim, as Oscar Cargill did, that Mencken anticipated the development and in his backhanded way sought to cultivate it. But there can be little question that within a few years, "Like Aaron's rod Mencken's goad had proved itself a symbol of fertility." [20] That Mencken pricked Southern awareness in more than one nerve was apparent from the frequency of references to him among the literary groups that were springing to life. Of late years, the Poetry Society of South Carolina noted in its first *Year Book* (1921), "it has not been *comme il faut* to wave the ensanguined chemise. . . . 'South-Baiting' from now on is going to be more of a dangerous sport than formerly, and will have to be carried on by matadors who wield a brand that does not too closely resemble the animal which they desire to slay." The Sahara had oases where the fig tree was not entirely barren, the *Year Book* asserted, and missiles from the editor of the *Smart Set* had "the irony of the boomerang." [21]

---

[18] James Branch Cabell, *Straws and Prayer Books* (New York, 1924), 93.

[19] This thesis is developed in Louis D. Rubin, Jr., *No Place on Earth: Ellen Glasgow, James Branch Cabell and Richmond-in-Virginia* (Austin, 1959), 56–67.

[20] Oscar Cargill, "Mencken and the South," *Georgia Review*, VI (1952), 372, 375.

[21] "The Worm Turns: Being in Some Sort a Reply to Mr. H. L. Mencken," in *The Year Book of the Poetry Society of South Carolina* (Charleston), I (1921), 14, 16.

The Poetry Society of South Carolina (mainly Charleston) stood in the vanguard of the Southern Renaissance. It grew out of weekly meetings at which two aspiring poets, DuBose Heyward, an insurance agent, and Hervey Allen, a high school teacher, submitted their verses to a "fanging" by their mentor, John Bennett, an established writer known chiefly for the children's classic, *Master Skylark* (1896). Formal organization came in the fall of 1920, and the first *Year Book* in the spring of 1921 revealed no small element of chauvinism in its effort to prove that "culture in the South is not merely an *ante bellum* tradition." Convinced that they represented "a force that needs only to be directed and coordinated in order to stimulate a genuine *south-wide* poetic renaissance," the Charlestonians set afoot a feverish campaign to awaken the literary South. "Their humorless intensity," said their historian, "would be almost laughable were it not for the fact that they succeeded." [22]

The group drew a miscellany of local poetasters, including some who achieved a degree of success: Josephine Pinckney, Beatrice Ravenel, Katherine Drayton Mayrant Simons, and from upstate, Henry Bellamann and Julia Peterkin. It brought in for lectures and readings outsiders such as Carl Sandburg, Harriet Monroe, Vachel Lindsay, and Robert Frost. It sponsored prize contests that afforded early recognition to young authors such as Donald Davidson, Robert Penn Warren, Olive Tilford Dargan, and others. Heyward, as secretary, neglected his business to carry afar a missionary campaign of lecturing, reading, and fomenting new poetry societies. Within a decade similar groups had sprung up in Maryland, Virginia, Georgia, Florida, Louisiana, and Texas, and active local groups in Norfolk, Suffolk, Nashville, Birmingham, Winter Park, and elsewhere.[23]

The quality of the Charleston group found expression in a

[22] Frank Durham, "South Carolina's Poetry Society," in *South Atlantic Quarterly*, LII (1953), 279.

[23] Addison Hibbard (ed.), *The Lyric South* (New York, 1928), xviii; *Year Book of the Poetry Society of South Carolina*, II (1922), 8; III (1923), 10–11; Ernest Hartsock, "Roses in the Desert: A View of Contemporary Southern Verse," in *Sewanee Review*, XXXVII (1929), 328–35; Josephine Pinckney, "Charleston's Poetry Society," *ibid.*, XXXVIII (1930), 50–56; Katherine H. Strong, "The Poetry Society of Georgia," in *Georgia Review*, VIII (1954), 29–40.

collection of verses by Heyward and Allen, *Carolina Chansons* (1922), a self-conscious effort to capture in lyric form the history and legends of the Low Country. It found more explicit expression the same year in *Poetry's* "Southern Number," which Heyward and Allen edited. They filled it mostly with Charleston authors and inserted an essay, "Poetry South," which predicted a coming Southern poetry "decidedly regional in spirit . . . strongly local in tone," based largely on local color, tradition, and legend.[24]

The Charlestonians betrayed a fatal addiction to the delicate tints of local color, but some of their contemporaries flaunted more garish hues of detached sophistication. At the beginning of 1921 a little group in New Orleans, intoxicated by the exuberance of revolt against Philistia, brought forth *The Double Dealer*—the title was explained by a cryptic quotation from Congreve's play of the same name: "I can deceive them both by speaking the truth." Julius Weis Friend and Basil Thompson were associate editors; later John McClure, newspaperman and poet, became editor. One "need not expect to find in these pages sympathy for presto change reforms, nor for syndicates for the propagation of brotherly love," the editors warned in the first issue; it would avail nothing to seek "an unground ax, a moral purpose, a political affiliation." Their concern was rather the "dissemination of good readable matter and the telling of the truth regardless of whom it disquiets." [25]

But they, too, felt the inexorable pull of regional loyalty. *The Double Dealer*, they said, wanted "to be known as the rebuilder, the driver of the first pile into the mud of this artistic stagnation which has been our portion since the Civil War . . . a movement, a protest, a rising up against the intellectual tyranny of New York, New England, and the Middle West." [26] In the sixth issue Basil Thompson championed a new Southern literature to replace "the treacly sentimentalities" of "lady fictioneers" and "the storied realm of dreams, lassitude, pleasure, chivalry and the Nigger." Hundreds of towns, he said, fairly bubbled "with the stuff of stories," with something "vital to the soil—the physical, mental

[24] Hervey Allen and DuBose Heyward, "Poetry South," in *Poetry* (Chicago), XX (1922), 35–48.
[25] *The Double Dealer* (New Orleans), I (1921), 2, 3.   [26] *Ibid.*, 126.

and spiritual outlook of an emerging people—the soul-awakening of a hardy, torpid race, just becoming reaware of itself." [27] In the seventh issue the slogan on the masthead changed from "A Magazine for the Discriminating" to "A National Magazine from the South." [28]

During its five years of existence *The Double Dealer* became the focus of a minor writers' colony. Its office in an unused third floor on Baronne Street, just outside the French Quarter, became a center for literary talk and beaux arts balls. In and out of the group moved Roark Bradford, Oliver LaFarge, E. P. O'Donnell, Lyle Saxon, the teen-aged Hamilton Basso and James K. Feibleman. For brief periods the exotic charm of the Vieux Carré drew Sherwood Anderson and William Faulkner into a kind of domestic expatriation in the Quarter. The place had, as Faulkner described it in a parody of Anderson's style, an "atmosphere of richness and soft laughter, you know . . . a kind of ease, a kind of awareness of the unimportance of things that outlanders like myself were taught to believe important." [29] There Faulkner wrote his first novel, *Soldiers' Pay* (1926), a story of postwar *Weltschmerz,* and gathered material for the second, *Mosquitoes* (1927), a caricature of the New Orleans Bohemians. After knocking about Europe and the Gulf Coast, he returned home to pursue Anderson's admonition that "all you know is that little patch up there in Mississippi where you started from," and Anderson after the success of *Dark Laughter* (1925) bought a farm near Marion, Virginia, thereby assuming residence at least on the fringes of the Southern literary pantheon.[30]

[27] *Ibid.,* 214.   [28] *Ibid.,* II (1921), 2.

[29] William Spratling and William Faulkner, *Sherwood Anderson & Other Famous Creoles: A Gallery of Contemporary New Orleans* (New Orleans, 1926). The foreword travestied an article Anderson wrote during a brief stay in 1922: "New Orleans, the Double Dealer and the Modern Movement in America," in *The Double Dealer,* III (1922), 119–26. See also Carvel Collins, "Introduction," in William Faulkner, *New Orleans Sketches* (New Brunswick, N.J., 1958), 12–25; Frances Jean Bowen, "The New Orleans *Double Dealer,* 1921–1926," in *Louisiana Historical Quarterly* (New Orleans), XXXIX (1956), 445–46, 449–50; and James K. Feibleman, "Literary New Orleans Between World Wars," in *Southern Review* (Baton Rouge) (N.S.), I (1965), 702–19.

[30] William Faulkner, "Sherwood Anderson: An Appreciation," in *The Atlantic,* CXCI (June, 1953), 29.

In May, 1926, *The Double Dealer* expired with the forty-third issue. Like many another such publication, it never paid for itself, but it performed better than most the little magazine's function of uncovering new talents. It printed some of the earliest work of Faulkner, Basso, Feibleman, Ernest Hemingway, Jean Toomer, Thornton Wilder, Hart Crane, Matthew Josephson, Malcolm Cowley, Edmund Wilson, and Kenneth Fearing, among others— surely achievement enough to justify one short-lived journal.[31]

Unlike the group that, in Mencken's phrase, ran amok in New Orleans, *The Reviewer* in Richmond maintained an air of rectitude befitting its locale where, one of its editors said, "the uncontrolled emotionalism of the Far South has been considered, always, slightly bad form." [32] Edited by Emily Clark, Hunter Stagg, Margaret Freeman, and Mary Dallas Street, the magazine first appeared in February, 1921. Like its contemporary, it "declared war" on mediocrity and the second rate.[33] Ellen Glasgow, Mary Johnston, and Cabell all contributed; Cabell quit his ivory tower long enough to edit three issues and advise on others. With the uncertain recompense of "payment in fame not specie," the magazine attracted leading writers of the literary establishment: Mencken, Hergesheimer, Galsworthy, Elinor Wylie, and others.[34]

The chief aim "should be to develop new Southern authors," Mencken advised the editors. "The South is beginning to emerge from its old slumber." And he cautioned: "Friend is failing in New Orleans because he is trying to print an imitation of the *Dial* and the *Smart Set*." [35] The Richmonders never conquered the impulse to court outland celebrities, but Emily Clark proclaimed a purpose "to build *The Reviewer* with Southern material insofar as this is possible." [36] Its roster of Southern "discoveries" included Frances Newman, a librarian who wrote reviews for the Atlanta

[31] Bowen, "The New Orleans *Double Dealer*, 1921–1926," *loc. cit.*, 454–56; Frederick J. Hoffman *et. al.*, *The Little Magazine: A History and a Bibliography* (Princeton, 1946), 12–13; Collins, "Introduction," in Faulkner, *New Orleans Sketches*, 15.

[32] Emily Clark, *Innocence Abroad* (New York, 1931), 29.

[33] "Foreword," *The Reviewer*, I (1921), 5.

[34] The phrase quoted appears in the advertising pages of *The Reviewer*, II (1921–1922).

[35] Quoted in Clark, *Innocence Abroad*, 112, 119.

[36] Emily Clark, "Beginning the Second Volume," in *The Reviewer*, II (1922), 40.

Constitution and staggered the home folk with a novel entitled *The Hard Boiled Virgin* (1926); [37] Julia Peterkin, whose early stories appeared there; Gerald W. Johnson, who ventured into its pages from the Greensboro *Daily News;* and Lynn Riggs, Oklahoma poet and dramatist. Late in 1924 *The Reviewer,* unable to pay its way, moved to Chapel Hill. Under the aegis of Paul Green and the University of North Carolina Press it survived one more year, then merged into *The Southwest Review.*[38]

In April, 1922, the first issue of *The Fugitive,* a little magazine devoted to poetry, issued forth to an unexpectant world from Nashville, Tennessee, and thus announced the existence of the most influential group in American letters since the New England Transcendentalists. In several respects the Fugitive poets differed from the transient groups in Charleston, New Orleans, and Richmond: they had a rigorously intellectual tone and academic connections with Vanderbilt; they sustained an intensive devotion to excellence; they were gestating the "New Criticism" that later worked a revolution in the English classroom; and quite ironically in the light of later developments, they were self-consciously cosmopolitan in attitude and opposed to the promotion of Southern literature as such.

At the time Vanderbilt's English department enjoyed a healthy diversity: Edwin Mims, New South progressive and inspirational champion of nineteenth-century literature; Walter Clyde Curry, author of the erudite *Chaucer and the Mediaeval Sciences* (1926); and John Crowe Ransom, who had just published his *Poems About God* (1919).[39] Ransom, in his thirties, was dean and mentor of the Fugitives, though never in any sense their leader. The beginning was in a group of faculty and student intellectuals that began to gather for discussions in 1915. Scattered by the war, the group reassembled in the fall of 1919 at sessions in the home of

[37] Her untimely death in 1928 cut short what Cabell and others thought a promising career. Her other books were *The Short Story's Mutations* (1924) and *Dead Lovers Are Faithful Lovers* (1928). See also Hansell Baugh (ed.), *Frances Newman's Letters* (New York, 1929).

[38] Hoffman *et al., The Little Magazine,* 263; Jay B. Hubbell, "Southern Magazines," in Couch (ed.), *Culture in the South,* 178–79.

[39] Randall Stewart, "The Relation Between Fugitives and Agrarians," in *Mississippi Quarterly,* XIII (1960), 55–56.

James Frank, around the chaise longue of his brother-in-law, Sidney Mttron Hirsch, an esoteric dilettante "whose doctrine skittered elusively among imaginary etymologies." [40] Gradually the discourse turned from philosophy to literature and then to biweekly reading and criticism.[41] At the end of 1921 there were seven members and eventually sixteen in all. Of these, four stood out in their ultimate commitment to literature as a profession: Ransom, Donald Davidson, Allen Tate, and Robert Penn Warren.[42]

Under the stimulus of discussions and critiques they began to create new poetry distinguished by attention to form and language, by complexity of content and allusion that yielded only to the closest study. The chief quality which set apart the poetry of the Fugitive group, their historian wrote, was "its embodiment of the fundamental beliefs of the society out of which it came." [43] But their "Southern quality" came through only later, for they started in revolt against the twin images of the sentimental traditionist and the New South booster. A literary phase "known rather euphemistically as Southern Literature has expired," Ransom announced in the first issue. "*The Fugitive* flees from nothing faster than from the high-caste Brahmins of the Old South." [44] In 1923, ruffled by *Poetry* editor Harriet Monroe's calls for a "strongly localized indigenous art" in a region "jewel-weighted with a heroic past," Davidson retorted that it was "not the province of any critic to dictate the material [Southern poets] shall choose" and expressed fear of too much stress "on a tradition that may be called a tradition only when looked at through the haze of a generous imagination." [45]

The "Southernness" of the Fugitives was least obtrusive in the

---

[40] Tate, "*The Fugitive,* 1922–1925: A Personal Recollection," *loc. cit.,* 76.

[41] The Fugitives' origins are traced in Louise Cowan, *The Fugitive Group: A Literary History* (Baton Rouge, 1959) , 3–42; and John L. Stewart, *The Burden of Time: The Fugitives and Agrarians* . . . (Princeton, 1965) , 3–21.

[42] The others were Hirsch, Frank, Curry, Merrill Moore, Laura Riding, Jesse Wills, Alec B. Stevenson, Stanley Johnson, William Yandell Elliott, William Frierson, Ridley Wills, and Alfred Starr. Cowan, *The Fugitive Group,* xvi.

[43] *Ibid.,* xx.

[44] "Forward," *The Fugitive,* I (1922) , 1.

[45] Harriet Monroe, "The Old South," in *Poetry* (Chicago) , XXII (1923) , 91; [Donald Davidson], "Merely Prose," *The Fugitive,* II (June–July, 1923) , 66.

poems of John Crowe Ransom, who perfected a personal style before any of the others and who, indeed, published few poems after his *Chills and Fever* (1924) and *Two Gentlemen in Bonds* (1927). "Antique Harvesters" did evoke the Agrarian myth of the Old South, which Ransom later espoused, in the picture of a fox hunt:

> . . . *The horn, the hounds, the lank mares coursing by*
> *Straddled with archetypes of chivalry.* . . .

The fieldworkers, who had paused to watch the gentry, he enjoined:

> *Resume, harvesters. The treasure is full bronze*
> *Which you will garner for the Lady.* . . .

And in the Lady Ransom evoked a semi-religious image of the South:

> *The sons of the fathers shall keep her, worthy of*
> *What these have done in love.*

"Necrological" was one among many examples of Ransom's gift for "the conjunction of a stylized, formal attitude of discourse and some of the most vicious, sanguinary subject matter in all of modern America." [46] In that poem a friar slipped away to view the carnage of a battlefield:

> *So still that he likened himself unto those dead*
> *Whom the kites of Heaven solicited with sweet cries.*

But the common qualities in Ransom's poems were those of a lofty yet unpretentious elegance, a blend of archaic and modern language, a "fury against abstractions," a dualism that dwelt upon the gap between human aspiration and achievement, a gentle and civilized irony that underscored the terrors which lie below the surface of life. In "Bells for John Whiteside's Daughter," whose "wars were bruited in our high window," the poet was

> . . . *sternly stopped*
> *To say we are vexed at her brown study,*
> *Lying so primly propped.*

[46] Louis D. Rubin, Jr., "The Poetry of Agrarianism," in his *The Faraway Country: Modern Writers of the South* (Seattle, Wash., 1963), 169.

In September, 1925, *The Fugitive* expired, less from want of support than from want of time.[47] Its founders had become busy authors with other outlets; some of them, including Tate and Warren, had left Nashville. They still thought themselves detached from the South, but an event remote from the realm of poetry, the Scopes trial, worked a sharp change in their thought. The Mencken-Darrow image of the benighted South stirred defensive attitudes and brought a dawning realization that they "shared pretty much the same assumptions about society, about man, nature, and God."[48] In 1926 Davidson produced an ambivalent essay in which he scored "civic boosters" and "the treacly lamentations of the old school," but called attention to certain Southern qualities: "Exuberance, sensitiveness, liveliness of imagination, warmth and flexibility of temper," which "properly realized, might display an affirmative zest and abandon now lacking in American art." Fundamentalism, he argued, expressed "a fierce clinging to poetic supernaturalism against the encroachments of cold logic; it stands for moral seriousness."[49] About the same time Ransom began to compose *God Without Thunder: An Unorthodox Defense of Orthodoxy* (1930), which used religious myth to counter the deification of science. Tate, in New York, had begun a search for roots, a search that led to biographies of Stonewall Jackson (1928) and Jefferson Davis (1929). In March, 1926, he wrote to Ransom, "I've attacked the South for the last time."[50] The next year Tate published "Ode to the Confederate Dead" and Davidson "The Tall Men," both poems about the Southerner's relation to—or rather alienation from—his heritage. By then the Agrarian Manifesto, *I'll Take My Stand* (1930), had begun to take shape in their minds; Warren and new allies from outside the Fugitive group were being drawn in.[51] The Fugitives, who had begun in flight from the South, stood finally at the very center of the new historical focus in Southern literature.

[47] Cowan, *The Fugitive Group*, 219–21.

[48] Donald Davidson, *Southern Writers in the Modern World* (Athens, Ga., 1958), 6.

[49] Davidson, "The Artist as Southerner," *loc. cit.*, 781–83.

[50] Cowan, *The Fugitive Group*, 244, gives the date as 1927. Virginia J. Rock, "The Making and Meaning of *I'll Take My Stand:* A Study in Utopian-Conservatism, 1925–1939" (Ph.D. dissertation, University of Minnesota, 1961), 222–23, gives the evidence for 1926.

[51] *Ibid.*, 246–47.

The four groups in Charleston, New Orleans, Richmond, and Nashville stood out, but other groups and little magazines germinated all across the South. By 1923, the South Carolina Poetry Society's *Year Book* asserted, the poetry movement resembled "the legendary matron who inhabited a discarded boot, and was confused by the multiplicity of her progeny." [52] In 1921 the Poet's Club in Norfolk began *The Lyric,* which outlived all the other little magazines but never deeply influenced developments. In Mississippi there was the short-lived *Blues: A Review of Modern Literature;* in Atlanta, *Bozart,* soon absorbed into *The Westminster Review;* in Dallas, *The Buccaneer;* in Charlotte, *The Journal of American Poetry,* which clung to verse "exalted in mood"; in Birmingham, *The Nomad,* a poetry journal, and The Loafers, a group of local writers.[53]

The magazines that survived were those with institutional support. Less modish, they nevertheless published some of the new authors and acknowledged the rising movements. *The Sewanee Review* at the University of the South, founded in 1892, and the *South Atlantic Quarterly* at Trinity College (Duke), founded in 1902, were the old standbys. More recently on the scene was *The Texas Review* at the University of Texas, founded by Stark Young in 1915 and converted into *The Southwest Review* at Southern Methodist in 1924, under Jay B. Hubbell. In 1925 James Southall Wilson founded *The Virginia Quarterly Review* at the University of Virginia.

In the Southwest, Texas and Oklahoma had their own nests of singing birds and a new group of fiction writers, but the activities that dominated the literary scene were the little theaters and a rising interest in folklore.[54] The little theater movement, which

[52] "Foreword," in *The Year Book of the Poetry Society of South Carolina,* III (1923), 9.
[53] Hoffman *et al., The Little Magazine,* 240–41, 262, 272, 283, 285–86; Ernest Hartsock, "Roses in the Desert, A View of Contemporary Southern Verse," in *Sewanee Review,* XXXVII (1929), 332; Federal Writers Program, *Alabama, A Guide to the Deep South* (New York, 1941), 133–34. See also Louis D. Rubin, Jr., "The Southern Muse: Two Poetry Societies," in *American Quarterly,* XIII (1961), 365–75.
[54] The writers are given brief treatment in Mabel Major *et al., Southwest Heritage: A Literary History and Bibliography* (Albuquerque, N.M., 1938), 109–17, 122–29. See also Benjamin A. Botkin (ed.), *The Southwest Scene: An Anthology of Regional Verse* (Oklahoma City, 1931); and Benjamin A. Botkin, "Folk-Say and Space," in *Southwest Review,* XX (1935), 322–23.

had originated in Chicago a decade earlier, entered the Sout.
when the road show collapsed after World War I. In 1929 one
authority located 133 in the Southern states and listed 10 of them
among the 35 "Leading Little Theaters" in the country.[55] Two of
these stood ahead of all the others: Le Petit Théâtre du Vieux
Carré (1919) under Walter Sinclair in New Orleans and the
Dallas Little Theater (1920) directed by Oliver Hinsdell. The
Dallas players in three successive years at the National Little
Theater Tournament, 1924–1926, won the David Belasco cup
with indigenous dramas: *Judge Lynch* by John William Rogers of
Dallas, *No 'Count Boy* by Paul Green of Chapel Hill, and *El
Christo* by Margaret Larkin of New Mexico. But the community
theaters were never very successful at stimulating creativity; to
win audiences they had to produce mostly standard classics or
Broadway hits.[56] The one native prodigy to arise from the
movement was Lynn Riggs of Oklahoma and New Mexico, whose
best known play, *Green Grow the Lilacs* (1931), later became the
musical *Oklahoma!*

The Southwest germinated one new theme of major literary
importance: a quickening search for folklore. This subject, like
the conscious literature, was just emerging from gentility. There
was a long-established interest in Negro spirituals and stories of
the Uncle Remus type, but the collection of white folklore
suffered from a tendency to reject materials not traceable to
English sources and analogues.[57] John A. Lomax's *Cowboy Songs*

[55] The count is from a map made by Harold A. Ehrensperger, editor of *The
Little Theater Monthly.* Kenneth MacGowan, *Footlights Across America: Toward
a National Theater* (New York, 1929), 10–11, 359–65. See also Major *et al., Southwest Heritage,* 132–33.

[56] Ula Milner Gregory, "The Fine Arts," in Couch (ed.), *Culture in the South,*
295; MacGowan, *Footlights Across America,* 346; John Rosenfield, "The Southwest
Amuses Itself," in *Southwest Review,* XVI (1931), 277–89. An interesting offshoot
was The Dallas Negro Players, who in 1930 presented Kathleen Witherspoon's *Jute,*
a play about racial conflict, before an audience of Negroes and whites in a community recently dominated by the Ku Klux Klan. Flora Lowrey, "The Dallas
Negro Players," in *Southwest Review,* XVI (1931), 373–82.

[57] Largely as a result of the classic Francis James Child, *The English and Scottish
Popular Ballad* (5 vols.; Boston and New York, 1882–1898), which strongly influ-
enced Cecil J. Sharp and Olive Dame Campbell, *English Folk Songs from the
Southern Appalachians* (Rev. ed., 2 vols.; London, 1932), and other works. One
student claimed that "there exists no such thing as American folklore, but only
European (or African, or Far Eastern) folklore on the American continent."
Alexander Haggerty Krappe, "American Folklore," in *Folk-Say,* II (1930), 291.

nd Other Frontier Ballads (1910) heralded a new interest in autochthonous and even primitive materials formerly beneath the notice of collectors: the sub-literary culture of the backwoods, slums, coal mines, lumber camps and oil fields, Negro blues and work songs, "bad man stuff" and "sinful songs." Lomax collaborated with Dorothy Scarborough and L. W. Payne, Jr., to found the Folk-Lore Society of Texas (1909) which, through its annual *Publications* (1916), edited by J. Frank Dobie (1923–1942), offered up rich stores of Southwestern folklore.[58]

In 1917 political upheaval at the University of Texas caused Lomax to seek other employment, but in 1931 he fled confinement in a Dallas bank to search the rural South, the prison camps, the red-light districts for folk songs, discovered Leadbelly (murderer and folk singer), and eventually became Curator of the Archive of American Folk Song at the Library of Congress. Lomax, according to one student, was the first collector of folk songs in English to use the phonograph in the field, and perhaps the most effective popularizer of all, who bequeathed the tradition finally to his son Alan.[59]

Meanwhile the academic archivists pursued more prudent careers in the Child-Sharp tradition of seeking out English ballads. C. Alphonso Smith, at the Universities of Virginia and North Carolina, was an extreme example, opposed to making the Virginia Folklore Society he had founded in 1913 "merely an agency for the loose record of all sorts of popular stuff," keeping the work "pointed steadily to the collection of these old world songs." [60] Reed Smith at South Carolina followed a similar line, but others, less purist, recorded popular tradition as they found it: Arthur Palmer Hudson at North Carolina, Frank C. Brown at Trinity (Duke), Arthur Kyle Davis, Jr., Smith's successor at Virginia.[61]

Others focused on the vital strain of folklore among Negroes.

[58] Robert Adger Law, "History of the Folk-Lore Society of Texas," in Stith Thompson (ed.), *Publications of the Folk-Lore Society of Texas*, I (Austin, 1916), 3–6.

[59] John A. Lomax, *Adventures of a Ballad Hunter* (New York, 1947); D. K. Wilgus, *Anglo-American Folksong Scholarship Since 1898* (New Brunswick, N.J., 1959), 158.

[60] Quoted in Arthur Kyle Davis, Jr., *Traditional Ballads of Virginia* (Cambridge, Mass., 1929), 54.

[61] Wilgus, *Anglo-American Folksong Scholarship Since 1898*, pp. 175–76.

One of the first to report at first hand was a sociologist more concerned with folk culture than folklore *per se*. Howard W. Odum, uninhibited by conventional judgments that Negro secular songs were worthless, published a quantity of them in 1911.[62] In 1925 he collaborated with Guy B. Johnson on *The Negro and His Songs* and the next year on *Negro Workaday Songs*. About the same time Dorothy Scarborough's *On the Trail of Negro Folk-Songs* (1925) explored new areas while the brothers James Weldon and Rosamond Johnson exploited a traditional field in *The Book of American Negro Spirituals* (1925). In 1928 Newman I. White of Duke produced *American Negro Folk-Songs*, the most comprehensive collection to that time, and in 1926 Newbell N. Puckett, sociologist, brought out his monumental *Folk Beliefs of the Southern Negro*.[63]

Some students sought to promote a union of folklore with high culture. In Oklahoma B. A. Botkin, a tenderfoot from Massachusetts who went to the state university in 1921, was swept up in the excitement of discovering folklore and new poets. In 1928 he became president of the state folklore society and in 1929 founded its short-lived annual, *Folk-Say*. Botkin coined the title to signify "literature *about* as well as *of* the folk and to center attention on oral, story telling phases of living lore conceived as literary material." [64] *Folk-Say* in its four issues became a sort of combined folklore journal and little magazine. In every age, Botkin expounded in the first issue, "literature moves on two levels—that of folk and that of culture; and . . . whenever the latter is in need of being strengthened and revitalized, it returns to the lower of the folk, to the source of all art in the wonder and faith that are also the mother of religion." [65]

But the oldest and most continuous activity at the nexus of folklore and literature was in Frederick Henry Koch's Carolina

[62] Howard W. Odum, "Folk-Song and Folk-Poetry as Found in the Secular Songs of the Southern Negroes," in *Journal of American Folk-Lore* (Boston), XXIV (July–September, 1911), 255–94; (October–December, 1911), 251–96.

[63] Other such works are cited in Richard M. Dorson, *American Folklore* (Chicago, 1959), 176–80.

[64] Botkin, "*Folk-Say* and *Space*," loc. cit., 324–25.

[65] Benjamin A. Botkin, "The Folk in Literature: An Introduction to the New Regionalism," in *Folk-Say: A Regional Miscellany*, I (Norman, 1920), 9.

Playmakers at Chapel Hill. Imported in 1918 from the University of North Dakota where he first developed his idea of folk drama, "Proff" Koch emphasized the experimental writing and production of dramas about the life of the people. "Write what you know," he preached. "If you observe the locality with which you are most familiar, and interpret it faithfully, it will show you the way to the universal." [66] The only male in his first playwriting class was an overgrown mountain boy from Asheville who was too young for the army, Thomas Wolfe. In March, 1919, the first bill of three experimental plays included Wolfe in the title role of *The Return of Buck Gavin,* his own tragedy of mountain people. The 1920 playbill included *The Last of the Lowries,* the first effort of a country boy from Harnett County, Paul Green, whose schooling had been interrupted by military service in France. In 1920 Koch produced at Raleigh his own *Raleigh, The Shepherd of the Ocean,* an outdoor historical pageant. It was the birth of a genre that eventually came to flower in Paul Green's *The Lost Colony* (1937).[67]

This was the beginning of a group whose work by 1942 led to the publication of five folk-play collections, two volumes of plays by single authors, annual playmaking festivals, and tours that carried the Carolina Playmakers into schoolhouses across the state.[68] Everywhere, Koch declared in 1922, there was "an awakening of the folk consciousness, which should be cherished in a new republic of active literature." [69] The Playmakers' influence on other dramatists would be difficult to establish, but one may guess that the sudden appearance of four plays about hillbillies in the Broadway season of 1923–1924 was not entirely unrelated: Lula Vollmer's *Sun-Up,* about reluctant mountaineers in World War I, later a favorite on the little theater circuit, and *The Shame Woman;* Hatcher Hughes' *Hell-Bent for Heaven,* a drama of

[66] Quoted in William Peery, "American Folk Drama Comes of Age," in *The American Scholar,* XI (1942), 149–50, 153.

[67] Samuel Selden and Mary Tom Sphangos, *Frederick Henry Koch: Pioneer Playmaker* (Chapel Hill, 1954), 13, 20–25; Arthur Hobson Quinn, *A History of the American Drama from the Civil War to the Present Day* (New York and London, 1927), 242.

[68] Peery, "American Folk Drama Comes of Age," *loc. cit.,* 151.

[69] Quoted in Paul L. Benjamin, "The Carolina Playmakers," in *Survey,* XLVIII (1922), 482.

mountain feuds and hypocrisy which took the Pulitzer Prize; and Percy MacKaye's *This Fine-Pretty World*.[70]

Paul Green, however, was the one early Playmaker who went on to a successful career as dramatist. Thomas Wolfe tried, then turned to the novel, and vented his disillusionment in one of his manuscripts: "A folk play is a play in which the people say 'Hit ain't' and 'that air.' "[71] Green, after graduate study at Cornell, returned to Chapel Hill as instructor in philosophy, but kept on writing plays.[72] In 1925 he published his first collection of one-act plays. In 1926–1927 the Provincetown Players of Greenwich Village performed *In Abraham's Bosom,* the full-lenth tragedy of a Negro man's ambition to uplift his people and his ultimate failure to overcome his own ignorance, the hostility of the whites, the inertia of the Negroes. The play ran only a little over two months, from December to March, but in May, 1927, it won the Pulitzer Prize for drama. During the same season Green's *The Field God,* a play about a white farmer's defiance of orthodox religion and neighborhood gossip, also had a short run in New York.

By 1928 Green had published three volumes of one-act plays: *The Lord's Will and Other Carolina Plays* (1925), *The Lonesome Road: Six Plays for the Negro Theater* (1926), and *In the Valley* (1928), mostly plays charged with compassion for humble rural Negroes and whites, the victims of prejudice and hypocrisy. *The House of Connelly* (1931) deviated from this pattern by treating a decadent aristocracy in a way that anticipated the more strident tones of Tennessee Williams. Green produced not only plays but poetry and prose in other forms, short stories and novels set in the "Little Bethel country," roughly the Cape Fear Valley of Eastern North Carolina. But the stage remained his chief interest, and he turned in the 1930's to the development of stylized "symphonic dramas" that utilized poetry, music, pageantry, pantomime, and the dance. The effects created in such plays as *Tread*

---

[70] Quinn, *A History of the American Drama,* 245–48; Alan S. Downer, *Fifty Years of American Drama, 1900–1950* (Chicago, 1951), 78–80. Both Vollmer and Hughes were from North Carolina, MacKaye from Oklahoma.

[71] Quoted in Richard S. Kennedy, *The Window of Memory: The Literary Career of Thomas Wolfe* (Chapel Hill, 1962), 48.

[72] Agatha Boyd Adams, *Paul Green of Chapel Hill* (Chapel Hill, 1951), is a brief biography.

the Green Grass (1932), *Roll, Sweet Chariot* (1934), and *Johnny Johnson* (1936), seemed too often only to mystify playgoers. But the experimentation was an unconscious apprenticeship for the creation of a new genre in *The Lost Colony* (1937), an outdoor pageant-drama produced at the Roanoke Island site from which Sir Walter Raleigh's colonists vanished and the forerunner of other historical extravaganzas enacted under summer skies.

The folk material used by the Carolina Playmakers became a major subject matter also for writers of fiction: Negroes and "poor whites," mountaineers and flatlanders. The types were familiar, long since exploited by local colorists in a humorous and senti-mental vein. Now they appeared in a different focus: the primitive-exotic Negro who never saw Marse Chan, the isolated moun-taineer or tenant, heir only to an oral tradition, often juxtaposed to a civilization encroaching upon his world—with strong implica-tions of his unspoiled wisdom.

"Literature in the South as well as trouble," Shields McIlwaine submitted, "seems to start with the 'darkey.' " [73] As it was with the local-color movement of the 1880's, so it sometimes seemed with the new revival. The difference was that, although stereo-types dogged the Negroes' footsteps, it was less as "darkies" and more as people that they were appearing. To be sure a hard core of lachrymose ladies perpetuated mammy and the pickaninnies; and successful humorists followed the advice of Irvin S. Cobb's Jeff Poindexter, "don't mess wid no race problem": men like Hugh Wiley, Arthur Akers, E. K. Means, and most notably Octavus Roy Cohen, a *Saturday Evening Post* regular, whose Florian Slappey perpetrated "a Negro dialect never heard on land or sea—compounded more of Dogberry and Mrs. Malaprop than of Birmingham Negroes." [74] Not far removed from this was Roark Bradford, whose *Ol' Man Adam and His Chillun* (1928) became a stage success as Marc Connelly's *Green Pastures* (1930), a travesty on Bible stories as they might be seen by unlettered Negroes.

In 1922 three authors broke sharply away from this pattern,

[73] Shields McIlwaine, *The Southern Poor-White from Lubberland to Tobacco Road* (Norman, 1939), 170.

[74] Sterling A. Brown, "Negro Character as Seen by White Authors," in *Journal of Negro Education*, II (1933), 189. See also Sterling A. Brown, *The Negro in American Fiction* (Washington, 1937), 84–92.

with problem novels of the aspiring Negro, novels of sociological realism strongly motivated by the urge to right wrongs. H. A. Shands' *White and Black* presented an ambitious Texas Negro sharecropper who was finally lynched for his pains. Clement Wood's *Nigger* took a strikingly new approach, the history of a Negro family from slavery in the Black Belt to bondage in the Birmingham slums, a story suffused with the futility of the former slave Jake's search for the "emancipation" he had heard of, at least for his grandchildren. T. S. Stribling's *Birthright*, the most successful of the three, announced a major new talent. It was the story of Peter Siner, Negro graduate of Harvard, who returned with missionary zeal to "Niggertown" in Hooker's Bend only to find himself cut off from his own people and swindled out of his school by a white banker who supported African missions. Eventually he fled North with Cissie, a girl who had been violated by a white rapist. A basic quality of the novel, which recurred in Stribling's later writings, was satiric irony directed at the racial double standard and at the white man's complacent assurance that he understood the Negro. Walter White's *The Fire in the Flint* (1924), motivated in part by the feeling that Stribling had not truly comprehended the Negro middle class, carried forward the author's antilynching crusade with the story of a Negro doctor lynched by Georgia crackers who could not understand his entry into a white home to save a girl's life.[75] In *Flight* (1926) White retold the classic story of "passing" by a near-white girl.

Other authors turned away from the older stereotypes to exploit themes from Negro folklore. Close to the Uncle Remus tradition were Ambrose Gonzales' stories from the South Carolina Gullahs: *Black Border: Gullah Stories of the Carolina Coast* (1922), *With Aesop Along the Black Border* (1924), and others. John B. Sales's *The Tree Named John* (1929) presented a collection of Mississippi folklore in dialect. R. Ernest Kennedy in *Black Cameos* (1924), *Gritny People* (1927), and *Red Bean Row* (1929) wove original stories about Louisiana Negroes, "unlettered folk who have not lost the gracious charm of being natural: wonderfully gifted and fairly tingling with poetic tendencies."[76] Howard

[75] White, *A Man Called White*, 65, explains his purpose.
[76] Quoted in Brown, *The Negro in American Fiction*, 125.

Odum amused himself with stories about Left Wing Gordon, a roguish character based on a highway worker Odum knew, an extroverted, one-armed roustabout who moved from place to place, from woman to woman in three books: *Rainbow Round My Shoulder* (1928), *Wings on My Feet* (1929), and *Cold Blue Moon* (1931). But the masterpieces of the genre were *Congaree Sketches* (1927) and *Nigger to Nigger* (1928), stories about Negroes in the Congaree swamps told by a Columbia physician, E. C. L. Adams. In tales and poems that ran from high comedy to satire on the white man's justice, Adams succeeded in permitting Negro characters to speak for themselves.

In 1921, not far from Adams' Congaree swamps, Julia Peterkin, mistress of Lang Syne Plantation, was hostess to Carl Sandburg, just up from a visit to the Poetry Society in Charleston. He urged her to write down stories of Negroes she had learned around the plantation. The result was a series of sketches, too strong for Mencken's *Smart Set,* that found outlet in *The Reviewer* and grew eventually into *Green Thursday* (1924). *Black April* (1927) and the Pulitzer-Prize winning *Scarlet Sister Mary* (1928) focused on the violent, amoral lives of Negroes in the quarters, struggling not against the injustice of white men but against an overpowering fate that hedged them in with superstition and helplessness: Black April, a plantation foreman with a gigantic appetite for battle and a fatal attraction for women; Scarlet Sister Mary, the feminine equivalent, a matriarch who, abandoned by a footloose husband, bred an indiscriminate brood and struggled against fate with unbending will. The characters were presented with sympathy and respect but with an uninhibited candor that shocked Julia Peterkin's neighbors who had not discovered what James Branch Cabell called the vicarious enjoyment of sin in literature. "I said things that no nice South Carolina lady ever says," she confessed, "and so I must be disciplined a bit even by my friends." [77]

In Charleston, meanwhile, DuBose Heyward followed the counsel of Sidney Lanier to "kill his Egyptian," fled the insurance business for the profession of letters, and poetry for higher achievement in the novel.[78] *Porgy* (1925), a novel about primitive

---

[77] Quoted in Clark, *Innocence Abroad,* 224.
[78] Frank Durham, *DuBose Heyward: The Man Who Wrote Porgy* (Columbia, S.C., 1954), 49.

Negroes brought "from the woods to town," differed from Julia Peterkin's works in its brooding awareness of history, in its suggestion of capturing the life of disappearing types: "Are they an aeon behind, or an aeon ahead of us?" Heyward had pondered in a 1923 article. "Who knows? But one thing is certain: the reformer will have them in the fullness of time." [79] A further contrast to Julia Peterkin was the rich tincture of romantic haze cast over a Golden Age "when men, not yet old, were boys in an ancient, beautiful city that time had forgotten before it destroyed." [80] But his characters, if somewhat romanticized, were believable people, with human hopes and emotions, drawn in such high colors as to constitute a gallery of unforgettable portraits: Porgy of the goat cart, Bess, Crown, and others. Popularized in a successful Broadway play (1927), then in George Gershwin's opera, *Porgy and Bess* (1935), the inhabitants of Catfish Row became more widely known than any other characters from the Southern literature of the decade.

Two other unforgettable characters appeared in *Mamba's Daughters* (1929): Mamba, outwardly a handkerchief-headed mammy, inwardly a sly old woman fanatically obsessed with her granddaughter's chances; and Hagar, the slow-witted giant of a daughter who did a man's work in the phosphate mines and finally submitted to her mother's will. But *Mamba's Daughters* added another dimension—a remarkable depiction of the new currents in Negro life. Lissa, beneficiary of Mamba's and Hagar's sacrifice, moved into the genteel circles of Charleston's Negro élite and finally on to triumph as a singer in New York. And Saint Julien Wentworth, willing instrument of Mamba's purpose, stood as the incarnation of "the dilemma of the liberal but nonrevolutionary Southern aristocrat confronted by a world he never made," unwilling to challenge the Southern racial credo but quietly helping in Lissa's triumph.[81]

Both Julia Peterkin and DuBose Heyward arrived at an opportune moment. For one thing it was what F. Scott Fitzgerald had labeled the Jazz Age, a time when the world was just becoming

[79] Heyward, "And Once Again—the Negro," *loc. cit.*, 42.

[80] DuBose Heyward, *Porgy* (New York, 1925).

[81] Durham, *DuBose Heyward*, 143. The quoted statement applied to Heyward himself, but describes the character of Wentworth.

aware of Negro music. The forms that were then working a revolution in the popular music of the nation were forms that had gestated for years in the Negro subculture of the South. There the sorrows—and joys—of the Negro experience had found one free outlet in the music of the people, and the makers of jazz were able to draw upon a rich heritage of African, European, and American elements; upon work songs, field hollers, blues, ragtime, minstrelsy, spirituals—and above all a fashion of wild improvisation.[82]

New Orleans was not the only incubator of jazz, but already by 1900, in the age of the legendary cornetist Buddy Bolden, something that might later have been recognized as jazz was being played by bands that marched in parades and played the street corners and dance halls. Occasionally one of the "spasm" or "jass" bands would venture forth for engagements elsewhere, or upriver on one of the excursion boats. By the early teens a few of the musicians had begun to drift into the gin mills of Chicago, which was destined to be the next major center of jazz.

But the Jazz Age may be dated from January, 1917, when a group of white musicians from New Orleans via Chicago, Nick LaRocca's "Original Dixieland Jass Band," hit solid at Reisenweber's Restaurant in New York. In March the Victor Talking Machine Company released their "Livery Stable Blues" and "Dixieland Jass Band One-Step" on the first commercial jazz record. The dissemination of jazz was soon under way in earnest; hundreds of Negro jazzmen joined the Great Migration. In 1917 Ferdinand "Jelly Roll" Morton, ex-piano-playing "professor" of the Tenderloin, left New Orleans for California. In 1918 Joseph "King" Oliver left for Chicago, whence in 1922 he summoned Louis Armstrong, his successor as cornetist with Edward "Kid" Ory. Kid Ory, meanwhile, had gone to California in 1919. W. C. Handy, "father of the blues," a native of Florence, Alabama, who had knocked about the Mississippi Valley as a bandleader and had already scored success as the composer of "Memphis Blues" (1912) and "St. Louis Blues"

[82] The above and the following are drawn chiefly from Marshall Stearns, *The Story of Jazz* (New York, 1956); Leonard Feather, *The Encyclopedia of Jazz* (New York, 1955); H. O. Brunn, *The Story of the Original Dixieland Jazz Band* (Baton Rouge, 1960); W. C. Handy, *Father of the Blues: An Autobiography* (New York, 1941); Alan Lomax, *Mister Jelly Roll* (New York, 1950); and Louis Armstrong, *Swing That Music* (London, New York, and Toronto, 1936).

(1914), moved from Memphis' Beale Street to Broadway in 1918 for a new career as music publisher. In 1920 Fletcher Henderson of Georgia finished Atlanta University with a major in chemistry and mathematics and went to New York for postgraduate study, but hired out to Handy as a pianist and launched a career as bandleader and arranger.

Soon the record companies discovered a Negro market for "Race Recordings" of hot jazz and blues singers like "Ma" Rainey and Bessie Smith of the Rabbit Foot Minstrels, often too "mean" and "low-down" for the uninitiated whites. But by 1924, when bandleader Paul Whiteman staged a "symphonic" jazz concert in New York's Aeolian Hall, with George Gershwin playing his own "Rhapsody in Blue," the new music had begun to achieve respectability and had moved along the way to recognition as perhaps the one truly original American contribution to the arts.

And as Southern Negroes poured into New York, they created in Harlem the largest center of Negro population in the world and mingled with others from the North, from Africa, from the West Indies. Harlem became a segregated melting pot out of which there boiled up a renaissance in Negro literature and the arts, a rediscovery of Africa and of the folk culture so often derogated by the black bourgeoisie—for many sensitive Negroes an emancipation not only from the genteel tradition but from the race problem itself.[83] Southern emigrés were at the center of the movement: Charles S. Johnson, editor of *Opportunity,* who opened its pages to much of the new writing; Zora Neale Hurston, folklorist and student of anthropology; Countee Cullen, poet and novelist, who explored the Negro past and present in "Heritage" and other poems; James Weldon Johnson, NAACP secretary and author, who rendered old-fashioned sermons in verse in *God's Trombones* (1927) and pictured the Negro mecca in *Black Manhattan* (1930).

After Carl Van Vechten presented a titillating picture of Negro cabaret life in *Nigger Heaven* (1926), adventurous whites in large numbers ventured into the "black and tan" night clubs of Harlem and other cities to sample forbidden fruits. With the Negro Renaissance, Eugene O'Neill's *Emperor Jones* (1921), Sherwood Anderson's *Dark Laughter* (1925), and the writings of Southern folk-

[83] See Locke, *The New Negro.*

lorists and novelists, the Negro as exotic primitive was for a few years all the rage—to the dismay of a scandalized Negro middle class. But it was, one critic remarked, "a shallow literary vein soon worked out." [84] Still, it wrought an emancipation from old stereotypes even by creating new; the old molds would never again be quite adequate.

In retrospect the supreme creation of the Negro Renaissance was Jean Toomer's novel *Cane* (1923), which a later critic counted among four "Major" novels by American Negroes.[85] Toomer, a grandson of Louisiana's Reconstruction Lieutenant-Governor P. B. S. Pinchback, was born in Washington, D.C., studied at the University of Wisconsin and the City College of New York, moved in a white literary clique devoted to mysticism, and before he wrote his book, made a pilgrimage to Georgia as a rural schoolteacher to establish contact with his Southern roots. The book, a disjointed collection of stories, vignettes, and poems, pictured with a sensitivity that transcended propaganda, the life of simple Negroes in Georgia's Black Belt and sophisticated Negroes in Washington's brown belt. Toomer's book, Waldo Frank asserted in a preface, was "a harbinger of the South's literary maturity," of its release from the racial obsession. Other writers, he said, escaped through "sentimentalism, exoticism, polemic, 'problem' fiction, and moral melodrama." Toomer wrote "not as a Southerner, not as a rebel against Southerners, not as a Negro, not as apologist or priest or critic," but "as a *poet*." [86] His book unfortunately was so strong in its experimental character that it met a cold reception and the rebuff caused Toomer to retire from further literary effort.

During the 1920's the mountaineer, popular as he was with ballad hunters, had little vogue in literature outside the folk plays; his day had come and gone with writers like Mary Noailles Murfree. DuBose Heyward, like all proper Charlestonians, had a summer home at Flat Rock in the North Carolina mountains and used that background for some of his poems and for one novel,

---

[84] McIlwaine, *The Southern Poor-White*, 170.

[85] Bone, *The Negro Novel in America*, 254.

[86] Waldo Frank, "Foreword," in Jean Toomer, *Cane* (New York, 1923), vii, ix. See also Bone, *The Negro Novel in America*, 81–89.

Angel (1926). But it was written hastily to capitalize on the reputation established by *Porgy*. Perhaps most successful in exploiting the folk mountaineer were Mary and Stanley Chapman, a Tennessean and her British husband who wrote as Maristan Chapman, in *The Happy Mountain* (1928) and *Weather Tree* (1932), which self-consciously utilized peculiarities in mountain speech and customs, usually to the disparagement of cultivated flatlanders.

T. S. Stribling, on the other hand, inverted the Chapman image and subjected the Tennessee hill people to devastating satire. He wrote, Shields McIlwaine said, "like an old-fashioned scalawag." [87] In *Teeftallow* (1926) and *Bright Metal* (1928) he reacted almost directly to the Scopes trial and flayed with mordant irony the stupid cruelties of religious fanaticism and hypocrisy. Stribling eventually would suffer neglect and obscurity at the hands of critics who derogated liberalism and social satire, but he was a significant innovator who opened up a broad range of the Southern experiences that novelists had never before explored. And his novels published in the 1920's, it turned out, were but preparation for a trilogy of the New South, his *magnum opus,* which appeared in the 1930's.

In contrast to Stribling's scalding satires of village life, the sociological novels of tenancy were sympathetic, and usually pointed the way to progressive reform. The salient example of the type was Dorothy Scarborough's *In the Land of Cotton* (1923), outstanding neither for qualities of artistry nor for its picture of local peculiarities of the Brazos River valley, but for its panoramic view of the cotton culture and of people entangled in an almost deterministic system. "If Job was a character today he'd be a cotton farmer," one rustic opined, "a share-cropper, I reckon." [88] One striking feature of the book was a foreshadowing of the New Deal farm programs in an outline of necessary reforms given by one of the characters: credit, tenant rehabilitation, crop limitation, warehouses, cooperation, diversification. Miss Scarborough's *Can't Get a Red Bird* (1929) —the title reflects her primary concern with folklore—further treated the cotton system and farm

[87] McIlwaine, *The Southern Poor-White*, 195.
[88] Scarborough, *In the Land of Cotton*, 364.

problems, while Jack Bethea in *Cotton* (1928) told about an Alabama tenant farmer's son who achieved an education and came back to promote co-operative marketing.

At the same time there developed a different artistic perception of the Southern poor-white, not as an object of satire or reform, but as a prototype of man's universal fate: his tribulations, his endurance, his limitations, his ultimate tragedy—a new treatment "compounded of sensibility and idealism in character and of rather hard realism in situation and background." [89] The new perception focused at first upon women characters, possibly because women authors led the way, possibly because the family was the basic Southern social unit and families become matriarchies— the natural superiority of woman is manifested repeatedly in Southern fiction and drama.

Ellen Glasgow's *Barren Ground,* while it did not deal with tenants, paralleled the development, but two ladies in Kentucky led it with remarkably similar novels: Edith S. Kelley's *Weeds* (1923) and Elizabeth Madox Roberts' *The Time of Man* (1926). *Weeds* traced the story of Judy Pippinger, a bright, tomboyish girl growing up in the Kentucky tobacco fields, a girl who somehow expected to escape the usual fate of tenant wives, old before their years, bowed down by inexorable fate. But it was not so ordained. Married to a tenant farmer, she finally bent under the burden of perennial defeat, the inability to have that good year that would put them ahead. In the end she arrived at quiet resignation: "peace was better than struggle, peace and a decent acquiescence before the things which had to be." [90]

The story of Ellen Chesser in Miss Roberts' *The Time of Man* was much the same, but told by an author of greater sensitivity and talent, largely from Ellen's own viewpoint. Ellen Chesser, more than Judy Pippinger or Dorinda Oakley, possessed a lively sensibility, filled with the wonder of earth and the things she had seen and heard. "Here I am," she cried out at the beginning. "I'm Ellen Chesser! I'm here." More than the others she longed for something better, something vaguely spiritual, but also for a home "fixed up, the shutters mended and the porch. . . . To sit on a

[89] McIlwaine, *The Southern Poor-White,* 199.
[90] Edith S. Kelley, *Weeds* (New York, 1923) , 330.

Saturday when the work is done. A vine up over the chimney. Once I saw a far piece from here. . . ." But again it was out of reach. The only surviving child of parents who were wagoners, then tenants, Ellen gradually moved from vernal exuberance through adolescent disillusionment to adult resignation as the wife of a tenant farmer unjustly accused of barn burning, forever on the move. The book ended as it began, with Ellen on a wagon, the shoddy accumulation of the years piled about, going she knew not where, listening to the children's talk—so much like her own in the years now dead. And yet the enduring hope of some fair land. "Some better country. Our own place maybe. Our trees in the orchard. Our own land sometime. Our own place to keep." [91]

Publication of *The Time of Man* disclosed the existence of still another major talent nourished apart from the little groups and movements elsewhere in the South. The talent bloomed late; Miss Roberts was forty-five when the novel appeared. In her youth, prevented by ill health and uncertain finances from continuing her studies at the University of Kentucky, she settled down to a career of spinster school marm conducting classes in the family's living room. But in 1917, with the assistance of interested friends and a sympathetic professor at the state university, she entered the University of Chicago at the age of thirty-six. There under new stimuli, her interests in philosophy and literature quickened and she began to write the poems collected in *Under the Tree* (1922). Its success stimulated her to finish *The Time of Man*, begun the same year. Often on the move to New York, Massachusetts, California, and Florida in search of health, she always returned to Springfield, in the center of the state and the "Pigeon River" country of her novels.[92]

Other books followed in the fifteen years that remained to her, but *The Time of Man* remained the best. Set in the Kentucky tobacco country of the early twentieth century, it had about it a quality of universality and timelessness in the central theme of man's eternal seeking. Her sensibility grew from a unique com-

[91] Elizabeth Madox Roberts, *The Time of Man* (New York, 1926), 81, 273, 382.
[92] Harvey M. Campbell and Ruel E. Foster, *Elizabeth Madox Roberts, American Novelist* (Norman, 1956), 3–79, presents a biographical sketch.

bination: a concrete sense of earth and soil and landscape mixed with a Berkeleian turn of philosophy in which ultimate reality resided in the spiritual, all woven together by a rich imagery "physicalizing the spiritual." [93] The language vibrated with music and poetry, the idiom of her Kentucky tenants colored by the English ballad themes of contemporary folklore scholarship. But with remarkable success Elizabeth Madox Roberts presented also scenes of violence: a scene in which Ellen experienced childbirth alone and unaided, and other scenes of realism that broke sharply with the genteel tradition and again marked the transition of the 1920's toward even starker scenes that would soon appear in Southern writing.

The first novel was followed by *My Heart and My Flesh* (1927), which explored themes of madness, incest, and miscegenation, from which the heroine finally emerged into greener pastures; *Jingling in the Wind* (1928), a piece of fantasy and social satire that ridiculed contemporary absurdities of religious prejudice, politics, and high pressure advertising; *A Buried Treasure* (1931), the lighthearted story of what happened to a farmer who discovered it; *The Great Meadow* (1932), which rivaled her first novel in its reception, a story of Harrodsburg pioneers with a sensitive heroine much like Ellen Chesser; *He Sent Forth a Raven* (1935), an allegory of the spirit triumphant over the evils of modern civilization; and *Black Is My Truelove's Hair* (1938), about the spiritual rebirth of a "ruined" woman in the discovery of true love.

With remarkable suddenness after 1920 Mencken's cultural Sahara had turned into a literary hothouse that germinated an increasingly prolific vegetation. With growing frequency after the South Carolina Poetry Society's first *Year Book* called for "a genuine *south-wide* poetic renaissance," the term renaissance appeared and reappeared in discussions of the Southern literary scene. Within two years the Poetry Society complacently confessed "that further assertion on our part that the South has brought forth a literary revival would be to stress the obvious." [94] By mid-

[93] *Ibid.*, 123.
[94] *The Year Book of the Poetry Society of South Carolina*, I (1921), 6; III (1923), 9.

decade the major literary journals were taking cognizance of the development in surveys of Southern writing by DuBose Heyward, Frances Newman, and Donald Davidson.[95] Mencken himself, who followed the scene closely, used the little magazines of the South as bush-league training grounds for *The American Mercury*. And in the *Mercury*'s first two years, he noted not without satisfaction, the South supplied fifty-five contributions from twenty-three authors while New England supplied only forty-one by twenty-four authors.[96]

And as the decade advanced there were signs that the flowering of the 1920's foretokened a harvest of ripened fruits in the future. Ellen Glasgow and Elizabeth Madox Roberts were in the full tide of creativity and books published in 1929 heralded the emergence of still other mature talents: Thomas Wolfe's *Look Homeward, Angel* and William Faulkner's *Sartoris* and *The Sound and the Fury*. "One may reasonably argue," wrote Howard Mumford Jones in 1930, "that the South is the literary land of promise today." [97]

[95] DuBose Heyward, "The New Note in Southern Literature," in *The Bookman*, LXI (1925), 153–56; Frances Newman, "On the State of Literature in the Late Confederacy," in *Books*, I (August 16, 1925), 1–3; Davidson, "The Artist as Southerner," *loc. cit.*, 781–83.

[96] Mims, *The Advancing South*, 197.

[97] Howard Mumford Jones, "Is There a Southern Renaissance?" in *Virginia Quarterly Review*, VI (1930), 185.

CHAPTER X

WHEN SOUTHERN LABOR STIRRED

ONE Saturday afternoon in the early 1920's, as the mill villagers thronged into downtown Greensboro, a local newsman witnessed a scene as poignantly symbolic of the changing South as any in the emergent fiction. A young couple with three small children pushed through the traffic to a store window where a many-colored display of silks cascaded to the floor. For a moment they stood there, faces vacant and pinched. "Languidly chewing gum and inspecting rich brocades woven for mistresses of empire and broad seas," the wife was "perhaps justly an object of derision," Gerald Johnson wrote. "But I pray you pardon me if I do not join in your mirth, for I am somehow not in the mood for laughter. I have seen the gleam in her eyes." [1] A barrier more substantial than plate glass separated such couples from the ever more visible promise of the New South. For such a family, with three children, the National Industrial Conference Board computed in 1920 that a "Minimum American Standard" of living at Charlotte, not far away, would require $1,438 a year. In 1919 the average textile worker's income in the state was about $730; in 1921 it was $624. [2]

Low wages, it often seemed, had become one of the cherished Southern traditions, the great magnet for outside capital, the foundation of industrial growth. The South was "the greatest, best, and cheapest labor market in the United States," a steel executive declared. [3] Moreover, the region had become the

---

[1] Johnson, "Greensboro, or What You Will," *loc. cit.*, 171–73.

[2] Herbert J. Lahne, *The Cotton Mill Worker* (New York and Toronto, 1944), 132–33; Blanshard, *Labor in Southern Cotton Mills*, 27–30.

[3] George Gordon Crawford, quoted in Neil M. Clark, "Birmingham—The Next Capital of the Steel Age," in *World's Work*, LIII (1926–1927), 534.

stanchest repository of the Anglo-Saxon myth, and in their own patronizing version of that grand vision many of the textile barons summed up the rationale of their labor policy. By offering sanctuary to the impoverished whites of the farms and mountain coves, the story went, they had brought salvation to the purest stock of native Americans. "The people we have are just as good Americans as any," one of them told a Northern visitor. "They are the people who made this country. Good, sturdy Anglo-Saxon stock." But, he added after a pregnant pause, "they are like children, and we have to take care of them." [4]

"Abundant supply of labor," the Macon, Georgia, Chamber of Commerce advertised in 1922, "thrifty, industrious, and one hundred per cent American." "Labor of purest Anglo-Saxon stock" Spartanburg, South Carolina, offered; "strikes unknown." *"Under no more than reasonably fair treatment of its help,"* the Kiwanians of Marion, North Carolina, explained, "every factory or branch of industry is certain to be able to secure adequate, satisfactory and contented labor." [5] In the booster rhetoric the patient docility of the Saxon churl became almost indistinguishable from that attributed to the African. "The workers are being offered on the auction block pretty much as their black predecessors were, and their qualities are enlarged upon with the same salesman's gusto," an exasperated Southern economist declared. "Native whites! Anglo-Saxons of the true blood! All English-speaking! Tractable, harmonious, satisfied with little! They know nothing of foreign born radicalism! Come down and gobble them up!" [6]

The regional wage differential was a tenacious reality. During the first three decades of the century the average annual wage reported by the census for ten Southern states hovered between 60 and 70 per cent of that for the rest of the country, except during the postwar boom of 1919 when it reached 73.9 per cent.[7] The

---

[4] Tannenbaum, *Darker Phases of the South*, 40.

[5] *Blue Book of Southern Progress, 1922*, p. 109; *1923*, p. 182; Kiwanis Club leaflet quoted in Sinclair Lewis, *Cheap and Contented Labor: The Picture of a Southern Mill Town in 1929* (New York, 1929) , 31.

[6] Broadus Mitchell, "Fleshpots in the South," in *Virginia Quarterly Review*, III (1927) , 169.

[7] Heer, *Income and Wages in the South*, 25. This is a rough measure, reached by dividing total wages by the average number of workers employed, but

ultimate source of cheap labor was an impoverished agriculture, which exerted a drag on wages all the way up the line. Monthly wages in Southern agriculture ranged from $21.35 in 1913 to a high of $45.46 in 1920 and back down to $30.75 in 1930, running from 60 to 65 per cent of the national averages.[8] Clarence Heer computed the annual net return of the independent Southern farmer in 1927 at $519. The factory indeed "held out a promise that the land had not fulfilled." [9] Average earnings in industry for 1927 ran up to $671 in cotton goods, $748 in lumber and timber, $849 in Southern industry as a whole. In 1928 average hourly earnings in cotton goods ran from 20.8 cents to 39.9, depending on skills; in hosiery and underwear from 22.6 to 63.5; in sawmills from 21.9 to 84.1; in foundries and machine shops from 28.5 to 79.4. At the higher levels of skilled labor, regional differentials tended to decrease, and disappeared altogether for blacksmiths, machinists, and bricklayers.[10]

Some of the organized crafts achieved an eight-hour day, but the ten- or eleven-hour day was more common for urban labor through the 1920's. In 1923 United States Steel dropped the twelve-hour day, but some of the independent iron and steel producers retained it even longer. It persisted here and more in other industries and the seven-day week was not unknown. It remained a widespread practice in the oil industry; as late as 1928 some Oklahoma oil-field workers were putting in a twelve-hour day and a seven-day week. Textiles, which employed more workers than any other one industry, usually operated on a ten- or eleven-hour day with a five-hour shift on Saturday to round out a week of fifty-five to sixty hours.[11]

---

substantially corroborated by other studies. The ten states include the South as herein defined excluding Kentucky, Oklahoma, and Texas.

[8] Herman Jay Brownhut, "Farm Labor Wage Rates in the South, 1909–1948," in *Southern Economic Journal*, XVI (1949–1950), 370–93.

[9] Harry Mortimer Douty, "The North Carolina Industrial Worker 1880–1930" (Ph.D. dissertation, University of North Carolina, 1936), 69.

[10] Heer, *Income and Wages in the South*, 37–41, 43–44, 59–60, 64–09. See also Simon Kuznets, *National Income: A Summary of Findings*, in National Bureau of Economic Research Twenty-Fifth Anniversary Series, I (New York, 1946), 23–25. Maurice Leven, *Income in the Various States: Its Sources and Distribution, 1920 and 1921*, in Publications of the National Bureau of Economic Research No. 7 (New York, 1925), 266–67.

[11] Abraham Berglund, et al., *Labor in the Industrial South* (Charlottesville, 1930), 24–29, 51, 71, 85; Jennings J. Rhyne, *Some Southern Mill Workers* and

Legislation regulating the conditions of labor remained in the rudimentary stages, barely established in principle. "The struggle for collective welfare against individualistic design in the South," a close student of the issue declared, "acted out, speech by speech, scene by scene" the battle for the British factory acts a century earlier.[12] One needed only substitute for Sadler, Oastler, and Shaftesbury the names of Edgar Gardner Murphy, Alexander J. McKelway, and Owen R. Lovejoy, the leaders of the National Child Labor Committee which had begun its efforts in 1904. By 1912 the movement had won restrictions on child labor in all the Southern states, although the age limits in six were only twelve or thirteen and numerous exemptions and inadequate enforcement virtually nullified the laws.[13] The failings of state action brought the Committee finally to the support of Federal legislation.[14] In 1916, with President Wilson's support, Congress passed the Keating-Owen Child Labor Act excluding from interstate commerce goods manufactured by children under fourteen. Against that measure as against state measures the textile manufacturers came forward as the chief opponents, parading before the Congress all the conventional defenses of child labor: its beneficial moral effects, the need to supplement family incomes, the desire of operatives to have their children work, the right to acquire a skill early in life.[15] "How long do you believe it is safe . . . to employ

---

Villages (Chapel Hill, 1930), 75; Horace B. Davis, *Labor and Steel* (New York, 1933), 75; Harvey O'Connor, *History of Oil Workers Intl. Union* (Denver, 1950), 5, 7–8, 27; *Official Proceedings of the Twenty Sixth Annual Convention of the Oklahoma State Federation of Labor* (n.p., n.d.), 38; Larson and Porter, *History of the Humble Oil & Refining Company*, 99; *Monthly Labor Review*, XXXI (1930), 181. See also reports of state labor departments.

[12] Mitchell, "Fleshpots in the South," *loc. cit.*, 173.

[13] The laws are summarized in *Child Labor Bulletin* (New York), I (August, 1912), 1–77. See also Alexander J. McKelway, "Ten Years of Child Labor Reform in the South," *ibid.*, II (February, 1914), 35–39. For examples of inadequate enforcement see Edward N. Clopper, "The Majesty of the Law in Mississippi," *ibid.*, 54–58.

[14] Another factor was the continuing fear that legislation would place any given state at a competitive disadvantage with its neighbors. McKelway, "Ten Years of Child Labor Reform in the South," *loc. cit.*, 35–38.

[15] The arguments are summarized in George S. Mitchell and Broadus Mitchell, *Industrial Revolution in the South* (Baltimore, 1930), 218–19; Davidson, *Child Labor Legislation in the Southern Textile States*, 255–63; and Alexander J. McKelway, "Another Emancipation Proclamation: The Federal Child Labor Law," in *Review of Reviews*, LIV (1916), 423–26. See also Richard Earl Walker, *The Problem of the Southern Cotton Mill: An Analysis of the Sociological Problem Which the*

a girl 12 years of age in a cotton mill?" a North Carolina mill doctor was asked. Not over ten or twelve hours, he responded.[16]

Both the Keating-Owen Act and a subsequent act of 1919 to accomplish the same purpose by a prohibitory tax were knocked down by the Supreme Court in cases instigated in North Carolina by David Clark, editor of the *Southern Textile Bulletin*.[17] A Constitutional amendment authorizing Federal child-labor legislation passed Congress in 1924 but was never ratified. As late as 1937 only three Southern legislatures had approved it; the rest had rejected it. In the struggle against it, textile interests joined forces with the National Association of Manufacturers and the American Farm Bureau Federation.[18] The amendment would take away parental control of children, they argued. It was "part of a hellish scheme laid in foreign countries to destroy our Government," said Mississippi's Senator Hubert D. Stephens. "It would destroy the state," said Georgia's secretary of state. "It would destroy the home. It would destroy a civilization based on the Bible." [19]

Successful Federal action awaited the New Deal, but there is some evidence that the persistent agitation bore fruit. In Alabama the proportion of children under sixteen among wage earners declined from 16.7 per cent in 1914 to 1.8 in 1919; in Georgia from 18.7 to 3.4; in South Carolina from 15.3 to 6.3; in North Carolina from 13.3 to 6.0. The figures compared not unfavorably

---

Southern Cotton Mill and the Operative Present to This Section of the Country (Winston-Salem, N.C., 1915); David Clark, "A Demand for a Square Deal," in *Child Labor Bulletin*, IV (May, 1915), 37–44; and "Proceedings of Twelfth Annual Conference on Child Labor, Asheville, N.C., February 3–6," *ibid.*, V (May, 1916), 42–43.

[16] Quoted in Douty, "The North Carolina Industrial Worker, 1880–1930," 343.

[17] Davidson, *Child Labor Legislation in the Southern Textile States*, 263–69.

[18] Richard B. Sherman, "The Rejection of the Child Labor Amendment," in *Mid-America: An Historical Review* (Chicago), XLV (1963), 3–17 (especially 10–11); Charles W. Pipkin, *Social Legislation in the South*, in *Southern Policy Papers*, No. 3 (Chapel Hill, 1936), 14; Elizabeth D. Brandeis, "Labor Legislation," in John R. Commons *et al.*, *History of Labour in the United States* (New York, 1935), III, 446. David Clark was again a leading figure in the campaigns. Katherine Du Pre Lumpkin and Dorothy Wolff Douglas, *Child Workers in America* (New York, 1927), 204–205.

[19] Brandeis, "Labor Legislation," *loc. cit.*, III, 445; S. G. McLendon, "Should the Twentieth Amendment Be Ratified?", in *Manufacturers' Record*, LXXXVI (October 2, 1924), 91.

to Rhode Island's 6 per cent, Massachusetts' 5.8, or Connecticut's
4.8; but they did not include children employed in Southern
agriculture. The proportion of children under sixteen in the over-
all textile work force declined from 15 per cent in 1914 to only 3.8
in 1930. By 1931 all Southern states forbade factory labor by
children under fourteen and night work under sixteen, and most
set an eight-hour limit for all under sixteen.[20]

The pressures were strong for all members of the family to
work, especially in textiles, nor was the practice unfamiliar in a
rural tradition. In the late 1920's an investigator in Gaston
County, North Carolina, mill villages found few children over
fourteen who were not either working or caring for younger
children while the mother worked.[21] A large proportion of
women worked. In 1920 over a third of all women in South
Carolina worked, and elsewhere from 13.2 per cent in Oklahoma
to 29.1 in Mississippi.[22] Most of them were in agriculture and
domestic service, but in Southern textiles they constituted more
than a third of the work force, working amid a monotonous din of
machinery that required constant attention, often in oppressive
humidity and in an atmosphere of dust and cotton fibers that gave
the workers their cognomen of "lintheads" and their susceptibility
to respiratory ills. The woman who could muster any strength for
household chores after ten or eleven hours in the mill must have
been rare.[23]

Legislation for the protection of women workers lagged behind
that for children. By 1931, however, all Southern states except
Alabama and Florida had set limits of nine to twelve hours a day
on the labor of women in manufacturing and some other occupations, but only Georgia and South Carolina had extended such
laws to cover men, ten hours in each case. There was no law

[20] Davidson, *Child Labor Legislation in the Southern Textile States,* 273; Lahne,
Cotton Mill Worker, 290; Lucy Randolph Mason, *Standards for Workers in Southern
Industry* (n.p., 1931) , 15.

[21] Rhyne, *Some Cotton Mill Workers and Their Villages,* 83. Fourteen was the
legal minimum in North Carolina after 1919.

[22] *Facts about Working Women,* Bulletin of the Women's Bureau of the Department of Labor, No. 46 (Washington, 1925) , 10.

[23] The cotton-mill workers' daily regimen is described in Rhyne, *Some Cotton
Mill Workers and Their Villages,* 9–17. See also Lahne, *Cotton Mill Worker,* 160,
290; and Otey, "Women and Children in Southern Industry," *loc. cit.,* 164.

against adult night work, however, except for women in South Carolina stores after 10 P.M.[24] No Southern state had minimum wage legislation.[25] Four had no workmen's compensation legislation.[26] A careful student rated only four Southern states as having adequate provision for enforcement of such laws as existed.[27] In 1929 a South Carolina legislative committee declared the state's enforcement officer alert only to "excuse practically every violation of labor laws." In three years he had instituted five prosecutions and levied a maximum fine of fifty dollars.[28]

The textile industry was the first in the South to have its labor policies brought under prolonged investigation because, if for no other reason, it was the harbinger of industrial revolution, "the first to break a thousand traditions of rural and handicraft civilization, the first to subject a large body of working people to the discipline of the machine, the first formally to employ women and children, the first to take people out of their homes to labor." [29] From the beginning of the century, the mills had come under a siege of criticism that developed an image of the mill baron as a greedy and dictatorial exploiter of women and children. During the 1920's another cycle of criticism focused upon the theme of a mill village isolation that threatened to develop an hereditary helot class.[30] So great had become "those multitudes of people who have a cotton mill complex" that one of them feared the mills' submergence under questionnaires and investigators; by the

---

[24] Mason, *Standards for Workers in Southern Industry*, 19. By 1931 all European countries except Turkey, Monaco, and Albania had outlawed night work for women, Miss Mason claimed. Lucy Randolph Mason to B. E. Geer, February 21, 1931, in Lucy Randolph Mason Papers (Manuscripts Division, Duke University Library).

[25] Shivers, "Social Welfare Movement in the South," 309–10. A Texas minimum wage law was repealed in 1921 and an Arkansas law was struck down in 1927 by the Supreme Court, which ruled against such legislation until 1937.

[26] John B. Andrews, "Workmen's Compensation Legislation in the South," in *Annals of the American Academy of Political and Social Science*, CLIII (1931), 189.

[27] Mason, *Standards for Workers in Southern Industry*, 19.

[28] South Carolina *House Journal*, 1930, p. 17.

[29] Harriet L. Herring, "Cycles of Cotton Mill Criticism," in *South Atlantic Quarterly*, XXVIII (1929), 123.

[30] Harriet L. Herring, *Passing of the Mill Village: Revolution in a Southern Institution* (Chapel Hill, 1929), 4–5; Tannenbaum, *Darker Phases of the South*, 39–73; Jeanette P. Nichols, "Does the Mill Village Foster Any Social Types?", in *Social Forces*, II (1923–1924), 350–57.

end of the decade a "tradition of attack and defense" had become "all but stereotyped." [31]

Various studies indicated that three quarters or more of the Southern textile workers lived in mill villages. Descriptions differed widely, from the "packing box on stilts" that Sinclair Lewis found in Marion, North Carolina, without running water or toilet, with newsprint for wallpaper and clapboards that could be pried off with a finger, to the "clean, architecturally pleasing . . . community, with modern plumbing, modern sewerage and all the conveniences of life" pictured by the South Carolina state health officer.[32] One inquirer found the workers "over tired and lacking in vigor or initiative . . . an ingrown population with little knowledge or contact with life." But another saw workmen going through a pine woods at Lyman, South Carolina, and thought of "the stuffy, crowded subways and the crowded elevated" and "could not find the frightful conditions about which he had read so much." [33]

The diversity of mill villages, "not more closely alike—nor less closely so—than the small country towns they hover near," was above all the product of evolution.[34] As late as 1916 almost half the village houses lacked modern conveniences: baths, sewerage, running water, and electricity. But during and after World War I mill profits and labor shortages prompted remodeling, the installation of plumbing, electric lights, sewers, sidewalks, and other improvements. The newer villages were often planned with more consciousness of variety and convenience and in some cases were attractive and substantial indeed.[35] In 1926 a survey of North

[31] Harriet L. Herring, "Morituri Te Salutamus," in *Social Forces*, III (1924–1925), 511; Herring, *Welfare Work in Mill Villages*, 2.

[32] Lahne, *Cotton Mill Worker*, 35; Rhyne, *Some Southern Cotton Mill Workers and Their Villages*, 122–25; Lewis, *Cheap and Contented Labor*, 18–19; Ashmun Brown, "Industry Is Giving Us a New South," in *Nation's Business*, XII (1924), 36.

[33] Lois MacDonald, *Southern Mill Hills: A Study of Social and Economic Forces in Certain Textile Mill Villages* (New York, 1928), 151; Lemert, *Cotton Textile Industry of the Southern Appalachian Piedmont*, 70.

[34] Herring, *Welfare Work in Mill Villages*, 3.

[35] Lahne, *Cotton Mill Worker*, 39; Berglund, *Labor in the Industrial South*, 118–19; M. S. Heiss, "The Southern Cotton Mill Village: A Viewpoint," in *Social Forces*, II (1923–1924), 345–46. For eulogistic treatments, see E. T. H. Shaffer, "A New South—The Textile Development," in *Atlantic Monthly* (Boston and New York), CXXX (1922), 562–66; Harry Shumway, *I Go South: An Unprejudiced Visit*

Carolina villages disclosed only 10 plants with 1,490 workers that still lacked modern conveniences, but 97 with 21,037 workers that provided lights, water, and inside toilets and 15 more with 3,789 workers that also had fully-equipped bathrooms.[36]

Even at its worst, one observer contended, "the company house is better built and far more liveable than the general run of mountain cabins." [37] When Frank Tannenbaum declared that "it were far better that textile workers had remained on the farm and scratched the soil with their nails," economic historian Broadus Mitchell challenged the idea that "the mountaineer or small cotton farmer who moves to the mill village is lost to the community." Tenancy "has been tried and has brought the South nothing," he argued. "A people who had no part in the life of the section are being brought back into its work and councils. . . . In any event, the judgement of the observer of their history a generation from now will be that, whatever their advantages or detractions as viewed from this angle or that, the mill villages were a natural and necessary stage in industrial upbuilding." [38]

Many features of the villages were highly exaggerated in the pattern of attack and defense. The company stores, a common target, existed only in a minority of the communities.[39] Labor mobility was a serious problem, but Jennings J. Rhyne discovered that the group of drifters, those who habitually moved more than once a year, were only about 20 per cent of the mill families in Gaston County. Moreover, the freedom to move offered some

---

to a Group of Cotton Mills (Boston and New York, 1930) ; and Marjorie A. Potwin, Cotton Mill People of the Piedmont: A Study in Social Change, in Columbia University Studies in History, Economics, and Public Law, CCXI (New York, 1927) .

[36] Rents were 25 to 50 cents a room per week. A rough estimate was that they represented a subsidy to the workers of $50–$200 a year for each dwelling. Herring, Welfare Work in Mill Villages, 31. For a full discussion of the evolution and variety of mill villages see ibid., 219–76.

[37] Frank T. de Vyver, "Southern Industry and the Southern Mountaineer," in American Federationist: Official Magazine of the American Federation of Labor (New York) , XXXV (1928) , 1319.

[38] Tannenbaum, Darker Phases of the South, 55, 70; Mitchell and Mitchell, Industrial Revolution in the South, 264–66.

[39] Herring, Welfare Work in Mill Villages, 187, 192; Gilman, Human Relations in the Industrial Southeast, 152–53.

degree of independence, one of the few means of protest at unsatisfactory conditions.[40]

On the other hand, the extent of welfare work was less than advertised. It increased during and after the First World War but declined greatly thereafter, and only a few of the largest mills had extensive programs. Most of 322 North Carolina plants surveyed by Harriet Herring in 1926 had contributed to the building or support of churches, but only 28 supplemented the income of schools, only 49 employed community workers, and only 40 had group insurance plans, although 127 supported baseball teams and many supplied wood and coal at low prices.[41] Another survey, covering 66 mills from Virginia to Alabama, disclosed only 37 with any kind of health program and 33 with group insurance.[42] There was evidence, further, that workers were indifferent or hostile to formal welfare programs where they existed, and would have preferred the equivalent in wages.[43]

However, to dwell upon social workers and other attributes of formal welfare programs would be to miss the point of paternalism, the obligation of every mill president to "take care of" his people. His business was making American citizens, a Georgia millowner declared, and running cotton mills to pay the expenses.[44] Whatever the motivation of the industrial leaders in the beginning, the concept of the owners as community benefactors was firmly entrenched, sometimes to the handicap of men who had to play their role in bad times as well as good. The extent of casual, personal welfare work probably would be difficult to exaggerate.[45] The trouble was, as Gerald Johnson succinctly

[40] Rhyne, *Some Southern Cotton Mill Workers and Their Villages*, 105–21; Gilman, *Human Relations in the Industrial Southeast*, 153–54; Blanshard, *Labor in Southern Cotton Mills*, 47–48.

[41] Herring, *Welfare Work in Mill Villages*, 27–31, 135.

[42] Berglund *et al.*, *Labor in the Industrial South*, 110, 113. For description of one of the most elaborate systems see Smith, *Mill on the Dan*, 245–53, 262–76.

[43] Blanshard, *Labor in Southern Cotton Mills*, 53.

[44] Arthur B. Edge, Jr., *Fuller E. Calloway (1870–1928): Founder of Calloway Mills* (New York, 1954), 27, cited in James A. Hodges, "The New Deal Labor Policy and the Southern Cotton Textile Industry, 1933–1941" (Ph.D. dissertation, Vanderbilt University, 1963), 114.

[45] Harriet L. Herring, "The Southern Mill System Faces a New Issue," in *Social Forces*, VIII (1929–1930), 352–53; Herring, *Welfare Work in Mill Villages*, 213–14, 217–18; Gilman, *Human Relations in the Industrial Southeast*, 157–59.

noted, that "in the sociological world Lady Bountiful has for years been a fallen woman." [46]

The consequence of paternalism was often an atmosphere of despotism. "We govern like the czar of Russia," said a candid manager in South Carolina. "We are monarchs of all we survey." [47] Criticism often brought self-incriminating outbursts of righteous indignation. "We had a young fellow from an Eastern seminary down here . . . and the young fool went around saying that we helped pay the preachers' salaries in order to control them," said one South Carolina textile baron. "That was a damn lie—and we got rid of him." [48] Challenges to the benefactors of the Piedmont became, in short, lèse majesté. Millmen refused to co-operate with what purported to be the most objective investigations. [49] In 1927 a public appeal to the industrial leaders of the South, sponsored by Bishop James Cannon, Jr., and signed by forty-two prominent church and public leaders, stated "the necessity for the improvement of certain social and economic conditions, especially in the textile industry," and called specific attention to long hours, low wages, the employment of women and children, the general absence of labor representation, and company control of mill villages. The signers were misinformed, said Richard Hathaway Edmonds, victimized by the "rank Socialism and Bolshevism" that had infiltrated ministerial organizations. They needed to learn "the fallacy of the so-called living wage theory," said NAM President John E. Edgerton of Tennessee. [50]

Belonging to a "generation which still stands waist deep in the notions of a society which was close to the soil," economist Claudius Murchison observed, the manufacturer—and most of his

[46] Gerald W. Johnson, "Service in the Cotton Mills," in American Mercury, V (1925) , 223.

[47] Quoted in MacDonald, Southern Mill Hills, 44.

[48] Quoted in Pope, Millhands & Preachers, 159–60.

[49] Thomas Tippett, When Southern Labor Stirs (New York, 1931) , 19–21, gives examples of rebuffs by North Carolina manufacturers to proposals for surveys by women's organizations and by Howard Odum's Institute for Research in Social Science at the state university. See also Nell Battle Lewis, "The University of North Carolina Gets Its Orders," in Nation, CXXII (1926) , 114–15.

[50] Manufacturers' Record, XCI (April 28, 1927) , 61, 66, 68; Southern Textile Bulletin, XXXII (March 31, 1927) , 22; Textile World (New York) , LXXI (1927) , 2493–94.

workers—had little or no conception of social groupings and social forces. The moving force in the human drama was the individual, and there was no philosophical basis for criticism of a "system." In the circumstances, how could a "survey" be regarded "as other than a personal thrust with all the insinuations of incompetency and turpitude?"[51]

Critics of labor conditions focused on textiles, but for patterns of paternalism or exploitation they could turn as readily to other areas. The lumber industry, which employed the next largest number of workers, had an even more varied pattern. In many places the "laborers were share-croppers last year, public laborers through the winter, croppers or wage-workers or floating labor the next season. A flexible folk, who could man a cant hook or hoe handle with equal languor."[52] Mostly they were not the footloose migrants of lumberjack tradition, but (at least in East Texas lumber camps) natives of the "piney woods" who married girls from the same region, whose children played in the pine-tree shade and grew up "with little to suggest the possibility of their entering other lines of work."[53] Situated in remote quarters, usually serving temporary operations, the camps lacked "many of the comforts and conveniences which even the dweller in the cotton mill village finds absolutely essential." Welfare work was "practically non-existent . . . an expensive luxury"; life was "at best a rude sort of existence."[54] At worst it was a kind of vassalage to corporate feudalism, as in the town of Kirbyville, Texas, where 90 per cent of the wages in the early teens were drawn in commissary money (sometimes called "robissary money") that suffered a severe discount outside the company store.[55] And company stores,

[51] Claudius T. Murchison, "Captains of Southern Industry," in *Virginia Quarterly Review*, VII (1931), 382, 388, 390–91.

[52] Harry Harrison Kroll, *I Was a Share-Cropper* (Indianapolis and New York, 1937), 240.

[53] Ruth A. Allen, *East Texas Lumber Workers: An Economic and Social Picture, 1870–1950* (Austin, 1961), 51, 196.

[54] Berglund, *Labor in the Industrial South*, 53–68, described a variety of camps. See also Allen, *East Texas Lumber Workers*, 143–49.

[55] George Creel, "The Feudal Towns of Texas," in *Harper's Weekly*, LX (1915), 76. A common device in lumber and other occupations was to pay cash wages at infrequent intervals, forcing workers meanwhile to draw scrip redeemable only at the company store or at a discount on pay-day.

more common than in textiles, charged heavy mark-ups.[56] The sixty-hour week prevailed, and in 1928 average weekly wages ran from $13.61 for common labor to $49.30 for sawyers.[57]

Similar patterns of isolation and corporate domination prevailed in the Appalachian coal fields. Geography dictated in most cases that companies develop their own towns, perched along the hillsides of narrow creek valleys; in 1923, 64 per cent of the Kentucky miners occupied company houses. In the captive mines of Ford, U.S. Steel, or International Harvester the houses might be substantial, well-maintained, and equipped with sanitary facilities; but at the average mine, beset by competition and price flurries (and steady decline after 1927), the housing became shabby, employment irregular and often rewarded in scrip. In most of the communities the schools, the churches, and law enforcement were under company control.[58]

The most highly developed system of company welfare was that unfolded in Alabama by George Gordon Crawford, president of Tennessee Coal and Iron after its acquisition by United States Steel in 1907. Well-planned and solidly built industrial communities like Westfield and Fairfield replaced much of the "shotgun" housing for steel and mine workers in the Birmingham district. Schools built and supported by the company totaled nine for whites and fourteen for Negroes in the mid-1920's. A Department of Health, organized in 1913, worked through medical, sanitary, dental, and hospital divisions, and complemented a Department of Social Science with education, welfare, physical education, and garden divisions. Standards of health, education, welfare, and efficiency rose, and there were other dividends: "All this gave the company a working force with which trade unionism could make little headway." [59] Vice-President Milton H. Fies of DeBardele-

[56] See for example an official investigation in Louisiana, cited in Vernon H. Jensen, *Lumber and Labor* (New York, 1945), 79–80.

[57] Berglund, *Labor in the Industrial South*, 46–47, 51.

[58] Glen Lawhon Parker, *The Coal Industry: A Study in Social Control* (Washington, 1940), 83; Bruce Crawford, "The Coal Miner," in Couch (ed.), *Culture in the South*, 361–66; Ross, *Machine Age Comes to the Hills*, 53–55.

[59] Rose Feld, "Way Down in Alabama," in *Success* (New York), VIII (1924), 53–56; Mims, *Advancing South*, 100–107; Arundel Cotter, *United States Steel: A Corporation with a Soul* (Garden City, N.Y., 1921), 171–72, 177–78; Ida M. Tarbell, *The Life of Elbert H. Gary: The Story of Steel* (New York, 1925), 309–14; Bond, *Negro*

ben Coal bluntly described his company's welfare program as a reward for "the Negro's contribution to non-union Alabama." [60]

Other industries did not so completely implant the sense of isolation and subordination. The more highly skilled furniture, cigarette, hosiery, or rayon worker, or the skilled artisan of the town might have some vague sense of higher status, but his living conditions were seldom much better. The rise of real-estate values put the middle-class suburbs beyond his reach. He resorted instead to "scrubby little suburbs located unpleasantly close to the garbage dump, the gas works, or railroad yards," moved into quarters with "a water spigot for every half-dozen shacks and an open privy for every two or three," or into downtown mansions abandoned by the gentry and converted into decrepit rooming houses. By 1930, W. J. Cash observed, "a large part of Southern labor, particularly in the greater and more rapidly developing towns, was living under slum or semi-slum conditions." [61] And in the background swarmed the masses of depressed rural workers, a wellspring of cheap labor that one pessimist predicted in 1931 "cannot be exhausted for the next fifty years." [62]

Labor unionism in the South was a feeble growth before the 1930's. Its nucleus was in the craft organizations of the towns, some of which antedated 1900. The aristocracy of the crafts were the railroad brotherhoods, which had gained general recognition after the government took over the lines during the war, but the typographers and the building trades, especially the carpenters and bricklayers, were the predominating core of some 160 city central unions that existed in the South in 1930. At that time the South had in all about six thousand locals affiliated with national unions and the American Federation of Labor.[63] In 1925 Texas

---

Education in Alabama, 240–42. Quotation from Spero and Harris, *Black Worker,* 247.

[60] Quoted from a speech before the Alabama Mining Institute, 1922, in Spero and Harris, *Black Worker,* 363.

[61] Cash, *Mind of the South,* 271–73. See also Harriet L. Herring, "The Industrial Worker," in Couch (ed.), *Culture in the South,* 348–49; and Blanshard, *Labor in Southern Cotton Mills,* 47–48.

[62] Tippett, *When Southern Labor Stirs,* 6.

[63] Marshall, "History of Labor Organizations in the South," 113–16; George S. Mitchell, "Labor Disputes and Organization," in Couch (ed.), *Culture in the South,* 631; Broadus Mitchell, "A Survey of Industry," *ibid.,* 90.

barbers, bricklayers, carpenters, electrical workers, musicians, painters, plumbers and steam fitters, and typographers each had more than five locals, while the garment workers had exactly five and the longshoremen four.[64] Reliable statements of union membership in the South before World War I seem unavailable, but an informed estimate in 1930 gave each of the Southern states an established craft membership of between five and thirty thousand. The Gulf states and South Carolina approached the smaller figure; Virginia, Kentucky, and Texas ranked highest.[65]

Over the years the craft unions had achieved a degree of legitimacy and public acceptance. Working in stable occupations that escaped the extremes of economic fluctuation and shielded by their skills against competition from the rural labor surplus, the members were usually conservative and business-minded, "their official thinking . . . almost compliant with small-town Rotary economics." Quietly active in politics, the unions gained occasional recognition in appointive or elective posts, and through their state federations worked for school, social, and labor legislation. From time to time the craft unions gave financial and moral support to sporadic agitations and strikes among industrial workers, but the more radical outlook of the industrial groups sometimes brought conflict within the state federations.[66]

The period of World War I and its aftermath brought significant new developments. It was a period of unusual expansion for the old-line craft unions, but also a time when thousands of industrial workers first experienced unionism. Southern textiles saw a widespread and protracted union activity after 1912, when an organizer for the United Textile Workers (UTW) established locals at Lynchburg, Danville, and Knoxville.[67] In 1913 the Knoxville local resolved "that the time is now ripe for an organizing campaign in the Southern states," and offered to share the expenses of an organizer; the national accepted the challenge.

[64] Ruth A. Allen, *Chapters in the History of Organized Labor in Texas,* in University of Texas *Publications,* No. 4143 (Austin, 1941), 153–58.

[65] Mitchell, "Labor Disputes and Organization," *loc. cit.,* 633.

[66] *Ibid.,* 632–34.

[67] Except where otherwise indicated, the following account of textile unionism is drawn from George S. Mitchell, *Textile Unionism and the South* (Chapel Hill, 1931), 32–56.

However, the activity through 1918 affected chiefly a few local situations. Unable to blanket the mills with organizers, the UTW encouraged local groups to seek immediate gains in the hope, after 1914, that rising wartime orders would put managements under pressure to reach agreements. In places it signed workers by the thousands, but the whole activity resulted in charters for only about forty Southern locals, mostly in South Carolina and Georgia, and a number of strikes in which the reinstatement of discharged union members was about the only victory, and that rare.

Employers generally assumed postures of implacable hostility. Unions, said John A. Law, Spartanburg mill president, only made their members "disloyal to their employers, shirkers of their work, breeders of discontent, invaders of the rights of others and usurpers of property rights." [68] The industrial South, Frederick B. Gordon of Columbus, Georgia, declared, "will never . . . allow itself to be bound hand and foot . . . by that *thing* which seeks to stab in the heart that inherent right of selective employment. . . . That unholy, foreign-born, un-American, socialistic, despotic *thing* known as *labor unionism.*" [69]

During 1919 union activity reached higher levels. Shortly after the war the UTW set February 3, 1919, as the date for achieving a 48-hour week. The movement was intended primarily for Northern industry, but Southern workers joined the walkout at Columbus, Chattanooga, Sherman, Texas, and in the Horse Creek Valley of South Carolina. The Columbus strike, joined by nearly the whole labor force of 7,000, brought serious disorders, the death of one worker, and the destruction of the union as an effective force; but the mills did reduce their work week of fifty-five hours. The union's main strength shifted to North Carolina, where a strike of 1,500 workers in North Charlotte won a reduction of the work week, incorporation of wartime bonuses in the wages, free house rent for the duration of the strike, and reinstatement of union members—but not union recognition. There followed a series of disputes, mostly settled on the same basis, in East Charlotte and at least eleven other communities of the Carolina Piedmont.

[68] John A. Law to William Watts Ball, November 29, 1916, in Ball Papers.
[69] *Manufacturers' Record,* LXXIV (November 21, 1918), 67–68.

Before September the UTW had chartered forty-three locals in North Carolina and claimed forty thousand members in that state and five thousand in South Carolina; many mills were 70 to 80 per cent organized, some as much as 95 per cent. But the momentum soon ran out. During the next twelve months only thirty more locals rose in the entire South and the movement remained concentrated in North Carolina. Postwar prosperity had built the unions; the slump of late 1920 and 1921 destroyed them. The mills began to curtail operations and cut wages by 30–50 per cent, and the union officials could not restrain the insistent demands for a strike, which the representatives of forty locals approved unanimously despite warnings that the national could provide only limited benefits. On June 1, 1921, about nine thousand workers went out. The mills, under little pressure to reopen, patiently waited for the union to collapse.

The *coup de grâce* was administered by a propaganda campaign of David Clark's *Southern Textile Bulletin* in Charlotte. "If the union has no funds," he asked, "what has become of the dues that have been paid in during these months and years that the textile workers have belonged to it?" Although the national officers had counseled against the strike, Clark accused them of having "deceived and betrayed the mill operatives of this section." [70] Late in August the strike began to crumble. At Concord and Kannapolis the state militia protected returning workers. The wage cuts remained in effect, and unionists could not even win guarantees of reinstatement. After the North Carolina debacle, the union effort collapsed. If the movement demonstrated a stronger urge to collective action than ever before, it left a lingering suspicion that union leaders had somehow misled and deserted the Southern workers. [71]

Meanwhile other groups manifested a new militancy. In September, 1917, representatives of oil-field locals recently formed by the

[70] *Southern Textile Bulletin*, quoted in Mitchell, *Textile Unionism and the South*, 53.

[71] On the activity in North Carolina textiles, 1919–1921, see Douty, "North Carolina Industrial Worker," 279–89; Harley E. Jolley, "The Labor Movement in North Carolina, 1880–1922" in *North Carolina Historical Review*, XXX (1953), 371–75; and Gerald W. Johnson, "The Cotton Strike," in *Survey*, XLVI (1921), 646–47.

Texas state federation and the Houston Trades Council called upon the companies to discuss labor conditions in the light of rising oil prices.[72] The invitation met with indignant refusal. The Humble Oil Company, said Ross Sterling, could "see no reason why . . . it should confer with outsiders or strangers upon matters which solely concern our employees and ourselves." Consequently on November 1 approximately ten thousand workers in seventeen oil fields walked out, demanding an eight-hour day in place of the twelve- to fourteen-hour day, a change in the bonus system, a daily wage increase from $3.40 to $4.00, and union recognition.

The wartime strike dragged on for three months, severely handicapped by the influx of strikebreakers from the "Big Thicket" of agricultural East Texas and drought-ridden ranches of West Texas. Efforts at Federal mediation brought only an agreement that a committee of the Oil and Gas Association would investigate grievances and that the companies would not discriminate against union members, provided they were not "personally objectionable to the foreman or superintendent"; but there was no recognition of the union nor of collective bargaining. The union lost most of its membership as a result, and at the first meeting of the newly chartered Oil Field, Gas Well, and Refinery Workers at El Paso in November, 1918, only five Texas locals were represented with sixteen others in Oklahoma, Louisiana, and California.

During the war, however, oil workers gained in wages and hours. The standard two-shift, twelve-hour day began to yield to the eight-hour day, and by 1919 drillers were earning 38 per cent more and refinery stillmen 65 per cent more than in 1914.[73] But the wartime gains receded in the postwar depression, and by March, 1921, wage cuts were running from 10 per cent up; in the

[72] The following account is drawn from Allen, *Chapters in the History of Organized Labor in Texas*, 222–34; and O'Connor, *History of Oil Workers Intl. Union*, 4–8, 18–22. See also Loos, *Oil on Stream!*, 41–43; and Larson and Porter, *History of Humble Oil & Refining Company*, 66–71.

[73] Kendall Beaton, *Enterprise in Oil: A History of Shell in the United States* (New York, 1957), 152, citing chart submitted before hearings of the Temporary National Economic Committee and reproduced in *Petroleum Almanac* (New York, 1946), 200.

Caddo Field of Louisiana the eight-hour day was extended back to ten and twelve. By 1924, with only one Texas local, at Port Arthur, the union had ceased publication of its journal and given up its office. It continued for the time only a shadowy existence from the home of its secretary in Fort Worth. It was the only national union with headquarters in the South—but with most of its members in California.

Union activity, however, may have provoked a greater corporate attention to labor policy. Humble Oil liberalized an employee stock-purchase plan introduced in 1917, began construction of permanent bungalows for workers in the Goose Creek field in 1918 (a program much extended later), and during the 1920's introduced a variety of annuities and benefits, an employee representation program, and finally a personnel division. But not until 1928 did it introduce the six-day week, denounced as a "bolshevik idea" by the Shreveport superintendent, and not until 1930 a universal eight-hour day, after the example of firms like Carter Oil and Standard of Louisiana, which had achieved it by 1925.[74]

Tobacco workers also scored spectacular, but again temporary, advances in unionization. Before 1919 the Tobacco Workers International Union had maintained a Southern presence chiefly in a few small factories around Louisville that catered to the union-label trade. By early summer of 1919 an organizing drive in Winston-Salem had set up six strong locals which in August signed an agreement for a 48-hour week, a 20 per cent wage increase, and overtime pay. The movement then spread to Durham and Reidsville, but without the same success. Even in Winston-Salem the membership drifted away and the 1919 agreement lapsed; by 1922 membership was back to its prewar status.[75]

During the summer of 1917 the United Mine Workers, absent from the Alabama coal fields since a crushing defeat in 1908, reappeared in force to stage a strike that won (through Federal intervention) wage increases of 10 to 15 per cent, the right to have checkweighmen and tribunals to hear complaints, but no union

---

[74] Larson and Porter, *History of Humble Oil & Refining Company*, 70–71, 94–104, 384–85.

[75] Douty, "North Carolina Industrial Worker," 290–99.

Hitch-hiking Family near Macon, Georgia, 1937

Mississippi Planter and Negro Workers, 1936

Huey P. Long

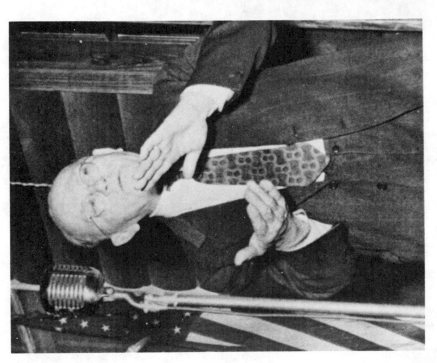

Theodore G. Bilbo

Loray Mill Strike, Gastonia, North Carolina, 1929

recognition.[76] Appeal for another raise in 1918 was denied, but the Alabama miners in November, 1919, joined a national bituminous coal strike which won a 14 per cent increase from a Presidential arbitration board. The operators accepted the award, but rejected the board's suggestion that they confer with union leaders. In September, 1920, after several local strikes to compel union recognition the UMW called a statewide walkout in which about 12,000 of the 27,000 miners joined. The coal companies resolved to "fight for their property right on high social, moral, and legal grounds" and to resist a union with a history "of associating the black man on terms of perfect equality with the white man." In their purpose they had the sympathy of the progressive Governor Kilby, who called the strike "illegal and immoral."

The strike at its peak engaged about 15,000 workers, mostly Negroes. Outbreaks of violence brought out the militia; four people were killed, one a company official, Negro workers were beaten and evicted from company houses, the governor threatened to destroy their tent colonies and finally compelled arbitration. A committee of three Montgomery businessmen appointed by Kilby ruled that it would not be "to the interest of the people of the State to recognize the United Mine Workers of America," but recommended that strikers be re-employed as rapidly as possible without displacing strikebreakers already at work—meanwhile, the union should support the unemployed. The strike wiped out the union in Alabama for another decade. Efforts to organize the steel industry in 1917 met failure even more quickly. Birmingham, as a result, played little part in the great national steel strike of 1919.[77]

The lumber industry saw a brief revival of unionism in the wake of the war. Two AFL unions, the International Timber Workers Union, and the United Brotherhood of Carpenters and Joiners united in efforts to organize the Great Southern Lumber

[76] The following account is drawn from Cayton and Mitchell, *Black Workers and the New Unions*, 317–20; Marshall, "History of Labor Organization in the South," 170–71; Spero and Harris, *Black Worker*, 359; *Manufacturers' Record*, LXXIX (March 31, 1921), 78. See also Emily Owen, "The Career of Thomas E. Kilby in State and Local Politics" (M.A. thesis, University of Alabama, 1942), 117–24.

[77] Spero and Harris, *Black Worker*, 247–49.

Company at Bogalusa, Louisiana, one of the largest in the region. During the summer of 1919 the sawyers and filers of Bogalusa joined the carpenters' union and other workers joined a timber workers' local, 75 per cent Negro. But the movement provoked a lockout and a mobilization of local vigilantes who ransacked the home of Sol Dacus, Negro vice president of the timber workers' local who fled into the Pearl River swamps; the vigilantes finally organized an attack on union headquarters in which the president of the Bogalusa Central Trades Assembly and three other union men died.[78]

By the end of 1921 the upthrust of unionism was over. In not a single case had it brought an important union recognition, and the feeble locals soon disappeared. Failure of a railroad shopmen's strike in 1922 left that group largely unorganized.[79] The other craft unions, which had shared in the growth, felt the severe impact of open-shop organizations that proliferated across the country after the war. In 1920 the eight largest cities of Texas had such groups, organized under the leadership of the Texas Chamber of Commerce, and from 1920 to 1927 membership in the Texas State Federation of Labor declined by approximately half, from 50,000 to 25,000. The Tulsa Open Shop Association enrolled 3,500 members. Reports of similar movements came from Alabama, Arkansas, Florida, Georgia, Kentucky, Louisiana, Mississippi, and Tennessee. In January, 1921, the local groups came together at a meeting in Chicago where the open shop was officially designated the "American Plan" of employment; in 1922 the American Plan–Open Shop Conference was organized.[80] In 1921 an Anniston manufacturer reported that the campaign had left fewer than a dozen "radical" union organizers and sympathizers in the community, "as they find that this city is not a fertile field for their disturbing endeavors." [81] "The open shop has done

[78] Jensen, *Lumber and Labor,* 91–94; Seligman, *Negro Faces America,* 196–201; Goodyear, *Bogalusa Story,* 133–35.

[79] Marshall, "History of Labor Organization in the South," 117.

[80] Selig Perlman and Philip Taft, "Labor Movements," in Commons (ed.), *History of Labour in the United States,* IV, 490–94; Richardson, *Texas: Lone Star State,* 417; Eugene Earnhardt, "The 'American Plan' to Disorganize Labor, 1919–1926" (unpublished seminar paper, University of North Carolina, 1963, in author's possession), 36–38.

[81] *Manufacturers' Record,* LXXX (July 7, 1921), 88.

more for the upbuilding of Oklahoma City than any one other factor," said a representative of the local Chamber of Commerce.[82] In Dallas a ten-year program left about 95 per cent of the city's employees under open-shop conditions in 1929; during the decade no industrial plant had faced a strike nor had any building job been tied up a single day by a labor dispute.[83] "The 'Solid South' means security for every manufacturer trembling under the whiplash of the anarchistic labor leaders," said the *Manufacturers' Record* in 1924, "to every manufacturer hovering under the rim of radical labor's volcano." [84]

But a subterranean turbulence simmered in the mill villages of the Piedmont. The collapse of textile unionism in 1921 left the depression wage cuts in effect, although the rates never quite sank to prewar levels. A male loom fixer in the South (the aristocrat of cotton-mill help) earned $32.88 for a full week's work in 1920 but only $21.41 in 1922 and $22.20 in 1928; the average for female weavers declined from $26.56 to $19.59 to $19.37. But full-time work was not always available, so that the loom fixer in 1928 actually averaged $18.38; the female weaver $12.05; and five other standard occupations brought less than $10, only $6.76 in the case of male frame spinners.[85]

Dissatisfaction engendered by the retreat from wartime prosperity was compounded by other factors. Continuing expansion kept up a flow of workers from field to factory, but strong evidences indicated that a cotton-mill caste was developing. The mills "will soon become independent of their reserve of tenant farmers," Jennings Rhyne suggested, and "the cotton mill population may . . . become in time a hereditary occupational group." [86] At the same time their social and psychological isolation was borne in upon the people themselves. Mill children went to mill schools; mill workers went to mill churches; and on Saturday afternoons

[82] George Garner, "American Plan Open Shop Conference of Nationwide Interest," in *Manufacturers' Record*, XCIII (February 9, 1928), 67.

[83] E. C. Wallis, "After Dallas Threw Off the Shackles of the Closed Shop," *ibid.*, XCVII (February 13, 1930), 53–54.

[84] *The South's Development*, 100.

[85] Berglund, *Labor in the Industrial South*, 95–96, 99. See also *Wages and Hours of Labor in Cotton Goods Manufacturing, 1910–1928*, U.S. Bureau of Labor Statistics Bulletin No. 492 (Washington, 1929).

[86] Rhyne, *Some Southern Cotton Mill Workers and Their Villages*, 76–77.

they met an ill-concealed contempt from the people downtown. The South "more than any other part of the country, retains the idea of the Gentry versus the Lower Classes," it seemed to Sinclair Lewis. "It doesn't take much to feel that you are in the Gentry. Owning a small grocery . . . will do it." [87] The sense of upward mobility from tenant farm to mill village gave way to a sullen class consciousness—not as a militant group but "as an isolated social group" acutely aware of the stigma attached to the mill village. "They ain't no difference," one resigned woman told a visitor, "they is all cotton mills." [88]

A widening gulf between workers and bosses increased the sense of alienation. Preoccupied with growing competition, mill presidents found it more and more difficult to maintain personal contact. A new generation of managers came under the spell of the "Yankee cult of the Great Executive" and surrounded themselves "with flunkies and mahogany and frosted glass." [89] Broadus Mitchell found in them tendencies away from the restraints of their fathers. "They are not burdened with a sense of *noblesse oblige*. . . . They are class-conscious and money-wise. . . . If you thrust your fingers into a downy wool of the lamb you feel beneath it the coarse bristle of the wolf." [90]

In a highly competitive industry, plagued by uncertainty and lacking agencies of stabilization, reduction of costs seemed the only solution—and labor represented a high proportion of the costs in textiles. In the mid-1920's "efficiency experts" began to appear, stop-watches in hand, to conduct time studies of Southern workers and introduce the "Bedeaux" system. Abrupt changes took place, sometimes without adequate planning and with little effort to explain. The result was the appearance, often the reality, of exploitation, of stepping up the pace, increasing the work load, reducing the work force.[91] The root of the trouble, Josephus Daniels maintained, was "the attempt to graft the New England

[87] Gilman, *Human Relations in the Industrial Southeast*, 163–67; Lewis, *Cheap and Contented Labor*, 14.

[88] Otey, "Women and Children in Southern Industry," *loc. cit.*, 166.

[89] Cash, *Mind of the South*, 270. See also Gilman, *Human Relations in the Industrial Southeast*, 201–205.

[90] Mitchell, "Fleshpots in the South," *loc. cit.*, 166–67.

[91] Gilman, *Human Relations in the Industrial Southeast*, 180–83; Lahne, *Cotton Mill Worker*, 156–57; Tippett, *When Southern Labor Stirs*, 18, 30–33.

efficiency system . . . on to our people, who work fifty-five and more hours a week at lower wages." [92] The workers expressed their reaction more succinctly; it was the "stretch-out."

The long quiet after the textile strike of 1921 was broken only here and there until 1927, when Henderson, North Carolina, staged a preview of the drama to follow. There, on August 4 some three hundred workers went out spontaneously, demanding the restoration of wages cut three years before. Organizers came, the state militia came, but withdrew after two days because there was no violence. The movement reached a climax with the eviction of nine families from company houses, and then collapsed, but not before Alfred Hoffman, a young organizer for the hosiery workers trained at Brookwood Labor College, had signed up five to six hundred members for the United Textile Workers.[93]

The Henderson affair stimulated new activity. The Georgia state federation in 1926 had commenced a campaign of reviving and reinvigorating local organizations, a program taken over and expanded in 1928 by the AFL. In the summer of 1927 the AFL sponsored the first Southern Summer School for Women Workers at Burnsville, North Carolina.[94] In January, 1928, under Alfred Hoffman's leadership a Piedmont Organizing Council launched a program of monthly meetings in the towns of the Carolinas, inspirited the craft unions, and encouraged efforts in tobacco and textiles. Virginians formed a similar Tidewater Labor Conference later in the year.[95] In October, 1928, delegates from six state federations met in Chattanooga to discuss the situation in coal and textiles, and in November Southern delegates to the AFL national convention in New Orleans secured a resolution to plan for an organizing drive in the South.[96]

[92] Quoted in Pope, *Millhands & Preachers*, 210–11.

[93] Harriet L. Herring, "12 Cents, the Troops and the Union," in *Survey*, LIX (1927–1928), 199–202; Douty, "North Carolina Industrial Worker," 300–303; Mitchell, *Textile Unionism in the South*, 61–62.

[94] Marshall, "History of Labor Organization in the South," 213–14; Lois MacDonald, "A New School in the Old South," in *Survey*, LIX (1927–1928), 96–97; Lois MacDonald, "Southern Labor Looks at Itself," *ibid.*, LXI (1928–1929), 358–60; Marion Bonner, "Behind the Southern Textile Strikes," in *Nation*, CXXIX (1929), 351–52.

[95] Marshall, "History of Labor Organization in the South," 215–16.

[96] Irving Bernstein, *The Lean Years: A History of the American Worker, 1920–1933* (Boston, 1960), 13. The Prologue, 1–43, gives the best general account of the textile revolt of 1929.

But the eruption of 1929 caught them unprepared to guide the onrush of events. It started at Elizabethton, an East Tennessee town thrust suddenly into the industrial age by the great German-owned American Bemberg and American Glantzstoff rayon plants which opened in 1926 and 1928.[97] In the town where Herbert Hoover extolled Southern prosperity during the 1928 campaign, an accumulation of grievances at low wages, the high cost of living in a mushrooming town, and growing work loads had brought sporadic troubles over a period of two years. On March 12, 1929, most of the 550 young women in the inspection department of the Glantzstoff mill walked out in protest at the demotion of a girl who had sought an increase in the average weekly wage of $8.96; six days later both plants were closed.[98] Local craftsmen helped the strikers form a textile local, and a week later Alfred Hoffman appeared with Matilda Lindsay of the Woman's Trade Union League. The management secured an injunction against picketing and other union activities, then from a compliant governor secured units of the militia in full military panoply—and paid by the company. But when a Federal conciliator appeared the management agreed to reinstate strikers on an open-shop basis, withdraw the injunction, recognize shop grievance committees, and grant a wage increase—or so it was reported on March 22. When the terms were published, however, President Arthur Mothwurf denied that the company had entered any agreement with union people.

In the uncertainty that followed, many of the strikers drifted back into the plants while both sides mobilized for a showdown. Meanwhile, local businessmen, alarmed at the trade-union threat to their benefactors, kidnapped Hoffman and Edward F. Mc-Grady, an AFL representative, dumped them separately in North Carolina and Virginia, and threatened both with harm if they

[97] Except where otherwise indicated, the account of the Elizabethton strike is drawn from James A. Hodges, "Challenge to the New South: The Great Textile Strike in Elizabethton, Tennessee, 1929," in *Tennessee Historical Quarterly*, XXIII (1964), 343–57; Tippett, *When Southern Labor Stirs*, 54–75; Bernstein, *Lean Years*, 13–20; and Duane McCracken, *Strike Injunctions in the New South* (Chapel Hill, 1931), 94–113.

[98] Paul J. Ayman, "Rayon Workers Strike Elizabethton," in *American Federationist*, XXXVI (1929), 546. See also Richard Woods Edmonds, "Southern Labor to Be Organized Say Leaders in Elizabethton Strike," in *Manufacturers' Record*, XCV (April 25, 1929), 52–53.

returned. Both returned, guarded by mountaineers with "veritable arsenals of Winchesters," and on April 7 President William Green addressed a mass meeting of workers, promising them support. The company then discharged members of union grievance committees and provoked another strike that closed both plants again on April 15. There followed a tumult of parades, picketing, machine guns on mill roofs, tear gas, and the dynamiting of the city water main.

Continued efforts at mediation finally brought an agreement on May 25. It was a total defeat for the strikers. Employees could apply for reinstatement; those not accepted could appeal to the new personnel officer, E. T. Willson, "presiding as an impartial person." Willson, who had a record of busting textile unions in New Jersey, announced that management did "not intend at any time to discuss any matters . . . with outside individuals or organizations." Inside the mills he formed a company union, commenced a welfare program, and blacklisted about a thousand workers. A protest strike by the blacklisted remnants in March, 1930, was dismissed by the company as "an unemployment demonstration." The county sheriff resigned—forced out, he said, by a group that insisted upon his shooting down strikers. His successor promised to drive the union leaders from the city.[99]

While Elizabethton seethed, a more spectacular revolt erupted at Gastonia in the North Carolina Piedmont.[100] The Loray Mill, largest in Gaston County, organized by local capital in 1900, had been acquired by the Manville-Jenckes Corporation of Rhode Island in 1923. Enlarged by the infusion of new capital, it specialized in the production of tire fabric. In 1927 the company sent in a new superintendent, G. A. Johnstone, who began arbitrarily to increase work loads, sometimes doubling them without the inconvenience of time studies or explanations to the em-

---

[99] Marshall, "History of Labor Organization in the South," 230.

[100] Except where otherwise indicated, the account of the Gastonia strike is drawn from Pope, *Millhands & Preachers*, 207–330; Bernstein, *Lean Years*, 20–28; Robin Hood, "The Loray Mill Strike" (M.A. thesis, University of North Carolina, 1932); and Tippett, *When Southern Labor Stirs*, 76–108. See also Benjamin U. Ratchford, "Economic Aspects of the Gastonia Situation," in *Social Forces*, VIII (1929–1930), 359–67. For a Communist view see William F. Dunne, *Gastonia: Citadel of the Class Struggle in the New South* (New York, 1931).

ployees. He discharged workers and replaced them with cheaper labor, reduced the force from about 3,500 to about 2,200, effected two wage cuts of 10 per cent each, and reduced costs by a half million dollars a year.

In March, 1928, weave-room workers walked out briefly, complaining of larger work loads and smaller wages. Some time later Loray workers paraded a coffin down Gastonia's main street. At intervals an effigy of the superintendent rose up to ask, "How many men are carrying this thing?" The group shouted "Eight." "Lay off two," the effigy responded; "six can do the work." The comedy masked a growing tension. As the situation deteriorated, word reached the management in Pawtucket and Johnstone was removed in November, 1928. The workers staged a jubilant parade and a new superintendent sought to allay discontent, but the situation soon moved beyond control.

In Gastonia the specter of communism for the first time took on flesh in the South. A new party line in 1928 dictated separate Communist-led unions, and before long organizers of a new National Textile Workers Union (NTWU) were fishing in the troubled waters of the Piedmont.[101] On the first day of 1929 Fred Beal arrived at Charlotte, worked quietly for two months organizing workers at neighboring mills, and finally went to Gastonia in mid-March. There he quickly developed a nucleus of NTWU members who were almost as quickly identified by an informer. On March 25 the mill discharged five union members and at an open meeting on March 30 a thousand voted for an immediate strike. On April 1 a majority of both shifts refused to work.

Union demands were unrealistic in the circumstances, but essentially of a trade union character. They included a minimum weekly wage of $20, a forty-hour week, equal pay for women and children, abolition of the stretch-out and piecework, better housing (screens and bathtubs), cheaper rents and electricity, and union recognition. The demands were "beyond reason," Superintendent J. A. Baugh declared. "If you do not like conditions here, you ought to go elsewhere, or put up your own mill if you can raise $7,000,000." Baugh refused to negotiate and trade unionism

[101] Paul Blanshard, "Communism in Southern Mills," in *Nation*, CXXVIII (1929), 500–501; Myra Page, *Southern Cotton Mills and Labor* (New York, 1929).

dissolved into "revolutionary" agitation. Agents of the Communist apparatus, including party secretary William Z. Foster, flocked in to make Gastonia a "citadel of the class struggle." "North Carolina," one of them said, "is the key to the South, Gaston County is the key to North Carolina, and the Loray Mill is the key to Gaston County." [102]

Scattered evidences of local sympathy quickly disappeared. The challenge to the very culture of the community, to its religion and mores—and its ambitions—supplied grist to the propaganda mills of the company and its supporters. The reds were giving Gastonia a bad name. The situation, said a Federal conciliator, was "not a strike" but "a form of revolution." Advertisements in the Gastonia *Gazette* warned against world revolution, irreligion, racial mixing, and free love. The strike, one advertisement proclaimed, was started "simply for the purpose of overthrowing this government and to kill, kill, kill." Faced with this barrage, strikers hesitated, withdrew, and began to drift back into the mill. Before the summer was out many had joined an active opposition to the union. [103]

Gastonia swirled into a vortex of turmoil and tragedy. A picket line scuffle became the occasion for the entry of state militia on April 4. Strikers and workers poured back into the mill, which by April 15 had returned to full operation. On April 20 the militia withdrew to be replaced by squads of newly sworn deputies. By the end of the month the strikers numbered probably not more than two hundred. An antiparading ordinance made even picketing illegal, but the NTWU defied it in continuing demonstrations. On May 7 the company evicted sixty-two families, whereupon the union established a tent colony in a nearby field. On the night of June 7 a parade designed to be the signal for another walkout (the union continued to win converts among the scabs) was broken up by deputies. Later the same night local officers proceeded to the tent colony to investigate reports of trouble. There a shooting incident left one unionist and four policemen

---

[102] Quoted in Edgar W. Knight, "The Lesson of Gastonia," in *Outlook and Independent*, CLIII (1929), 46.

[103] Don Wharton, "Poor White Capitalists," in *Outlook and Independent*, CLIII (1929), 252–53, 279.

wounded, Chief D. A. Aderholt mortally. Still later that night a mob raided the tent colony.

But the agony was not yet over. In August sixteen unionists went on trial at Charlotte for murder, but a mistrial occurred on September 9 when one terrorized juror became unhinged at the sight of a bloodstained dummy of Chief Aderholt, brought into the courtroom by Solicitor John G. Carpenter. Temporary failure of the prosecution inflamed a disappointed mob; and a caravan of more than a hundred automobiles, led by a motorcycle policeman, roamed through Gaston and adjoining counties, wrecked union property, and terrorized organizers. Another mob milled about the Mecklenburg County jail in Charlotte, where the defendants were held.[104]

The Communists responded with a call for a mass meeting of protest on September 14. A truckload of workers on the way from nearby Bessemer City was turned back as it approached Gastonia, and its path blocked by an automobile. A hail of shots poured into the truck and at workers fleeing through a cotton patch. Ella May Wiggins, twenty-nine-year-old mother of five who had sustained morale in the tent colony with her mountain-style "ballets," was killed, and the few who reached the meeting ground were dispersed. Mrs. Wiggins was buried at Bessemer City, and as the first clods fell on the cheap coffin a friend broke into one of her songs: [105]

We leave our home in the morning,
We kiss our children goodby.
While we slave for the bosses
Our children scream and cry.

. . . . . .

But understand, all workers
Our union they do fear,
Let's stand together, workers,
And have a union here.

[104] Nell Battle Lewis, "Anarchy versus Communism in Gastonia," in *Nation,* CXXIX (1929), 321–22.

[105] Margaret Larkin, "Ella May's Songs," *ibid.,* 383.

But the union died with Ella May. The strike was long since over; the demonstrations now ended. Her murder occurred in broad daylight, with no fewer than fifty witnesses; but the five Loray workers indicted for the killing (after special intervention by Governor O. Max Gardner) were acquitted. The second-degree murder conviction of seven unionists in the second Aderholt murder trial was anticlimax. Under party instructions Beal and his comrades stuck to the facts and avoided propaganda, but one witness flaunted revolution and atheism from the witness stand. With that opening the proceedings "turned into a heresy trial." "Do you believe in the flag of your country . . . ?", Solicitor Carpenter demanded in his summation. "Do you believe in North Carolina? Do you believe in good roads . . . ? [The union organizers] came into peaceful, contented Gastonia . . . bringing bloodshed and death, creeping like the hellish serpent into the Garden of Eden." It took the jury less than an hour to reach its verdict, and the defendants got from five to twenty years. Released pending appeal, they jumped bail and fled to the Soviet Union, but Beal slipped back into the United States in 1933 to write an autobiography in which he set forth his bitter disillusionment with Russian communism.[106] Captured in 1938, he served time in the North Carolina penitentiary until pardoned in 1942.

Before Gastonia's ordeal reached its climax, revolt broke out anew in Marion, North Carolina, where the Baldwin and Clinchfield mill villages presented an unsightly contrast amid vistas of the Blue Ridge.[107] Physical conditions, a visitor wrote, were "almost indescribably degrading." [108] Dilapidated millhouses, perched on brick pillars, lacked either running water or sewerage, and filth overflowed from outside privies while new pits were being dug in the summer of 1929. Wages below ten dollars a week were common. Women started as beginners without pay, and

[106] Pope, *Millhands & Preachers*, 302–306; Fred E. Beal, *Proletarian Journey: New York, Gastonia, Moscow* (New York, 1937).

[107] Except where otherwise indicated, the account of the Marion strike is drawn from Tippett, *When Southern Labor Stirs*, 109–55; Bernstein, *Lean Years*, 29–32; and "The Strike at Marion, North Carolina," in Federal Council of Churches of Christ in America, Department of Research and Education *Information Service* (New York), VIII (1929). See also McCracken, *Strike Injunctions in the New South*, 79–93.

[108] Benjamin Stolberg, "Madness in Marion," in *Nation*, CXXIX (1929), 463.

there was at least one case of a girl, fourteen, working more than twelve hours a day for five dollars a week.[109]

An attempt to install the stretch-out brought a bitter reaction and the nearby Asheville city central helped the workers get a charter from the UTW. An open meeting in June prompted the discharge of twenty-two members. Early in July a committee called on R. W. Baldwin, president of the Marion Manufacturing Community, to demand a reduction in hours from twelve to ten, reinstatement of discharged members, and a grievance committee. Baldwin refused. When Alfred Hoffman arrived, urgently summoned from Elizabethton, he tried to stave off a strike in the absence of relief funds but the committee brushed off his objection. "Hell! We've done struck," one of them said. John Peel, vice president of the North Carolina federation and UTW organizer, officially took charge of the 650 strikers, but little help came from either the AFL or the UTW. The main support came from Hoffman and others associated with the more militant Conference for Progressive Labor Action: A. J. Muste, Tom Tippett, and William Ross.

The progress of the strike paralleled the Elizabethton affair. Clinchfield employees joined the Baldwin workers in the protest. Picket line scuffles brought an injunction and the state militia, and a mediator—in this case L. L. Jenkins, banker and manufacturer of Asheville—arranged a settlement that the company almost immediately repudiated. Baldwin was reported to have agreed orally to a fifty-five hour week and reinstatement of all but twelve union members. Instead, he blacklisted more than a hundred and efforts to interview him further proved fruitless. In the early morning hours of October 2, workers who claimed harassment from the foreman walked out of the Baldwin Mill and tried to persuade the day shift to stay out. Sheriff Oscar E. Adkins fired tear gas into their ranks and his eleven deputies, apparently taking it as a signal, began to shoot at the backs of the scattering workers. Six eventually died, and twenty-five were seriously wounded.

No local minister was available for the funeral, but James Myers of the Federal Council of Churches spoke and Cicero Queens, a

[109] William B. Spofford, "Marion, North Carolina," in *Christian Century*, XLVI (1929), 1502–1503.

mountain preacher, dropped to his knees. "I trust, O God," he prayed, "that these friends will go to a better place than this mill village or any other place in Carolina." L. L. Jenkins brought flowers from Asheville, stammered out a few words, and left the speakers' stand, weeping. President Baldwin, whose conversation one reporter found "studded with . . . a sort of complicated ignorance and irrelevance," was interviewed at his home. "I read that the death of each soldier in the World War consumed more than five tons of lead," he remarked. "Here we have less than five pounds and these casualties. A good average I call it." [110]

In November, Alfred Hoffman and three strikers stood trial for leading a crowd of unionists to evict a strikebreaker who had moved into the former home of a striker. Hoffman got a fine of $1,000 and thirty days in jail; the other three got six months on the chain gang. A trial of Sheriff Adkins and his deputies for murder resulted in an acquittal on December 21, "so they could go home for Christmas," a juror said.

Elizabethton, Gastonia, and Marion were but the chief storm centers in a kaleidoscopic turbulence that swept the textile mills. Other strikes occurred in Pineville, Lexington, Bessemer City, Leaksville, and Charlotte, North Carolina; Thompson, Georgia; and elsewhere.[111] By early May an observer counted fifteen textile strikes in the South Carolina Piedmont.[112] Three days after the March walkout in Elizabethton, twelve hundred workers at Ware Shoals spontaneously left the plant to protest the stretch-out; the local efficiency expert discreetly left town. From Ware Shoals the contagion spread to Pelzer, Woodruff, Greenville, Central, Anderson, and elsewhere. But South Carolina was somehow different. "No," a striker said at Greenville's Brandon Mill, "we don't want no organizers from outside. . . . We're doin' this ourselves." Unlike the agents of absentee owners in Tennessee and

---

[110] Asheville *Advocate*, November 15, 1929.

[111] Marshall, "History of Labor Organization in the South," 260; Mary Heaton Vorse, "Gastonia," in *Harper's*, CLIX (1929), 700.

[112] The following account is drawn from Paul Blanshard, "One-Hundred Per Cent Americans on Strike," in *Nation*, CXXVIII (1929), 554–56; Richard Woods Edmonds, "Underlying Cause of Textile Strikes in the Carolinas," in *Manufacturers' Record*, XCV (April 18, 1929), 60–62; and Mitchell, *Textile Unionism and the South*, 78–80.

North Carolina, the operators in South Carolina received delegations and in nearly every case eliminated or modified the stretch-out to the workers' satisfaction.

"The presence of an outside labor leader would have challenged that philosophy of class partnership which is the corner-stone of South Carolina life," Paul Blanshard observed. "For the time being the weakness of these leaderless strikers is their strength." Moreover, they had a degree of political influence elsewhere lacking. Since 1921 the state had limited the factories to a fifty-five hour week while workers in surrounding states were still struggling to get it.[113] In 1929 it was the only state to conduct a legislative investigation of workers' grievances. The legislative committee, which included a former textile worker, Olin D. Johnston, found, among other things, that the mills had provoked the strikes "by putting more work on the employees than they can do." [114]

In times of crisis, Liston Pope asserted, social patterns often reveal themselves more starkly than in times of "normalcy" and peace.[115] The rebellion of 1929 revealed new elements in the Southern industrial pattern, but highlighted the prevalence of the old. If Southern workers had grown mutinous at class subordination, poverty, and the stretch-out amid prosperity hoopla, they remained close to their native culture. "At the core of the Southern mill workers' outlook on life," Paul Blanshard found, "are the Sunday school, the Star Spangled Banner, and personal friendship for the boss." [116] As historian Irving Bernstein summarized it, the Southern worker's "rural tradition, his ingrained individualism, his restless mobility, his apathy, his poverty, and his suspicions of northerners joined to impede his ability to act collectively." [117] He seized upon the union as an instrument of immediate protest rather than as an agency for long-range collective bargaining. Launched suddenly upon the whirlwind by hotspur workers, even in Gastonia, the organizers were ill-prepared to ride it.

[113] Lander, *History of South Carolina*, 92.
[114] South Carolina *House Journal*, 1930, pp. 11–25.
[115] Pope, *Millhands & Preachers*, 207n.
[116] Blanshard, "One-Hundred Per Cent Americans on Strike," *loc. cit.*, 556.
[117] Bernstein, *Lean Years*, 40.

If the millowners showed a dim perception of new forces in their often stumbling efforts at efficiency, they were far better prepared in crisis to fall back upon paternalism and the timeworn war cries of religion and individualism, to discharge and evict unionists, to deny labor's right to be consulted in matters of its own welfare. "We manufacturers naturally do not take kindly to the idea of a union," said Greensboro's Benjamin Cone, ". . . the laborer does not need the union. The union can do nothing for him." [118]

And if "uptown" elements sometimes expressed sympathy for the striker, they were mostly too far removed from his problems, too far gone in community promotion to see in him anything but a threat to local values and prosperity. Governors who dispatched the militia, deputies and police officers who attacked strikers, mobs that flogged them and destroyed their property, courts that rendered *ex parte* injunctions—all reflected the community hostility or indifference. "In every case where strikers were put on trial," wrote a North Carolina editor, "strikers were convicted; in not one case where anti-unionists or officers were accused has there been a conviction." [119] It would not be safe "for any so-called labor agitator to be caught nosing around here any time soon," the Gastonia *Gazette* warned. "The folks here are simply not going to put up with it any longer." When a strike occurred at nearby Bessemer City in 1930, the strikers themselves drove out both NTWU and AFL organizers who appeared on the scene.[120]

But as the storm passed, the signs of a painful reappraisal multiplied. "Gastonia shocked Southern editors out of their apathy," Mark Ethridge of the Macon *Telegraph* wrote; "editors began to agitate, to take sides, and some of them to demand of mill owners that they make such manifestations as Gastonia unnecessary and impossible." "A low wage scale will not prove an unmixed boon to the South," said George Fort Milton of the Chattanooga *News*. The call for reform was joined by such journals as the Mont-

[118] Bernard Cone, *Some Present Day Problems of the Textile Industry: An Address Delivered February 3, 1930, before the School of Commerce of the University of North Carolina* (n.p., n.d.) , [14].

[119] Weimar Jones, "Southern Labor and the Law," in *Nation*, CXXXI (1930) , 16.

[120] Gastonia *Gazette*, October 22, 1929, quoted in Ratchford, "Economic Aspects of the Gastonia Situation," *loc. cit.,* 363; Pope, *Millhands & Preachers,* 313.

gomery *Advertiser,* Greensboro *Daily News,* Asheville *Citizen,* Raleigh *News and Observer,* and Norfolk *Virginian-Pilot.*[121] Church bodies began to debate and pass resolutions on labor issues. A committee of the United States Senate investigated working conditions in Southern textiles.[122] Articles and books on the subject poured out through Howard Odum's *Social Forces,* the University of North Carolina Press, the *Virginia Quarterly Review,* and other outlets.[123] At the University of North Carolina, history professor Frank P. Graham wrote a "Statement on North Carolina Industry," signed by 415 other citizens of the state who defended the workers' right to civil liberties and collective bargaining; they called for a reduction of hours, elimination of night work, and a stronger child labor law.[124] Governor Gardner, himself a textile manufacturer, publicly declared for higher wages and shorter hours, and against night work and the mill village.[125]

Other manufacturers experienced a change. NAM President John E. Edgerton of Lebanon, Tennessee, admitted the existence of some employers "whose sense of justice is not as keen as it should be." The employer, he said, had an obligation not only to deal justly with his employees, "but as generously as the circumstances will permit."[126] In 1930 P. H. Callahan of the Louisville Varnish Company addressed the Southern Industrial Conference on Human Relations at Blue Ridge, North Carolina. "I trust," he said, "that the chivalrous spirit of the South . . . will remove from industry in the South the extravagances that have been a black mark in other sections of the world, and that . . . there will be infused . . . a determined purpose to improve the human relations of life in society, to make industry serve the lowest no less

[121] Mark Ethridge, "The South's New Industrialism and the Press," in *Annals of the American Academy of Political and Social Science,* CLIII (1931), 252–54.

[122] "Strike at Marion, North Carolina," *loc. cit.,* 11–15; U.S. Senate, Committee on Manufacturers, *Working Conditions of the Textile Industry in North Carolina, South Carolina, and Tennessee,* Senate Report No. 28, Part 2, 71 Cong., 1 Sess. (Washington, 1929).

[123] Much of this material appears in the bibliography of Pope, *Millhands & Preachers,* 337–57.

[124] Tippett, *When Southern Labor Stirs,* 286–88.

[125] New York *Times,* September 30, 1929.

[126] John E. Edgerton, "Obligations of the Manufacturer," in *Manufacturers' Record,* XCVI (August 22, 1929), 45.

than the highest among the people." [127] Donald Comer, Alabama textile manufacturer, addressed a convention of Northern mill-men in 1930: "We should join our friends in the best plans looking toward the elimination of night work for women, for care of, or pensions for aged employees, care of widow mothers, better compensation laws, sick, accident and death benefits, safe guards against unemployment. Child welfare, health and happiness programs." [128]

Some improvement occurred in the strike centers. Welfare work on a broad scale was instituted at Elizabethton; the work week at Marion was reduced six hours and the Clinchfield mill increased wages 5 per cent; mills in Gaston County reduced the work week to fifty-five hours at the same pay and the Loray mill extended its welfare program.[129] The burgeoning reappraisal among millmen brought on a movement to eliminate night work for women and children. Collective bargaining, however, was not a part of the manufacturers' program. The AFL, so irresolute in the strikes of 1929, finally launched a general Southern organizing drive in 1930, just in time for the Great Depression. Substantial improvement in working conditions awaited the New Deal.

[127] P. H. Callahan, "Where Is Southern Industry Headed?", *ibid.*, XCVIII (September 4, 1930) , 55.

[128] National Association of Cotton Manufacturers' *Transactions*, No. 128 (1930), 81–82.

[129] Tippett, *When Southern Labor Stirs*, 73–75, 156; Pope, *Millhands & Preachers*, 307–11.

CHAPTER XI

DEPRESSION AND DELIVERANCE

THE Great Depression of 1929 followed a sequence of crises in Southern agriculture and it afflicted most the very group that had shared least in the decade's prosperity, the farmers. In the fall of 1928 David R. Coker reported from Hartsville, South Carolina, "fifteen bank failures in this and the two counties adjoining, North and South, within the past month." Only three out of eight banks in Darlington remained open; only one of eight in Chesterfield. It was all because of the "persistent absence of farm profits the past nine years." Wet weather in 1929 caused severe crop failures in the area, and Coker himself suffered a loss.[1] Then, with the depression, farm receipts dropped faster and further than incomes in general. In 1932 farm incomes fell to 39 per cent of the 1929 level and receipts from cotton alone to 31 per cent; both far outdistanced the general decline of incomes to 58 per cent.[2]

After the bumper crops of 1925 and 1926 cotton prices mounted to an average of 20.19 cents in 1927, then drifted to 16.78 in 1929, and fell to 9.46 in 1930, 5.66 in 1931, and 6.52 in 1932. The 1931 production was 17,087,000 bales (only a little below the 17,978,-000 bales of 1926 and in June, 1932, the price slumped to 4.6 cents on the New Orleans Cotton Exchange, the lowest since 1894. Tobacco fell from 18.3 cents in 1929 to 12.8, 8.2, and 10.5 in the following years. In December, 1931, when the burley market at Owensboro, Kentucky, opened at prices about half those of the previous year, enraged farmers broke up the sale with angry shouts

[1] Simpson, *Cokers of Carolina*, 202–203.
[2] Hoover and Ratchford, *Economic Resources and Policies of the South*, 53–54. The figures refer to "production income," a category explained in the source.

and threats.[3] Louisiana's sugar country, still suffering the ravages of mosaic disease, experienced low production as well as low prices. In 1930 sugar fell below 3 cents a pound despite a 2-cent tariff imposed in 1930.[4]

The plight of D. A. Cowart, a cotton farmer of Banks, Alabama, was symptomatic. He had bought land during the price upswing of 1923. In 1931 he could not meet the payments. "When we bought the place the price of cotton was 35 cts a lb.," he wrote. "When we lost cotton was worth 5 cts. a lb. . . . In the meantime land values have decreased until there is no cash value on land." [5] Between 1927 and 1932 forced sales of Southern farms rose from 21 to 46 per thousand and as high as 99.9 per thousand in Mississippi; one day in April, 1932, a fourth of the entire area of Mississippi went under the hammer.[6]

In 1930 dry weather conspired with depression to unsettle the entire economy and credit system of the rural South. A drought that by weather bureau records easily took "first place in the climatological history of the country" parched fields in 1,057 counties of 23 states east of the Rockies and devastated especially the Southwest and Lower Mississippi Valley. Arkansas had only 35 per cent of its normal rainfall that summer. Early in January, 1931, a Red Cross worker who visited forty-four white and Negro homes in one Arkansas area found 60 per cent of them with food for less than forty-eight hours, five with no food at all. In a remote section of the Kentucky mountains drought and the shutdown of coal mines left a destitution "so great that many families had sold their beds and stoves to a junk man for a few cents. The relief workers found families sleeping on the floor, huddled together." [7]

[3] U.S. Bureau of the Census, *Historical Statistics of the United States,* 301, columns K-302 and K-303, column K-309; Boyle, *Cotton and the New Orleans Cotton Exchange,* 187–88; Robert, *Story of Tobacco in America,* 207.

[4] Sitterson, *Sugar Country,* 379–81.

[5] D. A. Cowart to Franklin D. Roosevelt, August 24, 1933, in Farm Relief 12, Files of the Secretary of Agriculture (National Archives). Courtesy of Professor Jack B. Key.

[6] Claudius T. Murchison, "Depression and the Future of Business," in Couch (ed.), *Culture in the South,* 95; "One-Fourth of a State Sold for Taxes," in *Literary Digest,* CXIII (May 7, 1932), 10.

[7] American Red Cross, *Relief Work in the Drought of 1930–1931: Official Report of Operations of the American National Red Cross* (Washington, 1931), 7–8, 10, 14,

With the support of President Hoover and a Federal Drought Committee under Secretary of Agriculture Arthur M. Hyde, the Red Cross mobilized a relief fund of $10,000,000, and in January, 1931, Congress appropriated $45,000,000 for seed, feed, and fertilizer loans in stricken areas. These were at best piecemeal measures. To treat the fundamental maladies of low prices and glutted markets the Hoover administration had two specifics: the Agricultural Marketing Act of 1929 and the Smoot-Hawley Tariff of 1930. The marketing act, passed in June, 1929, embodied the new President's idea of "orderly" co-operative marketing for agriculture, a logical extension of his trade association program for business stabilization; it included also a limited program for surpluses. The act created a Federal Farm Board which got a loan fund of $500,000,000 to assist co-operatives and authority to set up "stabilization corporations" to buy surpluses off the market. But the program got underway almost simultaneously with the onset of depression in October.

Farm Board activities were chiefly in wheat and cotton; operations in other fields, however, included efforts to revive the tobacco co-operatives, among others.[8] By March 2, 1931, the Board had extended loans of $136,269,887 to thirty-six co-operative associations in the Southern states.[9] Aid to cotton began in October, 1929, when the board offered loans of 16 cents a pound on lint delivered to the co-operatives, but when market prices fell below 16 cents in late January it undertook more drastic steps. By June, 1930, it had organized the Cotton Stabilization Corporation; in July it gave responsibility for handling the stocks purchased by the government to the American Cotton Cooperative Association, formerly the American Cotton Exchange. The Board took over about 1,250,000 bales from the co-operatives and by June 30, 1931, brought the total up to 1,300,000 bales.[10] Prices did not respond,

---

41–42. See also A. L. Schafer, "When Hunger Followed Drought," in *Survey*, LXV (1930–1931), 581–83; and C. W. Wilson, "Famine in Arkansas," in *Outlook and Independent*, CLVII (1931), 595–97.

[8] *Progressive Farmer*, XLV (1930), 430; Sarah McCulloh Lemmon, "The Public Career of Eugene Talmadge 1926–1936" (Ph.D. dissertation, University of North Carolina, 1952), 64–66.

[9] Saloutos, *Farmer Movements in the South*, 274.

[10] Benedict, *Farm Policies of the United States*, 259–66; Gee and Terry, *Cotton Cooperatives in the Southeast*, 205–208, 226, 227.

and early in the summer the Board called upon the governors of fourteen cotton states to lead a crop reduction movement. It suggested plowing under every third row; in return it promised to keep its own holdings off the market.[11]

Once again crop reduction schemes swept the South. Once again they failed. Huey Long advanced the most drastic plan. Summoning his obedient legislature into a one-day session, he secured unanimous passage of a law prohibiting the "planting, gathering, and ginning of cotton in 1932," and arose from his couch in a cotton nightshirt at 2 A.M. the morning of August 29, 1931, to sign the bill "in the presence of clicking news cameras."[12] The Louisiana plan, however, was too rigorous for the other states. In Texas Governor Ross Sterling sponsored a law limiting acreage in 1932 to 30 per cent of the previous year's, with a similar reduction in 1933. The governors of Arkansas, Oklahoma, and New Mexico endorsed the idea and reduction laws passed the Mississippi and South Carolina legislatures. All of the laws were contingent upon curtailment elsewhere and the other states did not fall in line. After the Texas Supreme Court declared Sterling's plan unconstitutional the movement fell through.[13] But the Southern mind was being prepared for a more meaningful reduction movement under the New Deal. "We believe the time is coming, if it is not already here," said the *Progressive Farmer* "when farmers will recognize the advantage of some form of public control of acreage in order to prevent the disastrous recurrence of overproduction and bankruptcy."[14] Meanwhile the Farm Board ceased its purchases and helplessly watched cotton sink into the slough.[15]

In his message to the special session of Congress that passed the marketing act, President Hoover also recommended limited upward revision of the tariffs, especially on agricultural products. What he got in 1930 was a general upward revision, on manu-

---

[11] Robert S. Simpson, *Interstate Compacts and the Regulation of Cotton,* 35.

[12] *Ibid.,* 30–31; Molyneaux, *Cotton South and American Trade Policy,* 21–22.

[13] Simpson, *Interstate Compacts and the Regulation of Cotton,* 32–34; Saloutos, *Farmer Movements in the South,* 279–80; Karl E. Ashburn, "The Texas Cotton Acreage Control Law of 1931–1932," in *Southwestern Historical Quarterly* (Austin), LXI (1957–1958), 116–24.

[14] *Progressive Farmer,* XLVI (1931), 694.

[15] Small quantities were sold from the stabilization stocks during 1932–1933. In July, 1932, Congress voted 500,000 bales to the American Red Cross for relief purposes. Gee and Terry, *Cotton Cooperatives in the Southeast,* 218–19.

factured goods as well as farm commodities. In the course of the struggle the traditional Southern low-tariff line wavered on several fronts and in the end 25 per cent of the Southern Representatives voted for the Smoot-Hawley Tariff; only 15 per cent had supported the Fordney-McCumber Tariff of 1922.[16] Even the majority who opposed the measure looked after their home districts. John Nance Garner, for example, took care to insert duties on goat hair and Bermuda onions; Cordell Hull suspected him of being "at heart as much a high-tariff man as Smoot or Hawley." [17] "I have heard Democrats from the South stand on the floor . . . for thirty years proclaiming the virtues of Jefferson, until it comes to protecting some little industry of their own States, when they betrayed the Jeffersonian doctrine every time," said Carter Glass. "Jefferson would not speak to one of them." [18] Nor, perhaps, would he have spoken to Glass who, within six months, joined thirteen other Southern senators in supporting tariff schedules for rayon and dyes.[19] In June, 1929, another Jeffersonian, Georgia's Commissioner of Agriculture Eugene Talmadge, deserted the pure doctrine to join a group of tariff advocates in Washington at a meeting called by John Kirby's Southern Tariff Association.[20]

In the Senate Furnifold M. Simmons led a forlorn coalition of Democrats and Republican insurgents against the Smoot-Hawley Tariff, but the lines broke when a Wyoming Democrat joined the sugar and citrus senators from Louisiana and Florida in supporting final passage.[21] John E. Edgerton predicted that the measure would stabilize business conditions, and a jubilant *Manufacturers' Record* foresaw great benefits to the South, particularly in the raw material schedules.[22] An economist, one among many, dissented.

[16] Hoover and Ratchford, *Economic Resources and Policies of the South*, 423.

[17] Timmons, *Garner of Texas*, 77–79; Hull, *Memoirs of Cordell Hull*, I, 133.

[18] "Address of Senator Carter Glass," in University of Virginia Institute of Public Affairs *Proceedings*, 1929, I, 47.

[19] *Manufacturers' Record*, XCVII (February 20, 1930), 50.

[20] *Ibid.*, XCV (June 27, 1929), 59–60; Lemmon, "Public Career of Eugene Talmadge," 60–63.

[21] Rippy (ed.), *Simmons: Memoirs and Addresses*, 59–60; Southern Tariff Association, Bulletin No. 131, April 23, 1930, in Drawer 37, Southern Pine Association Papers.

[22] "The Tariff as It Affects the South," in *Manufacturers' Record*, XCVII (June 26, 1930), 47.

"The fact is that the twentieth century South is still an agricultural South," wrote M. Ogden Phillips. "And the southern congressmen, who for so long have supported a low tariff policy, have represented the interests of their constituents."[23] In any case, the Smoot-Hawley Tariff did not stem the depression nor the decline of commodity prices.

Agriculture led the descent into the depths of depression; towns and industry and the buoyant Atlanta spirit followed not far behind. The Florida boom had passed in 1926, followed by Asheville and the other resorts, and an eerie silence echoed in the tourist hotels. The collapse of real estate values left promoters with uncompleted or unsalable subdivisions and banks with worthless mortgages, foreclosure on which was a futile gesture that preceded bankruptcy. In 1934 one economist guessed that 90 per cent of the money ventured in real estate speculation remained beyond recovery.[24] The far-flung villages that serviced agriculture suffered first, but the commercial centers gradually "took on the air of those old dead towns of Belgium and the Hanseatic League."[25] In Savannah wholesale trade fell by more than half between 1929 and 1933, retail sales and manufactures by almost half.[26] In 1932 Alabama department store sales were down 47.9 per cent from 1929 (49.6 per cent from the peak of 1928); automobile sales off 84.6 per cent; fertilizer, 71.9; life insurance, 50.4; gasoline, 23.4. In each category Alabama had dropped further than the country at large.[27]

By 1931 per capita income payments in the region sank to 67 per cent of 1929 payments, by 1932 to 55 per cent, as compared to

[23] M. Ogden Phillips, "The Tariff and the South," in *South Atlantic Quarterly*, XXXIII (1933), 385.

[24] Murchison, "Depression and the Future of Business," *loc. cit.*, 109.

[25] Cash, *Mind of the South*, 359.

[26] W. H. Steiner, "Changing Composition of the Savannah Business Community, 1900–1940," in *Southern Economic Journal*, X (1943–1944), 303–10.

[27] W. M. Adamson, *Industrial Activity in Alabama, 1913–1932*, in University of Alabama Bureau of Business Research *Mimeographed Series*, No. 4 (Tuscaloosa, 1933), 107. Of approximately 108,000 wage and salary earners in the Birmingham Congressional district, Representative George Huddleston reported, 25,000 were unemployed on January 5, 1932, and 60,000–75,000 were on short time. *Unemployment Relief*, Hearings before a Subcommittee of the Committee on Manufactures, United States Senate, 72 Cong., 1 Sess. (Washington, 1932), 239.

75 and 56 per cent for the non-South. Moreover, the South's was a descent from chronically lower incomes, from $372 in 1929 to $203 in 1932, as compared to a drop from $797 to $448 in the same years outside the South. Yet the Depression bottomed out more quickly in the South; from 1933 on per capita income in the South was higher *in relation to 1929* than it was in the rest of the nation.[28] Paradoxically Southern industry continued to improve its *relative* position in the nation. After 1931 Southern manufacturing dropped off proportionately less than that elsewhere.[29] During 1933, one investigator noted, the South's rate of industrial failures was only about a third of that in the rest of the country.[30] This peculiar situation arose from what at other times would seem a basic economic weakness—the concentration on nondurable consumer goods, compounded with a degree of competition that left manufacturers in those fields about as helpless as farmers to retrench by cutting production. In none of the major nondurable goods industries of the South—textiles, tobacco, food, and paper and pulp—did production in 1932 fall below 73 per cent of 1929, while for all manufactures in the country it fell to 52 per cent and for iron and steel to 24 per cent.[31]

Tobacco was the ideal depression-proof industry, the saying went: the product was cheap, habit-forming, soothing to jangled nerves, and quickly consumed. Cigarette prices held steady—and in 1931 Reynolds even raised the price of Camels when moisture-proof cellophane wrapping was introduced.[32] Moreover, the manufacturers gained an added bonanza in desperately low prices for raw tobacco. From 1926 to 1931 the annual bonus for President George Washington Hill of American Tobacco went up from $199,000 to $892,000. In 1930 and 1931, to the consternation of tobacco farmers, his total annual compensation exceeded a million

[28] Hoover and Ratchford, *Economic Resources and Policies of the South*, 48. There is a slight discrepancy between these figures and those given earlier for "production income."

[29] *Ibid.*, 117.

[30] Arthur Coleman, "The South's Chance at Industry," in *Nation's Business*, XXV (October, 1937), 116.

[31] Hoover and Ratchford, *Economic Resources and Policies of the South*, 117–18.

[32] Nicholls, *Price Policies in the Cigarette Industry*, 83–88.

dollars; total executive bonuses in the company exceeded three million.[33]

Textile mills, however, poured a surfeit of unwanted cloth into the market. Despite the drop in cotton prices, the gray goods manufacturers' margin fell between 1928 and 1932 from 19.60 to 12.05 cents per pound.[34] It was not enough to cover the costs, and after a temporary spurt of profits in 1927—in the wake of low cotton prices—textiles suffered absolute losses. A compilation for the years 1930–1932 showed a ratio of net loss to net worth in the entire industry of, respectively, 3.82, 1.53, and 1.05 per cent.[35]

King Cotton was sick, and the disease infected the whole organism, manufacturing as well as farming. In 1931 an economist at the University of North Carolina offered a lengthy case history and diagnosis.[36] The internal structure of the industry presented a pattern of the rawest competition, Claudius T. Murchison wrote. Its small, numerous, scattered units exhibited "the most extreme and the most tenacious form of individualism to be found in any of the major industries" and "a philosophy of independence which resisted vigorously any collective effort toward modifying individual behavior in the interest of the group as a whole." [37] Instead of one industry there was a whole series of industries waging a constant warfare of "economic bushwhacking": spinners, yarn merchants, weaving mills, converters, commission merchants, wholesalers, garment makers, and various forms of co-operative buying associations. Commission merchants, for example, were concerned primarily with the volume of sales. Mills which looked to their selling agents for financing, therefore, had to sell goods regardless of price or cost in order to meet bills payable.

[33] *Ibid.,* 73.

[34] "Gray goods" is a trade name for unfinished cloth. The margin represented the difference between the value of one pound of gray cloth and one pound of cotton. Kennedy, *Profits and Losses in Textiles,* 128.

[35] Blicksilver, *Cotton Manufacturing in the Southeast,* 99.

[36] Murchison, *King Cotton Is Sick.* For a summary of the book's major points see Claudius T. Murchison, "King Cotton Is Sick," in *Virginia Quarterly Review,* VI (1930), 48–64. See also Blicksilver, *Cotton Manufacturing in the Southeast,* 100–18.

[37] Murchison, *King Cotton Is Sick,* 132.

The obvious solution, Murchison said, was vertical integration of control from spinning to market. A sound economic view, he argued, would look upon the agencies of distribution as the supreme arbiters, rather than subordinate to the means of production. There were already a few significant cases of integrated companies that had developed markets for standard brand names: Cannon Mills, Cone Mills, Riverside and Dan River Mills, Burlington Industries, Pacific Mills, and a few others. But the most that one could foresee for the time being was some degree of rationalization and co-operation along trade association lines.

The trade association movement, which Herbert Hoover encouraged as Secretary of Commerce, reached textiles in 1926 with the formation of the Cotton Textile Institute by manufacturers representing some fifteen million spindles, North and South. Its purpose at first was stabilization through the characteristic trade association research and publication on markets, new uses, reduction of waste, credits, freight rates, production, stocks on hand, shipments, improved methods, and other such matters. As the industry slid into depression the question of balancing production with demand more and more occupied the Institute's leaders—and action was spurred by the labor troubles of 1929. In January, 1930, the Institute proposed that cotton mills limit their operations to day and night shifts of fifty-five and fifty hours weekly; by 1932 about 82 per cent of the spindles in the industry were operating on the plan. In September, 1930, the Institute proposed the elimination of night work for women or children under eighteen; in June, 1931, about 85 per cent of the industry was reported to be co-operating.[38] "The exchange of statistics and the pursuance of policies based on lessons they convey require a largeness of viewpoint that is fortunately becoming more prevalent," said B. B. Gossett, president of the American Cotton Manufacturers Association; "our industry is being gradually revolutionized through the substitution of the principle of cooperation for cut throat competition."[39] For all that, the industry had not solved its problems.

[38] Boris Siniavsky, "The Cotton-Textile Institute, Inc., A Stabilizing Agency in the Cotton Textile Industry" (M.A. thesis, University of North Carolina, 1931), 32–35, 54–59, 61–63, 96–102; Michl, *Textile Industries*, 260–63.

[39] B. B. Gossett, "A Review of the South's Cotton Industry," in *Manufacturers' Record*, CII (January, 1933), 19.

Market fluctuations for both raw materials and finished products, Murchison said, still exhibited "a perfect carnival of violence and unrestraint." [40]

For an even more perfect carnival of violence and unrestraint one could look to Oklahoma City and East Texas, drowning in a flood of oil. The inundation commenced with the discovery that Oklahoma's capitol stood above one of the state's richest oil fields. After the first discovery in December, 1928, derricks sprouted in back lots and front yards all over town. On March 26, 1930, the "Wild Mary Sudik" well blew in and ran uncontrolled for twelve days, the wind spreading oil over farms as far as Norman, twelve miles away.[41]

Other runaway menaces followed periodically. Then came the climactic East Texas field, the most gigantic yet. In September, 1930, C. M. "Dad" Joiner, a wildcatter near the end of his resources, opened the field with a well in the unpromising piney woods of Rusk County. When it flowed he paled, leaned against the derrick, and said, "I always dreamed it, but I never believed it." [42] Even in his worst dreams it is doubtful that Joiner could have envisioned the nightmare he released on the oil industry. In February, 1931, the field produced a daily average of 25,062 barrels; by the middle of August an entire countryside was spewing over a million barrels daily, one third of the nation's requirements. It was more than the majors could cope with. Wildcatters grabbed leaseholds, pumped oil as fast as they could, and sold it below posted prices to the "tapping" and "skimming" plants (crude refineries) that sprang into existence. At one point the price hit a record low of 2½ cents a barrel.[43] "If some arch enemy of the petroleum industry had sought to do it the greatest possible injury," said Jersey Standard's journal, *The Lamp,* "he could scarcely have hit upon a more diabolical scheme"—a new field "larger in size than any previously discovered, with prolific wells of comparatively shallow depth, and leaseholds vested in hundreds of small ownerships in the hands largely of people who . . . had

[40] Murchison, "King Cotton Is Sick," *loc. cit.,* 58.   [41] Rister, *Oil!,* 250–64.

[42] Richardson, *Texas: Lone Star State,* 346.

[43] Charles A. Warner, *Texas Oil and Gas since 1543* (Houston, 1939), 72; Richardson, *Texas: Lone Star State,* 398; Forbes, "Passing of the Small Oil Man," *loc. cit.,* 208.

no interest in the oil industry. Control and orderly production under such circumstances appeared almost beyond hope." [44]

The embryonic conservation and proration laws of Oklahoma and Texas collapsed under the surfeit of "hot oil" (amounts above the allowables), and the governors of both states resorted to martial law in August, 1931. William H. "Alfalfa Bill" Murray of Oklahoma ordered the militia to close all prorated wells until "the price hits one dollar." In October the wells were permitted 5 per cent of their allowables and the troops were withdrawn a short time later, only to return from June, 1932, until April, 1933. Murray could not attend the inauguration of a new President because of "a military oil control that I dare not leave with the Lieutenant Governor." [45] In mid-August, 1931, Governor Sterling sent the militia into the East Texas field, closed down the wells temporarily, and then reopened them under strict daily limitations of 225 barrels each. Martial law remained in effect six months and prices advanced to 67 cents; but after a Federal court ordered the troops removed, hot oil began to flow again. Despite fears of depletion, the field in 1932 spouted more oil than Spindletop had in thirty-one years.[46] Before the flood ended it had swept oil men ever more strongly toward the concept of stabilization, just as overproduction had impelled textile leaders and cotton farmers to similar movements. "It was not until the epochal discovery of the East Texas field . . ." said a Texas oil leader, "that the real science of modern conservation began to crystallize." [47]

For some years regulation to prevent physical waste had been accepted; it was an easy step from that to the prevention of

[44] "East Texas Drowns Itself in Oil," reprinted from *The Lamp* (June, 1931), *Review of Reviews*, LXXIV (August, 1931) , 78.

[45] Rister, *Oil!*, 264–65; William H. Murray to Franklin D. Roosevelt, February 1, 1933, in William H. Murray Papers (University of Oklahoma Library, Norman).

[46] Warner, *Texas Oil and Gas*, 72–73; Rister, *Oil!*, 319–22. For a discussion of Sterling's imposition of martial law and all the legal vicissitudes see Mills, "Public Career of a Texas Conservative," 275–315.

[47] E. O. Thompson, quoted in Rister, *Oil!*, 316. Thompson, who joined the Texas Railroad Commission in 1932, was perhaps the individual most responsible for persuading Texas oil men to accept strict regulation. Douglass Cater, "The General and the Umbrella," in *The Reporter: A Fortnightly of Facts and Ideas* (New York) , XVI (March 21, 1957) , 11–15.

"economic waste" by limiting output in accordance with the market. The somewhat oblique reasoning was that production in excess of demand led to physical waste through deterioration, leakage, or evaporation of oil in storage. Economic stabilization, therefore, could masquerade as conservation—which in part it was. From 1915 Oklahoma had authorized proration to prevent both physical and economic waste. Limitation to fit market demand, however, had been applied only rarely until the Corporation Commission issued its first statewide order in 1928. Out of the Oklahoma City chaos finally came in 1932 a decision of the United States Supreme Court upholding the prevention of economic waste; in 1932 a new state law strengthened the Commission's powers. In Texas, which had a strong antitrust tradition, the movement encountered cries of monopoly and price-fixing. In 1931 the state strengthened its existing law against physical waste, which dated from 1919, but not until 1932 did the legislature permit production allowables on the basis of market demand. The other oil states gradually perfected their proration laws through the 1930's.[48] Proration restrictions at last brought to an end the brawling boom towns of flush production; the last stand of the "Wild West" was finally over.

Movements for production control and stabilization yielded no relief from the general economic slump. Railroads afforded one basic index. Of twenty-one Class I railroads in the South only four earned as much as their fixed charges in 1931, in 1932 only one, the Clinchfield. As a group they failed to meet fixed charges by $22,000,000 in 1931 and by $48,000,000 in 1932. By July 1, 1933, seven of the twenty-one roads that controlled more than a quarter of the mileage in the region were in receivership.[49] Banking resources provided another index of the malaise. The South's proportion of the nation's banking resources declined from 9.7 per cent in 1929 to 8.7 in 1934, a total decline from $6,995,000,000 to

[48] Section of Mineral Law of the American Bar Association, *Legal History of Conservation of Oil and Gas* (Chicago, 1938), 16–27, 60–74, 91–100, 110–288. On Texas see also Warner, *Texas Oil and Gas,* 60–63, 70–74; and Larson and Porter, *History of Humble Oil & Refining Company,* 246–57, 316–26, 446–87.

[49] C. K. Brown, "The Financial Condition of Railroads in the South in 1933," in *Southern Economic Journal,* I (January, 1934), 14. However, in 1933 railroad freight revenues began to pick up more quickly in the South than outside it. *Ibid.,* 17.

$4,844,000,000—or 30.7 per cent while national banking resources went down 21.3 per cent. Southern banks were particularly vulnerable to economic distress because of the large number of small state banks, poorly supervised and regulated, lacking experienced and competent management. Many failed, an Atlanta banker said, "because the community in which they operated failed." From 1921 through 1929 bank suspensions in the South numbered 1,776 in a national total of 5,641. In 1928, 1929, and 1930 the South's proportion of failures was more than three times its proportion of resources. After 1929 the proportion declined, because of rising distress elsewhere, but the total number increased.[50]

The most spectacular cycle of failures was set in motion across the mid-South by the collapse of Caldwell and Company at Nashville in November, 1930. Founded in 1917 by Rogers Caldwell as a municipal bond house specializing in Southern issues, the company had grown into a classic example of the "madhouse banking of the 1920's."[51] Rising on the tide of economic and governmental development in the 1920's, this "Morgan of the South" brought some $120,000,000 into the region through the sale of Southern securities and large additional sums of working capital through loans from Eastern banks, newspapers, an investment trust (Shares-in-the-South), and a variety of enterprises ranging from textiles to the Kentucky Rock Asphalt Company, producers of "Kyrock." Altogether they represented assets of more than a half billion dollars.

After 1927 Caldwell became associated with Colonel Luke Lea, former senator and would-be kidnapper of the Kaiser, later a Nashville publisher and businessman, in the purchase of various banks and newspapers and finally in dubious political operations. Governor Henry H. Horton, a close ally and pliant tool, removed a highway commissioner who refused to specify Kyrock for Tennessee highways and a tax commissioner who refused favors to financiers, deposited millions of state funds in their banks,[52] and

[50] Hoover and Ratchford, *Economic Resources and Policies of the South*, 169–71; William J. Carson, "Banking in the South: Its Relation to Economic and Industrial Changes," in *Annals of the American Academy of Political and Social Science*, CLIII (1931), 213.

[51] The following account is drawn from McFerrin, *Caldwell and Company*, an excellent detailed study of the company and its connections.

[52] Benjamin U. Ratchford, *American State Debts* (Durham, N.C., 1941), 413–16.

built a road through Lea's property to increase its value. In 1930, however, the decline of stock and property values brought growing difficulties. Caldwell arranged a merger with the Banco Kentucky Company of Louisville, which ruled a lesser empire, mainly for the purpose of milking its banks. The scramble for cash to meet pressing obligations involved Lea and Caldwell in more and more questionable manipulations, to no avail. On November 7, 1930, their chief subsidiary, the Bank of Tennessee, went into receivership; on the twelfth another subsidiary bank in Knoxville failed to open; and on the thirteenth Caldwell and Company itself admitted bankruptcy. Affiliated banks fell like dominoes. Within two weeks the resultant panic carried down approximately 120 banks in seven states; a number of others survived only by hasty mergers. At Asheville, North Carolina, the collapse sent one bank president to the penitentiary and caused the removal and subsequent suicide of the mayor who had lost public funds in a futile effort to prop up the tottering banks.[53] The downfall of the "politico-bunko-busto-banko" coalition prompted an unsuccessful effort to impeach and remove Governor Horton and criminal prosecutions in Tennessee, Arkansas, and Kentucky. But only Luke Lea and Luke Lea, Jr., actually served time, with the Asheville bank president, for conspiracy and misuse of bank funds in North Carolina. In the debacle the state of Tennessee lost approximately $6,500,000 and avoided bankruptcy only by getting emergency loans from local and New York banks.[54] Common unsecured claimants against Caldwell and Company recovered only .4129 per cent, and secured depositors fared little better: Mead County, Kentucky got only $400 on a $20,500 deposit and Mobile, Alabama, $1,250 on $100,000.

Bank failures and the decline of revenues brought a day of reckoning for communities that had plunged into debt during the 1920's. A wave of defaults by governmental units that had begun in Florida after the boom now spread to other states in the Depression. During the 1930's the South had a majority of the nation's delinquent governmental units. South Carolina was temporarily

---

[53] Daniels, *Tar Heels*, 226–27. Thomas Wolfe used the incident in his novel *You Can't Go Home Again* (New York, 1940), 359–72.

[54] Ratchford, *American State Debts*, 407–28.

in arrears, but Arkansas in 1932 was the only state to default.[55] There a proliferation of special road districts, characterized by inefficiency and graft, had run up a sizable debt, much of which the state assumed in 1927. A state road program, started at the same time, brought "an era of prodigality, an interlude of fortune," and insolvency in 1932. An indifferent legislature, obviously eager to evade obligations, finally enacted in 1934 a refunding measure that spread payments of $288,211,960 in principal and interest over a period of years from 1936 to 1977—with no loss of principal but some loss of interest to bondholders.[56]

The financial necessities of the Depression abruptly halted the expansive impulse of business progressivism, but at the same time spurred action for efficiency, centralization, and new revenues. The accumulation of deficits brought reform measures to tighten the supervision of local debt administration. Virginia in 1930 empowered Governor John Garland Pollard to cut appropriations, which he did by more than seven million dollars; the Texas legislature in 1933 reduced appropriations about 21 per cent, while other states sought savings through rationalization as well as retrenchment.[57] Richard B. Russell, Jr., elected governor of Georgia in 1930 on pledges of economy and efficiency, sponsored a reorganization that reduced ninety-odd state agencies to nineteen departments, with a resultant saving of a million dollars.[58] During 1931 North Carolina, the exemplar of business progressivism, undertook several ventures in state centralization under Governor O. Max Gardner. The state brought the three major institutions of higher education under the Consolidated University of North Carolina and assumed complete responsibility for public roads and a six-month school term. Tax cuts reduced local property taxes approximately $12,000,000, while salary cuts and other economies reduced the total cost of government about $7,000,000.[59]

[55] Hoover and Ratchford, *Economic Resources and Policies of the South*, 218–19.
[56] Ratchford, *American State Debts*, 383–406. See also Martin, *Southern State and Local Finance Trends and the War*, 76–78.
[57] Matthew Page Andrew, *Virginia: The Old Dominion* (Garden City, N.Y., 1937), 588; Richardson, *Texas: Lone Star State*, 324–25.
[58] Buck, *Reorganization of State Governments*, 78–81. See also Cullen B. Gosnell, *Government and Politics of Georgia* (New York, 1936), 97–114.
[59] O. Max Gardner, "One State Cleans House," in *Saturday Evening Post*, CCIV (January 2, 1932), 23, 72–74.

State assumption of local responsibilities, together with new state responsibilities later, reversed the relative position of state and local governments in the tax structure; Southern state governments in 1932 got 42 per cent of the combined state and local revenues; in 1942, 60 per cent.[60] The desperate search for revenues awakened an interest in the general sales tax. Georgia had one temporarily, 1929–1931, and Kentucky and Mississippi in 1930 adopted low-rate sales taxes of negligible importance; but in 1932 Mississippi's success in raising revenues 25 per cent by a 2 per cent sales tax generated a national interest. By the end of 1933 North Carolina and Oklahoma had joined the sales-tax states and serious movements had developed in six more Southern states, accompanied by massive demonstrations of hostility from retail merchants and others. The sales tax was "a perversion of the equitable basis of taxation," one student pointed out, which disregarded "the ability to pay." [61] But it had one overpowering pragmatic merit—it worked.

Beset by the struggle with debts, scarcely able to retain existing public services, state and local governments were neither prepared nor able to cope with human distress. On the face of inadequate statistics, it would seem that the South experienced less absolute unemployment than the rest of the nation. In the South Atlantic states, the monthly average employment in manufacturing had dropped by 1933 to 72.1 per cent of the 1929 figure, a level higher than for any other census regions. But in the East South Central states the level was 54.3 per cent and in the West South Central states 55.9 per cent, somewhat below the national level.[62] In 1930 total unemployment reported by the census in the Southeast was 253,000, only 1.6 per cent of the work force. That, however, was before the full impact of industrial decline and the agricultural distress that, in any case, would be inadequately reflected by

[60] Hoover and Ratchford, *Economic Resources and Policies of the South,* 199.

[61] Alfred W. Garner, "A Note on the Mississippi Sales Tax," in *Southern Economic Journal,* I (January, 1934) , 24–27; Carl Shoup, *The Sales Tax in the American States* (New York, 1934) , 145–210. Kentucky, Mississippi, North Carolina, and Oklahoma adopted sales taxes, and efforts were mounted in Arkansas, Georgia, Texas, and Virginia. See also Josephine L. Doughton, "Passage of the Sales Tax Law in North Carolina, 1931–1933" (M.A. thesis, University of North Carolina, 1949) .

[62] Anne Page, *Employment and Unemployment, 1929–1935,* Office of National Recovery Administration, Division of Review, No. 45, Part B (Washington, 1936) , 27.

unemployment figures. By 1937 the increase of job seekers and the displacement of farm workers had brought the total in the Southeast to 1,988,000 or 10.4 per cent of the work force, as compared to 11.8 per cent in the nation. But the Southeast had 15 per cent farm unemployment as compared to 11.2 per cent in the nation.[63]

The individualistic outlook of the region yielded only with difficulty to a recognition of collective social and economic forces. If people "do not . . . practice the habits of thrift and conservation," John E. Edgerton asked, "or if they gamble away their savings in the stock markets or elsewhere, is our economic system, or government, or industry to blame?"[64] Governor Ross Sterling of Texas suggested that much suffering was caused by the improvidence of people who had "not the right idea of using what means they may have." "The big trouble," his friend and fellow banker, J. W. Hoopes of Dallas, explained, "is that we are playing too damn much and working too damn little."[65] The owner of a feed mill in Denison informed Sam Rayburn that "most of the men on the road are hoboes just because they want to be and this unemployed publicity has made it easy for them."[66] "The phenomenon of a whole major section of American citizens remaining blindly and selfishly aloof while a fifth of the population struggled desperately against actual starvation is one which the future historian will no doubt view with the appropriate incredulous scorn," wrote a Duke University folklorist who had struggled to organize a local relief project.[67]

But in Durham and countless other cities conscientious burghers rallied to the cause of relief only to have their resources devoured by the needs of the destitute. One striking exception was Alfred I. DuPont, family rebel and adopted citizen of Jacksonville,

[63] Rupert B. Vance and Nadia Danilevsky, "Population and the Pattern of Unemployment in the Southeast, 1930–1937," in *Southern Economic Journal*, VII (1940–1941), 187–203. The inclusion of Texas and Oklahoma would raise the figures to 366,160 for 1930 and 2,331,859 for 1937.

[64] *Proceedings of the Thirty-Fifth Annual Meeting of the National Association of Manufacturers, New York City, October 6-7-8-9, 1930* (New York, 1930), 14–15.

[65] Both quoted in Mills, "Public Career of a Texas Conservative," 162.

[66] George C. Knaur to Sam Rayburn, April 8, 1932, in Legislative File, 1932, Sam Rayburn Library (Bonham, Tex.).

[67] Newman I. White, "Labor Helps Itself: A Case History," in *South Atlantic Quarterly*, XXXII (1933), 360–61.

who sent out trucks to pick up the jobless for work in public parks at $1.25 a day. With daily payrolls as high as $400 he kept it up until New Deal agencies took over in 1933.[68] Made-work in public parks became a favorite device. Birmingham voted a bond issue of $500,000 in January, 1931, for the purpose, but by September nearly half of it had evaporated in wages of 25 cents an hour. In Little Rock an emergency relief appropriation of $20,000 in January, 1931, was supplemented by $25,000 in contributions; the funds provided work for as many as 600 during one week but by the end of March the money was gone. A similar effort in Louisville lasted from November, 1930, to April, 1931, providing jobs for 1,641 in all. Atlanta, New Orleans, Birmingham, and other cities depleted their funds for family relief early in 1932.[69]

Other schemes were as useless in stemming the tide of adversity. Fantasies of an agricultural safety valve, a "back-to-the-farm" movement for the urban unemployed, engaged the imaginations of a people still rooted in a rural culture. "The great opportunity for Southern agriculture is in providing homes and a good living for the surplus population of the North and West," David R. Coker wrote.[70] In Charleston William Watts Ball envisioned an Arcadia of factory-farm life, the South's answer to industrial megalopolis.[71] John H. Kirby, Texas lumberman and foe of enlarged government, nevertheless proposed a $50,000,000,000 bond issue to acquire unused lands for sale in small tracts on long-range terms.[72] "The best solution of the problem," the Atlanta

[68] Marquis James, *Alfred I. DuPont: The Family Rebel* (New York, 1941) , 474.

[69] Joanna C. Colcord, *Emergency Work Relief as Carried Out in Twenty-Six American Communities, 1930–1931, with Suggestions for Setting Up a Program* (New York, 1932) , 42–47, 114–26; "How the Cities Stand," in *Survey*, LXVIII (1932), 71–75; John Dean Minton, "The New Deal in Tennessee, 1932–1938" (Ph.D. dissertation, Vanderbilt University, 1959) , 74–78.

[70] Simpson, *Cokers of Carolina*, 209.

[71] William Watts Ball to the Editor of *Liberty*, November 9, 1931; Ball to Oswald Garrison Villard, June 15, 1932; Ball to D. L. Chambers, September 20, 1932; Ball to Hugh McRae, April 5, 1933, in Ball Papers. Ball planned but never finished a book on the subject. See also "Address by Governor Franklin D. Roosevelt of New York on State Planning," in University of Virginia Institute of Public Affairs *Proceedings*, 1931, pp. 660–61.

[72] John H. Kirby, "A Relief for Unemployment and an Aid in the Pursuit of Happiness," address to the Southern Pine Association, New Orleans, March 22, 1932, in Southern Pine Association Papers.

371

Journal agreed, "is to send these unemployed back to the farms. . . . Georgia's 50,000 abandoned farms offer a haven for those who are dispiritedly walking the streets." [73] A few efforts were made. The Atlanta Chamber of Commerce sponsored a program to settle some fifty to sixty families on Georgia farms. The Department of Labor and the Red Cross placed forty-two destitute families on abandoned farms near Greenville, South Carolina. Muscogee County, Georgia, and Houston tried similar projects on a small scale.[74] In 1931 North Carolina's Governor Gardner raised the old cry of diversification again in a lively "live-at-home" campaign. With a surplus of cotton and tobacco, the Charlotte *Observer* noted, North Carolina still imported dairy products, canned goods, grain, hay, and feedstuffs to the tune of $160,000,-000 a year.[75]

For all that such campaigns invoked mystic strains of agrarianism, they ran headlong into a migration that was going the other way—except briefly during 1932.[76] A survey of families on relief in 1932 disclosed only in the Appalachian and Ozark areas any substantial number that had shifted to agriculture from other employment, mostly people who were already living in open country. Throughout the cotton belt farm families in large numbers had moved into towns and cities in search of work or relief.[77] The towns rather than the country promised sanctuary for the distressed.

A minor variation on the back-to-the-farm theme was devised by the Atlanta Black Shirts, or American Fascisti, who paraded up

---

[73] Atlanta *Journal*, December 1, 1932, quoted in Troy J. Couley, *Agrarianism: A Program for Farmers* (Chapel Hill, 1935), 69.

[74] Conkin, *Tomorrow a New World*, 29–30.

[75] Charlotte *Observer*, September 7, 1931, quoted in Gee and Terry, *Cotton Cooperatives in the Southeast*, 16.

[76] Rupert B. Vance with Nadia Danilevsky, *All These People: The Nation's Human Resources in the South* (Chapel Hill, 1945), 131; Carter Goodrich *et al.*, *Migration and Economic Opportunity: The Report of the Study of Population Redistribution* (Philadelphia, 1936), 503–19.

[77] P. G. Beck and M. C. Forster, *Six Rural Problem Areas: Relief—Resources—Rehabilitation: An Analysis of the Human Material Resources in Six Rural Areas with High Relief Rates*, Federal Emergency Relief Administration Research Monograph I (Washington, 1935), 66–67. See also W. S. Thompson, *Research Memorandum on Internal Migration in the Depression* (New York, 1937), 29–30.

Peachtree Street in 1930 with banners warning, "Niggers, back to the cotton fields—city jobs are for white folks." Newspaper exposures and official hostility suppressed the nascent "fascism" but the policy of displacing Negroes caught on—and reached a dramatic climax in the arrest of Atlanta's Negro bellhops on charges of selling liquor and in some cases of "attempted rape," for which they were fined $100! [78] Racial discrimination extended from jobs to relief, on the theory that Negroes could live on less. Houston authorities refused to take applications from either Mexican or Negro families: "They are being asked to shift for themselves." [79]

As local relief funds trickled away, Southern Congressmen began to join the cry for Federal aid. In December, 1931, George Huddleston of the Birmingham district demanded an appropriation of $50,000,000 for relief to the unemployed. His colleague, William B. Bankhead, however, assured the country that the Democrats would behave responsibly.[80] But soon Bankhead himself was urging that some old bridges be burned; one of the first, he suggested, would have to be the prejudice against direct relief.[81] Early in 1932 Representative Wright Patman of Texas proposed a kind of selective Federal relief—immediate full payment of the veterans' bonus due in 1945. His bill from the beginning faced opposition in the Senate and the certainty of a Presidential veto; it was voted down in July during a remarkable demonstration by unemployed veterans, the "Bonus Army." [82]

Hoover meanwhile supported measures of Federal intervention to shore up the corporate and financial structure: the Reconstruction Finance Corporation (RFC), chartered in January, 1932, to make loans to corporations; the Federal Home Loan Bank Act of July to refinance home loans and prevent foreclosures; and other

[78] Arthur Raper and Ira DeA. Reid, *Sharecroppers All* (Chapel Hill, 1941), 122–26; Edwin Tribble, "Black Shirts in Georgia," in *New Republic*, LXVI (1930), 204–206. A similar group of "Blue Shirts" appeared briefly in Jacksonville.

[79] Broadus Mitchell, *Depression Decade: From New Era through New Deal, 1929–1941* (New York, 1947), 103–104, Vol. IX of Henry David *et al., The Economic History of the United States.*

[80] Thomas L. Stokes, *Chip Off My Shoulder* (Princeton, 1947), 280.

[81] Walter J. Heacock, "William B. Bankhead and the New Deal," in *Journal of Southern History*, XXI (1955), 350.

[82] Arthur M. Schlesinger, Jr., *The Crisis of the Old Order* (Boston, 1957), 256–65; Bernstein, *Lean Years*, 437–55.

measures. Gradually circumstances pushed a reluctant administration toward Federal relief. Speaker John Nance Garner of Texas, with his own eye cocked to the White House, proposed a billion dollar bond issue for public works, another billion for RFC loans to state and local public works projects, and $100,000,000 for distribution to the needy. Senator Robert F. Wagner of New York proposed even larger appropriations, but the Wagner-Garner bill that came out of a conference committee met a veto. Then, on July 21, 1932, Hoover signed a revised Emergency Relief and Construction Act giving the RFC $300,000,000 for relief loans to the states and appropriating $322,224,000 for Federal public works.[83]

By the fall of 1932 RFC loans, administered through the states, began to pump life back into welfare and relief agencies. Mississippi, without any state welfare organization, accepted as a condition of its loan the appointment of a relief director by the RFC. Aubrey Williams, native of Alabama and social worker, spent three months organizing work programs to give each head of a family on relief three dollars worth of work per week. He faced continuous abuse from Jackson editor Fred Sullens as "this fellow who was sent in here by Hoover." [84] A new State Board of Public Welfare finally took over the responsibility. By the spring of 1933 about 30 per cent of the state's families had received $3,709,962 of RFC funds in sums that averaged $1.80 per week; 75 per cent of the total amount went to work-relief at rates averaging less than a dollar a day. In Tennessee the state highway department used the relief money mostly in a road work program at 12½ cents an hour. By April, 1933, Kentucky had received $5,162,166 from the RFC; Louisiana $7,602,506; Alabama $2,800,000; North Carolina $5,-074,000; South Carolina $3,801,815; Texas $5,513,089, to be expended by various agencies, usually special relief commissions, on a variety of direct allocations and work relief.[85]

[83] Bernstein, *Lean Years*, 468–71.
[84] Aubrey Williams, "Memoirs," 9–13. Typescript examined by courtesy of author.
[85] Joanna C. Colcord, and Russell H. Kurtz (eds.), "Unemployment and Community Action," in *Survey*, LXIX (1933), 168–70, describes the state programs. For over-all totals see Edward Ainsworth Williams, *Federal Aid for Relief*, in Columbia University *Studies in History, Economics, and Public Law*, No. 452 (New York, 1939), 50.

Relief was renewed, state and Federal governments entered the field, but the tide of distress continued to rise. It overflowed in a desperate wandering, a movement not back to the farm but from place to place in a futile search for escape. In San Antonio the young county tax collector, Maury Maverick, estimated that each Southern Pacific freight from New Orleans brought in fifty to a hundred transients, those from Los Angeles and El Paso almost as many. With two companions Maverick set out in December, 1932, on a hobo trip through Texas, Oklahoma, and Louisiana. They "slept in jungles, got lousy, and, what was worse, got preached and lectured at by fourflushing racketeers," and gagged on mission food. In Dallas and Fort Worth, he estimated, as many as two thousand passed through in a day—more in New Orleans or Oklahoma City. Mostly displaced tenants and farm workers, they also included businessmen, salesmen, doctors, and lawyers. About a fourth were women and children, including unattached boys as young as eleven or twelve. "I saw enough to make anyone sick for a long time," Maverick wrote. "There was promiscuity, filth, degradation. . . . Men and families slept in jails, hot railroad urinals, cellars, dugouts, tumble-down shacks." Back in San Antonio he organized relief stations at the freight depots, provided cheap meals and freight schedules, and out of remnants of the Bonus Army encamped at the fair grounds organized a self-help colony on land donated by Humble Oil.[86]

It was not until the South's labor surplus was thus greatly augmented by depression that the torpid AFL mobilized to meet the challenge of the Piedmont textile revolt. On October 7, 1929, three days after the burial of the Marion massacre victims and a little over two weeks before the Wall Street panic, the AFL held its annual meeting in Toronto. After hearing a report on the "Awakening South" the delegates voted on a high pitch of enthusiasm for a Southern organizing drive.[87] A plan emerged later to have each national union supply an organizer and financial assistance. Southerners at the planning conference, led by W. C.

[86] Maury Maverick, *A Maverick American* (New York, 1937), 152–76.
[87] *Report of Proceedings of the Forty-Ninth Annual Convention of the American Federation of Labor, Held at Toronto, Ontario, Canada, October 7th to 18th, inclusive, 1929* (Washington, 1929), 199, 265–83.

Birthright of Tennessee, urged a bold and militant program, but more conservative counsels prevailed.

The campaign started in January, 1930, with a mass meeting at Charlotte and the opening of headquarters in Birmingham. Directing such agents as the national and state federations could spare, the organizing committee usually had about forty, never more than eighty, organizers.[88] The drive fell into two major parts: standard organizing techniques plus an effort to persuade businessmen and the public that responsible unionism would contribute to economic stabilization. During 1930 President William Green made two Southern speaking tours during which he flayed the Communists and emphasized AFL moderation. "We come preaching doctrine of cooperation and good will," he said. On his heels came Geoffrey Brown, the union's efficiency expert, to explain the stabilizing effect of union-management co-operation. "The millowners," a contemporary observer wrote, "listened politely to Mr. Brown's speeches, informed him that they were perfectly well able to manage their plants without assistance, and ushered him out the door." [89]

By October organizers reported the formation of 112 new locals mostly in Alabama, Georgia, and the Carolinas, 25 in textiles. The appeal to respectability, one observer wrote, deprived the movement of "those inspirational and dramatic qualities which alone can rally the rank and file about the union banner"; [90] yet a major problem was to curb the militancy of workers itching to strike against hopeless odds. At Danville, Virginia, it became impossible, and the campaign reached its calamitous end. Until 1930 President H. R. Fitzgerald of Dan River and Riverside Cotton Mills had enjoyed a reputation as a good employer.[91]

[88] Although 105 had been proposed. George S. Mitchell, "Organization of Labor in the South," in *Annals of the American Academy of Political and Social Science,* CLIII (1931) , 186. Even smaller numbers appear in Bernstein, *Lean Years,* 35; and Marshall, "History of Labor Organization in the South," 279.

[89] Jean Carol Trepp, "Union-Management Co-operation and the Southern Organizing Campaign," in *Journal of Political Economy* (Chicago) , XLI (1933) , 602–24.

[90] *Ibid.,* 623.

[91] The following account of the Danville strike draws on Marshall, "History of Labor Organization in the South," 281–88; Bernstein, *Lean Years,* 36–40; Tippett, *When Southern Labor Stirs,* 210–69; and Smith, *Mill on the Dan,* 245–394. See also Julian R. Meade, *I Live in Virginia* (New York, 1935) , 5–23, 37–49, 58–73.

Wages exceeded the Southern average, the work week was fifty-five hours, the welfare program elaborate, and since 1919 the company had sponsored a representative system of "Industrial Democracy." In 1930, however, the workers' representatives refused to accept a 10 per cent wage cut, whereupon Fitzgerald abolished the system and imposed it anyway. The workers turned to the United Textile Workers, who sent their Vice President Francis Gorman to organize the mills. Gorman disclaimed any intention of a strike, proposed instead a scheme of union-management co-operation for efficient production. But Fitzgerald remained convinced that the union proposed to usurp management prerogatives. "What can such a movement do for you that you do not already have," he asked the workers, *"except to take your money in dues to pay a lot of foreign agitators . . . ?"*

When the company began discharging union members, replacing them from the pool of floating labor in the Piedmont, the UTW either had to retire or strike; on September 29 the workers walked out. The ensuing drama followed a standard script. Fitzgerald got injunctions against picketing, refused an offer of mediation from Governor Pollard, and reopened the mills on November 24. The workers responded with mass picketing, the militia appeared, Fitzgerald evicted union members from company houses, and the strike dragged out a familiar course to defeat. On January 29, 1931, Gorman called it off. Fitzgerald, he said, was taking back former strikers without regard to union membership, thereby respecting a fundamental principle of organized labor. But it was a poor sham. The Southern organizing drive was over.

But if depression hampered orthodox unionism it invited radical agitation. Gastonia had revealed a susceptibility to extremist leadership and the Communist activity around Loray Mill had left cadres of followers in the textile towns.[92] Late in the summer of 1930 a renewed activity was heralded in Birmingham by the appearance of the *Southern Worker,* "the communist paper for the South," which continued a spasmodic career through the

[92] The party secretary claimed that a Southern conference of the National Textile Workers' Union in Charlotte, October 12–13, 1929, drew 287 delegates from 75 mills, 35 cities, and 5 states and a concurrent conference of the Trade Union Unity League by 40 delegates from 17 cities in 8 states. William Z. Foster, "The Historic Southern Conference," in *Labor Defender* (New York), IV (1929), 223, 238.

1940's. "The hitherto guerrilla warfare," the *Manufacturers' Record* exclaimed, "is announced now as a deliberate invasion by a horde of reds determined to destroy the peace, to wreck the prosperity and to subjugate the Americanism of the American Southern States."[93] Birmingham, the stagnant center of heavy industry, became the pivot of the new campaign. From its office there the party undertook to develop four chief types of agencies: branches of the party, affiliated industrial unions, an organization of sharecroppers, and unemployed councils. Its agitations met ruthless hostility by the police and vigilante groups and the party made little headway, but the activity around Birmingham and Bessemer continued through the decade.[94]

Scattered reports of activity came from other places. In May, 1930, Atlanta police arrested six Communists on a charge of insurrection.[95] In the summer of 1932 Angelo Herndon, a Negro Communist sent into Atlanta to organize a demonstration of the unemployed, was arrested, convicted of insurrection under a law of 1866, and sentenced to from eighteen to twenty years. His defense attorney, Benjamin J. Davis, Jr., son of Georgia's Republican national committeeman, later asserted that he had been turned toward communism himself by the bigotry of a judge who addressed him as "nigger." After a protracted litigation Herndon finally won his freedom in 1937 with a ruling by the United States Supreme Court that the Georgia law violated the Fourteenth Amendment guarantee of due process.[96]

The University of North Carolina became another focal point during the year 1931–1932. Some half-dozen Reds enrolled as students, but they found it difficult to agitate, Virginius Dabney observed, "for the requisite persecution was denied them." They did not return the next session.[97] In Oklahoma, on the other

[93] *Manufacturers' Record*, XCVIII (September 4, 1930), 42, 43.

[94] Wilson Record, *The Negro and the Communist Party* (Chapel Hill, 1951), 72; Virginius Dabney, "Reds in Dixie," in *Sewanee Review*, XLII (1934), 418–22; Cayton and Mitchell, *Black Workers and the New Unions*, 337–40.

[95] Baker, *Negro-White Adjustment*, 110.

[96] The case is detailed in David Entin, "Angelo Herndon" (M.A. thesis, University of North Carolina, 1963). Herndon's own story appears in Angelo Herndon, *Let Me Live* (New York, 1937). See also Benjamin J. Davis, Jr., "Why I Am a Communist," in *The Phylon Quarterly* (Atlanta), VIII (1947), 107.

[97] Dabney, "Reds in Dixie," *loc. cit.*, 418.

hand, unemployed councils instigated by the Communists were said to number about eighty locals and thirty thousand members in 1933.[98] In Tampa the Tobacco Workers Industrial Union, headed by Juan Hidalgo and affiliated with the Trade Union Unity League, organized an unemployed council and attempted a parade on November 7, 1931, fourteenth anniversary of the Bolshevik Revolution. Policemen and American Legion volunteers broke it up and the employers, who already had their stock of Christmas cigars, easily defeated a protest strike and reopened under open-shop conditions.[99]

The most persistent activity was in the Share Croppers' Union, organized chiefly among Negroes in counties east and south of Birmingham. Following the dictates of the Moscow Congress of the Communist International in 1928, the American party had accepted the theoretical policy of a Negro nation in the South, "self-determination of the black belt."[100] A program adopted in 1930, however, called for an emphasis upon immediate demands in the course of which Negroes would be prepared for revolutionary action under Communist leadership.[101]

On the night of July 16, 1931, the sheriff of Tallapoosa County and two deputies clashed with a picket outside a country church in which the SCU was meeting near Camp Hill; the clash provoked rioting, the death of one and probably two Negroes, the wounding of three Negroes and two white officers. More than thirty Negroes were arrested, but eventually were released, apparently through the intervention of the Interracial Commission.[102] Probably not one in ten of the croppers knew that the organizers were Communists, William Pickens of the NAACP said, and probably not

[98] Jamieson, *Labor Unionism in American Agriculture*, 265.

[99] Marshall, "History of Labor Organization in the South," 294–96.

[100] John Beecher, "The Share Croppers' Union in Alabama," in *Social Forces*, XIII (1934–1935), 124.

[101] "Draft, Program for the Negro Laborers, in the Southern States," in *Communist*, IX (1930), 246–47, cited in Record, *Negro and the Communist Party*, 68.

[102] The account is drawn from Beecher, "Share Croppers' Union in Alabama," *loc. cit.*, 124–32; Baker, *Negro-White Adjustment*, 100–105; New York *Times*, July 18, 1931; Jamieson, *Labor Unionism in American Agriculture*, 295–302; *Southern Farm Leader* (New Orleans), I (July, 1936), 4; and Olive Matthews Stone, "Agrarian Conflict in Alabama: Sections, Races, and Classes in a Rural State from 1800 to 1938" (Ph.D. dissertation, University of North Carolina, 1939), 522–26.

one in a hundred would know the meaning of the word. They simply responded to people who offered to help. Finally in December, 1932, officials identified one of the local leaders in the nearby Reeltown area, served a writ of attachment against some of his livestock, and provoked another riot when neighbors tried to resist the seizure. How many died in that incident cannot be known but at least two succumbed to wounds. The International Labor Defense put the bodies of the martyrs on display in Birmingham and a great crowd, including many whites, attended the funeral. Trials of other leaders in the county seat of Dadeville revealed a tenacious spirit of resistance among Negroes who appeared in numbers that overflowed the courthouse. In the spring of 1933 the union said it had some 3,000 members; in the fall 5,500. It continued for another three years, spreading into counties south of Montgomery, but the positive achievements were meager. Even the Communists claimed to have won only the right to cultivate gardens and the continuance of food allowances through the slack seasons.

The SCU got little attention outside its immediate vicinity, but the party reaped an unexpected propaganda windfall in Jackson County, to the northeast. On March 25, 1931, a group of white itinerants hopped a freight at Chattanooga. They included two young women on their way back to Huntsville after an overnight hobo escapade. When a number of Negroes boarded the train at Stevenson a fight occurred and seven of the white men were thrown or jumped from the train. An alarm went ahead to Paint Rock where officers took into custody nine young Negroes and the three remaining whites, one man and the two girls. What happened between Chattanooga and Paint Rock is clouded in the confusion of the trials and the *cause célèbre* that followed, but the nine Negroes, aged thirteen to twenty, were charged with raping the girls atop a gondola car of gravel.[103]

All were convicted in a hasty trial at Scottsboro, the county seat,

[103] There is no adequate history of the Scottsboro case. Useful accounts appear in Files Crenshaw, Jr., and Kenneth A. Miller, *Scottsboro: The Firebrand of Communism* (Montgomery, Ala., 1936); Haywood Patterson and Earl Conrad, *Scottsboro Boy* (New York, 1950); Arthur Garfield Hays, *Trial by Prejudice* (New York, 1933); Quentin Reynolds, *Courtroom: The Story of Samuel S. Leibowitz* (New York, 1950); and Allan Knight Chalmers, *They Shall Be Free* (Garden City, N.Y., 1951).

amid an atmosphere of mob hostility, with an unprepared defense counsel appointed by the local court and a lawyer hastily summoned from Chattanooga by the local Negro ministerial union. All but the youngest were sentenced to the electric chair on the dubious and uncorroborated testimony of two profligates, the alleged victims, one of whom later repudiated her statement. The Communist-led International Labor Defense (ILD) suddenly entered the case with a telegram informing the judge that he would be held "personally responsible unless the nine defendants are immediately released." [104] That prefaced a flood of protests to the governor and state officials. The ILD quickly shouldered aside the NAACP, the Interracial Commission, and other groups that sought to help. It persuaded the boys and their parents that only "mass action" could save them. Communist groups staged demonstrations of protest in the North and in Europe and collected funds for the "defense of the Scottsboro boys and for mass protest against the ruling class." [105] "If the Communists want these lads murdered," W. E. B. Du Bois protested, "then their tactics of threatening judges and yelling for mass action . . . is calculated to insure this." [106]

For four long years the defense remained in the hands of the ILD and dragged its way through a maze of appeals and retrials. Twice it went to the United States Supreme Court, which ruled in 1932 that the failure to provide adequate counsel had denied due process and in 1935 that the systematic exclusion of Negroes from Alabama juries had denied equal protection of the law—a principle that had significant and widespread impact on Southern courts.[107] Samuel S. Leibowitz, a celebrated New York lawyer, who became the chief defense counsel in 1933, prepared the way for the jury ruling. But Leibowitz, who accepted neither fees nor expense money, eventually rebelled against Communist manipula-

[104] Walter White, "The Negro and the Communists," in *Harper's Magazine*, CLXIV (1931–1932) , 64–65.

[105] Reynolds, *Courtroom*, 302; White, "Negro and the Communists," *loc. cit.*, 68.

[106] *The Crisis*, XXXVIII (1931) , 314. See also "A Statement by the N. A. A. C. P. on the Scottsboro Case," *ibid.*, 82–83.

[107] Powell *v.* Alabama, 287 U.S. 45 (1932) ; Norris *v.* Alabama, 294 U.S. 587 (1935) . See also Mangum, *Legal Status of the Negro*, 333–34.

tions—the party, he said, had made the case a "three-year-meal-ticket"—and formed a separate defense committee in 1935. Shortly afterward a new turn in the party line opened a period of "united front" against fascism, and the ILD agreed to yield direction of the case to a coalition Scottsboro defense committee chaired by Dr. Allen Knight Chalmers of the Broadway Tabernacle in New York. With the assistance of an Alabama committee the group carried through the long and grubby task of securing freedom for the "Scottsboro Boys."

It was a ticklish situation. For a people "too much obsessed with fears of race and sex Scottsboro became the symbol of a nation's opprobrium," Rupert Vance wrote. "All the sickness of the South's regional culture is summed up under that symbol, and it came to feel it could justify itself to itself only by a legal execution of the defendants." [108] It demonstrated again "the folly of needless clash with the emotional symbols of a people," wrote George Fort Milton, who assisted the defense committee. "To the initial racial phobia have been superadded two others: The prejudice against 'outsiders' and the even more important prejudice against Communists—'Reds.' " [109] Nevertheless, the NAACP's *Crisis* gave the devil his due. "An important legal victory has been won against the lily-white jury system. As far as propaganda is concerned the whole Negro race is far ahead of where it would have been had the Communists not fought the case in the way they did." All this could be admitted, but it left one basic question: "did they have the right to use the lives of nine youths, who, unlike Angelo Herndon, did not know what it was all about, to make a propaganda battle . . . ?" [110] Moving quietly and cautiously, the Scottsboro defense committee eventually secured the release of eight prisoners between 1937 and 1950, in some cases by decisions to drop further prosecution, in others by parole. The ninth prisoner escaped in 1948.

In the Kentucky mountains the party found another unforeseen but less profitable outlet. That story, a reporter wrote, was "one of

[108] Rupert B. Vance, *The South's Place in the Nation*, Public Affairs Pamphlets, No. 6 (Washington, 1936) , 18–19.
[109] George Fort Milton to Norman Thomas, February 8, 1936, in Milton Papers.
[110] *The Crisis*, XLII (1935) , 369.

desperate, hungry, unemployed or partially employed men rallying to anybody who promised aid." [111] By 1931 Eastern Kentucky afforded some of the bleakest scenes of depression. After 1927 coal prices sank steadily and the operators' struggle to reduce costs put a continuing squeeze on wages. Miners with whom Reinhold Niebuhr talked at Pineville in 1932 received thirty cents a ton for seven to eight tons daily, and averaged a day and a half of work per week; few earned as much as five dollars weekly.[112] Hunger and petty thievery were endemic. A common diet was beans, cornbread, "bulldog gravy" (flour, water, and a little grease), perhaps a few vegetables in summer. "Milk was regarded as medicine," one observer reported; "when the children were sick they tried to borrow a few cents to buy a little." Disease stalked on the track of hunger: pellagra, tuberculosis, and "flux"—a bleeding dysentry caused by starvation.[113] "Thirty-seven babies died in my arms in the last three months of 1931," Aunt Molly Jackson, ballad-singing midwife of Straight Creek, said. "Their little stomach busted open":

> *Dreadful memories! How they linger;*
> *How they pain my precious soul.*
> *Little children, sick and hungry,*
> *Sick and hungry, weak and cold.*[114]

Successive wage cuts, the decline of employment, the rising asperity of bosses under pressure to slash costs brought the miners to the verge of revolt.[115] On March 1, 1931, two thousand turned out for a mass meeting of the United Mine Workers (UMW) in Pineville and two coal companies fired more than two hundred for attending. Eleven thousand walked out in spontaneous protest and one pit after another closed down. Violence flared; hungry workers looted commissaries; families were evicted; deputies assaulted strikers. Harlan County deputies threatened to "shoot up"

[111] Louis Stark in New York *Times,* September 28, 1931.

[112] Bernstein, *Lean Years,* 360–61.

[113] Adelaide Walker, "Living Conditions in the Coal Fields," in Theodore Dreiser *et al., Harlan Miners Speak: Report on Terrorism in the Kentucky Coal Fields* (New York, 1932), 85.

[114] John Greenway, *American Folksongs of Protest,* Philadelphia, (1953), 273–74.

[115] Caudill, *Night Comes to the Cumberlands,* 118–91.

the town of Evarts, where many evicted strikers had taken refuge; and on May 4, a score of miners stopped several carloads of deputies armed with rifles and machine guns. In the "Battle of Evarts" that followed one miner and three deputies died.[116] Governor Flem D. Sampson sent in the National Guard two days later. The union claimed he had agreed that no outside labor should be sent in, that food and relief would be supplied, and that mine guards would be disarmed and their commissions as deputies revoked. The sheriff said he knew of no such agreement. Arrests of union leaders continued and scabs arrived under guard. The UMW discreetly repudiated the hopeless strike, leaving the miners convinced that the governor had "let them down" and the union had "sold them out." [117]

On June 19 Don Brooks of the National Mine Workers Union (NMWU) entered Harlan; soon afterward Jessie Wakefield of the ILD followed. Within a few weeks they claimed four thousand members. The remainder of 1931 saw a reenactment of Gastonia and Camp Hill, but on a greater scale. Harlan and Bell counties became armed camps, and the violence redoubled. Miners were cowed and intimidated, their homes invaded, property destroyed, meetings broken up, an NMWU soup kitchen dynamited. In retaliation tipples were burned and head mine houses blown up. Two news reporters in the area were shot and wounded; two men killed at a union soup kitchen; between May and September the mine war cost about a dozen lives—no exact count was possible.[118] "What is the law?" a Harlan woman was asked amid the disorders. "The law," she replied, "is a gun thug in a big automobile." [119]

Into the midst of the terror came delegations of writers and intellectuals. In November, 1931, Theodore Dreiser led a group sponsored by the National Committee for the Defense of Political Prisoners. In February, 1932, Waldo Frank brought a committee

[116] John Dos Passos, "Harlan: Working under the Gun," in *New Republic*, LXIX (1931–1932), 63.

[117] Charles Rumford Walker, "Organizing a Union in Kentucky," in Dreiser *et al.*, *Harlan Miners Speak*, 45.

[118] Dos Passos, "Harlan," *loc. cit.*, 63; Herbert Abel, "Gun Rule in Kentucky," in *Nation*, CXXXIII (1931), 306–307; Boris Israel; "I Got Shot," in *New Republic*, LXVIII (1931), 256–58; Louis Stark in New York *Times*, September 28, 1931.

[119] Melvin P. Levy, "Class War in Kentucky," in Dreiser *et al.*, *Harlan Miners Speak*, 35n.

of New York writers: Edmund Wilson, Malcolm Cowley, Mary Heaton Vorse, Quincy Howe, and others. Vigilantes escorted them across the Tennessee state line and seriously hurt two in a physical assault. Herndon Evans, Pineville editor whom they identified as one of the assailants, suggested that they hurt themselves "alighting from the autos." Other delegations of ministers and students followed and one from the American Civil Liberties Union. The publicity brought a Senate investigation in the spring of 1932, but the terror continued.[120]

The Communist union made one final gesture of calling a general strike on January 1, 1932, and then expired, soup kitchens and all, to be succeeded by the American Friends' Service Committee, dispensing what aid it could to hungry children and attempting to rehabilitate the unemployed in handicraft shops and on abandoned farms.[121] There is strong evidence that, in the end, the union was killed as much by the rock-ribbed fundamentalism of the miners as by guns and whips. One active member of the Holiness Church, sent north for union training, returned with the horrifying testimony that "they demanded their members to teach their children there is no God; no Jesus; no Hereafter. . . . I heard them . . . denounce our government and our flag and our religion." [122] The miners were ready for revolt, but not for revolution. In the next few years they turned back to the UMW.

In the crisis of the Depression there was desperate but nebulous talk of "revolution." "Folks are restless," Governor Bilbo told reporters in 1931. "Communism is gaining a foothold. Right here

[120] Lawrence Grauman, Jr., " 'That Little Ugly Running Sore': Some Observations on the Participation of American Writers in the Investigation of Conditions in the Harlan and Bill County, Kentucky, Coal Fields in 1931–1932," in *Filson Club Historical Quarterly*, XXXVI (1962), 340–54; Evans, quoted in *Time*, XIX (February 22, 1932), 16.

[121] Oakley Johnson, "Starvation and the 'Reds' in Kentucky," in *Nation*, CXXXIV (1932), 141–43; Tess Huff, letter, *ibid.*, CXXXV (1932), 37–38; Ross, *Machine Age Comes to the Hills*, 189–211; Malcolm Ross, "Permanent Part-Time," in *Survey Graphic*, XXII (1933), 266–68; Morris, *Plight of the Bituminous Coal-Miner*, v, 33–39, 105–106, 113, 202–203, 209–10; Tess Huff, letter in *Nation*, CXXXV (1932), 37–38.

[122] Morris, *Plight of the Bituminous Coal Miner*, 134–37; Ross, *Machine Age Comes to the Hills*, 182–85.

in Mississippi some people are about ready to lead a mob. In fact, I'm getting a little pink myself." [123] But a year later he was committed to the Presidential candidacy of Franklin D. Roosevelt. Deliverance, when it appeared on the horizon, came under the familiar banner of the Democracy and in the person of the Dutch squire of the Hudson Valley. Roosevelt brought to his campaign a background of pastoral gentility and an accent better attuned to Southern ears than Al Smith's East Side twang. Moreover he was a part-time Georgian, a fact that he did not permit Southerners to overlook. Drawn to Warm Springs, Georgia, for treatment after his polio attack, he had established the Warm Springs Foundation in 1926 and in 1932 built a cottage nearby.[124]

His campaign for the nomination, like Wilson's, enlisted Southern support from the beginning. In 1931 circumstances conspired to cast him in the role of the candidate best situated to deliver the party from the menace of Al Smith and John J. Raskob. Early that year Chairman Raskob called a meeting of the Democratic National Committee, apparently confident of his control. The purpose was to seek Democratic endorsement of prohibition repeal and the protective tariff, and incidentally to impede Roosevelt's campaign by forcing the liquor issue into the foreground. Under the leadership of Cordell Hull, Southern regulars rallied to the opposition. Faced with the risk of a disruptive controversy and probable defeat, Raskob retreated.[125]

It was the first major coup of the campaign, and from that time forward Southern party leaders for the most part enlisted in the Roosevelt cause, which ironically soon led to the repeal of prohibition. At the end of March, 1931, a poll of delegates to the 1928 convention revealed that he was the choice of thirty-nine state delegations, including every Southern state except Arkansas.[126] By the time of the 1932 convention Roosevelt had carried primaries in

[123] Hilton Butler, "Bilbo—The Two-Edged Sword," in *North American Review*, CCXXXII (1931), 496.

[124] Frank Freidel, *Franklin D. Roosevelt: The Ordeal* (Boston, 1954), 193–98.

[125] Frank Freidel, *Franklin D. Roosevelt: The Triumph* (Boston, 1956), 177–82; Hull, *Memoirs of Cordell Hull*, 140–45.

[126] New York *Times*, March 30, 1931. The limitations of such a poll will be obvious; only one Virginia delegate to the 1928 convention responded.

Georgia, Alabama, and Florida, and had won the support of every Southern delegation except three that supported favorite sons: Speaker John Nance Garner of Texas, Harry F. Byrd of Virginia, and "Alfalfa Bill" Murray of Oklahoma.[127]

Only Garner had any chance to become a serious candidate, but he seemed to have few illusions. "There are no presidential bees buzzing around my office," he wrote. In Texas his campaign manager, Sam Rayburn, told Roosevelt's manager, "I have believed for some time that Franklin D. Roosevelt was the man in our present situation and I still believe he will in all probability be nominated."[128] But after a Garner delegation headed by William Gibbs McAdoo won the California primary on May 4, the Garner forces were in a position to deadlock the Chicago convention and stop Roosevelt short of the necessary two-thirds majority. However, the memory of 1924 was still strong; the party could not afford another Madison Square Garden. When Rayburn described the situation on the telephone, Garner replied, as he later told a reporter, "All right, release my delegates. . . . Hell, I'll do anything to see the Democrats win one more national election."[129]

Garner's reward was the vice-presidential nomination. It was "a kangaroo ticket," one Texan complained. "Stronger in the hind quarter than in the front."[130] One of the minor curiosities of the campaign was a widespread fear of Garner's "radicalism" among Eastern businessmen. It apparently arose from his long history of support for the income tax, his opposition to the Mellon tax program of the 1920's, and especially his efforts for Federal relief in 1932.[131] Some Republican leaders, at least, were still haunted by the ghost of Bryan, apprehensive, as Henry L. Stimson noted in

[127] Freidel, *Franklin D. Roosevelt: The Triumph*, 276–81; Roy V. Peel and Thomas C. Donnelly, *The 1932 Campaign: An Analysis* (New York, 1932), 72–79.

[128] Sam Rayburn to T. W. Davidson, January 26, 1932, in 1932 Political File, Rayburn Library.

[129] Timmons, *Garner of Texas*, 152–67; C. Wright Dorough, *Mr. Sam* (New York, 1962), 203–10; Freidel, *Franklin D. Roosevelt: The Triumph*, 245–47, 287–88, 308–10.

[130] Quoted in Timmons, *Garner of Texas*, 167.

[131] A. G. Hopkins to Sam Rayburn, July 29, 1932; Rayburn to J. Andrew West, October 26, 1932, in Rayburn Library.

his diary, of "the full power which Roosevelt will produce in the field to the radical elements of the West and the South."[132]

There were, indeed, a few leaders in the South who were pushing Roosevelt at least gently to the left. "For one," young Claude Pepper had written him from Tallahassee in 1928, "I want the Democratic party genuinely to become the liberal party of this Nation."[133] In 1932 O. Max Gardner wrote to warn the governor, after he had held a series of conferences with prominent Eastern business leaders, that the conservative vote was "going to Hoover, and in my judgment it is less powerful today than at any time in this century . . . the people are either going to follow a liberal leadership or they are going to develop it themselves." Huey Long telephoned to protest vigorously his consorting with conservatives.[134] Nevertheless, Roosevelt's candidacy had gained its earliest success through the cultivation of party regulars. He had not appeared, like Bryan, as the leader of popular uprising and protest. That would come later. His Southern support, in fact, had as yet little relation to the Depression.

When victory came in November, 1932, it came as "hope and confidence riding under the banner of the Democratic Party, over what appeared to be the emaciated corpse of the Republican Party, under whose rule catastrophe had arrived," W. J. Cash wrote. "For the South, in truth, it was almost as though the bones of Pickett and his brigade had suddenly sprung alive to go galloping up that slope to Gettysburg again and snatch victory from the Yankee's hand after all."[135] But in March, 1933, the New Deal arrived under a cloud of national crisis that overshadowed all other concerns. If, as Cash insisted, the South rallied more enthusiastically than any other region, Roosevelt's administration arrived without the marveling reports of Southern accents that greeted the New Freedom twenty years before. The new cabinet

[132] Stimson diary, July 5, 1932, quoted in Freidel, *Franklin D. Roosevelt: The Triumph*, 325.

[133] Claude Pepper to Franklin D. Roosevelt, December 22, 1928, in Franklin D. Roosevelt Library.

[134] Freidel, *Franklin D. Roosevelt: The Triumph*, 331. Roosevelt had Hull relay to Daniels the assurance: "Put it down that my administration will be progressive with a big P." Frank Freidel, *F. D. R. and the South* (Baton Rouge, 1965), 42.

[135] Cash, *Mind of the South*, 365. See also Ben Robertson, *Red Hills and Cotton: An Upcountry Memory* (New York, 1942), 273–74, 286–87.

included only three Southerners, none of whom participated significantly in framing domestic policies: Secretary of State Cordell Hull of Tennessee, Secretary of the Navy Claude A. Swanson of Virginia, and Secretary of Commerce Daniel C. Roper of South Carolina. Roosevelt's Brain Trust, developed during the campaign, included only one Southerner, South Carolina's Senator James F. Byrnes, as political adviser.[136]

Yet the President himself, in his biographer's words, knew the South "uncommonly well, loved it, and aspired to bring it a richer, more noble future." He mingled on friendly terms with the region's politicians and with the plain people around Warm Springs. In Georgia he organized the Warm Springs Foundation, developed nearby timber land, demonstrated diversified agriculture and cattle breeding to the neighboring farmers. Repeatedly, as President, he would refer to Georgia experiences that activated his thinking. The high light bills at Warm Springs, he said, set him on the road to the TVA. Inadequate schools impelled him to the conviction that the supreme challenge of the South was poverty, the root of countless deficiencies.[137] As early as the summer of 1931, after he had addressed a conference on regionalism at the University of Virginia, Roosevelt talked informally, and prophetically, with a smaller group about land planning, agricultural resettlement, part-time farming for urban workers, the South's deficiency in milk production, and other such issues.[138]

Roosevelt's cordial relationships with Southerners proved indispensable on Capitol Hill, where Southern Democrats once again entered into their heritage of seniority. During the lean years of the 1920's the Congressional party had been predominantly Southern. In 1933 Southerners headed nine of fourteen major Senate committees and twelve of seventeen in the House, a pattern that varied only in detail until 1945.[139] For leadership on the floor, as well, Roosevelt depended on Southerners. In the Senate, Joseph T. Robinson of Arkansas, Democratic floor leader

[136] Raymond Moley, 27 *Masters of Politics: In a Personal Perspective* (New York, 1948), 252–53.
[137] Freidel, *F. D. R. and the South*, 1–25. Quotation from p. 1.
[138] H. C. Nixon, *Possum Trot* (Norman, 1941), 149–50.
[139] Dewey W. Grantham, Jr., "An American Politics for the South," in Charles G. Sellers, Jr. (ed.), *The Southerner as American* (Chapel Hill, 1960), 163n.

since 1923, served until his death in 1937, to be succeeded by Alben W. Barkley of Kentucky. In the House Joseph Byrns of Tennessee became floor leader, followed by William B. Bankhead of Alabama and Sam Rayburn of Texas; each became Speaker in turn, in 1935, 1936, and 1940.

In the bustle of the Hundred Days, when legislation passed in an atmosphere of crisis, Congressional leadership had little influence on policy, and even afterward much of the legislation that would bear the names of Congressional sponsors originated down the Mall from the Capitol. But the administration utilized the parliamentary skills of loyal Southerners. And Arthur Schlesinger, Jr., has argued that the Congress "played a vital and consistently underestimated role in shaping the New Deal." [140] Southern influence was important especially in agricultural legislation; to a considerable degree representatives of cotton and tobacco wrote their own ticket. The Federal deposit insurance system, proposed in the Wilson years by Morris Sheppard of Texas, was inaugurated at the insistence of Representative Henry Steagall of Alabama, chairman of the House Banking and Currency Committee. On occasion radical pressures from Southern members would move Roosevelt as they had Wilson: when Elmer Thomas pushed inflation, when Hugo Black precipitated the NRA, or when Huey Long gave impetus to tax and social security legislation.

But if the influence of the South on the New Deal would be less than on the New Freedom, the impact of the New Deal on the South would be far greater. Unlike Wilson's New Freedom, Roosevelt's New Deal would shake the social and economic power structure of the region, and would thereby generate an opposition such as Wilson never had. But on March 4, 1933, that remained in the future. Richmond's response to the new administration was indicative. At 8:30 A.M. on inauguration day all the city's factory whistles blew to herald a ten-day "Confidence in Roosevelt" observance proclaimed by the mayor. At 12:50 the Richmond Howitzers fired a 21-gun salute in honor of the new President. Newspaper advertisements and placards in shop windows proclaimed, "America Awakens! Roosevelt Says 'Let's Go!' " [141]

[140] Schlesinger, *The Coming of the New Deal*, 554.
[141] Richmond *Times-Dispatch*, March 4, 1933.

CHAPTER XII

THE TRANSFORMATION
OF AGRICULTURE

SOUTHERN agriculture, for all the advice to diversify and live at home, was geared to the market place. Its leaders viewed the farm problem chiefly in terms of commercial agriculture. The protracted McNary-Haugen debates, the Farm Board experiments, the long years of adversity, all focused attention upon markets and prices. Moreover, they had defined the problem in terms of national responsibility, and the failure of crop limitation attempts caused Southern farmers to look with growing urgency to Washington for solutions. "I shall vote for Roosevelt now," a North Carolina farmer told Clarence Poe at the polls in 1932, "yet if things do not improve greatly by 1936, this whole country will go Socialist." [1] Edward A. O'Neal of Alabama, president of the American Farm Bureau Federation, suggested a greater urgency: "unless something is done for the American farmer," he told a senate committee in January, 1933, "we will have a revolution in the country-side in less than 12 months."[2]

It was an admonition, not a threat. *Fortune* later hailed O'Neal as "quite the most spectacular farm leader in the U.S.," but he was an improbable candidate for revolutionary leadership. He approached more nearly the stereotype of a cultivated planter. Brought up near Florence on the plantation of his grandfather, a Confederate general and once governor, he attended Washington and Lee and returned from a postgraduate "Grand Tour" of Europe inspired by the idea of scientific agriculture. Drawn into

[1] *Progressive Farmer,* XLVII (1932) , 26.
[2] Quoted in Theodore Saloutos, "Edward A. O'Neal: The Farm Bureau and the New Deal," in *Current History,* XXVII (1955), 358.

the Alabama Farm Bureau at the beginning, he reached the national presidency in 1931. Aggressive, earthy, supremely self-confident, a consummate politician, he forged a potent alliance of the corn and cotton belts and identified the Farm Bureau so closely with New Deal agricultural policy as to make it the dominant farm organization of the 1930's.[3]

In the beginning, however, Southern leaders had little direct part in formulating the plan for attack on surpluses. The domestic allotment plan was the brainchild of several men; it was advanced most cogently by M. L. Wilson of Montana State College. Yet the idea, if not the practice, of crop limitation was a venerable Southern tradition, and Southern Congressmen hastened to its support.[4] The Department of Agriculture produced an omnibus farm bill in consultation with farm leaders; the President urgently submitted it on March 16, 1933; and Marvin Jones of Texas dropped it into the House hopper. It was guided through the Senate by John H. Bankhead, Jr., who functioned as the administration's leader on farm policy in lieu of the irascible agriculture chairman, Ellison D. "Cotton Ed" Smith.[5]

The bill passed the house quickly, but in the Senate it faced a renewed agrarian insurgency. John A. Simpson of Oklahoma, the antithesis of O'Neal, president of the Farmers' Union, "a spiritual successor of the Greenbackers and Populists," proposed in vain a plan to guarantee farmers the "cost of production." When he had to give way to the crop limitation program, he echoed all the more loudly the old battle cry of inflation (or "reflation") raised by his

[3] *Ibid.*, 356–61; "The Farm Bureau," in *Fortune*, XXIX (June, 1944), 156; Kile, *Farm Bureau through Three Decades*, 172; Christiana McFadyen Campbell, *The Farm Bureau and the New Deal: A Study of Making of National Farm Policy, 1933-1940* (Urbana, Ill., 1962), 57–58. See also McConnell, *Decline of Agrarian Democracy*, 62–83.

[4] W. J. Spillman of the Department of Agriculture, Beardsley Ruml of the Rockefeller Foundation, and John D. Black of Harvard contributed to it. Fite, *George N. Peek*, 229–33. Theodore Saloutos argues that Southern farm movements pioneered not only the crop limitation idea but also the "basic commodity" and "parity" concepts. Saloutos, *Farmer Movements in the South*, 282–87.

[5] Henry A. Wallace, *New Frontiers* (New York, 1934), 161–67; Kile, *Farm Bureau through Three Decades*, 198–99; Saloutos and Hicks, *Agricultural Discontent in the Middle West*, 453–67; Benedict, *Farm Policies of the United States*, 281–84; Montgomery *Advertiser*, December 3, 1933.

fellow Oklahoman, Senator Elmer Thomas.[6] In 1932 Thomas had joined Representative John E. Rankin of Mississippi in sponsoring an inflation bill; now he had a package of inflationary measures to insert in the farm bill, and for a time the ghost of Bryan stalked the Capitol. The White House, alarmed at growing sentiment for the measure in the West and South, finally accepted an amendment whereby the President got optional but not mandatory powers to issue additional greenbacks and silver currency and to devalue the gold dollar.[7]

The Agricultural Adjustment Act, signed into law on May 12, 1933, contained nearly every major device that had been advanced for farm relief. Its core was the plan of voluntary acreage reductions for which farmers would get benefit payments designed to restore them to "parity," or the same level of purchasing power they had had in the golden age of 1909–1914 (1919–1929 for tobacco). Seven "basic commodities" were defined, including the Southern staples of cotton, rice, and tobacco; nine more were added later, including cattle, peanuts, and sugar cane. But the act also included an element of McNary-Haugenism in the authority to subsidize exports and arrange marketing agreements with processors.[8]

When Congress acted the growing season was already advanced. "Wherever we turn," said George N. Peek, first head of the Agricultural Adjustment Administration (AAA), ". . . we have in prospect a race with the sun." [9] The most urgent problem was the prospect of another bumper cotton crop in the face of prices near five cents. A plan was reluctantly but quickly adopted for an emergency plow-up to prevent an intolerable glut. Late in May, following the appointment of Cully A. Cobb, a Georgia farm editor, as chief of the Cotton Production Control Section, the AAA reached

[6] Fite, "John A. Simpson," *loc. cit.*, 563–84.

[7] Eric Manheimer, "The Public Career of Elmer Thomas" (Ph.D. dissertation, University of Oklahoma, 1953), 91–114; Schlesinger, *Coming of the New Deal*, 41–42, 200–201.

[8] Provisions of the act and some subsequent legislation are outlined in Edwin G. Nourse, Joseph S. Davis, and John D. Black, *Three Years of the Agricultural Adjustment Administration* (Washington, 1937), 32–50; and U.S. Department of Agriculture, *Agricultural Adjustment: Report of Administration of Agricultural Adjustment Act, May 1933–February 1934* (Washington, 1934), 4–11.

[9] Fite, *George N. Peek*, 254.

a fateful decision that the need to hasten the program into the field dictated use of the Extension Service's existing machinery. The decision was probably inevitable, but its result was to entangle the program with the interlocking politics of land grant colleges and farm bureaus, both closely associated with the county agents.[10]

After conferences of state extension directors and cotton leaders the AAA mobilized an organization of some 22,000 workers. A Mississippi editor, acquainted with past reduction campaigns, warned that it would be "necessary to 'put a bee on the boys' to make them sign up," but farmer resistance proved to be negligible. More trouble came from balky mules, trained to avoid trampling the crop, and occasionally from stubborn tenants.[11] Altogether 10,400,000 acres were taken out of production; the crop was reduced to 13,177,000 bales, about 4,000,000 below the estimate; and farmers got about $112,000,000 in benefit payments.[12] To destroy a growing crop was "a shocking commentary on our civilization," Secretary of Agriculture Henry A. Wallace lamented. "I could tolerate it only as a cleaning up of the wreckage from the old days of unbalanced production." [13]

It worked temporarily. Prices went above 11 cents in July (parity was 12.7), but sagged to between 8 and 10 as the crop came in. The rise "came in cotton when we farmers had none to sell," a Mississippi grower wrote; "it has gone down just as we begin to sell." [14] By late summer such complaints bulged Congressional letter files. The only alternative to inflation, Senator Bankhead wrote the President, would be to restrict the amount ginned, perhaps 50 to 60 per cent of the 1931 production on each

[10] Paul A. Porter to Marvin H. McIntyre, memorandum on the cotton program, July 20, 1933, in Official File (OF) 258, Franklin D. Roosevelt Library; Saloutos, "Edward A. O'Neal," loc. cit., 358.

[11] Frederick Sullens to Franklin D. Roosevelt, telegram, July 6, 1933, in OF 258, Roosevelt Library; David L. Cohn, The Life and Times of King Cotton (New York, 1956), 256.

[12] Porter to McIntyre, memorandum, July 20, 1933, loc. cit.; U.S. Department of Agriculture, Agricultural Adjustment, 1933–1934, 19.

[13] Wallace, New Frontiers, 174–75.

[14] W. A. Cole to Henry A. Wallace, August 24, 1933, in Farm Relief, 12, 1933, Secretary of Agriculture Files (National Archives, Washington). Courtesy of Professor Jack B. Key.

farm: "If industrial employees are to be benefitted . . . by compulsory action, I sincerely hope you can see your way clear to extend the same doctrine to the protection of the cotton producers." The President was not prepared to go so far; he feared too drastic a reduction, he replied, and questioned the constitutionality of the scheme.[15] Others preferred the quicker solution of inflation. "People of whole state are urging expansion of currency to bolster price of cotton," Sam Rayburn wired from the Texas Red River country. Similar messages poured in from elsewhere. "Commodity prices have got to go up," Senator Pat Harrison of Mississippi asserted. "I favor some sort of rational inflation. We've got to do more than we are doing."[16]

In October, to appease the inflationists, Roosevelt began to purchase gold in quantity and in January, 1934, reduced the gold content of the dollar. It had little effect on commodity prices, and in March the neo-populists rallied to a "Farm-Silver Bill" introduced by a young agrarian radical from Texas, Representative Martin Dies, Jr. With some changes in the Senate the Silver Purchase Act passed in June, 1934; it required the Treasury to acquire silver at prices above the market until its holdings equaled a third of the gold reserve. Again the effect on prices was negligible, but it was a bonanza for a minor Western industry, a subsidy of nearly one and a half billion dollars over the next fifteen years, substantially more than was spent to support farm prices in other ways.[17]

Effective relief for cotton came neither from gold manipulation nor silver purchases, but from a large-scale holding operation supported by government loans. The father of the program was Oscar Johnston, AAA director of finance and manager of the South's largest cotton plantation, the British-owned Delta and Pine Land Company of Scott, Mississippi. In October, 1933, the President established the Commodity Credit Corporation (CCC) under the Reconstruction Finance Corporation, and CCC loans to farmers pegged the cotton price at ten cents during 1933 and at twelve

[15] John H. Bankhead, Jr., to Roosevelt, August 21, 1933; Roosevelt to Bankhead, September 18, 1933, in OF 258, Roosevelt Library.
[16] Quoted in Schlesinger, *Coming of the New Deal*, 236–37.
[17] Gellerman, *Martin Dies*, 42–44; Schlesinger, *Coming of the New Deal*, 250–52.

cents during the following year. Ultimately the CCC extended price-support loans on other storable commodities such as corn, wheat, naval stores, tobacco, and peanuts. In 1939 it was transferred to the Department of Agriculture and achieved permanent status as the keystone of price-support programs.[18]

Like the radicals of the Wilson era, Southern agrarians kept pushing the New Deal toward increased governmental intervention. Senator Bankhead continued to champion stricter controls and by December, 1933, had developed two bills for compulsory marketing quotas on cotton, to be enforced by a prohibitive tax of 50 per cent on all cotton sold beyond the allotment. An agriculture department questionnaire showed support for marketing controls from 98 per cent of the AAA committeemen, 99 per cent of the county agents, and 93 per cent of the crop reporters. Their testimony, together with other reports of "overwhelming sentiment" for controls finally brought the administration around. "My study of the various methods of securing crop limitation suggested leads me to believe that the Bankhead bills in principle best cover the situation," the President wrote to the agricultural chairmen of Congress in February, 1934.[19] On April 21 he signed into law the Bankhead Cotton Control Act under which cotton farmers received a total quota of 10,000,000 bales in 1934 and 10,500,000 in 1935.[20]

AAA programs for other commodities were fundamentally the same as for cotton, but differed in detail. There was no plow-up of any other crop, but the distress of tobacco farmers brought quick

[18] Jesse H. Jones with Edward Angly, *Fifty Billion Dollars: My Thirteen Years with the RFC, 1932–1945* (New York, 1951), 88–103. See also Oscar Johnston to George N. Peek, September 22, 1933, and "Resolution of Delegates Appointed by Governors of Alabama . . . [and other cotton states] in Convention Washington, 18 September 1933," in OF 258, Roosevelt Library; Benedict, *Farm Policies of the United States*, 333; Murray R. Benedict and Oscar C. Stine, *The Agricultural Commodity Programs: Two Decades of Experience* (New York, 1958), 10; Montgomery *Advertiser*, September 23, 1933. According to the last source, the President rejected a demand by the cotton states' conference for a fifteen-cent loan but agreed to ten.

[19] Henry I. Richards, *Cotton and the Agricultural Adjustment Act: Developments up to July, 1934*, in Brookings Institution *Pamphlet Series*, No. 15 (Washington, 1934), 186; Birmingham *Age-Herald*, July 19, 1934, clipping in John H. Bankhead, Jr., Papers.

[20] Benedict, *Farm Policies of the United States*, 313.

action by other means. Early in August, 1933, Georgia and South Carolina markets opened at prices around ten cents a pound, seven cents below parity, whereupon the Raleigh *News and Observer* commenced a campaign to shut the markets entirely. On August 31, two days after the North Carolina auction began, a meeting of tobacco growers in Raleigh demanded a closing under martial law. The governors of both Carolinas complied.[21] "The growers are not receiving anything but the wages of a peon and a slave," North Carolina's Governor J. C. B. Ehringhaus said. "That condition cannot be permitted to go on indefinitely." [22]

During a three-week market holiday the AAA hastened to sign up 95 per cent of the growers for acreage limitations in 1934 and negotiated a marketing agreement with the leading buyers, who promised to pay an average price of seventeen cents for flue-cured tobacco, approximately parity. Manufacturers were influenced not only by popular pressures but also by the appearance of competitive cheap brands of cigarettes that capitalized on low prices. Similar agreements were made for burley and five other types, and the markets reopened, stabilized at a higher level. In the next two years voluntary acreage allotments were supplemented by marketing quotas under the Kerr-Smith Tobacco Control Act of 1934, similar to the Bankhead Act for cotton.[23] Other marketing agreements applied to peanuts, rice, watermelons and strawberries, citrus fruits, canned foods, dried fruits and nuts; and ultimately restrictions on rice and peanut production developed.[24]

Sugar cane was a special case. An exotic growth even in Louisiana and Florida, it survived only because of tariff protection. After an unsuccessful attempt at marketing agreements in 1933, the President recommended a quota system to protect existing sugar production but "provide against further expansion of this neces-

[21] Harold B. Rowe, *Tobacco under the AAA*, in Brookings Institution, Institute of Economics *Publications*, No. 62 (Washington, 1935), 100–103; *Newsweek: The Magazine of News Significance* (New York), IV (August 11, 1934), 25.

[22] Quoted in Robert, *Story of Tobacco in America*, 209.

[23] Rowe, *Tobacco under the AAA*, 103–31; Edwin G. Nourse, *Marketing Agreements under the AAA*, in Brookings Institution Institute of Economics *Publications*, No. 63 (Washington, 1935), 76–88; Raleigh *News and Observer*, September 26, 1933.

[24] See Nourse, *Marketing Agreements under the AAA*, 88–95, 107–18, 120–26, 148–95.

sarily expensive industry." [25] The result was the Jones-Costigan Act of 1934 which provided acreage adjustments and benefit payments for sugar, assigned Louisiana and Florida cane 260,000 tons and domestic beets 1,550,000 tons of the total national requirements (6,476,000 tons), and gave quotas for the rest to offshore areas.[26]

Under the Sugar Act of 1937 the Louisiana-Florida quota rose to 420,000 tons, although Secretary of State Hull warned of damage to commercial relations with Cuba and other areas. Despite the increased quota, cane growers remained unhappy with their limited share of the market; they were the only substantial group of Southern agriculturists who regarded the New Deal restrictions as more harmful than otherwise. They particularly resented Secretary Wallace's description of their specialty as an "inefficient industry" that should be exposed "to the winds of world competition." [27]

Critics of the farm program decried the deliberate scarcity, the effort to extort higher prices from consumers, and some denounced it as "regimentation"—but few who did were farmers. Where was the "liberty," Clarence Poe asked, in the right to plant more cotton and further depress prices? "The Bankhead Law," he said, "represents an historic attempt to win new frontiers for democracy—to carry into economic life the same . . . willingness of the individual to bow to the will of the majority, that has distinguished our political democracy." [28] "I've seen too much rugged individualism," Ed O'Neal told a county farm bureau at Independence, Missouri. "We must have a national plan for

[25] Sitterson, *Sugar Country*, 383.

[26] Chiefly Cuba, Hawaii, the Philippines, Puerto Rico, and the Virgin Islands.

[27] Sitterson, *Sugar Country*, 381, 383–93; Virginius Dabney, *Below the Potomac: A Book about the New South* (New York and London, 1942), 77–78; Cordell Hull to Pat Harrison, March 1, 1937 (copy); and Washington *Evening Star*, September 2, 1937, in John H. Overton Papers (Department of Archives, Louisiana State University). Senator Overton took the position that "any permanent policy relative to sugar should provide unrestricted production of sugar in the United States," but found this in conflict with a Cuban trade agreement of 1934 and other obligations of the government. "Sugar 2/8/37," mimeographed release by the Department of State, *ibid.*

[28] Clarence Poe, "The Bankhead Act and Democracy," in *South Atlantic Quarterly*, XXXIII (1934), 321–33.

agriculture." [29] M. L. Wilson, now in the Department of Agriculture, late in 1934 found "every reason to believe that a majority of actual cotton producers desire to have the Bankhead Act enforced." [30] As late as 1936 the *Texas Weekly* cited "the confirmed opinion of many of the southern farmer's leaders that without the Bankhead Act the A.A.A. would be ineffective, so far as cotton was concerned." [31] When cotton farmers had to give formal approval, a referendum late in the fall of 1934, approximately 90 per cent of the cotton farmers voted in favor of continuing compulsory controls.[32]

Not long afterward a visiting professor of economics expressed surprise at the delight with which a public affairs conference at Southern Methodist received criticism of the cotton program. "Are you the dirt farmers who voted so decisively in favor of continuing the program," he asked, "or are you an entirely different group—ginners, transport men, cotton merchants, brokers and manufacturers of the fleecy staple." One speaker had ridiculed the "fanciful doctrine of getting rich by creating scarcity." "What did industry do?" the professor asked. Scarcity was "about the surest way to get rich," he suggested. "It is the source of all monopoly profits." [33]

Complaints from manufacturers that the processing tax penalized the consumer made an awkward argument for a protected industry. The people of the South "never got their fair share of the national income and have been exploited by the New England tariff policy in a damnably unfair way," Secretary Wallace blurted

[29] Kansas City *Times*, March 7, 1934, in Scrapbook, in Edward A. O'Neal Papers (Alabama Department of Archives and History).

[30] M. L. Wilson to Elmer Thomas, August 16, 1934, in Thomas Papers.

[31] Texas *Weekly*, January 11, 1936, 4, quoted in Lionel V. Patenaude, "The New Deal and Texas" (Ph.D. dissertation, University of Texas, 1953), 237.

[32] Richards, *Cotton and the Agricultural Adjustment Act*, 189–90. Of the estimated goal of eligible voters, 57 per cent voted: 1,361,418 in favor and 160,536 against. More than 90 per cent in each of the cotton states voted affirmatively. Opposition was concentrated in a few Oklahoma and Texas counties and was probably influenced by concern over the export market and the possibility of freezing production in the Southeast.

[33] Jack Johnson, comment on A. B. Cox, "Evaluating the Government's Program," in S. D. Myres, Jr. (ed.), *The Cotton Crisis: Proceedings of Second Conference, Institute of Public Affairs . . . Southern Methodist University, Dallas, Texas, January 31, and February 1, 1935* (Dallas, 1935), 137.

out to a Maine audience in 1935. The strongest objections, in fact, came from New England textile men. The American [Southern] Cotton Manufacturers Association resolved in 1935 that the AAA "must be guarded, treasured, and made permanent." [34]

But the cotton trade was never reconciled to crop restrictions, price pegging, or government operations in the market. "If experience teaches anything," said Will Clayton, cotton exporter of Houston, "it is that nature's method of automatic regulation through price, arrived at by competitive trading in free markets, is the only system which ever works in world commodities like cotton." [35] "As you doubtless know," a small town dealer wrote Sam Rayburn, "ninety percent of the cotton in the Southwest goes for export due to the high cost of freight to the mill centers of the Southeast and it looks to us if we lose our foreign business that this part of the country will be in very bad shape." [36] Nor was the sentiment confined to the Southwest. At Birmingham the Southeastern Chamber of Commerce resolved against tariff and farm policies that damaged the export market for cotton.[37] The advocates of a larger cotton production had "other reasons than their concern for the welfare of the farmers," a Texas farm journal asserted. "It isn't the fear that the South will lose its hold on the markets of the world that motivates these gentlemen. . . . They prefer a large volume of cotton at any price because their profits depend largely upon the number of bales passing through their hands." [38]

The directors of the farm program were not indifferent to exports. "We wish to retain our foreign market, and this means that

[34] Richards, *Cotton and the AAA*, 250–52.

[35] Quoted from a 1935 statement in Harris Dickson, *The Story of King Cotton* (New York and London, 1937), 294–95.

[36] T. R. Davis and Co. (Greenville, Tex.) to Sam Rayburn, November 17, 1934, in Rayburn Library. See also M. M. Brooks to Rayburn, November 23, 1934, *ibid.*

[37] Copy of resolution enclosed with Walter Parker to Louis McHenry Howe, November 21, 1934, in OF 258, Roosevelt Library.

[38] *Farm and Ranch*, May 15, 1934, p. 8, quoted in Patenaude, "New Deal and Texas," 236. For other expressions of fears for the export market see letters of Walter Parker, Marvin Jones, and H. Renfer in OF 258, Roosevelt Library; W. L. Clayton, "Our Vanishing Markets," in Myres (ed.), *Cotton Crisis*, 25–39; Peter Molyneaux, "Economic Nationalism as a Cause," *ibid.*, 43–62; Montgomery *Advertiser*, November 10, 1934. *The Cotton Trade Journal* was constantly exercised over the question.

we must continue to supply it at moderate prices," said Henry A. Wallace. "But we do not wish to keep prices ruinously low on the assumption that any improvement through the elimination of the surplus will cause a loss of our foreign markets." [39] In an effort to meet the problem, however, the administration shifted cotton loans from twelve to nine cents in 1935 and inaugurated for the first time parity payments on cotton, to make up the difference between the farmer's selling price and twelve cents.[40]

But the decline of the South's share in the world cotton market resulted from forces more deep-seated than the domestic farm program. The causes, many argued, were the transition of the United States from a debtor to a creditor nation during the First World War and a nationalistic tariff program that created a shortage of American dollars in world trade channels.[41] Louis H. Bean, AAA economist, however, found the causes in factors beyond the reach of American policy: expansion of acreage overseas, monetary and trade policies of foreign governments, the correlation of cotton consumption with industrial activity rather than prices. Tracing world production after the Civil War, Bean found that a projection of earlier trends yielded the actual pattern in 1937. "Apparently foreign production especially in the newer countries has responded more to other factors than volume and low price competition from American cotton," he concluded.[42]

Whatever the causes, the American share of world markets shrank drastically in the twentieth century. In 1911 American cotton constituted about 60 per cent of all that was used abroad,

[39] Henry A. Wallace, in U.S. Department of Agriculture, *Yearbook of Agriculture,* 1935 (Washington, 1935), 41.

[40] Jones, *Fifty Billion Dollars,* 94.

[41] John H. Bankhead, Jr., "The Cause of Lost Cotton Exports," in *Manufacturers' Record,* CIV (July, 1935), 45–54; Molyneaux, *Cotton South and American Trade Policy,* 29–30, 37–40, and *passim.*

[42] Louis H. Bean, "Changing Trends in Cotton Production and Consumption," in *Southern Economic Journal,* V (1938–1939), 442–59. A more detailed study that supports the Bean thesis is Royall Brandis, "Some Factors Affecting American Cotton Exports, 1929–1948" (Ph.D. dissertation, Duke University, 1953). See also Abraham Berglund, "The Effect of Current International Trade Conditions and Foreign Agricultural Developments on Southern Agriculture," in *Southern Economic Journal,* II (January, 1936), 61–68; and John Richard Huber, "The Effects of German Clearing Agreements and Import Restrictions on Cotton, 1934–1939," *ibid.,* VI (1939–1940), 419–39.

by 1921 the proportion had dropped to 50 per cent, by 1931 to 45, by 1936 to 30, and by 1937 to 23.[43] In these circumstances the New Deal farm program did what John H. Kirby and all the protectionists had never accomplished. It introduced Southern farmers to economic nationalism, not by walling them off from foreign competition but by walling them in with a plan to adjust their production mainly to domestic requirements. "The processing tax and benefit payments are the only effective tariff the cotton farmer has ever had," Henry A. Wallace asserted.[44]

This did not, of course, mean a sudden dissipation of cherished doctrine. As Secretary of State, Cordell Hull—whose economic thinking was "a blend of Adam Smith and the cotton South," and who deeply believed that international trade served the cause of international understanding—promoted the idea of reciprocity. In March, 1934, with the endorsement of the administration and almost solid support of his party in Congress, Hull won passage of the Reciprocal Trade Agreements Act providing for mutual tariff reductions by international agreement.[45] Later in the same year, after Hull addressed the Farm Bureau convention in Nashville, the Bureau endorsed the trade agreements principle, a significant break from its earlier policy of protectionism.[46] The cotton trade gave wholehearted support and the Southern press was almost unanimously favorable.[47]

It is difficult to trace the effects of Hull's program through the complex factors that affected world trade in subsequent years. Agreements had been made with fourteen countries by the end of

[43] Benedict, *Farm Policies of the United States*, 400.

[44] Henry A. Wallace, "The Cotton Program Carries On," address at Atlanta, April 13, [1935], copy in Ransdell Papers (Department of Archives, Louisiana State University), 13.

[45] Hull, *Memoirs of Cordell Hull*, I, 352–77; William Allen, "The International Trade Philosophy of Cordell Hull, 1907–1933," in *American Economic Review* (Princeton), XLIII (1953), 101–16.

[46] Kile, *Farm Bureau through Three Decades*, 214; Campbell, *Farm Bureau and the New Deal*, 140–55. "I don't see how it is possible for the cotton producer to stand for nationalism," Ed O'Neal wrote in 1936. Quoted *ibid.*, 143.

[47] Will Clayton to George Fort Milton, October 15, 1937, in Milton Papers. Milton had gone into the Department of State temporarily to handle public relations, *i.e.*, to build up public support for the program.

1935, with twenty-nine by 1945. The program did not regain world markets for Southern cotton, nor did it arrest a decline in the relative importance of exports to the Southern economy. By the postwar period, 1945–1948, exports equaled only about 4.2 per cent of total income payments in the South in contrast to 12 per cent in the late 1920's. The peculiar regional stake in foreign trade was disappearing. Total Southern exports in the postwar period nearly equaled those of the late 1920's in value, but they amounted to only 12.6 per cent of the nation's exports, whereas they had been about 30 per cent in the late 1920's.[48]

The farm program, on the other hand, clearly helped the South more than any other region in benefits, prices, and income. The greatest relative gains, according to three economists who studied the program carefully, probably occurred in the tobacco areas and the second greatest in the cotton belt, where they affected more people.[49] In May, 1935, when the program seemed threatened by a textile challenge to the processing tax, three or four thousand Southerners, together with a few Mid-Westerners, signified their support in a "plowman's pilgrimage" to Washington; they were led by a Texas farmer, Clifford H. Day.[50] Regions that produced less of the staple crops evidenced less support. The results of a Gallup poll published on January 5, 1936, showed 59 per cent of the nation's voters opposed to the AAA; the South was the only region in which supporters constituted a majority: 57 per cent.[51]

The day after publication of the figures, the Supreme Court held that the processing tax served the unconstitutional purpose of regulating agricultural production, a matter reserved to the states.[52] Southern press reaction was mostly hostile. If the general welfare clause of the Constitution meant anything, said the Chat-

[48] Schlesinger, *Coming of the New Deal*, 259; Ratner, *American Taxation*, 511; Hoover and Ratchford, *Economic Resources and Policies of the South*, 425–31.

[49] Nourse, Davis, and Black, *Three Years of the Agricultural Adjustment Administration*, 325.

[50] Campbell, *Farm Bureau and the New Deal*, 85–87; Saloutos and Hicks, *Agricultural Discontent in the Middle West*, 501.

[51] Dallas *Morning News*, January 5, 1936. There were also strong manifestations of support in Kansas, Iowa, and North Dakota.

[52] United States *v.* Butler, 297 U.S. 1 (1936).

tanooga *News,* "the Congress must be able to spend Federal funds for the general welfare of the people of the United States." [53] Congress could and would have to find some way of overcoming the decision, Douglas Southall Freeman of the Richmond *News Leader* wrote.[54] "It would be lamentable," said the Dallas *Morning News* if no way could be found to preserve the program even though in many ways it "smacked of coercion" and "worked largely to the benefit of large land owners." [55]

The government responded to the decision with haste. Congress repealed the Bankhead and Kerr-Smith acts, but within six weeks devised a new plan for agriculture in the Soil Conservation and Domestic Allotment Act. The new act omitted processing taxes and acreage quotas, but provided benefit payments for soil conservation practices: withdrawing land from soil-depleting crops—chiefly the staples covered by AAA—and putting it into soil-building grasses and legumes, together with other measures to check erosion and restore fertility. Thus, crop limitation occurred under the rubric of soil conservation.[56]

At the same time the act boosted a developing conservation movement. The AAA worked closely with the Soil Conservation Service, created in 1935 and directed by Hugh H. Bennett, a husky and genial North Carolinian who had promoted the cause in the Department of Agriculture since 1903. The work had a particular pertinence for Bennett's native region. Since colonial days the open-row crops and heavy rainfall, together with a frontier indifference that tenancy perpetuated, had sapped the fertility of the land and released the topsoil into muddy rivers. Vast running sores in the land consumed fields and even tenant shacks. In 1930, Bennett estimated that 4,000,000 of the 9,000,000 acres under cultivation in Alabama were largely denuded of top soil. His

[53] Chattanooga *News,* January 7, 1936, quoted in Francis Pickens Miller (ed.) , *The Southern Press Considers the Constitution,* in Southern Policy Papers, No. 6 (Chapel Hill, 1936) , 14.

[54] Douglas Southall Freeman to John Stuart Bryan, telegram, January 6, 1936, in Douglas Southall Freeman Papers (Division of Manuscripts, Library of Congress) .

[55] Dallas *Morning News,* January 8, 1936.

[56] Chester C. Davis, "The Development of Agricultural Policy since the End of the World War," in U.S. Department of Agriculture, *Farmers in a Changing World: Yearbook of Agriculture,* 1940 (Washington, 1940) , 318–19; *Farm Policies of the United States,* 349–52.

estimates for other Southern states ran from 1,500,000 acres in Virginia to 5,000,000 in Georgia; a single county in the South Carolina Piedmont had lost 277,000 acres. Even these terrifying figures did not include the acres totally decimated by erosion (some 97,000,000), bottomlands lost by the filling of stream beds and subsequent overflow, lands strewn with sand and gravel washed down from above, and soil depleted for want of prudent cultivation. The impoverished Southern land consumed more fertilizer than all the rest of the nation, at a cost of $2.71 per acre in contrast to 30 cents in the Middle states.[57]

For thirty years Bennett proclaimed the gospel of conservation in a wilderness of indifference; only the Western drought of 1934–1936 and the great dust storms, one of which providentially sifted into Washington as Bennett testified before a Congressional committee, created the necessary sense of urgency. In the Soil Conservation Act of 1935 a national reponsibility was assumed. Building upon experiments begun by the Bureau of Soils in 1930 and demonstrations begun by the Soil Erosion Service in 1933, Bennett set about establishing a national program. In 1937 six Southern states passed legislation authorizing soil conservation districts to work with Bennett's new Soil Conservation Service (SCS), and by 1940 all the Southern states had acted. Working through contracts with farmers and tenants, the SCS laid out plans for land use, crop rotation, grasses, woodlands, contour plowing, terracing, strip cropping, ponds, drainage, and the planting of legumes like soybeans, kudzu, and lespedesa. Altogether 272,889 plans were devised and 26,732,812 acres treated in the South before the end of 1946.[58] Incidental benefits accrued in the process: new cash crops of soybeans and sorghum; turpentine, timber, and pulpwood; hay and forage for livestock. Before the

[57] Odum, *Southern Regions of the United States*, 339–41. See also Stuart Chase, *Rich Land, Poor Land: A Study of Waste in the Natural Resources of America* (New York and London, 1936), 49–53, 90–99.

[58] Hugh H. Bennett, in *Study of Agricultural and Economic Problems of the Cotton Belt: Hearings before Special Subcommittee on Cotton of the Committee of Agriculture, House of Representatives, 80 Cong., 1 Sess., Part 2* (Washington, 1948), 1123–40. See also Wellington Brink, *Big Hugh: The Father of Soil Conservation* (New York, 1951); and Peter Farb, "Hugh Bennett: Messiah of the Soil," in *American Forests* (Washington), LXVI (January, 1960), 18–19, 40, 42.

end of the decade, Julian Street has written, one could "observe the magnitude of the change in farm lay-outs and cropping practices" merely by flying over the South in an airplane. Because of "its comprehensive scope and . . . the significant educational impact which it had within the region," he asserted, the transformation wrought by Hugh Bennett was "one of the lasting benefits of the emergency program of the thirties." [59]

An almost unqualified success as an engineering and educational project, soil conservation was a failure as a device for limiting production. With their worst lands taken out of cultivation, farmers could work the more fertile acres intensively. In 1936 droughts kept the first uncontrolled cotton crop down to 12,399,-000 bales, and demand held the average price up at 12.36 cents; but 1937 brought an all-time record crop of 18,946,000 bales in conjunction with a business recession. The price fell to 8.41 cents and farmers swamped the Commodity Credit Corporation with demands for loans that depleted its resources. [60] By August 1, 1939, the carry-over exceeded 13,000,000 bales, more than a year's supply, a drug on the market until 1941. [61]

Once again the demand for controls mounted. In August, 1937, Marvin Jones announced that members of his House agriculture committee were in full accord with the desire for new legislation. [62] In December the Texas Agricultural Association demanded "a compulsory control of production law applicable to cotton, corn, peanuts and rice." [63] In the Senate "Cotton Ed" Smith held out for something like McNary-Haugenism, but John H. Bankhead returned to a special session in the fall confident of support for a compulsory program. "The cotton exporters for

[59] Street, *New Revolution in the Cotton Economy*, 48–50.

[60] U.S. Bureau of the Census, *Historical Statistics of the United States*, 301, columns K-302 and K-303; Jones, *Fifty Billion Dollars*, 96. The cotton trade would have preferred parity payments as in 1935, but farmers demanded CCC loans as high as twelve cents. The loan level was finally set at nine cents because, the President declared, a higher level would have damaged American cotton in the world market. Pat Harrison to Franklin D. Roosevelt, August 11, 1937; Theodore G. Bilbo to Roosevelt, August 19, 1937; Roosevelt to Bilbo, September 3, 1937, in OF 258, Roosevelt Library.

[61] Benedict, *Farm Policies of the United States*, 390, 407n. Until 1945 carryovers ranged from 10,500,000 to 13,000,000 bales.

[62] Statement of Representative Marvin Jones, August 4, 1937 (news release), in OF 2960, Roosevelt Library.

[63] Quoted in Patenaude, "New Deal and Texas," 249.

more than two years have been engaged in a widespread propaganda campaign in an effort to continue the use of cotton farmers for their special benefit as they have done for many long years," he wrote the President. But early in October Alabama farmers at meetings in every county voted 92 per cent in favor of controls, and their delegates to a statewide meeting at Auburn declared enthusiastically for "compulsory acreage control in every year when necessary to hold the supply of cotton down to effective demand." At about the same time a meeting of Tennessee farmers in Nashville voted unanimously for such action. Ed O'Neal and Southern Congressmen and governors joined in the cry.[64]

Disagreements stalled legislative action during the fall, but in the next regular session Congress passed the second Agricultural Adjustment Act and the President signed it on February 16, 1938. The new act substantially re-established the program that had evolved from 1933 through 1936, with certain additions but without processing taxes. Acreage allotments for the basic staples were revived; they were not compulsory, but no farmer could receive soil conservation payments unless he co-operated. Marketing quotas were compulsory but subject to approval by two thirds of the farmers affected. Parity payments were authorized, subject to annual appropriations by Congress. Crop insurance was provided for wheat beginning in 1939, and extended to cotton in 1941.[65]

Within a month of the act's passage cotton farmers voted 92.1 per cent in favor of marketing quotas, a stronger support than in 1934.[66] Tobacco farmers also approved the imposition of controls in 1938, but the burley and flue-cured growers had fared so well for several years that they failed to muster a two-thirds majority in

[64] John H. Bankhead to Franklin D. Roosevelt, telegram, October 12, 1937; Lister Hill to Roosevelt, telegram, October 11, 1937; Carl E. Bailey to Roosevelt, October 11, 1937; Edward A. O'Neal to Roosevelt, telegram, October 12, 1937, in OF 258, President's Personal File (PPF) 419-A, and PPF 1362, and PPF 4471, Roosevelt Library.

[65] Benedict, *Farm Policies of the United States,* 375–81, 384; Kile, *Farm Bureau through Three Decades,* 236–43; U.S. Department of Agriculture, *Agricultural Adjustment, 1937–1938: Report of Activities Conducted by the Agricultural Adjustment Administration* . . . (Washington, 1938), 17–21, 97–107.

[66] *Progressive Farmer,* LIII (May, 1938), 14; U.S. Department of Agriculture, *Agricultural Adjustment, 1937–1938,* 111. California, by less than 1 per cent, was the only state in which cotton farmers failed to poll a two-thirds majority or better for controls.

1939. During that year the acreage of flue-cured increased 40 per cent which, together with rising yields, gave a record crop of 1,159,000,000 pounds. The glut coincided with the start of World War II in Europe, and when British buyers suspended purchases the average price for flue-cured fell from 22.2 cents in 1938 to 14.9 in 1939. The growers escaped ruin only by means of loans from the Commodity Credit Corporation, and they hastened to approve a quota for the following year. The unforgettable lesson left tobacco farmers more strongly attached to the principle of controls than any other farm group.[67]

Meanwhile, the cotton market remained in the shadow of the carry-over. Bankhead and other cotton senators came together temporarily behind a plan advanced by "Cotton Ed" Smith to sell farmers the government holdings of loan cotton in return for acreage reductions, in effect to let farmers have cotton without the trouble of growing it. The administration countered with a proposal to dump the government cotton in the foreign market and finally compromised on a plan to subsidize foreign sales from the 1939 crop.[68] Between July 27 and December 4 such sales amounted to 4,344,354 bales, subsidized at 1.5 cents a pound, an amount thereafter reduced because of limited funds. At the same time the government undertook to unload some of its own swollen stocks. During the summer of 1939 Congress approved a barter of 600,000 bales to Great Britain for 85,000 tons of rubber, 175,000 bales went to France and Switzerland for cash, and the RFC extended credits to Spain for the purchase of 250,000 bales. As a result exports rose from 3,326,800 bales in 1938 to 6,162,900 in 1939, but the outbreak of war cut them back to 1,111,900 in 1940. Fortunately, when the foreign market collapsed, the domestic market improved because of the national defense effort and the capture of foreign textile markets from the belligerents.[69]

[67] U.S. Department of Agriculture. *Agricultural Adjustment, 1937–1938,* 113; *1938–1939,* 65; *1939–1940,* 45, 48–49; Benedict and Stine, *Agricultural Commodity Programs,* 66–67; Hoover and Ratchford, *Economic Resources and Policies of the South,* 348–49.

[68] *Progressive Farmer,* LIV (January, 1939) , 4; (February, 1939) , 14; (May, 1939) , 16; (June, 1939) , 14; Charleston *News and Courier,* February 10, 1939.

[69] Arthur P. Chew, "Conditions in Agriculture," in *The American Year Book: A Record of Events and Progress,* 1939 (New York, 1940) , 443–44; New York *Times,* July 28, August 8, 18, December 8, 12, 1939; Jones, *Fifty Billion Dollars,* 218; Hoover

The end of the 1930's came, like the end of the 1920's, with agriculture still the chief occupation of the South and still in distress. Briefly it had seemed that farm income, which led the descent into depression, was destined to lead the way back. Cash receipts from farm marketing had sunk in 1932 to 37 per cent of the 1929 receipts; in 1933 they reached 45 per cent and by 1937, 74, but during 1939 and 1940 they sank back to 58 per cent. Receipts from cotton in 1939 were only 39 per cent of those in 1929, the lowest point since 1933.[70]

The chief victim of chronic distress was the man farthest down, where the torrent of New Deal spending ran out into a trickle. It might be, Rupert Vance wrote in 1934, "that the greatest efficiency of the southern planters consists in securing government subsidy to uphold a system that might otherwise break down of its own weakness. . . . With one hand the cotton landlord takes agricultural subsidies and rental benefits from his government, with the other he pushes his tenant on relief." [71] The problem of tenancy was nothing new. For generations the rural South had sunk into the morass. In 1880 tenants operated 36.2 per cent of all Southern farms; in 1920, 49.6 per cent; in 1930, 55.5 per cent. By 1935 the proportion had dropped to 53.5 but the numbers had risen to a climactic 1,831,475 among 3,421,923 farm operators. Increasingly the typical tenant was white, two out of three in 1935. Nearly half of all white farm operators were tenants; more than two thirds of the Negro. Nearly a fourth of the white tenants and more than half of the Negro were sharecroppers, lacking even a plug mule or any other semblance of capital. In all, tenant families included perhaps five and a half million whites and more than three million Negroes, about one of every four Southerners.[72]

---

and Ratchford, *Economic Resources and Policies of the South,* 308; Benedict and Stine, *Agricultural Commodity Programs,* 26.

[70] Hoover and Ratchford, *Economic Resources and Policies of the South,* 54.

[71] Rupert B. Vance to William Watts Ball, September 15, 1934, in Ball Papers.

[72] U.S. Bureau of the Census, *Historical Statistics of the United States,* 278, Series K-23 and K-27; Johnson, Embree, and Alexander, *Collapse of Cotton Tenancy,* 4–5. The figures are for the sixteen-state Census South. In the thirteen-state South tenants were a majority of farm operators in all but four states: Florida, Kentucky, North Carolina, and Tennessee.

The long shadow of slavery still reached the vassals of King Cotton, white and black. The prerogatives all rested with the landlord: the choice of crop, its cultivation and marketing, the conditions of credit, the bookkeeping, the final settlement. On the other side the system bred dependence and servility; on both sides insecurity and distrust. A vast folklore grew up about landlords who kept books with "crooked pencils" and about the proverbially shiftless and unreliable tenants. "The tenant and cropper system . . . has bred a race of people who are without the slightest conception of consequence . . . who live in a poverty which makes any cultivation of a sense of responsibility impossible," wrote the artist and traveler Thomas Hart Benton. The rare bonanza of cash that came their way vanished in immediate pleasures; experience too often taught that prudent investment in land or mules only went to settle accounts the next bad year.[73]

But the cash nexus seldom appeared in that feudal pattern. From the days of slavery, world cotton markets had dictated an iron law of wages that pushed the producers to the margins of survival. The tenant sold his labor for a share of the crop, a share often consumed in advance by the cost of "furnish" from the country merchant or plantation commissary. In 1934 interest charges on these advances in three cotton counties of Texas and Mississippi ranged from 16.1 to 25.3 per cent; higher "credit prices" made the total cost more than 50 per cent. Among 1,022 Alabama farm households surveyed in 1933, a sociologist found that 89 per cent of the years spent in sharecropping resulted in breaking even or taking a loss; in most cases the "loss" meant a decline of status and increased dependency—there were so few material possessions to forfeit. Among three thousand Alabama cropper families, 80 per cent had an indebtedness to the landlord of more than a year's standing.[74] A survey of seven cotton states in 1934 showed an average net income (cash and "furnish") of $180 to wage hands, $312 to croppers, and $417 to

---

[73] Thomas Hart Benton, *An Artist in America* (New York, 1937), 196; Johnson, Embree, and Alexander, *Collapse of Cotton Tenancy*, 7–11; Raper, *Preface to Peasantry*, 159–63.

[74] Harold Hoffsomer, *Landlord-Tenant Relations and Relief in Alabama*, FERA Research Bulletin Series II, No. 9 (Washington, 1935), 2.

other share tenants. Other studies varied in detail, but all confirmed the fact that tenants eked out a gaunt subsistence.[75]

Except for the most fortunate, home was a dilapidated, unpainted, weatherbeaten frame cabin leaning out of plumb on rock or brick pilings—unceiled, unscreened, covered with a leaky roof. Families of six to ten often occupied two or three rooms separated by flimsy walls.[76] Wintry winds blew under the floors and through a wallpaper of newsprint. The summer sun beat down on unshaded roofs, for the imperatives of the cash crop required planting to the door. For all the years of diversification propaganda, landlords often discouraged garden plots. In 1932, when Aubrey Williams sought to require gardens as a condition of RFC relief in Mississippi, he stirred the active opposition of Delta planters, who feared a dangerous precedent of independence and initiative.[77] The diet was the ubiquitous "hog and hominy," or the "three M's": salt meat, meal, and molasses. Despite the long sanitation campaigns, open surface privies were still common and a fourth to a third of all rural households had not even those.[78] "After all, Miss," an Arkansas landlord told a newcomer who had innocently supplied outhouses on her plantation, "all that a sharecropper needs is a cotton patch and a corn cob." [79]

The Southern tenant lived in one of the stagnant backwaters of Western civilization. "Depressions and booms, good times and bad times have affected them little—nor has the advance of civilization," said the Montgomery *Advertiser*. "Poverty, disease, illiteracy have been their companions." [80] Their cultural landscape afforded a "miserable panorama of unpainted shacks, rain-gullied fields, straggling fences, rattle-trap Fords, dirt, poverty, disease, drudgery, and monotony that stretches for a thousand miles across

[75] T. J. Woofter, Jr., *et al.*, *Landlord and Tenant on the Cotton Plantation*, WPA Research Monograph V (Washington, 1936) , 220, 223. See also Johnson, Embree, and Alexander, *Collapse of Cotton Tenancy*, 11–13, 75–77; Raper, *Preface to Peasantry*, 33–58; William R. Amberson, "Report of Survey," in Norman M. Thomas, *The Plight of the Share-Cropper* (New York, 1934) , 19–24; Johnson, *Shadow of the Plantation*, 12.
[76] Raper, *Preface to Peasantry*, 52–54, 59–65.
[77] Aubrey Williams, manuscript Memoirs, 11–12.
[78] Woofter *et al.*, *Landlord and Tenant on the Cotton Plantation*, 228.
[79] Quoted in Howard Kester, *Revolt of the Sharecroppers* (New York, 1936) , 41.
[80] Montgomery *Advertiser*, May 26, 1937.

the cotton belt." [81] The circumstances of peasants under the Tsar of Russia, wrote an English visitor who had seen them, "were greatly superior to those of the negro share-cropper and the 'poor white' in South Carolina. . . . Here an old economy, based on slavery, had collapsed, and nothing had taken its place. The human wreckage released by the collapse had been allowed to drift aimlessly about for sixty years." [82] In none of the European democracies, a French visitor asserted, "is the lot of the agricultural tenant as wretched, his prospects as hopeless, and his rights as unprotected as in the Southern regions of America." [83]

For peak seasons and odd jobs landlords could tap a pool of floating wage laborers who moved in and out of sharecropping. In 1940 they numbered 842,525 in the Southeast alone, working at daily wages of less than a dollar, sometimes as low as fifty cents or less.[84] Tenancy, although a static system, constantly stirred farm workers to move in search of improvement or debt evasion; in 1935 a majority of Southern tenants had been resident on the same farm a year or less.[85] On the fringes of the cotton belt, moreover, a new system of migratory casual labor arose with the advent of good roads after World War I. Reclamation of the Florida Everglades opened "winter gardens" employing some fifty thousand workers by the late 1930's. This created a year-round produce market in the East and a system of migratory labor, drawn largely from Southern farms, that followed the seasons from Florida to Maine. From the Gulf Coast a cycle of strawberry pickers followed the spread of the "pink rash" up the Mississippi Valley, into Michigan, and as far east as the "Del-Mar-Va" peninsula. Among 10,945 of them interviewed for the relief administration in 1934, estimates of annual earnings ran from $108.24 to $424.02. The "big swing" in Texas constituted the third major cycle of nomads, mostly Mexican-Americans, who followed the cotton crop north-

---

[81] Quoted in Johnson, Embree, and Alexander, *Collapse of Cotton Tenancy*, 14.

[82] Price, *America after Sixty Years*, 213.

[83] Odette Keun, *A Foreigner Looks at the TVA* (New York and Toronto, 1937), 30.

[84] Vance, *All These People*, 216; Braunhut, "Farm Labor Wage Rates in the South," *loc. cit.*, 192–93.

[85] President's Special Committee on Farm Tenancy, *Farm Tenancy* (Washington, 1937), 100.

ward from the Rio Grande and swung back into the southern counties for winter vegetables.[86]

The farm labor system presented the AAA with two thorny problems: the difficulty of assuring the tenant a share in the benefits, and the danger of displacing him by acreage reductions. In the cotton plow-up of 1933 displacement was not an acute problem since the tenant was entitled to the same rights in the benefits as he had in the crop.[87] Yet certain devices conveyed the lion's share to the landlord. "Our landlord wouldn't plow up any of our cotton," a South Carolina tenant complained. "He plowed up his own so that he could get the pay for it." Wage hands had no claim on the benefit payments and tenant payments sometimes went to cover indebtedness to the landlord or passed directly from the county agents to merchants for past or future supplies.[88] In 1934 Professor Calvin B. Hoover of Duke underscored the problem in a report to the AAA. In a number of cases, Hoover noted, landlords had failed to seek the consent of tenants or made no mention of tenants before signing the contract. Tenants, he concluded, sometimes got the amount due, sometimes less, "depending upon the charitableness or unscrupulousness of the landlord." [89]

The AAA was designed to raise farm prices. It had neither the organization nor the mandate to reform the landlord-tenant relationship. Furthermore, landlords dominated the local committees that administered the program. Long-established attitudes made it almost impossible for the government to deal directly with the tenant and such attitudes permeated Cully Cobb's Cotton Section.[90] The AAA, therefore, moved with circumspection. Setting

[86] McWilliams, *Ill Fares the Land*, 168–76, 182, 149–64, 230–31; U.S. Department of Labor, *Migration of Workers: Preliminary Report* (Washington, 1938), 1–2, 91, 97; Grubbs, "Story of Florida's Migrant Farm Workers," *loc. cit.*, 103–107.

[87] Nourse, Davis, and Black, *Three Years of the Agricultural Adjustment Administration*, 342.

[88] Johnson, Embree, and Alexander, *Collapse of Cotton Tenancy*, 51–55.

[89] Calvin B. Hoover, "Human Problems in Acreage Reduction in the South" (March, 1934; typed copy in Duke University Library), 7–8. See also Calvin B. Hoover, *Memoirs of Capitalism, Communism and Nazism* (Durham, 1965), 156–57.

[90] Harold Hoffsomer, "The AAA and the Cropper," *Social Forces*, XIII (1934–1935), 495–96; David Eugene Conrad, *The Forgotten Farmer: The Story of Sharecroppers in the New Deal* (Urbana, 1965), 52–53.

too high a proportion of benefits for tenants would entail the risk of losing landlord support or having tenants displaced by wage labor. Consequently the acreage contracts for 1934 and 1935 limited the cropper to about 11 per cent of the benefits and the share tenant to about 15. Provisions covering displacement were vague. The contracts specified that landlords should spread acreage reduction "as nearly ratably as practicable among tenants" and should "insofar as possible, maintain . . . the normal number of tenants and other employees." [91] In 1935, after many complaints, a group in the AAA led by Jerome Frank tried during a temporary absence of Administrator Chester Davis to issue a directive that the landlord must keep the *same* tenants. However, the order was countermanded as impracticable and the Frank group dismissed.[92]

The issue entered the headlines early in 1934, when Socialist leader Norman Thomas, after a visit to the Arkansas Delta, charged that "under the operation of the AAA hundreds of thousands . . . are either being driven out on the roads without hope of absorption into industry or exist without land to cultivate by grace of the landlord in shacks scarcely fit for pigs." [93] As this and other indictments reverberated across the country, the AAA became a scapegoat for sins not altogether its own, for a tragedy that had developed over the years, a rural poverty that existed long before the AAA brought it into the spotlight. The situation might well have been more critical without the stabilization that protected the old cotton belt against the competition of cheaper production in the Southwest.

Indeed, statistical evidence showed that the total number of tenants and farm operators increased substantially from 1930 to 1935.[94] The reason, however, may have been some Depression movement back to subsistence farming, particularly near the cities, plus the fact that any stranded worker tilling three acres counted as a tenant. A study of 593 counties in seven states placed

[91] Richards, *Cotton and the Agricultural Adjustment Act,* 140.

[92] Conrad, *Forgotten Farmers,* 136–53.

[93] *American Guardian* (Oklahoma City), March 2, 1934, quoted in Richards, *Cotton and the Agricultural Adjustment Act,* 149n.

[94] U.S. Bureau of the Census, *Historical Statistics of the United States, 1789–1945* (Washington, 1949), 96, Series E 43–60.

the increases in predominantly noncotton and nontobacco counties, and therefore in areas least affected by the AAA. Displacement, however, did occur in the areas most affected: 170 cotton counties showed a decrease of 1.1 per cent in tenants and 11.6 per cent in croppers. Even so, one cannot attribute all the displacement to the AAA. In 1934 a study of 825 dispossessed farm families in Eastern North Carolina revealed that about three fifths had lost out in the Depression years 1929–1932. The AAA found, in 1934, that tenants and former tenants of farms covered by cotton contracts in fifty-two counties constituted only 32.6 per cent of all tenants or former tenants on relief.[95]

For many of those who stayed on the farms, New Deal credit agencies and crop programs improved conditions. But for great numbers the 1930's were years of perilous insecurity, mobility, and shifting tenure status. The tenant farmer, so long an object of scholarly study and alarm, at last entered the arena of public controversy. The AAA provided the focus for this belated discovery, but it derived from other sources as well. The popularity of Erskine Caldwell's *Tobacco Road* (1932) inspired a sharecropper fashion in the literature of the decade. The vogue ran through such works as Herbert Harrison Kroll's *Cabin in the Cotton* (1931) and *I Was a Sharecropper* (1937); Charlie May Simon's *The Share-Cropper* (1937): and many a forgotten book commemorated in the files of *The New Masses*. The masterpiece of "proletarian" novels on rural displacement was John Steinbeck's *Grapes of Wrath* (1939), which pictured the wanderings of the uprooted "Okies" and "Arkies" in the Odyssey of the Joad family, drawn by the illusory promise of a California already overloaded with farm labor. The most sensitive and effective evocation of tenant life, James Agee's *Let Us Now Praise Famous Men* (1940), with photographs by Walker Evans, got little notice at the time but gradually made its way to recognition as a unique masterpiece of documentation and art.

[95] Woofter *et al., Landlord and Tenant on the Cotton Plantation,* 154, 155, 236; Fred C. Frey and T. Lynn Smith, "The Influence of the AAA Cotton Program upon the Tenant, Cropper, and Laborer," in *Rural Sociology,* I (1936), 495, 498; Gordon W. Blackwell, "The Displaced Tenant Farm Family in North Carolina," in *Social Forces,* XIII (1934–1935), 69; Richards, *Cotton and the Agricultural Adjustment Act,* 152.

Scholarly investigations benefited from the support of New Deal farm and relief agencies.[96] Outstanding independent studies included Charles S. Johnson's *The Shadow of the Plantation* (1934), based on a survey of Negro life in Macon County, Alabama; and Arthur F. Raper's *Preface to Peasantry* (1936), a comparative study of Greene and Macon counties, Georgia. Most important of all in its immediate effect was a little book by Charles S. Johnson, Edwin Embree, and Will Alexander, *The Collapse of Cotton Tenancy* (1935). Supported by the Rockefeller Foundation, it summarized in graphic form the statistical and field investigations of students under Johnson at Fisk University and Rupert B. Vance at Chapel Hill and recommended a Federal program for small farm ownership. The book's impact was heightened by a skilled press agent who put it on front pages across the nation. "The country believed, by George, that this cotton tenancy had collapsed," Alexander said later. "It was one of the most effective pieces of publicity ever done." Some time later the President remarked to Secretary Wallace: "Henry, Will Alexander and those fellows wrote the best book that has been written on Southern Agriculture." Wallace: "They gave the A.A.A. the devil." Roosevelt: "That's why I liked it." [97]

For forty years or more, sociologist Edgar T. Thompson remarked, teachers and leaders had been discussing tenancy. "What distinguishes present from past discussion of share-tenancy is the implication of the present discussion for action." [98] What even more conspicuously distinguished it was that inarticulate tenants found voice through their own organization, the Southern Tenant Farmers' Union (STFU), which arose from unique circumstances in northeastern Arkansas, where for three decades large areas had been opened to farming by lumbering operations and by drainage projects under the direction of engineer A. E. Morgan. The lure of fertile bottom lands had drawn in a surplus of labor, but the

[96] Some are cited in this chapter. A bibliography of many others may be found in C. E. Lively and Conrad Taeuber, *Rural Migration in the United States*, WPA Research Monograph XIX (Washington, 1939), 177–83.

[97] "Reminiscences of Will W. Alexander," 372–82, 391, 394; Louise Ware, *George Foster Peabody: Banker, Philanthropist, Publicist* (Athens, Ga., 1951), 240–41.

[98] Edgar T. Thompson, "The Natural History of Agricultural Labor in the South," in David K. Jackson (ed.), *American Studies in Honor of William Kenneth Boyd, by Members of the Americana Club of Duke University* (Durham, 1940), 112.

traditions of dependency were less deeply rooted on the newer plantations than in the older cotton lands.[99] Depression, the AAA, and mechanization created an extreme instability of tenure. During 1934–1935 about 25 per cent of all tenant complaints to the AAA came from the area.[100]

The Delta town of Tyronza was an improbable place for a Socialist party local, but one was organized in 1932 by H. L. Mitchell, a former sharecropper who ran a cleaning business, and H. Clay East, town constable and owner of a filling station. Early in 1934 they invited Norman Thomas to meet at the high school with a group of displaced tenants; soon afterward Thomas delivered his public attack on the AAA and promoted a study of the area by Dr. William R. Amberson of Memphis. Amberson's findings confirmed the reports of extensive displacement.[101] On the night of July 11, 1934, stimulated by the Socialist activity, a small group of tenant farmers, white and Negro, gathered in the dim light of kerosene lamps at Sunnyside School near Tyronza to organize the union. "Are we going to have two unions," a voice asked, "one for the white and one for the colored?" A seventy-year-old Negro, a veteran of the Negro union smashed by the Elaine Massacre of 1919, rose. "The same chain that holds my people holds your people too," he said. "If we're chained together on the outside we ought to stay chained together in the union." The group decided to welcome white and Negro tenants, sharecroppers, and wage laborers. "Nothing will win the battle quicker than by having members of all races, creeds and colors united in one strong Union," H. L. Mitchell wrote later.[102]

The union turned to Mitchell and East for assistance; J. R.

[99] F. Raymond Daniell in New York *Times*, April 15, 1935; "Reminiscences of H. L. Mitchell," 53. Donald Hughes Grubbs, "The Southern Tenant Farmers' Union and the New Deal" (Ph.D. dissertation, University of Florida, 1963), is an excellent and full secondary account. See also Jamieson, *Labor Unionism in American Agriculture*, 306–26; Kester, *Revolt among the Sharecroppers;* and Oren Stephens, "Revolt on the Delta," in *Harper's*, CLXXXIII (1941), 656–64.

[100] Richards, *Cotton and the AAA*, 148.

[101] "Reminiscences of H. L. Mitchell," 19–21; Amberson, "Report of Survey," in Thomas, *Plight of the Share-Cropper*, 19–34.

[102] Kester, *Revolt among the Sharecroppers*, 55–56; C. T. Carpenter, "King Cotton's Slaves," in *Scribner's*, XCVIII (1935), 196; Ward Rogers "Sharecroppers Drop Color Line," in *The Crisis*, XLII (1935), 168–69, 178; H. L. Mitchell to Nathan Wiley, November 21, 1935, in Southern Tenant Farmers Union Papers (Southern Historical Collection, University of North Carolina).

Butler, ex-teacher, sharecropper, and sawmill hand ("just an Arkansas Hill Billy") came down from the Ozarks to help and became president; Oscar Ameringer of Oklahoma City, a Socialist veteran, provided advice on the constitution. Three ministers, all Vanderbilt alumni infused with a social gospel, joined the organizing drive: Ward H. Rodgers, a Methodist who left Pumpkin Center in the Ozarks to run a relief school for adults, Howard Kester of Reinhold Niebuhr's Committee on Economic and Racial Justice, and Claude Williams from the radical Commonwealth College at Mena, Arkansas.[103] In Washington the union came to be represented, officially in 1936, by Gardner Jackson, a wealthy young New Dealer with a penchant for humanitarian causes.[104]

Planters refused to take the union seriously at first. The Socialists and Republicans (Negroes) were getting together, they remarked in amusement. But as the organization spread, their reaction turned to shock and outrage.[105] Organizers were arrested on charges of anarchism, "interfering with labor," barratry, and other crimes. As moving time approached, January 1, 1935, union members began to receive eviction notices. Evictions from the Hiram Norcross Plantation became a test case, but a court ruled that tenants were not parties to the 1935 AAA contracts and therefore had no right to sue. Secretary Wallace would not intervene and the issue gave rise to the controversy that ended with the firing of the Jerome Frank group. Mitchell led a delegation to protest in Washington but won only a promise that the Department of Agriculture would send an investigator. An inquiry by Mrs. Mary Connor Myers apparently confirmed charges of widespread evictions and intimidation, but her report was suppressed and disappeared from the files.

Opposition, however, aroused further militancy: mass meetings, speeches, parades accompanied by the union song, "We Shall Not Be Moved." The spring of 1935 blossomed amid scenes of violence in the Arkansas Delta: meetings dispersed, union members ar-

[103] Kester, *Revolt among the Sharecroppers*, 66–69; H. L. Mitchell, letter in *New Republic*, LXXX (1934), 218. Cedric Belfrage, *A Faith to Free the People* (New York, 1944), is a biography of Claude C. Williams.

[104] "Reminiscences of H. L. Mitchell," 63–64; *The Sharecroppers' Voice* (Memphis), February 1, May 1, 1936.

[105] Mitchell, letter in *New Republic*, LXXX (1934), 218.

rested and turned off the land, relief cut off, bullets fired into tenant shacks and into the home of C. T. Carpenter, union lawyer at Marked Tree, highways watched by armed vigilantes.[106] "I don't know, though, but what it would have been better to have a few no-account shiftless people killed at the start than to have had all this fuss raised up," remarked the Reverend Abner Sage of Marked Tree's First Methodist Church. "We have had a pretty serious situation here, what with the 'mistering' of the niggers and stirring them up to think the Government was going to give them forty acres." [107] During March Norman Thomas toured the area. At Birdsong in Mississippi County an armed mob of planters and deputies drove him from the platform: "We don't need no Gawd-damn Yankee Bastard to tell us what to do with our niggers." [108] Thomas returned East to address a national radio audience. "There is a reign of terror in the cotton country of eastern Arkansas," he said, but his complaints in Washington produced no action. "I know the South," Roosevelt told Thomas, "and there is arising a new generation of leaders in the South and we've got to be patient." [109]

Eventually the union weathered the attacks; terrorism subsided under the glare of publicity, and the union continued to grow. In the fall of 1935 its day laborers staged a cotton pickers' strike, demanding a dollar per hundred pounds, but the effort soon waned.[110] In May, 1936, the union called a general strike of cotton choppers and demanded a dollar a day or ten cents an hour. Outbreaks of violence occurred again. When Claude Williams and Willie Sue Blagdon, STFU agents, sought to investigate the disappearance of a Negro tenant falsely rumored to have been beaten

[106] Kester, *Revolt among the Sharecroppers*, 82–85; [Howard Kester] to Clarence Senior, February 24, 1935, in Socialist Party Collection (Manuscripts Division, Duke University Library).

[107] F. Raymond Daniell in New York *Times*, April 16, 1935.

[108] Kester, *Revolt among the Sharecroppers*, 80–81; "Reminiscences of Norman Thomas" (Oral History Research Office), 82–83; Norman Thomas to Franklin D. Roosevelt, telegram, March 15, 1935; and Chester Davis to Roosevelt, March 19, 1935, in Roosevelt Library.

[109] "Reminiscences of Norman Thomas," 99–100.

[110] Jamieson, *Labor Unionism in American Agriculture*, 309–10; "Reminiscences of H. L. Mitchell," 49–50. A similar strike with similarly unsuccessful results was staged by the Share Croppers' Union during August.

to death, they were seized and beaten themselves. Negro strikers were arrested and convicted of vagrancy; others were released when they agreed to go back to work. Governor Marion J. Futrell called out the militia and after personal investigation pronounced the hubbub "much ado about nothing," the work of "agitators." One of the union marches was broken up by Paul Peacher, town marshal of Earle; thirteen strikers were arrested and forced to work on his farm. For this action he was later convicted of peonage, fined $3,500, and sentenced to two years in the penitentiary. The strike won only scattered concessions, mostly from small landowners, but the union once again caught national attention, and its stormiest period was over. Publicity focused upon the violence (motion picture cameras recorded the strike for a "March of Time" short subject), and the conviction of Peacher inhibited further use of illegal tactics.[111]

From Arkansas the movement reached into surrounding states. By the time of its third annual convention at Muskogee, Oklahoma, in January, 1937—a unique gathering of whites and blacks, Mexicans and Indians—the STFU listed a membership of 30,827 in 328 locals, mostly in Arkansas but scattered through seven states from North Carolina (1 local) to Oklahoma (76).[112] But that was the peak. A major factor in subsequent decline was an ill-fated affiliation with the Congress of Industrial Organizations in July, 1937, as a subsidiary of the United Cannery, Agricultural, Packing and Allied Workers of America (UCAPAWA). The UCAPAWA did not respect STFU autonomy, Mitchell and other leaders charged. Communist elements dominating the larger group tried first to take over the STFU and then to undermine confidence in it after it withdrew from the affiliation in March, 1939.[113] Thereafter the STFU lived on the contributions of outside church and labor agencies.

[111] Jamieson, *Labor Unionism in American Agriculture,* 310–13. An interesting by-product of the 1936 strike was the Delta Cooperative Farm at Hillhouse, Bolivar County, Mississippi, set up by Sherwood Eddy and others as a refuge for dispossessed tenants. Leonard G. Pardue, "The Delta and Providence Farms: 1936–1942" (Seminar paper, University of North Carolina, 1963, copy in author's possession).

[112] Jamieson, *Labor Unionism in American Agriculture,* 314n; Edward Levinson, *Labor on the March* (New York, 1938), 242.

[113] Jamieson, *Labor Unionism in American Agriculture,* 316–18, 320–22; "Reminiscences of H. L. Mitchell," 74–117.

Probably the greatest factor in the STFU's decline was a growing sense of futility. A third strike during the cotton picking season of 1938 did not meet with the violence of 1935 and 1936, but failed all the same. "We were paupers trying to bargain with paupers," Mitchell told the Little Rock convention of the STFU in 1941. "No method can be devised whereby an organization of economically insecure people such as tenant farmers, sharecroppers, and farm laborers on southern plantations can bargain with an industry that is disorganized, pauperized and kept alive only by Government subsidy." [114] But the executive council voted to continue as a trade union and in 1946 the remnants joined the AF of L as the National Agricultural Workers Union.[115]

If it failed as a bargaining agency, it could lay claim to some positive achievements. These included, according to a union bulletin in 1940, exposures of peonage and forced labor, governmental investigations of conditions, greater recognition of constitutional guaranties of civil liberties, government benefits and grants, WPA jobs, better contracts with planters, election of union members to AAA committees, free textbooks for Negro school children.[116] However, the greatest achievement was to focus attention on the plight of the sharecropper. Scholarly investigations had been helpful, but "it was the sensationalism of the S.T.F.U.'s actions that made the situation known to the whole population." [117]

Thrust unavoidably before the public, the situation by its very contrast rekindled Jeffersonian images of rural independence, reinvigorated the farm community ideas of the 1920's and the back-to-the-land movement of the Depression. Return to the land, Senator Bankhead wrote in 1933, offered not only a means of relief but a means of restoring "that small yeoman class which has been the backbone of every great civilization." [118] New Deal receptivity to social experimentation opened the way to modest trials of new approaches.

[114] Quoted in Stephens, "Revolt on the Delta," *loc. cit.*, 664.
[115] *Ibid.*; "Reminiscences of H. L. Mitchell," 149.
[116] Jamieson, *Labor Unionism in American Agriculture*, 325.
[117] Stephens, "Revolt on the Delta," *loc. cit.*, 664.
[118] John H. Bankhead, "The One Way to Permanent National Recovery," in *Liberty* (New York), X (July 22, 1933), 18, quoted in Conkin, *Tomorrow a New World*, 87.

The first experiment embodied the concept of factory-farm living, which indeed was already practiced in much of Southern industry. In 1933 Senator Bankhead inserted a provision in the National Industrial Recovery Act authorizing $25,000,000 for a program of subsistence homesteads to "provide for aiding in the redistribution of the overbalance of population in industrial centers." [119] Except for a few communities built as refuges for stranded workers and submarginal farmers, the subsistence homesteads sprang up near industrial centers with the idea of permitting urban workers to keep one foot on the soil. The experiment paid off handsomely in the Senator's home state. Of the 34 completed projects, 5 were at Birmingham and Jasper, the latter his home town; 20 were located in the South, numbering from 20 to 159 units each, generally with an average of 2 to 5 acres per homestead.[120]

More directly relevant to farm distress was the Federal Emergency Relief Administration's (FERA) rural rehabilitation program, which ultimately evolved into the largest New Deal effort to cope with rural poverty. It originated in the activities of Colonel Lawrence Westbrook, engineer, agriculturist, politician, and Texas director of the FERA. In January, 1934, Westbrook undertook permanent rehabilitation of a hundred families by transferring them from the Houston relief rolls to the Woodlake community a hundred miles north where they lived in modest homes with subsistence plots and worked two co-operative farms. The following month Westbrook became head of the FERA Division of Rural Rehabilitation and Stranded Populations. Most of its funds went into distress loans and grants enabling farmers to keep off relief rolls. However, it undertook twenty-eight rural communities, exactly half of them in the South. Some resembled the subsistence homesteads, but most were farming communities, including the largest of all New Deal communities, the Dyess Colony near Wilson, Arkansas, with ultimately 275 units, and

<hr>

[119] Conkin, *Tomorrow a New World*, 87–88.

[120] *Ibid.*, 93–130, 332–34; Paul W. Wager, *One Foot on the Soil: A Study of Subsistence Homesteads in Alabama* (University, Ala., 1945), 47, 51. See also Russell Lord and Paul H. Johnstone (eds.), *A Place on Earth: A Critical Appraisal of Subsistence Homesteads* (Washington, 1942).

Pine Mountain Valley, near Warm Springs, Georgia, an especial favorite of President Roosevelt.[121]

The mushroom growth of such programs led to a regroupment into Rexford G. Tugwell's Resettlement Administration (RA), established by Executive Order of April 30, 1935. The unified agency took on a threefold responsibility: rural rehabilitation, land use planning and the retirement of submarginal lands, and rural and suburban resettlement communities.[122] The RA completed most of the communities, ninety-nine in all, of which sixty-one were in the Southern states. In some cases, but not typically, the communities experimented with collective farming that strongly resembled (depending upon who described it) either Soviet collectives or the larger Southern wage-hand plantations with co-operative associations substituting for landlords.[123] But the communities totally failed to shake the individualism of rural Southerners. "I believe a man could stay around here for five or six years," a resident of one confided to Will Alexander, "and save enough money to go out and buy him a little hill farm all his own." [124]

Through some magnetic attraction the community experiments seemed to hold the greatest fascination for both critics and defenders of the RA, yet they remained among the least important of its responsibilities. Far more effort was made to salvage farmers by rehabilitation loans and grants than to settle them in communities.[125] The aid went for supplies, equipment, tools, and debt adjustment to keep farm families off relief. It was not designed to aid tenants and laborers in the purchase of land, but gradually the forces gathered behind that one ultimate remedy, which fitted so

[121] Conkin, *Tomorrow a New World*, 131–42; James G. Maddox, "The Farm Security Administration" (Ph.D. dissertation, Harvard University, 1950), 8–14.

[122] Maddox, "Farm Security Administration," 29–30; Resettlement Administration, *Resettlement Administration Program*, Senate Document 213, 74 Cong., 2 Sess. (Washington, 1936), 2.

[123] Conkin, *Tomorrow a New World*, 143–82.

[124] Quoted in Dykeman and Stokely, *Seeds of Southern Change*, 220.

[125] Resettlement Administration, *Resettlement Administration Program*, 11. Net encumbrances to April 15, 1936, were $77,403,814 for rural rehabilitation, $47,400,809 for land use, $22,143,520 for resettlement communities, and $26,143,689 for administration. In total funds available communities somewhat exceeded land use but not rehabilitation.

well the folklore of rural virtue. "Would you favor government loans . . . to enable farm tenants to buy the farms they now rent?" Gallup pollsters inquired late in 1936; 83 per cent of the respondents answered in the affirmative and an even greater proportion in every Southern state except Virginia and North Carolina (81 per cent each) —Georgia and Alabama were 91 per cent favorable.[126]

In 1935 Senator Bankhead introduced a bill to authorize a $1,000,000,000 Federal corporation for tenant purchase loans. "The Bankhead tenant share cropper bill is not only one of the most constructive bills that has been before Congress this session," Mississippi's Senator Bilbo wired the President, "but with it we can drive Huey Long out of the South." [127] It passed the Senate but died in the House agriculture committee. In 1936 the President appointed a Special Committee on Farm Tenancy, chaired by Secretary Wallace. Its report early in 1937 outlined the evidences of rural poverty. "We find the unwholesome spectacle of men, women, and children . . . moving from farm to farm each year," the committee declared"; . . . rural children caught in this current . . . find their schooling periodically interrupted, if not made impossible; they suffer from mental as well as economic insecurity." [128] The committee recommended a new Farm Security Administration as successor to the RA with a program expanded to include purchase and sale of land to tenants on easy terms; the main goal, the group urged, should be the privately owned family farm. However, W. L. Blackstone, representing the STFU, challenged the "small homestead provision" as "an economic anachronism, foredoomed to failure." A more realistic remedy, he urged in a dissenting statement, would be "cooperative effort under enlightened Federal supervision." [129] But the yeoman tradition was too deeply rooted.

Senator Bankhead introduced a new bill embodying the committee's recommendation for a tenant purchase corporation, but Marvin Jones preferred outright land purchase loans without

[126] Birmingham *News*, December 13, 1936.
[127] Theodore G. Bilbo to Franklin D. Roosevelt, August 18, 1935, in OF 1403, Roosevelt Library.
[128] President's Special Committee on Farm Tenancy, *Farm Tenancy*, 6–7.
[129] *Ibid.*, 10–27.

governmental supervision. Eventually a conference committee reconciled the viewpoints and the Bankhead-Jones Farm Tenant Act of July, 1937, provided for purchase loans repayable over forty years at 3 per cent but embodied the Senate principle of supervision and a five-year prohibition against sale. The law authorized $10,000,000 for purchases the first year, $25,000,000 the second, and $50,000,000 thereafter.[130] On September 1, 1937, Secretary Wallace changed the RA to the Farm Security Administration (FSA) and endowed the agency with the responsibility for the new program. Headed by the dean of Southern liberals, Will Alexander, who had succeeded Tugwell at the end of 1936, the FSA continued the fight against rural poverty. Misconceptions pursued it as they had the RA. The impression carried over that resettlement communities were its principal activity, while in other quarters responsibility for administering the Bankhead-Jones Act left the impression that it was mainly concerned with tenant purchase loans; and Steinbeck's *Grapes of Wrath* left an exaggerated impression of extensive migratory labor camps.[131] The FSA undertook all these and a number of other activities, but the less spectacular and less understood program of rural rehabilitation remained its chief preoccupation.[132]

The core of the program was the rehabilitation loan of livestock, capital, equipment, supplies, and family necessities. FSA sought to add the magic ingredient of planning and supervision. "We felt that the guidance and adult education of these people were essential to everything that was done," Will Alexander later said. "Ultimately, we thought, there ought to be a large program of government credit to enable the best tenants to become owners. . . . Our idea was about as simple at that." [133] Often the supervisors worked against frustrating odds. Their job was to salvage human failures; they advised unsuccessful farmers who seldom saw a county agent, extended credit to those who could not qualify for other loans, and extended a variety of helps: a volun-

---

[130] Conkin, *Tomorrow a New World*, 183–84. "Reminiscences of Will W. Alexander," 586–96, discusses the various sources of support for the plan.

[131] Steinbeck's camps were in California, but a large number also were located in Florida.

[132] Maddox, "Farm Security Administration," 86.

[133] Dykeman and Stokely, *Seeds of Southern Change*, 213.

tary debt adjustment service, a program for written contracts and better arrangements with landlords, encouragement to the formation of co-operatives, and a health and sanitation service which formed medical care co-operatives with the assistance of country doctors.

Most of the program focused on the South, where the problems were most difficult. Alexander's chief lieutenants were two Southerners: Calvin B. ("Beanie") Baldwin of Virginia, who succeeded him in 1940, and R. W. ("Pete") Hudgens of South Carolina. More than half the rehabilitation loans went to Southern farmers: 505,124, or 56.6 per cent of the total number, comprising $456,-472,625, or 47.1 per cent of the total amount.[134] An even larger proportion of the tenant purchase loans went to the South: 30,809, or 69.5 per cent, at an average of about $5,400 each.[135] The purchase loans were scattered across the region, but they were concentrated in the plantation areas of northeastern Arkansas, the Mississippi Delta, and northern Alabama. The South, James G. Maddox, an FSA official and later its historian, wrote, "probably felt the impact of the whole FSA effort more than any other area of the country." [136]

But in the grand strategy of agricultural change the FSA was only a minor factor, overwhelmed by problems beyond its resources. It was, in the words of Grant McConnell, "the residual legatee of nearly every human problem of rural life that was not solved by increasing the prices of a few 'basic' commodities." [137] Its constituency was mostly unorganized and politically impotent. It was eyed with suspicion and hostility by the agricultural establishment: the Department of Agriculture, the Extension Service, the land-grant colleges, the Farm Bureau. They "had the attitude that the medicine man in Africa would have toward someone who came in and tried to give penicillin for boils," Alexander said.[138] But FSA's goal of the family farm was already an anachronism. Its chief function in the end was to provide relief, to tide over destitute farmers through the persistent Depression. During World War II it became a casualty of conservative reaction.

[134] Computed from Maddox, "Farm Security Administration," 175–76.
[135] *Ibid.*, 424.   [136] *Ibid.*, 179.
[137] McConnell, *Decline of Agrarian Democracy*, 93.
[138] "Reminiscences of Will W. Alexander," 547.

Effective power in farm politics gravitated to the American Farm Bureau Federation. In 1931, when Edward A. O'Neal just became president, the alliance of cotton and corn rested more upon the hope than the reality of strength in the South. Southern membership, located chiefly in Alabama and Tennessee, slid from a peak of 25,476 in 1930 to 7,771 in 1933, while national strength slipped from 321,196 to 163,246.[139] But at that point O'Neal took the initiative in mobilizing support for the New Deal programs and, what was more important, reaped an organizational windfall from the cotton program. The necessity for using the Extension Service to put the AAA into the field led to a reliance upon local farm bureaus, which were closely associated with county agents, to organize committees and marshal support. In unorganized areas, county agents recruited committeemen into the Farm Bureau. An inevitable confusion between the Farm Bureau and the AAA arose in many farmers' minds; some believed that they could not get benefit checks unless they joined.[140]

In 1935 Farm Bureau strength in the South reached 29,705— about a tenth of total membership, half of which was located in Alabama. In 1936 O'Neal launched a membership drive throughout the South with full co-operation from the Extension Service, which granted some of its agents leaves of absence to serve as organizers.[141] In 1938 the national convention was held at New Orleans "in order to cement more closely the working alliance between the Midwest and the South." [142] By 1940 the Southern membership of 113,031 constituted more than a fourth of the total, and agriculture's "working alliance" had a solid if not a mass base in the cotton and tobacco belts.[143]

The situation was a compound of ironies. An alliance of the South and West, promoted by generations of agrarian mavericks,

[139] Tontz, "Membership of General Farmers' Organizations, United States, 1874–1960," loc. cit., 156. See also Ralph Russell, "Membership of the American Farm Bureau Federation, 1926–1935," in Rural Sociology, II (1937), 30–31.

[140] Saloutos, "Edward A. O'Neal," loc. cit., 358; Baker, County Agent, 75–76, 141–42; McConnell, Decline of Agrarian Democracy, 73–76; Wesley McCune, The Farm Bloc (Garden City, N.Y., 1943), 190–91.

[141] Campbell, Farm Bureau and the New Deal, 88–102; McConnell, Decline of Agrarian Democracy, 76–77; Richardson, Texas: Lone Star State, 378.

[142] Edward A. O'Neal to Franklin D. Roosevelt, October 6, 1938, in PPF 1011, Roosevelt Library.

[143] McConnell, Decline of Agrarian Democracy, 185.

achieved a degree of stability and status through the Farm Bureau, which soon assumed a conservative stance. "I've seen too much rugged individualism," O'Neal said in 1934; he welcomed "co-operation instead of competition . . . mutual welfare instead of cut-throat practices . . . a sense of fairness and fair play instead of harmful and reactionary practices." [144] But the farm program was the product of the first New Deal of stabilization and recovery, not the second New Deal of reform and social democracy. The Farm Bureau's orientation toward landlords (albeit most of them small farmers) led it eventually into opposition to New Deal programs for farm and urban labor.

Meanwhile, the Farmers' Union made a belated and forlorn re-entry into Alabama where, reorganized in 1934, it comprised a dissonant mixture of small farmers, tenants, and laborers, both white and Negro, in the Gulf, Wiregrass, and northern areas. In 1937 it made an agreement with the Share Croppers' Union whereby it absorbed farm owners from that organization while the tenants and laborers went into another group soon absorbed by the UCAPAWA. By 1940 the Farmers Union survived only among the small farmers of Baldwin County and near a few industrial centers where it had the support of organized labor. Activity in Louisiana, begun in 1936, led to a similar short-lived experience. The UCAPAWA, short on resources, soon abandoned the fields to concentrate on processing workers in the towns. No group, it turned out, had the durability or influence to offer an alternative to what the *Louisiana Union Farmer* called the "company union" headed by "Ed O'Neal, big Alabama cotton planter." [145]

A larger revolution than that in farm politics emerged from the rural travail of the 1930's. The "bizarre incident" of the 1933 plow-up marked " a sharp cleavage in cotton history," Thomas D. Clark has written. "Depression closed the old style ledger on the

---

[144] Kansas City *Times*, March 7, 1934, in Scrapbook, 1934–1938, O'Neal Papers; Edward A. O'Neal, "The New Agricultural Philosophy," radio address over the National Farm and Home Hour, National Broadcasting Company, October 12, 1935, enclosed with S. G. Rubinow to Marvin McIntyre, October 18, 1935, OF 1350, Roosevelt Library.

[145] *Louisiana Union Farmer* (New Orleans), III (November, 1939), 1, 4: *Southern Farm Leader*, I (July, 1936), 4; Jamieson, *Labor Unionism in American Agriculture*, 290–92, 322–23; Stone, "Agrarian Conflict in Alabama," 516–22.

industry. A phase of history dating back to Whitney's invention of the gin was ended." [146] The rising tide of foreign production and the growing competition of paper, rayon, and other synthetics eroded the foundations of the Cotton Kingdom. In 1938 Oscar Johnston led representatives of the industry in establishing at Memphis the National Cotton Council, designed chiefly to salvage their markets by aggressive publicity and searches for new uses and new outlets.[147] But no such counter-revolution could ever again restore King Cotton to his toppled throne.

At the same time controls released Southern farmers from their old compulsion to grow cotton; harvested acreage in the South declined from 44,768,000 in 1929 to 22,800,000 in 1939. Tobacco acreage held its own, only to decline in the 1940's. Corn acreage declined, too, although it remained in 1939 greater than that of any other single crop. Other feed and food crops gained significantly. Workstock retreated before the encroachments of the tractor, but cash receipts from cattle, dairy products, hogs, and poultry rose from 27.6 per cent of total farm marketing receipts in 1929 to 36.7 per cent in 1939. Cotton remained the chief cash crop but declined in relative position from 46 per cent of cash receipts in 1929 to 29.2 per cent in 1939 and 21 in 1946, while increases were registered by tobacco, corn, peanuts, soybeans, truck crops, rice, sugar, forest products, citrus fruits, peaches, and some other crops.[148] There is evidence, moreover, that farmers were not only diversifying into new commercial specialties but realizing a greater potential for living at home. By 1939 the Southeast led all other regions in the proportion of farms with hogs and pigs (70.3 per cent), poultry (88.2), and garden vegetables for household use (about 83); it lagged, however, in the proportion with milk cows (71.9 against a national average of 76) and led in its dependence upon commercial fertilizer (over 60 per cent of the farmers).[149]

---

[146] Thomas D. Clark, *The Emerging South* (New York, 1961), 51.

[147] *Proceedings of the Committee on Organization, National Cotton Council of America, Hotel Peabody, Memphis, Tennessee, November 21, 1938* (n.p., n.d.); *The Record of the National Cotton Council of America* (Memphis, 1955).

[148] Hoover and Ratchford, *Economic Resources and Policies of the South*, 63, 95, 101, 103, presents the picture in some statistical detail. See also John Leonard Fulmer, *Agricultural Progress in the Cotton Belt since 1920* (Chapel Hill, 1950).

[149] Vance, *All These People*, 189–95.

Mechanization paralleled diversification; tractors facilitated the development of new crops such as grains, wheat, and soybeans, as well as pasturage. In ten cotton states the number of tractors nearly quadrupled in the 1920's, from 29,100 to 111,900; in the 1930's they doubled again to 223,300; and despite wartime shortages nearly doubled again by 1945, to 407,400 or 16.8 per cent of all farm tractors in the United States. The general trend was rapid development on the Oklahoma and Texas plains and gradual eastward movement, but the introduction of the smaller Farmall tractor about 1925 encouraged greater use on the small farms and hilly lands of the Southeast. After 1925 the rate of increase was above the national average, but that reflected a later start in mechanization and left a continued lag behind national ratios of tractors to land and workers.[150]

The traditional staples, cotton and tobacco, and to a lesser degree corn, resisted mechanization in cultivation and harvesting. The abundance of cheap labor tended to inhibit mechanical processes even in breaking land, preparing seed beds, harrowing, or planting. However, the 1930's brought the mechanization of cotton within the range of technical possibility. The use of rotary hoes and sweep blades for cultivation was supplemented late in the decade by the flame cultivator.[151] Far more important was the cotton picker developed by the Rust brothers, John D. and Mack. A 1935 magazine article brought the machine and its sociological implications sharply to public attention.[152] In 1931 a Rust spindle picker harvested one bale of cotton in a day; in 1933, five. Newspapers and journals echoed with forebodings of labor displacement that would convulse the cotton belt. The Rust brothers themselves were troubled by the paradox of technological unemployment. The imminent emancipation of millions from backbreaking toil meant "in the share-cropped country, that 75 percent of the labor population would be thrown out of employment," John said. "We

[150] Street, *New Revolution in the Cotton Economy*, 157–63. The ten cotton states excluded Kentucky, Virginia, and Florida.
[151] *Ibid.*, 139–41.
[152] Oliver Carlson, "The Revolution in Cotton," in *American Mercury*, XXXIV (1935), 129–36: condensed and reprinted in *Reader's Digest* (Pleasantville, N.Y.), XXVI (March, 1935), 13–16. For several years limited production took place in a development shop at Memphis.

are not willing that this should happen." [153] First they tried to adapt the machine to smaller farmers, then to sell it under restrictions to guarantee favorable working conditions, and finally to make it available first in co-operative communities. In 1937 they undertook to channel part of the profits into a foundation to assist displaced farmers and encourage co-operative farming.[154]

Technological defects, however, slowed development of the machine, and in the early 1940's the Rust brothers liquidated their Memphis operations. In 1942 the International Harvester Company announced its readiness to begin commercial production of a spindle picker, and in 1944 the Allis-Chalmers Company secured rights under the Rust patents. Other firms were ready soon after the war. Meanwhile, still other manufacturers had developed cotton strippers which removed the cotton, burr and all, and became practical with improvements in ginning and cleaning machinery. Still, costs, difficult terrains, and the continued presence of a large labor supply after World War II slowed the spread of machinery. In 1946 the National Cotton Council estimated that not more than 1,802 strippers and 107 spindle pickers were available for the harvest, and in 1953 only 18,587 strippers and 15,550 pickers. As late as 1955 less than a fourth of the cotton was harvested mechanically, mostly in the Mid-South and farther west, only 2 per cent in the Southeast.[155]

To the Cassandras of the late 1930's it was not yet apparent that the greatest crisis of agricultural transition was already passing. The shock of later changes would be cushioned by the manpower needs of World War II and the economic growth that followed. Tenancy had reached its peak somewhere between 1930 and 1935. In the next five years various forces conspired to reduce the numbers from 1,831,475 to 1,449,293 and the total number of

[153] Quoted in *Time*, XXVII (March 23, 1936), 60.

[154] John Rust, "The Origin and Development of the Cotton Picker," in *West Tennessee Historical Society Papers* (Memphis), VII (1953), 38–56; Gilbert C. Fite, "Recent Progress in the Mechanization of Cotton Production in the United States," in *Agricultural History*, XXIV (1950), 19–20; Street, *New Revolution in the Cotton Economy*, 126–28.

[155] Street, *New Revolution in the Cotton Economy*, 115, 133, 167. Mid-South here means Arkansas, Louisiana, Mississippi, Missouri, and Tennessee. The most highly mechanized harvest was in California (67 per cent).

farm operators from 3,421,923 to 3,007,170.[156] Continuing acre-age reductions and failures in staple crops displaced some; higher yields and the shift to less labor-intensive crops, others. Many sank to the status of wage laborers, whose numbers in eleven South-eastern states rose from 573,271 to 842,525 in the second half of the decade.[157] Many others were drained off by relief projects, industry, and out-migration. Most of the change represented a renewed exodus of Negroes; the number of white farm operators actually increased. "Mechanization," Oscar Johnston said in 1947, "is not the cause, but the result of economic change in the area." [158] Until 1945, at least, the machine tended to follow rather than precede the flight from the land.[159]

[156] *Statistical Abstract of the United States*, 1941, p. 682.
[157] Vance, *All These People*, 216.
[158] Oscar Johnston, "Will the Machine Ruin the South?" in *Saturday Evening Post*, CCXIX (May 31, 1947) , 37.
[159] Fite, "Recent Mechanization of Cotton Production in the United States," *loc. cit.*, 28.

CHAPTER XIII

DILEMMAS OF A COLONIAL ECONOMY

THE AAA posed dilemmas of crop controls and export trade, of cash crops and rural poverty. The National Industrial Recovery Act posed other dilemmas of the regional economy. Its purposes, briefly stated, were twofold: to stabilize business by codes of "fair" competitive practice, and to get more purchasing power into the markets by assuring employment, defining labor standards, and raising wages. Southern businessmen at first joined in the national enthusiasm for the effort. Already many of them had entered voluntary arrangements to restrain "cut-throat" competition. Stabilization by trade associations like the Cotton Textile Institute or the Southern Pine Association promised manifest advantages of more predictable costs, prices, and markets, as well as more stable employment and wages.

Yet the doctrine of stabilization, at least as it appeared in the Depression years, was largely the restrictive doctrine of a mature economy that had reached substantially all its frontiers of expansion. Both in theory and practice it ran headlong into conflict with the creed of the New South, the doctrine of industrial growth that was written in the prophets. The Tennessee Coal and Iron Company offered a case in point. Its acquisition by United States Steel in 1907 had afforded stability and orderly development, but the over-all considerations of management obstructed the growth that Birmingham might have achieved under competitive conditions. Voluntary co-operation posed a similar danger. One South Carolina textile man, for example, withdrew from the Cotton Textile Institute in 1929 precisely because it held an umbrella

433

over all the mills. Night operations in the South hurt New England, "and for this I am not sorry," he confessed. "If we should discontinue night operations in South Carolina, overproduction would immediately stop, but as a consequence, New England would start up all of her idle spindles." [1] In Oklahoma an oilman conveyed the point more brusquely in a protest against restraints in 1931. If a poor cotton farmer should find oil under his land, E. W. Marland wrote, "CALL OUT THE MILITIA! He must not be permitted to sell it. He will ruin the vested interests of the petroleum industry. . . . What matters if he wants to produce his oil this year? Buy the old woman a new dress . . . give the old mule a full feed just once? No, he must not do it." [2]

NRA labor standards created a parallel dilemma, but they too got a favorable reception at first. "Previously business recovery was looked for following a depression when industry was fortunate enough to make a profit, after which payrolls were increased," a writer noted in the *Manufacturers' Record*. "The process is reversed in the new plan because of the emergency of employing the idle and avoiding a desperate winter." [3] Yet higher standards soon collided with the low-wage philosophy of the New South. Any movement to raise Southern wages, the reasoning went, threatened the region's supreme competitive advantage, hampered industrial development, and therefore contributed to the very poverty it was supposed to relieve. This argument repeatedly arose against efforts to improve labor conditions: the NRA, relief, unionism, and wages and hours legislation. In each case Southern employers demanded, and usually got, a "favorable" wage differential.

Like the AAA the recovery act had many fathers, but the only significant Southern contribution was peripheral: Bankhead's subsistence homesteads. The measure was hastened into being when Senate passage of Hugo Black's thirty-hour bill evinced a mood of impatience at unemployment. The administration quickly submitted another bill that emerged on June 16, 1933, as the Na-

---

[1] A. F. McKissick to William Watts Ball, July 31, 1929, in Ball Papers.

[2] Quoted in Matthews, *Life and Death of an Oilman*, 210–11.

[3] Howard L. Clark, "United America," in *Manufacturers' Record*, CII (August, 1933), 14–17.

434

tional Industrial Recovery Act, the three major parts of which dealt with recovery, public works, and relief. The new chief of the National Recovery Administration, General Hugh S. Johnson, immediately turned to the existing trade associations for help in drafting the codes of fair practice.[4]

George A. Sloan of the Cotton Textile Institute quickly submitted a plan that became the basis for the cotton textile code, approved on July 9. It was "dear to my heart," Johnson wrote later. "It was Code No. 1. It came at a time when the whole of industry was wavering as to whether it would submit codes at all." [5] Its labor provisions were the heart of the code, an important feature of stabilization in an industry for which labor was the most important cost. Maximum hours went down from the 55–50 that the Institute had tried to impose to a standard 40-hour week. The minimum weekly wage of $12 in the South ($13 elsewhere) more than doubled earnings in some cases. And at Johnson's insistence the code eliminated the labor of children under sixteen. Announcement of that provision set off roars of applause in the code hearing room. It did "in a few minutes what neither law nor constitutional amendment had been able to do in forty years," Johnson said; it permitted "employers to do by agreement that which none of them could do separately and live in competition," the President noted.[6] "I believe that they are pleased that they have been driven to do what is sensible," a Charleston editor wrote.[7] The code also imposed restrictions on plant expansion, limited operations to not more than eighty hours per week, required reports on operations and production every four weeks, and included Section 7 (a) of the recovery act which guaranteed the right of collective bargaining.[8]

[4] Schlesinger, *Coming of the New Deal*, 87–102.

[5] Hugh S. Johnson, *The Blue Eagle from Egg to Earth* (Garden City, N.Y., 1935), 315.

[6] *Ibid.*, 233; Samuel I. Rosenman (comp.), *The Public Papers and Addresses of Franklin D. Roosevelt, with a Special Introduction and Explanatory Notes by President Roosevelt* (New York, 1938), II, 275. By September, 1933, twenty-two of the thirty codes concluded prohibited child labor. A. J. Nichol, "Child Labor Provisions in the Codes," in *South Atlantic Quarterly*, XXXIV (1934), 229.

[7] William Watts Ball to [D. C. Heyward], November 11, 1933, in Ball Papers.

[8] *A Handbook of NRA: Laws, Regulations, Codes* (Washington and New York, 1933), 97–103. Summaries of the code appear in Backman and Gainsbrugh, *Eco-*

The economic roller-coaster had conditioned textiles for acceptance. "The law of life," said one of the leading trade journals, "is
co-operation and not selfish cut-throat competition"; "as for our
industry," said the president of the American Cotton Manufacturers Association, "we want no slackers in its field." "We
heartily endorse the principles of the N.I.R.A.," his association
resolved.[9] Probably no industry in the South received its code
with more enthusiasm than textiles, yet none illustrated better the
regional dilemmas of stabilization. Immediately prior to the code,
average hourly wages in the North were 38.5 per cent above those
in the South, a difference reduced to 15.9 per cent in August,
1933.[10] The 80-hour limit on operations curtailed activity in the
South while New England mills expanded their production.[11]
One mill at Easley, South Carolina, reduced its total operating
hours from 128 in May to 80 in August. Its total payroll went up
from $10,131.40 to $11,889.40, but its working force dropped
from 1,399 to 1,036. "We have more unemployment in our
villages now than we have ever had before," its vice president
wrote. George A. Sloan, he suspected, was controlled by Eastern
influences bent upon curbing the growth of Southern industry.[12]

Business improved substantially during the early months of the
code when producers and buyers anticipated higher costs. But
when stocks began to accumulate again the code proved inadequate as a solution to the problem of overproduction. Before the
end of 1933 many leaders of the industry were seeking to limit
machines temporarily to sixty hours a week and workers to thirty.
The code authority effected this during December, but the threat

nomics of the Cotton Textile Industry, 217–18; and Leverett S. Lyon et al., The
National Recovery Administration: An Analysis and Appraisal, in Brookings Institution Institute of Economics Publications, No. 60 (Washington, 1935), 305–306.

[9] Cotton: Serving the Textile Industries (Dalton, Ga.), XCVII (June, 1933), 38;
American Cotton Manufacturers' Association, Proceedings of 38th Annual Conven-
tion . . . 1934, 40, 41, 52–55, 106, cited in Blicksilver, Cotton Manufacturing in the
Southeast, 119–20, 141; Charleston News and Courier, April 21, 1934.

[10] Michl, Textile Industries, 272.

[11] The hours each active loom was operated in New England increased 7 per cent
in the last half of 1933 over the first half. Blicksilver, Cotton Manufacturing in the
Southeast, 120.

[12] A. F. McKissick to William Watts Ball, September 25, 1933, and February 26,
1934, in Ball Papers.

of another curtailment in the spring of 1934 set off a wave of labor unrest that generated a major textile strike.[13] The honeymoon of Southern textile men with NRA was soon over. Higher wages, higher cotton prices, and processing taxes drove up costs, and the burden of restrictions and reports began to tell on the nerves of millmen. After working for nearly two months on machinery reports, Elliott White Springs wrote from South Carolina, "[my auditor] has developed spots before his eyes, and has gone to a sanitarium for a rest." His own temper was getting the better of a "formerly sweet disposition and time-tested patience," Springs asserted. "When I reach my home at night . . . my children dash frantically out of the home to hide in the barn." [14]

In May, 1935, when the Supreme Court struck down the NRA, there were few laments from textile men, but some apprehension of renewed chaos. Prodded by the Cotton Textile Institute, manufacturers representing a majority of the Southern spindles resolved to maintain the code's labor standards. Except in a few of the smaller and weaker mills, it turned out, the NRA had worked a permanent change in labor standards: the 40-hour week, the $12 minimum, and the elimination of child labor remained in effect.[15] "Mill managers in our area are rather proud of their record of compliance," a textile official remarked in 1938.[16] Another consequence of the NRA was the impetus that increased costs gave to efficiency and modernization. Expansion was restricted, but the NRA did permit the replacement of outmoded and worn-out machinery.[17]

Without the 80-hour limit on operations, the graveyard shift re-

---

[13] James Andrew Hodges, "The New Deal Labor Policy and the Southern Cotton Textile Industry, 1933–1941" (Ph.D. dissertation, Vanderbilt University, 1963), 201–202.

[14] Elliott White Springs to George A. Sloan, December, 20, 1933; Springs to Walter Gayle, May 30, 1934, both quoted in Elliott White Springs, *Clothes Make the Man* (n.p., 1949), 65, 70–71.

[15] Hodges, "New Deal Labor Policy and the Southern Cotton Textile Industry," 342–51.

[16] W. M. McLaurine, Secretary of the American Cotton Manufacturers' Association, in American Cotton Manufacturers' Association, *Proceedings of 42nd Annual Convention . . . 1938*, 27, quoted in Blicksilver, *Cotton Manufacturing in the Southeast*, 121.

[17] Blicksilver, *Cotton Manufacturing in the Southeast*, 122–24.

appeared in many mills, and Southern textiles soared to new records of production in time for the business recession of 1937, which sent the enterprise into a new decline. In 1939 the print-cloth group of the industry sought to reduce output voluntarily by 25 per cent, but the arrangement lasted only two months. The group encountered a lawsuit from an administration that had re-discovered the antitrust laws.[18] The NRA had established new standards of decency for labor, but it had not ended overproduction.

For oil, however, NRA was a major step toward regulated production. The oil code, formulated under the eye of Petroleum Administrator Harold L. Ickes, included provisions for stabilizing business practices, marketing, and competition, together with recommendations of quotas to state prorating agencies. Its labor standards required a 36-hour week (or 72 every two weeks) for field and plant operatives, 40 for clerical, and 48 for service-station workers, and minimum wages ranging from 45 cents (Southern) to 52 cents hourly and from $12 to $15 weekly in service stations.[19]

The most nettlesome problem was the flow of "hot oil," amounts in excess of the state allowables, which continued despite the strengthening of state laws from 1931 to 1933.[20] Under Section 9 (c) of the NIRA the shipment of hot oil in interstate commerce became a Federal offense, and Federal investigators became active in the last half of 1933. In 1934 a new policy of requiring state and Federal certificates of clearance before shipment was introduced. In June, 1934, a Texas state tender board began passing on tenders for crude oil and in October a Federal board, but in January, 1935, Section 9 (c) of the NIRA was declared unconstitutional. Within a few weeks, however, Congress passed the Connally Act which re-established the Federal Tender Board under provisions that obviated the objections of the court.[21]

[18] *Ibid.,* 121.

[19] The code and its operation are summarized in Watkins, *Oil: Stabilization or Conservation?,* 62–97. See also René de Visme Williamson, *The Politics of Planning in the Oil Industry under the Code* (New York, 1936).

[20] See Chapter XI. See also Louis Howe to Sam Rayburn, May 15, 1933, transmitting letter of Governor Miriam Ferguson on the problem, in OF 56-A, Roosevelt Library.

[21] The issue involved what the court called an excessive grant of discretionary authority to the President in the law. Panama Refining Co. *v.* Ryan, and American

Meanwhile, a movement developed for over-all Federal regulation, and a series of bills to that end appeared in Congress. Oilmen, however, began to look with more favor upon a growing movement for an interstate compact. The idea had been discussed for some years, but the effective initiative came from E. W. Marland of Oklahoma. Elected governor in 1934, Marland immediately sought negotiations with Governors James V. Allred of Texas and Alfred M. Landon of Kansas. "I'm governor of the state," he answered a critic who pointed out the inconsistency with his former defense of free enterprise. "I'm not an oilman any more." [22] After many vicissitudes, including a clash between Marland and Allred over the doctrines of economic versus physical waste as the basis for controls, the Interstate Compact to Conserve Oil and Gas was concluded at a conference in Dallas in February, 1935, ostensibly on the basis of Allred's principle of conservation to prevent physical waste. Ratified by Texas, Oklahoma, New Mexico, Kansas, Colorado, and Illinois, the "Treaty of Dallas" was approved by Congress and the President in August, 1935. By 1945 seventeen states had entered the agreement.[23]

The compact set up an interstate Oil Compact Commission to propose standard legislation and practices and to make recommendations on state allowables. Its findings were not mandatory, but its moral influence was bolstered by the prospect of Federal action if the arrangement failed. Despite the emphasis upon physical conservation, however, state proration laws were clearly administered with an eye to the market place.[24] Like Marland, independent producers gradually came to accept the advantages of that system over the chaos that gave them temporary advantages but ultimately threatened their destruction. "It used to be when I went to East Texas they would meet me with shotguns," General Ernest O. Thompson, who joined the Texas Railroad Commission

---

Petroleum Corp. *v.* Ryan, 293 U.S. 389 (1935) ; Warner, *Texas Oil and Gas,* 74–75; Watkins, *Oil: Stabilization or Conservation?,* 99–101.

[22] Mathews, *Life and Death of an Oilman,* 241–42.

[23] Blakely M. Murphy, "The Oil States Advisory Commission, A Predecessor of the Compact," in American Bar Association, *Conservation of Oil and Gas,* 545–55; and Murphy, "Formation of the Interstate Compact to Conserve Oil and Gas," *ibid.,* 556–70.

[24] Blakely M. Murphy, "The Interstate Compact to Conserve Oil and Gas: The Interstate Oil Compact Commission, 1935–1948," *ibid.,* 571–96.

in 1932, said years later. "Now they give a barbecue for me." [25]

In coal mining, too, high levels of operation had brought industrial disorder, market gluts, and low standards for workers. "No code in the history of the NRA," Lewis L. Lorwin asserted, "gave rise to more procedural crises, perplexities, and struggle than did the bituminous coal code." [26] Coal was the last major industry to agree on a code, approved September 18, 1933, and then only under threat of compulsion by the President. The internal fissures of the industry were reflected in an unusual administrative plan for five semiautonomous geographical divisions under the code authority. Efforts to stabilize prices foundered on regional rivalries and widespread violations.[27]

Efforts to raise labor standards ran up against the same problem. The original wage scale was based upon what came to be known as the Appalachian Agreement, negotiated by the United Mine Workers with operators in that field. It provided a minimum daily wage of $4.60 in the northern Appalachians and $4.20 in the southern, but only $3.40 in the Alabama division where the union had just begun to reorganize. Dissatisfaction with the differential contributed to a snowballing drive for union organization in Alabama, in which the union held out the hope of a $4.60 wage. The threat of a nationwide coal strike on April 1, 1934, hastened action; General Johnson reduced the work week to thirty-five hours and increased Appalachian wages to $5.00 and Alabama wages to $4.60, which nearly eliminated the differential. His action in turn provoked a fierce response from businessmen. "Sherman's march to the sea was no more destructive than the NRA is going to be on the South," warned Theodore Swann, Alabama chemical manufacturer. "Before it is over, we may have secession." [28] Many of the Alabama and Georgia owners closed their

---

[25] Quoted in Cater, "General and the Umbrella," *loc. cit.*, 11. The name of the Texas Railroad Commission was not changed after new responsibilities, including proration, were added.

[26] Lyon *et al.*, *National Recovery Administration*, 431.

[27] Parker, *Coal Industry*, 105–10, 125, 131–33. The main Southern fields were embraced in Divisions I (northern and southern Appalachians) and III (Alabama, southern Tennessee, and Georgia).

[28] Washington *Post*, April 19, 1934, quoted in Mitchell and Cayton, *Black Workers and the New Unions*, 99n. Advertisements in the Birmingham papers declared

mines, sought an injunction against Johnson's order, and finally got an NRA directive holding the minimum at $3.80 while raising it to $5.00 in the northern Appalachians and $4.60 in the southern. But the directive was almost immediately nullified by the success of thirty-four Kentucky operators in getting an injunction against it that still stood until the NRA ended in 1935.[29]

After the NRA fell, Congress hastened into being the Guffey-Snyder Coal Conservation Act of 1935 establishing for coal alone what came to be called a "Little NRA." But, it too fell before the Supreme Court in 1936 and never became operative. The Guffey-Vinson Coal Conservation Act of 1937 established a Bituminous Coal Commission which enforced compliance with minimum prices and certain fair marketing rules, but that act expired in 1943.[30] Yet, through all the struggle, NRA had established a new vision of labor standards. The thirty-five hour week remained and child labor disappeared. The work of stabilizing labor requirements was continued thereafter by the United Mine Workers, who had recruited 95 per cent of the country's miners in 1935 and conquered even "Bloody Harlan" in 1938.[31]

Southern lumbering had developed a remarkably dense thicket of competition, with its thousands of peckerwood mills scattered through the Southern woods. For years trade associations of pine and hardwood producers had worked toward standard grades and "open competition" through the dissemination of statistics, so the concept of stabilization, at least, was not absent. Indeed, the Southern Pine Association afforded one ready-made agency for administration of the code in a field covering seventeen states.[32] On August 25–26, 1933, more than six hundred pine producers gathered in New Orleans at sessions "marked by a display of

---

Southern industries were to be "economically lynched" by Northern interests. *Ibid.*, 322.

[29] Lyon *et al.*, *National Recovery Administration*, 432–33; Charles Frederick Roos, NRA Economic Planning, in Cowles Commission for Research in Economics Monograph No. 2 (Bloomington, Ind., 1937), 216–18.

[30] Parker, *Coal Industry*, 143–49.

[31] *Ibid.*, 74–75.

[32] Including Delaware, Maryland, Missouri, and West Virginia in addition to the thirteen-state South. The following description is drawn from James Boyd, "Southern Pine Association History," in Drawer 77, Southern Pine Association Papers.

enthusiasm" to pledge unanimously their support for the lumber code, which included standards like those in which the trade associations had pioneered: inspection and grading, statistics, uniform terms of sale, allocations of production, and various requirements of ethical practices. Moreover it fixed wages in the Southern forests at a minimum of twenty-four cents and the work-week at forty hours.

New Deal projects, as well as a general upswing in 1933, opened new markets for the sawmills. Within nine months after the code became effective some three thousand mills had resumed operations after closing in the Depression, even though the output had never declined to the level of consumption. Renewed overproduction and a flood of demands for allocation followed. After the first flurry of enthusiasm, disillusionment gradually settled upon the lumbermen. At an SPA meeting in the spring of 1935 Chairman Charles Green of the Southern Pine Division's Steering Committee summarized the growing objections: excessive wage and hour standards; ineffective cost protection; excessive allocations; demands that mills that had tried to take care of their communities give up allocations to mills that had shut down or to newcomers; and poor enforcement. If the government were to continue "a policy of lax enforcement," the SPA's general counsel suggested, ". . . then we had better get rid of the whole thing." The group so resolved, a month before the NRA fell. "Prohibition . . . and then the Lumber Code," the Association's bulletin declared, "have demonstrated that regulations governing hundreds of daily transactions of thousands of people scattered throughout the country are impossible of enforcement." [33] The AAA may have demonstrated the contrary, but the rout of the NRA in Southern lumber was almost complete. [34]

As recovery began to seep back, eroding the cement of fear, the daily annoyances of code enforcement inspired a growing hostility. Charges mounted that the larger corporations dominated the code

[33] "Robinson-Patman Price Discrimination Act," Supplement to *Southern Pine Bulletin*, I (September, 1936), in Southern Pine Association Papers.

[34] See W. Averell Harriman to Franklin D. Roosevelt, February 16, 1938, in OF 2730, Roosevelt Library. Harriman stated his belief that all members of the NRA board considered the lumber code a failure in the South.

authorities, that allocations froze the existing industrial structure, that price-fixing robbed small producers of chances for competition. In the South the complaints assumed a sectional tone. Donald Comer, Alabama textile man, made a computation that showed only 181 Southerners among 2,033 industrial leaders on 210 code authorities. Among the major authorities only that for cotton textiles had a majority of Southerners.[35] "You know," George Fort Milton wrote the secretary of commerce in the fall of 1934, "that a great many of our Southern industrialists suspect . . . that much of the glee about NRA is because it is going to permit . . . obsolete units of the north and east to better themselves at the expense of the South." [36] No region stood "to gain more than the Gulf Southwest in any sound policy which has for its aim the expansion of industry based upon fair competition," the *Texas Business Review* remarked. "Conversely no region would stand to suffer greater loss if a policy of permanent restriction were to be adopted." [37]

The root of the trouble, however, was in the labor standards. "Now, we are referred to in other parts of the country as the low-wage section," former NAM President John E. Edgerton said. "As a matter of fact the N. R. A. was devised, to a very large extent, to reform the South . . . General Johnson practically told me that when he said, 'We don't propose to allow the Negro labor of the South to debase the living standards of the rest of the country.' " [38] Actually, a clause in the recovery act permitted differentials "according to the locality of employment" and in about half the codes businessmen included variant wage minimums according to geographical or population differences.[39] Among the forty-six

[35] Rupert B. Vance, "Planning the Southern Economy," in *Southwest Review*, XX (1934–1935) , 122.

[36] George Fort Milton to Daniel C. Roper, September 13, 1934, in Milton Papers.

[37] *Texas Business Review*, June 29, 1934, quoted in Patenaude, "New Deal and Texas," 291.

[38] "Address of J. E. Edgerton, President, Southern States Industrial Council, at annual meeting of the Southern Pine Association, March, 1937," in Southern Pine Association Papers.

[39] Lyon *et al.*, *National Recovery Administration*, 326; there were 261 out of 515 codes with differentials. That number covered some four fifths of the employees under codes.

codes covering "manufacturing products," eleven set lower minimums for the South.[40] The President expressed qualified acceptance of the practice in a statement on the coal agreement of 1934: "It is not the purpose of the Administration, by sudden or explosive change, to impair Southern industry by refusing to recognize traditional differentials. On the other hand, no region has any right, by depressing its labor, wages, and hours, to invade with its cheaper produce an area of higher wages and hours and thus to impose its lower standards on an area of higher standards." [41] Despite the differentials, code wages had a decided impact on the South, generally lifting rates by 50 to 100 per cent, according to the *Manufacturers' Record,* and reducing the gap to something like the $12–13 differential set in the textile code. In one case, South Carolina lumbering, wages rose (theoretically, at least) 70 per cent while in some of the Western states they gained only 5 per cent.[42]

Such increases generated an organized opposition. In December, 1933, John E. Edgerton took the lead in founding the Southern States Industrial Council (SSIC) "to protect the South against discrimination"—that is, against higher wages. The SSIC was "a child of the N.R.A.," Edgerton told a senate committee. "It sprang into . . . spontaneous existence, immediately after the codes began to become operative" to agitate for wider differentials.[43] Low pay, he said elsewhere, would "preserve labor's racial purity, that is foreign labor will not be attracted to the Southland." [44] The code scales, the *Manufacturers' Record* declared, would "hamper present manufacturing activity, industrial development and the fullest utilization of Southern resources in the future."

[40] *Ibid.,* 329. In only two codes were the definitions of the "South" identical. The rationale offered may be illustrated by the provision in the iron and steel code attributing geographical differentials to "differences in living costs and general economic conditions and the ability adequately to man the industries in the respective localities." *Handbook of NRA,* 131.

[41] Quoted in Lyon *et al., National Recovery Administration,* 328n.

[42] "Wage Discrimination," in *Manufacturers' Record,* CIII (January, 1934), 13; Roos, *NRA Economic Planning,* 164.

[43] Quoted in John Dean Minton, "The New Deal in Tennessee, 1932–1938" (Ph.D. dissertation, Vanderbilt University, 1959) , 135–36.

[44] Quoted in Hood, "Some Basic Factors affecting Southern Labor Standards," *loc. cit.,* 57.

Businessmen whose comment the magazine sought agreed. "I do not believe that any section has responded more enthusiastically to the requirements of the Industrial Recovery Act than has the South," an Augusta industrialist wrote, "nor paid more heavily for the response." The sole dissent came from a Memphis lumberman who opposed the differential because he believed the South needed better wages and more purchasing power.[45]

Edgerton urged a restoration of pre-code differentials. But, according to an NRA economist who endorsed his viewpoint, he secured only limited support from Southern industrialists. Opposition to the code standards remained muted, partly because recovery made higher wages possible and partly because evasions and outright violations of standards were easy.[46] Men who would have scorned to take advantage of their competitors in any illegal or underhanded way, fudged on wages and hours of their employees in the calm conviction that it was only a way of redressing a wrong against themselves," W. J. Cash noted. He claimed personal knowledge of cotton and hosiery mills that maintained the fifty-five hour week and wages as low as three dollars below the minimum.[47]

By 1935 the NRA had gained more critics than friends in Southern business. Among representative Southern manufacturers polled late in 1934 more than three fourths wanted the NRA either abolished (43.4 per cent) or modified (34.2 per cent). Only 22.4 per cent expressed satisfaction. The most common complaint was the inflexibility of wage and hour standards, although a good majority accepted the principle of maximum hours (67.1 per cent) and minimum wages (70.2 per cent). Other

---

[45] "Wage Discrimination," *loc. cit.*, 13, 53, quoting F. W. Dugan of the Dugan Lumber Company, Memphis, and W. A. Riggsbee of the Lombard Iron Works and Supply Company, Augusta. See also "The Condition of Southern Manufacturing under N.R.A.," in *Manufacturers' Record*, CIII (March, 1934), 21, 56.

[46] Roos, *NRA Economic Planning*, 164–65, 165n. For an over-all analysis of differentials see also *ibid.*, 165–72.

[47] Cash, *Mind of the South*, 385. Some retail enterprises developed the ingenious device of putting out their employees as independent peddlers or contractors, not subject to the codes. The manager of the Southern Ice and Utilities Company, Denison, Texas, described practices of this sort in William J. Rylee to Sam Rayburn, February 27, 1935, in Rayburn Library. See also, on noncompliance, Cayton and Mitchell, *Black Workers and the New Unions*, 341.

objections included Eastern domination of code authorities, the complexity of the codes, poor administration, and price-fixing. Provisions for ethical trade practices were generally approved.[48]

When the NRA died in May, 1935, struck down by the "sick chicken" suit in New York, few paused to mourn. The experiment was generally put down as a failure, but it left a permanent mark on the South. The labor provisions of the codes, with dramatic suddenness, established new standards from which it was difficult to retreat altogether, and encouraged modernization of machinery and methods as a means of meeting the new costs. Moreover, the recognition of collective bargaining in Section 7 (a) spurred the rise of the labor movement in the South. The codes advanced tendencies toward stabilization and rationalization that were becoming the standard practice of the business community at large and that, despite misgivings about their effect upon industrial growth, would be further promoted by trade associations and outright integration.

The eclectic philosophy of the New Deal embraced more than the restrictive approaches of the NRA. The creation of the Tennessee Valley Authority was a salient contrast. Among the measures of the First Hundred Days, mostly defensive efforts to salvage the wreckage of depression, TVA became a massive monument of economic growth and development, albeit not cast in the New South mold of industry-hunting. The TVA idea was the product neither of a single imagination nor of a doctrinaire concept, but of discussion and controversy that had evolved for years. In 1916, when the government authorized power and nitrate plants at Muscle Shoals, national defense was the justification. New objectives unfolded in succession: fertilizers, industrial development, and Senator George W. Norris' concept of cheap public power as a "yardstick" to measure private utilities. Waterpower development pointed inevitably to problems of navigation, of controlling stream flow for both power and flood control, and in turn to conservation of soils and forests. The chain of connections led ultimately to a concept of over-all planning for an entire

[48] "Southern Manufacturers Urge Changes in NRA," in *Manufacturers' Record*, CIV (January, 1935) , 23. It should be noticed that the survey was conducted by the Southern States Industrial Council.

watershed, a total drainage area of 40,569 square miles overlapping seven states, four-fifths the size of England.[49]

"Muscle Shoals gives us the opportunity . . . of setting an example of planning, not just for ourselves but for generations to come, tying in industry and agriculture and forestry and flood prevention, tying them all into a unified whole over a distance of a thousand miles," Franklin D. Roosevelt declared at Montgomery on January 21, 1933, after visiting the site with Senator Norris.[50] On April 10, 1933, Roosevelt asked Congress to create the TVA as a multipurpose public corporation; on May 18 he signed the TVA Act. It extended to the entire Valley Norris' plan for a Muscle Shoals corporation with authorization for electrical power, navigation, flood control, and fertilizer production, and also for "surveys of and general plans for said Tennessee basin and adjoining territory . . . for the general purpose of fostering an orderly and proper physical, economic, and social development of said areas." [51]

The act, therefore, supplied an opportunity for social as well as physical engineering; and the first appointee to the TVA board, Chairman Arthur E. Morgan, had propensities for both. President of Antioch College in Ohio and a self-made engineer who had developed a great flood control project for Dayton, Ohio, Morgan also had a utopian bent, manifested in years of

[49] C. Herman Pritchett, *The Tennessee Valley Authority: A Study in Public Administration* (Chapel Hill, 1943), 18. The states were Kentucky, Virginia, North Carolina, Tennessee, Georgia, Alabama, and Mississippi. On the development of the multipurpose concept of river valley development, see Johnny Booth Smallwood, Jr., "George W. Norris and the Concept of a Planned Region" (Ph.D. dissertation, University of North Carolina, 1963); and Hubbard, *Origins of the TVA*. Good general treatments of TVA include Willson Whitman, *God's Valley: People and Power along the Tennessee River* (New York, 1939); Joseph Sirera Ransmeier, *The Tennessee Valley Authority: A Case Study in the Economic of Multiple-Purpose Stream Planning* (Nashville, 1942); Clarence Lewis Hodge, *The Tennessee Valley Authority: A National Experiment in Regionalism* (Washington, 1938); and Donald Davidson, *The Tennessee* (New York, 1948), II, 213–333.

[50] Rosenman (comp.), *Public Papers and Addresses of Franklin D. Roosevelt*, I, 888–89.

[51] 48 U.S. Statutes 69, quoted in Gordon R. Clapp, *The TVA: An Approach to the Development of a Region* (Chicago, 1955), 183. On passage of the act see Judson King, *The Conservation Fight: From Theodore Roosevelt to the Tennessee Valley Authority* (Washington, 1959), 267–76.

labor on a biography of Edward Bellamy. Engineering was not enough, he told a group of TVA employees. Years before he had directed a gigantic drainage project in Arkansas on the philosophy "that if you give people the means of creating wealth and comfort they will work out the situation without further help. Yet today that most fertile land in America is the locus of the most miserable sharecropper tenantry, where poverty and bitterness are general, and violence appears." TVA, he wrote elsewhere, should not merely "duplicate here on the Tennessee the industrial set-up that has broken down in Detroit and Pittsburgh. . . . We must try to get another picture of what to do about the two million people in this watershed." [52]

The picture he projected, however, seemed nebulous and vaguely archaic: handicraft industries, self-help co-operatives that would issue their own currency, the restoration of lost folkways. At the same time he left a personal impression of beneficent paternalism that aroused suspicion among his associates and the people of the Valley. Towns, transportation, forests, land policy, and industry—all should come under a master plan in his vision. Land laws, he suggested, might penalize farmers who failed to co-operate with conservation measures.[53] "These outlanders seemed to have come down here to reform an illiterate, godless lot who would not wear shoes," Chattanooga editor George Fort Milton recalled later. "This is unfortunate," he wrote to one of Morgan's colleagues at the time, "for there is no more resistant group to be found anywhere in America than the East Tennessean, and once he thinks that outsiders are coming in to 'improve' him he is going to be rather ugly about it." [54]

Arthur Morgan's associates had a less exalted conception of the TVA but a greater finesse and flexibility in public relations. Their

[52] J. Charles Poe, "The Morgan-Lilienthal Feud," in *Nation*, CXLIII (1936), 386; Arthur E. Morgan, "Bench-Marks in the Tennessee Valley, I. The Strength of the Hills," in *Survey Graphic*, XXIII (1934), 8.

[53] Morgan, "Bench-Marks in the Tennessee Valley, III. Planning for the Use of the Land," in *Survey Graphic*, XXIII (1934), 233–37, 251; Morgan, "Bench-Marks in the Tennessee Valley, IV. Roads to Prosperity in the TVA," *ibid.*, 548–52, 575–76; Poe, "Morgan-Lilienthal Feud," *loc. cit.*, 386.

[54] George Fort Milton, "A Consumer's View of the TVA," in *Atlantic Monthly*, CLX (1937), 656; Milton to David E. Lilienthal, August 15, 1933, in Milton Papers.

views more than his ultimately determined its evolution. David E. Lilienthal, a young lawyer plucked from the Wisconsin Power Commission, brought to the board a profound distrust of the private utilities and a single-minded determination to pursue the Norris vision of cheap and plentiful public power. Harcourt A. Morgan, president of the University of Tennessee, a native of Ontario who had won acceptance as a Southerner in a long career of promoting agricultural work, was concerned chiefly with the land. The board seemed a complementary group, and a practical division of functions was agreed upon. Engineering fell to Arthur Morgan, fertilizers and agriculture to Harcourt Morgan, power policy and the legal division to Lilienthal. But mutual disagreements with the chairman thrust the other two into alliance and each won virtual autonomy in his own field by support of the other.[55]

The rationale that eventually displaced the chairman's concept of superplanning grew out of Harcourt Morgan's experience in agriculture and his respect for the resistant powers of the ordinary farmer. He envisioned progress through "leading and teaching and hoping," through the demonstration techniques to which his career as agriculturist had been devoted.[56] TVA's farm program, he told a Congressional committee, should animate the personal initiative of farmers and "in the interest of efficiency . . . should be projected through the medium of existing agencies . . . which enjoy the confidence of the farmers." Consequently he turned to the land-grant colleges of the seven TVA states for an agreement to co-ordinate programs of research, extension, land-use planning, and educational activities. As a result the program was geared to the agricultural establishment and carried into the field chiefly by the county agents.[57]

In fertilizer research and production, on which both the Muscle Shoals controversy and the TVA Act had focused attention, Morgan steered away from nitrates and toward phosphates. Two factors induced the decision: first, advances in nitrogen technology

[55] Pritchett, *Tennessee Valley Authority*, 148–51, 155–56.
[56] Jonathan Daniels, "Three Men in a Valley," in *New Republic*, XCVI (1938), 37.
[57] Norman I. Wengert, *Valley of Tomorrow: The TVA and Agriculture*, in University of Tennessee Record *Extension Series*, XXVIII, No. 1 (Knoxville, 1952), 70–73. Morgan quoted on p. 70.

had rendered the Muscle Shoals plants obsolete; second, phosphates in Morgan's view better fitted the multipurpose goals of the new agency. Nitrates, he reasoned, served to increase the yields of annual row crops and contributed to the old habit of plundering the soil. Farmers should be urged instead to manufacture their own nitrogen by growing legumes, which would contribute to crop-rotation and diversified farming as well as water control and soil conservation. At the same time soils in the area were deficient in phosphate, natural rock phosphate was available in Tennessee; and existing facilities could be converted to process it. Phosphates, therefore, offered a fulcrum for agricultural reform. By 1935 the experimental production of phosphates was sufficient to begin promoting them through test-demonstration farms, and by 1937 quantities were being supplied to the AAA for use outside the Valley.[58]

From Harcourt Morgan's extension-demonstration tradition Lilienthal elaborated a theory of "grass-roots democracy" to explain their departure from the idea of overhead planning. The farm program, he argued, avoided the danger of fastening upon people "a system that would inevitably sap their initiative . . . substitute armchair brains for their own, discourage a wholesome and necessary diversity of ideas and practical experimentation, and weaken an already undernourished system of State and local research and educational leadership." [59] In other fields as well, "grass-roots democracy" required collaboration with local agencies, public and private: with health departments, libraries, power boards, co-operatives, businessmen, and labor unions—a titanic stimulus to local initiative and an antidote to the "poison of overcentralization." [60] The theme of "democracy on the march," as orchestrated by Lilienthal, had a galvanic effect. "It's strange," a visitor recently back from Germany remarked. "I've never noticed it anywhere before in America. But all these men you meet in the TVA talk about democracy with the same solemn but casual devotion as you will get from all sorts of people in Germany about the Nazi program." [61]

---

[58] *Ibid.*, 24–29.   [59] Quoted *ibid.*, 88–89.
[60] David E. Lilienthal, *TVA: Democracy on the March* (New York, 1944) , 150–51. See also *ibid.*, 139–49.
[61] Daniels, "Three Men in a Valley," *loc. cit.*, 36–37.

But the slogans of democracy also served to mask dubious aspects of the policy. To some degree they functioned as a "protective ideology" behind which Lilienthal agreed to an "informal cooptation" of the TVA Agricultural Relations Department by the Farm Bureau-Extension-land-grant-college axis in return for its support of his public power program.[62] TVA came to reflect the hostility of the agricultural establishment toward such agencies as the Soil Conservation Service and the Farm Security Administration, which threatened to build competing administrative structures. TVA policy neglected nitrogen, the "poor man's fertilizer," for phosphate. But the "cooptation" worked both ways; TVA stimulated local institutions to new perspectives and bought political insurance by cultivating local support.

The public power program brought conflict enough, within the board and with outside adversaries, chiefly Wendell Willkie, president of the Commonwealth and Southern Corporation (C & S), holding company for the most important operating utilities in the Valley. At the outset there was only Wilson Dam at Muscle Shoals, already supplying a trickle of electricity to Alabama Power, but in October, 1933, construction began on Norris Dam above Knoxville and before the year was out on Wheeler Dam, just above Wilson, at the President's request to provide unemployment relief. By 1936 three more were underway, and the board had developed a master plan for nine high dams on the main river, which would obliterate its shores under the "Great Lakes of the South," and other dams on the tributaries.[63]

In the beginning Arthur Morgan engineered the dams but power distribution fell to Lilienthal.[64] The proper policy, in his view, was to develop markets as rapidly as possible. Since the TVA Act dictated preference to nonprofit agencies, this meant an aggressive program of encouraging municipal systems and rural co-

---

[62] This thesis is developed at length in Selznick, *TVA and the Grass Roots,* which should be balanced by reference to Wengert, *Valley of Tomorrow.* See also Rexford G. Tugwell and E. C. Banfield, "Grass Roots Democracy—Myth or Reality?" in *Public Administration Review* (Chicago), X (1950), 47–55.

[63] On the physical development of TVA see John H. Kyle, *The Building of TVA: An Illustrated History* (Baton Rouge, 1958).

[64] The power controversy is traced in Schlesinger, *Politics of Upheaval,* 363–71; Joseph Barnes, *Willkie: The Events He Was Part of, the Ideas He Fought for* (New York, 1952), 60–78, 96–148; and in the general treatments of TVA cited above.

operatives. Such a program, however, set TVA on a collision course with the utilities and, as Arthur Morgan saw it, endangered his own vision of human engineering, which did not include Lilienthal's passion for public power. "I am not going to fight the power companies," he said at the outset, but his desire for accommodation was repeatedly frustrated by events.[65] At first, early in 1934, a truce was arranged. Contracts were signed to purchase distribution properties from subsidiaries of Willkie's C & S in northeastern Mississippi and northern Alabama. In return TVA agreed to a division of territory; it would not sell power outside the ceded counties to any customer already supplied by C & S. The town of Tupelo, Mississippi, home of Representative John Rankin, one of the South's most fervent advocates of public power, signed the first contract for municipal distribution.

The truce, however, was short-lived. In September, 1934, a minority of preferred stockholders of Alabama Power, led by George Ashwander, challenged the constitutionality of power sales from Wilson Dam. The Ashwander suit hung over TVA until February, 1936, when the Supreme Court upheld its operations, but only with respect to Wilson Dam. Three months later nineteen utility companies, including several C & S affiliates, filed a suit attacking TVA's broader program and TVA operated under the shadow of that suit until 1939. Willkie meanwhile pursued a dual policy, negotiating but encouraging propaganda against TVA. Lilienthal followed his own dual policy, also negotiating but encouraging new outlets through municipal and co-operative systems. At places rival crews strung parallel lines into rural areas formerly neglected by the utilities. C & S, the Chattanooga *News* charged, was building "spite lines" to defeat TVA; in one place a militant Georgia farm woman fended off a C & S crew with a shotgun.[66]

In August, 1936, the Norris Dam power plant was completed, ninety days before the agreement on territorial division expired. Willkie proposed a new division following the Valley watershed line. Lilienthal, however, contended that this would violate the legal obligation to give preference to public agencies, and the

[65] King, *Conservation Fight*, 287.
[66] Poe, "Morgan-Lilienthal Feud," *loc. cit.*, 385.

board voted against further territorial limitations. Lilienthal countered with a proposal for a southeastern "power pool" with a single distribution system and uniform rates, with municipalities choosing between C & S and TVA. Discussions of a pool, however, broke off in December, 1936, after the power companies won a court injunction against any more TVA contracts for six months.

Meanwhile a parallel conflict within the TVA moved into the open. In 1936 Arthur Morgan tried to prevent the reappointment of Lilienthal and failed. Early in 1937 he complained of "people who are ruled by a Napoleonic complex, which leads them to use any method at hand, including intrigue, arbitrary force and appeal to class hatred." [67] The other two board members, in turn, suspected the chairman of negotiating behind their backs, of intrigues to weaken their position in court. Things had "come to a pass where . . . there must be a sharp conclusion one way or the other by somebody walking the plank," George Fort Milton wrote early in 1938.[68] The quarrel finally reached a climax when the board members demanded that the chairman document his public charges of malfeasance and dishonesty against them. When he refused and demanded a Congressional investigation instead, the President removed him for "insubordination and contumacy" in March, 1938.[69] The investigation that followed proved a disappointment to scandal-hounds who scented another Teapot Dome affair. The charges, a majority of the committee decided, were without foundation; the "malfeasance" of Lilienthal and Harcourt Morgan consisted of policy disagreements with the chairman.[70]

With the internal conflict resolved, Lilienthal's position was further strengthened by a Supreme Court decision in January, 1938, upholding the right of the Public Works Administration to make loans for the construction of municipal power systems. Knoxville, Chattanooga, Memphis, and other communities were

[67] T. R. B., "Washington Notes," in *New Republic*, LXXIX (1937), 410.
[68] George Fort Milton to Robert M. LaFollette, Jr., January 16, 1938, in Milton Papers. See also Milton to LaFollette, November 4, 1936, *ibid.*
[69] Rosenman (comp.), *Public Papers and Addresses of Franklin D. Roosevelt*, VII, 151–63.
[70] The controversy and hearings are summarized in Pritchett, *Tennessee Valley Authority*, 185–222.

enabled to pursue their plans to develop municipal systems with cheap TVA power.[71] In January, 1939, the Supreme Court finally handed down its decision in the power companies' challenge to TVA; there was no legal basis for a suit, the majority declared. On February 4 the sale of Tennessee Electric Power Company, a C & S affiliate, to TVA was announced. It was the largest single acquisition and, with a few additions, gave the TVA lines reaching most of Tennessee and large portions of Mississippi and Alabama, with smaller outlets in other Valley states.[72]

With the major controversies settled and TVA removed from legal jeopardy, its basic structure had taken shape by 1940. It never fulfilled the dream of regional planning and its leaders after Arthur Morgan carefully evaded use of the term, preferring "the ways of contract, persuasion, incentives, encouragement, methods based upon the people's confidence in TVA's comprehension, its good faith, and the quality of its technical leadership." [73] After 1936, Rexford Tugwell declared, it "should have been called the Tennessee Valley Power Production and Flood Control Corporation." [74]

TVA wrought a transformation nonetheless with its dams, lakes, and transmission lines. "Two million kilowatts cannot be turned loose in a Valley without some shocks being felt," C. Herman Pritchett remarked.[75] Cheap power transported farmers of the Valley from the age of kerosene to the age of electricity. "The women went around turning the switches on and off," said a farm bureau man who saw the transition. "The light and wonder in

[71] On local movements for public power see Cecil Buchanan, "Municipal Ownership of Public Utilities in Chattanooga, Tennessee" (M.A. thesis, Louisiana State University, 1941) ; and Ralph C. Hon, "The Memphis Power and Light Deal," in *Southern Economic Journal*, VI (1939–1940) , 344–75. George Fort Milton's Chattanooga *News* advocated municipal distribution. The Chattanooga *Free Press*, started by advocates of private power, took most of the advertising and forced the *News* to suspend publication.

[72] TVA acquisitions are mapped in Twentieth Century Fund, *Electric Power and Government Policy: A Survey of the Relations between the Government and the Electric Power Industry* (New York, 1948) , 609.

[73] Lilienthal, *TVA*, 202; Norman Wengert, "TVA—Symbol and Reality," *Journal of Politics*, XIII (1951) , 383.

[74] Tugwell and Banfield, "Grass Roots Democracy," *loc. cit.*, 50.

[75] Pritchett, *Tennessee Valley Authority*, 130–31.

454

their eyes was brighter than that from the lamps." [76] Refrigerators, freezers, electric sewing machines, chicken brooders, cream separators, feed grinders, and other labor-saving devices lightened the burden of country folks. TVA's first rural co-operative, the Alcorn County Electric Power Association, formed at Corinth, Mississippi, in 1934, pointed the way to the electrification of the nation's farms in the decade that followed. The Rural Electrification Authority, formed as a relief agency by Presidential order in 1935, achieved a permanent statutory basis in 1936. By 1940 it had granted loans of $321,306,114 for rural co-operatives.[77] Its activities were especially pertinent to the South, which got 41 per cent of all loans to 1953.[78] In five states across the lower South, where less than 3 per cent of the farms had electric service in 1935, the number increased within ten years to 18.7 per cent of all farms in Mississippi and 41.5 per cent in South Carolina. Tennessee Valley farms were about 75 per cent electrified.[79]

In other respects the influence of TVA reached beyond the Valley. It never became a "yardstick" by which to measure private utility rates (problems of allocating costs among navigation, flood control, and other purposes were too complex), but its experience in generating larger consumption by lower rates belied predictions that it could not find outlets, and awakened the beleaguered utilities to the value of mass consumer markets. Among the twelve original distributors of TVA power, Lilienthal reported, the average household use of electricity rose 146 per cent between 1934 and 1942. Drastic rate reduction by private utilities in adjacent areas produced similar increases. In another way TVA pointed the way to more aggressive marketing, by loans for appliances from the Electric Farm and Home Authority, established for the Valley

[76] Quoted in Russell Owen, "From 'Monkey Trial' to Atomic Age," in New York Times Magazine, July 21, 1946, p. 38.

[77] Harry Slattery, Rural America Lights Up (Washington, 1940), 77. See also Marquis Childs, The Farmer Takes a Hand: The Electric Power Revolution in Rural America (Garden City, N.Y.).

[78] Arthur Goldschmidt, "The Development of the U.S. South," in Scientific American (New York), CCIX (1963), 230.

[79] "Southeast Power Moves On," in U.S. Rural Electrification Administration, Rural Electrification News: A Summary of Rural Electrification Activities (Washington), XI (1945–1946), 12–14, 22; William E. Coles, "The Impact of TVA upon the Southeast," in Social Forces, XXVIII (1949–1950), 439.

region late in 1933 and later extended nationally. In the first year of its rate reduction, inaugurated late in 1933, Georgia Power sold more electric refrigerators and water heaters than any other company in the country and was second in electric ranges. Tennessee Electric Power stood first in ranges, second in refrigerators, and third in water heaters.[80]

Absolutist contentions for public power never greatly stirred the people of the Valley, although TVA won almost universal loyalty; "we are chiefly concerned about the economic development and social progress of the Valley and its people," George Fort Milton wrote. "The Tennessee Valley should become the American Ruhr." [81] That was scarcely the goal of the TVA Act, which gave industry a secondary priority, nor the intent of the President, who cautioned against creating competition for industries suffering depression. But industrial customers were accepted when legal barriers temporarily delimited other markets. The first large contract provided 50,000 kilowatts for a Monsanto chemical plant at Columbia, Tennessee, in 1936; Aluminum Company of America took 40,000 kilowatts in 1936 and 60,000 more in 1937.[82] By the fiscal year 1940 industry took nearly a third of the power sold, and the necessities of defense and war thereafter accelerated the growth of industrial users.[83] From 1940 through June, 1948, the Valley acquired 1,448 new manufacturing and processing plants. In 1933 15 of the 212 Valley counties had no manufacturing plants; by 1947 there were plants in all. Industrial employment rose from 49 per thousand population in 1929 to 80 in 1947, the Valley's proportion of the nation's wages and salary payments from .82 per cent to 1.28, its per capita income from about 40 to 60 per cent of the national average.[84] The most conspicuous

---

[80] Lilienthal, *TVA*, 22–24. See also Joseph S. Ransmeier, *Shadow and Substance in the TVA Power Controversy*, in *Papers of the Institute of Research and Training in the Social Science*, Vanderbilt University, I (Nashville, 1941).

[81] Milton, "Consumer's View of the TVA," *loc. cit.*, 654.

[82] Pritchett, *Tennessee Valley Authority*, 75.

[83] Twentieth Century Fund, *Electric Power and Government Policy*, 616.

[84] Cole, "Impact of TVA upon the Southeast," *loc. cit.*, 438. See also Lawrence L. Durisch, "The TVA Program and the War Effort," in *Journal of Politics*, VIII (1946), 531–37; and Gordon R. Clapp, "The Tennessee Valley Authority," in Merrill Jensen (ed.), *Regionalism in America* (Madison, Wis., 1956), 226–27.

employment growth was in chemicals, primary metals, food processing, leather, and furniture, each of which added more than five thousand workers, chemicals nearly twenty thousand.[85] Whatever other directions it took, TVA became fully oriented to the New South of industrial growth.

Viewing the broader scene toward the end of the 1930's a young historian detected a belated revival of what he called the New South romanticism of Henry Grady.[86] The Atlanta spirit lay dormant only for a brief winter of depression; before the end of the 1930's it was in as full bloom as ever in the flourishing 1920's. "Depression is forgotten in the South," *Business Week* reported at the end of 1936. "The industrial expansion is on again, full swing, and things are booming." [87] A business writer who traveled the Southern states in 1936 and 1937 was caught up in the spirit of expansion: "since 1935 the South has gone hog-wild . . . every where I went I found trains running full, hotels doing capacity business, buses loaded . . . residence and industrial construction going full blast, factories and mills running night and day, towns and cities filled with new cars." [88]

A year later *Fortune* suggested prospects for "serious modifications" in the pessimistic theories of economic "saturation." Even in a mature economy, it noted, certain industries would make relative progress and could direct some of their expansion to the South. But beyond that Southern potentialities were "a denial of saturation." Kraft paper and chemicals were "new industries, adding much more to the economy than they are taking away from older enterprises." It was likely, therefore, "that the further development of the South . . . may provide the evidences needed to disprove the theories of those who hold that industrial expansion has about reached its limit." In 1937, he noted, $135,000,000 of the $477,000,000 laid out for new industrial plants was spent in

[85] John V. Krutilla, "Economic Development: An Appraisal," in Roscoe C. Martin (ed.), *TVA: The First Twenty Years, A Staff Report* (University, Ala., 1956), 226–27.

[86] C. Vann Woodward, *The South in Search of a Philosophy* (Gainesville, Fla., [1938]), 19.

[87] *Business Week*, December 5, 1936, p. 37.

[88] Coleman, "South's Chance at Industry," *loc. cit.*, 33.

the Southeast. In 1936 and 1937, *Business Week* reported, the South had more investment in new and modernized plants than all the rest of the nation.[89]

The incarnation of the growth psychology was the Texas millionaire, already well ensconced in the national folklore, the living evidence that the "free individual with his own hands and mind could work economic miracles, benefitting himself and society." [90] The Texas way of life represented "an extension into the twentieth century of certain ideas that animated all Americans up to the First World War," Russell Davenport said. "Here is the land of opportunity, where anybody can rise to the 'top,' where tomorrow is unpredictable and yesterday unnecessary. Here the intrepid individual, the risk, the adventure, the fabulous reward, have somehow come to fruition in a world largely occupied with the less romantic problems of social 'security' and social 'science.' " [91]

The epitome of the Texas millionaire was Jesse H. Jones of Houston, a city that, handling rather than producing the glut of cotton and oil, "never knew the depression." [92] Starting as a farm boy, Jones had first entered lumbering, then moved to Houston where he laid his bets on real estate and branched out into other fields, including politics. By 1939 the value of his holdings in the city was estimated at $30,000,000, with half as much also in Forth Worth and Dallas. Appointed to the board of the Reconstruction Finance Corporation by Hoover in 1932, he became its chairman under Franklin D. Roosevelt in 1933 and built it into a major agency for salvaging insolvent corporations and an in-

[89] "Industrial South," in *Fortune*, XVIII (November, 1938) , 48, 126; "Diversification Goes South," in *Business Week*, February 12, 1938, p. 20. The investment reported was $186,000,000—$59,000,000 more than in the rest of the nation.

[90] Mills, "Public Career of a Texas Conservative," 3.

[91] Editors of *Fortune* with Russell Davenport, *U. S. A.: The Permanent Revolution* (New York, 1951) , 15. Contrary to the stereotype of Texas wealth, however, the state in 1940 ranked thirty-fourth in per capita income, which was $413 or 72 per cent of the national average, and stood behind two Southern states: Florida, thirtieth, and Virginia, thirty-first. Hoover and Ratchford, *Economic Resources and Policies of the South*, 50.

[92] "Texas," in *Fortune*, XX (December, 1939) , 87. The phrase, of course, is an exaggeration. In 1931 Jones himself organized local resources to save two banks on the verge of collapse. Bascom M. Timmons, *Jesse H. Jones: The Man and the Statesman* (New York, 1956) , 153–61.

vestor in business expansion that dwarfed private institutions. By 1938 it had disbursed ten billion dollars. Jones carried the Southern growth psychology into the New Deal, where it served as a counterpoise to the "saturation" theories of the Depression and "played an indispensable role in shifting the economic and financial direction of the country from the hard-money, gold-standard, coupon-clipping groups of the East to those who, for better or worse, were prepared to risk monetary inflation because they deeply believed in economic growth." [93]

At lower levels the growth psychology continued to inspire industry-hunting. Programs of tax exemption, bonuses in the form of favorable assessments and utility rates, and local participation in financing survived the hard times. Under the pressure of depression, however, the boosters leaned increasingly upon state and local governments in lieu of hard-pressed chambers of commerce.

The use of subsidies was extensive—how common, one cannot say precisely. But systematic evidence gathered in Tennessee revealed a complaisant indulgence of the practice, even legislative and judicial connivance in the face of constitutional interdiction. A TVA study of forty-one Tennessee towns, none larger than 25,000, uncovered eighteen that owned twenty factory buildings either completed or under construction in 1937. Municipal ownership in each case had occurred since 1930. Among eighty-six plants operating or under construction in the same communities, fifty had received public concessions, including temporary tax exemptions in twenty-seven. All but four of the thirty-six plants established after 1930 had been subsidized. Garment factories were the most numerous, followed by shoe and textile plants. A later study by the state planning commission disclosed that public bond issues for industrial subsidies in the state amounted to more than $2,500,000 over a ten-year period, 1935–1945.[94]

In their voracity for payrolls, small towns eagerly fell prey to unstable enterprises and fly-by-night garment factories. Among

[93] Schlesinger, *Coming of the New Deal*, 425–33.

[94] Robert E. Lowry, "Municipal Subsidies to Industry in Tennessee," in *Southern Economic Journal*, VI (1940–1941), 317–29; Tennessee State Planning Commission, "Subsidies for Industry in Tennessee" (Mimeographed; Nashville, 1947), cited in Ross, "Industrial Promotion by Southern States," 143.

thirteen factories built by community development companies in the 1920's, according to the TVA study, only two were occupied by the original tenants in 1937 and two were standing vacant.[95] One community was bamboozled by a swindler who occupied a municipal building rent-free, got city-paid help for a thirty-day "training period," and absconded with enough neckties for the Christmas trade. At Dickson a garment maker secured an agreement to pay his rent by deductions of 6 per cent from the employees' weekly wages, which averaged twelve dollars.[96]

The same fatal affinity for sweatshops afflicted other states. Mississippi, beset by the collapse of cotton and lumber, proved especially susceptible and contrived some bizarre innovations in the subsidy technique. By putting the label of "training school" on a new factory the communities found they could use Federal or local school funds for "vocational education" in the plant. At Vicksburg a shirt factory in flight from union standards in Indiana was presented an $80,000 plant and a five-year tax exemption. Girls who entered this "training school" worked without pay for six to twelve weeks, then went on the payroll at learners' wages. The "instructors," paid out of funds from the Office of Education, did the work of mechanics and operatives.[97] Five communities carried the process a step further, securing WPA funds to build their "industrial training schools." [98]

The name most prominently associated with community subsidies was that of Hugh L. White. The closing of his lumber operations at Columbia, the result of depression and depleted timber, blighted the local economy. Seeking to ease the shock,

[95] Lowry, "Municipal Subsidies to Industries in Tennessee," *loc. cit.*, 320.

[96] Tennessee State Planning Commission, "Subsidies for Industry in Tennessee," cited in Lepawsky, *State Planning and Economic Development in the South*, 71; Stokes, *Chip Off My Shoulder*, 513–15.

[97] William P. Mangold, "On the Labor Front," in *New Republic*, LXXVI (1936), 19.

[98] Stokes, *Chip Off My Shoulder*, 517–19; New York *Times*, February 20, 1936. The towns were Brookhaven, Columbia, Ellisville, Lumberton, and Philadelphia. See also Current Economics Association, Inc., "Mississippi—The Nation's Number One Sweatshop: From Agricultural Slum to Industrial Sweatshop—1932–1938" ([Brooklyn, N.Y.], [1938]), copy in Odum Papers. This publication cited several alleged cases of firms moving into Mississippi with local subsidies after losing contracts for prison labor in other states.

White organized a chamber of commerce, raised a subsidy of $80,000, and lured a vagrant garment factory to town. Soon two others moved in. Wages were low but the payrolls revived Columbia; by 1936 merchants' sales had gained 26 per cent over 1932. The "Columbia method" presently became the basis for the most celebrated state industrial program of the decade. In 1935 White was elected governor on the slogan, "Balance Agriculture with Industry," and in 1936 the state legislature enacted a BAWI program that set up a state industrial commission to screen applicants and authorize local bond issues for buildings to be leased or given to industries.

In four years the commission sponsored issuance of $980,500 in subsidy bonds and the establishment of twelve enterprises. In 1940 they provided an annual payroll of $3,314,645 and through the second quarter of 1943 had made total wage disbursements of $43,539,361; but more than two thirds of that amount came from a single war industry, the Ingalls Shipbuilding Corporation of Pascagoula.[99] Ended in 1940, the BAWI plan was revived in 1944; by 1947 the two programs had brought fifty-seven installations into the state, including thirty-one garment plants.[100] "All in all," an analyst of the first program concluded, "it cannot be said that the BAWI system was in itself the fundamental or decisive factor in determining many things that were ascribed to it. . . . Rather, its offer of aids was a marginal factor, serving to precipitate half-formed decisions of management."[101] It probably did more to promote "special inducements than . . . to promote industrial expansion," another critic felt.[102] Its chief direct accomplishment was to draw in low-wage garment plants. Even so, one economist reasoned, the central board showed excessive caution, "a smothering overprotectiveness" in screening applicants when Mississippi needed any industry it could get.[103]

[99] Ernest Jerome Hopkins, *Mississippi's BAWI Plan: Balance Agriculture with Industry: An Experiment in Industrial-Subsidization* (Atlanta, 1944), 11–13, 16–20, 22–24, 37, 53, 56–57.
[100] *Balancing Agriculture with Industry*, Second Report to the Legislature by the Mississippi Agricultural and Industrial Board ([Jackson], [1947]), 14–16.
[101] Hopkins, *Mississippi's BAWI Plan*, 37.
[102] Ross, "Industrial Promotion by Southern States," 93.
[103] John E. Moes, *Local Subsidies for Industry* (Chapel Hill, 1962), 71–80.

The BAWI plan was the precursor of other state industrial programs that followed in the next few years. Beginning with the Louisiana Department of Commerce and Industry (1936), which combined publicity and informational services with tax exemptions, new or expanded agencies appeared in Arkansas and North Carolina (1937), South Carolina (1938), Alabama (1939), Virginia and Texas (1940), Florida (1941), Tennessee (1942), and Oklahoma and Georgia (1943). By the end of 1943, only Kentucky lacked a state-financed industrial growth program.[104] None of the new agencies, however, adopted the Mississippi device of subsidized buildings. Their activities most often combined advertising with locational services and special privileges, among which tax favors were almost universal—only North Carolina and Texas omitted the device.[105]

Notwithstanding doubts that state efforts had more than peripheral influence upon plant location, the programs probably stood on a stronger base of popular support than any before.[106] An important factor was a growing public unrest over the South's tributary status, its undeveloped potentialities, its "colonial economy"—a phrase increasingly current.[107] Events of the Depression years had exposed the raw-material economy to violent fluctuations and had underscored the uses of even sweatshop industries in raising incomes. But the drive for industry raised another dilemma. The quest for capital and branch plants led inevitably to the imperial North, and thus to outside control and to the drain of profits and interest from the region. Yet little effort was expended to boost local development—in part, one observer thought, because of a persistent agricultural tradition and a "regional inferiority complex, where industry is concerned." The deficiency of capital in the South was aggravated by "the spectacle of . . . Southerners turning down industrial investments of a few thousand dollars that would return them many hundred per cent" for

[104] Ross, "Industrial Promotion by Southern States," 149–50; Barnett, "State Industrial Development Programs," 5, 50.

[105] Hoover and Ratchford, *Economic Resources and Policies of the South*, 374–80. See also Joe S. Floyd, Jr., *Effects of Taxation on Industrial Location* (Chapel Hill, 1952).

[106] The objections are surveyed in Moes, *Local Subsidies for Industry*, 221–37.

[107] The concept of the "colonial economy" is discussed in Chapter XVII.

investments in national corporations and in land "not . . . producing nearly enough to justify its valuation." [108] "The greatest opportunity for the region lies in the chance to begin manufacturing for itself," one student argued,[109] but no organized effort occurred until the Alabama development board in 1943 prepared a study, *Industrial Opportunity in Alabama,* suggesting possibilities for diversification into higher-wage and higher-value industries sponsored by local capital. This book was followed up with an eight-volume survey of *Alabama's Industrial Opportunities,* which was, however, but a conventional program of locational data aimed for a change at home-grown investors.[110]

Qualms about alien control or exploitation seldom deterred the Southern boosters. Large-scale development increasingly required large amounts of capital, and the South manifestly could not lift itself by its own bootstraps. The history of industrial development in the region was largely a story of imported capital; and if outside control brought restraints, as for Birmingham or Marland Oil, it more often speeded expansion, as for Alabama Power or Humble Oil. Large concerns brought technological and managerial know-how and the multiplier effects of markets, increased labor skills, and auxiliary industries. Growth bred diversification. Petroleum and gas brought in turn a multiplicity of chemicals; textiles lured machinery and garment plants; paper mills gave rise to pulpwood farms. The benefits did not all flow away in profits and interest.

Chemicals and paper provided the most spectacular movements toward diversity. In both a dynamic expansion began about 1936. The chemical industry, with its variety of products and customers, kept up a momentum of research and development through the Depression. The South benefitted not only from its climate and resources but also from enlarged markets in textiles, rayon, and kraft paper. In 1936, the peak year of plant construction during the decade, the industry put more than $33,000,000 into the South, more than twice the amount spent in the Eastern states. By 1939 the South produced 11 per cent of the value added by

[108] Coleman, "South's Chance at Industry," *loc. cit.,* 34, 116.
[109] Harriet L. Herring, *Southern Industry and Regional Development* (Chapel Hill, 1940) , 79.
[110] Ross, "Industrial Promotion by Southern States," 184–85.

chemical manufacturing and the momentum of growth made it "evident that the South was destined to become the great chemical production center of the country." [111]

Baton Rouge emerged in 1935–1936 as an important focal point for the industry, adding to its Consolidated Chemical sulphuric acid plant (1925) an $8,000,000 Solvay plant to produce soda ash, caustic soda, and chlorine, and the Ethyl corporation's main tetraethyl-lead plant, while the chemical-minded leaders of the Esso refinery encouraged the use of petroleum by-products. Elsewhere in Louisiana, where the known sulphur deposits had been exhausted in 1924, production was resumed for a time at the Jefferson Island salt dome (1932–1936) and more permanently at Freeport Sulphur's Grand Ecaille deposit (1936) in the delta marshes below New Orleans. In all, seven old domes were abandoned during the decade, but six new ones were tapped in Louisiana and Texas and shipments grew steadily after 1933. The Solvay alkali production supplemented plants already built by Mathieson at Lake Charles and Southern Alkali at Corpus Christi (in part to serve a new Pittsburgh Plate Glass mill) in 1934, and Mathieson's enlargement of its old plant at Saltville, Virginia, in 1930. At Texas City the first strictly chemical plant to utilize gas and petroleum by-products was built during the 1930's, and both Dow and Monsanto companies announced plans to enter the field.[112]

An important concentration developed in Louisiana and Texas, but other plants checkered the region. Chlorine production grew in new plants of Allied Chemical at Hopewell, Virginia (1936), and Hercules Powder at Canton, North Carolina (1938). DuPont opened new cellophane and acetate rayon plants in Virginia; Dow Chemical set up a bromine plant at Kure Beach, North Carolina; American Cyanamid opened production of aluminum sulphate and other heavy chemicals at Mobile, Chattanooga, and Georgetown, South Carolina.[113]

[111] Haynes, *American Chemical Industry*, V, 30–31, 52–53; Hoover and Ratchford, *Economic Resources and Policies of the South*, 127.

[112] Haynes, *American Chemical Industry*, V, 53, 73–75, 90–94; *Baton Rouge Morning Advocate*, April 22, 1956; Haynes, *Stone That Burns*, 237–56.

[113] Haynes, *American Chemical Industry*, V, 53, 90–94. For other examples of expansion in chemicals see "Industrial South," in *Fortune*, XVIII (November, 1938), 54; Williams Haynes, *Southern Horizons* (New York, 1946); and Haynes, *Cellulose*.

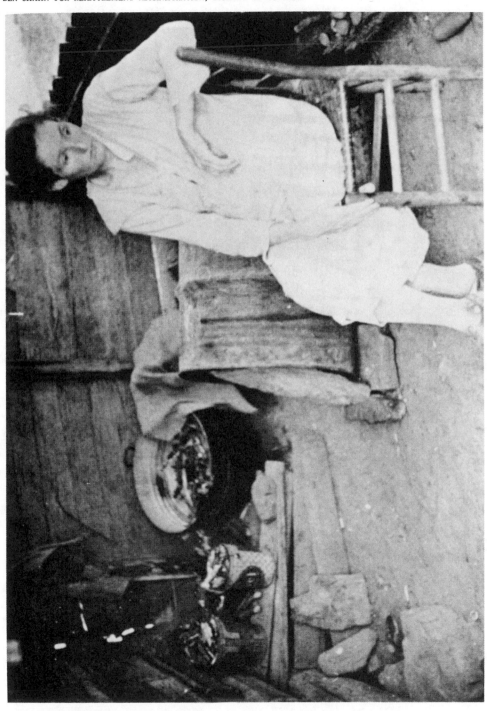

Arkansas Tenant Farmer's Wife, 1936

Birmingham Steel Mill and Workers' Homes, 1936

TVA's Douglas Dam under Construction, 1943

NAACP Annual Conference, Richmond, Virginia, 1939. Panel on Civil Rights. Speaking: Editor Peter B. Young of the Norfolk *Journal and Guide.* Seated, left to right: James M. Nabrit, Howard University; Hubert T. Delany, New York; Thurgood Marshall, NAACP; Mrs. Grace Towns Hamilton, Memphis; and Leon A. Ransom, Howard University.

Meanwhile, interest in the promise of chemistry was jogged by the "chemurgic" movement, which gave a new name to the old but expanded use of farm products in chemical production. The idea had been advanced during the 1920's in public lectures by George Washington Carver of Tuskegee and by Charles H. Herty and William J. Hale of the Chemical Foundation. It took form in Hale's *Chemistry Triumphant* (1932) and *The Farm Chemurgic* (1934), and National Farm Chemurgic Council (1935), and the first Southern Chemurgic Conference at Lafayette, Louisiana (1936). Victor Schoffelmayer, farm editor of the Dallas *Morning News,* and Peter F. Lawson, secretary of the Beaumont Chamber of Commerce, both converts of Herty, propagated the "chemurgic renaissance" around the Gulf Coast, prodding interest in tung oil, sweet potato starch, wood and cotton cellulose, naval stores, and a number of other projects in organic chemistry. In 1938, Senator Theodore G. Bilbo sponsored a rider to the Farm Relief Act that assigned $4,000,000 for four regional chemurgic laboratories, including one at New Orleans to seek new uses for cotton, peanuts, and sweet potatoes. The South, Williams Haynes noted, found itself in the position of the *bourgeois gentilhomme* who was astounded to learn that he spoke prose: "The South had been practicing chemurgy since colonial times." But the novelty of the term caused the movement to be greatly oversold as a solution to economic problems.[114]

In woodpulp and paper the "chemurgic renaissance" already was far advanced. In 1931 its prophet, Charles H. Herty, envisioned a day when the South "could escape domination of the Canadian paper manufacturers . . . through the blessings of sunlight, the creator of cellulose, the characteristic beneficence of our Southern territory."[115] Herty by then was already on the way to the crowning achievement of his long career, the making of news-

[114] Haynes, *American Chemical Industry,* V, 227, 229–34; William J. Hale, "The Farm Chemurgic Movement," *ibid.,* 486–90; Borth, *Pioneers of Plenty,* 134–39, 315–47; Benedict, *Farm Policies of the United States,* 380, 380n. See also columns by Victor Schoffelmeyer on a "Chemurgic Caravan" tour of Louisiana and Mississippi in Dallas *Morning News,* November 25, 27, 30, December 2, 4, 7, 9, 11, 14, 16, 1937.

[115] Herty speech to Southern Newspaper Publishers' Association, Asheville, N.C., 1931, quoted in Walter C. Johnson and Arthur T. Robb, *The South and Its Newspapers, 1903–1953: The Story of the Southern Newspaper Publishers' Association and Its Part in the South's Economic Rebirth* (Chattanooga, 1954), 217.

print from Southern pine. In 1932, with help from the Chemical Foundation and the Georgia legislature, he set up a laboratory in a Savannah warehouse. Starting with the simple observation that young slash pine was not highly resinous, by December, 1933, he had prepared enough woodpulp to make newsprint for a day's edition of nine Georgia papers. The remainder of his life was devoted to refining the process and finding support for a newsprint mill. In 1939, the year after his death, the Southland Paper Mills went up near Lufkin, Texas, with financial support from the RFC and thirty-two Southern newspapers from Virginia to Oklahoma. It began production early in 1940 with an annual capacity of fifty thousand tons and the next year inaugurated plans to double the capacity.[116]

In 1940 Southern papermaking entered another new field with the production of cigarette paper by Ecusta Paper Corporation near Brevard, North Carolina. The region already produced tissues, ledger, book, writing, and various other specialty types, as well as wall boards; but brown kraft paper remained the foundation of the industry. International Paper's subsidiary, Southern Kraft, incorporated in 1930, erected a new plant at Panama City, Florida (1934–1935).[117]

In 1936 a phenomenal expansion began when the Union Bag and Paper Company finished the first unit of a new plant near Savannah, and near the oak-lined avenue of old Hermitage Plantation. Additional units in 1937 raised Chatham County's payroll by two thirds.[118] Union's action was a goad to competitors, who entered a scramble to win priority at likely ports and subjugate the tributary woodlands. The old ports of Georgetown, Charleston, Savannah, Brunswick, Fernandina, Jacksonville, Port St. Joe,

[116] Johnson and Robb, *South and Its Newspapers*, 208–39; Borth, *Pioneers of Plenty*, 93–124. See also Jones, *Fifty Billion Dollars*, 188–89; *Newsweek*, XIII (February 13, 1939), 43; *Time*, XXXV (February 12, 1940), 48–49; and Eugene Wright, "The Tidewater South Goes Modern," in *Travel* (New York), LXXVIII (1941–1942), 32–24, 40.

[117] Mouzon, "Social and Economic Implications of Recent Developments within the Wood Pulp and Paper Industry of the South," 156–58, 167–68, 209–10; *Time*, XXXV (April 8, 1940), 74, 76; Curran, "The Paper Industry in the South," 142–43.

[118] Mouzon, "Social and Economic Implications of Recent Developments within the Wood Pulp and Paper Industry of the South," 122–26; "Union Bag and Paper Corporation," in *Fortune*, XVI (August, 1937), 122, 126, 132.

Mobile, and Houston, and sleepy inland towns of Virginia, North Carolina, Arkansas, and Louisiana quickened into new activity with the arrival of the mills. By the end of 1938 twelve new kraft mills had been added to the sixteen existing in 1935, and the South's share of national production bounded up from 12.4 per cent in 1935 to 17.2 in 1937. In all, Southern paper mills increased from twenty-nine in 1929 to forty-seven in 1939, representing an investment of over $200,000,000, about half of which came after 1935.[119] The peculiar significance of the development, a business writer noted, was that "the new industry has come to that particular part of the South—the pine barrens—which at the moment needs new industry more than any other part."[120] Moreover, it offered a use for cutover lands and an outlet for waste products of lumbering.

In the older Piedmont Industrial Crescent cotton textiles maintained their advantage over New England, with over-all losses only during 1930–1932 and with subsequent profits higher than the Northern industry, which took losses again in 1934, 1935, and 1938.[121] Continued expansion carried the South to even greater domination of the industry, by 19.3 to 9.7 million spindles in 1939 and 17.6 to 4.9 million in 1945. In active spindles the lead was even more commanding.[122] But the victory was soured by bitter realities. Increasing production of rayon and paper raised competition on the industry's flanks while foreign producers posed a more direct threat. Exports declined under the pressure of multiple forces: price-support programs, the processing tax, increased costs, depreciation of foreign currencies, and the rise of foreign production.

Southern victory in textiles, it began to appear, might be only a fleeting phase of the industry's migration. "From time immemo-

[119] Mouzon, "Social and Economic Implications of Recent Developments within the Wood Pulp and Paper Industry of the South," 168–69, 188, 207–208; William T. Hicks, "Recent Expansion in the Southern Pulp and Paper Industry," in *Southern Economic Journal*, VI (1939–1940), 440; James, *Alfred I. DuPont*, 495–98, 525–29.

[120] Lipscomb, "New Kind of Agriculture Comes to the Piney Woods," *loc. cit.*, 34–35.

[121] Blicksilver, *Cotton Manufacturing in the Southeast*, 99.

[122] Backman and Gainsbrugh, *Economics of the Cotton Textile Industry*, 16; Hoover and Ratchford, *Economic Resources and Policies of the South*, 142.

rial it has been the custom of each people to make its own tex-tiles," a manufacturer reminded his colleagues in 1935. A head start in the machine age was transitory, and millmen had "to recognize this tendency." [123] Reciprocal trade agreements could not counteract the trend, and exports of cotton cloth at the end of the 1930's were only about 40 per cent of those in the late 1920's. Meanwhile Japanese textiles began to make inroads on the do-mestic market. They amounted to only 1 per cent of domestic production, but they were concentrated in a narrow range of cloths and provoked alarm among domestic competitors. Demands for relief brought, in 1936, a Presidential order for tariff increases on certain textiles and, in 1937, the dispatch of an industry commission to Japan to negotiate a voluntary agreement limiting exports to the United States. The Japanese, it turned out, could not fill even those quotas because of military involvements in Asia. Still, in 1939 imports of textiles outweighed exports.[124]

The domestic industry itself remained a classic model of compe-tition, its instability only partially countered by the Cotton Tex-tile Institute and NRA. As one writer described the situation in 1940, "producers are numerous, small, and widely scattered . . . entrance is unobstructed . . . production shows little concentra-tion . . . prices are flexible and profits low." [125] As late as 1935 the four largest cotton textile producers controlled only 8 per cent of the output and the eight largest only 14.2 per cent,[126] but the process of integration was on the increase. One investigator found 220 acquisitions leading to horizontal combinations between 1931 and 1941 and 125 vertical combinations between 1930 and 1939, mostly "backward integrations" through the acquisition of pro-ducing firms by selling houses. Both forms of combination, how-ever, led to increased control by outside capital.[127]

[123] G. H. Dorr, President, Cotton Textile Institute, in American Cotton Manufac-turers' Association, *Proceedings of 39th Annual Convention . . . 1935,* quoted in Blicksilver, *Cotton Manufacturing in the Southeast,* 114.

[124] Blicksilver, *Cotton Manufacturing in the Southeast,* 110–17.

[125] Clair Wilcox, *Competition and Monopoly in American Industry,* U.S. Tem-porary National Economic Committee Investigation of Concentration of Economic Power . . . *Monograph No.* 21 (Washington, 1940), 31.

[126] By value of product. U.S. National Resources Planning Board, *The Structure of the American Economy: Part I. Basic Characteristics* (Washington, 1939), 258–59.

[127] Blicksilver, *Cotton Manufacturing in the Southeast,* 133–35; Jesse W. Mark-ham, "Integration in the Textile Industry," in *Harvard Business Review* (Boston),

Competition had long been absent in iron and steel, and management considerations dictated by existing Northern capacity still restrained expansion. In 1939 Alabama accounted for only 10.2 per cent of the national value added by blast furnaces, only .2 per cent above the region's proportion in 1900.[128] From 1904 to 1938 the South's proportion of steel ingot capacity stood constant at 3 per cent.[129] The picture began to brighten only toward the end of the 1930's. Attention was called sharply to Birmingham's disadvantage under the multiple basing point price system in 1935 when Senator John H. Bankhead and Representative George Huddleston introduced a bill for its abolition, and Southern newspapers and trade organizations mounted an intensive campaign against discrimination.[130] More effective, perhaps, were several other factors: the threat of renewed inquiries by the Federal Trade Commission and the Temporary National Economic Committee, the latter set up in 1938 to investigate economic concentration; an engineering firm's report to U.S. Steel that the practice of supplying Southern and Western markets from Northern and Eastern plants was wasteful, and the accession of a new U.S. Steel leadership under Benjamin Fairless. Failure to utilize Birmingham's cost advantage, the engineers estimated, cost a million dollars annually. In 1938 U.S. Steel reduced its Birmingham prices to a parity with Pittsburgh in most cases and built a modern tin plate mill in Birmingham on the basis of the engineers' recommendation that Birmingham could lay down the product on the Eastern seaboard for $2.48 a ton less than Pittsburgh. World War II soon followed, and the South's steel ingot capacity rose from 3 to 4 per cent of the total in 1945, its tin plate capacity from 5 to 12.[131]

XXVIII (January, 1950) , 78–80. See also Solomon Barkin, "Regional Significance of the Integration Movement in the Southern Textile Industry," in *Southern Economic Journal*, XV (1948–1949) , 395–411.

[128] Chapman, *Iron and Steel Industries of the South*, 116, 142–46. The figures for 1900 include production in Georgia and Tennessee, which was negligible by 1939.

[129] Stocking, *Basing Point Pricing and Regional Development*, 147–48.

[130] Birmingham *News*, March 12, 1935; John H. Bankhead to Marvin Pearce, March 15, 1935, in John H. Bankhead, Jr., Papers; Graves, *Fighting South*, 60–61.

[131] Stocking, *Basing Point Pricing and Regional Development*, 75–76, 105–108, 148–49. On the new pricing policy in 1938 see also "New Steel Price Structure Clicks," in *Business Week*, July 23, 1938, pp. 29–32. The multiple basing point system was entirely abandoned only in 1948.

The new price policy still did not fully exploit the manifest cost advantages of the Birmingham district. Economist George R. Stocking figured the cost of materials and labor per long ton of pig iron in 1939 at $11.633 in Alabama, at $17.508 in Pennsylvania. Nor was Tennessee Coal and Iron permitted by its parent firm the autonomy with which it might have exploited its advantage. In February, 1939, Birmingham supplied in its "natural market area" (the area in which its cost plus freight was below that of any other major producing area) less than half the shipments of plain drawn wire, wire rods, hot rolled sheets, hot rolled strip, structural shapes, and steel plates.[132] Severe criticism of U.S. Steel for retarding development continued into the post-World War II period. As late as 1952 one careful student lamented that outside ownership "tends to place regional interest in a decidedly subordinate position." The fear of endangering existing investments, he concluded, "frequently has blocked developments that seem logical in the region." [133]

But the industrial creed of the New South and the experience of the Southern businessman continued to nourish the growth psychology. Oilmen had feared that their resources were exhaustible, but repeated discoveries revealed greater reserves. Lumbermen had left trails of devastation up the mountainsides and across the coastal plains, but new growths refuted the pessimists. Southern industry had steadily gained on the rest of the nation. Not even the Depression, it turned out, could stop the relative growth of Southern industries. Devoted largely to nondurable consumer goods, they began to climb back from the bottom by 1931. A sharp upturn in 1933 was followed by a textile slump the next year; but by 1936 production was above 1929 levels in textiles, tobacco, and paper and pulp, and by 1937 in food processing, a recovery not achieved by durable manufactures until 1940.[134]

Each advance opened new horizons of diversity. Over the whole interwar period, 1919–1939, the fastest-growing fields were clothing (with a 383 per cent increase in value added), paper and printing (210), furniture (131), and chemicals (123).[135] Of

[132] Stocking, *Basing Point Pricing and Regional Development*, 84–98.

[133] Chapman, *Iron and Steel Industries of the South*, 371.

[134] Hoover and Ratchford, *Economic Resources and Policies of the South*, 118.

[135] H. W. Arndt, "Economic Development of the American South, 1929–1952," in *Indian Economic Review* (Delhi), III (1956–1957), 42.

these, chemicals and paper ranked high in the value added per wage earner. Textile mills, however, with their 476,000 wage earners in 1939, retained the lead in employment—and total value added—followed by lumber and timber products (203,000), and food products (126,000), the only categories with more than 100,000 workers. But in terms of value added chemicals had surged to third place, just behind food products, followed in order by lumber, tobacco, petroleum and coal, printing and publishing, paper, and clothing, each of which added a value of more than $100,000,000.[136]

By 1939 industrial production was about as high as it had been in 1929. Total wages were down 9.9 per cent and value added 2.3 per cent, but outside the South they were down about 20 and 22 per cent respectively. In relative terms the South had gained substantially, increasing its proportion of the nation's production workers from 15.1 to 17.3 per cent, of the nation's wages from 10.2 to 12.1, of value added from 10.2 to 12.7.[137] What is more, total income payments increased relatively after 1931 and absolutely after 1932. By 1940 they were one per cent above the 1929 level in the South, 10 per cent lower in the rest of the country. Per capita income payments were up from 55 per cent of the national average in 1929 to 59 per cent in 1940.[138]

The burden of the temporary business "recession" in 1937–1938 fell chiefly upon the metals industries, of which the South had few.[139] Consequently a drastic slump in cotton and tobacco markets during 1938 and 1939 was partially offset by lesser declines in income from manufacturing and from trade and services. Manufacturing alone did not, of course, account for the change. The only major source of income that registered a substantial absolute increase was, not surprisingly, government. Mainly by force of the New Deal the proportion of income payments from all governmental units in the South rose from 8.1 per cent in 1929 to 12.7 in 1940.[140]

The South was still poor by American standards, with a per

---

[136] Hoover and Ratchford, *Economic Resources and Policies of the South*, 126–27.
[137] *Ibid.*, 116.　　　　[138] *Ibid.*, 48, 50.
[139] Kuznets, *National Income and Its Composition*, 163, 578.
[140] Hoover and Ratchford, *Economic Resources and Policies of the South*, 60; Arndt, "Economic Development of the American South," *loc. cit.*, 32–33, 44. See also Goldschmidt, "Development of the U.S. South," *loc. cit.*, 228–30.

capita income of $340 in contrast to $575 for the nation, but rich by world standards, with an income level near that of Canada.[141] If the region was still far behind on the eve of the Second World War, the very knowledge of its deficiencies plus evidences of continued growth served to bolster the deeply rooted growth psychology. All the forces that worked to narrow the income gap would soon be accelerated in their operation. In 1940 the South was on the threshold of its greatest economic growth yet, amid the tragedy of another world war.

[141] Hoover and Ratchford, *Economic Resources and Policies of the South,* 50; O. J. Firestone, *Canada's Economic Development 1867–1953* (London, 1958) , 171.

CHAPTER XIV

THE UNEVEN PLACES: RELIEF, WELFARE, AND EDUCATION

THE relief of personal distress was an urgent necessity in 1933, and a major need until World War II. In the effort to meet the crisis New Deal agencies administered first-aid to the destitute, doctored the regional economy with injections of Federal money, raised the hopes of countless Southerners and won their devotion. Yet with the ineluctable fate that pursued it, the New Deal provoked divisions in Southern opinion and conjured up sectionalism in still another guise. In the end Federal relief left a heritage of welfare programs that further enlarged state functions and revolutionized Federal relations.

The Federal Emergency Relief Administration, created in May, 1933, with an authorization of $500,000,000, was the New Deal's first general relief agency. Headed by Harry L. Hopkins, who had directed Roosevelt's state relief program in New York, the FERA continued and expanded the assistance that had begun under Hoover's RFC, but with a difference: Federal moneys flowed to the states in grants rather than "loans." The FERA, however, continued to channel the aid through special agencies or welfare departments, for which all Southern states made provision.[1] Aid went to relief clients chiefly in direct payments; but Hopkins gradually developed special programs for education, college student aid, rural rehabilitation, and transient relief, all administered through the states.[2] By September, 1933, public relief reached

[1] Josephine Chapin Brown, *Public Relief, 1929–1939* (New York, 1940), 160–63, 170.

[2] Theodore E. Whiting, *Final Statistical Report of the Federal Emergency Relief Administration* (Washington, 1942), 59, 64–66, 70.

473

more than 20 per cent of all families in three Southern states: Florida, Oklahoma, and South Carolina—the only other state with so high a proportion was West Virginia. Three more had 15 per cent of all families on their rolls: Arkansas, Louisiana, and Alabama. Among the other states only Pennsylvania and Arizona counted so many. By October, 1933, 4,057,145 Southerners (more than one in every eight) were getting public relief; as late as March, 1935, there were still 1,517,561.[3]

The Civilian Conservation Corps and the Public Works Administration made contributions in another way, by taking up the slack in employment. Beginning on a cold, rainy day in April, 1933, when a caravan of motor trucks set out from Washington to put up the first CCC camp in Virginia's George Washington National Forest, hundreds of thousands of young men between eighteen and twenty-five took to the woods for a variety of projects improving forests, parks, and recreational areas. After 1935 Hugh Bennett's soil conservation projects utilized a major part of their labor; by 1941 the CCC operated, among other projects, 106 soil-saving camps scattered across the region from North Carolina to Texas.[4] The PWA—created by the National Industrial Recovery Act in June, 1933, and entrusted to Secretary of the Interior Harold Ickes—got underway more slowly because the nature of its responsibilities required it to take more pains, but it was soon making grants to state and local agencies for public improvements in addition to projects it administered directly. By the end of 1938 PWA had allocated to Southern states $504,133,922 of a total $2,142,508,520 designated for non-Federal projects.[5]

To a remarkable degree the Federal aid programs remained free from political manipulation, and the state relief offices operated

[3] Odum, *Southern Regions of the United States,* 86; New York *Times,* February 3, 1934; Works Progress Administration Division of Social Research, *Workers on Relief in the United States in March, 1935* (Washington, 1938), I, 68.

[4] James J. McEntee, *Now They Are Men: The Story of the CCC* (Washington, 1940), 12–13; *Annual Report of the Director of the Civilian Conservation Corps, 1940* (Washington, 1940), 56–57; *Annual Report of the Director of the Civilian Conservation Corps, 1941* (Washington, 1941), 37. See also Hubert Humphrey, "In a Sense Experimental: The Civilian Conservation Corps in Louisiana," in *Louisiana History,* V (1964), 345–67, and VI (1965), 27–52.

[5] *Congressional Record,* 76 Cong., 1 Sess., 927. See also Harold L. Ickes, *Back to Work: The Story of PWA* (New York, 1935).

under experienced administrators. In Georgia and Alabama the state directors were social workers throughout the program. In most Southern states except Alabama, Louisiana, and Florida, however, it was necessary to bring in supervisory personnel from outside and to recruit untrained social workers, a group that later supplied the cadre for permanent welfare staffs.[6] In Nashville, where in 1933 the new workers crowded pell-mell into a renovated apartment house, office wits insisted that a person who "learned to get in and out of the labyrinth of rooms and cubby holes without being lost . . . was ready to be promoted to a supervisor." But for experienced welfare agents who had toiled so long to make bricks without straw, one of them fondly recalled later, "bliss was it in that age to be alive but to be a social worker was heaven." FERA came "like a burst of bright sunlight after endless days of gloom." [7]

Freedom from politics, however, was not purchased without struggle. In three Southern states it became necessary to use a provision in the Emergency Relief Act of 1934 which permitted federalization of the state agencies whenever politics endangered standards: in Oklahoma (1934), where Governor "Alfalfa Bill" Murray demanded the right to spend funds without regard to Federal rules and regulations; in Georgia (1935), where Governor Eugene Talmadge repeatedly attempted to interfere; and in Louisiana (1935), where Huey Long's commission furnished its offices in a manner "befitting a Madison Avenue advertising firm," hired five lawyers at $7,500 each, and appropriated sums that vanished mysteriously in several banks.[8]

The New Deal's first large-scale experiment with work relief came with the Civil Works Administration during the winter of 1933–1934, when it became apparent that even the titanic

[6] Brown, *Public Relief*, 274, 279.

[7] Mildred Stoves, "Social Work in the Thirties," Elizabeth W. Nairm Memorial Paper, presented to the Middle Tennessee Chapter, National Association of Social Workers, March 11, 1964 (mimeographed; [Nashville], 1964), 1, 11. Courtesy of Professor and Mrs. Dewey W. Grantham, Jr.

[8] Williams, *Federal Aid for Relief*, 176–77. In his characteristic manner Huey Long told Aubrey Williams, Hopkins' assistant, "I am through with this whole goddam ———ing business. Hereafter it's your sucking bastard, and I'll be giving you and Hopkins and that ——— in the White House unshirted hell every day from now on." Aubrey Williams, typescript Memoirs, 28. See also Searle F. Charles, *Minister of Relief: Harry Hopkins and the Depression* (Syracuse, N.Y., 1963), 74–76.

largesse of FERA would not prevent widespread privation. The CWA, working through state relief agencies, provided work relief on a wage basis to those who needed jobs. It was conceived and implemented in great haste, and many of its projects were "made work" jobs of leaf-raking and ditch-digging; but it contributed a variety of more useful projects. In Tennessee, for example, the CWA built and repaired highways and public buildings, installed 14,023 outdoor privies, and provided sewing rooms, school lunch programs, office work, research, and teaching jobs that helped to keep the schools open through the winter.[9]

During the spring of 1934 the CWA was abandoned, having served its purpose of weathering the winter; but Roosevelt and Hopkins continued to be persuaded that work-relief was preferable to the "dole." In 1935 a long period of discussion and planning led finally to the establishment of the Works Progress Administration. The WPA provided relief for the unemployed, and the problem of relief for "unemployables" was left to the states, with Federal grants-in-aid for the purpose under the Social Security Act.

From January, 1933, through April, 1939, the FERA, CWA, and WPA poured $1,938,061,860 into the Southern states, providing relief and in the process engineering spectacular physical improvements. One of FERA's most imaginative projects renovated Key West and turned a bankrupt community into a successful winter resort. In 1934, 80 per cent of Key West's inhabitants were on the relief rolls when the state relief administration mobilized a work corps, cleaned up streets and beaches, improved sanitary facilities, developed cabanas, brightened up bars and restaurants with murals, stimulated handicrafts, and organized fetes and operas. The PWA contributed an overseas highway across the keys and some forty thousand visitors arrived the following winter.[10] In South Carolina, Charleston's energetic Mayor Burnet R. Maybank, having steered the city around the financial

[9] Minton, "New Deal in Tennessee," 91–94.
[10] Elmer Davis, "New World Symphony with a Few Sour Notes," in *Harper's Magazine*, CLXX (1934–1935), 641–52; Federal Writers' Project of the Works Progress Administration for the State of Florida, *Florida: A Guide to the Southernmost State* (New York, 1939), 199–200.

shoals of depression, seized upon the Federal emergency funds to buoy up its economy, tapped new water resources to bring in a paper mill, secured five public housing projects, a yacht-seaplane basin, restoration of the eighteenth-century Dock Street Theater, and finally accepted the chairmanship of the state Public Service Authority which, with WPA and PWA help, developed the Santee-Cooper project, South Carolina's "little TVA." [11]

In Baton Rouge Federal aid renovated the old state capitol, a Gothic artifact of the romantic age; in Montgomery and Raleigh it provided new depositories for state archives; on all sides an infinite variety of emergency projects mushroomed into schools, courthouses, city halls, sewage plants, hospitals, bridges, libraries, playgrounds, airports. Through Alabama and the Carolinas, an English visitor noted in 1938, one could hardly round a curve in the highway without encountering a sign, "WPA-Men at Work." [12] Special talents were put to use in art, music, and drama programs, in compiling state guide books, and in surveying historical records.

But catalogs of expenditures and improvements scarcely convey the human consequences of Federal relief. Like NRA wages, even relief payments established new levels of income for many. Among subsistence farmers and stranded miners in the Southern Appalachians, the Depression "actually served to raise standards for many families . . . who had lacked contact with the American standard of living." [13] In the foothills and coastal plains dispossessed whites and Negroes swarmed around the relief offices,

[11] LeRoy M. Want, "On the Job: Mayor of Charleston," in Charleston News and Courier, March 7, 1937; Edward B. Talty, "A New Leader in the New South," in Christian Science Monitor, March 30, 1940, clippings in Maybank Papers; "Reminiscences of J. Waties Waring," 94–109.

[12] Writers' Program of the Works Progress Administration in the State of Louisiana, Louisiana: A Guide to the State (New York, 1941), 257; Philip M. Hamer, "The Records of Southern History," in Journal of Southern History, V (1939), 13–14; Ursula Branston, "Mr. Roosevelt Helps the South," in The Spectator (London), CLXI (1938), 1084.

[13] Rupert B. Vance, "The Region: A New Survey," in Thomas R. Ford (ed.), The Southern Appalachian Region: A Survey (Lexington, Ky., 1962), 5. See also L. S. Dodson, Living Conditions and Population Migration in Four Appalachian Counties, Farm Security Administration and Bureau of Agricultural Economics Social Research Report No. III (Washington, 1937), 19.

seeking the miraculous leisure of a forty-hour week or less and luxury wages of nineteen dollars a month or more. "This is a rich country," one of them remarked. "I figger it ain't going to hurt the government to feed and clothe them that needs it." "The government is the best boss I ever had," said a North Carolina worker. Whenever "I hear the 'Star-Spangled Banner' I feel a lump in my throat," a North Carolina tenant farmer told a visitor to his quarters in an abandoned filling station. "There ain't no other nation in the world that would have sense enough to think of WPA and all the other A's." [14] In urban slum quarters the influx of relief clients created scenes of teeming squalor. W. J. Cash, who witnessed them, gave a vivid description: "In the morning the crazy porches were sprinkled with direct relief clients or the able-bodied who had not yet got on the WPA list, sunning themselves happily. And in the afternoon, once the brief WPA day was over, they were crowded with active men and women, laughing, sleeping, drinking cheap wine or corn whiskey, or dreaming restlessly of violence to relieve the monotony of their leisure. To the great disgust, naturally, of all Southerners of the superior orders, who never troubled to ask themselves how it had come about—but above all to that of the passing landowners." [15]

The reaction of gentlefolk could indeed be intense. Relief was undoing the spirit of self-reliance and crowding the towns with the less resolute workers in a region where land was so abundant that subsistence offered no problem, William Watts Ball wrote from Charleston.[16] What was worse, it jeopardized the great natural resource of cheap labor to the acute distress of planters and village nabobs. "Ever since federal relief . . . came in you can't hire a nigger to do anything for you," said a North Carolina landlord. "High wages is ruinin' 'em." And worst of all was the lessening of dependency. "I don't like this welfare business," another landlord told a relief worker. "I can't do a thing with my niggers. They aren't beholden to me any more. They know you all won't let

<hr />

[14] Ruth Durant, "Home Rule in the WPA," in *Survey*, LXXV (1939) , 275; Federal Writers' Project of the Works Progress Administration in North Carolina, Tennessee, and Georgia, *These Are Our Lives, as Told by the People* (Chapel Hill, 1939) , 15, 366.

[15] Cash, *Mind of the South*, 408.

[16] William Watts Ball to Henry Hazlitt, December 11, 1933, in Ball Papers.

them perish." [17] "I wouldn't plow nobody's mule from sunrise to sunset for 50 cents per day," an outraged farmer in Georgia wrote Eugene Talmadge, "when I could get $1.30 for pretending to work on a DITCH." Talmadge forwarded the letter to the President, who computed that farm labor at 50 cents a day, considering its seasonal nature, would come to about $75 a year. "Somehow," he wrote, "I cannot get it into my head that wages on such a scale make possible a reasonable American standard of living." But on second thought he asked Harry Hopkins to sign the reply.[18]

In the depths of the crisis many landlords, in fact, had encouraged their tenants to go on relief, and localities without funds welcomed a chance to dump the load on the Federal government. But in the early months of 1934 the authorities began to weed out the rural relief rolls and throw responsibility back on the landlords, even while rural unemployment increased. The CWA dismissed rural workers first of all on the theory that men having made seven or eight weeks' wages "should be able to go back to their farm and raise a crop without suffering." A downward trend in rural relief continued throughout the life of FERA, although it was somewhat balanced by the rise of the rural rehabilitation and resettlement programs.[19]

In 1936 Harry Hopkins began a practice of closing WPA projects and releasing workers during the cotton-picking season. His policy statement carried instructions that actual employment at standard wages should be available. The purpose was not to create an oversupply of labor, depress going wages, or force workers to accept substandard wages, the President assured a complainant, but soon it became apparent that officials in the mid-South had joined in a drive to undermine the Southern Tenant Farmers Union.[20] Several state relief agencies developed elaborate pro-

[17] Both quoted in Esther Morris Douty, "FERA and the Rural Negro," in *Survey,* LXX (1934), 215–16.

[18] Schlesinger, *Coming of the New Deal,* 274.

[19] Harold B. Myers, "Relief in the Rural South," in *Southern Economic Journal,* III (1936–1937), 282–83; Lumpkin and Douglass, *Child Workers in America,* 101.

[20] Gardner Jackson to Franklin D. Roosevelt, September 12, October 31, 1936; Roosevelt to Jackson, September 26, 1936; Jackson to Harry Hopkins, telegram, September 12, 1936, in OF 444-C, Roosevelt Library. The telegram to Hopkins mentions appeals of the Memphis Chamber of Commerce and similar bodies for the release of cotton pickers.

cedures to prevent the diversion of surplus farm workers to relief. In Louisiana regulations stipulated that relief offices should consider sharecroppers for WPA referral only after consultation with the plantation management or the usual source of credit.[21]

In 1937, when a bumper cotton crop required a sudden increase in pickers, WPA officials again required relief workers to accept offers of temporary employment in the fields. But the response was so inadequate that planters turned to the more co-operative local officials. The pattern was set at Anderson, South Carolina, where an obliging police chief rounded up laborers for the farms; from there it spread across the cotton belt. In Warrenton, Georgia, a mob entered town and drove Negroes to the fields, and in other places something like the old slave patrol was revived to prevent an exodus of workers.[22]

Relief, when granted, almost inevitably built in the existing regional differentials, sometimes in exaggerated form. Local pressures and the FERA policy of not granting help in excess of prevailing labor standards kept the rates painfully low. In July, 1933, when the national average monthly payment per family was $15.07, Southern averages ranged from $3.96 in Mississippi to $13.89 in Louisiana. By January, 1935, Southern payments averaged from $9.59 in Oklahoma to $25.99 in Louisiana, but the national level was $30.43. Averages for rural or Negro families ran considerably lower.[23] A typical rural relief family of the eastern cotton belt in the summer of 1935 consisted of a worker, about forty years old, attempting to feed and clothe a wife and two or three children on $10 a month if white, $7 if Negro.[24]

Similar differentials appeared in the work-relief programs. The PWA provided at the beginning a 40 cent hourly minimum in the

[21] Donald S. Howard, *The WPA and Federal Relief Policy* (New York, 1943), 506.

[22] Cash, *Mind of the South*, 409; Kennedy, *Southern Exposure*, 51–52. A similar drive had occurred with the bumper crop of 1931. Wilson, *Forced Labor in the United States*, 92; and Walter Wilson, "Cotton Peonage," in *New Republic*, LXIX (1931–1932), 130–32.

[23] Federal Emergency Relief Administration, *Monthly Report*, December 1 to December 31, 1933 (Washington, 1934), 64; *ibid.*, January 1 through January 31, 1935 (Washington, 1935), 31.

[24] Howard B. Myers, "Relief in the Rural South," in *Southern Economic Journal*, III (1936–1937), 283–84.

lower South, 45 cents in a central region including four upper South states, and 50 cents elsewhere. The CWA copied the PWA standard but dropped the minimum to 30 cents in the spring of 1934. After CWA ended, wages continued at that level under a limited FERA work program until November, when wages were set at the "prevailing rates," as determined by local committees, and fell to 12½, 15, and 20 cents throughout the South.[25] After 1935 the WPA based its "security wage" on a more complex system of four regions and five kinds of population-density areas within regions. This system yielded monthly wages ranging from $19 to $75 in the South and from $32 to $94 in other states. The underlying theory required wages to be above the relief rate and a decent minimum standard, yet below the prevailing level of private wages. But the theory left no middle ground for the WPA to occupy in much of the rural South, where private wages were near or even below relief levels.[26] In 1938 one WPA official noted that the $21 then paid to unskilled workers for 140 hours in the rural South was "about double the wage for the same amount of labor on a farm," and defended the practice as "good public policy in areas of extremely low living standards." [27]

But a policy of using relief programs to narrow regional differentials was never articulated or, apparently, seriously considered. On the contrary, one relief study after another showed that, as one put it, "not only were there many more families with very small incomes in the South than in other regions but a substantially larger proportion of these low-income families failed to receive relief." "Unmet need," the National Resources Planning Board

[25] Arthur E. Burns and Peyton Kerr, "Survey of Work-Relief Wage Policies," in *American Economic Review*, XXVII (1937), 713–15; J. Kerwin Williams, *Grants-in-Aid under the Public Works Administration: A Study in Federal-State-Local Relations*, in Columbia University *Studies in History, Economics, and Public Law*, No. 459 (New York, 1939), 189. According to Carter Glass, the PWA minimum of forty-five cents in Virginia was "in some instances more than double the prevailing rates, and it has disorganized all the common labor on all of the farms in that section of Virginia." Quoted *ibid.*, 191. After 1935 PWA rates were set "in accordance with local wage conditions." *Ibid.*, 193.

[26] Howard, *WPA and Federal Relief Policy*, 160–61; Burns and Kerr, "Survey of Work-Relief Wage Policies," *loc. cit.*, 720.

[27] Nels Anderson, *The Right to Work* (New York, 1938), 143–44. Anderson was Director of the WPA Section of Labor Relations.

concluded in 1942, "was the greatest in the southern regions." [28] Relief in the South was disproportionate even to population. With more than a fourth of the nation's inhabitants, the Southern states received less than a seventh of the FERA expenditures.[29] Of total expenditures for FERA, CWA, and WPA programs to April, 1939, they received less than a sixth.[30] In the Southeastern states alone (excluding Texas and Oklahoma) the recipients of public aid rose steadily from 12.4 per cent of the national total in September, 1937, to a high of 16.5 per cent in December, 1939, but the area had 21.5 per cent of the population; the number in all other regions remained near or above the proportion of population.[31]

Two factors accounted for the persistent discrepancies. One was the reluctance, or inability, of Southern states to contribute substantially to the programs. In the nation as a whole the Federal proportion of FERA obligations came to 62 per cent; it was above 90 in eight Southern states and over 80 in all but Texas, where it was 72.7.[32] The other factor was the inability to raise rates without arousing the hostility of employers, some of whom questioned relief itself. "Even God Almighty never promised anybody that he should not suffer from hunger," one Southern manufacturer declared. " 'No one in America shall starve.' When was it decided that that is the business of Federal government?" asked an incredulous *Manufacturers' Record*.[33] The pattern of regional differences was repeatedly explained by the folklore of lower living costs in the South. In 1938 the Atlanta *Constitution* uncovered statistics showing that the average Mississippian spent

[28] National Resources Planning Board Committee on Longe-Range Work and Relief Policies, *Security, Work, and Relief Policies*, 1942 (Washington, 1942), 156, 157. See also Howard, *WPA and Federal Relief Policy*, 73–85.

[29] Or $640,337,910 of a total of $4,819,225,130 expended or obligated by the time the program was completely liquidated in 1937. This includes state contributions. Whiting, *Final Statistical Report of the Federal Emergency Relief Administration*, 299–307.

[30] Corrington Gill, *Wasted Manpower: The Challenge of Unemployment* (New York, 1939), 281–307.

[31] National Resources Planning Board, *Security, Work and Relief Policies*, 104.

[32] Williams, *Federal Aid for Relief*, 216–20; Whiting, *Final Statistical Report of the Federal Emergency Relief Administration*, 308–22.

[33] New York *Times*, August 30, 1934; "Perversion of Government," in *Manufacturers' Record*, CV (June, 1926), 19.

only $70 a year in his retail stores and the New Yorker $297. This, according to the *Constitution*'s exegesis, demonstrated the lower costs in the South, the advantages of climate, "and the simplicity of life in Mississippi." A Southerner with $11 a week, the paper argued, would be better off than a New Yorker with $13.[34] The WPA discrepancy, however, was much greater. The conclusion is unavoidable that the differential, like so many other things, reflected differences not in the cost but in the standard of living.[35]

Relief policy, therefore, presented Southern Congressmen with another troublesome dilemma of the colonial economy. The low-wage philosophy of Southern expansionism pulled them one way; human need and the political potential of relief another. As sectional consciousness grew in the late 1930's they suddenly discovered that the differentials were susceptible to criticism as sectional "discrimination," although the censure sometimes masked a conservative attack on Federal expenditures. Senator James F. Byrnes of South Carolina, who proposed to cut back relief as social security expanded, tried unsuccessfully to reduce the appropriation in 1937. He noted that New York City alone had gotten 12.3 per cent of WPA expenditures through 1936 although it had only 5.6 per cent of the population and contributed only one half of one per cent of the project costs.[36]

In 1939 Richard B. Russell gave the Southern case against discrimination its fullest documentation. "I have always considered myself a liberal and progressive Democrat," he told the Senate, but "I am not as much an evangel of this philosophy . . . that we can spend our way out of the depression, as some of my colleagues appear to be." Lacking a better plan, however, he proposed to support continued outlays "if the funds were to be expended equally and fairly among all the people of the United States." But

[34] Atlanta *Constitution*, February 18, 1938.

[35] Burns and Kerr, "Recent Changes in Work-Relief Wage Policy," *loc. cit.*, 62.

[36] The President explained this on the dubious ground of more intense need, but also pointed out that New York State was giving to all relief $56 per capita while South Carolina was contributing only $8. "It occurs to me," he wrote Byrnes, "that due publicity should be given to this comparison when you speak on the floor of the Senate. . . . Or do you want me to do it?" James F. Byrnes to Franklin D. Roosevelt, June 8, 1937; Harry Hopkins to Roosevelt, June 2, 1937; Roosevelt to Byrnes, June 9, 11, 1937, in OF 444-C, Roosevelt Library; Byrnes, *All in One Lifetime*, 84–87; Charles, *Minister of Relief*, 160–65.

he marshaled charts of expenditures for relief, public works, and AAA to demonstrate "that it almost always follows that the State having the lowest income has received the lowest per capita expenditure of these funds through which we seek to help the underprivileged." [37]

Persistent complaint, and perhaps political considerations, eventually caused the gap to narrow. In 1938 Congress authorized increased spending to meet the business recession, and Southern members wangled a provision to put on the WPA rolls farmers who needed supplementary income. From July to November, 1938, the number of WPA workers in eleven Southern states grew from 461,000 to 641,000, about 40 per cent against a 10 per cent growth in the nation. Moreover, in June administrative action raised monthly earnings in the thirteen Southern states an average of about $5 and put the minimum at $26. No WPA worker should get less than a dollar a day, Hopkins said. "We felt for some time that our security wages in certain areas . . . were based on a standard of living below the levels of health and decency." [38]

During the excitement of that summer's primaries, many saw political expediency in the actions, but the new dispensation still left the South well behind in both wages and the amount of WPA employment. In 1939 further improvements accrued from a requirement in the relief appropriation that differentials should be no greater than differences in the cost of living. Definition was imprecise, but the Southern minimum rose to $31.20 and the Northern dropped to $39 in most states, and maximums reached $81.90 in most Southern and $94.90 in most Northern states. Another measure of change was an increase of average monthly earnings in Southern states. From 1935–1936 to 1941–1942 these grew by 93 per cent or more, as much as 135 per cent in Florida and 138 in Kentucky. [39] These changes brought WPA more nearly into line with manufacturing wage differentials, the 10 per cent

[37] *Congressional Record*, 76 Cong., 1 Sess., 910–30. See also remarks of Senator Josh Lee of Oklahoma, Alben Barkley of Kentucky, and Byrnes, *ibid.*, 8121–22, and Claude Pepper of Florida, *ibid.*, 10305.

[38] New York *Times*, June 27, 1938.

[39] Howard, *WPA and Federal Relief Policy*, 159–62, 182–84; Burns and Kerr, "Recent Changes in Work-Relief Wage Policy," *loc. cit.*, 58–59; *Time*, XXXII (July 4, 1938), 10.

differential for work on government contracts, and variations permitted by the Fair Labor Standards Act of 1938—and they came as relief benefits reached their peak in 1939.[40] But the reduction in differentials was confined to the direct Federal work program; their persistence in state and local relief programs remained a different, and neglected, matter.

Housing, like relief, presented patterns of inadequacy. Southerners, conditioned to think of slums in terms of Northern tenements, often failed to see their own. "We have become used to slums, and don't think of them as slums," a Mississippian wrote. "They're part of the scenery. They are principally the hovels in which most of our Negro population lives." [41] Negro shanties were prime investments in Southern towns; they required small outlays and bore low assessments but brought handsome returns from areas where neglect of sanitary provisions was "as proverbial as . . . exhorbitant rents." [42] For white workers as well, urbanization created "swarming warrens, with four or five persons herded into each room," conditions further aggravated by the influx of displaced persons in the 1930's: unemployed, relief clients, WPA workers—uprooted, poorly identified with the communities, enlarging the patches of disease and violence.[43]

The slum clearance projects of the Public Works Administration afforded a partial if inadequate answer to the problem. The program took life in Atlanta in September, 1933, when Harold L. Ickes cleared the way for the nation's first projects by symbolically blasting a shack on each of two sites near Georgia Tech and Atlanta University. On one arose Techwood Homes for whites, 2,124 rooms ready in August, 1936; on the other, University Homes for Negroes, 2,342 rooms opened in 1937.[44] In all, twenty-one of PWA's fifty-seven slum-clearance projects were located in

[40] Spartanburg (S.C.) *Journal and Carolina Spartan,* August 15, 16, 1939; National Resources Planning Board, *Security, Work and Relief Policies,* 104.

[41] Greenville (Miss.) *Delta Democrat-Times,* October 10, 1945, quoted in David L. Cohn, *Where I Was Born and Raised* (Boston, 1948), 236.

[42] *Ibid.,* 239–40; quotation from Lumpkin, *South in Progress,* 77.

[43] Cash, *Mind of the South,* 271–73, 412–17.

[44] Harold L. Ickes, *The Secret Diary of Harold L. Ickes* (New York, 1953), I, 199–200; Michael W. Straus and Talbot Wegg, *Housing Comes of Age* (New York, 1938), 190–91; Marion Luther Brittain, *The Story of Georgia Tech* (Chapel Hill, 1948), 222–25.

the Southern states.[45] After 1937, when the United States Housing Authority assumed responsibility, Southern legislatures and towns on the whole responded as favorably as the rest of the country. By 1940, 12 of the 34 states with legislation for housing authorities and 89 of the 204 authorities were Southern.[46] But if public housing replaced some of the blighted areas it was often too expensive for the displaced occupants. In 1938 the average monthly rent in Atlanta's Techwood Homes was $7.33 per room including service charges; in Charleston's Meeting Street Manor and Cooper River Court (both for Negroes), $5.89.[47] "I pay a negro man $10 a week and feed him," William Watts Ball of Charleston wrote. "On that wage he could not afford to rent one of those government houses. In other words, the negro houses are for the negro economic royalists." [48]

The problem of rural housing was even more formidable. Except for subsistence homesteads and the rare farm communities, experiments in the field made little progress before the Second World War. And compromises had to be made in many of those. Roosevelt wanted houses with modern plumbing, but the cost for most rural families was prohibitive. Brought up short by the economic realities, Will Alexander recalled, the President of the United States spent much of one forenoon sketching designs for the best possible outdoor privies.[49] The Wagner-Steagall Housing Act of 1937 made provision for rural authorities, and the USHA by June, 1941, had allocated almost $14,000,000 to them, mostly for regional and county authorities embracing 277 Southern counties. The largest grant of $1,594,000 went to 25 of South Carolina's 46 counties. But few of the projects materialized before war intervened, and most of the housing for war workers was around urban areas.[50]

Relief measures were temporary and public housing peripheral,

[45] Only three states had none: Arkansas, Louisiana, and Mississippi. Straus and Wegg, *Housing Comes of Age*, 103–10, 190–229.

[46] Lepawsky, *State Planning and Economic Development in the South*, 113.

[47] Straus and Wegg, *Housing Comes of Age*, 190, 196.

[48] William Watts Ball to Hunter A. Gibbes, January 12, 1938, in Ball Papers.

[49] "Reminiscences of Will W. Alexander," 505–507.

[50] M. H. Satterfield, "Trends in Rural Local Government in the South," in Taylor Cole and John H. Hallawell (eds.), *The Southern Political Scene, 1938–1948* (Gainesville, Fla., 1948), 513–14; Greenville (S.C.) *News*, April 9, 1941.

but the new welfare policy under the Social Security Act of 1935 had both a permanent and a material effect. Roosevelt himself called it the New Deal's "cornerstone" and "supreme achievement." [51] In common parlance "social security" came to mean the Old-Age and Survivors' Insurance, but the eleven titles of the act also established unemployment insurance and committed the Federal government to a broad range of welfare activities. The underlying theory was that "unemployables" who were ineligible for WPA work relief should remain a state responsibility. To that end the law inaugurated grants-in-aid for three public assistance programs—old-age assistance, aid to dependent children, aid to the blind—and for maternal, child-welfare, and public health services, but not for general relief.[52]

The discrepancies of the colonial economy pursued the South on into the emerging welfare state. Old-age insurance, oriented to an industrial society, did not cover agricultural workers and domestic servants, among others. Consequently by June, 1938, only 21.3 per cent of the Southeastern population had registered, in contrast to 30.6 per cent in the other states. In 1946 ten Southeastern states had only 68 beneficiaries among every thousand people over sixty-five, in contrast to 104 in the nation. The one Southern advantage arose from a formula weighted to favor workers with lower earnings, plus the larger number of young workers with time to build up protection; but the benefits were geared to earnings and therefore lower on the average in the South.[53] Unemployment insurance, administered by the states, showed variations in benefits as well as coverage. By 1937, all

[51] On its passage see Edwin E. Witte, *The Development of the Social Security Act: A Memorandum on the History of the Committee on Economic Security and Drafting and Legislative History of the Social Security Act* (Madison, Wis., 1962), quotation from Rosenman (comp.), *Public Papers and Addresses of Franklin D. Roosevelt*, IV, 324, 472.

[52] Brown, *Public Relief*, 306–12, 327–28. For greater detail see Paul H. Douglas, *Social Security in the United States: An Analysis and Appraisal of the Federal Social Security Act* (New York, 1939); and Lewis Meriam, *Relief and Social Security* (Washington, 1946), 16–140, 184–242.

[53] John J. Corson, "Old-Age Insurance and the South," in *Southern Economic Journal*, V (1938–1939), 324–29; E. J. Eberling, "Old Age and Survivors' Insurance and Old Age Assistance in the South," *ibid.*, XV (1948–1949), 57–58. The figures for 1946 cover the states east of the Mississippi River, including Louisiana.

Southern states had entered the program but it covered only a third of their labor force compared to a half in other states. In the second quarter of 1939, when unemployed workers realized a weekly compensation averaging $10.13 for all states combined, they got $8.68 in Kentucky and $5.88 in North Carolina—and the duration of benefits was shorter in Southern states.[54]

In 1938, when Virginia adopted all three of the public assistance programs, every Southern state had accepted the Federal welfare grants.[55] But the deficiencies of insurance coverage in the South threw a heavy burden upon the assistance programs, for which the hard-pressed states had to find matching funds. The South lagged in the numbers covered by old-age insurance, but it led in the proportion of its elderly citizens on the welfare rolls. In 1941 in the ten Southern states east of the Mississippi, 225 out of every 1,000 persons sixty-five or older were getting assistance, but only 217 in the nation; by 1946 the figures were 235 and 205. And because of the greater burden the grants were smaller.[56] In June, 1940, average monthly grants for old-age assistance ran from $7.47 in Arkansas to $37.95 in California, for the blind from $7.95 in Mississippi to $48.02 in California, and for dependent children from $12 in Arkansas to more than $45 in New York and California.[57] California could readily match the maximum Federal grants; Arkansas and Mississippi could not.

Still, the Federal money held out a compelling lure and expenditures for public welfare in the South expanded phenomenally. From a total of about $21,000,000 in 1929 (mostly for Confederate pensions), the outlay more than tripled to $74,000,000 by 1937–1938, doubled again to $155,000,000 by 1942, and nearly doubled again to $247,000,000 in 1946.[58] So widespread

[54] William R. Curtis, "Unemployment Compensation Experience in the South," *ibid.*, VII (1940–1941), 51, 53; William R. Curtis, "The Development of Unemployment Insurance in the South," *ibid.*, XV (1948–1949), 53.

[55] J. Alton Burdine, "Trends in Public Administration in the South," in Cole and Hallowell (eds.) *Southern Political Scene*, 426. Florida had no approved plan for aid to dependent children.

[56] Eberling, "Old Age and Survivors' Insurance and Old Age Assistance in the South," *loc. cit.*, 56, 58.

[57] National Resources Planning Board, *Security, Work, and Relief Policies*, 456.

[58] Hoover and Ratchford, *Economic Resources and Policies of the South*, 210–11. The figures include Federal, state, and local funds, which in 1946 constituted 50.6, 44.2, and 5.2 per cent, respectively, of the total. They include old-age assistance, aid

was the need and so much greater the participation that, despite the smaller individual benefits and the lower incomes of taxpayers, expenditures in proportion to population nearly equaled those in the nation: in December, 1948, $1.01 per capita in the South and $1.14 outside the region. For old-age assistance alone the Southern expenditure was greater by 76 cents to 70.[59] By fiscal 1948 pensions for the elderly accounted for the largest program of Federal grants-in-aid to the region: about $156,000,000 in a total of $475,000,000; highways ranked second at $105,000,000.[60]

Public health work entered a new period of expansion in the late 1930's, largely because of social security and the Venereal Disease Control Act of 1938, but partly as a result of mounting concern with public welfare in general. Local leadership and new support were significant in some states, as in Alabama and Arkansas, where new liquor taxes served to equalize the coverage in poorer counties. Only 49 new county health departments appeared in the Southeast between 1930 and 1935, but from 1935 to 1941 the total nearly doubled from 396 to 747, covering more than three fourths of all counties in the area and 44.7 per cent of all counties in the United States with such service. But if the Southeast had nearly half of the county health departments, it spent the least on public health. Six states of the region put out less than a dollar per capita in 1940, and only Louisiana, at $2.43, exceeded the national average of $1.90. At the same time the Southeast had one physician for every 1,101 persons, the nation had one for every 751. No Southeastern state reached the national average in hospital beds proportionate to population. In infant mortality, perhaps the most sensitive index of public health, the Southeastern rate fell from 87.4 per thousand live births in 1920 to 57.4 in 1940, the national rate from 85.8 to 47; only Arkansas did better than the nation at large.[61]

---

to dependent children, and aid to the blind, for which Federal grants were available, and general assistance or relief payments, responsibility for which reverted entirely to the states after the creation of WPA in 1935.

[59] *Ibid.*, 212–13.

[60] *Ibid.*, 225. However, Florida, Oklahoma, and Texas received about 55 per cent of the Federal grants to the region for old-age assistance.

[61] Allen, "Public Health Work in the Southeast," 399–400; Vance, *All These People,* 366–67, 371–73.

The welfare revolution of the 1930's—the permanent outgrowth of relief—created a new major function of state governments. In 1940 highways remained the largest field of state expenditures, with 30.1 per cent of the total, and education came second with 27.9; but welfare accounted for 10.2 per cent or 23.7 if unemployment compensation, public health, and hospitals were added.[62] And the over-all trend toward expanded state services kept up the pace that had been set during the progressive era. Total state expenditures in the South, excluding debt retirement, increased 316 per cent over two decades, from $555,000,000 in 1929 to $1,123,000,000 in 1942, and $2,311,000,000 in 1948. Federal contributions made up a growing proportion of the necessary revenues: 5.7 per cent in 1929, 15.3 in 1937, and 17.4 by 1948. Tax revenues improved with rising incomes, but a large proportion of the increase came from sales taxes on particular commodities, which brought more than half the tax collections in Southern states by 1937, 54.9 per cent by 1948. But despite the flurry of interest in the general sales tax during the early years of the Depression, Southern states relied less heavily upon it than others. Motor fuels outweighed all other sources of sales taxes, but became progressively less important as the states turned to heavier taxes on such minor vices as soft drinks, tobacco (except in North Carolina and Virginia, where the weed remained sacrosanct), and alcoholic beverages (even in prohibitionist Mississippi, which levied a "black-market" tax on illegal sales).[63] The situation yielded a painful irony. Social security was financed by state tax programs that tended to be regressive, to fall more heavily on the poor. Who could say, a troubled economist asked, "whether society gains or loses when, in order to give one aged person a pension of $120 a year, it takes

[62] Pierce et al., White and Negro Schools in the South, 327–28. By 1938 schools had replaced highways in the first place. Local expenditures scarcely changed during the period, either in amount or in purpose, the new developments being almost altogether state responsibilities. Hoover and Ratchford, Economic Resources and Policies of the South, 213–14.

[63] Hoover and Ratchford, Economic Resources and Policies of the South, 197–207. See also B. U. Ratchford, "Recent Economic Developments in the South," in Cole and Hallowell (eds.), Southern Political Scene, 275–78; and James W. Martin, "State and Local Taxation in the Southeast and the War," in Southern Economic Journal, XIV (1947–1948), 376–86.

$2 apiece from 60 families subsisting on incomes of $400 per year?" [64]

It was a heavy price to pay for the principle of state participation, but direct Federal programs would have met insurmountable political obstacles. "With our local policies dictated by Washington," the conservative Charleston *News and Courier* warned, "we shall not long have the civilization to which we are accustomed." [65] Southern Congressmen, with Senator Harry F. Byrd of Virginia in the lead, expurgated certain minimum standards from the Social Security Act before its passage, including administrative safeguards and a requirement for old-age assistance adequate to "a reasonable subsistence compatible with decency and health." Federal standards, Byrd told a Senate Committee, threatened "dictatorship" over the states, and behind his remarks loomed an apprehension expressed by the Jackson *Daily News:* "The average Mississippian can't imagine himself chipping in to pay pensions for able-bodied Negroes to sit around in idleness on front galleries." [66] In any case, standards above the barest minimum would have loaded an intolerable burden upon the poorer states in the absence of broader coverage by old-age insurance or some Federal effort to equalize the burden of public assistance for poorer states.

As it was, the program greatly enlarged the role of the Federal government and, together with other grant-in-aid plans, revolutionized its relations with the states. The pattern of the "new federalism" entailed an increasing collaboration of Federal, state, and local governments, with policies guided from Washington. States channeled their activities into programs for which Federal money was available and accepted the Federal standards for administrative structures, merit systems, and procedures. At the same time the states centralized control of their new activities in

[64] Clarence Heer, "Financing the Social Security Program in the South," in *Southern Economic Journal,* IV (1937–1938) , 299.

[65] Quoted in *Congressional Record,* 74 Cong., 2 Sess., 3938.

[66] Witte, *Development of the Social Security Act,* 143–45; New York *Times,* January 24, 1935; Jackson (Miss.) *Daily News,* June 30, 1935, quoted in William E. Leuchtenburg, *Franklin D. Roosevelt and the New Deal, 1932–1940* (New York, 1963) , 131.

order to qualify more quickly for Federal aid. The sprawling proliferation of new agencies in turn impelled renewed efforts toward integration of administrative structures. Kentucky in 1936, Tennessee in 1937, Alabama in 1939, and Louisiana in 1940 and 1942 undertook major reorganizations, and all of the states took steps toward executive budgets, merit systems, and retirement programs.[67]

Older programs, like the new welfare, drew sustenance from the Federal cornucopia. Relief and public works projects rejuvenated the highway movement, and state expenditures moved from about $54,000,000 in 1929 to $147,000,000 in 1946.[68] They did not quite keep pace with the over-all governmental expansion, partly because the major outlines of road systems were already established; but in some states the networks were not developed until the 1930's. In Louisiana Huey Long built upon the earlier work of his opponents, John M. Parker and Jared Y. Sanders, to outdo the other states in the rate of development. Parker took Louisiana "out of the mud"; Long put it on asphalt and concrete. Between 1928 and the end of 1935 the state extended its concrete highways from 296 to 2,446 miles, asphalt from 45 to 1,308, and graveled roads from 5,728 to 9,629. "We got the roads in Louisiana, haven't we?" the irrepressible Huey asked an inquisitive reporter. "In some states they only have the graft." [69] Mississippi was the last state to develop an over-all plan for highways when it earmarked $42,500,000 in 1936 for a system of primary and secondary roads connecting all eighty-two counties.[70]

A crowning achievement of roadbuilding was to bridge the lower Mississippi. The Harahan Bridge at Memphis dated from 1916; in 1930 another crossing was completed at Vicksburg and in

[67] Buck, *Reorganization of State Governments in the United States*, 110–15, 226–32; Burdine, "Trends in Public Administration in the South," *loc. cit.*, 432–37; Roscoe C. Martin, "Alabama's Administrative Reorganization of 1939," in *Journal of Politics*, II (1940), 436–47; Robert H. Weaver, *Administrative Reorganization in Louisiana*, in Louisiana State University Bureau of Government Research *Publications*, No. 17 (Baton Rouge, 1951).

[68] Hoover and Ratchford, *Economic Resources and Policies of the South*, 208–209.

[69] Sindler, *Huey Long's Louisiana*, 103–104; George E. Sokolsky, "Huey Long," in *Atlantic Monthly*, CLVI (1935), 526.

[70] Federal Writers' Project of the Works Progress Administration in Mississippi, *Mississippi: A Guide to the Magnolia State* (New York, 1938), 91.

1935 the Huey P. Long Bridge at New Orleans; by early 1940 three more were nearing completion—at Baton Rouge, Natchez, and Greenville, Mississippi. At the end of 1946 the Southern states had 116,093 miles of surfaced highways in their primary systems, 36.5 per cent of the nation's total; and a motorist could cross the region in any direction without leaving the pavement.[71] Highway development in turn stimulated the creation of state police systems, or highway patrols, in every Southern state during the decade 1929–1939.[72]

Public education endured a desperate famine in the early years of the Depression. Scholarship, one disheartened observer lamented, was "an unnecessary frill, something to be tolerated in times of prosperity, but to be left off at the first sign of hard times."[73] School boards abbreviated the terms, pruned salaries, and paid teachers in scrip or not at all. In the fall of 1931 salaries of Tennessee's elementary school teachers dropped almost 10 per cent.[74] In Mississippi, where the state treasury was nearly empty at the beginning of 1931, college employees had to subsist on the charity of their neighbors. New contracts at Mississippi State authorized percentage reductions in salaries at the board's discretion. In 1932 the University of South Carolina paid faculty salaries in scrip, some of which was not redeemed for thirteen years. South Carolina's general funds shrank 46.7 per cent from 1931–1932 to 1933–1934, and similar contractions were common in other state universities: 41.7 per cent at North Carolina, 25.6 at Kentucky, 20.8 at Virginia. Salary cuts varied from 5 per cent at Oklahoma to 45 at Mississippi.[75]

But renewal followed the lean years. During the year 1933–

[71] John A. Fox, "Bridging the Mississippi River," in *Manufacturers' Record*, CXI (February, 1940) , 28–29; Hoover and Ratchford, *Economic Resources and Policies of the South*, 209. The South, however, had a larger proportion of narrow roads.

[72] Weldon Cooper, "The State Police Movement in the South," in *Journal of Politics*, I (1939) , 415.

[73] W. T. Couch, "A University Press in the South," in *Southwest Review*, XIX (1933–1934) , 199–200.

[74] Andrew David Holt, *The Struggle for a State System of Public Schools in Tennessee, 1903–1936* (New York, 1938) , 390.

[75] Bettersworth, *People's College*, 297–99; Hollis, *University of South Carolina*, II, 332–33; William Burl Thomas, "The Educator and the Depression. II: The College Instructor," in *Nation*, CXXXVII (1933) , 213–15.

1934 grants from the FERA's Emergency Educational Program helped to keep open 34,992 rural schools throughout the South.[76] Under the heading of work relief for teachers FERA and WPA offered special programs of many kinds, from nursery schools and classes in literacy to vocational training and general adult studies. By October, 1936, the enrollment of 361,613 Southerners in WPA classes exceeded the enrollment of the region's colleges.[77] "The facts of the Emergency Education program speak for themselves," said the *Texas Weekly.* "Measured in terms of citizenship and general welfare, its impact will be felt . . . for years to come." [78] Library services revived and expanded with work projects that complemented a program of county library demonstrations by the Rosenwald and Carnegie foundations, 1929–1937. The number of people in Southeastern political units served by public libraries rose from 6,286,821 (27 per cent of the population) in 1926 to 17,426,948 (62 per cent) in 1941. By 1941 WPA had contributed $4,268,000, nearly double the state and local subventions.[79]

Under Harry Hopkins' assistant, Aubrey Williams, a native Alabamian, the National Youth Administration provided jobs to keep high school and college students in school and sponsored a variety of educational work activities. It placed twenty Negro girls in New Orleans' Flint Goodridge Hospital where they got experience in jobs from the switchboard to the operating room; it conducted soil-conservation demonstrations in Texas, built fish-rearing ponds in Tennessee, placed young people from relief

[76] Whiting, *Final Statistical Report of the Federal Emergency Relief Administration,* 112. This represented a great majority of the 45,220 schools aided. The largest number in any state was 5,492 in Mississippi.

[77] John S. Perkins, "Extent and Nature of the Federal WPA Educational Program," in *School and Society* (New York and Garrison, N.Y.), XLV (1937), 134–35. The figure is for the Census South. See also Brown, *Public Relief,* 271; Doak S. Campbell, Frederick H. Blair, and Oswald S. Harvey, *Educational Activities of the Works Progress Administration,* WPA Staff Study (Washington, 1939).

[78] *Texas Weekly,* June 27, 1936, quoted in Patenaude, "New Deal and Texas," 431. A WPA release of December 18, 1938, stated that the 50,000th Texan had begun learning to read and write and that more than 33,000 had already learned in the five years of the program.

[79] Louis Round Wilson, "The Role of the Library in the Southeast in Peace and War," in *Social Forces,* XXI (1942–1943), 463; Embree and Waxman, *Investment in People,* 60–67; Smith, *Builders of Goodwill,* 103–12; Beatrice Sawyer Russell, "Book Relief in Mississippi," in *Survey,* LXXI (1935), 73–74.

families in resident projects. For the first of these, begun at Southwestern Louisiana Institute in 1936, WPA built two $20,000 dormitories; and NYA brought in young men, previously out of school, for a variety of work experiences in horticulture, dairying, swine husbandry, farm shops, automobile mechanics, maintenance of buildings and grounds, and kitchens.[80] "If the Roosevelt Administration had never done another thing," said Lyndon B. Johnson of Texas, who at twenty-seven became the youngest NYA state administrator, "it would have been justified by the work of this great institution for salvaging youth."[81]

Emergency programs also expanded the regular educational plant. In the years 1934–1936, six Southern states built 314 new school buildings with relief workers and enlarged or modernized 1,225 more; Georgia alone got PWA help for 162. Before the end of the 1930's WPA and PWA contributed $9,708,921 for 1,758 school projects in Kentucky. Altogether, PWA alone poured about $200,000,000 into school construction in the South.[82] The front·ranks of relief advocates, Senator Byrnes noted, were crowded with college presidents "who seized the opportunity to have the federal government build football stadiums and libraries at no cost to the colleges."[83]

Stimulated first by the New Deal and then by wartime prosperity, state school expenditures resumed their upward trend, mounting from $344,283,681 in 1930 to $603,994,031 by 1946; again as in the 1920's the region surpassed the nation in the rate of increase.[84] Because the Depression ravaged country schools, sapping their sources of revenue first, it hastened the trend toward minimum programs supported by state equalization funds. In 1937, for example, Georgia established a minimum statewide seven-month term. North Carolina went further than any other

[80] Betty Lindley and Ernest K. Lindley, *A New Deal for Youth: The Story of the National Youth Administration* (New York, 1938), 48, 50–51, 86–88, 225–27.

[81] Booth Mooney, *The Lyndon Johnson Story* (New York, 1956), 33–34.

[82] Stanley High, "A Kind Word for the South," in *Saturday Evening Post*, CCX (January 8, 1938), 55; McVey, *Gates Open Slowly*, 243; Pierce *et al.*, *White and Negro Schools in the South*, 58.

[83] Byrnes, *All in One Lifetime*, 84.

[84] U.S. Bureau of Education, *Biennial Survey of Education in the United States*, 1928–1930, II, 76–77; U.S. Bureau of Education, *Biennial Survey of Education in the United States*, 1944–1946, II, 74.

state, with the assumption of state responsibility for a six-month term in 1931 and eight months in 1933, and became thereby the only state with "truly a state system of public education." [85]

In some quantitative measures Southern schools began to overtake national averages. In 1940 they enrolled a slightly higher percentage of school-age children than schools outside the South, respectively 85.4 and 85.2 per cent; and average attendance reached 86.8 per cent of that in the rest of the country. The length of term increased substantially, and the average number of days each pupil attended went from 113 in 1927–1928 to 144 in 1945–1946, or from 80 to 96 per cent of the national average.[86] But the long years of inadequacy still exerted their drag. In 1940 about 40 per cent of all Southerners over twenty-five had never gone beyond the sixth grade, but only 20 per cent of the non-Southerners. At higher levels the differential was less striking: 9.08 per cent of Southerners had some college training and 10.32 per cent of other Americans.[87] In 1945–1946 expenditures per pupil in every Southern state still ran well below the national average of $144.02. The highest was Texas with $134.41, but only three other states averaged more than $100—Florida, Louisiana, and Oklahoma—and Mississippi brought up the rear with $47.49. Yet the South, with about a third of the school children and less than a fifth of the country's income, was spending a higher proportion of its personal earnings for public education than the rest of the country, 1.78 per cent in contrast to 1.71.[88]

A possible response to the situation would have been Federal aid to help the poorer states, just as state aid helped the poorer districts. Relief programs did supply some Federal aid, but it was neither permanent nor geared systematically to needs. In 1938, however, a Presidential Advisory Committee on Education recommended a program of grants for special purposes and of general aid to be allocated according to the number of school-age children and the financial ability of the states. The report provoked a

[85] Pierce *et al.*, *White and Negro Schools in the South*, 58; Harry S. Ashmore, *The Negro and the Schools* (Chapel Hill, 1954), 24, 26–28; Dorothy B. Orr, *A History of Education in Georgia* (Chapel Hill, 1950), 38; Plemmons, "Extension and Equalization of Educational Opportunity in the South," *loc. cit.*, 33, 36.

[86] Hoover and Ratchford, *Economic Resources and Policies of the South*, 31, 210.
[87] *Ibid.*, 32.   [88] *Ibid.*, 210.

perennial, but fruitless, political controversy. Southerners, including Senators Harrison of Mississippi, Hill of Alabama, George of Georgia, and Representative Ramspeck of Georgia, rallied to the support of Federal-aid bills. Education in an age of mobility "is not a State problem alone; it is a national problem," Lister Hill declared in 1943. "It must be an accepted principle of American Government that wealth, income, and privileges should be taxed wherever found, and the revenue spent for public services wherever needed." But successive bills for aid to education perished in committees or expired on the calendars. A fatal impasse came in 1943 when a measure sponsored by Hill and Elbert Thomas of Utah was amended to require equitable distribution among segregated schools. Southerners deserted the bill and it was recommitted. Jim Crow once again had exacted his tribute.[89]

Still, the advance of state and local support resumed as depression faded and public school systems continued to absorb the pioneering programs of the General Education Board. In 1933 the GEB began a planned withdrawal from the support of special programs for public schools. At that time it began to terminate grants to state institutions for practice schools and by 1937 for special administrative divisions in state departments of education. However, it continued to support curriculum studies and work in the co-ordination of high school and college curricula, as well as summer schools and workshops on new materials and methods. But the GEB mission in the establishment and elaboration of state public school systems was drawing to an end.[90]

Its focus turned now to the special needs of higher education, a field in which the University of Virginia's Professor Wilson Gee had pointed up acute deficiencies. Because of inferior university salaries and facilities, heavy teaching loads, and the low quality of postgraduate centers, Gee reported in 1932, "a steady stream of the best in intellectual and leadership qualities has been pouring

---

[89] The efforts are outlined in Frank J. Munger and Richard F. Fenno, Jr., *National Politics and Federal Aid to Education* (Syracuse, N.Y., 1962), 7–8; Charles A. Quattlebaum, *Federal Aid to Elementary and Secondary Education* (Chicago, 1948), 41–48; and "The U.S. Congress and Federal Aid to Higher Education," in *Congressional Digest* (Washington), XXIII (1944), 38–41. The latter is in a special issue devoted to the question; Senator Hill is quoted *ibid.*, 51.

[90] Calkins, "Historical Review," *loc. cit.*, 38–40.

from out the borders of the South toward superior advantages elsewhere." Unless the conditions were remedied, he warned, the South was "forever doomed to mediocrity." [91] In 1934 a national survey by the American Council on Education underscored his findings. It identified only seven institutions in the South with departments "adequately staffed and equipped" for the doctorate. Of 661 such departments in the nation the South had only 42, of which 12 were at Texas and 11 at North Carolina; of 230 starred for "eminence" only 2 were Southern: genetics at Texas and sociology at North Carolina.[92] In 1935 Edwin R. Embree of the Rosenwald Fund asserted that not a single Southern institution could be considered eminent in scholarship. "Even one university of first rank would rally the intellectual forces of the region," he wrote. "A great university in the South is the insistent need in American scholarship to-day." [93]

That particular need remained unmet, but the advance of higher education brought a growing recognition that the standards set by the Southern Association of Colleges and Secondary Schools posed no challenge to the better institutions. The standards operated chiefly to distinguish colleges from high schools. In 1927, however, a Conference of Deans of Southern Graduate Schools had evolved from a Southern Association committee and in 1932 the Association's Committee on Standards had resolved that the stronger institutions should confer on "standards or regulations for graduate work, extension and correspondence study, and other matters not now covered by our requirements." The result was the Southern University Conference, formed at

---

[91] Gee, *Research Barriers in the South*, 165–69. See also Wilson Gee, "The 'Drag' of Talent out of the South," in *Social Forces*, XV (1936–1937), 343–46; Harold Loran Geiser, "The Trend of the Interregional Migration of Talent; The Southeast, 1899–1936," *ibid.*, XVIII (1939–1940) , 41–47; and Harry Estill Moore and Sidney R. Worob, "Place of Education and Residence of Eminent Southerners," *ibid.*, XXVII (1948–1949) , 408–12.

[92] American Council on Education, *Report of Committee on Graduate Instruction* (Washington, 1934) , 4–35. The seven institutions were Duke, North Carolina, Oklahoma, Peabody, Rice, Texas, and Virginia. The report was based on judgments by juries drawn from outside the South and perhaps favored "so-called prestige institutions" elsewhere. Pierson, *Graduate Work in the South*, 179n.

[93] Edwin R. Embree, "In Order of Their Eminence: An Appraisal of American Universities," in *Atlantic Monthly*, CLV (1935), 664.

Atlanta in 1935 with a membership of thirty-three institutions. The venerable Chancellor Kirkland of Vanderbilt, father of the earlier movement, sounded a new keynote: "We are not organized to meet any definite educational evils such as existed forty years ago. Our organization is rather to secure freedom for the study of problems peculiar to our own group that are forcing themselves upon our attention at the present time." The problems had moved beyond minimal standards; they involved a multiplicity of new programs and the quest for excellence.[94]

In that quest the GEB still performed a significant function. "Make the peaks higher" had been a favorite aphorism of Wickliffe Rose, GEB president in the 1920's; during the following decades the foundation's Southern policy moved more toward his ideal. The emphasis shifted to higher education and the programs turned from general endowment and buildings toward the improvement of quality, the introduction of new disciplines, the enlargement of opportunities for graduate study. One ill-starred effort encouraged the development of co-operative university centers for whites in Atlanta, Nashville, Richmond, and Durham-Chapel Hill on the model of Atlanta and Dillard universities for Negroes; but it never progressed beyond some exchanges of faculty and students, some co-ordination of library services, and the Joint University Libraries in Nashville. In 1938 the GEB initiated a more fruitful plan to stimulate training and research in fields especially related to Southern economic and social development: grants for studies of agriculture, rural sociology, forestry, fisheries, public administration, population, industry and marketing, and statistics, together with smaller grants for conferences and studies. The studies included pilot programs for education in health and nutrition and the preparation of materials for resource-use education. After 1940 the fellowships program expanded and during the following decade almost seven hundred students from Southern colleges sought advanced degrees under GEB fellowships. And in a gradual liquidation after 1947 the GEB devoted most of its re-

[94] Pierson, *Graduate Work in the South*, 78–87; Committee on Work Conferences on Higher Education of the Southern Association of Colleges and Secondary Schools, *Higher Education in the South*, 100; Southern University Conference, *Proceedings, Constitution, and By-Laws*, 1935, pp. 1–3.

maining resources plus additional sums from the Rockefeller Foundation to further "strategic advances" in the field of graduate education in the South.[95]

In the march of education Negro schools plodded far behind, still hobbled by discrimination. "Should the Negro pupil be given as much education as the white pupil?" 114 county and city superintendents in North Carolina were asked in 1930; 27 answered "No." As late as 1940 pollsters found about half the white Southerners opposed to educational equality for Negroes.[96] The "typical" Negro school of East Texas was described in 1934 as "a crude box shack, built by the Negroes out of old slabs and scrap lumber," with no blackboards or desks, and benches for only half the pupils.[97] Of 3,753 Negro schools in Mississippi, 1,440 held their sessions in churches, lodges, old stores, or tenant houses. Hundreds of rural schools had "just four blank, unpainted walls, a few old rickety benches, an old stove propped up on brickbats, and two or three boards nailed together and painted black for blackboards."[98] In St. Andrew's Parish, across the Ashley River from Charleston, Negro pupils sat on newspapers or on planks supported by bricks.[99]

One agent of Northern philanthropy found Negro schools "not a system but a series of incidents: bizarre, heroic, pathetic, romantic," and gave revealing evidence of the straws at which a sympathetic observer clutched when he felt his judgment "melted by the sudden singing of a spiritual" or the realization that an illiterate teacher in a room without desks or textbooks was "bringing the

[95] Calkins, "Historical Review," *loc. cit.*, 45–47; Fosdick, *Adventure in Giving*, 266–97, 309; Southern University Conference, *Proceedings, Constitution, and By-Laws,* 1939, pp. 26–75.

[96] Cooke, *White Superintendent and the Negro Schools in North Carolina*, 124; N. C. Newbold, "Has North Carolina Made Any Real Progress in Negro Education?" in *North Carolina Teachers' Record* (Raleigh), II (1931), 3; Dabney, *Below the Potomac,* 206.

[97] William R. Davis, *The Development and Present Status of Negro Education in East Texas,* in Columbia University Teachers' College *Contributions to Education,* No. 626 (New York, 1934), 56.

[98] P. H. Eason, "Negro Education," in *Biennial Report and Recommendations of the State Superintendent of Public Education to the Legislature of Mississippi for the Scholastic Years 1933–34 and 1934–35* (Jackson, 1935) 41.

[99] Frank A. DeCosta to William Watts Ball, November 26, 1936, in Ball Papers.

children along with her native wit and ingenuity." [100] But if discrimination continued, the older trend toward lesser shares for Negroes had ended. The gap in public expenditures had ceased to widen in the 1920's; it began to narrow slowly in the 1930's. Figures for six states show that the current expenditures per pupil rose from 29.6 per cent of the white average in 1931–1932 to 44.0 in 1941–1942 and 55.8 in 1945–1946. [101] Average teacher salaries for Negroes by 1939–1940 were more than half those for whites in the region, in contrast to about a third in 1930, and were on the eve of more rapid increases under the pressure of lawsuits for equalization. [102] The average length of term was almost equal to that of the whites, 153 days to 169. But in other measures, such as buildings, school buses, libraries, and laboratories, the Negro schools continued to lag. [103]

Foundation programs for Negro education unfolded in much the same way as those for whites, with differences in detail and timing. Assistance began at the lower levels and aid to higher education generally came later. [104] But as public support of Negro schools gained, the older programs tapered off. In 1932 the Rosenwald Fund terminated its school-building grants and focused its educational concern upon high schools, normal schools, and colleges; "the beginnings of a proper school system . . . in the Negro group may be regarded as established," its president reported. School buildings were no longer the crucial need they had once been. [105] In 1932 the GEB stopped its grants for Jeanes teachers and in 1934 for Slater schools. After 1939 its contributions for state agents of Negro schools dwindled away as the states assumed

[100] Edwin R. Embree, "Every Tenth Pupil," in *Survey Graphic*, XXIII (1934), 539.

[101] Ernst W. Swanson and John A. Griffin, *Public Education in the South Today and Tomorrow: A Statistical Survey* (Chapel Hill, 1955) , 63. The respective figures were 39.09 for whites and 11.56 for Negroes in 1931–1932, 51.67 and 22.76 in 1941–1942, and 80.29 and 44.84 in 1945–1946. The states were Alabama, Arkansas, Florida, Georgia, North Carolina, and South Carolina.

[102] Pierce *et al., White and Negro Schools in the South*, 207. Throughout the region in 1939–1940 salaries for whites averaged $960 and for Negroes $504.

[103] *Ibid.*, 216–22, 228–32, 235, 245–54.

[104] Calkins, "Historical Review," *loc. cit.*, 57–58.

[105] Edwin R. Embree, *Julius Rosenwald Fund: Review for the Two-Year Period 1931–1933* (Chicago, 1933) , 31; Embree and Waxman, *Investment in People*, 35, 55.

responsibility.[106] The Jeanes and Slater funds, however, united in 1937 as the Southern Education Foundation and continued their aid to rural Negro schools on a descending scale.[107]

In the Depression years the GEB directed larger grants to a number of promising state colleges and a smaller group of strategically located private colleges. Many of the grants were rescue operations, necessitated by the Depression; but most were arranged to prime various pumps—like the Mississippi legislature, which elevated Jackson State College from two- to four-year status in 1942 when the GEB and the Rosenwald Fund each gave $30,-000 toward a building program. Both foundations gave especial attention to the emerging Negro university centers: Atlanta, Dillard, Howard, Fisk, Hampton, Tuskegee, and the Meharry Medical School. The grants at first subsidized buildings, libraries, and laboratories, but after 1939 the GEB turned to the improvement of specific departments—a shift of emphasis made for white colleges some fifteen years before. By that time some of the Negro institutions were already prepared to participate in the new programs of research and training for regional development.[108]

After 1930 the Southern Association's practice of accrediting Negro schools offered some quantitative measure of their progress. A survey at the time disclosed eighty-five institutions of "postsecondary" grade for Negroes, but of sixty contacted only thirty-five filed complete reports with supporting data. Of these the Association ranked Fisk University as the only Class A institution and six others as Class B. By 1945 the Association had approved 28 Class A colleges, 16 Class B, 4 Class A junior colleges, 5 Class B, and 106 secondary schools.[109]

But the unmistakable signs of progress could not obscure the

[106] Calkins, "Historical Review," loc. cit., 57–58.

[107] Southern Education Foundation, Biennial Report for 1950–51, 1951–52 (Atlanta, 1952), 1–6. The coalition also included residual sums of the old Peabody Education Fund, left to the Slater trustees in 1914, and the Virginia Randolph Fund, representing small sums collected from the Jeanes teachers.

[108] Calkins, "Historical Review," loc. cit., 58–59; Fosdick, Adventure in Giving, 209–10, 268.

[109] Snavely, "Short History of the Southern Association of Colleges and Secondary Schools," loc. cit., 489–92. Class B colleges did not meet all requirements but were regarded as sufficiently qualified to warrant acceptance of their graduates in any program requiring the bachelor's degree for entrance.

cruel deficiencies. "The whole program of college education for Negroes" in South Carolina, a Peabody College report asserted in 1946, "is very seriously impaired and conditioned by the unsatisfactory type of elementary and secondary education which . . . Negroes have received up to this time." [110] If there were no universities of the first rank for whites there were none of any rank for Negroes, save in name. Negro institutions had to adapt to the preparation of their students. Not one offered the Ph.D. at the end of the 1930's, and many of the smaller schools remained travesties of higher education.[111] Faced with the necessity of appealing to white trustees or legislators, many a Negro president swallowed his pride and assumed the assigned role of servility, building in the hope of some future daybreak. But many another sank into the role of petty tyrant, a sycophant before his white overlords and a capricious despot in his own domain.[112]

By 1945 the foundations had substantially completed their original mission in Southern education. Uneven places were still sorely apparent, especially between rural and urban or between white and Negro schools, but a system existed to which every Southern child had access—and a superstructure of colleges and universities, four of which had achieved membership in the Association of American Universities.[113] The Southern Education Foundation still supported Jeanes teachers at the bottom while the GEB tried to raise the peaks at the top, but both worked with diminished resources. The Southern states, for the most part, were on their own in the field of public education.

The GEB, the great central directorate of educational develop-

---

[110] Division of Surveys and Field Services, George Peabody College for Teachers, *Public Higher Education in South Carolina* (Nashville, 1946) , 347.

[111] Fred McCuistion, "Graduate Instruction for Negroes," in *Proceedings of the Sixth Annual Meeting of the Association of Colleges and Secondary Schools for Negroes, 1939* (n.p., n.d.) , 66. For a comprehensive and caustic indictment of Negro institutions in one state see Lewis K. McMillan, *Negro Higher Education in the State of South Carolina* (Orangeburg, S.C., 1952) .

[112] Louis E. Lomax, *The Negro Revolt* (New York, 1962) , 190–92; J. Saunders Redding, *No Day of Triumph* (New York, 1942) , 121–24, 131–39. The most vivid descriptions are in novels; see Ralph Ellison, *Invisible Man* (New York, 1952) , and J. Saunders Redding, *Stranger and Alone* (New York, 1950) .

[113] Virginia (1904) , North Carolina (1922), Texas (1929), Duke (1938) . Pierson, *Graduate Work in the South*, 74–75.

ment, had nearly consumed its capital by 1946 and worked thereafter with periodic grants from the Rockefeller Foundation. During the forty-five years, 1902–1947, it had poured $126,774,765 into the Southern program from its total expenditures of $289,-406,144. Most of the Southern expenditures, or $104,615,527, went into universities and colleges. Much of this was for endowments; public school programs were used mainly to induce public expenditures, and were therefore smaller. For Negro education the board laid out $52,085,250, of which $7,118,452 went to public education in contrast to only $6,861,955 for white.[114] Working by the "slow processes of evolution" (another of Rose's aphorisms, dubbed S.P.O.E. by irreverent associates), the GEB had greatly enlarged its activities in public education of Negroes after 1919 and ultimately had given Negro schools the greater amount of expenditures in that field. Its guiding strategy was to wage war not against the inequity "that existed between the two races but that which distinguished the South from the other regions of the United States," the GEB's former president, Raymond B. Fosdick, wrote. Its program by-passed problems later considered fundamental. "But it led to many impressive achievements, not the least of which was its stimulating effects on Negro education." Out of the effort, Fosdick noted, came leadership that sparked the thinking of a later day.[115] And before the GEB made its exit into the wings of history an entirely new and vital force entered the stage—the NAACP's drive for equal opportunity in education.

[114] Calkins, "Historical Review," *loc. cit.*, 8–11.
[115] Fosdick, *Adventure in Giving*, 323–24.

CHAPTER XV

BUILDING UNIONS IN THE SOUTH

THE violent strikes of 1929 exposed a deep unrest in the industrial South, but the sporadic union activity that followed left behind only the shambles of defeat. Suddenly, in the spring of 1933, the moribund labor movement stirred anew, with a vitality that provoked combat on wider battlefronts than ever before. The National Industrial Recovery Act provided the psychological leverage to release pent-up frustrations into organized activity. Section 7 (a) demanded in every industry's code a declaration of the workers' right to bargain collectively, and alert unionists quickly translated the provision into a compelling summons: "The President wants you to join the union." "The United States Government Has Said LABOR MUST ORGANIZE," a handbill of the Kentucky State Federation of Labor asserted. "ALL WORKERS ARE FULLY PROTECTED IF THEY DESIRE TO JOIN A UNION." [1] The claims were exaggerated, but among workers the conviction grew that labor had a friend in the White House, that the government would protect unions, and that working men had a duty to join.

John L. Lewis of the United Mine Workers was among the first to exploit the spirit of the Blue Eagle. President of a union decimated by depression, he staked its remaining treasury on an intensive organizing campaign. Agents of the union thronged into the coal fields, raised the banner of the New Deal, and gathered members by the thousands. Antiunion defences crumbled before the sudden onslaught. On July 2, 1933, William Turnblazer, president of District 19 (Tennessee and eastern Kentucky) reported

---

[1] McAlister Coleman, *Men and Coal* (New York, 1943) , 148; Schlesinger, *Coming of the New Deal,* 139.

that 85 per cent of the mine workers in his area had enrolled during a two-week drive.[2] By the fall the union was strong enough throughout the mountains to secure code wages based upon a collective-bargaining contract, the Appalachian Agreement.[3]

Alabama required a more protracted siege. In June, 1933, William Mitch, newly arrived from Indiana, invited miners to revive the defunct District 20. His organizers invaded the fields, held up fistfuls of paper and silver dollars, asked miners when they had last seen cash money, and promised good wages as the outcome of organization.[4] On July 23 Mitch told a convention in Birmingham's City Auditorium that the union had signed 18,000 members in 85 locals. "There is a brighter day on the horizon for the mine workers of Alabama," he declared.[5] Through that fall a series of isolated strikes forced recalcitrant operators in the state to pay code wages. Mitch was ready for a bigger offensive in February, 1934, when most of Alabama's miners walked out to force union recognition. On March 14 about 85 per cent of the noncaptive mines signed an agreement for a voluntary check-off and other benefits.[6] Before the end of 1934 the UMW claimed 92 locals in Alabama and a membership of 23,000.[7] By April, 1935, the international union had enrolled an over-all paid membership of 541,-000, representing 95 per cent of the workers. By that time the only significant nonunion enclaves in the South were certain captive mines of United States Steel in Kentucky, the West Kentucky Coal Company, Harlan County, and the Acmar and Margaret mines of the Alabama Fuel and Iron Company, where Charles F. DeBardeleben fiercely protected his charges against becoming "the slaves of John L. Lewis." [8] In October, 1935, when union members attempted to march toward the company's mines

[2] Minton, "New Deal in Tennessee," 204.

[3] Coleman, *Men and Coal*, 74. On labor standards under NRA see Chapter XIII above.

[4] Cayton and Mitchell, *Black Workers and the New Unions*, 321–22.

[5] *United Mine Workers' Journal* (Indianapolis), XLIV (August 15, 1933), 12.

[6] *Ibid.*, XLV (April 1, 1934), 10. The captive mines had signed earlier.

[7] Cayton and Mitchell, *Black Workers and the New Unions*, 323.

[8] Walter Galenson, *The CIO Challenge to the AFL: A History of the American Labor Movement, 1935–1941* (Cambridge, 1960), 194–95; Daniels, *Southerner Discovers the South*, 286.

despite signs warning them off, the explosion of dynamite planted in the road killed one man and injured several others.[9]

The enthusiasm of the coal miners inspired the iron ore miners to join in a similar revival of the International Union of Mine, Mill and Smelter Workers. The Mine Mill union, heir to the militant tradition of the old Western Federation of Miners, operated chiefly in nonferrous metals; but during the summer of 1933 it responded to an invitation extended by James A. Lipscomb, a Bessemer lawyer, and began to organize the red ore miners. In May, 1934, the union directed a strike supported by nearly all the ore workers, a violent affair of two months' duration that won wage increases for all except common laborers, but not union recognition. In October, 1934, a district convention of Mine Mill workers drew delegates from sixteen locals, including a few in Tennessee, representing some 7,000 workers; it remained active in the area until 1949.[10]

During the NRA period the example of the two mine workers' groups centered at Birmingham and Bessemer made Jefferson County a peculiar focus of labor organization, ranging from company unions in the steel mills to the Communist party, which had made Birmingham its Southern headquarters in 1930. By 1934 the Communists had a following of probably fewer than 250 members and perhaps 1,500 fellow-travelers, but enough to attract a disproportionate attention by provoking radical demonstrations and retaliatory brutalities from police and vigilantes.[11] Union membership in the county swelled from something below 2,000 to an estimated 50,000 in the fall of 1934. The established railroad brotherhoods and city trades filled out their member-

[9] *Violations of Free Speech and Rights of Labor: Hearings before a Subcommittee of the Committee on Education and Labor, United States Senate,* 75 Cong., 2 Sess., Pt. 3 (Washington, 1937), 793–94, 969.

[10] The Mine Mill union fell prey to Communist infiltration and, eventually, domination. In 1949, the United Steelworkers, who had organized the iron ore miners elsewhere, picked off the Alabama Mine Mill membership. Vernon H. Jensen, *Nonferrous Metals Industry Unionism, 1932–1954: A Story of Leadership Controversy* (Ithaca, N.Y., 1954), 41–42, 233–40; Cayton and Mitchell, *Black Workers and the New Unions,* 323–24, 329–30.

[11] Cayton and Mitchell, *Black Workers and the New Unions,* 337–41; *Violations of Free Speech and Rights of Labor; Hearings,* 75 Cong., 2 Sess., Pt. 3, pp. 733–804.

ship, and new locals mushroomed among boilermakers, laundry employees, meat cutters and butchers, and workers in furniture, garment-making, cast iron pipe, cement and slag, and other fields. In steel, however, the movement failed. Neither the Mine Mill union nor the old Amalgamated Association of Iron, Steel and Tin Workers made much headway despite strenuous efforts.[12]

The intensity and diversity of unionism in the Birmingham district were unique, but craft unions rallied in most Southern cities, city centrals revived, some new ones appeared, and the existing ones grew stronger.[13] And the contagion spread among industrial workers. The Tobacco Workers' International Union, previously active only on the union-label fringes of the industry, strengthened its position in North Carolina, Virginia, and Kentucky, and in December, 1933, signed a two-year closed-shop agreement covering about 4,600 workers in the Brown and Williamson plants in Winston-Salem, Louisville, and Petersburg. The Big Four of the industry, however, held them off until 1937.[14] In the Southwest a clamor for membership in the International Association of Oil Field, Gas Well, and Refinery Workers drew Secretary John L. Coulter from a lonely headquarters in his home at Fort Worth to organize locals in East Texas. Before the end of 1934 the formerly dormant union held a convention at Fort Worth, its first since 1926, set up 175 locals, and signed one agreement with a major company, Sinclair; but it declined almost as fast after the end of NRA in 1935. By the time of its Tulsa convention in 1936 there were only 75 locals.[15]

Elsewhere there were scattered manifestations of labor militancy: the Southern Tenant Farmers' Union in Arkansas, an automobile workers' local in Atlanta, strikes of Gulf Coast longshoremen and seamen in 1934, 1935, and 1936. Altogether in the four years, 1933–1936, between 450,000 and 500,000 Southern workers went on strike.[16] The figure was greatly augmented by the most

[12] Cayton and Mitchell, *Black Workers and the New Unions*, 321–37.
[13] Douty, "Development of Trade-Unionism in the South," *loc. cit.*, 574.
[14] Herbert R. Northrup, "The Tobacco Workers' International Union," in *Quarterly Journal of Economics*, LVI (1941–1942), 611–12, 615.
[15] Allen, *Chapters in the History of Organized Labor in Texas*, 234–37; O'Connor, *History of Oil Workers' Intl. Union*, 30–38.
[16] Lumpkin, *South in Progress*, 121, 125–27.

spectacular incident of the period, the general textile strike of 1934, which carried out more than 400,000 workers including perhaps 200,000 in the South.

The United Textile Workers, potentially the largest industrial union in the South, had a record of repeated defeats. It had reached a nadir of about 15,000 dues-paying members early in 1933. But energized by the New Deal spirit, it regained a foothold in Southern textiles for the first time since 1921. By September, 1933, the UTW claimed an over-all membership of 40,000; by August, 1934, 270,000; from July, 1933, to August, 1934, it issued 600 local charters.[17]

Lessons of the past, however, dictated caution. The leadership sought to moderate worker militancy and to channel complaints through the grievance machinery created under the textile code. A committee set up to investigate the stretchout became in August, 1933, the Cotton Textile National Industrial Relations Board. The CTNIRB undertook to hear complaints and mediate disputes but, lacking enforcement powers, was helpless to prevent numerous violations of the code. Dissatisfaction stemmed chiefly from heavy work loads and the continuing pattern of part-time employment, for which many workers mistakenly expected the full-time code wage. Restlessness increased when after temporary curtailment in December, 1933, the code authority decided in May, 1934, to limit operations for twelve weeks to two 30-hour shifts at the same hourly rate. UTW Vice President Francis J. Gorman threatened a general strike unless the industry maintained the existing weekly wages. But on June 2 the union, still uncertain of its strength, accepted a temporary compromise that postponed the issue pending a study of the industry's ability to absorb the cost. Meanwhile the curtailment began on June 4.

The summer of 1934 was a period of festering dissension. In July the editor of the *Textile World* declared: "Not one shred of cooperation, sympathy or mutual understanding exists between

---

[17] Hodges, "New Deal Labor Policy and the Southern Cotton Textile Industry," 208–209. For a description of the textile strike of 1934 and its antecedents see pp. 207–99; Lahne, *Cotton Mill Worker*, 224–31; and John Wesley Kennedy, "The General Strike in the Textile Industry, September, 1934" (M.A. thesis, Duke University, 1947).

southern manufacturers and textile labor organizers." [18] In August a government representative who had visited mills in four states reported: "Labor leaders in each state . . . tell me . . . their only recourse is through the use of their economic strength." [19] Eventually the prudence of the national leaders yielded to the militancy of the Southern workers. On July 18 a strike erupted in northern Alabama, where before the end of August about twenty-three thousand workers walked out of twenty-eight mills demanding a $12 minimum for the 30-hour week and other concessions. Union President Thomas McMahon "killed the other strike," said one worker, alluding to the June compromise; "we are not going to let him kill this one." [20] On August 16 about two thousand more workers went out in Columbus, Georgia, on a complaint of intimidation and discharge of union members.[21]

Already, on the day before the Georgia walkout, the rising tide of Southern passion had swept a national convention in Philadelphia. Southern delegates presented fifty strike resolutions. The lack of union funds did not dampen their spirits, a delegate from Newberry, South Carolina, asserted. "I have been wounded in the head and shot in the leg," one of the Alabama strikers declared, "but I am ready to die for the union." [22] On August 15 the convention resolved for a general strike. Union demands announced by Gorman included a 30-hour week without wage reductions, elimination of the stretchout, reinstatement of union members who had been discharged, union recognition, and the creation of an effective arbitration agency.

"President Roosevelt is the only person in God's green world who can stop a general strike," McMahon said.[23] But Roosevelt did not intervene directly and, after futile efforts to bring the

[18] *Textile World,* LXXXIV (1934) , 74.

[19] Frank E. Coffee to Lloyd K. Garrison, August 9, 1934, in National Recovery Administration, Records of the Cotton Textile National Industrial Relations Board, National Archives, quoted in Hodges, "New Deal Labor Policy and the Southern Cotton Textile Industry," 265.

[20] Alexander Kendrick, "Alabama Goes on Strike," in *Nation,* CXXXIX (1934) , 233–34.

[21] Kennedy, "General Strike in the Textile Industry," 26.

[22] W. N. Adcock of Huntsville, quoted in *Newsweek,* IV (August 25, 1934) , 9.

[23] McMahon, quoted *ibid.*

mills into negotiations, the general strike began on September 1. Textile workers responded in numbers that startled the skeptical managers. As strike director, Gorman reinforced their enthusiasm by skillful showmanship. He dispatched "sealed orders" to the locals and then, with dramatic flourish, telegraphed the effective dates. He scored unprecedented success in making the news columns and using the radio. And he planned the tactic of "flying squadrons," boisterous caravans of strikers who persuaded or forced workers to close down mills that remained open.[24]

It was the largest single strike in American history to that time, its scope a new experience for Southern mills; but it developed according to the familiar pattern, featuring the militia, armed guards and deputies, and flashes of violence at the plant gates. The worst outburst erupted on September 6 at Honea Path, South Carolina, where most of the workers in the Chiquola Mill commuted from farms and opposed the strike. An attempt to bar them by mass picketing provoked a clash in which policemen and deputized workers killed seven strikers.[25] State militia were called out in the Carolinas, Alabama, and Georgia. On September 12 Governor Talmadge declared martial law in the Georgia strike areas to deal wtih "armies of insurrectionists imported and coming in to the affected areas." At Fort McPherson in Atlanta he set up a "concentration camp" to impound participants in flying squadrons behind barbed wire.[26]

Knowing the condition of humble people "forced in some mills to work for long hours for compensation below proper sustenance," Josephus Daniels wrote President Roosevelt, "it makes me heart-sick to see soldiers beat them down, even when they make demands greater than the industry can stand in days of weak demand for their goods." [27] Daniels' lament identified the strikers' essential weakness, their inability to put economic pressure on an

[24] Jonathan Mitchell, "Here Comes Gorman!" in *New Republic*, LXXX (1934), 203.
[25] Writers' Program of the Works Progress Administration in the State of South Carolina, *South Carolina: A Guide to the Palmetto State* (New York, 1941) , 80, 420.
[26] Lemmon, "Public Career of Eugene Talmadge," 180–81; Benjamin Stolberg, "Buzz Windrip—Governor of Georgia," in *Nation*, CXLII (1936) , 270.
[27] Josephus Daniels to Franklin D. Roosevelt, September 17, 1934, in President's Personal File 86, Roosevelt Library.

overextended industry. On September 16 Southern mills began a movement to reopen; four days later about 150,000 Southern workers remained out but "force and hunger," the union said, were driving them back. On September 20 a mediation board, appointed fifteen days earlier, presented its report. The board, headed by former New Hampshire Governor John G. Winant, condemned the practice of referring complaints to the industry-dominated code authority, but its recommendations called for little more than the creation of other boards to study wages, hours, and workloads.[28]

President Roosevelt asked the union to end the walkout on the basis of the report, and with the strike clearly crumbling, the union decided to yield before it collapsed. On September 22 the UTW called off the strike and Gorman hailed the Winant report as an "overwhelming victory." "Our triumph is one of the greatest in all labor history," he told the members, "and your officers salute and congratulate you." The report only postponed the issues and, before anything came of it, the NRA was defunct. Undeceived by claims of victory, United Textile Workers members drifted away. By the beginning of 1937 the union represented only 60,500, of whom only about 20,000 were in cotton mills and practically none in the South. As late as 1960, a long-time textile organizer said, the memory of Gorman's shoddy pretense still retarded unionization.[29]

Defeat in textiles and the death of the NRA prefaced a dormant period in Southern unionism, but in 1935 two significant national developments heralded a period of renewed growth: the enactment of the National Labor Relations Act and the formation of the Committee for Industrial Organization. The labor act, sponsored by Senator Robert F. Wagner of New York, provided enforceable restraints in place of the ineffectual Section 7 (a). It outlawed "unfair labor practices" of discrimination or intimidation by employers, provided for referendums among workers to determine their collective-bargaining agents by majority vote,

[28] Board of Inquiry for the Cotton Textile Industry, *Report . . . to the President* (Washington, 1935).

[29] Interview with Franz Daniel, July 26, 1960, Washington, D.C., quoted in Hodges, "New Deal Labor Policy and the Southern Cotton Textile Industry," 298.

required that employers bargain with these agents, and set up a National Labor Relations Board to administer the provisions.[30]

Senators Joseph T. Robinson of Arkansas and Pat Harrison of Mississippi were cool to the measure and sought vainly to enlist the President's support for a postponement. In the House, after the President had endorsed it, conservative Representatives Howard Smith of Virginia and Eugene Cox of Georgia warned that it proposed, in Cox's words, to use "the commerce clause of the Constitution . . . to the extent of ultimately striking down and destroying completely all State sovereignty." [31] But the opponents mustered few votes. The measure passed both houses overwhelmingly with a majority of the Southerners in support, some of them perhaps anticipating an adverse court ruling.[32] Southern conservative influence, however, secured one fateful amendment, a provision sponsored by Representative Robert Ramspeck of Georgia that limited collective bargaining elections to groups no larger than an "employer unit." The amendment eliminated any chance of compulsory industry-wide bargaining and condemned textile unionists to protracted struggles against isolated plants. Even so there was little compliance until the Supreme Court upheld the act in 1937.[33]

Meanwhile, continued neglect of the demand for industrial unions provoked a rebellion against the craft-oriented AFL leaders. In December, 1935, the insurgent unions formed the Committee for Industrial Organization, headed by John L. Lewis, and in 1936 the AFL expelled the CIO unions, which went on to form a permanent structure in 1938 as the Congress of Industrial Organizations.[34] From the outset the CIO had a strong foothold in the Southern mining districts, and resolutions of support by state federations in Alabama, Kentucky, Tennessee, Virginia, and Georgia reflected the influence of Lewis' mine workers.[35] More-

---

[30] The act's legislative history appears in Irving Bernstein, *The New Deal Collective Bargaining Policy* (Berkeley and Los Angeles, 1950) , 112–28. For text see *ibid.*, 153–60.

[31] *Congressional Record,* 74 Cong., 1 Sess., 9679, 9693.   [32] *Ibid.,* 7681, 9731.

[33] National Labor Relations Board *v.* Jones & Laughlin Steel Corp., 301 U.S. 1 (1937) .

[34] For origins of the CIO see Galenson, *CIO Challenge to the AFL,* 3–74.

[35] *Ibid.,* 21.

over, certain other affiliated unions had toeholds in the region: in oil, textiles, iron ore, and garment-making.

The CIO's major organizing drives, in automobiles and steel, begun in 1936, touched the South but little. During the NRA period the AFL had organized a number of Federal unions in the auto plants; out of these grew the United Automobile Workers, which affiliated with the CIO.[36] Beginning in 1934 a militant local maintained a precarious existence in the Fisher Body and Chevrolet plants at Atlanta and in November, 1936, staged the first sit-down in the industry to protest the discharge of four members. The affair lasted a day and a night and ended when the company agreed to stay closed. Finally, in February, 1937, after more lengthy sit-downs in Michigan and elsewhere, General Motors recognized the union in an agreement that covered the Atlanta workers. The event had more than local significance, for Atlanta's automobile workers, like the miners, bred a corps of seasoned leaders who directed other union offensives in the Southeast.[37]

Soon after General Motors gave in, United States Steel capitulated to the Steel Workers Organizing Committee (later United Steelworkers of America). In March, 1937, the company's major subsidiaries, including Tennessee Coal and Iron, signed contracts giving SWOC the right to represent its membership. But membership in Birmingham lagged, despite the vigorous efforts of William Mitch, who led the SWOC drive. The union concentrated on the major Northern centers until 1941–1942, when a large contingent of organizers prepared the Birmingham district for a series of elections beginning in December, 1942. These won for the steel union sole bargaining rights for all workers and brought in their

[36] The Federal union was a device to pool workers until they were drawn off by the established craft unions, but in this case it followed a different development. The story appears in Sidney Fine, *The Automobile under the Blue Eagle: Labor, Management, and the Automobile Manufacturing Code* (Ann Arbor, 1963), Chapters V, IX, XII, and *passim*. For the CIO period see Galenson, *CIO Challenge to the AFL*, 123–92.

[37] Marshall, "History of Labor Organization in the South," 367–69; *United Automobile Worker* (Detroit), I (May, 1936), 3; (November, 1936), 11; Fine, *Automobile under the Blue Eagle*, 153, 213, 301, and *passim*; Lucy Randolph Mason, *To Win These Rights: A Personal Story of the CIO in the South* (New York, 1952), 33–38.

train recognition by most of the smaller iron and steel companies and many foundries, pipe shops, and fabricating concerns. But the steel workers in the South never matched the vigor of the mine workers. For one thing, they tried to copy the miner's formula of racially mixed locals, but the pattern worked less well in an industry that had more job segregation and wider wage differentials between the skilled and unskilled; for another their union was virtually handed to them in the national settlement of 1937.[38]

No such easy victory awaited other unions. Their Southern campaigns assumed, rather, the character of guerrilla actions punctuated by occasional victories. The old Oil Field, Gas Well, and Refinery Workers joined the CIO with the new name of Oil Workers International Union. In March, 1937, they agreed to the establishment of a Petroleum Workers Organizing Committee, which sent twenty-one organizers into the field. But the returns were meager, and by June, 1938, only two organizers remained active. A lengthy and unsuccessful strike against the Mid-Continent Petroleum Company at Tulsa ran from December, 1938, to March, 1940, and nearly bankrupted the union. Membership drifted below 20,000 in 1940. The oil workers, more than some other groups, suffered the common handicap of unions in the South; they sought "laborers from a farming frontier naively individualistic in philosophy and untrained to organized cooperation in any aspects of life." [39]

Refinery workers proved somewhat more receptive; in 1941 a new organizing drive concentrated on them, and a union that originated in the fields became primarily a refinery union. The first big victory came in bargaining elections at the Texas City Pan-American plant in June, 1942, followed by other coups at Port Arthur and on the west coast. The officers reported to the 1942 convention twenty-eight working agreements in Texas and Louisiana and by 1944 claimed to be leading the fastest growing international in the CIO, with 50,000 members as against 18,000 three

[38] Frederick H. Harbison, "Steel," in Harry A. Millis (ed.), *How Collective Bargaining Works* (New York, 1945), 523; Herbert J. Northrup, "The Negro and Unionism in the Birmingham, Ala., Iron and Steel Industry," in *Southern Economic Journal*, X (1943-1944), 35-40.

[39] Allen, *Chapters in the History of Organized Labor in Texas*, 240.

years before. In most places, however, the oil workers remained stubbornly attached to local and independent unions that evolved from earlier company unions.[40]

In 1936 the United Rubber Workers entered the South at Gadsden, Alabama, and Memphis and Clarksville, Tennessee. The effort encountered violence, especially around the Goodyear plant in Gadsden, where thugs invaded a union meeting and attacked the URW's President Sherman Dalrymple in the presence of a sheriff who offered only perfunctory protection. Within a year three organizers were beaten in downtown Gadsden and the union headquarters wrecked by marauders.[41] Similar violence met a renewed drive in 1941 at the Memphis Firestone plant, but the antiunion citadels both fell in 1943. By 1944 the rubber workers had eleven agreements and nine locals in six Southern states.[42]

As early as 1935, shortly after the invalidation of the NRA, the Amalgamated Clothing Workers of America began organizing efforts in the South, followed presently by the International Ladies Garment Workers Union and the United Garment Workers. These drives were in response to the problem of "runaway" garment firms that sought local subsidies and cheap labor and thereby threatened the standards of union members in the North. There were some successes, especially where unions had gone before—a notable example was at La Follette, Tennessee, where militant mine workers supported the organization of their wives in a shirt plant. But scattered plants posed a more difficult problem of organizing than the concentrated needles trade of New York City. By 1938 the ACWA had approximately 4,500 Southern members in sixteen locals and the UGW had union-label contracts

[40] Ibid., 237–45; O'Connor, History of Oil Workers' Intl. Union, 37–43, 46–50; Douty, "Development of Trade Unionism in the South," loc. cit., 578–79; Herbert Werner, "Labor Organization in the American Petroleum Industry," in Harold F. Williamson et al., The American Petroleum Industry: The Age of Energy, 1899–1959 (Evanston, Ill., 1963), 835–39, 844–45.

[41] Violations of Free Speech and Rights of Labor: Hearings, 75 Cong., 2 Sess., Pt. 8, pp. 3002–3005; Maxwell Stewart, "Gadsden Is Tough," in Nation, CXLV (1937), 69–70.

[42] Marshall, "History of Labor Organization in the South," 365–67; Douty, "Development of Trade-Unionism in the South," loc. cit., 578.

with ten shops, but the ILGWU claimed only 678 members in the region.[43]

The momentum of organization among tobacco workers during the NRA period carried them after 1937 to agreements involving most of the plants of American, Liggett and Myers, Peter Lorillard, and Philip Morris. By January, 1943, TWIU-AFL membership exceeded 20,000, the largest in its history. Only Reynolds remained outside the fold.[44]

However, textiles were the touchstone of Southern unionism, and on that critical test the CIO faltered. The first targets of CIO strategy were the concentrations of heavy industry, mostly outside the South. The resultant delay caused textile unionism once again to run full-tilt into a business slump, just as it gathered momentum. The decision for a textile drive was not taken until March, 1937, when the foundering UTW entered an agreement with the CIO whereby a new Textile Workers Organizing Committee virtually absorbed the old union.[45] Chairman of the new group was Sidney Hillman, president of the Amalgamated Clothing Workers, a labor leader with a rare experience of co-operation with businessmen.

Hillman sought to exploit his record by offering the TWOC as an instrument of stability in textiles, as the ACWA had been in garment-making. A firm wage base, he argued, would shield legitimate enterprise from sweatshop competition. The textile workers could "assume a correlative responsibility in stabilizing the industry and in eliminating unnecessary stoppages and interruptions in production." "We are going to present a constructive program," he said, "a program which needs from management as much organization as from labor." [46] He clearly meant industry-

[43] Marshall, "History of Labor Organization in the South," 359–65; Frank T. de Vyver, "The Present Status of Labor Unions in the South," in *Southern Economic Journal*, V (1938–1939), 488.

[44] Northrup, *Organized Labor and the Negro*, 111.

[45] For text of the agreement see Textile Workers' Organizing Committee, *Building a Union: Report of Two Years' Progress* (New York, 1939), 10–11.

[46] Raleigh *News and Observer*, April 5, 1937; *Newsweek*, IX (April 10, 1937), 6. See also Sidney Hillman, "Why Textile Unionism Means Profits," in *Barron's National Business and Financial Weekly* (Boston), XVII (September 20, 1937), 18.

wide bargaining, but textile bosses rejected the idea. "The industry will make no counterorganization," said Claudius T. Murchison, new head of the Cotton Textile Institute. "Its first answer to the challenge of the C. I. O. is that if there is to be a battlefront, it will . . . develop into as many as 1,184 battle fronts." [47]

The Southern drive began early in April. From the offices of UTW Vice President John Peel in Roanoke, Virginia, and former Georgia State Federation President A. Steve Nance in Atlanta, TWOC organizers fanned out through the textile South. By the end of the year Nance presided over thirty offices with three or four agents each, most of whom were Southerners, a policy adopted to counter charges that they were "outside agitators." They moved cautiously, usually discouraged strikes, undertook to use the election machinery of the NLRB, and promised to collect no dues until they delivered contracts.[48]

On May 17, 1937, TWOC claimed its first Southern victory, an agreement covering three plants of the Marlboro Mills in McColl and Bennettsville, South Carolina. The contract yielded wage increases up to 22 per cent and a check-off for union dues.[49] But the Marlboro victory was deceptively quick and easy. Other attempts were more prolonged and often violent, but the union on September 3 claimed to have contracts covering 20,000 workers in the South. In the following ten months it won forty-three bargaining elections involving 23,000 and lost nineteen involving 5,800; the elections occurred in eight states from Virginia to Texas.[50]

In the fall of 1937, however, a business recession began to retard the momentum of the campaign. Union income dropped, and shifts in leadership caused further setbacks. In the fall Hillman stepped aside because of illness and in the spring Nance died in Atlanta; Emil Rieve and Roy Lawrence, respectively, took their places.[51] In the fall of 1938 Francis Gorman, dissatisfied with a

[47] Raleigh *News and Observer*, March 30, 1937.

[48] Richmond *Times-Dispatch*, April 1, 1937; Raleigh *News and Observer*, April 5, 1937; Herman Wolf, "Cotton and the Unions," in *Survey Graphic*, XXVII (1938), 147. The dues policy was modified later in some locals to permit payments after victory in a representative election.

[49] Raleigh *News and Observer*, May 18, 1937.

[50] Textile Workers' Organizing Committee, *Building a Union*, 22.

[51] *Ibid.*, 25; New York *Times*, April 4, 1938.

subordinate position in the new group, began to revive the old UTW, which the AFL rechartered in the spring of 1939. By 1941 it claimed 42,000 members, though few in the South.[52] Whatever opportunity TWOC may have had to sweep textiles was lost in the recession. The union could not even prevent widespread wage cuts in 1938, and the textile industry did not fully recover until World War II approached.

In May, 1939, the TWOC assumed permanent form as the Textile Workers' Union of America in a convention at Philadelphia. On the fourth day of the convention 111 delegates from 92 Southern and Border State locals massed on the steps of the convention platform for a demonstration pledging the TWUA to the paramount task of organizing Southern textiles. "When the South is organized, my friends," said Franz Daniel, assistant to Roy Lawrence, "much of the trouble of the textile workers of this country is over." [53]

But the textile workers had only established a beachhead. To expand it required a struggle that met hostility at every turn. The bosses knew that when textiles were organized "every other industry will be organized in the South," Hillman told the clothing workers' convention in 1938. "That is why we are meeting . . . such vicious opposition from all of the southern Tories." [54] Huntsville, Alabama, and Gaffney, South Carolina, afford two case studies of the enmity facing the union.

In the spring of 1937 the Dallas Manufacturing Company, with one of three big mills at Huntsville, signed a contract with the TWOC but the mill closed in October. In December the Merrimack and Lincoln mills closed. In March, 1938, the Dallas mill undertook to reopen with an entirely new labor force recruited through the state employment service. Governor Bibb Graves demanded a postponement, whereupon the community became

---

[52] Hodges, "New Deal Labor Policy and the Southern Cotton Textile Industry," 407–409.

[53] *Proceedings, First Constitutional Convention, Textile Workers Union of America, May 15–19, 1939* . . . (New York, 1939), 126–39, 146–47, 208–209; New York *Times*, May 19, 1939.

[54] Amalgamated Clothing Workers of America, *Report of the General Executive Board and Proceedings of the Twelfth Biennial Convention, 1936–1938* (New York, 1938), 399.

aroused over the prospect of losing the payrolls permanently. "You will be blacklisted until your dying day," the local editor warned union members. "If you turn back to the farm there is no hope for you." The mayor proclaimed April 20, 1938, "Save Huntsville Day." "Huntsville and Madison County are confronted with the most serious and tragic situation in our history," he announced. Places of business and public offices closed for the day, and a thousand inflamed citizens joined a motorcade to Montgomery to demand state troops.

The movement followed the celebrated "Mohawk Valley Formula," first used in 1936 by Remington Rand in upstate New York: arouse the citizenry against "outside agitators," then stage a back-to-work movement under armed guard. This time it failed to work. Governor Graves refused to co-operate and the affair dragged out until October 12, when the mill finally reached an agreement with the union, nearly a year after it had closed. Twelve days later workers in the Merrimack Mills voted overwhelmingly for the union and the company signed a contract on December 3. Shortly thereafter the Lincoln Mill capitulated.[55]

Gaffney, for its more unseemly tactics, won a reputation after 1937 as the "roughest place this side of Harlan County." Efforts to organize the Hamrick, Alma, and Limestone mills ran the gauntlet of tested methods that included "good fellowship clubs," discriminatory firings, deputized thugs paid by management, a co-operative sheriff, sandbag barricades and machine guns at the mills, and rattlebrained preachers hired to talk against the unions. "It is heart-rending," a trial examiner for the NLRB wrote in 1940, "to see one witness after another—come to the witness chair, start to tell his story—catch Hamrick's eye—and then stutter his or her answers until courage returns." But the NLRB on April 8, 1940, directed the mills to cease and desist from antiunion activities and re-employ twenty-four workers (twenty-two with back pay). By 1942 the union was firmly entrenched, strong enough to

[55] Whitman, God's Valley, 165–75; Textile Workers Organizing Committee, Building a Union, 31; Lucy Randolph Mason to Carroll Kilpatrick, April 20, 1928; Mason to Eleanor Roosevelt, November 28 and December 9, 1938, in Lucy Randolph Mason Papers (Manuscripts Department, Duke University).

send its candidates to the legislature and to elect a textile worker sheriff of Cherokee County by eight votes.[56]

In 1941–1942, by way of contrast, the Dan River Mills were successfully organized in a campaign that the local paper said "was marked by no distressing incident" and "devoid of any spirit of recrimination." Management claimed it had fully accepted the union, and the first contract, signed in 1943, became something of a pattern for the Southern texile industry as a whole.[57] Other important mills such as Erwin and Kendall mills came into the fold, but such antiunion strongholds as Bibb, Cannon, Burlington, and Avondale remained outside. In 1946 the TWUA still could claim to represent only 20 per cent of Southern cotton and rayon workers.[58] But textile unionism was an established fact, and with influence on wages and working conditions beyond the mills in which it was recognized. Meeting union standards became a common tactic to keep the union out.

The laggard pace in textiles denied the CIO a major victory in the South like the swift conquest of autos and steel in the North. But with dogged determination the CIO organizers built a labor movement in Southern industry, one that was at last something more than a vehicle for sporadic revolt. And the AFL, spurred on by competition, quickened its tempo. In 1938 Frank T. de Vyver gathered union membership figures from eleven Southern states (excluding Oklahoma and Texas). The statistics were incomplete, but one may derive from them an estimate of 450,000–500,000 members.[59] This was a base from which unionism made further rapid gains during World War II. The spread of war industries encouraged the growth established in the environment of the

[56] John Wesley Kennedy, "A History of the Textile Workers' Union of America, C. I. O." (Ph.D. dissertation, University of North Carolina, 1950), 133–37; Selden Menefee, *Assignment: U.S.A.* (New York, 1943), 46–47.

[57] Kennedy, "History of the Textile Workers' Union of America," 147–50; Smith, *Mill on the Dan,* 491–502.

[58] Textile Workers' Union of America, *Executive Council Report to the Fourth Biennial Convention . . . , Atlantic City, N.J., April 24–27, 1946* (n.p., 1946), 49.

[59] de Vyver, "The Present Status of Labor Unions in the South," *loc. cit.,* 485–98. The estimate is in Milton Derber, "Growth and Expansion," in Milton Derber and Edwin Young (eds.), *Labor and the New Deal* (Madison, Wis., 1957), 28.

Wagner Act, a favorable climate that continued under the friendly auspices of the War Labor Board.[60]

In 1948 de Vyver resurveyed the field and produced an estimate of more than a million union members in the region. In 1938 he listed only seven unions that numbered more than 15,000; in 1948 he listed fifteen among fifty-nine unions for which figures were available. Of these fifteen, six counted more than 40,000 members each: the Carpenters and Joiners (92,827), TWUA (89,557), UMW (87,500), National Maritime Union (60,000), United Steelworkers (49,651), and Railway Clerks (42,630). And the figures omitted certain other unions with a sizable membership in the South: the AFL Operating Engineers, Teamsters, and Longshoremen, and the CIO Longshoremen—nor did they include Texas, where wartime expansion precipitated a rapid growth of unionism. Unionism had secured strong footholds in aluminum, cement, electrical utilities, transit systems, pulp and paper, butchering, shipbuilding, and newspaper printing and publishing in addition to the fields already mentioned.[61]

Membership growth in the decade after 1938 kept pace with that in the nation, perhaps exceeded it slightly; yet the phenomenal expansion of unions left untouched vast areas of small-town and rural industries. Food processing, lumbering, and furniture, as well as many service trades and miscellaneous manufacturing industries, experienced almost no activity. The South remained predominantly nonunion and largely antiunion. In this tenacious pattern strong impediments to labor organization persisted.[62] The prevalence of an impoverished agriculture was fundamental. "If labor in the South is going to get anywhere, we've got to do something about these tenant folks," A. Steve

[60] Wartime union growth is traced in Marshall, "History of Labor Organization in the South," 390–93.

[61] Frank T. de Vyver, "Present Status of Labor Unions in the South—1948," in *Southern Economic Journal*, XVI (1949–1950), 1–22; Frederick Meyers, "The Growth of Collective Bargaining in Texas—A Newly Industrialized Area," in *Proceedings of Seventh Annual Meeting of Industrial Relations Research Association* (Madison, Wis., 1954), 286–97.

[62] F. Ray Marshall, "Impediments to Labor Union Organization in the South," in *South Atlantic Quarterly*, LVII (1958), 409–18; Douty, "Development of Trade Unionism in the South," *loc. cit.*, 100–102; Gilman, *Human Relations in the Industrial Southeast*, 237, 303–307.

Nance said shortly before his death. "The real threat to the American standard of living . . . [comes] from the poor whites of the South." Unionism alone, he admitted, could not do the job: "We're working about as far down as you can go right now." [63]

It was not simply the availability of cheap labor. In the Southern workers' agrarian heritage lurked a fateful paradox, a fierce and petulant individualism combined with attitudes of dependency and obeisance. The worker often "appreciated" his job and deferred to the leadership of the gentry. The personal nexus of industrial relations, at least in textiles, was consciously cultivated after the shattering events of 1929. Southern textile managers in the 1930's successfully combined the personal relationships of an agrarian society with modern personnel methods, re-established channels of communication with their "people," tutored overseers to shun arbitrary command, and cultivated in the factory an environment of living folkways. In that congenial climate the worker found less need to seek the protective shelter of a union.[64]

The agrarian heritage had erected mental barriers to unionism, and the effort to escape that heritage had generated another: the belief that cheap and docile labor offered the most effective lure for industry. In the late 1930's the upthrust of unionism paralleled the resurgence of industry-hunting. And labor leaders found themselves ironically "performing, in the minds of the Southerners (small businessmen, professionals, farmers, and even workers) . . . the role of 'yankee carpet-baggers' attempting to keep all Southerners from tasting the sweet fruit of industrialization in higher incomes." Organized labor became "the symbol of the *only* opposition to economic progress in the South." It created an atmosphere into which industry would be unwilling to enter; more than that, it endangered the continuation of existing industry. "If you join the CIO," a Tupelo editor threatened when the union entered in 1937, "you will be endorsing the closing of a factory." [65]

[63] Daniels, *Southerner Discovers the South,* 295–96.

[64] Gilman, *Human Relations in the Industrial Southeast,* 222–48, 303–10.

[65] Marvin E. Lee, "Southern Economic Conditions and the Failure of Trade Union Organizing Policies in the Southeast," paper presented to the Graduate Seminar in Economics, University of North Carolina, February 18, 1958 (mimeographed copy in author's possession) , 22; Tupelo *Daily News,* July 10, 1937, clip-

Certain other peculiarities of the regional culture reinforced the conditioning of rural life and industry-hunting. Industrial unionism was especially vulnerable to racist attacks, since the mass organization of labor, to be fully effective, demanded the inclusion of Negro workers. Orthodox or fundamentalist religion fostered an other-worldly perspective, even fatalism and submissiveness. Its use as a deliberate antiunion tactic to direct the workers' attention away from immediate grievances may easily be exaggerated, but it sometimes assumed incredible forms. The letters "CIO," an evangelist in Greenville, South Carolina, told his flock, meant "Christ is Out"; "in the beginning of the Bible," one C. E. "Preacher" Parker informed the workers at Gaffney, "it tells us to be satisfied with our wages." [66] The traditional hostility to outsiders loaded another burden upon the organizers. Even if they were born and bred in the brier patch they became "outsider agitators" when they entered a new community.

Hostility to unions permeated public institutions. "You people in New York," a TWOC worker wrote to Sidney Hillman, "don't know what it means to have the politicians, the local and state administrations, the press and the public lined up with the employers and against the workers." [67] Local and state police often stood at the disposal of management. A colonel of the Georgia militia revealed a customary role of state troops when he remarked during a textile conflict: "With the arrest of these 25 strikers we believe that the backbone of the strike is broken." [68] Local and state authorities co-operated by adopting repressive legislation. Macon, Georgia, forbade the distribution of "any handbill, circular, pamphlet, poster, postcard, or literature of any kind." Birmingham permitted the authorities to hold a person

---

ping attached to Lucy Randolph Mason to Claude F. Clayton, April 18, 1938, in Mason Papers.

[66] Walter Davenport, "All Work and No Pay," in *Collier's*, C (November 13, 1937), 72; C. B. Whittemore (NLRB trial examiner), letter in *Textile Labor* (Philadelphia), I (February, 1940), 4, quoted in Kennedy, "History of the Textile Workers' Union of America," 135.

[67] Lucy Randolph Mason to Sidney Hillman, September 11, 1937, in Mason Papers.

[68] Atlanta *Journal*, January 8, 1935, quoted in Lumpkin, *South in Progress*, 112.

indefinitely without charge.[69] An Alabama state law went so far as to forbid picketing altogether, but the Supreme Court struck it down in 1940 on the ground that it violated the constitutional protection of free speech. A later Texas law that required labor organizers to register fell under a similar judgment.[70]

Community sentiment supported, or at least acquiesced in, the use of extralegal force and violence. Arbitrary arrests occurred without any color of legality, or on unfounded charges of vagrancy. Newspapers published veiled and even direct incitements to violence. In a "Note to the CIO" at the beginning of the TWOC drive Frederick Sullens of the Jackson *Daily News* warned: "The Mississippi National Guard has been mustered up to 2,300. . . . The boys know how to shoot guns and are not afraid to do it when the command to fire is given." [71] "Citizens of Tupelo . . . have politely asked organizers to leave the city," a Tupelo editor declared, ". . . and if it takes bloodshed to accomplish the removal of agitators then they stand ready for action." [72] Soon afterward, an ILGWU organizer, Ida Sledge, was politely dragged down the hotel steps and escorted from town. About a year later Charles Cox, local leader of the textile unionists, was taken into the country and beaten.[73]

These were neither the first nor the last instances of kidnapping, which became a standard practice. At Barnesville, Georgia, on July 28, 1938, kidnappers seized Miss Billye Bailey, an ILGWU organizer, and deposited her sixty miles away with orders never to return. Businessmen who led the mob told her they had guaranteed protection against unions when they secured industries for the town.[74] At Fitzgerald, Georgia, on August 8, 1938, Wither-

---

[69] Dabney, *Below the Potomac*, 129.

[70] Thornhill *v.* Alabama, 310 U.S. 88 (1940); Thomas *v.* Collins, 323 U.S. 516 (1944).

[71] Quoted in Marshall, "Impediments to Labor Union Organization in the South," *loc. cit.*, 413.

[72] Tupelo *Daily News*, July 10, 1937, clipping attached to Lucy Randolph Mason to Claude F. Clayton, April 18, 1938, in Mason Papers.

[73] Charles F. Cox, "The Famous Struggle at Tupelo," in Highlander Folk School, *Let Southern Labor Speak* (Mimeographed; Monteagle, Tenn., 1938), 40–44; Whitman, *God's Valley*, 153–64; Lucy Randolph Mason to Mrs. Eleanor Roosevelt, April 16, 1938, in Mason Papers.

[74] Billye Bailey to Franklin D. Roosevelt, July 9, 1938, copy in Mason Papers.

spoon Dodge, a former Presbyterian minister who had become a TWOC organizer, was seated on the porch of the Lee-Grant Hotel talking with the president of the Fitzgerald Cotton Mills when a band of men seized him, beat him with a blackjack, threw him into a truck, dumped him in the country, and threatened him with death if he returned. A Federal grand jury indicted fifteen men, including the mill president, but all were acquitted in what Federal attorneys called "a complete abortion of justice, extending all the way from the United States District Attorney's office in Savannah through the jury and the presiding judge of the court." [75] At Vicksburg, in 1943, Claude Welch of the International Woodworkers of America was seized, taken into the country, and beaten. "If it wasn't for people like the CIO," said a company guard in the mob, "we could still have slavery and get along without working." [76]

Professional spying agencies and munitions manufacturers found a bull market on the Southern industrial frontier of the 1930's. In a series of hearings from 1936 to 1939 a Senate subcommittee on civil liberties, headed by Robert M. La Follette, Jr., piled up a mountainous documentation of their activities. From 1933 to 1937 the Pinkerton National Detective Agency from offices in five Southern cities planted spies in twelve international unions. One of these operatives, Lyle Letteer, served as an officer of the Atlanta auto local, reported daily on its activities, and copied union records for the agency. He played his part so well that the Chevrolet plant at one point discharged him for union activity. In the same period, 1933–1937, twenty-seven Southern firms laid out nearly $800,000 for spying and strikebreaking services. In all, the La Follette Committee recorded seventy-eight Southern firms that used such services, twenty of them in textiles and six in oil, not including national steel corporations which were also listed.[77]

---

[75] *Textile Labor*, I (March 6 and October 1, 1940) , cited in Galenson, *CIO Challenge to the AFL*, 339.

[76] Menefee, *Assignment: U.S.A.*, 57–58.

[77] Lumpkin, *South in Progress*, 107, gives computations from *Violations of Free Speech and Rights of Labor*, in Senate Repts., 75 Cong., 2 Sess., No. 46, Pt. 3, pp. 75–121. On Lateer see *Violations of Free Speech and Rights of Labor: Hearings*, 75 Cong., 2 Sess., Pt. 5, pp. 1532–45. The La Follette Committee grew directly out of

Among eighty companies identified as buyers of more than $1,000 worth of tear and sickening gas in the period nine were Southern textile firms, two were textile subsidiaries of rubber companies, and one an employers' association in Alamance County, North Carolina.[78] In addition to $1,722.55 worth of tear gas, the West Point Manufacturing Company in 1934 purchased four machine guns, borrowed three more, and hired professional strike guards. Immediately deputized by local officials in Chambers County, Alabama, they proceeded to barricade public roads and assault union sympathizers. Flying squadrons stayed away.[79]

Certain communities won special recognition for antilabor violence. In June, 1937, the American Civil Liberties Union listed eleven major "centers of repression" during the previous twelve months. Six of the eleven were in the South: Harlan County, the eastern Arkansas sharecropper country, Tampa, Atlanta, Birmingham, and New Orleans. The following year the ACLU dropped Arkansas, Atlanta, Birmingham, and New Orleans, but added Memphis and San Antonio.[80] In Memphis Boss Edward H. Crump feared the CIO as a threat both to his easy relationships with the AFL and to his ambitions for industrial development of the town. In September, 1937, Mayor Watkins Overton announced that "CIO agitators, Communists, and highly paid professional organizers are not wanted in Memphis." "We will not tolerate these foreign agitators," the police commissioner asserted. "We know Norman Smith [a CIO organizer] and his whereabouts and will take care of that situation very soon." Two days later Smith was badly beaten, whereupon the police commissioner announced that "the city government is opposed to violence." But antilabor violence and arbitrary jailings of union men did not cease until Eleanor Roosevelt delivered a severe criticism in a

---

efforts by Gardner Jackson to get an investigation of conditions in the Arkansas sharecropper country, but the committee never delved into that situation because of opposition from Southern senators, La Follette told H. L. Mitchell. Jerold S. Auerbach, "The La Follette Committee: Labor and Civil Liberties in the New Deal," in *Journal of American History*, LI (1964–1965), 438; "Reminiscences of H. L. Mitchell," 64–65.

[78] *Violations of Free Speech and Rights of Labor*, in *Senate Repts.*, 76 Cong., 1 Sess., No. 6, Pt. 3, p. 65.

[79] *Ibid.*, Pt. 1, pp. 41–46.   [80] Dabney, *Below the Potomac*, 127–28.

speech at Richmond in 1940 and the White House brought indirect pressure to bear on Boss Crump.[81]

Until 1938 Harlan County, Kentucky, held unquestioned supremacy in the science of intimidation.[82] Almost wholly dependent upon mining, the county included thirty company towns that housed 45,000 people. In typical communities the company owned the houses, the streets, the stores, the medical services, even in some cases the roadway into town, which could be blocked by gates or guards. One company maintained a privately owned jail, administered by a deputy on its own payroll. A preponderance of the county's deputies belonged to the coal companies, and the inauguration of a "reform" sheriff, Thomas R. Middleton, to replace the notorious J. H. Blair in 1934 left the situation unchanged. In a little over three years the new sheriff increased his private fortune from $10,000 to $100,000 on a salary of $5,000; in the same period he appointed thirty-seven deputies who had served sentences for murder, manslaughter, malicious shooting with intent to kill, robbery, burglary, and grand larceny. Three had served terms in Federal penitentiaries and sixty-four had been indicted at one time or another. The total number was above 369, the precise figure being unknown because of haphazard records. The sheriff himself had served five months for bootlegging. Mine owners dominated the county through the Harlan County Coal Operators' Association, and concerted their antiunion activities through Deputy Ben Unthank, who served on their payroll as "field man." In the mines "far up the ravines off the main track where the workers live on the mineowners' property, conditions slip back into the old feudal horror," a visitor to the hills wrote President Roosevelt in 1937; "in that corner of Kentucky conditions can only be compared to Germany under Hitler." [83]

[81] Mason, *To Win These Rights,* 104–14; William D. Miller, *Mr. Crump of Memphis* (Baton Rouge, 1964), 202, 214–16; Lucy Randolph Mason to Eleanor Roosevelt, November 28, 1940; and Franklin D. Roosevelt to Kenneth McKellar, December 23, 1940, in Eleanor Roosevelt Papers (Roosevelt Library).

[82] The following account, except where otherwise indicated, is drawn from *Violations of Free Speech and Rights of Labor,* in *Senate Repts.* 76 Cong., 1 Sess., No. 6, Pt. 2, pp. 17–114.

[83] Chester A. Arthur, III, to Franklin D. Roosevelt, August 31, 1937, in PPF 4343, Roosevelt Library.

The first tide of mine unionism broke in futility against that bastion of terror. In the sudden flood of 1933 the UMW somehow got a contract with the operators' association, but the agreement became ineffective long before its expiration in 1935. Unthank's mercenaries harassed, threatened, and assaulted unionists until the incipient organization disappeared. A renewed drive in the summer of 1935 met another barrage of violence climaxed by the assassination of a maverick county attorney who suggested a grand jury investigation. But the persistent unionists returned in January, 1937, whereupon ruffians dynamited and tear-gassed a hotel in which they were staying, then ambushed a carload of organizers and seriously wounded one of them. Three boys who saw the incident were hidden by their parents, and their father was shot and killed when they were subpoenaed by the La Follette Committee. Marshall A. Musick, a union organizer, fled the county on the warning that he was marked for attack and in his absence shots fired into his home killed his son. A deputy who rebelled at the excesses was shot by two others and left for dead.

The terrorists had finally overreached themselves. From March until May, 1937, hearings by the La Follette Committee turned the glare of publicity on "Bloody Harlan," and in September a Federal grand jury returned indictments against forty-seven company officials and deputies for conspiracy to violate the Wagner Act. The trial ended with a hung jury on August 1, 1938, but on August 19 the Harlan County Coal Operators' Association, faced with a cease-and-desist order from the National Labor Relations Board and a threat of renewed prosecution by the Department of Justice, signed with the union. In 1939 the association balked at renewing the contract, but yielded under the threat of another trial. Harlan's reign of terror was at last over.[84]

Labor violence left a bloody trace across the history of the 1930's, but the number of fatalities, if not of assaults, declined after the birth of the CIO. According to figures gathered by Arthur Raper seven strikers and one police chief were killed in the period 1929–1931; twenty-four persons died in the labor upheavals of 1934, thirteen of them in the textile strike; during the two-year period 1934–1935 forty-two of eighty-eight labor fatal-

[84] *CIO News*, May 22, July 24, 1939.

ities occurred in the South. That was the peak period; during 1936–1937 there were only five fatalities; during 1938–1939 fourteen; and during 1940–1941 six—a total of seventy-five deaths over the whole period 1929–1941, but only twenty-five after 1935.[85]

The attitudes of employers perforce changed with the arrival of permanent unionism. Moreover, after 1935 they fell under legal obligation to bargain and to desist from union-busting tactics. In 1938, after a tour of fifty-six textile mills, Frank T. de Vyver reported that Southern millmen were "managing labor with more finesse than formerly." [86] Many of the younger executives, he discovered, could treat labor problems as dispassionately as the purchase of cotton. Not that they had come to an acceptance of unions; "southern employers generally do not yet consider unions as even a mixed blessing," de Vyver wrote in 1949, after a new survey.[87]

Public opinion followed a similar course. Strikes, labor-management disputes, and union activity became so familiar as to attract less and less attention; and people drifted toward a degree of indifference. Punitive action by vigilante groups or police and the use of troops in labor disputes diminished as the South moved into the 1940's. The larger newspapers came to accept the existence of unions and to comment on their activities in more restrained tones.[88] In 1937 the CIO's publicity director in Atlanta complained that there was not "a single editor in Georgia to whom I can go without the danger of having all that I say used against our work." But in 1940 she reported that the Atlanta *Constitution* had moved from "raw hostility" to "a pretty complete forebearance." Other papers were, if not friendly, at least willing to report labor news objectively, including such journals as the Raleigh *News and Observer*, the Charlotte *News*, the Richmond *Times-Dispatch*, the Chattanooga *Times*, the Birmingham *Age-*

---

[85] Dabney, *Below the Potomac*, 131. See also Raper and Reid, *Sharecroppers All*, 169–70, 173–76.

[86] Frank T. de Vyver, "Southern Textile Mills Revisited," in *Southern Economic Journal*, IV (1937–1938), 468.

[87] de Vyver, "Present Status of Labor Unions in the South—1948," *loc. cit.*, 16.

[88] Robert Grissom Schultz, "A Study of the Reactions of Southern Textile Communities to Strikes" (M.A. thesis, University of North Carolina, 1949), 203–204.

Herald, the Anniston *Star,* and two papers each in Spartanburg and Columbia, South Carolina.[89]

Union propaganda itself effected some changes. In the Southeast Lucy Randolph Mason was the central agent in the interpretation of unionism to the public. A former worker for the YWCA and the National Consumers' League, in 1937 she joined the textile organizing headquarters in Atlanta as public relations director and, when it moved to Charlotte in 1940, stayed on as a CIO employee. For a unionist she had a unique protective coloration, a Virginia ancestry like a genealogist's dream, including among others George Mason, author of the Virginia Bill of Rights. She interpreted her duties so broadly as to become a kind of "roving ambassador" for the unions—traveled, spoke, wrote, kept in contact with editors, ministers, civic leaders, public officials, women's groups, maintained a congenial relationship with Eleanor Roosevelt, acted as trouble-shooter in delicate negotiations, soothed ruffled antagonists with womanly charm. "Madam," said a hostile Virginian after hearing a recitation of her lineage, "I don't know what the C.I.O. pays you, but I am sure you are worth it." [90]

The development of unions and changes in public opinion eased the way for some liberalization of labor legislation, but the moving force in the 1930's was the Federal government.[91] Under the stimulus of Federal aid all Southern states by 1940 provided for unemployment insurance and public employment services. Secretary of Labor Frances Perkins and her department's Division of Labor Standards promoted improvements and offered technical help in drafting legislation and improving procedures. Between 1935 and 1941 six Southern states established or reorganized labor departments; by 1941 only Florida and Mississippi lacked such an

[89] Lucy Randolph Mason to Sidney Hillman, September 11, 1937; and Mason to Emil Rieve, May 19, 1940, in Mason Papers.

[90] Mason, *To Win These Rights,* xii and *passim;* Lucy Randolph Mason, "The Middle Class and Organized Labor," *loc. cit.,* 5–7; Margaret E. Lee, "Lucy Randolph Mason: 'Roving Ambassador' for Textile Unions in the South, 1937–1940" (Seminar paper, University of North Carolina, 1965). The Mason Papers at Duke reflect Miss Mason's active career.

[91] For surveys of labor legislation see Addison T. Cutler, "Labor Legislation in Thirteen Southern States," in *Southern Economic Journal,* VII (1940–1941), 297–316; Marian D. Irish, "The Proletarian South," in *Journal of Politics,* II (August, 1940), 241–45; and Charles F. Sharkey and Marian L. Mel, "State Labor Legislation in the South," in *Monthly Labor Review,* LXIII (1946), 535–54.

agency. By 1935, when South Carolina and Florida passed work-men's compensation legislation, only Mississippi and Arkansas lacked such protection for injuries or fatalities on the job—in part because lawyers and workingmen hoped for better settlements from juries. In such matters as regulation of wages and hours, safety standards, and the protection of women and children, the record was more uneven.

A contemporary economist who surveyed the field concluded that during the years 1935–1939 the Southern states made note-worthy progress toward overcoming the regional lag in labor legislation. In administrative structure and in the power to make safety rules, state labor bodies approached national standards. In such fields as wage and hour legislation and child labor, however, the South still fell behind. Only Kentucky had an operative minimum wage law, for women and minors, passed in 1938. Both North and South Carolina raised the minimum age to 16 and both moved to limit the hours of labor. In 1937 North Carolina adopted a 9-hour day, 48-hour week for women and a 10-hour day, 55-hour week for men. In 1938 South Carolina set an 8-hour day and 40-hour week for textiles, a 12-hour day, 56-hour week for other workers—but the law was contingent upon similar limita-tions in the adjoining states of Georgia and North Carolina.

That proviso embodied a fundamental impediment to labor legislation, the fear of competition from other states. In 1937, when the question was raised in connection with a proposed North Carolina hours law, the Raleigh *News and Observer* erupted: "Men everywhere in the nation grow tired of the profession of State powerlessness before competition with which decent labor laws are year after year defeated in State legislatures." A state "which will not adopt decent standards," the editorialist warned, "may have decent standards imposed upon it." [92] Already, after the end of the NRA codes, Congress had moved to impose mini-mum standards for all work under government contracts. The Walsh-Healey Act of 1936 set a 40-hour week, forbade child labor under sixteen, and required payment of "prevailing wages in the locality" as determined by the Secretary of Labor.[93]

[92] Raleigh *News and Observer*, January 29, 1937.
[93] Brandeis, "Organized Labor and Protective Labor Legislation," in Derber and Young (eds.) *Labor and the New Deal*, 208–10.

In 1937 the way seemed open for more general wages and hours legislation after the Supreme Court upheld state minimum wage legislation and the Wagner Act, the latter on the basis of the interstate commerce power. Secretary Perkins dug out a bill that rested in her files and submitted it to legal assistants for reworking. On the appeal of Grace Abbott, former chief of the Children's Bureau, they added a provision against child labor under sixteen. On May 24, 1937, Hugo Black of Alabama introduced the bill in the Senate and William P. Connery, Jr., of Massachusetts in the House; but it was more than a year before the bill ran the legislative gauntlet and emerged as the Fair Labor Standards Act.[94] Once again the Capitol reverberated with defenses of the regional differential. "Any man on this floor who has sense enough to read the English language," Cotton Ed Smith declaimed to his fellow senators, "knows that the main object of this bill is, by human legislation, to overcome the splendid gifts of God to the South." [95] It should be entitled, Sam F. Hobbs of Alabama suggested, "A bill to enslave labor, to increase unemployment . . . to kill all labor unions and collective bargaining, to shut down all business and industries competing with the tariff-protected and freight-rate-favored East, to drive western and southern businessmen and industrialists back between the plowhandles—looking at the east end of a west-bound mule." It was another step toward Federal despotism. "I have never known a Board in Washingon to be fair to the South," Hobbs wrote to a friend. Sooner or later, the multiplication of Federal agents would lead to a movement to enforce the Reconstruction Amendments.[96]

Southern lumbermen became the spearhead of opposition. To set a 40-hour week and a 40-cent minimum wage, a Virginia producer estimated, would raise the cost of lumber $8–12 per thousand feet and leave the South at the mercy of the mechanized West Coast industry.[97] In June, 1937, leaders of the industry formed the Southern Pine Industry Committee to combat the bill

---

[94] See Orme W. Phelps, *The Legislative Background of the Fair Labor Standards Act* (Chicago, 1939).

[95] *Congressional Record*, 75 Cong., 1 Sess., 7882.

[96] *Ibid.*, 75 Cong., 2 Sess., 1494; Sam F. Hobbs to Col. Harry M. Ayers, August 3, 1937, in Sam F. Hobbs Papers, University of Alabama Library (Tuscaloosa).

[97] J. L. Camp, Jr., to Sam F. Hobbs, June 28, 1937, in Hobbs Papers.

by publicity and pressure tactics.[98] Farmers as well as business-men became particular targets of propaganda. By the end of July, a disturbed friend wrote to Black, the effort was making inroads among his rural supporters. "The worst offenders of all against industrial decency in this state—the lumbermen—are the ones who are doing most of the agitating." [99] The Black Connery bill, the Selma *Times-Journal* warned, would cause price advances that would wipe out gains from the New Deal farm programs.[100] In the spring of 1938 President Roosevelt read to one of his press conferences portions of a full-page advertisement inserted by the Southern Pine Association in a number of papers. "If a wages and hours bill . . . goes through," it warned, "you farmers . . . will have to pay $3.00 a day to your field labor." "That is a lie," the President barked, "and every editor who ran that ad knew it was a lie." [101] The bill exempted labor in agriculture and in a number of other categories, chiefly in trade and services.

The clamor of the bill's opponents gave an impression of gen-eral hostility in the region. "It is my firm belief that the vast majority of Alabama Democrats are unalterably opposed to the passage of the Black Connery labor standards bill," Democratic State Chairman John D. McQueen wrote in July, 1937. Mary Louise Kendall, Mississippi National Committeewoman, pre-dicted "grave dissension" in the national party if it passed. Secre-tary C. C. Gilbert of the Southern States Industrial Council, claimed a constituency of seventeen thousand industrialists in fourteen states, "practically every one of whom is opposed to the Black Connery labor control bill." [102] The Gallup poll, however, recorded Southerners as 51 per cent favorable to minimum wage legislation in December, 1935; 56 per cent in May, 1937, and again in May, 1938.[103]

[98] Boyd, "Southern Pine Association History," *loc. cit.*, 57.

[99] Charles B. Crow to Hugo L. Black, July 20, 1937, copy in John Bankhead, Jr., Papers.

[100] Selma *Times-Journal*, n.d., clipping in Hobbs Papers.

[101] "Press Conferences," II (April 21, 1938) , 340, in Roosevelt Library.

[102] John D. McQueen to James A. Farley, July 26, 1937; Mary Louise Kendall to Farley, July 30, 1937; C. C. Gilbert to Farley, July 27, 1937, all enclosed with Farley to Franklin D. Roosevelt, August 3, 1937, in OF 2730, Roosevelt Library.

[103] Hadley P. Cantril and Margaret Strunk (eds.), *Public Opinion, 1935–1946* (Princeton, 1951) , 1018, 1021.

But the bill's opponents held strategic positions in Congress. After it passed the Senate on July 31, 1937, conservative Southern Democrats like Howard W. Smith of Virginia and Eugene E. Cox of Georgia joined Republicans to bottle it up in the House Rules Committee. In December its supporters by strenuous effort secured enough signatures on a discharge position to get the bill on the floor. But it lacked wholehearted support from union leaders, most of whose members were well above the proposed minimum, and the House voted by a close margin to recommit the measure.

It appeared to be entombed permanently, but the startling returns from two Southern primaries induced a sudden resurrection in the spring. In January, 1938, Lister Hill of Alabama, who campaigned as a supporter of the wages and hours bill, easily overcame Thomas J. Heflin for the seat Hugo Black had left to join the Supreme Court. In May the issue came more sharply into focus in Florida's senatorial primary. There Claude Pepper, a thorough New Dealer in the short term he was then serving, won a clear majority over four opponents, including Representative James Wilcox, an outspoken critic of labor-standards legislation. On May 6, 1938, three days after Pepper's triumph, a discharge petition became available for signatures and Congressmen disrupted proceedings in a rush to get on the "honor roll." "The people of the South are for the minimum wage bill," said Maury Maverick of Texas, "and there is plenty of proof of this." On May 24 the House passed the bill, 314 to 97.[104]

Differences between the House and Senate versions had to be ironed out before final disposition. In the conference committee Southern advocates of a regional differential made their last stand, but finally yielded to a provision that no minimum wage rate should be fixed solely on a regional basis.[105] The Fair Labor Standards Act, signed by the President on June 25, provided a 40-hour week and a minimum wage of 40 cents, both to be achieved by gradual steps: a 44-hour week effective October 24, 1938, to be reduced by 2 hours in each of the two successive years; the wage minimum to start at 25 cents and gradually rise to 40 cents in 1945. However, the wages and hours administrator (head of a new

[104] Congressional Record, 75 Cong., 3 Sess., 7292, 7449–50.
[105] Frances Perkins, The Roosevelt I Knew (New York, 1946), 264.

division in the labor department) could advance rates ahead of schedule upon recommendation of industry committees, in order to reach the 40-cent minimum "as rapidly as is economically feasible without substantially curtailing employment." [106] By 1942 forty industry committees had been appointed and thirty-five minimum wage orders issued on this principle.[107] In textiles, which had the first industry committee, the rate rose to 32.5 cents in 1939, 37.5 in 1941, and 40 in 1942, more than three years ahead of schedule.[108]

The law had its greatest impact on the marginal industries, and therefore mainly on workers in the South. In July, 1938, shortly after its adoption, a survey of selected industries showed that in the South entrance rates were less than the 25-cent minimum for 17 per cent of the common laborers in fertilizer, 27 per cent in brick and tile, and 43 per cent in sawmills. In the cottonseed crushing industry during the 1937–1938 season 55 per cent of all labor earned less than the minimum; in August, 1938, about 11 per cent of employees in cotton goods and 26 per cent in seamless hosiery.[109] Yet the minimum standards brought no catastrophe to such industries. Here and there a prudent lumberman closed his sawmills; but in November, less than a month after the effective date of the law, Wage and Hour Administrator E. F. Andrews estimated that not more than thirty to fifty thousand had been affected by layoffs, about 90 per cent of whom were concentrated in a few Southern industries: pecan shelling, tobacco stemming, lumber, and bagging.[110]

The more common result of the law was pressure upon industrial managers to consider problems of costs and efficiency: improved machinery, processes, scheduling, the use of labor. In some cases the effect was direct and immediate. In October, 1938, for

[106] "Federal Wage and Hour Law of 1938," in *Monthly Labor Review*, XLVII (1938), 107–12.

[107] John C. Shinn and John I. Kolemainen, "Time-Table of Minimum Wage Procedure under the Fair Labor Standards Act," in *Social Forces*, XXI (1942–1943), 231.

[108] Kennedy, "History of the Textile Workers' Union of America," 163, 166–67.

[109] Edward K. Frazier and Jacob Perlman, "Entrance Rates of Common Laborers, July, 1938," in *Monthly Labor Review*, XLVIII (1939), 170–73; John F. Moloney, "Some Effects of the Federal Fair Labor Standards Act upon Southern Industry," in *Southern Economic Journal*, IX (1942–1943), 17–18.

[110] *Time*, XXXII (October 31, 1938), 9–10; (November 21, 1938), 16.

instance, the little pecan industry of San Antonio closed down temporarily for the installation of shelling machinery. When it reopened only two to three thousand employees were needed instead of the twelve thousand formerly hired at peak seasons, but the 25-cent wages were 500 per cent higher.[111] Re-examination of labor policies in the cottonseed industry brought general abandonment of that rare anachronism, the 12-hour shift, even though the act specifically exempted cottonseed from the hours provision. A number of mills made substantial improvements in machinery; and gross hourly wages rose 6 per cent, but employment declined.[112]

In most cases it was difficult to separate effects of the Fair Labor Standards Act from other influences: the NRA, unions, the increasing complexity of industry, and various economic forces. But there was evidence of significant progress toward lessening the regional wage differential in such fields as fertilizer, seamless hosiery, and cotton garments. In some cases this was accompanied by reduced employment—for example, in seamless hosiery and cottonseed oil. Yet in others substantial increases came in both wages and employment. From 1939 to 1941 the differential in men's cotton garments declined by about a third, but employment rose more rapidly in the South than in the North. From 1937 to 1941, the differential in wood furniture went down 8 per cent, but employment rose 26 per cent in the South while it declined in the North.[113] Coal offered one of the most startling cases. By 1941 the United Mine Workers had eliminated the regional differential altogether; yet the South, which had the most rapid rate of technological change, also had gains in employment against substantial declines in Northern fields.[114] Such experiences, Richard A. Lester, an economist at Duke, said in 1946, "taught that the answers are often just the opposite from what some economists expected and some industrialists feared. . . . We must think

[111] Grannenberg, "Maury Maverick's San Antonio," *loc. cit.*, 423-24.

[112] Moloney, "Some Effects of the Federal Fair Labor Standards Act upon Southern Industry," *loc. cit.*, 19-20.

[113] Richard A. Lester, "Must Wages Differ North and South?" in *Virginia Quarterly Review*, XXII (1946), 21-22.

[114] Milton S. Baratz, *The Union and the Coal Industry*, in Yale *Studies in Economics*, IV (New Haven, 1955), 123; Galenson, *CIO Challenge to the AFL*, 219-25.

through our economic problems anew unencumbered by past prejudices and shibboleths, if the South is to make rapid strides in its economic affairs." [115]

A significant factor, however, was that the minimum-wage law preceded a period of defense and war prosperity. Amid the rising demand for labor, minimum-wage determinations became irrelevant. By 1945 the South would reach a stage of development in which growing markets and new uses for Southern raw materials began to outweigh the availability of labor in the dynamics of industrial growth. Two economists who studied the immediate postwar situation concluded in 1949 that it was "no longer necessary to base promotional efforts on low wage rates." [116]

The travail of the New Deal years had brought into such focus as never before the aspirations and the needs of Southern workers. It left a legacy of permanent unionism and minimal standards set by legislation. Still, the changes of those years worked no revolutionary transformation. Unionism involved a minority of workers and the legal standards exempted vast numbers from their application. The high rate of population growth continued steadily to expand the labor supply and the wage differential remained a stubborn reality. It varied "widely and irrationally from industry to industry, from locality to locality, and from firm to firm." It nearly disappeared for skilled workers in such lines as iron and steel, paper and pulp, and the building trades; in some low-wage industries decidedly affected by wage minimums, such as textiles, the differential became greater in skilled occupations. In some fields it hardly existed at all: automobiles, railroads, aircraft, oil, paper, seamless hosiery, and garments. In others Southern wages

[115] Lester, "Must Wages Differ North and South?" *loc. cit.*, 31. In a number of articles Lester developed his position that the effects of wage-hour legislation were generally beneficial. For citations see Hoover and Ratchford, *Economic Resources and Policies of the South*, 399. The orthodox position that wage-hour legislation impeded economic growth is developed by economist John V. Van Sickle in his *Planning for the South* (Nashville, 1943), 186–91; and Van Sickle, "Industrialization and the South," in *Southern Economic Journal*, XV (1948–1949), 412–24, and in other writings.

[116] Glenn E. McLaughlin and Stefan Robock, *Why Industry Moves South: A Study of Factors Influencing the Recent Location of Manufacturing Plants in the South*, National Planning Association Committee of the South *Report* No. 3 (Washington, 1949), 120.

ran at least 25 per cent below Northern: lumber, furniture, rubber, fertilizer, soft drinks, and food.[117] Yet there was an over-all improvement. The average annual wage per production worker in the South in 1937 was 63.2 per cent of that in the non-South, in 1939, 64.4 per cent, and in 1947, 74.1 per cent.[118] Whether this was a temporary phenomenon of wartime prosperity or the evidence of a trend toward closing the gap remained to be seen.

[117] Lester, "Must Wages Differ North and South?" *loc. cit.*, 21–22.
[118] Hoover and Ratchford, *Economic Resources and Policies of the South*, 136.

CHAPTER XVI

NEW DIRECTIONS IN NEGRO LIFE

I N the South . . . the Negro has a genuine place in society,"
South Carolina's poet laureate Archibald Rutledge wrote in
1932. "It is secondary, but it is certain. He lives and moves
and has his being in the security of a definite status." [1] Such comfortable assurance became more difficult to maintain in the decade
that followed. Indeed the Negro's status was never so definite as the
cherished legend would have it. The etiquette of race relations encompassed a "welter and chaos of codes," one Negro scholar noted.
The "very complexity and uncertainty" of segregation practices,
another testified, became "abundant sources of confusion and
discontent." [2]

"From the beginning . . . the attempt has been made to fix
permanently the status of the Negro and so remove the subject
from public discussion and agitation," Tuskegee's President
Robert R. Moton wrote in 1929. "But it refused to stay fixed." [3]
"New questions have arisen over [Negroes'] entrance into industry and politics, questions which may become more widespread in
the future," President Hoover's Committee on Recent Social
Trends reported in 1930. "The relationship of white and Negroes
will raise continuing problems." [4] Moreover, a perceptive Virginian, R. Charlton Wright, noted, white Southerners had abandoned the issue to drift, under the complacent illusion that it was

[1] Archibald Rutledge, "The Negro in the North," in *South Atlantic Quarterly*,
XXXI (1932), 62.

[2] Bertram Wilbur Doyle, *The Etiquette of Race Relations in the South* (Chicago,
1937), 160; Charles S. Johnson, *Patterns of Negro Segregation* (New York, 1943), 6.

[3] Moton, *What the Negro Thinks*, 48–49.

[4] President's Research Committee on Recent Social Trends, *Recent Social Trends
in the United States* (2 vols.; New York, 1933), I, xli.

settled, while Negroes were "well organized for advancement" on the "higher levels" and in the North. "If the white man still believes his race, alone, can impose inequitable ex parte judgments, without reference to the Negro's interests," Wright concluded, "he is kidding himself." [5]

Certain forces already had begun to loosen the patterns fixed at the turn of the century: the Great Migration, the New Negro movement, the NAACP, the interracial movement and new concepts in anthropology, which undermined the intellectual respectability of racism. And no longer could one equate "the Negro problem" and "the Southern problem," a habit of bygone times. By 1930, 21.3 per cent of American Negroes lived in the North, where the most aggressive race leaders established their citadels. Negro immigrants followed their European counterparts into the ethnic politics of the North, and in 1928 sent Republican Oscar DePriest to Congress.

In 1930 a dramatic episode signified the Negro political renaissance: the battle against Senate confirmation of Judge John J. Parker for the Supreme Court. When President Hoover nominated the North Carolinian, somebody supplied the NAACP a yellowed clipping which quoted Parker's statement, as Republican candidate for governor in 1920, that Negro participation in politics was "a source of evil and danger." After an unanswered inquiry to the judge, the organization filed a protest with the Senate Judiciary Committee and mounted a campaign of publicity and pressure; it was conducted, W. E. B. Du Bois said, "with a snap, determination, and intelligence never surpassed in colored America and very seldom in white." However, the defeat of Parker, by a close vote of 41–39, resulted from a convergence of unlikely allies: the NAACP; the AFL, which boggled at a Parker decision upholding a "yellow dog" contract; insurgent Senators who found him too conservative; and Southern Democrats disinclined to reward a Southern Republican. The NAACP's contribution to the outcome, therefore, was one of several imponderables. Nevertheless, the campaign operated "to give the American Negro a consciousness of his voting power." It assumed signifi-

[5] R. Charlton Wright, "The Southern White Man and the Negro," in *Virginia Quarterly Review*, IX (1933), 179, 180, 191.

cance as the first instance of Negro political impact on Congress since Reconstruction.[6]

It signified, also, a growing disillusionment with the party of Lincoln. Neither Harding nor Coolidge had restored Negro patronage to pre-Wilson levels, and in 1928 Hoover by-passed the regular black-and-tan organizations to cultivate white support in the South. Negro Republicans like Robert Church of Memphis declined service on the national advisory committee, and others like Thomas E. Miller of Charleston openly supported Al Smith, as did Negro papers like the Chicago *Defender,* the Baltimore *Afro-American,* and the Norfolk *Journal and Guide.*[7] After the election Hoover proposed to develop in the South a lily-white Republicanism "of such character as would commend itself to the citizens of those states."[8] Government offices and cafeterias remained segregated; the War Department jim-crowed Negro Gold Star mothers traveling to their sons' graves in France; the President ignored race problems, even lynching, in his messages to Congress. He made "fewer first-class appointments of Negroes to office than any President since Andrew Johnson," W. E. B. Du Bois asserted; and Walter White tagged him "the man in the lily-White House."[9]

Meanwhile Democrats in Northern cities courted and on occasion won the Negro vote. As early as 1924 the Democratic national committee established a Negro division, which reappeared in subsequent campaigns. Rebuffs from Hoover put Negroes in a rebellious state of mind. In 1932, beset by depression, Negroes had much the same reasons as white citizens to seek new leadership.

[6] Richard L. Watson, Jr., "The Defeat of Judge Parker: A Study in Pressure Groups and Politics," in *Mississippi Valley Historical Review,* L (1963–1964), 213–34; White, *A Man Called White,* 104–15; Ovington, *The Walls Came Tumbling Down,* 255; Heywood Broun, "The Black Voter," in *The Crisis,* XXXVII (1930), 369. In subsequent years Judge Parker established a liberal record in both racial and labor cases.

[7] John G. Van Deusen, *The Black Man in White America* (Rev. ed.; Washington, 1944), 133–34; Franklin, *From Slavery to Freedom,* 513.

[8] Hoover statement, March 26, 1929, quoted in Work (ed.), *Negro Year Book, 1931–1932,* p. 93.

[9] Van Deusen, *The Black Man in White America,* 134; Arthur Krock, "Did the Negro Revolt?" in *Opportunity,* XI (1933), 19; Du Bois, "Hoover," in *The Crisis,* XXIX (1932), 362; White, *A Man Called White,* 102–19.

One significant augury was the defection of Robert L. Vann, publisher of the *Pittsburgh Courier*. "My friends, go home and turn Lincoln's picture to the wall," he told Negro voters. "That debt has been paid in full." [10] Still, most Negroes held to the old fealty; some feared "for the welfare of their race with the 'solid south' in the saddle." Consequently the defections were limited to a minority. But Roosevelt got an estimated 23 per cent of Chicago's Negro vote in 1932 and 36.7 per cent of Detroit's. In Atlanta he carried three of four Negro wards.[11]

At first Negroes accepted Roosevelt with guarded optimism. "A liberal in politics and in economics might well be expected to be a liberal in race relations," said *Opportunity*, organ of the Urban League. "As he assumes his duties, he will carry the hopes of millions of Negroes." [12] Like Wilson, Roosevelt did not assign a high priority to Negro affairs, but he tolerated in his official family men who did. The first initiative, however, came from outside the administration. In the spring of 1933 three men descended on the bustling capital, convinced that the dynamics in Washington afforded opportunities for a new stage of Negro advancement: Will Alexander of the Interracial Commission, Edwin Embree of the Rosenwald Fund, and Charles S. Johnson of Fisk University. They concluded that someone in government should have a special responsibility to look after Negro interests in the new programs. With assent from the White House they approached Secretary of the Interior Harold L. Ickes, former president of Chicago's NAACP, who appointed as an advisor Clark Foreman, a white Atlantan who had worked with both Alexander and Embree. The Rosenwald Fund promised to pay his salary. Negroes, however, protested that such a position should go to a Negro. Soon Foreman acquired an assistant: Robert C. Weaver, a young Negro econo-

[10] Work (ed.), *Negro Year Book, 1937–1938*, p. 101; Vann, quoted in Joseph Alsop and Richard Kintner, "The Guffey, Biography of a Boss, New Style," in *Saturday Evening Post*, CCX (March 26, 1938), 6.

[11] "The Election," editorial in *Opportunity*, X (1932), 368; Myrdal, *An American Dilemma*, 494–95; Atlanta *Daily World*, May 3, 1933, quoted in Rollin Chambliss, *What Negro Newspapers of Georgia Say About Some Social Problems, 1933* (Athens, 1934), 49.

[12] "The Election," *loc. cit.*, 369.

mist at North Carolina Agricultural and Technical College. Daniel C. Roper, a South Carolinian, made Eugene Kinkle Jones of the Urban League an advisor in Commerce.[13]

Gradually Negro advisors appeared in other agencies: Robert L. Vann in Justice, Henry Hunt in the Farm Credit Administration; William H. Hastie, assistant solicitor in Interior; Ambrose E. Caliver in the Office of Education; Lawrence W. Oxley in Labor; later Mrs. Mary McLeod Bethune in NYA and Ira De A. Reid in Social Security. Opportunities multiplied for Negro employment in professional and white-collar jobs. By 1936, when Weaver succeeded Foreman, the "Black Cabinet" of Negro advisors numbered between thirty and forty.[14] They worked doggedly against repeated frustrations, often without authority, usually relying on persuasion. Forrester B. Washington, after spending six weary months answering thousands of complaints at the FERA, quit in disgust.[15] Others persisted.

One of their first problems was the ironic backlash of recovery programs against the man at the bottom. Under AAA Negro tenants and sharecroppers suffered first from crop limitations. Under NRA, whites displaced Negroes when wages suddenly rose; some Negroes sardonically rendered the letters NRA into "Negro Removal Administration."[16] The Atlanta Chamber of Commerce suggested lower standards to protect Negro jobs and a Selma manufacturer circulated leaflets demanding a "subnormal" wage scale of $6 to $9.50 weekly for Negroes.[17] None of the codes ever carried a racial differential, but many were dotted with loopholes:

[13] Dykeman and Stokely, *Seeds of Southern Change,* 192–96; Allen Francis Kifer, "The Negro Under the New Deal, 1933–1941," (Ph.D. dissertation, University of Wisconsin, 1961), 218–20, 232; Rosenwald Fund, *Annual Report, 1934,* pp. 214–15.

[14] Dykeman and Stokely, *Seeds of Southern Change,* 197; Kifer, "The Negro Under the New Deal," 220–23; Leslie H. Fishel, "The Negro in the New Deal Era," in *Wisconsin Magazine of History,* XLVIII (1964–1965), 115. Work (ed.), *Negro Year Book, 1937–1938,* pp. 112–14, lists fifty-five major Negro appointments in 1933 and 1934.

[15] Kifer, "The Negro Under the New Deal," 233.

[16] Roos, *NRA Economic Planning,* 172–73, cites estimates of 500,000 Negroes thrown on relief directly or indirectly by code wages; Robert C. Francis, "The Negro and Industrial Unions," in *Social Forces,* XV (1936), 274.

[17] Raper and Reid, *Sharecroppers All,* 241–42; J. F. Ames, *The Subnormal Negro; Discussion of Reasons Showing the Imperative Necessity for Code for Subnormal Labor,* pamphlet in Samuel H. Hobbs Papers (University of Alabama). See also Cayton and Mitchell, *Black Workers and the New Unions,* 437–38.

Southern laundry workers had an hourly minimum of 14 cents; the lowest rates in two Southern steel districts were 25 to 27 cents; cotton textiles exempted cleaners and outside workers; petroleum permitted 10 per cent of the Southern employees to get less than the minimum; in one artful dodge Negro workers were designated "executives." [18]

In July, 1933, John P. Davis, a young Negro lawyer, became secretary of the Joint Committee on National Recovery, set up by the NAACP and other Negro groups to plead the Negroes' case. NRA officials, Davis wrote later, met all appeals "with an unpardonable sophistry." [19] Of almost a thousand Negro employees in the NRA not one rose above the rank of messenger except Mabel Byrd, a labor specialist employed to study the problems of Negro labor. After a few months in a Jim-Crow corner, she was released. It was "preposterous," Hugh Johnson said, to have such a study made by a Negro.[20] In February, 1934, Foreman and Ickes developed an interdepartmental committee on Negro affairs to examine displacements under both AAA and NRA, but it yielded no solutions. Agriculture Secretary Wallace merely advised them to be cautious. And the NRA offered poor choices: either lower minimums, or racial differentials, or displacement cushioned by relief. Negro organizations and individuals consulted in meetings across the South rejected differentials. A policy of drift, therefore, conceded displacement or evasion.[21]

Inexorably discrimination stalked Negroes in every Federal program. Although real benefits flowed from the New Deal bounty, Federal agencies dared not challenge entrenched habits. More could be gained by "inching along," TVA Chairman Morgan told Negro critics, than by sudden steps calculated to provoke hostility. TVA therefore conformed to Jim Crow, excluded Ne-

[18] John P. Davis, "A Survey of the Problems of the Negro under the New Deal," in *Journal of Negro Education*, V (1936), 10; Alfred L. Barnheim and Dorothy Van Doren (eds.), *Labor and the Government: An Investigation of the Role of the Government in Labor Relations* (New York and London, 1935), 300–302.

[19] John P. Davis, "Blue Eagles and Black Workers," in *New Republic*, LXXXI (November 14, 1934), 7–9. See also John P. Davis, "What Price National Recovery?" in *The Crisis*, XL (1933), 272.

[20] Cayton and Mitchell, *Black Workers and the New Unions*, 102.

[21] Kifer, "The Negro Under the New Deal," 220–30; Roos, *NRA Economic Planning*, 172–73; Raper and Reid, *Sharecroppers All*, 241.

groes from model towns like Norris, put "white" and "colored" signs over water fountains and employment offices, hired whites first for skilled jobs, and segregated most work crews. On the other hand, in March, 1934, the personnel director proclaimed a policy of employing Negro workers in "a proportion commensurate with their part of the population," about 10 per cent in the Valley. A year later, during a sample two-week period, Negroes constituted 11 per cent of the work force, drawing 9.5 per cent of the payroll. The proportion remained fairly constant through the decade. Few, however, worked in clerical or supervisory positions.[22]

Other agencies were bolder only by contrast. Even Harold Ickes, who desegregated Interior Department cafeterias, would not challenge segregated housing. But about half the Federal housing projects in the South were for Negroes, and beginning with the first, Atlanta's Techwood Homes, PWA housing contracts stipulated the employment of Negro workers. Failure to pay colored workers a specified percentage of the payroll, as determined by the occupational census, constituted *prima facie* evidence of discrimination. It was a small matter at first, but it set the precedent for like safeguards in contracts let by the United States Housing Authority, the Federal Works Agency, later the various war agencies, and ultimately all Federal contracts.[23] On the other hand, the Federal Housing Administration, which insured mortgages on private homes, emphasized "ordinary business principles," actively encouraged racial covenants, and collaborated in planning white suburbs that encircled Negro ghettoes in the central cities.[24]

The greatest windfall was public relief, which became during the 1930's one of the major Negro occupations, surpassed only by

[22] Charles H. Houston and John P. Davis, "TVA: Lily White Reconstruction," in *The Crisis*, XLI (1934), 290–91, 311; John P. Davis, "The Plight of the Negro in the Tennessee Valley," *ibid.*, XLII (1935), 294–95, 314–15; Cranston Clayton, "The TVA and the Race Problem," in *Opportunity*, XII (1934), 111–12; Whitman, *God's Valley*, 112; Pritchett, *The Tennessee Valley Authority*, 285–86.

[23] Robert C. Weaver, "The New Deal and the Negro," in *Opportunity*, XIII (1935), 202; Robert C. Weaver, "Racial Policy in Public Housing," in *Phylon*, I (1940), 153–54; Herbert R. Northrup, *Organized Labor and the Negro* (New York, 1944), 29.

[24] Sterner, *The Negro's Share*, 321–16. The FHA did not have a division of race relations.

agriculture and possibly by domestic service.[25] The incidence and benefits varied from place to place, determined by local verdicts on projects and allocations, but the recipients were numerous and the total sums large. In urban areas, both North and South, the proportion of Negroes on the relief rolls was greater than in the population. The proportions lagged in Southern rural areas, where traditional attitudes were more intense. In either case, however, Negroes had to meet more severe means tests. A study of representative Southern towns and cities in the mid-1930's disclosed among nonrelief Negro families about a third with annual incomes under $500 and a significant number under $250. "I ask the government people for help," a young mother wrote the President from Dillon, South Carolina. "But they would not. They help the white people. But not many negroes." [26]

Moreover, allotments in the South almost always reflected discrimination. Jacksonville at one point devised a formula for dividing relief funds according to population. Although Negro relief families outnumbered the white three to one, they got only 45 per cent of the funds.[27] In May, 1935, the average general relief benefit in Atlanta was $32.66 monthly for whites and $19.29 for Negroes; in Houston $16.86 for whites and $12.67 for Negroes. In sample counties of the eastern cotton area in 1935 monthly benefits averaged $11 for rural whites and $7 for Negroes; in the western cotton area $10 and $8.[28] Even with the best intentions relief agencies faced an insoluble dilemma: how to provide adequate allotments that would not exceed prevailing wages. "For these people to be getting $12 a week—at least twice as much as common labor has ever been paid before," an FERA agent reported from Georgia early in 1934, "is an awfully bitter pill for Savannah people to swallow." [29]

WPA wages after 1935 were, if anything, more offensive. In

[25] The following discussion, except where otherwise indicated, is based on Sterner, *The Negro's Share*, 213–53, 271–94; and Myrdal, *An American Dilemma*, 235–363.

[26] Katherine Bethea to Franklin D. Roosevelt, May 8, 1934, quoted in Kifer, "The Negro Under the New Deal," 215.

[27] Fishel, "The Negro in the New Deal Era," *loc. cit.*, 113.

[28] "Relief Benefits of Rural Negroes in Eastern and Western Cotton Areas," in *Monthly Labor Review*, XLII (1936), 63.

[29] Lorena Hickock, quoted in Schlesinger, *The Politics of Upheaval*, 433.

eight of the thirteen Southern states, however, Negroes were more numerous on the work relief rolls than in the population, although less numerous generally in proportion to the unemployed. Discrimination in work relief took the form of geographical wage differentials and classification into unskilled occupations. In May, 1940, fourteen Southern and Border States had only 11 Negroes among 10,344 WPA supervisors. Moreover, the transition to work relief imposed a hardship on Negro women, who had more difficulty getting either WPA jobs or welfare grants under the new social security programs.

The discrepancies carried over into special programs for youth: the Civilian Conservation Corps and the National Youth Administration. At the outset local agencies often excluded Negroes altogether from the CCC. Georgia's director of selection claimed they were needed "for chopping cotton and for planting other produce"; Florida's relief director found Negroes unqualified to meet the standards; in Arkansas the director indignantly denied charges of discrimination—three Negroes had been chosen; in Texas recruiters simply told Negroes "this work is for whites only." During the summer of 1933 the Department of Labor's Director of CCC Selection W. Frank Persons, under pressure from Will Alexander, gradually began to wrest concessions from local officials. At the end of January, 1934, Negro enrollments were only 5.3 per cent of the total; a year later only 6.1. By January, 1936, however, they rose to 9.9 and thereafter fluctuated between 9 and 11 per cent. Negroes were underrepresented only in the Fourth Corps Area, which covered eight Southern states.

In 1934 CCC Director Robert Fechner, a Tennessean, ordered complete segregation of the camps, although he permitted exceptions where Negro enrollees were few, chiefly in New England. In 1935 he set a policy of selecting Negroes only for vacancies in existing Negro companies—a policy in which Roosevelt acquiesced while asking that his name "be not drawn into the discussion." But in 1936 CCC began to employ Negro supervisors and in 1938 decided to replace all white supervisors in Negro camps. The limited selection policy, however, stood until 1941, when Fechner's successor, James McEntee, authorized larger Negro quotas to boost enrollments that sagged with the defense boom. When the CCC ended in 1942, some 350,000 Negroes had served, about 14 per cent of the total—a tally deceptively high because of the belated increase of quotas.[30]

The NYA chief was a Southerner altogether different from Fechner: Aubrey Williams, an Alabamian and a professional social worker, Harry Hopkins' deputy in FERA. Almost from the beginning in 1935, his agency had a Division of Negro Affairs. As its director Williams named Mrs. Mary McLeod Bethune, probably the most celebrated member of the "Black Cabinet," a formidable lady from a South Carolina farm who had founded Bethune-Cookman College in Daytona Beach and had become a national leader in Negro life. Under her resolute guidance the NYA by 1940 had twenty-seven state supervisors of Negro affairs and avoided the racial controversies that churned the CCC. At the end of 1939 Negro secondary and college students in every Southern state received aid in proportions substantially greater than their numbers—except in South Carolina, where the proportion was nearly equal. Since there was no regional or racial differential in NYA aid, this meant substantially higher sums. However, it did not alter the fact that relatively fewer Negroes were students. And in the out-of-school work program, Negroes were underrepresented in every Southern state, although overrepresented in the nation as a whole. The difficulty was to find eligible sponsors where Negro service organizations were scarce and white-control governments reluctant.[31]

In every category of relief, however, the national pattern, and in some cases the regional pattern, showed overrepresentation of Negroes in proportion to population, although clearly not in proportion to need. In October, 1933, Negroes, about 10 per cent of all Americans, constituted 18 per cent of the relief population. In January, 1935, Negro families on relief represented about 26 per cent of all Negro families and about 15 per cent of all relief recipients. WPA rolls usually showed about the same proportion. In the NYA and CCC representation ran somewhat closer to the proportion of Negro youth (around 11 per cent) : about 12 per

[30] John A. Salmond, "The Civilian Conservation Corps and the Negro," in *Journal of American History*, LII (1965–1966), 78–88; Kifer, "The Negro Under the New Deal," 5–21, 66–68; Sterner, *The Negro's Share*, 254–61; Kenneth Holland and F. E. Hill, *Youth in the CCC* (Washington, 1942), 83, 257–58.

[31] Rackham Holt, *Mary McLeod Bethune: A Biography* (Garden City, N.Y., 1964), 194 and *passim;* Sterner, *The Negro's Share*, 261–70.

cent of the NYA rolls in February, 1939, and about 10 per cent of the CCC in February, 1941, for example. In rural rehabilitation Negro clients were nearly 13 per cent of the total accepted, 1935–1939, a figure close to the percentage of Negro farm operators. Under the Social Security welfare programs recipients of old-age assistance were about 14 per cent Negro in 1938–1939 (against 5.6 per cent of the population sixty-five or over), aid to the blind 25 per cent (against 16 per cent of the blind population), and aid to dependent children 15 per cent (against 11 per cent of the children under sixteen). In the last category, however, Negroes were again underrepresented in the Southern states. And in each category they got smaller allotments.[32] But despite evidences of discrimination against which Negro leaders railed in the pages of *The Crisis* and *Opportunity,* relief reached greater proportions of Negroes than of whites, especially in the North where they voted more freely. "Even with their failures," *The Crisis* admitted, relief officials "made great gains for the race in areas which heretofore have set their faces steadfastly against decent relief for Negroes." [33]

If Negroes derived comfort from relief, they derived little from the Congressional performance on civil rights proposals—which meant, in the context of the times, antilynching bills. After 1922, when a Senate filibuster killed the Dyer bill, the issue became dormant in national politics; a decline of mob violence after 1926 encouraged complacency. But depression reversed the trend; in 1930 mobs dispatched twenty-one victims. That year the Commission on Interracial Cooperation responded with two new projects. A Southern Commission on the Study of Lynching under George Fort Milton backed an intensive study of the 1930 lynchings by Arthur Raper of the Interracial Commission and Walter Chivers of Morehouse College, another study of lynching and the law by James H. Chadbourn of the University of North Carolina. Both appeared in 1933.[34] At the instigation of Mary McLeod Bethune

[32] National Resources Planning Board, Committee on Long-Range Work and Relief Policies, *Security, Work, and Relief Policies* (Washington, 1945), 116–17, 159–60.

[33] "The Campaign," in *The Crisis,* XLIII (1963), 337.

[34] Arthur Raper, *The Tragedy of Lynching* (Chapel Hill, 1933); James Harmon Chadbourn, *Lynching and the Law* (Chapel Hill, 1933). See also George Fort Milton, "The Impeachment of Judge Lynch," in *Virginia Quarterly Review,* VIII (1932), 247–56.

and under the direction of Jessie Daniel Ames, the Commission also sponsored the Association of Southern Women for the Prevention of Lynching, to combat "the claim of . . . mobsters that they were acting solely in defense of womanhood." The men were making studies, Mrs. Ames quipped, "so the women had to get busy . . . to stop lynching!" By 1939 the Association, numbering 39,391 women, had pledged 1,229 police officers to resist mobs, and had influenced many others. With a card file of members in her office, Mrs. Ames could mobilize women to influence officials in any Southern county where violence threatened and thereby forestall trouble.[35]

The NAACP answered the renewed carnage with a renewed campaign for Federal legislation. Late in 1933 that association drafted an antilynching bill, which Democratic Senators Edward P. Costigan of Colorado and Robert Wagner of New York introduced at the next session. Like the Dyer bill it proposed Federal trials of mobsters when states failed to act, punishment of derelict officers, and damage claims against lynching counties. The bill lay dormant until the session ended. Then a resurgence of lynching revived it. One case, the death of Claude Neal in October, 1934, provoked an unusually fierce revulsion when the NAACP circulated a detailed account by Howard Kester. Neal, accused of murdering a white girl in Marianna, Florida, was taken for safekeeping to a county jail across the line in Alabama. The mob that brought him back staged a carnival of sadism. Death followed incredible tortures and mutilations, after which a car dragged the corpse through the streets, where crowds including children inflicted further indignities, and finally hanged it on the courthouse lawn. The next day a mob ran amuck, threatening both Negroes and policemen until the militia restored order. The Federal "Lindbergh Law" against interstate kidnapping did not apply, the attorney-general ruled, since the purpose was not monetary gain.[36]

[35] Lewis T. Nordyke, "Ladies and Lynching," in *Survey Graphic*, XVIII (1939), 683–86; Dykeman and Stokely, *Seeds of Southern Change*, 141–52. See also Ames Papers.

[36] Robert L. Zangrando, "The NAACP and a Federal Antilynching Bill," in *Journal of Negro History*, L (1965), 106–107, 114. [Howard Kester], "The Lynching of Claude Neal," pamphlet dated November 30, 1934, copy with Walter White to

Southern editorialists reacted with shock: "we have to admit that the Marianna incident has shaken us materially," the Birmingham *Age-Herald* conceded. "This brutality simply cannot go on," the Macon *Telegraph* asserted; ". . . the federal anti-lynching bill appears to be the answer." The Interracial Commission for the first time endorsed Federal legislation.[37] When Costigan proposed to take up his bill in April, 1935, however, Southern senators manned their stations and turned it back. Connally, Byrnes, Bankhead, and others in turn filled the time. It was a force bill, Josiah Bailey asserted. "The American people cannot be coerced." It was a disguised antilabor measure, Hugo Black suggested. Cotton Ed Smith invoked "the virtue of our women" and rehearsed the legendary Reconstruction "horrors which confronted . . . one of the most cultured, refined and progressive States of the Union." Majority Leader Robinson co-operated with timely motions to adjourn. After six days of bombast the Senate shelved the bill.[38]

Again lynchings increased after the bill was laid aside. During 1936 Senator Van Nuys proposed an investigation of these incidents, but his resolution died in the Audit and Control Committee, which Chairman James F. Byrnes refused to convene.[39] By 1937 a number of leading Southern dailies endorsed Federal action—in Atlanta, Chattanooga, Columbia, Louisville, Greensboro, Knoxville, San Antonio, El Paso, Houston, Fort Worth, New Orleans, Danville, Memphis, and other cities. "As long as State and local officials are indifferent to these barbarities they will continue to occur," Douglas Southall Freeman wrote in the Richmond *Times-Dispatch*. "We see no alternative but to enact a Federal law with teeth in it." Southerners, Virginius Dabney thought, were ready to accept Federal legislation; the Gallup poll in November found them 53 per cent in favor.[40]

Eleanor Roosevelt, December 14, 1934; White to Eleanor Roosevelt, February 28, 1936, in Eleanor Roosevelt Papers.

[37] Birmingham *Age-Herald*, November 1, 1934; Macon *Telegraph*, February 15, 1935; Dabney, *Below the Potomac*, 184.

[38] Franklin L. Burdette, *Filibustering in the Senate* (Princeton, 1940), 179–81; *Congressional Record*, 75 Cong., 1 Sess., 5749, 6616.

[39] Ovington, *The Walls Came Tumbling Down*, 261; Walter White to Franklin D. Roosevelt, June 2, 1936, in OF 93A, Roosevelt Library.

[40] Dabney, *Below the Potomac*, 185; Ovington, *The Walls Came Tumbling Down*, 185; Richmond *Times-Dispatch*, February 2, 1937.

But when Joseph A. Gavagan of New York sponsored a new antilynching bill in the House, Hatton W. Sumners of Texas bottled it up in his Judiciary Committee. It finally reached the floor by discharge petition in April, 1937, and passed, 277 to 120. Two days earlier a mob at Duck Hill, Mississippi, guaranteed passage when they lynched two Negroes with a new refinement of cruelty —a blowtorch. The sheriff could not identify any of those who took the prisoners, but commended their "orderly" behavior. "Maybe you are right," Sumners confided to Walter White in a Capitol corridor. "Maybe we will have to have an anti-lynching bill after all." [41]

But efforts to consider a Senate bill failed in August and again in November, during a special session. The bill was postponed until January 6, 1938, and for six weeks thereafter a filibuster again occupied the chamber, the most protracted since forgotten battles of the 1890's.[42] Led by Tom Connally, Southern senators talked in relays and perpetrated the reading of lengthy and irrelevant documents. Louisiana's Allen J. Ellender descanted for most of six calendar days on race laws, Father Divine, the history of Egypt, India, and Haiti, and sundry other topics. The struggle for white supremacy "was costly; it was bitter, but oh, how sweet the victory!" he exclaimed. "We shall at all cost preserve the white supremacy of America." Mississippi's Bilbo expounded his scheme of African colonization for Negroes. Harrison punctuated the talk with a warning to Northern Democrats: "Is the faith of the South to be broken? Is its love for the Democratic party to be shattered . . . ?" "The South may just as well know . . ." said Byrnes, "that it has been deserted by the Democrats of the North." [43]

A majority favored the bill, but two attempts to invoke cloture failed. Not even a simple majority, much less the required two-thirds, was ready to abandon what Republican leader McNary called the "full, untrammelled opportunity for argument . . . the last palladium . . . the last barrier to tyranny." On February 21 the Senate turned to other business. If there had been a deter-

[41] *Congressional Record*, 75 Cong., 1 Sess., 3532, 3563–3564; *Time*, IX (April 24, 1937), 12; White, *A Man Called White*, 124.

[42] Burdette, *Filibustering in the Senate*, 5–6.

[43] *Ibid.*, 195–97; New York *Times*, January 11, 1938; *Time*, XXXI (January 24, 1938), 9.

mination to hold sessions around the clock, Tom Connally declared later, the bill might have passed. But only two night sessions occurred during the entire discussion.[44] In other ways the bill's advocates proved irresolute, failing to enforce rules that would inconvenience the opposition. But the debate yielded political advantage for both sides.

It also reversed the trend of public opinion. In November, 1937, the Gallup poll found the nation 72 per cent favorable and the South 57 per cent. In January, during the filibuster, the national percentage in favor dropped to 53. A majority in the South, together with the Rocky Mountain and Pacific Coast regions were by then opposed.[45] After "the statesmen from Dixie had shaken the Capitol rafters for two weeks with apostrophes to the fair name of Southern womanhood," Virginius Dabney noted two years later, ". . . there were alarms from Harper's Ferry to Eagle Pass, and the excitement hasn't fully subsided yet." [46]

Nevertheless, the mob spirit subsided, as though satiated by excess, with eight lynchings in 1936, eight in 1937, six in 1938, three in 1939. A number of factors operated: agitation for a Federal law, the editorial attitude of Southern dailies; the Interracial Commission and Mrs. Ames' Association of Southern Women; good roads; better communications; state police systems; New Deal programs that occupied the destitute of both races; rising levels of education; and, some claimed, the lessened contacts between races because of segregation.[47] Whatever the reasons, the end of a bloody trail seemed near, although some charged that lynching had gone "underground," that white papers suppressed stories or disguised mobs as "posses." [48] Efforts to revive the anti-lynching bill in 1939 and 1940 yielded to more pressing matters of legislation—or at least that offered a convenient pretext.[49]

[44] Connally, *My Name Is Tom Connally*, 170–72.

[45] *Newsweek*, XI (January 31, 1938) , 13.

[46] Virginius Dabney, "Civil Liberties in the South," in *Virginia Quarterly Review*, XVI (1940) , 86.

[47] The last point was made by William Watts Ball, "Improvement in Race Relations in South Carolina: The Cause," in *South Atlantic Quarterly*, XXXIX (1940), 390.

[48] Jessie Daniel Ames, *The Changing Character of Lynching* (Atlanta, 1942) , 2–5.

[49] Zangrando, "The NAACP and a Federal Antilynching Bill," *loc. cit.*, 114–15.

Throughout the controversy Roosevelt kept publicly aloof. Once, in December, 1933, after the governor of California had condoned the lynching of two white men, he seized the chance to denounce mob murder without invoking race or sectionalism. "We do not excuse those in high places or in low who condone lynch law," he told the Federal Council of the Churches of Christ.[50] But he never endorsed Federal legislation. From the beginning Negro leaders had difficulty penetrating the White House secretariat. Colonel Edwin M. "Pa" Watson, the military aide, Stephen Early and Marvin McIntyre, secretaries, all contrived to insulate the President. "What do you *boys* want?" one staff member greeted a delegation that called in 1933; the group never got beyond the waiting room.[51]

Walter White, however, found an intermediary in Mrs. Roosevelt, who indeed associated publicly with Negro groups and thereby served her husband both as go-between and as lightning rod for criticism. In May, 1934, she arranged an audience at which White and the President discussed the issue for more than an hour. "I did not choose the tools with which I must work," Roosevelt told him. ". . . Southerners, by reason of the seniority rule in Congress, are chairmen or occupy strategic places on most of the . . . committees. If I come out for the anti-lynching bill now, they will block every bill I ask Congress to pass to keep America from collapsing. I just can't take that risk." [52] Yet a month later Mrs. Roosevelt told White that the President authorized sponsors of the bill to say he would "be glad to see the bill passed and wishes it passed" provided it could be brought to a vote during a lull. The message was conveyed to Joe Robinson, but elicited no response.[53] In 1935, however, Roosevelt persuaded Robinson to permit a motion for consideration. "I . . . am not clear in my own mind as to whether that is absolutely the right

[50] News Release, December 6, 1933, in OF 93A, Roosevelt Library.

[51] Charles H. Houston to Stephen T. Early, August 16, 23, 1933, in OF 93A, Roosevelt Library. See also Stephen T. Early to Mrs. [Malvina] Scheider, memorandum, August 3, 1935, in Eleanor Roosevelt Papers.

[52] White, *A Man Called White*, 169–70. Although White dated the interview in the spring of 1935, historian Frank Freidel believes it occurred a year earlier. Freidel, *F. D. R. and the South*, 85.

[53] Freidel, *F. D. R. and the South*, 87.

way to attain the objective," he told a press conference. "However, I told them to go ahead and try to get a vote on it." [54] This back-handed endorsement was the most he ever gave.

Yet, for all his caution, Roosevelt—and especially his wife—communicated to Negroes a sense of concern. "People like you and me are fighting . . . for the day when a man will be regarded as a man regardless of his race," he once told Mrs. Bethune. "That day will come, but we must pass through perilous times before we realize it." [55] Among American citizens, he told students at Howard University, "there should be no forgotten men and no forgotten races." [56] For many Negroes, John Hope Franklin suggested, his physical handicap was an inspiration. "He had overcome his; perhaps, some day, they could overcome theirs." [57] But more than anything else, New Deal relief shattered the Republican allegiance of Negro voters; for millions it meant survival. If discrimination persisted, the Black Cabinet signified an interest shown by no other administration within memory.

By 1934 the new allegiance of Negro voters effected Democratic upsets in Pennsylvania and in Louisville, Kentucky. In Chicago Arthur W. Mitchell toppled Oscar DePriest to become the first Negro Democrat in Congress.[58] In 1936 twelve states, including Kentucky and West Virginia, sent Negro delegates or alternates to the Democratic convention, thirty in all.[59] When a Negro minister opened one session with prayer, Cotton Ed Smith exclaimed, "My God, he's black as melted midnight," and stormed out. Later, when Congressman Mitchell spoke, he left for South Carolina. "I cannot and will not be a party to the recognition of the Fourteenth and Fifteenth Amendments," he told reporters.[60] But in the campaign Northern Democrats diligently courted Negroes. The director of the effort in the East was Julian D. Rainey of

[54] Schlesinger, *The Politics of Upheaval,* 438.
[55] Mary McLeod Bethune, "My Secret Talks with FDR," in *Ebony,* IV (April, 1949), 44.
[56] Rosenman (comp.), *Public Papers and Addresses of Franklin D. Roosevelt,* V, 538.
[57] Franklin, *From Slavery to Freedom,* 516.
[58] "New Congressmen," in *The Crisis,* XLI (1934), 359.
[59] Work (ed.), *Negro Year Book, 1937–1938,* p. 102.
[60] *Ibid.,* 102–103; Charleston *News and Courier,* June 25, 1936; "Mr. Roosevelt's Party," in *Fortune,* XVII (June, 1938), 88.

Boston, son of a Reconstruction Congressman from South Carolina.[61] On September 21 thousands traveled from Harlem to Madison Square Garden for a Roosevelt rally. Similar rallies of Negro Democrats occurred in twenty-five other cities that night.[62] In former times, Senator Wagner told Secretary Ickes, Negroes would not turn out to see any Democratic candidate. When Roosevelt visited New York they lined the streets.[63] Ickes, who among cabinet members stood highest with Negroes, spoke to many audiences. Under Roosevelt, he told the Chicago Urban League, Negroes had a special New Deal of their own.[64] In November, for the first time, a majority of the Negro voters cast Democratic ballots, 76 per cent of those later interviewed in a Gallup poll.[65]

In the South, as in the North, the Democratic trend was evident. "Every Negro I have registered so far has said he would vote for President Roosevelt," a registrar in Columbia, South Carolina, testified. "They say Roosevelt saved them from starvation, gave them aid when they were in distress." [66] Negroes continued to participate in local elections and referendums, here and there in Democratic primaries, but they remained few in number. In 1936 Raleigh Democrats sent a Negro delegate to the party's state convention. At Durham more than four thousand Negroes voted in November, in contrast to about five hundred in previous national elections. Later, Negroes voted with little difficulty in AAA and collective bargaining referendums of the late 1930's.[67] But when the decade ended, according to estimates by Ralph J. Bunche, twelve Southern states had registered only about 250,000 Negro voters—from a few hundred in Mississippi to perhaps 50,000 each in Texas, Oklahoma, Tennessee, and North Carolina; Kentucky, if included, would add some 80–100,000.[68]

[61] *Time,* XXVIII (August 17, 1936), 11.
[62] New York *Times,* September 22, 1936.
[63] Ickes, *The Secret Diary of Harold L. Ickes,* I, 689.
[64] New York *Times,* February 27, 1936.
[65] Guzman (ed.), *Negro Year Book, 1941–1946,* p. 279; Earl Brown, "How the Negro Voted in the Presidential Election," in *Opportunity,* XIV (December, 1936), 359.
[66] New York *Times,* August 22, 1936.
[67] George C. Stoney, "Suffrage in the South, Part II. The One Party System," in *Survey Graphic,* XXIX (1940), 205.
[68] Myrdal, *An American Dilemma,* 488n.

These voted mainly in general elections. The white primaries remained mostly intact despite vigorous assaults in the courts. Twice the Supreme Court struck down white primary statutes in Texas as violations of equal protection under the Fourteenth Amendment: first, in Nixon *v.* Herndon (1927), a state law excluding Negroes, and second, in Nixon *v.* Condon (1932), a rule of the party committee sanctioned by state law. But the legislature rose to the challenge. It repealed the law, and the Democratic state convention on its own initiative limited party membership to white only. This the high court accepted in Grovey *v.* Townsend (1935) as the action of a voluntary political association and not the state. Similar suits arose in other states, but without success except in Virginia, where a Federal district court in West *v.* Bliley (1930) struck down a party rule, but in this case one sanctioned by the state legislature. The Circuit Court of Appeals upheld the decision and party officials dropped the matter. Few Negroes tried to invade the primaries.[69]

The Grovey opinion clearly made it possible for the Democratic party of any state to exclude Negroes. But it stood only nine years and it marked the end of major decisions that, since the Slaughterhouse Cases of 1873, had successively narrowed application of the Reconstruction Amendments. Already a different trend had appeared in the review of state criminal procedures. In 1931 a circuit court in a Georgia rape case reaffirmed the precedent of the Elaine cases (1923) that a verdict secured in a mob atmosphere was invalid.[70] Two important precedents arose from the Scottsboro case. The first verdict failed because the lack of counsel denied the defendants due process; appointing "all of the members of the bar" to defend the accused Justice Sutherland pronounced "little more than an expansive gesture imposing no substantial or definite obligation upon anyone."[71] In 1935 a later verdict in the same case fell because "long continued, systematic and arbitrary exclusion of Negroes from jury service" violated the guarantee of equal protection.[72] This principle became one of the chief bases

[69] Nelson, *Fourteenth Amendment and the Negro Since 1820,* pp. 36–41.
[70] Moore *v.* Dempsey, 261 U.S. 86 (1923); Downer *v.* Dunaway, 53 Fed. 586 (1931).
[71] Powell *v.* Alabama, 287 U.S. 45 (1932).
[72] Norris *v.* Alabama, 294 U.S. 587 (1935). The Maryland Court of Appeals had reached a similar decision in Lee *v.* State, 161 Atl. 284 (1932).

for challenging the conviction of any Negro, to such a degree, o.ᵣᵉ authority declared twenty-five years later, that "jury cases constitute the largest single category of litigation involving equal protection . . . since 1935." [73] Police brutality also came under Federal scrutiny in two cases rising from Mississippi in 1936 and Florida in 1940. In each the high court overruled a conviction obtained by forced confessions. In the Florida case Justice Black invoked "the historic truth that the rights and liberties of people accused of crime could not be safely intrusted to secret inquisitorial processes." [74]

A more significant development was the gathering determination to test the "separate but equal" doctrine. Compulsory segregation, Robert R. Moton wrote in 1929, always met "uncompromising protest" from Negroes, who anticipated a decision against it whenever the question should be "placed properly and squarely before the Supreme Court." Yet, he confessed, many Negroes were prepared to accept segregation "and perhaps in some instances adopt voluntary separation for the advantage it will give . . . in fortifying the race to meet the issue of inferiority." [75] This was the essence of the old Hampton-Tuskegee-Booker T. Washington design, and to some it seemed by the early 1930's that W. E. B. Du Bois had veered toward the philosophy of his old adversary. Washington and Du Bois were "never very far apart in their basic philosophies," Ralph Bunche later remarked. "Both confined their thinking within the periphery of race." [76] Actually there was a difference; Du Bois' ideas issued from an undercurrent of black nationalism that always stirred in his mind. Disillusioned by the slow progress toward equality, he counseled Negroes to turn inward, by "self segregation" to establish "such economic foundations as would enable the colored people of America to earn a liv-

[73] Robert J. Harris, *The Quest for Equality: The Constitution, Congress, and the Supreme Court* (Baton Rouge, 1960), 110, and pp. 111–15. See also Carl Brent Swisher, "The Supreme Court and the South," in Cole and Hallowell (eds.), *Southern Political Scene*, 284–86, for additional cases and the continuing practice of exclusion or tokenism.

[74] Brown *v.* Mississippi, 297 U.S. 278 (1936); Chambers *v.* Florida, 309 U.S. 227 (1940).

[75] Moton, *What the Negro Thinks*, 114, 150, 183.

[76] Ralph J. Bunche, "The Programs of Organizations Devoted to the Improvement of the Status of the American Negro," in *Journal of Negro Education*, VIII (July, 1939), 541.

ing, provide for their own social uplift." [77] These foundations would be manufacturers' and consumers' co-operatives "beyond race prejudice and trust competition," accompanied by rejuvenated educational, religious, and social institutions to prepare a distant day when Negroes could advance toward integration into American Society.

Early in 1934 Du Bois advanced his program of Negro self-sufficiency in the editorial columns of *The Crisis,* and a simmering dispute within the NAACP came to a boil. The controversy finally bubbled over from the pages of *The Crisis* into the board of directors, where Du Bois met such fierce opposition that in August he resigned as editor of the journal he had founded in 1910.[78] He had already returned to Atlanta University as visiting professor. There he stayed ten years more, his vigor undiminished, produced among other things his *Black Reconstruction* (1935), and founded *Phylon* (1940), a quarterly "Review of Race and Culture."

James Weldon Johnson, former NAACP secretary who was teaching creative writing at Fisk, explored the issues in a slender volume: *Negro Americans, What Now?* The alternatives, he wrote, were five: Exodus, Physical Force, Revolution, Isolation, or Integration. The first three, he argued, were impractical. Of the latter two he favored Integration; "wisdom and farsightedness and possibility of achievement demand that we follow the line that leads to equal rights," he wrote. "The seeming advantages of imposed segregation are too costly to keep." [79]

Already the NAACP had begun to mount a campaign against inequalities in education. In 1930, with a grant from the American Fund for Public Service, the Association hired Nathan R. Margold, a New York attorney, to formulate a legal campaign against "specific handicaps facing the Negro." Charles H. Houston of the Howard Law School, aided by his associates and students, prepared the plans on education. When the Depression reduced

[77] Du Bois, *Dusk of Dawn,* 296.

[78] Du Bois, "Segregation," in *The Crisis,* XLI (1934), 20; and "The N.A.A.C.P. and Race Segregation," *ibid.,* 52–53; J. E. Spingarn *et al.,* "Segregation—A Symposium," *ibid.,* 79–82; "Dr. Du Bois Resigns," *ibid.,* 245–46. The controversy is detailed in Broderick, *W.E.B. Du Bois,* 166–75; and Rudwick, *W.E.B. Du Bois,* 276–85.

[79] James Weldon Johnson, *Negro Americans, What Now?* (New York, 1934), 3–18.

available funds, this became the focus. In 1934 Houston became the first full-time head of the legal department and resolved to attack first the problem of graduate and professional education. At that time no state institution for Negroes provided such training; only two Border States, West Virginia and Missouri, provided out-of-state tuition grants. Inequality was obvious; distracting social problems presumably would be less acute at the post-graduate level, and the cost of separate facilities would be so prohibitive that a demand for equality might breach the color line itself.[80]

So it did, eventually. In 1933, however, the first effort failed when a Negro candidate for admission to the University of North Carolina's School of Pharmacy proved to have qualifications too doubtful for his attorneys to press the claim.[81] The first break came in two Border States, Maryland and Missouri. In 1936 Donald Murray, a Negro graduate of Amherst, won admission to the University of Maryland Law School when the Maryland Court of Appeals ruled that an out-of-state scholarship failed to meet the requirement of equal protection.[82] Murray's lawyer was Thurgood Marshall, former student of Houston and later his successor as head of the NAACP legal department. Murray was graduated and took up practice in Baltimore. In 1938 the United States Supreme Court, on appeal from Missouri courts, upheld the right of Lloyd L. Gaines to attend the University of Missouri Law School. "The admissibility of laws separating the races in the enjoyment of privileges afforded by the State rests wholly upon the equality of the privileges which the laws give to the separated groups within the State," Chief Justice Hughes asserted in the majority opinion. Again an out-of-state grant failed to meet the test, this time in the Federal court.[83] For the first time the Supreme Court had reexamined the "separate but equal" fiction. It did not overthrow

[80] Thurgood Marshall, "An Evaluation of Recent Efforts to Achieve Integration in Education Through Resort to the Courts," in *Journal of Negro Education*, XXI (1952), 316–17; *Annual Report of the National Association for the Advancement of Colored People*, 1930, p. 17; *ibid.*, 1931, p. 13; *ibid.*, 1934, p. 22; White, *A Man Called White*, 141–43; Dewey Allen Stokes, Jr., "Negro Education and Federal Courts," (M.A. thesis, University of North Carolina, 1955), 36, 38.

[81] White, *A Man Called White*, 156–58; Durham *Morning Herald*, March 29, 1933; Thomas Houck, "Newspaper History of Race Relations in Durham," (M.A. thesis, Duke University, 1941), 60.

[82] University of Maryland v. Murray, 169 Maryland 478 (1936).

[83] Missouri ex. rel. Gaines v. Canada, 305 U.S. 337.

the doctrine, but the Gaines case became the first milestone on the road to desegregation. However, a long and difficult journey still lay ahead, and Gaines himself never made it. Missouri hastily improvised a separate law school in which he refused to register. Before his lawyers could resolve the issue, he disappeared mysteriously and was never found.[84]

The earliest lawsuits originated in state courts. After the Gaines case, applicants in seven states filed petitions in Federal courts.[85] None of them secured admission to white schools, but their challenges quickened progress within the bounds of segregation. Theoretically it seemed a movement to get Negroes into state universities, the Norfolk *Journal and Guide* noted at the outset. "But realistically, it is a movement to procure for colored people educational needs which they are now denied." [86] President Harmon W. Caldwell of the University of Georgia laid the available options before the Southern University Conference: desegregation, separate graduate schools, separate classes in state universities, or state support to private Negro colleges. He preferred a fifth plan, regional institutions supported by the states, but expressed doubt that the courts would countenance them as substitutes for equal opportunity within each state.[87]

The states responded mainly with belated programs for out-of-state tuition grants. Before the Gaines decision only five states offered such grants; by 1943 eleven, by 1948 seventeen—including all the Border States.[88] At most they were temporary stopgaps, already judged inadequate in the very decision that prompted them. But for another decade there was little more except makeshift graduate and professional curriculums added to state institutions

[84] *Newsweek*, XIV (October 2, 1939) , 32–33; Florence Murray (ed.) , *The Negro Handbook, 1942* (New York, 1942) , 40–41.

[85] Stokes, "Negro Education and Federal Courts," 53, citing Charles Stuart Holloway, *The Fourteenth Amendment and Negro Education* (Washington, 1942) , 55n.

[86] Norfolk *Journal and Guide,* August 31, 1935.

[87] Southern University Conference, *Proceedings*, 1939, pp. 90–95. The idea of regional support to build strong fields in selected institutions finally produced the Southern Regional Education Board in 1948, but ostensibly not as an agency to preserve segregation. Redding S. Sugg and George Hilton Jones, *The Southern Regional Education Board* (Baton Rouge, 1960) .

[88] Florence Murray (ed.) , *The Negro Handbook,* 1949 (New York, 1949) , 130.

as emergencies arose. Before the Gaines decision only two state Negro institutions in the South enrolled graduate students: Virginia State and Prairie View State in Texas.[89] In 1939 the North Carolina legislature, at the recommendation of a study commission, initiated graduate programs at North Carolina College and the Agricultural and Technical College. North Carolina College utilized professors from Duke and Chapel Hill. By 1948 ten states had made gestures toward separate graduate and professional programs for Negroes. In addition six private institutions offered such work. But none, public or private, awarded the Ph.D. degree.[90]

Another battlefront in Houston's legal offensive was an attack upon unequal salaries for public school teachers.[91] The average Negro teacher's compensation in 1930 was 42 per cent of the white's; in 1940, 55 per cent. In 1942 the NAACP estimated that Negro teachers in fifteen states lost more than $25,000,000 annually because of the discrepancy.[92] Action began in 1936, after a study of Maryland salaries; near the end of the year a teacher filed suit in Montgomery County. In 1937 the governor announced steps toward salary equalization. In 1937 a Florida teacher brought suit, only to lose his job. The first case to reach a decision arose in Anne Arundel County, Maryland; in 1939 a Federal district court ruled that Negro teachers there should receive no less than the minimum paid to whites.[93] Nine Maryland counties meanwhile

[89] Fred McCuistion, *Graduate Instruction for Negroes in the United States* (Nashville, 1939), 5.

[90] George N. Redd, "Present Status of Negro Higher and Professional Education: A Critical Summary," in *Journal of Negro Education*, XVII (1948), 403, 406. The ten states that acted were Alabama, Florida, Georgia, Louisiana, North Carolina, South Carolina, Tennessee, Texas, Virginia, Missouri. The private institutions were Atlanta, Fisk, Hampton, Howard, Xavier, and Meharry Medical College. See also special issue of *Journal of Negro Education*, XVII (Summer, 1948); and Pierson, *Graduate Work in the South*, 144–76.

[91] Detailed accounts may be found in Stokes, "Negro Education and Federal Courts," 48–61; and Nelson, *The Fourteenth Amendment and the Negro Since 1920*, pp. 127–35.

[92] Stokes, "Negro Education and Federal Courts," 61; Marion T. Wright, "Some Educational and Cultural Problems and Needs of Negro Children and Youth," in *Journal of Negro Education*, XIX (1950), 311; NAACP, *Teachers' Salaries in Black and White* (New York, 1942), 4.

[93] Mills *v.* Board of Education of Anne Arundel County, 30 Fed. Supp. 245b (1939).

had settled out of court, and in 1941 the Maryland legislature adopted an equalization law.

Virginia teachers began their campaign at the 1937 meeting of the State Teachers Association. In 1940 Norfolk's Melvin O. Alston won the first unqualified victory when a Federal circuit court declared salary differentials "as clear a discrimination on the ground of color as could well be imagined," and demanded equal pay for equal qualifications and experience.[94] By that time fifty-three city and county boards in Virginia had agreed to equalize rather than face litigation.[95] The movement spread across the South, with court victories by 1943 in five more states. Statewide equalization was nearly accomplished in Maryland and Oklahoma and programs had begun in Kentucky, Tennessee, Texas, and North Carolina, while other states had taken first measures toward narrowing the gap. When the NAACP closed its salary campaign in 1948 to concentrate upon segregation itself, Negro salaries had risen to 79 per cent of the white.[96]

The drive for equalization aroused little excitement, even in the Deep South. The tedious pace, the limited results, the manifest equity of the claim prevented any profound shock or alarm. The specter of integration was scarcely visible, the word itself hardly known. In a special senatorial race of 1941, the Atlanta *Journal* noted, South Carolina's Olin D. Johnston "shouted that he was against the coeducation of whites and blacks. A profound silence greeted his declaration and he dropped the matter like a hot potato. His hearers knew that the State Constitution, like that of Georgia, prohibited such coeducation and that the statement was not only irrelevant but silly." [97] However, communities would have to equalize not only salaries but school facilities in general, wrote William Watts Ball, Charleston's conservative editor. "If

[94] Alston *et al. v.* School Board of City of Norfolk *et al.,* 112 Fed. Rep. (2d Series) 992 (1940).

[95] Stokes, "Negro Education and Federal Courts," 51–54; "Progress in the Elimination of Discrimination in White and Negro Teachers' Salaries," in *Journal of Negro Education,* IX, (1940), 1–4.

[96] C. S. Johnson, *Into the Main Stream* (Chapel Hill, 1947), 137–51; Wright, "Some Educational and Cultural Problems and Needs of Negro Children and Youth," *loc. cit.,* 311.

[97] Atlanta *Journal,* September 18, 1941.

white children shall ride to school in buses, negro children will not walk." [98] "The nation's tribunal of last resort has spoken on the subject," declared Frederick Sullens, firebrand of the Jackson *Daily News.* "Whether you like the decision or not doesn't matter. It must be obeyed." [99]

Such statements hardly represented a revolution. But in 1942 John A. Rice, a white professor in his fifties, wrote: "The Southerner's attitude toward the Negro is incredibly more humane than it was in the South I knew as a child." [100] The currents were moving, if almost imperceptibly, to erode the old Southern credo, as Howard Odum called it—the unexamined belief that "the Negro is a Negro, and nothing more." [101] Certain intellectual forces of the twentieth century weakened the credibility of old shibboleths: the rise of educational levels, a new anthropology that challenged doctrines of racial inferiority, the increased emphasis upon environmentalism in the social sciences. Moreover, social forces worked in the same direction: the declining need for mudsill labor in agriculture; the rising example of a talented Negro minority; the growing boldness of Negro demands; the reaction against the Ku Klux Klan and other extremists, including now the Nazi example; the Great Migration and the resultant Negro political influence in the North, which in turn rendered the Federal government less indifferent; the impact of the New Deal, which highlighted inequities, occasionally challenged them, and quickened liberal thought; the accelerated communication of ideas through the mass media.[102]

Finally, certain traditional factors tempered viewpoints. The white Southerner's adherence to what Gunnar Myrdal called the "American creed" of equality implanted a fundamental am-

---

[98] Charleston *News and Courier,* February 6, 1941.

[99] Quoted in Dabney, *Below the Potomac,* 208–209.

[100] John A. Rice, *I Came Out of the Eighteenth Century* (New York, 1942), 195. Rice was a child in Columbia, South Carolina, in the late 1890's.

[101] Howard W. Odum, *Race and Rumors of Race* (Chapel Hill, 1943), 22.

[102] George B. Tindall, "The Central Theme Revisited," in Charles G. Sellers (ed.), *The Southerner as American* (Chapel Hill, 1960), 104–29; C. Vann Woodward, *The Strange Career of Jim Crow* (New York, 1955), 108–24; I. A. Newby, *Jim Crow's Defense: Anti-Negro Thought in America, 1900–1930* (Baton Rouge, 1965), 191–92, 197–98; Myrdal, *An American Dilemma,* 998–1004.

bivalence in his attitude. And the religiosity of the region inspired a moral consciousness that provoked uneasiness about discrimination. Scattered reports testified to widespread, if seldom coordinated, interracial activities in missionary, settlement house, and educational work, particularly by women's organizations. From time to time major church bodies and journals spoke out against lynching and the more flagrant discriminations.[103] In 1938 the Baptist World Alliance met in Atlanta without segregation and few Southern churchmen protested.[104] In 1939 the Plan of Union for the Northern and Southern wings of Methodism brought remonstrance from an unexpected source, the Southern Methodist Women's Missionary Council, because its structure of segregation fell "far short of Jesus' ideal for the Kingdom." [105] Yet a majority of white and Negro Christians remained isolated from each other; despite the resolutions, editorials, and formal interracial work, white ministers normally preserved a discreet silence in the local congregation. Even in Catholic churches, theoretically open to all, Negroes usually attended separate services.[106]

Negro churches were, if anything, less inclined to reach across the racial barriers. The most prevalent organization in Negro communities, they retained their hold on the people; but they operated largely in a context of fundamentalism that excluded the social and economic issues of the day. On these they often functioned as agencies of accommodation. "We are the policemen of the Negroes," one Negro preacher confessed in 1941. "If we did not keep down their ambitions and divert them into religion, there would be upheaval in the South." [107]

During the 1930's Will Alexander continued to plant the

[103] Robert Moats Miller, "The Attitudes of American Protestants Toward the Negro, 1919–1939," in *Journal of Negro History*, XLI (1956) , 119, 224–25; Johnson *et al., Into the Main Stream*, 281–312; Mason Crum, *The Negro in the Methodist Church* (New York, 1951) , 71–74, 84–90.

[104] Johnson *et al., Into the Main Stream*, 288.

[105] Quoted in Dwight W. Culver, *Negro Segregation in the Methodist Church* (New Haven, 1953) , 76.

[106] Myrdal, *An American Dilemma*, 868–72. J. A. Cotton to Howard W. Odum, June 7, 1933, in Odum Papers, reported unsegregated attendance of Negroes at the Catholic Church in Henderson, North Carolina.

[107] Myrdal, *An American Dilemma*, 858–78. Quotation on p. 876n.

seeds of change through the Interracial Commission and a variety of other activities. In 1928 he helped initiate a program of Rosenwald Fellowships that for twenty years supported advanced study and creative work by 999 Negroes and 538 Southern whites, and contributed to the development of leaders in scholarship, medicine, journalism, the fine arts, and many other fields. From 1930 to 1948 Alexander served as a trustee of the Rosenwald Fund.[108] His other concerns included the unification of Atlanta and Dillard universities (he was the first president of the latter), efforts to influence New Deal Negro policy, propaganda for the amelioration of farm tenancy, and service in the Resettlement-Farm Security Administration programs.

Most of the Interracial Commission's resources, by deliberate policy, went into research and educational work, to the neglect of local and state committees, which functioned only intermittently. In 1938, when the Commission undertook to revive that work, only three state committees remained.[109] Meanwhile, the publicity work continued and a special grant from the Carnegie Corporation invigorated the educational work. In 1931 a meeting of educators at Peabody College organized the Peabody Conference on Education and Race Relations, which undertook the following year to augment race relations study in formal curriculums. In 1933 it sponsored a conference of school administrators, including eight state superintendents, who endorsed the program and recommended analysis of textbook treatments of Negroes. Findings from several states appeared later in a pamphlet, *Schoolbooks and Racial Antagonism,* with suggestions for improvement. In addition, the program sponsored visiting Negro speakers and musical groups in white schools, joint meetings of high school clubs, in one case participation of white students in a Negro high school orchestra. In 1935 and 1936 twenty-five college professors went to Peabody each summer for an intensive six-week study of race relations. By 1938 the Interracial Commission's files showed people in

[108] Dykeman and Stokely, *Seeds of Southern Change,* 182–87; Alexander, "Reminiscences of Will W. Alexander," 275–81; Embree and Waxman, *Investment in People,* 132–61. See pp. 238–61 for a list of the fellows.
[109] Myrdal, *An American Dilemma,* 844.

260 colleges co-operating in some way, and many state and local superintendents.[110] As early as 1931, 106 Southern white colleges offered studies of Negroes and race relations, 39 in special courses; ten years later the numbers had increased to 187 and 53 respectively; 20 sponsored research in the field, 80 supplemented courses with lectures and concerts, and 58 had some kind of student interracial activity.[111]

But the programs at best reached an elite minority. Interracial meetings were painfully formal experiences. "Everybody present is overpolite in a strained way," a Memphis Negro complained. "The whites are hell-bent upon being broadminded. The Negroes affect to take it all as a matter of course. But nobody present ever dares to speak the blunt truth. They drift on clouds of sentimentality. They pass meaningless resolutions." [112] A North Carolina Negro editor expressed a less indulgent view: "the old guards are always there, and stand ready to throttle any move which might result in accomplishing something. . . . 'Uncle Tom' Epps; N. C. Newbold, the great white father; Cap'n Howard Odum and many others of their kind are always on the scene to prevent their Negro wards from getting others off the right track." [113] The "right track" was still the slow route of education and contacts among the "best people" of both races. It would be too heavy a burden, Odum wrote, "to place upon one or two generations the task of changing the powerful folkways of the centuries." [114] Even so, Gunnar Myrdal attested, it was a monumental accomplishment merely *"to have rendered interracial work socially respectable in the conservative South."* [115]

The NAACP, for all the momentum of its legal program, remained almost as much an upper-class elite as the Interracial Commission; "we recognize our lack of skill at mass appeal," *Crisis*

[110] "Education Program Commission on Interracial Cooperation, Inc.," typewritten report with Emily H. Clay to Howard W. Odum, October 24, 1938, in Odum Papers. Examples of high school programs are cited in E. H. Garinger to Odum, May 15, 1933; L. R. Johnson to Odum, May 11, 1933; and C. W. Phillips to Odum, May 11, 1933, all in Odum Papers.

[111] Johnson *et al, Into the Main Stream*, 153.

[112] Quoted in Cohn, *Where I Was Born and Raised*, 280.

[113] Durham *Carolina Times*, November 3, 1934.

[114] Odum, *Southern Regions of the United States*, 483.

[115] Myrdal, *An American Dilemma*, 847.

editor Roy Wilkins admitted in 1941. The Southern branches were anemic, lacking money and leadership, and often ephemeral. The Urban League, with twelve of its forty-six branches in the South, moved even more circumspectly, heavily dependent upon white approval for Community Chest support in some cities and for its main function of placing Negro workers in all. For a time after 1936 another group, the National Negro Congress (NNC), briefly promised to show strength. An outgrowth of New Deal critic John P. Davis' Joint Committee on National Recovery, it proposed a united front of Negro organizations to arouse the Negro masses for a broad social and economic program of Negro advancement. With Davis' co-operation as secretary, however, Communists played an important role from the beginning and in 1940 converted the Congress into an undisguised party front, ousted A. Philip Randolph as president, and forfeited the support of most Negro organizations. In 1937 the NNC sponsored the Southern Negro Youth Congress, organized at a meeting in Richmond. For a while that group captivated militant educated youths, impatient with the NAACP, but it established little contact with the lower strata. By 1940, Ralph Bunche reported, it was "a flame that flickers only feebly in a few Southern cities"—like its parent organization, a Communist front.[116]

Here and there the sparks of militancy kindled brushfires in Negro communities, but little sustained combustion. The record for South Carolina in the 1930's, compiled by a patient student from fugitive sources, was mainly an inventory of futility. At Greenville early in 1931 a biracial Unemployed Council staged protest demonstrations and demanded relief. Before the year ended, harassment by the police and Klansmen stifled the organization. In 1937 separate chapters of the Worker's Alliance, a union of WPA workers, appeared. The white group soon faded, but the Negro chapter claimed two thousand members in 1939. That year it joined the local NAACP and the Negro Youth Council in a voter registration drive, which exploited resentment at the city's rejection of low-cost housing. But intimidation quickly ended that

---

[116] Wilson Record, *Race and Radicalism: The NAACP and the Communist Party in Conflict* (Ithaca, 1964), 93–100; Record, *The Negro and the Communist Party*, 152–66, 192–96; Myrdal, *An American Dilemma*, 817–42.

episode; among other things, authorities arrested and convicted the youth council leader on the improbable charge of telephoning a white girl for a date. When the decade opened the NAACP had three unobtrusive branches in Charleston, Columbia, and Greenville. When it closed there were four more, sparked mainly by the drive for antilynching legislation. In 1939 the branches organized a South Carolina Conference of the NAACP. The total membership was less than a thousand.[117]

For most Negroes life imposed more urgent necessities. "The escape that the Negro mass seeks is one from economic deprivation, from destitution and imminent starvation," Ralph Bunche observed. "To these people, appealing for livelihood, the N.A.A.C.P. answers: give them educational facilities, let them sit next to whites in street-cars, restaurants, and theaters. They cry for bread and are offered political cake." [118]

In the Depression years the safety valve of out-migration almost ceased to function, although movement picked up again in the late 1930's. Negro unemployment, greater than the white everywhere, ran constantly higher in the North than in the South.[119] From 1930 to 1940, therefore, the proportion of American Negroes living in the South declined only from 78.7 to 77 per cent. In net migration the Southeast lost 424,924 or 5.4 per cent of its Negro population in contrast to 615,000 or 8.2 percent in the 1920's.[120]

Meanwhile Negroes continued to leave the farm; 37.3 per cent of the Southern Negroes were town dwellers by 1940. There, as on the farm, earlier trends in employment persisted. Their relative position deteriorated, even in the traditional "Negro jobs." It was not until after World War I, William Watts Ball remarked, that he saw white waitresses in South Carolina hotels and restaurants.

[117] Edwin D. Hoffman, "The Genesis of the Modern Movement for Equal Rights in South Carolina," in *Journal of Negro History*, XLIV (1959), 346–69.

[118] Ralph J. Bunche, "Extended Memorandum on the Programs, Ideologies, Tactics, and Achievements of Negro Betterment and Interracial Organizations," microfilm of typescript, 1940, in Schomburg Collection, New York Public Library, 144.

[119] Vance, *All These People*, 328; Myrdal, *An American Dilemma*, 297–303. The point must be qualified by recognizing that much unemployment goes unreported in agricultural areas.

[120] Vance, *All These People*, 119, 126; Davie, *Negroes in American Society*, 92. Over-all proportion for the Census South.

"One sees them now," he wrote in 1940. "As boy and young man in my village I not often saw a white carpenter, cabinetmaker, bricklayer or blacksmith. The Negro artisans are now relatively few. The garage mechanic has taken the place of the blacksmith and is a white man." [121] Even in laundering and personal services the proportion of Negroes declined. Among twenty-one categories of employment listed by Gunnar Myrdal, Southern Negroes lost ground in all but seven during the 1930's. The gains were mostly in fields that employed relatively few: chemicals; pulp and paper; printing and publishing; automobile sales and service; trade; finance, insurance, and real estate; and professional services. In some categories losses were not only relative but absolute: railroads, coal mining, iron and steel.[122]

Union restrictions still limited Negro opportunities. As late as 1944 Herbert Northrup counted twelve unions that specifically excluded Negroes by constitution or ritual, seven that habitually did so by tacit consent, and ten that gave Negroes only segregated auxiliary status, with little or no voice in policy. Others tolerated, if they did not sanction, discrimination by local bodies. All were craft unions, mostly affiliated with the AFL. Only four could be found that had dropped racial restrictions previously adopted. The earlier history of Negro displacement on the railroads continued through the 1930's. From 1931 to 1934 another period of terror swept the Mississippi Valley, with ten Negro firemen and trainmen dead and twenty-one wounded; further declines occurred in employment elsewhere, and further refinement of the rules excluded Negro firemen altogether from Diesel locomotives, except on the Florida East Coast and Louisville and Nashville lines.

Nevertheless there were fresh currents in the labor movement, as elsewhere in Negro life. Habitual practices did not go unchallenged. After 1929, when the AFL granted A. Philip Randolph's Brotherhood of Sleeping Car Porters a Federal charter, Negro workers had a spokesman in AFL conventions. In 1936 the

[121] Ball, "Improvement in Race Relations in South Carolina: The Cause," *loc. cit.*, 389.

[122] Myrdal, *An American Dilemma*, 288–91, 1079–1124. See also Northrup, *Organized Labor and the Negro*, 18–19.

porters' union became a full-fledged international. Randolph repeatedly assailed exclusionist policies. In 1934 he demanded expulsion of any AFL union maintaining the color bar. He got, instead, a committee to investigate and report. The committee recommended strong action, but at the next convention an innocuous call for "education" was substituted for its report. Even that came at ten P.M. of the eleventh day and was never implemented. Still Randolph continued to hammer at the issue year after year; occasionally he got harmless resolutions against discrimination, but never any substantive action against recalcitrant unions.[123]

The CIO, however, exhibited a different spirit from its birth in 1935. Unlike the craft unions, whose strength depended upon strategic skills, the industrial unions sought power in numbers, by organizing all the workers in an industry. Moreover, some of the leading unions in the new group, like the United Mine Workers, brought to the CIO long records of interracial amity. Among miners the interracial character of employment in the pits compelled interracial solidarity in the union. In Alabama, where Negroes constituted 53.2 per cent of the miners, the UMW developed a standard pattern of mixed locals in which the two races shared the offices. The president was usually white and Negro members usually sat apart. But they participated in the meetings and experienced friendly if sometimes awkward relations with their white brethren. Their sessions, a visitor reported, struck a delicate balance "between adherence to and departure from traditional southern ways." Many unions copied the "miners' formula," particularly metal unions in the Birmingham district, but never with such conspicuous success.[124] The CIO and its affiliates gave more than lip service to the policy of universality. No CIO national excluded Negroes and none shunted them into Jim-Crow locals. The

[123] Northrup, *Organized Labor and the Negro,* 8–14; Taft, *The A.F. of L. From the Death of Gompers to the Merger,* 439–48; Galenson, *The CIO Challenge to the AFL,* 625–31.

[124] Herbert R. Northrup, "The Negro and the United Mine Workers of America," in *Southern Economic Journal,* IX (1942–1943), 313–26; Cayton and Mitchell, *Black Workers and the New Unions,* 342–68. See also Harold Preece, "The South Stirs. I. Brothers Under the Skin," in *The Crisis,* XLVIII (October, 1941), 317–18, 322.

single exception to this rule apparently was the Textile Workers' Union of America, which sometimes accepted the expedient of separate locals in the South where the numbers were large. Other CIO unions, moreover, hesitated to demand equalitarian practices in promotions.[125]

New themes appeared in every department of Negro life. But up the back alleys and down the by-paths of the South, Negroes still lived in a world remote from the battlefronts of social and economic issues—"set aside as a subject group by social prejudice and government sanction," as the Cheraw, South Carolina, branch of the NAACP put it in a 1939 manifesto.[126] The static character of their world at its base was delineated by myriad sociologists who invaded it to analyze its economic and social problems, its stratifications of caste and class.[127] A sense of inertia in Negro society permeated Jay Saunders Redding's *No Day of Triumph*, the contemporary travel account that most successfully captured the life of the Negro masses.[128] All of the observers, however, recorded a process of acculturation to middle-class standards, a stimulus from outside influences in remote communities, and undercurrents of defiance among people who could no longer "ignorantly accept their 'place' as once they could." [129]

Few Negroes had yet entered the paths of upward mobility that millions of Southern whites traveled during the early decades of the twentieth century. In the poignant words of William Faulkner, "they endured." But underneath the stagnant surface of Negro life new forces stirred, new directions emerged, new expectations quickened. Gunnar Myrdal, the Swedish scholar who at the

---

[125] Northrup, *Organized Labor and the Negro*, 14–16, 120.

[126] Quoted in Hoffman, "The Genesis of the Modern Movement for Equal Rights in South Carolina," *loc. cit.*, 368.

[127] The classics of this literature are two community studies of Indianola, Mississippi, and one of Natchez, respectively John Dollard, *Caste and Class in a Southern Town* (New Haven, 1937); Hortense Powdermaker, *After Freedom: A Cultural Study in the Deep South* (New York, 1939); and Allison Davis, Burleigh B. Gardner, and Mary R. Gardner, *Deep South: A Social Anthropological Study of Caste and Class* (Chicago, 1941). The static image, however, may have derived in part from the theory and methodology of the investigators. Myrdal, *An American Dilemma*, 1129–32.

[128] Jay Saunders Redding, *No Day of Triumph* (New York, 1942).

[129] Dollard, *Caste and Class in a Southern Town*, 68.

573

end of the decade was immersed in a comprehensive study of Negro America, concluded that the age of segregation "was only a temporary balancing of forces which was just on the verge of being broken." [130] The course of events confirmed his prophecy.

[130] Gunnar Myrdal, "The Negro Problem: A Prognosis," in *New Republic*, CXLVII (July 9, 1962), 11. For the original prognosis, see Myrdal, *An American Dilemma*, 997–1024, especially p. 1022.

CHAPTER XVII

SOUTHERNERS REDISCOVER THE SOUTH: REGIONALISM AND SECTIONALISM

TWO conflicting images of the South had dominated the outlook of the 1920's: one, that of the benighted (or the embattled) South; the other, that of the progressive New South. Both originated earlier and both persisted into subsequent years. In the words of William Faulkner's character, Gavin Stevens, there was the North, which suffered "gullibility: a volitionless, almost helpless capacity and eagerness to believe anything about the South not even provided it be derogatory but merely bizarre enough and strange enough." [1] And in the words of Howard Odum, there was the "pale print of the sensitive South" which darkened into livid rage at every affront.[2] Secretary of Labor Frances Perkins was the first but not the last New Deal functionary to incur its wrath. In May, 1933, in a maladroit appeal for more purchasing power, she suggested that the South was "an untapped market for shoes." "A social revolution will take place," she said, "if you put shoes on the people of the South." Reaction from "the barefoot South" echoed through the rest of her tenure. "Why . . . even the mules in the South wear shoes," North Carolina's Josiah Bailey archly informed the Senate. Not only that, the Jackson *Daily News* insisted, "even Huey Long, when he is at home, wears shoes sometimes." [3]

Few Southerners, when provoked, could suppress the rising

---

[1] William Faulkner, *Intruder in the Dust* (New York, 1948) , 153.

[2] Odum, *An American Epoch*, 341.

[3] *Congressional Record*, 73 Cong., 1 Sess., 4155–56; Jackson *Daily News*, quoted in New York *Times*, June 4, 1933.

gorge. Texas' New Dealer Maury Maverick, one of the fiercest critics of Southern quackery, found himself on the Capitol steps one day in the 1930's abruptly scolding New Yorkers from the League Against War and Fascism after a heckler demanded to know about " 'southern justice,' hissing out the 'S' like a stage villain." "Where were Sacco and Vanzetti tried?" Maverick shot back. "In Alabama? In what prison do we find Tom Mooney? The Texas Penitentiary?" There was, he concluded, "likely more sectional prejudice in Manhattan than . . . in the South." [4] So it went, the old ritual of attack and counterattack, embellished from time to time with new detail.

A happier if somewhat romantic picture was that of the progressive New South. In 1929, when the American Historical Association held its annual meeting in Durham, Robert D. W. Connor of the University of North Carolina depicted a rehabilitated South that had "shaken itself free from its heritage of war and Reconstruction. Its self-confidence restored, its political stability assured, its prosperity regained, its social problems on the way to solution. . . ." [5] But two months before Connor spoke, prices on the New York Stock Exchange had broken sharply; in the aftermath the image he projected became badly blurred.

In the Depression years two new and disparate views of regional life emerged, both with the novel feature of academic trappings and affiliations: agrarianism and regionalism, one centered at Vanderbilt, the other at Chapel Hill. In 1930 the Vanderbilt Agrarians first captured public attention with their manifesto, *I'll Take My Stand,* an eloquent celebration of the rural virtues by Twelve Southerners.[6] The volume fired a double-barreled volley: against the modern idea of Progress, meaning chiefly industrialism, and against the pretensions of modern science, meaning chiefly positivism. By fortuitous circumstance the book appeared just as industrial capitalism verged on collapse, indeed almost on the very day that Nashville's Caldwell and Company tottered into

---

[4] Maverick, *A Maverick American,* 15–17.

[5] Robert D. W. Connor, "The Rehabilitation of a Rural Commonwealth," in *American Historical Review,* XXXVI (1930–1931), 62.

[6] Twelve Southerners, *I'll Take My Stand: The South and the Agrarian Tradition* (New York, 1930).

bankruptcy. But the timing, if opportune, was accidental. The book originated not in the Depression but in the years before 1929, in the twofold revulsion of Fugitive poets against both Menckenism and the Atlanta Spirit, in the quest for a viable Southern tradition amid relentless change. John Crowe Ransom, Allen Tate, and Donald Davidson formed a triumvirate that planned the work. The other nine contributors included one Fugitive, Robert Penn Warren, one Ransom student, Andrew Nelson Lytle, and three others in the field of literature: Stark Young, John Gould Fletcher, and John Donald Wade. One historian, Frank L. Owsley, a psychologist, Lyle Lanier, a political scientist, H. C. Nixon, and a journalist, Henry Blue Kline, rounded out the list.[7]

The "Introduction: A Statement of Principles," drafted by Ransom, summarized the pivotal themes: "The capitalization of the applied sciences has now become extravagant and uncritical; it has enslaved our human energies to a degree now clearly felt to be burdensome." [8] The modern world had embarked on an aimless quest of change for its own sake, and the Cult of Science ignored the fact that applied science had brought industrialism with all its attendant evils. "We receive the illusion of having power over nature, and lose the sense of nature as something mysterious and contingent." [9] The book expressed a revolt against the modernity that crowded out tradition, against the philosophy of secular progress that nurtured liberalism, pragmatism, relativism, and centralization of authority.

For the Agrarians, capitalism and communism represented an identical menace because both were aspects of the same evil: "it is simply according to the blind drift of our industrial development

[7] The definitive study is Virginia J. Rock, "The Making and Meaning of *I'll Take My Stand*: A Study in Utopian-Conservatism, 1925–1939," (Ph.D. dissertation, University of Minnesota, 1961). Other useful studies are John L. Stewart, *The Burden of Time: The Fugitives and Agrarians* . . . (Princeton, N.J., 1965); and Alexander Karanikas, *Tillers of a Myth: Southern Agrarians as Social and Literary Critics* (Madison, Wis., 1966). On the origins see also Allen Tate, "The Fugitive," in *Princeton University Library Chronicle*, III (1942), 84; and Donald Davidson, " 'I'll Take My Stand': A History," in *American Review*, V (1935), 301–21.

[8] Twelve Southerners, *I'll Take My Stand*, xi.

[9] *Ibid.*, xiv. See also Louis D. Rubin, Jr., "The Concept of Nature in Modern Southern Poetry," in *American Quarterly*, IX (1957), 63–71.

to expect in America at last much the same economic system as that imposed by violence upon Russia in 1917." [10] The real choice lay not between capitalism and communism but between industrialism and agrarianism, and the Agrarians endorsed "the Southern way of life against what may be called the American or prevailing way; and all as much as agree that the best terms in which to represent the distinction are contained in the phrase, Agrarian *versus* Industrial." [11]

Their utopia was a society "in which agriculture is the leading vocation, whether for wealth, for pleasure, or for prestige." [12] Only in such a society could men find a right relation with nature and cultivate the traditional amenities: personal relations, manners, conversation, hospitality, leisure, family life, breeding culture, art, religion. Their ideal of the traditional virtues took on the texture of myth in the image of the agrarian South, although it never became altogether clear whether the Agrarians were extolling the aristocratic graces or rustic simplicity. Ransom wrote of the "squirearchy" and Fletcher denounced mass education. "The inferior," he wrote, "whether in life or in education, should exist only for the sake of the superior." [13] But Lytle glorified the common man and criticized tendencies that led farmers "deeper into the money economy instead of freeing them." [14] Owsley, the historian, later directed graduate studies that rediscovered the antebellum yeoman farmer.

I'll Take My Stand was "the most audacious book ever written by Southerners," *Sewanee Review* editor William S. Knickerbocker wrote, "the most challenging book published since Henry George's *Progress and Poverty*." The book was deliberately provocative, and it prompted outrage and ridicule from contemporaries who hailed its authors as "unreconstructed rebels," "Young Confederates," "a socially reactionary band," "typewriter agrarians," "tower-of-ivory agrarians." [15] "Have they never been in the modern South . . . ?" asked Gerald Johnson. "Have they been completely oblivious to the Vardamans, the Bleases, the Heflins, the Tom Watsons . . . ? Are they unaware of pellagra and hook-

[10] Twelve Southerners, *I'll Take My Stand*, xiii–xiv.   [11] *Ibid.*, ix.
[12] *Ibid.*, xix.   [13] John Gould Fletcher, "Education, Past and Present," *ibid.*, 119.
[14] Andrew Nelson Lytle, "The Hind Tit," *ibid.*, 216.
[15] Quoted in Rock, "The Making and Meaning of *I'll Take My Stand*," 331.

worm, two flowers of Southern agrarianism?" [16] The "Agrarian Habakkuks," H. L. Mencken dubbed them. "Left to the farmers of Tennessee, they would be clad in linsey-woolsey and fed on side-meat, and the only books they could read would be excessively orthodox." [17] "If the South in its industrialization is going to preserve some of its distinctive characteristics, it must consciously attempt to deal with the existing situation," wrote historian W. B. Hesseltine. "The South has the opportunity to regulate industry before industry gets a strangle hold on the section. It . . . can profit from the experience of the rest of the nation in such matters as the relations of capital and labor. . . . None of these results can be obtained by a policy of obscurantism, or by fostering a spirit of reaction." [18]

There were friendly critics, fewer and less influential, who applied to the book such epithets as "radical," "passionate," "committed," "conservative and rational," "a call to arms." Donald Davidson singled out John Temple Graves of the Birmingham *Age-Herald* as the journalist who offered the most consistent editorial support.[19] And even unfriendly critics occasionally found in the book something of value. "All around us we see the qualities which gave distinction to Southern life threatened and disappearing," wrote Howard Mumford Jones. "It is at least important that this voice has been raised." [20] "When Agrarians, prompted by a love of their region, most devoutly wish that the towns of the South may not become barbarized middletowns," sociologist Dudley Wynn asserted, "every liberal is with them." [21]

The manifesto, Richmond Croom Beatty wrote later, "precipitated more widespread controversy . . . than has attended any southern book ever printed." [22] In the first year after publication it provoked several oral debates, the first at Richmond on Novem-

[16] Gerald W. Johnson, "The South Faces Itself," in *Virginia Quarterly Review*, VII (1931), 157.

[17] H. L. Mencken, "The South Astir," *ibid.*, XI (1935), 53.

[18] W. B. Hesseltine, "Look Away, Dixie," in *Sewanee Review*, XXXIX (1931), 102.

[19] Rock, "The Making and Meaning of *I'll Take My Stand*," 331.

[20] Howard Mumford Jones, "The Future of Southern Culture," in *Southwest Review*, XVI (1930–1931), 159.

[21] Dudley Wynn, "A Liberal Looks at Tradition," in *Virginia Quarterly Review*, XII (1936), 78.

[22] Richmond Croom Beatty, "Fugitive and Agrarian Writers at Vanderbilt," in *Tennessee Historical Quarterly*, III (1944), 17.

ber 14, 1930, between Ransom and Stringfellow Barr, professor of history and editor of the *Virginia Quarterly,* before an audience of more than three thousand. Subsequently Ransom debated W. S. Knickerbocker in New Orleans, Barr again in Chattanooga, and William D. Anderson of Macon's Bibb Manufacturing Company in Atlanta. Davidson challenged Knickerbocker in Columbia, Tennessee. Barr and Knickerbocker both came down on the side of a regulated industrialism. "I accept the weather and I accept industrialism," Barr said in Richmond. "Both are inevitable in the world today." "Neither Barr nor anybody else," Ransom declared in the same debate, "will ever succeed in regulating into industrialism the dignity of personality, which is gone as soon as the man from the farm goes in the factory door." For stable prosperity, he said in Atlanta, "the state should assist people to go back to the land. . . . Walks, machines, streets, and noise are abstractions." Both Ransom and Davidson stubbornly rejected industry under any circumstances. To argue for regulation, Davidson said, was like opening the house to a dragon and then deciding whether he should eat in the kitchen or dining room.[23]

For a time the Agrarians envisioned a popular movement, at least an Agrarian magazine, or perhaps a county weekly, with an associated publishing house and chain of bookstores; but none of these ever materialized.[24] They found outlets for their doctrine, instead, in established periodicals and especially in two new quarterlies which opened their pages to Agrarian writings: the *American Review* (1933–1937) in New York and the *Southern Review* (1935–1942) at Louisiana State University. The latter was edited by Robert Penn Warren and Cleanth Brooks, a younger Vanderbilt graduate and Fugitive-Agrarian disciple.[25]

In 1936 several of the original group contributed to a volume edited by a convert, Herbert Agar, editor of the Louisville *Courier-Journal,* and Allen Tate: *Who Owns America?* In the new

---

[23] Rock, "The Making and Meaning of *I'll Take My Stand,*" 349–59.

[24] *Ibid.,* 347–49.

[25] Albert E. Stone, Jr., "Seward Collins and the *American Review:* Experiment in Pro-Fascism, 1933–37," in *American Quarterly,* XII (1960), 3–19; Cleanth Brooks and Robert Penn Warren, "Introduction," in Brooks and Warren (eds.), *Stories from the Southern Review* (Baton Rouge, 1953), xi–xvi.

book they focused their attack more clearly on large property. "Effective ownership ceases at the point where a certain kind of effective control ceases," Tate argued. "So, a defender of the institution of private property will question not only the collectivist State, but also large corporate property." [26] "Whatever restores small property, fosters agrarianism, and curtails exaggerated industrialism is on the side of regional autonomy," and contributes to "the end of colonialism," said Donald Davidson.[27] Lytle and Ransom celebrated the yeoman farmer, and a young recruit, George Marion O'Donnell, assailed planters who had deserted the agrarian economy "deliberately in order to share in the great profits of a money economy dominated by finance-capitalism." [28]

In 1937 Davidson added to the Agrarian bibliography a collection of his essays, *The Attack on Leviathan,* which dwelt on themes of regionalism and sectionalism.[29] But the most thoroughgoing Agrarian of all was T. J. Cauley, an economist at Georgia Tech who worked independently of the Vanderbilt group. In 1935 Cauley contributed a curious artifact to the Agrarian lore, *Agrarianism,* a little book that championed the subsistence economy. "Chiefly it meets the problem" he wrote, *"by reducing the number and variety of material wants."* [30]

One central irony of the movement was its disengagement from the events of the times, not only in that it stated a program impossible for the twentieth century, but in that it had no practical effect even on current programs to help small farmers. Except for H. C. Nixon, a populist fallen among conservatives, the Agrarians, having said their piece, retired to their studies and left the darkling plain of struggle to the Farm Bureau, the tenant farmers' unions, the foundations, the sociologists, and the New Deal agencies. Donald Davidson shied away from the ill-fated effort to make owners out of tenants because he feared that Will Alexander

[26] Allen Tate, "Notes on Liberty and Property," in Hebert Agar and Allen Tate (eds.), *Who Owns America? A New Declaration of Independence* (Boston, 1936), 81.

[27] Donald Davidson, "That This Nation May Endure—The Need for Political Regionalism," *ibid.,* 133–34.

[28] George Marion O'Donnell, "Looking Down the Cotton Row," *ibid.,* 162.

[29] Donald Davidson, *The Attack on Leviathan: Regionalism and Nationalism in the United States* (Chapel Hill, 1937).

[30] T. J. Cauley, *Agrarianism* (Chapel Hill, 1935), 112–13.

would make it "a lever for an equalitarian program or, if that falls through . . . the cooperative idea." [31]

But the significance of the Agrarians lay elsewhere, not in any specific program but in the spirited discussion they provoked about fundamental problems, about the vulgarity and failures of modern industrialism, about the aimlessness of undirected "progress," about Southern traditions that even their critics could value. They were true radicals, Allen Tate maintained, working at "cutting away the overgrowth and getting back to the roots." [32] They offered a vantage point, outside the main currents of the times, for social criticism. Their image of the agrarian South provided "a rich, complex metaphor," through which they "presented a critique of the modern world," Louis Rubin has said. "In contrast to the hurried, nervous life of cities, the image of the agrarian South was of a life in which human beings existed serenely and harmoniously." Their critique of the modern frenzy "has since been echoed by commentator after commentator." [33] Their vantage point also was one from which there issued a literature conscious of "the past within the present." Their philosophy "proved to be an excellent discipline for the historical novelist"—and for the poet and critic as well. [34] The motivating force of the group came from the Fugitive poets and their literary allies, who soon returned to their first love, literature, and to superior achievements in that field.

One major contribution of their quest for tradition was a revival of concern with the regional identity. Soon other explorers ventured out where "the broad stream of southern life, muddy and turbulent and torrential," went stubbornly on its way. In 1934 the University of North Carolina Press, obviously galvanized by the Agrarians, brought out a monumental symposium, *Culture*

[31] Donald Davidson to William Watts Ball, January 10, 1937, in Ball Papers. See also Donald Davidson, "A Sociologist in Eden," in *American Review*, VIII (1936–1937), 385–417.

[32] Allen Tate, "Remarks on Southern Religion," in Twelve Southerners, *I'll Take My Stand*, 175.

[33] Louis D. Rubin, Jr., "Introduction to the Torchbook Edition," in Twelve Southerners, *I'll Take My Stand* (Torchbook ed., New York, 1962), xiv, xvii. See also *Mississippi Quarterly*, XIII (Spring, 1960), a special issue on the Fugitives and Agrarians.

[34] Lively, *Fiction Fights the Civil War*, 38.

in the South: essays by thirty-one authors (including two of the original Agrarians) which ranged over the entire Southern scene, economic, political, and cultural. The complexity of the life they revealed, press director W. T. Couch wrote, challenged an "easy reduction of southern life to opposing 'agrarian' and 'industrial' forces." [35]

Within the university at Chapel Hill academic exploration of the South already pointed toward new perspectives on regionalism. For more than a decade the term "regionalism" had occupied the pages of literary journals and "little magazines" in the South and elsewhere; geographers had discussed it even before that and the term became increasingly current among social scientists; it attracted a more technical consideration under the heading of "regional planning" for metropolitan areas. Meanwhile, Howard W. Odum had been building an academic empire in Chapel Hill. Brought in to head the new School of Public Welfare and Department of Sociology in 1920, he went on to found the *Journal of Social Forces* in 1922 and the Institute for Research in Social Science in 1924. In 1925 he edited a symposium on *Southern Pioneers in Social Interpretation,* which sought out the "Southern Promise" in a tradition of social analysis and reform.[36]

As early as 1929, his protégé and colleague Rupert B. Vance produced the first major work of the regional school in his description of the culture complex of cotton, *Human Factors in Cotton Culture.* Three years later Vance's *Human Geography of the South* appeared, an exhaustive guide to the Southern scene at that time. There Vance set forth in some detail the "eclectic tasks" of a new regionalism, which would look to intellectual leaders nurtured in the universities, "the more cultured of the industrialists," some of the "inheritors of the old traditions," and other public-spirited citizens. Renouncing Chamber of Commerce "Neo-Mercantilism" and the Agrarian "Neo-Confederacy," regionalists would look to "both orderly industrial development and agricul-

[35] Couch (ed.), *Culture in the South,* vii, x.

[36] For greater detail see George B. Tindall, "The Significance of Howard W. Odum to Southern History: A Preliminary Estimate," in *Journal of Southern History,* XXIV (1958), 285–307. On the early development of regionalism see Vernon Carstensen, "The Development and Application of Regional-Sectional Concepts, 1900–1950," in Jensen (ed.), *Regionalism in America,* 99–118.

tural reform." Research and planning would be the key to a material and cultural renaissance of the South, although it might well be that "as an effective sentiment around which to rally a genuine regional movement," the Agrarians' "nostalgia for the old South" would "prove of more avail than the formulae of technicians and the undifferentiated aspirations of southern liberals." [37]

The theme was stated by Vance, but the leadership fell to Odum. In 1930 Odum published *An American Epoch: Southern Portraiture in the National Picture,* the subtitle of which foreshadowed his more mature regionalism. The book grew from a creative insight that pictured the evolution of folk life with a skill few historians could muster. Through two semifictional characters, "Uncle John" and "the old Major," and their numerous progeny, Odum presented an impressionistic view of the Southern folk through four generations. Critical of the South's shortcomings, it was none the less a hopeful book, looking for "a colorful picture of an achieving region." [38] It was in this spirit that Odum approached his supreme opportunity in 1931, when the General Education Board made a grant to the Social Science Research Council for a Southern regional study. The following year the Council put the project under the general direction of Odum with a committee chaired by historian Benjamin B. Kendrick. From a series of co-operative investigations Odum finally evolved his *Southern Regions of the United States* (1936), the Bible of the new regionalism. A weighty compendium of facts and figures, written in the turbid prose that his students labeled "Odumesque," the book presented a panorama of the contemporary South, outlined a program of regional development, and groped toward regional planning.

Odum's distinction between the new "regionalism" and the old "sectionalism" became one of his fundamental tenets. Sectionalism, as described by Frederick Jackson Turner, was manifestly a valid interpretation of the American past which supplied a historical foundation for Odum's structure of regionalism, but it did not for him provide an acceptable vision of the future. Sectionalism abounded in conflict; it drew off into controversy talents bet-

---

[37] Vance, *Human Geography of the South,* 482–511.
[38] Odum, *An American Epoch,* 341.

ter spent on rational study and planning. Regionalism was the magic word that exorcised the evil spirits of sectionalism. It would promote integration of the region into the nation, permitting diversity, but only in a larger framework of the national welfare.[39] The distinction became one of many points of difference between Regionalists and Agrarians, and one of the most trenchant criticisms of Odum's approach came from Donald Davidson. "Odum," he wrote, "will not escape the political aspects of Southern economic and cultural problems simply by insisting that he has a regional, not a sectional, program." What, he asked, if the TVA should make it possible to produce furniture more cheaply in Tennessee than in Grand Rapids? "The bricks will fly, for one reason or another. . . . Sectionalism offers the political approach, which is the natural approach that our history and governmental habits invite." [40]

But regionalism was more than an attack on sectionalism. It was a frame of reference in which to synthesize the social sciences and, to some extent, the humanities and natural sciences. Its multiple implications appeared in *Southern Regions* and later more explicitly in *American Regionalism* (1938) by Odum and Harry E. Moore. Regionalism was also a practical point of departure from which to pursue social planning. Odum did not content himself with regionalism as a purely academic exercise. He "never concealed the fact that he was a sociologist," said two of his colleagues, "and that certain social theories implied certain appropriate social action." [41] In June, 1936, shortly after *Southern Regions* appeared, he presided over a ten-day Institute on Southern Regional Development and the Social Sciences at Chapel Hill sponsored by the General Education Board to consider the implications of the findings. The Institute in turn chose a committee chaired by Odum to consider a co-ordinated program of regional research and planning.

In Odum's mind the implementation of regionalism gradually

[39] Howard W. Odum, *Southern Regions of the United States* (Chapel Hill, 1936), 253–59.

[40] Donald Davidson to [John Donald] Wade, March 3, 1934, copy in Odum Papers.

[41] Rupert B. Vance and Katherine Jocher, "Howard W. Odum," in *Social Forces*, XXXIII (1955), 207.

took form in a Council on Southern Regional Development, an independent agency to be financed by foundations and individuals. The Council would operate in four general fields: race relations, land tenure and farm relations, economics and labor relations, and public relations and administration. In January, 1938, a conference of businessmen, educators, labor leaders, and other public figures, assembled by Odum's committee in Atlanta, endorsed the plan. In February the Commission on Interracial Cooperation (Odum was then its president) agreed to merge with the new group. Odum confidently projected a twelve-year program with a budget of at least two million dollars, most of which he expected to get from the major foundations, several of which gave tentative assurances. And he planned to bring Will Alexander back South from his post as Farm Security Administrator to direct the work.[42]

The Council on Southern Regional Development would have been the crowning achievement of Odum's regionalism, but it ran afoul of confusing cross-currents in the late 1930's: a revival of the sectionalism that Odum feared and the appearance of "so many diversified groups in the South, each one bent on doing the whole job in its own way." "Between the Right Honorable FD," Odum wrote a friend in August, 1938, "the Southern Conference for Human Welfare, and twenty other groups that are literally taking the lead to do what the Council ought to do, I think I'll presently go heat-wave hay-wire." For the time being, he finally wrote Will Alexander, they would have to continue "cheerfully but stubbornly, using a punting game, and develop good teams and strategy."[43]

Among the diversified groups in the field the New Deal state planning boards offered a fleeting promise of regional planning. In 1932 Franklin D. Roosevelt had emphasized planning in his one major campaign speech in the South, at Oglethorpe Univer-

[42] "Resolution Passed by Interim Advisory Committee, at Atlanta Biltmore, January 15, 1938"; "Commission on Interracial Cooperation, Inc. Meeting of the Executive Committee," mimeographed minutes of meeting held February 27, 1938; Odum to Frank P. Graham, January 18, 1938; Odum to Francis P. Miller, June 13, 1938; Odum to Will W. Alexander, March 10, 15, 23, 1939; all in Odum Papers.

[43] Odum to Prentiss M. Terry, August 15, 1938; Odum to Emily H. Clay, August 15, 1938; Odum to Will W. Alexander, February 17, 1940, in Odum Papers.

sity in Atlanta. Drawing upon his experience in New York and his knowledge of Georgia, he had suggested programs in each state with over-all national co-ordination. In July, 1933, Harold L. Ickes established a National Planning Board to assist in preparing the public works program, and in several stages the Board grew into a Federal agency concerned with more comprehensive activities: successively the National Resources Board, National Resources Committee, and the National Resources Planning Board which expired in 1943, a casualty of World War II.

In 1933 the Board and the PWA offered funds for consultants in state planning agencies that could meet certain standards. By January, 1935, all Southern governors had appointed boards and by March, 1938, all Southern states had created statutory boards. The purpose, as set forth by the Arkansas board in 1936, was the "common sense principle of directing the future physical development of a state in accordance with a comprehensive long-term coordinated plan" which would "take into account many social and economic considerations." In 1940 the governors of seven states established a Southeastern Regional Planning Commission to correlate their several programs. However, the promise of comprehensive plans never materialized. The state boards had scarcely moved beyond general surveys and research before the pressure for economic development in the late 1930's and the 1940's caused their transformation or absorption into industry-hunting agencies.[44]

Odum's vision of regional planning never materialized, but his ideas exerted a broad influence. Certain piecemeal programs of local and state planning, certain efforts of the TVA, doubtlessly received inspiration from his emphasis on planning. In December, 1939, the Southern Governors' Conference set forth a ten-year program based largely on his design; the New Deal tenant programs owed much to the investigations of Rupert Vance; and Odum encouraged the research and development emphasis of the Southern Association for Science and Industry, founded in 1941

[44] Lepawsky, *State Planning and Economic Development in the South,* 8–33; Lepawsky, "Governmental Planning in the South," in *Journal of Politics,* X (1948), 536–67; National Resources Board, *State Planning a Review of Activities and Progress* (Washington, 1935) ; National Resources Planning Board, *Regional Planning,* Pt. XI, *The Southeast* (Washington, 1942) .

by George D. Palmer of the University of Alabama.[45] But such programs as developed were so narrow in scope as to fall short of what Odum envisaged.

Odum's chief contribution was that he, like the Agrarians, provided the impetus of an idea. Agrarianism quickened a generation of writers with its vision of Southern tradition beset by change. Regionalism quickened a generation of social scientists with its vision of the "problem South," a region with obvious deficiencies but with potentialities that demanded constructive study and planning. Through the disciples of Odum, and agencies of the New Deal, the vision inspired a profusion of social science monographs and programs for reform and development. Odum's own *magnum opus, Southern Regions,* enjoyed such wide popularity as a textbook that a large part of a generation of college students became familiar with the general outline of his ideas. One undergraduate in Chapel Hill at the time remembered later a prevalent "attitude of service to the South." [46]

The emergence of antithetic philosophies at Vanderbilt and the University of North Carolina were the most conspicuous manifestations of regional consciousness in Southern universities. But academic explorations of the region went beyond those two institutions and beyond the devotees of literature and sociology. The concern manifested itself in the proliferation of regional academic societies and journals. A Southern Society for Philosophy and Psychology dated from 1904, the Association for the Study of Negro Life and History from 1915, the Southeastern Library Association from 1920. In rapid succession now came the South Atlantic Modern Language Association (1928), the Southern Political Science Association (1929), the Southern Economic Association (1929), the Southern Historical Association (1934), the Southeastern Chapter of the American Musicological Society (1934), Southern Sociological Society (1935), the South Central Modern Language Association (1939), and the Southeastern Regional Conference of

---

[45] William Pruett, "The Southern Association of Science and Industry," in *Manufacturers' Record,* CXXVI (July, 1957), 49–56.

[46] Alexander Heard, quoted in Dykeman and Stokely, *Seeds of Southern Change,* 303.

the College Art Association (1941).[47] The new regionalism in academia inspired such new periodicals as the *Southern Economic Journal* (1933), the *Journal of Southern History* (1935), the *Southern Speech Journal* (1935), the *Southern Folklore Quarterly* (1937), and the *Journal of Politics* (1939).

Somewhere between academic treatise and belles lettres fell a literature of social exploration and descriptive journalism that formed the Southern expression of what Alfred Kazin called the "now innocent, now calculating, now purely rhetorical, but always significant experience in national self-discovery" that occurred in the 1930's.[48] The New Deal, through the WPA Federal Writers' Project contributed to the collection of a "vast granary of facts" in its state guidebooks, catalogs of archives, collections of folklore and folksongs, even its record of tombstone inscriptions. In *These Are Our Lives* the Writers Project in North Carolina, Tennessee, and Georgia gathered case histories of workers, sharecroppers, and Negroes in a form that Charles A. Beard called "literature more powerful than anything I have read in fiction, not excluding Zola's most vehement passages." [49] A new genus of literature that combined social reportage with photographic illustration often focused on the South: Erskine Caldwell and Margaret Bourke-White, *You Have Seen Their Faces* (1937) and *Say, Is This the USA?* (1941); Dorothea Lange and Paul S. Taylor, *An American Exodus* (1939); Archibald MacLeish, *Land of the Free* (1938); and James Agee and Walker Evans, *Let Us Now Praise Famous Men* (1941). Under the direction of Roy Stryker the Farm Security Administration built up a unique photographic documentation of the life of the people, making familiar in the credits such

[47] J. O. Bailey and Sturgis E. Leavitt (comp.), *The Southern Humanities Conference and Its Constituent Societies*, Bulletin No. 2, The Southern Humanities Conference (Chapel Hill, 1951), 37–57; Walter J. Matherly, "The History of the Southern Economic Association, 1927–1939," in *Southern Economic Journal*, VII (1940–1941), 225–40; "News and Notes," in *American Journal of Sociology*, XLI (1935), 105; Charles H. Wesley, "Carter G. Woodson—as a Scholar," in *Journal of Negro History*, XXXVI (January, 1951), 12–24.

[48] Alfred Kazin, *On Native Grounds: An Interpretation of Modern American Prose Literature* (New York, 1942), 485.

[49] Quoted on book jacket of Federal Writers' Project, *These Are our Lives* (Chapel Hill, 1939).

names as Lange, Rothstein, Shahn, Post, and Vachon.[50] Pare Lorenz pioneered the motion picture documentary in *The Plow That Broke the Plains* and *The River*.

"Here was America," Kazin wrote—and mostly it was the South —"the cars on the unending white ribbon of road; the workers in the mills; the faces of farmers' wives and their children in the roadside camp, a thousand miles from nowhere; the tenant farmer's wife with her child sitting on the steps of the old plantation mansion . . . the Okies crossing the desert in their jalopy . . . the Baptist service in the old Negro church. Here was the greatest creative irony the reportorial mind could establish—a picture of Negro farmers wandering on the road, eating their bread under a billboard poster furnished by the National Association of Manufacturers—'America Enjoys the Highest Standard of Living in the World.' Here was the migrant family sleeping on sacks in the roadside grass, above them the railroad legend, 'Travel While You Sleep.' " [51]

In more conventional form, too, Southern journalists delineated the profile of the region. In 1935 Clarence Cason, who taught journalism at the University of Alabama, put together a collection of essays partly descriptive, partly analytical, a personal view of Southern problems under the title, *90° in the Shade*. Though quite genteel, the essays were mildly critical. The South, Cason asserted, "would profit from a nice, quiet revolution . . . a revision of the region's implanted ideas, a realistic and direct recognition of existing social problems." [52] It was no more than thousands of other Southerners were saying in those difficult years, but Cason brooded so long over the possibility of hostile reception by his colleagues that he committed suicide a few days before the book's publication. In 1937 Jonathan Daniels of the Raleigh *News and Observer* set forth on a six-week exploration of the region for his book, *A Southerner Discovers the South*. "And such a South as I found!" he wrote. "Mountain and Piedmont and Coastal Plain, I rode it. . . . I talked with Governors and professors, with male

[50] Beaumont Newhall, *The History of Photography from 1839 to the Present Day* (Rev. ed., New York, 1964), 148–49.

[51] Kazin, *On Native Grounds*, 497.

[52] Clarence Cason, *90° in the Shade* (Chapel Hill, 1935), 185–86.

and female patriots, with labor leaders and industrialists, educators and uplifters, engineers and chemists, and foresters and physicians. . . . But I also talked to hitch hikers and tenant farmers, to filling station operators, hill billies and Delta planters, to poets and bartenders, to Syrians in Vicksburg and Cajuns in Louisiana." [53] Again it was a picture of people caught up in social change. In 1942 Virginius Dabney, out of resources gathered in many years of service on the Richmond *Times-Dispatch,* produced a more generalized view in *Below the Potomac: A Book About the New South* and the next year John Temple Graves of the Birmingham *Age-Herald* produced a more personal view of *The Fighting South.*

But the supreme contribution by a journalist came from a little-known editorialist on the Charlotte *News,* Wilbur J. Cash, who wrote *The Mind of the South* (1941), one of the classics of Southern history. "Sleepy" Cash, a bookish and introverted youth from Gaffney, South Carolina, had grown up in Boiling Springs, North Carolina, where his father managed a hosiery mill. From the time when, as an undergraduate at Wake Forest, he heard Professor C. C. Pearson discourse on "The Mind of Virginia" and "The Mind of North Carolina" he had become obsessed with the idea that was to become his own book. Through the entire decade of the 1930's he labored with the agonizing persistence of a perfectionist, threw away more pages than he kept, and persevered through cycles of depression and confidence; he worked at first in a vacant room adjoining the Boiling Springs post office in between freelance articles for Mencken's *American Mercury* and other publications, then in time snatched from his job at the Charlotte *News.*[54]

His book was the product of exhaustive reading, perceptive observation, and a creative insight that transcended the limitations of his own and the historian's professions. It was, in the words of the *Atlantic Monthly,* a "literary and moral miracle." The region, Cash wrote, was like "a tree with many age rings, with its limbs

[53] Daniels, *A Southerner Discovers the South,* 9.

[54] Joseph L. Morrison, "The Obsessive 'Mind' of W. J. Cash," in *Virginia Quarterly Review,* XLI (1965), 266–86; Marshall W. Fishwick, *Sleeping Beauty and Her Suitors: The South in the Sixties* (Macon, Ga., 1961), 45–48.

and trunk bent and twisted by all the winds of the years, but with its tap root still in the Old South." The best way to begin was "by disabusing our minds of two correlated legends—those of the Old and the New Souths." He rejected both: the stage piece of rose gardens and dueling grounds and the picture of a progressive and modernized South. The "man at the center" was the yeoman farmer of the old South and his descendants, the people from whom Cash himself sprang. And the changing South was the South still: at its best "Proud, brave, honorable by its lights, courteous, personally generous, loyal, swift to act, often too swift." But its characteristic vices remained: "Violence, intolerance, aversion and suspicion toward new ideas, an incapacity for analysis . . . an exaggerated individualism and a too narrow concept of social responsibility, attachment to fictions and false values, above all too great attachment to racial values and a tendency to justify cruelty and injustice in the name of those values." [55]

The book ended on a note of pessimism. Soon, he wrote, the South would "have to prove its capacity for adjustment far beyond what has been true in the past." [56] But adjustment required leadership and a willingness to grapple with problems. And despite all the multifarious activity of the literati in rediscovering, analyzing, interpreting the South, a broad chasm separated them from the masses of the people. "If Southern people of the ruling orders read the Southern novelists but little . . . they read the studies . . . which were concerned with the questions directly involved in the cotton-population-unemployment quandary of the South hardly at all," and dismissed them as "the work of busy-body theorists bent on raising disturbing issues." [57] The desperate need was "an active and practical political and economic leadership . . . able and willing to serve as a liaison force"; but "there was no articulation between the new intellectual leaders and the body of the South, and it is in this that the tragedy of the South as it stood in 1940 centrally resided." [58]

One organized effort was mounted to remedy the defect, the Southern Policy Committee, but it never exerted much influence. It grew from an effort of the Foreign Policy Association to form a

[55] Cash, *Mind of the South*, ix–x, 428–29.
[56] *Ibid.*, 429.
[57] *Ibid.*, 420–21.
[58] *Ibid.*, 421.

kindred National Policy Committee for study and discussion of domestic affairs. The organizer, Francis Pickens Miller, a liberal attorney from Charlottesville, Virginia, undertook to form also a regional committee with affiliated groups in local communities. The purposes of the group, founded at a conference in Atlanta in April, 1935, were to draw in people "whose minds are open to facts and who are aware of their responsibility for discovering and serving the general public interest," to facilitate the exchange of ideas, to encourage formation and recommendation of desirable public policies, and by public discussions to prepare "the general body of citizens for more intelligent and socially-minded political action." H. C. Nixon, one of the original Agrarians then teaching at Tulane, chaired the conference and the permanent organization.[59]

Significant activity by the group lasted only about two years. After 1938 it was overshadowed by the larger Southern Conference for Human Welfare, which attracted some of its leading participants. But it did draw together concerned citizens for discussions of public policy and added to the body of literature on Southern problems a series of ten *Southern Policy Papers* published by the University of North Carolina Press.[60] Strong disagreements between Agrarians and their opponents marked the Atlanta meeting and a second conference at Lookout Mountain in 1936, which featured a sharp exchange between Allen Tate and the Socialist William R. Amberson, who was associated with the Southern Tenant Farmers' Union. Both meetings produced statements of policy, sprinkled with minority reports, on various Southern problems. The one policy on which the group secured general agreement was support for the Bankhead Farm Tenant Bill. A group of SPC members who met regularly in Washington, led by Alabama's Representative Lister Hill, helped to mobilize support for its passage as the Bankhead-Jones Farm Tenant Act. But as a liaison agency between the intellectuals and the masses, the SPC failed.

[59] *Southern Policy*, Report of the Southern Policy Conference in Atlanta, April 25–28, 1935 (n.p., n.d.) ; T. J. Woofter, Jr., *Southern Population and Social Planning*, Southern Policy Paper No. 1 (Chapel Hill, 1936) , statement inside back cover.

[60] *Southern Policy Papers*, No. 1–10 (Chapel Hill, 1936–1937) . The Southern Conference for Human Welfare is discussed in Chapter XVIII.

"Where are the laymen?" Donald Davidson asked after the Chattanooga meeting. A fourth of the delegates were college professors and most of the others represented newspapers, the government, labor unions, and various other interest groups. The whole cast of the meeting, Davidson noted, was "urban" and "intellectualist." [61]

"Only one force has ever drawn the Southern states together for a vast concerted effort," Davidson argued, "and that is the lusty force of strong sectional feeling. If Mr. Odum, knowing what he knows, were a Huey Long in temperament, the sound trucks would be on the road tomorrow, to translate the deficiency indices into the language of the 'ignorant man.' " [62] Neither Odum nor Davidson was a Huey Long, but on one idea the force of sectional feeling united them with many Southerners of divergent viewpoints—the idea that the South's fundamental handicap was its "colonial economy." Odum's deficiency indices pointed ultimately to a source in poverty and that, in turn, to a source in the one-crop agriculture and one-crop industry of the region. The South, Odum wrote, had been "essentially colonial in its economy," suffering "the general status of an agricultural country engaged in trade with industrial countries." [63]

The concept of the colonial economy, thus expressed in rudimentary form, in effect summarized an earlier treatment by Rupert Vance, whose *Human Geography of the South* gave currency to the term. In one chapter of that book Vance had traced the region's evolution through successive conquests of new frontiers, the development of an extractive economy that progressively exploited natural resources and cheap labor without any appreciable accumulation of capital, that looked to outside financing and exported much of the return.[64] In the beginning the "colonial economy" was defined basically in the distinction between primary and secondary production. The South produced chiefly raw materials and industrial roughage for the market-oriented indus-

[61] Francis P. Miller (ed.), *Second Southern Policy Conference Report*, Southern Policy Paper No. 8 (Chapel Hill, 1936) ; Donald Davidson, "Where are the Laymen! A Study in Policy-Making," in *American Review*, IX (1937), 456–81; Daniels, *A Southerner Discovers the South*, 81–87.

[62] Davidson, *The Attack on Leviathan*, 308.

[63] Odum, *Southern Regions of the United States*, 353.

[64] Vance, *Human Geography of the South*, 442–81.

tries of the North, and as a primary producer remained in a dependent and tributary status, performing those functions that brought smaller rewards in a modern economy.

But in its further development the colonial concept grew almost into a conspiracy thesis of a region deliberately and systematically plundered by outside forces. This, of course, was not a novel idea. In different ways it had inspired antebellum sectionalism, the industrial creed of the New South, the populistic, Bryanite, and progressive attacks on the corporations. Issues of freight rates and Pittsburgh-plus pricing in steel kept it alive in the 1920's. By the early 1930's an acute realization developed that an economic revolution in distribution was squeezing retail merchants; one prime contributor to the process had been Clarence Saunders of Memphis, who in 1919 began to develop a chain of self-service markets, the Piggly Wiggly Stores. Not only chain stores, but chain movie houses and service stations, direct manufacturers' outlets, and the penetration of outside capital into department stores aroused independent merchants and citizens who feared a drain on community spirit as well as profits.[65]

William K. ("Hello World") Henderson, who owned and operated a number of business enterprises in Shreveport, Louisiana, including radio station KWKH, achieved a temporary notoriety by exploiting the apprehension: "Hello—World! Hello, you lil' ole doggone North American continent!" he would announce in personal talks that had eager listeners across the South. "Haven't you got sense enough to know that if you give your money to chain organizations which immediately send it out of your town that it won't be long before we have a hell of a country to live in?" [66] Memberships poured into his Merchants' Minute Men, and Henderson briefly was a national phenomenon.

The anti-chain store cause became a national issue, strongly supported by independent merchants all over the country, especially in the South. It brought about state legislation hiking license fees

[65] Walter Prescott Webb, *Divided We Stand: The Crisis of a Frontierless Democracy* (New York, 1937), 86–125; John Brooks, "A Corner in Piggly Wiggly," in *The New Yorker*, XXXV (June 6, 1959), 118–40.

[66] Margery Land May, *Hello World Henderson, The Man Behind the Mike* ([Shreveport, La.], 1930), 7, 72. See also Philip Lilber, "National Chain Systems," in *Manufacturers' Record*, XCVI (November 7, 1929), 65–67. Lilber was a Shreveport businessman who inspired Henderson's war on the chains.

and otherwise restricting the chains; the Price Discrimination Chain Store Act of 1936, sponsored by Representative Wright Patman of Texas and Senator Joseph T. Robinson of Arkansas, to restrict price discriminations by the chains; and the Miller-Tydings Resale Price Maintenance Act of 1937 to legalize under the Federal antitrust laws "fair trade" agreements establishing minimum prices for the resale of commodities in order to forestall price-cutting by the chains.[67]

In 1937 Walter Prescott Webb, historian at the University of Texas, elaborated the larger theme of the "colonial economy" in his *Divided We Stand: The Crisis of a Frontierless Democracy.* In Webb the scholar fused with the polemicist, who identified with dramatic skill the villains of the piece. They were the great corporations with their patent controls, their discriminatory pricing systems, their restrictive licensing arrangements, their insurance-company investments in Northern industry, their deliberate measures to subjugate the South and West under "economic imperial control by the North." [68] Their allies were the economic carpetbaggers and scalawags of America's new feudalism: lawyers, insurance men, branch managers, chain-store executives, lobbyists, journalists, governors, legislators.

The political agent of economic oppression, Webb argued, was the Republican party, with its policies of tariffs, subsidies, patents, and regionalized freight rates. Emancipation would have to come through the only truly national party, the Democratic, through which the outlying regions might combine with the workers and small tradesmen of the East against their common oppressors. A program for the abeyance of sectionalism would involve the dispersal of industry, Federal charters for interstate corporations, an overhaul of the patent system, checks on the licensing of patented machinery, and a drastic revision of freight rates.[69]

<hr/>

[67] 49 *U.S. Stat.,* 1526; 50 *U.S. Stat.,* 693. On the North Carolina chain store tax see *Business Week* (September 14, 1929), 15; *ibid.* (January 8, 1930), 13.

[68] Webb, *Divided We Stand,* 12.

[69] Walter Prescott Webb, *Divided We Stand: The Crisis of a Frontierless Democracy* (Revised and abridged ed., Austin, 1947), 94–95. For a later treatment of the colonial economy theme see A. G. Mezerik, *The Revolt of the South and West* (New York, 1946).

The publishers omitted from the first edition one lengthy account of outside malevolence because they feared a lawsuit, but Webb printed it in later editions after the story appeared on the record of the Temporary National Economic Committee.[70] This was the tragedy of a milk bottle factory in Santa Anna, Texas, whose owners discovered that the Hartford Empire Glass Company claimed rights to machinery they had bought from another company. Under threat of lawsuit the Texas firm sold the machines and leased them on a royalty basis, only to have the agreement expire after six months. Eventually a Hartford licensee acquired the plant and dismantled it. As a crowning irony the National Association of Manufacturers erected on the site a billboard that carried the inscriptions "I'm glad I'm an American" and "Free Enterprise and Opportunity."

Variations on Webb's theme resounded in periodicals and public discussion for more than a decade. The region's lack of specialty enterprises, economist C. T. Murchison noted, "leaves the South with the worst form of economic disadvantage, that of having to exchange a few bulky staple products for the myriads of highly manufactured specialty goods which she must consume." [71] The South's adverse balance of trade, a Southern editor told David Cushman Coyle in 1937, was probably a billion dollars annually.[72] The debit was balanced by selling property to outside investors, by borrowing, by going bankrupt, or by exhausting lands and timber for immediate cash. "The South actually works for the North," Maury Maverick declared; "mortgage, insurance, industrial, and finance corporations pump the money northward like African ivory out of the Congo." [73] "We are confronted with a paradox more amazing and ironical than any ever conjured by the

[70] Webb, *Divided We Stand* (Revised and abridged ed.) , 53–64. Webb said that pressures forced the original publisher to declare it out of print with undue haste, although in subsequent editions fifteen thousand copies were sold up to 1958. Walter Prescott Webb, "History as High Adventure," in *American Historical Review*, LXIV (1958–1959) , 276.

[71] C. T. Murchison, "Depression and the Future of Business," in Couch (ed.) , *Culture in the South,* 103.

[72] David Cushman Coyle, "The South's Unbalanced Budget," in *Virginia Quarterly Review*, XIII (1937) , 192.

[73] Maury Maverick, "Let's Join the United States," in *Virginia Quarterly Review*, XV (1938) , 64.

imagination of Gilbert and Sullivan," B. B. Kendrick told the
Southern Historical Association in his 1941 presidential address.
"The people of the South, who all their lives had suffered deprivation, want, and humiliation from an outside finance imperialism,
followed with hardly a murmur of protest leaders who, if indirectly, were nonetheless in effect agents and attorneys of the im-
perialists." [74]

A kind of climax to the literature of the colonial economy came
in the *Report on Economic Conditions of the South* (1938), sponsored by the National Emergency Council. Clark Foreman of Atlanta, then an official of the Public Works Administration and
formerly advisor to Harold Ickes on Negro affairs, persuaded the
President to request the report and largely directed its preparation
by a group of Southerners in Federal service, active in the Washington unit of the Southern Policy Committee.[75] Many hands
contributed to the final result, but it was essentially a synopsis of
existing analyses by Vance, Odum, Webb, and others. "The paradox of the South is that while it is blessed by Nature with immense
wealth, its people as a whole are the poorest in the country," the
report declared. "Lacking industries of its own, the South has been
forced to trade the richness of its soil, its minerals and forests, and
the labor of its people for goods manufactured elsewhere." [76] The
document proceeded in sixty-four pages and fourteen sections to
detail problems of soil and water resources, population, income,
education, health, housing, labor, tenancy, credit, natural resources, industry, and purchasing power. It particularly condemned damage to the regional economy by tariffs, regional freight
rates, monopoly, and absentee ownership.

The report placed the Roosevelt administration squarely behind the sectional rebellion against colonial bondage and strongly
implied administration support for a co-ordinated effort of regional development. Moreover, the President deliberately linked
it to his effort for a political realignment in 1938. In August, when

[74] B. B. Kendrick, "The Colonial Status of the South," in *Journal of Southern History*, VIII (1942), 19.

[75] Clark Foreman, "The Decade of Hope," in *Phylon*, XII (1951), 140.

[76] National Emergency Council, *Report on Economic Conditions of the South*
(Washington, 1938), 8.

he launched the ill-fated campaign to "purge" Georgia's Senator Walter F. George, he announced the publication of the report, and repeated a part of his earlier remarks to the report's sponsoring committee.[77]

"It is my conviction," the President had said in July, "that the South presents right now, in 1938, the Nation's No. 1 economic problem."[78] The report went forth, coupled with that catch phrase, so well tailored to the headlines, but so easily misinterpreted as another purblind stereotype of the benighted South. It was almost as if the President had rung a bell that activated the conditioned reflex of the sensitive South. The region had accomplished much in the past seventy-five years, North Carolina's Senator Josiah W. Bailey declared indignantly, because of "our forefathers who rebuilt the South after the Civil War." What the South needed most, Senator John E. Miller of Arkansas asserted, was to be left alone.[79] "This section has been unwisely characterized as the economic problem No. 1 of the nation," the *Manufacturers' Record* protested. "Quite the opposite is true. The South represents the nation's greatest opportunity for industrial development."[80] In the clamor of that political summer the import of the President's commitment to regional development was lost, and his effort to harness the power of sectional feeling to the New Deal cause failed completely.

Insofar as the colonial-imperialistic thesis became a political force it ran in a narrow channel, finding outlet in one specific grievance, discriminatory freight rates. "This freight rate business is the heart of the whole Southern problem," Governor Bibb Graves of Alabama asserted. "It explains nearly everything. Poverty. Low wages. Bad housing. We can't move till we get free."[81] The attack on freight-rate discriminations became the sectional crusade of its day, like cotton mills, schools, and public health at

[77] The "purge" campaign is treated in Chapter XVIII.
[78] National Emergency Council, *Report on Economic Conditions of the South,* 1.
[79] Richmond *Times-Dispatch,* July 10, 1938.
[80] "The South—Its Abundant Resources for Development and National Defense," in *Manufacturers' Record,* CIX (September, 1940), 36.
[81] Quoted in Daniels, *A Southerner Discovers the South,* 266.

other times. The fight enlisted universal support in the South and powerful allies in the administration.[82]

The problem in its essence was simple, a ready-made issue for Southern politicians, a "tailored defense for more deep-rooted sectional ills." [83] In detail, however, freight rates constituted an esoteric mystery revealed only to a cult of commissioners, rate experts, and railway men. But certain conspicuous features manifested themselves to outsiders. The nation was divided into five rate territories: "Official" (roughly north of the Ohio and east of the Mississippi but including most of Virginia and West Virginia), Southern (the South east of the Mississippi), Southwestern (the South west of the Mississippi and southeastern New Mexico), Western Trunk Lines, and Mountain Pacific. Estimates on the variations of class rates disagreed, but they ranged somewhere around those given in a TVA report of 1937: Southern rates were 139 per cent of Official; Southwestern, 175; Western Trunk Lines, 147; and Mountain Pacific, 171.[84] This was for *intra*territorial rates. *Inter*territorial rates were a blend of these, according to formulas that approximated the application of *intra*territorial rates to the distance traveled in a given territory.

However, a producer who shipped in quantity could secure "exception" rates, and most of the freight moved on such exceptions. Among these, the "commodity" rates, designed for bulk cargo, were most significant for the South, and on these the region had advantageous arrangements. The rate structure therefore favored the existing pattern of shipping out raw materials for refinement in the Northeast. Any manufacturer who wanted to move into new specialties, on the other hand, had to labor against discriminatory class rates until he could establish the bargaining power to secure exception rates. "Freight rates do not exist ahead of indus-

[82] The following account is derived chiefly from Robert A. Lively, *The South in Action: A Sectional Crusade Against Freight Rate Discrimination* (Chapel Hill, 1949) ; and William H. Joubert, *Southern Freight Rates in Transition* (Gainesville, Fla., 1949). For a brief survey of the background see David M. Potter, "The Historical Development of Eastern-Southern Freight Rate Relationships," in *Law and Contemporary Problems* (Durham), XII (1947), 416–48.

[83] Lively, *The South in Action*, 19.

[84] J. Haden Alldredge, *The Interterritorial Freight Rate Problem of the United States,* in *House Documents*, 75 Cong., 1 Sess., No. 264, p. 13.

try, they follow it," said Birmingham coal shipper Alvin Vogtle. "They are made in response to demand." [85] Since the South already had a favorable rate structure for its established industries, the issue resolved itself partly into a quarrel between present and future, between the advocates of economic growth—shippers, small businessmen, political leaders, and economists—and the firmly seated "industrial Bourbons," who preferred not to rock the boat.

Rumblings of discontent began to rise about 1934, when the Southern Traffic League, a federation of shippers' organizations, began representations to the Interstate Commerce Commission (ICC) and the carriers. The Southeastern Association of Railroad and Utilities Commissioners joined the complaint in 1935, but the effort reached no conclusive results. By 1934 Southern members of Congress had begun to introduce bills for investigations or changes, and in 1935 Atlanta's Robert Ramspeck proposed to have all rates determined at the "destination level," so that shipments into Official Territory would pay the rates prevalent there and *vice versa*—an ingenious device to reverse the advantage held by the East.

The crusade gathered its full momentum when the Southern governors began to push it. As early as November, 1934, a group of nine governors and governors-elect discussed the problem with President Roosevelt at Warm Springs; in December they organized the Southeastern (later Southern) Governors' Conference.[86] In May, 1937, after discussions in Washington and Atlanta the governors filed a complaint with the ICC—the Southern Governors' Case, or the Commodities Case—sponsored by their chairman, Bibb Graves of Alabama.[87] That same month the cause gained force from a report on regional discriminations by TVA's chief transportation economist, J. Haden Alldredge, who translated the issues "from economics to English." [88] Two additional

---

[85] Quoted in Lively, *The South in Action,* 78.

[86] Walter R. McDonald, *The Southern Governors' Conference: A Brief History* (Raleigh, [1959]) .

[87] The State of Alabama *et al. v.* the New York Central Railroad Company *et al.,* ICC Docket No. 27746, "Complaint."

[88] Lively, *The South in Action,* 24; Alldredge, *The Interterritorial Freight Rate Problem of the United States.*

TVA reports in subsequent years provided still more impetus.[89]

In various ways the administration evinced sympathy. The President received the Southern governors in January, 1938—immediately afterward the governors endorsed wage-hour legislation, a not unrelated gesture since New England governors argued that low wages in the South justified the freight rate differential. Later in the year Harry Hopkins and Eleanor Roosevelt made statements in favor of revision, still later, Henry A. Wallace; the *Report on Economic Conditions of the South,* in a section that drew on the Alldredge report, declared the differential rates "a manmade wall to replace the natural barrier long since overcome by modern railroad engineering." [90] More substantive help came with Roosevelt's appointment of new ICC commissioners from the South and West.[91]

In 1939 the Southern Governors' Case, which focused on alleged discriminations in the commodity rates, came to a favorable decision, by five to four, on ten items out of fourteen commodity groups on which complaint had been filed.[92] The governors celebrated their victory in a meeting timed to coincide with Atlanta's world première of *Gone With the Wind.* At the Atlanta meeting they admitted Arkansas, Oklahoma, and Texas, changed their name from the Southeastern to the Southern Governors' Conference, and adopted a general ten-point plan for "Balanced Prosperity, 1940–1950." In annual meetings thereafter they concerned themselves with a broader range of regional problems.[93]

---

[89] J. Haden Alldredge, *Supplemental Phases of the Interterritorial Freight Rates Problem of the United States,* in *House Documents,* 76 Cong., 1 Sess., No. 276; Harry B. Kline (ed.), *Regionalized Freight Rates: Barrier to National Productiveness,* in *House Documents,* 78 Cong., 1 Sess., No. 137.

[90] National Emergency Council, *Report on Economic Conditions of the South,* 59.

[91] Between 1933 and 1945 four from Southern Territory, including J. Haden Alldredge, and one from Southwestern (Texas). Of the forty-four who served before 1933, twenty-four had come from Official, only five from Southern, and one from Southwestern (Oklahoma). In 1933 a majority were from Official; when the Southern Governors' Case was decided in 1939 a majority were from the Southern and Western Territories. Lively, *The South in Action,* 81–82.

[92] These were stoves, stone, enameled iron or steel plumber's goods, cast-iron pipe fittings, iron-body valves, fire hydrants, brass pipe fittings, soapstone, talc, and papeteries. Lively, *The South in Action,* 47.

[93] McDonald, *The Southern Governors' Conference: A Brief History;* H. C. Nixon, "The Southern Governors' Conference as a Pressure Group," in *Journal of*

In 1939 Senate and House committees for the first time held hearings on the freight-rate problem, with the consequence that the Wheeler-Truman Transportation Act of 1940 included a Hill-Ramspeck proposal for an ICC investigation of rate differentials and for adding "regions," "districts," and "territories" to the categories of persons, places, and things protected against discrimination in the Interstate Commerce Act. Already, in 1939, the ICC had announced a class-rate investigation which met the demands of the act, but the study dragged out until 1945. Georgia's Governor Ellis Arnall applied the pressure that helped to end the delay when, in 1945, he got the Supreme Court to accept jurisdiction of a suit on behalf of Georgia and Georgia shippers charging that the railroads' rate-making bureaus violated the antitrust laws. The case never reached a decision—in 1948 the Reed-Bulwinkle Bill relieved the bureaus from application of the antitrust laws—but the ICC decision on class rates followed in two months. "Perhaps the apples were ready to fall from the tree anyway," the Birmingham *News* commented. "Perhaps not. The Supreme Court action gave the tree a strong shake. The pippins began to drop and they were all for the Southern governors' basket." [94]

Moreover, the ICC discovered that railroad costs in the South differed little from those in the East—insofar as they did, they ran slightly lower. This undermined the chief rationale for rate differentials. On May 15, 1945, seven commissioners (all but one from the South or West) endorsed a declaration that class rates east of the Rockies were "unjust and unreasonable," that the rate structure reacted "to the disadvantage" of the South and West and restricted "growth and expansion" in those areas. [95] The majority, therefore, ordered immediate inauguration of a uniform classification system east of the Rockies and the ultimate establishment of uniform class rates. Pending this, it raised class rates in Official Territory 10 per cent and lowered them 10 per cent in Southern, Southwestern, and Western Trunk Lines. [96]

Politics, VI (1944), 338–45. Membership later embraced the border states of West Virginia (1946), Maryland (1946), and Delaware (1951).

[94] Birmingham *News*, February 23, 1945, quoted in Lively, *The South in Action*, 69.

[95] *Class Rate Investigation, 1939* and *Consolidated Freight Classification*, 262 ICC 447 (Washington, 1946).

[96] *Ibid.*, 270–73.

The decree brought victory in principle, although it was not completely effective until May 31, 1952.[97] But it did not signal a massive migration of industry to the South. Other factors were more important: men, materials, markets, and, before 1952, the impact of World War II and postwar conversion. The decision, nevertheless, removed an irritating obstacle to Southern development. And the struggle demonstrated again the potency of economic growth as a battle cry—the cause, said Mark Ethridge, inspired "a unity more striking than even that of our Confederate days." [98] The Southern governors, Professor Lively declared, "pooled their resources for ten years, and . . . so worried at the heels of the ICC, Congress, and the nation that they . . . won their point" by "consistent advocacy of specific action . . . for a more prosperous southern future . . . despite the concerted opposition of the most powerful industrial forces of the region." [99]

In retrospect economists have discounted regionalized freight rates as only a minor barrier to Southern development, and one that gradually would have yielded in any case.[100] In other respects, too, they have challenged the analyses of the 1930's. "The colonial-imperialistic thesis of conspiracy," Clarence Danhof has written, "must be considered an unfortunate episode—a resurgence of crude sectionalism—that diverted the attention of some of the South's ablest men from constructive approaches to the region's problems." [101]

Much of the colonial revolt against the imperial East did echo old battle cries of Jeffersonian agrarianism and populism, but with a significant difference: the rebels looked not back to Arcadia but forward to an industrial South. They geared the force of sectional feeling to a different theme, the theme of economic growth. Few of them were professional economists, but to a significant degree

[97] When uniform class rates became effective east of the Rockies. New York *Times*, May 31, 1952.

[98] Mark Ethridge, "The Second Reconstruction," in *Southern Association Quarterly*, III (1939), 374.

[99] Lively, *The South in Action*, 90.

[100] Hoover and Ratchford, *Economic Resources and Policies of the South*, 78–84.

[101] Clarence H. Danhof, "Four Decades of Thought on the South's Economic Problems," in Melvin L. Greenhut and W. Tate Whitman (eds.), *Essays in Southern Economic Development* (Chapel Hill, 1964), 50.

they anticipated concepts later developed by economists. The economic report of 1938, Arthur Goldschmidt has noted, "covered to a remarkable extent the same range of problems discussed by experts . . . reviewing similar underdeveloped segments of the world for the United Nations, the World Bank or U. S. foreign-aid agencies" in later years.[102] The report afforded a wider perspective than the conventional New South concept of industry-hunting. It set economic development in a broader framework: agricultural readjustment, governmental policies, education, resource development, human welfare, purchasing power. It took a long step toward an understanding that economic development was related to the entire social and cultural milieu.

"The South is in greater ferment than I have ever known it to be," editor Mark Ethridge remarked in 1939. "To me the feverish restlessness of the moment is the highest evidence that . . . the germ of Southern culture has not died. . . . Mental revival always precedes economic revival; the South is in the first stage of an awakening that can conceivably take her civilization to heights it has never known."[103] A Bassett or a Trent, historian Paul Buck asserted in 1940, "would have no reason to complain today about the absence of free and rational discussion in the South about the South."[104] But the discussion had a way of slipping back into time-worn channels. "What is happening is a revivification of Turner's sectionalism," Howard Odum lamented as early as 1934, when he experienced the growth of sectional animosity even within his regional study committee. "What is happening in many cases . . . is a resurgence of the 'old sectionalism' rationalized as regionalism."[105] The South, moreover, seemed bent on proving repeatedly "that it cannot get along with itself."[106]

If by 1940 the South was substantially united on the freight-rate crusade it was more disunited otherwise on ideology and policy than it had been since the Populist era. The very dissonance per-

[102] Arthur Goldschmidt, "The Development of the U.S. South," in *Scientific American*, CCIX (September, 1963) , 226.

[103] Ethridge, "The Second Reconstruction," *loc. cit.,* 374–75.

[104] Paul H. Buck, "The Genesis of the Nation's Problems in the South," in *Journal of Southern History,* VI (1940), 469.

[105] Howard W. Odum to George Fort Milton, February 8, 1934, in Odum Papers.

[106] Odum to Charles S. Johnson, September 21, 1938, *ibid.*

haps was evidence of vitality, the rise of new ideas to challenge the old. But the concurrent trends of disunity and sectionalism increasingly characterized the regional awakening. The region's political leaders, in detachment from its intellectual leaders, more and more exploited the resurgent sectionalism, fought for equalization of freight rates, pursued defense and war industries, argued issues of race that assumed new urgency during World War II, opposed New Deal labor and welfare measures. The new regionalism gradually dissolved into the old sectionalism, from which Southern conservatives forged destructive weapons against the New Deal.

CHAPTER XVIII

SOUTHERN POLITICS AND
THE NEW DEAL

IF the Southern intellectuals failed to make contact with the masses, Franklin D. Roosevelt was quite another matter. His personality and his programs aroused a devotion that ran stronger in the South than in any other region, persistently so to the end of the 1930's.[1] "The popularity of President Roosevelt not only is general but it is unprecedented in intensity," a Texas editor asserted one year after his inauguration; "the clod-busters in this neck of the woods will probably remain as loyal to the President as a Methodist minister to fried chicken," a Houston labor journal declared shortly afterward.[2] "Roosevelt," a North Carolina mill worker blurted to an anti-New Deal reporter, "is the only man we ever had in the White House who would understand that my boss is a sonofabitch."[3]

In 1934 the President's heterogeneous support from all classes strongly impressed an Englishman who visited Gainesville, Georgia, where he found evidences of sympathy for public power and of liberal opinion on race.[4] In Alabama at the end of 1935 Representative Joe Starnes estimated "conservatively" that 80 per cent of the people in his district wanted Roosevelt re-elected.[5] Mississippi was "standing squarely behind the New Deal," Jackson ed-

[1] Hadley Cantril, *Public Opinion, 1935–1946* (Princeton, 1951) ; 754–760.

[2] Peter Molyneaux in New York *Times*, March 4, 1934; Houston *Labor Messenger*, June 1, 1934, quoted in Patenaude, "The New Deal and Texas," 372, 381.

[3] Quoted in Eric Goldman, *Rendezvous with Destiny: A History of Modern American Reform* (New York, 1952) , 345.

[4] M. Phillips Price, *America After 60 Years* (London, 1936) , 204.

[5] Joe Starnes to Marvin H. McIntyre, December 1, 1935, in OF 300—Alabama, 1933–37, Roosevelt Library.

itor Fred Sullens reported early in 1936. "An overwhelming majority of the people are for it, stronger than horseradish." [6] In North Carolina, as the 1936 election neared, Senator Josiah W. Bailey observed that "the masses of the people are very strong for [Roosevelt], and while he has lost support with a limited number of business men, he has gained very greatly with the smaller business man, the farmers, clerks, and general run of the voters." [7]

Such massive support inhibited those Congressmen who, like Bailey, harbored doubts about the new directions in government. Roosevelt, like Wilson, cultivated the Congressional leaders and bent them to his program. In many ways the New Deal duplicated the Wilsonian experience of a Southern leadership bound by party loyalty, by the need to make a constructive record, by the taste of power and recognition—but even more at first by Roosevelt's overwhelming popularity and the national crisis. The only way to surmount the danger, North Carolina's Representative Robert Lee Doughton wrote to a constituent in 1933, was "to follow the leadership which has inspired and encouraged the American people, as has not been done in many years." [8]

"Muley Bob" Doughton himself exemplified those Southern leaders on whom Roosevelt leaned heavily. A taciturn farmer and horsetrader from the mountains, he had first attracted national notice in his eleventh term by leading the opposition to Hoover's sales tax proposal. Seventy years old in 1933, he became chairman of the Ways and Means Committee, which he headed throughout the Roosevelt years. By hard work, long hours, and tenacious mastery of detail, Doughton faithfully steered through the House the New Deal fiscal measures and such innovations as the NRA and social security. He never deviated from the administration line until 1941, when he voted to retain the Neutrality Act. [9]

The successive majority leaders and speakers embodied a kin-

[6] "The South is Still Solid/Six Editors Render A Report," in *Review of Reviews*, XCIII (1936) , 39.

[7] Josiah W. Bailey to James A. Farley, July 21, 1936, in OF 300—1936 Campaign, Roosevelt Library.

[8] Robert Lee Doughton to Lee R. Blackwelder, March 16, 1933, in Robert Lee Doughton Papers (University of North Carolina Library, Chapel Hill) .

[9] Gerald Movins, "He'll Take a Bite Out of You," in *Saturday Evening Post*, CCXIV (January 17, 1942) , 27, 53; "Farmer Bob," in *Newsweek*, III (January 13, 1934), 20.

dred loyalty. In 1933 Tennessee's homespun Joseph W. Byrns brought to the leadership a reputation for ultra-conservatism but worked quietly behind the scenes to expedite Roosevelt's New Deal.[10] Alabama's more urbane William B. Bankhead, first as Rules Committee chairman, then as majority leader and speaker, operated in much the same manner: "the conciliator, the patient, workmanlike statesman." [11] In contrast to his predecessors, Sam Rayburn of Texas was austere and reserved; but he wielded more power, and he probably favored more genuinely the New Deal measures. As chairman of the Committee on Interstate and Foreign Commerce he guided to passage some of the basic economic reforms: the Securities Act (1933), the Securities Exchange Act (1934), the Public Utility Holding Company Act (1935), and the Rural Electrification Act (1936) before he became majority leader in 1937 and speaker in 1940.[12]

Rayburn epitomized certain characteristics common among the Southern leaders: "small-townish, agrarian, nationalistic, individualistic, anti-Wall Street," men of rural background and humble origin who had struggled hard for an education, who felt an instinctive sympathy for the "little fellow," who "savored the honors and prestige associated with Congressional leadership," and who observed party regularity as an article of faith. Some of them enjoyed their relationships with bankers and utilities executives, Frank Freidel has noted. But most, in the progressive tradition, idealized small property and supported restraints against financial abuses. The utilities, Rayburn, who earned their hostility, once said, could "produce more noise and fewer votes than any crowd I ever saw." [13]

More nearly than Rayburn perhaps, Joseph T. Robinson of Arkansas, Roosevelt's first majority leader in the Senate, conformed to the standard pattern of Southern leaders. "I think I am

[10] *Newsweek,* IV (December 22, 1934), 8–9.

[11] Montgomery *Advertiser,* n.d., quoted in Walter J. Heacock, "William B. Bankhead and the New Deal," in *Journal of Southern History,* XXI (1955), 348.

[12] C. Dwight Dorough, *Mr. Sam* (New York, 1962), 219–47.

[13] Ray Tucker, "Texas Annexes the United States," clipping in Rayburn Scrapbooks, June 23, 1936–March 2, 1937 (Sam Rayburn Library, Bonham, Texas); Freidel, *F.D.R. and the South,* 54–55; author interview with Sam Rayburn, July 2, 1959.

what the public generally terms conservative," he wrote in 1937, "although I regard myself as a liberal." A country boy who had worked his way through the state university, an adroit trial lawyer (closely related to the utilities through his law partnership), a bombastic orator, and an officeholder most of his adult life, Robinson had been a Senator twenty years and minority leader ten when the New Deal arrived. On March 9, 1933, he put the Emergency Banking Act through the Senate in seven hours and thereafter pushed administration measures so faithfully that one Washington newsman called him "a veritable slave driver, keeping the Senate's nose to the grindstone." [14]

Mississippi's Pat Harrison, like Robinson, was an effective tactician. In the 1932 convention he held the Mississippi delegation for Roosevelt at a critical point and later, as chairman of the Senate Finance Committee, guided administration measures to passage: NIRA, reciprocal trade agreements, social security, and revenue acts. In 1939 a *Life* panel of Washington correspondents voted him the most influential man in the upper house, "the cunning fox," "the best wangler in the Senate"—an eminence they conceded despite his being "downright lazy." [15]

The same correspondents ranked the dapper James F. Byrnes a close second in influence. The man who toppled Cole Blease from the Senate in 1930, Byrnes became political advisor to Roosevelt's brain trust in 1932 and thereafter the President's confidant and liaison man in the Senate. He "rendered yeoman service to the new administration," Raymond Moley testified. "I seriously doubt that any other man on Capitol Hill could have achieved the parliamentary victories realized by Byrnes." Roosevelt certified him "a man of excellent common sense—a liberal and not of a radical or conservative predilection." Drawn into a national orbit, he became South Carolina's most influential Senator since Calhoun—and like

[14] Franklyn Waltham, Jr., in Washington *Post,* April 19, 1934; and Joseph T. Robinson to unknown addressee, n.d. (Spring, 1937), both quoted in Nevin Emil Neal, "A Biography of Joseph T. Robinson" (Ph.D. dissertation, University of Oklahoma, 1958), 390, 472; "The Senator from Arkansas," in *Fortune,* XV (January, 1937), 88–90ff.

[15] C. O'Neal Gregory, "Pat Harrison and the New Deal" (M.A. thesis, University of Mississippi, 1960); *Life,* VI (March 20, 1939), 14, 16. Among the ten "ablest" senators, Harrison ranked lowest in integrity, intelligence, and industry.

Calhoun, a Presidential prospect fatally hampered by his political base.[16]

Kentucky's Alben W. Barkley, as Robinson's lieutenant, played a secondary role in Roosevelt's first term. Having led farmer and labor opposition to his state's racetrack, liquor, and coal "Combine," he assumed a moderately liberal posture. After Robinson's death in 1937, therefore, he became the President's logical choice as successor over the more conservative Harrison. Elected majority leader by one vote, he carried on the Kentucky tradition of great compromisers, Border State senators who, like Clay and Crittenden, were "trained in the task of holding the North and the South together within their own states." [17]

Conservative elements were reduced at first to sporadic sniping. Mainly the fire came from a senatorial trio: Carter Glass and Harry F. Byrd of Virginia and Josiah W. Bailey of North Carolina, all true believers in economic orthodoxy who viewed with alarm the new heresies. As early as 1932, in response to a Roosevelt dictum that economic laws "are made by human beings," Bailey protested: "the accepted doctrine for 150 years is that fundamental economic laws are natural laws, having the same source as physical laws." [18] Bailey's credo impelled him to oppose both the AAA and the NRA.[19] "It is un-American to prescribe by law what a farmer may sell, a manufacturer shall make or a consumer shall pay," he wrote later. "It denies Liberty, which is the breath of our Republic's life. There is no half-way ground. We will stick to Liberty or go over to Communism." [20] But in 1930 Bailey had run as the champion of party regularity against the apostate Furnifold Simmons, and after 1933 he carefully dodged any collision with New Dealers in North Carolina. New Deal

[16] Raymond Moley, 27 Masters of Politics in a Personal Perspective (New York, 1949), 250–54; Byrnes, All in One Lifetime, 64–81 and passim; Franklin D. Roosevelt to John G. Winant, September 8, 1934, in OF 716-B, Roosevelt Library.

[17] John H. Fenton, Politics in the Border States (New Orleans, 1957), 48–52, 221; Alben W. Barkley, That Reminds Me— (Garden City, N.Y., 1954), passim.

[18] Josiah W. Bailey to James A. Farley, August 13, 1932, quoted in John Robert Moore, "Josiah W. Bailey of North Carolina and the New Deal, 1931–1941" (Ph.D. dissertation, Duke University, 1962), 86–87.

[19] Ibid., 95–97, 195.

[20] Josiah W. Bailey, "Liberty vs. Communism," in Manufacturers' Record, CIII (April, 1934), 16.

policies, he declared in 1934, were justified by the emergency. "We will return to reliance upon private enterprise and individual initiative, but not to greed, not to unconscionable profits, not to speculation. . . . This, as I understand, is the essence of the New Deal." [21] In 1936, when he ran for re-election, Bailey grabbed onto the President's coattails.

An invulnerable machine made Virginia's Senators more independent—and more outspoken. The methods of the New Deal, Glass wrote before it was six months old, "have been brutal and absolutely in contravention of every guaranty of the Constitution and of the whole spirit of sane civilization." The Blue Eagle, he told Hugh Johnson, was a "bird of prey" that created "a reign of terror among thousands of struggling small industries." "The New Deal," he declared publicly in 1934, ". . . is not only a mistake; it is a disgrace to the Nation." Few Southern politicos were ever so blunt in their hostility; none so early. Roosevelt, who maintained cordial relations through it all, dubbed Glass an "unreconstructed old rebel." [22]

Byrd, who entered the Senate by appointment in 1933, backed some New Deal measures on the grounds of emergency, but "watched with much apprehension the growing tendency toward centralization of government in Washington." [23] Economy had been his watchword as governor; it became his obsession as Senator. "I do not believe a government can borrow and spend its way to prosperity any more than an individual can enrich himself by living beyond his income," he declared.[24] Similar concerns gave Glass and Byrd a potent ally in Douglas Southall Freeman, editor of the Richmond *News-Leader*.[25]

There were other skeptics who, like Bailey, avoided a complete

[21] Raleigh *News and Observer*, July 8, 1934.

[22] Carter Glass to Walter Lippmann, August 10, 1933; and Washington *Post*, April 8, 1934, clipping, in Glass Papers; "Washington Diary—1931–33," in Henry M. Hyde Papers (University of Virginia Library, Charlottesville) ; Palmer, *Carter Glass: Unreconstructed Rebel*, 256.

[23] Harry Flood Byrd, "Shall We Destroy the Foundation?" in *Manufacturers' Record*, CIII (July, 1934) , 18.

[24] Harry Flood Byrd, "Return to Sound Principle," in *Manufacturers' Record*, CIV (March, 1935) , 23.

[25] Douglas Southall Freeman to Harry F. Byrd, June 29, July 10, September 18, 1935; Byrd to Freeman, June 27, 1935, in Douglas Southall Freeman Papers (Manuscripts Division, Library of Congress) .

break: Walter F. George of Georgia, Tom Connally of Texas, Ellison D. "Cotton Ed" Smith of South Carolina, who waxed irascible over crop controls. Oklahoma's Thomas P. Gore, however, went the whole way. The New Deal, he warned, was "going too far too fast." He criticized crop limitations, the NRA, Federal relief, and old-age pensions. "A paternalistic government is bound to destroy the self-reliance and self-respect of the people," he said; "the dole spoils the soul." In 1936 the old populist and progressive went down to humiliating defeat, running third in a senatorial primary won by New Dealer Josh Lee, a spellbinding professor of speech.[26]

No Southern Congressman, however, was disposed to enter a conservative coalition during Roosevelt's first term. When a rumor spread in 1934 that Glass, Byrd, Bailey, and Gore were about to join the American Liberty League in such a move, they denied it. "I have had no conferences with Republicans or Democrats about this matter," Carter Glass protested, and Byrd asserted that he would not "join in any movement to obstruct or embarrass President Roosevelt in his efforts to end the deplorable conditions which resulted from twelve years of Republican misrule." [27]

If any real threat to Roosevelt existed in those early years, it arose on the left, in the person of Louisiana's unorthodox Senator Huey Pierce Long, Jr.[28] Without his help in the 1932 convention, some thought, Roosevelt might have lost the nomination. Shortly after the election Long invaded Roosevelt's suite at Washington's Mayflower Hotel and emerged to inform reporters, "He told me, 'Huey, you're a-goin' to do just what I tell you'; and that's just what I'm a-goin' to do." But the role of faithful retainer was never Huey's forte, and a breach developed quickly. In June, 1934, he explained his position. He had opposed Roosevelt on such matters as banking, economy, the NIRA, silver purchase, the 30-hour week, income and inheritance taxes; he had supported him on in-

[26] Monroe Billington, "Senator Thomas P. Gore," in *Chronicles of Oklahoma,* XXXV (Autumn, 1957), 282–87; Washington *Post,* June 18, 1934, clipping in Thomas P. Gore Papers (University of Oklahoma Library, Norman).

[27] George Wolfskill, *The Revolt of the Conservatives: A History of the American Liberty League, 1934–1940* (Boston, 1962), 16, 31–32.

[28] The following account, except where otherwise indicated, is taken from Long, *Every Man a King: The Autobiography of Huey P. Long;* Kane, *Louisiana Hayride,* 100–102, 116–19; Sindler, *Huey Long's Louisiana,* 83–87; Schlesinger, *The Politics of Upheaval,* 52–68; Albert Edward Cowdrey, "Huey Long in National Politics" (M.A. thesis, Johns Hopkins University, 1957).

flation, home loans, farm relief, deposit insurance, repeal, TVA, regulation of securities markets. "Whenever the administration has gone to the left I have voted with it, and whenever it has gone to the right I have voted against it." [29]

But it was not solely an ideological clash. What probably counted for more were Long's mercurial temperament, his ambition, and Roosevelt's instinctive distrust. Long was one of the two most dangerous men in the country, the President told Rexford Tugwell.[30] The administration, therefore, channeled patronage to his Louisiana opponents and reactivated an investigation of his income tax returns. And Joseph T. Robinson, whose Arkansas bailiwick Long had invaded in 1932 to campaign for Senator Hattie Caraway, encouraged a senatorial investigation into the election of a new Longite Senator from Louisiana, John H. Overton. Long responded with a growing ferocity, insulted the President by keeping his hat on through an interview, and coined ludicrous nicknames for administration leaders: Lord Corn Wallace; Ickes, the Chicago Chinch Bug; Sitting Bull Hugh Johnson; Prince Franklin, Knight of the Nourmahal—a reference to the President's vacationing on Vincent Astor's yacht.

In Louisiana, a fiefdom assigned to his vassal Governor O. K. Allen, Huey moved to buttress his control. During 1934 new laws reinforced his domination of the election machinery and the state militia invaded the enemy stronghold of New Orleans to supervise elections. From August, 1934, through September, 1935, seven special sessions of a servile legislature whipped through laws that destroyed virtually all local government. By 1935 hardly any town or parish officeholder could keep his place without Long's favor. An obliging supreme court upheld the legislation. In return the state's benevolent despot continued to deliver tax favors, roads, schools, free textbooks, charity hospitals, a strongly supported state university, and generally better public services at the cost of corruption and dictatorship.

Louisiana, however, had become only the base from which to conquer other worlds. The vehicle for that purpose was Long's Share-Our-Wealth program, unveiled in March, 1932, and carried

---

[29] *Congressional Record*, 73 Cong., 2 Sess., 11451–11452.

[30] The other was Douglas MacArthur. Rexford Guy Tugwell, *The Democratic Roosevelt* (Garden City, N.Y., 1957), 349.

through numerous emendations during the next three years. In one version, he proposed to liquidate large personal fortunes, guarantee every American family an allowance of $5,000 and every worker an annual income of $2,500, grant an "adequate" pension to the aged, reduce the hours of labor, pay veterans' bonuses, and assure a college education for all qualified students. In 1933 Long secreted himself for six weeks to write *Every Man a King*, a slender volume designed to enhance the program's appeal. In January, 1934, he launched the nationwide Share-Our-Wealth Clubs and named as his chief lieutenant Gerald L. K. Smith, fundamentalist exhorter and rabble-rouser. By February, 1935, Long claimed 27,431 clubs and a file of 7,500,000 names.

A canvass by the Democratic National Committee indicated that he could get perhaps five to six million votes as a third-party candidate for President, that at the least he might use his influence to defeat Robinson and Harrison, and establish political sway over the Lower Mississippi Valley and parts of the West. In the spring of 1935 Roosevelt began to talk of the need to "steal Long's thunder," which he did in part with the "soak-the-rich" tax of 1935, which sharply lifted the surtax on large incomes and levied a graduated corporation income tax, in part with the Social Security Act.[31] But one night in September, 1935, Long's threat suddenly evaporated. Dr. Carl Austin Weiss, who apparently had brooded over Long's effort to oust one of the state's few independent judges, his father-in-law B. J. Pavy, accosted the Senator in a corridor of his skyscraper capitol at Baton Rouge. Suddenly he fired one shot, whereupon Long's bodyguards riddled the assassin. Thirty-one hours later the Kingfish was dead.[32]

Before the assassination Georgia's Governor Eugene Talmadge was rumored to be negotiating an anti-New Deal alliance with Long.[33] Politics has made stranger bedfellows, but Talmadge belonged to a different breed of firebrand. He embraced a philos-

[31] Farley, *Behind the Ballots*, 249–50; Moley, *After Seven Years*, 305.

[32] T. Harry Williams, "Louisiana Mystery—An Essay Review," in *Louisiana History*, VI (1965), 287–91, explores several theories about the assassination.

[33] Hamilton Basso, "Our Gene," in *New Republic*, LXXXVI (1936), 35–37. The following account is based on Sarah M. Lemmon, "The Public Career of Eugene Talmadge, 1926–1936" (Ph.D. dissertation, University of North Carolina, 1952); and Willis Anderson Sutton, Jr., "The Talmadge Campaigns: A Sociological Analysis of Political Power" (Ph.D. dissertation, University of North Carolina, 1952).

ophy as orthodox as that of the most hidebound Senators. In 1926 the "Wild Man from Sugar Creek" had burst upon the Georgia voters as the winning candidate for commissioner of agriculture. Fingering the red galluses that became his trademark, glowering through horn-rimmed spectacles, shaking an unruly shock of black hair, the successor of Tom Watson flaunted a populistic rhetoric against railroads, monopolies, and Wall Street, and championed the virtues of work, thrift, individualism, and piety. In a state whose county-unit system favored rural areas, he later boasted that he never campaigned in a county that had a streetcar.

Six years as commissioner of agriculture were a rehearsal for the governorship. Talmadge established a firm control, cut expenses, reactivated the Bureau of Markets, endorsed panaceas like the tariff and the cotton holiday, wrangled with the legislature, warred on Hoover's Farm Board, and weathered a threat of impeachment for financial irregularities. His governorship, 1933–1937, spanned four more years of tumult. He slashed expenditures, found legal authority to reduce legislative appropriations, ran the state without any at all in 1935 and 1936, starved public services, and left a surplus in the state treasury. In part he did it by using Federal road and school moneys so as to divert state funds to other uses. The state militia put strikers behind barbed wire and brought a recalcitrant highway commission to heel, an executive order reduced all license tags to three dollars, new laws lowered the property levies. Talmadge replaced the entire personnel of the Public Service Commission, which then reduced telephone, railroad, gas, and power rates.

Yet powerful businessmen soon recognized an unsuspected ally. His doctrine of frugal and limited government matched their own convictions. "Whenever you have a rich government," he declared, "you usually have a poor citizenry." He therefore vetoed extravagances like C. H. Herty's experiments with pine newsprint, old-age pensions, free textbooks, and a seven-month school term. Meanwhile, the Georgia Power Company, which had suffered a rate reduction at his hands, more than recovered the loss on three dollar tags for its trucks and the property-tax cut. On the tags Georgia farmers saved five or ten dollars and on the property tax an average of fifty-three cents a year. By the beginning of his second term in 1935 "Our Gene" led an incongruous coalition of moguls and rustics. "He is perhaps lacking in the elegancies, politeness, and very sensitive refinements," President Arkwright of the Georgia Power Company wrote a colleague, "but he is sound and strong, determined and courageous. . . . I am a great admirer of his and I am for him." [34]

From the beginning Talmadge fulminated against the New Deal: its relief, wage, and highway policies, the NRA, the AAA. It was all a "combination of wet nursin', frenzied finance, downright Communism an' plain dam-foolishness." His pastiche of rugged individualism and bucolic appeal captivated John H. Kirby, Texas lumberman and chronic conservative. In January, 1936, Kirby's Southern Committee to Uphold the Constitution sponsored a "Grass Roots Convention" in Macon to rally the anti-New Dealers and incidentally start a Presidential boom for Talmadge. Invitations went to "Jeffersonian Democrats" in seventeen Southern and Border States, but the show played to a half-empty auditorium. The cast included Talmadge, Gerald L. K. Smith, and Thomas Dixon, author of *The Clansman*. On every seat was a copy of the *Georgia Woman's World* which featured what Vance Muse, Kirby's propaganda director, called "a picture of Mrs. Roosevelt going to some nigger meeting, with two escorts, niggers, on each arm." They were ROTC cadets at Howard Univerity.

The affair discredited its sponsors and embarrassed contributors such as John J. Raskob, Alfred P. Sloan, and Henry du Pont, who were later identified by Hugo Black's Special Committee to Investigate Lobbying Activities. It backfired even in Georgia, where Talmadge made a try for the Senate. Entering the lists against Richard B. Russell, he promised to uphold the constitution, oppose the income tax, reduce the budget, take the government out of business, and refuse dictation from boards and bureaus that had Negro members. The farmers, reporters noted, listened pensively to attacks on farm policy, apparently torn between personal loyalty and benefit checks. Russell in turn extolled Roosevelt and accused Talmadge of unholy alliance with Republicans and Liberty Leaguers. In the same primary gubernatorial candidate E. D.

---

[34] Preston Arkwright to William Chamberlain, May 20, 1935, quoted in Lemmon, "Public Career of Eugene Talmadge," 243n.

Rivers promised a "little New Deal." The magic combination of "the three R's," Roosevelt, Russell, and Rivers, overpowered the Talmadgeites, and Russell led by more than 100,000 votes.

"When we fail to stand by President Roosevelt," Georgia's Senator Walter F. George declared during the campaign, "we shall be ready to forsake the best of our friends." [35] Until 1936 to oppose Roosevelt was to court political suicide. Piecemeal efforts to stop his renomination fell as flat as the grass-roots movement.[36] Yet the administration slowly gathered enemies. Sectional feeling, which had sustained the progressive coalitions of Bryan and Wilson, increasingly plagued Roosevelt. Crop limitations antagonized the cotton trade, codes and labor standards annoyed industrialists, relief policies and the NRA raised the issue of wage differentials. All touched on racial discrimination and all threatened existing relationships in the social power structure.

The roots of disaffection lay in the county-seat "élites," in the "banker-merchant-farmer-lawyer-doctor-governing class." For them the New Deal jeopardized a power that rested on the control of property, labor, credit, and local government.[37] Relief projects reduced dependency; labor standards raised wages; the farm program upset landlord-tenant relationships; government credit bypassed the bankers; new Federal programs skirted the county commissioners and sometimes even state agencies. "My honest opinion," a wholesale grocer in Greenville, Texas, wrote to Sam Rayburn in 1935, "is that sentiment is growing—growing against regimentation more and more." [38]

The trends became more ominous in 1935, when the "Second New Deal" swung from recovery to reform with such measures as the WPA, social security, the Wagner Act, the "Soak-the-Rich" tax, and later, the Farm Tenant and Housing acts of 1937 and the

[35] Atlanta *Journal*, n.d., clipping with James A. Farley to Franklin D. Roosevelt, August 13, 1936, in OF 300-Georgia, Roosevelt Library.

[36] Wolfskill, *The Revolt of the Conservatives*, 179–81; Farley, *Behind the Ballots*, 249–52.

[37] Jasper Berry Shannon, *Toward a New Politics in the South* (Knoxville, 1949), 38–53. See also McGill, *The South and the Southerner*, 161.

[38] Hal C. Horton to Sam Rayburn, April 6, 1935, in Rayburn Papers, 1935-Legislation. See also F. C. Dillard to Rayburn, April 5, 1935, *ibid.*

Fair Labor Standards Act of 1938. "Northernization" of the Democratic party in the wake of overwhelming victories aggravated the tensions. In 1936 the Democratic convention eliminated the two-thirds rule for nominations, thereby removing the South's veto power, and seated Negro delegates. Later, at a meeting in Detroit, a small number of digruntled Southerners helped organize an abortive movement of "Jeffersonian Democrats." The "Jeffersonians" put out separate electoral tickets in several states and made their biggest display in Texas, where they stressed anti-Negro and anti-Communist themes, but with little effect on the electorate.[39]

An opposition did not coalesce until Roosevelt provoked a constitutional crisis in 1937. For two years, through 1935 and 1936, the Supreme Court had been striking down New Deal measures: the NRA, the AAA, the Guffey Coal Act, among others, usually by a narrow construction of the Federal power to regulate interstate commerce. When the court ruled against the NRA in 1935, Senator Byrd expressed surprise that anyone should have expected any other outcome. The decision merely "re-affirmed fundamental principles." But the administration's drive to extend Federal power, he predicted, would bring a conflict on the issue of local self-government, which might come on the commerce clause, the Tenth Amendment, a change in the amending process, or the court's power of judicial review.[40] Through 1936 public discussion turned mostly on the commerce clause. "The nation still needs its states and its states' rights," John Temple Graves wrote in the Birmingham *News*. "But it has grown too small and related to get along without a certain uniformity of economic rules." [41] This position had widespread support in the Southern press and in 1936 the Democratic platform endorsed an amendment to

---

[39] Patenaude, "The New Deal and Texas," 138–70; McKay, *Texas Politics*, 397–413; Alexander Heard, *A Two-Party South?* (Chapel Hill, 1952), 158, 257–58; Knoxville *Journal*, August 29, 1936, clipping with W. V. Bishop to Stephen A. Early, September 4, 1936, in OF 300-Tennessee, Roosevelt Library.

[40] Richmond *Times-Dispatch*, June 11, 16, 1935.

[41] John Temple Graves, quoted in Francis P. Miller (ed.), *The Southern Press Considers the Constitution*, in Southern Policy Papers, No. 6 (Chapel Hill, 1936), 13.

broaden the commerce power, but Roosevelt decided upon another, and unexpected, course.[42]

In February, 1937, he proposed to create up to fifty new Federal judges, including six justices, to assist any judge who had served ten years and remained on the bench six months after his seventieth birthday. Two Texas Congressmen expressed the divergent reactions to his stratagem. "Boys, here's where I cash in," Hatton W. Sumners told Congressional leaders as they emerged from the conference in which the President sprang his plan. But at the Capitol Maury Maverick seized a mimeographed copy of the proposal, wrote his name at the top, and tossed it into the House hopper as his own.[43] Speaker Bankhead, however, demanded that the Senate take up the issue first, lest it endanger the seats of too many Representatives. Privately he expressed to Lindsay Warren his personal opposition. "Lindsay," he asked, "wouldnt [sic] you have thought that the President would have told his own party leaders what he was going to do? He didnt [sic] because he knew that hell would break loose." [44]

The "court-packing" maneuver handed new issues to men who previously had shunned a fight with Roosevelt. It was too patently disingenuous. Its implications of senility among judges angered the elder statesmen of Congress. It ran headlong into the accustomed veneration of the courts and aroused the fear of a dangerous precedent. Southern opponents touched the mystic chords of sectional tradition: it threatened the sanctity of the Constitution, states' rights, white supremacy. Carter Glass immediately denounced this "frightful proposition." [45] On March 29 he sounded the alarm over the radio, speaking, he said, "from the depths of a soul filled with bitterness against a proposal . . . utterly destitute

[42] Miller (ed.), *The Southern Press Considers the Constitution*. See also Caleb Perry Paterson, *The Supreme Court and the Constitution*, in *Arnold Foundation Studies in Public Affairs*, IV (Winter, 1936); and James Ernest Pate, *The Decline of States' Rights*, *ibid*. (Spring, 1936).

[43] Joseph Alsop and Turner Catledge, *The 168 Days* (Garden City, N.Y., 1938), traces the entire controversy. See also Kenneth Harrell, "Southern Congressional Leaders and the Supreme Court Fight of 1937" (M.A. thesis, Louisiana State University, 1959).

[44] L[indsay] C. W[arren], "Memo," dated "Sunday Feb. 7th, 1937, 2 P.M.," in Lindsay C. Warren Papers (University of North Carolina Library, Chapel Hill).

[45] *Newsweek*, IX (February 13, 1937), 7–9; (February 20, 1937), 18.

of moral sensibility." "Political janizaries" of the administration were parading the states, whipping up support. Did those who applauded Harold Ickes in Raleigh know, Glass asked, "that he recently reproached the South for providing separate public schools for the races; that he urged repeal of segregation; that he practically committed the administration . . . to a new Force Bill for the South. . . ?" If such "visionary incendiaries" helped choose the "six proposed judicial sycophants, very likely they would like to see the reversal of those decisions of the Court that saved the civilization of the South." [46] Once compromise the independence of the judiciary, Josiah Bailey predicted, and "it would be violated again and again; and our people would be reduced to the very conditions under which our forefathers suffered." [47]

The Republican minority shrewdly stood aside while the Democrats plunged into a family squabble. For the first time the administration's opponents achieved a degree of organized cohesion. At a dinner given by Millard E. Tydings of Maryland they named a steering committee of ten, including four Southerners— Bailey, Byrd, George, and Conally. Its composition was heavily conservative, but Burton K. Wheeler, the old progressive from Montana, became chairman.[48] Yet before the end of March fifteen Southern Senators had endorsed the bill, while only seven opposed and four remained uncommitted. This hardly represented a rebellion against Roosevelt; none of the outright opponents had ever been closely identified with him.[49] A few rallied with conviction and force: Hugo Black, Claude Pepper, Theodore G. Bilbo ("100% for"), Morris Sheppard, Alben Barkley. But the regulars for the most part acted without enthusiasm. Pat Harrison, who announced his support early and said no more, put in a character-

---

[46] *Congressional Record,* 75 Cong., 1 Sess., Appendix, 661.

[47] Josiah W. Bailey to Hon. W. P. Horton, President of the Senate, and Hon. R. G. Cherry, Speaker of the House, the General Assembly of North Carolina, April 17, 1937, copy in John H. Overton Papers (Department of Archives, Louisiana State University, Baton Rouge).

[48] Connally, *My Name Is Tom Connally,* 189.

[49] Washington *Post,* March 25, 1937. Those committed against the bill were Bachman of Tennessee, Bailey, Byrd, Connally, George, Glass and Smith. The uncommitted senators were Andrews of Florida, Bankhead, Overton, and Russell.

istic performance.[50] Majority Leader Robinson acted partly, at least, in the hope of a court appointment. Speaker Bankhead publicly announced his support but privately expressed preference for a constitutional amendment. Vice President Garner decamped for Texas.

Word from home disclosed sharp divisions. In the Gallup poll, 53 per cent of the nation's voters opposed the plan, but a majority supported it in all Southern states except Kentucky and Oklahoma. The proportion ran from 51 per cent in North Carolina to 76 per cent in South Carolina. Legislatures in the Carolinas and Oklahoma, and the Georgia Senate, resolved in favor. But in Texas the Senate expressed opposition and the House tabled a favorable resolution.[51] The bar association in every Southern state objected and editorial pages exhibited a growing dissent. "I have been surprised," William Watts Ball wrote, " by the almost unanimous opposition of the South Carolina press." [52] One electoral test occurred during the debate. In a special congressional election for the Austin, Texas, district, the young state director of the NYA, Lyndon B. Johnson, made his support for the court plan "the major issue" in a winning campaign.[53]

No direct vote ever tested senatorial convictions. Several unexpected events blunted the drive to reform the courts. A sequence of Supreme Court decisions upheld a state minimum wage law and several New Deal measures including the Wagner Act. Chief Justice Hughes wrote a letter explaining that the court had kept up with its docket. And conservative Justice Van Devanter resigned, giving Roosevelt his first appointment. In mid-July the sudden death of Senator Robinson demoralized the President's supporters and precipitated a divisive struggle for the leadership between Harrison and Barkley. Barkley won by a single vote, with the President's support, but the court bill went back to the Judiciary Committee, which had reported it unfavorably. Finally

[50] Gregory, "Pat Harrison and the New Deal," 84.

[51] Washington *Post*, March 25, 1937.

[52] Harrell, "Southern Congressional Leaders and the Supreme Court Fight of 1937," 77; William Watts Ball to John W. Davis, March 19, 1937, in Ball Papers.

[53] Patenaude, "The New Deal and Texas," *loc. cit.*, 189, 223. Quotation from Lyndon B. Johnson to Patenaude, October 7, 1952.

Vice President Garner arranged a compromise that provided reforms in court procedures and more generous retirement provisions, but no new judges.

The struggle had an ironic epilogue. When the President appointed one of the most consistent New Dealers, Senator Hugo Black, to fill the court vacancy, Ray Sprigle of the Scripps-Howard newspaper publicized what was common knowledge in Alabama—that Black had joined the Ku Klux Klan a dozen years before. Black had no choice but to confess his guilt, but pointed to his subsequent record in mitigation. "After all," said the Montgomery *Advertiser*, "the enemies that Hugo Black made as a Senator came to hate him, not because he was once a Klansman, but for quite other reasons. . . . They hate him because of what he said as a Senator . . . about social and economic conditions. They hate him because he has been a Rooseveltian and because Roosevelt appointed him to the bench." [54] Roosevelt later claimed he had lost the battle but won the war. If so, it was a pyrrhic victory that divided the Democratic party and blighted his own prestige. For the first time Southern Congressmen in large numbers deserted the leader and the opposition found an issue on which it could openly take the field. Things were never again quite the same.

Meanwhile rebellion erupted on other fronts even while the court bill pended. Sit-down strikes that swept the auto industry early in 1937 represented to Garner and many like him an intolerable defiance of property rights. The sit-downs, a former Senator from South Carolina wrote to James F. Byrnes, represented "the most dangerous development that has come about in our National Life in recent years." [55] With Garner's tacit support, Byrnes introduced a resolution censuring the sit-downs. It was defeated, but during the debate Garner gave public affirmation to his reported part in the affair by walking over and putting his arm around Byrnes. At the same time Garner, Byrnes, Harrison, Robinson, and Rayburn expressed alarm over spending policies and the unbalanced budget. They demanded a reduction in relief

[54] John Frank, *Mr. Justice Black* (New York, 1949), 99–107; Montgomery *Advertiser*, October 3, 1937.

[55] Christie Benet to James F. Byrnes, April 8, 1937, in James F. Byrnes Papers (Clemson University Library, Clemson, S.C.).

requests, but the administration pushed through its demand for $1,500,000,000. Then Byrnes and Robinson sought to put upon local communities a specified percentage of the relief costs. Byrnes asked 10 per cent, and Robinson 25, but neither proposal passed.[56] "I fear that Roosevelt has lost a great deal of strength in the last six months," Virginius Dabney wrote in the fall of 1937; "I fear he has lost some of his political sagacity." [57] Stalemate in a special session of Congress that fall seemed to bear out the evaluation. Congress passed not a single measure the President sought: a new farm act, wage-hour legislation, administrative reorganization, and regional planning.[58]

Sectional issues continued to mount. The attack on economic colonialism and freight-rate discriminations grew. Conservatives in the Farm Bureau assailed the tenant program and the demands of organized labor. Antilynching bills once again provoked filibusters. In the New Deal coalition Southern Democrats had become uneasy bedfellows with organized labor and Negroes. Consequently some of them drifted toward countercoalition with conservative Republicans. Before the court battle ended in 1937 the rapprochement was apparent. During the special session that fall the conservatives edged toward an open alliance. Shortly after Congress convened, Senator Byrd summoned ten Democrats and Republicans to a quail luncheon at which they discussed a combination against Roosevelt. Continuing exchanges finally induced Josiah Bailey, aided by Republicans Arthur Vandenberg and Warren Austin, to draft a ten-point "conservative manifesto" that called for revision of the undistributed-profits and capital-gains taxes, a balanced budget, states' rights, and reliance "upon the American system of private enterprise and initiative." But the newspapers got the text and published it prematurely, whereupon Bailey denied that it represented any coalition attempt. The document, he said, was merely "a statement of views and policies that anyone in America may espouse or reject." Few Democrats

[56] Alsop and Catledge, *The 168 Days,* 129–32; Harrell, "Southern Congressional Leaders and the Supreme Court Fight of 1937," 99–104.

[57] Virginius Dabney to Samuel Chiles Mitchell, September 24, 1937, in Mitchell Papers.

[58] Rosenman (comp.), *Public Papers and Addresses of Franklin D. Roosevelt,* VI, 490–500.

chose to espouse it: Southerners like Smith, George, Byrd, and Glass, together with a few Northerners like Royal Copeland of New York and Peter Gerry of Rhode Island.[59]

Nevertheless, a conservative bloc, if unorganized and mutable, had appeared. The administration still secured several major measures in the regular session of 1938: the second Agricultural Adjustment Act, a spending act to fight the recession, the Fair Labor Standards Act, the establishment of the Temporary National Economic Committee to investigate monopoly. But Democrats wandered freely off the reservation. The opposition stymied a reorganization bill amid cries that it would open the way to executive dictatorship and Senators Harrison and Byrnes secured a drastic cut in the undistributed-profits and capital-gains levies to help restore business "confidence."[60] The House established a Committee on Un-American Activities, proposed and chaired by Martin Dies of Texas. Dies, who earlier had inveighed against international bankers and aliens, now took to the warpath against Communists. Soon he began to brand New Dealers as Red dupes. "Stalin baited his hook with a 'progressive' worm," Dies wrote in 1940, "and New Deal suckers swallowed bait, hook, line, and sinker."[61]

Yet despite the dissonance on Capitol Hill, the election year of 1938 opened on a more agreeable note for the New Deal. Primary victories by Lister Hill in January and Claude Pepper in May signaled a new liberalism in Southern politics, or so it seemed.[62] Heartened by the revival of fortunes, the White House ripened a new idea as momentous as the court plan—a program to reshape the Democratic party in the image of the New Deal. In that project the South occupied a strategic position.

As the political season of 1938 advanced, Roosevelt unfolded an

[59] John Robert Moore, 'Senator Josiah W. Bailey and the 'Conservative Manifesto' of 1937," in *Journal of Southern History,* XXXI (1965), 21–39; *Congressional Record,* 75 Cong., 2 Sess., 1936–1940; New York *Times,* December 17, 1937.

[60] Leuchtenburg, *Franklin D. Roosevelt and the New Deal,* 254–57, 262–63; Gregory, "Pat Harrison and the New Deal," 119–26.

[61] Martin Dies, *The Trojan Horse in America* (New York, 1940), 285; August Raymond Ogden, *The Dies Committee* (Washington, 1943), 38–46 and *passim.*

[62] Lee Collier, "The Solid South Cracks," in *New Republic,* XCIV (March 23, 1938), 185–86.

interpretation of regional problems to sustain his political design. On March 24 at Gainesville, Georgia, he addressed a crowd gathered to celebrate the town's recovery from a disastrous tornado two years before. "Georgia and the lower South may just as well face the facts," he said, "the purchasing power of the millions of Americans in this whole area is far too low." Better things "will not come to us," he continued, ". . . if we believe in our hearts that the feudal system is still the best system." The people needed representatives with minds "cast in the 1938 mold and not in the 1898 mold." [63] To Aubrey Williams, who commended the speech, he responded: "One difficulty is that three-quarters of the whites in the South cannot vote—poll tax, etc. Even at that I am sure that if the basic issue is soundly and strongly presented, the South will react to the morals of the situation just as fast as any other part of the country." [64]

Sometime during the spring Clark Foreman won the President's approval for the *Report on Economic Conditions of the South,* which appeared in August. Publication amounted to an administration endorsement of Southern revolt against economic colonialism. It offered a chance to direct a growing sectionalism into New Deal channels. But its potential was not effectively exploited in the political campaigns of the summer. Instead of a blueprint for regional development, the report became an occasion for political division.

On June 24 the President announced his purpose to intervene in Democratic primaries as the party leader, "charged with the responsibility of carrying out the definitely liberal declaration of principles set forth in the 1936 Democratic platform." [65] On July 7 he commenced a transcontinental tour that finally led back via the Panama Canal through the Deep South. At Covington's Latonia Race Track he told Kentuckians it would take "Happy" Chandler "many, many years to match the national knowledge, the experience and the acknowledged leadership" of Alben Bark-

[63] Rosenman (comp.), *Public Papers and Addresses of Franklin D. Roosevelt,* VII, 167–68.

[64] Franklin D. Roosevelt to Aubrey Williams, March 28, 1938, in Aubrey Williams Papers. Courtesy of Aubrey Williams.

[65] Rosenman (comp.), *Public Papers and Addresses of Franklin D. Roosevelt,* VII, 399.

ley.[66] Skirting the Senatorial contest in Tennessee, he made passing reference to his "old friend" Hattie Caraway in Arkansas and endorsed Elmer Thomas in Oklahoma. Because of Barkley's prominence as majority leader, national attention focused on Kentucky. Chandler, a successful and popular governor with a potent state organization, "a man of action and not of words," pursued a vigorous campaign; but Barkley turned him back with a surprisingly comfortable majority. Meanwhile both Mrs. Caraway and Thomas had carried their states.[67]

To that point the effort was to retain New Deal officeholders. Not until Roosevelt disembarked at Pensacola and entered Georgia did he challenge an incumbent, Senator Walter F. George. On August 11, while dedicating a new REA plant at Barnesville, he announced publication of the *Report on Economic Conditions of the South* and quoted his previous designation of the South as "the Nation's No. 1 economic problem." This he coupled with a plea for more progressive representation; on most public questions, the President said, he and George did "not speak the same language." [68]

Georgia became the pivotal battleground, and one on which the administration's tactical position was weak. The New Deal candidate, Lawrence Camp, former legislator, state party chairman, and district attorney, was relatively unknown. In the absence of a strong personality to focus the issues, Roosevelt's speech served mainly to fire the resentment of George's supporters. The Senator's next speech, a few days later at Waycross, set the tone of the campaign. The President, he charged, had been misinformed; as a consequence he had undertaken a "second march through Georgia." The Senator's forces vigorously stirred indignation against outside meddling, while George himself carefully avoided a frontal attack on Roosevelt or the New Deal. He had favored much of the President's program, he said, and compilation of his

---

[66] *Ibid.,* 438.

[67] Stokes, *Chip Off My Shoulder,* 493–94; Jasper B. Shannon, "Presidential Politics in the South: 1938," in *Journal of Politics,* I (1939), 146–70, 278–300, remains the best comprehensive account of Presidential intervention in the 1938 primaries.

[68] Rosenman (comp.), *Public Papers and Addresses of Franklin D. Roosevelt,* VII, 64–69.

voting record corroborated the claim. In 1933 he had opposed no major administration proposal and since that time only ten, but they included such key measures as the public utilities holding company bill, the wages and hours bill, and what probably piqued Roosevelt most, the Supreme Court plan.[69] No one considered George a New Dealer, columnist Ray Clapper noted, but he had supported so many basic New Deal measures that one had to render a Scotch verdict, "guilty, but not proven." In the returns George garnered a plurality of popular votes and a majority of the county unit votes. Camp ran a poor third, behind Talmadge. Fully 65 per cent of the vote, journalist Ralph Smith wrote the President later, was cast by people "whose admiration and faith in you is unshaken." The outcome merely showed that Senator George spoke "the language of Georgia," Smith wrote in the Atlanta *Journal*. But the result was a damaging setback for the administration.[70]

Roosevelt's following could not be transferred to Camp. Nor could it carry the day for Olin D. Johnston, South Carolina's "mill boy" governor, who had announced his Senatorial candidacy from the White House lobby. Stopping briefly in Greenville, Roosevelt declared that he did not believe the voters would support a man who believed fifty cents a day an adequate wage. Taken literally, the reference misconstrued an illustrative use of figures by "Cotton Ed" Smith in opposing the wage-hour law, although it did not misrepresent the Senator's low-wage philosophy. Again intervention fired resentment. Again the opposition charged that the President had been misled. Again local circumstances blurred ideological issues. Byrnes, temporarily at odds with the administration, quietly mobilized Federal officeholders behind Smith. Both Smith and Johnston descended into a white-supremacy campaign, featured by Cotton Ed's account of his walkout in "Phillydelphy." [71] On the night after his victory, Smith exultantly led a

[69] New York *Times*, August 12, 1938.

[70] David Nolan Thomas, "Roosevelt versus George: The Presidential Purge Campaign of 1938" (M.A. thesis, University of North Carolina, 1953), 37–39, 59–60, 72. Ralph Smith to Franklin D. Roosevelt, September 16, 1938, in OF 300-Georgia S, Roosevelt Library.

[71] Shannon, "Presidential Politics in the South: 1938," *loc. cit.*, 286–89; William Watts Ball to John W. Davis, September 23, 1938, in Ball Papers; Harry Ashmore, *An Epitaph for Dixie* (New York, 1957), 100.

red shirt parade to the Wade Hampton statue on the State House grounds. "No man dares to come into South Carolina and try to dictate to the sons of those men who held high the hands of Lee and Hampton," he shouted. "I am sure you are rejoicing," a professor at the nearby state university wrote to an old friend the next day, "that State's rights, white supremacy, Bourbonism, low wages, long hours, and the right to ignorance, prejudice and superstition are no longer in jeopardy in S. C." [72]

If the primary returns proved anything, it was the difficulty of dislodging an incumbent. The administration ousted only one opponent, John O'Connor of New York, chairman of the House Rules Committee. The opposition displaced Senator James Pope of Idaho. The Southern returns showed no general rebellion against the President. A summation of the Senatorial vote in nine Southern primaries, including Maryland, gave the margin to New Dealers by 53.4 to 46.6 per cent. At about the same time two thirds of the Southern voters expressed approval of the President in a Gallup poll. [73]

The Southern masses had "come to include Roosevelt in their tradition as they include the Democratic party itself," John Temple Graves wrote in 1939; ". . . he is their man; they believe in his good intentions; they suspect his enemies." [74] But administration defeats in Georgia, South Carolina, and Maryland came late in the season; they broke the spell of Presidential invincibility. Again, as in the court fight, Roosevelt had committed his prestige while handing his adversaries persuasive issues. His opponents tagged his intervention an attempted "purge"; the word evoked visions of Nazi dictatorship.

Charges of dictatorship also accompanied claims of political intervention by the WPA. Harry Hopkins' assistant, Aubrey Williams, furthered the accusation when he exhorted WPA workers in June: "Keep your friends in power." [75] During the campaign,

---

[72] Charleston *News and Courier*, August 31, 1938; Josiah Morse to Samuel Chiles Mitchell, August 31, 1938, in Mitchell Papers.

[73] Shannon, "Presidential Politics in the South: 1938," *loc. cit.*, 296–97. The states were Alabama, Arkansas, Florida, Georgia, Kentucky, Maryland, Oklahoma, South Carolina, and Tennessee.

[74] John Temple Graves, II, "The South Still Loves Roosevelt," in *Nation*, CXLIX (July 1, 1939), 13.

[75] *Time*, XXXII (July 4, 1938), 10.

Scripps-Howard reporter Thomas Stokes charged that "the whole atmosphere and tone of WPA in Kentucky" was political. Hopkins denied all but two of twenty-two specific accusations, but Stokes' articles provoked an inquiry by Senator Morris Sheppard's Campaign Expenditures Committee. The committee condemned scattered instances of corruption in Tennessee and Pennsylvania, as well as Kentucky, but revealed no evidence that the WPA central office or any Senatorial candidate was involved. In Kentucky, Chandler's campaign forces collected more from state employees than Barkley's from Federal workers. And the returns showed no correlation between the Barkley vote and WPA employment. The probe, however, prompted the Hatch Act of 1939, which prohibited political activity by Federal employees but left state and local officeholders to their own devices.[76]

The elections of November, 1938, handed the administration another setback, a result partly of the friction among Democrats, partly of the current economic recession. The Democratic margin in the House fell from 229 to 93, in the Senate from 56 to 42.[77] The majorities were still large, but the President headed a restive and divided party. The Southern leadership on which he had leaned during his first term had become undependable, and some of it hostile. The Democratic losses, Senator George warned, were a "danger signal from sober-minded American voters calling us back to common sense in legislation."[78] During 1939 the administration won some extension of social security and finally put through its reorganization plan with the help of Byrnes and North Carolina's Representative Lindsay C. Warren. But the opposition, behind disaffected Southern leaders like Byrnes and Harrison, now cut relief expenditures, eliminated the Federal Theater Project, rejected Roosevelt appointments, abolished the undistributed-profits tax. The House set up an investigation of the NLRB

---

[76] Stokes, *Chip Off My Shoulder*, 534–37; Charles, *Minister of Relief*, 195–98; Shannon, "Presidential Politics in the South: 1938," *loc. cit.*, 166–70; *Investigation of Senatorial Campaign Expenditures and Use of Governmental Funds*, in Senate Report, 76 Cong., 1 Sess., No. 1.

[77] U.S. Bureau of the Census, *Historical Statistics of the United States, Colonial Times to 1937*, 691, Columns Y-139-144.

[78] Atlanta *Constitution*, November 13, 1938.

chaired by the hostile Howard W. Smith of Virginia and attempted to lessen the coverage of the wage-hour law.[79] The conservative coalition and the administration had reached a standoff.

On the last day of the 1939 session, Claude Pepper rose in the Senate to "decry the unrighteous partnership of those . . . who hate Roosevelt and what Roosevelt stands for." Conservatives, he said, had formed a "designing alliance" with "the benficiaries of special privilege, who hate in their hearts the man who has tried to lighten the burden of toil on the back of labor." [80] But no historian has yet documented the existence of a "designing alliance." The coalition was neither organized nor coherent. Nor was it sponsored by "Wall Street" and "international bankers," as Pepper charged. It represented instead a meeting of minds among Congressmen from rural and small-town constituencies that did not adjust readily to the urban liberalism of labor, welfare, and housing programs.[81] In the 1930's, as one writer expressed it, "Southerners had not changed a great deal, but the Northern Democrats had. The South remained pro-Populist; the North became social democratic." [82] Even so, a careful student of the coalition found that while Southerners contributed the largest sectional group of Democratic mutineers in the 1939 session, they still gave the administration less opposition than either the East or Midwest, where Republicans had scored substantial gains.[83]

There is much truth in Marian Irish's judgment that Roosevelt found both "his staunchest supporters and his strongest opponents within the ranks of his own party south of the Mason-Dixon

[79] *Time,* XXXIII (April 3, 1939), 12; Gregory, "Pat Harrison and the New Deal," 127–36.

[80] *Congressional Record,* 76 Cong., 1 Sess., 11165, 11166.

[81] James Tyler Patterson, III, "Conservative Coalition in Congress, 1933–1939," (Ph.D. dissertation, Harvard University, 1964), 567–79.

[82] Norman R. Phillips, "The Question of Southern Conservatism," in *South Atlantic Quarterly,* LIV (1955), 3.

[83] Patterson, "Conservative Coalition in Congress, 1933–1939," 563–64. Based on a study of votes in the House; in the Senate about half the Southerners remained loyal to the New Deal. *Ibid.,* 501. See also William G. Carleton, "The Conservative South—A Political Myth," in *Virginia Quarterly Review,* XXII (1946), 179–92; *idem,* "The Southern Politician 1900 and 1950," in *Journal of Politics,* XIII (1951), 215–31; Phillips, "The Question of Southern Conservatism," *loc. cit.,* 1–10.

line." [84] The New Deal provoked more than one kind of rebellion in the South. It "precipitated an extraordinary popular agitation over political and economic issues," one historian has written. "It frightened the conservatives . . . promoted the growth of organized labor, and encouraged the spread of liberal ideas." It induced "the first real stirring of the southern 'proletariat'— submerged elements like the sharecropper, the textile worker, and the Negro domestic servant." [85]

The President's concern for Southern problems and his diversified programs presented a new challenge and a new opportunity to the scattered tribe of Southern liberals. A small, literate, middle-class group for the most part, they comprised the growing corps of relief and welfare workers, the new labor leaders, women active in club work and civic affairs, and solitary idealists: professors, writers, lawyers, professional men, aberrant planters and industrialists. A pivotal figure was Will W. Alexander of the Interracial Commission, who kept in touch with all the current movements in the region.

The liberals were strongest among the professors and journalists of the upper South. Among the university people probably the most influential was the University of North Carolina's President Frank P. Graham, a man who, according to Francis B. Simkins, "signed enough liberal manifestoes to put the South in the reformer's paradise." [86] A number of the university liberals, including the Regionalists, taught in Chapel Hill, but many served elsewhere: Wilson Gee at Virginia, Edwin Mims at Vanderbilt, Clarence E. Cason at Alabama, Charles W. Pipkin at Louisiana State, H. C. Nixon at Tulane, Walter Prescott Webb at Texas. A fair sampling of the newsmen would include Mark Ethridge of the Louisville *Courier-Journal,* Virginius Dabney of the Richmond *Times-Dispatch,* George Fort Milton of the Chattanooga *News,* Silliman Evans of the Nashville *Tennessean,* and Jonathan Daniels of the Raleigh *News and Observer,* who, W. J. Cash asserted, sometimes waxed "almost too uncritical in his eagerness

[84] Marian D. Irish, "The Southern One-Party System and National Politics," in *Journal of Politics,* IV (1942) , 90.

[85] Dewey W. Grantham, Jr., *The Democratic South* (Athens, Ga., 1963) , 69–70.

[86] Francis B. Simkins, *A History of the South* (3rd ed.; New York, 1963) , 607.

to champion the underdog: surely a curious charge to bring against a Southern editor." [87]

The main strategic function of Southern liberals, Gunnar Myrdal contended, had been liaison with Northern philanthropy. Their power came "from outside the South," through donations for education, welfare, public health, and interracial work.[88] But in the 1930's they found a new patron, the Federal government, and new responsibilities for implementing Federal programs, in which they found spheres of independence from local and state politics. The new outlets emboldened them, increased their influence and numbers, and broadened their vision of regional welfare into the economic and political realms. Moreover, they had an unprecedented entree in Washington. But they remained generals without an army, leaders with little influence among the masses of workers, farmers, and middle class, and with almost no foothold in politics. The New Deal lifted a few of their persuasion to political prominence—Maury Maverick of Texas, Lister Hill of Alabama, and Claude Pepper of Florida stood out, but as exceptions that proved the rule.

Generally moderate and cautious by necessity, Southern liberals shaded off into a radical fringe that championed the proletarian causes of the 1930's. The Highlander Folk School near Monteagle, Tennessee, became a mecca for this group. Founded in 1932 by a young idealist, Myles Horton of Tennessee, assisted by Don West of Georgia, the school grew from a "settlement house in a rural setting" into a regional center of worker educaton. Among the woodcutters and miners of Grundy County its small staff organized unions, co-operatives, and political activities. At times the school extended assistance to strikes and organizing drives elsewhere in eastern Tennessee. In 1937 the CIO commissioned Highlander to train Southern unionists. In residence terms of four to six weeks, or in briefer "workshops" and weekend conferences, the students received instruction in labor history, economics, strike tactics, public speaking, current events, and parliamentary law. By 1947 Highlander had trained more than 6,900 and had reached more than 12,300 through field or extension classes. Over the years it weathered successive onslaughts by conservative news-

[87] Cash, *Mind of the South*, 373.   [88] Myrdal, *An American Dilemma*, 466.

papers and the Grundy County Crusaders, antiunion vigilantes organized by a reactionary mine operator.[89]

A similar school, the older Commonwealth College at Mena, Arkansas, had a more turbulent career. Founded as a workers' college at the utopian colony of Newllano, Louisiana, two years before it moved to Arkansas in 1925, Commonwealth repeatedly splintered into ideological factions. In 1931 a new director, Lucien Koch, made a sharp turn toward radical militancy, and after 1934 the school emphasized work with the Southern Tenant Farmers' Union. In 1935 it endured a hostile but inept legislative investigation, then folded in 1940 after a state court seized its property in a suit brought on charges of anarchy, failure to fly the American flag during school hours, and the display of an "illegal emblem" (the hammer and sickle). Like Highlander, Commonwealth disclaimed any party affiliation; but unlike the Tennessee school, it drifted toward the Communist orbit in the late 1930's. Its last director, after 1937, was Claude Williams, an unfrocked Presbyterian minister who veered off toward the social gospel and united-front causes.[90]

Among the little group of Christian radicals, however, the central figure was Howard "Buck" Kester. During the 1920's, after graduation from Vanderbilt, Kester had worked for the Fellowship of Reconciliation in student interracialism. During the 1930's he worked for Reinhold Niebuhr's Committee on Economic and Racial Justice, which freed him to wander the Southern states, organize tenant farmers, investigate lynchings and labor strife, write and speak in colleges and seminaries. In 1934, Kester assembled a group of like-minded men at Monteagle to found the Fellowship of Southern Churchmen.[91] Niebuhr, who was present at the first meeting, became "the spiritual god-father of the Fellowship"; Kester became its secretary. This dedicated band sought "to set the redemptive gospel of Christ to work in the midst of a society floundering in economic chaos, political uncertainty and

[89] H. Glyn Thomas, "The Highlander Folk School: The Depression Years," in *Tennessee Historical Quarterly*, XXIII (1964), 358–71.

[90] William H. Cobb, "Commonwealth College: A History" (M.A. thesis, University of Arkansas, 1963); Cedric Belfrage, *South of God* (New York, 1941), and *A Faith to Free the People* (New York, 1944).

[91] Known until 1936 as the Younger Churchmen of the South.

spiritual dry-rot." Its members reasoned that the social conservatism of the South was "rooted in its religious conservatism and that there can be little or no alteration or amelioration of social conditions until the basic religious pattern has been radically and fundamentally changed." [92]

The Fellowship itself excluded "known communists or fellow-travellers," at a time when "the 'united front' was the liberal's religion." [93] But some Southerners drifted into united-front attitudes. "I refuse to ask saint or sinner, Pharisee or Publican, 'What are your politics?' before I sit down to work with him," said the Reverend Claude Williams.[94] I personally happen to dislike Communists [sic] tactics," Lucy Mason wrote. "But I cannot see myself saying I will never cooperate with a Communist for a good cause and by good, legitimate means." [95] In December, 1934, in conferences at Monteagle and Chattanooga, Socialist party members from four Southern states (North Carolina, Tennessee, Kentucky, and Alabama) undertook to form a united front with Communists "and other working class groups" on a program of "joint struggle for the immediate needs of the southern masses." [96] But the movement was stillborn and parties to the agreement later became bitter critics of Communist influence in other organizations. Nevertheless, in that golden age of the popular front Southern Communists emerged openly into civic action. The party encouraged members to become active in churches and clubs. In 1937 Alabama Communists distributed petitions against the sales tax and local merchants expressed their gratitude; in Pratt City they boasted that they helped bring street lights to the

[92] David Burgess, "The Fellowship of Southern Churchmen, Its History and Promise," in *Prophetic Religion* (Chapel Hill, N.C.), XIII (Spring, 1953), 3–11; Thomas B. Cowan, "History of the Fellowship of Southern Churchmen," mimeographed (*ca.* 1937); and Howard Kester to Elisabeth Gilman, February 16, 1942, in Fellowship of Southern Churchmen Papers (University of North Carolina Library, Chapel Hill).

[93] Burgess, "The Fellowship of Southern Churchmen, Its History and Promise," *loc. cit.*, 6.

[94] Belfrage, *A Faith to Free the People*, 238.

[95] Lucy Randolph Mason to Roger Baldwin, July 4, 1942, copy in Eleanor Roosevelt Papers.

[96] New York *Daily Worker*, January 5, 1935; Birmingham *Southern Worker*, January, 1935.

town. In September, 1937, Communists held a regional conference at Chattanooga, with more than a hundred delegates from Alabama, Florida, Kentucky, Louisiana, North Carolina, and Tennessee.[97]

In 1938 the spirit of the New Deal inspired the one regional group that ever effected a broad coalition of liberals and radicals: the Southern Conference for Human Welfare (SCHW). The idea originated with Joseph S. Gelders, Southern Secretary of the National Committee for the Defense of Political Prisoners, formerly a physicist at the University of Alabama. Late in 1936, after he was kidnapped and brutally assaulted at Birmingham, Gelders projected a Southwide conference on the civil rights of workers and Negroes. The idea gestated until the spring of 1938, when Lucy Mason arranged for him to meet Eleanor Roosevelt who in turn arranged a conference with her husband. The President, already involved in plans to transform the Democratic party, endorsed the idea, and urged upon Gelders an anti-poll-tax campaign. Gelders then induced members of the Alabama Policy Committee to collaborate on arrangements. Meanwhile the *Report on Economic Conditions of the South* appeared and the conference planners, after consulting Clark Foreman, broadened the agenda to include problems of economic "colonialism." [98]

In November, 1938, with H. C. Nixon as field secretary and W. T. Couch as program chairman, the SCHW assembled an imposing array of talent at Birmingham's Municipal Auditorium. Sponsors and participants included Senator Lister Hill and Congressman Luther Patrick, Democratic National Committeeman Brooks Hays of Arkansas, Governor and Mrs. Bibb Graves, George Fort Milton, Clarence Poe, Virginius Dabney, Ralph McGill, Mark Ethridge, Mary McLeod Bethune, and others of like stature. Eleanor Roosevelt, Aubrey Williams, Senators Bankhead and Pepper, and Justice Hugo Black addressed the group. Frank Graham became its first chairman. Gunnar Myrdal, who visited the sessions, wrote later that "for the first time in the history of the region . . . the lonely Southern liberals met in great numbers—

[97] Thomas A. Krueger, *And Promises to Keep: The Southern Conference for Human Welfare, 1938–1948* (Nashville, 1967), 72–73.
[98] *Ibid.*, 25–29; Foreman, "The Decade of Hope," 138–39.

actually more than twelve hundred"; they "experienced a fore-taste of the freedom and power which large-scale political organization and concerted action give." [99]

In a way, Clark Foreman later wrote, the SCHW marked "the peak of the New Deal, as it was so clearly the outgrowth of the efforts of President Roosevelt to help the people of the South escape . . . feudal economic conditions." [100] But the Conference envisioned escape less in designs of economic development than of reform "so that the full advantage of the natural wealth of the South may accrue to the workers of the South." [101] Representing chiefly a coalition of the CIO unions and middle-class activists, the organization looked more toward political action than to the academic studies and planning proposed by men like Howard Odum. Consequently many discreet liberals shied away, regarding it as unwise and divisive in effect. "It will stir up a great deal of enthusiasm and do some good work over a period of a few years," the University of Virginia's Wilson Gee prophesied, "and then, as is true of so many organizations of that nature, it will likely dwindle and pass off the stage." [102]

From the beginning the SCHW was branded a racial-equality group. After two unsegregated sessions, Birmingham's police commissioner, Eugene "Bull" Connor, imposed the local segregation ordinance. Delegates complied, but the group resolved against segregated meetings in the future. The Associated Press erroneously reported this as a "condemnation of the South's Jim Crow laws." It was not precisely that, but the convention's gesture contrasted with the accustomed caution of Southern liberals who dodged open challenges to racial barriers. The SCHW blazed a new trail, but not without cost to itself. The Conference "began in tragic mistake," the Raleigh *News and Observer* lamented, "when action was taken which resulted in placing emphasis upon the one thing certain angrily to divide the South." [103]

---

[99] Myrdal, *An American Dilemma*, 469.

[100] Foreman, "The Decade of Hope," *loc. cit.*, 137.   [101] *Ibid.*, 146.

[102] Wilson Gee to Howard Odum, October 11, 1938, in Odum Papers. See also Odum to Will W. Alexander, November 30, 1938, *ibid.*

[103] Krueger, *And Promises to Keep*, 33; Raleigh *News and Observer*, November 26, 1938.

More damaging, however, was the presence of Communists. The group originated in the activities of Joseph S. Gelders, whose connections placed him in the party's orbit. And delegates from the party itself participated in SCHW activities. However, if they expected to control the organization, they failed miserably. In 1947 the House Committee on Un-American Activities branded the organization a Communist front, but its report was a masterpiece of logical fallacies, quotations out of context, and guilt-by-association techniques.[104]

Nevertheless, the Communist issue absorbed much of the organization's energy and weakened its effectiveness. In 1940 the second meeting at Chattanooga pursued the theme of "Democracy in the South," but attention focused on a resolution against the current Soviet aggression in Finland. The conference finally condemned aggression "by all fascist, nazi, communist, and imperialist powers alike," but the resolution provoked a tense debate that threatened to erupt in fisticuffs.[105] Two years later, at Nashville, however, the members coalesced in support of the war effort. The meeting's theme was "The South's Part in Winning the War."

United by the war, the SCHW after 1942 emphasized programs for the postwar South, established several state committees, and projected others. With support from unions and foundations the group anticipated financial stability and a secure existence. By mid-1946 it claimed six thousand members, by the end of that year ten thousand. But disintegration followed quickly. The CIO concentrated its energies on job-conscious organizing drives in the postwar "Operation Dixie," and union support dwindled. Internal disagreements over administration split the leaders. The last convention, at New Orleans in November, 1946, mustered only 269 official delegates—fewer than at Nashville in 1942. Charges of Communist influence mounted. During 1947 and 1948, Clark

---

[104] *Report on Southern Conference for Human Welfare,* 80 Cong., 1 Sess., House Report No. 592 (Washington, 1947); Walter Gellhorn, "Report on a Report of the House Committee on Un-American Activities," in *Harvard Law Review,* LX (1947), 1193–1234. The report was hastily concocted apparently to discredit an SCHW meeting addressed by Henry A. Wallace. Curiously, it omitted altogether Gelders' role in the origins of the organization.

[105] Foreman, "The Decade of Hope," *loc. cit.,* 142; Record, *The Negro and the Communist Party,* 200–201.

Foreman, chairman since 1942, and other leaders flirted with Henry Wallace's Progressive movement. In November, 1948, it finally disbanded, but left behind an offshoot, the Southern Conference Education Fund under James Dombrowski, which concentrated its efforts on civil rights for Negroes in subsequent decades.[106]

During its decade of existence, the SCHW exerted an imponderable influence. Like the Southern Sociological Congress of the teens, it featured sessions on a variety of regional problems: Southern youth, religion and democracy, rural life, industrial life, citizenship, civil liberties, wage and freight-rate differentials, poverty and landlessness, mob violence, educational and health facilities, social welfare, and housing.[107] On occasion the group sponsored special programs, and through its periodical, *Southern Patriot,* circulated news and information. It did not, however, spark a political movement. It represented not so much the peak of the New Deal as the epilogue, coming after the period of reform legislation and hard on the heels of the ill-fated "purge."

Its one oustanding achievement was to thrust into national debate a rising protest against the poll-tax requirement for voting. But the SCHW was not the only agency in that campaign, which flared spontaneously in the New Deal atmosphere. The Southern Policy Committee, AFL and CIO unions, farm groups, women's and civic clubs, and other organizations had spoken out earlier.[108] In two states repeal had already come. In 1934 Huey Long destroyed Louisiana's poll tax chiefly to increase his own support and to thwart opposition sheriffs who mobilized voting blocs with poll-tax receipts. Similar considerations motivated Florida's repeal in 1937, a move supported by the Pepper faction but spearheaded by a beleaguered legislator from Miami, where gambling and racing interests bought up poll-tax receipts. In 1938 repeal became an issue in Arkansas and Tennessee. President Roosevelt endorsed the movement in a letter to Brooks Hays, one of the Arkansas

---

[106] Krueger, *And Promises to Keep, passim.*

[107] Gellhorn, "A Report on a Report of the House Committee on Un-American Activities," 1226–28.

[108] Frederic D. Ogden, *The Poll Tax in the South* (University, Ala., 1958) , 250–51; Lumpkin, *The South in Progress,* 219–21.

leaders, but in November Arkansas voters defeated a repeal amendment. In Tennessee the Crump forces stalled off repeal, after ex-
pressing support, in part because their adversary, editor Jennings
Perry of the Nashville *Tennessean,* sponsored it.[109] In 1939
eight states retained the poll-tax requirement: Alabama, Arkansas,
Georgia, Mississippi, South Carolina, Tennessee, Texas, and Virginia. In different states the amount varied from $1 to $25, but
four (Alabama, Mississippi, Virginia, and Georgia) imposed a cumulative liability, up to $36.00 in Alabama and $47.00 in Georgia.
All but South Carolina demanded payment for primaries as well as
general elections.[110] Originally advanced as a device to disfan-
chise Negroes, the poll tax also raised a suffrage barrier against
impoverished whites.

Its abolition, therefore, assumed priority among liberals as a
prerequisite to further reform. The "only hope for progressive
democracy in the South lies in the lower economic groups—
particularly the wage earner," Lucy Mason wrote to Eleanor
Roosevelt. "Yet this is the group so largely disfranchised by the
poll-tax requirements of eight southern states." [111] Conservatives,
too, suspected that such analysis had validity. Repeal "would arm
the dispossessed with a political power that the responsible citizens
cannot afford to grant," the Montgomery *Advertiser* editorialized
in 1938. It "would invest the pauperized thousands of our people
with the balance of power in Alabama politics." [112]

In February, 1939, the SCHW Executive Board created a Civil
Rights Committee, which concentrated on the poll tax. Sparked
by Mrs. Virginia Foster Durr of Alabama, the committee drafted a
bill for Federal abolition and after futile search for a Southern
sponsor got Representative Lee E. Geyer, California Democrat, to
introduce it. Reintroduced later, the Geyer bill lay in committee

---

[109] Ogden, *The Poll Tax in the South,* 179–85, 193–97, 224–26; Jennings Perry,
Democracy Begins at Home: The Tennessee Fight on the Poll Tax (Philadelphia
and New York, 1944) ; George C. Stoney, "Suffrage in the South, Part I. The Poll
Tax," in *Survey Graphic,* XXIX (January, 1940) , 5–9, 41–43.

[110] Key, *Southern Politics in State and Nation,* 579–82.

[111] Lucy Randolph Mason to Eleanor Roosevelt, February 11, 1938, in Mason
Papers.

[112] Montgomery *Advertiser,* n.d., quoted in Lumpkin, *The South in Progress,*
218.

until discharged by petition and passed by the House in October, 1941. In the Senate Claude Pepper proposed to declare the tax an unconstitutional qualification for voters in either primaries or general elections. "I envisage a South where the feudal system will remain a beautiful romantic legend," Pepper told his colleagues, "but where democracy shall practically be a functioning institution." In 1942 the Senate Judiciary Committee substituted his bill for Geyer's, but the other Southern Senators sounded the battle cries of states' rights, white supremacy, and anticommunism until the bill was abandoned. The House again passed anti-poll-tax bills in 1943, 1945, 1947, and 1949. All of them stagnated in the Senate.[113]

During 1941 Mrs. Durr transformed the SCHW Civil Rights Committee into a National Committee to Abolish the Poll Tax. Another group, founded the same year, worked mainly for state action: the Southern Electoral Reform League, headed by Moss A. Plunkett of Virginia, with subsidiaries in Virginia and Georgia. Virginia remained loyal to the Byrd forces, which prevented action, but Georgia experienced a sudden conversion. When Governor Ellis Arnall proposed a poll-tax study in 1944, Eugene Talmadge abruptly took the initiative by endorsing repeal. Arnall then demanded action and the legislature moved quickly in February, 1945.[114] In the late 1940's the anti-poll-tax groups lapsed into inactivity, but efforts for national and state action continued. Ventilation of the issue inspired a growing public sentiment against the restriction.[115]

The frustration of the Southern Conference ultras was characteristic among those who demanded ideological consistency in American statecraft. The spectacle of one-party politics in the Southern states still defied logic, with its personality cults, its undisciplined legislatures, its kaleidoscopic factions, and the resul-

[113] Ogden, *Poll Tax in the South,* 241–49; Francis P. Locke, "Claude D. Pepper 'Champion of the Belligerent Democracy,'" in Salter, *Public Men in and out of Office,* 267.

[114] Ogden, *Poll Tax in the South,* 185–88.

[115] *Ibid.,* 251–53. Two more states acted later: South Carolina in 1951, Tennessee in 1951 and 1953. The Twenty-Fourth Amendment (1964) eliminated the poll tax in Federal elections and a Supreme Court decision, Harper *v.* Virginia Board of Elections, 383 U.S. 663 (1966), ruled it out in others.

tant difficulty of defining policies. Yet all Southern states felt the effect of the New Deal programs in their administrations and some, notably Oklahoma under E. M. Marland and Georgia under E. D. Rivers, attempted "Little New Deals" at home.

Marland, an oil magnate who lost out to the House of Morgan in 1930, found that his grudge against the "wolves of Wall Street," his former philanthropies, and his generosity toward labor afforded bridges to the common man and the New Deal. Elected to Congress in 1932, he asked the voters in 1934 to make him governor and "bring the New Deal to Oklahoma." "We are coming to a new thought," he proclaimed before his inauguration. "It is the duty of the government to provide every man able to work . . . with employment and to take care of those unable to work." [116]

His inaugural address elaborated a vision of public works, subsistence homesteads for the unemployed, a network of multiple-purpose dams, state-owned mills to process native resources and provide staple goods for the indigent. But in the end his main achievement was the Interstate Oil Compact. The legislature in 1935–1936 gave him a planning board, a new highway patrol, additional help for the schools, and a sales tax to match Federal welfare funds. But an economy-minded House dominated by Speaker Leon C. "Red" Phillips, the next governor, refused money for other new programs and slashed appropriations for existing departments. The next legislature ran up a record of extravagance more embarrassing to Marland than the earlier obstruction and ran wild with patronage in the highway, tax, and welfare areas until, in the case of the latter, Federal standards forced replacement of precinct workers by "sorority sisters"—trained welfare workers. Oklahoma like other Southern states was ill-prepared for sudden transition from an agrarian, patronage-minded commonwealth to the new welfare state. And Marland perpetuated the state's tradition of inept governors.[117]

Georgia experienced more elaborate reforms, but a kindred disappointment, after Eurith D. "Ed" Rivers broke with Tal-

[116] Quoted in Scales, "Oklahoma Politics," 362, 374.

[117] *Ibid.*, 356–93; McReynolds, *Oklahoma: A History of the Sooner State*, 368–76.

madge and rode Roosevelt's coattails into the governorship in 1936. Abruptly Rivers thrust Georgia into the new era. He wangled amendments securing the supreme court against gubernatorial dictation and permitting the General Assembly to convene itself. He pushed through state guarantee of a seven-month school term, free textbooks, and welfare programs; reorganized state education, health, and welfare agencies; moved to comply with Federal standards in highway construction; set up new state employment, housing, and planning boards; extended homestead and property tax exemptions. But revenues were inadequate to the burden, even with increased income taxes, new liquor levies, a graduated scale on automobile licenses, and a chain store tax. After Rivers' re-election in 1938 the bills came due but rising calls for "no more taxes" blocked additional levies.

In its last year the Rivers administration disintegrated. An effort to divert highway funds to schools led Rivers to use the Talmadge tactic of martial law until the state supreme court ruled against him. Investigation of the highway department brought Federal indictments against Hiram Evans, once Imperial Wizard of the Klan, now an asphalt dealer and highway department purchasing agent. The granting of wholesale pardons rounded out the picture. In 1940 Georgia yielded again to Talmadge and returned the bucolic leader to office—temporarily, it turned out.[118]

In most states, however, the division was not drawn so sharply along New Deal lines. South Carolina's Olin D. Johnston became a "New Deal" governor in 1935, but his rise from bobbin boy to governor stemmed from local factors: Upcountry hostility to alleged frauds in Charleston and to a highway department in alliance with the "Barnwell Ring," patrician opposition to Cole Blease, Johnston's appeal to Blease's mill-village constituents. Johnston, like Talmadge, mobilized the militia against the highway department, but lost the battle in the legislature and the courts. He was more successful in other moves: a liberalized workmen's compensation law, a forty-hour week for textiles, free textbooks, reduced prices on automobile tags, prison reform, and entry into social security

[118] Roy E. Fossett, "The Impact of the New Deal on Georgia Politics, 1933–1941" (Ph.D. dissertation, University of Florida, 1960), 207–69; E. Merton Coulter, *Georgia: A Short History* (Chapel Hill, 1947), 440–43.

programs. "My election," he declared belligerently, ". . . did not meet with the approval of the blue-bloods and aristocrats of this State, to whom I was obnoxious simply because I had come from poor but honorable parentage." [119]

His successor, Burnet R. Maybank, however, was a New Dealer of another stripe, a blue-blood of ancient vintage, a descendant of Robert Barnwell Rhett. Allied with Byrnes, Maybank as mayor of Charleston and chairman of the Santee-Cooper power project wielded a golden touch with the New Deal to bring the Low Country out of the doldrums. As governor he continued to stress economic development. The state needed more industries before it could finance "the progressive reforms we need in the fields of old age pensions, housing, public health and education," he said. "I don't propose to get them here by offering cheap labor and tax subsidies. Therefore we've got to sell ourselves with cheap power and other natural advantages." [120]

Governors of whatever persuasion, like Maybank, tapped the reservoir of Federal aid. Even Talmadge used Federal money to balance his budget and David Scholz of Florida, otherwise undistinguished, gained repute as a New Dealer by his receptivity to Washington's largess.[121] Occasionally an editorialist would note the inconsistency between the rush for Federal money and the rhetoric of states' rights. "Where in the entire nation is there a commonwealth that seeks to maintain its rights by the simplest, most effective method—that of discharging its duties?" the Richmond *News Leader* asked. "Virginia now sees her Governor riding to Washington and waiting on a bureaucrat—not to say what Virginia will undertake for the protection of her needy but to ask how little she must do in order to have federal agents dispense federal funds!" [122]

[119] John E. Huss, *Senator for the South: A Biography of Olin D. Johnston* (Garden City, N.Y., 1961), 65–80; Henry Steele Commager, "A South Carolina Dictator," in *Current History*, XLIII (1936), 568–72.

[120] Edward B. Talty, "A New Leader in the New South," in *Christian Science Monitor*, March 30, 1940; and LeRoy M. Want, "On the Job: Mayor of Charleston," Charleston *News and Courier*, March 7, 1937, both in Maybank Scrapbooks (South Carolina Department of Archives and History).

[121] Merlin G. Cox, "David Sholtz: New Deal Governor of Florida," in *Florida Historical Quarterly*, XLIII (1964–1965), 142–52.

[122] Richmond *News-Leader*, April 20, 1934.

Virginia was one of three states, with North Carolina and Tennessee, where fairly cohesive majority factions retained their strength by bending in the winds of change. Senator Byrd headed Virginia's machine, which he had perfected in his reorganization of state government during the 1920's. Key figures in the organization were E. R. Combs, state comptroller and chairman of the state compensation board, whose power over the incomes of county officials kept them in "an understanding and sympathetic frame of mind," and the circuit judges, named by the General Assembly, who appointed the electoral boards. In 1935, however, Lieutenant Governor James H. Price startled the oligarchy by announcing for governor in 1937. To a network of personal friends Price added reformers and New Dealers. The organization, after a protracted silence, accepted him rather than risk a bruising fight. In 1938 Governor Price took Virginia into the Social Security system, which a reluctant legislature had refused to join, and gained recognition as chief dispenser of Federal patronage. In 1939, however, Senators Byrd and Glass prevented confirmation of a Price candidate for Federal judge, and in 1940 a hostile legislature defeated his proposals for reorganization. In 1941 the oligarchy regained undisputed control under Governor Colgate Darden, one of its abler and more progressive leaders.[123]

North Carolina's peculiar blend of progressive conservatism continued under the "Shelby Dynasty" that supplanted the "Simmons Machine" after the old Senator's apostasy in 1928. In 1932 Governor O. Max Gardner picked J. C. B. Ehringhaus as successor. Factional struggle assumed a sectional form: a dominant organization in the mountain, Piedmont, and the northeastern counties versus agrarian insurgents in the eastern tobacco belt. But it involved also a fundamental difference of philosophy, the machine supporting Gardner's program of centralization and efficiency, the rebels emphasizing home rule and democracy. Under Ehringhaus the insurgents focused their attack on the administration's sales tax, and in 1936 backed a young legislator, Dr. Ralph

[123] Herman L. Horn, "The Growth and Development of the Democratic Party in Virginia Since 1890" (Ph.D. dissertation, Duke University, 1950), 423-43; Key, *Southern Politics in State and Nation*, 19-23; George W. Spicer, "Gubernatorial Leadership in Virginia," in *Public Administration Review*, I (1941), 441-57.

McDonald of Winston-Salem, former professor at Salem College, who had fired enthusiasm by his attacks on the levy. McDonald promised a "Little New Deal" for North Carolina, but the organization rallied to Clyde R. Hoey, Gardner's brother-in-law, turned back the challenge, and made a clean sweep of state offices.[124]

Tennessee also presented a pattern of playing both ends against the middle. Edward H. Crump, long a power in Memphis and its impregnable boss after 1928, delivered a solid bloc of votes from Shelby County. His junior partner, Senator Kenneth McKellar, dispensed Federal patronage to Democrats in East Tennessee, where Republicans dominated local governments. With these bases of operation and a rare gift for maneuver, timing, and invective, Crump backed and probably determined the winner in every gubernatorial primary from 1930 through 1946—in turn, Henry Horton, Hill McAlister, Gordon Browning, Prentice Cooper, and Jim Nance McCord. Through it all Crump and McKellar maintained good relations with the national administration. The opposition, however, usually mustered a substantial vote and Tennessee's majorities usually represented shifting alliances rather than a coherent faction.[125]

In Louisiana the death of Huey Long delivered the state to a plunderbund that confirmed the martyr's prophecy: "If them fellows ever try to use the powers I've given them, without me to hold them down, they'll all land in the penitentiary." Robert S. Maestri, New Orleans Longite and conservation commissioner, quickly seized command of the organization and endorsed Richard W. Leche, who was elected governor in 1936 with Huey's brother Earl as his lieutenant governor. In New Orleans Maestri presently accepted capitulation by the Choctaw Ring and became mayor. The machine jettisoned the Share-Our-Wealthers, restored diplomatic relations with Washington, and calmed the local opposition by assuming a more conservative stance—among other things the

[124] Puryear, *Democratic Party Dissention in North Carolina, 1928–1936.*

[125] Stanley J. Folmsbee, Robert E. Corlew, and Enoch L. Mitchell, *History of Tennessee* (4 vols.; New York, 1960), II, 350–60; Key, *Southern Politics in State and Nation,* 58–75; Miller, *Mr. Crump of Memphis, passim.*

new regime sponsored a sales tax. Meanwhile the WPA and PWA strewed buildings, hospitals, bridges, and grade crossings around the state.

Halcyon days of plunder lasted until 1939, when James A. Noe, a disaffected Longite, tipped reporters that a Leche supporter was using materials and men from Louisiana State University to construct a new home. The WPA began to inquire into university policies, whereupon Leche resigned because of "arthritis with complications" and LSU President James M. Smith absconded just ahead of revelations that he had used university bonds as collateral to speculate in wheat futures. Both eventually landed in prison. Other revelations followed in rapid succession: violations of the hot-oil act, padded accounts, "dee-ducts" that flew into the organization's coffers, "double-dipping" (double payment for services or materials), bribes, kickbacks, outright embezzlement. The boodlers rested secure in their control of state courts until O. John Rogge of the Justice Department found an ingenious charge to establish Federal jurisdiction: use of the mails to defraud. "Major criminals," he said, "should not commit minor crimes." [126]

In 1940 Sam Houston Jones, a conservative lawyer from Lake Charles, ran to victory over Earl K. Long. Earl tried to dissociate himself and Huey from The Scandals and called on the commoners to reject "High Hat Sam . . . the guy that pumps perfume under his arms." But in vain. Under Jones and his designated successor, Jimmie H. ("You Are My Sunshine") Davis, the "better element" gave Louisiana eight years of reform government. But Longism outlived its founders. Sam Jones refused to repudiate Huey—"My pappy was for Huey," he said—and retained Huey's program of services for the people. Yet the Long faction kept its identity, harassed and frustrated Jones and Davis. The reign of the Kingfish left the state an enduring bifactionalism so strong as to approximate a party system. Both sides were chastened and moderated by experience but they still presented Louisiana

[126] The succession and the scandals are most fully covered in Kane, *Louisiana Hayride*, 147–426. See also Sindler, *Huey Long's Louisiana*, 117–39, and W. V. Holloway, "The Crash of the Long Machine and Its Aftermath," in *Journal of Politics*, III (1941), 348–62.

voters the dilemma of choice between buccaneering "liberals" and standpat "reformers." [127]

Texas, too, was moving toward an enduring bifactionalism. "The confluence of the anxieties of the newly rich and the repercussions of the New Deal," V. O. Key later wrote, "pushed politics into a battle of conservatives versus liberals, terms of common usage in political discourse in the state." [128] But the emergent bifactionalism manifested itself most clearly in the quadrennial jockeying of pro- and anti-New Dealers for advantage of Presidential conventions and campaigns. Texas began the New Deal era with another period of Fergusonism—Ma Ferguson served again with Pa's help from 1933 to 1935. In 1935 the state promoted its capable young Attorney General, James V. Allred, to the governor's chair for the first of two terms. His administration was marked by the end of prohibition, the Interstate Oil Compact, and the state's entry into the Social Security system. But the legislature dragged its heels about supplying adequate revenues for the program and a growing demand for old-age pensions became the focal issue in the state.

In 1938 the issue elevated to fame one of the more engaging mountebanks of the period, W. Lee "Pass the Biscuits, Pappy" O'Daniel: flour salesman extraordinary, impresario of the Light Crust Doughboys (a radio hillbilly band), and composer of "Beautiful Texas." As gubernatorial candidate O'Daniel championed the Ten Commandments, businesslike government, and pensions for everybody over sixty-five. Masterfully vague about revenues, he garnered a majority in the first primary. True to his promise to oppose a sales tax, he proposed instead a "transaction tax." Few could comprehend the distinction but the legislature rejected it anyway, while extending the pension rolls. By the end of his term the needy aged had smaller allowances than before, but the voters blamed the legislature and re-elected "Pappy" overwhelmingly. In 1941 a new legislature, faced by a $25,000,000 deficit and the probable loss of Federal funds, passed an omnibus

[127] Sindler, *Huey Long's Louisiana*, 140–80 and *passim*; Kane, *Louisiana Hayride*, 427–55. See also Gerald W. Johnson, "Live Demagogues or Dead Gentlemen?" in *Virginia Quarterly Review*, XII (1936), 1–14.

[128] Key, *Southern Politics*, 255.

tax bill that tapped oil and gas production and a variety of other sources. In 1941 Pappy moved on to a new field. In a special senatorial election for a successor to the deceased Morris Sheppard, he edged out Lyndon B. Johnson, Roosevelt's "old, old friend," by 1,311 votes. Already he had shifted to a new specialty that would distinguish his senatorial tenure: "Communistic labor leader racketeers." In 1942 he won a full term.[129]

In surveying the period one is impelled to conclude that state politics in Texas, and in the South, became a kind of shadow-boxing with issues that were determined elsewhere. The essential decision for pensions was made in Washington, not in Texas. The issue made O'Daniel, not O'Daniel the issue. Oklahoma and Georgia had "Little New Deals," the Virginia machine experienced the Price rebellion, largely because the previous leaders had obstructed Federal programs that other states accepted more quietly. The welfare revolution in the states was engineered in Washington, not in Austin or Richmond or Little Rock. The administration did force new issues into state politics and did lure the states into new commitments. Yet if the New Deal fundamentally altered Federal-state relations, Roosevelt, like Wilson, failed in any fundamental way to reshape the amorphous factionalism below the Potomac.

[129] Richardson, *Texas; The Lone Star State,* 322–31, 419; Seth Shepard McKay, *Texas Politics, 1906–1944* (Lubbock, 1952), 240–390; Seth Shepard McKay, *W. Lee O'Daniel and Texas Politics, 1938–1942* ([Lubbock], 1944).

CHAPTER XIX

TRADITION AND TRANSITION: THE SOUTHERN RENAISSANCE

SOUTHERN writers discovered regionalism before the sociologists. In the 1920's they laid the foundations for regional rediscovery; by the 1930's they were charting the intricate designs of meaning in the transition of Southern life. The resultant structure of Southern literature was, as George Marion O'Donnell wrote of William Faulkner's work, "built around the conflict between traditionalism and the anti-traditional modern world in which it is immersed." [1] With maturation the literary groups and little magazines of the 1920's passed from view. Only the Fugitive-Agrarian poets retained a degree of cohesion—enough indeed to form a central directorate that promulgated the orthodox canons of the Southern Renaissance—but they had scattered from Nashville. Southern literature thenceforth grew mainly from the solitary cultivation of individual genius.

In 1929 two vital figures emerged: Thomas Wolfe, with *Look Homeward, Angel,* and William Faulkner, with his first Yoknapatawpha novels, *Sartoris* and *The Sound and the Fury.* Fame rushed in first upon Wolfe. His book, Leo Gurko said, "was the nearest thing to a literary thunderbolt in the twentieth century." [2] The appraisal was excessive, but the shock of recognition electrified Wolfe's native Asheville, which became in the last golden October of the 1920's a classic example of the scandalized community. "Most of the Asheville people who appear in the novel wear their most unpleasant guises," a local reviewer warned.

---

[1] George Marion O'Donnell, "Faulkner's Mythology," in *Kenyon Review,* I (1939), 285.

[2] Leo Gurko, *The Angry Decade* (New York, 1947), 29.

"Against the Victorian morality and the Bourbon aristocracy of the South," Wolfe had "turned in all his fury," his former classmate, Jonathan Daniels wrote. "North Carolina and the South are spat upon." [3]

The reaction was not an uncommon response to products of the Renaissance, created by authors who, like Wolfe, had experienced separation from their origins, had "outgrown the dimensions" of their communities, and looked back from new perspectives acquired in travel and education.[4] After 1916, when Wolfe had left for the University of North Carolina, he returned to Asheville only for brief visits. He studied at Harvard under John Livingston Lowes and George Pierce Baker, tried to market plays in New York, taught English at New York University, made several trips to Europe, had a tumultuous love affair, and began his first book in London in 1926. After its publication, a Guggenheim Fellowship and income from writing freed him from teaching. He wandered through Europe and America, returning always to home base in New York, until in 1938 he fell ill during a Western tour and died in the Johns Hopkins Hospital, not yet thirty-eight years old.[5]

The far-flung scenes of his adult life, and of his books, made Wolfe in many ways more cosmopolitan than regional. He "was born in the South," Maxwell Geismar wrote, "but he shared with it little except the accident of birth." [6] To those who read his exposures of tawdry hypocrisy, his condemnation of the South's "murderous entrenchment against all new life," his picture of the "stricken, wounded 'Southness' of cruelty and lust," the relationship seemed one of rejection. Wolfe himself thought he was more American than Southern and laid ambitious plans to produce a national epic, yet that in turn led back to his origins. "The people

[3] Quoted in Elizabeth Nowell, *Thomas Wolfe: A Biography* (Garden City, N.Y., 1960), 151. See also George W. McCoy, "Asheville and Thomas Wolfe," in *North Carolina Historical Review*, XXX (1953), 200–17.

[4] See Louis D. Rubin, Jr., *The Faraway Country: Writers of the Modern South* (Seattle, 1963), 3–20.

[5] Nowell, *Thomas Wolfe: A Biography,* is the only full-length biography, but relies heavily on the autobiographical character of the novels. See also Kennedy, *The Window of Memory.*

[6] Maxwell Geismar, *Writers in Crisis* (Boston, 1942), 196.

of North Carolina are like that wonderful earth," he wrote to his editor. "I am going to *tell the truth* about these people and, by God, it is the truth about America." [7]

So, for all his Gargantuan lust for experience and knowledge, his daemonic drive to escape the encircling hills for the "fabled" world outside, his agonized search for some "lost lane-end into heaven," Wolfe never completely severed his roots. *Look Homeward, Angel*, his first novel, remained his most successful; it was the lyrical and agonized biography of Eugene Gant's (actually Wolfe's) youth in Altamont (Asheville). It established him as "the giant among American writers of sensitive youth fiction." [8] Three subsequent books, two edited posthumously from a mountain of manuscript, traced his subsequent wanderings as Eugene Gant in *Of Time and the River* (1935) and as George Webber in *The Web and the Rock* (1939) and *You Can't Go Home Again* (1940). *The Hills Beyond* (1941) contained fragments of an unfinished effort to recapture his mountain heritage.

More perhaps than any contemporary Southern writer, Wolfe was reared amid the experience of change: in boom-town Asheville, in his tumultuous family, in the emergent university at Chapel Hill. From the first book he was obsessed with the passage of time, the existence of the past in the present. In *The Web and the Rock* he exemplified the Southern Renaissance in George Webber's image of the Southern people who had come out of an old house "into a kind of sunlight of another century. . . . They heard wheels coming and the world was *in,* yet they were not yet wholly of that world."

Wolfe was a Southerner, Hugh Holman has noted, "torn by the tensions and issues that thoughtful Southerners feel, oppressed . . . with the tragic nature of life, and feeling . . . a sense of guilt that demands some kind of expiating action." [9] The qualities in his writing that retained the most powerful and lasting appeal were his dual genius for the concrete image on the one hand and

[7] Thomas Wolfe to Maxwell Perkins, December, 1930, in Elizabeth Nowell (ed.), *Letters of Thomas Wolfe* (New York, 1956), 283.

[8] Bradbury, *Renaissance in the South*, 92.

[9] C. Hugh Holman, " 'The Dark, Ruined Helen of His Blood': Thomas Wolfe and the South," in Louis D. Rubin, Jr. and Robert D. Jacobs (eds.), *South: Modern Southern Literature in Its Cultural Setting* (Garden City, N.Y., 1961), 197.

transcendent rhetoric on the other. His books reflected the penchant of Southern writers for the immediate, concrete incident, scene, or character to such an extent that they impressed formalist critics as not novels at all, but vast undisciplined compendia of sensuous impressions. He had the gift—and curse—of total recall, infused with a vitalism that gave his scenes and characters a quality of life beyond life.[10] The rhetoric, however, was a feature more often perceived as associated "with something in the tradition of Southern culture." Alfred Kazin found in it the quality that linked Wolfe to his most significant contemporary, Faulkner. "It is their rhetoric, a mountainous verbal splendor, that holds these writers together," he wrote. "In Faulkner and Wolfe the extravagant and ornamental tradition of Southern rhetoric is manifest." [11]

Faulkner himself ranked Wolfe first among contemporary novelists because he "made the best failure. . . . My admiration for Wolfe is that he tried his best to get it all said; he was willing to throw away style, coherence, all the rules of preciseness, to try to put all the experience of the human heart on the head of a pin, as it were." [12] Faulkner's own achievement, more than Wolfe's, was rooted in the world that produced him. Born in New Albany, Mississippi, in 1897, he grew up in Oxford, Lafayette County, which he transmuted into Jefferson, Yoknapatawpha County, in his fiction.[13] The family fortunes had waned since the days of his tempestuous great-grandfather, Colonel William C. Falkner, Mexican and Civil War veteran, railroad builder, and author of a melodramatic romance, *The White Rose of Memphis* (1880),

[10] Bela Kussy, "The Vitalist Trend and Thomas Wolfe," in *Sewanee Review*, L (1942), 306–24.

[11] Kazin, *On Native Grounds*, 468; Joseph Warren Beach, *American Fiction, 1920–1940* (New York, 1960), 211. See also Floyd C. Watkins, "Rhetoric in Southern Writing: Wolfe," in *Georgia Review*, XII (1958), 6–9.

[12] Quoted in Richard Walser (ed.), *The Enigma of Thomas Wolfe* (Cambridge, 1953), vii.

[13] Except where otherwise noted, biographical details are from Margaret Patricia Ford and Suzanne Kincaid, "Biographical Sketch," in *Who's Who in Faulkner* (Baton Rouge, 1963), 3–12. See also Ward Miner, *The World of William Faulkner* (Durham, N.C., 1952); and Robert Coughlan, *The Private World of William Faulkner* (New York, 1954). It should be remembered that Faulkner defended his privacy and exhibited a perverse disdain for routine fact in answering questions about himself.

who was finally shot down by a former business partner turned political rival. The author's father quietly ran a livery stable and hardware store, then served as secretary and business manager of the state university.

After brief wartime service with the Royal Air Force in Canada, Faulkner passed the postwar decade in what seemed to his fellow townsmen an aimless drifting. Admitted to the university as a special student, he soon dropped out, worked at odd jobs, wrote poems and stories, wandered about in an abstracted manner, affected a kind of aristocratic disdain for community opinion, became a town eccentric, "Count No-count" to the local wags. In 1921 he worked briefly in a New York bookshop, then returned for a disastrous tenure as university postmaster. In 1924 he brought out *The Marble Faun,* a book of verse, and in 1925 went to New Orleans, where he wrote *Soldiers' Pay* (1926) and collected material for *Mosquitoes* (1927). He then shipped out for a brief expatriation in Europe, and, after knocking around the Gulf Coast, finally returned to Oxford.

It was there, in writing *Sartoris,* that he began to discover that his "own little postage stamp of native soil was worth writing about" and that he "would never live long enough to exhaust it." [14] *Sartoris* (1929) introduced Yoknapatawpha County and many of its inhabitants who peopled later novels. In this book a postwar Waste Land unlike that of *Soldiers' Pay* stood out the more starkly against a legend of past glory in the Sartoris family. Young Bayard Sartoris, a veteran denied the romantic end that befell his twin brother who was shot down over France, pursued a kind of gallant death-wish by automobile and airplane until he found release in a plane crash. In the very sound of the name Sartoris, Faulkner wrote, there was "death . . . a glamorous fatality, like silver pennons downrushing at sunset, or a dying fall of horns along the road to Roncevaux."

With *Sartoris* and the creation of his mythical kingdom, Yoknapatawpha, Faulkner kindled a blaze of creative energy. Next, as he put it, he wrote his guts into *The Sound and the Fury.* Again it was the story of a demoralized family, told from the

[14] Malcolm Cowley (ed.), *Writers at Work: The Paris Review Interviews* (New York, 1958), 141.

viewpoints of three brothers: one an idiot, another near suicide from brooding over his sister's seduction, the third soured and avaricious, driving his illegitimate niece to flight with the money he had stolen from her. In its complexity and gradual unfolding of meaning the book made few concessions to the reader, but it immediately struck critics as a successful experiment in form and technique.

But the critical acclaim buttered no parsnips and Faulkner, recently married, by his own confession decided to invent a "cheap idea . . . deliberately conceived to make money." [15] The result was *Sanctuary,* so terrifying that his publisher hesitated to print it. Meanwhile Faulkner, while shoveling coal on the power plant's night shift, rigged up a wheelbarrow desk and in six weeks wrote *As I Lay Dying* (1930) during the quiet hours from midnight to 4 A.M. This story turned on the pilgrimage of the poor-white Bundrens, grimly determined to honor their promise to bury their wife and mother in Jefferson, despite repeated misadventures. Then the *Sanctuary* galleys came and Faulkner rewrote them, "trying to make something which would not shame *The Sound and the Fury* and *As I Lay Dying* too much." [16] But every page, Clifton Fadiman asserted in a review, was "a calculated assault on one's sense of the normal." [17] The book featured violence, murder, nymphomania, lynching, rape perpetrated with a corncob by the impotent Popeye, and the utter corruption of the victim, teenaged Temple Drake. Faulkner had correctly judged the market. The book sold well, the author exhumed unpublished stories from his archives and published a baker's dozen as *These 13* (1931). Hollywood made a movie of *Sanctuary,* and Faulkner soon discovered that he could support his family by selling himself intermittently into bondage as a Hollywood script writer.

The creative frenzy diminished temporarily with the completion of *Light in August* (1932). Here the central plot revolved about the torment of Joe Christmas, bastard and probably part

[15] William Faulkner, "Introduction," in *Sanctuary* (Modern Library ed., New York, 1932), v.
[16] *Ibid.,* vii.
[17] Quoted in Frederick John Hoffman and Olga W. Vickery (eds.), *William Faulkner: Three Decades of Criticism* (East Lansing, Mich., 1960), 17.

Negro (the uncertainty was part of his torment), pursued by a perverse Calvinism and racism to his death as a fugitive after he killed his mistress, the daughter of a carpetbagger. A parallel plot dealt with Lena Grove, a bovine poor-white girl, who arrived at the beginning to seek the father of her unborn child and left at the end with Byron Bunch, her stolid protector.

It was three years before another novel, *Pylon* (1935), a tale of barnstorming flyers in New Orleans. In 1936 Faulkner began filling in the earlier history of Yoknapatawpha with *Absalom! Absalom!*, a story which unfolded slowly through the fog of history as Quentin Compson, in a series of midnight conversations with Shreve McCannon, his Canadian roommate at Harvard, attempted to reconstruct the story of Sutpen's Hundred from bits and pieces he had picked up. Thomas Sutpen, central figure of the plot, was a mountaineer from western Virginia who made a fortune in Haiti and conceived the "design" of founding a great dynasty in Yoknapatawpha. He brought in a horde of wild slaves to carve his plantation out of a wilderness wrested from the Indians. But the appearance of his mulatto son, born in Haiti, set in motion a fatal train of events that thwarted the "design," and finally left only a half-witted and part-Negro great-grandson to howl through the ashes and run away when the house burned in 1909.

In *The Unvanquished* (1938) Faulkner returned to the Compson family of the Civil War-Reconstruction period. In *The Wild Palms* (1939) Faulkner departed from Yoknapatawpha again to give in alternate chapters the stories of a runaway wife, smitten with a medical student, and a runaway convict, unwillingly swept away in a Mississippi flood with a pregnant woman he had been sent to rescue.

A good many of Faulkner's earliest reviewers and critics interpreted him as the exemplar of a new school of Gothic horror. He seemed the leader in a new "cult of cruelty," one among a group who "set themselves up in a rather profitable literary business with unmitigated cruelties and abnormalities as their regular stock in trade." Faulkner's world, Granville Hicks said, echoed "with the hideous trampling march of lust and disease, brutality and death." All this he compounded with excessive obscurity, slow unfolding of meaning, convoluted syntax, and runaway rhetoric. *Absalom!*

William Faulkner in the Early Thirties

Thomas Wolfe with His Manuscript

President Roosevelt Calls for the Defeat of Senator George, Barnesville, Georgia, August 11, 1938. Senator George is at the center in dark coat.

Student Demonstration Against Eugene Talmadge, Atlanta, 1941. Effigy of Talmadge is being hoisted atop statue of Tom Watson on State Capitol grounds.

Assembly Line, B-24 Liberators, Consolidated Aircraft Corporation, Fort Worth, Texas, 1942

Absalom!, Clifton Fadiman said, exploited the "Non-Stop or Life Sentence," a method of "Anti-Narrative, a set of complex devices used to keep the story from being told." [18] As Faulkner was linked to Wolfe by a common gift of rhetoric, it was his fate to be linked to Erskine Caldwell for other qualities. He and Caldwell were twin apostles of depravity, twin delineators of the benighted South, the authors of novels scandalous in a sense that transcended Wolfe's exposé of Asheville.

Out of the subculture of Southern poverty Erskine Caldwell created a fantastic literary world all his own. Born at White Oak, Georgia, in 1903, the son of an Associate Reformed Presbyterian preacher, he grew up in small towns of the Southeast, worked at odd jobs, ran off to New Orleans in his second year at Erskine College, and later attended the University of Virginia where, in the growing compulsion to write, he neglected his assignments and never finished. After a year on the Atlanta *Journal* he left in 1926 for Maine, where he collected rejection slips and supported his family by raising potatoes and selling review copies of books. Persistence conquered when, in 1929, he sold his first stories and published two novelettes: *The Bastard* and *Poor Fool*. The next year he brought out *American Earth,* a collection of stories with both Southern and New England locales.[19]

But his first triumph was *Tobacco Road* (1932), in which he recaptured the Old Southwest's literary tradition of poor-white depravity and humor. The idea first came to him one midsummer afternoon, Caldwell said, when he walked a dusty road through "clusters of stunted, scrawny, scraggly cotton plants trying vainly to exist in the depleted soil" and saw groups of apathetic people leaning against their "two-room shacks with sagging joists and roofs," waiting for the cotton to mature.[20] In the novel, Jeeter Lester and his family caricatured a people disinherited by agricultural collapse and brutalized by deprivation. The story was sordid and oppressive, but in the very absurdity of the characters' be-

[18] Alan Reynolds Thompson, Granville Hicks, and Clifton Fadiman, quoted in Hoffman and Vickery (eds.), *William Faulkner*, 2, 3. 20.

[19] Erskine Caldwell, *Call It Experience* (New York, 1951), 5, 11–90.

[20] Erskine Caldwell, "Introduction," in *Tobacco Road* (Modern Library ed., New York, 1940).

havior it evoked a kind of grim comedy. Drawn sympathetically, Robert Cantwell suggested, the characters would have made Caldwell's picture but a copy of "An Elegy in a Country Churchyard"; "as comic characters, they make that poverty unforgettable." [21] The book got favorable notices, but sales moved slowly until it became a Broadway play in 1933. Then it became an immediate *succès de scandale,* shocking and titillating millions in the form of stage play, motion picture, and book.

Books and stories thereafter rolled from Caldwell's typewriter in profusion, most of them set in that outrageous world around Tobacco Road. In *God's Little Acre* (1933) the atmosphere was less oppressive and the comedy more zestful, but the lunacy much the same: Ty Ty Walden's gold fever, Will Thompson's satryriasis, the climactic scenes in which Thompson forcibly took Griselda, the object of his lust, then proceeded in his exaltation to a foredoomed effort to seize and operate a mill from which the workers were locked out. The attempt resulted in his death at the hands of a mill guard. *Journeyman* (1935) was chiefly the story of Semon Dye, itinerant evangelist and lecher, who exploited the emotional starvation of rural Georgia. *Trouble in July* (1940) was a classic picture of a remote community in the throes of a lynching crisis. *Georgia Boy* (1943), in contrast to most of the earlier books, was pure comedy for its own sake: a boy's account of his father's zany escapades. *Tragic Ground* (1944) returned to more familiar themes with the Spence Douthits, migrants to the city whose incompetence repeatedly foiled the welfare department.

Caldwell had "one of the most fertile humorous imaginations in American literature." [22] His comedy radiated a peculiar quality of the absurd, the unexpected, the ridiculous, the grotesque. His characters lived mostly in a setting of limited instincts, and their ignorance of the larger world afforded much of the comic surprise. They displayed a perverse indifference to the most desperate situations, a guiltless amorality, a fanatical determination to pur-

[21] Robert Cantwell, "Caldwell's Characters: Why Don't They Leave," in *Georgia Review,* XI (1957), 253.

[22] Robert Cantwell, *The Humorous Side of Erskine Caldwell* (New York, 1951), xxi.

sue hopeless projects. But Caldwell's vehicle of comedy carried also a heavy burden of tragedy and social criticism. *Tobacco Road* became a byword for rural poverty and established a vogue of tenant literature for a decade. "If conditions are ever better in the South, if the treatment of the colored man is ever more humane," wrote Oscar Cargill, "we are going to owe a very great debt to Erskine Caldwell." [23]

By 1945, through dogged attention to his typewriter, Caldwell had produced twenty-four books: novels, stories, and documentaries. But favorable reviews gradually gave way to the charge that he had taken to grinding out paperback dreadfuls to formula.[24] The decline in critical esteem, however, ran counter to a steady rise in popularity that made him the most widely read American writer of the twentieth century. By 1955 *God's Little Acre* ranked third among the best sellers since 1895, with more than 6,500,000 copies sold; six other Caldwell books had sold more than 2,000,000 each.[25] There could be no question that much of this represented a triumph of prurience and shock. Success came, John Donald Wade asserted, because he presented "the detached, nervous, thrill-goaded metro-cosmopolitans of his day" with characters they could "at once most envy and marvel over and deplore." Early reviewers, Wade noted, "recognized his insistence on sex with the discernment of a Sahara-dweller in recognizing the sun." The wardens of public morals only added spice with attempts at suppression.[26]

Among literary stars of the first magnitude T. S. Stribling blazed most briefly, then flickered out. His most mature and successful work was in his historical trilogy: *The Forge* (1931), *The Store* (1932), and *Unfinished Cathedral* (1934). A quartet of earlier novels, set in his native Tennessee, had established him as a kind of Southern Sinclair Lewis, exposing the vacuity of the vil-

[23] Oscar Cargill, *Intellectual America: Ideas on the March* (New York, 1941), 396.

[24] See, for example, Willard Thorp, *American Writing in the Twentieth Century* (Cambridge, 1960), 262: "The inevitable Caldwell novel or collection of stories (there is a new one on the racks every few months) repeats the earlier shootings and shack-ups."

[25] Alice Payne Hackett, *60 Years of Best Sellers* (New York, 1956), 12.

[26] John Donald Wade, "Sweet Are the Uses of Degeneracy," in *Southern Review*, I (1935–1936), 453, 466. The earliest attempt at censorship was against *God's Little Acre* by the New York Society for the Suppression of Vice in 1933. Caldwell, *Call It Experience*, 137–38. See also *Publisher's Weekly*, CLV (1949), 1312.

lage South. Now he undertook an historical panorama of northern Alabama that stretched in time from the 1860's to the 1920's. The fundamental context was economic progression from the downfall of slavery in the first volume through the rise of sharecropping and the country merchant in the second to urbanization and the Muscle Shoals boom in the third. Within that pattern Stribling wove stories of families which represented the plantation tradition, the rising middle class, hill people, storekeepers, poor whites, and Negroes. The unusually prolonged lives of Miltiades Vaiden, eventually the town banker, and his quadroon half-sister, Gracie, provided a unifying device. Two themes established in the earlier novels ran through the trilogy: the constricting effect of the provincial mind and the injustice of Southern race relations. Stribling's forte was an irony that exposed contradictory, irrational, and often violent turns of the Southern mind, which showed up most strikingly in the double standards of race relations.

The Store won the Pulitzer Prize and *Unfinished Cathedral* elicited fanfares from the literary reviews; but then, after two unsuccessful novels on social problems in the North, Stribling's springs ran dry. In retrospect his work lacks artistry: his characters were social types, his missionary zeal betrayed him, plot and satire almost alone carried the burden of the novels. Stribling's Tennessee Valley exhibited a shallow and rootless society, and he quarreled with its lack of logic and human sympathy. But few would question the later judgment that, compared with Faulkner and Caldwell, Stribling was "the one most rooted in daily actuality." [27]

Almost the same phrase was used to characterize Hamilton Basso's "quality of genuine intellect, rooted in actuality." [28] Basso, Alfred Kazin wrote in 1939, "belongs to that small and earnest group of young Southern novelists who have not only heard of Appomattox, but are quite willing to forget it." His South was "an old, run-down but still charming house, slightly

[27] George J. Becker, "T. S. Stribling: Pattern in Black and White," in *American Quarterly*, IV (1952), 203.

[28] Evelyn Scott, Review of *Days Before Lent*, in *Saturday Review of Literature*, XX (August 5, 1939), 7.

seedy and fearful, but one in which men can still live." [29] Born in New Orleans, Basso as a Tulane student had circulated in the *Double Dealer* group. Off and on during the 1930's he lived in the North Carolina mountains, but wandered off to Aiken, New York, Europe, and other places. Louisiana and South Carolina were the favorite settings for his fiction; he created no mythical kingdom like Faulkner's Yoknapatawpha or Stribling's Tennessee Valley. *Cinnamon Seed* (1934), set on a plantation near New Orleans, was the story of Dekker Blackheath, a young man torn between the old ways and the new. *In Their Own Image* (1935) explored the small-town narrowness that frustrated a young liberal who tried to help a Negro physician start a hospital. *Days Before Lent* (1939) placed against a backdrop of New Orleans' Mardi Gras the story of Dr. Jason Kent's decision to stay and serve rather than pursue glittering opportunities, and *Sun in Capricorn* (1943) was based on Huey Long's career. Through all this Basso supported himself by newspaper and periodical journalism. None of his books scored a commercial success until *The View From Pompey's Head* (1954).[30]

Basso, Stribling, and Ellen Glasgow, the pioneer realist who was still exploring the life and manners of Queenboro, grappled with problems of the village and urban South. But they and other writers omitted the Southern factory worker from any significant role in fiction. The current fashion of the "proletarian novel" found little expression in the South except in a brief freshet of books set off by the Gastonia strike. The most successful of these were Olive Tilford Dargan's *Call Home the Heart* (1932), published under the pseudonym of Fielding Burke, and Grace Lumpkin's *To Make My Bread* (1932); both books followed the movement of mountain people to the mill village and their conversion to radicalism in strikes that paralleled the Gastonia affair. Both exploited mountain dialect and folkways to such a degree

[29] Alfred Kazin, Review of *Days Before Lent*, in *New York Times Book Review*, August 6, 1939, p. 5.

[30] Obituary in New York *Times*, May 14, 1964. See also Stanley J. Kunitz (ed.), *Twentieth Century Authors: First Supplement* (New York, 1955), 54; and Malcolm Cowley, "The Writer as Craftsman," in *Saturday Review*, XLVII (June 27, 1964), 17–18.

that they became "in effect local-color fiction performed with a radical purpose." [31] But the larger realities of Southern labor would not fit the Procrustean bed of Marxism, and the theme quickly played out.

However, serious writers like Faulkner, Stribling, Caldwell, and Basso frequently brought Negroes and problems of race relations into the foreground, and Negro-centered fiction became a common vehicle of social criticism.[32] Gilmore Millen of Memphis in *Sweet Man* (1930) created the prototype of many novels in which the Negro protagonist suffered oppression and injustice from the white man's world until driven to outbursts of hatred and violence. Welbourn Kelley's *Inchin' Along* (1932) and Robert Rylee's *Deep Dark River* (1935) offered indictments of wrongs against Negro tenants. Julian Meade's *The Back Door* (1938) dealt with a Negro tobacco worker dying of tuberculosis while the white community argued about a sanatorium. James Saxon Childers' *A Novel About a White Man and a Black Man in the Deep South* (1936) focused on two men denied a normal friendship because of community pressures that finally precipitated tragedy. Other books, most notably Lillian Smith's best-seller, *Strange Fruit* (1944), exploited in new variations the old theme of a white man's liaison with a pale mulatto girl.

The local color Negro retreated before the advance of the new types, but lingered in such books as Lyle Saxon's *Children of Strangers* (1937), a treatment of relations between light and dark Negroes on a Louisiana plantation; Gertrude Shelly and Samuel Stoney's *Po Buckra* (1930), about a young man's foredoomed attempt to rise out of the mixed-blood "brass ankle" group in South Carolina; and Nan Bagby Stephens' *Glory* (1932), which centered around a Negro church in a small Georgia town and a

---

[31] Walter B. Rideout, *The Radical Novel in the United States, 1900–1954* (Cambridge, 1956), 173. Other novels based at least in part on the Gastonia strike were Mary Heaton Vorse, *Strike!* (1930); Sherwood Anderson, *Beyond Desire* (1932); Myra Page, *Gathering Storm* (1932); and William Rollins, *The Shadow Before* (1934). See also William Cunningham, *The Green Corn Rebellion* (1935).

[32] Numerous examples may be found in Bradbury, *Renaissance in the South*, 140–50; Hugh M. Gloster, *Negro Voices in American Fiction* (Chapel Hill, 1948), 196–251; and Sterling Brown, *The Negro in American Fiction*, (Washington, 1937), 151–206.

lecherous preacher who betrayed his congregation. Traditional attitudes were more obtrusive in Mrs. L. M. Alexander's *Candy* (1934), a story of primitive exotics interspersed with laments at the ingratitude of Negroes lured from the plantation to wicked Harlem; in Ronald Kirkbride's *Dark Surrender* (1933), in which a Negro graduate of Harvard informed his old South Carolina boss that Negroes with aspirations were not "true negroes" and were doomed to unhappiness; and in Archibald Rutledge's Low Country pastorals such as *It Will Be Daybreak Soon* (1939).

Negro novelists, the few who reached publication, moved sharply away from jazz exoticism toward themes of protest and explorations of the American Negro's tradition: slavery, folk culture, the Great Migration, the black ghettoes of the North.[33] Arna Bontemps, librarian at Fisk University, based his *Black Thunder* (1936) on the Virginia slave insurrection of 1800 with its leader, Gabriel Prosser, as the hero. The novel eulogized the slaves' yearning for freedom, but its power resided in the theme of tragedy and in the spent passion of a lost cause—if a cause rarely celebrated in Southern fiction.

Racial conflict did not obtrude into *Ollie Miss* (1935) by George Wylie Henderson, an Alabama emigré to New York. It was a plantation pastoral about a Negro woman's obsessive desire for a man; only two incidental white characters entered. And few whites appeared in treatments of the rural folk culture by Zora Neale Hurston, who combined the talent of a writer with the training of an anthropologist. Native of an all-Negro town, Eatonton, Florida, she left home as maid to a Gilbert and Sullivan Company, attended Howard University where Alain Locke drew her into the Negro Renaissance, served as secretary to Fannie Hurst, and studied anthropology under Franz Boas at Columbia.[34] A serious student of folklore, she published the results of extensive investigations in Louisiana, Florida, and the West Indies and exploited her knowledge to produce novels with a unique flavor. *Jonah's Gourd Vine* (1934), the first, projected the odyssey

---

[33] Robert Bone, *The Negro Novel in America* (Rev. ed.; New Haven, 1965), 118–19. Bone cited only twelve novels by Negro authors in the 1930's.

[34] Zora Neale Hurston, *Dust Tracks on A Road: An Autobiography* (Philadelphia, 1942).

of John Buddy Pearson, preacher and philanderer, against a vivid background of Negro life. *Their Eyes Were Watching God* (1937), the second and more successful, written in the afterglow of a love affair, told the haunting story of the high-spirited Janie, a dreamer who endured life with two lumpish husbands but found fulfillment in two short years with Tea Cake, a happy-go-lucky vagabond.

The preeminent novel about the Great Migration was *Blood on the Forge* (1941) by William Attaway, himself the son of a doctor who moved from Mississippi to Chicago. It pursued the history of the Moss brothers—Mat, Chinatown, and Melody—shipped North in a boxcar "like hogs headed for market" and their failure to adjust from an agrarian to an industrial setting in the steel mills. But the supreme genius among Negro novelists was another Mississippi migrant to Chicago: Richard Wright. Born on a plantation near Natchez, the son of a matriarch whose husband deserted the family, Wright grew up in the course of moving from town to town, ended his formal schooling with the ninth grade, worked in Memphis and greedily devoured books he borrowed on a white friend's library card, all the while saving up to go North. In Chicago, where he arrived on the eve of the Depression, the Federal Writers' Project gave him an opportunity to perfect his talent, and his effort to be a Communist from 1934 to 1944 gave him an intellectual framework of Marxism—which, however, did not overpower his fierce independence.[35] His first book, *Uncle Tom's Children* (1938), a collection of four novellas, and his autobiographical *Black Boy* (1945) revealed in the very rebellion against racial injustice his ties to the South, for, he wrote, "there had been slowly instilled into my personality and consciousness, black though I was, the culture of the South."[36]

Native Son (1940), his masterpiece, was set in the Chicago he had come to know. It was the story of Bigger Thomas, a product of the Negro ghetto, a man hemmed in and finally impelled to murder by forces beyond his control. "They wouldn't let me live and I killed," he said unrepentantly at the end. Somehow Wright

[35] Bone, *The Negro Novel in America*, 140–44; Richard Wright, *Black Boy: A Record of Childhood and Youth* (Cleveland, 1945).
[36] Wright, *Black Boy*, 298.

managed to sublimate into literary power his bitterness and rage at what he called "The Ethics of Living Jim Crow," in itself an art he never mastered. In the Negro, he wrote, America had "a past tragic enough to appease the spiritual hunger of even a James; and . . . in the oppression of the Negro a shadow athwart our national life dense and heavy enough to satisfy even the gloomy broodings of a Hawthorne." [37]

For an audience long conditioned by attacks on the Benighted South and by the liberation from gentility, Southern literature seemed in the 1930's to be operating still in the context of those themes. In a society convulsed by economic depression and the New Deal, its thrust seemed to be at best a liberal critique of contemporary error, at worst a sensational exposé of degradation that made Cabell's phallicism seem mild by contrast. "Thirty years ago I objected to the evasive idealism in American novels," Ellen Glasgow wrote in 1935. "Nowadays I object to the aimless violence." In the South "we remain incurably romantic," she said. "Only a puff of smoke separates the fabulous Southern hero of the past from the fabulous Southern monster of the present—or the tender dreams of James Lane Allen from the fantastic nightmares of William Faulkner. . . . Has Southern life—or is it only Southern fiction—become one vast, disordered sensibility?" The new quality she labeled "Southern Gothic"—a less elegant Mississippian would later call it the "privy school of literature." [38]

For Gerald Johnson the trends spelled vindication. His prophecy twelve years earlier that the new Southern literature "may wallow in filth" was a "lallapaloosa," he said in 1935. "Above the Potomac and west of the Mississippi . . ." he wrote, "the impression is general that the characteristic Southerners are the horror-mongers," chief among them Stribling, Wolfe, Faulkner, and Caldwell. "These are they who drive the conservative Confederates into apoplexy"—and they very nearly overwhelmed Johnson. *Sanctuary,* he admitted, put him "under the weather for thirty-six hours." But, those who saw only "the morons, the

[37] Richard Wright, "How Bigger Was Born," in *Saturday Review of Literature,* XXII (June 1, 1940), 20.

[38] Ellen Glasgow, "Heroes and Monsters," in *Saturday Review of Literature,* XII (May 4, 1935), 3–4; Rubin, *The Faraway Country,* 14.

perverts, the idiots, the murders, the satyriasis and nymphomania, the lust and lues" overlooked "the horror and pity these things have aroused in some of the best minds of the South . . . the fierce determination that the South . . . shall stand, like Faust, and for her own soul's salvation, gaze into perdition." [39]

The explication of Southern authors in terms of exposure and reform, however, scarcely plumbed the depths of their perception, their historical consciousness, their awareness of the past in the present. Most of them betrayed in some degree a sense of yearning backward from the rootlessness of a changing world, seeking if not finding some anchor in the past. For the Fugitive poets turned Agrarian this assumed the proportions of a conscious movement to seize upon and celebrate tradition—indeed ultimately to create in literature a new tradition. By the late 1930's the fires of agrarianism had flickered out in the pages of the *American Review* and in the last two manifestoes, *Who Owns America?* (1936) and Donald Davidson's *The Attack on Leviathan* (1937). But the glow lingered on in the pages of the *Southern Review* (1935–1942) at Louisiana State; then in the *Kenyon Review* (1939——), begun by John Crowe Ransom after he left Vanderbilt in 1938, and the *Sewanee Review*.

Of the major figures only Donald Davidson remained at Vanderbilt after 1938, and only he remained an unreconstructed Agrarian. By 1945 Ransom looked back on agrarianism as "phantasy," for "without . . . division of labor, and hence modern society, we should have not only no effective science, invention, and scholarship, but nothing to speak of in art." Yet, he wrote, "the agrarian nostalgia was very valuable to the participants, a mode of repentance not itself to be repented." [40] By a kind of paradox befitting their canons the Fugitives carried agrarianism to triumph not in society but in literature. "The practical movement never materialized," John M. Bradbury observed, "but the critical doctrines . . . the negative social verdicts and the positive aesthetic creeds, proved viable products." [41] It was Ransom who created

[39] Gerald W. Johnson, "The Horrible South," in *Virginia Quarterly Review*, XI (1935), 201, 203, 211, 214, 216.

[40] John Crowe Ransom, "Art and the Human Economy," in *Kenyon Review*, VII (1945), 686–87.

[41] John M. Bradbury, *The Fugitives: A Critical Account* (Chapel Hill, 1958), 258.

a name for the new approach, already far advanced, in the title of his book, *The New Criticism* (1941). Tate, Warren, Brooks, and R. P. Blackmur led in its development; in many ways they paralleled English critics like T. S. Eliot, I. A. Richards, and William Empson.

The New Criticism, therefore, while not strictly Southern, was closely associated with the Fugitive-Agrarians. It was, Alfred Kazin suggested, a retreat into literature to secure by a "rarified aesthetics" at least one last citadel for the traditionalists' sense of propriety and order. The New Critics' "preciosity was not an 'escape' from anything," Kazin wrote; "it was a social pressure, subtle and militant in its despair, working against the positivism of the age and sustained by a high contempt for it; a despair in the face of contemporary dissolution and materialism and irreligion that found its locus in the difficulty of modern poetry and prized that difficulty as the mark of its alienation and distinction." [42] Modern writers, in a phrase Brooks borrowed from Eliot, suffered a "dissociation of sensibility"—that is, a separation of their own outlook from the kind of overarching myth or moral order available to writers of other ages. If Agrarians could not establish such an order, they could at least defend literature from the disordering influences of modernity.

Against the claims of science Tate and Ransom advanced the claim for literature, and especially poetry, as a discrete branch of knowledge, imaginative or "mythic" knowledge—in the phrase of Tate's Confederate Ode, "knowledge carried to the heart." The fundamental value of a literary work inhered in the work itself. The proper study of a poem, therefore, focused upon the poem and not upon its author, its historical context, or other external factors. This led to an intense concern with image, symbol, "meaning," technique, the "structural properties" of literature—and an equally intense disapproval of romantic abandon and historical or impressionistic criticism. [43]

The Fugitives' contribution to the new canons developed

---

[42] Kazin, *On Native Grounds*, 426.

[43] For a summary see C. Hugh Holman, "The Defense of Art: Criticism Since 1930," in Floyd Stovall (ed.), *The Development of American Literary Criticism* (Chapel Hill, 1955), 229.

through a succession of essays collected in Ransom's *The World's Body* (1938) and *The New Criticism* (1941), and in Tate's *Reactionary Essays on Poetry and Ideas* (1936) and *Reason in Madness* (1941). Cleanth Brooks undertook a synthesis in *Modern Poetry and the Tradition* (1938), and in *The Well Wrought Urn* (1947) explored such typical concerns of "formalism" as irony, paradox, ambiguity, dramatic context, and organic structure. With Warren he edited *Understanding Poetry* (1938) and *Understanding Fiction* (1943), and with Robert B. Heilman, *Understanding Drama* (1948). By the end of the 1940's the New Critics had so swept the field that one dissenter, poet Robert Hillyer, envisioned a vast conspiracy of critics "wholly concerned with irony, the meaning of meaning, paradoxes, ambiguities, ambivalences, dichotomies—and, indeed, any double-talk," who had left "in the history of American literature . . . a quarter-century of desert where once the aesthetes sterilized the soil." [44]

If that petulant appraisal undervalued the new traditionalists' contribution to a broader awareness of writers and a sharper focus of critics, it gauged correctly their ascendancy in the world of letters. And their canons excluded whole categories of Southern writing. Wolfe's vitalism, for example, and his romantic urge to self-expression only compounded his sin of formlessness. "Shakespeare merely wrote Hamlet," Robert Penn Warren explained; "he was not Hamlet." [45] Caroline Gordon found Wolfe lacking "artistic intelligence," and John Donald Wade convicted him of having abandoned Southern tradition.[46] Wolfe got in some counterblows against the "lily-handed" intellectuals who sought refuge in universities from which they issued "very precious magazines which celebrated the advantages of an agrarian society." [47] Yet, in drawing back toward his heritage, Floyd C. Watkins suggested, "in the end he was much closer to their opinions than even he would

[44] Robert Hillyer, "The Crisis in American Poetry," in *American Mercury*, LXX (1950), 65, 67.

[45] Robert Penn Warren, "The Hamlet of Thomas Wolfe," in Walser (ed.), *The Enigma of Thomas Wolfe*, 132.

[46] Caroline Gordon, quoted in Betty Thompson, "Thomas Wolfe: Two Decades of Criticism," *ibid.*, 305–306; John Donald Wade, "Prodigal," in *Southern Review*, I (1935–1936), 198.

[47] Thomas Wolfe, *The Web and the Rock* (New York, 1939), 242–43.

admit, and closer than any of the Nashville critics have yet realized." [48]

One could not say as much for Caldwell and Stribling. Caldwell carried vitality to the point of "animal burlesque," Brooks charged, and, afflicted with "modern literary sociologism," let his sympathies sap his art.[49] Warren pronounced the anathema on Stribling, and consigned him to "a paragraph in the development, or conceivably the decline, of . . . critical realism." Stribling's books represented "a strange compound of hick-baiting, snobbery, and humanitarianism: in a word, disordered liberalism." [50]

Meanwhile Faulkner's reputation flourished in the climate of the New Criticism. In 1935 Ransom called him the most exciting figure in contemporary literature, adept at modern techniques, "much too bold to content himself with any safe or consistent craftsmanship," and possessing "a sense, the opposite of revolutionary, of society as a fixed order which goes on though private persons err and suffer." Warren and Davidson bestowed similar accolades.[51] But the critical discovery of Faulkner may be dated from 1939, when two significant essays by George Marion O'Donnell and Conrad Aiken began an exploration into the qualities of traditionalism and formalism that Ransom had recognized.[52]

In Ransom's *Kenyon Review,* O'Donnell challenged the view of Faulkner as the leader in a cult of cruelty and nihilism. He was, instead, "really a traditional moralist, in the best sense." The principle unifying his work was "the Southern social-economic-ethical tradition which Mr. Faulkner possesses naturally, as a part of his sensibility," and the conflict between tradition and the modern world. The conflict took form in a central dramatic ten-

[48] Floyd C. Watkins, "Thomas Wolfe and the Nashville Agrarians," in *Georgia Review,* VII (1953), 423.

[49] Cleanth Brooks, "What Deep South Literature Needs," in *Saturday Review of Literature,* XXV (September 19, 1942), 8–9.

[50] Robert Penn Warren, "T. S. Stribling: A Paragraph in the History of Critical Realism," in *American Review,* II (1933–1934), 463, 476.

[51] John Crowe Ransom, "Modern with a Southern Accent," in *Virginia Quarterly Review,* XI (1935), 197–98; Warren, "T. S. Stribling," *loc. cit.,* 479–86; Donald Davidson, "The Trend of Literature," in W. T. Couch (ed.), *Culture in the South,* 193.

[52] O'Donnell, "Faulkner's Mythology," *loc. cit.,* 285–99; Conrad Aiken, "William Faulkner: The Novel as Form," in *The Atlantic Monthly,* CLXIV (1939), 650–54.

sion between the Sartorises and Snopeses (by whatever name in the various novels), one family acting "traditionally," the other having "no ethical code." The Sartoris world faced doom because "in our time the values of Mr. Faulkner's tradition are available to most men only historically." Faulkner, however, had not created mere social types. His characters' humanity was "not limited, ultimately, by their archetypal significance." [53]

This thematic interpretation seemed thoroughly vindicated by the appearance of *The Hamlet* (1940). A sprawling novel, reworked in large part from previously published stories, it followed the rise of Flem Snopes and his myriad relatives from the time his father, Ab Snopes, first appeared in Frenchman's Bend. Later novels, *The Town* (1957) and *The Mansion* (1959), would trace Flem's continued rise to dominance as the town banker in Jefferson. The theme was continued in *Go Down, Moses* (1942), a collection of stories mostly about the relations between the white McCaslins, another "traditional" family, and their colored kin. The collection included "The Bear," a brooding story about the destruction of the wilderness by lumbering and the white man's civilization.

O'Donnell's essay commenced an investigation of Faulkner's myth that other critics fruitfully extended and qualified. Delmore Schwartz, for example, used it to explain the violence in the novels: "the conflict between the idea of the Old South and the progressive actuality of the New South brought Faulkner to the extreme where he can only seize his values, which are those of the idea of the Old South, by imagining them being violated by the most hideous crimes." [54] A valuable correction came in Malcolm Cowley's Introduction to *The Portable Faulkner* (1946), which further elaborated the legend of Yoknapatawpha County, but emphasized that Faulkner hardly qualified as a Bourbon, testing everything against the tradition of the antebellum aristocrats. "They had the virtue of living single-mindedly by a fixed code; but there was also an inherent guilt in their 'design,' their way of life; it was slavery that put a curse on the land," slavery and the

[53] O'Donnell, "Faulkner's Mythology," *loc. cit.,* 285–86, 292, 299.

[54] Delmore Schwartz, "The Fiction of William Faulkner," in *Southern Review,* VII (1941), 156.

other crimes of seizing the Indians' land and despoiling the wilderness.[55]

When *The Portable Faulkner* appeared, all of the books were out of print except *Sanctuary*, but Cowley's preface started a revival that brought Faulkner the Nobel Prize in 1950. But for Cowley, Faulkner remarked, he probably would have been remembered as "the man with the corncob." [56] A lengthy review by Robert Penn Warren reinforced Cowley's effect. "No land in all fiction lives more vividly in its physical presence than this mythical county . . ." he wrote of Yoknapatawpha. Faulkner had "taken our world, with its powerful sense of history, its tangled loyalties, its pains and tensions of transition, and elevated it to the level of a great moral drama on the tragic scale." [57]

The Fugitive-Agrarian-New Critics themselves, despite the diffusion of their activities, continued their contributions to creative literature. In fact they remained the only poets of much consequence. Ransom, to be sure, became so absorbed in teaching, editing, and criticism that in his *Selected Poems* (1945) he added only five poems written after 1927. Davidson remained a polemical essayist to the neglect of both poetry and criticism, but in 1938 brought out a new volume of verse, *Lee in the Mountains and Other Poems*, that included a revised version of "The Tall Men" and reflected his continuing quarrel against a New South which had

> . . . *no faith, even to die. Only a smoulder,*
> *Only an evil burning and a smoke*
> *That hardly lifts even for winds of spring.*[58]

Amid the steel and brick of Nashville, he still cherished, like his Lee in the mountains, a hope that the merciful God waited

---

[55] Malcolm Cowley, "Introduction," in *The Portable Faulkner* (New York, 1945), 14.

[56] C. Hugh Holman, "The Proper Audience of the Critic," in *Georgia Review*, XI (1957), 269.

[57] Robert Penn Warren, "Cowley's Faulkner," in *New Republic*, CXV (1946), 176; Warren, speech at the University of Virginia, quoted in Louis D. Rubin, Jr., "All the King's Meanings," in *Georgia Review*, VIII (1954), 434.

[58] Donald Davidson, "Aunt Maria and the Grounds," in *Lee in the Mountains and Other Poems* (Boston, 1938), 10.

Brooding within the certitude of time,
To bring this lost forsaken valor
And the fierce faith undying
And the love quenchless
To flower among the hills to which we cleave
To fruit upon the mountains whither we flee. . . .[59]

In contrast to Davidson's lyricism, Tate spoke "the crabbed line" as one of poetry's high priests of obscurity and arcane allusions. If Davidson found at least a personal anchor in the past, Tate seemed to embody the modern man unable to lay hold effectively upon his past. An ironic contrast was offered by the traditional order—for Tate in the thirties an aristocratic version of the Old South myth. His "Ode to the Confederate Dead," which he continued to revise for a decade after 1925, was " 'about' solipsism," he said, "a philosophical doctrine . . . that we create the world in the act of perceiving it," about modern man's incapacity to "function objectively . . . under a unity of being." [60] It was not the nostalgic celebration of the Confederacy that one might get from Davidson, but the musing of a modern man in a Confederate cemetery, cut off by time from "the vision" and "the arrogant circumstance" of those who fell, "seeing only the leaves flying, plunge and expire," certain only of "the grave who counts us all." [61] In "The Mediterranean," however, the poet pursued a quest for tradition that led him back to the travels of Aeneas, then forward until

Now, from the Gates of Hercules we flood

Westward, westward till the barbarous brine
Whelms us to the tired land where tasseling corn,
Fat beans, grapes sweeter than muscadine
Rot on the vine: in that land were we born.[62]

The modern world had become a hell of abstractionism and positivism. Like Lewis Carroll's Alice, man had passed into a wonderland from which

[59] Davidson, "Lee in the Mountains," *ibid.,* 7.
[60] Allen Tate, "Narcissus as Narcissus," in *The Man of Letters in the Modern World: Selected Essays: 1928–1955* (New York, 1955) , 334.
[61] Allen Tate, *Poems, 1922–1947* (New York, 1948) , 20–21, 23.   [62] *Ibid.,* 4.

We too back to the world shall never pass
Through the shattered door, a dumb shade-harried crowd
Being all infinite, function depth and mass
Without figure, a mathematical shroud.

Hurled at the air—blessed without sin!
O God of our flesh, return us to Your wrath,
Let us be evil could we enter in
Your grace, and falter on the stony path! [63]

Warren carried further than any of the Fugitives the ironic effect of the "Tennessee accent to the classic phrase." But Warren, the youngest of the original group, moved gradually from musings over the past toward the world of action that appeared in his novels. In the "Kentucky Mountain Farm" sequence, dating from 1928 to 1931, the third section, "History Among the Rocks," stated the modern man's inability to understand why

In these autumn orchards once young men lay dead. . . .
Their reason is hard to guess and a long time past. . . .

And the final section, "The Return," rejected retreat to the past:

So, backward heart, you have no voice to call
Your image back, the vagrant image again.

How glimmering a buried world is lost
In the water's riffle, the wind's flaw. . . .[64]

"The Return: An Elegy," first printed in 1934, put the theme into more personal form, the inability to recapture childhood. The theme appeared again in "History," with pioneers hesitating in sight of the promised land, looking back, but then descending into the valley: "The act Alone is pure." [65] In the *Selected Poems* "History" was followed by "Question and Answer," in which no key could be found to the riddle of the universe:

What has availed
Or Failed?
Or will avail? [66]

---

[63] Allen Tate, "The Last Days of Alice," *ibid.*, 116.
[64] Robert Penn Warren, *Selected Poems, 1923–1943* (New York, 1944), 80, 83.
[65] *Ibid.*, 32.   [66] *Ibid.*, 34.

The Selected Poems, 1923–1943 began with "The Ballad of Billie Potts," a long narrative about a Kentucky boy, brought up in an atmosphere of evil, returning home rich to be killed and robbed by parents who failed to recognize him. A series of other poems followed the theme most explicitly stated in the title of "Original Sin: A Short Story." All of these coincided with Warren's increasing drift toward narrative and the novel as his favorite form, in which an outstanding theme again would be man's unfailing instinct for evil: "Original Sin."

Such other Southern poets as won favorable notice in the 1930's were affiliated with the Nashville group either directly or by sympathy. John Gould Fletcher, who returned to his native Arkansas in 1933 after fifteen years in England, had already contributed to the Agrarian Manifesto and after his return strongly defended regional tradition in prose and in his later poems, particularly in *South Star* (1941).[67] William Alexander Percy had been quietly writing poetry at Greenville, Mississippi, since the teens, and while his poetic themes were not peculiarly regional, he wrote in his autobiography, *Lanterns on the Levee,* the most revealing self-portrait of a cultivated Southern conservative anywhere in the literature of the South.[68] John Peale Bishop, a native of West Virginia who resided in New York after a decade in France, went through many phases, one as a "Southern" poet, revealing an affinity for the moral and traditional problems stated in Fugitive-Agrarian verse.[69]

Unique among the poets of the period was Jesse Stuart, the one horny-handed agrarian among them, six feet tall and over two hundred pounds, who emerged from W-Hollow in Kentucky's Greenup County to work on a paving gang, join a carnival, labor in a Birmingham steel mill, then work his way through Lincoln Memorial University in the Tennessee mountains and miss an M.A. at Vanderbilt when his thesis burned in a dormitory fire. As

[67] John Gould Fletcher, *Life Is My Song* (New York, 1937).

[68] William Alexander Percy, *Lanterns on the Levee* (New York, 1941). See also Phinizy Spalding, "A Stoic Trend in William Alexander Percy's Thought," in *Georgia Review*, XII (1958), 241–51.

[69] J. Max Patrick and Robert Wooster Stallman, "John Peale Bishop: A Checklist," with a Preface by Robert Wooster Stallman, in *Princeton University Library Chronicle*, VII (1946), 56, 64.

principal of the Greenup County High School, where he threw the fear of God into the rowdies, Stuart was possessed by the fury to write. In 1934 he brought out *Man With a Bull-Tongue Plow*, 703 sonnets written in eleven months, followed two years later by a book of stories, *Head o' W-Hollow*, about his mountain neighbors and kin. The popularity of his novel, *Taps for Private Tussie* (1943), finally established him as a professional writer who could give up the teaching that had cut down his production from thirty to ten thousand words a day.[70]

In the main, Southern poetry revolved around the Fugitive-Agrarian axis; so too did much of the fiction. By the mid-1940's Robert Penn Warren had emerged as one of the most versatile of twentieth-century American writers, with contributions to fiction, biography, and drama, as well as poetry and criticism. The most flexible of the Fugitives, the least captivated by doctrine, he stood forth as the supreme creative prodigy of the group; "his work," Tate wrote in 1924, ". . . will have what none of us can achieve —power." [71] And one writer later advanced an extravagant theory that the Fugitive movement eventually would be "interesting only as historical background for the writing of Robert Penn Warren." [72]

Devoted to poetry at Vanderbilt, Warren undertook his first substantial short story at Oxford in 1930 on the suggestion of an editor: "Prime Leaf," later the basis for his first novel.[73] His apprenticeship to fiction continued through the *Southern Review* period, but the early stories were not collected until 1947.[74] Meanwhile his first three novels had appeared, all "pegged to the realism of historic events, to recognizable localities and people." [75] The first, *Night Rider* (1939), was set in the Black Patch

[70] Jesse Stuart, *Beyond Dark Hills: A Personal Story* (New York, 1938); *Time*, XXXI (April 18, 1938), 77; *Time*, XXXII (November 7, 1938), 62–63; Stanley J. Kunitz and Howard Haycraft (eds.), *Twentieth Century Authors: A Biographical Dictionary of Modern Literature* (New York, 1942), 1367.

[71] Quoted in Cowan, *The Fugitive Group*, 150.

[72] John T. Westbrook, "The Fugitives Overhauled," in *Southwest Review*, XLIV (1959), 343.

[73] Warren in Cowley (ed.), *Writers at Work*, 191.

[74] Robert Penn Warren, *The Circus in the Attic and Other Stories* (New York, 1947).

[75] Bradbury, *The Fugitives*, 202.

War of 1907–1908, the revolt of Kentucky farmers against the tobacco trust in Warren's home county. The second, *At Heaven's Gate* (1943), exploited somewhat less directly the financial manipulations of Luke Lea and Rogers Caldwell, with suggestions of Sergeant York and the Carmack murder of 1908. In *All the King's Men* (1946) the historical underpinning was the rise and fall of Huey Long. But Warren reordered historical circumstances to fit his fictional purposes. He did not undertake a history of the South in either the realistic pattern of Stribling or the mythical pattern of Faulkner. Instead he dealt with the moral dilemmas of individuals in the modern South. *Night Rider* was primarily "about" Percy Munn, a young man newly out of law school who in the defense of what seemed to him a just cause drifted into crimes of violence and eventually met death at the hands of his adversaries. *At Heaven's Gate* was "about" the rootlessness of life in a modern city much like Nashville in the 1920's. There was no single protagonist, but a series of individuals vainly seeking identity: Susan Murdock, the "lady sweet" to whom the title ironically alluded, the daughter of Bogan Murdock, a figure representing the rootless abstraction of finance capitalism, and Susan's lovers—Jerry Calhoun, a figure of decadent agrarian background who became Murdock's protegé; Slim Sarrett, an avant-garde esthete and homosexual; and Sweetwater, a labor leader who had rejected a heritage of good family for Marxism. In her "emancipation" Sue was left spiritually empty, prey to an abortionist and finally to murder. At the end her death coincided with the collapse of Murdock's financial empire. The only character who showed moral responsibility was Ashly Windam, a poor-white fundamentalist on the fringes of the plot. It was, in short, an Agrarian judgment on the city.

The historical incidents behind the first two novels were relatively obscure, but the parallels to Huey Long's career caused serious misunderstandings of *All the King's Men*. Judged as history, it would not pass muster, although Willie Stark more nearly embodied the spirit of Long than any of several other fictional impersonators.[76] But, as Robert B. Heilman put it, "the author

---

[76] See Rubin, "All the King's Meanings," 422–34.

begins with history and politics, but the real subject is the nature of man: Warren is no more discussing American politics than Hamlet is discussing Danish politics." [77] Politics, Warren himself said, merely provided the framework in which the deeper concerns worked themselves out.[78] The book was "about" Jack Burden, its first-person narrator,* a sensitive young journalist of scholarly temperament caught up in Willie Stark's machine and moving like Percy Munn from idealistic commitment to guilty implication. It was the story of a man drawn half-unwillingly into the public world of action, drawn "out of the house . . . into the awful convulsion of the world, out of history into history and the awful responsibility of Time." In the end Burden decided that "all knowledge that is worth anything is maybe paid for by blood. Maybe that is the only way you can tell that a certain piece of knowledge is worth anything. . . ." And with his discovery, unlike Percy Munn or Sue Murdock, Jack Burden ultimately found his painful way to redemption.

Certain major themes ran through the three novels: the theme of self-discovery in the toils of moral responsibility, the theme of guilt in one's involvement, and the condition of Original Sin, which found its modern expression in the rejection of humanity for some disembodied abstraction—whether a tobacco cooperative, art for art's sake, an ideal of social justice, finance capitalism, or an image of political greatness.[79]

Andrew Nelson Lytle, a native of Murfreesboro, Tennessee— "in itself a career in Southern tradition" [80]—a Vanderbilt undergraduate among the last to join the original Fugitive group, became a writer chiefly of fiction. After drama studies at Yale and some acting on the New York stage, he turned to teaching and writing, and in 1942–1943 was editor of the *Sewanee Review*.

[77] Robert B. Heilman, "Melpomene as Wallflower; or, The Reading of Tragedy," in *Sewanee Review*, LX (1947), 155.

[78] Robert Penn Warren, "A Note to *All the King's Men*," in *Sewanee Review*, LXI (1953), 480.

[79] Everett Carter, "The 'Little Myth' of Robert Penn Warren," in *Modern Fiction Studies* (Lafayette, Ind.), VI (1960–1961), 6–8; and Thorp, *American Writing in the Twentieth Century*, 252–54.

[80] Lively, *Fiction Fights the Civil War*, 25.

677

Drawn into the Agrarian movement, like Warren and Tate he undertook a Civil War biography—of Nathan Bedford Forrest.[81] *The Long Night* (1936), his first novel, was also set against a Civil War background, the episodic story of a young Alabamian beset by the moral dilemma of desire for revenge against the persecutors of his father and his larger duty in the war, a story that rose to its climax in the Battle of Shiloh. The second novel, *At the Moon's Inn* (1941), turned far back to the Southern adventures of de Soto, using him as foil to Indian "agrarianism." Lytle also wrote stories, one of the most effective of which was "Jericho, Jericho, Jericho" (1936), the story of a stubborn old matriarch reviewing her guilty career on her deathbed.

Allen Tate also ventured into fiction with two short stories and one novel, *The Fathers* (1938), a story of the Civil War era set in Virginia. Through both the elderly narrator of *The Fathers* and one of its characters, George Posey, an ineffectual figure unable to fulfill the code of his society, Tate transposed a modern dissociation of sensibility well back into the nineteenth century.

Tate's wife, Caroline Gordon, became the earliest and most prolific of the Fugitive-Agrarian novelists. Never technically a member of either group, she was related to them by marriage and by disposition, and her fiction embodied the Agrarian and formalist principles at their purest. Readers who wanted to learn Southern ways "should go to school to her fiction," Willard Thorp wrote. "She knows the life cycle of the quail, how a house grows from a dog-trot cabin to a mansion with a portico, how the Tennessee walking horse is trained, how often the boys at Sawney Webb's school were birched, how crops and animals were bred out of the land, and how nature had to be propitiated if there was to be fertility." [82] And each of her novels provided a new experiment with form.

Penhally (1931), a novel of a Kentucky family and plantation, traced through three generations the story of family disintegration in the disruption of agrarian culture. *Aleck Maury, Sportsman*

---

[81] Andrew Nelson Lytle, *Bedford Forrest and His Critter Company* (New York, 1931). Tate wrote biographies of Stonewall Jackson and Jefferson Davis, Warren one of John Brown.
[82] Thorp, *American Writing in the Twentieth Century*, 249–50.

(1934) was the story of an old man recalling his lifetime pursuit of nature and its secrets, the inner struggle between intellectual and sportsman. *None Shall Look Back* (1937) was a Civil War story of military action, of bereaved women and family disruption in the violence that swept the South. *The Garden of Adonis* (1937) followed the career of a young tenant who returned from Detroit to resume farming, failed in a struggle against drought, lost his fiancée to a prosperous bootlegger, and finally committed a senseless murder of his landlord. *Green Centuries* (1941) treated the Indian and white societies of the eighteenth century, seen through the stories of two brothers, one of whom was captured by the Indians and entered into their life. Each of her frontiersmen, Lytle said, became a "homespun Dr. Faustus," whereas the Indians represented identity with the power of nature.[83] *The Women on the Porch* (1944) centered on a modern Southern woman who fled from New York to her childhood home when she discovered her husband's infidelity and who drifted into the purposelessness of that agrarian backwater, committing an infidelity of her own, until her penitent husband came like Orpheus to return her to the world of the living.

The Fugitive-Agrarians, for all their emphasis upon form and restraint, sometimes skirted perilously close to the line that separated their traditionalism from that of the plantation myth and the costume novel. One Agrarian deliberately and successfully straddled the line: Stark Young. Born the same year as Stribling (1881), he represented a far different viewpoint. A native of Como, Mississippi, Young finished his undergraduate work at Ole Miss in 1901 and took an M.A. at Columbia. After teaching English at Mississippi, at Texas (where he started the *Texas Quarterly* in 1915), and at Amherst, he became a New York drama critic and on the side wrote poetry, plays, and essays.[84] His four novels were all set in the Natchez area, but his Adams County stood at an immense distance from Yoknapatawpha. It was one of the few places where the plantation reality had once approached

---

[83] Andrew Nelson Lytle, "Caroline Gordon and the Historic Image," in *Sewanee Review*, LVII (1949), 570–72.

[84] Virginia Rock, "The Twelve Southerners: Biographical Essays," in Twelve Southerners, *I'll Take My Stand* (Torchbook ed., New York, 1962), 383–85.

the legend. In the Young saga it appeared first in *Heaven Trees* (1926), which celebrated the art of living in a bewildering profusion of aunts, uncles, cousins, breeding, good manners, gay parties, fine homes, and *noblesse oblige*. The next two novels presented a more characteristic Agrarian theme, the conflict of tradition with the modern world. In *The Torches Flare* (1928) Eleanor Dandridge, a Mississippi girl who succeeded on the New York stage and became involved in an illicit love affair, found that back home the traditional code reasserted itself over Bohemianism. In *River House* (1929), however, her brother found that he could not go home again. "There are no codes to follow anymore," old Major Dandridge mused. "There's only the individual case, you decide it for yourself." The final novel of Natchez, *So Red the Rose* (1934), portrayed the travail of a cultivated Unionist community caught up in secession, war, and postwar occupation. Toward the end one of the characters, Hugh McGehee, summarized his social philosophy: "Democracy, a good theory, a great human right, which works out none too well; slavery, a great human wrong, which works out none too badly. . . . Mr. Mack [a Yankee speculator] and his crew won't consume me . . . these men just haven't enough life behind them to match me. I mean by 'life' tradition, forefathers, and a system of living. . . . It's as if I stood on the ground and they didn't."

That *So Red the Rose* became a best-seller bespoke the abiding popularity of the plantation myth, and while Stark Young escaped the designation of costume novelist, the greatest popular triumph of the decade was a novel squarely in that tradition. Yet Margaret Mitchell's *Gone with the Wind* (1936) was not made precisely to formula either. Produced by the quiet accretion of manuscript over the period of a decade, backed up by extensive reading in original and secondary sources, built around characters unusual in Lost Cause romance—the tempestuous Scarlett O'Hara and the cynical Rhett Butler—it conveyed an impression not of sentimentality but of compelling power. For a time Margaret Mitchell's one book outdistanced in sales even the scandalous works of her one-time Atlanta *Journal* colleague, Erskine Caldwell. Indeed, "*GWTW*" became a unique phenomenon of publishing history by the suddenness of its success; a million copies were in print by the end of 1936, a half year after publication. The search for a screen actress to play Scarlett absorbed the public for two years. And from December, 1939, when Atlanta saw the glittering spectacle of a Hollywood première, through the following June, the film version, running nearly four hours at advanced prices, played to a total audience of 25,000,000.[85]

New talents, untutored and cultivated in isolation from any group, kept cropping up. One of the finest, Katherine Anne Porter, eluded definition by any category. She was, Willard Thorp wrote, "a roving regionalist" who knew, as she herself remarked, "a borderland of strange tongues and commingled races." [86] The outlines of her biography, which she has guarded with a jealous reserve, remain uncertain. Born sometime during the 1890's in Indian Creek, Texas, educated in convent schools until she eloped at sixteen for a short-lived marriage, she worked on newspapers in Chicago, Fort Worth, and Denver, and sojourned at various times in New York, Mexico, Bermuda, Spain, Germany, Switzerland, and France. In the 1930's she lived in Baton Rouge as the wife of Albert Erskine, Jr., English professor and business manager of the *Southern Review*.[87] She may be identified with the Fugitive-Agrarian school not by ideological commitment but by resolute devotion to form and craftsmanship, to the inner life and "historic memory" of the individual. "My whole attempt," she once wrote, "has been to discover and understand human motives, human feelings. . . . I am passionately absorbed with these individuals . . . these beings without which, one by one, all the 'broad movements of history' could never take place." [88]

She established and sustained one of the highest reputations on one of the smallest bodies of published work, without a single full-length novel before *Ship of Fools* (1962). The reputation was established by *Flowering Judas* (1930), the title piece of which told the story of an American girl who, torn between her Catholic faith and the Mexican Revolution to which she had given her

[85] Finis Farr, *Margaret Mitchell of Atlanta: The Author of Gone with the Wind* (New York, 1965); *Margaret Mitchell Memorial Issue, The Atlanta Historical Bulletin*, No. 34 (May, 1950).

[86] Thorp, *American Writing in the Twentieth Century*, 258.

[87] George Hendrick, *Katherine Anne Porter* (New York, 1965), 11–27.

[88] Katherine Anne Porter, *The Days Before* (New York, 1952), 127–28.

support, finally betrayed both. *Pale Horse, Pale Rider* (1939) was the most "Southern" of her books in subject matter. "Old Mortality" introduced Miranda, a sensitive adolescent haunted by family legends which she could not fully enter into or even grasp: "At least I can know the truth about what happens to me, she assured herself silently, making a promise to herself, in her hopefulness, her ignorance." Miranda, something of a proxy for Miss Porter, reappeared in the story, "Pale Horse, Pale Rider," as a young woman in Denver, in love with a soldier who was swept away by the influenza epidemic of 1918 while she endured the feverish nightmare of a near-fatal attack.

The Miranda stories continued in *The Leaning Tower and Other Stories* (1944), which explored the girl's childhood and the history of her grandmother. "To the reviewer Miss Porter is baffling because one cannot take hold of her work in any of the various ways . . ." Edmund Wilson complained. "There is no place for general reflections; you are to live through the experience as the characters do. And yet the writer has managed to say something about the values involved in the experience. But what is it?" [89] The answer, Robert Penn Warren suggested, was in the two propositions about which all her work revolved: the necessity for moral definition and the difficulty of moral definition. They were elusive themes and the quality of elusiveness created in her devotees the atmosphere of a mystery cult. The flavor of "exquisiteness and snobbery" clung to her reputation. But, Warren contended, she belonged to the very small group "who have done serious, consistent, original, and vital work in the form of short fiction." [90]

Eudora Welty was similar in her devotion to style and personal experience. Indeed the *Southern Review* printed seven of her earliest stories and Miss Porter wrote a laudatory introduction to her first collection, *A Curtain of Green* (1941). "I believe in the

[89] Edmund Wilson, "Katherine Anne Porter," in *The New Yorker*, XX (September 30, 1944), 72.

[90] Robert Penn Warren, "Introduction," in Edward Schwartz, "Katherine Anne Porter: A Critical Bibliography," in *Bulletin of the New York Public Library*, LVII (May, 1953), 212, 215; Robert Penn Warren, "Katherine Anne Porter (Irony with a Center)," in *Kenyon Review*, IV (1942), 29, 41.

rightness of Miss Welty's instinctive knowledge that writing cannot be taught," she said, "but only learned, and learned by the individual in his own way, at his own pace." [91] Eudora Welty grew up and continued to live in a middle-class milieu in Jackson, Mississippi. After undergraduate study at Mississippi State College for Women and at Wisconsin, she studied advertising at Columbia University, worked for a radio station, and then did publicity for the Mississippi relief programs. Meanwhile she pursued a serious interest in writing and photography—and critics have suggested a relationship of the two in her capacity to capture in writing a given moment, suspended in time.

Her first story was published in 1936 and by 1941 she was absorbed in a writing career.[92] *The Robber Bridegroom* (1942), a novelette, was her second volume, followed by another collection, *The Wide Net* (1943), and another novel, *Delta Wedding* (1946), and many subsequent writings. She sometimes dealt in fantasy and occasionally created rather grotesque characters— Katherine Anne Porter cited a Bostonian who remarked that he would not care to meet them socially.[93] But the characteristic world of her writing was not the Southern Gothic but what Louis Rubin called the "other Mississippi," as distinguished from Faulkner's: "a tidy, protected little world, in which people go about their affairs, living, marrying, getting children, diverting themselves, dying, all in tranquil, pastoral fashion." [94]

Two other women successfully exploited peculiar regional worlds of their own: Caroline Miller and Marjorie Kinnan Rawlings. Both, like Stribling and Margaret Mitchell, earned wide popularity and won Pulitzer Prizes. Caroline Miller, a high-school graduate in Waycross, utilized the oral traditions of south Georgia to weave the story of a girl's growth to maturity in the piney-woods frontier of the nineteenth century: *Lamb in His Bosom* (1934), a book reminiscent of Elizabeth Madox Roberts' *The*

[91] Katherine Anne Porter, "Introduction," in Eudora Welty, *A Curtain of Green* (Garden City, N.Y., 1941), xii.

[92] Ruth M. Vande Kieft, *Eudora Welty* (New York, 1962), 15–24.

[93] Porter, "Introduction," in Welty, *A Curtain of Green*, xvi.

[94] Rubin, *The Faraway Country*, 131.

Time of Man. But she produced only one other novel, *Lebanon* (1944), which repeated many of the themes but not the success of her first.[95]

Marjorie Kinnan Rawlings' world lay still farther south, in the hammock and scrubland of north-central Florida. Born in Washington, D. C., Miss Rawlings had written for the newspapers in the North before 1928, when she bought a Florida orange grove and began a new life. There, as she related in *Cross Creek* (1942), she set out to know the bypaths and waterways, the people and the customs of a primitive region and to re-create them in fiction. After many failures with short stories and an indifferent success with a novelette, "Jacob's Ladder" (1931), published in *Scribners*, her first full-scale novel became a Book-of-the-Month Club selection: *South Moon Under* (1933). This was the story of scrub-country people who wrested a bare existence from the recalcitrant land and from moonshining. *The Yearling* (1938), her Pulitzer Prize novel, was a minor classic of boyhood and growing up. It told the story of Jody Baxter and a pet fawn he brought home. His father was indulgent, but his mother's forebodings were realized when the yearling deer destroyed the plant beds and she had to shoot it. Jody ran away but eventually came back to reality, himself no longer a yearling but a man who "took it for his share and went on." [96]

By virtue of birth in New Orleans and her use of Southern themes, Lillian Hellman belongs in any list of major Southern writers during the period—the one successful Broadway dramatist before Tennessee Williams' *The Glass Menagerie* (1945). Although her family moved to New York when she was five, Miss Hellman later returned often for long summers with relatives. She scored her first Broadway triumph with *The Children's Hour* (1935), which had shock value for its references to lesbianism but was really, its author insisted, about a schoolgirl's malicious falsehood. Miss Hellman's next success was *The Little Foxes*

[95] Kunitz and Haycroft (eds.), *Twentieth Century Authors*, 959; Kunitz (ed.), *Twentieth Century Authors: First Supplement*, 670.

[96] Kunitz and Haycroft (eds.), *Twentieth Century Authors*, 1150–51; Bradbury, *Renaissance in the South*, 99–100.

(1939), which portrayed a middle-class Southern family at the turn of the century—the Hubbards, who were much like Faulkner's Snopeses. It was a drama of greed and malice among the grasping *nouveaux riche* who had supplanted an aristocracy and who contemptuously rejected its values. It owed part of its success to a convincing performance by Tallulah Bankhead as the venomous Regina. After two anti-Fascist plays, *Watch on the Rhine* (1941) and *The Searching Wind* (1944), Lillian Hellman returned to the Hubbard family's background in *Another Part of the Forest* (1946) and later to other Southern themes.[97]

Still another major talent appeared with Carson McCullers' *The Heart Is a Lonely Hunter* (1940), a surprisingly mature performance for an author only twenty-two. The theme of the title, which the publishers suggested as a clue to meaning, became the central obsession of her writing: the spiritual isolation, the ultimate loneliness of the individual. In the novel, a small Southern town much like her native Columbus, Georgia, was peopled with characters striving to communicate and fulfill their lonely yearnings: the deaf-mute Singer, whom the others endowed with mystic wisdom, himself obsessed by the loss of his friend Antonopolous; an ineffectual cafe proprietor; a frustrated labor leader; a Negro physician misunderstood by his own people; an adolescent tomboy, Mick Kelley, forced to abandon her dream of the concert stage for a Woolworth counter. *Reflections in a Golden Eye* (1941), set on a peacetime army post (the author knew Fort Benning and Fort Bragg), earned classification as the purest Southern Gothic by its grotesque and perverted characters. The book had a quality of unity and control that the first lacked, but the theme of human isolation was almost lost in a chamber of horrors. But five years later she demonstrated in *The Member of the Wedding* (1946) a capacity to treat her theme with both control and tenderness in the story of Frankie Addams, a motherless girl on the threshold of adolescence, who was not a "member" of any-

---

[97] Moss Hart, "Miss Lily of New Orleans: Lillian Hellman," in Margaret C. Harriman (ed.), *Take Them Up Tenderly* (New York, 1944); Jacob H. Adler, "The Rose and the Fox: Notes on the Southern Drama," in Rubin and Jacobs (eds.), *South*, 221–47; Jean Gould, *Modern American Playwrights* (New York, 1966), 168–85.

thing and who vainly sought identity through the coming marriage of her older brother.[98]

In the decades after 1920 the Southern Renaissance became the most extraordinary literary development of twentieth-century America, a regional phenomenon unequaled since the flowering of New England a century before. "From the peculiarly historical consciousness of the Southern writer has come good work of a special order," Allen Tate wrote in the *Virginia Quarterly*'s tenth anniversary number in 1935; "but the focus of this consciousness is quite temporary." His comment, he noted ten years later, "was written at the height of the Southern literary renascence. That renascence is over." [99] But the continuing rise of new talents testified to a persistent capacity for renewal. Still other figures were just beginning to emerge; Randall Jarrell, James Agee, Tennessee Williams, if little noticed as yet, had all published books before the end of 1945. Waiting now, just offstage, were Truman Capote, Peter Taylor, Elizabeth Spencer, William Styron, Flannery O'Connor, and a host of others. Thomas Wolfe was gone, DuBose Heyward died in 1940, Elizabeth Madox Roberts in 1941, Ellen Glasgow in 1945; but most of the major figures in the Renaissance were still flourishing and still productive. The "New Critics" were moving toward their conquest of the classroom from the historical scholars. By 1945 the South, whatever deficiencies it might suffer in other fields, was far advanced toward, if indeed it had not already seized, triumphant "possession of the American literary world." [100]

---

[98] Oliver Evans, *Carson McCullers: Her Life and Work* (London, 1965), *passim;* Oliver Evans, "The Theme of Spiritual Isolation in Carson McCullers," in Rubin and Jacobs (eds.), *South*, 333–48.

[99] Allen Tate, "The Profession of Letters in the New South," in *Virginia Quarterly Review*, XI (1935), 175; Tate, "The New Provincialism," *ibid.*, XXI (1945), 262.

[100] C. Hugh Holman, "The Southerner as American Writer," in Sellers (ed.), *The Southerner as American*, 181.

CHAPTER XX

WORLD WAR II:
THE TURBULENT SOUTH

I N the late 1930's when the storm of war swept Asia and Europe, the main focus of American politics moved abruptly from domestic to foreign affairs. Once again, as twenty years before, a Democratic administration built its foreign policy on a foundation of Southern support. "The South's legislative role," one writer has said, "was not only marginally decisive; it furnished the bedrock of support without which United States policy might well have been paralyzed." [1] It furnished also the cement that bound together a divided party; the phenomenon of "internationalism" spanned the entire spectrum of Southern politics from Carter Glass to Claude Pepper.

The region's devotion to a vigorous foreign policy arose from a number of factors: traditional, ethnic, economic, psychological, and political. Sentimental identification with the British, and to a lesser degree with the Chinese (because of the missionary impulse), merged with economic interests. German conquests menaced the cotton and tobacco trade with Europe and Britain. Japanese textiles, if they used Southern cotton, competed with Southern mills. The region's population included few of the German, Italian, or Irish elements that formed anti-British or isolationist nuclei in other areas. Moreover, Southern history had bred a psychology of danger and defense, and a military-patriotic tradition. The basic explanation of regional attitudes, Carter Glass said, was the Southerner's "superior character and exceptional

---

[1] Paul Seabury, *The Waning of Southern "Internationalism"* (Princeton, 1957), 2.

understanding of the problem." The explanation, Erskine Caldwell said, was the Southerner's ignorance.[2]

For whatever reasons, as the world crisis deepened, Southerners more than other Americans favored measures against Nazi, Fascist, and Japanese expansion. In the years before the Pearl Harbor attack they repeatedly displayed in the opinion polls a greater conviction that the United States would be drawn into war again, that overseas events were vital to American interests, that the nation should help France, Britain, China, and ultimately Russia, that the army and navy should be enlarged, that young men should be drafted, that neutrality legislation should be revised or repealed.[3] In October, 1941, the Gallup poll found 88 per cent of the Southerners convinced that the defeat of Germany was more important than keeping out of war; in other regions from 63 to 70 per cent thought so.[4] The isolationist America First Committee, despite persistent efforts, made little headway in the South.[5]

For many senior Democrats the Wilsonian legacy remained a living force. In 1919–1920 they had gone the last mile with Wilson on the Versailles Treaty. In the end they had been frustrated by the partisan machinations of Henry Cabot Lodge, arch-foe of the South, one-time sponsor of the 1890 "Force Bill." The resultant failure to join the League of Nations led in time to the collapse of collective security and new threats to world peace.[6]

[2] Various writers at the time and since have elaborated explanations for the distinctive Southern outlook on world affairs, most of which revolve about the factors mentioned above. See especially Alfred O. Hero, Jr., *The Southerner and World Affairs* (Baton Rouge, 1965) ; Seabury, *The Waning of Southern "Internationalism,"* 2–18; Alexander De Conde, "The South and Isolationism," in *Journal of Southern History,* XXIV (1958) , 332–46; John Temple Graves II, *The Fighting South* (New York, 1954) , 5–18; and James Boyd, "The South and the Fight," in *Atlantic Monthly,* CLXXIII (February, 1944) , 53–59. Quotation from Graves, *The Fighting South,* 7.

[3] Hero, *The Southerner and World Affairs,* 91–103, cites evidence in detail from the files of the American Institute of Public Opinion.

[4] *Public Opinion Quarterly,* VI (1942) , 150–51.

[5] Wayne S. Cole, "America First and the South, 1940–1941," in *Journal of Southern History,* XXII (1956) , 36–47.

[6] "I was convinced that he detested our President with such a deadly hate that if Wilson had opposed the League of Nations, Lodge would have supported it," Tom Connally of Texas said years later. His animosity stemmed from jealousy of Wilson's academic achievements and the fact that Wilson "was born in Virginia and Lodge had a deep-seated hatred of the South." Tom Connally, as told to Alfred Steinberg, *My Name Is Tom Connally,* 100. See also the fictional Southern congressmen in Robert A. Dahl, *Congress and Foreign Policy* (New York, 1950) , 18–19.

The memory reached across the interwar decades. In 1921 Carter Glass contemptuously dismissed Republican proposals in the Washington Conference "to scrap a few obsolete vessels and to leave the principal nations of the world with more powerful navies than they had before they entered the last war." The Kellogg-Briand Pact to "outlaw" war, he declared in 1929, would "confuse the minds of many good and pious people who think that peace may be secured by polite professions of neighborly and brotherly love." [7] In 1925 Southern Senators led by Virginia's Claude A. Swanson backed President Coolidge's proposal to join the World Court, but partisanship reasserted itself on other measures, in the absence of world crisis. Southern support waned on most proposals that Republican Presidents made for defense or international participation.[8]

Through the early 1930's Southern Congressmen drifted in the current of complacency about foreign affairs. In 1935–1937 most of them voted for neutrality legislation to embargo arms shipments and keep Americans out of war zones, although Tom Connally of Texas protested against the doctrine that America should refuse "either to bring peace or to prevent the outrage of the weak and the defenseless by the powerful and by the aggressor." [9] But after 1937, when war erupted in Asia, President Roosevelt was able once again to invoke the party loyalty of Southern Democrats, including conservative dissenters. As the emphasis shifted from domestic to foreign affairs the administration found its main support among Southerners while many liberals of the North and West remained staunch isolationists.[10]

---

[7] Carter Glass to Bernard Baruch, November 19, 1921, in Carter Glass Papers (University of Virginia Library); *Congressional Record*, 70 Cong., 2 Sess., 1728.

[8] Grassmuck, *Sectional Biases in Congress on Foreign Policy*, 40–42, 59–82, 152–54, and *passim*.

[9] Marian D. Irish, "Foreign Policy and the South," in Cole and Hallowell (eds.), *The Southern Political Scene, 1938–1948*, 306; *Congressional Record*, 74 Cong., 1 Sess., 14433.

[10] One suggested that party loyalty "intensified on international issues perhaps because many Southerners opposed Roosevelt's domestic policies." Grassmuck, *Sectional Biases in Congress on Foreign Policy*, 152–53. Some writers argue that Roosevelt deliberately abandoned reform after 1938 in order to cultivate Southern support on foreign policy. But a more valid interpretation seems to be that the de-emphasis of reform resulted from New Deal losses in the 1938 elections and the growing emphasis on events overseas. See, however, Tugwell, *The Democratic Roosevelt*, 476.

In January, 1938, Southern Democrats furnished the solid foundation for a majority that narrowly defeated the Ludlow Amendment, which would have required a referendum for the declaration of war.[11]

In 1939 the challenge to isolation began in earnest. That spring, after Hitler took Czechoslovakia, Roosevelt sought revision of the neutrality legislation to eliminate the embargo on sales of arms to belligerents. To let the Western democracies buy arms in case of war, he reasoned, might discourage aggression. But the Senate Committee on Foreign Relations blocked the move. In September war began in Europe, and the President asked a special session of Congress to reconsider. The embargo clearly imposed a handicap on Britain and France and, as North Carolina's Josiah Bailey put it, was not required to maintain strict neutrality according to international law. The House quickly adopted the change. During the Senate debate the President discreetly kept in the background and entrusted the measure to Tom Connally and to Jimmy Byrnes, who symbolized renewed party unity. Only Robert R. Reynolds of North Carolina and Overton of Louisiana voted against the Neutrality Act of 1939, which passed by 63 to 30.[12]

Until the spring of 1940 Southern Congressmen sustained a perfunctory lip service to neutrality and noninvolvement. But when the Nazi *blitzkrieg* overran Western Europe, Florida's Senator Claude Pepper passionately championed aid to the Allies. In May, when Hitler's forces reached the English channel, Pepper demanded the sale of American aircraft to the desperate Allies. "It is not written in the holy writ of Americanism," he asserted, "that America should be a mere spectator at Armageddon." When Paris fell he demanded mobilization. In September he defended Roosevelt's swapping American destroyers for Atlantic and Caribbean

---

[11] Robert A. Divine, *The Illusion of Neutrality* (Chicago, 1962) , 220–21; New York *Times*, January 11, 1938. Louis Ludlow, Indiana Democrat, also sponsored a Federal antilynching bill.

[12] Divine, *The Illusion of Neutrality*, 229–36; *Congressional Record*, 76 Cong., 2 Sess., 1024, and Appendix, 184; Irving Howards, "The Influence of Southern Senators on American Foreign Policy from 1939 to 1950" (Ph.D. dissertation, University of Wisconsin, 1955) , 43; Josiah Bailey, mimeographed statement for release October 2, 1939, with A. Hand James to Franklin D. Roosevelt, October 5, 1939, in PPF 2518, Roosevelt Library.

bases. A year later, in October, 1941, he declared his readiness to vote for an American expeditionary force.[13] As early as the spring of 1941, Carter Glass, honorary chairman of the Fight For Freedom Committee, favored "doing everything possible to bring about the downfall of Hitler and his gang."[14]

Pepper and Glass were in the vanguard. But Southern Congressmen successively recorded their abandment of neutrality in votes for interventionist measures. In August and September, 1940, only Senator "Cotton Ed" Smith and three Republican representatives from Kentucky and Tennessee voted against the first peacetime draft.[15] Conscription was necessary, Alabama's Luther Patrick said, "to keep our Southern boys from filling up the army."[16] On the Lend-Lease Act of 1941 all the Representatives from seven Southern states and a majority from the rest recorded favorable votes; in the Senate only Reynolds of North Carolina registered opposition.[17] Indeed the aberrant Reynolds was the only Southerner among the twenty-six Senators who voted most consistently as isolationists on Roosevelt's proposals.[18] In August, 1941, only Smith and W. Lee O'Daniel joined him in voting against renewal of the draft. In the House Speaker Rayburn barely forestalled reconsideration of a 203–202 vote for extension, and thus preserved the new army just four months before the attack on Pearl Harbor.[19]

Whatever measure is applied, the result is the same: in the late 1930's and early 1940's Southern Democrats ranked above all

[13] Francis P. Locke, "Claude D. Pepper 'Champion of the Belligerent Democracy,'" in J. T. Salter (ed.), *Public Men in and out of Office* (Chapel Hill, 1946), 257–76; *Congressional Record*, 76 Cong., 3 Sess., 6474; Claude Pepper to Franklin D. Roosevelt, August 2, 1940, in PPF 4773, Roosevelt Library.

[14] Carter Glass to W. Glenn Elliott, May 16, 1941, in Glass Papers.

[15] Irish, "Foreign Policy and the South," 312. The count does not include Oklahoma.

[16] Quoted in Graves, *The Fighting South*, 5; see also p. 82. From January through June, 1940, enlistments from the thirteen Southern states were 31,390 of 74,579, or 42 per cent of the total. *Congressional Record*, 76 Cong., 3 Sess., 11119–20.

[17] Marian D. Irish, "The Southern One-Party System and National Politics," in *Journal of Politics*, IV (1942), 93–94.

[18] Kenneth W. Colegrove, *The American Senate and World Peace* (New York, 1944), 202–209. The test was a vote on at least seven of nine measures.

[19] David L. Cohn, "Mr. Speaker," in *Atlantic Monthly*, CLXX (October, 1942), 77–78.

other regional and party groups in their devotion to intervention and internationalism. V. O. Key, for example, in his classic study of Southern politics, recorded an analysis of thirty-four foreign policy votes in the Senate, divided into four categories. On reciprocal trade agreements, on preparedness and neutrality, on the lend-lease program, and later, on the United Nations and international bank agreement in 1945, Southerners recorded more solid support than other Democrats or Republicans.[20] Without their overwhelming support the administration would have lost on neutrality revision in 1939 and 1941, the Lend-Lease Act, draft extension, and authorization for seizing foreign and arming American merchant ships.[21]

In 1940 the world crisis subdued the impulse of Democratic rebels to replace Roosevelt with a conservative candidate. Their main hope had been Vice President John Nance Garner, the village nabob of Uvalde, Texas, epitome of the small-town élite. At odds with Roosevelt on sit-down strikes, court reform, government spending, and the attempted "purge," he became the symbolic head of the opposition. In December, 1938, friends gathered at his log-cabin birthplace on Blossom Prairie to start a Garner-for President boom. A year later he announced his candidacy. The polls repeatedly showed him the leading choice of Democratic voters—on the assumption that Roosevelt would not run for a third term.[22]

The President cultivated party unity behind his foreign policy and maintained a sphinx-like silence on his political intentions. Amid the uncertainty no other candidate rose high enough to challenge him. Garner was past seventy and had provoked strong opposition. He was, John L. Lewis said in 1939, a "poker-playing, whiskey-drinking, evil old man" whose knife was "searching for the quivering, pulsating heart of labor." [23] When the convention met in Chicago, he was scarcely more than Texas' favorite son, and even Texas delegates had instructions not to join any stop-

[20] Key, *Southern Politics*, 352–54.

[21] Howards, "The Influence of Southern Senators on American Foreign Policy from 1939 to 1950," 157; Cole, "America First and the South, 1940–1941," *loc. cit.*, 36.

[22] Bascom N. Timmons, *Garner of Texas* (New York, 1948), 246–67.

[23] *Time*, XXXIV (August 7, 1939), 13.

Roosevelt movement. Cordell Hull was in frail health and lacked a following. James A. Farley, who opposed a third term, was a Catholic and Al Smith's defeat was a recent memory. Nobody else loomed as a man of the necessary stature. Crisis, therefore, reconciled Southern conservatives to the man whose foreign policy, at least, they approved. After Alabama's Lister Hill put his name before the convention, Roosevelt won the nomination with only scattered opposition: 946½ votes to 72½ for Farley, 61 for Garner, 9½ for Tydings, 5½ for Hull.[24]

But querulous delegates vented their frustration on his vice-presidential choice, Henry A. Wallace, for whom Roosevelt by-passed Southern possibilities: Speaker Bankhead, Sam Rayburn, James F. Byrnes, Jesse Jones. Wallace, a former Republican with more reputation for mysticism than politics, was anathema to the professionals. A dedicated New Dealer who denounced racism, he offended conservatives. The opposition gravitated to Speaker Bankhead, but Roosevelt threatened to withdraw if the delegates rejected his choice. On the convention floor, Jimmy Byrnes strode the aisles asking: "For God's sake, do you want a President or a Vice-President?" Finally the convention named Wallace, 628 votes to 329 for Bankhead and a scattering for others. In the eleven former Confederate states Bankhead took 193 of 248 potential votes and Wallace only 44. In Bankhead's total of 329 votes, 247½ came from sixteen Southern and Border States, which gave Wallace only 88½.[25]

Despite much grumbling, few Southern Democrats bolted the ticket. Cotton Ed Smith decided to go fishing.[26] Other South Carolina rebels formed a Jeffersonian Democratic party to support Wendell Willkie and at the same time "hold to the time tested principles of the Democratic party." [27] Texas rebels formed the

---

[24] Jasper B. Shannon, "Presidential Politics in the South," in Cole and Hallowell (eds.) , *The Southern Political Scene, 1938–1948*, 471–72; New York *Times*, July 18, 1940; McKay, *Texas Politics, 1906–1944*, 422. For a full account of the third-term nomination see Bernard F. Donahoe, *Private Plans and Public Dangers: The Story of FDR's Third Nomination* (Notre Dame, Ind., 1965) .

[25] Shannon, "Presidential Politics in the South," in Cole and Hallowell (eds.) , *The Southern Political Scene, 1938–1948*, 473.

[26] Charleston *News and Courier*, July 20, 1940.

[27] Greenville (S.C.) *News*, July 21, 1940.

No-Third-Term Democratic party, pledged to Willkie as the only "real Democrat." [28] But Roosevelt carried both states overwhelmingly. In the eleven former Confederate states he got 300,000 more votes than in 1936, although the Republican proportion increased somewhat in all the states except Mississippi, Georgia, and North Carolina.[29]

World War II activated another cycle of change in the South. To a greater degree than the previous war it put people on the move: to shipyards, war plants, training camps, and far-flung battlefields. It intensified established trends: in economic development, race relations, and politics. The initial impact of the defense effort was defined by President Roosevelt in December, 1940, when he received newsmen aboard ship in Charleston Harbor. Asked what distinctive role the South could play in national defense, he responded: "of these million four hundred thousand people that are going to be trained, how many are going to be trained in the South?" [30] Before the war ended Texas alone had accommodated over a million.[31] Once again the climate and open spaces of the region were the magnet for training camps and airfields. Altogether more than four billion dollars went into military facilities in the South, some 36 per cent of the total for the continental United States. In six states—Florida, Georgia, Mississippi, the Carolinas, and Virginia—the expenditure exceeded that for war plants.[32]

Early in 1941 *Time* printed a marveling report on the "Defense Boom in Dixie": the construction of new training camps, powder mills, shipyards, activity in such established fields as steel and

[28] McKay, *Texas Politics, 1906–1944,* 337.

[29] Shannon, "Presidential Politics in the South," in Cole and Hallowell (eds.), *The Southern Political Scene, 1938–1948,* 473–76.

[30] Press Conference," XVI (December 14, 1940, on board the USS *Tuscaloosa,* Charleston Harbor) , 349, in Roosevelt Library.

[31] Seth S. McKay, *Texas and the Fair Deal, 1945–1952,* (San Antonio, 1954) , 15–16.

[32] Frederick L. Deming and Weldon A. Stein, *Disposal of Southern War Plants,* National Planning Association Committee of the South, Report No. 2 (Washington, 1949) , 17. These figures, for July, 1940–June, 1945, understate the total awards to the South since $1,600,000,000 of $11,800,000,000 were not allocated to individual states. Of the $10,200,000,000 allocated, the South got $4,200,000,000 or about 41 per cent.

textiles, payrolls that "bounced from one merchant's cash register to another."[33] The "whole draft business is just a Southern trick . . . put over by Southern merchants to hold the big trade they get from the training camps," an irate New Jersey trainee blurted to a reporter in Alabama that summer.[34]

The defense effort, however, held a potential for economic development more fundamental than an "ice-cream-and-powder-mill-boom." In September, 1940, the Southern Governors' Conference urged decentralization of defense industry and called on the government to utilize the South's "vast reservoirs of natural resources and available labor."[35] In March, 1941, after hearing Chester C. Davis of the National Defense Advisory Commission, the governors appointed a committee to wait on the President and the Office of Production Management. "Nothing short of the most rigorous and most positive efforts to achieve recognition . . . will suffice," Davis asserted. To March 1, he noted, plans for 302 defense plants included only 24 in the former Confederate states. From June, 1940, through January, 1941, those states had received only 7 per cent of the $7,500,000,000 in defense contracts; "we have followed the same pattern of regional concentration that was followed in 1917 and 1918."[36] Davis' figures, however, omitted shipbuilding and supplies. During the first year of activity after the National Defense Act of June, 1940, the eleven Southeastern states got 11.7 per cent of the $16,824,065,000 in defense contracts, a proportion below their 21.5 per cent of the population but about equal to their proportion of existing industrial capacity.[37]

Throughout the war the South remained more campground than arsenal, but war production increasingly moved southward. In the early period urgent need dictated that defense contracts go to areas that had the established facilities and skills. When those areas became saturated, defense production spread, partly to utilize new resources and labor, partly to decentralize for traffic and secu-

[33] *Time*, XXXVII (February 17, 1941) , 75–80.
[34] Quoted in Graves, *The Fighting South*, 104.
[35] *Congressional Record*, 77 Cong., 1 Sess., Appendix, 1415–16.
[36] New York *Times*, March 16, 1941.
[37] Ralph C. Hon, "The South in the War Economy," in *Southern Economic Journal*, VIII (1941–1942) , 294. The period was the fiscal year ending June 30, 1941.

rity reasons.[38] But no policy was ever established to exploit the war effort for region building.

However, Roosevelt, who had favored shipyards in the South since his World War I experience, backed arguments by the National Resources Planning Board in favor of using the "large numbers of workers . . . available for unskilled work or for training" in "a low-income area" which needed "supplementary employment opportunity." [39] Shipyards mushroomed around the Atlantic and Gulf coasts, even at some inland points. Newport News Shipbuilding and Dry Dock Company, the oldest in the country, experienced at making all kinds of vessels up to battleships and aircraft carriers, became the major Southern producer, chiefly for the navy. But the Norfolk and Charleston navy yards and private yards at Houston and Orange, Texas, added substantial contributions.[40] And the Maritime Commission, a civilian agency, sponsored new or greatly enlarged shipyards in 1940 at Norfolk, Tampa, Mobile, Pascagoula, Beaumont, and Orange; in 1941 at Wilmington, New Orleans, and Houston; in 1942 at Brunswick, Jacksonville, and Panama City.[41]

Unseasoned managers struggled with green workers to produce steel, concrete, and wooden vessels: Liberty ships, tugs, barges, landing craft, and other types. J. A. Jones, a general contractor from Charlotte, operated the Brunswick and Panama City yards with a labor force that included farmers, several prize-fighters, one Ph.D., thirteen clergymen, and in one of the pipe-welding departments an entire colored troupe, "The Original Silas Green New Orleans Shows." [42] At Pascagoula, Mississippi, Robert Ingersoll Ingalls, steel manufacturer of Birmingham, took over a dilapidated World War I shipyard and in 1940 launched the first arc-welded cargo ship, made of steel from the parent company. Pascagoula boasted the champion woman welder of the world.[43]

[38] Hoover and Ratchford, *Economic Resources and Policies of the South*, 59.
[39] Quoted in Frederic C. Lane, *Ships for Victory* (Baltimore, 1951), 49–50.
[40] Gerald J. Fischer, *Statistical Summary of Shipbuilding under the Maritime Commission during World War II*, Historical Reports of War Administration United States Maritime Commission, No. 2 (Washington, 1949), 164.
[41] Lane, *Ships for Victory*, 33–38, 51, 59, 142, 148.   [42] *Ibid.*, 250.
[43] Hodding Carter and Anthony Ragusin, *Gulf Coast Country* (New York, 1951), 186–96.

The most celebrated miracle-worker was Andrew Jackson Higgins, a former lumberman who had made motorboats in New Orleans before the war and who specialized in smaller craft for the army and navy. One of his many exploits was to deliver finished lighters at Norfolk in 1941 two weeks after the order, having had them painted on flat cars en route.[44] When the war ended, seventeen Southern yards had accounted for $6,092,000,000 or nearly 23 per cent of the cost of vessels delivered by seventy principal shipyards.[45]

Parallel to the shipyards, a line of aircraft plants sprang up, mostly at inland points from Dallas–Fort Worth, where Consolidated-Vultee began making B-24 Liberators in 1942, to Marietta, Georgia, where Bell Aircraft brought its first B-29 Superfortresses off the line in December, 1943. Important component or assembly plants appeared at Dallas, Tulsa, New Orleans, Nashville, Birmingham, and Miami.[43] The production of ships and planes gave the South its greatest industrial thrust. In value added the census category of "transportation equipment, except automobiles" jumped suddenly from fifteenth place among Southern industries in 1939 to third place in 1945; in the number of wage earners from fourteenth to second, exceeded only by textiles.[47]

In chemicals and related processes, war production catalyzed many new developments. By the opening of 1942 the landscape was sprouting ordnance plants that made smokeless powder and other explosives from cotton linters, wood cellulose, and petroleum products. Every Southern state participated—in six (North Carolina, Alabama, Arkansas, Kentucky, Mississippi, and Tennessee) ordnance plants were the largest item in the war expansion; in four (Louisiana, Oklahoma, Texas, and Virginia) they placed second. The largest plant was the du Pont Alabama

[44] Hermann B. Deutsch, "Shipyard Bunyan," in *Saturday Evening Post,* CCXV (July 11, 1942), 22–23, 60–62; "The Boss," in *Fortune,* XXVIII (July, 1943), 101–102, 210–14.

[45] Fischer, *Statistical Summary of Shipbuilding,* 164.

[46] Frank J. Taylor and Lawton Wright, *Democracy's Air Arsenal* (New York, 1947), 76, 83, 86; H. Parker Lowell, "Bell Builds B-29's in Georgia," in *Manufacturers' Record,* CXIII (November, 1944), 42–43, 68; Knight, *Fort Worth,* 215.

[47] Deming and Stein, *Disposal of Southern War Plants,* 8, 22. For the 1945 figures the authors relied on *The Blue Book of Southern Progress;* there was no *Census of Manufactures* between 1939 and 1947.

Ordnance Works at Childersburg, near Birmingham. Other significant operations were the Holston Works at Kingsport, the Radford Works in Virginia, the Oklahoma Works at Choteau, and the Volunteer Works at Chattanooga. These were supplemented by loading plants and lesser amounts of gun and ammunition manufacture.[48] In a class by itself, and greatest of all, was the Oak Ridge plant of the Manhattan District, twenty miles northwest of Knoxville, which processed uranium for the atomic bombs that ended the war with Japan. Altogether, the project employed some 110,000 construction workers from 1942 to 1945; peak employment in the plant was 82,000 in May, 1945.[49]

Petroleum refineries faced a need to convert from automobile fuel to high-octane aviation gasoline, fuel oils, butadiene and styrene for synthetic rubber, toluene for explosives, and alcohol for explosives and rubber. The need for high-octane gasoline hastened conversion to a new catalytic cracking process. More than half the nation's synthetic rubber capacity centered near the petroleum resources in Louisiana and Texas, with another concentration around Louisville. The co-ordination of refinery and chemical plants suggested further potentialities for the future. Oil requirements in the East, and the operations of submarine "wolf-packs" against tankers offshore, hastened the completion of new pipelines. The Plantation line from Baton Rouge to Greensboro and the Southeastern line from Panama City to Chattanooga began to flow in 1941. In January, 1943, the "Big Inch" (24 inches) was completed from Longview, Texas, to Norris City, Illinois, and by August it extended to Philadelphia. In December, 1943, the "Little Big Inch" (20 inches) was completed from Beaumont to Linden, New Jersey.[50]

[48] S. A. Lauver, "The South's War Effort and Private Industry: Ordnance," in *Manufacturers' Record*, CXI (January, 1942), 20–21, 60; Deming and Stein, *Disposal of Southern War Plants*, 44–56; Haynes, *Cellulose*, 66; Haynes, *Southern Horizons*, 233.

[49] George Oscar Robinson, *The Oak Ridge Story* (Kingsport, Tenn., 1950), 45–46 and *passim;* Richard G. Hewlett and Oscar E. Anderson, Jr., *The New World 1939/ 1946* in *A History of the United States Atomic Energy Commission*, I (University Park, Pa., 1962), *passim.*

[50] Harold F. Williamson *et al., The American Petroleum Industry: The Age of Energy, 1899–1959* (Evanston, Ill., 1963), 747–94; J. Stanley Clark, *The Oil Century: From the Drake Well to the Conservation Era* (Norman, Okla., 1958), 141–45; Haynes, *Southern Horizons* 233ff.; Jesse Jones, *Fifty Billion Dollars: My Thirteen*

An important growth occurred also in nonferrous metals. At Texas City a subsidiary of Jesse Jones's Reconstruction Finance Corporation built the world's largest tin smelter.[51] Magnesium production issued from new plants at Freeport, and Austin, Texas, and Lake Charles, Louisiana.[52] In aluminum war broke the ALCOA monopoly, which dated from 1893. In 1940 Robert S. Reynolds, whose aluminum foil plant at Richmond was an off-shoot of the family's tobacco business, secured loans from the RFC for alumina plants at Listerhill, Alabama (named for the Senator, who urged expansion), and Longview, Washington. After the war, Reynolds Metals Company acquired government-owned plants at Louisville and at Hurricane Creek and Jones Mill, Arkansas, as part of a deliberate program to encourage competition in the industry. Kaiser Aluminum Company, a new entry after the war, took over a government plant at Baton Rouge. ALCOA itself greatly expanded production in Tennessee and North Carolina, and established a new plant at Mobile.[53]

The total expenditure for Southern war plants was some $4,-442,000,000, or 17.6 per cent of the national total—less than the region's share of the population but more than its portion of prewar industry. Nearly a billion of this was private investment, and one study estimated another $600,000,000 in private investments not reported or not connected with the war effort.[54] The over-all investment in the end exceeded that for military facilities, but much of it occurred later at inflated prices. The geographical balance of new capacity tilted heavily toward the Gulf Southwest. More than half the total investment went into Texas, Louisiana,

---

Years with the RFC, 1932–1945 (New York, 1951), 415; Deming and Stein, *Disposal of Southern War Plants,* 41.

[51] Jones, *Fifty Billion Dollars,* 436. [52] Toulmin, *Diary of Democracy,* 98.

[53] "Aluminum Reborn," in *Fortune,* XXXIII (May, 1946), 104–105; Toulmin, *Diary of Democracy,* 84–85; Special Committee to Investigate the National Defense Program, *Report on Aluminum Investigation,* I, 2–3 and *passim,* in *Senate Documents,* 77 Cong., 1 Sess., No. 480; Paul T. Hendershot, "The Aluminum Industry of the United States, 1940–1947" (Ph.D. dissertation, Louisiana State University, 1947), 63–70, 123–62, and *passim.*

[54] Deming and Stein, *Disposal of Southern War Plants,* 11, 17; *Study of Agricultural and Economic Problems of the Cotton Belt,* Hearings before Special Sub-Committee on Cotton of the Committee on Agriculture, House of Representatives, 80 Cong., 1 Sess. (Washington, 1947), 678.

and Alabama, in that order; more than a fourth into Texas alone, or some $1,435,000,000. Indeed, the South Atlantic states below Virginia ranked behind all those farther west, except Mississippi, which ranked last with $64,000,000. Virginia was fifth, after Tennessee. In 1945 Texas temporarily displaced North Carolina as the leading Southern state in value added by manufacturing.[55]

"A bird's-eye view of large-scale Southern industry makes you feel that the South has rubbed Aladdin's lamp," War Production Board Chairman Donald M. Nelson told an Atlanta audience in 1944. Within the next generation, he suggested, Southern resources, skills, and capital would "bring the South into the vanguard of world industrial progress." The region, he noted, had the country's largest combination powder and explosive plant near Birmingham, the largest repair and supply depot at San Antonio, the largest bomber and modification plant in Marietta, one of the largest airplane factories at Dallas, the largest chemical warfare plant at Huntsville.[56] But the catalog suggested a serious imbalance, a preponderance of capacity ill-suited to peacetime. The region got about 43 per cent of the war-plant expenditure for chemicals and coal and petroleum products (mainly synthetic rubber and aviation gas), 36 per cent of that for ordnance, 12 for guns and ammunition, 24 for ships and aircraft, and 21 for nonferrous metals, but only about 8 per cent of the investment in iron and steel plants, 3 in machinery and electrical equipment, 1 in vehicles.[57]

Much of the expansion, therefore, proved ephemeral, especially in the shipyards, aircraft plants, and ordnance works. Still, the war boom created permanent assets. If the South later slid back from the wartime peaks, it remained on a plateau higher than ever before. In all, Hoover and Ratchford estimated, the wartime expansion raised the region's effective industrial capacity about 40 per cent. From 1939 to 1947 the number of manufacturing establishments grew from 26,516 to 42,739, the value added from $3,124,000,000 to $10,744,000,000 and from 12.7 to 14.4 per cent

[55] Deming and Stein, *Disposal of Southern War Plants*, 13, 22.
[56] Donald M. Nelson, "The South's Economic Opportunity," in *American Mercury*, LIX (1944), 423, 427.
[57] Deming and Stein, *Disposal of Southern War Plants*, 15–16.

of the national total. The number of production workers swelled from 1,349,000 to 2,835,000 in November, 1943, and remained at 2,023,000 in 1947. After reconversion, therefore, the South retained about half the addition to its factory force.[58]

The significance of wartime growth did not lie in expanded capacity alone. The war introduced new dynamics of economic growth. Income payments in the South multiplied about two and a half times during the war—in 1944 governmental payments accounted for a quarter of the total, but the over-all rise continued after they slacked off.[59] The new prosperity drew industries oriented to the market. The newly developed pool of skilled workers and experienced managers drew others. In addition the South had accumulated some amounts of local capital. More important than physical assets, perhaps, were the intangibles: the demonstration of industrial potential, new habits of mind, a recognition that industrialization demanded community services. The South had acquired certain essential ingredients of economic "take-off." [60]

But it acquired them at a heavy cost of wartime tribulation. Agnes Meyer of the Washington *Post,* who visited Southern war towns from Texas to North Carolina in 1943, entitled her account *Journey through Chaos.* Mobile offered an extreme example of a community overrun by war boom. Serving two major shipyards and a new ALCOA plant, plus an overflow from Pascagoula, it grew from 114,906 in 1940 to 201,369 in 1944. An influx of "primitive, illiterate backwoods people . . . hostile, defiant, suspicious, and terrified," swarmed into shacks, tent colonies, trailer camps. Hotels filled, old buildings became dormitories that rented "hot beds" in shifts, and abandoned tenant shacks in the country filled with war workers. By the spring of 1943, John Dos Passos reported, Mobile looked "trampled and battered like a city that's

---

[58] Hoover and Ratchford, *Economic Resources and Policies of the South,* 116, 120–25.

[59] *Ibid.,* 57–61.

[60] Glenn E. McLaughlin and Stefan Robock, *Why Industry Moves South: A Study of Factors Influencing the Recent Location of Manufacturing Plants in the South,* National Planning Association Committee of the South, Report No. 3 (Washington, 1949), which focuses on the postwar years, emphasizes these points. See also Deming and Stein, *Disposal of Southern War Plants,* 41–43.

been taken by storm. Sidewalks are crowded. Gutters are stacked with litter. . . . Garbage cans are overflowing. Frame houses on treeshaded streets bulge with men in shirtsleeves. . . . Cues wait outside of movies and lunchrooms." [61] Community services collapsed. Housewives kept water taps open to catch the trickle. The police force of nineteen was overwhelmed. Murphy High School, built for 2,200, had 3,650 in double shifts; it reported 1,688 absences the first twelve days of April. Juvenile delinquents ran wild; gangs robbed stores, teen-aged girls pursued sailors and war workers. Discontent wracked the shipyards with absenteeism, strikes, and racial conflict. Not until mid-1944 did federally aided services and housing begin to catch up with the problem. But somehow ships were built.[62]

Panama City, Florida, a small paper mill town, served nearby navy and coast guard stations, an AAF gunnery school at Tyndall Field, and the Wainwright Shipyard. The J. A. Jones Construction Company built houses and cafeterias for shipyard workers, even delivered milk and ice to their families, but Panama City remained essentially a town of 20,000 trying to accommodate 60,-000.[63] Pascagoula, which grew from 4,000 to 30,000, got a head start on war housing and community services in 1940, but had to unload surplus population on Mobile.[64] Wilmington had a more favorable situation; many of the shipyard workers commuted from their farms. Still, the population of New Hanover County grew from 48,000 to 60,000 in two years.[65]

Other communities seethed with anarchy, in greater or lesser degree. Every war town, Marvin Schlegel noted in his account of Norfolk, had its uniform-crazy "V-girls" who became "VD-girls" through their contribution to morale. Norfolk itself, a center of naval and shipbuilding activity, achieved an unequaled reputation

[61] Agnes E. Meyer, *Journey Through Chaos* (New York, 1944), 210; John Dos Passos, *State of the Nation* (New York, 1944), 92–93. Population figures for metropolitan area.

[62] Meyer, *Journey Through Chaos*, 202–13; Menefee, *Assignment: USA*, 51–56; Lane, *Ships for Victory*, 438–40.

[63] Lane, *Ships for Victory*, 438; "The Deep South Looks Up," in *Fortune*, XXVIII (July, 1943), 100, 218.

[64] Lane, *Ships for Victory*, 437; Meyer, *Journey Through Chaos*, 193–201.

[65] Lane, *Ships for Victory*, 440–41.

for squalor, perhaps because it was so easily reached by Eastern muckrakers. Walter Davenport of *Collier's* started the exposés in 1942 with "Norfolk Nights," which reported, among lesser sensations, a "girlie" trailer camp with Hollywood titles over the doors: "It Happened One Night," "All That Money Can Buy." *American Mercury* tagged Norfolk "Our Worst War Town." *Architectural Record, PM, Business Week,* and *Domestic Commerce* joined the indictment. When a reporter appeared from Baltimore the local paper announced wearily, "The *Sun* also rises." In 1943 the notoriety finally brought a Congressional investigation which sparked belated action on housing, vice, and other problems. Norfolk, like Mobile, began to overtake its problems before the war ended.[66]

Estimates based on war ration books showed that from 1940 to 1943 civilian population in the South shrank by 1,422,000. Nevertheless thirty-nine of forty-eight metropolitan areas gained. Savannah grew 29 per cent, Charleston 37, Norfolk 57, Mobile 61. Over the decade to 1950 urban population rose 35.9 per cent. Military service and war plants drew off people long chained to the farm, broadened their horizons, gave them new skills. From 1940 to 1945 the South's farm population decreased by 3,347,000, or 20.4 per cent, with the greatest losses in Depression problem areas: the Ozark-Ouachita region, the Eastern and Western upland cotton areas, the North-South border region, and to lesser degree, the Appalachians. Meanwhile farm owners increased and the number of tenants dropped, though less sharply than farm population, from 1,449,293 to 1,165,279. A substantial number flowed into the stream of out-migration.[67]

But those who stayed on the land enjoyed a rare prosperity. Farm prices rose steadily after a period of sharp uncertainty in the

[66] Marvin Wilson Schlegel, *Conscripted City: Norfolk in World War II* (Norfolk, Va., 1951), 186–90, 250–57, 328–35.
[67] All figures for the Census South. Street, *The New Revolution in the Cotton Economy,* 184–85, 187; U.S. Bureau of the Census, *Historical Statistics of the United States, Colonial Times to 1957,* 278, K-27; Rudolf Heberle, *The Impact of the War on Population Redistribution in the South,* Papers of the Institute of Research and Training in the Social Services, Vanderbilt University, No. 7 (Nashville, 1945), 33; U.S. Bureau of the Census, *Historical Statistics of the United States, 1789–1945,* 96, E-52, E-59.

fall of 1939. Tobacco went from 15.4 cents per pound in 1939 to 42.6 cents in 1945; cotton from 9.89 to 22.52 cents.[68] Tobacco farmers, after their disastrous experiment with *laissez-faire* in 1939, stabilized production at a level somewhat below the bumper crop of 1939 until 1944 and 1945, when the crop reached nearly two billion pounds in each year.[69] In the cotton market domestic needs offset a decline in exports, and production stayed around eleven to twelve million bales until bad weather brought a drop to nine and then eight and a half million in 1945 and 1946. However, the stabilization reflected improved yields, for the acreage dropped from 22,811,000 in 1939 to 17,584,000 in 1945.[70] Army camps and industrial complexes offered outlets for foodstuffs and spurred expansion in dairying and truck farming. Heightened demand for oilseed products raised the production of peanuts, especially in Georgia, Alabama, and Texas. In the Black Belts of Alabama and Mississippi the transition to livestock, spurred first by the boll weevil, got new impetus.[71]

But the failure to diversify further was the story of an opportunity lost. "The outstanding example of misused . . . resources in agriculture during the war effort," Walter W. Wilcox wrote afterward, "occurred in the Cotton Belt." [72] Despite an urgent demand for foods, despite a domestic carry-over that never fell much below 10,500,000 bales, despite labor shortages, cotton still absorbed vast amounts of manpower and fertilizer. The wartime drive for diversification assumed the familiar character of exhortation. "There's no sense in continuing to pile up cotton," Secretary of Agriculture Claude A. Wickard told a Memphis audience in September, 1941. "The country needs milk and eggs and meat a lot worse." "We cannot eat surplus cotton," Georgia Farm Bureau

[68] U.S. Bureau of the Census, *Historical Statistics of the United States from Colonial Times to 1957*, 301–302, K-303, K-309.

[69] *Ibid.*, 302, K-308; Hoover and Ratchford, *Economic Resources and Policies of the South*, 350–52; Walter W. Wilcox, *The Farmer in the Second World War* (Ames, Iowa, 1947) , 235–42.

[70] U.S. Bureau of the Census, *Historical Statistics of the United States from Colonial Times to 1957*, 301, K-301-302.

[71] Street, *The New Revolution in the Cotton Economy*, 72–76. See also John Leonard Fulmer, *Agricultural Progress in the Cotton Belt Since 1920* (Chapel Hill, 1950) , 193.

[72] Wilcox, *The Farmer in the Second World War*, 64.

President R. L. Wingate said in 1944. "We cannot eat tobacco. . . . We have got to grow food." The Department of Agriculture publicized a system of "goals" for "essential war crops" and Congress extended price support to such crops, but continued the same support for "basic" crops like cotton. Cotton farmers, therefore, preferred to stay with the familiar rather than risk the unknown.[73]

War prosperity offered a chance to redress the balance sheet from two decades of distress, and cotton-belt Congressmen fought through the war to raise both floors and ceilings on farm prices. One cycle of controversy turned on Commodity Credit Corporation policies. In 1941 House Agriculture Chairman Hampton P. Fulmer of South Carolina sponsored a bill to prevent sale of CCC wheat and cotton stocks, but the President vetoed it and the CCC thereafter used the opportunity gradually to feed out its cotton holdings, at some profit.[74] After early 1942 a program of food subsidies, administered chiefly through the CCC, met persistent but futile opposition from farm organizatons which favored Ed O'Neal's principle of "parity in the marketplace." [75] The farm bloc, led by Senator Bankhead, was more successful at winning adjustments in CCC loan rates which rose from 85 per cent of parity in the spring of 1941 to 90 per cent in 1942 (92.5 for cotton), and finally to 95 per cent in 1944.[76]

This was a cushion against postwar deflation. The more immediate issue turned not on price supports but on price controls. To give farmers real parity, Bankhead argued, would require prices above parity: "If parity is the ceiling point, practically all cotton will be sold below that point." [77] The controversy began in July, 1941, when the President sought enforcement powers for the new

[73] Ibid., 64–67; Bela Gold, Wartime Economic Planning in Agriculture (New York, 1949) , 124–26; Street, The New Revolution in the Cotton Economy, 66–69.

[74] Rosenman (comp.) The Public Papers and Addresses of Franklin D. Roosevelt, X, 341–43; Edwin M. Watson to John H. Bankhead, August 25, 1941, in OF 258, Roosevelt Library.

[75] Rosenman (comp.) The Public Papers and Addresses of Franklin D. Roosevelt, XII, 278–90; XIII, 72–75; Benedict, Farm Policies of the United States, 1790–1950, 419–30.

[76] Wilcox, The Farmer in the Second World War, 217.

[77] Birmingham News, April 28, 1942, clipping in Bankhead Papers (Alabama Department of Archives, Montgomery) .

Office of Price Administration. The debate dragged on through the fall, but the coming of war in December changed the picture. Even so, when Congress passed the Emergency Price Control Act in January, 1942, it included a Bankhead Amendment that required approval of the Secretary of Agriculture for any farm ceilings and set the minimum level at 110 per cent of parity, or whichever was the highest of three other standards.[78]

"The plain fact is that a majority of our upper chamber . . . sold out to a pressure group of profiteers," the New York *Herald-Tribune* fulminated. The alternative standards, Roosevelt claimed, set farm ceilings at 116 per cent of parity on the average and 150 per cent on some commodities. In September, 1942, he demanded elimination of the provision. "Did you ever read the *Merchant of Venice?*" he wrote to Bankhead. "I remember something about a fellow who wanted his pound of flesh." [79]

A new Stabilization Act of October, 1942, let the President reduce ceilings to parity or the highest price, January 1–September 15, 1942, with a further proviso that the President could go below the latter if necessary to correct "gross inequities." On the other hand, under an amendment by Senator Barkeley, he could raise ceilings to reflect labor and other cost increases.[80] Victory remained with the President, but not without flank attacks designed to change the definition of parity. Early in 1943 Bankhead put through a bill to exclude government subsidy or other payments in computing parity. This was already the practice, but the requirement was vetoed.[81] From 1943 until the end of the war, Elmer Thomas and Georgia's Representative Stephen Pace spearheaded an unsuccessful drive to include rises in farm-labor

[78] Benedict, *Farm Policies of the United States*, 410–11; McCune, *The Farm Bloc*, 39–40; John H. Bankhead, "The Price Control Bill," in Montgomery *Advertiser*, January 25, 1942, clipping in Bankhead Papers.

[79] New York *Herald-Tribune*, February 27, 1942; Rosenman (comp.) *Public Papers and Addresses of Franklin D. Roosevelt*, XI, 356–68; Franklin D. Roosevelt to John H. Bankhead, August 31, 1942, in OF 258, Roosevelt Library.

[80] Benedict, *Farm Policies of the United States*, 415; McCune, *The Farm Bloc*, 58–73.

[81] Rosenman (comp.) *Public Papers and Addresses of Franklin D. Roosevelt*, XII, 135–43; Benedict, *Farm Policies of the United States*, 425; Kile, *The Farm Bureau Movement*, 299; Edward A. O'Neal to John H. Bankhead, February 11, 1943, in Bankhead Papers.

costs.[82] Bankhead, however, did get one change: a requirement in the Stabilization Extension Act of 1944 that no ceiling price should reflect a price *to the farm producers* below parity.[83]

The parity battle was only one manifestation of a tetchy spirit that troubled the countryside with complaints against "regimentation" and labor shortages. "A prosperous farmer's the most conservative man on earth," an Alabama farmer told John Dos Passos. "We were plenty sick for a while. Now we feel about ready to throw away our crutches. Just leave us alone. Get us good prices and let us produce." [84] With a preponderance of political power in the South, John Temple Graves observed, "the farmer was apparently swinging it against his New Deal patrons and being encouraged by the industrialists, most of whom were long-standing anti-New Dealers." [85] As late as 1937 Ed O'Neal was calling Virginia's Senators "reactionary"; by the early 1940's he was joining Harry Byrd in attacks on the Farm Security Administration (FSA).[86]

The FSA, as an independent power structure, became a prime target of the agricultural establishment. It came under attack for its co-operative farms, mostly inherited from the Resettlement Administration, for its loans to land-leasing and land-purchasing associations, for its tenant-rehabilitation and tenant-land-purchase programs, for helping Negro farmers. "Now comes the New Deal," a Mississippi Delta planter wrote in 1942, ". . . with a law to acquire our plantations . . . and divide the land up again into family sized farms of 40 acres and a mule—the same promise the other Yankees made to the negroes during the other Civil War." [87]

Will Alexander, FSA's first administrator, was an "off-color

---

[82] McCune, *The Farm Bloc*, 55; Backman and Gainsbrugh, *Economics of the Cotton Textile Industry*, 220; Edward A. O'Neal to Bankhead, March 22, 1943; Bankhead to Roy E. Loper, April 3, 1946, in Bankhead Papers.

[83] Wilcox, *The Farmer in the Second World War*, 217–18; Bankhead to Atticus Mullin, July 10, 1944; Montgomery *Advertiser*, July 13, 1944, clipping, in Bankhead Papers.

[84] Dos Passos, *State of the Nation*, 75.   [85] Graves, *The Fighting South*, 245.

[86] Campbell, *The Farm Bureau and the New Deal*, 186.

[87] O. F. Bledsoe, III, "The Political Aspect of the Delta and Plantation System," political broadside on behalf of James O. Eastland for the Senate, enclosed with Franklin D. Roosevelt to Eleanor Roosevelt, June 9, 1942, in OF 93, Roosevelt Library.

politician," Georgia's Representative Eugene Cox said.[88] Calvin B. "Beanie" Baldwin, a small-town businessman from Virginia who succeeded him in 1940, grew into an intransigent liberal, inept at maneuver, unwilling to compromise. Baldwin's FSA became increasingly militant in defense of small farmers, tenants, and laborers, but unequal to the growing attack.[89] In 1942 FSA assumed responsibility for most of the wartime farm labor programs, through which it undertook to move workers from submarginal lands to areas of labor shortage and sought to assure minimum standards for its recruits. Among other things, it found jobs for displaced members of the Southern Tenant Farmers Union. Instead of "devoting your efforts to the development of agriculture in the South," Georgia's Representative Malcolm C. Tarver stormed at Baldwin, "you are going out after this fly-by-night program of trying to move some hundreds of thousands, if not millions, of farmers and their families out of the South." [90]

The attack built slowly to a crescendo during the war. In 1942 Harry Byrd investigated the FSA for extravagance and Kenneth McKellar asserted flatly, "I think Mr. Baldwin is a Communist." [91] An Alabama judge created a momentary sensation with a charge that FSA provided funds for poll-tax payments. Closer scrutiny revealed only that it included poll taxes in its clients' family budgets.[92] In truth, FSA's fatal weakness was the absence of an organized political constituency. Yet it did not altogether lack defenders, including John Bankhead, who quarreled with the Farm Bureau on this point. Clarence Poe's *Progressive Farmer* accused Ed O'Neal of "a tragic mistake in joining hands with those elements that are seeking to destroy the Farm Security Administration" and driving "a wedge of bitterness between land-owning

[88] Conkin, *Tomorrow a New World*, 386–92; Maddox, "The Farm Security Administration," 480–94.

[89] Stokely and Dykeman, *Seeds of Southern Change*, 277–28; Albertson, *Roosevelt's Farmer*, 274.

[90] Wilcox, *The Farmer in the Second World War*, 89–90; Menefee, *Assignment: USA*, 252–53; Mitchell, "The Reminiscences of H. L. Mitchell," *loc. cit.*, 135–38; Albertson, *Roosevelt's Farmer*, 366–67.

[91] Conkin, *Tomorrow a New World*, 392.

[92] Montgomery *Advertiser*, January 3, 1942, cited in Gardner Jackson to Stephen Early, February 12, 1942, in OF 1638, Roosevelt Library. The Greensboro (Ala.) *Watchman* first aired the charge.

farmers and other farmers all over the South." [93] In a public letter leaders of several farm, labor, and church organizations charged that the attacks came "solely from farm interests committed to the high-price-through-scarcity concept" and defended FSA on the ground that it would contribute to war food production.[94] In 1943 this rather dubious idea became the basis of a desperate effort by Baldwin to save FSA by enmeshing it with the Agriculture Department's credit and war production programs.[95]

Meanwhile a conservative-minded Congress whittled away his powers. In 1942 it slashed the FSA budget by 30 per cent, most heavily in the migratory labor camp and tenant purchase programs; forbade further loans to co-operatives; prohibited direct land purchases, collective farming, and homestead associations; and required reports every six months on liquidation of the resettlement program. Early in 1943 North Carolina's Representative Harold D. Cooley put through a resolution for an investigation. Witnesses paraded their charges before his committee while the Farm Bureau and its allies kept up a drum-fire of opposition. Oscar Johnston's National Cotton Council joined the fray with charges of "mismanagement, waste of funds, decreased production, and Communistic activities," and requested that "general rumors" of this nature be forwarded to the council.[96] "But how can they call a program to build up the family-size farm communistic?" John Dos Passos asked an Alabama dairy farmer. "Well, around here communism's anything we don't like," the man replied. "Isn't it that way everywhere else?" [97]

In 1944 the Cooley Committee published its inventory of FSA sins: farm collectives, stretching executive orders, uprooting families, deception, loans to unqualified persons, backing industry in competition with business, and enlarged and inefficient organiza-

[93] *Progressive Farmer*, LVII (March, 1942) , 6.

[94] Gardner Jackson *et al.* to Marvin McIntyre, June 25, 1942, in OF 1568, Roosevelt Library.

[95] Albertson, *Roosevelt's Farmer*, 341–42, 349–52.

[96] Stetson Kennedy, *Southern Exposure*, (New York, 1946) , 277; *Agricultural Department Appropriation Bill for 1944*, Hearings before the Subcommittee of the Committee on Appropriations, House of Representatives, 78 Cong., 1 Sess. (n.p., n.d.) , 1616–32.

[97] Dos Passos, *State of the Nation*, 82.

tion.[98] But the report was anticlimactic. Late in 1943 Baldwin had resigned under pressure to be replaced by a "safe" administration under former Representative Frank Hancock of North Carolina. Liquidation proceeded apace and in 1946 Congress replaced FSA with the Farmers Home Corporation, which administered a reduced tenant purchase program.[99]

Commercial farmers who, like businessmen, had manpower problems of their own, viewed labor in much the same perspective. The price-control and food-subsidy disputes set them against urban workers as rivals for shares of the national income. "Farmers resent the efforts of organized labor leaders to influence agricultural policies that are intended to force farmers to toil and sweat unlimited hours at price levels far below industrial wages and industrial prices," Ed O'Neal said.[100] Labor shortages and rising wages came closer home. From 1940 to 1945 the average rate for picking seed cotton rose 211 per cent, from 62 cents a hundred pounds to $1.93.[101] The American war worker "has so much money he doesn't know what to do with it," O'Neal complained. "How can the farmer compete for labor. . . ?" The protest broadened out into generalized attacks. "We must realize that the present administration is not a Democratic party," Mississippi Farm Bureau President Ransom Aldrich told a Greenville meeting. "It is a New Deal party, a labor government. We are letting creep in with the labor policy of the government a lot of communism and state socialism." [102] President Craig Smith of the Alabama Cotton Manufacturers Association, speaking to the Talladega Kiwanians, denounced efforts by metropolitan papers and "professional labor leaders" to portray farmers as war profiteers.[103]

Organized labor, despite substantial gains during the war, remained too weak to temper the rural orientation of most Southern

[98] *Report of Select Committee on Agriculture to Investigate the Activities of the Farm Security Administration,* in *House Miscellaneous Documents,* 78 Cong., 2 Sess., No. 1430.

[99] Conkin, *Tomorrow a New World,* 597–98; Maddox, "The Farm Security Administration," 501–502; Kile, *The Farm Bureau Movement,* 272.

[100] Edward A. O'Neal to all Members of Congress, June 23, 1942, copy in OF 1568, Roosevelt Library.

[101] Street, *The New Revolution in the Cotton Economy,* 204.

[102] O'Neal and Aldrich, quoted in McCune, *The Farm Bloc,* 179, 188.

[103] Quoted in Graves, *The Fighting South,* 244–45.

politicos. Quite the contrary, the antilabor obsession quickened movements for antiunion legislation. In Houston Vance Muse, whose "Christian American Association" had explored thin veins of racial and religious prejudice since 1936, finally struck pay-dirt in the antiunion cause. In 1941, after Governor O'Daniel put through a law forbidding violence or threats on the picket line, they began to promote "Anti-Violence-in-Strikes" laws, "God-Given Right-to-Work" laws, and union registration laws. In 1942 Mississippi adopted an antiviolence law on the Texas model. In 1943 Texas, Alabama, and Florida enacted restrictions that required union financial statements and licenses for union agents; limited union fees; prohibited jurisdictional strikes, secondary boycotts, and mass picketing; regulated union elections and the expulsion of members; and banned union political contributions. In 1944 Arkansas and Florida by constitutional amendment set in motion a wave of right-to-work legislation that would crest in 1947 when Georgia, North Carolina, Tennessee, Texas, and Virginia adopted laws against the closed shop and other union security devices. Once started, the movement developed its own momentum, but Vance Muse admitted collecting $67,873.49 to ballyhoo the Arkansas amendment and confessed to significant influence on labor legislation in Alabama, Florida, Mississippi, and Texas.[104]

But the most inflammable issue ignited by the war was the question of Negro participation in the defense effort. From the beginning Negro leaders kept up an unremitting demand for full recognition. In September, 1940, Walter White, A. Philip Randolph, and T. Arnold Hill presented at the White House a program for full integration of Negroes into the armed forces and defense industries. Soon thereafter White House Press Secretary Stephen Early announced a policy of receiving Negroes into the Army in proportion to population, but in separate units. Walter White indignantly denied the implication that the Negro group

[104] Walter Davenport, "Savior from Texas," in *Collier's* XCVI (August 18, 1945) , 13; Kennedy, *Southern Exposure*, 249–55; John Roy Carlson, *The Plotters* (New York, 1946), 270–71; Victor H. Bernstein, "The Antilabor Front," in *Antioch Review*, III (1943) , 334–37; Harry A. Millis and Emily Clark Brown, *From the Wagner Act to Taft-Hartley* (Chicago, 1950) , 321–29; Sanford Cohen, *State Labor Legislation, 1937–1947* (Columbus, Ohio, 1948) , *passim;* Helen Fuller, "The Christian American Cabal," in *New Republic*, CVIII (January, 1943) , 115–17.

had endorsed this. Such units as were authorized, he protested, were mainly service and supply units. And the Navy had openings only for Negro mess attendants, stewards, and cooks.[105]

A few significant appointments did little to quiet the outcry. In October, 1940, shortly before the election, Benjamin O. Davis became the first Negro brigadier general, and Negro assistants were named for the Secretary of War and the Director of Selective Service. But as the armed forces grew, Negroes did find a greater variety of positions than in any previous war. Eventually about a million served, in every major branch and in every theater. But they served under circumstances that mirrored the society from which they came, usually in segregated units. In April, 1942, the Navy began to accept Negroes for general service and because it lacked traditional Negro units developed a variegated pattern that ranged up to fairly thorough integration in places. In 1944 the Navy began to commission Negro officers.

But most Negroes served in the Army, which maintained its tradition of separate units through the war. Every camp had its little Harlem, its separate facilities, its periodic racial "incidents." The most publicized departure from the pattern was a 1944 order that banned segregation in recreational and transportation facilities on Army bases, an order honored chiefly by evasion. More important was a 1940 decision to give up segregation in all officer candidate schools except those for Air Force cadets. A separate flight school at Tuskegee, Alabama, trained about six hundred Negro pilots, many of whom saw action over Europe. The nearest approach to integration in ground combat forces occurred during the Battle of the Bulge early in 1945, when the Army distributed platoons of Negro volunteers from the Service of Supply, about 2,500 in all, among eleven white divisions. They fought through the subsequent drive across Germany.[106]

War industries were even less accessible to Negro influence and

[105] Walter White to Eleanor Roosevelt, October 4, 1940, in Eleanor Roosevelt Papers; STE [Stephen T. Early] to General Watson, confidential memorandum, September 19, 1940, in 2538, Roosevelt Library; White to Harold Ickes, October 16, 1940; and Roosevelt to White, October 25 1940, in 93, *ibid.*; Walter White, "It's Our Country Too," in *Saturday Evening Post*, CCXIII (December 14 1940), 27.

[106] Charles Dollard and Donald Young, "In the Armed Forces," in *Survey Graphic*, XXXVI (1947), 66–68, 111–16; Franklin, *From Slavery to Freedom*, 560, 564–73; White, *A Man Called White*, 249–50.

pressure than the armed forces, although government policy theoretically opposed discrimination. In July, 1940, the National
Defense Advisory Commission appointed Robert C. Weaver to the
staff of its Labor Division and in August it urged employers not to
discriminate, but buried the recommendation in a long statement
on labor policy. In October an appropriation act prohibited
discrimination in defense training, but local officials in the South
frustrated enforcement with the sophism that Negroes should get
training only for jobs already open to them.[107] As the defense programs advanced, Negroes saw little evidence that nondiscrimina-
tory policies were implemented. During the fall of 1940 A. Philip
Randolph conceived the idea of a mass march on Washington
to dramatize job demands and in February, 1941, a meeting in
New York organized the March on Washington Movement, with
July 1 as its target date. As the movement grew, its leaders
promised to mobilize 100,000 marchers. The Office of Production
Management, in a letter signed by Sidney Hillman but not by his
colleague William S. Knudsen of General Motors, again called
upon defense contractors to hire Negro workers, and Roosevelt
demanded "immediate steps to facilitate the full utilization of our
manpower." [108] Negro leaders rejected these as empty gestures
and the administration, alarmed at the prospect of a mass descent
on Washington, maneuvered desperately to forestall the march.
Finally, a series of conferences produced a recommendation for a
Presidential directive against discrimination and the establishment of a grievance committee. This Randolph's group accepted.
On June 25 President Roosevelt issued Executive Order 8802
which forbade discrimination in defense industries and training
programs, required a nondiscrimination clause in defense contracts, and established the Committee on Fair Employment Practice (FEPC).[109]

Chaired first by Mark Ethridge, publisher of the Louisville

[107] Louis Ruchames, *Race, Jobs, & Politics: The Story of FEPC* (New York, 1953),
11–14; Charles S. Johnson, *Patterns of Negro Segregation* (New York, 1943), 107–108;
Rosenman (comp.), *The Public Papers and Addresses of Franklin D. Roosevelt*, IX,
420.

[108] Rosenman (comp.), *The Public Papers and Addresses of Franklin D. Roosevelt*,
X, 216.

[109] Herbert Garfinkel, *When Negroes March: The March on Washington Movement*
(Glencoe, Ill., 1959), 37–61.

Courier-Journal, the FEPC wielded chiefly a moral influence, since it had no power to enforce directives and refused to recommend the ultimate weapon, cancellation of defense contracts. Moreover, it initiated investigations only upon complaint.[110] Its first major action was to seek information and publicize the President's policy through regional hearings: in Los Angeles, Chicago, New York, and Birmingham. At Birmingham in June, 1942, Ethridge under-took to mollify Southern whites with the assurance "that Executive Order 8802 is a war order, and not a social document." It was to the South's interest, he said, "even to our economic salvation, that we give our people skills while we can and while they are needed." But in a widely quoted paragraph he denied any inten-tion to challenge segregation: "there is no power in the world—not even in all the mechanized armies of the earth, Allied and Axis—which could now force the Southern white people to the abandon-ment of the principle of social segregation." [111]

Birmingham itself accepted the three-day hearings with surpris-ing equanimity, Brooks Atkinson reported to the New York *Times* two weeks later.[112] The Birmingham *News,* after noting statements by FEPC representatives that the community had less discrimination than any other Southern town, commented: "Bir-mingham and the committee seem well met." Other newspapers in the South, however, called the hearings a "three-day inquisi-tion" and wrote of "Roosevelt racial experts," "halo-wearing mis-sionaries of New Deal socialism," "a group of snoopers," and "dat cummittee fer de purtechshun uv Rastus & Sambo." The commit-tee's most outspoken defenders were CIO and Negro organiza-tions, whose voices were lost in a storm of hostility.[113]

The FEPC assumed a low status among war agencies. It can-celled hearings in El Paso because the State Department feared the revelation of discrimination against Spanish-Americans. After the Birmingham hearings the President transferred the committee from the jurisdiction of the War Production Board to the War

[110] The account of FEPC is taken chiefly from Ruchames, *Race, Jobs, & Politics.*
[111] Louisville *Courier-Journal,* June 21, 1942.
[112] New York *Times,* July 2, 1942.
[113] Ruchames, *Race, Jobs, & Politics,* 43–45; Kesselman, *The Social Politics of* FEPC (Chapel Hill, 1948) , 168.

Manpower Commission and in January, 1943, WMC Chairman Paul V. McNutt "indefinitely postponed" hearings on complaints against Southern railroads and unions. This brought the resignation of three members, including Ethridge, and the organization of a new committee.

In May, 1943, Roosevelt established a second FEPC in the Executive Office of the President under, first, Monsignor Francis J. Haas, then Malcolm Ross, with six other members. It still lacked enforcement powers but enlarged the staff, established twelve regional offices (at Dallas and Atlanta in the South), and worked closely with the WMC Minority Groups Branch under Will Alexander. It immediately faced a crisis over an earlier directive that grew out of the Birmingham hearings. On May 24 the Mobile shipyard promoted twelve Negroes to jobs as welders. The next day white workers rioted and more than twenty people were injured before an army detachment quelled the disturbance. In this case the FEPC managed to negotiate an agreement setting aside four segregated shipways on which Negroes could win promotion. In September the committee held the delayed railroad hearings and in November directed the roads and brotherhoods to cease discrimination. But the Southern roads defied the order, the FEPC certified the cases to President Roosevelt, and he, faced by the exigencies of war and politics, permitted the issue to expire in a special mediation committee.

Still the FEPC persisted, hounded by hostile investigations and impassioned critics—"Oh! This is the beginning of a communistic dictatorship," [114] Mississippi's John Rankin erupted—until it expired for want of funds in June, 1946. One measure of its effectiveness was the fact that the very maintenance of a regional office in downtown Atlanta was a major victory over local efforts to have it removed; another, that the Atlanta and Dallas offices spent much of their time fighting discrimination in other governmental agencies such as the War Manpower Commission and the United States Employment Service. Among 1,108 complaints handled by the Southern offices only 227 were successfully adjusted. Scattered reports attested to significant employment gains by Negroes in

[114] *Congressional Record*, 78 Cong., 2 Sess., 5054.

shipyards, ordnance, aircraft and other defense plants, but more because of intense demand and willing employers like A. J. Higgins in New Orleans than because of governmental policy—and mostly in the "h jobs": hot, heavy, and hard.[115]

In their drive for wartime participation Negroes broadened the front on which battle had already developed against lynching, discrimination, educational inequalities, and voting restrictions. Before the war ended, the great sectional compromise of 1877, which had left the white South unhampered in developing its institutions of white supremacy, faced challenge. And segregation itself became, at last, an open question. "It was as if some universal message had come through to the great mass of Negroes," Howard Odum wrote in 1943, "urging them to dream new dreams and to protest against the old order." [116]

New attitudes were reflected in reports of young Negroes testing barriers at soda fountains, in railroad dining cars, and elsewhere, in stories of Negro defiance like that of a soldier telling his white tormentors: "If I've got to die for democracy, I might as well die for some of it right here and now." On a Southern trip Sterling A. Brown found among Negroes "a sense of not belonging, and protest, sometimes not loud but always deeply felt. . . . The protest I heard ranged from the quietly spoken aside, through twisted humor and sarcasm, to stridency." [117] If protest was more voluble in the North, J. Saunders Redding warned, it was only because "the Negro North has always been the tongue of the black South." [118]

The rising wind of Negro aspirations soon fanned the flames of racist reaction. On July 22, 1942, one month after the Birmingham hearings, Horace C. Wilkinson, a lawyer-politician and former Klansman, stoked the fires with a speech to the Bessemer

[115] Fair Employment Practice Committee, *Final Report* (Washington, 1947), 33–36; Robert C. Weaver, *Negro Labor: A National Problem* (New York, 1946), 84–88; Johnson, *Into the Main Stream*, 108–109, 111–12. For the story of FEPC's last chairman see Malcolm Ross, *All Manner of Men* (New York, 1948).

[116] Howard W. Odum, *Race and Rumors of Race* (Chapel Hill, 1943), 171.

[117] Sterling A. Brown, "Count Us In," in Rayford W. Logan (ed.), *What the Negro Wants* (Chapel Hill, 1944), 314–15.

[118] J. Saunders Redding, "A Negro Speaks for His People," in *Atlantic Monthly*, CLXXI (March, 1943), 60.

Kiwanis Club. He began with the story of a Birmingham bus driver who said, pointing to a group of Negroes, "Right there, mister, is where our next war will break out, and it may start before this one is over." This prophecy introduced a sequence of atrocity stories: Negroes who resisted Jim Crowism on buses and trains, took white men's jobs at Republic Steel, threw kisses at white college girls, "practically took over" a liquor store in Dothan, and brought suit to force Negro posts on the Alabama American Legion. "If there is room for a National Association for the Advancement of Colored People," Wilkinson declaimed, "there is need of a League to Maintain White Supremacy." Soon afterward Governor Frank Dixon, with a flourish of publicity, refused to have Alabama convicts supply cloth for the Defense Supplies Corporation because the contract included a standard clause forbidding discrimination.[119] After that Senator Bankhead found the situation so inflamed that he urged the Army to train Northern Negroes only in Northern camps.[120] By September Martin Dies had smelled out a plot: "throughout the South today," he told the House of Representatives, "subversive elements are attempting to convince the Negro that he should be placed on social equality with the white people; that now is the time for him to assert his rights." [121]

Rumor mills went into overtime production, fabricating tales of insolence in crowded buses, warnings that Negroes planned to "take over" white women, and wild fantasies that they were gathering ice picks for a mass insurrection. The stories followed time-worn patterns, different mainly in their prevalence and the urgent significance assigned them. But there was one ingenious original: the legend of the "Eleanor Clubs," named for Mrs. Roosevelt, groups of domestics organized to put "a white woman in every

[119] Graves, *The Fighting South*, 121–24, 135; Menefee, *Assignment: USA*, 163.

[120] Mobile *Register*, August 3, 1942, clipping in Bankhead Papers. Chief of Staff George C. Marshall replied that "the only sound basis upon which we can proceed . . . is to station our troops in accordance with the dictates of military necessity." Birmingham *News*, August 13, 1942, *ibid.*

[121] *Congressional Record*, 77 Cong., 2 Sess., 7457. Others detected a different plot, "to drive a wedge between tne southern people and the administration" and win a Senate seat for Dixon. James A. Dombrowski to Marvin McIntyre, August 20, 1942, in OF 4952, Roosevelt Library.

kitchen." Diligent search never uncovered a single one, but the stories had a foundation in labor shortages created by the war boom. White women might not understand the danger of Hitler, Will Alexander remarked, "but white women in the South certainly recognized what a crisis the loss of a cook is." [122]

For Southern liberals tutored in the interracial school the "rumor crisis" threatened a cataclysm. "Indeed," Jonathan Daniels wrote Eleanor Roosevelt, "I have never known a time when well informed friends of the colored people in the South and elsewhere were so alarmed about the situation." [123] One after another such people counseled caution. Segregation "is not an argument in the South," John Temple Graves admonished. "It is a major premise." "A small group of Negro agitators and another small group of white rabble-rousers are pushing this country closer and closer to an interracial explosion," Virginius Dabney wrote. "Let them beware," warned David L. Cohn. "He who attempts to change [the mores of a people] by law runs risks of incalculable gravity." [124] In 1944 W. T. Couch, director of the University of North Carolina Press, having invited fifteen Negro leaders to explain *What the Negro Wants,* felt impelled to cushion the shock of revelation with a "Publisher's Introduction" in which he argued that a sudden end to segregation "would be disastrous for everyone and more so for the Negro than the white man." [125]

Inevitably the tensions challenged the old Commission on Interracial Cooperation, which had sprung from the crisis of another war. But the Commission, Will Alexander had decided

---

[122] Alexander, "The Reminscences of Will W. Alexander," *loc. cit.,* 699. Odum, *Race and Rumors of Race,* is based on some two thousand rumors collected in the Southeastern states. See also Thomas Sancton, "Trouble in Dixie I. The Returning Tragic Era," and "Trouble in Dixie III. Race Fear Sweeps the South," in *New Republic,* CVIII (1943), 11–14, 81–83.

[123] Jonathan Daniels to Eleanor Roosevelt, August 28, 1942, in Eleanor Roosevelt Papers.

[124] Graves, *The Fighting South,* 120; Virginius Dabney, "Nearer and Nearer the Precipice," in *Atlantic Monthly,* CLXXI (January, 1943), 94; David L. Cohn, "How the South Feels," in *Atlantic Monthly,* CLXXIII (January, 1944), 50. During 1943, Dabney, however, participated in a campaign to repeal Virginia's law for segregation of common carriers. See Nancy Armstrong, *The Study of An Attempt Made in 1943 to Abolish Segregation of the Races on Common Carriers in the State of Virginia,* in Phelps-Stokes Fellowship Papers, No. 17 (Charlottesville, Va., 1950).

[125] W. T. Couch, "Publisher's Introduction," in Logan (ed.), *What the Negro Wants,* xx.

with uncommon detachment, had outlived its generation. William E. Cole, a University of Tennessee sociologist whom Alexander secured to make an analysis, reinforced the judgment. The staff, Cole said, had grown jaded and inefficient. Negro leaders felt that the Commission was "static, colorless . . . not charged with social action . . . 'Uncle Tomish' in nature." He suggested a revival of Howard Odum's proposed Council on Southern Regional Development.[126]

Meanwhile, Mrs. Jessie Daniel Ames, one of the Commission's stalwarts, had unknowingly provided the way. Fearing the reaction that Northern "radicals" might provoke, she had prodded Gordon B. Hancock, dean of Virginia Union University, to call a conference of Southern Negroes which met at Durham in October, 1942, to challenge the "cooperation of that element of the white South who express themselves as desirous of a New Deal for the Negroes." [127] In December a committee of the Durham Conference published a statement detailing demands for the ballot, civil rights, employment opportunity, and access to public services. In April, 1943, 115 whites meeting in Atlanta issued a response and proposed a joint conference which convened in Richmond on June 16. The Richmond Conference in turn undertook to plan a new interracial organization and on February 16, 1944, the Southern Regional Council (SRC) replaced the Committee on Interracial Cooperation in Atlanta. Howard W. Odum, its first president, and Guy B. Johnson, its executive secretary, laid plans for a broad program of regional development, with commissions on race relations, economic affairs, community life and welfare, cultural development, and public affairs.[128]

But dissenters plunged them unwillingly into segregation con-

[126] William E. Cole, "Report on the Commission on Interracial Cooperation, 1942–1943," typed report in Commission on Interracial Cooperation Papers (Atlanta University), 29, cited in William C. Allred, Jr., "The Southern Regional Council, 1943–1961" (M.A. thesis, Emory University, 1966), 16. Stokely and Dykeman, *Seeds of Southern Change*, 283; Alexander, "Reminiscences of Will W. Alexander," *loc. cit.*, 656–57.

[127] Southern Regional Council, *The Southern Regional Council: Its Origin and Purposes* (Atlanta, 1944), 4. Mrs. Ames, who confessed to feeling like "the frustrated Cassandra," assured Hancock that "only Southern Negroes can save the situation for themselves as for the Nation." Jessie Daniel Ames to Mark Ethridge May 25, 1942; Ames to Gordon B. Hancock, July 1942, in Ames Papers.

[128] Southern Regional Council, *The Southern Regional Council*, 8–12.

troversies. "The habit of thought that would tear the Negro problem out of its national context is a southern habit of thought," J. Saunders Redding asserted in the little magazine, *Common Ground,* "and . . . it is potentially more harmful than beneficial." The only appropriate strategy, he argued, was "to storm and defend advanced positions . . . so that when the forces of the native enemy build themselves up for the counterattack, no retreat will be made beyond the lines now—in the spring of 1944—held." [129] "Do we want the tangled race skein completely unraveled? Or don't we?" Lillian Smith asked. "Are we merely trying to avoid . . . more 'tensions' which embarrass white folks, or are we trying to secure for the Negro his full human rights?" [130] *"Common Ground,"* Odum fumed, "like a good many of the others, seems to think that when they set up an argument and get people to split among themselves, they are doing something liberal." [131]

On the other side Birmingham columnist John Temple Graves proposed a conference "of Southerners of just plain decency and enlightenment, *plus power,* to do something big for the Negro this side of the segregation line." Odum demurred. "If we could just stop talking about social equality and segregation and go to work," he wrote Graves, "it would be a day for us, wouldn't it?" [132] Several militant groups, North and South, "insist that we must declare ourselves on what they assume to be the one definitive issue," he told the SRC's first membership meeting in December, 1944. He proposed to work for more equal facilities, full equality before the law, and economic opportunities, but not "to go on record as approving the principles and philosophy, the practice and pattern of legal segregation." [133] Carter H. Wesley, Negro publisher of Houston, introduced a resolution endorsing Odum's position: "We shall center our efforts on gaining equal facilities as

[129] J. Saunders Redding, "Southern Defensive—I," in *Common Ground* (New York), IV (Spring, 1944), 36–38, 42.

[130] Lillian E. Smith, "Southern Defensive—II," *ibid.,* 43.

[131] Odum to Guy B. Johnson, June 20, 1944, in Odum Papers. See also Johnson to Odum, June 20, 1944, *ibid.*

[132] John Temple Graves, II, column, unidentified clipping with Odum to Graves, August 4, 1944 in Odum Papers. See also Graves to Odum, July 13, August 1, 8, 1944; and Odum to Graves, July 17, August 3, 1944, *ibid.*

[133] *Southern Frontier,* V (December, 1944), 4.

provided by law and equal opportunities for all people of the South." [134]

At the same meeting the members endorsed a program for equal employment opportunity, Negro policemen and firemen, equalization in education and public transportation, Negro voting, and increased public financing for medical and dental care. The organizational program, like the resolutions, emphasized racial considerations. As it evolved, the SRC continued on the paths developed by the Interracial Commission. During 1945 it revived interracial groups in ten states, surveyed bus segregation in Atlanta, prompted the use of Negro police, established a Veterans Service project to promote equal treatment for returned servicemen, provided informational services, began the periodical *New South,* and advised an official Kentucky Commission for the Study of Negro Affairs, which recommended the abolition of segregation in higher education.

A Conference on the South's Postwar Economy, which met in Atlanta, April 11–12, 1945, drew little attention because it adjourned on the day President Roosevelt died.[135] This and a survey of reconversion problems constituted the only significant departures from interracial activities. Racial controversy and the failure to secure broad support frustrated the SRC in its larger plans. "It seems foolish," Odum wrote Johnson early in 1945, ". . . to talk about getting the South back of the movement when there is no indication anywhere of leadership or of business and professional people following," not even "that brilliant coterie of liberals we counted on." Many of the liberals still had confidence in the Southern Conference for Human Welfare, which experienced a sudden membership growth in 1945, but it virtually collapsed in 1946 and disbanded in 1948. Nevertheless, the SRC survived, essentially as a reincarnation of the Commission on Interracial Cooperation.[136]

---

[134] Quoted in Guy B. Johnson to Editor, in Norfolk *Journal and Guide,* July 21, 1945. See also *ibid.,* July 7, 1945.

[135] Guy B. Johnson to Edwin R. Embree, March 2, 1946, in Odum Papers, gives a report on activities in 1945 and plans for 1946. See also Southern Regional Council, *The South, America's Opportunity Number One* (Atlanta, 1945) .

[136] Odum to Johnson, January 13, 1945, in Odum Papers. In 1947 George S. Mitchell succeeded Johnson and in 1951 the SRC finally committed itself in opposition to racial segregation.

In politics the gathering storm of wartime discontent—with Negro demands, price controls, labor shortages, rationing, and a hundred other petty vexations—reinforced the prevailing winds of conservatism. In 1942 the Congressional elections registered a national swing against the New Deal. Republicans gained forty-six Representatives and nine Senators, chiefly in the Middle States farm areas.[137] In Oklahoma they defeated the arch-New Deal Senator Josh Lee.[138] Democratic losses outside the South strengthened the Southern delegation's position within the party, and the delegation itself reflected a conservative trend in Southern primaries. In 1942 Arkansas and Mississippi added John L. McClellan and James O. Eastland to the rebel forces in the Senate. Conservative incumbents Bailey, Glass, and O'Daniel returned; only O'Daniel faced serious opposition. Many primary campaigns mirrored the growing obsession with race. In the Little Rock Congressional district Brooks Hays had to fend off the charge that he had attended unsegregated meetings of the Southern Conference for Human Welfare. In Louisiana, E. A. Stephens, senatorial candidate against Ellender, conjured up eerie visions of "colored organizations . . . sitting around midnight candles." In South Carolina, Eugene S. Blease, Cole's brother, accused the NAACP of backing Maybank and promised to reform Washington, where "white ladies are ordered to call Negro officials Mister." [139]

But the cry of white supremacy alone was not enough, as Eugene Talmadge discovered to his dismay. In Georgia Talmadge had set the stage during 1941, when he had purged the state's board of regents in order to dismiss five men from Georgia institutions on vague and unsupported charges of advocating "racial equality." Instead of political profit he reaped a whirlwind of

[137] U.S. Bureau of the Census, *Historical Statistics of the United States,* 691, Y-140, Y-143.

[138] Carroll Kilpatrick, "Will the South Secede?" in *Harper's,* CLXXXVI (1943), 420. A year later former Governor Leon Phillips announced his bolt to the Republican party. "I expect the party that I affiliate with will make American plans instead of New Deal plans," he said. Leon C. Phillips, "A Southern Democrat Renounces the New Deal Party," in *Manufacturers' Record,* CXII (August, 1943), 32–33, 60.

[139] Alexander Heard and Donald S. Strong, *Southern Primaries and Elections 1920–1949* (University, Ala., 1959), 33, 86, 100–101, 179, 202; Charles S. Johnson, *To Stem This Tide* (Boston, 1943), 63–66.

opposition. The Southern Association of Colleges and Secondary Schools withdrew accreditation from state institutions and in the 1942 gubernatorial race students, parents, and an aroused press rallied to the support of Ellis G. Arnall, the young attorney-general, who defended academic freedom and took care to neutralize Talmadge's racist appeal in the boondocks: "Over in west Georgia, where I live," said Arnall, "we don't need any governor to keep Negroes out of our white schools." [140] During his four-year term Arnall restored the independence of the state university system, increased teacher pay, put through a new state constitution, reformed the state's penal and parole systems, cut the voting age to eighteen, sponsored the first state law for soldier voting, and personally argued before the Supreme Court the suit that precipitated action against regionalized freight rates. The "liberal majority within the Democratic Party," he wrote before leaving office, should "retain control of the party; make it the vehicle for acceptance of new ideas; and utilize it for that experimentalism required to solve our problems." [141]

But Georgia under Arnall moved against the political currents. In January, 1943, the "Victory Congress" convened, with Southern Democrats in revolt. In the House Southerners dominated the party caucus, took four additional seats on the steering committee to secure a majority, and rejected a proposal to give the American Labor party's Vito Marcantonio a committee seat for service to New York Democrats. In the Senate Southerners maneuvered deftly to downgrade Bronx Boss Edward J. Flynn by demanding that he quit both the national chairmanship and the national committee before being considered as Ambassador to Australia and then blocking confirmation.[142]

These steps were but the prelude to more substantive assaults on New Deal policies and agencies. "Government by bureaucrats," said Eugene Cox, "must be broken, and broken now." [143]

[140] Quoted in Sutton, "The Talmadge Campaigns," 256. See also Ralph McGill, "It Has Happened Here," in *Survey Graphic*, XXX (1941), 449–53.

[141] Ellis G. Arnall, *The Shore Dimly Seen* (Philadelphia and New York, 1946), 301–302. The book gave Arnall's own story of his administration.

[142] J. Donald Kingsley, "Congress and the New Deal," in *Current History*, IV (1943), 28–31.

[143] *Congressional Record*, 78 Cong., 1 Sess., 10.

While Bankhead led the farm bloc against food subsidies and price controls, Harold Cooley investigated the FSA, Virginia's Howard W. Smith chaired a "Special Committee to Investigate Acts of Executive Agencies Beyond the Scope of their Authority," and Harry F. Byrd led a drive by the Joint Committee on Non-Essential Expenditures (established in 1941) to eviscerate "nonessential" New Deal agencies. During 1943 Congress abolished the WPA, the NYA, and the CCC, brought the FSA to heel, and liquidated the National Resources Planning Board by refusing it funds. Tom Connally and Howard Smith sponsored antistrike legislation which authorized the government to seize struck plants, required pre-strike plebiscites, and outlawed union political contributions. Martin Dies produced a list of forty "irresponsible, unrepresentative, crackpot, radical bureaucrats," and won passage of an appropriation amendment against paying the salaries of three alleged radicals. Mississippi's John Rankin, previously known as a friend of inflation, public power, and veterans, now emerged as the foe of bureaucrats, labor unions, and the "Communist-Jewish world plot" while his senatorial colleague, Theodore G. Bilbo, on most things a New Dealer, warred against the FEPC and proposed to resettle American Negroes in Africa.[144]

After the 1942 elections two Deep-South governors, Dixon of Alabama and Jones of Louisiana, tentatively lofted trial balloons of insurgency. The position of Southern Democrats was "anomalous in the extreme," Dixon told the Southern Society of New York in December. "It is their own party that is dynamiting their social structure. . . . Ways and means are being discussed daily to break our chains": a Southern party, unpledged electors. The South had gotten better treatment from the Republican party, Sam Jones declared in New Orleans.[145] "The fact is," he said in a *Saturday Evening Post* article, "that political booby trap known as the 'Solid South' . . . is about to fall apart of its own absurdity." New Deal "worthies, perhaps with the best intentions in the

[144] Vance Johnson, "The Old Deal Democrats," in *American Mercury*, LIX (1944), 51–53; Russel Whelan, "Rankin of Mississippi," *ibid.*, 31–37; Young, *Congressional Politics in the Second World War*, 107–108, 115–17, and *passim*; Gellerman, *Martin Dies*, 245–46; Green, *The Man Bilbo*, 100–105.

[145] New York *Times*, December 12, 1942; Thomas Sancton, "Trouble in Dixie II. The Bloody Shirt Once More," in *New Republic*, CVIII (1943), 50–51.

world, are doing the Negro race a grave long-term disservice." War industries went mostly to the North, New Dealers were "blind and deaf" to freight-rate differentials, the South carried a disproportionate burden of education, Federal grants went mostly to "the pampered and protected industrial North and East," public housing was for Northern slums, and the New Deal had tried to wipe out rice and sugar production.[146] Both Jones and Dixon raised the banner of insurgency again at the Southern Governors Conference in Tallahassee in the spring of 1943.[147]

What was happening, Thomas Sancton wrote in the *New Republic,* was a duplication of the strategy that beat the Populists. Negroes could not vote. The whites had been poisoned against Negroes. Farmers and laborers were set at odds. "At all events, the New Deal in the South is dead," he concluded. "And this is where the New Deal helped the most." [148] Other observers agreed. Columnist Paul Mallon found "all of the Southern and border states, with the possible exception of Florida . . . in an extreme condition of psychological political revolution." But reports of the New Deal's demise were premature. Reporter Seldon Menefee decided during wartime travels that the great majority of the people, unlike the "nostalgic upper-class Southerners," supported the administration wholeheartedly, "with far less 'beefing' over minor restrictions than I had grown used to hearing in Washington." [149] A Gallup poll in mid-summer, 1943, showed 80 per cent of the Southern voters in favor of Roosevelt's renomination.[150]

Events early in 1944 charged the political atmosphere with additional tensions. In February came a rebellion against an administration request for a tax increase to combat inflation and finance the war. Instead of the $10,500,000,000 the Treasury demanded, the finance committees headed by Robert Doughton and Walter George put through a measure that yielded an additional $2,300,000,000. The President responded with a biting veto; it was, he said, "a tax relief bill . . . not for the needy, but for the

[146] Sam Jones, as told to James Aswell, "Will Dixie Bolt the New Deal?" in *Saturday Evening Post,* (March 6, 1943) , 20–21, 42, 45.

[147] Johnson "The Old Deal Democrats," *loc. cit.,* 55.

[148] Sancton, "Trouble in Dixie II. The Bloody Shirt Once More," *loc. cit.,* 51.

[149] Menefee, *Assignment: USA,* 66.

[150] Johnson, "The Old Deal Democrats," *loc. cit.,* 56.

greedy." Alben Barkley angrily resigned as Majority Leader, only to be re-elected unanimously. Both houses promptly overrode the veto by large votes despite Claude Pepper's plea that such a vote would "alter the understanding of the Nation concerning the fundamental spirit . . . of the Democratic Party" and persuade the public "that we are no longer the crusading party." [151]

The reverberations from this incident still echoed when, in March, the question of soldier voting came to a decision. Proposals for a simplified Federal soldier ballot raised the prospect of increased voting by Negroes and by young people likely to support New Dealers. In 1942 a limited law provided for distribution of postal cards with which servicemen could request state absentee ballots. It even abrogated state registration and poll-tax requirements, but came so late that only 28,000 voted under it. The President appealed for a simple and uniform servicemen's ballot in 1944, but a states' rights bloc led by Mississippians in each house, Eastland and Rankin, sidetracked the proposal for a truncated version that required the consent of the state. The President let the bill become law without his signature. That fall twenty states accepted some 111,773 Federal ballots, and probably more than four million servicemen cast state absentee ballots.[152]

With spring the focus centered more sharply on Negro voting. On April 3, in the case of Smith v. Allwright, the Supreme Court reversed Grovey v. Townsend (1935) and struck down the Texas white primary on grounds that it was part of the election procedure and subject to the Fifteenth Amendment.[153] Texas Democrats, who had fought the issue for two decades, yielded. But the Allwright opinion seemed to offer a loophole by suggesting that the party acted as an agency of the state because the state regulated primary procedures. South Carolina's Governor Olin D. Johnston, therefore, summoned a special session of the legislature to repeal all laws pertaining to the primary and turn the Demo-

---

[151] Barkley, *That Reminds Me*, 169–82; *Congressional Record*, 78 Cong., 2 Sess., 2049.

[152] Young, *Congressional Politics*, 82–89. See also Shannon, "Presidential Politics in the South," in Cole and Hallowell (eds.), *The Southern Political Scene, 1938–1948*, 478; and Rosenman (comp.), *The Public Papers and Addresses of Franklin D. Roosevelt*, XIII, 53–60, 111–16. In 1944 servicemen's votes were 5.6 per cent of the total Presidential vote.

[153] Smith v. Allwright, 321 U.S. 649 (1944).

cratic party into a "private club." Should this prove inadequate, he warned, "we South Carolinians will use the necessary methods to retain white supremacy in our primaries and to safeguard the homes and happiness of our people." [154]

The South, Senator Maybank said the day before Johnston's message, would handle the problem as it saw fit "regardless of what decisions the Supreme Court may make and regardless of what laws Congress may pass." [155] In May the Senate faced an anti-poll tax bill, a wartime perennial. Again, as in 1942, the Senators buried it, this time after a subdued debate and a pre-arranged cloture vote that was foredoomed to failure. Allen Drury, a young Texan covering the Senate for the United Press, recorded his impressions in his diary: "We seem to be perched on a cliff, in Washington, above a vast and tumbled plain that stretches far away below us: the South, unhappy, restless, confused, embittered, torn by pressures steadily mounting. As far as the eye can see there is discontent and bitterness, faint intimations of a coming storm like a rising wind moving through tall grass." [156]

Spring primary victories by Lister Hill in Alabama and Claude Pepper in Florida, however, suggested that the New Deal retained some vitality in the South. In South Carolina, where Roosevelt did not intervene again, Olin D. Johnston finally toppled the aging Cotton Ed Smith. But in each case the New Deal candidate deemed it prudent to reaffirm his allegiance to white supremacy. Pepper assured the voters that Florida primaries would be "kept white," and Johnston came to the campaign fresh from his effort to circumvent the Supreme Court.[157]

As the spring advanced, anti-Roosevelt conservatives attempted to mobilize a rebellion in the national convention. In May a movement that came to be known as the "Texas Regulars" captured that state's Democratic convention and named anti-

---

[154] South Carolina *House Journal*, 1944, pp. 115–57. The arrangement lasted until 1947, when District Judge J. Waties Waring declared the primary still a part of the election process. Elmore *v.* Rice., 72 Fed. Supp. 516 (1947).

[155] Allen Drury, *A Senate Journal, 1943–1945* (New York, 1963), 138 (entry for April 13, 1944).

[156] *Ibid.*, 141.

[157] Shannon, "Presidential Politics in the South," *loc. cit.*, 480; Locke, "Claude D. Pepper 'Champion of the Belligerent Democracy,'" *loc. cit.*, 270.

Roosevelt delegates and an anti-Roosevelt electoral slate. Aroused conservatives greeted Lyndon Johnson with cries of "Throw Roosevelt's pin-up boy out of there." Mississippi's convention took similar action.[158] But it was abundantly clear, more so after the Normandy invasion began in June, that Roosevelt the war leader was impregnable. The anti-New Deal campaign then focused on the more vulnerable Wallace, who as vice president had swung increasingly toward the liberal-labor wing of the party but had antagonized the harassed President in 1943 by a bitter embroglio with Secretary of Commerce Jesse Jones over rubber and quinine stockpiling. Wallace, however, carried the battle to the enemy with a bold proclamation in the convention: "The future belongs to those who go down the line unswervingly for the liberal principles of both political democracy and economic democracy regardless of race, color or religion. . . . The poll tax must go. Equal educational opportunities must come. The future must bring equal wages for equal work regardless of sex or race." [159]

Wallace earned the enmity of both Southern conservatives and Northern city bosses who feared the rising CIO Political Action Committee. Yet he retained a substantial degree of Southern support, 43 per cent of the voters, the Gallup poll reported as late as June 6. But in the convention he commanded only the vote of Ellis Arnall's Georgia delegation, about half the Florida votes, and scattered support in Alabama, which voted as a unit for favorite-son John Bankhead. Roosevelt, who won easily over scattered votes for Harry Byrd, apparently considered and rejected James F. Byrnes, since 1943 head of the Office of Economic Stabilization which supervised civilian war agencies, because Byrnes had the fatal opposition of organized labor, Negroes, and city bosses who feared the effect of his early departure from the Catholic church. The outcome, amid complicated maneuvers for the Presidential nod, was a convergence upon Missouri's Harry S. Truman, who had established a solid reputation as chairman of the Senate War Investigating Committee, and was acceptable to Southern conservatives because of his Confederate antecedents and his Border-State background. Even so the Republicans under Thomas E.

[158] McKay, *Texas Politics, 1906–1944*, 391–466. Before the election loyal slates appeared in both states.
[159] Lord, *The Wallaces of Iowa*, 533.

Dewey gained an increased percentage of the vote in every Southern state except Texas, where the unpledged Texas Regulars drew a substantial portion of the anti-Roosevelt vote.[160]

Roosevelt had hardly begun his brief fourth term in January, 1945, before he provoked one of the sharpest major political battles of his era—and the last—by proposing to replace Jesse Jones with Henry A. Wallace as Secretary of Commerce. This, Roosevelt said, was the former vice president's expressed preference as a reward for services rendered in the 1944 campaign. The controversy that followed, said the London *Times*, might come to rank "with the Hayne-Webster debate as pregnant with significance in the future," for it involved "all those mighty issues which agitate men's minds when they look forward to the world after the war . . . the true function of Government in a democratic state; the yearning to be rid of the scourge of unemployment; the conflict between the social conscience and the nostalgia for the old days." Senators Bailey and George led the fight against Wallace, and only Pepper among the Southerners rallied to his defense. The argument raged on through February while Roosevelt flew off to the Yalta Conference with Churchill and Stalin, and reached its end in March when the Senate approved Wallace only after the post was separated from control of the Federal Loan Agency and the Reconstruction Finance Corporation.[161] In a similar battle during March a conservative coalition blocked confirmation of Aubrey Williams as head of the Rural Electrification Administration.[162]

But unity on foreign affairs persisted through the war. Several Southerners in Congress stood forth as champions of internationalism: Claude Pepper, Lister Hill, William Fulbright, and Tom Connally. In 1943 Hill joined with Senators Hatch, Ball, and Burton to sponsor the "B_2H_2 Resolution" that called for a strong international organization with a military force of its own. In the House, Fulbright, "the Rhodes scholar from the Ozarks," pushed a resolution for "appropriate international machinery with power adequate to establish and maintain a just and lasting peace." The House passed the Fulbright Resolution, 360 to 69. Then Tom

[160] Shannon, "Presidential Politics in the South," *loc. cit.*, 481–86.
[161] Lord, *The Wallaces of Iowa*, 496–514.
[162] New York *Times*, January 23, March 3, 24, 1945.

Connally, chairman of the Senate Foreign Relations Committee, worked out a compromise, the Connally Resolution, which reaffirmed the principles of national sovereignty, a proviso designed to fend off isolationist attacks. Roosevelt worked closely with Connally in cultivating Senate Republicans in order to avoid partisan divisions like those which had undermined Wilson's postwar program, and Connally himself ultimately participated in the San Francisco Conference that formulated the Charter of the United Nations.[163]

But on April 12, 1945, two weeks before the charter conference convened, Franklin D. Roosevelt quietly and unexpectedly passed away in his cottage at Warm Springs, Georgia. In Knoxville the next day a TVA driver who took David E. Lilienthal to his plane for a sad mission to Washington ventured a few words about the dead President. "I won't forget what he done for us, beginning with the NRA," said the man, who had been a textile worker at sixteen cents an hour. But, he asked, "Who are the little people like me going to have to take their part?" [164] Roosevelt's death indeed "cast the southern liberals adrift," and the accession of Truman heartened the conservatives who had helped to engineer his nomination. "President Truman," the Speaker of Mississippi's House of Representatives wrote in May, "has begun well and is making rapid progress towards returning this country to Fundamental Americanism." [165]

But Truman's domestic policies remained unformulated while he wrestled with problems of world affairs and peacemaking, a responsibility in which Southern leaders participated significantly —among them James F. Byrnes, who became Secretary of State in July, 1945. Truman, however, gave one early clue to his character, when he renominated Lilienthal in May for chairman of the TVA over the opposition of Tennessee's Senator McKellar, who resented Lilienthal's independence.[166] A more significant clue to his policies came on September 6, 1945, four days after the

[163] Irish, "Foreign Policy and the South," *loc. cit.,* 318–21.

[164] Lilienthal, *The TVA Years, 1939–1945,* 691.

[165] Grantham, *The Democratic South,* 75; Walter Sillers to James O. Eastland, May 28, 1945, copy in John H. Bankhead, Jr., Papers.

[166] Jonathan Daniels, *The Man of Independence* (Philadelphia and New York, 1950), 291–92.

Japanese surrender, when he sent Congress a comprehensive peacetime program which, in effect, proposed to continue and enlarge the New Deal. Its twenty-one points included expansion of unemployment insurance, extension of the Employment Service, a higher minimum wage, executive reorganization, a permanent FEPC, slum clearance and low-rent housing, regional development of the nation's river valleys, and a public works program.[167] The message signaled a revival of conservative antagonism toward the White House.

In 1945 the South emerged from the war, as H. C. Nixon had foretold, "with more social change and more unfinished business than any other part of the country," with fewer sharecroppers but more pipe-fitters and welders, with less plowing and hoeing but more mowing and sowing, with less rural isolation and more urban sophistication, with nearly a million people in the ranks of organized labor and a growing movement for antiunion laws, with veterans returning from new experiences beyond the seven seas, and with "a standard of living for the common man that was undreamt of in its prewar philosophy." [168] The region was more an integral part of the Union and of the world than ever before. But its political leaders, internationalist and parochial at the same time, embodied a curious paradox. In foreign affairs they had advanced boldly toward new horizons in their support of plans for "winning the peace." But in domestic affairs they had retreated back within the parapets of the embattled South, where they stood fast against the incursions of social change. The inconsistency could not long endure, and a critical question for the postwar South, facing eventful issues of economic and racial adjustment, was which would prevail, the broader vision or the defensive reaction.

[167] Harry S. Truman, *Years of Decision* (Garden City, N.Y., 1955), in *Memoirs of Harry S Truman*, I, 481–85; *Public Papers of the Presidents of the United States: Harry S. Truman, 1945* (Washington, 1961), 263–309.

[168] H. Clarence Nixon, "The South After the War," in *Virginia Quarterly Review*, XX (1944), 321–34.

CRITICAL ESSAY ON AUTHORITIES

THE following essay calls attention to selected materials of major significance, but does not supply a bibliography of all items consulted or cited. Readers seeking a fuller critical bibliography of secondary works may turn to Arthur S. Link and Rembert W. Patrick (eds.), *Writing Southern History: Essays in Historiography in Honor of Fletcher M. Green* (Baton Rouge, 1965), in which three essays span the period 1913–1945.

MANUSCRIPT COLLECTIONS

The available manuscript sources for the period are already voluminous, and they grow at an increasing pace. Most of the major collections are listed in Philip M. Hamer (ed.), *A Guide to Archives and Manuscripts in the United States* (New Haven, 1961), and in a continuing series: *The National Union Catalog of Manuscript Collections, 1959–1961* (Ann Arbor, 1962); *ibid.,* 1962 (Hamden, Conn., 1964); *ibid.,* 1963–1964 (Washington, 1965); *ibid.,* 1965, with index for 1963–1965 (Washington, 1966); and *Index, 1959–1962* (Hamden, Conn., 1964). The *Journal of Southern History* (Baton Rouge, Nashville, Lexington, Ky., Houston, 1935———) and other historical journals report recent acquisitions.

In the use of manuscripts the impulse to exhaust all resources yielded to the need for synthesis in a period so recent. Manuscripts, therefore, were sampled to season the store of information rather than provide the basic staple. The collections most exploited for the purpose were those of the Division of Manuscripts, Library of Congress; the Southern Historical Collection, University of North Carolina at Chapel Hill; the Manuscript Department, Duke University Library; the Department of Archives, Louisiana State University; the Alabama Department of Archives and History; the Columbia University Oral History Research Office; and the Franklin D. Roosevelt Library at Hyde Park, New York.

733

The collections run heavily to political affairs. The papers of political leaders in the Manuscripts Division, Library of Congress, include those of Woodrow Wilson, William Jennings Bryan, Josephus Daniels, Thomas W. Gregory, and William Gibbs McAdoo. Useful in relation to Wilson's Negro policies were the papers of Mary Church Terrell, Robert H. Terrell, and Booker T. Washington. Important political collections at the University of North Carolina are those of Claude Kitchin, Braxton Bragg Comer, John M. Parker, Robert L. Doughton, and Lindsay Warren; at Duke University, those of Furnifold M. Simmons, Josiah W. Bailey, John M. Grace, and the Socialist party; in the Alabama Department of Archives and History, the papers of Oscar W. Underwood, John H. Bankhead, Sr., John H. Bankhead, Jr., and William B. Bankhead; and at Louisiana State University, those of Edward J. Gay, John H. Overton, Joseph E. Ransdell, and Jared Y. Sanders, and a small collection of John M. Parker Papers.

Useful political collections at other depositories are the Oscar B. Colquitt Papers at the Eugene C. Barker Texas History Center, University of Texas; the papers of Thomas P. Gore, William H. Murray, and Elmer Thomas at the University of Oklahoma; the Charles H. Brough Papers at the University of Arkansas; and the papers of Henry D. Clayton and Samuel F. Hobbs at the University of Alabama. The Burnet R. Maybank Papers, now at the South Carolina Archives Department, were sampled while still located at the College of Charleston. The James F. Byrnes Papers were available only in small part at Clemson University, where the remainder are to be deposited eventually.

The massive collections of the Franklin D. Roosevelt Library contain materials relevant to many aspects of Southern life, mainly but not altogether in the New Deal period. They are unusually well arranged and fully cross referenced. The Eleanor Roosevelt Papers there were examined by permission of the late Mrs. Roosevelt, chiefly for materials pertinent to Negro and labor history. The Aubrey Williams Papers, including his unpublished memoirs, were examined while still in his possession in Montgomery, Alabama. Materials in the Sam Rayburn Library, Bonham, Texas, relate chiefly to the period after 1937, but some earlier items have survived.

The papers of newsmen and editors often prove more pithy and pungent than those of politicos. Two such collections proved unusually rich: the papers of William Watts Ball, conservative editor of the Charleston *News and Courier*, at Duke University, and the papers of George Fort Milton, progressive editor of the Chattanooga

News, at the Library of Congress. Other useful papers of journalists, in addition to those of Josephus Daniels, mentioned above, were those of his son Jonathan and those of W. D. Robinson at the University of North Carolina; and the papers of Santford Martin at Duke University, Douglas Southall Freeman in the Library of Congress, and Henry M. Hyde at the University of Virginia.

For social and cultural history the Southern Historical Collection, University of North Carolina, is especially useful. The Howard W. Odum Papers illuminate Odum's concept of regionalism, the interracial movement, and many other aspects of Southern life. The Jessie Daniel Ames Papers are a small collection dealing with interracial work. In the Joseph Goldberger Papers one recaptures the excitement of Goldberger's pellagra discoveries. The Southern Education Papers and the papers of Charles W. Dabney, Frank P. Graham, and S. C. Mitchell have materials on many current movements; and the papers of the Southern Tenant Farmers' Union, the Fellowship of Southern Churchmen, and the Delta and Providence Farms give information on liberal movements of the 1930's. The Library of Congress has the papers of Alexander J. McKelway, crusader against child labor and a journalist who commented on the Washington scene in the Wilson era, and George Foster Peabody, philanthropist.

The voluminous Southern Pine Association Papers in the Department of Archives, Louisiana State University, include a typescript history of the organization and yield much on the trade association, reclamation, and tariff movements. The Lucy Randolph Mason Papers and the George S. Mitchell Papers, both at Duke University, contain chiefly materials on the labor movement in the 1930's. Materials on agricultural matters for different periods are in the Reuben Dean Bowen Papers at Duke University, the Aubrey H. Strode Papers (on the Tri-State Tobacco Co-operative) at the University of Virginia, and the Edward A. O'Neal Papers in the Alabama Department of Archives and History.

The pioneering effort of the Columbia University Oral History Research Office has produced several important interviews relevant to the South, and especially to Southern agriculture. The most significant are the reminiscences of H. L. Mitchell, a founder of the Southern Tenant Farmers' Union, and Will W. Alexander, director of the Commission on Interracial Cooperation and head of the Farm Security Administration. The reminiscences of Norman Thomas shed light on the Southern Tenant Farmers' Union, those of Samuel B. Bledsoe and John B. Hutson on New Deal farm policies, and those of

735

Louis J. Taber on the revival of the Grange in the South. The reminiscences of J. Waties Waring have much on politics in Charleston and in South Carolina.

GOVERNMENT PUBLICATIONS

The most useful guide through the maze of Federal documents is the *Monthly Catalog of United States Government Publications* (Washington, 1895——), which has an annual index. For materials to 1940 one will find somewhat fuller listings in the *Catalog of the Public Documents of the United States* (Washington, 1893–1940). For detailed statistics the historian must turn to the decennial censuses, but many of his questions will be answered in the United States Bureau of the Census, *Historical Statistics of the United States, Colonial Times to 1957* (Washington, 1960), which gives few figures on a regional basis but lists and evaluates other more detailed statistical series. The annual *Statistical Abstract of the United States* (Washington, 1878——) offers fuller data.

A variety of useful items was found in the *Bulletins* of the Department of Agriculture (Washington, 1913——) and the Bureau of Labor Statistics (Washington, 1912——), and in the United States Public Health Service's *Public Health Reports* (Washington, 1878——). The *Biennial Survey of Education* (Washington, 1921——) was used mainly for statistics. Among the Department of Agriculture's *Yearbooks of Agriculture* (Washington, 1895——), the most valuable, for its articles on agricultural history and policy, is *Farmers in a Changing World: Yearbook of Agriculture, 1940* (Washington, 1940).

A few examples of special reports or decisions by governmental agencies will suffice to indicate the wealth of such materials. An early consideration of tenancy appears in *Industrial Relations: Final Report and Testimony Submitted to Congress by the Commission on Industrial Relations*, 11 vols. (Washington, 1916), IX, 8949–9056; X, 9057–9290. The question of basing-point pricing is treated in *Federal Trade Commission* vs. *United States Steel Corporation, et al.*, Docket 760 (Washington, 1924); and basic documents on regionalized freight rates are J. Haden Alldredge, *The Interterritorial Freight Rate Problem of the United States*, in *House Documents*, 75 Cong., 1 Sess., No. 264; and Harry B. Kline (ed.), *Regionalized Freight Rates: Barrier to National Productiveness, ibid.*, 78 Cong., 1 Sess., No. 137. Several pertinent cases found in the ICC Dockets are cited in Chapter XVII.

Studies and reports of New Deal agencies accelerated the growth of documents. Examples of special series, with parallels in other agencies, are the Federal Emergency Relief Administration's *Research Bulletins* (Washington, 1933–1936), and *Monthly Reports* (Washington, 1933–1936), and the Works Progress Administration's *Research Monographs* (Washington, 1935–1943). Special attention should be given to two publications of the National Resources Planning Board: *Security, Work, and Relief Policies* (Washington, 1942), and *Regional Planning,* Part XI: *The Southeast* (Washington, 1942). Perhaps the most significant, certainly the most celebrated, single document for Southern history in the period was the National Emergency Council's *Report on Economic Conditions of the South* (Washington, 1938).

Congressional hearings and reports often focused on Southern affairs. *The Ku Klux Klan,* Hearings Before the Committee on Rules, House of Representatives, 67 Cong., 1 Sess. (Washington, 1921), recorded testimony that publicized, while it discredited, the Klan. Two significant Senate committees of the 1930's, headed by Hugo Black and Robert M. La Follette, Jr., recorded testimony in *Investigation of Lobbying Activities,* Hearings before a Special Committee to Investigate Lobbying Activities, 74 Cong., 1 Sess., Pts. 1–6 (Washington, 1935–1936); and *Violations of Free Speech and Rights of Labor,* Hearings before a Subcommittee of the Committee on Education and Labor . . . , 74 Cong., 2 Sess., through 76 Cong., 3 Sess. (Washington, 1936–1940). Findings of the La Follette Committee appeared in *Violations of Free Speech and Rights of Labor,* in *Senate Reports,* 75 Cong., 2 Sess., No. 46, and *ibid.,* 76 Cong., 1 Sess., No. 6. Particularly valuable for brief monographs by experts in various fields were the hearings of a committee first headed by Representative Stephen Pace of Georgia: *Study of Agricultural and Economic Problems of the Cotton Belt,* Hearings before Special Subcommittee on Cotton of the Committee on Agriculture, House of Representatives, 80 Cong., 1 Sess. (Washington, 1947–1948).

Official documents of the states, including legislative journals and reports of state officials, are given detailed listing in the *Monthly Checklist of State Publications, Library of Congress* (Washington, 1910——). Data on voting have been assembled conveniently in several nonofficial publications: Alexander Heard and Donald S. Strong (eds.), *Southern Primaries and Elections, 1920–1949* (University, Ala., 1950); Donald R. Matthews and Associates, *North Carolina Votes: General Election Returns by County* . . . (Chapel Hill, 1962); and Jasper B. Shannon and Ruth McQuown, *Presidential Politics in Kentucky, 1824–1948: A Compilation of Election Statistics and an Analysis*

737

of Political Behavior (Lexington, Ky., 1950). See also Cortez A. M. Ewing, *Primary Elections in the South: A Study in Uniparty Politics* (Norman, 1953).

AUTOBIOGRAPHIES, MEMOIRS, AND PUBLISHED PAPERS

Autobiographical works of Southern political figures include Alben W. Barkley, *That Reminds Me . . .* (Garden City, N.Y., 1954); James F. Byrnes, *All in One Lifetime* (New York, 1958); Tom Connally as told to Alfred Steinberg, *My Name Is Tom Connally* (New York, 1954); Josephus Daniels, *The Wilson Era: Years of Peace, 1910–1917* (Chapel Hill, 1944), and *The Wilson Era: Years of War and After, 1917–1923* (Chapel Hill, 1946); *The Memoirs of Cordell Hull,* 2 vols. (New York, 1948); Jesse H. Jones with Edward Angly, *Fifty Billion Dollars: My Thirteen Years with the RFC, 1932–1945* (New York, 1951); *Every Man a King: The Autobiography of Huey P. Long* (New Orleans, 1933); J. Fred Rippy (ed.), *F. M. Simmons, Statesman of the New South: Memoirs and Addresses* (Durham, 1936); and Oscar W. Underwood, *Drifting Sands of Party Politics* (New York and London, 1928). Ellis G. Arnall, *The Shore Dimly Seen* (Philadelphia and New York, 1946), is largely the story of Arnall's governorship, 1943–1947. David E. Lilienthal tells about his Southern experiences in *The Journals of David E. Lilienthal,* Vol. I: *The TVA Years, 1939–1945* (New York, 1964).

Felicitous defenses of conservatism appear in William A. Percy, *Lanterns on the Levee: Recollections of a Planter's Son* (New York, 1941), and William Watts Ball, *The State That Forgot: South Carolina's Surrender to Democracy* (Indianapolis, 1932). A liberal gives her apologia in Katharine Du Pre Lumpkin, *The Making of a Southerner* (New York, 1947). Radical viewpoints are represented in the recollections of an old-time Socialist, *If You Don't Weaken: The Autobiography of Oscar Ameringer* (New York, 1940), and two one-time Communists: Fred E. Beal, *Proletarian Journey: New England, Gastonia, Moscow* (New York, 1937), and Angelo Herndon, *Let Me Live* (New York, 1937).

Leaders of the NAACP tell their stories in W. E. B. Du Bois, *Dusk of Dawn: An Essay Toward an Autobiography of a Race Concept* (New York, 1940); James Weldon Johnson, *Along This Way* (New York, 1933); Mary White Ovington, *The Walls Came Tumbling Down* (New York, 1947); and *A Man Called White: The Autobiography of Walter F. White* (New York, 1948). Negro life in various perspectives may be seen in Zora Neal Hurston, *Dust Tracks on a*

Road: An Autobiography (Philadelphia, 1942) ; Robert R. Moton, *Finding a Way Out: An Autobiography* (Garden City, N.Y., 1921) ; Haywood Patterson and Earl Conrad, *Scottsboro Boy* (New York, 1950) ; J. Saunders Redding, *To Make a Poet Black* (Chapel Hill, 1939) ; and Richard Wright, *Black Boy: A Record of Childhood and Youth* (Cleveland, 1945). Allan Knight Chalmers, *They Shall Be Free* (Garden City, N.Y., 1951), tells about the effort to free the Scottsboro boys.

A number of newsmen have produced personal accounts, largely autobiographical in character: David L. Cohn, *Where I Was Born and Raised* (Boston, 1948) ; Ralph E. McGill, *The South and the Southerner* (Boston, 1963) ; Julian R. Meade, *I Live in Virginia* (New York and Toronto, 1935) ; Clayton Rand, *Ink on My Hands* (New York, 1940) ; Ben Robertson, *Red Hills and Cotton: An Upcountry Memory* (New York, 1942) ; Thomas L. Stokes, *Chip Off My Shoulder* (Princeton, 1940) ; and James H. Street, *Look Away!: A Dixie Notebook* (New York, 1936).

Memoirs that enrich our knowledge of the literary renaissance include: James Branch Cabell, *Quiet, Please* (Gainesville, Fla., 1952), and *As I Remember It* (New York, 1955) ; Erskine Caldwell, *Call It Experience* (New York, 1951) ; Emily Clark, *Innocence Abroad* (New York, 1931) ; John Gould Fletcher, *Life Is My Song* (New York, 1937) ; Ellen Glasgow, *The Woman Within* (New York, 1954) ; John A. Lomax, *Adventures of a Ballad Hunter* (New York, 1947) ; Jesse Stuart, *Beyond Dark Hills: A Personal Story* (New York, 1938) ; and Stark Young, *The Pavilion* (New York, 1951). Rob Roy Purdy (ed.), *Fugitives' Reunion: Conversations at Vanderbilt, May 3–5, 1956* (Nashville, 1959), records nostalgic discussions by members of the Fugitive and Agrarian groups.

Other facets of cultural and social history are illuminated by Richard L. Watson, Jr. (ed.), *Bishop Cannon's Own Story: Life As I Have Seen It* (Durham, 1955) ; and *Center of the Storm: Memoirs of John T. Scopes*, with James Presley (New York, 1967). Unique and moving accounts of life among workers, tenants, and the unemployed appear in Federal Writers' Program of the Works Progress Administration, *These Are Our Lives* (Chapel Hill, 1939).

The period 1913–1945 is too recent for many collections of correspondence and papers to have been published. The documentation cites various editions of the public papers of the Presidents. One definitive collection has not yet reached the period in the two volumes so far available: Arthur S. Link and Associates (eds.), *The Papers of*

739

Woodrow Wilson (Princeton, 1966———). The North Carolina Department of Archives and History has published the public papers of all North Carolina governors in the period. A comparable private publication is Mrs. Allie H. Peay (comp.), *Austin Peay, Governor of Tennessee, 1923–1925, 1925–1927, 1927–1929: A Collection of State Papers and Public Addresses . . .* (Kingsport, Tenn., 1929). Other examples of occasional papers are Anthony Harrigan (ed.), *The Editor and the Republic: Papers and Addresses of William Watts Ball* (Chapel Hill, 1954); and Milton Terris (ed.), *Goldberger on Pellagra* (Baton Rouge, 1964). Selected letters of three writers appear in Blair Rouse (ed.), *Letters of Ellen Glasgow* (New York, 1958); Hansell Baugh (ed.), *Frances Newman's Letters* (New York, 1929); Elizabeth Nowell (ed.), *The Letters of Thomas Wolfe* (New York, 1956); and John S. Terry (ed.), *Thomas Wolfe's Letters to His Mother* (New York, 1943).

TRAVEL AND DESCRIPTION

An extensive survey of travel literature now exists: Thomas D. Clark (ed.), *Travels in the New South: A Bibliography*, 2 vols. (Norman, 1962); Volume II, *The Twentieth Century South, 1900–1955*, includes sections on English-language travel accounts by Rupert B. Vance and on foreign-language accounts by Lawrence S. Thompson. An editor's preface and introductions by both contributors make observations on general trends, and each of the 627 entries carries a brief description. In the twentieth century travelers once again included the South in the "grand tour" and many accounts concentrated on the region. Increasingly they gave attention to themes of change: social, political, and economic.

The rise of Southern resorts and tourism occasioned or influenced such accounts as Mildred Cram, *Old Seaport Towns of the South* (New York, 1917); John Martin Hammond, *Winter Journeys in the South* (Philadelphia and London, 1916); Julian L. Street, *American Adventures: A Second Trip "Abroad at Home"* (New York, 1917); and numerous guidebooks. Among the accounts of the Florida boom the most rewarding is T. H. Weigall, *Boom in Florida* (London, 1931), by an English newsman who became a part of the Coral Gables promotion. But see also Kenneth L. Roberts, *Florida* (New York, 1926); and Cecil Roberts, *Gone Sunwards* (New York, 1936). Marjorie Kennan Rawlings, *Cross Creek* (New York, 1942), gives a contrasting view of the Florida scrub country.

Relatively few critical evaluations of Southern life appeared before

740

the Depression. Important and sharply contrasting exceptions were Maurice S. Evans, *Black and White in the Southern States: A Study of the Race Problem in the United States from a South African Point of View* (London and New York, 1915) ; and Stephen Graham, *The Soul of John Brown* (New York, 1920), by a British visitor who chose Frederick Law Olmsted as his model in following the color line across the Southeast just after World War I. In *America Comes of Age* (New York, 1927), André Siegfried, a French writer, viewed with alarm prohibition, fundamentalism, racism, and the Ku Klux Klan.

During the Depression and New Deal years themes of the "problem South" came more strongly to the fore. The most informative panorama of the South in those years is Jonathan Daniels, *A Southerner Discovers the South* (New York, 1938). Ursula Branston, *Let the Band Play "Dixie"!* (London, 1940), offers the interesting, if scarcely profound, observations of an inquiring Englishwoman. M. Phillips Price, *America after Sixty Years* (London, 1936), in which the author retraced the travels of his father, is better, but touches only Georgia and the Carolinas in the South.

An entirely new genre appeared in two community studies of Indianola, Mississippi, sponsored by the Yale Institute of Human Relations: John Dollard, *Caste and Class in a Southern Town* (New Haven, 1937) ; and Hortense Powdermaker, *After Freedom: A Cultural Study in the Deep South* (New York, 1939). Another classic of the type is Allison Davis, Burleigh B. Gardner, and Mary R. Gardner, *Deep South: A Social Anthropological Study of Caste and Class* (Chicago, 1941), on Natchez and Claiborne County, Mississippi. Earlier accounts of the mountain people, by authors who took up permanent residence among them, were Horace Kephart, *Our Southern Highlanders* (New York, 1913) ; and John C. Campbell, *The Southern Highlander and His Homeland* (New York, 1921). The Kentucky coal-mining region was treated by a man who did relief work there in Malcolm H. Ross, *Machine Age in the Hills* (New York, 1933). A rosy view of textile mill villages is given in Harry I. Shumway, *I Go South: An Unprejudiced Visit to a Group of Cotton Mills* (New York, 1930).

A number of excellent accounts treat various aspects of Southern life. Odette Keun, *A Foreigner Looks at the TVA* (New York and Toronto, 1937) ; and Willson Whitman, *God's Valley: People and Power along the Tennessee River* (New York, 1939), give informative accounts of TVA and its region. James Agee, *Let Us Now Praise Famous Men* (Boston, 1941), with pictures by Walker Evans, recounts in poetic prose a sojourn of several weeks with Alabama tenant families. Two books by Erskine Caldwell and Margaret Bourke-White also combine photography and prose to describe the life of the people: *You Have Seen Their Faces* (New York, 1937), and *Say, Is This the USA?* (New York, 1941). Thomas Hart Benton, *An Artist in America* (New York, 1937), used sketches and paintings instead of photographs. Russell Lord, *Behold Our Land* (Boston, 1938), is valuable for its description of soil erosion and conservation. Carl Carmer, *Stars Fell on Alabama* (New York, 1934), gives observations on different kinds of Alabamians, with an emphasis on folklore. J. Saunders Redding, *No Day of Triumph* (New York and London, 1942), focuses on Negro life in the region.

During World War II a number of writers reported on turbulence in Southern war towns: John Dos Passos, *State of the Nation* (Boston, 1944); Selden Menefee, *Assignment: USA* (New York, 1943); Agnes E. Meyer, *Journey Through Chaos* (New York, 1944); and Alden Stevens, *Arms and the People* (New York and London, 1942).

CONTEMPORANEOUS ANALYSES

With the rise of Southern universities social criticism became a standard academic exercise, so that many of the most trenchant critiques of Southern problems came from the campuses, especially after 1930. The trend found earlier expression in Frank Tannenbaum, *Darker Phases of the South* (New York, 1924), a Columbia University historian's somber view of current problems; and Edwin Mims, *The Advancing South: Stories of Progress and Reaction* (New York, 1926), a Vanderbilt English professor's sanguine view of men and movements. Also somewhat optimistic was William J. Robertson, *The Changing South* (New York, 1927). Broadus Mitchell and George S. Mitchell, *The Industrial Revolution in the South* (Baltimore, 1930), reproduced the occasional papers of two academic economists. In *The War on Modern Science: A Short History of the Fundamentalist Attacks on Evolution and Modernism* (New York, 1927), Maynard Shipley gave much detail on fundamentalism in the South.

Henry L. Mencken, nemesis of the benighted South, collected his essays in the six volumes of *Prejudices* (New York, 1921–1927), but left others scattered through the issues of the Baltimore *Sun*. The most scathing critique of Southern barbarities, however, was produced by an oldtime Alabama Populist: William H. Skaggs, *The Southern Oligarchy: An Appeal in Behalf of the Silent Masses of Our Country Against the Despotic Rule of the Few* (New York, 1924). Other muckraking critiques are Walter Wilson, *Forced Labor in the United*

States (New York, 1933) ; Allan A. Michie and Frank Ryhlick, *Dixie Demagogues* (New York, 1939), in which few Southern politicos escape designation as demagogues; and Stetson Kennedy, *Southern Exposure* (New York, 1946).

Much of the analytical and controversial literature of the 1930's revolved around agrarianism and regionalism. The Agrarian Manifesto was Twelve Southerners, *I'll Take My Stand* (New York, 1930), followed by Herbert Agar and Allen Tate (eds.), *Who Owns America? A New Declaration of Independence* (Boston, 1936) ; and Donald Davidson, *The Attack on Leviathan: Regionalism and Nationalism in the United States* (Chapel Hill, 1937). The most uncompromising defense of a subsistence agriculture was T. J. Cauley, *Agrarianism* (Chapel Hill, 1935). The first major work of the Regionalist school was Rupert B. Vance, *Human Geography of the South* (Chapel Hill, 1932), but the Regionalist Bible was Howard W. Odum, *Southern Regions of the United States* (Chapel Hill, 1936). The idea of regionalism was further explored in Odum and Harry E. Moore, *American Regionalism* (New York, 1938). A good sampling of Odum's ideas may be found in Howard W. Odum, *Folk, Region, and Society: Selected Papers,* arranged and edited by Katharine Jocher and others (Chapel Hill, 1964). See also Odum's *American Epoch: Southern Portraiture in the National Picture* (New York, 1930), an impressionistic folk history, and his *The Way of the South: Toward the Regional Balance of America* (New York, 1947). A later survey of Southern problems was Rupert B. Vance and Nadia Danilevsky, *All These People: The Nation's Human Resources in the South* (Chapel Hill, 1945).

Katharine Du Pre Lumpkin, *The South in Progress* (New York, 1940), preserves the flavor of liberalism in the 1930's. Virginius Dabney, editor of the Richmond *Times-Dispatch,* sought out a liberal tradition in *Liberalism in the South* (Chapel Hill, 1932), and gave his own informed survey of the contemporary scene in *Below the Potomac: A Book About the New South* (New York, 1942). Similar surveys by newsmen were Clarence Cason, *90° in the Shade* (Chapel Hill, 1935) ; John Temple Graves, II, *The Fighting South* (New York, 1943). Walter Prescott Webb, *Divided We Stand: The Crisis of a Frontierless Democracy* (New York, 1937), was the major polemic against economic colonialism. The Southern Policy Committee's *Southern Policy Papers,* in ten numbers (Chapel Hill, 1936–1937), dealt with many of the current issues. Jasper B. Shannon, *Toward a New Politics in the South* (Knoxville, 1949), is especially valuable

743

for its chapter on "The Governing Class of a Southern County Seat."
Many other contemporary analyses of particular problems are given
below under the appropriate headings.

NEWSPAPERS

Newspaper files for the twentieth century have grown so mountainous that they were sampled only sparingly to add color, and occasionally to check out specific points. In locating files the standard Winifred
Gregory (ed.), *American Newspapers, 1821–1936: A Union List of
Files Available in the United States and Canada* (New York, 1937),
may be supplemented by George A. Schwegmann, Jr. (comp.), *Newspapers on Microfilm* (5th ed., Washington, 1963), and [Armistead S.
Pride], *Negro Newspapers on Microfilm: A Selected List* (Washington, 1953).

Some overview may be gained from Frank Luther Mott, *American
Journalism: A History of Newspapers in the United States Through
250 Years, 1690 to 1940* (New York, 1941); Thomas D. Clark, *The
Southern Country Editor* (Indianapolis, 1948); Walter C. Johnson
and Arthur T. Robb, *The South and Its Newspapers, 1903–1953: The
Story of the Southern Newspaper Publishers' Association and Its Part
in the South's Economic Rebirth* (Chattanooga, 1954); and Louis T.
Griffith and John E. Talmadge, *Georgia Journalism, 1763–1950*
(Athens, 1951). See also Gerald W. Johnson, "Journalism below the
Potomac," in *American Mercury*, IX (1926), 77–82; Gerald W. John-
son, "Southern Image Breakers," in *Virginia Quarterly Review*, IV
(1928), 508–19; and John D. Allen, "Journalism in the South," in
W. T. Couch (ed.), *Culture in the South* (Chapel Hill, 1935), 126–
58.

Several lively histories of individual papers exist: Sam Acheson,
35,000 Days in Texas: A History of the Dallas News and Its Forebears
(New York, 1938); Earl L. Bell and Kenneth C. Crabbe, *The Augusta
Chronicle: Indomitable Voice of Dixie, 1785–1960* (Athens, 1960);
Lenoir Chambers and Joseph E. Shank, *Salt Water & Printer's Ink:
Norfolk and Its Newspapers, 1865–1965* (Chapel Hill, 1967); Thomas
Ewing Dabney, *One Hundred Great Years: The Story of the Times-
Picayune from Its Founding to 1940* (Baton Rouge, 1944); Herbert
Ravenel Sass, *Outspoken: 150 Years of the News and Courier* (Colum-
bia, 1953); and Robert Talley, *One Hundred Years of the Commercial
Appeal* (Memphis, 1940).

In the Upper South the Richmond newspapers, which had strong
editorial direction during the period, proved very useful: the *News*

Leader (1868——, title varies), edited by Douglas Southall Freeman throughout most of the period, 1915–1949; and the *Times-Dispatch* (1850——, title varies) under Virginius Dabney after 1936. Similarly strong direction characterized the Norfolk *Virginian-Pilot* (1865——) under Louis I. Jaffe after 1919. In Louisville the *Courier-Journal* (1868——) retained the high standard set by Marse Henry Watterson when it passed under the ownership of Judge Robert W. Bingham and his son Barry after 1919. Leading papers in Tennessee include the Memphis *Commercial Appeal* (1869——), long edited by C. P. J. Mooney, 1908–1926; the Nashville *Tennessean* (1907——, title varies); the Nashville *Banner* (1876——); the Chattanooga *Times* (1869——); and the Chattanooga *News* (1888–1939), which succumbed to competition inspired by editor George Fort Milton's strong support of public power. In North Carolina the Raleigh *News and Observer* (1872——) under Josephus Daniels and his son Jonathan persisted in its liberalism and Democratic party regularity. Other North Carolina papers consulted were the Greensboro *Daily News* (1905——, title varies); the Charlotte *Observer* (1869——, title varies); the Asheville *Citizen* (1885——, title varies); and the Asheville *Times* (1892——, title varies).

In the Lower South the Charleston *News and Courier* (1803——, title varies) was distinguished for its outspoken conservatism under William Watts Ball, 1927–1951. The Columbia *State* (1891——), under the Gonzales family, was also edited by Ball, 1913–1923. Valuable for their wide coverage of the Southeast were the Atlanta *Constitution* (1868——) and Atlanta *Journal* (1883——). During the 1920's reputations for unusual vigor were gained by the Columbus *Enquirer-Sun* (1828–1930) under Julian Harris, 1923–1929, and the Macon *Telegraph* (1860——), under Mark Ethridge, 1925–1933, who later served the Richmond *Times-Dispatch* and the Louisville *Courier-Journal*. Of special value for Alabama affairs are the Montgomery *Advertiser* (1850?——), long under Grover C. Hall, 1926–1941; and the Birmingham *Age-Herald* (1887——). A few issues of the Birmingham *Southern Worker* (1930——?) were examined, together with the New York *Daily Worker* (1922——, title varies) for communist activities in the region. In Mississippi the Jackson *Daily News* (1892——, title varies) stands out for the fiery editorials of Frederick Sullens, its editor throughout the period.

For Louisiana affairs the New Orleans *Times-Picayune* (1837——, title varies) was consulted; and for the Southwest, the Dallas *Daily News* (1885——), with good coverage of economic and cultural developments. Other leading dailies include the Houston *Press* (1911————) ; the Houston *Post* (1880————) ; and the Fort Worth *Star-Telegram* (1896————). Standard newspapers for Oklahoma and Arkansas are the capital city papers: the Oklahoma City *Daily Oklahoman* (1894————) ; and the Little Rock *Arkansas Gazette* (1865————). For Florida see the Tallahassee *Daily Democrat* (1915————) ; the Jacksonville *Times-Union* (1875————, title varies) ; and the Miami *Daily News* (1896————).

Negro newspapers with long runs in the period include the Norfolk *Journal and Guide* (1901————) ; the Atlanta *Daily World* (1928————), the only Negro daily; the Houston *Informer* (1919————) ; and the Oklahoma City *Black Dispatch* (1915————). The Washington *Bee* (1882–1922) was consulted on the Negroes' response to Woodrow Wilson.

The most useful single newspaper, however, was the fully-indexed New York *Times* (1851————). Other New York papers consulted for material on the South were the *Tribune* (1841–1924), which united with the *Herald* (1835–1924) ; and the *World* (1860–1931).

PERIODICALS

More comprehensive coverage of periodicals than of newspapers was undertaken to secure greater yield for the investment of time; the most significant events and issues usually found their way into the magazines. Many specific articles are cited in the footnotes, but few of those titles are repeated in this essay. The chief finding aid for periodicals currently is Edna Brown Titus (ed.), *Union List of Serials in the United States and Canada*, 5 vols. (3rd ed., New York, 1965). For an overview see Jay B. Hubbell, "Southern Magazines," in Couch (ed.), *Culture in the South*, 159–82.

Among regional periodicals the old standbys were the *Sewanee Review* (Sewanee, Tenn., 1892————), which emphasized literature, and the *South Atlantic Quarterly* (Durham, 1902————), on which see also William B. Hamilton (comp.), *Fifty Years of the South Atlantic Quarterly* (Durham, 1952). Major new regional periodicals were the *Texas Review* (Austin, 1915–1924), which became the *Southwest Review* (Dallas, 1924————) ; the *Virginia Quarterly Review* (Charlottesville, 1925————) ; and the *Southern Review* (Baton Rouge, 1935–1942, new series, 1965————). More recent entries include the *Georgia Review* (Athens, 1947————), and the *Mississippi Quarterly* (State College, Miss., 1948————).

In addition to the older *Southwestern Historical Quarterly* (Austin,

1897——), a number of scholarly journals with regional focus began publication during the period under consideration: the *Southwestern Political Science Quarterly* (Austin, 1920——); Howard W. Odum's *Journal of Social Forces* (Chapel Hill, 1922——, title varies); the *Southwestern Social Science Quarterly* (Norman, 1932); the *Southern Economic Journal* (Chapel Hill, 1933——); the *Journal of Southern History* (Baton Rouge, Nashville, Lexington, Ky., Houston, 1935——); and the *Journal of Politics* (Gainesville, Fla., 1939——). The standard historical journals were consulted, including state journals for every Southern state. Titles of these may be found in *American Association for State and Local History, Directory of Historical Societies and Agencies in the United States and Canada, 1965–1966* (Nashville, 1965). The *Southern Association Quarterly* (Durham, 1937——), is the organ of the Southern Association of Colleges and Secondary Schools.

The major "little magazines" of the literary renaissance were the *Year Book of the Poetry Society of South Carolina* (Charleston, 1921–1926); the *Double Dealer* (New Orleans, 1921–1926); the *Reviewer* (Richmond, Chapel Hill, 1921–1925), which merged with the *Southwest Review* in 1926; the *Fugitive: A Journal of Poetry* (Nashville, 1922–1925); the *Lyric* (Norfolk, 1921——); and *Contempo* (Chapel Hill, 1931–1934). On others see Chapter IX above and Frederick J. Hoffman *et al., The Little Magazine: A History and a Bibliography* (Princeton, 1947). A unique magazine edited by Lillian Smith and Paula Snelling promoted both literature and liberalism under three successive titles: *Pseudopodia* (Atlanta, 1936–1937); *North Georgia Review* (Atlanta, 1937–1941); and *South Today* (Atlanta, 1941–1945).

The *Manufacturers' Record* (Baltimore, Atlanta, 1882–1958), which merged with *Industrial Development* (Atlanta, 1954——), and its annual *Blue Book of Southern Progress* (Baltimore, Atlanta, 1909——), provide indispensable sources for economic history. Of especial interest is *The South's Development,* a supplement to the *Manufacturers' Record* issue of December 11, 1924. For various aspects of economic development the following were consulted: the *Southern Textile Bulletin* (Charlotte, 1911——, title varies); *Textile World* (New York, 1888——); *Cotton: Serving the Textile Industry* (Atlanta, 1908——, title varies); *Cotton Trade Journal* (New Orleans, 1921——); *Progressive Farmer* (Raleigh, 1886——, title varies); *Southern Agriculturist* (Nashville, 1869——); *Business Week* (Greenwich, Conn., and New York, 1929——); *Fortune* (New York;

747

1930———) ; *Nation's Business* (Washington, 1912———) ; *United Mine Workers' Journal* (Indianapolis, 1891———) ; *Textile Labor* (Philadelphia, 1939———) ; *American Federationist* (Washington, 1894———) ; and the *CIO News* (Washington, 1937———) .

The *Southern Workman* (Hampton, Va., 1872–1939) reflected the Hampton-Tuskegee philosophy, and *Phylon: The Atlanta University Review of Race & Culture* (Atlanta 1940———) reflected that of its founder, W. E. B. Du Bois. Items on Southern affairs appeared frequently in *The Crisis: A Record of the Darker Races* (New York, 1910———) , and *Opportunity: A Journal of Negro Life* (New York, 1923–1949) , organs of the NAACP and the Urban League, respectively. Materials both contemporaneous and retrospective in content have appeared in the *Journal of Negro History* (Lancaster, Pa. and Washington, 1916———) , and the *Journal of Negro Education* (Lancaster, Pa., 1932———) . *Southern Frontier* (Atlanta, 1940–1945) , the organ of the Commission on Interracial Cooperation and the Southern Regional Council, was superseded by *New South* (Atlanta, 1945———) .

National weeklies of news and opinion provided a useful guide to important events: the *Literary Digest* (New York, 1890–1938) ; the *Nation* (New York, 1865———) ; the *New Republic* (New York, 1914———) ; *News-Week* (Dayton, Ohio, 1933———) ; and *Time: The Weekly News Magazine* (New York, 1923———) . Among the national periodicals, the following often carried articles about the South: *Annals of the American Academy of Political and Social Science* (Philadelphia, 1890———) ; the *American Mercury* (New York, 1924———) ; the *Atlantic Monthly* (Boston, 1857———, title varies) ; *Current History* (New York, 1914———, title varies) ; *Forum* (New York, 1886–1930) ; *Harper's* (New York, 1850———) ; the *Independent* (New York, Boston, 1848–1928) ; *Outlook* (New York, 1870–1935) ; *Review of Reviews* (New York, 1890–1937, title varies) ; *Saturday Evening Post* (Philadelphia, 1821———) ; *Saturday Review of Literature* (New York, 1924———, title varies) ; *Survey* (New York, 1897–1952) ; *Survey Graphic* (New York, 1921–1948) ; and *World's Work* (New York, 1900–1932) .

This listing should not end without at least passing notice to a home magazine that circulated widely in the South: *Holland's Magazine* (Dallas, 1876———) .

BIOGRAPHIES

Few Southerners of the recent period have yet been the subjects of critical biographies. Most of the scholarly studies treat figures prominent early in the period 1913–1945. Such biographies of political figures include Francis B. Simkins, *Pitchfork Ben Tillman: South Carolinian* (Baton Rouge, 1944); C. Vann Woodward, *Tom Watson: Agrarian Rebel* (New York, 1938); Dewey W. Grantham, Jr., *Hoke Smith and the Politics of the New South* (Baton Rouge, 1958); George C. Osborn, *John Sharp Williams: Planter-Statesman of the Deep South* (Baton Rouge, 1943); Joseph L. Morrison, *Josephus Daniels: The Small-d Democrat* (Chapel Hill, 1966); Lawrence W. Levine, *Defender of the Faith, William Jennings Bryan: The Last Decade 1915–1925* (New York, 1925); and William D. Miller, *Mr. Crump of Memphis* (Baton Rouge, 1964). Alex M. Arnett, *Claude Kitchin and the Wilson War Policies* (Boston, 1937), is redolent of World War I revisionism.

Relatively uncritical but useful treatments include Sam Hanna Acheson, *Joe Bailey: The Last Democrat* (New York, 1932); A. Wigfall Green, *The Man Bilbo* (Baton Rouge, 1963); John Frank, *Mr. Justice Black* (New York, 1939); Aubrey Lee Brooks, *Walter Clark: Fighting Judge* (Chapel Hill, 1944); Marquis James, *Mr. Garner of Texas* (Indianapolis and New York, 1939); Bascom N. Timmons, *Garner of Texas: A Personal History* (New York, 1948); James E. Palmer, Jr., *Carter Glass: Unreconstructed Rebel* (Roanoke, Va., 1938); Harold B. Hinton, *Cordell Hull: A Biography* (Garden City, N.Y., 1942); John E. Huss, *Senator for the South: A Biography of Olin D. Johnston* (Garden City, N.Y., 1961); Bascom M. Timmons, *Jesse H. Jones: The Man and the Statesman* (New York, 1956); John Joseph Mathews, *Life and Death of an Oilman: The Career of E. W. Marland* (Norman, 1951); and C. Dwight Dorough, *Mr. Sam* (New York, 1962).

A number of valuable biographical Ph.D. dissertations remain unpublished: Escal Franklin Duke, "The Political Career of Morris Sheppard, 1875–1941" (University of Texas, 1958); Warner E. Mills, Jr., "The Public Career of a Texas Conservative: A Biography of Ross Shaw Sterling" (The Johns Hopkins University, 1956); Robert M. Burts, "The Public Career of Richard I. Manning" (Vanderbilt University, 1957); John Robert Moore, "Josiah Bailey of North Carolina and the New Deal" (Duke University, 1962); Sarah M. Lemmon, "The Public Career of Eugene Talmadge, 1926–1936" (University of North Carolina, 1952); A. Graham Shanks, "Sam Rayburn and the New Deal, 1933–1936" (University of North Carolina, 1964); and Alexander R. Stoesen, "The Senatorial Career of Claude D. Pepper" (University of North Carolina, 1964).

The field of biography is richer in studies of nonpolitical figures. Educational leaders are treated in Dumas Malone, *Edwin A. Alderman: A Biography* (New York, 1940); Rackham Holt, *Mary McLeod Bethune: A Biography* (Garden City, N.Y., 1964); Willard C. Gatewood, *Eugene Clyde Brooks: Educator and Public Servant* (Durham, 1960); Benjamin Brawley, *Dr. Dillard of the Jeanes Fund* (New York, 1930); and Ridgely Torence, *The Story of John Hope* (New York, 1948).

Two great leaders in Negro life have not yet received definitive study, but excellent critical evaluations exist in Samuel R. Spencer, Jr., *Booker T. Washington and the Negro's Place in American Life* (Boston, 1955); Francis L. Broderick, *W. E. B. Du Bois: Negro Leader in a Time of Crisis* (Stanford, 1959); and Elliott M. Rudwick, *W. E. B. Du Bois: A Study in Minority Group Leadership* (Philadelphia, 1960). Biographical sketches of many Negro leaders appear in Richard Bardolph, *The Negro Vanguard* (New York, 1959), which has an extensive bibliographical essay.

Leaders in business, except for those active in politics—such as Jones, Marland, and Sterling—have mostly been neglected. See, however, LeGette Blythe, *William Henry Belk: Merchant of the South* (Chapel Hill, 1950); Charles Howard Candler, *Asa Griggs Candler* (Emory University, 1950); George Lee Simpson, *The Cokers of Carolina: A Social Biography of a Family* (Chapel Hill, 1956), which treats a family active in business, agriculture, and intellectual pursuits; John W. Jenkins, *James B. Duke: Master Builder* (New York, 1927); and John K. Winkler, *Tobacco Tycoon: The Story of James Buchanan Duke* (New York, 1943).

Robert P. Parsons, *Trail to Light: A Biography of Joseph Goldberger* (Indianapolis, 1943), tells about the conquest of pellagra, and Wellington Brink, *Big Hugh: The Father of Soil Conservation* (New York, 1951), tells about another crusade. Two Southern humanitarians are sympathetically portrayed in Wilma Dykeman and James Stokely, *Seeds of Southern Change: The Life of Will Alexander* (Chicago, 1962), and Wilma Dykeman, *Prophet of Plenty: The First Ninety Years of W. D. Weatherford* (Knoxville, 1966). One churchman is treated with great severity in Virginius Dabney, *Dry Messiah: The Life of Bishop James Cannon, Jr.* (New York, 1949); but others are the subjects of more congenial treatments: Alfred M. Pierce, *Giant Against the Sky: The Life of Bishop Warren Akin Candler* (Nashville, 1948); Powhatan W. James, *George W. Truett: A Biography* (New York, 1939); Eugene Schuyler English, *Robert G. Lee: A Chosen*

Vessel (Grand Rapids, Mich., 1949) ; and Cedric Belfrage, *A Faith to Free the People* (New York, 1944), which eulogizes Claude Williams, Presbyterian and united front activist.

Biographies of Southern writers, other than sketches in critical works, include Louis D. Rubin, Jr., *No Place on Earth: Ellen Glasgow, James Branch Cabell, and Richmond-in-Virginia* (Austin, 1959) ; Charlie May Simon, *Johnswood* (New York, 1953), a personal memoir by Mrs. John Gould Fletcher; Frank M. Durham, *DuBose Heyward: The Man Who Wrote Porgy* (Columbia, S.C., 1954) ; Oliver W. Evans, *Carson McCullers: Her Life and Work* (London, 1965) ; Elizabeth Nowell, *Thomas Wolfe: A Biography* (Garden City, N.Y., 1960) ; Richard S. Kennedy, *The Window of Memory: The Literary Career of Thomas Wolfe* (Chapel Hill, 1962) ; and Joseph L. Morrison, *W. J. Cash: Southern Prophet. A Biography and Reader* (New York, 1967).

GENERAL STUDIES

Few general histories of the United States give much attention to the twentieth-century South. Some exceptions are Arthur S. Link, *Woodrow Wilson and the Progressive Era* (New York, 1954) ; William E. Leuchtenburg, *Franklin D. Roosevelt and the New Deal* (New York, 1963) ; and three volumes so far published in Arthur M. Schlesinger, Jr., *The Age of Roosevelt* (Boston, 1957———).

Wilbur J. Cash's classic, *The Mind of the South* (New York, 1941), has qualities of both a secondary and primary work, since much of the last part rests upon personal observation. The same point applies to two works by Thomas D. Clark: *The Emerging South* (New York, 1961), which explores social, economic, and political change after 1920; and *Three Paths to the Modern South: Education, Agriculture, and Conservation* (Athens, 1965). Helpful surveys of Southern history include Francis B. Simkins, *A History of the South* (3rd ed., New York, 1963) ; W. B. Hesseltine and David L. Smiley, *The South in American History* (Englewood Cliffs, N.J., 1960) ; John S. Ezell, *The South since 1865* (New York, 1963) ; and Thomas D. Clark and Albert D. Kirwan, *The South since Appomattox: A Century of Regional Change* (New York, 1967).

The state histories most useful for the period after 1913 are Matthew Page Andrews, *Virginia: The Old Dominion* (New York, 1937) ; Hugh T. Lefler and Albert Ray Newsome, *North Carolina: The History of a Southern State* (Rev. ed., Chapel Hill, 1963) ; D. D. Wallace, *The History of South Carolina*, 4 vols. (New York, 1934) ; Ernest M.

Lander, *A History of South Carolina, 1865–1900* (Chapel Hill, 1960);
E. Merton Coulter, *Georgia: A Short History* (Chapel Hill, 1947);
J. E. Dovell, *Florida: Historic, Dramatic, Contemporary,* 4 vols. (New
York, 1952); Alfred Jackson Hanna and Kathryn Abbey Hanna,
Florida's Golden Sands (Indianapolis, 1950); Stanley J. Folmsbee,
Robert E. Corlew, and Enoch L. Mitchell, *History of Tennessee,* 4
vols. (New York, 1960); Albert B. Moore, *History of Alabama* (Uni-
versity, Ala., 1934); David Y. Thomas, *Arkansas and Its People: A
History, 1541–1930* (New York, 1930); Edwin C. McReynolds, *Okla-
homa: A History of the Sooner State* (Norman, 1954); and Rupert
Norval Richardson, *Texas: The Lone Star State* (New York, 1943).

Studies of local and urban history tend to be superficial, but some
exceptions stand out: Gilbert E. Govan and James W. Livingood, *The
Chattanooga Country, 1540–1951* (Rev. ed., Chapel Hill, 1963);
Thomas J. Wertenbaker, *Norfolk: Historic Southern Port* (Durham,
1931; 2nd ed., edited by Marvin W. Schlegel, Durham, 1962); Marvin
W. Schlegel, *Conscripted City: Norfolk in World War II* (Norfolk,
1951); William Kenneth Boyd, *The Story of Durham: City of the
New South* (Durham, 1925); Charles G. Summersell, *Mobile: History
of a Seaport Town* (University, Ala., 1949); William D. Miller,
Memphis During the Progressive Era, 1900–1917 (Memphis, 1957);
Oliver Knight, *Fort Worth: Outpost on the Trinity* (Norman, 1953);
James Howard, *Big D Is for Dallas: Chapter in the Twentieth-
Century History of Dallas* (Austin, 1957); and Angie L. Debo, *Tulsa:
From Creek Town to Oil Capital* (Norman, 1943). H. C. Nixon's
Possum Trot: Rural Community, South (Norman, 1941) is a happy
combination of social history and memoir.

One should not overlook the Federal Writers' Program of the
Works Progress Administration, *American Guide Series,* with volumes
on each state and several cities; nor the *American Folkways* series,
which includes such volumes as Hodding Carter and Anthony Ragusin,
Gulf Coast Country (New York, 1951); nor the *Rivers of America*
series, in which one of the best is Donald Davidson, *The Tennessee,*
2 vols. (New York, 1946–1948).

POLITICAL STUDIES

Dewey W. Grantham, Jr., *The Democratic South* (Athens, 1963),
offers a thoughtful and informative introduction to Southern political history. V. O. Key, Jr., *Southern Politics in State and Nation*
(New York, 1949), gives greater detail but focuses on the 1940's—not
without much historical background. One very useful survey and

analysis is a reprint from the *Journal of Politics:* Taylor Cole and John H. Hallowell (eds.), *The Southern Political Scene, 1938–1948* (Gainesville, Fla., 1948). T. Harry Williams, *Romance and Realism in Southern Politics* (Athens, 1961), emphasizes the hypnotic effect of legend and rhetoric.

Among monographic works on various aspects of politics Frederick D. Ogden, *The Poll Tax in the South* (University, Ala., 1958), is a thorough study. Thomas A. Krueger, *And Promises to Keep: The Southern Conference for Human Welfare, 1938–1948* (Nashvil'e, 1967), is both thorough and sprightly. Paul Lewinson, *Race, Class & Party: A History of Negro Suffrage and White Politics in the South* (New York, 1932), is still a useful reference on Negro participation and nonparticipation; but see also Hugh D. Price, *The Negro and Southern Politics: A Chapter of Florida History* (New York, 1957); and William A. Mabry, *The Negro in North Carolina Politics since Reconstruction* (Durham, 1940). The distinctive regional impact on the woman suffrage movement is the subject of one chapter in Aileen Kraditor, *The Ideas of the Woman Suffrage Movement, 1890–1920* (New York, 1965); greater detail may be found in A. Elizabeth Taylor, *A Short History of the Woman Suffrage Movement in Tennessee* (Nashville, 1943), and in numerous articles by Professor Taylor. On prohibition see James B. Sellers, *The Prohibition Movement in Alabama, 1702 to 1943* (Chapel Hill, 1943); and Daniel Jay Whitener, *Prohibition in North Carolina, 1715–1945* (Chapel Hill, 1945).

Among the better state studies are Albert D. Kirwan's *Revolt of the Rednecks: Mississippi Politics, 1876–1925* (Lexington, Ky., 1951); Elmer L. Puryear, *Democratic Party Dissension in North Carolina, 1928–1936* (Chapel Hill, 1962); Paul Isaac, *Prohibition and Politics: Turbulent Decades in Tennessee, 1885–1920* (Knoxville, 1965); John H. Fenton, *Politics in the Border States . . . Maryland, West Virginia, Kentucky, and Missouri* (New Orleans, 1957); and three books on Louisiana: Harnett T. Kane, *Louisiana Hayride: The American Rehearsal for Dictatorship, 1928–1940* (New York, 1941); Perry H. Howard, *Political Tendencies in Louisiana, 1812–1952* (Baton Rouge, 1957); and Allan P. Sindler, *Huey Long's Louisiana: State Politics, 1920–1952* (Baltimore, 1956). Uncritical but useful is William T. Cash, *History of the Democratic Party in Florida . . .* (Tallahassee, 1936). Thorough factual treatments are given in three volumes by Seth S. McKay: *Texas Politics, 1906–1944, With Special Reference to the German Counties* (Lubbock, 1952); *W. Lee O'Daniel and*

753

Texas Politics, 1938–1942 (Lubbock, 1944); and *Texas and the Fair Deal, 1945–1952* (San Antonio, 1954).

A number of good state studies remain in the form of unpublished Ph.D. dissertations: Joseph F. Steelman, "The Progressive Era in North Carolina, 1884–1917" (University of North Carolina, 1955); James A. Tinsley, "The Progressive Movement in Texas" (University of Wisconsin, 1953); Charles G. Hamilton, "Mississippi Politics in the Progressive Era, 1904–1920" (Vanderbilt University, 1958); James R. Scales, "Political History of Oklahoma, 1907–1949" (University of Oklahoma, 1949); Lionel V. Patenaude, "The New Deal and Texas" (University of Texas, 1953); John Dear. Minton, "The New Deal in Tennessee, 1932–1938" (Vanderbilt University, 1959); and Roy E. Fossett, "The Impact of the New Deal on Georgia Politics, 1933–1941" (University of Florida, 1960).

Other studies treat regional politics in national or international perspectives: unpublished studies on the Wilson era by John Wells Davidson, Dewey W. Grantham, Jr., and Anne Firor Scott, cited in Chapter I; Seward W. Livermore, *Politics Is Adjourned: Woodrow Wilson and the War Congress, 1916–1918* (Middletown, Conn., 1966); Lee N. Allen, "The Underwood Presidential Movement of 1924" (Ph.D. dissertation, University of Pennsylvania, 1955); Julius Turner, *Party and Constituency: Pressures on Congress* (Baltimore, 1951); and James Tyler Patterson, III, "Conservative Coalition in Congress, 1933–1939" (Ph.D. dissertation, Harvard University, 1964), a superior study scheduled for early publication. A pioneering essay on the South and foreign affairs is Paul Seabury, *The Waning of Southern "Internationalism"* (Princeton, 1957). Fuller treatments include George L. Grassmuck, *Sectional Biases in Congress on Foreign Policy* (Baltimore, 1951); Timothy G. McDonald, "Southern Democratic Congressmen and the First World War, August, 1914–April, 1917: The Public Record of Their Support for or Opposition to Wilson's Policies" (Ph.D. dissertation, University of Washington, 1962); Irving Howards, "The Influence of Southern Senators on American Foreign Policy from 1939 to 1950" (Ph.D. dissertation, University of Wisconsin, 1955); Charles O. Lerche, Jr., *The Uncertain South: Its Changing Patterns of Politics in Foreign Policy* (Chicago, 1964); and Alfred O. Hero, Jr., *The Southerner and World Affairs* (Baton Rouge, 1965).

AGRICULTURE

There is no comprehensive history of Southern agriculture in the twentieth century, but Theodore Saloutos, *Farmer Movements in the*

South, 1865–1933 (Berkeley and Los Angeles, 1960), covers more than its title indicates. The effects of the New Deal and World War II are pursued in James H. Street, *The New Revolution in the Cotton Economy: Mechanization and Its Consequences* (Chapel Hill, 1957), which may be supplemented by John L. Fulmer, *Agricultural Progress in the Cotton Belt since 1920* (Chapel Hill, 1950). Anthony M. Täng, *Economic Development in the Southern Piedmont, 1860–1950: Its Impact on Agriculture* (Chapel Hill, 1958), shows how industry benefited agriculture. Willard Range, *A Century of Georgia Agriculture, 1850–1950* (Athens, 1954), is a unique state study.

The culture complex of cotton is vividly described in Rupert B. Vance, *Human Factors in Cotton Culture: A Study in the Social Geography of the American South* (Chapel Hill, 1929). There is no adequate history of either cotton or rice, but two other Southern staples are covered in excellent works: Nannie May Tilley, *The Bright Tobacco Industry, 1860–1929* (Chapel Hill, 1948); Joseph C. Robert, *The Story of Tobacco in America* (New York, 1949); and J. Carlyle Sitterson, *Sugar Country: The Cane Sugar Industry in the South* (Lexington, Ky., 1953). See also David L. Cohn, *The Life and Times of King Cotton* (New York, 1956); and James E. Boyle, *Cotton and the New Orleans Cotton Exchange* (Garden City, N.Y., 1934).

Very useful for general reference are Murray R. Benedict, *Farm Policies of the United States, 1790–1950* (New York, 1953); Murray R. Benedict and Oscar C. Stine, *The Agricultural Commodity Programs: Two Decades of Experience* (New York, 1958); and three period studies: James H. Shideler, *Farm Crisis, 1919–1923* (Berkeley, 1957); B. H. Hibbard, *Effects of the Great War upon Agriculture in the United States and Great Britain* (New York, 1919); and Walter W. Wilcox, *The Farmer in the Second World War* (Ames, Ia., 1947).

The farmers' drift from agrarian rebellion to "businesslike" procedures is the subject of an interpretive work by Grant McConnell, *The Decline of Agrarian Democracy* (Berkeley, 1953). There is no adequate over-all history of any farm organization in the period, but see Robert L. Hunt, *A History of Farmer Movements in the Southwest, 1873–1925* (College Station, Tex., 1935); Commodore B. Fisher, *The Farmers' Union* (Lexington, Ky., 1920); Orville M. Kile, *The Farm Bureau Movement* (New York, 1921); Orville M. Kile, *The Farm Bureau through Three Decades* (Baltimore, 1948); Christiana McFadyen Campbell, *The Farm Bureau and the New Deal: A Study of the Making of National Farm Policy, 1933–1940* (Urbana, Ill., 1962), which is more critical; and Stuart L. Noblin, *The Grange in*

North Carolina, 1929–1954: A Story of Agricultural Progress (Greensboro, N.C., 1954).

The co-operative movement gets sympathetic treatment in Robert H. Montgomery, *The Cooperative Pattern in Cotton* (New York, 1929); and Wilson Gee and Edward A. Terry, *The Cotton Cooperatives in the Southeast,* in University of Virginia Institute for Research in the Social Sciences Monographs, No. 17 (New York and London, 1933). Histories of two successful co-operatives are James T. Hopkins, *Fifty Years of Citrus: The Florida Citrus Exchange, 1909–1959* (Gainesville, Fla., 1960); and W. G. Wysor, *The History and Philosophy of Southern States Cooperative* (Richmond, 1940).

An example of the earlier literature on tenancy is E. A. Goldenweiser and Leon Truesdell, *Farm Tenancy in the United States* (College Station, Tex., 1921). Among the many studies of the New Deal era the most intensive treatments are two books by Arthur F. Raper: *Preface to Peasantry: A Tale of Two Black Belt Counties* (Chapel Hill, 1936); and *Tenants of the Almighty* (New York, 1943). Other valuable studies are T. J. Woofter, Jr., *et al., Landlord and Tenant on the Cotton Plantation,* Works Progress Administration Research Monograph V (Washington, 1936); Charles S. Johnson, *Shadow of the Plantation* (Chicago, 1934); Margaret Jarman Hagood, *Mothers of the South: Portraiture of the White Tenant Farm Woman* (Chapel Hill, 1939); and William C. Holley *et al., The Plantation South* (Washington, 1940). A treatment that called attention sharply to the problem was Charles S. Johnson, Edwin R. Embree, and W. W. Alexander, *The Collapse of Cotton Tenancy: A Summary of Field Studies & Statistical Surveys, 1933–35* (Chapel Hill, 1935). New Deal policies may be pursued in Paul K. Conkin, *Tomorrow a New World: The New Deal Community Program* (Ithaca, 1959); David Eugene Conrad, *The Forgotten Farmers: The Story of Sharecroppers in the New Deal* (Urbana, Ill., 1965); and James G. Maddox, "The Farm Security Administration" (Ph.D. dissertation, Harvard University, 1950), by a former official of the FSA. On farm unions see Stuart N. Jamieson, *Labor Unionism in American Agriculture,* in Bureau of Labor Statistics *Bulletin* No. 836 (Washington, 1945); and Donald H. Grubbs, "The Southern Tenant Farmers' Union and the New Deal" (Ph.D. dissertation, University of Florida, 1963), an exhaustive study.

MANUFACTURING AND COMMERCE

A brief but helpful sketch of achievements and needs is Gerald D. Nash, "Research Opportunities in the Economic History of the

South after 1880," in *Journal of Southern History*, XXXII (1966), 308–24. The best over-all treatment of the Southern economy and its problems in the period is Calvin B. Hoover and Benjamin U. Ratchford, *Economic Resources and Policies of the South* (New York, 1951). The colonial-imperialistic thesis is traced and challenged in Clarence H. Danhof, "Four Decades of Thought on the South's Economic Problems," in Melvin L. Greenhut and W. Tate Whitman (eds.), *Essays in Southern Economic Development* (Chapel Hill, 1964), 7–68.

Southern efforts to promote industry get attention in Yoshimitsu Ide, "The Significance of Richard Hathaway Edmonds and His *Manufacturers' Record* in the New South" (Ph.D. dissertation, University of Florida, 1959); Albert Lepawsky, *State Planning and Economic Development in the South* (Washington, 1949); John V. Van Sickle, *Planning for the South: An Inquiry into the Economics of Regionalism* (Nashville, 1943); Paul Barrett, *An Analysis of State Industrial Development Programs* (Knoxville, 1944); and Ernest J. Hopkins, *Mississippi's BAWI Plan, Balance Agriculture with Industry: An Experiment in Industrial Subsidization* (Atlanta, 1944). Harriet L. Herring, *Southern Industry and Regional Development* (Chapel Hill, 1940), advocated a more balanced economy. Much solid information on industrial development during and immediately after World War II is in National Planning Association Committee of the South, Report Nos. 2 and 3: Frederick L. Deming and Weldon A. Stein, *Disposal of Southern War Plants* (Washington, 1949); and Glenn E. McLaughlin and Stefan Robock, *Why Industry Moves South: A Study of Factors Influencing the Recent Location of Manufacturing Plants in the South* (Washington, 1949). On urbanization, see Rupert B. Vance and Nicholas J. Demerath (eds.), *The Urban South* (Chapel Hill, 1954).

The problem of freight-rate discrimination is covered in two first-rate studies: William H. Joubert, *Southern Freight Rates in Transition* (Gainesville, Fla., 1949); and Robert A. Lively, *The South in Action: A Sectional Crusade Against Freight Rate Discriminations* (Chapel Hill, 1949). The issues of freight-rate and price discriminations receive critical attention in George R. Stocking, *Basing Point Pricing and Regional Development: A Case Study of the Iron and Steel Industry* (Chapel Hill, 1954). Studies of competition in tobacco are Reavis Cox, *Competition in the American Tobacco Industry, 1911–1932: A Study of the Partition of the American Tobacco Company by the United States Supreme Court*, in Columbia University *Studies in History, Economics, and Public Law*, No. 381 (New York, 1933);

757

William H. Nicholls, *Price Policies in the Cigarette Industry: A Study of "Concerted Action" and Its Social Control, 1911-1950* (Nashville, 1951); and Richard B. Tennant, *The American Cigarette Industry: A Study in Economic Analysis and Public Policy* (New Haven, 1950). An excellent study of efforts at stabilization in textiles became available after this book was written: Louis Galambos, *Competition and Cooperation: The Emergence of a National Trade Association* (Baltimore, 1966).

The books on cotton and tobacco by Cohn, Tilley, and Roberts, given above, cover manufacturing as well as agriculture. For other industries, good syntheses are Jack M. Blicksilver, *Cotton Manufacturing in the Southeast: An Historical Analysis* (Atlanta, 1959); James A. Morris, *Woolen and Worsted Manufacturing in the Southern Piedmont* (Columbia, 1952); Herman H. Chapman *et al.*, *The Iron and Steel Industries of the South* (University, Ala., 1953); Carl Coke Rister, *Oil! Titan of the Southwest* (Norman, 1949); H. E. Klontz, "An Economic Study of the Southern Furniture Manufacturing Industry" (Ph.D. dissertation, University of North Carolina, 1948); Olin T. Mouzon, "The Social and Economic Implications of Recent Developments within the Wood and Paper Industry in the South" (Ph.D. dissertation, University of North Carolina, 1940); and J. E. Mills (ed.), *Chemical Progress in the South* (New York, 1930). Williams Haynes, *American Chemical Industries*, 6 vols. (New York, 1945–1954), reflects the author's interest in the South, as do several of his other books: *The Stone that Burns: The Story of the American Sulphur Industry* (New York, 1942); *Cellulose: The Chemical that Grows* (Garden City, N.Y., 1953); and *Southern Horizons* (New York, 1946), on the region's promise in chemicals. The history of transportation in the period has been neglected generally, but there is one good state study of road building: Cecil K. Brown, *The State Highway System of North Carolina* (Chapel Hill, 1931). See also Albert N. Sanders, "State Regulation of Public Utilities by South Carolina, 1879–1935" (Ph.D. dissertation, University of North Carolina, 1956).

One of the very best corporation histories is Henrietta M. Larson and Kenneth W. Porter, *History of Humble Oil & Refining Company: A Study in Industrial Growth* (New York, 1959). John L. Loos, *Oil on Stream! A History of Interstate Oil Pipe Line Company, 1909–1959* (Baton Rouge, 1959), is a work of substantial merit. Several other oil-company histories, cited in the text, touch upon the South. In other fields corporation histories are scarce and usually thin. One outstanding exception is Robert S. Smith, *Mill on the Dan: A His-*

tory of Dan River Mills, 1882–1950 (Durham, 1960), thorough but formidable. More effervescent is E. J. Kahn, Jr., *The Big Drink: The Story of Coca-Cola* (New York, 1960), first published in the *New Yorker*. John B. McFerrin, *Caldwell and Company: A Southern Financial Empire* (Chapel Hill, 1939), covers the "Morgan of the South."

For private utility companies nothing exists but "official" histories, and few of those. One is noteworthy because its author was a leader in the company: Thomas W. Martin, *Forty Years of Alabama Power Company, 1911–1951* (New York, 1952). By contrast, the Tennessee Valley Authority has been the subject of many sound studies. For its genesis, see Preston J. Hubbard, *Origins of the TVA: The Muscle Shoals Controversy, 1920–1932* (Nashville, 1961), a superior study. The best survey of its early years is still C. Herman Pritchett, *The Tennessee Valley Authority: A Study in Public Administration* (Chapel Hill, 1943). Philip Selznick, *TVA and the Grass Roots: A Study in the Sociology of Formal Organization* (Berkeley, 1949), develops the thesis of a TVA-Farm Bureau alliance and should be balanced by reference to Norman I. Wengert, *Valley of Tomorrow: The TVA and Agriculture*, in University of Tennessee Record *Extension Series*, XXVIII, No. 1 (Knoxville, 1952). Other works on TVA are cited in the documentation for Chapter XIII.

LABOR, RELIEF, AND WELFARE

A valuable contemporary survey is Abraham Berglund, George T. Starnes, and Frank T. de Vyver, *Labor in the Industrial South: A Survey of Wages and Living Conditions in Three Major Industries of the New Industrial South* (University, Va., 1930). A later survey is H. M. Douty (ed.), *Labor in the South* (Washington, 1946), reprinted from the *Monthly Labor Review*, LXIII (1946), 481–586.

A full survey for one industry is Herbert J. Lahne, *The Cotton Mill Worker* (New York, 1944). Studies of textile mill villages include Jennings J. Rhyne, *Some Cotton Mill Workers and Their Villages* (Chapel Hill, 1930); Lois MacDonald, *Southern Mill Hills: A Study of Social and Economic Forces in Certain Textile Mill Villages* (New York, 1928); and Marjorie A. Potwin, *Cotton Mill People of the Piedmont: A Study in Social Change,* in Columbia University *Studies in History, Economics, and Public Law,* CCXI (New York, 1927), which is relatively uncritical. Management policies in textiles are the subject of Harriet L. Herring, *Welfare Work in Mill Villages: The Story of Extra-Mill Activities in North Carolina* (Chapel Hill,

1929) ; Harriet L. Herring, *Passing of the Mill Village: Revolution in a Southern Institution* (Chapel Hill, 1949) ; and Glenn Gilman, *Human Relations in the Industrial Southeast: A Study of the Textile Industry* (Chapel Hill, 1956).

The protracted troubles of the 1930's prompted several books on the coal miners: McAlister Coleman, *Men and Coal* (New York, 1943) ; Homer L. Morris, *The Plight of the Bituminous Coal Miner* (Philadelphia and London, 1934) ; and Malcolm H. Ross, *Machine Age in the Hills* (New York, 1933). See also the impressionistic but fervid account in Harry M. Caudill, *Night Comes to the Cumberlands: A Biography of a Depressed Area* (Boston, 1963).

Special aspects of labor are treated in Clarence Heer, *Income and Wages in the South* (Chapel Hill, 1930) ; Katharine Du Pre Lumpkin and Dorothy Wolff Douglas, *Child Workers in America* (New York, 1927) ; Elizabeth H. Davidson, *Child Labor Legislation in the Southern Textile States* (Chapel Hill, 1939) ; Virginia H. Brown, *The Development of Labor Legislation in Tennessee* (Knoxville, 1945) ; Lucy Randolph Mason, *Standards for Workers in Southern Industry* (n.p., 1931) ; and Addison T. Cutler, "Labor Legislation in Thirteen Southern States," in *Southern Economic Journal,* VII (1941), 297–316.

State studies include two excellent works by Ruth A. Allen: *Chapters in the History of Organized Labor in Texas* (Austin, 1941) ; and *East Texas Lumber Workers: An Economic and Social Picture, 1870–1950* (Austin, 1961). Other state studies are George T. Starnes and John E. Hamm, *Some Phases of Labor Relations in Virginia* (New York, 1934) ; Harry M. Douty, "The North Carolina Industrial Worker, 1880–1930" (Ph.D. dissertation, University of North Carolina, 1936) ; and Grady L. Mullenix, "A History of the Texas State Federation of Labor" (Ph.D. dissertation, University of Texas, 1955).

There is no comprehensive history of unionism in the South, but F. Ray Marshall, "History of Labor Organization in the South" (Ph.D. dissertation, University of California at Berkeley, 1955), is a useful guide, though spotty. The following general histories make some references to the South: Philip Taft, *The A.F. of L. in the Time of Gompers* (New York, 1957) ; Philip Taft, *The A.F. of L. from the Death of Gompers to the Merger* (New York, 1959) ; and Walter Galenson, *The CIO Challenge to the AFL: A History of the American Labor Movement, 1935–1941* (Cambridge, 1960). Histories of unions active in the South include Harvey O'Connor, *History of Oil Workers Intl. Union (CIO)* (Denver, 1950) ; Milton S. Baratz, *The Union and the Coal Industry,* in Yale *Studies in Economics,* IV (New Haven, 1955) ; and John W. Kennedy, "A History of the Textile

Workers' Union of America, C.I.O." (Ph.D. dissertation, University of North Carolina, 1950).

The best secondary account of the 1929 labor upheavals is in Irving Bernstein, *The Lean Years: A History of the American Worker, 1920–1933* (Boston, 1960), 1–43. Thomas Tippett, *When Southern Labor Stirs* (New York, 1931), is a report by a union activist. The best account of the Gastonia strike is in Liston Pope, *Millhands & Preachers: A Study of Gastonia* (New Haven, 1942). See also Paul Blanshard, *Labor in Southern Cotton Mills* (New York, 1927). George S. Mitchell, *Textile Unionism and the South* (Chapel Hill, 1931), sketches early efforts. For the New Deal era see James A. Hodges, "New Deal Labor Policy and the Southern Cotton Textile Industry, 1933–1941" (Ph.D. dissertation, Vanderbilt University, 1963).

On Negro labor see Charles H. Wesley, *Negro Labor in the United States* (New York, 1927); Sterling D. Spero and Abram L. Harris, *The Black Worker: The Negro and the Labor Movement* (New York, 1931); Horace R. Cayton and George S. Mitchell, *Black Workers and the New Unions* (Chapel Hill, 1939); Herbert R. Northrup, *Organized Labor and the Negro* (New York and London, 1944); and F. Ray Marshall, *The Negro and Organized Labor* (New York, 1965).

An excellent account of the welfare movement remains unpublished: Lyda Gordon Shivers, "The Social Welfare Movement in the South: A Study in Regional Culture and Social Organization" (Ph.D. dissertation, University of North Carolina, 1935). For one state see Virginia Wooten Gulledge, *The North Carolina Conference for Social Services: A Study of Its Development and Methods* (n.p., 1942). On penal reform see Hilda Jane Zimmerman, "Penal Systems and Penal Reforms in the South since the Civil War" (Ph.D. dissertation, University of North Carolina, 1947); and for an overview of the public health movement see Francis R. Allen, "Public Health Work in the Southeast, 1872–1941: The Study of a Social Movement" (Ph.D. dissertation, University of North Carolina, 1946). T. J. Woofter, Jr., and Ellen Winston, *Seven Lean Years* (Chapel Hill, 1939), is an account of human distress in the Depression years. Standard works in the field of health and welfare devote some space to the South: Josephine Chapin Brown, *Public Relief, 1929–1939* (New York, 1940); Donald S. Howard, *The WPA and Federal Relief Policy* (New York, 1943); Edward Ainsworth Williams, *Federal Aid for Relief*, in Columbia University *Studies in History, Economics, and Public Law*, No. 452 (New York, 1939); and Lewis Meriam, *Relief and Social Security* (Washington, 1946).

The Southern Sociological Congress of the teens published papers given at its meetings in several volumes edited by James E. McCulloch: *The Call of the New South* (Nashville, 1912); *The Human Way: Addresses on Race Problems* (Atlanta, 1913); *The South Mobilizing for Social Service* (Atlanta, 1913); *Battling for Social Betterment* (Memphis, 1914); *The New Chivalry: Health* (Houston, 1915); *Democracy in Earnest* (Washington, 1918); and *"Distinguished Service" Citizenship* (Knoxville, 1919).

NEGROES AND RACE RELATIONS

The basic book is Gunnar Myrdal, with the assistance of Richard Sterner and Arnold Rose, *An American Dilemma: The Negro Problem and Modern Democracy*, 2 vols. (New York and London, 1944), a monumental survey backed up by numerous typescript monographs deposited in the Schomburg Collection, New York Public Library, and available on microfilm. Basic reference works are the *Negro Year Book* (Tuskegee, Ala., 1912———, title varies), published at irregular intervals; and the *Negro Handbook*, 1942, 1944, 1946, 1949 (New York, 1912———). The standard history is John Hope Franklin, *From Slavery to Freedom: A History of American Negroes* (Rev. ed., New York, 1956). Another useful synthesis is E. Franklin Frazier, *The Negro in the United States* (Rev. ed., New York, 1957), by a sociologist who is aware of historical forces.

I. A. Newby, *Jim Crow's Defense: Anti-Negro Thought in America, 1900–1930* (Baton Rouge, 1965), explores racist thought among whites. August Meier, *Negro Thought in America, 1880–1915: Racial Ideologies in the Age of Booker T. Washington* (Ann Arbor, 1963), barely reaches the period under consideration, but see Earlie E. Thorpe, *The Mind of the Negro: An Intellectual History of Afro-Americans* (Baton Rouge, 1961), which is a miscellany of essays. Important contemporaneous statements of Negro aspirations include Robert R. Moton, *What the Negro Thinks* (Garden City, N.Y., 1929); James Weldon Johnson, *Negro Americans, What Now?* (New York, 1934); and Rayford W. Logan (ed.), *What the Negro Wants* (Chapel Hill, 1944).

C. Vann Woodward, *The Strange Career of Jim Crow* (New York, 1955), effectively outlines the history of racial segregation. Earlier sociological studies are Bertram W. Doyle, *The Etiquette of Race Relations in the South* (Chicago, 1937); Charles S. Johnson, *Patterns of Negro Segregation* (New York, 1943); and Charles S. Johnson and Associates, *Into the Main Stream: A Survey of Best Practices in Race Relations in the South* (Chapel Hill, 1947). Legal aspects of race relations may be explored in Charles S. Mangum, Jr., *The Legal Status of the Negro* (Chapel Hill, 1940); Bernard H. Nelson, *The Fourteenth Amendment and the Negro Since 1920* (Washington, 1946); and Robert J. Harris, *The Quest for Equality: The Constitution, Congress and the Supreme Court* (Baton Rouge, 1960).

The most intensive study of lynching and its causes is Arthur F. Raper, *The Tragedy of Lynching* (Chapel Hill, 1933); but see also Walter F. White, *Rope and Faggot: A Biography of Judge Lynch* (New York, 1929); and James H. Chadbourn, *Lynching and the Law* (Chapel Hill, 1933). The drive for a Federal antilynching law is covered in Robert Lewis Zangrando, "The Efforts of the National Association for the Advancement of Colored People to Secure Passage of a Federal Anti-Lynching Law, 1920–1940" (Ph.D. dissertation, University of Pennsylvania, 1963). The fullest general account of the 1919 race riots is in Arthur I. Waskow, *From Race Riot to Sit-In, 1919 and the 1960's: A Study in the Connections between Conflict and Violence* (Garden City, N.Y., 1966).

For Negro migration see Frank Alexander Ross and Louise V. Kennedy, *A Bibliography of Negro Migration* (New York, 1935); U.S. Department of Labor, Division of Negro Economics, *Negro Migration in 1916–17* (Washington, 1919); and Emmett J. Scott, *Negro Migration During the War* (New York, 1920). See also *Scott's Official History of the American Negro in the World War* (Chicago, 1919). Alain Le Roy Locke (ed.), *The New Negro: An Interpretation* (New York, 1925), is an anthology of the Negro renaissance. The most valuable survey of the New Deal years yet available is Leslie H. Fishel, Jr., "The Negro in the New Deal Era," *Wisconsin Magazine of History*, XLVIII (1964–1965), 111–26. Richard Sterner, *The Negro's Share* (New York, 1943), considers the economic status of Negroes in those years.

The most satisfactory general study of Negro improvement and protest organizations is still an unpublished monograph written for the Myrdal study: Ralph J. Bunche, "Programs, Ideologies, Tactics and Achievements of Negro Betterment and Interracial Organizations." There is no satisfactory history of the National Urban League, and the first scholarly history of the NAACP appeared only as this book went to press: Charles Flint Kellogg, *NAACP: A History of the National Association for the Advancement of Colored People*, Vol. I, 1909–1920 (Baltimore, 1967). On the mainly futile effort to recruit Negroes to communism see two books by Wilson Record: *The Negro and the Communist Party* (Chapel Hill, 1951), and *Race and*

Radicalism: The NAACP and the Communist Party in Conflict (Ithaca, 1964). The story of the interracial movement is given in Dykeman and Stokely, *Seeds of Southern Change;* and Edward F. Burrows, "The Commission on Interracial Cooperation in the South" (Ph.D. dissertation, University of Wisconsin, 1955). A contemporary survey of interracial efforts is Paul E. Baker, *Negro-White Adjustment: An Investigation and Analysis of Methods in the Interracial Movement in the United States* (New York, 1934). For statements by moderates active in the Commission see T. J. Woofter, Jr., *The Basis of Racial Adjustment* (New York, 1925); and Willis D. Weatherford and Charles S. Johnson, *Race Relations: Adjustment of Whites and Negroes in the United States* (Boston, 1934).

Two excellent studies of Negro efforts to achieve recognition during World War II are Herbert Garfinkel, *When Negroes March: The March on Washington Movement in the Organizational Politics for FEPC* (Glencoe, Ill., 1950); and Louis Ruchames, *Race, Jobs & Politics: The Story of the FEPC* (New York, 1953). In *Race and Rumors of Race: Challenge to American Crisis* (Chapel Hill, 1943), Howard W. Odum examined the wartime rumor mills. Ulysses Lee, *The Employment of Negro Troops,* in *U.S. Army in World War II: Special Studies,* Number 8 (Washington, 1966), became available too late for use in the preparation of this volume.

CULTURAL AND SOCIAL HISTORY

A monumental survey of Southern culture and society in the period is W. T. Couch (ed.), *Culture in the South* (Chapel Hill, 1935), which has thirty-five essays on different facets of Southern life. Several volumes of essays pursue that elusive but enduring question of the Southern identity: Benjamin B. Kendrick and Alex M. Arnett, *The South Looks at Its Past* (Chapel Hill, 1935); Louis D. Rubin, Jr., and James J. Kilpatrick, *The Lasting South: Fourteen Southerners Look at Their Home* (Chicago, 1957); Charles G. Sellers, Jr. (ed.), *The Southerner as American* (Chapel Hill, 1960); Frank E. Vandiver (ed.), *The Idea of the South: Pursuit of a Central Theme* (Chicago, 1964); C. Vann Woodward, *The Burden of Southern History* (Baton Rouge, 1960); and Francis B. Simkins, *The Everlasting South* (Baton Rouge, 1963).

Charles W. Dabney's *Universal Education in the South,* 2 vols. (Chapel Hill, 1936), remains the standard work but does not reach far into the period under consideration. However, a number of state histories do: Horace Mann Bond, *Negro Education in Alabama: A*

Study in Cotton and Steel (Washington, 1939); Andrew D. Holt, *The Struggle for a State System of Public Schools in Tennessee, 1903–1936*, in Teachers College, Columbia University, *Contributions to Education*, No. 753 (New York, 1938); Frank L. McVey, *The Gates Open Slowly: A History of Education in Kentucky* (Lexington, Ky., 1949); and Dorothy B. Orr, *A History of Education in Georgia* (Chapel Hill, 1950).

For the philanthropic foundations the official proceedings constitute the basic sources. Histories written by foundation leaders include Raymond B. Fosdick, *Adventure in Giving: The Story of the General Education Board* (New York, 1962), which seeks to counter the interpretation in Louis R. Harlan, *Separate and Unequal: Public School Campaigns and Racism in the Southern Seaboard States, 1901–1915* (Chapel Hill, 1958); Edwin R. Embree and Julia Waxman, *Investment in People: The Story of the Julius Rosenwald Fund* (New York, 1949); and Robert M. Lester, *Forty Years of Carnegie Giving . . .* (New York, 1941).

Efforts to improve Negro schools and colleges are the subject of Ullin Whitney Leavell, *Philanthropy in Negro Education* (Nashville, 1930); Dwight O. W. Holmes, *Evolution of the Negro College* (New York, 1934); Lance G. E. Jones, *The Jeanes Teacher in the United States, 1908–1933: An Account of Twenty-Five Years' Experience in the Supervision of Negro Rural Schools* (Chapel Hill, 1937); S. L. Smith, *Builders of Goodwill: The Story of the State Agents of Negro Education in the South, 1910 to 1950* (Nashville, 1950); Horace Mann Bond, *The Education of the Negro in the American Social Order* (New York, 1934); and Willard Range, *The Rise and Progress of Negro Colleges in Georgia, 1865–1949*, in University of Georgia *Phelps-Stokes Fellowship Studies*, No. 15 (Athens, 1951). Major surveys of Negro schools in the period are Thomas Jesse Jones, *Negro Education: A Study of the Private and Higher Schools for Colored People in the United States* (Washington, 1917); Arthur J. Klein, *Survey of Negro Colleges and Universities*, U.S. Bureau of Education *Bulletin*, 1928, No. 7 (Washington, 1928); and Doxey A. Wilkerson, *Special Problems of Negro Education*, in U.S. Advisory Committee on Education *Staff Studies*, No. 12 (Washington, 1939).

Some perspectives on developments in higher education may be gained from Wilson Gee, *Research Barriers in the South* (New York and London, 1932); Mary Bynum Pierson, *Graduate Work in the South* (Chapel Hill, 1947); and Guy E. Snavely, *A Short History of the Southern Association of Colleges and Secondary Schools* (Durham?, 1945?), reprinted from the *Southern Association Quarterly*, IX (1945), 423–549. The many institutional histories vary widely in quality. Some of the best are identified and evaluated in Horace H. Cunningham, "The Southern Mind Since the Civil War," in Link and Patrick (eds.), *Writing Southern History*, 395–99. Two histories of merit appeared too late for mention there: Earl W. Porter, *Trinity and Duke, 1892–1924: Foundation of Duke University* (Durham, 1964); and Charles G. Talbert, *The University of Kentucky: The Maturing Years* (Lexington, 1965).

A significant contribution to the neglected field of religious history is Kenneth K. Bailey, *Southern White Protestantism in the Twentieth Century* (New York, 1964). For other studies see Nelson R. Burr, *A Critical Bibliography of Religion in America* (Princeton, 1961). Other works in the field include Victor I. Masters, *Country Church in the South* (2nd ed., Atlanta, 1917); Edmund deS. Brunner, *Church Life in the Rural South: A Study of the Opportunity of Protestantism Based upon Data from Seventy Counties* (New York, 1923); Pope, *Millhands & Preachers,* on Gastonia; Paul N. Garber, *The Methodists Are One People* (Nashville, 1939); and William Wright Barnes, *The Southern Baptist Convention, 1845–1935* (Nashville, 1954). There is a superabundance of works on fundamentalism and the Scopes trial, among which some of the best are Norman F. Furniss, *The Fundamentalist Controversy, 1918–1931* (New Haven, 1954); Ray Ginger, *Six days or Forever? Tennessee v. John Thomas Scopes* (Boston, 1958); and Jerry R. Tompkins (ed.), *D-Days at Dayton: Reflections on the Scopes Trial* (Baton Rouge, 1965). A superb state study is Willard B. Gatewood, Jr., *Preachers, Pedagogues and Politicians: The Evolution Controversy in North Carolina, 1920–1927* (Chapel Hill, 1966).

The best studies of the Ku Klux Klan in the South are two overlapping books by Charles C. Alexander: *The Ku Klux Klan in the Southwest,* and *The Ku Klux Klan in Texas, 1920–1930* (Houston, 1962). Good studies that are broader in scope include David Chalmers, *Hooded Americanism: The First Century of the Ku Klux Klan, 1865–1965* (New York, 1965); and Arnold S. Rice, *The Ku Klux Klan in American Politics* (Washington, 1962).

The twentieth-century South has made major contributions to the fine arts in two fields: music and literature. For music the starting point is Marshall W. Stearns, *The Story of Jazz* (New York, 1956), which includes a bibliography by Robert George Reisner that is expanded in the Mentor paperback edition (New York, 1958). See also George P. Jackson, *White Spirituals in the Southern Uplands* (Chapel Hill, 1933); D. K. Wilgus, *Anglo-American Folksong Scholarship since 1898* (New Brunswick, N.J., 1959); Maud Cuney-Hare, *Negro Musicians and Their Music* (Washington, 1936); Louis Armstrong, *Swing That Music* (New York, 1936); William C. Handy, *Father of the Blues: An Autobiography* (New York, 1941); and Alan Lomax, *Mister Jelly Roll* (New York, 1950).

There is as yet no definitive history of the literary renaissance, but John M. Bradbury, *Renaissance in the South: A Critical History of the Literature, 1920–1960* (Chapel Hill, 1963), touches all the bases and gives an exhaustive list of Southern writers. In addition to literary memoirs and biographies listed above, critical works often illuminate the history of the renaissance. See especially two collections of essays edited by Louis D. Rubin, Jr., and Robert D. Jacobs: *Southern Renascence: The Literature of the Modern South* (Baltimore, 1953); and *South: Modern Literature in Its Cultural Setting* (Garden City, N.Y., 1961), which includes a checklist by James B. Meriwether of books by, and writings about, thirty-six major writers; and Louis D. Rubin, Jr., *The Faraway Country: Writers of the Modern South* (Seattle, 1963). One enduring fashion in Southern writing is traced in Shields McIlwaine, *The Southern Poor White: From Lubberland to Tobacco Road* (Norman, 1939).

Negroes as authors and subjects are treated in Sterling A. Brown, *The Negro in American Fiction* (Washington, 1937); Sterling A. Brown, *Negro Poetry and Drama* (Washington, 1937); Hugh M. Gloster, *Negro Voices in American Fiction* (Chapel Hill, 1948); and Robert A. Bone, *The Negro Novel in America* (New Haven, 1958), the last here being the best.

The Fugitive-Agrarian-New Critics have received more attention than any other literary group and have been the subject of some of the best critical-historical studies. A personal view by one of the group is Donald Davidson, *Southern Writers in the Modern World* (Athens, 1958). The basic surveys are Louise Cowan, *The Fugitive Group: A Literary History* (Baton Rouge, 1959); Virginia J. Rock, "The Making and Meaning of *I'll Take My Stand*: A Study in Utopian-Conservatism, 1925–1939" (Ph.D. dissertation, University of Minnesota, 1961), a definitive work if ever there were one; John L. Stewart, *The Burden of Time: The Fugitives and Agrarians* . . . (Princeton, 1965); and Alexander Karanikas, *Tillers of a Myth: Southern Agrarians as Social and Literary Critics* (Madison, Wis., 1966).

To include critical studies of individual authors would extend this essay beyond reasonable bounds. On other subjects, too, the listing here falls short of exhausting the possibilities. The reader wishing to pursue further any particular topic should utilize the bibliographies mentioned above and consult the documentation at pertinent points in the text of this volume.

INDEX

Abbott, Grace, on child labor, 533
Adams, E. C. L., 308
Adamson, William C., 16
Adamson Eight Hour Act, 17
Aderholt, D. A., 346, 347
Adkins, Oscar E., 348, 349
Advancing South, The, 216
Advertising, in the 1920's, 99
Agar, Herbert, 580
Agee, James, 415, 589, 686
Agrarianism, 581
Agrarian Manifesto, 216, 299, 576–82. *See also* Fugitive group, New Criticism
Agrarian myth, 125. *See also* Back-to-the-farm movement, Factory-farm living
Agrarian "radicals," bank reforms of, 13; reform programs of, 17; and socialism in Southwest, 26
Agricultural Adjustment Act, first, 393; ruled unconstitutional, 403; second, 407; effect of, on Negroes, 544; and Negro voting, 557; mentioned, 611, 625
Agricultural Adjustment Administration, Cotton Production Control Section of, 393; and emergency plow-up of cotton, 393–94; program for tobacco farmers, 396–97; South's support of, 403; and farm labor system, 413–15
Agricultural Marketing Act of 1929, p. 356
Agriculture, as source of cheap labor in South, 320; crises in, prior to Depression, 354; effect of 1930 drought on, 355–56; diversification in, during 1930's, 429; influence of mechanization on, 430, population decreases in, 703;

prosperity of, during World War II, 703–704; and preference of farmers for basic crops, 705
Aiken, Conrad, 669
Aircraft industry, in World War II, 697
Akers, Arthur, 306
Alabama, Progressive reforms in, 19; statewide prohibition legislation in, 19; power production in, 73; Mobile harbor development, 102; real estate boom in, 102; diversification in, 123; Negro longshoremen in, 165; anti-Catholicism in, 188–89; Ku Klux Klan in, 194; abolition of convict leasing in, 213; business progressivism in, 227–28; decrease of child labor in, 322; United Mine Workers in, 336–37, 506; price declines in, during Depression, 359; Share Croppers' Union in, 379–80; antitariff sentiment in, 400; need for soil conservation in, 404; farmers support agricultural production controls, 407; favors farm tenant loans, 424; Farmers' Union in, 428; and TVA, 452; relief percentages in, 474; 1938 antilabor violence in Huntsville, 519–20
Alabama Power Company, 73, 241, 463
Alderman, Edwin A., 50, 266
Aldrich, Ransom, 710
Alexander, H. Q., 47
Alexander, Mrs. L. M., 663
Alexander, Will W., heads Interracial Commission, 177–78; on newspapers and racial progress, 180–81; warns Interracial Commission against over-com-

Division of Negro Economics of Department of Labor, 150
Dixie Highway, 105
Dixon, Frank, 717, 724
Dixon, Thomas, 186, 617
Dobie, J. Frank, 302
Dodd, William E., 17, 65
Dodge, Witherspoon, antiunion attack on, 525–26
Doheny, Edward L., 242
Dombrowski, James, 639
Dorsey, Hugh M., cites racial atrocities in Georgia, 181; and Leo Frank case, 186; mentioned, 212
Dorsey, W. F., 49
Dos Passos, John, 701, 707, 709
Double Dealer, The, 293–95
Doughton, Robert Lee, 608, 725
Dow, Grove S., 201
Dreiser, Theodore, 384
Du Bois, W. E. B., as new major voice of Negro race, 158; and "self segregation," 559–60; mentioned, 169, 381, 541, 542, 559
Du Bose, Bishop H. M., 246
Duke, James B., and beginnings of Duke Power Company, 72; Duke endowment, 265–66; mentioned, 78
Duke University, expansion of, 265–66
DuPont, Alfred I., relief efforts of, 370–71
du Pont, Henry, 617
Durham Conference of Negroes, 719
Durr, Mrs. Virginia Foster, 640, 641
Dyer, L. C., 174
Dyer antilynching bill, 174, 550, 551

Eagle, Joseph H., 10
Early, Stephen A., 555, 711
East, H. Clay, 417
Eastland, James O., 722
Economic development, boosted by wartime industries, 56, 697; Negro's disproportionate share in, 162–65. *See also* BAWI, Industrial promotion, Industrial development, *Report on Economic Conditions of the South,* Tennessee Valley Authority

Edgerton, John E., elected president of National Association of Manufacturers, 71; heads Southern States Industrial Council, 444; seeks restoration of pre-NRA wage differentials, 445; mentioned, 328, 352, 358, 370, 443
Edmonds, Richard Hathaway, prophet of industrial New South, 70; mentioned, 328
Education, Southern progress in, during 1920's, 262; Depression status of, 493; segregation and Federal aid to, 497; higher education in the South, 498; of Negroes, 500; discrimination in Negro, 500–501; in Negro colleges, 503; separate, 562–63
Education movement, state and local governments assume responsibility for, 262; and increase of higher education institutions in South, 264–65; philanthropy in, 265; neglects Negro education in first two decades, 268; renewal of, 493–94; state expenditures in, 495. *See also* Carnegie Foundation, General Education Board, Jeanes Fund, Rosenwald Fund
Ehringhaus, J. C. B., 397, 645
Eighteenth Amendment, 220–21
Elaine massacres, circumstances surrounding, 152–54; mentioned, 558
"Eleanor Clubs," 717–18
Eleazer, Robert B., Jr., racial education reform efforts of, 182–83
Electrical development, in the South in 1920's, 71–75; consolidation of companies in, 74; innovations in interconnections, 74. *See also* Muscle Shoals, Tennessee Valley Authority, Santee-Cooper project
Eliot, T. S., 667
Elizabethton, Tenn., Hoover speech in, 252; textile workers strike in, 342–43
Ellender, Allen J., 553, 722
Embree, Edwin R., on Southern educational institutions, 498; mentioned, 416, 543
Emergency Banking Act, 610
Emergency Price Control Act, Bankhead Amendment to, 706

799

ment in, 436; overproduction in, 436–38; major strike in, 437; continued Southern expansion in, in the 1940's, 467; domestic market of, threatened by Japan, 468; competition and instability in, 468; efforts to integrate, 468; minimum wage rates in, raised by Fair Labor Standards Act, 536

Textile workers, average income of, 318

Textile Workers Organizing Committee, absorbs United Textile Workers, 517; organizing campaign of, 518; Southern successes of, 518; business recession retards growth of, 518

Textile Workers Union of America, formation of, 519; hostility toward, 519; in Huntsville, Ala., 519–20; in Gaffney, S.C., 520; mentioned, 573

These Are Our Lives, 589

Thirty Years of Lynching, 173

Thomas, Elbert, 497

Thomas, Elmer, sponsors inflation bill, 393; adds inflationary measures to 1933 farm bill, 393; mentioned, 390, 627, 706

Thomas, Norman, criticizes AAA for labor displacement, 414, 417; tours Arkansas Delta, 419

Thompson, Basil, 293–94

Thompson, Edgar T., 416

Thompson, Ernest O., 439

Thorp, Willard, on Caroline Gordon, 678; on Katherine Anne Porter, 681

Tillman, Benjamin R. "Pitchfork Ben," 20, 21

Tippett, Tom, 348

Tobacco industry, and price collapse of 1920, p. 112; early success of co-operative movement in, 118; membership in co-operatives in, 119; reasons for failure of co-operative movement in, 119–120; Depression price declines in, 354; as Depression-proof industry, 360–61; farmers support acreage controls in, 407; price collapse of 1939 in, 408

Tobacco Growers' Cooperative Association, 119–20

Tobacco Road, 415

Tobacco Workers Industrial Union, Unity League of, 379; and Communist activity in Tampa, Fla., 379

Tobacco Workers International Union, strength of, 508; mentioned, 336

Toomer, Jean, 295, 312

Trade association movement, in lumbering, in textile industry, 362

Trinity College, becomes Duke University, 265–66

Tri-State Cooperative. *See* Tobacco Growers' Cooperative Association

True Americans, 189

Truman, Harry S., 603, 728, 730–31

Tugwell, Rexford, and Resettlement Administration, 423; on TVA, 454; mentioned, 614

Tulane University, 265

Turnblazer, William, 505

Turner, Frederick Jackson, 584

Tuskegee Institute, 274. *See also* Moton, Robert R.

Twelve Southerners, named, 577

Tydings, Millard E., 621

Tyler, Mrs. Elizabeth, publicizes KKK, 189, 195

Tyronza, Ark., Southern Tenant Farmers' Union organizes in, 417–18; Hiram Norcross Plantation test case in, 418; violence in, 418–19

Ucker, Clement S., and Federal land reclamation program, 129

Underwood, Oscar W., attacks Ku Klux Klan, 242; seeks Democratic Presidential nomination, 242–43; mentioned, 9, 19, 194, 238

Underwood-Simmons Tariff Act, income tax provision of, 11; revision of, in House and Senate, 11; mentioned, 17

Unemployment, during Depression, 369–70; and racial discrimination, 373

Unionism, beginnings of, 331–32; craft unions gain public acceptance, 332; increased activity in textiles, 332–34, 521; Southern, 1930, p. 332; in oil industry, 334–36, 515; in tobacco industry, 336, 517; in steel industry, 337; in lumber industry, 337–38; failure of, in the teens, 338–39; upsurge of activity in